Symbols used on the maps

CONSTRUCTED FEATURES

Built-up area - tour centre..................... **BUNBURY** ①

Town, village or other selected stopping place..................... **Bunton** ③

Other town or village..................... Lower Bunfield

Selected route.....................

Isolated building..................... ■

Motorway.....................

A or B road.....................

Under construction {
Motorway.....................
A or B road.....................
}

Other metalled road.....................

Unmetalled road or track, footpath.....................

Gradients: 1 in 5 to 1 in 7, steeper than 1 in 5; toll..................... *Toll*

Bridges, roundabout, level crossing.....................

Road number..................... **M 4   A 27   B 3845**

Town off route and distance..................... →BUNBURY 6 MILES

Course of Roman or other historical route..................... **ICKNIELD WAY**

Roman wall.....................

Railway, station, viaduct and tunnel.....................

Hotel (route identification)..................... **HOTEL**

Public House (route identification)..................... **PH**

Parking area..................... P

Toilets..................... WC

Telephone (route identification)..................... **T**

Radio or TV mast.....................

Airfield.....................

PHYSICAL FEATURES

Hill and height above sea level..................... *2160 ft • Bunbury Tor*

Other features..................... *Bunbury Forest*

River or canal and lake..................... *Waterfall   Dam   Lock*

Coast.....................

SELECTED SITES

Castle or house usually open to the public..................... 血

Castle or house in ruins..................... ⌘

Gardens..................... ❀

National Trust property..................... **NT**

Museum..................... ♟

Church or chapel..................... ✝

Other ecclesiastical building..................... ⛪

Archaeological site..................... ⊓

Tumulus or earthworks..................... ✳

Roman antiquity..................... ⚛

Industrial monument..................... ⚙

Monument, memorial or other site..................... •

Site of battle..................... ✕

Lighthouse..................... ⚑

Windmill..................... ✹

Observatory..................... ◠

Viewpoint (arc of view)..................... ≋

Camping & Caravan site (AA approved)..................... ⛺

Caravan site only (AA approved)..................... ⛺

Camping site only (AA approved)..................... ⛺

Picnic area..................... ⚘

Nature reserve..................... ✿

Nature/Forest trail..................... 🐾

Golf course..................... ⛳

Zoological gardens..................... 🐘

Bird Sanctuary..................... 🐦

Historical railway..................... 🚂

Craft centre..................... ⚒

Gliding..................... ✕

Sailing..................... ⛵

Canoeing..................... ✎

Motor racing..................... 🏎

Motor-cycle racing..................... 🏍

Surfing..................... 🏄

Water ski-ing..................... 🎿

Racecourse..................... 🐎

Highland Games..................... ⚜

Ski-ing..................... ⛷

Parachuting..................... ☂

THE MAPS OF THE TOURS HAVE BEEN DERIVED FROM ORDNANCE SURVEY MATERIAL WITH THE SANCTION OF THE CONTROLLER OF HER MAJESTY'S STATIONERY OFFICE (CROWN COPYRIGHT RESERVED)

CARTOGRAPHERS: FAIREY SURVEYS LTD, MAIDENHEAD

© THE READER'S DIGEST ASSOCIATION LIMITED

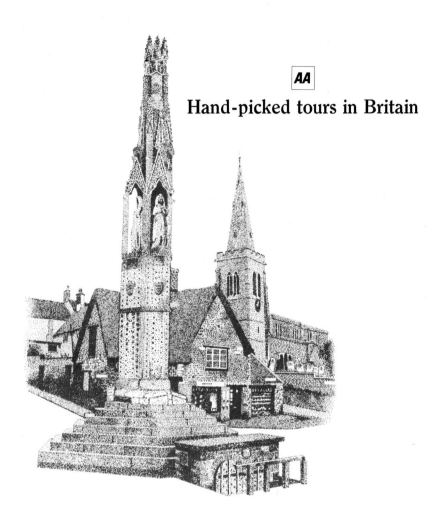

AA

Hand-picked tours in Britain

AA Hand-picked tours in Britain

Day drives along quiet roads through all parts of the countryside, with halts in historic villages and towns and visits to castles, gardens, follies and other selected places of interest

Published by Drive Publications Limited for the Automobile Association, Fanum House, Basingstoke, Hampshire RG21 2EA

AA HAND-PICKED TOURS IN BRITAIN
was edited and designed by
The Reader's Digest Association Limited
for Drive Publications Limited,
Berkeley Square House, London W1X 5PD

First AA Edition Copyright © 1977
Drive Publications Limited

Printed in Great Britain

Contributors

The publishers would like to thank the following people for major contributions to this book

AUTHORS

His Grace The Duke of Atholl
Dorothy Bacon
Joan Bates
Bill Bawden
Robert John Berkeley
John Burke
Martyn F. Chillmaid
Neil Cossons
Herbert Coutts
His Grace The Duke of Devonshire
Arthur Eperon
Nigel Finch
Ross Finlay
Charles Greenwood
Nigel Hamilton
Beryl Hedges
Harry Hopkins
George Howard

Malcolm Livingston
Philip Llewellin
Barbara Long
Colin Luckhurst
Hamish Mackinven
The Very Reverend Fenton Morley
Sylvie Nickels
Trefor M. Owen
Dr Franklyn Perring
Charles Puddle
Roger Redfern
Ronald Stevens
Noel Turnbull
Air Commodore A. H. Wheeler

PHOTOGRAPHERS

Malcolm Aird
Philip Dowell
Phillip Evans
Tony Evans
Michael Wells
Trevor Wood

ARTISTS

David Baird
Terry Callcut
Michael Craig
Terry Hadler
Gillian Kenny
Robert Micklewright
Peter Morter
Linda Nash

Contents

Where England comes to an end in beauty and antiquity

Scalloped with white sandy bays, two coastlines run to reach a joint conclusion at Land's End. On one side the Atlantic rolls and pounds upon sweeping surf beaches. On the other, calmer Channel waters wash into pretty fishing ports. An essentially Celtic land of tiny villages and epic myths, forced to abandon its two most prosperous industries, mining and smuggling, it has swiftly developed into a year-round holiday playground.

(1) Penzance to Mousehole Leave the town on the seafront road, following the signpost to Newlyn. Cross the bridge and turn left, skirting Newlyn Harbour and following the signpost to Mousehole. Continue on the coast road and into Mousehole.

(2) Mousehole to Land's End In the village turn right by the Ship Inn, following the signpost to Paul. In Paul turn left by the church to follow the signpost to St Buryan. At the junction turn left on to the B3315, and after 1¼ m. turn right, again signposted to St Buryan. Follow the road to St Buryan and at the T-junction in the village turn left on to the B3283, following the signpost to Porthcurno. After just over 1 m. this road becomes the B3315. Follow the road through Treen and on to the junction with the A30, turn left and continue to Land's End.

(3) Land's End to Chûn Castle Return to the A30 and follow the road through Sennen. At the next major junction turn left on to the B3306, following the signpost to St Just. Pass Land's End airport on the left and at the T-junction turn left on to the A3071 and continue into St Just where the A3071 joins the B3306. Leave the town on the B3306, following the signposts to St Ives. After about 3 m. go through Morvah and almost immediately turn right, following the signpost to Penzance. After 1 m. turn right to Chûn Castle and Chûn Quoit. Mên-an-tol can be reached by the lane opposite the one leading to Chûn Castle.

(4) Chûn Castle to Zennor From the castle return to the Penzance road, turn left and then follow the road to the B3306 and turn right, following the signposts to St Ives. After about 4 m. turn left to Zennor.

(5) Zennor to Hayle Return to the B3306 and turn left, following the road to the outskirts of St Ives. Here, turn right on to the B3311, again following the signpost to Penzance. After 2½ m., in the village of Cripplesease, turn left to follow the road signposted to Hayle. Bear right at a fork in the road signposted to Hayle, passing Trencrom Hill and, at its foot, the car park. At the next T-junction turn right and then right again on to the A3074. Almost immediately bear left and turn left again on to the A30, and continue into Hayle.

(6) Hayle to Tolgus Tin Mill Leave Hayle on the B3302, signposted to Helston, and immediately turn left by the White Hart Hotel. Follow the road to a staggered crossroads by a railway arch and keep straight ahead, following the road through Angarrack. After about 1½ m. turn left, crossing the A30 and continuing into Gwithian. In the village turn right on to the B3301, following the signpost to Portreath. Leave Portreath on the B3300, following the signpost to Redruth. Tolgus Tin Mill is signposted on the right about 1 m. from Portreath.

(7) Tolgus Tin Mill to Godolphin House Just beyond the tin workings turn right to follow the signpost to Illogan. At the road junction in Illogan go straight ahead, keeping to the road signposted to Pool. At the junction 1 m. further on, turn left, go under the A30 and after ½ m. cross the A3047, following the sign to Four Lanes. After 1 m. there is a turning to the right, signposted to Treskillard, where there is a carriage museum. Continue into Four Lanes, turn right on to the B3297 and right again on to the B3280, following the signpost to Penzance. Go straight across the B3303 and the B3302, following the road into Townshend. In the village turn left on to the road signposted to Helston. After just under 1 m. Godolphin House is on the right.

(8) Godolphin House to Goldsithney Return by the same route to Townshend and turn left on to the B3280. Follow the road to Goldsithney.

(9) Goldsithney to St Michael's Mount Leave the village on the B3280, and on meeting the A394 turn right following the signpost to Penzance, and after ¼ m. enter Marazion for St Michael's Mount.

(10) St Michael's Mount to Penzance Return to the A394 and follow the signposts to Penzance. At the junction with the A30 keep straight ahead along the seafront road and into Penzance.

INFORMATION

Places of interest *Godolphin House:* June and July, Thur., 2-5 p.m.; Aug. and Sept., Tues. and Thur., 2-5 p.m. *Goldsithney:* West Cornwall Museum of Mechanical Music, Easter weekend to end Sept., weekdays, Sun. afternoons. *Hayle:* Bird Paradise, daily, Paradise Railway, Apr. to Oct. *Lelant:* model village, Apr. to Oct., daily; Nov. to Mar., weekends. *Penzance:* Man-of-War Display, Apr. to Oct., weekdays, 10.30 a.m.-6.30 p.m. *Pool:* Cornish engines, Apr. to mid-Oct., daily. *Porthcurno:* Minack Cliffside Theatre, end June to early Sept. *St Michael's Mount:* Castle, conducted tours only, Mon., Wed. and Fri., all year; also Tues., July to Oct. *Tolgus Tin Mill:* Easter to end May, daily except Sat.; June to end Sept., daily; Oct., daily except Sat., 9.30 a.m.-6 p.m. Rest of year by appointment. *Treskillard:* Carriage Museum, daily, 11 a.m. to dusk. *Zennor:* Wayside Cottage Folk Museum, Spring Bank Hol. to end Oct., daily.

Information Alverton Street, Penzance (Tel. Penzance 2341 or 2207).

Towns with easy access to Penzance:

Falmouth	26 m.	Penryn	24 m.
Helston	13 m.	Redruth	18 m.

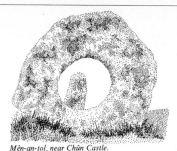

Mên-an-tol, near Chûn Castle.

CHÛN CASTLE
Overlooking the coast and moorland are the remains of a circular Iron Age hill-fort with two concentric stone walls surrounded by a large ditch. The fort faces Chûn (pronounced 'Choon') Quoit, a small burial chamber dating from the period 2500-500 BC. Near by is Mên-an-tol, meaning the stone with the hole, thought to be part of another burial chamber. At one time children suffering from rickets were passed through the hole in the belief that this would cure them.

LAND'S END
Granite cliffs plunge 200 ft to the sea at this most westerly point on the English coast. Land's End is best at dawn or dusk, when it is less crowded. From the cliff-top, Longships Lighthouse can be seen rising 120 ft from the sea. On a fine day the Scilly Isles are also visible on the horizon 25 miles to the south-west. More dramatic cliffs can be seen at close quarters on the little-used footpath between Land's End and Porthcurno.

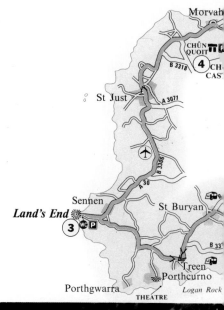

Gannets at Mousehole bird hospital.

MOUSEHOLE
Colour-washed cottages crowded into a steep valley attract many artists to Mousehole and its small but busy fishing harbour. The RSPCA sea-bird hospital was kept busy during the *Torrey Canyon* disaster of 1967, when a huge oil slick from the wreck took a heavy toll of sea birds. Mousehole (pronounced 'Mowsel' by the local people) was sacked by Spanish raiders in 1595. The sword with which Jenkin Keigwin fought the invaders, and the cannonball that killed him, are on display in Penzance museum.

SCALE

0   1   2   3   4   5 MILES

HAYLE

This is a pleasant old market town whose prosperity dwindled with that of the tin-mining industry. Hayle now attracts visitors through its situation on the sandy Hayle Estuary. In the town is Bird Paradise, a 7 acre garden devoted to exotic birds, including pairs of several endangered species such as the white-eared pheasant and the thick-billed parrot. Two miles from Hayle is the Lelant model village, where each exhibit is a miniature of buildings in villages and towns in the countryside round Hayle.

ZENNOR

A windswept village 350 ft above the sea, Zennor huddles around its 15th-century church. A mermaid holding a comb and mirror is carved on the end of one of the pews. She is said to have lured Matthew Trewhella, a local man whose singing she admired, down into the sea at nearby Pendour Cove. Two miles south of Zennor there is an Iron Age village with one house roofed with overlapping stones.

The mermaid of Zennor.

TOLGUS TIN MILL

The mill here still extracts tin from stone by the methods used in the 18th and 19th centuries. All the processes are open to the public, and there is a museum of tin mining, a mineral house and a craft centre. By appointment, it is possible to 'prospect' for tin under the guidance of a local expert. A few miles away, at Pool, the National Trust have preserved two engine-houses which recall the heyday of the industry. One of them, East Pool Whim, houses the machinery which used to haul men and ore from the workings 1300 ft below. The pump engine near by drained the mine at a rate of 27,000 gallons of water an hour.

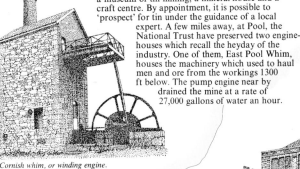

Cornish whim, or winding engine.

Inner courtyard, Godolphin House.

GODOLPHIN HOUSE

Parts of the house date from the 15th century but the north front, with its mullioned windows and large granite columns, was built in the early 16th century. It belonged, for about 200 years, to the Godolphin family.

GOLDSITHNEY

The museum of mechanical music, opened at Goldsithney in 1972, houses a remarkable collection of instruments dating from the early 19th century to the 1930s. Among the exhibits are a decorated mechanical piano dating from 1886, a singing bird and several mechanical violins. The most prized exhibits are the reproducing pianos, which play pieces exactly as the original pianists recorded them. All the instruments are kept in working order so that visitors can hear them.

Mechanical singing bird, Goldsithney.

PENZANCE

The pirates of Penzance, famed in the Gilbert and Sullivan opera, were no mere figment of the playwright's imagination. Pirates from France and the Barbary coast used to raid the town until the mid-18th century. Penzance is now a holiday resort and transport centre for the Cornish and Scilly Isles flower industry. On the seafront are the Morrab Gardens, where sub-tropical plants flourish and some flowers bloom even in winter. The main street, Market Jew Street, is dominated by Market Hall, built in 1836. In front of it stands a statue of Sir Humphry Davy, inventor of the miner's safety lamp, who was born in Penzance in 1778.

Penzance harbour.

St Michael's Mount from Marazion.

ST MICHAEL'S MOUNT

The island is impressive when viewed from the road above Marazion, and may be reached from the town on foot at low tide. The present castle was built in the 19th century but incorporates the old rectory of the 12th-century monastery and rooms dating from 1650.

Ghosts of the packet ships in the land of the Furry Dance

Seafaring traditions abound along the rugged coast, cut by creeks and valleys, on either side of Falmouth. Here, in rocky caves and village inns, the villains of a lawless age plied the twin trades of smuggling and looting wrecked ships. Sir Walter Raleigh and most of the great Elizabethan sea-dogs knew the natural harbour of the Carrick Roads. From a hilltop at Poldhu in 1901 Marconi made his first transatlantic wireless transmissions, not far from the Goonhilly Downs satellite communication station.

1 Falmouth to Porth Navas Leaving the town centre, drive down into Market Strands and turn right, parallel with the quays. The road passes the dock entrance. At the roundabout keep straight ahead, and turn left into Castle Drive. Follow this road around the peninsula and past the entrance to Pendennis Castle, and bear left above the seafront to pass to the right of Queen Mary Gardens. Continue downhill and bear left alongside Swan Pool. Follow the road inland and, at the T-junction beside the pitch-and-putt green, turn left and immediately right towards Penjerrick. Turn left at the next T-junction and pass Penjerrick Gardens on the right. Follow the road about another 1½ m. into Mawnan Smith. Turn left at the T-junction facing the post office and shop, to follow the signpost for Porth Navas. Continue on this road for about 3 m. to Porth Navas.

2 Porth Navas to Goonhilly Continue on the same road out of Porth Navas for about 2 m. to Constantine village centre. Turn left past the church, following the signpost for Gweek. Turn left at the T-junction on to the B3291 and continue about 1 m. to Gweek. Pass through the village and turn left on to the B3293, following the sign for Goonhilly Downs. At the junction with the other arm of the B3293 turn left, following the Goonhilly signs. After about 2 m. reach the giant parabolic aerial complex of the Goonhilly Downs satellite communication station. It can deal with nearly 3000 inter-continental messages at the same time by means of satellites 22,000 miles out in space.

3 Goonhilly to Lizard Beyond the aerial site, at the next crossroads turn right, following the Lizard signpost on to an unusually straight road over the downs. In Kuggar turn right, still following the Lizard signs, and right again at the next crossroads. Join the A3083, turning left, and enter Lizard village. A narrow road leads south towards Lizard Point.

4 Lizard to Poldhu Cove Return along the A3083 about 3½ m. to Penhale, and turn left on to the B3296, following the signposts for Mullion Cove, through Mullion and Trenance. The cove is a much painted and photographed miniature harbour with Mullion Island and Gull Rock out to sea. From Mullion Cove, return to the village and turn left to visit Poldhu Cove.

5 Poldhu Cove to Helston Continue on the same road. Pass through Cury, keeping the church on the right, and ½ m. beyond the village turn left on to the road opposite a telephone kiosk. After 1½ m., at the junction with the A3083, turn left following the Helston signposts. After about 1 m. reach the Culdrose Fleet Air Arm station. At the A394, signposted to Penzance, turn left for Helston town centre.

6 Helston to Wendron Forge Leave the town by the A394, following the Truro signs, and after a few hundred yards turn left on to the B3297, following the signs for Redruth. After about 2 m. enter Wendron, a former tin-mining centre, with its forge-museum of old industries and crafts at the far end of the village.

7 Wendron Forge to Truro Near Wendron Forge, turn right and continue just over 1 m. to Porkellis. In Porkellis village, turn right at the T-junction and continue about 1½ m. to Carnkie. Beyond Carnkie, follow the signs to Stithians and go through the village. Follow the road for another 1½ m. to the junction with the A393. Cross the A393 into Perranwell Station, and continue for about 2 m. to the A39 at Carnon Downs. There turn left and continue for just over 3 m. to the centre of Truro.

8 Truro to Trelissick Gardens Leave the city centre back along the A39 in the Falmouth direction and, after about 2½ m., just past the village of Playing Place, turn left on to the B3289 and left again at the next crossroads, remaining on the B3289. After just over 1 m. reach Trelissick. The entrance to the gardens is on the right.

9 Trelissick Gardens to Falmouth Return along the B3289 to the crossroads, and continue straight ahead for about another 1½ m. to Carnon Downs. Turn left here to rejoin the A39, and continue on it for just over 3 m. to the junction with the A393 and A394. Follow the A39 to the left and continue for about 3 m., through Penryn to Falmouth.

INFORMATION

Places of interest *Porth Navas:* Glendurgan gardens; Apr. to Sept., Mon. and Wed., also Fri. in Apr. and May. *Helston:* Borough museum, Mon. to Sat., except Wed. afternoon. *Lizard Lighthouse:* Mon. to Sat., afternoons, except in fog. *Pendennis Castle:* All year, weekdays, Sun. afternoons.

Craft workshop *Wendron:* Forge, daily. *Penryn:* Davey & Jordan, Commercial Road, Wrought ironwork, daily, Sat. mornings.

Events *Falmouth:* Folk Festival, mid-Aug. *Helston:* Flora Day and Horse Show, early May; Carnival, late Aug.; Harvest (Plum) Fair, early Sept. *Truro:* Antiques Fair, late June; Antique Collectors' Fair, early Oct.

Information *Newquay:* Morfa Hall, Cliff Road (Tel. Newquay 2119/2716).

Towns with easy access to Falmouth:

Newquay	27 m.	St Austell	25 m.
Penzance	26 m.	St Ives	25 m.

TRURO

Cornwall's administrative centre received its city status only in 1877, and completed its cathedral in 1910, incorporating part of the old 16th-century parish church. In earlier days it was described as 'in the pocket' of the Earls of Falmouth, the Boscawens, after whom the main thoroughfare is named. The adjoining streets, Lemon Street and Quay Street, have some of the best-preserved examples of Georgian architecture in Britain. The Lander monument in Lemon Street commemorates two Truro brothers, Richard and John, who in 1830 were the first explorers to trace the course of Africa's River Niger. The county museum contains a fine collection of Cornish prehistoric relics, minerals, flora, fauna, art and historical exhibits.

Beam engine, Wendron Forge.

WENDRON FORGE
Amid ancient graves and earthworks, holy wells and relics of old chapels on the moors, this little village of Wendron on the River Cober is best known for its early 19th-century forge. Modern craftsmen still work there, spending much of their time restoring the antique machines preserved in the forge museum. The old exhibits include such survivals as an 1850 pumping engine which was in constant use until 1959, and ornate hand-printing presses made in the 1840s which were used until 1968.

The annual Helston Furry Dance.

HELSTON
A market town of steep streets and attractive stone houses, Helston was an important port until the 13th century. Then a bank of sand and shingle, the Loe Bar, finally silted up the harbour mouth. Behind the Bar there is now a pretty inland lake. Helston was also a Stannary town, or administrative centre for the tin-mining industry. Every May the town echoes to the sound of the Furry Dance. No one knows why it is called the Furry Dance. It may be a corruption of 'fleur' or flower: hence the famous Cornish Floral Dance.

SCALE

| 0 | 1 | 2 | 3 | 4 | 5 MILES |

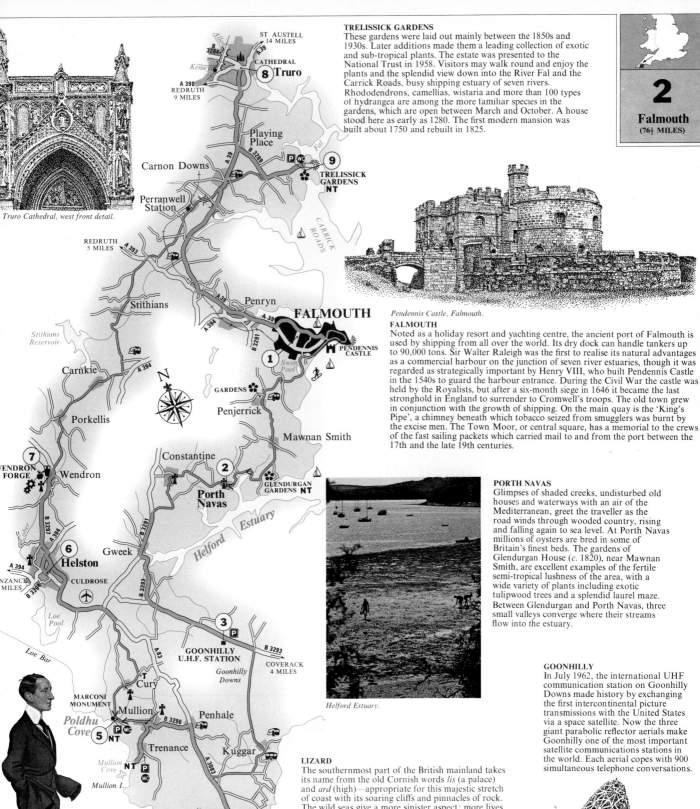

Truro Cathedral, west front detail.

TRELISSICK GARDENS

These gardens were laid out mainly between the 1850s and 1930s. Later additions made them a leading collection of exotic and sub-tropical plants. The estate was presented to the National Trust in 1958. Visitors may walk round and enjoy the plants and the splendid view down into the River Fal and the Carrick Roads, busy shipping estuary of seven rivers. Rhododendrons, camellias, wistaria and more than 100 types of hydrangea are among the more familiar species in the gardens, which are open between March and October. A house stood here as early as 1280. The first modern mansion was built about 1750 and rebuilt in 1825.

Pendennis Castle, Falmouth.

FALMOUTH

Noted as a holiday resort and yachting centre, the ancient port of Falmouth is used by shipping from all over the world. Its dry dock can handle tankers up to 90,000 tons. Sir Walter Raleigh was the first to realise its natural advantages as a commercial harbour on the junction of seven river estuaries, though it was regarded as strategically important by Henry VIII, who built Pendennis Castle in the 1540s to guard the harbour entrance. During the Civil War the castle was held by the Royalists, but after a six-month siege in 1646 it became the last stronghold in England to surrender to Cromwell's troops. The old town grew in conjunction with the growth of shipping. On the main quay is the 'King's Pipe', a chimney beneath which tobacco seized from smugglers was burnt by the excise men. The Town Moor, or central square, has a memorial to the crews of the fast sailing packets which carried mail to and from the port between the 17th and the late 19th centuries.

PORTH NAVAS

Glimpses of shaded creeks, undisturbed old houses and waterways with an air of the Mediterranean, greet the traveller as the road winds through wooded country, rising and falling again to sea level. At Porth Navas millions of oysters are bred in some of Britain's finest beds. The gardens of Glendurgan House (c. 1820), near Mawnan Smith, are excellent examples of the fertile semi-tropical lushness of the area, with a wide variety of plants including exotic tulipwood trees and a splendid laurel maze. Between Glendurgan and Porth Navas, three small valleys converge where their streams flow into the estuary.

Helford Estuary.

GOONHILLY

In July 1962, the international UHF communication station on Goonhilly Downs made history by exchanging the first intercontinental picture transmissions with the United States via a space satellite. Now the three giant parabolic reflector aerials make Goonhilly one of the most important satellite communications stations in the world. Each aerial copes with 900 simultaneous telephone conversations.

Guglielmo Marconi (1874–1937), the radio pioneer.

POLDHU

Only a stone remains to record the part this little cove has played in human affairs. Marconi carried out his first successful long-distance wireless transmission between here and Newfoundland, 3000 miles away, in 1901. Later, a permanent station was set up from which many new developments were pioneered. Until 1922 daily news bulletins were sent to ships at sea. In 1912 Poldhu received the news of the Titanic disaster. The remains of the old station lie behind the monument.

LIZARD

The southernmost part of the British mainland takes its name from the old Cornish words lis (a palace) and ard (high)—appropriate for this majestic stretch of coast with its soaring cliffs and pinnacles of rock. The wild seas give a more sinister aspect; more lives have been lost by shipwreck here than on any other part of the Cornish coast. In winter, when gales blow or mist settles, the land takes on an eerie quality. But from May or June, the downs burst into life with gorse and blossom. Fishing villages dot the coves. The lighthouse dates from the last century. The Lizard parish is officially Landewednack, with its granite and serpentine church of St Winwallo, a short distance from Lizard village. Nearby Kynance Cove, preserved by the National Trust, has magnificent cliff scenery.

Polished serpentine.

Television transmitter-receiver, Goonhilly Downs.

Woolcraft and witchcraft in the country of Camelot

Tintagel, Camelford, Slaughterbridge . . . names steeped in the legends of King Arthur and his Knights, and the Camelot immortalised by Tennyson. The early saints often left more tangible evidence of their influence in villages with names such as St Mawgan. Interspersed with the romance and history are man-made wonders like a bridge built on bales of wool, and the immense slate quarry at Delabole.

(1) Wadebridge to Port Isaac Leave the town on the A39, following the signpost to Bude, and turn left after the bridge, keeping on the A39. After ½ m. turn left on to the B3314, following the signpost to Port Isaac. Continue on the B3314 past St Endellion, then turn left on to the B3267 and follow the road into Port Isaac.

(2) Port Isaac to Delabole From the car park at the top of the village turn left and follow the road through Port Isaac past the beach at Port Gaverne. Continue to the junction with the B3314. Here turn left and follow the road into Delabole. To visit the quarry, turn right in the centre of the village, following the signpost to Pengelly.

(3) Delabole to Tintagel Return to Delabole and turn right. Just beyond the village turn left, following the signpost to Trebarwith. After ¼ m. turn right to follow the signpost to Trebarwith Strand. At the junction with the B3263 turn left, following the signpost to Tintagel. Continue through Trewarmett and into Tintagel, turning left at the T-junction to visit the castle.

(4) Tintagel to Boscastle Leave the village on the B3263, following the signpost to Boscastle. Continue through Bossiney, just beyond which are two attractive walks. A path to the left leads down Rocky Valley, an oasis of luxuriant greenery in this otherwise bare and rocky coast. On the right another path leads to St Nectan's Waterfall, a 40 ft drop in a small river. King Arthur's Round Table is, according to legend, buried in Bossiney Mound and rises from the ground on Midsummer's Eve. Continue into Boscastle.

(5) Boscastle to Slaughterbridge Return along the B3263 and turn left on to the B3266, following the signpost to Camelford. After about 3½ m., just before Camelford, turn left, following the signpost to Davidstow and reaching Slaughterbridge after 1 m.

(6) Slaughterbridge to Bodmin Return to the B3266 and follow the road through the outskirts of Camelford to the junction with the A39. Here turn right and then left on to B3266 again, following the signpost to Bodmin. From here the road skirts Bodmin Moor, with Rough Tor and Brown Willy, the highest points on the moor, dominating the skyline to the left of the road. Keep on the B3266 for about 10 m., then turn left on to the A389 signposted to Bodmin, and left again on to the A30 to Bodmin.

(7) Bodmin to St Mawgan Leave the town on the A30, following the signpost to Redruth, but at the de-limit sign turn right, following the signpost to Nanstallon. As the road bears right turn left, skirting Nanstallon and keeping on the road signposted to Ruthernbridge. At Ruthernbridge, cross the 14th-century bridge, following the signpost to Wadebridge, and keep on the road up into St Breock Downs. The rough heathland is reputedly haunted by Jan Tregeagle, steward to the Robartes family in the 17th century, who had an evil reputation for his treatment of the poor.

Turn left at the T-junction, following the signpost to Rosenannon. Go straight on at the crossroads in Rosenannon, and at the T-junction turn right to follow the signpost to St Columb Major. Go straight ahead on meeting the B3274, following the signpost to Padstow, but turn left through Tregamere. Turn left on to the A39 signposted to St Columb Major, but just before the town turn right. After ½ m. bear left, following the signpost to St Mawgan, keeping straight ahead to the T-junction. Here turn left and left again, following the road into St Mawgan.

(8) St Mawgan to Bedruthan Steps Leave the village on the road signposted to Mawgan Porth, turning left at the T-junction and down to the attractive beach. Leave Mawgan Porth on the B3276, following the signpost to Padstow through the village of Trenance. The entrance to Bedruthan Steps is about 1 m. along the road on the left.

(9) Bedruthan Steps to Padstow Return to the B3276, turning left and following the road to the centre of Padstow.

(10) Padstow to Wadebridge Leave Padstow on the A389. Turn left on to the A39 and follow this road back to Wadebridge.

INFORMATION

Places of interest *Bodmin:* Great Western Society Railway Museum, all year, Sat. and Sun., 12-5 p.m. Military Museum, all year except Mar. and Bank hols., Mon. to Fri., 9 a.m.-12.30 p.m. and 2-4.45 p.m. *Boscastle:* Museum of witchcraft and black magic, Easter to Oct., 10 a.m.-9 p.m. or dusk. *Delabole museum:* May to Oct., daily. *Padstow:* Bird garden, all year, daily, 10.30 a.m. to dusk. *Tintagel:* Castle, daily except Sun. mornings in winter. King Arthur's Hall of Chivalry, Easter to Oct., daily. Old Post Office, April 1 to Oct., weekdays, 11 a.m.-1 p.m., 2-6 p.m.; Sun., 2-6 p.m. *St Tudy:* Tremeer Gardens, Apr. and May, Sun. 2-6 p.m.

Events *Wadebridge:* Royal Cornwall Agricultural Show, early June. Traction-engine rally, weekend in mid-June. *St Endellion:* Music Festival, early Aug. *St Columb Major:* Shrove Tues. celebrations.

Information *Newquay:* Morfa Hall, Cliff Road (Tel. Newquay 2119/2716).

Towns with easy access to Wadebridge:

Bude . . . . 30 m.		Newquay . . . . . . 16 m.	
Launceston . . . . 27 m.		Redruth . . . . 30 m.	
Liskeard . . . . . . 20 m.		Truro . . . . 24 m.	

PADSTOW

This old-fashioned town on the Camel Estuary is thought to have been in existence before the arrival of St Petroc in the 6th century. It was certainly a busy port until the mid-19th century, when the silting occurred that produced Doom Bar and prevented larger ships from using the harbour. Among the more interesting buildings are Prideaux Place, a privately owned castellated Tudor house, and 16th-century Raleigh Court House, headquarters of Sir Walter Raleigh when he was Warden of Cornwall. One of the highlights of a visit to Padstow in spring is the May Day 'Hobby Hoss' celebration, in which colourfully dressed characters perform a dance and pantomime around a maypole in the market square—an old folk custom associated with fertility rites.

Padstow harbour.

BEDRUTHAN STEPS

This astonishing beach, 300 ft below the gorse-covered cliffs, is always deserted since there is no safe path down the crumbling shale. A series of stacks, or rocks, some as high as 200 ft, range across the sands, and are said to be the stepping-stones of the giant Bedruthan. At the northern end is a rock said to look like the profile of Elizabeth I.

ST MAWGAN

In the lovely vale of Lanherne the village sprawls round what was once the seat of the Arundel family. Lanherne House was given to a group of Carmelite nuns in the early 18th century, and is still a nunnery. Near by is the church of St Mawgan, where a fine lantern cross, elaborately carved, stands in the churchyard. There is also a monument in wood, like the stern of a boat, on which are the names of ten shipwrecked seamen whose frozen bodies were swept ashore at nearby Mawgan Porth in 1846.

Lantern cross, St Mawgan.

SCALE

0   1   2   3   4   5 MILES

PORT ISAAC
The old part of the village is a jumble of fishermen's cottages squeezed into a steep combe which runs down to the harbour. The old fish cellars, where fish were salted down and stored for export, are still in existence. Strict control of traffic and building has helped Port Isaac to retain much of its charm, and curiosities in house-building make the small streets and alleys the subject of fascinating exploration. Second to tourism, lobsters are the most important local industry, and the pots may often be seen in special pools in the attractive harbour.

The Padstow 'Hobby Hoss'.

DELABOLE
The slate quarry near Delabole is believed to have been worked continuously for over 350 years. It is no longer open to the public, but a path leads round to a viewing point from which to look into the 400 ft depths. The circumference is over a mile. Slate is still split by hand, and demonstrations may be seen at a nearby museum devoted to the history of slate quarrying in the district.

Delabole slate quarry.

The Old Post Office, Tintagel.

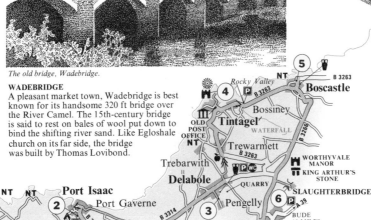

The old bridge, Wadebridge.

WADEBRIDGE
A pleasant market town, Wadebridge is best known for its handsome 320 ft bridge over the River Camel. The 15th-century bridge is said to rest on bales of wool put down to bind the shifting river sand. Like Egloshale church on its far side, the bridge was built by Thomas Lovibond.

TINTAGEL
The remains of Tintagel Castle lie on a wild headland, part of which has been almost severed from the mainland through weathering. As well as the ruined walls of a 12th-century castle, the area is strewn with the remains of a 6th-century Celtic Christian settlement. The setting teems with romance, and it is not surprising that Tintagel is a strong claimant to the title of King Arthur's legendary Camelot. Apart from the castle, the village's most interesting building is the Old Post Office, a miniature 14th-century manor house with an attractively uneven stone roof. It is now the property of the National Trust.

BOSCASTLE
A little harbour tucked away at the bottom of a steep glen gives a special charm to Boscastle. The inlet winds round two tall cliffs, and the harbour is protected by a breakwater built in 1584. From the rocks beyond the stone jetty it is possible to see and hear the famous blow-hole through which the sea grumbles and spouts at certain stages of the tide. The village is 400 ft above the harbour, and boasts a museum of witchcraft. Despite its name, there is no castle in the village; it is named after the Boscastle family who once lived there.

Blow-hole, near Boscastle.

SLAUGHTERBRIDGE
The Arthurian legend clings to many parts of Cornwall, even in this obscure spot. It is said that King Arthur fought his last battle with Mordred on the spot where a bridge of flat stones, with no arch, spans a tributary of the River Camel. In a grotto is a stone with a barely legible Latin inscription, translated as 'Here lies Latinus, son of Athorus'. The curious quiet of the grotto lends authenticity to the legend. The nearby market town of Camelford also lays claim to the Arthurian legend on the assumption that Camelot was sited by the River Camel.

BODMIN
Situated between a lovely valley and the moor which bears its name, Bodmin has a long history. St Guron the hermit is said to have lived here in the 6th century; a fountain, bubbling from the mouths of two stone heads in the walls of St Petroc's Church, is named after him. St Petroc's is the largest church in Cornwall and houses a remarkable 12th-century stone font. Five pillars, four of which are surmounted by angels, support an elaborately carved bowl almost 3 ft in diameter. Also in the church is a carved ivory casket, probably of oriental origin and dating from the 12th century, in which the bones of St Petroc were returned to Bodmin after they had been stolen by a monk in 1177. The regimental museum of the Duke of Cornwall's Light Infantry, which has a fascinating collection of guns, is near the station.

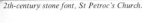

12th-century stone font, St Petroc's Church.

A land of Celtic saints—and smugglers

The Fowey and Looe rivers rise in the granite starkness of Bodmin Moor before cutting through green wooded valleys to their namesake ports on the English Channel. The land between the rivers abounds with evidence of Cornwall's pious Celtic past—churches and villages named after native saints, wayside crosses and even a holy well. The coast has a different history, in which wreckers and smugglers take the leading roles.

(1) Fowey to Polruan Take the car ferry across the Fowey River to Bodinnick, a small village straggling up a steep hill. On landing, follow the road left away from the quay and turn right on the road signposted to Polruan. Turn right at the T-junction at the foot of the hill and continue to Polruan.

(2) Polruan to Lansallos Return from the village and at the next junction keep right on the road signposted to Polperro. On the right of this lane there is access to several cliff walks and National Trust beaches. After 3 m., at the T-junction, turn right following the signpost to Lansallos.

(3) Lansallos to Polperro Drive on through the village, passing the church, and turn right at the T-junction following the Polperro signpost. Then take the next turn left and continue to the junction with the A387, where there are two large car parks. These must be used in summer because cars are forbidden to go further into the village. The centre of Polperro is about 400 yds from the car park.

(4) Polperro to Looe Leave Polperro on the A387 signposted to Looe, which is reached 4½ m. later.

(5) Looe to Murrayton Leave the town on the A387 following the Plymouth signpost. After ¼ m. turn right on to the B3253 signposted to Hessenford. After 2 m. turn right off this road on to a minor road signposted to Seaton. Turn right again, following the signpost to Murrayton. Drive into the village. The Woolly Monkey Sanctuary is signposted.

(6) Murrayton to St Cleer Return to the B3253, turn right and after 1¼ m. turn sharp left on to the A387 and into Widegates. Follow the A387 for ¼ m., then fork right on the road signposted to Liskeard. After ½ m. turn right on to the B3252, again signposted Liskeard. At the next crossroads turn right on to the B3251 signposted Menheniot. After 1 m. cross the A38, still following the Menheniot signpost. In the village keep ahead on the road signposted to Merrymeet. After ½ m., at the T-junction, turn left following the St Cleer signpost and soon afterwards take the left fork. Follow the road and keep left at the junction just before the A390. Go straight across the A390 on to the road signposted to St Cleer, and after 1 m., as the road bears right, turn left across the B3254. At the next crossroads turn right into St Cleer.

(7) St Cleer to King Doniert's Stone Follow the road through St Cleer, keeping right at the end of the village, and at the T-junction turn left, following the sign to Dobwalls. King Doniert's Stone is ¼ m. along the road on the left.

(8) King Doniert's Stone to Lanhydrock House Continue on the road past the stone and after ½ m. turn right on the road signposted to Bolventor and then left, across a bridge following the signpost to Draynes. Follow the road through the village and across moorland to a T-junction and turn right on the road signposted to St Neot. Turn right again and into St Neot. The church there has 15 stained-glass windows which are almost 500 years old. These contain 300 figures and tell the stories of Noah, St George and St Neot himself. Continue through St Neot on the road signposted to Mount. Immediately after leaving Mount, fork left, and at the next junction turn left, following the signpost to Bodmin. Turn left at the next T-junction and follow the road to the junction with the A38 and turn left, signposted Liskeard. After ½ m., by a Celtic cross, turn right on the road signposted to Lostwithiel. At the junction with the B3268 is the entrance to Lanhydrock House.

(9) Lanhydrock House to Lostwithiel Turn left on to the B3268 which 3 m. later runs into Lostwithiel. The 13th-century church in the town has a Breton look, showing the close links between Cornwall and Brittany.

(10) Lostwithiel to Restormel Castle Join the A390 going east towards Liskeard, and just beyond the town centre the road to Restormel Castle goes off to the left. The castle is just over 1 m. up the road.

(11) Restormel Castle to Fowey Return to the centre of Lostwithiel and leave on the A390 signposted to St Austell. After 1½ m. turn left on to the B3269 signposted to Fowey. On this road there are views of the white-china clay heaps of St Austell in the distance. After 4 m. join the A3082 and follow it into Fowey.

INFORMATION

Places of interest *Fowey:* St Catherine's Fort, daily, 9 a.m. to dusk. *Lanhydrock House:* Apr. to Oct., daily; Gardens only, Nov. to Mar., daily until dusk. *Looe:* Cornish museum, Easter weekend, May to end Sept., daily. Paul Corin Playing Musical Collection, May to Sept., daily; Oct. to Apr., Sat., Sun. afternoons. *Polperro:* Smugglers' museum. May to mid-Oct., weekdays, 10 a.m.-6 p.m., Sun., 2-5.30 p.m. *Restormel Castle:* Weekdays, Sun. afternoons; May to Sept., daily. *Murrayton:* Woolly Monkey Sanctuary, Apr. to mid-Oct., daily.

Craft workshops *Fowey:* Foye Forge, copper, pewter and silver jewellery, Mon. to Fri. *Polperro:* Paula Humphris Pottery Workshop, Mill Hill. Call at workshop or Rose Cottage any reasonable time.

Information *Plymouth:* Municipal Offices (Tel. Plymouth 68000).

Towns with easy access to Fowey:

Falmouth	30 m.	St Austell	9 m.
Newquay	25 m.	Tavistock	37 m.

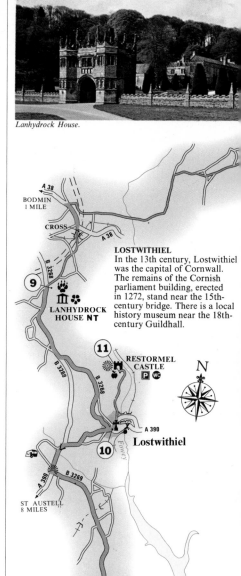

Lanhydrock House.

LOSTWITHIEL
In the 13th century, Lostwithiel was the capital of Cornwall. The remains of the Cornish parliament building, erected in 1272, stand near the 15th-century bridge. There is a local history museum near the 18th-century Guildhall.

FOWEY
There is an opulent air among the narrow streets and attractive houses of Fowey that is unusual in a Cornish coastal town. For, though small, it is a thriving commercial port which since the Middle Ages has supported trade rather than fishing. Now it is expanding to accommodate both the continuing world demand for Cornish china clay and the upsurge in yachting for pleasure. Close to the quay is Trafalgar Square, containing the town hall, the old gaol, the aquarium and the museum. Another museum, devoted to Cornish domestic life, is housed in Noah's Ark, the oldest house in the town, in Fore Street. Place House, near by, is where the townsfolk are said to have held out against the French who raided Fowey in 1457. In 1838 the mansion was made more impressive by the addition of a granite tower higher than that of the nearby 14th-century church of St Fimbarrus.

SCALE
0   1   2   3 MILES

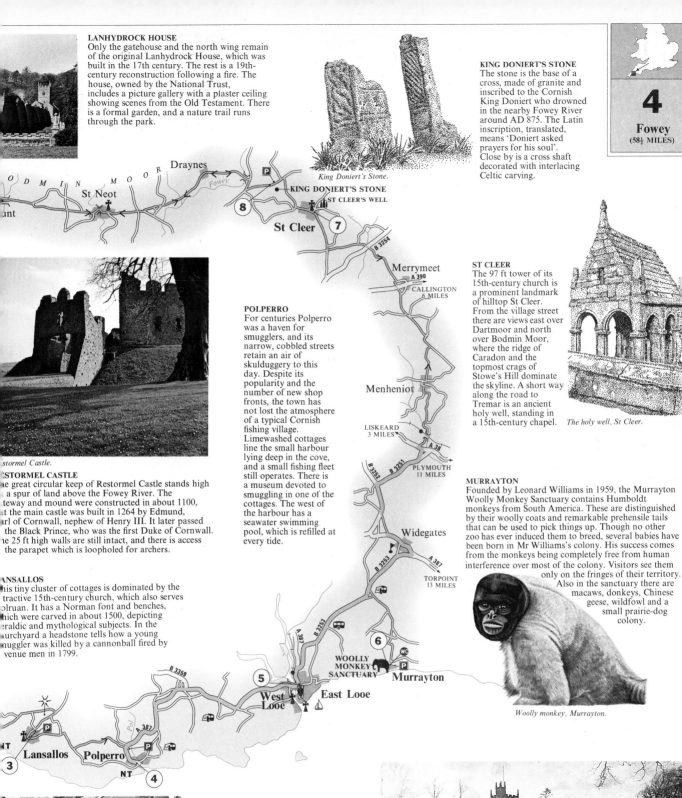

LANHYDROCK HOUSE
Only the gatehouse and the north wing remain of the original Lanhydrock House, which was built in the 17th century. The rest is a 19th-century reconstruction following a fire. The house, owned by the National Trust, includes a picture gallery with a plaster ceiling showing scenes from the Old Testament. There is a formal garden, and a nature trail runs through the park.

King Doniert's Stone.

KING DONIERT'S STONE
The stone is the base of a cross, made of granite and inscribed to the Cornish King Doniert who drowned in the nearby Fowey River around AD 875. The Latin inscription, translated, means 'Doniert asked prayers for his soul'. Close by is a cross shaft decorated with interlacing Celtic carving.

stormel Castle.

RESTORMEL CASTLE
The great circular keep of Restormel Castle stands high on a spur of land above the Fowey River. The gateway and mound were constructed in about 1100, but the main castle was built in 1264 by Edmund, Earl of Cornwall, nephew of Henry III. It later passed to the Black Prince, who was the first Duke of Cornwall. The 25 ft high walls are still intact, and there is access to the parapet which is loopholed for archers.

LANSALLOS
This tiny cluster of cottages is dominated by the attractive 15th-century church, which also serves Polruan. It has a Norman font and benches, which were carved in about 1500, depicting heraldic and mythological subjects. In the churchyard a headstone tells how a young smuggler was killed by a cannonball fired by revenue men in 1799.

POLPERRO
For centuries Polperro was a haven for smugglers, and its narrow, cobbled streets retain an air of skulduggery to this day. Despite its popularity and the number of new shop fronts, the town has not lost the atmosphere of a typical Cornish fishing village. Limewashed cottages line the small harbour lying deep in the cove, and a small fishing fleet still operates. There is a museum devoted to smuggling in one of the cottages. The west of the harbour has a seawater swimming pool, which is refilled at every tide.

ST CLEER
The 97 ft tower of its 15th-century church is a prominent landmark of hilltop St Cleer. From the village street there are views east over Dartmoor and north over Bodmin Moor, where the ridge of Caradon and the topmost crags of Stowe's Hill dominate the skyline. A short way along the road to Tremar is an ancient holy well, standing in a 15th-century chapel.

The holy well, St Cleer.

MURRAYTON
Founded by Leonard Williams in 1959, the Murrayton Woolly Monkey Sanctuary contains Humboldt monkeys from South America. These are distinguished by their woolly coats and remarkable prehensile tails that can be used to pick things up. Though no other zoo has ever induced them to breed, several babies have been born in Mr Williams's colony. His success comes from the monkeys being completely free from human interference over most of the colony. Visitors see them only on the fringes of their territory. Also in the sanctuary there are macaws, donkeys, Chinese geese, wildfowl and a small prairie-dog colony.

Woolly monkey, Murrayton.

LOOE
East and West Looe are joined by a seven-arched bridge built in the last century. West Looe centres on St Nicholas's Church, much of which was built in the last century from the timbers of wrecked ships. Near by is a 16th-century inn, The Jolly Sailors, thought to have been a favourite haunt of smugglers. East Looe has a 16th-century guildhall which houses a museum on the upper floor. The ground floor, which was used as a gaol, still contains the town stocks and pillory. St Martin's Church, which retains some Norman features, notably the north door, is a mile from the town centre on the road towards Murrayton.

Church of St Martin, East Looe.

lruan, seen from Fowey.

POLRUAN
This is a village whose inhabitants have traditionally been fishermen and boat-builders. From the quay there are excellent views of Fowey. On a rocky outcrop are the ruins of the 15th-century blockhouse, from which a chain was stretched across to Fowey to block the river mouth protecting pirates from the authorities.

By towering cliffs along England's sternest coast

Vast subterranean upheavals millions of years ago squeezed this Devon and Cornwall borderland into tucks and folds. The Atlantic breakers slashed into it, to bare the jumbled strata in spectacular cliffs. It is an eccentric area, with villages like Clovelly, where the milk is delivered by donkeys; Great Torrington, where Scandinavian craftsmen shape Dartington glass; and Morwenstow, where a poet-priest had his vicarage chimneys made to look like the church towers of his former parishes.

(1) Bude to Coombe Valley Leave the town on the road signposted to Poughill, going past the golf course. In Poughill (pronounced 'Poffil') the ancient St Olaf's Church has a lock in the south door nearly 2 ft long. Keep straight ahead through the village, and at the next crossroads turn left, following the signpost for Coombe Valley. After just under 2 m., in the hamlet of Stibb, turn left at the T-junction. After ½ m. there is a road to the left leading to the beach at Sandy Mouth. Follow the road right to reach Coombe Valley, where a nature trail starts close to the old mill.

(2) Coombe Valley to Morwenstow Continue along the same road northwards for about 2 m., passing the UHF transmission dish aerials on the left. Turn left at the T-junction and into Morwenstow.

(3) Morwenstow to Welcombe Mouth Return along the same road, keeping ahead at the junction. After just under 1 m. bear right at the fork in the road and into the quaintly named village of Shop. Turn left here at the T-junction, following the signs for Kilkhampton. After about 1½ m. turn left on to the A39 to follow the signs for Bideford. After about 1½ m., shortly after crossing the county boundary into Devon, turn left, following the signpost to Welcombe. Bear left by the common, and at the bottom of the descent turn sharp left on to a rough but serviceable track to Welcombe Mouth.

(4) Welcombe Mouth to Hartland Return along the track to the road and turn left. After about 2½ m. enter the village of Elmscott and turn left to follow the signpost for Stoke. Continue for about 1 m. to pass through Lymebridge, and at the next crossroads turn right, then fork left. At the following T-junction, turn left to follow the signs for Stoke and Hartland Quay. To visit Hartland Quay turn left at the T-junction in Stoke and continue to the picnic site overlooking the sea. Return by the same road to Stoke, and keep straight ahead at the junction to follow the signposts for Hartland. The road passes, on the left, the site of the old Hartland Abbey, and continues to the village. To visit Hartland Point, as the road bears sharp right to enter the village centre, turn left. Follow this road to the right. Soon afterwards turn left to follow the Hartland Point signpost. Cross the bridge and turn right. After 2½ m. reach Hartland Point with its car park and lighthouse. Return by the same road to Hartland.

(5) Hartland to Clovelly Go through the village and continue straight ahead to join the B3248. After 3 m., where the road bears sharp right, turn left to follow the sign for Clovelly. Turn left at the T-junction on to the B3237, and continue to the car park above Clovelly which, with its steep, cobbled streets, has remained virtually unchanged for more than 100 years.

(6) Clovelly to Great Torrington Return along the B3237 and turn left on to the A39. After ¼ m. turn right to follow the sign for Woolfardisworthy. After just over 1 m., at the Kennerland Cross crossroads, turn left to follow the signposts for Parkham. After 3½ m. turn left at the T-junction and into Parkham village, turning right by the Bell Inn to follow the Buckland signpost. Turn left at the crossroads to follow the signpost for Bideford and continue along the River Yeo Valley. After just over 3 m. cross the river and turn right, following the signpost to Monkleigh. Turn right at the T-junction on to the A388 and into Monkleigh. Here turn left, and immediately bear right to follow the sign for Great Torrington. After 1½ m. turn left at the T-junction and right on to the A386. After 1 m. enter Great Torrington. (The road to the Dartington Glassworks is opposite the church.)

(7) Great Torrington to Holsworthy Return along the A386 and turn left on to the B3227, following the Holsworthy signposts. After just under 5 m. the B3227 merges into the A388 and continues for about 6 m. into Holsworthy.

(8) Holsworthy to Stratton Leave the town by the A3072, following the signposts to Bude. After about 8 m. the road crosses a bridge and enters Stratton.

(9) Stratton to Bude Return across the bridge and immediately turn right down Howard Lane. Follow the road, bearing right at a junction and turn right at the crossroads into Marhamchurch. Turn left by the Bullers' Arms Inn to follow the signpost for Week St Mary. After 1 m. turn sharp right to follow the signpost to Widemouth Bay. Go straight across the A39 to visit the bay. Continue on this road through the village and follow the coast for 3 m. back into Bude.

INFORMATION

Places of interest *Bude:* Ebbingford Manor, summer, Tues., Wed., Thur.; also July to Sept., Sun., 2-5.30 p.m. *Coombe Valley:* Nature trail.

Events *Bideford:* Andrews Dole, Jan.; Manor Court, Sat. after Easter. *Bude:* Blessing of the sea, Aug. *Great Torrington:* Fair Celebrations, May.

Information West Country Tourist Board, Trinity Court, Southernhay East, Exeter (Tel. Exeter 76351).

Towns with easy access to Bude:

Barnstaple	35 m.	Camelford	19 m.
Bideford	26 m.	Launceston	19 m.

Rocks at Hartland Point.

WELCOMBE MOUTH
Although it is over the Devon boundary, Welcombe village remains entirely Cornish in character. Close to the church, dedicated to the Celtic St Nectan, is a holy well. At Welcombe Mouth, the cliffs have been eroded to expose a cross-section of the contorted rock formations, which show up as clearly as a geological chart. A 5 mile coastal lane leads north through clifftop scenery to Hartland Quay.

Pelican and young, roof boss in Morwenstow church.

MORWENSTOW
Morwenstow, Cornwall's northernmost parish, was once the base of wreckers who signalled ships to their doom on the perilous Hartland Point rocks in order to plunder their cargoes. One of the memorials in the churchyard is the figurehead of the Scottish ship *Caledonia*, wrecked in 1843 with the loss of over 40 of her crew, who were buried there. The vicar, who made a point of giving Christian burial to many an unknown sailor washed ashore near his church, was the poet R. S. Hawker, who wrote the song with the line 'and shall Trelawney die?' The chimneys of his vicarage are miniatures of the church towers of his previous parishes.

BUDE
The main attraction of Bude is as an outdoor holiday centre. The Atlantic breakers that pound on its beaches, half a mile from the town, make it a surfing centre comparable with Australia's Bondi Beach. The canal which links it, via the River Neet, with Holsworthy was once a busy shipping lane. Now it is used only for boating and fishing, but the towpath offers an interesting walk of 2 or 3 miles. The castle, now occupied as council offices, was built by the inventor Sir Goldsworthy Gurney, who drove the first mechanical vehicle to run on a British road—a 15 mph steam coach. He laid a bed of concrete, as a foundation for the castle, on the shifting sands just above highwater mark; it is due to his skill that the castle still stands after 130 years. Ebbingford Manor, once the home of the geographer Sir Dudley Stamp, is open to the public.

SCALE

0   1   2   3   4   5   MILES

HARTLAND

This small village on the Devon side of the border is a convenient stopping place from which to explore the coast reaching out to Hartland Point, at the entrance to the Bristol Channel. Here many a ship, trapped by an onshore wind, has been dashed to pieces on the rocks that litter the sea beneath soaring cliffs. The lighthouse, perched 120 ft up on the point, flashes its warning of this seaman's graveyard. It is open to the public in the afternoons when the weather is clear. Hartland is 1 mile east of the site of what little remains of Hartland Abbey, founded in the 11th century and converted into a private house by Henry VIII's wine cellarer after the Dissolution of the Monasteries. St John's Church, which stands on the site of the old town hall, has one of England's earliest pendulum clocks, made in 1622 by John Morcombe. Hartland Quay, 2½ m. beyond the village, was a fishing community until storms wrecked the quay in the 19th century.

A street in Clovelly.

CLOVELLY

'A village like a waterfall' is how it has been described. This is Clovelly, where the stepped streets tumble to the sea so precipitously that the ground floor of one cottage may be level with its neighbour's roof. If a villager moves house, the furniture has to be shifted on sledges. Donkeys pick their way over the narrow cobbled alleyways bringing the daily deliveries to and from the shops. Visiting motorists must leave their cars at the park overlooking the rooftops, but there is a local Land-Rover service between there and a point closer to the village to cut down the walking. Clovelly, claimed to be like no other village in the country, descends to a tiny harbour sheltered by a stone quay from which boat trips can be made. The church, approached by a fine avenue of yews, stands on the clifftop, and near by is Clovelly Dykes, an Iron Age hill-fort of concentric banks separated by ditches.

Emperor dragonfly

COOMBE VALLEY

The 1½ mile nature trail which begins in this wooded and peaceful spot passes a pre-Roman earthwork known locally as Buberchurch. A 12th-century castle, whose ruins can be seen, is believed to have been built illegally and consequently demolished by order of Henry II. A mill at the beginning of the trail, built in 1842, was in use until recently.

GREAT TORRINGTON

A market centre since Saxon times, Great Torrington is sited on a hill between its castle and the River Torridge. During the Civil War it was the scene of fierce fighting, and the church was used as a lock-up for several hundred Royalists captured by Cromwell's troops. The troops used it also as a gunpowder store, until an explosion blew it to pieces. The disaster is commemorated by an inscribed stone in the present church, which was built in 1651. Great Torrington's best-known local industry is the Dartington Glassworks.

HOLSWORTHY

Wednesday is the best time to see Holsworthy for visitors who enjoy the bustle of a typical market town. Its major claim to fame is that in 1861 it was the last place in England where a man was sent to the stocks. The church of St Peter and St Paul dates from about 1250, and stands on the site of a 12th-century Norman chapel. Additions and alterations were made in 1366 and during the 19th century. The tall, pinnacled tower was added in about 1450. The most striking feature of the church is the carillon, which plays tunes to mark the hours. An entry in the parish register records that in 1722 John Gimlett was paid 5s. 'for keeping ye dogs from ye church'.

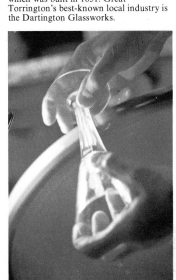

Glass-blower, Great Torrington.

STRATTON

Much older than its twin town of Bude, Stratton probably dates from Roman times and was a centre of the salt industry in the Middle Ages. It is a jumble of narrow streets and quaint houses. St Andrew's Church, dating from 1348, was originally Bude's church also. It has a number of later additions and has been substantially restored. A large brass commemorates Sir John Arundel, a Lord of the Manor, and his two wives. He lived through the reigns of six sovereigns, from Henry VII to Elizabeth I, without falling from favour. But the village's most famous resident was the 7 ft 4 in. 'Cornish Giant' Anthony Payne, who lived and died at the local Tree Inn and who led Royalist troops at the Battle of Stamford Hill in 1643.

Along the Tamar Valley to the sound of Drake's Drum

Bleak Dartmoor dips down into the winding Tamar Valley to form the intriguing landscape centred on Tavistock. This is a country which bred gallant men and wild robber bands. Sir Francis Drake was born here, and his famous drum is preserved at stately Buckland Abbey. In Lydford Gorge, in the 17th century, the Gubbins Gang hid from a law which was branded locally with the slogan 'Hang now, try later'.

1 Tavistock to Sheepstor Leave Tavistock following the signs to Princetown. Join the B3357, and after the cattle-grid turn right at the crossroads following the signpost to Horrabridge. Bear right at the fork and keep ahead at the next crossroads. Take the left fork after Plasterdown Army Camp and at the next crossroads keep ahead, following the signpost to Walkhampton. Bear left in the village, following the signpost to Dousland, cross the B3212 and just beyond Dousland turn left to follow the signpost to Burrator. Keep ahead at the junction by the dam and follow the perimeter road right round the reservoir. There is a succession of excellent views from this road and it is possible to park and walk among the surrounding woods. At the T-junction turn left into Sheepstor.

2 Sheepstor to Lee Moor Leave Sheepstor on the road past the church and bear right at the fork. At the crossroads turn right, following the signpost to Meavy, and at the T-junction turn left into Meavy. In the village turn left and left again just after the church. At the crossroads turn left, following the signpost to Ivybridge, and at the next crossroads turn left, again following the signpost to Ivybridge. Take the next turning right, and at the junction by Cadover Bridge bear left. After ¼ m. a track leads off to the left to Trowlesworthy Warren Nature Trail. Keep straight on and after 1½ m. reach Lee Moor spoil tips.

3 Lee Moor to Dartmoor Wildlife Park Keep along the same road as far as Cornwood and turn right at the Cornwood Inn, following the signpost to Sparkwell. Turn right again and after 1½ m. the entrance to Dartmoor Wildlife Park is on the right.

4 Dartmoor Wildlife Park to Saltram House Return to the road and turn right, following the road through Sparkwell as far as Plympton. At the T-junction by the railway bridge turn left, following the signpost to Plymouth. After the bridge turn right and right again on to the A374, again signposted Plymouth. After ½ m. turn left at the signpost to Saltram House, and at the T-junction turn right. Saltram House is on the right.

5 Saltram House to Buckland Abbey Retrace the route back to Plympton. Here turn left at the signpost to Shaugh Prior. Turn left at the crossroads at Beatland Corner and follow the road through Shaugh Prior. Bear right just beyond the bridge, and then right again, following the signpost to Yelverton. Turn right at a T-junction into Clearbrook and after crossing the river turn left to follow the signpost to Meavy. At the next crossroads turn left, signposted Yelverton. At the junction with the A386 turn left, signposted Plymouth, and immediately right, signposted Buckland Abbey. Follow the road through Crapstone and 1 m. later, just beyond the crossroads, turn right to the abbey.

6 Buckland Abbey to Morwellham On leaving the abbey turn sharp left, following the signpost to Buckland Monachorum. At the T-junction turn left and shortly afterwards take the left fork. Turn right to cross the bridge, go uphill and turn right again 1 m. later following the signpost to Tavistock. At the T-junction by the milestone turn right and, bearing left, follow the road across the hill. As the road re-enters woodland turn sharp left at the crossroads and follow the road into Morwellham.

7 Morwellham to Cotehele House Return to the crossroads and turn left. At the junction with the A390 turn left, following the signpost to Callington. Go through Gunnislake and ½ m. after the railway bridge turn left at the signpost to Cotehele House. Turn left at a crossroads and follow the road through Norris Green. Turn right after the village, and then left. Follow the road to Cotehele House.

8 Cotehele House to Lydford Return to the A390 and turn left, following the signpost to Callington. After 1 m. turn right on to the B3257, signposted to Launceston. Turn right at the signpost to Stoke Climsland, follow the road through Downgate and bear right, still following the signpost for Stoke Climsland. Go through the village and turn right at the next crossroads. Bear left after the bridge at Horsebridge and immediately right to follow the signpost to Lamerton. After ½ m. turn left at the crossroads and follow the road through Sydenham Damerel. Go straight over the A384 and the three following crossroads. At the T-junction by Brent Tor turn left and follow the road for 3½ m. into Lydford.

9 Lydford to Tavistock Continue through Lydford and at the junction with the A386 turn right, signposted to Tavistock. Follow the road for 8 m. and enter Tavistock.

INFORMATION

Places of interest *Buckland Abbey:* Good Friday to end Sept., weekdays, Sun. afternoons; rest of year, Wed., Sat., Sun., 3-5 p.m. *Cotehele House:* Apr. to end Oct., daily; garden, winter, daily. *Dartmoor Wildlife Park:* All year, daily, 10 a.m. to dusk. *Saltram House:* Apr. to end Oct., daily; garden, Nov. to March, daily.

Information *Plymouth:* Municipal Offices, Armada Way (Tel. Plymouth 68000).

Towns with easy access to Tavistock:

Bodmin	32 m.	Plymouth	15 m.
Exeter	34 m.	Torquay	35 m.

COTEHELE HOUSE
Almost unaltered since the early 17th century, Cotehele House is a good example of an early Tudor manor house. It was built by Richard Edgecumbe, who led a local rebellion against Richard III and fought for Henry VII at Bosworth Field. Richly furnished, the rooms are lined with tapestries, and there is an impressive array of armour, weapons and hunting trophies in the great hall. The estate slopes down to the River Tamar and contains a nature trail just over a mile long.

Cotehele House.

Morwellham Quay at the turn of the century.

MORWELLHAM
Once the busiest port west of Exeter, Morwellham ceased to function at the beginning of this century after 900 years of activity. Now its quays on the River Tamar, which once shipped ore from Devon's copper and manganese mines, have been restored and turned into an outdoor museum and recreation centre. There are marked trails round the quays and out to the 1½ mile long Tavistock Canal tunnel which carried ore to the harbour.

Model of the Golden Hind, Buckland Abbey.

BUCKLAND ABBEY
Built by Cistercian monks in 1278, Buckland Abbey was converted into a private house by Sir Richard Grenville, the sea captain renowned for his gallant fight against a Spanish fleet in his tiny ship, *Revenge*, in the 16th century. Sir Francis Drake bought the abbey in 1581, after returning from his voyage round the world in the *Golden Hind*. The house incorporates the tower of the original abbey church. Drake's drawing-room, with a portrait of fellow voyager, Sir John Hawkins, over the fireplace, and the Elizabethan hall are preserved. Among many relics of the famous seaman is the legendary Drake's Drum, and a model of the *Golden Hind* forms part of a collection of model ships. There is also an exhibition of local folk industry and a carriage museum in a 14th-century tithe barn, all set in beautiful gardens.

SCALE

0   1   2   3   4   5 MILES

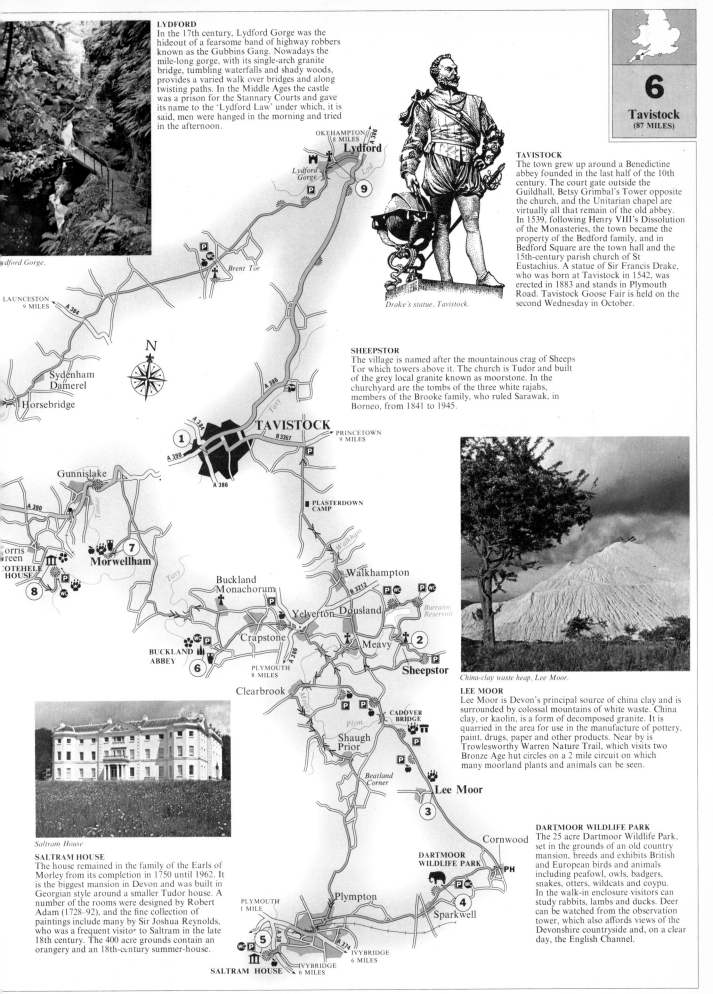

LYDFORD

In the 17th century, Lydford Gorge was the hideout of a fearsome band of highway robbers known as the Gubbins Gang. Nowadays the mile-long gorge, with its single-arch granite bridge, tumbling waterfalls and shady woods, provides a varied walk over bridges and along twisting paths. In the Middle Ages the castle was a prison for the Stannary Courts and gave its name to the 'Lydford Law' under which, it is said, men were hanged in the morning and tried in the afternoon.

...ydford Gorge.

TAVISTOCK

The town grew up around a Benedictine abbey founded in the last half of the 10th century. The court gate outside the Guildhall, Betsy Grimbal's Tower opposite the church, and the Unitarian chapel are virtually all that remain of the old abbey. In 1539, following Henry VIII's Dissolution of the Monasteries, the town became the property of the Bedford family, and in Bedford Square are the town hall and the 15th-century parish church of St Eustachius. A statue of Sir Francis Drake, who was born at Tavistock in 1542, was erected in 1883 and stands in Plymouth Road. Tavistock Goose Fair is held on the second Wednesday in October.

Drake's statue, Tavistock.

SHEEPSTOR

The village is named after the mountainous crag of Sheeps Tor which towers above it. The church is Tudor and built of the grey local granite known as moorstone. In the churchyard are the tombs of the three white rajahs, members of the Brooke family, who ruled Sarawak, in Borneo, from 1841 to 1945.

China-clay waste heap, Lee Moor.

LEE MOOR

Lee Moor is Devon's principal source of china clay and is surrounded by colossal mountains of white waste. China clay, or kaolin, is a form of decomposed granite. It is quarried in the area for use in the manufacture of pottery, paint, drugs, paper and other products. Near by is Trowlesworthy Warren Nature Trail, which visits two Bronze Age hut circles on a 2 mile circuit on which many moorland plants and animals can be seen.

Saltram House

SALTRAM HOUSE

The house remained in the family of the Earls of Morley from its completion in 1750 until 1962. It is the biggest mansion in Devon and was built in Georgian style around a smaller Tudor house. A number of the rooms were designed by Robert Adam (1728–92), and the fine collection of paintings include many by Sir Joshua Reynolds, who was a frequent visitor to Saltram in the late 18th century. The 400 acre grounds contain an orangery and an 18th-century summer-house.

DARTMOOR WILDLIFE PARK

The 25 acre Dartmoor Wildlife Park, set in the grounds of an old country mansion, breeds and exhibits British and European birds and animals including peafowl, owls, badgers, snakes, otters, wildcats and coypu. In the walk-in enclosure visitors can study rabbits, lambs and ducks. Deer can be watched from the observation tower, which also affords views of the Devonshire countryside and, on a clear day, the English Channel.

Sand, surf and rocky coves on Devon's Atlantic coast

From ancient Barnstaple, a busy town for more than 1000 years, the tour takes in part of Devon's Atlantic coast. At Saunton and Woolacombe there are long stretches of sand, ideal for bathing and surfing. Further east, there are tiny beaches with rock pools in coves between high cliffs, and wooded streams which rush down rocky paths from Exmoor to the sea at Woody Bay and Lynmouth. Inland, there is a great country estate, Arlington, held in trust for the nation.

(1) Barnstaple to Braunton Leave Barnstaple on the A361 signposted to Ilfracombe. There are good views of the River Taw Estuary to the left. In Braunton, go straight ahead at the traffic lights to see the church, which is just off the A361 to the right.

(2) Braunton to Croyde From the traffic lights in Braunton, take the B3231 signposted to Croyde. On the left is the 300 acre Braunton Great Field, which was still cultivated under the medieval system of strip tenure into the 1960s. It is now largely a bulb farm. Beyond it is Braunton Burrows National Nature Reserve, which has two marked 1½ m. nature trails, one exploring the extensive sand dunes and the other, the seashore. The road passes through Saunton, with downland rising to 528 ft on the right and the flat broad 3 m. stretch of Saunton Sands running southwards to the left. The road then bears right round the headland which forms the southern boundary of Croyde Bay, and into Croyde. Turn left in the centre of the village to visit Croyde Bay and Baggy Point.

(3) Croyde to Woolacombe Return to the B3231 and turn left following the signpost to Woolacombe. The road passes through Georgeham and rises to 630 ft, giving good views over Woolacombe Down to Morte Bay. About 1½ m. from Georgeham, turn left on to a minor road which leads steeply down to the village of Woolacombe.

(4) Woolacombe to Ilfracombe Follow the sea front road north through Woolacombe as it climbs steeply to the adjoining village of Mortehoe. This lies a short distance inland from Morte Point, owned by the National Trust. Go through Mortehoe and at the junction with the B3343 bear left, following the Ilfracombe signpost. Cross the disused railway line, bear left on to the B3231 and then turn left on to the road signposted to Lee. At the junction with the A361, bear left into Ilfracombe.

(5) Ilfracombe to Combe Martin Leave the centre of the town on the A399 signposted to Lynton, but turn off right on to the road signposted to Barnstaple (the B3230, but not marked on the signpost). At the T-junction turn left, still on the B3230, and at the crossroads 1 m. further on, turn left on to the B3343. After 2¼ m., where the B3343 turns right, bear left, then right, downhill to Combe Martin. Turn left at the T-junction with the A399, down the main road to the sea.

(6) Combe Martin to The Valley of Rocks Return from the sea front, and just before the Pack of Cards Inn turn left up Shute Lane, which rises steeply up to the plateau of Exmoor. After 2½ m. turn left at the crossroads, signposted Hunter's Inn. As the road nears the sea, passing between Holdstone and Trentishoe Downs, there are good views over the Bristol Channel. The road soon dips into an oak-wooded valley which joins the deep coastal valley, cut by the River Heddon, at Hunter's Inn. A nature trail leads from here to the coast. Turn left in front of the hotel up a steep winding road signposted to Martinhoe. Turn left at the T-junction, bear right through Martinhoe and bear left to Woody Bay. Bear right to Slattenslade and, 1½ m. beyond it, join the toll road to Lynton. Pay the toll at Lee Bay and continue past Lee Abbey into The Valley of Rocks.

(7) The Valley of Rocks to Lynton Carry on through the valley—watch out for the White Lady, a gap in the rocks on the left—and into Lynton.

(8) Lynton to Waters Meet Turn sharp left on to the B3234 and into Lynmouth. Leave Lynmouth on the A39 signposted to Barnstaple, following the wooded gorge of the East Lyn to Waters Meet.

(9) Waters Meet to Arlington Court About ¾ m. beyond the Waters Meet car park, turn left on to the B3223 signposted to Simonsbath. In Simonsbath, turn right on to the B3358 signposted to Barnstaple. Go through Challacombe, and after 2 m. turn right at the T-junction on to the B3226 signposted to Blackmoor Gate. In just over 1 m., before the junction with the A39, turn left down a minor road and stay on this for 2 m. before turning right to visit Arlington Court.

(10) Arlington Court to Barnstaple Return from Arlington Court to the minor road, turn right, go through Loxhore Cott, turn right at the T-junction and follow this road down the valley of the River Yeo to Barnstaple.

INFORMATION

Places of interest *Arlington Court:* Apr. to end Oct., daily, 11 a.m.-1 p.m., 2-6 p.m. Gardens, Nov. to March, daily. *Barnstaple:* St Anne's Chapel Museum, Spring Bank Hol. to mid-Sept., daily, 10 a.m.-1 p.m., 2-5 p.m. *Croyde:* Gem, Rock and Shell Museum, daily. *Ilfracombe:* Chambercombe Manor, Easter to Sept., weekdays (except Sat.), Sun. afternoons. Museum, daily, from 10 a.m.

Information West Country Tourist Board, Trinity Court, Southernhay East, Exeter (Tel. Exeter 76351).

Towns with easy access to Barnstaple:

Bideford	9 m.	Exeter	40 m.
Crediton	32 m.	Minehead	38 m.
Dulverton	31 m.	South Molton	12 m.

Woolacombe Bay.

WOOLACOMBE
Two miles of flat, broad, bathing and surfing sands stretch southwards from Woolacombe, open to the Atlantic breakers. On the inland side, the sands are overlooked by the dunes and rising downland of Woolacombe Warren, owned by the National Trust. The coastal scene rapidly changes to one of rocks, little pools and rocky inlets as the road climbs to the old and charming village of Mortehoe. Its 13th to 14th-century church contains some good 16th-century bench-ends and a remarkable 20th-century mosaic of angels. A path from the church leads to the cliffs at Morte Point.

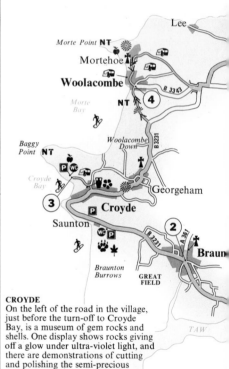

CROYDE
On the left of the road in the village, just before the turn-off to Croyde Bay, is a museum of gem rocks and shells. One display shows rocks giving off a glow under ultra-violet light, and there are demonstrations of cutting and polishing the semi-precious stones found on Devon's beaches.

BRAUNTON
The most interesting part of the town is on the hillside, east of the main road, where narrow streets are lined with 17th and 18th-century houses. By tradition, the town's patron saint, the 6th-century Irish monk St Brannoc, was directed in a vision to build a chapel where he found a sow and her young. In Braunton church, where he is buried, a roof boss shows the sow and piglets, and one of the 16th-century carved pew-ends, which are said to be among England's finest, depicts the saint with one of the beasts. Parts of the church are Norman: the rest are 13th century and later. It is large, with a single-span roof and a 15th-century lead-shingled spire.

St Brannoc, Braunton.

SCALE
0   1   2   3   4   5 MILES

ILFRACOMBE

Until the beginning of the 19th century, Ilfracombe was a small fishing port and market town. It is now North Devon's largest seaside resort. It has 11 small cove beaches—two reached by tunnels through the rocks. The old harbour area remains the centre of the town, where yachtsmen mingle with local fishermen. On Lantern Hill above the pier the Chapel of St Nicholas still burns a light for sailors. It has probably done so since it was built some 700 years ago, but its 'lighthouse' status dates only from the 18th century. There are fine parks and gardens with flowers in bloom all the year round. The Torrs Walks to the west of the valley town give access to magnificent views over the cliffs and the rocky shore line.

St Nicholas's Church, Ilfracombe.

LYNTON AND LYNMOUTH

Lynton was no more than a hamlet and Lynmouth a quiet little fishing village at the beginning of the 19th century. Hotel turrets and gables now give Lynton a Victorian-seaside look; but Lynmouth, with its tiny harbour, whitewashed cottages and weather-boarded villas, retains an older atmosphere. The poet Shelley came to Lynmouth in 1812, and lived here for a while with his schoolgirl bride. The two resorts are joined by a cliff railway, opened in 1890 and virtually unchanged since then. Two railcars alternate between Lynmouth and Lynton, 500 ft above, the top car taking on water ballast so that it descends by force of gravity, hauling up the other car from below.

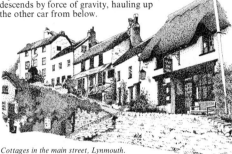

Cottages in the main street, Lynmouth.

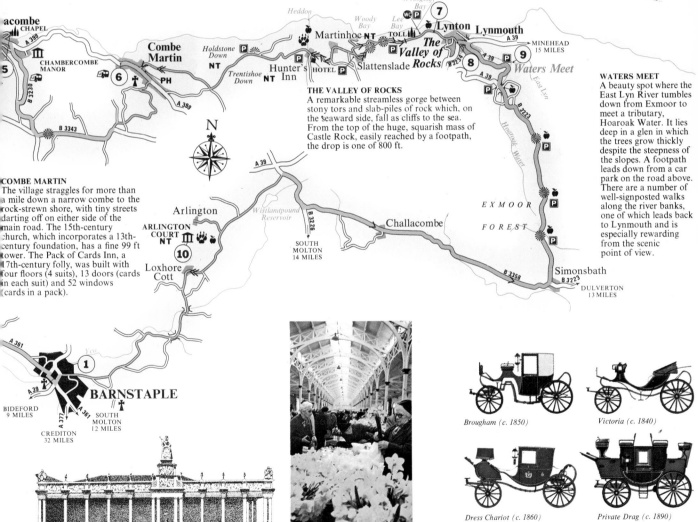

THE VALLEY OF ROCKS

A remarkable streamless gorge between stony tors and slab-piles of rock which, on the seaward side, fall as cliffs to the sea. From the top of the huge, squarish mass of Castle Rock, easily reached by a footpath, the drop is one of 800 ft.

WATERS MEET

A beauty spot where the East Lyn River tumbles down from Exmoor to meet a tributary, Hoaroak Water. It lies deep in a glen in which the trees grow thickly despite the steepness of the slopes. A footpath leads down from a car park on the road above. There are a number of well-signposted walks along the river banks, one of which leads back to Lynmouth and is especially rewarding from the scenic point of view.

COMBE MARTIN

The village straggles for more than a mile down a narrow combe to the rock-strewn shore, with tiny streets darting off on either side of the main road. The 15th-century church, which incorporates a 13th-century foundation, has a fine 99 ft tower. The Pack of Cards Inn, a 17th-century folly, was built with four floors (4 suits), 13 doors (cards in each suit) and 52 windows (cards in a pack).

Queen Anne's Walk, Barnstaple.

Covered Market, Barnstaple.

Brougham (c. 1850)

Victoria (c. 1840)

Dress Chariot (c. 1860)

Private Drag (c. 1890)

BARNSTAPLE

Tradition says that Barnstaple was granted a charter by King Athelstan in 930, making it one of the oldest boroughs in Britain. It was minting its own coins at the end of the 10th century. At the centre of the busy market town is the oddly twisted 17th-century timber-and-lead spire of the parish church. Within strolling distance are Butcher's Row, an unusual arcade of little identical shops, and the covered Pannier Market. Nearer the river is Queen Anne's Walk, a colonnaded, much-carved building 70 ft long by 12 ft wide. In the 17th and 18th centuries, before the silting-up of the River Taw reduced Barnstaple's importance as a port, this was the meeting place of merchants and shipowners. In front of the colonnade is the Tome Stone where they sealed their agreements. The Barnstaple pottery near by, founded in 1879, continues to produce many traditional lines in red clay as well as modern ovenware. Visitors can see the potters at work.

ARLINGTON COURT

The Arlington Court estate of 3471 acres, including three hamlets and 13 farms, was presented to the National Trust in 1946. The house, in simple Regency style dating from 1822, contains collections of model ships, shells, pewter and snuff boxes. In the stables there is a large collection of 19th and early-20th-century horse-drawn carriages, including Queen Victoria's pony-drawn bath-chair. The Trust has planned and signposted an hour-long nature walk through the park and woods, passing the lake. Herons and their nests can be seen, and a nesting island has been built in the lake to encourage wild duck to breed.

The deep south of Devon where palm trees wave

The sea probes between the wooded hills to meet rivers in wide estuaries. Here the Dart runs to the tide, past Dartington with its Cider Press Craft Centre, on through the once-walled Saxon town of Totnes, and out at Dartmouth, home of the Royal Naval College. Across country is the Kingsbridge Estuary, where gardens of semi-tropical plants and palm trees flourish in the mild climate at the southern tip of Devon.

(1) Kingsbridge to Salcombe Leave the town on the A381 signposted to Salcombe. Follow the road, with its fine views over the Kingsbridge Estuary, into Salcombe.

(2) Salcombe to Hope Cove Leave the town on Fore Street, which runs parallel with the harbour, and fork left down Cliff Road, following the signpost to Bolt Head. Continue on the coast road past North and South Sands bays. (To visit Sharpitor gardens, which contain semi-tropical plants, turn left on to a minor road at the T-junction beyond South Sands.) Follow the road as it turns sharp right, signposted to Malborough. At the next junction bear left on to the road signposted to Soar. Turn right at the T-junction and after ¾ m. turn left, following the signpost to Hope Cove. Turn left in Bolberry and follow the road through Inner Hope to the car park at Outer Hope, from which Hope Cove may be explored on foot.

(3) Hope Cove to Modbury Leave Outer Hope on the road signposted to Malborough. At the crossroads, where the Malborough road bears right, keep straight ahead, following the signpost to Kingsbridge. Turn left at the T-junction on to the A381. After 1½ m. turn left on to the B3197, following the Plymouth signpost, and continue through Aveton Gifford into Modbury.

(4) Modbury to Totnes At the far end of the town turn right on to the B3207 (not marked), following the signpost to Dartmouth. Keep on the road as it bears left and becomes the B3196. After about 2 m. turn right at the crossroads on to the B3210. At the next T-junction turn right, keeping on the B3210 (formerly the B3372). Cross Avonwick Bridge and take the second road to the right, following the signpost to Harberton. Go straight ahead at the crossroads and bear right at the next fork. Continue into the village of Harberton and turn left on to the A381, following the signpost to Totnes. Turn right at the traffic lights on to the A385 to Totnes.

(5) Totnes to Dartington Leave the town on the A385 signposted to Dartington. After 1 m. turn right on to the A384, and take the first road right into Dartington.

(6) Dartington to Dartmouth Return to the A384, turn left and at the junction with the A385 go straight ahead on to a minor road and into Cott. Continue through the village and turn right on to the A381. After 1 m. turn left on to the road signposted to Tuckenhay then bear left at a fork. After 1 m. turn right at the crossroads and, at the bottom of the hill, left in front of the inn by Bow Bridge. Follow the road through Tuckenhay and turn left at the T-junction, following the signpost to Cornworthy. Continue through the village and turn left at the T-junction on to the road signposted to Dittisham. Keep bearing left and in the village of Dittisham bear right, following the signpost to Dartmouth. At the crossroads turn left on to the B3207. On the outskirts of Dartmouth the road joins the A379, which leads to the town centre and Dartmouth harbour.

(7) Dartmouth to Slapton Sands Leave the town centre on the B3205, signposted to Dartmouth Castle, shortly passing Bayard's Cove, in which stand the remains of Bearscore Castle. (Where the road bears right there is a minor road straight ahead, signposted to One Gun Point and leading to Dartmouth Castle.) Continue on the B3205, following the signpost to Kingsbridge. Turn left at the T-junction on to the A379. Go through Stoke Fleming and Strete and on to Slapton Sands.

(8) Slapton Sands to Kingsbridge Continue past Slapton Sands and follow the A379 through Torcross to Stokenham. At the end of the village turn left to follow the signpost to East Portlemouth. After 5 m., by a water tower, turn right and enter the village of East Portlemouth. (To explore the beaches and coves of the Kingsbridge Estuary, turn left along the shore road.) From East Portlemouth continue bearing right along the shore road to the ford. (During spring tides this road is liable to flooding. To avoid this, turn right, before East Portlemouth, off the coast road to Holset. Here follow the road left to rejoin the coast road just beyond the ford.) Past the ford, turn sharp left, following the road signposted to South Pool, and continue bearing left. Turn right at a T-junction into South Pool, and follow the road through the village to Frogmore. Here turn left on to the A379 and continue to Kingsbridge.

INFORMATION

Places of interest *Dartington Hall:* Grounds, daily. *Dartmouth:* Agincourt House, weekdays, Sun. afternoons. Butterwalk Museum, May to Sept., Mon. to Sat., 11 a.m.-5 p.m.; Oct. to April, afternoons. Castle, weekdays, Sun. afternoons. *Kingsbridge:* William Cookworthy Museum, Easter to Oct., Mon. to Sat., 10 a.m.-5 p.m. (groups in winter). *Sharpitor gardens:* Daily. Museum, Apr. to end Oct., daily. *Totnes:* Castle, weekdays. Guildhall, Apr. to Sept., weekdays except Sat. afternoons. Motor Museum, Easter to mid-Oct., daily.

Event *Salcombe:* Regatta, Aug.

Information *Kingsbridge:* The Quay (Tel. Kingsbridge 3195). *Salcombe:* Shadycombe Road (Tel. Salcombe 2736).

Towns with easy access to Kingsbridge:

Ashburton	20 m.	Plymouth	21 m.
Exeter	38 m.	Teignmouth	28 m.
Newton Abbot	22 m.	Torquay	21 m.

MODBURY

The unusual steeple of St George's Church appears to rise straight from the ground and can be seen from miles around the town. There is no visible break between the tower and the steeple. This design dates from the 14th century, and after a fire in 1621 the tower and steeple were rebuilt in exactly the same style. Modbury is sited on a hill so steep that one of the streets has an iron handrail on one pavement and steps to ease the climb. The half-timbered Exeter Inn was first licensed in 1563. Another attractive building is Olde Traine House, a 16th-century farmhouse with a cobbled courtyard. A number of houses have tiled fronts and arched doorways. Much of the town is included in the conservation area for South Hams.

Inner Hope at Hope Cove.

HOPE COVE

The cove is sheltered by the headland of Bolt Tail and its sandy beach, rock pools and small harbour are set against a background of gently rolling hills. There are two villages at the cove. The larger one, Outer Hope, is a holiday centre. Inner Hope is much smaller, with a village square surrounded by whitewashed and thatched cottages. There is a pleasant walk from the cove to Bolt Head, where the clifftops are carpeted with bluebells, gorse and campion in spring and summer. From the headland the cliff path, past Bolberry Down all the way to Bolt Head, is National Trust property.

Salcombe from the Kingsbridge Estuary.

SALCOMBE

This popular sailing centre and holiday resort lies at the mouth of the Kingsbridge Estuary and is the most southerly town in Devon. The mild climate encourages semi-tropical shrubs, flowers and palm trees, and these can be seen in both public and private gardens. Exotic plants and good views make Sharpitor gardens attractive to visitors. Overbeck House, now a youth hostel but with parts housing a museum of model ships, is also at Sharpitor. Overlooking Salcombe harbour is Fort Charles, a Tudor castle which has been in ruins since the Civil War, when it was held for the king for four months and surrendered only when the citizens had been promised safety. A walk from the castle along the cliffs to Bolt Head provides fine views of the estuary. Regular ferries go across the estuary to the pretty beaches at Southpool Creek.

SCALE
0 1 2 3 4 5 MILES

Totnes harbour.

TOTNES

In Norman times the Saxon village of Totnes was turned into a walled town covering ten acres. Two of the old town gates still stand, though the East Gate has been altered many times. Near to it is Rampart Walk, built over the old wall, and at the end of this is the Guildhall, which includes a courtroom built in 1553. An attractive shopping area is formed by the 18th-century Butter and Poultry Walks where farmers used to sell their produce under the overhanging upper storeys of the buildings. The 13th-century keep and bailey of the castle overlook Totnes. A motor museum, where the exhibits include a 1933 Lagonda and a 1924 Voisin C3, is beside the river, adjoining the steamer quay.

1907 Mercedes Simplex, Totnes Motor Museum.

DARTINGTON

A succession of houses has stood on the site of Dartington Hall since the 9th century. The present building dates from the 14th and 16th centuries, and now forms the centre of a social and industrial experiment intended to revitalise a declining area of Devon. It was begun in 1925 by the Elmhursts, an American couple who bought and restored Dartington Hall. The trust since formed runs forestry estates, sawmills and small industries, including a textile mill. There is also a school and an art college. Parts of the estate and the mill are open to the public.

Agincourt House, Dartmouth.

DARTMOUTH

The deep-water harbour at Dartmouth has been the assembly point of many fleets, including those of two crusades, in 1147 and 1190, and the 485 ships of the American Navy which took part in the 1944 invasion of Normandy. The Royal Naval College is visible from many parts of the River Dart, but it is not normally open to the public. The elegant Butterwalk, built in the 1630s and restored in 1954, is among the many historic buildings. Four shops with overhanging upper storeys now house the borough museum. Agincourt House is a wealthy merchant's house built in 1415. Dartmouth has three castles. Two date from the 15th century and face each other across the Dart. The third, at Bayard's Cove, was built by the townsfolk in 1537.

Bluethroat

SLAPTON SANDS

During the Second World War the 2½ miles of raised beach at Slapton were used as a training ground for troops taking part in the Normandy invasion. An obelisk commemorates the event stands on the beach. Behind the beach are The Leys, a series of freshwater lagoons which are a nature reserve for wild fowl and rare species of marsh birds. In the village of Slapton, which lies in a hollow near The Leys, is a slate tower, all that remains of a church built in 1373 by Sir Guy de Brien, one of the first Knights of the Garter.

Kitchen range, Cookworthy Museum, Kingsbridge.

KINGSBRIDGE

Perched on a steep hill at the head of a long estuary, Kingsbridge was two royal estates in the 13th century. It still has two parishes, Dodbrooke and Kingsbridge, facing each other across the River Dod. The quayside, from which graceful clippers once sailed, has a long car park and a miniature railway. The Shambles, a long building with an overhanging upper storey supported on crude pillars, was built in 1585 and remodelled in the 18th century. The Cookworthy Museum is housed in the Old Grammar School, founded in 1670. It is named after William Cookworthy (1705–80), a local chemist who discovered how to make porcelain from china clay. The museum features, among other things, a reconstruction of a Victorian kitchen, with an iron range cast in the old Kingsbridge iron foundry.

23

Wild ponies and peaceful rural villages in Dartmoor

The exposed heathland of Dartmoor is dotted with outcrops of oddly shaped granite rocks and the remains of Bronze and Iron Age settlements. Its wildness is home for the hardy Dartmoor pony and a fitting backdrop for 'The Moor', the prison at Princetown. The lush valley of the River Dart is a reminder of the gentler side of rural Devon, as are the many villages of thatched cottages cupped in protective hollows on the moor. Other surprises include Buckfast Abbey, built in this century, and St Pancras Church at Widecombe, best known for its fair once attended by 'Uncle Tom Cobleigh and all'.

(1) Ashburton to Dart Valley Railway Leave the town centre on the road signposted to Buckfast Abbey. On the outskirts of the town, cross the B3357, following the signpost to Buckfast Abbey. At the next junction turn right, again following the Buckfast Abbey signpost. The Buckfastleigh station terminus of the Dart Valley Railway is on the left, ½ m. after Dart Bridge.

(2) Dart Valley Railway to Buckfast Abbey Return towards Ashburton and where the road turns right keep straight ahead for Buckfast Abbey.

(3) Buckfast Abbey to Princetown Return to the road and turn right. Turn right again at the junction, following the signpost to Holne. Go past Hembury, where a nature trail starts opposite the car park. About 1 m. further on fork left, following the Holne signpost, and left again at the T-junction. Go through Holne, birthplace of Charles Kingsley, the Victorian novelist. To the right of the road lies the Upper Dart Valley. The road soon goes into Dartmoor Forest and through Hexworthy. Here, bear right and go downhill, crossing the West Dart, and turn left on to the B3357 signposted Princetown. At Two Bridges, turn left on to the B3212 and into Princetown village. Dartmoor Prison lies through the village on the B3357.

(4) Princetown to Postbridge Return to Two Bridges and turn right. Just after Two Bridges turn left and continue on the B3212 for about another 4 m. to reach Postbridge. To visit the clapper bridge, use the car park on the left. Guided walks on to the moor start from the car park.

(5) Postbridge to Grimspound Stay on the B3212 and, after crossing the East Dart and the Postbridge cattle grid, turn right on to the road signposted to Widecombe. The road skirts Soussons Down, where a small stone circle stands in a clearing to the left of the road. Turn left at the next junction, following the signpost for Moretonhampstead. Turn left at the T-junction. After about 1 m. Grimspound, the remains of an ancient settlement, is reached. The site is on the hillside to the right of the road.

(6) Grimspound to Moretonhampstead Follow the same country road beyond Grimspound for about 1½ m. and turn right on to the B3212. Continue for just over 4 m. into Moretonhampstead.

(7) Moretonhampstead to Widecombe Leave the town on the B3212, signposted Exeter, passing the 17th-century almshouses.

After 2 m., at a five-road junction, take the second on the right, signposted to Christow. After ½ m., by Blackingstone Rock, turn right to follow the Christow sign. (To visit Blackingstone Rock, take the second on the right and park below the tor.) Follow the Christow road between two reservoirs and then keep straight ahead, following the signpost for Ashton. Turn right at the next T-junction and right again on to the B3193, following the signpost for Chudleigh. After 1 m., at Knowle Cross, turn right and follow the signpost for Hennock. Bear left at the fork and keep straight ahead at crossroads to Five Lanes junction. To visit Hazelwood Garden, turn sharp right here. To continue the main route, turn sharp left instead, following the Bovey Tracey signpost, and in just under 1 m., at the second crossroads, turn right. At the junction with the B3344, turn right into Bovey Tracey. Bear left into the village and continue to the end of the main street. There, bear left again on to the A382, and by the Dartmoor Hotel turn right on to the B3344, following the Widecombe signpost. After ½ m., turn left for Haytor. The 1491 ft summit of Haytor Rocks is an excellent viewpoint. But it is possible to see the sea, 12 m. distant, even from the car park. From here the road drops down to Widecombe in the Moor.

(8) Widecombe in the Moor to Buckland Leave Widecombe on the road signposted to Buckland. After 1 m., turn left. Then take the first turning right for the attractive village of Buckland in the Moor.

(9) Buckland to Ashburton Driving straight through the village, the road leads back to Ashburton. To visit Buckland Beacon, take the first on the left—½ m. beyond the village—and after ¾ m. a track on the left leads up to the 1282 ft summit. Return down the hill, and at the junction turn left to continue back to Ashburton.

INFORMATION

Places of interest *Ashburton Museum:* mid-May to Sept., Tues., Thur., Fri., Sat. 2.30-5 p.m. *Buckfast Abbey:* Church only, daily. House of Shells, Easter to mid-Nov., daily. *Buckfastleigh:* Dart Valley Railway, mid-Apr. to mid-Sept., daily.

Events *Ashburton:* Ale-tasting and bread-weighing, July. Carnival, July. *Widecombe:* Fair, second Tues. in Sept.

Information West Country Tourist Board, Trinity Court, Southernhay East, Exeter (Tel. Exeter 76351).

Towns with easy access to Ashburton:

Exeter	20 m.	Tavistock	20 m.
Kingsbridge	20 m	Torquay	14 m.
Plymouth	24 m.	Totnes	9 m.

Engraving of Dartmoor Prison when completed in 1810.

PRINCETOWN
The largest village on Dartmoor, and also the bleakest in bad weather, it is not at all forbidding when the sun shines. At 1400 ft above sea level, however, it is a seasonal victim of wind, rain, fog and snow. Princetown's fame today centres on Dartmoor Prison, built between 1806 and 1810 to hold French prisoners taken in the wars against Napoleon. By the mid-19th century it was being used to house dangerous criminals, or men serving long sentences. The village, where most of the prison staff have their homes, is a good centre for exploring the considerable prehistoric remains on Dartmoor. There are good Bronze Age relics at Merrivale, Great Mis Tor and near Two Bridges.

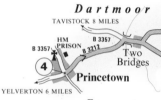

Ponies on Dartmoor.

DARTMOOR
The 350 square miles of Dartmoor National Park form the largest tract of unenclosed land in southern England. Though all the land is privately owned—much by the Duchy of Cornwall—there is public access to wide areas. The landscape varies from barren summits, many above 1500 ft, through heather-clad moorland to marsh and bog. Four national nature reserves and 20 other protected sites within the park preserve a variety of the plants and wildlife found on the moor. The ponies which roam the moor are not strictly wild, for they belong to the local farmers. They should not be petted or fed.

SCALE

0   1   2   3 MILES

POSTBRIDGE

The hamlet gets its name from the splendid surviving example of a clapper bridge which spans the East Dart. Clapper bridges were built in the 13th century to connect tin mines and farms with the towns bordering the moor. The one at Postbridge, with three 15 ft slabs on tall piers, is the largest left and is perfectly safe to use. It stands high enough to clear the stream when sudden storms bring floods.

GRIMSPOUND

This is a fine example of a Bronze Age shepherd settlement, of which a number remain on Dartmoor. Inside the stone compound, built to keep out wild animals and other marauders, are the remains of 24 huts. Door lintels and stone sleeping shelves still survive. Sir Arthur Conan Doyle used Grimspound as the location for Watson's hiding place during Sherlock Holmes's investigation of the *Hound of the Baskervilles*. The stone walls originally supported roofs of turf laid on branches.

Bronze Age hut remains, Grimspound.

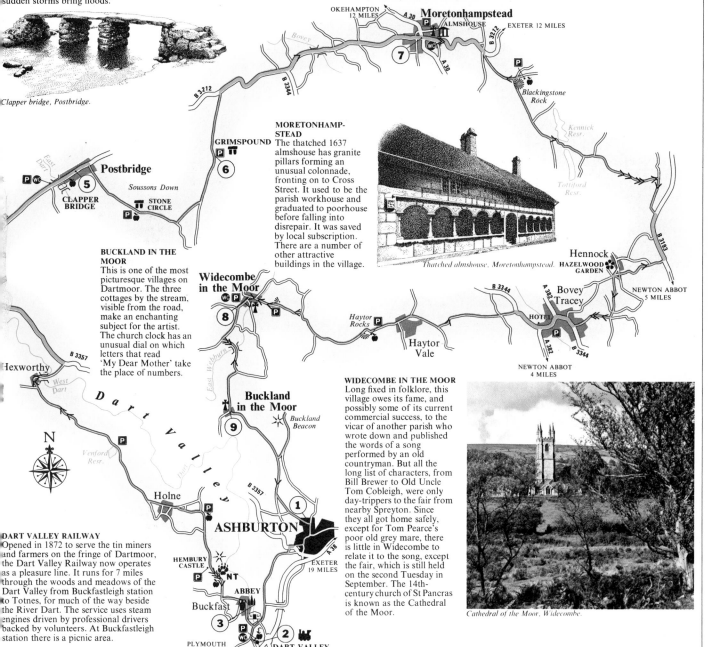

Clapper bridge, Postbridge.

MORETONHAMPSTEAD

The thatched 1637 almshouse has granite pillars forming an unusual colonnade, fronting on to Cross Street. It used to be the parish workhouse and graduated to poorhouse before falling into disrepair. It was saved by local subscription. There are a number of other attractive buildings in the village.

Thatched almshouse, Moretonhampstead.

BUCKLAND IN THE MOOR

This is one of the most picturesque villages on Dartmoor. The three cottages by the stream, visible from the road, make an enchanting subject for the artist. The church clock has an unusual dial on which letters that read 'My Dear Mother' take the place of numbers.

WIDECOMBE IN THE MOOR

Long fixed in folklore, this village owes its fame, and possibly some of its current commercial success, to the vicar of another parish who wrote down and published the words of a song performed by an old countryman. But all the long list of characters, from Bill Brewer to Old Uncle Tom Cobleigh, were only day-trippers to the fair from nearby Spreyton. Since they all got home safely, except for Tom Pearce's poor old grey mare, there is little in Widecombe to relate it to the song, except the fair, which is still held on the second Tuesday in September. The 14th-century church of St Pancras is known as the Cathedral of the Moor.

Cathedral of the Moor, Widecombe.

DART VALLEY RAILWAY

Opened in 1872 to serve the tin miners and farmers on the fringe of Dartmoor, the Dart Valley Railway now operates as a pleasure line. It runs for 7 miles through the woods and meadows of the Dart Valley from Buckfastleigh station to Totnes, for much of the way beside the River Dart. The service uses steam engines driven by professional drivers backed by volunteers. At Buckfastleigh station there is a picnic area.

BUCKFAST ABBEY

The abbey—home of Buckfast Tonic Wine—was built mainly between 1906 and 1932, after a religious community unearthed the foundations of an ancient monastery dissolved by Henry VIII. The entire re-creation was carried out by a workforce of monks never stronger than six at a time. The monks, who run their own farm, tend one of the biggest honey-bee colonies in the country. Close by is a museum of ornaments made from shells.

The House of Cards, Ashburton.

ASHBURTON

Chartered in 1285, Ashburton was originally one of four 'Stannary' towns, or administrative centres of the tin industry. Granite gives parts of the town a severe appearance. An ironmonger's shop in North Street has a Norman arch. The shop was once an inn, and during the Civil War was used as headquarters by the Cromwellian general, Sir Thomas Fairfax. Playing-card symbols carved in the wall outside a nearby grocer's shop date from the 17th century, when the building was a gaming house. Close to the road, as the route leaves the town, is St Gudula's Well. Water from the well was once believed to cure the blind. Close by is a Saxon cross which was discovered being used as a farm gatepost.

Around an ancient city between the moors and the sea

Lying between the moors and the sea, the gentle countryside round Exeter has long supported a comfortable way of life. The many castles round the route—reminders of sterner times—are now castles only in name. Some have fallen into ruin, some have been converted into fine mansions, and the most formidable 'baronial stronghold' of them all, Castle Drogo, was built in 1910 as a country house.

(1) Exeter to Fingle Bridge Leave by the A30, following the signposts for Okehampton. Soon after leaving the city, bear left on to the B3212, following the signs towards Dunsford, and on to Dartmoor. Stay on the B3212 for 6 m. then, ¼ m. past the junction with the B3193, turn right into Dunsford. At the T-junction turn left for Drewsteignton. After 5½ m., at the next T-junction, turn left for Fingle Bridge.

(2) Fingle Bridge to Castle Drogo Return to the junction and bear left into Drewsteignton and there go straight on. After ½ m. take a left turn, signposted for Chagford, and after ½ m. reach Castle Drogo.

(3) Castle Drogo to Chagford Leave the house and continue on the same road. At the crossroads go straight across the A382, and at the junction turn right into Chagford.

(4) Chagford to Berry Pomeroy Leave the town by turning left at the T-junction by Market House and taking the first right on to the Princetown road. After 2 m. turn right on to the B3212 and immediately left on to the B3344, following the Bovey Tracey signpost. Go through Manaton, pass Becky Falls, and after 2 m. reach Yarner Wood Nature Reserve (access by permit, although there are parking areas). Just after Dartmoor National Park boundary turn right, following the Haytor signs, and go straight on at the crossroads. At the T-junction turn left, following the Bovey Tracey signpost, and then first right and right again into Liverton. At the T-junction in Liverton turn right, following the signs for Haytor Vale. After ¼ m. turn left and at the next crossroads keep straight ahead into Sigford. There turn left towards Ashburton, keep straight ahead at the next crossroads and take the left fork. Cross the A38, following the Denbury signpost, bear right past the Rising Sun Inn, and at the next crossroads turn right. At the following crossroads go straight ahead, and at the next one turn left and take the first on the right, signposted to Staverton. At the next crossroads, turn left into Broadhempston. There turn left at the junction by the Church House Inn and take the first on the right signposted for Totnes. Keep ahead at the crossroads and after ¾ m. bear right towards Littlehempston. At the next junction go right, under the railway, cross the A381 and fork right into Afton. Beyond Afton bear right for Berry Pomeroy Castle.

(5) Berry Pomeroy Castle to Torbay Aircraft Museum Leave the castle and return along the same road, taking the first turning on the right signposted to Collaton. Go straight ahead at the crossroads to the museum, which is about 1 m. from the castle.

(6) Torbay Aircraft Museum to Compton Castle Return to the crossroads and turn right, following the Marldon signpost. After 1½ m., at the crossroads, turn left into Marldon village. At the T-junction turn right, go right again at the next T-junction, and after a few hundred yards turn left at the crossroads for Compton and its castle.

(7) Compton Castle to Newton Abbot Leave the castle and continue on the same road to Kingskerswell for about 2 m. There turn left on to the A380 signposted to Newton Abbot.

(8) Newton Abbot to Teignmouth Return along the A380 towards Torquay, and turn left on to the B3195 to Shaldon at the mouth of the River Teign. Take the A379 across the bridge, and turn right at the traffic lights for the centre of Teignmouth.

(9) Teignmouth to Powderham Castle Leave Teignmouth on the B3192 signposted to Exeter. After 2½ m., by Little Haldon National Trust car park, turn right at crossroads and follow the signposts for Ashcombe. Keep straight ahead at the crossroads and continue through the woodland. As the woods end, bear right at the fork towards Dawlish. At the T-junction turn right, then fork left and at the next crossroads keep straight ahead, following the signpost for Exeter. Carry on through the Black Forest and straight on over the B3381. At the next crossroads turn right, following the signpost to Kenton. Go through Kenton village and turn left on to the A379, signposted to Exeter. After 1½ m., turn right at the crossroads for Powderham Castle.

(10) Powderham Castle to Exeter Return to the A379 and turn right, following it back to the edge of Exeter, joining the A38 for the city centre.

INFORMATION

Places of interest *Berry Pomeroy Castle:* Daily. *Castle Drogo:* Apr. to Oct., daily, 11 a.m.- 1 p.m., 2-6 p.m. *Compton Castle:* Apr. to Oct., Mon., Wed., Thur., 10 a.m.-12 noon and 2-5 p.m. *Exeter:* Guildhall, Mon. to Sat. Maritime Museum, daily. St Nicholas's Priory, Mon. to Sat. Rougemont House Museum, weekdays, 10 a.m.- 1 p.m., 2-5.30 p.m. *Powderham Castle:* May to beginning Sept., Sun. to Thur., afternoons. *Shaldon Children's Zoo:* Spring Bank Hol. to Oct., daily, weekends in winter. *Torbay Aircraft Museum:* Daily.

Events *Exeter:* Air show, July. *Paignton:* Grand Oggie Fair, July. Regatta Fair, Aug.

Information *Exeter:* Paris Street (Tel. Exeter 77888 and 72434). *Newton Abbot:* Sherborne Road.

Towns with easy access to Exeter:

Barnstaple	40 m.	Taunton	32 m.
Honiton	17 m.	Tavistock	34 m.
Okehampton	23 m.	Torquay	22 m.

FINGLE BRIDGE
This beautiful Elizabethan, arched granite bridge spans the fast-flowing upper reaches of the River Teign between steep hills. Set amid attractive woodland, it is a popular beauty spot, but solitude can be found along the river banks with a little effort. East of the bridge, on the north side of the stream, is the Iron Age hill-fort called Prestonbury Castle, which is one of the surviving relics of the prehistoric inhabitants of Dartmoor.

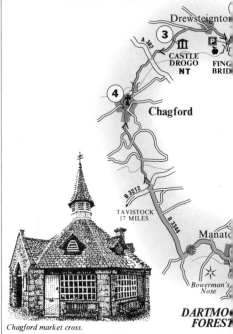

Chagford market cross.

CHAGFORD
The name comes from Old English, meaning a ford in gorse-covered country. In 1305 this attractive little town was made one of the three 'Stannary' towns to administer the Dartmoor tin mines. Later, it became important in the wool trade, but it is now an agricultural market town. The Three Crowns Hotel, with thatched roof and mullioned windows, dates back to the 16th century.

A wooded valley leads up to the heights of Dartmoor.

DARTMOOR
The south-eastern edge of Dartmoor is a softer, kinder country than the high, wild plateau further inland. It is an area of fields, woods, country lanes and picturesque villages of cob and thatch, broken by occasional hills clad with heather and bracken and rising to 1000 ft or more. Majestic and exhilarating country on a good day, Dartmoor should not be treated lightly in bad weather.

SCALE

0   1   2   3   4   5 MILES

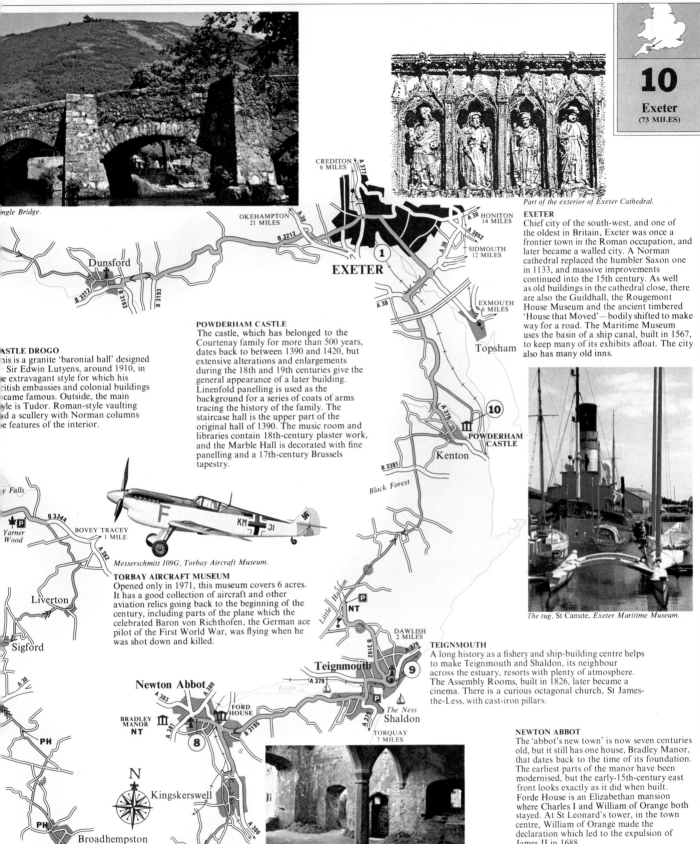

...ngle Bridge.

Part of the exterior of Exeter Cathedral.

EXETER
Chief city of the south-west, and one of the oldest in Britain, Exeter was once a frontier town in the Roman occupation, and later became a walled city. A Norman cathedral replaced the humbler Saxon one in 1133, and massive improvements continued into the 15th century. As well as old buildings in the cathedral close, there are also the Guildhall, the Rougemont House Museum and the ancient timbered 'House that Moved'—bodily shifted to make way for a road. The Maritime Museum uses the basin of a ship canal, built in 1567, to keep many of its exhibits afloat. The city also has many old inns.

CREDITON 6 MILES

OKEHAMPTON 21 MILES

Dunsford

EXETER

HONITON 14 MILES

SIDMOUTH 12 MILES

EXMOUTH 6 MILES

Topsham

POWDERHAM CASTLE
The castle, which has belonged to the Courtenay family for more than 500 years, dates back to between 1390 and 1420, but extensive alterations and enlargements during the 18th and 19th centuries give the general appearance of a later building. Linenfold panelling is used as the background for a series of coats of arms tracing the history of the family. The staircase hall is the upper part of the original hall of 1390. The music room and libraries contain 18th-century plaster work, and the Marble Hall is decorated with fine panelling and a 17th-century Brussels tapestry.

...ASTLE DROGO
...his is a granite 'baronial hall' designed ...r Sir Edwin Lutyens, around 1910, in ...e extravagant style for which his ...ritish embassies and colonial buildings ...came famous. Outside, the main ...yle is Tudor. Roman-style vaulting ...d a scullery with Norman columns ...e features of the interior.

POWDERHAM CASTLE

Kenton

Black Forest

...y Falls

Yarner Wood

BOVEY TRACEY 1 MILE

The tug, St Canute, *Exeter Maritime Museum.*

Messerschmitt 109G, Torbay Aircraft Museum.

TORBAY AIRCRAFT MUSEUM
Opened only in 1971, this museum covers 6 acres. It has a good collection of aircraft and other aviation relics going back to the beginning of the century, including parts of the plane which the celebrated Baron von Richthofen, the German ace pilot of the First World War, was flying when he was shot down and killed.

Liverton

Sigford

Little Haldon

DAWLISH 2 MILES

TEIGNMOUTH
A long history as a fishery and ship-building centre helps to make Teignmouth and Shaldon, its neighbour across the estuary, resorts with plenty of atmosphere. The Assembly Rooms, built in 1826, later became a cinema. There is a curious octagonal church, St James-the-Less, with cast-iron pillars.

Teignmouth

Newton Abbot

FORD HOUSE

Teign

The Ness Shaldon

BRADLEY MANOR NT

TORQUAY 7 MILES

N

Kingskerswell

NEWTON ABBOT
The 'abbot's new town' is now seven centuries old, but it still has one house, Bradley Manor, that dates back to the time of its foundation. The earliest parts of the manor have been modernised, but the early-15th-century east front looks exactly as it did when built. Forde House is an Elizabethan mansion where Charles I and William of Orange both stayed. At St Leonard's tower, in the town centre, William of Orange made the declaration which led to the expulsion of James II in 1688.

Broadhempston

PAIGNTON 3 MILES

CASTLE Compton

Berry Pomeroy Castle.

BERRY POMEROY CASTLE
After the Norman Conquest, a place named Beri was given to Ralf de Pomerai. By the end of the 13th century, records refer to a hall and other buildings, but not until 1497 is there a definite record of a castle. In 1548 the building was sold to the Lord Protector Somerset, in whose family, the Seymours, it has remained. By the middle of the 17th century a mansion had been built within the castle but it was destroyed by fire after about 50 years.

Marldon

TOTNES 4 MILES

Afton

BERRY POMEROY CASTLE

BRIXHAM 8 MILES

TORBAY AIRCRAFT MUSEUM

COMPTON CASTLE
When Compton came into the Gilbert family by marriage, around 1329, only the Great Hall stood. By the beginning of the 16th century, through the constant threat of French raids, towers and other defences had turned it into a fortified manor. Today's buildings have changed little since Elizabethan statesmen were visitors, and would probably still be recognised by Sir Walter Raleigh, who was closely related to the Gilberts.

27

The rich pastures and red cliffs of east Devon

The countryside around Exmouth is one of Britain's richest agricultural areas. The gently rolling landscape is punctuated by the rivers Otter, Sid, Exe and Axe which flow to a coastline of beaches and red cliffs. It is an unspoilt countryside which offers much to the lover of nature. Many of its towns and villages awaken memories of the days of sailing ships, and of the seafaring men of Sir Walter Raleigh's era.

1 Exmouth to Budleigh Salterton Leave Exmouth on the A376, following this road to the sea front in Budleigh Salterton, with its towering red cliffs around the bay.

2 Budleigh Salterton to East Budleigh Return by the same route and turn right on to the B3178 signposted to East Budleigh. On the left at this junction is the entrance to Leeford, a Georgian house with 40 acres of wooded gardens open to the public. Turn left at the T-junction with the A376, and left again at the Rolls Arms Inn and into the village of East Budleigh, where 1½ m. up the lane opposite the Sir Walter Raleigh Inn is Raleigh's birthplace, Hayes Barton.

3 East Budleigh to Bicton Gardens Return to the A376 and turn left towards Colaton Raleigh. After just over 1 m. the entrance to Bicton Gardens is on the left.

4 Bicton Gardens to Branscombe Return along the A376 and turn left at the crossroads, by a brick pillar. Follow this road through Otterton bearing left towards Sidmouth and turning right ¾ m. outside Otterton. Turn left by the cricket ground, on to the road signposted to Exeter, and then right, following the Lyme Regis signposts. Just after crossing the River Sid turn right on to a minor road, following the signpost to Salcombe Regis. In the village, fork left at the war memorial, then turn right on to the A3052 signposted to Seaton. After ¼ m. turn right and follow the signposts to Branscombe.

5 Branscombe to Colyton Go through the village on the road signposted to Seaton, and at the junction with the B3172 bear left. Continue on this road, through Seaton. Just after crossing the River Axe, on the outskirts of Seaton, a coast walk called the Landslips starts. Follow the road through Axmouth, and turn left on to the A3052 signposted to Colyford. Turn right on to the B3161 to Colyton.

6 Colyton to Axminster Follow the B3161 out of the village to Shute. There turn right on to the road signposted to Kilmington. On this corner stands the medieval manor of Shute Barton, the grounds of which are open to the public. After 1 m., at the crossroads, turn left and at the junction with the A35 turn right, following the signposts into Axminster.

7 Axminster to Honiton Leave the town on the minor road signposted to Membury. Go over the level crossing and at the junction ¾ m. later bear right, still following the signposts for Membury. After 2½ m. turn left at the crossroads into Membury village. Follow the road through the village,

keeping the church on the right, and after 1½ m. turn right on to the road signposted to Kilmington. Cross the old packhorse bridge of Beckford, and at the next junction turn right on to the road signposted to Stockland. On the outskirts of Stockland, turn left on to the road signposted to Dalwood. Bear left at the fork, and keep straight on at the crossroads. Follow this road to the left where it is signposted to Dalwood, and at Ham turn right on to the road signposted to Ridge. Go straight ahead at the crossroads by the radio mast, and bear left at the next junction following the signposts to Cotleigh. Go straight on at the staggered crossroads in Cotleigh, following the signposts to Honiton. At the next junction turn right and then left on to the road signposted to Honiton. Pass under the railway, turn left on to the A30 and continue into Honiton town centre.

8 Honiton to Farway Countryside Park Leave Honiton by the road almost opposite the church, signposted to Honiton station. Drive under the railway, and at the top of the hill, by Honiton golf course, turn right on to the road signposted to Farway. At the B3174 turn left and, after ¼ m., left again for the entrance to Farway Countryside Park.

9 Farway Countryside Park to Ottery St Mary Return to the B3174 and turn right. Go straight across the A375 and into Ottery St Mary. To see Cadhay Manor House, take the B3176 signposted to Tiverton. The house is on the left after 1 m.

10 Ottery St Mary to Exmouth Return to Ottery St Mary and leave on the B3174 signposted to Exeter. Just after crossing the River Otter, turn left on to the B3177. Turn left at the next T-junction on to the B3180, signposted to Exmouth, and cross the A3052. Turn right at the junction with the B3179, keeping on the B3180, and after 1 m. turn right down Summer Lane to A la Ronde. Beyond the house, turn left on to the A377 and follow it back to Exmouth.

INFORMATION

Places of interest *Bicton Gardens:* End Mar. to end May, first half Oct., afternoons; Easter weekends, end May to end Sept., daily. *Budleigh Salterton:* Fairlynch Arts Centre and Museum, Easter to end June, and Oct., afternoons; July to end Sept., weekdays, Sun. afternoons. *Farway Countryside Park:* Good Friday to early Oct., daily.

Information West Country Tourist Board, Trinity Court, Southernhay East, Exeter (Tel. Exeter 76351). *Exmouth:* Alexandra Terrace (Tel. Exmouth 3744).

Towns with easy access to Exmouth:

Exeter	11 m.	Taunton	36 m.
Lyme Regis	27 m.	Torquay	30 m.

OTTERY ST MARY
The poet Samuel Taylor Coleridge, who wrote 'The Ancient Mariner', was born in the town, where his father was vicar of the rambling 14th-century church. He is commemorated by a plaque on the church wall. Cadhay, a fine Tudor manor a mile to the north-west of the town, features a courtyard with patterned stonework and statuettes of Henry VIII.

Interior of A la Ronde, Exmouth.

EXMOUTH
The red cliffs and wide beaches of the resort attracted the rich and fashionable in the 18th century. Lady Nelson and Lady Byron were among its visitors. Two remarkable spinster sisters, Jane and Mary Parminter, built the A la Ronde, or Round House, in 1798. Actually 16-sided, it is styled on the church of San Vitale at Ravenna in Italy. The two ladies decorated it with feathers, shells and pictures made from sand and seaweed, and filled the house with curious items from their travels abroad. The top of the house is lantern-shaped, and the interior is decorated in the Parminter sisters' unique manner with shells and feathers. Although Exmouth's reputation as a fashionable resort waned during the 19th century, the town has since developed its facilities for family holidays. It has exceptional views across the Exe, and cruises can be made up the river.

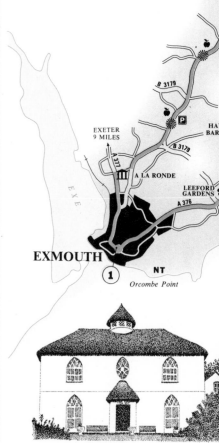

Fairlynch, Budleigh Salterton.

SCALE

0   1   2   3   4   5 M

FARWAY COUNTRYSIDE PARK

Overlooking the beautiful Coly Valley, the 70 acre park is a reserve for several rare breeds of cattle, sheep, pigs and goats, which roam freely. They include the Chartley cattle, a breed older than the Roman occupation; long-horned West Highland cattle, descendants of a Stone Age breed; St Kilda sheep, brought to Britain by the Vikings; and red, hairy Tamworth pigs. Six of Britain's native breeds of pony give rides to children, for whom there is also a 'pets' corner'. Nature trails have been laid around the park which are not difficult even for children. From the trails it is possible to observe deer, badgers and other animals, many species of birds and the very varied shrubs and trees of the park.

Chartley bull, Farway Countryside Park.

HONITON

The town's long main street is chiefly late Georgian: the earlier town was destroyed by fires during the 18th century. Honiton is famous for its lace, which has been made there since Elizabethan times. Queen Victoria's wedding veil was made of Honiton lace. In the Honiton and All Hallows Museum, by the church, a collection of lacework can be seen and its evolution traced through various styles and patterns. In the main street there are workshops where pottery is still handmade in the town's 200-year-old tradition. Visitors are invited to walk round at any time in normal working hours.

Honiton lace.

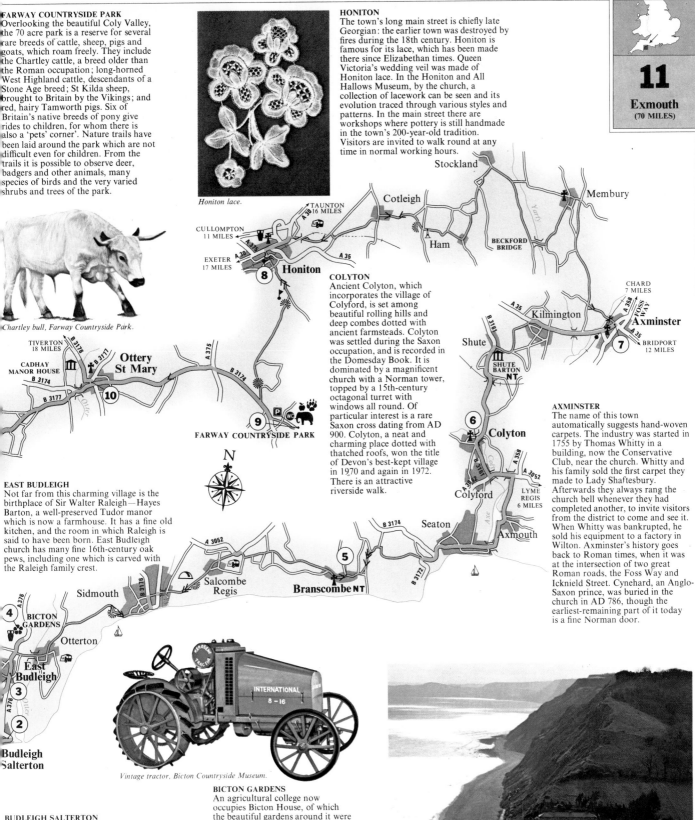

COLYTON

Ancient Colyton, which incorporates the village of Colyford, is set among beautiful rolling hills and deep combes dotted with ancient farmsteads. Colyton was settled during the Saxon occupation, and is recorded in the Domesday Book. It is dominated by a magnificent church with a Norman tower, topped by a 15th-century octagonal turret with windows all round. Of particular interest is a rare Saxon cross dating from AD 900. Colyton, a neat and charming place dotted with thatched roofs, won the title of Devon's best-kept village in 1970 and again in 1972. There is an attractive riverside walk.

AXMINSTER

The name of this town automatically suggests hand-woven carpets. The industry was started in 1755 by Thomas Whitty in a building, now the Conservative Club, near the church. Whitty and his family sold the first carpet they made to Lady Shaftesbury. Afterwards they always rang the church bell whenever they had completed another, to invite visitors from the district to come and see it. When Whitty was bankrupted, he sold his equipment to a factory in Wilton. Axminster's history goes back to Roman times, when it was at the intersection of two great Roman roads, the Foss Way and Icknield Street. Cynehard, an Anglo-Saxon prince, was buried in the church in AD 786, though the earliest-remaining part of it today is a fine Norman door.

EAST BUDLEIGH

Not far from this charming village is the birthplace of Sir Walter Raleigh—Hayes Barton, a well-preserved Tudor manor which is now a farmhouse. It has a fine old kitchen, and the room in which Raleigh is said to have been born. East Budleigh church has many fine 16th-century oak pews, including one which is carved with the Raleigh family crest.

Vintage tractor, Bicton Countryside Museum.

BUDLEIGH SALTERTON

This quiet, attractive resort, with red cliffs, a pebble beach and a fine sea view over Lyme Bay, is the setting of the painting 'The Boyhood of Raleigh' by John Millais. The Victorian artist lived for some time in a house called The Octagon, on South Parade. Fairlynch, an 18th-century thatched house, is an arts centre and museum. It has a collection of exhibits of local historical interest, natural history, archaeology and costumes ranging from the 18th century. Among many interesting houses is Little Hill, once the property of General Simcoe, first Lieutenant-Governor of Upper Canada.

BICTON GARDENS

An agricultural college now occupies Bicton House, of which the beautiful gardens around it were once the private grounds. The oldest part of the grounds, the Italian Gardens, were laid out in 1735 to a design by André le Nôtre, gardener to Louis XIV and creator of the gardens at Versailles. Several conservatories include a tropical house, a cactus house and a palm house. An ornamental lake is overlooked by a fairy-tale 19th-century summerhouse called the Hermitage. The gardens include a countryside museum; among the exhibits is a collection of early farming equipment and an 1894 traction engine.

Branscombe cliffs and beaches.

BRANSCOMBE

A huddle of whitewashed cottages of great charm distinguishes the village, which is separated from the sea by a narrow valley. The church, set away from the road, is mainly Norman, and opposite is an old house, Church Living, built about the 15th century. Near the centre of the village stands an ancient thatched forge, a mill and the Mason's Arms Inn, a mainly 17th-century building with parts that date back three centuries.

BATH

This tour begins from the heart of Roman Bath, where visitors can drink the mineral water from the hot springs discovered nearly 3000 years ago. Bath is a small city, and the walk covers most of its outstanding features.

THINGS TO SEE IN THE CITY

1. Abbey, Roman Baths and Pump Room. Open daily.

2. Abbey Green, site of early-Saxon abbey. Crystal Palace Inn, used by Nelson as a junior naval officer.

3. Lilliput Alley. Buildings include Sally Lunn's House (1480).

4. Linley House, Pierrepont Place, where Emma Hart (later Lady Hamilton, Nelson's mistress) was a maid.

5. South Parade, built 1740. Novelist Sir Walter Scott lived at No. 6.

6. Parade Gardens, fashion hub of Beau Nash's Bath. Plaque to John Palmer, originator of the mail coach.

7. Pulteney Bridge (1770), with tiny shops along the sides.

8. The 18th-century Guildhall. Open on application to the porter.

9. Trim Street. No. 5, home of General Wolfe (1727–59), hero of Quebec.

10. Original (1804) Theatre Royal front in 18th-century square.

11. Queen Square, planned 1729–36 to resemble a palace forecourt. Novelist Jane Austen lived at No. 13.

12. Cottages of 18th-century sedan chairmen, who waited in Queen's Parade for fares.

13. Royal Crescent. No. 1 is a museum reproducing an 18th-century Georgian interior. Open Mar. to Oct., weekdays except Mon., Sun. afternoons.

14. The Circus. Former residents include William Pitt the Elder (Nos. 7–8), Dr Livingstone (13), Clive of India (14), Thomas Gainsborough (17).

15. Assembly Rooms and Museum of Costume, Bennet Street, open daily. Contains fine 18th-century chandeliers.

16. Palladian-style buildings dating from about 1750.

17. The Octagon, built as a chapel in 1767. Open when not in use. Milsom Street, shopping area of distinguished buildings.

CAR PARKS: Charlotte Street, Kingsmead (enter Avon Street and bear left at approach to Monmouth Street), Broad Street, Walcot Street, South Parade, Sawclose, Ham Gardens (turn south from Henry Street and circle bus station), Avon Street (south, towards river), Green Park station (opposite junction of Charles Street–James Street West).

INFORMATION: Tourist Centre, Abbey Churchyard, opposite Pump Room entrance (Tel. Bath 62831).

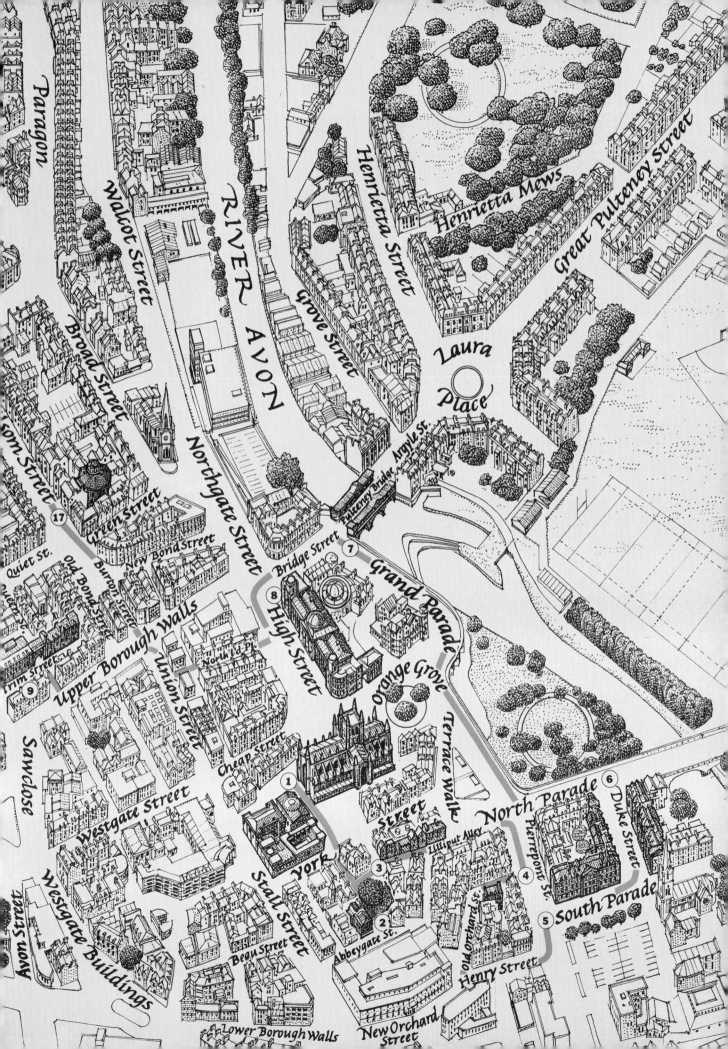

BATH

Gorgon's head, temple of Minerva.

Bath is a city of superlatives. Its Roman remains, health-giving hot springs and wealth of Georgian architecture combine to create an atmosphere of refinement and elegance unequalled in Britain.

CRITICAL OBSERVER *The cartoonist Rowlandson took a jaundiced view of Bath's 18th-century visitors.*

According to legend, Bath's origins go back to 800 BC when a Celtic prince named Bladud contracted leprosy. Having been banished from his father's court, he became a swineherd. His pigs also suffered from a skin disease, but it vanished after they had wallowed in a pool of hot, muddy water. The prince was so impressed that he plunged in and he, too, was cured. Later, he established a spa on the site of the miracle, dedicating the springs to the Celtic god, Sul.

Certainly the Roman conquerors of Britain in the 1st century AD were quick to realise the potential of Bath's hot springs. These still gush forth 500,000 gallons of water a day at a constant temperature of 120°F. They named the city they founded Aquae Sulis—'Waters of Sul'—and their buildings, including the Great Bath, which was rediscovered opposite the abbey in the 19th century, came to cover 25 acres by the end of the 3rd century. A temple was dedicated to Sulis Minerva—a combination of the original Celtic god and the Roman goddess of healing—and even pilgrims from the Continent flocked there. Centuries of neglect and decay followed the Roman withdrawal from Britain. It was not until the 9th century that Bath again rose to fame: this time it was its abbey—not its baths—which was the focal point.

The abbey the Saxons built, parts of which survive in Abbey Green, became an important religious centre. In 973 it was used for the coronation of Edgar, the first king of all England. The ritual performed by Archbishop Dunstan on that occasion became the basis for all future coronations.

But the abbey as it exists today was the work of Oliver King, Bishop of Bath and Wells, who ordered its construction in 1499. King was inspired by a dream in which angels climbed and descended ladders between heaven and earth, while voices urged 'a king to restore the church'. The dream was later immortalised in stone on the turrets at the western end of the church.

Progress on the building was painfully slow, despite the fact that King incorporated fragments of a cathedral the Normans had built into his grand design. When Elizabeth I visited Bath in 1574, she ordered nationwide collections to be made for the next seven years to speed the work. Despite these and other efforts, the nave was roofless until the 17th

RESTORED *Lined with lead and fed by a hot spring, the Great Bath was built by the Romans and rediscovered in the 19th century.*

TOWARDS COMPLETION *Among the gifts given to help to complete Bath Abbey was the West Door, presented by Sir Henry Montagu in 1617.*

century. And it was not given its breathtaking fan-vaulting until the end of the 19th century—400 years after the original masons had promised Bishop King the finest vault in England or France.

Queen Elizabeth's visit helped to put Bath back on the map in another way. Interest in the health-giving properties of the springs slowly reawakened.

Both Charles II and James II visited the city, but it was another queen, Anne, who really began the trend when she 'took the waters' at Bath in 1703. Where royalty led, society followed. And among the throng who flocked to the spa was Richard 'Beau' Nash, a 30-year-old adventurer who was to dominate Bath for over a generation.

Nash's wit, extravagant clothes and personality had already established him in high society. Now he set about organising Bath. There was much to do. There were few decent lodgings, no adequate assembly rooms and the filthy streets were a footpads' paradise. Even the baths themselves were dirty—as the 17th-century diarist Samuel Pepys recorded.

Having won himself the title of 'Master of Ceremonies', Nash dominated both the town council and the visitors. Even royalty quailed before his frown. Princess Amelia, a daughter of George II, was curtly refused one more dance after Nash had signalled the orchestra to stop.

Nash's passion for order and discipline in all things was shared by the architects he encouraged. Chief among them was John Wood

ELEGANCE *A court dress made of cream silk and embroidered with sprays of flowers. It dates from about 1760 and is now in the Museum of Costume.*

ACROSS THE AVON *The Ponte Vecchio in Florence was the inspiration behind Adam's Pulteney Bridge named after William Pulteney, 1st Earl of Bath.*

the Elder, who came to the city in 1727, the year that his equally talented son, John Wood the Younger, was born. The elder Wood greatly admired the Palladian style of architecture, named after the 16th-century Italian architect Andrea Palladio, and drew up plans to sweep away the jumble of medieval streets and transform Bath into a spacious Roman city.

Wood's work would have been impossible without the encouragement of Ralph Allen, for whom he built Prior Park and a town house in Old Lilliput Alley. Allen's quarries supplied Wood with the golden stone which he used to cover Bath and its surrounding hills in a succession of fine Palladian buildings.

Wood's finest monuments were Queen Square and the Circus which, with its diameter of 318 ft, was inspired by the Colosseum in Rome. Tuscan, Ionic and Corinthian columns adorn the houses, and more than 800 motifs symbolising the arts and sciences form a frieze above the ground-floor windows.

Work on the Circus did not begin until 1754—the year of Wood's death. It was his son who saw the building through to its conclusion and who, in his turn, gave Bath the glorious Royal Crescent. This was the first crescent to be built in England. He also designed new Assembly Rooms—now the home of the Museum of Costume. These cost £20,000, and were hailed as the finest in Europe.

Many other architects helped to create the Georgian city. Robert Adam was responsible for the Florentine-style Pulteney Bridge that spans the Avon just above its foaming weir. Thomas Baldwin, the City Architect, created

PRESERVED *It took John Wood the Younger seven years to build the 30 houses of Royal Crescent (above). This masterpiece was the first development of its kind to be built in England. Its only adornment is 114 giant columns attached to the first and second storeys of the façade. The drawing-room of No. 1 (left) has been furnished and decorated in the pure and elegant style of George III, to re-create a residence of Bath's Georgian heyday.*

Great Pulteney Street, often considered to be the most impressive street in the city. Baldwin also built the Pump Room, which was opened in 1796 and has the words 'Water is best' carved above its entrance in Greek.

Yet the splendour of Bath lies less in such individual triumphs of architecture than in the total effect—from the glories of the Royal Crescent to the city's many secluded, unpretentious little streets. Throughout the entire city the world of the 18th century still lives on —even though the fashionable aristocrats who once thronged the streets have long since vanished. But a legacy of their presence survives in the work of the artist Thomas Gainsborough, the greatest British portrait painter of the 18th century.

No one captured the glittering world of Bath more effectively. His move to the city in 1759 proved to be the turning-point in his career. There, he took a studio-shop opposite the abbey and soon won the patronage of the richest and most fashionable in the land—men like the Duke of Bedford and the Earl of Radnor. In a very short time, he was able to raise his price for a portrait from five to 40 guineas for a half-length and 100 guineas for a full-length view of the sitter. And the portraits he produced, such as his painting of Countess Howe, took on a new depth of beauty. So the unique atmosphere of Bath goes far beyond its buildings. It can now be seen in picture galleries all over the world.

WIDE HORIZONS *Among Bath's many museums is one devoted to American life and art from which this 17th-century sampler comes.*

CAPITAL OF FASHION

Dr William Oliver.   *Richard 'Beau' Nash.*

In the 18th century Bath was the leisure capital of England. Every summer the leaders of high society gathered in the city to take the waters—and to be seen.

The man chiefly responsible for transforming Bath into a fashionable resort was Richard 'Beau' Nash, for 40 years the uncrowned 'King of Bath'. Described by his friend, the author Oliver Goldsmith, as having 'too much merit not to become remarkable' but 'too much folly to arrive at greatness', he ruled both city and visitors with a rod of iron. The pattern of daily life he laid down had to be rigidly observed, always beginning with three glasses of water in the Pump Room.

Here another Bath character, Dr William Oliver, presided. He and Nash were close friends—though the beau as a rule was distrustful of doctors. When asked by one if he had followed his prescription, he answered: 'Egad! If I had I should have broken my neck, for I flung it out of the window.' Oliver won fame in his lifetime as an authority on rheumatism. But his most lasting legacy was a biscuit he invented as part of his treatment for patients. This was the Bath Oliver.

Queen Charlotte.

The Pump Room saw many notable patients. Among those who came to take the waters was Queen Charlotte, the wife of George III. She lived at 93 Sydney Place, a few doors away from the home of the Duke of Clarence, who later became William IV. And a future emperor of France—Napoleon III—lived for some time in Great Pulteney Street.

The Circus also attracted many illustrious residents. Among them were Clive of India, the artist Thomas Gainsborough, and William Pitt, 1st Earl of Chatham. Chatham's son, William Pitt the Younger, also lived in Bath. He became Prime Minister at the age of 24.

Bath was also immortalised by authors such as Jane Austen and Charles Dickens, whose character Sam Weller remarked that the waters tasted like 'warm flat-irons'. Nor did his master, Mr Pickwick, fare much better when he faced the ordeal of a game of bridge with two formidable dowagers.

But it was an earlier artistic visitor, the 18th-century playwright Richard Brinsley Sheridan, who brought true literary glory to Bath by setting one of his most famous comedies in the city. His characters in his masterpiece 'The Rivals', which was produced in 1775, are obviously based on the people his acute eye observed on his visits to the baths or the assembly rooms. One of them, Mrs Malaprop, gave a new term to the English language—malapropism. However, Sheridan found time for more than observation during his stay, for he eloped to France with Elizabeth Linley, the beautiful daughter of Thomas Linley, Bath's musical director.

Exmoor: natural setting for the pageant of the seasons

Seasons parade their passing moods and colours upon this landscape where wild, high moorland will suddenly plunge down wooded valley sides to river torrents. Among the thatched and whitewashed villages are relics of more ancient settlements of monks and Norman barons. Here, wild deer and ponies roam in herds, reminders of a still more ancient past when this was one great forest tract.

(1) Dunster to Cleeve Abbey Leave Dunster by the A396, following the Minehead signs. At the T-junction with the A39 turn right towards Bridgwater, and continue for about 4½ m. to the village of Washford. In the village turn right on the road signposted to Cleeve Abbey, founded in 1198 and once the most flourishing monastery in Somerset. Well-preserved cloisters, refectory, chapterhouse and common-room still remain.

(2) Cleeve Abbey to Tarr Steps Return to the road and turn left, in just over ¼ m. bear right on the road signposted to Roadwater. Bear right again at the White Horse Inn to enter Exmoor National Park, and on into Roadwater. Beyond Roadwater fork right and continue to Kingsbridge. In Kingsbridge turn right over the bridge, on the road signposted for Timberscombe. Climb uphill to Luxborough and turn right at the T-junction. Pass Luxborough church and after ½ m. turn left on to the road signposted to Timberscombe. Turn left again at the crossroads, following the road signposted Dulverton, right at the next crossroads and almost immediately fork left towards Winsford. Turn right on to the A396 following the Dunster signpost and almost immediately turn left, crossing the river. At the T-junction turn left and enter Winsford, keeping straight ahead on the road signposted to Dulverton. Turn right at the T-junction on to the A396. About 5 m. later turn right on to the B3222 and into Dulverton. After bearing left in the village, turn right on to the B3223, signposted to Tarr Steps. After about 3½ m. turn left into Liscombe. There turn left following the signpost to Tarr Steps, a beauty spot with a primitive bridge over the River Barle.

(3) Tarr Steps to Oare Cross the river by the ford beside the Steps and continue into Hawkridge. By the church, turn right and immediately take the right fork. Turn right at the T-junction, following the Withypool signpost, and after ½ m., at the next junction, turn right on to the road signposted to Withypool, one of many moorland villages famous for fly-fishing. Cross the river and turn left by the Royal Oak Inn. Fork right on to the road signposted to Exford, and at the T-junction turn left on to the B3223. After 300 yds turn right and into Exford. Leave Exford on the B3224, signposted to Simonsbath. The road merges into the B3223 after about 1 m. Follow the road to Simonsbath and go through the village, staying on the B3223. After 5½ m., where the road hairpins left, turn right, following the signpost to Brendon. Pass the church and go through Rockford into Brendon. Keep straight ahead at the crossroads in Brendon on the road signposted to Malmsmead (a footpath from the village leads into the hills of the secluded Doone Valley). In Malmsmead turn left and cross the bridge or go through the ford, following the signpost to Oare, whose village church was the setting for Lorna Doone's violent wedding.

(4) Oare to Porlock Weir Continue through the village, past the church, and after 2½ m. turn right on to the A39. After ½ m. choose whether to turn left and follow the scenic toll-road into Porlock, or to stay on the main road and follow the notoriously steep Porlock Hill road down into the town. In Porlock itself turn left on to the B3225 to Porlock Weir, a village of thatched cottages.

(5) Porlock Weir to Allerford Return along the B3225 through Porlock, and turn left on to the A39 signposted to Minehead. But as soon as the road bears sharp right, on the outskirts of the village, keep straight ahead on the minor road signposted to Bossington. As the road goes downhill turn left into the village, which is only ½ m. from the sea, and is noted for its views and walks. At the T-junction in the village turn right, and at the next junction follow the sign to Allerford, one of the most picturesque spots in the region.

(6) Allerford to Selworthy At the T-junction with the A39 turn left following the Minehead signpost. After ¾ m., past Brandish Street and Holnicote, turn left on to the road signposted to Selworthy. The road leads uphill to the parish church.

(7) Selworthy to Dunster Continue through Selworthy and at the crossroads with the A39 go straight across towards Tivington and Wootton Courtenay. After 2 m. bear left into Wootton Courtenay. Continue past the ancient parish church, which has a distinctive saddleback roof, and after about 3 m. turn left on to the A396 to arrive back in Dunster.

NATURE NOTES
Exmoor rises to a high point of 1750 ft. The open moorland is covered with heather, bilberry and western gorse, a low bush which flowers in the autumn. On the northern fringe of the moor there are oak woodlands. Porlock Marsh is an area with reed beds and shallow pools.

INFORMATION

Places of interest *Cleeve Abbey:* May to Sept., daily; Oct. to Apr., weekdays, Sun. afternoons. *Dunster Castle:* Bank Hols.; Easter Mon. to end Sept., daily (except Mon. and Sat.), 11 a.m.-5 p.m.; Oct. to Nov., Tues., Wed., Sun., 2-4 p.m.

Information West Country Tourist Board, Trinity Court, Southernhay East, Exeter (Tel. Exeter 76351). *Minehead:* Market House (Tel. Minehead 2624).

Towns with easy access to Dunster:

Barnstaple	40 m.	Taunton	22 m.
Bridgwater	25 m.	Tiverton	27 m.

Thatched cottages at Porlock.

PORLOCK WEIR
Pretty cottages fringe a little harbour dotted with fishing boats and pleasure craft. The view across Porlock Bay towards Hurstone Point and South Wales can be excellent in clear weather. In the 1850s iron ore was found in the Barle Valley. A mining company planned a railway which was to take the ore to Porlock Weir for shipment to the steel furnaces of Wales. But the railway was never completed, and the harbour has remained unspoilt. Near the village Culbone church, claimed by some to be the smallest surviving medieval church in England. It can be reached only on foot.

Head-shaped piscina, Oare.

OARE
The little church here, celebrated in fiction as the place where Lorna Doone was shot during her marriage ceremony, is more than 800 years old, and serves a village mentioned in the Domesday Book. R. D. Blackmore, the barrister-turned-author who wrote *Lorna Doone*, was the grandson of a 19th-century rector of Oare. His characters are named after local people, and as recently as 1925 one of the churchwardens was a John Ridd—the name of the hero of the novel. But Blackmore himself was not a local man: he lived and worked in a London suburb.

Exmoor: the setting for Lorna Doone

SCALE

0   1   2   3   4   5 MILES

Packhorse bridge, Allerford.

ALLERFORD

An old packhorse bridge and a thatched village school are two of the elements that contribute to the old-world charm of Allerford. Around the village there are deep green woods and rewarding walks with fine views such as that from Selworthy Beacon. Much of the village is protected by the National Trust. The setting, below Selworthy and Bossington Hills, enhances Allerford's air of seclusion and peace.

DUNSTER

Dominated by a castle built only four years after the Norman Conquest, and still in good repair, Dunster is often claimed to be the most beautiful village on Exmoor. The castle, begun by the Norman Baron de Mohun, has been in the hands of the Luttrell family since 1376. At the other end of the main street is Conygar Hill, with a tower built in 1775 as a landmark for shipping. The main street is wide and full of old-world houses, with a 17th-century yarn market recalling the once-important cloth trade. The nearby Luttrell Arms, dating in part from 1400, was reputedly the residence of the Abbots of Cleeve. Behind the church is a Norman dovecote where, until just over 100 years ago, pigeons were reared for the table.

Old yarn market, Dunster.

Cleopatra: detail from 17th-century Dutch leather panel, Dunster Castle.

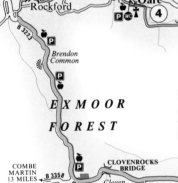

EXMOOR

Dramatic sea cliffs, hillside woods cut by fierce torrents, quiet valleys with trout and salmon streams . . . this is Exmoor, teeming with wildlife and studded with places of interest. It is ideal walking and riding country, but its roads also give the motorist access to some of the most absorbing survivals of centuries of British history. Most of the moor is now a National Park, spanning the Somerset-Devon borders. For centuries it was a royal forest, and until the 1800s it was remote and a virtual wilderness. Herds of red deer and wild ponies, descended from the ancient stock, still roam the moor. It is not hard to imagine that outlaws, like the Doones, came to this wild country to seek refuge from law and authority. Yet monasteries, churches and great houses show that civilised and orderly living existed here from earliest times.

SELWORTHY

White-painted thatched cottages rise towards a sturdy church set on a wooded hillside on the edge of Exmoor. Near the old cottages on the village green is a 14th-century tithe barn. Paths through the woods lead to Minehead and Allerford.

EXMOOR FOREST

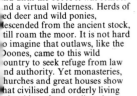

TARR STEPS

This ancient packhorse crossing of the River Barle is believed to date back to prehistoric times. The rough original stones must have been brought to the spot, since they are not of a local rock. Floods have often swept the crossing away but it has constantly been rebuilt. There is now a ford alongside it.

Ancient river crossing, Tarr Steps.

Carved ceiling, Cleeve Abbey.

CLEEVE ABBEY

The abbey, founded by Cistercian monks in 1198, took more than a century to complete, and minor additions were made for some time after that. The parts that remain are chiefly 13th century, plus a gatehouse remodelled by the last abbot before the Dissolution of the Monasteries.

Land of peat, willow and England's last battle

From bustling Bridgwater with its growing industrial and housing estates, the tour runs deep into the heartland of Somerset. Drainage in the 18th and 19th centuries has made rich and fertile the land of King's Sedge Moor, where the last battle on English soil ended the Monmouth Rebellion in 1685. Beyond the ridge of the Polden Hills, peat is still dug and processed. From Meare, country retreat and fish larder for the monks of Glastonbury, the route goes to the great ruined abbey of Glastonbury, over the hills to quiet little Somerton and down again to the southern reaches of West Sedge Moor where, by the River Parrett, willow plants are harvested for basket-making and wickerwork.

(1) Bridgwater to Chedzoy Leave the town on the A39 following the signpost to Glastonbury. Immediately after crossing the M5, turn right on to the road signposted to Chedzoy.

(2) Chedzoy to Shapwick In the village, turn left at the T-junction with Front Street, past the church on the left. After 1½ m. of flat road, turn left to Stawell. Go through the village and carry on straight over the crossroads to Moorlinch. Turn left at the T-junction in the village, follow the road to Greinton and turn left on to the A361 signposted to Glastonbury. After 1 m. turn left on to an unsignposted road uphill through Pedwell. At the junction of this road with the A39, turn left and then immediately right to Shapwick.

(3) Shapwick to Meare Go straight ahead over the crossroads in the village of Shapwick, descending now on the gentle northern slope of the Polden Hills. The signposts are for Wedmore, but in Westhay turn right on to the B3151, signposted to Meare/Glastonbury. Stay on this road to Meare.

(4) Meare to Glastonbury Soon after Meare, the road—still the B3151—runs flat and straight, part of the way alongside the River Brue, for some 3 m. to Glastonbury.

(5) Glastonbury to Somerton Leave Glastonbury on the A39 signposted to Street. Wearyall Hill is on the left. Near its summit once grew the original Glastonbury Thorn, said to have sprung from the staff of St Joseph of Arimathea when he came to Britain. The tree was destroyed during the Civil War, but a thorn in the abbey grounds is believed to be from a cutting. Just before Street, bear left on to the B3151. At the top of the hill on the right, just beyond the southern limits of Street, the National Trust properties of Ivy Thorn and Walton Hill run to the west of the road, from parts of which there are fine views over King's Sedge Moor. Stay on the B3151 and, after nearly 4 m., turn right on to the B3153, over a bridge, and right again into Somerton.

(6) Somerton to Muchelney Take the B3153 westwards from Somerton and, after about 4 m., turn left on to the A372 and into Huish Episcopi. Turn right by the church and immediately left for Muchelney.

(7) Muchelney to Bridgwater In the village bear right by the church. The abbey ruins are on the left after 100 yds. Continue on this road through Drayton and at the junction with the A378 turn left, then ¼ m. later turn right at the crossroads in Curry Rivel and past the church. Turn left at the T-junction and right at the next T-junction. Within 200 yds is the entrance to the National Trust property of Red Hill, on the south-eastern edge of West Sedge Moor. From these 2½ acres of hilltop there are views to Glastonbury Tor, the Quantocks and the Mendips. The road now descends to West Sedge Moor. Many of the fields in this area, watered by the River Parrett, are planted with willow saplings for the wickerwork industry. Up to 17,000 plants can be grown to each acre, and they are 'cropped' at different stages of growth according to the use for which they are required. Those cut at the largest size are used as the legs of wicker chairs. Just after the road passes over a big railway bridge, bear left and follow the river, passing through Stathe, where there is a willow-processing plant. Go through Burrow Bridge, where the road meets the A361. Turn right, over the bridge. At the top of the hillock on the right, Burrow Mount, accessible from the road, gives views in all directions. On the summit, a late-18th-century chapel was built over the foundations of an earlier one, but left unfinished. Leave the A361, turning left on the riverside road running away from the Mount to the north-west. After 2¼ m., at a T-junction, turn right to Westonzoyland. The parish includes most of the battlefield of Sedgemoor. The site is marked by a memorial stone at the end of a drove road at the northern end of the village. Westonzoyland was the headquarters of James II's army. From Westonzoyland, take the A372 westwards and follow this road back to Bridgwater.

INFORMATION

Places of interest *Bridgwater:* Admiral Blake Museum, daily, Tues., mornings only. *Glastonbury:* Abbey, daily. Lake Village Museum, The Tribunal, daily. *Meare:* Abbot's Fish House, open at any reasonable time, key available from Mrs Look of Manor Farm. *Muchelney:* Priest's House, by written appointment with the tenant, Priest's House, Muchelney, Nr. Langport, Somerset.

Craft workshop *Langport:* Muchelney Pottery, Mon. to Fri., Sat. mornings.

Events *Glastonbury:* Order of Bards, Ovates and Druids ceremonies, May 5; Pilgrimage to Glastonbury Abbey ruins and Parish Church, end June; plays in abbey ruins, beginning July to beginning Aug.; Tor Fair, second Mon. in Sept.

Information Central Library, Corporation Street, Taunton (Tel. Taunton 84077/5342).

Towns with easy access to Bridgwater:

Bristol	32 m.	Taunton	11 m.
Minehead	27 m.	Yeovil	23 m.

Bridgwater Guy Fawkes Carnival, 1899.

BRIDGWATER
This lively town in the fertile plains of west Somerset grew up as a river crossing. Its name is a simple slurring of 'Bridge of Walter', from the name of Walter of Douai, Lord of the Manor after the Conquest. Formerly a busy port on the tidal River Parrett, with a waterfront and quay, Bridgwater still has a small coastal trade, but it is now a town of mixed industries with three industrial estates. Continuous building has left only one great reminder of its medieval history, the cathedral-like parish church of St Mary, with its early-14th-century tower and slender 175 ft high spire added in 1367. From the tower, the rebel Duke of Monmouth surveyed Sedgemoor on the eve of battle in 1685. Robert Blake, who became Cromwell's admiral and one of the greatest names in Britain's naval history, was born in Bridgwater in 1599. Among exhibits in his house, now a museum, are his sea chest and compass. Behind the house are the Blake Memorial Gardens. There are some elegant Georgian houses in King Square, where a great medieval castle once stood. Two big events of Bridgwater's year, drawing thousands of visitors, are the four-day St Matthew's Fair in September and the Guy Fawkes Carnival, held on the Thursday nearest to November 5. There are tableaux processions and the firing of 500 'Bridgwater Squibs'—specially made fireworks 18 in. long

CHEDZOY
It was from Chedzoy that the supporters of Monmouth's rebellion, against the newly crowned James II, saw the king's army approaching over the flat lands of Sedgemoor in 1685. The tower of the parish church still shows the marks where they sharpened improvised weapons before going into battle. Every 20 years, a little less than an acre of land, bequeathed to the church in 1499, is auctioned to provide for church repairs, going to the last bidder before a ½ in. candle burns out. The next auction is in 1988.

SHAPWICK
The village overlooks Shapwick Heath, famous for its peat, once used for fuel, now processed for gardeners. The parish church has a central tower, rising from 13th-century arches. A heronry, with seven pairs of birds at the latest count, can be seen on the left of the road about a mile beyond the village.

Heron

King's Sedge Moor, site of the Battle of Sedgemoor, 1685.

Abbot's Fish House, Meare.

MEARE
When the mere from which the neat village took its name was a reality, lively with fish and waterfowl, it supplied the Glastonbury monks with the fish for their Friday and Lenten meals. The Fish House, a substantial early-14th-century house, was the home of the abbot's fisher bailiff. Manor Farm was a 14th-century country retreat for the Glastonbury abbots. The farm is not open to the public, but keys to visit the Fish House can be obtained there.

Joseph of Arimathea window, St John's, Glastonbury.

SOMERTON
No very busy roads pass through this quiet little town, and trains do not stop here now. The buildings round the market-place, with its 17th-century octagonal market cross, make up one of the most pleasant townscapes in Somerset. The towered 13th-century church and some 16th-century houses face the 18th-century town hall, built on the site of now-vanished Somerton Castle. There are mullioned windows to be seen, and Georgian houses in Broad Street.

GLASTONBURY
Only fragments remain of Glastonbury Abbey, set among trees and well-kept lawns. After the Dissolution in 1539, stone was 'quarried' from the abbey for buildings in the town, many of which still stand. Among the best preserved of the monastic ruins is the Abbot's Kitchen, built in the 14th century. A stained-glass window in St John's Church tells the story of Joseph of Arimathea, who is said to have brought the Holy Grail to Glastonbury from Jerusalem.

Abbot's Kitchen, Glastonbury.

WEST SEDGE MOOR
The route runs through West Sedge Moor, where willows are planted and cropped as withies for the basket-making and wickerwork trades. There are between 800 and 900 acres of basket willows in the area. Most of the crop is sent to basket-makers elsewhere, but some basket and chair-making is done locally and can be seen at Burrow Bridge. Darker colours are produced by boiling the shoots with the bark on. Paler withies are cut and stripped as their sap is rising.

Withy harvester.

Priest's House, Muchelney.

MUCHELNEY
Opposite the church in Muchelney is one of the oldest inhabited Priest's Houses in England, built as a vicarage to the church in the 14th century. It can be seen by appointment. The nave of the church has a rare, 17th-century painted wooden ceiling. The best relic of the nearby abbey, a Saxon foundation, is the abbot's house. This is mainly early 15th century, with the basic simplicity of the rooms set off by arcading, and there is a distinctive fireplace. The foundations of the Saxon abbey church have been recently uncovered. Many stones from the abbey have been built into farmyard walls in the village.

The meadows and hills that tumble to the Dorset coast

From high in the downlands, the hills tumble to the coast, over meadow and woodland, by rivers and clear brooks, where tiny thatched villages have stayed as unspoilt as the surrounding countryside. It is an ancient landscape, dotted with the settlements of Iron Age men. Beside the sea, prehistory is entombed in sandstone cliffs, and since the beginnings of the 18th century antiquarians have reaped from them a rich harvest of fossils.

(1) Lyme Regis to Forde Abbey Leave the town on the A3052, which is signposted to Bridport. In about 1½ m., turn left on to the road signposted to Axminster and keep straight ahead at the crossroads signposted to Wootton Fitzpaine. Follow the road over the A35, through a small wood and, in 1 m., turn left into Wootton Fitzpaine. Turn right at the T-junction which is signposted to Whitchurch Canonicorum, passing the 15th-century Wootton church on the right. Take the second turning on the left, signposted to Marshwood. Turn right at the crossroads for the entrance to Lambert's Castle, an Iron Age hill-fort, which is on the left. Return to the crossroads and turn right on the road signposted to Fishpond Bottom. At the T-junction, detour left to visit the Wootton Hill picnic site and forest trail, or turn right to Hawkchurch, to continue the tour. The road passes through pleasant woodlands until the junction with the B3165. Turn right following the signpost to Beaminster. Go through Marshwood and Bettiscombe and, at the crossroads by the Rose and Crown, turn left on to the minor road signposted to Thorncombe. Go straight ahead at the Thorncombe crossroads. After 1½ m., on the left, is Forde Abbey.

(2) Forde Abbey to Beaminster Leave the abbey, turning left. Immediately after crossing the River Axe, turn right for Winsham. At Winsham, turn right on to the B3162, going through Drimpton to Broadwindsor. Leave the village on the B3163 for Beaminster.

(3) Beaminster to Eggardon Hill Leave the village on the B3163, which is signposted to Evershot. After just over 1½ m., turn right towards Hooke, but continue on this road to pass the Mount Pleasant crossroads. Shortly afterwards, fork right and, ¾ m. later, pass under the railway. Soon the road skirts the 800 ft hill topped by Eggardon hill-fort.

(4) Eggardon Hill to Abbotsbury Continue on this road and, after 1½ m., turn left to Askerswell. Go through the village, and at the junction with the A35 turn left following the signpost to Dorchester. The road runs along a ridge of hills giving wide views on both sides. After 1½ m., turn right on the road signposted to Litton Cheney, down the hill and left at the junction. Go through the village to Long Bredy and turn left, following the signpost to Littlebredy. Just under ¾ m. later note, on the right, Kingston Russell House, birthplace of Admiral Sir Thomas Hardy, Nelson's flag captain at the Battle of Trafalgar. Go through the gateposts and into Littlebredy. Here fork right, following the signposts to Portesham. At the next junction turn right and after ½ m. right again. On the left is Admiral Hardy's monument. Go ahead at the cross-roads and down the hill into Portesham. Turn right on to the B3157, signposted to Abbotsbury. St Catherine's Chapel, on the summit of Chapel Hill, signals the village of Abbotsbury. In the village, turn left off the B3157 on to the road which leads down to the Abbotsbury Swannery, where there is a car park. To visit the gardens, return to the B3157 and turn left through the village, following the signposts to Bridport. The road to the gardens and Chesil Beach is on the left.

(5) Abbotsbury to Burton Bradstock Return to the B3157 and turn left. There are wide views of the coast from this road, taking in much of Lyme Bay. Go through Swyre and into Burton Bradstock.

(6) Burton Bradstock to West Bay Continue through the village on the B3157 and, after 1 m., turn left to West Bay.

(7) West Bay to Bridport Return to the B3157 and turn left, following the road into Bridport. The museum here contains an interesting collection of dolls belonging to Dr Donald Omand, international circus padre.

(8) Bridport to Whitchurch Canonicorum Leave the town on the A35, following the signposts to Charmouth. In Chideock village, a turning left leads to the attractive hamlet of Seatown. Continue along the A35 and, just before Morecombelake, turn right, following the signpost into Whitchurch (or Whitechurch) Canonicorum.

(9) Whitchurch Canonicorum to Charmouth Continue along the lane, turn right on reaching the A35 and follow the road into Charmouth.

(10) Charmouth to Lyme Regis In the village, Stonebarrow Lane, on the left, leads up to the clifftop National Trust estate. Continue through Charmouth on the A35 and then turn left on to the A3052 back to Lyme Regis.

INFORMATION

Places of interest *Abbotsbury:* Sub-Tropical Gardens, mid-Mar. to end Sept., weekdays, Sun. afternoons. Swannery, May to mid-Sept., weekdays, Sun. if fine. *Bridport Museum:* June to Oct., Mon. to Sat., 10.30 a.m.-1 p.m., afternoons 2.30-4.30 p.m. (except Thur. and Sat.). *Charmouth:* Barney's Fossil Museum, Easter to end Sept., daily, 10 a.m.-10 p.m. *Forde Abbey:* May to Sept., 2-6 p.m., Wed. and Sun., also Bank Hol. Mon.

Information West Country Tourist Board, Trinity Court, Southernhay East, Exeter (Tel. Exeter 76351). *Lyme Regis:* The Guildhall, Bridge Street (Tel. Lyme Regis 2138).

Towns with easy access to Lyme Regis:

Axminster	6 m.	Taunton	28 m.
Dorchester	24 m.	Weymouth	29 m.
Exmouth	27 m.	Yeovil	25 m.

Umbrella Cottage, Lyme Regis.

LYME REGIS
Ringed by steep hills and flanked by multi-coloured cliffs, the ancient borough of Lyme Regis is one of the best-loved beauty spots on the Dorset coast. Layers of lime and clay give the cliffs a tiered-cake effect. The highest, which rises 617 ft, has a cap that turns golden in sunlight. From these strata have been dug the prehistoric fossils for which the region is famous. But the instability of the cliffs has brought the town close to disaster. Twice the old parish register kept in St Michael's Church has recorded 'earthquakes' followed by ruinous tides. The harbour, protected by The Cobb, a massive breakwater, has silted up. Now it caters only for pleasure craft and lobster fishing boats. Novelist Jane Austen was a frequent visitor here.

Lyme Regis harbour.

Ammonite from Barney Hansford's fossil collection, Charmouth.

CHARMOUTH
Barney Hansford, the Charmouth amateur geologist who achieved worldwide fame for the fossils he unearthed in the district, now keeps his collection on show in the town Charmouth, though by-passed by history, has had two dramatic royal visits. Catharine of Aragon walked through the Tudor doorway of a hotel in the main street to rest, on her way to meet her future husband, Henry VIII. Charles II passed a fretful night in the same building during his flight from defeat at the Battle of Worcester in 1657. He had planned to embark from Charmouth Beach, but was thwarted by his boatman's wife who hid her husband's trousers, thus forcing the king to resume his flight by road.

SCALE

| 0 | 1 | 2 | 3 | 4 | 5 MILES |

façade of Forde Abbey.

[FO]RDE ABBEY

... beside the River Axe and surrounded by landscaped gardens where [ave]nues of trees troop across clipped lawns dotted with ponds, Forde [Ab]bey dates back to the 12th century, when a group of Cistercian [mo]nks were offered the site to found a new monastery. The building ... mixture of architectural styles of the 13th, 16th and 17th centuries. ... restored interiors are hung with valuable tapestries.

BEAMINSTER
Three disastrous fires have swept the old linen and wool town of Beaminster, each one destroying more of its fine heritage of early buildings, until today there are scant remains of the once important trading and market town. The centrepiece of the town, however, has withstood the flames: the soaring golden sandstone tower of St Mary's Church still stands. Built in the early 16th century as an addition to the older church, it has a peal of eight bells. About a mile south of the town is the Tudor manor house of Parnham. Many of the antique or decorative fittings originated in other houses. The stained glass in the dining-room came from Nonsuch Palace in Surrey, and the linenfold panelling in the Oak Room came from Sir Walter Raleigh's bedroom.

Iron Age fort, Eggardon.

EGGARDON HILL
Eggardon Down rises up to the hill-fort which was described by the Victorian novelist Thomas Hardy as 'a shape and form as near indestructible as any found in nature'. Like Dorset's other famous hill-fort, Maiden Castle, it is said to be haunted. Myth-makers speak of hounds baying at the ghosts of Roman soldiers and, more recently, of flying saucers landing. The fort is surrounded by massive earthworks of Iron Age men: Coney's Castle, Pilsdon Pen, Abbotsbury Castle and Lambert's Castle. This last was used as a racecourse from Roman times until recently. They all provide high points on the edge of the chalk country, where the land rolls out in waves to the west and down to the sweeping coastline in the south.

BURTON BRADSTOCK
This low-lying village, because it is set back from the seafront behind a ridge, has been left untouched by the local holiday trade. The old cottages crowd in upon the narrow streets and the 14th-century church. Just over the ridge is a beach and car park, where the River Bride flows out into the sea.

(Map spanning the central portion of the page shows the route through Winsham, Drimpton, Broadwindsor, Beaminster, Hooke, Eggardon Hill, Whitchurch Canonicorum, Bridport, Burton Bradstock, Abbotsbury, Lyme Regis, Charmouth, West Bay, and surrounding places, with numbered waypoints 1–10.)

[BRI]DPORT
[Th]e broad pavements of Bridport were [on]ce drying tables for the thousands of [mil]es of rope demanded of the town ... the Royal Navy ever since the time ... King John. Not only ships' ropes, but [ro]pes for every purpose—including the [gal]lows—were made at Bridport, and ... hangman's noose earned the [nic]kname of the 'Bridport Dagger'. [Mu]ch of the old industry has [dis]appeared. Now the town is given [ov]er to netmaking, and is the biggest [pr]oducer of industrial, fishing and [mu]lti-purpose netting in Europe, if not [the] world.

WEST BAY
In 1446 the Archbishops of England and Wales launched a fund-raising drive throughout the kingdom to build a harbour at Bridport. They set a target of £3000 but raised only £61. A sarcastic Henry VI directed it to be spent on the town's educational facilities. Bridport stayed without a harbour for 300 years, but one was finally built at West Bay in the 18th century. It flourished for about 100 years, and all but died as a cargo port when the railway arrived in 1884. Now it is a holiday harbour, but still has its fleet of fishing boats and the occasional ship carrying a cargo of timber.

WHITCHURCH CANONICORUM
The village, set on hillsides bordering a brook called The Char, takes its unusual name from the days when the canons of Wells and Salisbury divided the tithes between them. The 13th-century church of St Candida and the Holy Cross has a shrine dedicated to St Wite, a Christian Saxon woman who, according to local tradition, was killed by marauding Danish invaders. The holes bored in her stone coffin allowed a crippled pilgrim to insert his afflicted limb and so hope for a cure.

Peacock in the tropical gardens, Abbotsbury.

ABBOTSBURY
A huge medieval tithe barn, 282 ft long and 31 ft high, where the monks of the ancient abbey received and stored their dues in produce from the tenants who farmed their estate, is one of the few remains of this important monastic settlement. The rest of the abbey has been reduced to scattered foundations. There are two fine relics of the old abbey: St Catherine's Chapel, built on a hill above the village in the 15th century, and The Swannery. Here, mute swans, once bred for the monastery table, are now protected and allowed to breed. About 500 swans nest here each year and feed in the shallow waters of the Fleet. Near by are the tropical gardens open to the public, where exotic peacocks, turkeys and wildfowl strut among flowering shrubs and trees. Abbotsbury is a convenient stopping place from which to visit Chesil Beach. Extending to Portland, the beach is 16 miles long, banked with shingle 35 ft high in places.

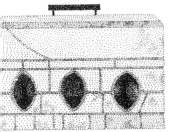

... shrine of St Wite.

Cottage gardens, and the hilltop where King Arthur held court

The last resting place of the poet T. S. Eliot, the legendary site of the Court of King Arthur, a unique museum of naval aircraft, Elizabethan architecture at its best, and an exotic zoo are some of the highlights of this surprising part of Somerset. Villages of golden stone, thatched roofs and old churches lie on every road, tempting the visitor to stop and linger over their peaceful charm and the atmosphere of a bygone age.

(1) Yeovil to East Coker Leave Yeovil by the A30, following the signposts for Dorchester. On the outskirts of the town, turn left to join the A37, still following the Dorchester signs. After 1½ m. turn right, and right again at the next junction. This leads into East Coker village.

(2) East Coker to Montacute Follow the same road through the village and into nearby North Coker. (Note the local Ham Hill limestone, revealed by roadside cuttings.) Turn right at the T-junction signposted Yeovil, and left on to the A30, going into West Coker. On the left, in Manor Street, is the 14th-century manor house. Follow the A30 to the outskirts of East Chinnock, and opposite the church turn right, following the signposts to Odcombe. At the crossroads in Odcombe turn left. Turn right at the next crossroads, following the Montacute signpost. When the lane meets the A3088 turn left into Montacute. The entrance to Montacute House is opposite the market square.

(3) Montacute to Cricket St Thomas Leave by continuing along the A3088. Go through Stoke sub Hamdon, and after 1 m. turn left on to the B3165, which is signposted to Crewkerne. After 2½ m. turn right, along a road signposted Hinton St George. In Merriott, the next village, turn right, still following the Hinton St George signs, and at the T-junction with the A356 turn right again. After about 200 yds turn left down a minor road into Hinton St George. The Poulett Arms in the village has a curious free-standing wall, built for a long-dead local version of the game of fives. Turn left at the crossroads at the start of the village, and after 1¼ m., at the A30, turn right towards Chard. After about 2 m. cross Windwhistle Hill and arrive at the entrance to Cricket St Thomas Wild Life Park, in the grounds of Cricket House, one of the most beautiful estates in the West Country.

(4) Cricket St Thomas to Chard Return to the A30 and turn left. Chard is another 2½ m. along the road. Two streams run in open culverts on either side of the High Street. One goes north to the Bristol Channel, and the other south to the English Channel.

(5) Chard to Barrington Court Turn right at the end of Chard High Street on to the A358, following the Ilminster signs. After just over 3 m. turn right on to the A3037 and into Ilminster. By the market cross, turn left on to the A303 and immediately right to the B3168, signposted to Langport. Go through Puckington and, where the road bears sharp left, keep right and into Barrington. Barrington Court is on the left at the end of the village.

(6) Barrington Court to Martock At the crossroads about ¾ m. beyond Barrington, turn left on the road signposted to Shepton Beauchamp. Go through Shepton Beauchamp and West Lambrook, then at the next junction turn right for East Lambrook and the hamlet of Coat. At the crossroads in Coat turn right, following the signposts to Martock. At the B3165 turn right again to enter Martock.

(7) Martock to Lyte's Cary Go back along the B3165 for 4½ m. to Long Sutton. At the A372 turn right, following the sign to Wincanton. After about 3 m., at the crossroads with the B3151, turn left and almost immediately right, following the signposts into Kingsdon. Continue through the village. The medieval manor of Lyte's Cary is opposite the next T-junction.

(8) Lyte's Cary to Fleet Air Arm Museum Return to the T-junction and, with the house behind, turn left. After about 1 m. turn left on to the A372. Cross the A37, on to the road signposted Wincanton, and continue for about 2 m. to the junction with the A303. There turn right; the Fleet Air Arm Museum is on the left after about 1 m.

(9) Fleet Air Arm Museum to South Cadbury Return along the A303 in the Wincanton direction. Pass through Sparkford and, about 2 m. later, turn right by a thatched chapel to South Cadbury. From the village, a track goes up to the Cadbury Castle site.

(10) South Cadbury to Yeovil Leave the castle and continue along the road into Sutton Montis. Turn left at the T-junction following the sign for Queen Camel. At the A359 turn left for the return to Yeovil through Marston Magna and Mudford.

INFORMATION

Places of interest *Barrington Court:* Wed., 10.15 a.m.-12.15 p.m., 2-6 p.m. (winter, 4 p.m.). *Cricket St Thomas:* Wild Life Park, daily. *Lyte's Cary:* Mar. to Oct., Wed. and Sat. afternoons. *Montacute House:* Apr. to Sept., Wed. to Mon., 12:30-6 p.m.; Mar., Oct., Nov., Wed., Sat., Sun., 2-6 p.m. (or dusk). *Yeovil:* Wyndham Museum, Mon. to Sat. (except Thur.). *Yeovilton:* Fleet Air Arm Museum and Concorde, 10 a.m. (Sun., 12.30) 5.30 p.m., closed last fortnight in December.

Craft workshops *Crewkerne:* The Pottery. Most days. Telephone first (Crewkerne 3630).

Events *Chard:* Carnival Week, Nov. *Crewkerne:* Fair, beginning Sept. *Ilminster:* Carnival, Sept. and Oct. *Yeovil:* Market days, Mon. and Fri.

Information *Taunton:* Central Library, Corporation Street (Tel. Taunton 84077/5342).

Towns with easy access to Yeovil:

Bridgwater	.... 26 m.	Shaftesbury	.... 22 m.
Dorchester	.... 20 m.	Taunton	...... 26 m.

Lyte's Cary House.

LYTE'S CARY
This medieval manor house, begun in 1343, was the home of the Lyte family for 500 years. The Great Hall was added in 1450, and the quadrangle buildings in 1535. Here Sir Henry Lyte, the Elizabethan botanist, translated a Dutch treatise which became famous as *Lyte's Niewe Herball*. The house passed from the Lyte family in the 18th century and fell into decay. It was bought in 1907 by Sir Walter Jenner, who restored it and bequeathed it to the National Trust in 1948. He also collected the 17th-century oak furniture with which many of the rooms are furnished in keeping with their original design.

MARTOCK
The Treasurer's House was, until the last century, the home of the rectors of Martock, who held the office of treasurer of Wells Cathedral. The mainly Perpendicular-style church has a lofty nave and a 16th-century angel roof, saved by massive restoration. Outside the church, the medieval village stocks still survive, and so does the 17th-century market cross.

BARRINGTON COURT
The present house, built around 1520 on the site of an earlier mansion, was sold and resold many times in the next 200 years, and ended up as a dilapidated farm. Rescued by the National Trust, it was restored by a philanthropist in the 1920s. The most unusual feature is its E-shaped front face.

[Map showing the Ilminster, Hornsbury, Chard, Honiton 13 MILES A 30, Axminster 7 MILES A 358, Cricket St Thomas area with roads A303, A358, A30, B3162, B3165.]

CHARD
Chard, granted its charter in 1234, became a royal borough in 1285. But only a few years later the town was begging to be relieved of the duty of sending two representatives to Parliament—the citizens said they could not afford the expense. There are many old and interesting buildings, including the 15th-century church with its gargoyles, the Grammar School, the Manor House, the Guildhall and Chough's Hotel, an Elizabethan mansion which was the home of the inventor John Stringfellow. He flew the first heavier-than-air machine—a steam-powered model aircraft—at Chard in 1843.

North American wood duck Cricket St Thomas.

CRICKET ST THOMAS
The wildlife park, in the middle of a 1000 acre estate, includes llamas, bison, wapiti, wallabies and flamingoes. A variety of ducks can be seen on the lakes, which were made by damming the stream in the parkland. There is also a 16 acre terraced garden laid out with rare shrubs and trees, and an early-19th-century house.

SCALE

0   1   2   3   4   5 MILES

FLEET AIR ARM MUSEUM
Since the Royal Naval air station HMS *Heron* was commissioned at Yeovilton in 1940 as the fighter training school for the Fleet Air Arm, the village has had both flying and naval associations. In recent years, the official museum of the Fleet Air Arm was also established there, and it is now possible to see historic aircraft, equipment, photographs and documents concerned with the flying branch of the Royal Navy since its formation in 1914. The aircraft on view include examples of the Swordfish, Sea Fury and Sea Vampire. There are also foreign machines, such as the Fokker Triplane used by the German air force in the First World War. The museum attracts some 130,000 visitors a year. There is also an open day and flying display in summer.

First World War Fokker Triplane.

SOUTH CADBURY
The reputed site of Camelot, the meeting place of King Arthur's Knights of the Round Table, Cadbury Castle is an ancient strongpoint on an isolated hilltop. Recent excavations have produced evidence of occupation going back nearly 6000 years, and defensive works erected in the Iron Age from about 600 BC and later remodelled. Some of the discoveries of military equipment suggest that there may have been a workshop here for its manufacture. There is also a pre-Roman shrine, and signs that the Romans occupied the place and destroyed the defences. In Saxon times, King Ethelred the Unready established a mint here and also built new fortifications. Coins from Cadbury are still in existence, some of them bearing the mark of a maker who was known as 'God at Cadbury'. King Canute closed down the mint in the 11th century and once again the defences were demolished. A fresh start was made on a new hilltop fort in the 13th century, but this building was never finished.

Ancient coin minted at Cadbury.

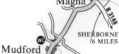

YEOVIL
The town on the River Yeo dates back to the Romans. But neither they, nor the Saxons, Danes or Normans who succeeded them, left many mementoes. The church of St John the Baptist was built of limestone and local Ham stone during the 14th century to replace one put there 200 years before. The museum attached to Henford Manor House has exhibits of local interest and a good collection of firearms. A big livestock market, held twice a week, serves the surrounding farming area.

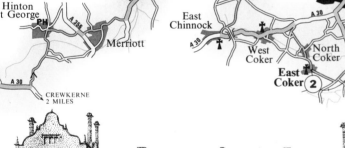

Montacute House; back elevation, facing extensive lawns and gardens.

A wall-hanging at Montacute.

MONTACUTE
The main attraction of the old village, overlooked by an 18th-century folly tower on St Michael's Hill, is the Elizabethan Montacute House, one of the stateliest of stately homes. The village dates back to before King Canute and gets its name from Latin words describing the 'pointed hill' near by. The house was built between 1588, the year of the Armada, and 1601, and is a splendid example of Elizabethan flamboyance. It contains valuable furnishings, china, portraits, tapestries, plasterwork and panelling. The formal gardens are among the most complete survivals of their period, and in summer there is a fine display of old-fashioned roses. Close by is the gatehouse of the Cluniac priory founded on the land in 1102. The priory itself came to grief at the Dissolution of the Monasteries by Henry VIII, when the land passed to Sir Edward Phelips, who built the present house.

Dampier memorial plaque, East Coker.

EAST COKER
Perhaps best known as the title of a poem by T. S. Eliot, this little village is Eliot's last resting place. A stained-glass window in the parish church, given by the Eliot family, records that one of the poet's forbears left the village some centuries ago and founded the American branch of the family. A plaque in the church also commemorates the 17th-century navigator and West Indies buccaneer William Dampier, born in the local manor house. Dampier wrote authoritative books on seamanship and navigation while he preyed on Spanish ships carrying treasure from the Americas.

A butterfly farm in the land of an ancient giant

From Sherborne, with its warm-stone abbey church and stately home built as a country retreat by Sir Walter Raleigh, the route takes in one of Britain's most unusual farms, where the livestock are butterflies. Then comes clay country, with little streams cutting through dairy pastures and sometimes flowing across minor roads in water-splashes. Quiet villages hide in the valleys of the chalk uplands, one brooded over by the 1500-year-old Giant of Cerne. To round off the tour, there is a look at the typical Dorset market town of Sturminster Newton, and a visit to the gabled show-place manor house of Purse Caundle.

(1) Sherborne to Sandford Orcas Leave Sherborne on the B3148, signposted to Marston Magna. After 2½ m. turn right at the crossroads, following the signpost to Sandford Orcas. At the T-junction turn right, down a rocky gorge, into the village. Turn left in the village to visit the church and manor house.

(2) Sandford Orcas to Over Compton Return to the village centre and turn right on to the road signposted to Trent. Cross the B3148, turning right and immediately left, following the Mudford signpost. At the next crossroads turn left towards Trent. Turn right at the T-junction ¾ m. later, then left at the next junction and into Trent. Pass the church, and at the T-junction turn left to Over Compton. To visit the butterfly farm, turn right and bear immediately left in Over Compton. Turn left on to the A30; after about ¼ m., turn left to the butterfly farm.

(3) Over Compton to Chetnole Return to the A30 and turn right. After ¼ m. turn left to Bradford Abbas. Go straight over the crossroads into the village and over the railway bridge. Turn left at the T-junction, then immediately right and over the hump-backed bridge. After about 1 m. turn right on to the road signposted to Yetminster. Turn left through the village, bearing left over the railway bridge. Turn right on the road signposted to Leigh about 1 m. later. In Leigh, by the village cross, turn right for Chetnole.

(4) Chetnole to Sydling St Nicholas At the junction by the post office in Chetnole, turn left and at the next junction in ½ m. turn left again, signposted Batcombe. Continue south to the T-junction in 1¼ m. and turn left, signposted Batcombe. Shortly, as the road bears sharply left by a junction, turn right and go up the valley. At the T-junction at the top of Batcombe Hill turn right. At the crossroads with the A37 keep straight ahead on the minor road signposted to Evershot. Take the first left in Evershot and go straight over the crossroads to Rampisham. Go over the crossroads here and up to the crossroads with the A356. Go straight over on the road signposted to Kingcombe. At the next crossroads, turn left through Higher Kingcombe and Lower Kingcombe into Toller Porcorum. Turn left at the T-junction in Toller Porcorum, following the signpost to Maiden Newton, and at the junction with the A356 turn right into Maiden Newton. In the village turn left, signposted Cattistock, and almost immediately bear right. Carry on across the A37, following the Sydling St Nicholas signpost. Turn right at the T-junction and turn right again at the crossroads into Sydling St Nicholas.

(5) Sydling St Nicholas to Cerne Abbas Return through the village, but fork right over the bridge by the chapel and right again at the T-junction by the ford. Follow the road signposted Cerne Abbas, and cross the A352 into the village.

(6) Cerne Abbas to Mappowder Return to the A352 and turn right through Minterne Magna. After 4 m., at Middlemarsh, turn right signposted Glanvilles Wootton. Go straight over the crossroads, and at the T-junction with the B3146 turn right, signposted Buckland Newton. At the crossroads with the B3143 go straight over on the minor road signposted to Mappowder. Turn left at the T-junction, right at the next T-junction and right again to visit Mappowder church.

(7) Mappowder to Sturminster Newton Return from the church and turn left, signposted Hazelbury Bryan. At the T-junction in Hazelbury Bryan turn right, signposted Woolland, and at the next T-junction turn left and immediately right by the church. At the next T-junction turn right. After about 1¾ m. turn left, signposted to Okeford Fitzpaine. Where the road bears left into Ibberton, keep straight ahead steeply uphill on the road signposted Bulbarrow. At the summit, turn left along the brow of Bell Hill. At the T-junction at the bottom of the hill turn right to Okeford Fitzpaine, and 1 m. after the village turn left on to the A357. After about 2 m. turn right on to the B3092 into Sturminster.

(8) Sturminster Newton to Purse Caundle Return to the A357 and turn right, signposted to Sherborne. About 1 m. beyond Lydlinch, turn left on the road signposted to Stourton Caundle. After another ¾ m. turn left into the village. Beyond the church, turn left. Enter Purse Caundle after 2½ m.

(9) Purse Caundle to Sherborne Go through the village to the A30 junction; there turn left following the signpost for Sherborne.

INFORMATION

Places of interest *Cerne Abbey:* Daily. *Over Compton:* Worldwide Butterflies Ltd, daily, 10 a.m.-5 p.m. ex. Christmas Day. *Purse Caundle Manor:* Mar. to Oct., Wed., Thur., Sun. and Bank Hols., 2-5 p.m. *Sherborne:* Castle, Easter to Sept., Thur., Sat., Sun. and Bank Hol. Mon. *Sandford Orcas:* Manor House, daily, 11 a.m.-5 p.m.

Information West Country Tourist Board, Trinity Court, Southernhay East, Exeter (Tel. Exeter 76351).

Towns with easy access to Sherborne:
Blandford Forum 20 m.　　　Shaftesbury .... 16 m.
Dorchester .... 19 m.　　　Yeovil .... 6 m.

British Large Blue butterfly   Underwings

OVER COMPTON
Just south of the grey-stone village, with its 15th-century church and well-preserved houses, is a farm where butterflies and moths are reared. The insects are bred as items for collection, or for release in flower gardens. A showroom and an exhibition of species from all over the world are open all year round. From May to August, there are conducted tours to see the breeding rooms; live butterflies and moths in cages; caterpillars in plastic rearing containers, and some stock in fine net cages on the trees outside. The British Large Blue butterfly is near extinction in the wild, and the farm's owners are experimenting to find a method of rearing it in captivity. In some cases, the release of 'farm' butterflies has been known to boost natural populations.

Water-splash road, Chetnole

SYDLING ST NICHOLAS
The village is sunk in a sheltered, wooded valley below the bare downs, with the hills rising to almost 700 ft on either side. There are some well-preserved chalk-and-cob cottages with thatched roofs. At the south end of the little High Street are three fine old houses in a row: The Old Vicarage, built in 1640, and the middle house, about 100 years later, are both of flint-banded stone with mullioned windows. East House is the odd one out. It is of red brick, with wide windows and a huge central chimneystack, built around 1780. Near by is the old Blacksmith's House and next to that a working smithy. The church of St Nicholas, mainly 15th and 16th century, was built independently of the tower (1430), two buttresses of which can be seen in the nave. The village also has a big tithe barn, of flint with stone buttresses.

SCALE
0　　1　　2　　3　　4　　5 MILES

SANDFORD ORCAS

The main feature of this little village in a valley, which is approached through high-banked lanes, is a small, complete Tudor manor house. An arched gatehouse leads into a stable courtyard, where a barn and the gabled house itself stand side by side. All three are built of honey-coloured Ham Hill stone. The Knoyle family, who once owned the village, are represented in the church by a tablet of 1607. It shows William Knoyle with his two wives, Fillip and Grace, and their children.

Gatehouse, Sandford Orcas.

Detail of the porch, Sherborne Abbey.

SHERBORNE

Although it is the busy centre of the district's dairy-farming industry, Sherborne, with its imposing abbey church, public school and 16th and 17th-century inns and houses, all in warm Ham Hill stone, has the air of a little cathedral city. The abbey church, rebuilt between 1425 and 1504 after a fire, contains elements which date back to Saxon bishops of the 8th century; and the beautiful 15th-century fan vaulting rests on Norman shafts and arches. Sherborne School, adjoining the church, was refounded in 1550, but can claim it is the successor to the Saxon school founded by the first bishop of Sherborne, St Aldhelm, in 705. Sherborne Old Castle, now in ruins, was once owned by Sir Walter Raleigh, who built the present Sherborne Castle in 1594. It was bought by Sir John Digby in 1617, and his descendants still live there. The castle, which is set in 20 acres of parkland, has fine collections of paintings, furniture and porcelain.

PURSE CAUNDLE

The many-gabled Purse Caundle Manor, with its mullioned windows and steep, stone-slated roofs, is one of Dorset's best-known smaller show places. The 15th and 16th-century house has a Great Hall, with minstrels' gallery and windows overlooking a paved courtyard, and a Great Chamber with a wagon roof and fine oriel window. Excellent period furniture includes two four-poster beds—one Jacobean, the other 18th-century French.

Purse Caundle Manor.

STURMINSTER NEWTON

The approach from the main road to this prosperous livestock and shopping centre is over a six-arched 15th-century bridge. The attractive streets and triangular market-place, where 18th and 19th-century brick intermingles pleasantly with 15th and 16th-century stone, are quiet, except on Mondays when they are thronged with Stour farmers and their families. On a grassy mound overlooking the river are the remains of a 14th-century manor house.

MAPPOWDER

This compact village in Blackmoor Vale clusters around a 15th-century stone church, with large windows of clear glass. Inside is a rare miniature effigy of a crusader. T. F. Powys (1875–1953) the Dorset novelist, lived in the cottage nearest the churchyard entrance.

CHETNOLE

The roads in and around the village are cut by water-splashes through the River Wriggle. This is typical well-watered 'cow country' in a narrow belt of clay, and ploughland is rare. Chetnole's church, surrounded by a walled area of sward, has a tower built in 1580, with four large gargoyles at the corners—one of an animal with human heads for eyes.

Map labels

MARSTON MAGNA 1 MILE · WINCANTON 9 MILES · Sandford Orcas MANOR · Milborne Port · SHAFTESBURY 11 MILES · Purse Caundle MANOR · STALBRIDGE 2 MILES · Sturminster Newton · SHAFTESBURY 8 MILES · BLANDFORD FORUM 7 MILES · Stourton Caundle · Lydlinch · Okeford Fitzpaine · Trent · Over Compton · SHERBORNE · CASTLE · CASTLE · BUTTERFLY FARM · YEOVIL 2 MILES · Bradford Abbas · Blackmoor · Glanvilles Wootton · Hazelbury Bryan · Ibberton · Woolland · Mappowder · PUDDLETOWN 10 MILES · Yetminster · Leigh · MIZ MAZE · Chetnole · YEOVIL 8 MILES · Wriggle · Melbury Bubb · Middlemarsh · Minterne Magna · MANOR GARDENS · Batcombe · Batcombe Hill · THE GIANT NT · Cerne Abbas · DORCHESTER 7 MILES · Evershot · Sydling St Nicholas · TITHE BARN · Rampisham · STRIP LYNCHETS · Maiden Newton · DORCHESTER 8 MILES · CREWKERNE 9 MILES · Lower Kingcombe · Frome · DORCHESTER 8 MILES · Higher Kingcombe · Toller Porcorum

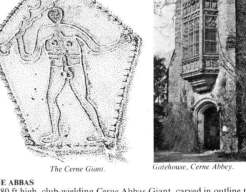

The Cerne Giant.

Gatehouse, Cerne Abbey.

CERNE ABBAS

The 180 ft high, club-wielding Cerne Abbas Giant, carved in outline through the turf of the chalk hillside north-east of the village, has been connected with local fertility legends. As late as the beginning of the 19th century, women believed that sleeping out on the hillside could cure barrenness. But the fact that it was almost certainly carved during the Roman occupation some 1500 years ago has led to the suggestion that it may be a representation of the Roman demigod, Hercules—possibly identified at the time with some local god. In the village, a tithe barn, a guest house and a beautiful 15th-century gatehouse with an intricately carved, two-storey oriel window, are all that remain of a Benedictine abbey originally founded here in the 10th century.

Thatched cottages, Sydling St Nicholas.

A land of ghosts—and royal relaxation beside the sea

If ghosts walked by day, this would be a tour on which one might expect to meet plenty. It begins with a look at the 'haunted' lodgings where Judge Jeffreys returned to sleep after condemning 292 men to the gallows in one day. It visits a Stone Age fort where the spectres of long-dead warriors are said to have wandered for up to 4000 years. It pauses by the village green where in 1834 the Tolpuddle Martyrs held the meeting that was to mark the birth of the trade union movement. And it looks in on the resort where a king discovered the pleasures of bathing in the sea.

(1) Dorchester to Higher Bockhampton Leave the town on the A35, signposted to Poole. After 1½ m. turn right on to the road signposted to Bockhampton. At the next crossroads, turn left for Higher Bockhampton. Take the first right and then right again to the woodland car park at Higher Bockhampton. From here a footpath leads to Hardy's Cottage.

(2) Higher Bockhampton to Athelhampton Hall Return along the same route to the crossroads and turn left on to the road signposted to Tincleton. After 1½ m. turn left through Puddletown Forest and into Puddletown. Turn right on to the A35 signposted to Poole. In about ¾ m., Athelhampton Hall is on the left.

(3) Athelhampton Hall to Tolpuddle Stay on the A35, which runs through Burleston and straight into Tolpuddle.

(4) Tolpuddle to Weymouth In the town turn right by the Martyrs' Tree to Affpuddle and, at the junction with the B3390, turn right, following the signpost to Weymouth. The road runs through heath and woodlands to Warmwell, a town set in rustic scenery with a Jacobean manor house. Beyond Warmwell, keep straight ahead at the roundabout on to the A353 signposted to Weymouth. (To visit Ringstead Bay, turn left for Ringstead just after the A353 bears sharp right, and continue through Upton village to the bay.) The A353 runs on to Osmington, where the giant figure of George III, cut into the chalk downs, rides away from Weymouth. Go through Osmington and into Preston. There turn right opposite the Ship Inn, down Sutton Road and into Sutton Poyntz. Bear left in the village and left at the T-junction, on the road signposted to Weymouth. On the left of this loop is Chalbury's ancient hill-fort. Turn left at the next T-junction, and at the A353 turn right. (To visit the remains of the small Roman temple on Jordan Hill, turn left where the road bears right at the sea front.) The A353 continues straight on and into Weymouth.

(5) Weymouth to Chesil Beach Leave on the A354 following the Portland signpost, crossing the bridge by the harbour. (To visit Sandsfoot Castle, the 16th-century blockhouse built to guard the harbour, turn left where the A354 bears sharp right.) The A354 continues on to Wyke Regis. Follow the road left and out on to Chesil Beach.

(6) Chesil Beach to Isle of Portland Follow the A354 along the beach and on to the Isle of Portland.

(7) Isle of Portland to Maiden Castle At the roundabout keep to the A354, which is signposted to Fortuneswell. (To see Henry VIII's Portland Castle, which stands beside the heliport within the naval base, keep ahead as the road turns sharp right.) Continue through Fortuneswell on the A354, which soon becomes the B3154 and enters Easton. (To visit Church Ope Cove, the site of William Rufus's castle and one of the few places on the island able to support trees, take the lane on the left.) Keep straight ahead to Southwell and, at the Eight Kings Inn, turn left for the Bill of Portland, where Pulpit Rock splits the breakers that roll upon it. Three lighthouses mark the Bill, but only one is working now. Built in 1906, it is 136 ft high. It has a car park and is open to visitors. One of the disused lighthouses is now a bird observatory.

Return along the route and rejoin the A354 to Wyke Regis where, as the A354 bears sharp right, go straight ahead on the B3157, which is signposted to Chickerell. Turn left at the junction, still on the B3157, and left again at the next T-junction. Continue through Chickerell and into Portersham, boyhood home of Admiral Sir Thomas Hardy, Nelson's Flag Captain at Trafalgar. In the village turn right on the road to Martinstown, up the hill and right at the next crossroads. The road passes Hardy's 70 ft monument. Turn right on to the B3159 to go through Martinstown and continue to Upwey. Turn left into Ellwell Street and then left on to the A354, signposted to Dorchester. On the outskirts of Dorchester, follow the signpost left for Maiden Castle.

(8) Maiden Castle to Dorchester Return to the A354 and turn left into Dorchester.

INFORMATION

Places of interest *Athelhampton Hall:* Apr. to Oct., Wed., Thur., Sun., Good Friday, Bank Hol. Sun. and Mon., 2-6 p.m. *Dorchester:* County Museum, Mon. to Sat., 10 a.m.-1 p.m., 2-5 p.m. Dorset Military Museum, weekdays, 9 a.m.-1 p.m., 2-5 p.m. Old Crown Court, Mon. to Fri. (not Sat. afternoons in winter). *Hardy's Cottage:* Exterior, Mar. to Oct., 11 a.m.-6 p.m., interior by appointment with tenant. *Portland:* Castle, Apr. to Sept., weekdays, Sun. afternoons. Museum, summer, Mon. to Sat. and Sun. afternoons; winter, weekdays except Tues. *Weymouth:* 2 and 3 Trinity Street, Easter Sat. to end Sept., Wed., Sat., Bank Hol. Mon. 2.30-5 p.m. *Sandsfoot Castle:* daily, 7.30 a.m.-dusk.

Information West Country Tourist Board, Trinity Court, Southernhay East, Exeter (Tel. Exeter 76351). *Weymouth:* The Esplanade (Tel. Weymouth 72444).

Towns with easy access to Dorchester:
Bournemouth . . . 27 m.   Taunton . . . . 41 m.
Lyme Regis . . . . 24 m.   Yeovil . . . . 20 m.

Ramparts of Maiden Castle.

MAIDEN CASTLE
Some say this vast earthen fort is haunted. It has a right to be. Set upon a saddleback hill 1000 yds long, its history stretches as far back as 2000 BC, when Stone Age farmers settled at the eastern knoll. After they left, it became the site of an enormous funeral monument: an earthen mound or barrow 1760 ft long. From then it was abandoned until 300 BC and the arrival of men of the Iron Age, who swiftly expanded it into a township that covered the entire hill. At first they ringed it with one ditched rampart, later adding two more to meet the threat of the new long-range sling-shot weapons. Thus defended, they met the full force of the Roman army in AD 43, and were totally overwhelmed. Soon after, Maiden Castle was abandoned for the last time. A mass burial ground containing the remains of the massacred defenders was excavated in the 1930s.

CHESIL BEACH   Portesh
A 20 mile long bank of shingle running from Abbotsbury to the Isle of Portland, Chesil Beach is like a sea wall, but formed by the sea itself. Strong currents constantly sift the stones, and local fishermen claim they can tell exactly where they are along the beach by the size of the stones. The smaller stones are found at the western end, and the size gradually increases all the way to the biggest ones at Portland. These are sifted again by 'beachcombers' who value the rounded shapes and brilliant colours.

ABBOTSBU 1 MILE

Pulpit Rock—Portland.

SCALE
0   1   2   3   4   5 MIL

DORCHESTER

Infamous Judge Jeffreys gave Dorchester its blackest day in 1685 when, presiding over a court in the back of the Antelope Hotel, he condemned 292 men to death for high treason in the Monmouth rebellion. Seventy-four of those convicted in this 'Bloody Assize' died on the gallows on the South Walks. The rest were transported to the sugar plantations of the West Indies. The hangman's cottage still stands on the banks of the River Frome. The ghost of Judge Jeffreys is still believed to haunt his former lodgings in a house in High West Street— a stone's throw from the old Crown Court that later saw equal injustice handed out to the Tolpuddle Martyrs. In 1613 fire swept across the old town. St Peter's was the only church that survived the flames. Its churchyard holds a statue to the poet William Barnes. The Dorset County Museum in High West Street has a large collection of local antiquities including finds from Maiden Castle.

Thomas Hardy's cottage.

17
Dorchester
(67 MILES)

HIGHER BOCKHAMPTON

All Dorset is Hardy country, but Higher Bockhampton is its heart. He was born in the village in a low, thatched cottage on June 2, 1840. He grew up there, and later returned to write *Far From the Madding Crowd* and *Under the Greenwood Tree*. Built with composition walls 2 ft thick, the cottage stands deep at the end of a lane running beside Yellowham Wood, an ideal location for his stonemason-grandfather's sideline as a brandy smuggler. The house now belongs to the National Trust, and visitors can, by appointment, see the room where Hardy wrote at a desk with a view over the heathland which figured in so many of his novels.

Judge Jeffreys.

The drawing-room, Athelhampton Hall.

ATHELHAMPTON HALL

This ancient house, set in 10 acres of formal and landscaped gardens and circled by the River Piddle, is among the finest examples of 15th-century domestic architecture in Britain. The oak-panelled rooms are furnished with antiques, such as the 18th-century harpsichord in the Great Chamber. The Great Hall has a magnificent timber roof. In the grounds is a 16th-century dovecote with a tiled roof.

Athelhampton Hall, exterior.

TOLPUDDLE

In the centre of the village stands the sycamore tree under which six local farm workers met in 1834 to form a society to fight starvation wages. For this they were transported to Australia. Later they were triumphantly reprieved and became the Tolpuddle Martyrs, 'saints' of the British trade union movement. In 1934 the Trades Union Congress built a row of six cottages in the village as a memorial. Every year, in July, there is a memorial service and parade in Tolpuddle.

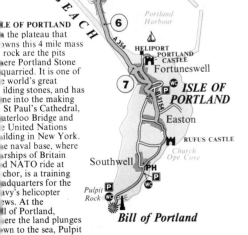

ISLE OF PORTLAND

... the plateau that ... owns this 4 mile mass ... rock are the pits ... ere Portland Stone ... quarried. It is one of ... e world's great ... ilding stones, and has ... ne into the making ... St Paul's Cathedral, ... aterloo Bridge and ... e United Nations ... ilding in New York. ... e naval base, where ... rships of Britain ... d NATO ride at ... chor, is a training ... adquarters for the ... avy's helicopter ... ews. At the ... l of Portland, ... ere the land plunges ... wn to the sea, Pulpit ... ck commands ... eeping views of the ... rset coastline.

Weymouth harbour as it was in 1822.

WEYMOUTH

To the strains of the National Anthem played by a brass band, a horse-drawn bathing machine carried the king down the sands and into the water of Weymouth Bay. The year was 1789 and the king was George III, the first British monarch to take up sea bathing. His plunge set the course for Weymouth's development into a health and holiday resort. A house built by King George's brother, the Duke of Gloucester, is now part of the Gloucester Hotel, which forms a section of the half-mile-long terrace of Georgian and Victorian houses that fronts the bay. Protected from southerly seas, the beach offers safe bathing. Restored Tudor houses at 2 and 3 Trinity Street are open to the public.

Haunted church, hidden village and a fortress with a view

Roe and fallow deer still warily trot out at night from coverts and plantations to graze on pastures which have replaced the great forests of Cranborne Chase, where their ancestors were hunted by King John. At Knowlton a haunted church stands on a prehistoric site and a fine tower folly looks over Horton. The route also passes Badbury Rings, a great fortress that the Romans took over from its tribal builders; and Milton Abbas, a village that was 'hidden' from the sight of its lordly 18th-century owner.

(1) Blandford Forum to Iwerne Minster Leave Blandford on the A354 signposted to Salisbury. After 1 m. turn left towards Shaftesbury. At the crossroads, $4\frac{1}{2}$ miles further on, turn left to the village of Iwerne Minster. (Pronounced 'Yewerne'.)

(2) Iwerne Minster to Fontmell Magna Take the A350 north in Iwerne, passing through the little village of Sutton Waldron, with its 19th-century Gothic church prominent on rising ground, to the village of Fontmell Magna.

(3) Fontmell Magna to Tollard Royal From Fontmell Magna, take the road signposted to Ashmore and at the crossroads turn left. Go through Melbury Abbas, keeping the towered church on the left, and take the first road on the right. In about $\frac{1}{2}$ m. turn sharp right on to the B3081 and follow this road through to Tollard Royal.

(4) Tollard Royal to Knowlton church Stay on the B3081 and after 1 m. turn right on to the road signposted for Farnham. After about 1 m. turn right into the village of Farnham. Turn left at the Museum Hotel and go straight over the crossroads. The road veers sharply left and through Chettle, where the early-18th-century manor house, seen on the right, is a good example of theatrical baroque architecture. After about $\frac{3}{4}$ m., at the T-junction, turn left on to the A354 towards Salisbury and then take the first right, signposted to Horton. After $1\frac{1}{2}$ m. bear left into Gussage St Michael, turn right at the T-junction in the village, past the 13th-century flint church with its Norman tower, and carry on to Gussage All Saints. The church here, to the left of the road at the head of the village, is fairly large and neat and has been described as like a Victorian church on a prosperous estate—but it is genuinely 14th century. At the crossroads just beyond the village, turn left, and take the first right downhill and over a little stream just past some farm buildings. Knowlton church can be seen on the left of the road.

(5) Knowlton church to Cranborne Turn left on to the B3078 and stay on this road to the small town of Cranborne, which is set amid trees beside the River Crane. Cranborne Manor is the home of the Marquis of Salisbury.

(6) Cranborne to Horton Returning along the B3078 from Cranborne, turn left after about 4 m. to Horton.

(7) Horton to Wimborne Minster Fork right at the church in Horton. Take the left fork after passing Horton Tower on the left. Turn right at the crossroads and go through Hinton Martell. At the T-junction, turn left on to the B3078 and follow this road to Wimborne Minster.

(8) Wimborne Minster to Badbury Rings Leave the town on the B3082, following the tree-lined avenue, and after about $3\frac{1}{4}$ m. the entrance to Badbury Rings is on the right.

(9) Badbury Rings to Milton Abbas Return along the B3082 and turn right to Sturminster Marshall. Sturminster has an attractive row of thatched cottages and is the location of one of the world's largest cheese factories. Bear right by the church on to the road signposted Blandford. Go straight across the A350 towards Almer and join the A31 towards Dorchester by the Stag Gate of Charborough Park. After about 3 m. turn right and go through Anderson and Winterborne Kingston. The village of Anderson is usually included among the villages of the Winterborne river, which joins the Stour at Sturminster Marshall. The Winterborne is a bourne, burn or streamlet which runs more strongly in winter, and occasionally dries up altogether in summer.

Turn right in Kingston, and first left to Winterborne Whitechurch. Go straight across the A354 and carry on to Milton Abbas. Turn left into the village, to descend between the cottages to the lake. Turn right at the bottom to Milton Abbey church, beside which is Abbey House, built in the late 18th century.

(10) Milton Abbas to Blandford Forum Returning from the church, turn left and up the hill through Milton Abbas. At the junction at the top of the village turn left, and after $\frac{1}{2}$ m. fork right to Winterborne Stickland. In the village, turn left on the road signposted to Blandford Forum. Turn right just beyond the village and follow the signposts back to Blandford Forum.

INFORMATION

Places of interest *Chettle House:* Interior only, by appointment. *Cranborne Manor:* Gardens, Apr. to Oct., first Sat. (all day) and Sun. (afternoons) in month, and Bank Hols. (all day). Garden Centre, all year, daily. *Shaftesbury:* Abbey Ruins Museum, Easter to end Sept., weekdays, Sun. afternoons only. *Wimborne Minster:* Model town, all year, daily. Priest's House Museum, Easter to end Sept., Mon. to Sat.

Events Shaftesbury and Blandford Forum, market day Thur.

Information Westover Road, Bournemouth (Tel. Bournemouth 28321).

Towns with easy access to Blandford Forum:

Bournemouth . . . 16 m.	Salisbury . . . . . . 24 m.
Dorchester . . . . . 16 m.	Shaftesbury . . . . 12 m.

FONTMELL MAGNA

The village, at the foot of a chalk escarpment, is a mixture of thatched cottages and big Victorian houses. It stands on a clear stream once used by both a mill and a brewery, but now the home of ducks and swans. The main body of the church was largely rebuilt in the middle of the last century; but parts of the embattled tower, which carries a peal of six bells, date back to the 15th century. There is a Norman font.

Iwerne Minster: village pump.

IWERNE MINSTER

Early in this century, Iwerne was transformed into a 'model' village by a rich owner: old houses were weatherproofed, and new ones built with diamond-paned windows and half-timbering. There is no single owner now, but the village is still uniformly pleasant. The parish church has one of the few spires to be found in Dorset.

MILTON ABBAS

The old village of Abbey Milton was destroyed and flooded by Lord Milton between 1773 and 1779—because he wanted a lake view from his home near the abbey. He had Milton Abbas built on a hillside out of his sight to rehouse the displaced villagers. Today's charming village is still largely that creation. There is a good museum of rural relics in the village.

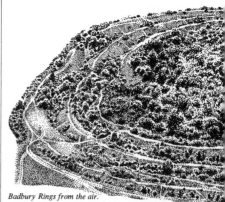

Badbury Rings from the air.

BADBURY RINGS

The Iron Age fort of Badbury Rings consists of three great ramparts rising to a plateau with a view of three counties and the sea. This tribal centre was occupied and strengthened by the Romans, who led four roads to it. In the centuries that followed their withdrawal, a town grew up within the ancient rings. It has been gone for 1000 years, and Badbury is now a vast picnic site.

SCALE

0   1   2   3   4   5 M

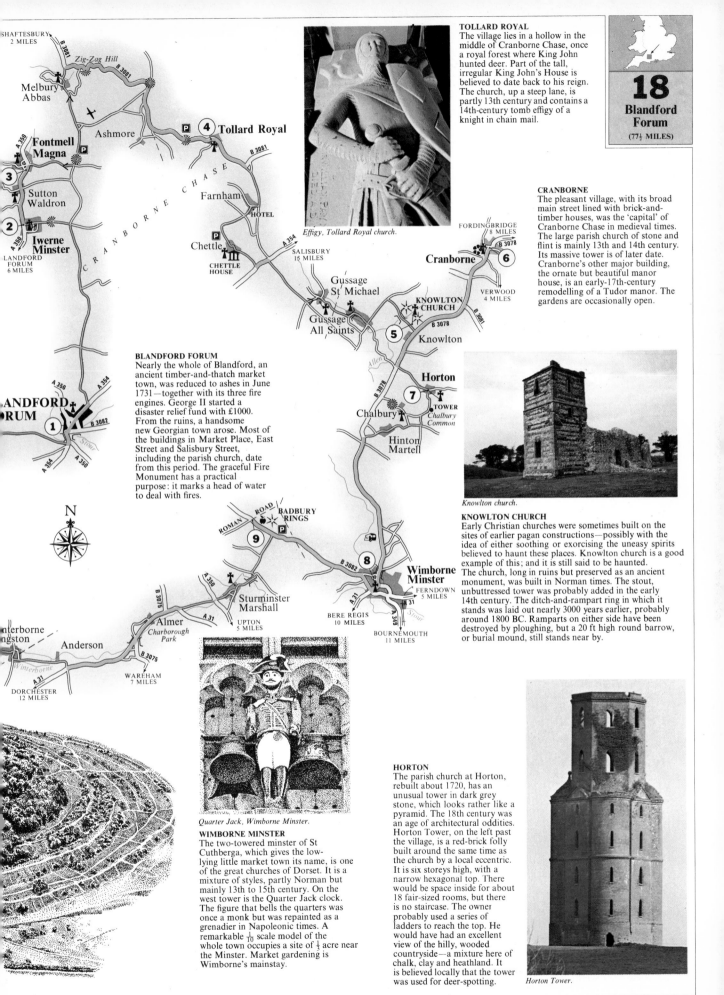

TOLLARD ROYAL

The village lies in a hollow in the middle of Cranborne Chase, once a royal forest where King John hunted deer. Part of the tall, irregular King John's House is believed to date back to his reign. The church, up a steep lane, is partly 13th century and contains a 14th-century tomb effigy of a knight in chain mail.

Effigy, Tollard Royal church.

CRANBORNE

The pleasant village, with its broad main street lined with brick-and-timber houses, was the 'capital' of Cranborne Chase in medieval times. The large parish church of stone and flint is mainly 13th and 14th century. Its massive tower is of later date. Cranborne's other major building, the ornate but beautiful manor house, is an early-17th-century remodelling of a Tudor manor. The gardens are occasionally open.

BLANDFORD FORUM

Nearly the whole of Blandford, an ancient timber-and-thatch market town, was reduced to ashes in June 1731—together with its three fire engines. George II started a disaster relief fund with £1000. From the ruins, a handsome new Georgian town arose. Most of the buildings in Market Place, East Street and Salisbury Street, including the parish church, date from this period. The graceful Fire Monument has a practical purpose: it marks a head of water to deal with fires.

Knowlton church.

KNOWLTON CHURCH

Early Christian churches were sometimes built on the sites of earlier pagan constructions—possibly with the idea of either soothing or exorcising the uneasy spirits believed to haunt these places. Knowlton church is a good example of this; and it is still said to be haunted. The church, long in ruins but preserved as an ancient monument, was built in Norman times. The stout, unbuttressed tower was probably added in the early 14th century. The ditch-and-rampart ring in which it stands was laid out nearly 3000 years earlier, probably around 1800 BC. Ramparts on either side have been destroyed by ploughing, but a 20 ft high round barrow, or burial mound, still stands near by.

Quarter Jack, Wimborne Minster.

WIMBORNE MINSTER

The two-towered minster of St Cuthberga, which gives the low-lying little market town its name, is one of the great churches of Dorset. It is a mixture of styles, partly Norman but mainly 13th to 15th century. On the west tower is the Quarter Jack clock. The figure that bells the quarters was once a monk but was repainted as a grenadier in Napoleonic times. A remarkable $\frac{1}{10}$ scale model of the whole town occupies a site of $\frac{1}{3}$ acre near the Minster. Market gardening is Wimborne's mainstay.

HORTON

The parish church at Horton, rebuilt about 1720, has an unusual tower in dark grey stone, which looks rather like a pyramid. The 18th century was an age of architectural oddities. Horton Tower, on the left past the village, is a red-brick folly built around the same time as the church by a local eccentric. It is six storeys high, with a narrow hexagonal top. There would be space inside for about 18 fair-sized rooms, but there is no staircase. The owner probably used a series of ladders to reach the top. He would have had an excellent view of the hilly, wooded countryside—a mixture here of chalk, clay and heathland. It is believed locally that the tower was used for deer-spotting.

Horton Tower.

The hills, heath and coast where Hardy's heroes lived

Wild heathland, mellow stone villages and an often dramatic coastline typify the landscape described so vividly in the novels of Thomas Hardy. Many of the villages are easily identified as the homes of his heroes and heroines. Winfrith Heath, too, despite the incursion of an atomic energy station, remains the wild Egdon Heath of Tess of the D'Urbervilles. *The area also has close connections with T. E. Lawrence—Lawrence of Arabia—who spent the last years of his life at Clouds Hill near Bovington Army Camp.*

(1) Wareham to Wool Leave the town on the A352 going towards Weymouth. After 2 m. turn left on to the B3070 to East Lulworth. Cross the River Frome and after $\frac{1}{2}$ m. turn right on to the road to Wool. After $2\frac{3}{4}$ m., where the road bears sharp right towards the railway line, the entrance to Bindon Abbey is on the right. The remains of this 13th-century Cistercian abbey lie in a broad belt of trees and should be recognised by readers of Thomas Hardy as the place where Angel Clare buried Tess of the D'Urbervilles while walking in his sleep. Continue past the abbey and follow the road around to the left and into Wool.

(2) Wool to Bovington Camp In the village, turn right on to the B3071 and then right again on to the A352 going towards Wareham. Woolbridge Manor Farm can be seen on the left. Cross the river and turn left, and after $\frac{1}{4}$ m. turn left again to visit the tank museum at Bovington Camp.

(3) Bovington Camp to Winfrith Newburgh Continue on the road past the camp and just before the T-junction, on the right, is Clouds Hill, a small cottage hidden among the trees, which was used by T. E. Lawrence when he was a soldier stationed at Bovington. At the T-junction turn left on to the road signposted to Dorchester. At the next crossroads turn left on to the B3390 towards Moreton. Cross the River Frome again and turn left into Moreton, where Lawrence is buried in the parish churchyard. In Moreton, turn right at the T-junction, follow the road past the cemetery on the right, and after just over 1 m. fork right, passing the Winfrith Atomic Energy Station. Turn right on to the A352, and after 2 m. turn left to West Chaldon. Follow the road through to East Chaldon and on to Winfrith Newburgh, a village on the fringe of the heath.

(4) Winfrith Newburgh to Lulworth Cove At the junction by the village church, turn right and follow the road to West Lulworth. Here turn right to visit beautiful Lulworth Cove.

(5) Lulworth Cove to Creech Grange Return to West Lulworth and follow the road towards Wareham. After 1 m. turn right to remain on the B3070. Just before the village of East Lulworth fork right, signposted to Whiteway Hill, and right again on to a gated road. The road rises steeply into the Purbeck Hills. Rings Hill, a fortified prehistoric camp on the cliff edge, can be seen to the right. After just over 2 m. turn left at the T-junction on a hairpin bend. The arch known as Bond's Folly is on the right and Creech Grange is further down the hill on the left.

(6) Creech Grange to Corfe Castle Turn right on to the road opposite the entrance to Creech Grange, and follow it to the village of East Creech. Follow the road through the village, and at the next T-junction turn right and then right again towards Church Knowle. At the next crossroads turn left and go through Church Knowle to Corfe Castle.

(7) Corfe Castle to Worth Matravers At the T-junction near the castle ruins, turn right on to the A351 and follow the road through Corfe Castle village. At the end of the village turn right on the B3069 signposted for Kingston. Continue through Kingston, where the road turns sharply left, and then turn right for Worth Matravers. No car access to chapel.

(8) Worth Matravers to Swanage In the village, take the right fork and at the T-junction turn right on to the B3069. Pass through Langton Matravers, and at the next junction turn right on to the A351 and follow it into the seaside resort of Swanage.

(9) Swanage to Studland In Swanage take the sea-front road, and after about 2 m. turn right on to the B3351 for Studland.

(10) Studland to Wareham Leave Studland on the B3351 going towards Corfe Castle. At the castle crossroads, turn right on to the A351 going towards Wareham. After $\frac{1}{2}$ m. turn right on to the road signposted to Arne. Bear right at the next junction and continue into Arne, where a bridlepath from the village leads to Poole Harbour and a nature trail. Return to Arne and keep straight ahead to Stoborough. Here turn right and follow the A351 back into Wareham.

INFORMATION

Places of interest *Bovington Camp:* Tank museum, daily. Clouds Hill, Apr. to Sept., Wed., Thur., Sun. and Bank Hols., 2-6 p.m., winter, Sunday, 2-4 p.m. *Corfe:* Castle, summer, 10 a.m. to dusk; winter afternoons weather permitting. *Wareham:* The Priory of Lady St Mary, gardens only, May to Sept., Wed. and third Sun. in month, 10 a.m.-6 p.m.

Craft workshops *Swanage:* The Owl Pottery, 108 High Street. Daily ex. Thur. afternoon and Sun.

Event *Swanage:* Carnival/Regatta, Aug.

Nature trails *Studland Heath Nature Reserve:* Leaflet from car park, off Ferry Road.

Information West Country Tourist Board, Trinity Court, Southernhay East, Exeter (Tel. Exeter 76351). *Swanage:* The White House, Shore Road (Tel. Swanage 2885).

Towns with easy access to Wareham:

Bournemouth	14 m.	Ringwood	21 m.
Dorchester	17 m.	Weymouth	19 m.

Lych gate, Winfrith Newburgh.

WINFRITH NEWBURGH
In the trees surrounding the parish church of St Christopher there is a large rookery which has existed for well over 100 years. The village itself is comparatively unspoilt, and is situated on the fringe of Winfrith Heath. A small stream called the Winfrith, meaning 'happy stream' in Celtic, rises in the village and crosses the heath towards the Frome. It is now swallowed up by the atomic-energy establishment, an incongruously modern complex surrounded by high wire fences.

Fossilised tree trunk, Lulworth Cove.

LULWORTH COVE
The lake-like beauty of the cove, almost enclosed by hills, is best appreciated out of season, when the holiday crowds have gone. Over the cliffs to the east is a 'forest' of fossilised tree stumps. On the west side is Stair Hole, where students of geology can see clearly how the rock strata have at some time been violently distorted and then eroded by the sea. A walk westwards along the cliffs is rewarded by the sight of Durdle Door, a limestone arch worn away by the sea and providing an almost theatrical backdrop to the sweep of Man o' War beach. In time it is likely that the top of the arch will collapse, leaving a pillar similar to many others formed in this way along the coast.

SCALE

0   1   2   3 MILES

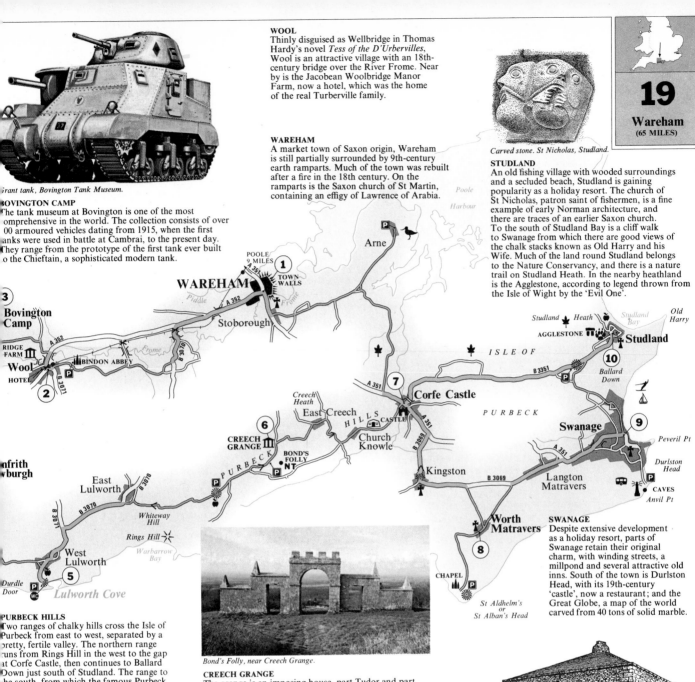

Grant tank, Bovington Tank Museum.

BOVINGTON CAMP
The tank museum at Bovington is one of the most comprehensive in the world. The collection consists of over 100 armoured vehicles dating from 1915, when the first tanks were used in battle at Cambrai, to the present day. They range from the prototype of the first tank ever built to the Chieftain, a sophisticated modern tank.

WOOL
Thinly disguised as Wellbridge in Thomas Hardy's novel *Tess of the D'Urbervilles*, Wool is an attractive village with an 18th-century bridge over the River Frome. Near by is the Jacobean Woolbridge Manor Farm, now a hotel, which was the home of the real Turberville family.

WAREHAM
A market town of Saxon origin, Wareham is still partially surrounded by 9th-century earth ramparts. Much of the town was rebuilt after a fire in the 18th century. On the ramparts is the Saxon church of St Martin, containing an effigy of Lawrence of Arabia.

Carved stone. St Nicholas, Studland.

STUDLAND
An old fishing village with wooded surroundings and a secluded beach, Studland is gaining popularity as a holiday resort. The church of St Nicholas, patron saint of fishermen, is a fine example of early Norman architecture, and there are traces of an earlier Saxon church. To the south of Studland Bay is a cliff walk to Swanage from which there are good views of the chalk stacks known as Old Harry and his Wife. Much of the land round Studland belongs to the Nature Conservancy, and there is a nature trail on Studland Heath. In the nearby heathland is the Agglestone, according to legend thrown from the Isle of Wight by the 'Evil One'.

PURBECK HILLS
Two ranges of chalky hills cross the Isle of Purbeck from east to west, separated by a pretty, fertile valley. The northern range runs from Rings Hill in the west to the gap at Corfe Castle, then continues to Ballard Down just south of Studland. The range to the south, from which the famous Purbeck marble was quarried, starts at Durlston Head in the east and continues to Worbarrow Bay near East Lulworth.

Bond's Folly, near Creech Grange.

CREECH GRANGE
The grange is an imposing house, part Tudor and part William and Mary, set in beautiful grounds which command excellent views of Creech Heath and the distant Corfe Castle. To the right of the road is Creech Grange Arch, popularly known as Bond's Folly. Built in the 18th century, the arch appears to have no other purpose than the self-aggrandisement of its owner, though the site makes an excellent viewpoint.

Corfe Castle.

CORFE CASTLE
The name Corfe means gap. It is appropriate, since the castle is situated in a gap in the Purbeck Hills. In ruins since an attack by Cromwell and his troops in 1646, Corfe Castle remains grandly aloof from the mellow stone-and-brick village on the slopes below. It was on this site in 987 that the 18-year-old King Edward the Martyr was murdered at the instigation of his stepmother. Near by is a model of the village and the castle as it once looked. In Corfe Castle village there is also a small local-history museum which is open daily. Most of the stone houses in the two streets that comprise the village are 17th and 18th century.

SWANAGE
Despite extensive development as a holiday resort, parts of Swanage retain their original charm, with winding streets, a millpond and several attractive old inns. South of the town is Durlston Head, with its 19th-century 'castle', now a restaurant; and the Great Globe, a map of the world carved from 40 tons of solid marble.

St Aldhelm's Chapel, Worth.

WORTH MATRAVERS
Worth and Langton Matravers were two of the main quarry villages for the famous Purbeck marble used to build or to adorn most of the English cathedrals. Worth is now far removed from any commercial bustle, but it has a charm of its own, enhanced by one of the oldest churches in Dorset. From here it is easy to visit St Aldhelm's Head, an unspoilt vantage point giving striking views across the sea. The chapel there, built as a memorial to St Aldhelm, the first Bishop of Sherborne, also served as a beacon, where a fire could be lit as a warning to ships in danger of being wrecked on the rocky coasts.

Underground, overground, man made his mark in the Mendips

The route passes the rock fissure in the Mendips where, in the 18th century, the Rev. Augustus Toplady wrote the hymn 'Rock of Ages' while sheltering from a thunderstorm. The same hills had been a place of refuge for thousands of years before the hymn was sung, for prehistoric man lived in the caverns around Wookey Hole and Cheddar. Today some of these caves, ablaze with electric lights, are open to visitors. At the other end of the scale of human achievement is the magnificent cathedral at Wells.

(1) Wells to Wookey Hole Leave Wells by the A371 signposted to Cheddar, but on the outskirts of the town turn right and after 1¼ m. there is the car park for Wookey Hole. For a worthwhile detour to the Ebbor Gorge National Nature Reserve, a memorial to Sir Winston Churchill, take the right fork on the road that runs past Wookey car park. After about ½ m. there is a car park and picnic area adjoining the reserve. Waymarked footpaths run through the gorge area, where there are several small caverns. In these, remains have been found of reindeer, bears, wolves, lemmings and Neolithic man.

(2) Wookey Hole to Cheddar If the detour to Ebbor Gorge has been made, return towards Wookey Hole and turn right on the road that runs steeply down to Easton. If the detour has not been made, join this road directly from Wookey Hole. It is signposted to Easton, together with the gradient—1 in 7. In the village of Easton, turn right on to the A371. The road runs placidly along the south-western flank of the Mendip Hills, giving no hint of the mighty gorge that cuts into those hills from the village that lies ahead—Cheddar.

(3) Cheddar to Wrington Turn right in Cheddar on to the B3135, for the gorge and cave entrances. Follow the road as it winds between the towering limestone cliffs—at 450 ft they are nearly three times higher than Nelson's Column—and past the start of the 1½ m. long Black Rock Nature Trail. After 1½ m., fork left on to the B3371 for Burrington Combe. Keep on to the crossroads with the B3134 and turn left on to this road. The 'combe' or gorge on the approach to Burrington is a smaller and less precipitous version of that at Cheddar. It was while sheltering from a thunderstorm in a rocky cleft in this gorge that the Rev. Augustus Toplady wrote the hymn 'Rock of Ages'. Continue through Burrington Combe and, at the junction with the A368, turn right, through Rickford and into Blagdon. Turn left in Blagdon. As the road descends to Blagdon Lake there are good views over this Bristol Waterworks reservoir. As the road bears away from the lake, turn left and, after 1 m., fork right. Turn left on to the A38, towards Taunton, and take the second road on the right into Wrington.

(4) Wrington to Clevedon Take the road westwards from Wrington, towards Yatton. At the crossroads junction with the A370, a detour can be made to the nature reserve at Goblin Combe. Turn right on to the A370 to the village of Cleeve. In the village, turn right down Cleeve Hill Road and park in the quarry on the left. The 32 acre reserve,

privately owned, is leased to the Somerset Naturalists' Trust. Permits are issued on site, but there is a public footpath at the bottom of the dry, steep-sided limestone valley. Returning from the reserve, turn left on to the A370 and at the crossroads turn right to Yatton. If this detour is not taken, go straight over the crossroads from Wrington and turn right on to the B3133. Go through Yatton, North End and Kenn, crossing the M5 motorway and the River Kenn before entering Clevedon.

(5) Clevedon to Chew Magna In Clevedon, turn right by the clock on to the B3130 and follow this road east to Clevedon Court, which is on the left just before the M5 motorway. Return from Clevedon Court on the B3130 and after ½ m. take the turning on the right, signposted Portishead. After ½ m. turn right for Clapton-in-Gordano. At the T-junction in the village, turn right on the road to Wraxall. The road rises steeply and goes over the M5. Turn left on to the B3128 for Bristol and, after about ½ m., turn right for Wraxall. At the T-junction with the B3130 in Wraxall, turn left. Follow the B3130 under the A370 and after 1½ m. turn right on to the A38. After ½ m. turn left, rejoining the B3130 through Winford to Chew Magna, a pretty village where there are several streams crossed by stone bridges dating back to the 15th and 16th centuries.

(6) Chew Magna to Wells Take the B3114 from the western outskirts of the village, to Chew Stoke. Keep on this road past the Chew Valley Lake and follow it as it bears right just before West Harptree. At the crossroads with the A368, go straight over. Take first turning right, go over the crossroads and at the Castle of Comfort Inn, bear left on to the B3134 towards Wells. At the crossroads with the B3135, go straight ahead on the minor road which leads across the Mendips. At the junction with the A39, turn right for Wells.

INFORMATION

Places of interest *Blagdon:* Beam engine, by written appointment with Bristol Waterworks. *Cheddar Caves:* Gough's Cave, daily. Cox's Cave, Waterfall Cave and Jacob's Ladder, April to mid-Oct. *Clevedon Court:* April to Sept., Wed., Thur., Sun. and Bank Hol. Mon. 2.30-5.30 p.m. *Wells:* Museum, Apr. to Sept., Mon. to Sat., 10 a.m.-6 p.m. (also Sun. afternoons July to Sept.); Oct. to Mar., 2-4 p.m. *Wookey Hole:* Caves, Madame Tussaud's Store Room, and Lady Bangor's Fairground Collection, daily.

Information *Weston-super-Mare:* Beach Lawns (Tel. Weston-super-Mare 26838).

Towns with easy access to Wells:

Bath	21 m.	Bristol	28 m.
Bridgwater	21 m.	Yeovil	24 m.

WRINGTON
The parish church here is said to have one of the finest of Somerset's Perpendicular church towers (mid-14th to mid-16th century). It is visible for miles around. John Locke, the famous 17th-century philosopher, was born here. His ideas of a 'social contract' with the state were taken up by later revolutionary leaders in France and the United States. There is a memorial tablet to him in the churchyard wall.

Jacob's Ladder, Cheddar.

CHEDDAR
There are more than 400 caves or holes in the Cheddar Gorge area. Two of the largest, Gough's and Cox's, have been developed as public attractions. Their limestone formations have such fanciful names as Pixie Forest, Ladye Chapel, and The Archangel's Wing. The action of minerals on the limestone rock has produced a variety of colours, including red (from iron), grey (lead), and green (copper). The Cheddar Caves Museum contains flint implements more than 20,000 years old. Jacob's Ladder is a flight of over 300 steps up the cliff face of the gorge to a viewing tower.

WOOKEY HOLE
Not a single cavern, but rather a group of caves, Wookey Hole was worn in the limestone by the River Axe over a period of 60,000 years. The main attraction for visitors is the Great Cave, known for centuries as a natural wonder. It is now floodlit, and the lights pick out every detail of its colourful walls and fantastic arrays of stalagmites and stalactites. The Witch of Wookey is a massive stalagmite in the first of three chambers open to the public: the Witch's Kitchen. A museum shows cave finds, including implements dating from the Roman occupation. On the approach to the caves, Lady Bangor's collection of painted and gilded fairground figures can be seen.

Fairground cock, Wookey.

The Witch's Kitchen, Wookey Hole.

SCALE

0   1   2   3   4   5 MILES

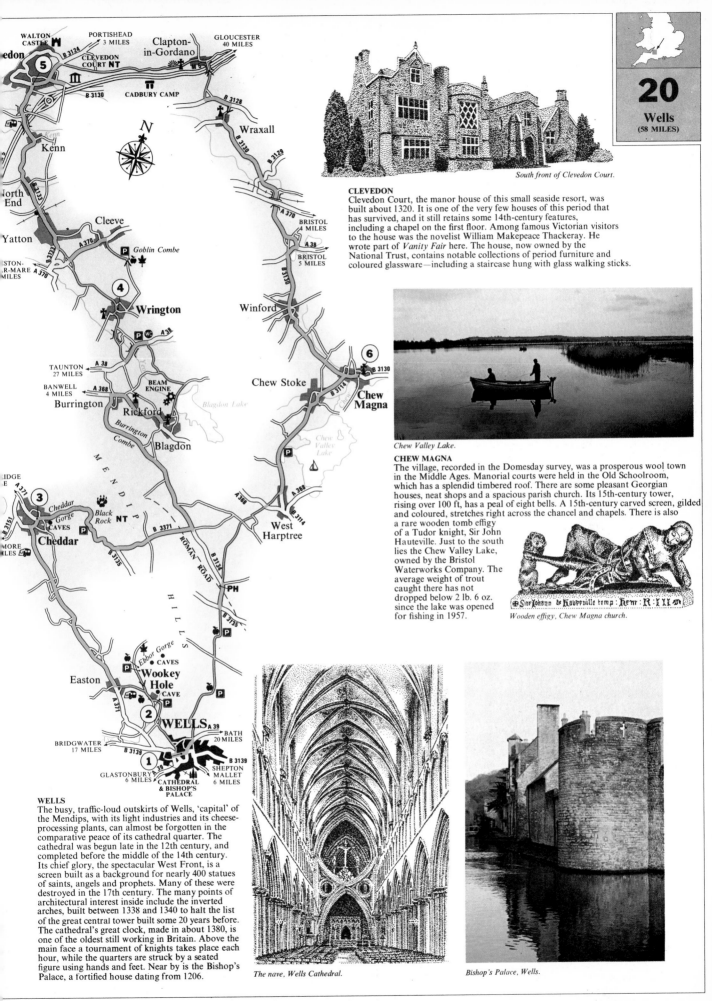

South front of Clevedon Court.

CLEVEDON

Clevedon Court, the manor house of this small seaside resort, was built about 1320. It is one of the very few houses of this period that has survived, and it still retains some 14th-century features, including a chapel on the first floor. Among famous Victorian visitors to the house was the novelist William Makepeace Thackeray. He wrote part of *Vanity Fair* here. The house, now owned by the National Trust, contains notable collections of period furniture and coloured glassware—including a staircase hung with glass walking sticks.

Chew Valley Lake.

CHEW MAGNA

The village, recorded in the Domesday survey, was a prosperous wool town in the Middle Ages. Manorial courts were held in the Old Schoolroom, which has a splendid timbered roof. There are some pleasant Georgian houses, neat shops and a spacious parish church. Its 15th-century tower, rising over 100 ft, has a peal of eight bells. A 15th-century carved screen, gilded and coloured, stretches right across the chancel and chapels. There is also a rare wooden tomb effigy of a Tudor knight, Sir John Hauteville. Just to the south lies the Chew Valley Lake, owned by the Bristol Waterworks Company. The average weight of trout caught there has not dropped below 2 lb. 6 oz. since the lake was opened for fishing in 1957.

Wooden effigy, Chew Magna church.

WELLS

The busy, traffic-loud outskirts of Wells, 'capital' of the Mendips, with its light industries and its cheese-processing plants, can almost be forgotten in the comparative peace of its cathedral quarter. The cathedral was begun late in the 12th century, and completed before the middle of the 14th century. Its chief glory, the spectacular West Front, is a screen built as a background for nearly 400 statues of saints, angels and prophets. Many of these were destroyed in the 17th century. The many points of architectural interest inside include the inverted arches, built between 1338 and 1340 to halt the list of the great central tower built some 20 years before. The cathedral's great clock, made in about 1380, is one of the oldest still working in Britain. Above the main face a tournament of knights takes place each hour, while the quarters are struck by a seated figure using hands and feet. Near by is the Bishop's Palace, a fortified house dating from 1206.

The nave, Wells Cathedral.

Bishop's Palace, Wells.

51

The countryside flourishes where motorways meet

At the south-western end of the Cotswolds, north of Bristol and Bath and close to the Severn Estuary, is an area which retains its essentially rural nature despite the recent arrival of two motorways, the M4 and the M5. The area contains the three largest houses in Gloucestershire and these can be seen in much the same setting as that in which they were built during the 18th century. The Severn Road Bridge, built in 1966, presents a very different but equally impressive form of architecture.

(1) Chipping Sodbury to Iron Acton Leave town on the B4060 signposted to Yate. Go through Yate and at the T-junction signposted A432 Bristol and Iron Acton, turn right. Cross the railway bridge and turn right on to the B4059, signposted Iron Acton. After 1 m. turn left into the centre of Iron Acton. The church with the memorial cross is on the left of the road.

(2) Iron Acton to Severn Bridge Continue past the church and at the T-junction turn right. At the crossroads go straight ahead signposted to Thornbury. Go through Latteridge, where the road becomes the B4427. Just after the road crosses the M5 note the tower of Old Church Farm on the left. The tower is all that is left of a church that formerly stood on the site. At the T-junction with the A38 turn left, following the signpost to Bristol. After 1¼ m., at a point where pylons cross the road, turn right to Tockington. In the village bear right, following the signs for Thornbury, and at the T-junction immediately afterwards turn left for Olveston. Go through Olveston on the B4461. The largely 14th-century church is on the left at the end of the village. Follow the road for about 3 m. into the Aust Services beside the Severn Bridge.

(3) Severn Bridge to Dyrham Park Join the M4 signposted to London and after 15 m. leave the motorway at junction 18, joining the A46 signposted for Bath. The entrance to Dyrham Park is on the right after 1½ m.

(4) Dyrham Park to Dodington House Rejoin the A46 and return towards the M4, only this time cross the motorway. Immediately after the roundabout the entrance to Dodington House is on the left.

(5) Dodington House to Great Badminton Leave the grounds of Dodington House on the north side, turning right on to the A432. After ¼ m., at the traffic lights by the Cross Hands Hotel, go straight ahead on to the B4040, signposted Malmesbury. (If Dodington House is not visited, continue past the entrance on the A46 to the traffic lights at Cross Hands and turn right on to the B4040.) In the fields to the left, note the smoke-blackened airshafts of the 2½ m. long Chipping Sodbury railway tunnel. After 3 m. fork right, still on the B4040, into Acton Turville. At the T-junction shortly afterwards, turn left and follow the road through the village to Great Badminton.

(6) Great Badminton to Somerset Monument Leave the village by the road to Little Badminton, skirting the park of Badminton House. Go through Little Badminton, noting the circular dovecote alone in a field on the left, and in 1¼ m. cross the A46 for Hawkesbury Upton. Go through the village on the road signposted to Hillesley and Wotton-under-Edge. After about ¼ m. the Somerset Monument is on the right.

(7) Somerset Monument to Horton Court Return to Hawkesbury Upton, and just after passing the village sign turn right, by the pond, on the road signposted to Hawkesbury. (Note: for the next 5½ m., through Horton and Little Sodbury until joining the A432, most of the route is on narrow lanes with occasional passing places.) Follow the road through Hawkesbury, and at the fork beyond the church turn left (no signpost) for Horton. After 1 m. the road goes right and left round Horton church, and Horton Court is on the left.

(8) Horton Court to Chipping Sodbury Continue along the road into Horton. At the T-junction in the village turn left (no signpost); after 300 yds bear right following the signpost to Little Sodbury. After ½ m. turn right at the T-junction and soon afterwards the entrance to Little Sodbury Manor is on the left. Set on the hillside above the village, the manor is an imposing Tudor building of Cotswold stone with mullioned windows. William Tyndale, who made the first translation of the Bible into English and was later martyred, lived here from 1521 to 1523. He was the tutor of the children of Sir John Walsh, and the attic bedroom, thought to have been his, remains much as it was when Henry VIII and Anne Boleyn stayed at the manor as Sir John's guests. At the church turn left, signposted Old Sodbury. Take the next turning on the left, also signposted Old Sodbury. After 1 m., at the T-junction with the A432, turn right, signposted Yate. At the roundabout on the outskirts of Chipping Sodbury turn right into the town. The prefix 'Chipping' derives from the Saxon word for a market-place.

INFORMATION

Places of interest *Badminton House:* June to Sept. 7, Wed. afternoons and May 28-30. *Dodington House:* Apr. to Oct., daily. *Dyrham Park:* Apr. to Oct., afternoons and Bank Hols.; Park, May to Sept., daily, Oct., Nov. and Mar. to Easter, Wed., Sat., Sun.. afternoons. *Horton Court:* Apr. to Oct., Wed. and Sat. afternoons. *Little Sodbury Manor:* Apr. to Sept., by appointment.

Event *Badminton:* Horse Trials, June.

Information Abbey Churchyard, Bath (Tel. Bath 62831).

Towns with easy access to Chipping Sodbury:
Bath	15 m.	Chippenham .... 15 m.
Bristol	12 m.	Gloucester ..... 29 m.

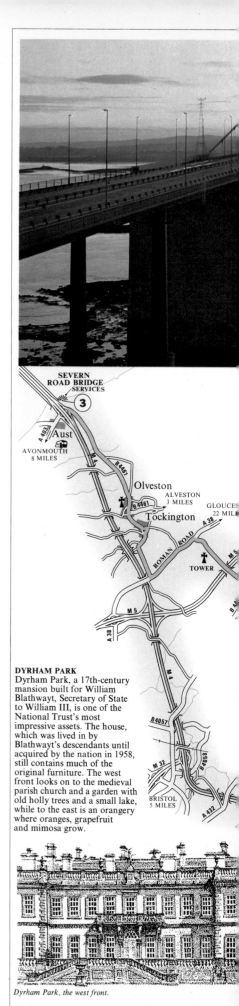

SEVERN ROAD BRIDGE SERVICES

DYRHAM PARK
Dyrham Park, a 17th-century mansion built for William Blathwayt, Secretary of State to William III, is one of the National Trust's most impressive assets. The house, which was lived in by Blathwayt's descendants until acquired by the nation in 1958, still contains much of the original furniture. The west front looks on to the medieval parish church and a garden with old holly trees and a small lake, while to the east is an orangery where oranges, grapefruit and mimosa grow.

Dyrham Park, the west front.

SCALE
0   1   2   3 MILES

Severn Road Bridge at sunset.

SEVERN ROAD BRIDGE
The opening of the Severn Suspension Bridge in 1966 enabled the people of Bristol to picnic in the Forest of Dean. And with the completion of the M4, South Wales is in closer contact not just with Bristol and Bath, but with London and the south-east. The huge, but seemingly delicate, structure has a main span of 3240 ft supported on two 400 ft towers. It can be viewed from a special platform at the Aust Services on the M4.

The ambulatory at Horton Court.

HORTON COURT
Horton Court was built between 1100 and 1150 and with its Norman hall is one of the oldest inhabited buildings in the west of England. The house was handsomely embellished in the 16th century, and an Italian-style ambulatory, or covered walk, unusual because it is completely detached from the rest of the building, was added at this time.

CHIPPING SODBURY
There have been markets on the site of Chipping Sodbury since Saxon times. In the early 13th century, by which time the town was well known for its cloth and cheese, it was granted a weekly market and became a fully-fledged market town. Georgian and older houses line the broad main street where weathered brickwork blends with Cotswold stone. The church, with its tall, pinnacled tower, contains a rare canopied pulpit exquisitely carved by 17th-century stonemasons. In the 1760s Edward Jenner, the pioneer of the modern technique of vaccination, was apprenticed to an apothecary in the town.

The Somerset Monument.

SOMERSET MONUMENT
This ornate tower was built in 1846, by the architect Lewis Vulliamy, as a memorial to General Lord Robert Somerset, a hero of Waterloo who was MP for Gloucestershire from 1803 until 1829. Standing on a hilltop, close to the road, the tower commands panoramic views over six counties.

IRON ACTON
The sculptured torso of a knight in armour rests on the parapet of the majestic tower of the 14th-century church, and in the churchyard is a curiously elaborate memorial cross, erected in about 1400. Several picturesque old buildings adorn the village, including Iron Acton Court, an Elizabethan manor house.

Memorial cross, Iron Acton.

The horse trials at Badminton.

GREAT BADMINTON
Now famous as the home of the annual Horse Trials, the elegant Palladian mansion which is Badminton House has also given its name to the game played with a shuttlecock, which was originally devised in the house. Built in the 17th century, the house, which has always belonged to the Dukes of Beaufort, contains an impressive collection of English, Dutch and Italian paintings, and carvings by Grinling Gibbons. Close to the house are extensive stables and hunt kennels.

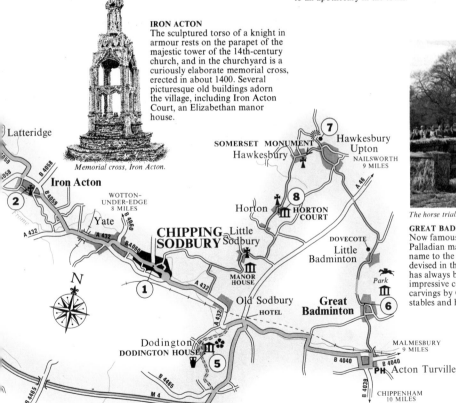

Travelling chariot, Dodington Carriage Museum.

DODINGTON HOUSE
Set in 700 acres of parkland laid out by Capability Brown, Dodington House is a striking 18th-century house built in Classical style by the architect James Wyatt. As well as the house—which has a small church, St Mary's, attached to it—and the grounds which are subtly landscaped around the headwaters of the River Frome, Dodington has a carriage museum which also offers carriage rides round the estate's other attractions. These include a garden and tropical-fish centre, a narrow-gauge railway and a children's adventureland.

53

A conducted tour of Salisbury Cathedral and Close
SALISBURY CATHEDRAL

Salisbury is the only ancient cathedral in England built to a single design. While Canterbury and the others grew throughout the Middle Ages, Salisbury, started in 1220, was complete except for the tower and spire by 1258. Planned on a grand scale, it has the tallest spire and the biggest close. It is a marvel of engineering as well as design. The Dean, the Very Reverend William Fenton Morley, tells its story.

When I came to Salisbury, the thing that struck me about the cathedral was its almost feminine grace. Alone among Britain's old cathedrals, it was built in little over a single generation. Unlike the others, it is the realisation of a single vision, a supreme example of that early-English Gothic.

True, the west façade, the cloisters and chapter house were not built until a few years after the consecration in 1258, and the spire was not started for more than a half century after that. But by 1380 all was done; and the effect was the wonderful unity you see today.

The 404 ft spire, the highest in Britain, is our most famous feature. Those medieval masons took a tremendous risk. The four central piers, which carry a load of 6400 tons, rest on foundations just 5–6 ft down, in swampy ground. No modern architect would dream of doing such a thing. Perhaps the old builders just put their trust in God. Anyhow, they brought it off brilliantly, against all the odds.

There was plenty of anxiety for three centuries or so. In fact, almost all the additions to the cathedral, such as the flying buttresses, have been designed to strengthen the structure. Even so, today, if you look up beneath the tower, you can see the Purbeck marble columns buckling slightly under the strain.

Leaning spire

In 1668 the Bishop, Seth Ward, asked Sir Christopher Wren to make a survey—his report is in the cathedral library. Wren found that the spire was leaning $29\frac{1}{2}$ in. to the south-west, and he advised putting in iron tie-rods and bands to strengthen it. Almost 70 years later the spire was checked again with a plumbline from the apex. A small brass plate in the floor, inscribed 'AD 1737 the centre of the tower', marks the spot where it touched the ground. No further movement had taken place—nor had it in 1951 when this check was repeated and Wren's rusted tie-rods renewed. But we never relax our vigilance. Something like 200 check marks are examined regularly.

Salisbury is unique in another way. As the cathedral was here before the town, the authorities had to house both the clergy and the builders. So they planned a great square—the largest and finest cathedral close in Britain. It is a walled village within a city, covering half a square mile, with 200 residents

CONSTABLE'S CATHEDRAL *John Constable painted this view of the cathedral from the garden of the Bishop's Palace. The small figures near the bottom left-hand corner are the artist's friend and patron John Fisher, who was Bishop of Salisbury from 1807 to 1825, and Mrs Fisher.*

SALISBURY CATHEDRAL

SUPPORTING THE SPIRE *The view up inside the spire shows the web of struts which have supported the 404 ft structure for more than 600 years. The weight of the spire has given it a slight tilt and bent its supporting pillars.*

WINDLASS *This wheel was built into the top of the tower to haul up the stone that went into the building of the spire. The wheel is operated by two men hauling on the enormous rim to wind up a rope. It is still used occasionally by workmen carrying out repairs.*

in addition to the students in term-time. It is claimed that there are as many pillars in the cathedral as hours in the year, as many windows as days. Most visitors are astonished at the lavish way our builders used space and height—the building is almost 450 ft long and rises to 81 ft. Some people find the cathedral a little austere, even cold. But they should remember that in medieval times the windows were ablaze with stained glass, the walls were red, with black tracery, the pillar capitals were gilded. The cathedral, in those pre-Reformation days, was a riot of colour.

Now there is only a streak of paint here and there—for instance on the wooden tombchest in the nave which carries the stone effigy of William Longespee, Earl of Salisbury. He laid one of the foundation stones in 1220 and, in 1226, was the first man to be buried in the new, rising cathedral. Half-brother of King John, he was one of the witnesses at the signing of Magna Carta at Runnymede in 1215. The copy that he brought back has, except for a brief interlude in the Second World War, been in the cathedral library since 1225. Its black characters, inscribed on vellum, are as regular and precise as print, and without a single correction.

The library also contains many medieval missals, some of them magnificently illuminated, and a remarkable collection of early medical works. This came about because Bishop Seth Ward (1617–89), mathematician, astronomer and founder-member of the Royal Society, collected medical books, and seems to have been an amateur physician. His notebook in the library has pages of prescriptions written in a neat hand, including one for gout which begins: 'Take an old fat cat and flea it and draw forth the guts . . .'

The world's oldest clock

There is plenty to fire the imagination in the cathedral. In the north aisle of the nave we have what is almost certainly the earliest complete working clock in the world, dating from 1386. Sunk into the floor of the Morning Chapel there is a brass plaque commemorating Bishop Robert Wyvil, who died in 1375, an aggressive prelate who was involved in a dispute over his ownership of Sherborne Castle in Dorset. Since bishops were not supposed to fight, the brass shows him praying in the castle while his champion stands in the gateway armed from head to foot, ready to fight for him.

Some small details can throw a light on an age. For instance, there is a tomb in the north aisle which displays an effigy of a 16th-century cathedral precentor. The corpse is lying on a woollen shroud, since it was then the law that everyone, unless excused, must be buried in wool—a measure to boost the wool trade.

We know little of the medieval masons, but what interests me is their obvious humour and lively minds. There is a superb example of this in the chapter house, which has a series of small stone tableaux, involving around 200 figures, round the walls—a sort of medieval strip cartoon recounting the Old Testament story. It is brilliantly done, and full of robust humour.

Music is a great tradition at Salisbury. The cathedral has always had a Song School, and

WEST FRONT *Graceful lancet windows and pointed arches housing statues decorate the West Front. It was the last part of the cathedral to be built and is far more elaborately ornamented than the rest of the building. The statues are arranged in five tiers, rising to Christ in Majesty at the summit. The original statues were destroyed and the present figures are Victorian. The craftsmen who carved and laid the original stones 'signed' their work, after the custom of the time, with a 'mason's mark', similar to the 17th-century tradesman's mark, reproduced on the left.*

NOAH AND THE FLOOD *A detail from one of the 60 carved Old Testament tableaux round the walls of the chapter house. These are fine examples of medieval craftsmanship.*

OLDEST CLOCK *Made in 1386, this wrought-iron clock has neither hands nor face—it tells the time by chiming the hours. The clock was built to summon the bishops to services. It was formerly housed in the bell tower in the close, and is reputed to be the oldest working clock in the world.*

THE NAVE *From the main entrance in the West Front there is an uninterrupted view of the full length of the 230 ft long nave—the main body of the cathedral.*

MOMPESSON HOUSE *Started in 1680, the house was given a stone façade and sash windows in about 1700. The cypher of Charles Mompesson, C.M., is worked in the wrought-iron gates.*

ORNATE INTERIOR *Early 18th-century panelling and plasterwork that can be seen on the main staircase in the hall of Mompesson House on the north side of the close.*

WALTON CANONRY *Izaac Walton, son of the great angler and a canon of the cathedral, lived in this house in the close in the early 18th century. The close, the largest in England, was a self-contained town in itself before the city of Salisbury began to spring up outside its walls. The King's House, with its mullioned windows, dates from Elizabethan times and is now a teacher-training college.*

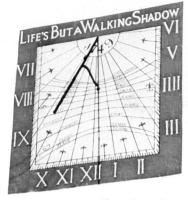

MALMESBURY HOUSE *The sundial on the wall of the house is inscribed 'Life's but a walking shadow', a quotation from Shakespeare's* Macbeth. *It was put there by James Harris, a wealthy MP and author, who lived in the house in the North Walk during the late 18th century.*

GEORGIAN LIBRARY *The library of Malmesbury House reflects the taste of James Harris, who refurbished the house in the 18th century.*

there are still choral services every day. The choir has six permanent, paid men singers, the lay vicars, and 16 boys who undergo a long and arduous musical education at the cathedral choir school in the old bishop's palace in the close. It was here that John Constable painted some of his many famous Salisbury pictures.

The remarkable array of 70 or so old buildings around the close range from simple 14th-century cottages to Elizabethan mansions. The stylish Matrons' College was erected by Bishop Seth Ward for clergymen's widows, and was probably designed by his friend Sir Christopher Wren.

The Old Deanery, which is a part of the college, has a superb medieval hall, and the Old Canonry has wonderful gardens that run down to the river.

The building of the Bishop's Palace was not begun until the 13th century. Charles II set up his court there during the Great Plague. The palace is used now by the boys of the cathedral school. The bishop is more modestly accommodated in the South Canonry.

The town houses

There have always been a number of private residents in the close. In the summer two of the grander town houses are open to the public. One of these, Mompesson House, stands imposingly on Choristers' Green, a small square within the close. The Mompessons were an old Wiltshire merchant family. Sir Richard, who died in 1627, and his wife Katherine, lie side by side in the cathedral in the most ornate of our tombs, brightly coloured and gilded. Mompesson House, until recently the bishop's residence, is now owned by the National Trust.

Malmesbury House was built as a humble dwelling around 1327. It was later purchased by the Harris family, and between 1640 and 1749 a rich new interior and Queen Anne façade were added.

One should not be surprised at how the religious and the secular mingle in Salisbury, for the town grew from the cathedral close. Workmen and tradesfolk as well as clergy had to be housed, and in 1258 Bishop Richard Poore drew up one of the first 'town planning' schemes. It provided for houses to be built in small squares, called 'chequers', radiating from the close. These are still in use, and the names of some of them, such as Guilder Lane (recalling the gilders' craft), still reflect the bond between the city and the cathedral.

1 *Library*
2 *Matron's College*
3 *Mompesson House* **NT**
4 *Choristers' Green*

WHEN TO VISIT SALISBURY

The city of Salisbury is the starting point of Hand-Picked Tour No. 25, which is described on pages 64–65.

Opening times Cathedral: Daily, tours of tower 11 a.m. and 2.30 p.m. Library: May to Oct., daily; winter, Mon., Wed. and Fri. Malmesbury House: May to Oct., Wed., Thur. afternoons. Mompesson House: May to Oct., Wed., Sat. afternoons.

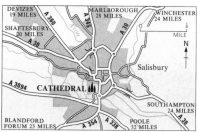

A rural ride through Stonehenge country

William Cobbett, the social reformer who put the English countryside under his microscope, was a pioneer along this trail. It was here that he gathered much of the material for his book, Rural Rides, *in the 19th century, and many of the stopping points are little changed since his time. They include the field where William the Conqueror disbanded his invading army, a statue of a mailcoach guard who came to a nasty end, and a church with a fire-engine inside. The Longleat lions are a modern novelty, but Stonehenge stands as a symbol of much that has remained untouched by time.*

(1) Warminster to Longleat House Leave Warminster by the A362, following the signpost for Frome. After 2 m. the entrance to Longleat House is on the left. The way in to the game park where the lions roam is slightly further along the A362 to the left, and is clearly signposted.

(2) Longleat House to Horningsham Return to the Longleat House entrance on the A362 and turn right, signposted to Horningsham. After 2½ m. turn right at the T-junction and ¾ m. later bear right into Horningsham. The Meeting House, believed to be the oldest-surviving Dissenters' chapel in the country, is signposted up a road on the left. To complete a circuit of the village, continue to the end of this road and turn left.

(3) Horningsham to Wylye Return to the Longleat junction, but there carry straight on along the road signposted to Shear Water. At the next T-junction turn left, and almost immediately left again. Pass the Shear Water lake on the left and, about ½ m. further on, turn left on to the A350. After about 1 m. turn off to the right and continue 2½ m. to Sutton Veny. Join the B3095 and go straight through the village, over the crossroads and continue into Tytherington. Carry on past Tytherington church and follow the road along the valley of the River Wylye through Corton, Boyton and Sherrington to Stockton. Stockton House was the home of an Elizabethan cloth merchant, John Topp, who founded the nearby Topp Almshouses. From Stockton the road continues to Wylye.

(4) Wylye to Great Wishford In Wylye, turn right on to the road signposted to Great Wishford. This road runs alongside the railway for 4 m. to Great Wishford. The villagers of Great Wishford have the unusual privilege of dancing before the High Altar of Salisbury Cathedral on Oak Apple Day (May 29). Nowadays the dance is actually performed on the cathedral lawns. The ceremony commemorates Charles II's escape from the Roundheads and restoration to the throne after hiding in an oak tree during the English Civil War in the 17th century, but the event may also derive from ancient tree-worship. The colourful ceremony provides an annual night out for the villagers.

(5) Great Wishford to Old Sarum From the church, cross the river and turn left on to the A36. Almost immediately, turn off it again to the right, beside the Swan Inn, and take the road signposted to Woodford. Cross the A360, continue into Middle Woodford and turn right, following the signpost for Lower Woodford. Follow the road for about 2½ m.; just after crossing the River Avon, turn left and follow the road round to the right, signposted Old Sarum. Turn right on to the A345 for the entrance to Old Sarum, which is on the right. There are multiple earthworks on the 56 acre site, the earliest of them Iron Age.

(6) Old Sarum to Stonehenge Go back along the A345 for 2½ m. and turn left at the crossroads, following the signpost for Durnford. At the second junction keep right and cross the Avon into Upper Woodford. Immediately after the bridge turn right, and after 3½ m., at a junction, turn left for Stonehenge on a road which soon merges into the A303. Just under 1 m. further on, fork right on to the A334. Almost immediately on the right is the entrance to Stonehenge.

(7) Stonehenge to Warminster Leave Stonehenge on the A344, which merges into the A360, and continue on to Shrewton, where 'Flood' cottages recall the great flood in 1841 when the River Till inundated the village. There are many bridges over small streams in the village. Just beyond the village bear left on to the B390 and follow the road for about 5 m. to Chitterne. Chitterne House, a 17th-century building close to the road, conceals, behind a stone gateway, a courtyard on old French lines, flanked on three sides by half-timbered wings in stone and flint. Continue on the B390 and after about 4 m. fork right on to the A36 and follow this along the upper Wylye Valley back to Warminster.

NATURE NOTES

Although the heathland around Longleat has been planted with conifers, some native heathland plants, such as bilberry and heath milkwort, may still be found. The lakes at Longleat and Shear Water attract large numbers of ducks in winter, and finches may also be seen.

INFORMATION

Places of interest *Longleat House and Safari Park:* daily (except Christmas Day), Easter to Oct., 10 a.m.–6 p.m., rest of year 10 a.m.–4 p.m. *Stonehenge:* Weekdays, Sun. afternoons. *Warminster:* The Dewey Museum, Sat.

Craft workshop *Heytesbury:* M. and P. Mullen. Bridgefoot, Mantles Lane. Traditional rush and chair caning of antique and modern furniture. Open most of the time, but telephone first (Tel. Sutton Veny 544).

Event *Stonehenge:* Midnight vigil by the Druids, June 21.

Information 10 Endless Street, Salisbury (Tel. Salisbury 4956).

Towns with easy access to Warminster:

Bath	19 m.	Salisbury	21 m.
Devizes	18 m.	Yeovil	32 m.

Old Bell Hotel, Warminster.

WARMINSTER

Military camps surround Warminster, home of the Army's School of Infantry. The name comes from the Saxon 'Church on the River Were'. William Cobbett, the 19th-century social reformer, wrote of it as being 'full of everything solid and good'. The town was once the greatest corn-marketing centre in southern England, and was also important in the wool trade. Many of it buildings look much as they did in Cobbett's tim including 200 year old houses, the 14th-century parish church and the colonnaded Old Bell Hote

Pink Library, Longleat House.

LONGLEAT HOUSE

Family home of the Marquises of Bath, Longleat is one of the greatest of the 'stately homes' and also a focal point for West Country tourists. It is still owned by the descendants of John Thynne, who completed the building of the house in 1580 on the site of a burnt-down Augustinian priory. The present Lord Bath, who opened the house to the public and introduced the lions to the park, prefers to live in a small modern house near by. Cley Hill, reached by a signposted track, and crowned by an Iron Age hill-fort, is on the prehistoric Ridgeway which runs from South Devon to the Wash.

HORNINGSHAM

The old thatched Meeting House in the village was built around 1566 on the orders of John Thynne, an ancestor of the Marquis of Bath. Its purpose was to provide a place of worship for Scottish Dissenters employed as workmen on Thynne's new house at nearby Longleat.

WYLYE

A stone figure of a man blowing a horn stands in the river, below the bridge in this little village, as a sinister reminder that travel had its hazards long before the motor-car age. The figure is a memorial to a mailcoach guard who was drowned here about 200 years ago. Wylye, tucked into a valley against a wooded background, is the setting for quaint cottages and stone houses of that period. The main road passes the Jacobean Bell Inn close to the parish church, where the parson preaches from a wooden pulpit carved in 1628.

SCALE

0   1   2   3   4   5 MILES

Sunset at Stonehenge.

'The wizard Merlin building Stonehenge' as depicted in a 12th-century history.

STONEHENGE

Britain's most famous ancient monument was built over a period of almost 1000 years up to 1250 BC. The only sure deduction about its purpose is that it was the sanctuary of a religious cult who regarded the sun as important—either to mark the seasons or as an object of worship. Though dwarfed from a distance against the vast backdrop of Salisbury Plain, the biggest of the stones stands 21 ft high. The oldest part of the construction is the outer ditch. Within it is a double circle of 80 bluestones believed to have been brought more than 200 miles from the Prescelly Hills of Wales by raft along rivers—and by sled overland. About 1650 BC these stones were replaced by two rings of 'sarsen' (from Saracen or foreign) stones from the Marlborough Downs. The stones which survive today are of this generation, the uprights and lintels being slotted together. Set at the very centre of the complex is the Altar Stone. From it the eye is drawn to the Heelstone, or Sunstone, over whose tip the sun rises on the longest day, June 21.

More than 300 barrows—ancient burial mounds—lie within easy walking distance of Stonehenge.

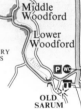

Horse-drawn fire-engine, Great Wishford.

GREAT WISHFORD

A series of plaques set into the east wall of the village churchyard sorrowfully records the rising price of bread since great-great-grandmother's day until 1971. The first entry shows that it cost 3s 4d in 1800 to buy a gallon of dough, to be cut up and baked into loaves at home. A horse-drawn fire-engine, in use 100 years ago, is kept in the church.

Old Sarum from the air.

OLD SARUM

Four years after winning the English crown at the Battle of Hastings, William the Conqueror assembled his victorious army at Old Sarum, paid off the soldiers and demobilised them. The scene was set in the Iron Age hill-fort to which an earlier invading army, the Romans, built four converging roads. Visitors can see the outline of the original cathedral, later replaced when the church authorities, quarrelling with the military occupiers over a water shortage, moved down to the Avon and founded New Sarum—the modern Salisbury. Old Sarum was one of the notorious 'rotten boroughs' until the 1832 Reform Act. A plaque commemorates William Pitt the Elder, the 18th-century statesman who was one of the two MPs returned by Old Sarum, which at that time had an electorate of only ten people.

William Pitt the Elder, MP for Old Sarum.

Landscape where the first photographer worked

Archaeology, aviation and photography all owe something to the pioneering instincts of those who peopled this fertile part of the Wiltshire downs. Their achievements started so long ago that the area can claim the biggest prehistoric monuments of their kind in Europe. At Malmesbury a monk made a pair of wings and tried to fly—with unfortunate results—in the year 1010. At Lacock a scientist took what is possibly the world's first photograph in 1835. Even without a scientific outlook it is impossible on this tour not to enjoy some of the loveliest scenery and villages in England.

(1) Malmesbury to Castle Combe Leave the town on the A429 signposted to Chippenham. After 6 m., just before the motorway, turn right on to the road signposted to Stanton St Quintin (not Lower Stanton St Quintin, which precedes it on the main road). Go through the village, and after 1 m. bear right, following the signpost for Grittleton. Turn left at the T-junction and go through Grittleton. After about 2 m. turn left on to the B4039, following the signpost to Chippenham and Castle Combe. Take the next turning on the right and then turn right again and continue into Castle Combe, which once held the title of the prettiest village in England.

(2) Castle Combe to Corsham Follow the road through the village. Turn left at the signpost to Ford and Chippenham, and after 2 m. turn left on to the A420 signposted to Chippenham. After 1 m. turn right into Biddestone. There is a 17th-century manor house here; the White Lion Inn, built in 1672; and a church with an unusual old bell-tower. Beyond Biddestone, go straight across the A4 and into Corsham.

(3) Corsham to Lacock Leave the town centre by the B3353, following the signpost for Melksham. At the edge of the town, where the B3353 swings to the right, keep straight on past Corsham Park, following the signpost to Lacock. After about 2½ m. at the A350, turn right, and almost immediately left into Lacock, an ancient village owned by the National Trust.

(4) Lacock to Calne Leave the village, taking the road signposted to Calne and climbing Bowden Hill, with its fine view to the right. At Sandy Lane, turn right on to the A342 and then first left, following the signpost for Heddington. After ½ m. turn left again, following the signpost for Calne which is reached after about 3 m.

(5) Calne to Cherhill Down Take the A4, following the Marlborough signpost. After about 3 m. the road goes through Cherhill village. About ¼ m. further on, a short track on the right leads to Cherhill Down.

(6) Cherhill Down to Silbury Hill Leave the Down and turn right on to the A4 again going towards Marlborough. Pass the site of the former Yatesbury RAF station on the left. Stay on the A4 at Beckhampton roundabout and pass through Beckhampton village. After about 1 m. Silbury Hill is on the left of the road. West Kennett Long Barrow, a prehistoric burial chamber, is 600 yds further along the A4 on the right.

(7) Silbury Hill to Avebury Continue on the A4 for about 1 m. to West Kennett village, there turn left on to the B4003. Travel along an avenue of ancient stones to Avebury village, encircled by the biggest prehistoric remains in Europe.

(8) Avebury to Dauntsey Leave Avebury by the A361, following the Swindon signpost, and after 4 m. turn left on to the B4041 signposted to Wootton Bassett. Go through Broad Hinton and, at the end of the village, turn left into a lane leading to Clyffe Pypard. The village church here contains an 18 ft marble figure commemorating a local carpenter who made his fortune in London. Keep left through Clyffe Pypard, following the signpost for Bushton and Lyneham. At the crossroads in Bushton continue straight ahead, through Tockenham, and 1 m. beyond the village turn left on to the A420. After just under 2 m. enter the outskirts of Lyneham. Stay on the A420 by-passing Lyneham town centre, and about 2 m. later pass through Dauntsey Lock, where the road crosses the railway. After 1 m., where the A420 swings left, turn right on to the road signposted to Dauntsey. Continue over the M4 motorway into Dauntsey.

(9) Dauntsey to Malmesbury Leave Dauntsey, continuing on the same road, and after about 1 m., at Great Somerford, turn right following the signpost to Little Somerford. Bear left in the village, following the Malmesbury signpost, and turn left at the junction on to the B4042, still following the signpost for Malmesbury. On the outskirts of Malmesbury, go straight across the A429 for the town centre.

INFORMATION

Places of interest *Avebury:* Alexander Keiller Museum, daily. Manor House, May to Aug., Wed. to Mon., 2-6 p.m.; Apr. and Sept., weekends 2-6 p.m.; Bank Hols., 10 a.m.-6 p.m. *Calne:* Bowood House, Apr. to mid-May, mid-June to Sept., Sun., Tues. to Thur., Bank Hols., 2-6 p.m. *Corsham Court:* Apr. to Oct., Wed., Thur., Bank Hols.; also Fri. to Sun., mid-July to mid-Sept. and daily during Bath Festival, 11 a.m.-12.30 p.m., 2-6 p.m. *Lacock Abbey:* Apr. to Oct., daily (except Mon., Tues., Apr., May, Oct.), Bank Hols., 2-6 p.m.

Craft workshops *Lacock:* Graham Watling, 23 Church Street: gold and silverware, daily, 10 a.m.-6 p.m. The Pottery, Tanyard: most days.

Event *Lacock:* Spring Folk Festival, Apr.

Information West Country Tourist Board, Trinity Court, Southernhay East, Exeter (Tel: Exeter 76351).

Towns with easy access to Malmesbury:

Bath	22 m.	Gloucester	24 m.
Bristol	26 m.	Marlborough	24 m.

MALMESBURY
Two rivers, the Avon and the Ingleburn, flank this old hilltop market town, which claimed to be the first borough in England. The charter giving it borough status was granted in the year 880. Only 130 years late a monk, wearing a pair of home-made wings, tried to fly from the roof of the 7th century abbey. He managed to glide about 200 yds before crashing and breaking both his legs. What is left of the abbey is now the parish church, which contains some fin carvings. The 16th-century roofed market cross was built 'for poore folks to stande dry when rayne cummith'. There is an attractive riverside walk, clearly marked, which starts from the Flying Monk Hotel on the Tetbury road.

Main street and market cross, Castle Combe.

CASTLE COMBE
No one seeing Castle Combe for the first time is likely to be surprised that it was chosen for the filming of 'Dr Doolittle' in the 1960s. Quaint old houses and shops shelter beneath mossy roofs. The hotel, which bustled with off-location film stars, was a 17th-century manor house. A 15th-century market cross recalls the village's years as a prosperous weaving centre. The brook mirrors an ancient arched bridge, and the church contains the 13th-century tomb and effigy of Sir Walter de Dunstanville, the knight who built the long-defunct castle from which the village took its name. The setting, in a steep sided and wooded valley, greatly enhances the mellow stone and irregular rooftops of a village which was once voted the prettiest in England.

Corsham Court.

CORSHAM
Weavers' cottages, built 200 years ago of warm, hone coloured stone, recall the quieter days of this town centre. Corsham Court, owned by the Methuen famil for more than 200 years, was begun in 1582 and alter by John Nash in 1800. The park with its fine elm aven was landscaped by Capability Brown, the most famo of the 18th-century garden planners.

SCALE

0   1   2   3   4   5 MILES

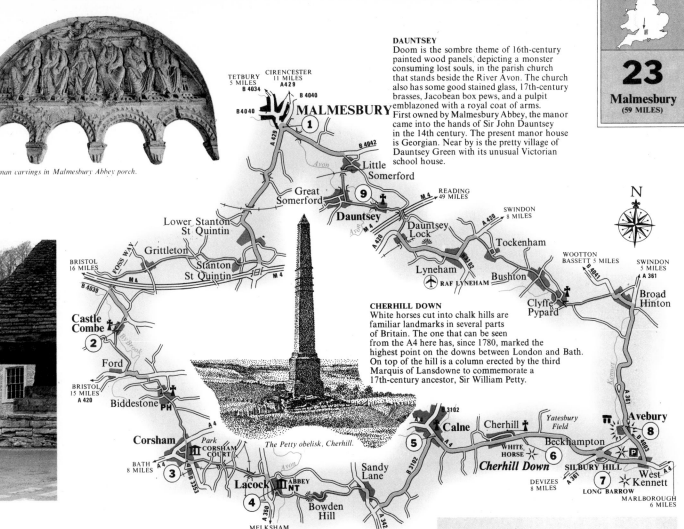

man carvings in Malmesbury Abbey porch.

DAUNTSEY
Doom is the sombre theme of 16th-century painted wood panels, depicting a monster consuming lost souls, in the parish church that stands beside the River Avon. The church also has some good stained glass, 17th-century brasses, Jacobean box pews, and a pulpit emblazoned with a royal coat of arms. First owned by Malmesbury Abbey, the manor came into the hands of Sir John Dauntsey in the 14th century. The present manor house is Georgian. Near by is the pretty village of Dauntsey Green with its unusual Victorian school house.

23
Malmesbury
(59 MILES)

TETBURY 5 MILES B 4034 — CIRENCESTER 11 MILES A 429 — B 4040

B4040

MALMESBURY
①

A 429

B 4042

Avon

Little Somerford

READING 49 MILES

Great Somerford

⑨

M 4

Dauntsey

Dauntsey Lock

SWINDON 8 MILES

A 420

Lower Stanton St Quintin

Tockenham

WOOTTON BASSETT 5 MILES

SWINDON 5 MILES A 361

Grittleton

FOSS WAY

M 4

Stanton St Quintin

M 4

Lyneham

RAF LYNEHAM

Bushton

B 4102

Clyffe Pypard

Broad Hinton

BRISTOL 16 MILES

B 4039

CHERHILL DOWN
White horses cut into chalk hills are familiar landmarks in several parts of Britain. The one that can be seen from the A4 here has, since 1780, marked the highest point on the downs between London and Bath. On top of the hill is a column erected by the third Marquis of Lansdowne to commemorate a 17th-century ancestor, Sir William Petty.

Castle Combe
②

By Brook

Ford

A 361

BRISTOL 15 MILES A 420

Biddestone PH

B 3102

A 4

A 361

Kennet

Calne
⑤

Cherhill

Yatesbury Field

Avebury
⑧

B 4003

Corsham

Park CORSHAM COURT

Beckhampton

P

A 4

BATH 8 MILES

A 4

③

B 3353

WHITE HORSE

⑥

Cherhill Down

SILBURY HILL

West Kennett

A 4

Lacock
ABBEY NT

④

A 350

Sandy Lane

B 3102

Avon

The Petty obelisk, Cherhill.

DEVIZES 8 MILES

⑦

LONG BARROW

A 361

MARLBOROUGH 6 MILES

MELKSHAM 2 MILES

Bowden Hill

A 342

DEVIZES 4 MILES

CALNE
A modern bacon factory is likely to be the dominant impression of anyone driving straight through Calne. But for those with time to linger, such places as the 15th-century church of St Mary and the 200 year old coaching inn, the Lansdowne Arms, will afford more historic interest. Near the church are Dr Townson's Almshouses, built in 1682, the 17th-century Church House, and the youth hostel, housed in a fine building of the same period. Some of the best Georgian buildings are round the green and in the nearby strand.

4000 year old stones, Avebury.

AVEBURY
A great ditch encloses the village of Avebury, and Europe's biggest layout of prehistoric ritual stones. Little is known of the origins of Avebury except that it was built about 4000 years ago, and that it was some sort of temple for worship rather than a settlement to be lived in. It remained unmentioned in written histories until 1648, when the diarist John Aubrey reported that it excelled Stonehenge as did a cathedral a parish church. Much of what is known, and what excavations have revealed, can be studied at the local museum. Some of the stones are incorporated in the older houses in the village.

lbot (right) photographic pioneer.

LACOCK
The entire village was given to the National Trust in 1944 by the then lady of the manor, Miss Matilda Talbot. No building in Lacock is later than the 18th century; many date from very much earlier, such as the 14th-century tithe barn and the church of St Cyriac, with its notable vault and Sir William Sharington's tomb and monument. Lacock Abbey, the manor house, was the last religious foundation to be dissolved at the Reformation. It was converted to a private residence by Sir William Sharington, Treasurer of the Bristol Royal Mint, who acquired it in 1540. The 13th-century cloister, sacristy and nuns' chapter house still remain. So do the later additions of Sharington's Tudor mansion, with its twisted chimneys and octagonal tower, and the 16th-century brewery, now restored. The house was 'modernised' in neo-Gothic style about 1753, and further alterations were made in 1828. The abbey is mentioned in 19th-century scientific records as the scene of W. H. Fox Talbot's pioneering experiments with light-sensitive materials in 1835, which later formed the basis for modern photography. Talbot's first recognisable photograph shows a detail of a corner of the abbey.

cock Abbey, corner Talbot photographed.

Silbury Hill—man-made mystery mound.

SILBURY HILL
A 130 ft high man-made mound of chalk rubble, 200 yds in diameter, forms a striking and slightly puzzling landmark on this part of the Wiltshire downs. It looks as if it could be an outsize barrow, or burial cairn, but excavations have failed to confirm this. What is fairly certain is that the mound has some connection with nearby Avebury.

Warm stone of Wiltshire withstands the toll of time

The short space of about 50 miles spans centuries of history in some of the most visually satisfying places in England. A great white horse marks a victory by Alfred the Great, and there are relics of the Iron Age, of medieval prosperity in the wool trade and the great age of canal building. The mellow stone that enshrines the history of the area, is best seen in the many old buildings at Steeple Ashton and Bradford-on-Avon. For good measure, there are two fascinating places in which to catch up on natural history— The Tropical Bird Gardens at Rode and Brokerswood Woodland Park.

(1) Devizes to Steeple Ashton Leave the town by the A361, following the signposts for Trowbridge, and after 3 m. at the junction with the A365, bear left to remain on the A361. Go through the village of Seend, and 2 m. further on turn left into Great Hinton. At the crossroads immediately beyond the village carry straight on, and 1 m. later turn left at the T-junction to enter Steeple Ashton (originally Staple Ashton, because of its importance in the local wool trade).

(2) Steeple Ashton to Bradford-on-Avon Return to the T-junction but keep straight ahead. Then take the first on the left, which is signposted to Trowbridge and Hilperton. Go straight across the A350 at the next crossroads, turn left on to the A361 at the entrance to Hilperton and almost immediately right on to the B3105, signposted to Staverton. Cross the Kennet and Avon Canal and the railway into Staverton, then cross the River Avon and bear left. After ½ m., at the B3107, turn left and continue straight on for about 1 m. into Bradford-on-Avon, with its Saxon and medieval buildings.

(3) Bradford-on-Avon to Westwood Leave the town southwards by the B3109 following the signs for Frome. (The road to the magnificent old Bradford tithe barn is signposted to the right on the outskirts of the town.) After 1 m. fork right and follow the sign for Westwood. Turn right at the T-junction to enter Westwood village, where there is an early-15th-century manor house.

(4) Westwood to Farleigh Castle Leave Westwood by the road past the church, and continue straight ahead for 1½ m. to turn right on to the A366 for the castle entrance. Standing on a grassy hill over the River Frome, the castle dates back to the 14th century.

(5) Farleigh Castle to Rode Leave the castle and turn left on to the A366. After 1½ m. turn right at the crossroads on to the B3109, following the Rode signposts. On the approach to Rode turn right, downhill, and cross the River Frome to the tropical bird gardens.

(6) Rode to Brokerswood Park Leave the bird gardens, turning to the right, and on meeting the A36 in Woolverton turn left. After just under 2 m., in Beckington, turn left and continue to Rudge, bearing left there to follow the sign for North Bradley. Turn left again at the next junction and straight over the next crossroads 1 m. further on. The entrance to Brokerswood Woodland Park is on the left.

(7) Brokerswood Park to Westbury Hill Leave the park and return to the crossroads. Turn left and follow the Westbury signposts. After 2 m. fork left on to the B3099, still signposted Westbury and, 300 yds further on, left again on to the A3098, which runs into the town. Westbury has an attractive Georgian market place and a Georgian cloth mill. Leave the town by the B3098, heading northeast, following the signs for Bratton. About ½ m. from the centre, on the outskirts of the town, turn right to follow the signs to Westbury White Horse.

(8) Westbury Hill to Edington From the top of the hill turn left along a track which goes past the castle earthworks. Follow this down to Bratton—which has a prehistoric hill fort—and the junction with the B3098. There turn right to Edington.

(9) Edington to Urchfont Stay on the B3098 through Erlestoke and Little Cheverell, across the A360 and through Market Lavington, Easterton and Eastcott to Urchfont.

(10) Urchfont to Potterne Leave the village, turning left to follow the Potterne sign. Continue along this lane for 3 m. to the A360. There turn right into Potterne village.

(11) Potterne to Devizes Leave the village on the A360, reaching Devizes 2 m. later.

INFORMATION

Places of interest *Bradford-on-Avon:* Barton Tithe Barn, at any reasonable time. *Bratton:* Castle and White Horse, at any reasonable time. *Brokerswood:* Woodland Park and Phillips Countryside Museum, daily, 10.30 a.m. to dusk. *Devizes:* Museum, Tues. to Sat. 11 a.m.-5 p.m. *Farleigh Castle:* Weekdays, Sun. afternoons. *Potterne:* Porch House, by appointment. *Rode:* The Tropical Bird Gardens, daily, 10.30 a.m.-7 p.m. (or dusk). *Westwood Manor:* Apr. to Sept., Wed. 2.30-6 p.m.

Craft workshops *Bratton:* White Horse Spinners and Weavers. Mon. to Fri. Phone first (Tel. Bratton 382). *Brokerswood:* Woodland Park. Wooden furniture and ornaments. Daily.

Events *Devizes:* Canoe Race, Devizes to Westminster, Good Friday. Cattle and agricultural machinery market, Thur. *Edington:* Fair and Festival of English Cathedral Music, Aug.

Information West Country Tourist Board, Trinity Court, Southernhay East, Exeter (Tel. Exeter 76351).

Towns with easy access to Devizes:

Bath	19 m.	Newbury	33 m.
Bristol	32 m.	Salisbury	27 m.
Marlborough	15 m.	Swindon	20 m.

WESTWOOD
The manor house was built in the early 15th century by Thomas Horton, a wealthy cloth merchant of Bradford-on-Avon. The house was altered in 1610, and has remained virtually unchanged since then. In the Kings' Room are portraits of the 22 English kings up to Charles I. There is a modern topiary garden.

FARLEIGH CASTLE
Two tall round towers and the outer wall are all that remain of the fortifications of Farleigh Castle, built in about 1380 by Sir Thomas de Hungerford. But the castle chapel survives in good order and contains family tombs, a collection of arms and armour and other fascinating relics of the Hungerfords, who held the castle for more than 300 years.

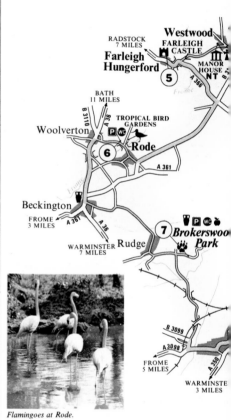

Flamingoes at Rode.

RODE
Tucked away here, between two main roads, is one of Britain's leading Bird Gardens. Originally opened in 1962 The Tropical Bird Gardens have established a unique breeding record for nearly 200 different species ranging from cranes and cassowaries to tiny finches. The free-flying flock of macaws, many of which are home-bred, is one of its unique features.

BROKERSWOOD WOODLAND PARK
Eight walks, ranging in distance from just over a mile to a mere 270 yds, wend their way through the 120 acres of woodland that make up this fascinating park. More than 50 different types of tree grow in the woods, and many birds, including woodpeckers, pheasants, nightingales and wrens, make their homes there. And on the lake herons and kingfishers may be seen. There is also a countryside museum.

Ash

SCALE
0   1   2   3 MILES

Chapel on the bridge, Bradford-on-Avon.

BRADFORD-ON-AVON

The warm beauty of the stonework rising steeply above the River Avon helps to make this one of the most visually beguiling towns in England. The bridge has two 14th-century arches and a lock-up which used to be a wayside chapel used by pilgrims on the way to Glastonbury. In Church Street is the Saxon church of St Laurence, built about AD 700 and rediscovered in the 1870s when it was in use as a house and school. The great tithe barn, once a granary for Shaftesbury Abbey, dates from the 14th century. The town's prosperity was founded on the wool trade and dates from the same period, but the last woollen mill closed in 1905 when the rubber industry took over.

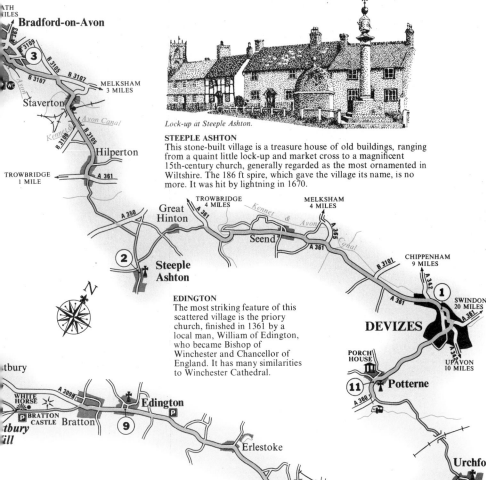

Devizes: flight of locks on the canal.

Lock-up at Steeple Ashton.

STEEPLE ASHTON

This stone-built village is a treasure house of old buildings, ranging from a quaint little lock-up and market cross to a magnificent 15th-century church, generally regarded as the most ornamented in Wiltshire. The 186 ft spire, which gave the village its name, is no more. It was hit by lightning in 1670.

EDINGTON

The most striking feature of this scattered village is the priory church, finished in 1361 by a local man, William of Edington, who became Bishop of Winchester and Chancellor of England. It has many similarities to Winchester Cathedral.

DEVIZES

A Norman church, 16th-century cottages and imposing Georgian houses are among the elements which create the mellow atmosphere of this old market town. Devizes grew up in the shelter of a castle built by the Bishop of Salisbury early in the 12th century on the boundaries of two manors. Tradition says the name is a corruption of 'ad divisas', Latin for 'at the boundaries'. The castle was destroyed during the Civil War. On the northern side of the town a remarkable series of 29 locks carries the Kennet and Avon Canal 230 ft over Caen Hill. The longest flight of double-gated locks in Britain, they were built in 1810 but are now abandoned. However, it is planned to have them back in operation by the late 1970s.

Porch House (left) and cottages, Potterne.

POTTERNE

Owned by the bishops of Salisbury before the Norman Conquest, Potterne appears in the Domesday Book. There are many half-timbered 15th-century houses, including the Porch House which has spy holes as well as windows in the upper storey.

URCHFONT

The name comes from the old word for a spring never known to run dry. There is still a pond here, near the 14th-century church and a house once owned by William Pitt the Elder, the 18th-century Prime Minister.

WESTBURY HILL

The huge White Horse, carved in the chalk of Westbury Hill, is the biggest of the Wiltshire White Horses. It is 175 ft long from head to tail and stands 107 ft at the shoulder. In its present form it dates back to 1778. In that year it was superimposed on an earlier horse which legend says was cut in the 9th century to celebrate Alfred the Great's victory over the Danes at Bratton Castle, the Iron Age stronghold which still remains on the hilltop. The victory ended Danish efforts to conquer England. Georgian cottages, cloth mills and the market-place now give the town a pleasant 18th-century flavour.

Westbury white horse.

West from New Sarum to the heights of Cranborne Chase

Salisbury, or New Sarum as it was called in its 13th-century charter, is surrounded by the lush meadows and valleys of the Nadder and Ebble rivers. To the west, rolling hills rise to Win Green, the highest point of Cranborne Chase, and continue into Dorset and the ancient hilltop town of Shaftesbury. The countryside is dotted with picture-book villages and some of the finest country houses in the south of England, including Stourhead.

(1) Salisbury to Win Green Leave the city on the A354, following the signs to Blandford. After 4 m., in Combe Bissett, turn right and continue westwards along the valley of the River Ebble. Just before Ebbesbourne Wake fork right, following the signpost to Shaftesbury. Continue through Alvediston and on to Berwick St John, which is overlooked on the left by the impressive Iron Age earthworks of Winkelbury Hill. There is a memorial in Berwick church to 'Jackie' Fisher, the admiral of the First World War, known as the father of the battleship. His motto, carved on the memorial, was 'Fear God: Dread Nought'. In the village, turn right and after 2 m. turn left on to the A30. After 1 m., in Ludwell, turn left and follow the road climbing between Charlton Down and Win Green. At the top of the ascent, a path to the left leads up to the National Trust viewpoint on Win Green Hill.

(2) Win Green to Shaftesbury At the top of the ascent, turn sharp right on to the B3081, which descends in steep hairpin bends known as Zig-Zag Hill. At the next T-junction, on Cann Common, turn right, keeping on the B3081, and then turn left on to the A30. At the next roundabout follow the signs for the centre of Shaftesbury, an imposing old stone-built town, with an abbey founded by Alfred the Great.

(3) Shaftesbury to Stourhead Leave the town on the B3081 and on the outskirts turn right, following the signpost to Motcombe. Go through Motcombe and continue across country towards Mere. After just over 6 m. enter Mere, a village with two old coaching inns, The Old Ship and The Talbot, and a richly decorated church. Here turn left and, passing under the A303, follow the B3092 signed for Stourton and Stourhead. After almost 1½ m. turn left to visit Stourhead.

(4) Stourhead to Maiden Bradley Return to the B3092 and turn left, following the road past White Sheet Downs and into Maiden Bradley.

(5) Maiden Bradley to Tisbury In the village turn right to follow the signpost to Kingston Deverill. Here turn left on to the B3095 and after ½ m., where the road swings left, keep straight ahead, following the signpost to Hindon. At the next junction turn right on to the A350 and then right again on to the A303. Almost immediately turn left, back on to the A350. After ½ m. turn left on to the B3089 and into Hindon, which was a flourishing market town before the coming of the railway. Here turn right and pass through the hamlet of Greenwich and on to Tisbury, where one of the oldest trees in Britain still grows in the parish churchyard.

(6) Tisbury to Dinton Just after The Cross public house bear left, going downhill and across the river, and follow the road to the right by Place Farm. In Lower Chicksgrove follow the road slightly to the left, and after 1 m., where the road swings left, go straight on and into Fovant. The village lies in a narrow valley and flanks a large pond. The chalk skin of Fovant Downs, to the south of the village, is carved with regimental badges of troops stationed at Fovant during the First World War. Leave Fovant on the road signposted to Dinton and follow the road through Fovant Wood across the River Nadder and into Dinton, crossing the B3089.

(7) Dinton to Wilton Leave Dinton on the B3089, following the signpost to Barford St Martin, a village with Tudor thatched cottages. In the village keep left on to the A30 and follow the road into the carpet town of Wilton.

(8) Wilton to West Harnham Continue through Wilton and turn right at the roundabout, keeping on the A30. After just over ¼ m. turn right on to the A3094. Cross the River Nadder and bear left with the road, after the long straight stretch, and into the village-suburb of West Harnham.

(9) West Harnham to Salisbury In the village, turn left along Upper Street and right on to Middle Street, which leads back to the A3094. Here turn left and follow the A3094 back into Salisbury.

INFORMATION

Places of interest *Dinton:* Philipps House. Apr. to Sept., Wed., 2-6 p.m., or dusk. *Salisbury:* Church House, all year, Mon. to Fri., 9 a.m.-5 p.m. North canonry, Apr. to Oct., daily, 9 a.m.-6 p.m. Old Deanery, Aug., Tues. to Sat., 2-5 p.m. Salisbury and South Wilts Museum, May to Sept., 10 a.m.-5 p.m.; Oct. to Apr., 10 a.m.-4 p.m., Sun. afternoons all year. *Shaftesbury:* Abbey ruins museum, Easter to Sept., Tues. to Sat., 10 a.m.-12.50 p.m., 2-7 p.m. Sun. 2-7 p.m. *Stourhead House:* Apr. to Sept. daily (except Mon., Tues., Apr. and Sept.), and Bank Hol., 2-6 p.m.; Mar., Oct., Nov., Wed., Sat., Sun., 2-6 p.m., or dusk if earlier. Gardens, all year, daily. *Wilton House:* Apr. to beginning Oct., Tues. to Sat. and Bank Hols., 11 a.m.-6 p.m., Sun. 2-6 p.m.

Craft workshops *Salisbury:* Rose Villa Pottery, 4-5 Water Lane.

Event *Salisbury:* Arts festival, Sept.

Information *Salisbury:* 10 Endless Street (Tel. Salisbury 4956).

Towns with easy access to Salisbury:

Blandford		
Forum . . . . . . 23 m.	Hungerford . . . . 31 m.	
Bournemouth . . . 30 m.	Southampton . . . 23 m.	
Devizes . . . . 25 m.	Winchester . . . . . 24 m.	

The garden lake, Stourhead.

STOURHEAD
Colin Campbell designed Stourhead house in the Palladian style, and it was completed in 1722 for the banker Henry Hoare. It is now a setting for Chippendale furniture, Grinling Gibbons carvings, and paintings by Gainsborough and Reynolds. The landscaped gardens were laid out in the 1740s by Henry Hoare's son. They feature bridges, ornamental lakes, a Classical temple and the market cross which had stood in Bristol from 1373. The estate covers over 2500 acres.

'Chevy Chase' sideboard, Shaftesbury.

TISBURY

A large village overlooking the upper reaches of the River Nadder, Tisbury contains some fine houses, including Old House and Gaston House, both built in the 17th century. Rudyard Kipling and his parents are buried in St John's churchyard, where the famous Tisbury yew, hundreds of years old, grows round a huge boulder. On the edge of the village is Place Farm, a collection of medieval buildings which were once the grange to Shaftesbury Abbey. Among these is a tithe barn, 200 ft long and reputed to be the largest thatched barn in England.

Little Clarendon, Dinton.

DINTON

The village green at Dinton is dominated by a fine square-towered church, near which is Hyde House, built in the 16th century and one of four village properties belonging to the National Trust. The only one open to the public is Philipps House, built in the Palladian style in 1815. Little Clarendon is an attractive Tudor house, and near by is Lawes Cottage, a 17th-century house roofed with stone shingles.

WILTON

A former capital of the ancient kingdom of Wessex, Wilton is now synonymous with carpets, the manufacture of which was introduced in the 17th century by the Earl of Pembroke. Wilton House is the family seat of the Earls of Pembroke, and was rebuilt by Inigo Jones after a fire in 1647.

The lower gallery, Wilton House.

MAIDEN BRADLEY

All Saints' Church in Maiden Bradley dates from the 12th century, though additions continued to be made up to the 1850s. The church houses a skeleton found in a lead coffin near by in 1965, and believed to be about 1500 years old.

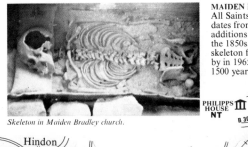

Skeleton in Maiden Bradley church.

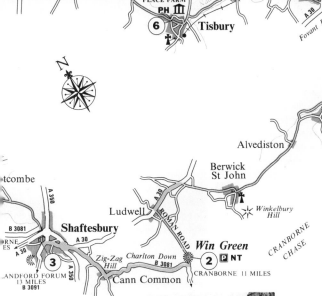

WEST HARNHAM

In the midst of Salisbury's modern suburbs, West Harnham has retained its village atmosphere. Outstanding among its buildings is the Old Mill, now a hotel and believed to have medieval origins. The house is surrounded by water, and is accessible only by a small footbridge.

SALISBURY

Situated at the meeting point of the Avon and Nadder rivers, the city of Salisbury has great charm, though this is often overshadowed by the famous cathedral. Salisbury was granted its first charter in 1227, and the city centre retains much of its medieval atmosphere. Among the notable buildings are Mompesson House, built in 1701 for a local merchant; the 14th-century Old George Hotel, praised in Samuel Pepys's diary; the Poultry Cross, at the junction of Silver Street and Butcher's Row; and the Joiner's Hall, which features fine examples of the wood-carver's art. (See p. 54.)

SHAFTESBURY

Built on a sandstone ridge 600 ft above sea level, this is one of the highest towns in southern England. One of the most striking streets is Gold Hill, buttressed on one side and steeply terraced on the other. Park Walk, a terrace in front of the ruined abbey founded by King Alfred in AD 880, commands views of Blackmoor Vale. In the 18th-century Grosvenor Hotel there is a 10th-century sideboard carved from a single block of oak, and depicting battle scenes from 'The Ballad of Chevy Chase'.

Gold Hill, Shaftesbury.

WIN GREEN

This much-admired viewpoint is 910 ft above sea level and is owned by the National Trust. It is the highest point of Cranborne Chase, a former royal forest and hunting-ground. The rolling hills and the remaining belts of forest are spread out below, and it is possible on a clear day to see as far as the Isle of Wight.

The Poultry Cross, Salisbury.

Relics of prehistoric man around a royal forest

Kings once hunted in Savernake Forest, where today motorists can drive through a long avenue of majestic beeches. Stage coaches rumbled over the cobbles in stately Marlborough, whose old inns still retain the character of the days of post horn and four-in-hand. The rolling chalk downs of Wiltshire, chiselled by wind and weather into curious contours and outcrops, yielded the material from which hill-forts and burial chambers—and part of Stonehenge—were built in prehistoric times. Tourists following this route are brought almost up to date at Crofton, where a steam pump-house, built in 1812 to supply water to the Kennet and Avon Canal, can be seen in action.

(1) Marlborough to Barbury Castle Leave Marlborough on the A345 signposted to Swindon. On the outskirts of the town, where the road swings right, keep straight ahead, following the signpost for Wootton Bassett. The road crosses the rolling Marlborough Downs to the crest of Hackpen Hill, a good viewpoint. After 6½ m. turn right on to the A361 and follow the road into Wroughton. Here, turn right on to the B4005 signposted for Chiseldon. After 1¼ m., where the road swings sharp left, keep straight ahead and follow the road for 3 m. to Barbury Castle.

(2) Barbury Castle to Aldbourne Return to the B4005 and turn right. Turn right again at the junction with the A345 in Chiseldon, and then left almost immediately on to the road signposted to Hinton Parva. The road passes the grassy earthworks of Liddington Castle on the right. Shortly afterwards, turn right on to the A419 and follow it into Aldbourne.

(3) Aldbourne to Savernake Forest Leave Aldbourne on the A419 signposted for Hungerford. After 2 m. turn right to follow the signpost for Ramsbury. At the crossroads on the way into the village, turn right into Oxford Street and follow it through the village. Follow the road along the Kennet Valley to the crossroads just beyond Axford. Here, turn left. Cross the river, follow the road round to the right, and almost immediately afterwards fork left up the hill. At the junction with the A4 turn right, following the signpost for Marlborough. After 1 m. turn sharp left on to the unmarked Grand Avenue and follow it into Savernake Forest.

(4) Savernake Forest to Great Bedwyn Continue along the Grand Avenue and turn left at the end. Take the second turning on the right signposted to Great Bedwyn and follow the road into the village.

(5) Great Bedwyn to Crofton In Great Bedwyn turn right at the signpost for Crofton and keep straight ahead at the junction on the edge of the village. After 1 m. the road reaches Crofton. The pumping station is on the left, just beyond the village.

(6) Crofton to Milton Lilbourne Follow the road across the canal and turn left at the T-junction. After ¾ m. turn right on to the A338, and follow it for 1¼ m. to the crossroads. There, go straight across on to the B3087 signposted for Pewsey. After 2½ m. turn left into Milton Lilbourne.

(7) Milton Lilbourne to Pewsey Return to the B3087, turn left and follow the road for 1½ m. into Pewsey.

(8) Pewsey to Pewsey Downs Nature Reserve Leave the centre of Pewsey on the A345 signposted for Salisbury. After crossing the River Avon on the outskirts of the town, keep straight ahead where the main road bears right. Swing right almost immediately following the signpost for Everleigh. The road runs between Pewsey Down on the right and Pewsey Hill on the left. After 5 m. turn right at the junction with the A342 in Everleigh, and go left almost immediately, following the signpost to Haxton. At the crossroads in Haxton turn right, and follow the lane up the valley of the River Avon. After 3 m., at the junction with the A342, keep straight ahead, following the signpost for Upavon. Turn right on to the A345 in Upavon, following the signpost for Pewsey. At the crossroads, 1½ m. later, keep straight ahead on to the minor road signposted to Woodborough. Follow the road round to the right at the next junction and just after the road crosses the railway keep straight ahead, following the signpost for Alton and Lockeridge. Keep straight ahead through Alton Barnes and cross the Pewsey Downs Nature Reserve.

(9) Pewsey Downs Nature Reserve to Lockeridge Follow the road on into Lockeridge.

(10) Lockeridge to Fyfield Leave Lockeridge on the road signposted for Marlborough. Turn right at the junction with the A4 and enter Fyfield.

(11) Fyfield to Marlborough Follow the A4, signposted for Marlborough, for 2 m. and go into the town.

INFORMATION

Places of interest *Crofton*: beam-engines, Sun. Dates of steaming from Crofton Society, 273 East Grafton, Burbage, Wilts. (Tel. Burbage 575).

Craft workshops *Marlborough*: Leathercraft, Hughendon Yard, High Street.

Nature trail *Savernake Forest*: Postern Hill Walk, starts from picnic site on A346. Guidebook on site and from Forestry Commission, Flowers Hill, Bristol.

Events *Marlborough*: Little Mop Fair, early Oct.; Big Mop Fair, late Oct. Market day, Sat.

Information *West Country Tourist Board*: Trinity Court, Southernhay East, Exeter (Tel: Exeter 76351).

Towns with easy access to Marlborough:

Andover	21 m.	Salisbury	28 m.
Bath	31 m.	Swindon	12 m.

Town Hall and church, Marlborough.

MARLBOROUGH
This home of the well-known public school is an outstanding example of the traditional English country town. Its broad High Street is little changed since the middle of the last century, when the town was a popular stopping place for stagecoaches. Handsome Georgian buildings look down on the brightly coloured stalls of the open-air market held every Saturday. Fine churches stand at either end of the main street. In one of them, St Peter and St Paul, Cardinal Wolsey was ordained priest in 1498.

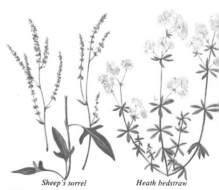

Sheep's sorrel   Heath bedstraw

FYFIELD
North of Fyfield village, a 612 acre nature reserve occupies a tract of chalk downland. The area is littered with blocks of sandstone, known as sarsens, and speckled with pockets of soil formed by erosion. Plants such as sheep's sorrel and heath bedstraw, which could never flourish in the surrounding chalkland, grow quite freely in the acid soil that has built up in these pockets. There is a public right of way across the downland but a permit is required for further exploration.

Sarsen stones near Lockeridge.

LOCKERIDGE
From a distance, the grassland to the left of the road that approaches the beautiful little village of Lockeridge appears to be filled with large sleeping sheep. The 'sheep' in fact are sarsens, massive boulders of a kind used in the building of Stonehenge and Avebury. They are thought to be formed by the erosion of the sandstone cap that once covered the chalk of the downs. The name derives from *saracen*, a 17th-century word for alien or strange. Because of their resemblance to sheep, the sarsens are also known locally as grey wethers.

SCALE

0   1   2   3   4   5 MILES

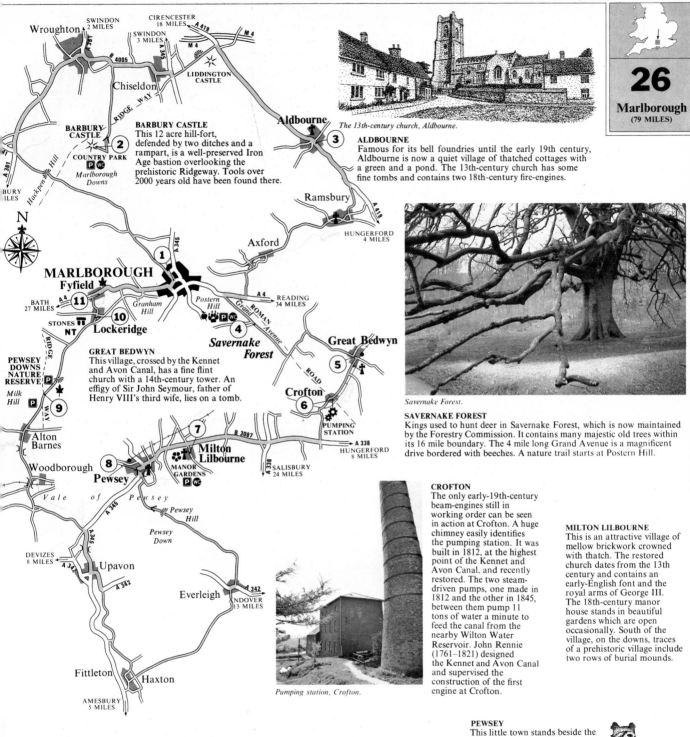

The 13th-century church, Aldbourne.

BARBURY CASTLE
This 12 acre hill-fort, defended by two ditches and a rampart, is a well-preserved Iron Age bastion overlooking the prehistoric Ridgeway. Tools over 2000 years old have been found there.

ALDBOURNE
Famous for its bell foundries until the early 19th century, Aldbourne is now a quiet village of thatched cottages with a green and a pond. The 13th-century church has some fine tombs and contains two 18th-century fire-engines.

GREAT BEDWYN
This village, crossed by the Kennet and Avon Canal, has a fine flint church with a 14th-century tower. An effigy of Sir John Seymour, father of Henry VIII's third wife, lies on a tomb.

Savernake Forest.

SAVERNAKE FOREST
Kings used to hunt deer in Savernake Forest, which is now maintained by the Forestry Commission. It contains many majestic old trees within its 16 mile boundary. The 4 mile long Grand Avenue is a magnificent drive bordered with beeches. A nature trail starts at Postern Hill.

CROFTON
The only early-19th-century beam-engines still in working order can be seen in action at Crofton. A huge chimney easily identifies the pumping station. It was built in 1812, at the highest point of the Kennet and Avon Canal, and recently restored. The two steam-driven pumps, one made in 1812 and the other in 1845, between them pump 11 tons of water a minute to feed the canal from the nearby Wilton Water Reservoir. John Rennie (1761–1821) designed the Kennet and Avon Canal and supervised the construction of the first engine at Crofton.

Pumping station, Crofton.

MILTON LILBOURNE
This is an attractive village of mellow brickwork crowned with thatch. The restored church dates from the 13th century and contains an early-English font and the royal arms of George III. The 18th-century manor house stands in beautiful gardens which are open occasionally. South of the village, on the downs, traces of a prehistoric village include two rows of burial mounds.

PEWSEY
This little town stands beside the River Avon in the middle of the broad Vale of Pewsey. The 12th-century church has altar rails made of timber from the *St Josef,* a ship captured by Nelson off St Vincent in 1797. A statue of Alfred the Great stands at the crossroads.

PEWSEY DOWNS NATURE RESERVE
A man called Jack the Painter was paid £20 in 1812 to cut the white horse on Milk Hill. He absconded with the money and, so it is said, was hanged. The nature reserve has a wealth of chalk-loving plants, including field fleawort and bastard toadflax. It is also famous for chalk-hill blue and brown butterflies. The prehistoric Ridgeway track crosses the reserve.

King Alfred's statue, Pewsey.

Alton white horse.

67

A thousand years of history in the New Forest

This ancient Crown Forest, created by William the Conqueror, has preserved its riches and its individuality down through the ages. Its people, living in hamlets nestled down in forest clearings, have clung to their own customs, laws and court, dealing with forest matters. The landscape covers moor, marsh and heath, stream and path, where wild animals and the famous New Forest ponies roam. At Bucklers Hard, the maritime museum shows how forest oak helped to make Nelson's Navy.

(1) Lyndhurst to Exbury In the town, take the A35, following the signposts to Southampton, but on leaving the High Street, turn right on to the B3056, following the Beaulieu signpost. Cross the railway at Beaulieu Road station and then turn left on to the road signposted to Hythe. Go straight on at the crossroads, and turn right on to the A326, following the signpost to Fawley. Turn right at the roundabout on to the B3054 then, after 2 m., turn left then immediately right and, after 2½ m., left again into Exbury.

(2) Exbury to Beaulieu Continue along the main road and, at the T-junction, turn left into Lepe. Return to the B3054 and turn left. The road passes the abbey gatehouse, crosses the bridge and then enters the village of Beaulieu. Continue on through the village, and at the T-junction turn right on to the B3056 for the entrance to the motor museum, abbey and Beaulieu Palace House.

(3) Beaulieu to Bucklers Hard Return along the B3056 to the T-junction and carry straight on to the B3054, following the Lymington signpost, and then left to Bucklers Hard.

(4) Bucklers Hard to Lymington Return to the B3054 and turn left towards Lymington. Fork left to keep on the B3054 at Hatchet Pond. After 4½ m., cross the bridge over the river and into the town of Lymington.

(5) Lymington to New Forest At the T-junction turn left on to the A337 and go through the town centre. At the next T-junction turn left again, keeping on the A337, following the signpost to Bournemouth. In Everton village turn left on to the B3058 signposted to Keyhaven, and then left again, following the Hurst Castle signpost. At the T-junction turn left into Keyhaven. From this yacht basin, regular ferries run out to Hurst Castle, one of a network of coastal forts built by Henry VIII against the possibility of invasion. Follow the road round the coast, bearing right at the spit of land which holds Hurst Castle on its tip. Follow the road inland and turn left at the T-junction into Milford on Sea. The Dane Stream flows through this village, which has an attractive beach with good bathing facilities. (If the road into Milford is flooded, return to the junction at Keyhaven and follow the signposts to Milford.) Turn left on to the B3058. The road rises up to Hordle Cliff, opening on to views over Christchurch Bay. As it bears inland, turn right into Downton Lane. Go straight on, crossing the A337, and into Hordle. Go straight on at the crossroads, following the signpost to Sway. Turn right at the T-junction and, after ½ m., turn left to Sway, passing the Sway Tower. This 213 ft building, also known as Peterson's Folly, was erected in 1870 to prove the builder's faith in concrete as a high-rise building material. Turn right on to the B3055, through Sway, over the railway and left at the crossroads, following the signpost to Burley. Here the road enters the New Forest.

(6) New Forest to Minstead After 2 m. turn left and then bear right, passing under the A35 and into the forest village of Burley. Continue through the village following the Ringwood signpost and, just beyond Burley Street, bear right. At the junction with the A31 turn left. On the outskirts of Ringwood, turn right on the road signposted to Moyles Court. This was the home of Dame Alicia Lisle who, at the age of 70, was condemned to death by Judge Jeffreys at the so-called 'Bloody Assizes' following the Monmouth rebellion. She was beheaded in 1685. Keep straight ahead on the middle of three roads, by the ford, through wooded country and, bearing right, join the A31. There turn left, following the Winchester signpost. After 4 m. turn left to the Rufus Stone. This stone, on the left, marks the site where William II, nicknamed Rufus, was killed by an arrow while hunting in 1100. It is not known for certain who fired the arrow and whether the king was murdered or died by accident. Continue on the road past the stone and turn right on to the B3078, following the Cadnam signpost. At the A31/M27 roundabout go straight ahead, and at the next roundabout take the third exit to join the A337, following the Lyndhurst signpost. After 1 m., turn right to Minstead. Follow the road left, and at the T-junction turn right into the village of Minstead.

(7) Minstead to Lyndhurst Return to the junction with the A337, turn right and follow the road back to Lyndhurst.

INFORMATION

Places of interest *Beaulieu:* Abbey, Palace House and National Motor Museum, daily. *Bucklers Hard:* Maritime Museum, daily. *Exbury Gardens:* Early Apr. to mid-June, daily, 2-7 p.m. *Hurst Castle:* Weekdays, Sun. afternoons.

Events *Beaulieu:* Steam festival, May; Christie's sale of vintage cars, July; Fire-engine fair, Aug.; Autojumble and automart, Sept.; Steam happening, Oct.; Fireworks fair, Nov. Various car club rallies, weekends in summer. Pony auction sales, Aug., Sept., Oct. and Nov. *Lymington:* Offshore Power Boat Race, May.

Information Southern Tourist Group, Canute Road, Southampton (Tel. Southampton 20438).

Towns with easy access to Lyndhurst:

Andover	31 m.	Salisbury	19 m.
Bournemouth	20 m.	Southampton	9 m.
Romsey	10 m.	Winchester	19 m.

New Forest pony

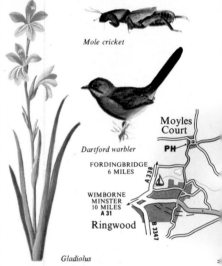

Mole cricket

Dartford warbler

Moyles Court

PH

FORDINGBRIDGE 6 MILES

WIMBORNE MINSTER 10 MILES

Ringwood

Gladiolus

NEW FOREST
For 900 years this sprawling 90,000 acre forest has been a wildlife preserve. At first its protection was ensured by savage laws, which could direct a man to be blinded for much as disturbing a deer in the royal hunting ground. Today, the forest is guarded by the Verderers' Court, whose green-jacketed Agisters mount constant horseback patrols to keep the forest teeming with wildlife. Some 2000 ponies run wild with herds of donkeys and deer. Birds that have fled other parts of the country flock here: the Dartford warbler, Montagu harrier and pied flycatcher are among them. Foxes, badgers and otters, Carolina grey squirrels, the yellow-necked field mouse and the rare mole cricket populate the undergrowth. In season, the whole forest bed is splashed by bog orchids, wild gladioli, bellflowers and other wild flowers.

Agister patrolling the New Forest.

SCALE

0   1   2   3   4   5 MILES

LYNDHURST

From this town, roads radiate out to all parts of the forest. It is the administrative capital, where the Verderers' Court still sits to deliberate. This court, partly elected and partly appointed by the Crown and other official bodies, dates back to 1388, and is charged with the maintenance and care of the whole forest. The court sits in the 17th-century Queen's House, before a masssive and primitive criminal dock. The stirrup that hangs over the fireplace was once used to gauge the size of forest-dwellers' dogs. If a dog could not pass through it, it was judged a danger to game. The parish church of St Michael, built in 1863, contains stained-glass windows by William Morris. In the churchyard is the grave of Mrs Alice Hargreaves who, when a girl, inspired Lewis Carroll to write *Alice in Wonderland*.

ined glass by William Morris.

Cannstatt-Daimler 1898

Hispano-Suiza 1912

BEAULIEU

The National Motor Museum, centred on the collection of veteran and vintage cars built up by Lord Montagu of Beaulieu, now contains more than 300 cars, motorcycles, buses, tractors and bicycles. They are housed in the museum complex opened in the grounds of the Beaulieu Estate in 1972, and are laid out to tell the story of motoring right up to modern times. The library holds a collection of motoring books and photographs. The museum stands close by the ruins of the Cistercian abbey founded in 1204. This became one of the most important monasteries in Britain, but was demolished in the Dissolution. Lord Montagu lives in nearby Palace House, at one time the gatehouse to the abbey, which together with its fine gardens is also open to the public. The old abbey refectory has been restored and converted and is now the village church. The village of Beaulieu faces Palace House across the river at the point where it opens out into an estuary.

Furzey folk cottage.

MINSTEAD

Hidden deep in the woods, the little village of Minstead was once the home of Sir Arthur Conan Doyle, creator of Sherlock Holmes, who now lies buried in the churchyard. In the church is a luxury pew, complete with its own fireplace. Furzey Gardens provide a setting for a cottage built in 1560.

EXBURY

Set in towering oakwoods, Exbury parish contains two fine old manor houses. Exbury House is the home of the Rothschilds, and the centrepiece of the famed 250 acre rhododendron and azalea gardens which are open to the public during the flowering season from April to mid-June. The other manor is Inchmery House, near Lepe, the old Roman port where goods destined for the Continent were first ferried over to the Isle of Wight, and there loaded on to waiting ships. There is now a country park here which overlooks the Solent, the Isle of Wight and isolated beaches.

Figurehead in the maritime museum.

BUCKLERS HARD

Georgian cottages line the main street of the tiny village that runs down to the Beaulieu River, where ships of the 18th-century Royal Navy were built and launched. Giant oaks felled in the New Forest were hauled to the yards, where they were cut and shaped into the massive timbers of 64-gun ships of the line, like Nelson's favourite, HMS *Agamemnon*. The industry declined and disappeared in the 19th century, and the villagers returned to farm and forestry work. But the maritime museum, built into the converted New Inn, is stocked with records and mementoes. Bucklers Hard is now a harbour for small boats. The most famous of these are *Gipsy Moth III* and *Gipsy Moth IV* of the late Sir Francis Chichester. This was the home port where he began and ended his single-handed voyage around the globe in *Gipsy Moth IV*. A nature trail leads from the Hard to Beaulieu, and river trips can be arranged.

MINGTON

s once bustling shipbuilding centre is now a nt backwater. A cobbled lane runs beneath windows down to the river and the ferry ch carries passengers and cars out to the Isle Wight. A street market sets the town bustling ry Saturday morning, as locals mix with the tsmen whose boats crowd the harbour.

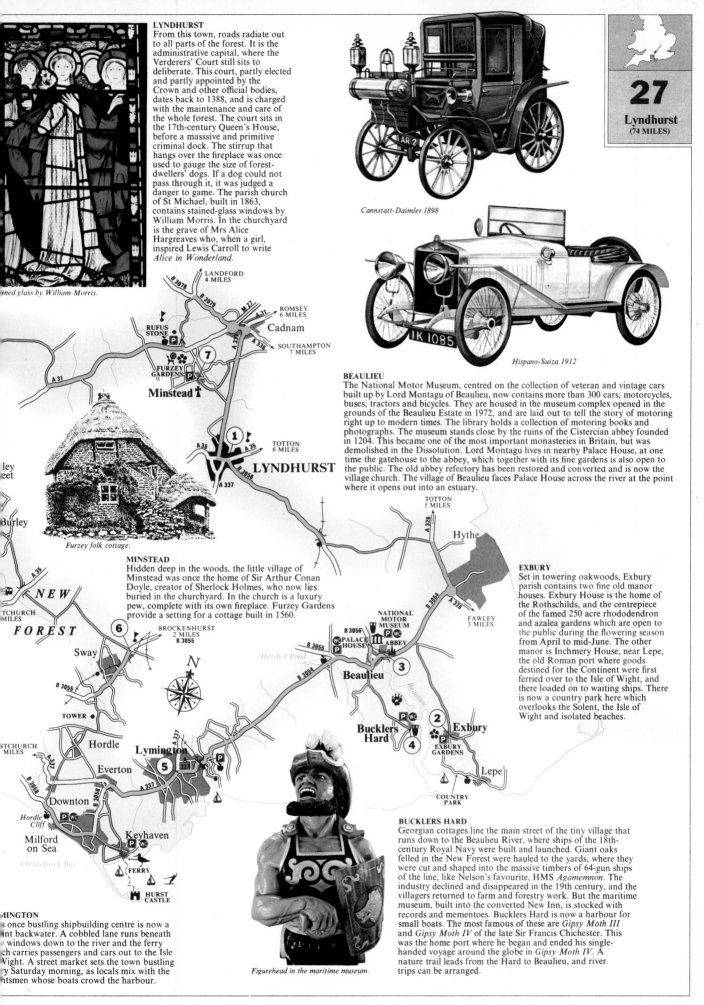

History and holidays . . .
the island of contrasts

A coastline dotted with popular holiday resorts, fringing downlands speckled with old-world villages and historic remains, make a well-planned tour in the Isle of Wight as varied as any on the mainland. Seven nature trails provide walks where plants and wildlife found in few other parts of the British Isles may be seen. By contrast, the island's many fascinating survivals of a historic past include Carisbrooke Castle, where Charles I was a prisoner before being taken to London for his execution.

(1) Yarmouth to Alum Bay Leave the town —terminus for the Lymington car ferry from the mainland—on the A3054, following the signposts for Totland. In Totland keep straight ahead on to the B3322 into Alum Bay.

(2) Alum Bay to Brook Return along the B3322 and, as it bears sharp left, keep right, following the signposts for Freshwater Bay. Where the road bears sharp left, by the High Down Inn, turn right to the National Trust car park for Tennyson Down. Return to the main road, turn right and continue into Freshwater Bay. Follow the road along the shore, joining the A3055, and after 3 m. turn left into Brook.

(3) Brook to Blackgang Continue through the village, and turn right on to the B3399, following the signposts for Newport. The road goes through Hulverstone and then on to Mottistone, with its 16th-century manor house and even older church. Continue through the village to Brighstone, with its thatched cottages, and on into Shorwell. Turn right at the church—which is said to have been built in Edward III's time—still on the B3399, and into Chale. Turn left at the T-junction on the A3055, following the signposts for Ventnor. After ½ m. turn right and into Blackgang.

(4) Blackgang to Ventnor Return the same way, turning right on to the A3055 towards Ventnor. In Niton turn right, keeping on the A3055 and, after ½ m., right again to visit St Catherine's Lighthouse and the 16th-century Buddle Inn, a tavern once deeply involved in the local smuggling trade. Return to the A3055, turn right and continue into Ventnor.

(5) Ventnor to Wroxall Leave the town on the B3327, which is signposted to Wroxall. Appuldurcombe House is signposted on the left in the village.

(6) Wroxall to Godshill Go through the village on the B3327 and 1 m. later turn left on to the A3020 signposted to Godshill, which is reached just over 1 m. later.

(7) Godshill to Newport Stay on the A3020 through Blackwater—starting point for walks across St George's Down on the eastern side of the Medina Valley—and into Newport.

(8) Newport to Carisbrooke Castle Leave Newport on the B3323, following the signposts for Carisbrooke. At the war memorial fork left on to the B3341, following the signposts for Carisbrooke Castle. At the next road junction, keep straight ahead, up Castle Hill to the castle, the island's major fortress.

(9) Carisbrooke Castle to Cowes Return down the hill and turn left, down Cedar Hill to Carisbrooke High Street. Here turn left on to the B3323, and right by the church. This church, built on the site of a heathen temple founded about AD 530, is considered the most important ecclesiastical building on the island. Go through Gunville and at the T-junction with the A3054 turn right towards Parkhurst, passing the Albany Steam Museum which is on the right. Turn left on to the A3020, following the signposts for Cowes and, after 2 m., bear left on to the B3325 by the Horseshoe Inn. Follow the road to the sea front in Cowes.

(10) Cowes to Newtown After visiting the town, and perhaps watching the hover-craft coming and going, follow the coast road towards Gurnard. As the road bears left inland, turn right down Solent View Road. Cross the bridge and follow the road inland. Turn right on to the road which is signposted for Yarmouth, and follow the signs into Porchfield. Go through the village and, after 1½ m., turn right into Newtown.

(11) Newtown to Yarmouth Follow the road round in a loop and at the next junction turn right. After ¾ m. turn right on to the A3054 and follow the road to Yarmouth.

NATURE NOTES
The cream-spot tiger moth and the Glanville fritillary butterfly breed in chines on the island's south coast.

INFORMATION

Places of interest *Albany Steam Museum:* Easter to Oct., 10 a.m.-6 p.m. By arrangement in winter. *Appuldurcombe House:* Weekdays, Sun. afternoons. *Blackgang Chine and Museum:* Apr. to Sept., daily. *Carisbrooke Castle:* Weekdays, Sun. afternoons. *Newtown:* Old Town Hall, Easter to Spring Bank Hol., Wed., Sun., afternoons; Spring Bank Hol. to Sept., afternoons except Mon., Fri. and Sat. August, afternoons. *Yarmouth Castle:* Weekdays, Sun. afternoons. *St Catherine's Lighthouse:* Weekdays from 1 p.m. Closed in fog.

Events *Cowes:* Cowes Week, Aug. 1-9; Starting point, Round the Island Yacht Race, June; Power Boat Round the Island Race, Aug.; Power Boat Race, Cowes to Torquay and back, Aug.

Information *Newport:* 21 High Street (Tel. Newport 4343). *Ventnor:* 34 High Street (Tel. Ventnor 853625). *Yarmouth:* The Quay (Tel. Yarmouth 760015).

Ferry services to the Isle of Wight
Lymington–Yarmouth: Tel. Lymington 3301; Yarmouth 213
Portsmouth–Fishbourne: Tel. Portsmouth 2251; Wootton Bridge 432
Southampton–Cowes: Tel. Southampton 22042; Cowes 2101.
It is advisable to book both ways well in advance for journeys on Fridays, Saturdays and Sundays, particularly between March and September.

NEWTOWN
Formerly Franchville, or 'freetown', Newt gets its modern name from the fact that it w rebuilt after a French raid in 1337. It was c important as a centre of the salt industry a the cultivation of oysters. The Old Town I dating from 1699, is open to visitors, and houses several relics of the town's past. It w derelict until 1934, when a group of anonyr masked philanthropists calling themselves Ferguson Gang handed it over to the Natic Trust, with a gift of £1000 towards its repa

YARMOUTH
The favourite son of this unspoilt little port is Sir Ro Holmes, who captured a Dutch ship off the coast of Guinea and brought its cargo of bullion home to be coined into the first golden guineas. A memorial to h in the town dates from a 17th-century raid on a Frenc ship carrying an unfinished statue of Louis XIV to Pa Sir Robert seized the statue and forced the sculptor t finish it with his head instead of the French king's. It can be seen now in St James's Church. The ruined castle was part of the fortress chain built by Henry V From the causeway, great liners can be seen passing ir out of Southampton. The town itself has one of the r up-to-date lifeboats in the world.

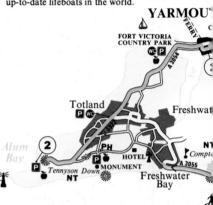

Alum Bay.

ALUM BAY
The cliffs around the bay are veined with more than 2 shades of sandstone, which vary in colour from chocolate-brown to strawberry-pink. The cliffs were formed under water before the island emerged from th sea 50 million years ago. Visitors to the cliffs can colle the sand but, to avoid erosion and accidents, people are asked not to scramble up the cliffs in search of their own specimens. Stalls at the clifftop sell the sands already bottled in layers. A cable car runs from the beach to the clifftops. The sand is firm and the bathin good, although tides which race in the Needles Channe can be dangerous. A monument records Marconi's historic experiments in wireless transmission at the end of the 19th century.

SCALE
0   1   2   3 MILES

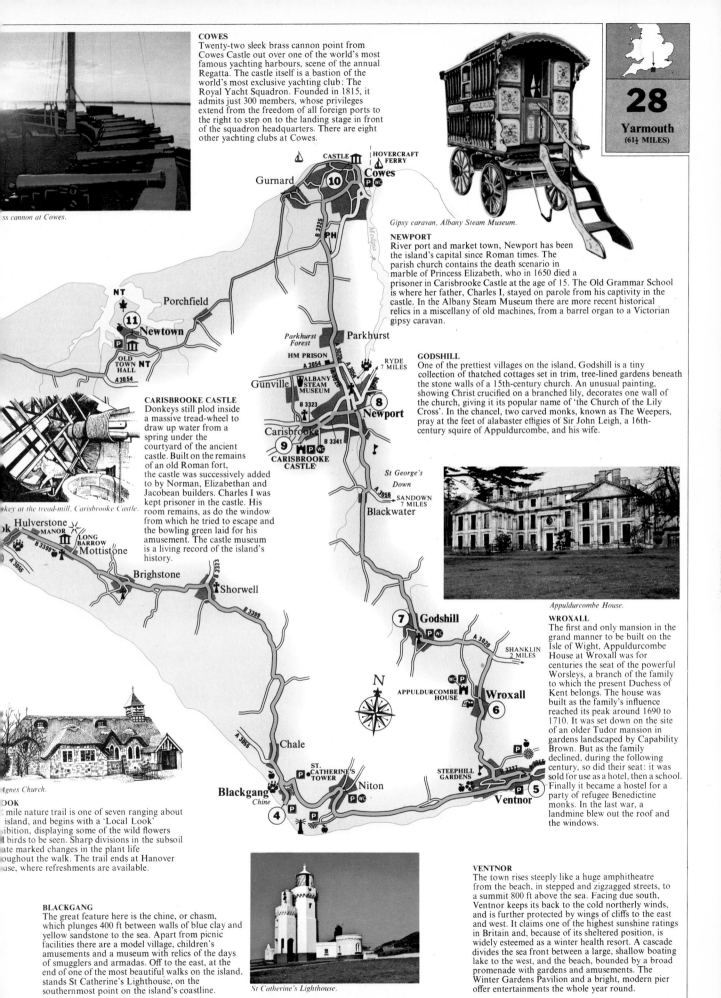

COWES

Twenty-two sleek brass cannon point from Cowes Castle out over one of the world's most famous yachting harbours, scene of the annual Regatta. The castle itself is a bastion of the world's most exclusive yachting club: The Royal Yacht Squadron. Founded in 1815, it admits just 300 members, whose privileges extend from the freedom of all foreign ports to the right to step on to the landing stage in front of the squadron headquarters. There are eight other yachting clubs at Cowes.

ss cannon at Cowes.

Gipsy caravan, Albany Steam Museum.

NEWPORT

River port and market town, Newport has been the island's capital since Roman times. The parish church contains the death scenario in marble of Princess Elizabeth, who in 1650 died a prisoner in Carisbrooke Castle at the age of 15. The Old Grammar School is where her father, Charles I, stayed on parole from his captivity in the castle. In the Albany Steam Museum there are more recent historical relics in a miscellany of old machines, from a barrel organ to a Victorian gipsy caravan.

CARISBROOKE CASTLE

Donkeys still plod inside a massive tread-wheel to draw up water from a spring under the courtyard of the ancient castle. Built on the remains of an old Roman fort, the castle was successively added to by Norman, Elizabethan and Jacobean builders. Charles I was kept prisoner in the castle. His room remains, as do the window from which he tried to escape and the bowling green laid for his amusement. The castle museum is a living record of the island's history.

key at the tread-mill, Carisbrooke Castle.

GODSHILL

One of the prettiest villages on the island, Godshill is a tiny collection of thatched cottages set in trim, tree-lined gardens beneath the stone walls of a 15th-century church. An unusual painting, showing Christ crucified on a branched lily, decorates one wall of the church, giving it its popular name of 'the Church of the Lily Cross'. In the chancel, two carved monks, known as The Weepers, pray at the feet of alabaster effigies of Sir John Leigh, a 16th-century squire of Appuldurcombe, and his wife.

Appuldurcombe House.

WROXALL

The first and only mansion in the grand manner to be built on the Isle of Wight, Appuldurcombe House at Wroxall was for centuries the seat of the powerful Worsleys, a branch of the family to which the present Duchess of Kent belongs. The house was built as the family's influence reached its peak around 1690 to 1710. It was set down on the site of an older Tudor mansion in gardens landscaped by Capability Brown. But as the family declined, during the following century, so did their seat: it was sold for use as a hotel, then a school. Finally it became a hostel for a party of refugee Benedictine monks. In the last war, a landmine blew out the roof and the windows.

Agnes Church.

OOK

mile nature trail is one of seven ranging about island, and begins with a 'Local Look' ibition, displaying some of the wild flowers birds to be seen. Sharp divisions in the subsoil ate marked changes in the plant life oughout the walk. The trail ends at Hanover use, where refreshments are available.

BLACKGANG

The great feature here is the chine, or chasm, which plunges 400 ft between walls of blue clay and yellow sandstone to the sea. Apart from picnic facilities there are a model village, children's amusements and a museum with relics of the days of smugglers and armadas. Off to the east, at the end of one of the most beautiful walks on the island, stands St Catherine's Lighthouse, on the southernmost point on the island's coastline.

St Catherine's Lighthouse.

VENTNOR

The town rises steeply like a huge amphitheatre from the beach, in stepped and zigzagged streets, to a summit 800 ft above the sea. Facing due south, Ventnor keeps its back to the cold northerly winds, and is further protected by wings of cliffs to the east and west. It claims one of the highest sunshine ratings in Britain and, because of its sheltered position, is widely esteemed as a winter health resort. A cascade divides the sea front between a large, shallow boating lake to the west, and the beach, bounded by a broad promenade with gardens and amusements. The Winter Gardens Pavilion and a bright, modern pier offer entertainments the whole year round.

Where Queen Victoria found peace and solitude

Greatly loved by Queen Victoria, who spent much of her long widowhood here, the north-east corner of the Isle of Wight has escaped industrialisation. It retains its rural peace and charm, broken only by the sophistication of Cowes and the popularity of Ryde with summer holidaymakers. This tour is studded with impressive views and informal picnic spots. It takes in Robin Hill Country Park, the quiet cloisters of old Quarr Abbey, and the intricate mosaics at the Roman villa in Brading.

(1) East Cowes to Arreton Manor Leave East Cowes on the A3021, following the signpost to Newport. At the roundabout beyond Whippingham take the A3054 for Newport. Join the A3020 at the roundabout on the outskirts of Newport and follow that road, signed for Shanklin, through the town. In Blackwater keep left, joining the A3056 signposted to Sandown. After 2 m., where the A3056 turns sharply to the right, keep straight ahead, following the signpost to Downend. The entrance to Arreton Manor, a fine Jacobean mansion, is on the right.

(2) Arreton Manor to Robin Hill Country Park Continue along the same road into Downend. Go past the Hare and Hounds Inn and, as the road forks, the entrance to Robin Hill Country Park is on the right.

(3) Robin Hill Country Park to Brading Return to Downend and turn left at the Hare and Hounds Inn, following the signpost to Brading. From this road there are excellent views down to the coast on the right. After 2½ m. bear right, following the signpost to Brading. Here there are more views, and lay-bys in which to stop and enjoy them. Follow the road for 2½ m. to the T-junction. Here turn left and bear left at the junction with the A3055. Go on to the car park at the end of Brading's main street. To visit Nunwell House go past the car park and the church and turn left down Coach Lane, which is signposted to Ashey. At the T-junction turn right—the entrance is on the left. To see the Roman villa, take the A3055 south through the town, following the signposts for Sandown. After the crossroads, where the B3395 leads off to the left, take the second turning on the right and the first on the left.

(4) Brading to Bembridge Return to Brading and leave on the B3395 signposted to Bembridge. (To visit the National Trust properties of Bembridge Down and Culver Down, turn right after 1 m. These hills, with views over the sea, are ideal for picnicking. On Culver Cliff there is a bird sanctuary.) Follow the road past Bembridge Airport, and at the next crossroads turn left. The road passes the windmill and continues into the centre of the town, a favourite haunt of anglers and yachtsmen.

(5) Bembridge to Ryde Follow the road round Bembridge Harbour, noticing the sandy spit across the mouth of the inlet. This is known as The Duver, and at the northern end of it are the ruins of a small church from which, it is said, sailors used to take 'holy stone' rocks to scour the decks of their ships. The road leads into St Helens, a traditional haven of smugglers. Here the village green is

surrounded with old houses, and in Upper Green Street a plaque marks the early home of Sophie Dawes, a fisherman's daughter who was called 'the Chantilly Queen' when in the early 19th century she became the mistress of a French duke. At the T-junction with the B3330 in St Helens turn right, following the signpost to Ryde. Stay on the B3330 for 3 m. and at the junction with the A3055 on the outskirts of Ryde turn right for the centre of the town, the pier and the esplanade.

(6) Ryde to Quarr Abbey Leave Ryde on the A3054, signposted to Newport. Keep straight on through Binstead. The entrance to old Quarr Abbey, named after the local stone quarries, will be seen on the right soon after passing through Quarr Hill. Continue past the ruins to see the modern abbey.

(7) Quarr Abbey to Whippingham Continue on the A3054 to Wootton Bridge. Here, where the shallow tidal estuary of Wootton Creek dwindles to a small stream, a dam has been built, creating an attractive freshwater lake fringed with woods. Boats can be hired, and there is a swimming pool. After 1½ m. bear right at the roundabout on to the A3021, following the sign to East Cowes. After 1 m., turn left at the signpost to Whippingham church, which is reached after ½ m.

(8) Whippingham to East Cowes Continue along the same road, turn left at the T-junction and follow the road to the centre of the town.

NATURE NOTES
The Glanville fritillary, a butterfly found only on the Isle of Wight, may be seen in sheltered coastal areas in May and June. Black-tailed godwits, migratory wading birds, inhabit Newhaven marsh in winter. Golden samphire, an aromatic plant which is used in the making of pickles, grows on the shingle.

INFORMATION

Places of interest *Arreton Manor:* Apr. to Nov., weekdays, Sun. afternoons. *Bembridge:* Windmill, Easter Sun. and Mon., then Spring Bank Hol. Mon. to Oct., daily. *Brading:* Nunwell House, Spring Bank Hol. to Sept., afternoons (except Fri. and Sat.). Roman villa, Easter to Sept., daily. Osborne-Smith's Wax Museum, daily. *East Cowes:* Osborne House, Easter Mon. to Oct., Mon. to Fri., 11 a.m.-5 p.m. *Quarr Abbey:* Chapel only, daily.

Events *Bembridge:* Air show, July. *Ryde:* Regatta, July. Carnival, Aug. *St Helens:* Carnival, Aug. Antique Fair, Sept.

Information Information Centre, Esplanade, Ryde (Tel. Ryde 62905).

Ferry services to the Isle of Wight See Yarmouth tour, p. 70.

Whippingham Church.

WHIPPINGHAM
The unusual church at Whippingham, with its central tower and excellent stained glass, was designed by Prince Albert and completed in 1862. The church was attended by Queen Victoria when she lived at Osborne, and her chair can still be seen in the Royal Chapel. Also in this chapel is a white marble reredos depicting the Last Supper. It was given to the church by Edward VII in memory of his mother.

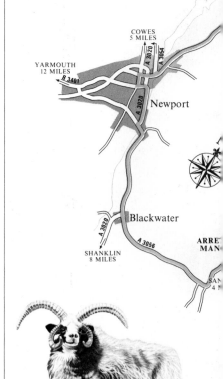
Jacob sheep, Robin Hill Country Park.

ROBIN HILL COUNTRY PARK
At Robin Hill is the island's Country Park, 8 acres of fields and woods filled with wildlife. park is open to the public and is the starting for a nature trail. There is a special area well stocked with amusements for younger childre a commando assault course for older childre and a jungle house with tropical animals. A Roman villa in the process of excavation can seen, and from the picnic gardens there are extensive views of the eastern end of the islar

SCALE
0   1   2 MILES

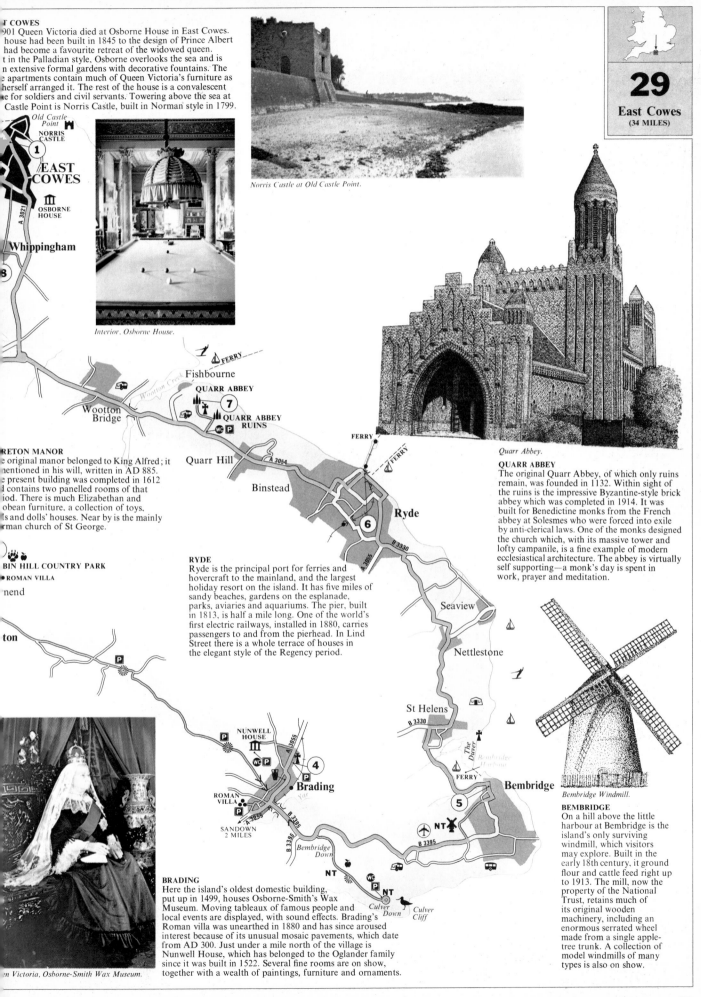

[EAS]T COWES
[In 1]901 Queen Victoria died at Osborne House in East Cowes. [The] house had been built in 1845 to the design of Prince Albert [and] had become a favourite retreat of the widowed queen. [Buil]t in the Palladian style, Osborne overlooks the sea and is [set i]n extensive formal gardens with decorative fountains. The [stat]e apartments contain much of Queen Victoria's furniture as [she] herself arranged it. The rest of the house is a convalescent [hom]e for soldiers and civil servants. Towering above the sea at [Old] Castle Point is Norris Castle, built in Norman style in 1799.

Norris Castle at Old Castle Point.

Interior, Osborne House.

[B]RETON MANOR
[Th]e original manor belonged to King Alfred; it [is m]entioned in his will, written in AD 885. [Th]e present building was completed in 1612 [an]d contains two panelled rooms of that [per]iod. There is much Elizabethan and [Jac]obean furniture, a collection of toys, [doll]s and dolls' houses. Near by is the mainly [No]rman church of St George.

[RO]BIN HILL COUNTRY PARK
[•] ROMAN VILLA
[Bra]nend

Quarr Abbey.

QUARR ABBEY
The original Quarr Abbey, of which only ruins remain, was founded in 1132. Within sight of the ruins is the impressive Byzantine-style brick abbey which was completed in 1914. It was built for Benedictine monks from the French abbey at Solesmes who were forced into exile by anti-clerical laws. One of the monks designed the church which, with its massive tower and lofty campanile, is a fine example of modern ecclesiastical architecture. The abbey is virtually self supporting—a monk's day is spent in work, prayer and meditation.

RYDE
Ryde is the principal port for ferries and hovercraft to the mainland, and the largest holiday resort on the island. It has five miles of sandy beaches, gardens on the esplanade, parks, aviaries and aquariums. The pier, built in 1813, is half a mile long. One of the world's first electric railways, installed in 1880, carries passengers to and from the pierhead. In Lind Street there is a whole terrace of houses in the elegant style of the Regency period.

Bembridge Windmill.

BEMBRIDGE
On a hill above the little harbour at Bembridge is the island's only surviving windmill, which visitors may explore. Built in the early 18th century, it ground flour and cattle feed right up to 1913. The mill, now the property of the National Trust, retains much of its original wooden machinery, including an enormous serrated wheel made from a single apple-tree trunk. A collection of model windmills of many types is also on show.

BRADING
Here the island's oldest domestic building, put up in 1499, houses Osborne-Smith's Wax Museum. Moving tableaux of famous people and local events are displayed, with sound effects. Brading's Roman villa was unearthed in 1880 and has since aroused interest because of its unusual mosaic pavements, which date from AD 300. Just under a mile north of the village is Nunwell House, which has belonged to the Oglander family since it was built in 1522. Several fine rooms are on show, together with a wealth of paintings, furniture and ornaments.

[Quee]n Victoria, Osborne-Smith Wax Museum.

Where dockland gives way to village greens

Along the Solent shore between Southampton and Portsmouth the business of shipping dominates the scene. But there is a sharp contrast between the commercial hustle of Southampton and the ordered calm of Portsmouth, the Royal Navy's major port. Inland among the chalk hills and lush valleys of Hampshire are villages which retain that essentially English atmosphere typified by the cricket at Hambledon and the pageant of architecture through the centuries. This is vividly displayed round the great square at Wickham, one of the finest villages in England.

(1) Southampton to Netley Abbey From Town Quay follow the A33 eastwards towards the docks. Where it turns left bear right, following the signposts to the 'Floating Bridge'. Cross the bridge to Woolston, noting the hovercraft terminal on the left. Join the A3025 signposted Portsmouth and, after 2 m., turn right at a minor crossroads signposted to Netley Abbey. Continue across the next crossroads, and at the T-junction overlooking Southampton Water, turn right into Netley Abbey.

(2) Netley Abbey to Titchfield Abbey Leave Netley Abbey by the same route, but at the first crossroads turn right, signposted Hamble, and then left at the T-junction. At the junction with the B3397 turn left, and follow the road to the junction with the A3025. There turn right, following the signpost to Bursledon. At the junction with the A27 turn right, signposted to Portsmouth. After 4½ m., at the bottom of a hill, take the turning left, signposted Titchfield Abbey, which is on the left after ½ m.

(3) Titchfield Abbey to Portchester Castle Return to the A27 and turn left. Continue through Fareham, and at the roundabout, 1½ m. after crossing the river, turn right, following the signpost to Portchester Castle. Turn right at the T-junction and continue into the castle car park.

(4) Portchester Castle to Portsmouth Return to the A27, keeping ahead at the junction in Portchester, and turn right, signposted to Portsmouth. There are excellent views of the castle and Portsmouth Harbour from this stretch of road. The road goes under the M27. At the next roundabout bear left. Another roundabout follows after ¾ m., at which turn right on to the A3 and follow it into Portsmouth.

(5) Portsmouth to Chalton Leave Portsmouth eastwards on the sea-front road past South Parade Pier. Turn left on to St George's Road and then right on to the A2030, signposted London. There are excellent views across Langstone Harbour on the right. At the roundabout, go right on to the A27, signposted Havant. Keep on the A27 through another roundabout. Then, at the next roundabout, go left on to the B2149 and in 3 m. turn right, following the Rowland's Castle signpost. Go through the village and under the railway bridge. After 1 m. turn left under the second railway bridge on to the road signposted to Finchdean. Take the left fork in the village signposted Chalton, which is reached after 3 m. Notice the ruined windmill on the hill to the left.

(6) Chalton to Hambledon Turn left at the fork by the church in Chalton and in 1 m. turn left at the T-junction with the A3. Soon afterwards turn right on the road signposted to Clanfield and follow the road into the village. Turn left in front of the church, noting the open belfry, and turn right, following the signpost to Hambledon. The road passes the Bat and Ball Inn and the cricket ground on Broadhalfpenny Down. As the road enters Hambledon the vineyard, one of the few in Britain, is on the right.

(7) Hambledon to Wickham At the T-junction in the village turn left on to the B2150. After ½ m. turn right and follow the road through World's End signposted Fareham. At the T-junction turn left on to the road signposted to Fareham, and at the junction with the A333, after 1 m., turn right, signposted Wickham. After 2½ m., at the crossroads with the A32, go straight over and into the centre of the village.

(8) Wickham to Bishop's Waltham Leave Wickham on the A333, signposted to Bishop's Waltham. Follow the road for 4 m. through Shedfield and Waltham Chase and into Bishop's Waltham.

(9) Bishop's Waltham to Southampton Leave Bishop's Waltham on the B3035, signposted to Botley. Pass through Curdridge, where William Cobbett, author of *Rural Rides*, lived and farmed, and soon afterwards turn right on to the A334. Follow the A334 through Botley, noting the memorial to William Cobbett in the attractive main street, and into Southampton.

INFORMATION

Places of interest *Bishop's Waltham Palace:* Weekdays (except Mon.), Sun. afternoons. *Portchester Castle:* Weekdays, Sun. afternoons; Apr. to Sept., all day Sun. *Portsmouth:* Dickens's Birthplace Museum, daily. HMS *Victory* and Royal Naval Museum, weekdays, Sun. afternoons. Royal Marines Museum, Mon. to Fri., 10 a.m.-4 p.m., Sat., Sun., 10-12 a.m. *Southampton:* Bargate Guildhall Museum, weekdays, except Mon., 11 a.m.-5 p.m., Sun. afternoons. God's House Tower, Netley Abbey, Tudor House and Maritime Museum, daily, except Mon. *Southsea Castle:* Daily. *Titchfield Abbey:* Weekdays, Sun. afternoons.

Events *Portsmouth:* Navy Days, Aug. Illuminations, May to Oct. *Southampton:* Show Jumping Championships, July. Boat Show, Sept. Fairs, Bank Hols. Carol ceremony, Bargate, May Day.

Information *Southampton:* Information Bureau, Civic Centre (Tel. Southampton 23855).

Towns with easy access to Southampton:

Basingstoke	30 m.	Salisbury	23 m.
Bournemouth	30 m.	Winchester	12 m.

Southampton docks.

SOUTHAMPTON

Southampton is now a huge urban complex surrounding Britain's most prosperous passenger port. But, as museum in the 15th-century God's House Tower illustrates, there have been settlements there since the Stone Age. The Romans and Saxons used place as a port, and the Normans b the old walled city which survives to though much added to and restored Inside the walls are a wealth of old buildings and monuments, including the Tudor House, a mansion comple in 1518, and the *Mayflower* memori The Bargate, which dominates the m street, is part Norman and houses th ancient Guildhall, now a museum.

A Saxon comb, God's House Tower Museum, Southampton.

NETLEY ABBEY

Netley was a Cistercian abbey founded in 1251 by Henry III and colonised by monks from nearby Beaulieu Abbey. After Henry VIII's Dissolution of the Monasteries in 1536, the church and cloister buildings were converted into a private house. The monastery fell into ruin in the early 18th century and subsequently attracted writers such as Thomas Gray and Horace Walpole as a romantic and lonely place. *Netley Abbey, An Operatic Farce,* appeared at Covent Garden in 1794 and signalled a new era of popularity for the abbey, with fashionable parties being held amongst the ruins.

Netley Abbey, a Victorian engraving.

SCALE
0   1   2   3   4   5 MILES

BISHOP'S WALTHAM

Bishop's Waltham Palace was built in the 12th century by King Stephen's brother, Henry de Blois, as a residence for the Bishops of Winchester. It housed many famous bishops including William of Wykeham, and in 1182 Henry II summoned his barons to the palace to obtain money for a crusade. In 1644 the palace was ruined by Roundheads, who forced the bishop to flee in a dungcart, and 200 Royalists to surrender after a siege.

HAMBLEDON

Hambledon is the cradle of cricket, for in the 1760s the Hambledon Cricket Club developed many of the rules of the present game. And the place still reeks of cricket, from the tiny old pub, The Bat and Ball, to the churchyard where four of Hambledon's greatest players are buried. The original ground is preserved and played on regularly, and the club is commemorated by the Boundary Stone. The Hambledon Vineyard produces over 3000 bottles of white wine each year.

Inn sign, Hambledon.

Vineyard, Hambledon.

CHALTON

The old world simplicity of Chalton reflects the fact that the size of its population has scarcely changed for three centuries. The Red Lion Inn, with its beams and thatch, is thought to be 15th century and the oldest inn in Hampshire. It takes its name from the lion crest of John of Gaunt, once Lord of the Manor. The small 13th-century church, which stands across the green from the inn, contains some excellent stained glass.

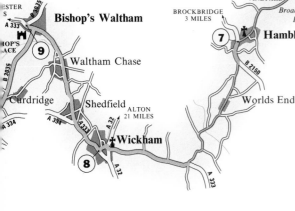

The Red Lion Inn, Chalton.

Titchfield Abbey.

TITCHFIELD ABBEY

Titchfield Abbey was built in the 13th century, dissolved in 1536 and then converted into a private house by the Earl of Southampton. Charles I spent his last night of freedom there in November 1647.

PORTCHESTER CASTLE

Portchester Castle is primarily a Roman fortress built in the 3rd century to form part of a chain of defences from The Wash to Southampton Water. It is the only Roman fort in northern Europe with its outer enclosure intact. In the 12th century, during the reign of Henry I, an impressive royal residence was constructed in one corner inside the Roman walls, while in the opposite corner a church was built to serve an Augustinian priory. In 1415 Henry V assembled his army at the castle before leaving for France and his victory at the Battle of Agincourt.

PORTSMOUTH

Still the principal port of the Royal Navy, Portsmouth was first used as a base for military missions soon after the Norman Conquest. Its importance grew until Henry VIII equipped it with an arsenal, a storehouse and sufficient docks to make it England's chief naval base. He also built Southsea Castle to protect it from the raids of the French. HMS *Victory*, Nelson's flagship at Trafalgar, stands out as the city's principal attraction. Close to the ship is the Royal Naval Museum, which houses many mementos of Nelson, as well as exhibits concerning many other aspects of naval history. Alongside its many ancient fortifications the town has some interesting houses. Among them is Charles Dickens's birthplace, now a museum furnished and decorated in period style. Buckingham House, a timber-framed 16th-century building, was the scene of the murder in 1628 of George Villiers, the 1st Duke of Buckingham and Charles I's principal adviser.

HMS Victory, *at Portsmouth.*

The downlands and forests of Hampshire's border country

Along quiet country lanes, this tour runs north to the Berkshire border over downlands, through forests and hop gardens. It is Jane Austen country. Here she worked on the novels that were to make her famous. The 18th-century naturalist Gilbert White spent a lifetime here producing his work on natural history; and here Charles Kingsley wrote The Water Babies, *which did so much to inspire Victorian social reform.*

(1) Petersfield to East Meon Leave the town on the A3, which is signposted to Portsmouth. After 2 m., just past the railway bridge, turn right on to the road signposted to East Meon. After 1 m., on the left of the road, is a farm track leading up to a footpath that climbs Butser Hill, high point of the South Downs. On the slopes of the hill archaeologists are recreating an Iron Age farm, and they occasionally open the site to the public. Continue on this road to the charming riverside village of East Meon.

(2) East Meon to West Meon Keep right, past the church in the village, and follow the signposts into West Meon.

(3) West Meon to Selborne Turn right on to the A32, which is signposted to Alton. After 8 m., the road enters East Tisted, a typically English village, with neat little cottages, a church spire that appears through the trees, and a cricket green. In this village, turn right on to the road signposted to Selborne. After 3 m. turn left on to the B3006 and into the centre of Selborne.

(4) Selborne to Chawton Leave the village on the B3006, which is signposted to Alton. After 3½ m. turn left and into Chawton, where Jane Austen lived.

(5) Chawton to Alton Continue on the road past Jane Austen's house to the roundabout. Go over the A31 and into Alton.

(6) Alton to Odiham Leave the town on the A339 signposted Farnham, turning left on the A31 at the roundabout on the outskirts. In Bentley, 4 m. later, turn left for Well. Where the road bears right, signposted to Crondall, keep straight ahead. Turn left at the T-junction and into Well. Go through Well and Long Sutton, and turn right on to the A32, following the signpost to Odiham. Turn right on to the A287 and into Odiham.

(7) Odiham to North Warnborough Return to the junction with the A32, and continue downhill on the A32 towards Basingstoke. At the roundabout in North Warnborough turn left and first right to the canal bank, where a footbridge leads across to Odiham Castle.

(8) North Warnborough to Eversley Return to the roundabout and turn left on to the A32. Pass over the M3 and into Hook. Here the half-timbered Raven House, formerly an inn, was built about 1650, and the White Hart, once a coaching inn, still displays a pair of giant stableyard doors. In the village, turn right on to the A30, and immediately left just past the White Hart Inn on to the A32, following the Reading signpost. After

4½ m. turn right on to the B3011, which is signposted to Bramshill, then left on to a minor road that runs through Bramshill village and forest. Here Bramshill House, a fine early-Jacobean house, was built on medieval foundations between 1605 and 1612. Once the seat of the Cope family, it is now a police college. Turn left at the crossroads and continue to Eversley on the A327.

(9) Eversley to Petersfield Return to the crossroads and go straight ahead towards Fleet. At the A30, go ahead over the staggered crossroads on the road signposted to Fleet. Turn right, following the signpost to Elvetham, and left on to the A323, which is signposted to Fleet. Pass under the M3 and then turn right, following the Dogmersfield signpost. Turn left at the T-junction by the Barley Mow and go through the village. Dogmersfield House, a much-restored Queen Anne building, with 18th-century dovecote, stands in the park of a former bishop's palace. Continue into Crookham village, and there turn right, following the signpost to Crondall. Turn left on to the A287 and, almost immediately, right and left on the road signposted to Crondall and Well. At the crossroads in Well, turn left on the road signposted to Bentley. After 1 m., turn right to Bentley. Cross the A31, which is signposted to Binsted, and after 1 m. turn right and follow the road into Binsted. The village has a 12th-century church which stands among some of the most attractive brick-and-timbered cottages in this part of Hampshire. Continue on the same road through Binsted, and cross the B3004 by turning left and right, following the signpost to Oakhanger. Go through Oakhanger and turn left at the T-junction signposted to Blackmoor. At the next T-junction, just past the church in Blackmoor, turn right, following the signpost to Petersfield, and immediately left. At the junction with the A325 opposite Woolmer Pond, turn right and follow the A325 back to Petersfield.

INFORMATION

Places of interest *Alton:* Curtis Museum, Mon. (except Bank Hols.) to Sat., 10 a.m.-1 p.m., 2-5 p.m. *Chawton:* Jane Austen's home, daily (except Mon. and Tues. Nov. to Mar.). *East Meon:* Court House, any time by appointment. *Selborne:* Gilbert White Museum and Oates Memorial Library, Mar. to Oct., daily, except Mon. (open Bank Hol. Mon.), 12 noon-5.30 p.m.

Events *Alton:* Show, Aug. *Petersfield:* Music Festival, Mar.

Information Southern Tourist Group, Canute Road, Southampton (Tel. Southampton 20438).

Towns with easy access to Petersfield:

Basingstoke	24 m.	Portsmouth	17 m.
Chichester	17 m.	Southampton	28 m.
Guildford	25 m.	Winchester	20 m.

Odiham Castle, North Warnborough.

NORTH WARNBOROUGH
The tumbled ruins of Odiham Castle, in this village, were the backdrop to the downfall of three kings. King John built the castle in 1207, and it was from there that he rode out to sign Magna Carta at Runnymede in 1215. In the following year it withstood a siege by the French Dauphin, later King Louis VIII, so frustrating his attempt to capture the English crown. Later, it became the prison of King David II of Scotland after his capture at the Battle of Neville's Cross in 1346.

Gilbert White's home at Selborne as it was in his day.

Detail of a memorial window to Gilbert White in Selborne church.

SELBORNE
One of the pioneers of natural history studies, the Rev. Gilbert White was born at Selborne in 1720. In the 175? he became curate of nearby Farringdon and began to compile his classic work *Natural History of Selborne*. It was published in 1789, just four years before his death, and is still regarded as one of the best accounts of the English countryside. Little change has come to the villa since. White's rambling old house, The Wakes, set clos? the church and village green, is now a museum and memorial library dedicated to both him and the Antarc? explorer, Captain Oates. Apart from exhibits that illustrate the lives and work of these two men, the muse? contains objects excavated from the ruins of a large church—part of an Augustinian priory founded near b? about 1233. Close by is the nature trail leading to the ? of the Hanger, a beech tree covered hill on what are no? National Trust lands west of the village. It was there th? White compiled those detailed, day-to-day observation of every aspect of local wildlife that fill his book. His grave is in the local churchyard. In the church, the mu? restored remainder of a 13th-century original, is a stain? glass window dedicated to White and showing St Franc? feeding birds. Outside is a yew tree said to be more tha? 800 years old.

SCALE

0   1   2   3   4   5 MILES

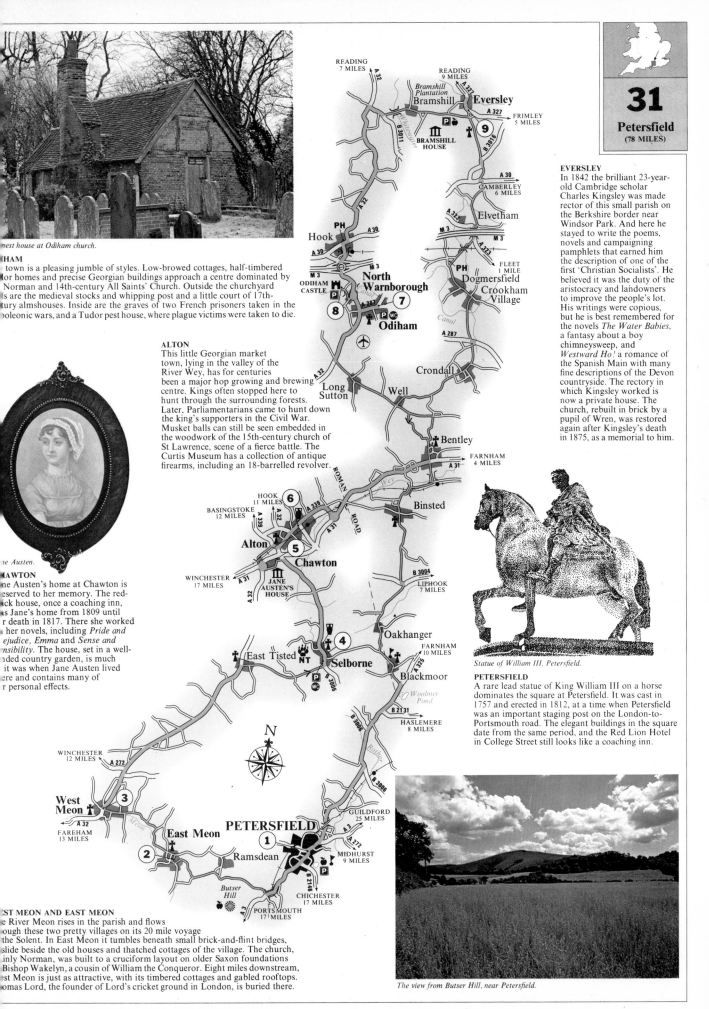

...pest house at Odiham church.

...HAM

...town is a pleasing jumble of styles. Low-browed cottages, half-timbered ...or homes and precise Georgian buildings approach a centre dominated by ... Norman and 14th-century All Saints' Church. Outside the churchyard ...s are the medieval stocks and whipping post and a little court of 17th-...ury almshouses. Inside are the graves of two French prisoners taken in the ...poleonic wars, and a Tudor pest house, where plague victims were taken to die.

ALTON

This little Georgian market town, lying in the valley of the River Wey, has for centuries been a major hop growing and brewing centre. Kings often stopped here to hunt through the surrounding forests. Later, Parliamentarians came to hunt down the king's supporters in the Civil War. Musket balls can still be seen embedded in the woodwork of the 15th-century church of St Lawrence, scene of a fierce battle. The Curtis Museum has a collection of antique firearms, including an 18-barrelled revolver.

...ne Austen.

...AWTON

...ne Austen's home at Chawton is ...eserved to her memory. The red-...ick house, once a coaching inn, ...as Jane's home from 1809 until ...r death in 1817. There she worked ... her novels, including *Pride and ...ejudice, Emma* and *Sense and ...nsibility*. The house, set in a well-...nded country garden, is much ... it was when Jane Austen lived ...ere and contains many of ...r personal effects.

EVERSLEY

In 1842 the brilliant 23-year-old Cambridge scholar Charles Kingsley was made rector of this small parish on the Berkshire border near Windsor Park. And here he stayed to write the poems, novels and campaigning pamphlets that earned him the description of one of the first 'Christian Socialists'. He believed it was the duty of the aristocracy and landowners to improve the people's lot. His writings were copious, but he is best remembered for the novels *The Water Babies*, a fantasy about a boy chimneysweep, and *Westward Ho!* a romance of the Spanish Main with many fine descriptions of the Devon countryside. The rectory in which Kingsley worked is now a private house. The church, rebuilt in brick by a pupil of Wren, was restored again after Kingsley's death in 1875, as a memorial to him.

Statue of William III, Petersfield.

PETERSFIELD

A rare lead statue of King William III on a horse dominates the square at Petersfield. It was cast in 1757 and erected in 1812, at a time when Petersfield was an important staging post on the London-to-Portsmouth road. The elegant buildings in the square date from the same period, and the Red Lion Hotel in College Street still looks like a coaching inn.

...ST MEON AND EAST MEON

...e River Meon rises in the parish and flows ...ough these two pretty villages on its 20 mile voyage ... the Solent. In East Meon it tumbles beneath small brick-and-flint bridges, ...slide beside the old houses and thatched cottages of the village. The church, ...inly Norman, was built to a cruciform layout on older Saxon foundations ... Bishop Wakelyn, a cousin of William the Conqueror. Eight miles downstream, ...st Meon is just as attractive, with its timbered cottages and gabled rooftops. ...omas Lord, the founder of Lord's cricket ground in London, is buried there.

The view from Butser Hill, near Petersfield.

From Brighton around Sussex by the sea

The road leaves Brighton—holiday playground, centre for political conferences and showpiece of Regency architecture—and climbs to more tranquil regions. From Devil's Dyke, Chanctonbury Ring and Ditchling Beacon it is possible on a clear day to see virtually the whole of 'Sussex by the sea' rolling down to the English Channel. There are many picnic spots on this tour, as well as stopping places with memories of the Knights Templar, a vicar with an anti-social cat, and a saint who pulled his mother around on a handcart.

(1) Brighton to Devil's Dyke Leave Brighton on the A23 signposted towards London, but at Patcham recreation ground, on the outskirts of the town, turn left on to the A2038 signposted Hove. There are good views across the downs from this road. After 1½ m. turn right at the signpost to Devil's Dyke and bear left twice to reach the summit and car park. From here there are excellent views.

(2) Devil's Dyke to Bramber Return along the same road and take the first turning left signposted to Poynings. Turn left at the T-junction and sharp left again at the signpost to Poynings. By the church, turn left through the village, following the sign to Fulking. Continue through Fulking, noticing the spring that eventually drives the mill wheel at Woods Mill. Pass through Edburton and at the junction with the A2037 turn left, following the signpost to Steyning. At Upper Beeding turn right on to the A283 for Bramber.

(3) Bramber to Steyning Continue along the A283, which reaches Steyning, once a sea port, after 1 m.

(4) Steyning to Chanctonbury Ring Follow the A283 as far as Washington. Turn left into the village and park the car. A footpath signposted to Chanctonbury Ring leads off to the left opposite the village, and reaches the Ring after 1¼ m.

(5) Chanctonbury Ring to Shipley Return to the A283 and turn left. At the roundabout take the A24 signposted to London. Almost immediately, turn left for Thakeham. After ½ m. bear left, passing Washington Common on the left. At the crossroads beyond the common turn right following the signpost to Thakeham. At the junction with the B2139 turn right, continue for 3 m. across the crossroads with the B2133, and turn right at the signpost to Shipley. At the T-junction turn right and soon afterwards left, then left again by the Countryman Inn signposted to Shipley. After the bridge, turn right on to a lane that leads past the windmill into the village.

(6) Shipley to Henfield Continue through the village and turn left at the junction with the B2224 signposted Southwater. At the junction with the A272 turn right, and after ¾ m. right again on to the A24. After another ¾ m. turn left on to the B2135 signposted Partridge Green. Follow the road through West Grinstead, and in Partridge Green turn left on to the B2116, following the signpost to Henfield. At the junction with the A281, turn right and drive 1¾ m. into Henfield.

(7) Henfield to Woods Mill Leave Henfield on the A2037 signposted Shoreham. Woods Mill is on the left after 1 m. close by a signpost to Hurstpierpoint.

(8) Woods Mill to Newtimber Place Take the road towards Hurstpierpoint; at the junction with the A281 turn right, following the signpost to Brighton. After 3 m., with the National Trust property of Newtimber Hill to the right, turn left at a minor crossroads signposted Newtimber. The church is on the right, and the entrance to Newtimber Place soon afterwards on the left.

(9) Newtimber Place to Clayton Continue along this road and turn right at the junction with the A23, which reaches Pyecombe after 1 m. The forge here was once renowned for its shepherds' crooks. It is still in operation, but the only crooks it makes now are for bishops. Just beyond this straggling village, turn left on to the A273, following the signpost for Burgess Hill. Clayton is reached after 1 m. A footpath leads up behind the church to the windmills.

(10) Clayton to Brighton Leave Clayton on the B2112 signposted to Ditchling, which is reached after 1½ m. As the village is entered, turn right at the signpost to Ditchling Beacon. There are spectacular views as the road rises almost to the summit of the Beacon, which at 813 ft is one of the highest points on the South Downs. A beacon lit here in 1588 announced the coming of the Spanish Armada. Follow this road down from the summit into Brighton.

INFORMATION

Places of interest *Bramber:* Castle, daily. House of Pipes, daily. *Shipley:* King's Mill, May to Oct., first Sat. and Sun. in month, Late Summer Bank Hol., afternoons. *Newtimber Place:* May to Aug., Thur. afternoons. *Henfield:* Woods Mill, Apr. to Sept., Tues. to Thur., Sat., 2-6 p.m., Sun. and Bank Hols., 11 a.m.-6 p.m.

Events London to Brighton: Run of Historic Commercial Vehicles, May. Veteran Car Run, 1st Sun. in Nov. Brighton Music and Arts Festival, July. London to Brighton Stock Exchange Walk, May. Milk Race, May. Brighton Motor Rally & Concours d'élégance, June. Brighton Carnival Week, end July. Brighton Races, May to Sept.

Nature trail *Woods Mill, Henfield:* Walk around grounds. Leaflets from Woods Mill.

Information *Brighton:* Marlborough House, Old Steine (Tel. Brighton 23755 or 26450).

Towns with easy access to Brighton:

Chichester . . . . . 32 m.	Petworth . . . . . . 29 m.
Horsham . . . . . . 23 m.	Reigate . . . . 33 m.
Newhaven . . . . . 9 m.	Tunbridge Wells 32 m.

The Shipley reliquary.

SHIPLEY
King's Mill at Shipley is West Sussex's only working smock windmill—a windmill whose upper floors are made of wood rather than stone. Built in 1879, it is maintained as a memorial to the poet and historian Hilaire Belloc, who owned it and lived near by from 1906 until 1953. St Mary's Church was built in the century by the crusading Order of Knights Templar. In a niche in the chancel is the Shipley reliquary, a 13th-century wooden casket decorated with Limoges enamel. It was probably made for the Templars by Byzantine craftsmen. The ruins of Knepp Castle lie to the south.

CHANCTONBURY RING
At nearly 800 ft, Chanctonbury Ring is one of the highest landmarks of the South Downs, and commands views for 30 miles around—north to Leith Hill in Surrey, and south to the English Channel. It is an Iron Age hill-fort, a 3½ acre area enclosed by a single bank and ditch, on top of which a local landowner planted a circle of beech trees in 1760. Inside the fort are the remains of a temple built by the Romans who occupied the fort in the 3rd and 4th centuries.

From Chanctonbury Ring most of Sussex can be seen.

SCALE

0   1   2   3   4   5 M

NEWTIMBER PLACE
There has been a house on the site of Newtimber Place since Saxon times, and the present house, built in the 17th century, is still surrounded by an ancient water-filled moat. The entrance is decorated with frescoes showing the animated figures of terra cotta goddesses and charioteers. These date from 1750 and there are tapestries and chair covers to match. The house belongs to the descendants of Earl Buxton (1835–1934), a Liberal politician and colleague of Gladstone. The many memorials to this family in the little 13th-century church near by include a mother and child finely sculptured in stone, to commemorate the earl's daughter who died in childbirth.

...e Cat House, Henfield.

...ENFIELD
...is is a large rambling village with a number of ...d buildings, some ancient inns and three ...mmons, on one of which the local cricket club ...s played since 1721. It is said that the metal ...ts adorning the walls of a 16th-century thatched ...ttage were put there long ago to ward off the ...car's cat after it had eaten one of the cottager's ...t birds. The church contains two notable ...asses. Old coaching inns recall when Henfield ...as a stop on the Brighton to London road.

WOODS MILL
In the 15 acres of grounds around Woods Mill there are a nature trail and a garden commemorating the 19th-century botanist William Borrer, who was a local man. The 18th-century water mill has been restored inside and contains an exhibition of plants and wildlife.

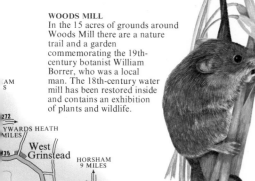
Harvest mouse

CLAYTON
Trains entering the Clayton railway tunnel on the London-to-Brighton line run under a pointed arch between two castellated turrets. This impressive folly, which includes a railwayman's cottage set right above the tunnel, was built in 1840. On the downs above Clayton are two windmills named Jack and Jill. Jack is a brick tower mill dating from 1876, while Jill is a wooden post mill built in Brighton in 1821 and dragged across the downs around 1850. The interior of Clayton church has a Saxon chancel arch and some remarkable medieval wall-paintings. There is a dispute as to whether these are of the 11th or 12th century, but the earliest date put on them is 1080. Above the chancel arch is a Christ in Judgment. On the walls of the nave, processions of kings, clerics and laymen are depicted, while the north wall represents the buildings of the New Jerusalem.

Entrance to the railway tunnel at Clayton.

BRIGHTON
The largest seaside resort on the south coast, Brighton is a holiday playground during the summer and a conference centre in winter. The town grew round its most famous building, the Royal Pavilion, built for the Prince Regent at the beginning of the 19th century. See feature, p. 80.

DEVIL'S DYKE
Legend has it that the V-shaped cleft in the downs known as the Devil's Dyke was dug by the Devil himself in an attempt to flood the Weald from the sea and drown its many churches. Mistaking an old lady's candle for the coming of dawn, he fled, leaving indentations in the hillside with his heels.

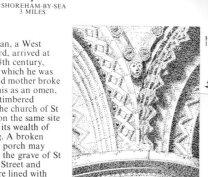
Norman carving, Steyning church.

...TEYNING
...When St Cuthman, a West ...Country shepherd, arrived at ...Steyning in the 8th century, ...he handcart on which he was ...ulling his invalid mother broke ...own. Taking this as an omen, ...e built a small timbered ...hurch. Today the church of St ...Andrew stands on the same site ...nd is noted for its wealth of ...Norman carving. A broken ...tone slab in the porch may ...ave come from the grave of St ...Cuthman. High Street and ...Church Street are lined with ...hatched and half-timbered ...ottages. Chantry Green House ...ates from 1547 and now ...ontains a collection of ...aintings and antiques.

BRAMBER
By the 13th-century bridge at Bramber is St Mary's, a timber-framed house built around 1480. It has a monks' walk, a Victorian music room and some fine panelling, including a complete room of 17th-century painted panels. The House of Pipes contains 25,000 smoking implements from 150 countries, their craftsmanship spanning 1500 years.

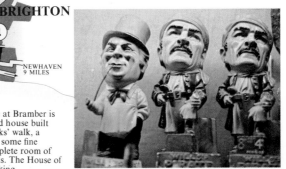
The House of Pipes, Bramber.

BRIGHTON

The largest seaside resort on the south coast, Brighton still retains the intimacy and elegance of its Regency origins. The map plots the route of a walk round the town, linking many of the places of interest that give the town its character. These places are numbered in the key below.

THINGS TO SEE IN THE TOWN

(1) The Lanes. Oldest part of Brighton, now mainly shops and restaurants converted from fishermen's cottages. Many of them are antique shops. Brighton Square, with its continental pavement café atmosphere, is in the centre.

(2) Royal Pavilion. Palace built for the Prince Regent. Fully furnished in the original style. Open daily except Christmas and three days before annual Regency Exhibition (July, Aug. and Sept.), during which the Banqueting Room is set as if for a banquet of George IV's time.

(3) The Dome. Built as royal stables and riding school, now an entertainment and conference hall.

(4) Museum and art gallery, housed in former Royal Pavilion stables. Open daily (except Mon. and Sun. morning).

(5) St Nicholas's Church. The parish church of old Brighton, built in the 14th century. Tombstones of characters in the town's history.

(6) Booth Museum of Natural History, with large collection of British birds displayed in their natural habitat. Daily (except Wed., Thurs. and Sun. mornings).

(7) Clifton Terrace. Built in 1850, after the death of George IV, but showing the continuing influence of the Regency style in domestic architecture.

(8) Regency Square. Planned in 1818, the square is a fine example of the Georgian terraces built by the wealthy on and near the sea front.

(9) Dolls in Wonderland. More than 300 lifelike characters in children's fairyland setting. Open daily.

(10) Palace Pier. Amusements. Terminus of sea-front railway which takes passengers to the Black Rock swimming pool and the new yachting marina.

(11) Aquarium, containing sea-lions, seals, turtles and tropical fish; there is also a licensed bar. Open daily. Dolphin performances morning and afternoon.

(12) Home of Mrs Maria Fitzherbert, the Prince Regent's morganatic wife, until her death in 1837. The house was built for her in 1804. It is now a Y.M.C.A. hostel.

CAR PARKS: North Street (near Pavilion Theatre), Bond Street and Gardner Street (between North Street and North Road), Church Street (opposite swimming baths), Dyke Road (near junction with Upper North Street), behind Regency Square (east side); five parks within area bounded by Esplanade, West Street, Western Road and Cannon Place; three near town hall (off Esplanade, approaching Palace Pier). Other parks in streets behind Marine Parade (east of Palace Pier).

BRIGHTON

Brighton, a fishing village that became a royal resort and then one of the nation's great holiday playgrounds, has something of each of these roles to show the visitor. There is no other town quite like it for its blend of old and new, Georgian grace and down-to-earth modern amenities.

A doctor brought the cult of the seaside to the South, and a prince made Brighton its temple.

The doctor was Richard Russell, born at Lewes in 1687. Sixty-three years later he published a book in which he prescribed 'the oceanic fluid' as a cure for many ills—not only for bathing in, but for drinking as well. His practice grew so rapidly that he built himself a seaside house, not far from Lewes, in the little fishing town of Brighthelmstone, on the spot where the Royal Albion Hotel now stands.

The prince was George, later George IV, who at the age of 21 paid his first visit to Brighthelmstone one Sunday in September 1783. He was so taken with the place that he bought a house there. In 1787 he had a mansion built, and later had it transformed into a fantastic palace—the Royal Pavilion. As the royal residence grew and was transformed, so was the little fishing town. Brighthelmstone developed into a new and exciting metropolis by the sea. Brighton had arrived.

Dr Russell could hardly have chosen a more promising location in which to launch his seawater treatment. Brighton lies at the foot of the rolling Sussex Downs, where the sun warms the south-facing chalk cliffs.

Little remains of the town he first knew, though The Lanes, which date from the 18th century, follow the street pattern of the original medieval village. These narrow byways are lined with tiny weatherboarded houses that were once fishermen's cottages. Many of them are now antique shops. In some parts people in the upstairs rooms can shake hands across the street. They form a quaint enclave close to Brighton Square, a traffic-free shopping centre with modern luxury flats.

A few minutes' walk leads to the Royal

'ONIONS' IN THE SKY *Bird's-eye view of the rooftops of the Royal Pavilion. Both inside and out, the palace is an expression of the prince's exotic taste.*

Pavilion, an extravaganza rising from tree-shaded lawns and topped by domes, minarets and green copper cupolas. This is the Prince Regent's pleasure house, first built as a Georgian mansion by Henry Holland in 1787. It was remodelled into an oriental palace by John Nash in 1822. The Royal Pavilion, with its furnishings, cost more than £500,000. The town bought it from the Crown in 1850 for £50,000.

At the beginning of the 19th century the prince commissioned William Porden to build stables and a riding school—the Dome. This is now a concert hall, the home of the Brighton Philharmonic Orchestra, and also a centre for political and trade union conferences.

The stable buildings facing Church Street were converted into a public library, art gallery and museum in 1873. The library has been enriched by gifts of many private collections, and the art gallery and museum contain old masters and exhibits of pottery, primitive art and Sussex natural history.

Brighton is well endowed with smaller and more specialised museums. Two of the most interesting on this walk are the Booth Museum

THE DOME *Conference hall, variety theatre, wrestling arena—the Dome owes its origin to the Prince Regent's love of riding. He had it built as stables early in the 19th century in a style inspired by the Indian mosques.*

THE MUSIC ROOM *This is one of the rooms entirely recreated by Nash when he rebuilt the Royal Pavilion. A resident royal orchestra, sometimes up to 70 in number, played here, and George himself sang to his guests.*

FOR DRINKS *Two of the exhibits in the museum and art gallery. Top: Chinese-enamelled posset pot made in Bristol in the late 17th century. Posset was a hot drink made of ale sweetened with honey and spiced with herbs. It was drunk through the spout. Bottom: The Hove Amber Cup, as it is known, was fashioned on a lathe from a single block of amber. The cup, just under 3 in. high, was excavated from a Wessex chieftain's grave at Hove in 1857. The cup was in an oak coffin along with a stone axe-head and a bronze dagger.*

of Natural History—the 'bird museum'—and Dolls in Wonderland on the sea front. The first displays a big collection of British birds in their natural surroundings as well as butterflies, minerals and other natural history exhibits. The doll museum is a treat for children—more than 300 lifelike dolls in a fairyland setting.

Bathers and dippers

When Dr Russell prescribed the healing properties of 'the oceanic fluid', sea bathing became a solemn and rigorous ritual, requiring stern attendants to ensure that doctor's orders—to get in the water and drink it—were faithfully obeyed. 'Bathers' supervised the men; 'dippers' saw to it that the women got wet. In these roles two characters achieved fame. The bather 'Smoaker' Miles is reputed to have rough-handled the Prince of Wales by pulling his ear; and Martha Gunn, first of a long line of dippers, lies in St Nicholas's churchyard.

St Nicholas's, the old parish church on the hill, dates from the 14th century. Another Brighton celebrity buried there was Captain Nicholas Tattersell, who took Charles II to France in his boat *Surprise* after the king's defeat at the Battle of Worcester in 1651.

Royal patronage made Brighton a centre of fashionable society, and elegant houses sprang up in the town that grew around the Royal Pavilion.

Many of the squares, crescents and terraces of Regency and Victorian days still contribute their elegance to the character of the modern town. Clifton Terrace, built in 1850, is one of many Victorian developments that contain almost as many buildings of the Regency style as were put up in areas such as Regency Square, which was laid out in 1818, when the Prince Regent lived in the town.

Tomorrow in the making

An easy stroll along the esplanade leads to the Palace Pier and aquarium. About halfway along, between the Grand Hotel and Kingswest, is the beginning of a £4 million conference hall, exhibition and entertainments complex to be called the Brighton Centre. A little further along, in Ship Street, are two of the town's oldest inns, The Old Ship—where the virtuoso Paganini once gave a violin recital—and the Cricketers Arms.

The Palace Pier is the younger of the town's two piers; it was built in 1899, 33 years after the West Pier. The gilded domes of the Palace Pier are in the style of the Royal Pavilion. The Chain Pier, the first pier in England, was built in 1823 and destroyed by a storm 63 years later. Close by, the aquarium, now more than 100 years old, contains thousands of fish, including tropical species, as well as sea-lions, seals and turtles. Dolphins perform their antics before upwards of 1000 spectators at a time.

On the way back to The Lanes in the Old Steine (pronounced steen) is the house of Mrs Maria Fitzherbert, morganatic wife of George IV. Although she had a drawing-room in the Royal Pavilion, she never lived there. Because of her lack of blue blood, her two previous husbands, and her Catholic faith, her marriage to the Prince Regent in 1785 was always officially denied. She lived discreetly in her own house which was built for her in 1804. It is now a Y.M.C.A. hostel. Mrs Fitzherbert died in 1837, and her monument in the church of St John the Baptist, not far from her house, shows her wearing three wedding rings.

DIPPER'S GRAVE *Tombstone of Martha Gunn in St Nicholas's churchyard. Martha was the 'queen' of the Brighton 'dippers', as the women seabathing attendants were known, and her portrait, by John Russell, R.A., hangs in Buckingham Palace. She practised her profession until her death.*

OSPREY *One of the birds in the Booth Museum of Natural History. The osprey, or fish hawk, was thought to be extinct in Britain until a pair were seen, the first for nearly half a century, near Loch Garten in Scotland. The Speyside nesting area has been declared a sanctuary, and the eagle-like birds and their eggs are jealously protected.*

REGENCY SQUARE *The bow fronts and canopied iron balconies are typical of the smaller houses that sprang up as Brighton's Regency vogue gathered momentum in the early 19th century. At the height of the building boom 500 similar houses were under construction at the same time.*

'THE OCEANIC FLUID' *Palace Pier seen across the sea from Marine Parade. Near the point from which this picture was taken, work has begun on a £30 million yachting marina.*

BRIGHTON ROCK *A shop window full of rock in all shapes, sizes and designs. Seaside rock was first made in 1868 by Ben Bullock, a Yorkshireman. Brighton visitors consume up to 10 tons a day.*

'DOLLS IN WONDERLAND' *With a unique collection of more than 300 dolls, this unusual museum is specially designed to appeal to children. The dolls are dressed in a variety of costumes and displayed in a fairyland setting. The museum contains a special children's postbox to Father Christmas.*

Art, history and life long ago on the rolling South Downs

One of the charms of the stately homes that are open to the public is that their art treasures can be appreciated in their natural setting. This is especially true of Petworth House, which contains one of the biggest and best collections of pictures in England, among them a series of landscapes by Turner, considered by many to be this country's greatest artist. He had a studio in the mansion in the 19th century, and two of his pictures are of the magnificent surrounding park. This tour of the South Downs also visits historic Arundel Castle, the remains at Bignor of one of Britain's biggest Roman villas, and an open-air museum which re-creates centuries of life and work in rural England.

(1) Arundel to Bignor Leave Arundel on the road signposted for London/Dorking and turn right on to the A284. At the roundabout after 3 m. take the A29 signposted for London/Dorking/Pulborough, and after 1½ m. turn sharp left on to a minor road signposted for Bignor and Roman Villa. After ½ m. bear left to Bignor.

(2) Bignor to the Weald and Downland Open Air Museum Leave Bignor on the road signposted to Sutton, and after ¾ m. take the left fork by The White Horse, following the signpost to Barlavington. After ¾ m. turn right at the T-junction, and follow the road for 1½ m. to the junction with the A285. Turn left, following the signpost to Chichester. After 2 m., just before the road curves to the left, turn right at the signpost to East Dean. Bear left in the village and carry straight on up the hill by the duckpond, following the signpost to Goodwood. After 1 m. turn right at the crossroads, following the signpost for Goodwood Racecourse, and continue past the main stand. Follow the road uphill, bearing sharp right and then left. After ¼ m. the entrance to Trundle picnic site is on the left. Follow the road for ¾ m. and turn sharp left through the gate to the museum.

(3) Weald and Downland Open Air Museum to West Stoke Leave the museum by the same gate, turn left, then turn left again at the T-junction with the A286. About 3 m. beyond West Dean, before the road curves left in Mid Lavant, turn sharp right, following the signpost to East Ashling and Funtington. In West Stoke turn right just past the church (no signpost). On the right is the car park for Kingley Vale Nature Reserve.

(4) West Stoke to Uppark Leave West Stoke on the same unsignposted road and follow it for 1½ m. to the junction with the B2146 in Funtington. Turn right into the village, and after 400 yds turn sharp right, still on the B2146, following the signpost to Petersfield. Drive through West Marden and Compton. After 7½ m. turn right at the signpost to Uppark. A track leads to Uppark House.

(5) Uppark to South Harting Leave Uppark by the exit which returns to the B2146 ½ m. on from the entrance. There, turn right and follow the road into South Harting.

(6) South Harting to Midhurst Leave South Harting on the road signposted for Midhurst, and follow it for 4½ m. through Elsted to the junction with the A272. Turn right, and after 2 m. enter Midhurst.

(7) Midhurst to Petworth Leave Midhurst on the A272 signposted to Petworth. The road passes Benbow pond on the left. After 1 m. turn sharp right at the signpost for Selham and Graffham. About ¼ m. beyond the pub in Selham, take the left fork as the road curves right, and continue to the A285. Turn left, following the signpost to Petworth. Petworth House is on the left after 2 m.

(8) Petworth to Stopham Leave Petworth on the A283 signposted to Pulborough. After 2¾ m. the road enters Stopham.

(9) Stopham to Amberley Follow the A283 into Pulborough and turn right on to the A29 signposted to Bognor. After 2 m., just past a school warning sign, turn sharp left, following the signpost to Greatham. Go through Greatham and, about 1 m. beyond the village, turn right at the signpost for Rackham and Amberley. Turn right again, 1 m. later, in Rackham, following the signpost to Amberley, which is reached ½ m. later.

(10) Amberley to Arundel Bear left through Amberley, and turn right at the junction with the B2139. Follow the road past Amberley railway station, and turn right just before the pub at Houghton, following the signpost to Bignor and Bury. After ¾ m. the road enters Bury. At the privately owned Bury House, John Galsworthy, author of the *Forsyte Saga*, died in 1933. At the crossroads in the village turn left, and soon afterwards left again at the junction with the A29 signposted to Arundel. After 1 m., at the roundabout, take the A284, following the signpost to Arundel, which is reached about 4 m. later.

INFORMATION

Places of interest *Arundel:* Castle, Apr. to May, Mon. to Thur. afternoons; June to end Sept., Mon. to Fri. afternoons, Sun. afternoons in Aug. Potters' Museum, daily, Easter to Oct., Sat. in winter. *Bignor Roman villa:* Mar. to end Oct., Tues. to Sun., Bank Hols., Mon. in Aug. *Cowdray Park:* May to Sept. *Petworth House:* Apr. to mid-Oct., daily (except Mon., Fri. and Tues. after Bank Hol.), and Bank Hol. Mon. *Uppark:* Apr. to Sept., Wed., Thur., Sun. and Bank Hol. Mon., afternoons. *Weald and Downland Open Air Museum:* Apr. to Sept., daily (except Mon.); Oct., weekends, Wed.; Nov. to Mar., Sun. afternoons (Mon. in Aug.).

Events *Goodwood Races:* May, end July, end Aug., Sept. Traffic heavy at July meeting.

Information Southern Tourist Group, Canute Road, Southampton (Tel. Southampton 20438).

Arundel is within easy reach of:

Brighton	21 m.	Horsham	23 m.
Chichester	11 m.	Worthing	10 m.

Yew, Kingley Vale.

KINGLEY VALE NATURE RESERVE
The nature reserve here was set up to preserve what is claimed to be the finest yew forest in Europe. The biggest and oldest trees, some nearly 500 years old, stand in a grove at the foot of the valley. Their smaller descendants—probably grown from seeds carried by birds—form a denser forest on the slopes. More than 70 species of birds have been seen among the surrounding woods, scrub and chalk heath. The area shelters roe deer, badgers and stoats, and has four 3500-year-old Bronze Age burial grounds.

St Andrew's Church, West Stoke.

WEST STOKE
St Andrew's Church at West Stoke is notable for its porch, which was added to the south side of the nave in the 13th century. It is two-storeyed, and proportioned to look like a low tower. The flint-and-rubble walls probably incorporate fragments of Roman brick from a villa that once stood to the west of the church.

SCALE

0   1   2   3   4   5 MILES

Petworth House, west front.

PETWORTH
The famous gardener Capability Brown landscaped the 2000 acre park surrounding Petworth House. The mansion was built by the 6th Duke of Somerset in 1688–96; it was given to the National Trust in 1947. The 320 ft long west front looks particularly impressive when mirrored in the lake. Perhaps more distinguished than the mansion itself is the fine collection of paintings it contains —works by such artists as Van Dyck, Titian, Gainsborough, Reynolds, Claude and especially Turner. Some of Turner's famous sea paintings are on view, featuring scenes on the Sussex coast. In the early 19th century Turner had a studio at Petworth, and the collection of his landscapes includes two of Petworth Park. The Carved Room displays fine wood carving by Grinling Gibbons.

Part of the Barttelot brass, Stopham church.

33
Arundel
(73 MILES)

STOPHAM
A fine collection of brasses can be seen in the parish church here. They commemorate 200 years in the history of the Barttelot family, owners of Stopham House since shortly after the Norman Conquest. The largest brass, dated 1614, shows Richard Barttelot in armour, with his two wives and nine children. The main feature of the village is its seven-arched bridge, which is so narrow that traffic has to cross in single file.

Thatched cottage, Amberley.

AMBERLEY
This is a village of deep-thatched cottages overlooked by the sprawling ruins of a castle built in 1380 for the Bishops of Chichester. During the Civil War the castle, held as a Royalist stronghold, was attacked by the Parliamentarians and later dismantled. Next to the ruin stands St Michael's Church, which contains a 15th-century brass effigy of a knight.

Roman pavement, Bignor.

BIGNOR
Remains of a Roman villa uncovered here are among the largest of their kind in Britain. Richly coloured mosaic pavements are preserved in their original settings.

UPPARK
Nelson's mistress, Lady Hamilton, once lived at Uppark House, a red-brick Queen Anne mansion standing in landscaped grounds from which there are views across the South Downs. The original flock wallpapers and damask curtains in the house provide a graceful background to a collection of period furniture and portraits.

Titchfield Market Hall at the Open Air Museum.

WEALD AND DOWNLAND OPEN AIR MUSEUM
This remarkable museum presents a vivid picture of rural life and craftsmanship over the centuries. Ancient buildings have been carefully dismantled on their original sites and re-erected here; they include an Elizabethan treadwheel, for drawing water; a 15th-century Kentish farmhouse; and a rare, early-17th-century market hall.

Arundel Castle from the air.

ARUNDEL
The massive keep and towers of Arundel Castle, built to defend the valley, have dominated the town since the Norman Conquest. The castle, home of the Dukes of Norfolk for 500 years, contains a collection of armour, tapestries and other treasures. The Norfolk Arms near by is a fine specimen of an 18th-century coaching inn.

A green belt that might have become a black country

Two beauty spots, popular with Londoners looking for a breath of country air, dominate the neighbourhood of Dorking. They are Box Hill and Leith Hill, where roads and railways follow the Mole Valley through the North Downs towards the sea. Beneath the hills are the towns and villages of Surrey and Sussex, with a life and history independent of the capital, and with the woodlands and gardens of the Weald to support their rural roots. Yet if coal had not been found in Wales and the Midlands, this might have been the dirty industrial heart of England.

(1) Dorking to Box Hill Leave the town on the A24, following the signpost for London. After ½ m., at the roundabout near the Burford Bridge Hotel, take the second exit to follow the signpost for Mickleham and Boxhill (spelt as one word). Turn right and climb the winding road which goes to the 690 ft summit of Box Hill, where there is a look-out platform.

(2) Box Hill to Brockham Pass the look-out platform, go down the hill, turn right at the road junction and right again on to the B2032, following the signpost to Dorking and Reigate. After 1 m. go over the level-crossing at Betchworth station, and at the roundabout follow the signpost to Betchworth. At the T-junction turn right and fork first left, then turn left again to enter Brockham.

(3) Brockham to Handcross Continue through the village, following the signpost to Newdigate. After 3 m. turn right, opposite the entrance to Brook Farm. After about 1½ m. turn right at the T-junction, continue through Newdigate and remain on the road for another 3½ m. to Rusper. In Rusper turn left and after about ½ m. take the first turning to the right, continuing for 1¾ m. to Faygate. Cross the railway, pass through the hamlet and cross the A264, continuing for 1 m. through woodland to Colgate. At the Dragon Inn junction turn left, following the signs for Pease Pottage, which lies 2¼ m. ahead beside the A23. At Pease Pottage turn right on to the A23, following the Brighton signpost. At the junction with the A279, bear left to enter Handcross. To visit Nymans Gardens, go through the village and turn left on to the B2114. Return by the same route to Handcross.

(4) Handcross to Wakehurst Place Leave Handcross village by turning right on to the B2110, following the signposts for Balcombe and East Grinstead. After 3½ m. along wooded roads turn left at the junction on to the B2036, and almost immediately right again to follow the resumed B2110 for just over 3 m. through luxuriant woodland and the beeches of Balcombe Forest to Turners Hill. At the crossroads turn right on to the B2028, following the signpost to Brighton, and continue for 2½ m. The entrance to Wakehurst Place gardens is on the right.

(5) Wakehurst Place to Ardingly Return to the B2028 and turn right, continuing gently downhill, past the South of England Agricultural Society showground, and after 1½ m. enter Ardingly.

(6) Ardingly to Balcombe In Ardingly village, turn sharp right and follow the signposts to Balcombe, ignoring any side roads, through a valley which may become a new reservoir. The road twists for 3 m. between hillsides and woodland before emerging in Balcombe village.

(7) Balcombe to Leith Hill At the T-junction in the village turn left towards Haywards Heath and follow the road which leads across the valley and under the railway bridge. After 3 m., on the outskirts of Haywards Heath, turn right, and continue 1 m. to Cuckfield. Turn right here to join the B2036, and then left on to the B2114/5. After about 1¼ m., at the next junction, turn right on to the B2114, and follow the road into Staplefield. From the crossroads on Staplefield village green turn left, following the signpost to Slaugham, passing under the A23, and after 1½ m. crossing the A279. After 4 m., at an unsigned junction with the A281, turn right and continue into Horsham. Follow the A281 through the town, following the signposts to Guildford as far as Broadbridge Heath. Turn right here on to the B2199, and continue 1½ m. to Warnham. After passing through Warnham bear left at the junction with the A24, following the signpost for Dorking. After 4 m., just before the village of Capel, turn left on to the B2126 and across Ockley Green, where Romans marched along the ancient Stane Street, and where in 851 King Ethelwulf and his son Ethelbald defeated the invading Danes and drove them back to their ships off the Isle of Thanet. After 1½ m. turn left on to the A29 and almost immediately sharp right to regain the B2126, following the signpost to Forest Green. The hills now appear on the right, dominated by Leith Hill tower. Turn right to follow the Leith Hill signpost. The road climbs through trees to the hilltop.

(8) Leith Hill to Dorking Return along the same road for a few hundred yards then fork left to follow the signpost to Coldharbour. Follow this road, and the signposts to Dorking, down through Abinger Forest, and after about 3 m. enter Dorking.

INFORMATION

Places of interest *Horsham:* Causeway House Museum, Tues. to Fri., afternoons, Sat., 10 a.m.-5 p.m. *Leith Hill:* Tower, Mar. to Oct., fine afternoons. *Nymans Gardens:* Apr. to Oct., Tues. to Thur., Sat., 2-7 p.m., Sun. and Bank Hols., 11 a.m.-7 p.m. *Wakehurst Place:* Garden, daily.

Information South-East England Tourist Board, Cheviot House, 4-6 Monson Road, Tunbridge Wells (Tel. Tunbridge Wells 33066).

Towns with easy access to Dorking:

Brighton	36 m.	Maidstone	42 m.
Guildford	12 m.	Windsor	27 m.
London	24 m.	Worthing	33 m.

Stepping-stones across the Mole at Box Hill.

BOX HILL
A popular beauty spot within easy reach of London. Box Hill gets its name from the box trees growing on its slopes. Since boxwood is exceptionally hard it was used for wood-engravers' blocks. The 1000 acres are cared for by the National Trust. At the foot of the hill, stepping-stones cross the River Mole on the line of the ancient Pilgrims' Way from Winchester to Canterbury.

DORKING
The irregularly shaped High Street, one side of which is higher than the other, follows the route of the Roman Stane Street. There is evidence that Saxons lived here and that Danes raided their settlement. Charles Dickens stayed at the White Horse Inn, parts of which date from the 16th century, and the 'Markis of Granby' in *The Pickwick Papers* is reputed to have been the King's Head, an inn which used to be at the North Street-High Street junction. Lord Nelson finally separated from his wife at the hotel in Burford Bridge, outside the town.

Bluebell time at Leith Hill.

LEITH HILL
The highest point in south-east England, Leith Hill has its natural 965 ft brought up to more than 1029 ft by the folly tower built on top in 1766 by Richard Hull of Leith Hill Place. Hull was buried beneath the tower upside down, believing that by Judgment Day the world would have spun round far enough for him to be facing his Maker.

SCALE

0   1   2   3   4   5 MILES

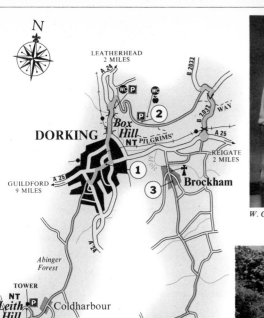

BROCKHAM

This is a delightful village with a triangular green, where the famous batsman W. G. Grace (1848–1915) frequently played cricket. The church butts up to one end of the green, and the backdrop to the other is Box Hill. A variety of houses surround the green, including the sedate Hope House with its typically Regency frontage. The 18th-century Brockham Court and Way House in Wheeler's Lane, a collection of estate cottages built in 1871, are of greater architectural interest. Feltons Farm on the south-west side of the village has a 17th-century farmhouse forming a quadrangle with its set of tarred Surrey barns.

W. G. Grace, a visitor to Brockham.

WAKEHURST PLACE

Now celebrated for its gardens, which are under the care of the Royal Botanical Society, the estate belonged from Norman times to the Wakehurst family. In 1454 it passed to the Culpepers after two Wakehurst heiresses eloped with the brothers of their Culpeper guardian. The present gabled stone house was built in 1590.

One of the formal parts of Nymans Gardens.

NYMANS GARDENS, HANDCROSS

The gardens were laid out by Ludwig Messel in 1885 and the work completed by his son. There is a fine topiary, a rose garden and a collection of exotic flowers, shrubs and conifers.

Richard and Elizabeth Wakehurst: brass in Ardingly church.

ARDINGLY

Though the village church is a mixture of styles and periods from the 14th century on, it has a number of interesting brasses and monuments, mainly to the Wakehursts and Culpepers who lived at Wakehurst Place near by. One commemorates a couple who had 18 children. Also in the village is the public school, Ardingly College.

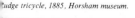

Rudge tricycle, 1885, Horsham museum.

HORSHAM

The town dates back to the 13th century, and may have even earlier origins. It was once so involved with the Sussex iron-smelting trade that a Tudor historian complained of the roads 'full of dirt and myre', because of ox-teams dragging timber through the town to the furnaces. Causeway, a wide street behind the Town Hall, is paved with massive stone flags, known as Horsham slabs, which were also used on house roofs. Causeway House Museum, a Tudor building, houses early bicycles, women's fashions from 1840 to 1930, reconstructions of rural workshops and relics of the Sussex iron trade. In Market Square is the turreted Town Hall, believed to date from the 17th century, where the assizes were held until 1830.

The Ouse viaduct, Balcombe.

BALCOMBE

Beech trees, a mill and a lake make this an attractive corner of Sussex. The most celebrated sight is the 1476 ft railway viaduct over the Ouse, built between 1838 and 1841 for the London, Brighton and South Coast Railway by John Urpeth Rastrick. It has 37 brick arches, each 30 ft wide, and increasing from 40 ft high at the ends to 96 ft in the middle. The parapets are of Caen stone and there are Classical pavilions at each end of the viaduct.

A tour timed by the blacksmith's hammer

This tour, seldom far from the picturesque valley of the quiet River Wey, takes a look at a plantation of rare trees, the mansion where the Queen Mother spent her honeymoon, and a little town in which harpsichords are still produced. At one village along the route, if the timing is lucky, a carved wooden blacksmith will hammer on a clock bell to strike the hour of the day, a reminder of the once busy clangour of many forges.

(1) Guildford to Hatchlands Leave the town on the A25/A246, following signposts for Dorking and Leatherhead. In Merrow turn sharp right by the church on to the A25. Continue on the A25 to Newlands Corner, a look-out point 567 ft above sea level with views far across Surrey and Sussex to the South Downs. Return along the A25 for 100 yds and turn right on to the A247, following the signposts towards West Clandon until the junction with the A246. (To visit Clandon Park, the 18th-century National Trust property with its collections of porcelain and antiques, continue straight across the A246. The park entrance is a few hundred yards down the road into the village.) Turn right on to the A246, following the signposts for Leatherhead. About 1 m. along this road is Hatchlands.

(2) Hatchlands to Polesden Lacey Continue on the A246 through to Great Bookham. Just past the turning signposted for the village and railway station, take the first turning right and follow the signs to Polesden Lacey.

(3) Polesden Lacey to Abinger Hammer Return through Great Bookham to Effingham and turn left at the traffic lights, following the signposts for Ranmore/Abinger. The road runs through woodlands and, after 3 m., meets the A25. Turn right, following the signposts for Guildford. The road runs to Abinger Hammer.

(4) Abinger Hammer to Shere Continue through the village to Gomshall. Just beyond the village turn left to Shere.

(5) Shere to Winkworth Arboretum In Shere, turn left down the village street, following the signpost for Peaslake/Ewhurst. Keep on this road, through Peaslake, and on to Ewhurst. In the village, turn right on to the B2127 and continue on this road to Cranleigh. Leave Cranleigh on the B2128, following the signposts for Wonersh and, at the end of the green, turn left on to the B2130, following the signposts for Hascombe. Cross the A281 and, still on the B2130, continue through Hascombe village and uphill (or right, following the signposts to the lower car park) to see the trees at Winkworth Arboretum.

(6) Winkworth Arboretum to Chiddingfold Return down the same road, through Hascombe village, for about 2 m. At the bottom of the slope turn right, following the signposts for Hydestile/Hambledon, bearing left at the junction 1½ m. later. Go past Hydestile Hospital and turn left at the crossroads towards Hambledon. Go through Hambledon and turn left on to the A283, reaching Chiddingfold after 2 m.

(7) Chiddingfold to Haslemere Continue on the A283 and, after 1¾ m., turn right, following the signposts for Haslemere. Turn right again on to the B2131 and into Haslemere.

(8) Haslemere to Frensham Great Pond Leave Haslemere on the B2131, following the signposts for Liphook. Continue under the railway bridge and, after 1 m., fork right on to the A286 and into Hindhead. In the village, turn right on to the A3, following the signposts for Guildford. The road runs round a deep cleft and into the Devil's Punch Bowl, a natural freak of erosion caused by spring water. After about 3½ m. turn left for Thursley. Go through the village and follow the signposts to Churt for about 4 m. In Churt turn right on to the A287. After 1 m. the road passes the Frensham Great Pond on the left.

(9) Frensham Great Pond to Farnham Continue on the A287 downhill and into Farnham, one of the least spoilt towns in Surrey. Elegant Georgian houses line Castle Street, and there are several Tudor houses.

(10) Farnham to Guildford Leave Farnham on the B3001, following the signposts for Godalming. At the corner opposite the gates which are the sole remains of Waverley Abbey turn left, following the signposts for Sandy Cross. Continue straight on over three crossroads and turn right on to the A31. After 3 m. turn left on to the B3000, following the signposts for Compton, through the underpass and left on to the A3. The road runs downhill, past the modern cathedral and university buildings, to Guildford.

INFORMATION

Places of interest *Clandon Park:* Apr. to mid-Oct., Tues. to Thur., Sat., Sun. and Bank Hol. Mon., 2-6 p.m. (closed Tues. after Bank Hol.). *Farnham Castle:* Wed. 2-4.30 p.m. Keep, Apr. to Oct., weekdays, Sun. afternoons. *Guildford:* Castle, Apr. to Sept., daily. *Hatchlands:* Apr. to Sept., Wed. and Sat., 2-5.30 p.m. *Polesden Lacey:* Mar. and Nov., Sat., Sun., 2-6 p.m. Apr. to Oct., daily (except Mon., Fri. and Tues. after Bank Hol.), and Bank Hol. Mon., 2-6 p.m. *Winkworth Arboretum:* Daily.

Craft workshop *Haslemere:* Arnold Dolmetsch Ltd, Kings Road, early musical instruments. Thurs., 11 a.m.-2.30 p.m. by appointment (Tel. Haslemere 51432).

Information Central Library, North Street, Guildford (Tel. Guildford 68496). South-East England Tourist Board, Cheviot House, 4-6 Monson Road, Tunbridge Wells (Tel. Tunbridge Wells 33066).

Towns with easy access to Guildford:

Chichester	34 m.	Reading	28 m.
Croydon	26 m.	Reigate	18 m.
London	29 m.	Winchester	38 m.

FARNHAM
Castle Street climbs between Georgian and early-Victorian façades to a crest where for 1000 years a castle belonging to the bishops of Winchester has stood. South of the river is The Jolly Farmer, birthplace in 1763 of William Cobbett, the radical politician and author of *Rural Rides* in which he recorded the life of the ordinary people. Just outside the town is Moor Park, where Jonathan Swift wrote *A Tale of a Tub* and met Esther Johnson, to whom he addressed his *Journal to Stella*.

FRENSHAM GREAT POND
Set in rolling acres of heather, its old lanes wandering down to the banks of the River Wey, Frensham is a favourite Surrey beauty spot. The village church, repeatedly restored from the Norman original, contains what is claimed to be the cauldron of Mother Ludlam, a medieval witch who lived in caves near Waverley Abbey. Outside the village lie the 780 acres of Frensham Country Park, a National Trust property. It completely encloses Great Pond which, despite its name, is one of the biggest lakes in southern England. The parish of Frensham includes Churt, where the First World War leader David Lloyd George made his home in the picturesque Old Barn, and in the orchards around it grew the strain of raspberries identified by his name.

Nightingale

Wood warbler

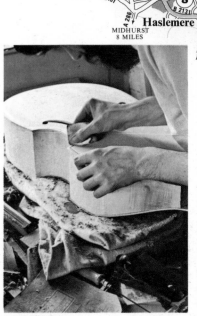

Dolmetsch workshop.

HASLEMERE
Many old crafts are practised in this quiet valley town. One of the more unusual is carried on by the Dolmetsch family, who make harpsichords, viols and other early instruments.

SCALE
0 1 2 3 4 5 MILES

Wharf on the River Wey, Guildford.

GUILDFORD
An ancient county town, and modern home of Surrey University, Guildford lies on a beautiful stretch of the River Wey, owned by the National Trust. The High Street, with its 17th-century Guildhall and old posting inn, The Angel, runs down to the river, where pleasure craft glide between locks and inlets lined by 18th-century mills and pubs.

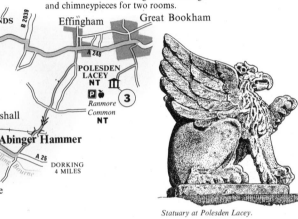
Drawing-room, Hatchlands.

HATCHLANDS
This red-brick house, begun in 1756, contains the first known decorative work of Robert Adam. He designed the ceilings and chimneypieces for two rooms.

SHERE
In the Tilling Bourne Valley, where weeping willows dip to the river, rests the village of Shere. Here Tudor, 17th-century and Victorian cottages have settled around the restored Norman church to form one of the prettiest villages in Surrey. High points on the timbered heathlands that surround it command sweeping views over the Weald to the South Downs.

Statuary at Polesden Lacey.

POLESDEN LACEY
This graceful Regency house, set in a 1000 acre estate, is now the property of the National Trust. It was the home of the dramatist Sheridan and, later, of Mrs Ronald Greville, intimate friend of Edward VII. She lent the house to the future King George VI and Queen Elizabeth for their honeymoon. It is filled with fine paintings, porcelain and furnishings bequeathed to the nation with the house.

CHIDDINGFOLD
Glass-making flourished at Chiddingfold in medieval times, producing windows for famous churches such as Westminster Abbey and St George's Chapel at Windsor. Some of the work of the early craftsmen is displayed in the 13th-century village church. The half-timbered Crown Inn, said to be the oldest licensed house in Surrey, was originally a 13th-century guest-house for travellers on the Pilgrims' Way between Winchester and Canterbury.

Crown Inn, Chiddingfold.

...worth Arboretum.

WINKWORTH ARBORETUM
This is a place for tree-lovers. A 95 acre hillside owned by the National Trust has been laid out to display rare trees which stand out among the common British species. The changes of season wash the Arboretum in a range of vivid colours. Apart from the spring and autumn leaf tints, there are bursts of blossom from a comprehensive range of flowering shrubs, including a large and varied collection of azaleas. Below the hill there is a lake which is well stocked with fish.

Blacksmith clock, Abinger Hammer.

ABINGER HAMMER
'Hammer' refers to the constant pounding of the village forges, long since silent. But the name is still appropriate because of a clock with a model blacksmith who hammers the hour on his bell. The village is now a centre for watercress growing.

Following history and trout streams out of Winchester

Around Winchester, ancient capital of England and living shrine of its history, two rivers break out to flow down valleys lined by water meadows. These are the famous trout streams of the Test and Itchen, where an angler can spend several hundred pounds for a season's fishing. When they invaded Hampshire, the Danes sailed up the rivers that now wind between the thatched and timbered cottages of the historic villages on their banks.

(1) Winchester to Farley Mount Leave the city on the A3090 following the signposts for Romsey. By the speed delimit sign, turn right into Kilham Lane and continue to the T-junction. Turn left, and after 1½ m. go straight ahead at the crossroads and continue for about 1½ m. to Farley Mount.

(2) Farley Mount to Romsey Leave the monument, return to the road junction and turn left. At the next junction turn left to Ashley. Go through Ashley and at the next junction turn left, continuing for 1½ m. into King's Somborne. Turn left at the T-junction in the village on to the road signposted to Braishfield. Keep straight ahead through Braishfield, following the Romsey signs. After about 2 m., at the T-junction with the A31, turn right into Romsey and right again on the A3057 to the town centre.

(3) Romsey to Mottisfont Abbey. Leave the town on the A3057, following the signs for Stockbridge. After 3½ m. turn left on to the road signposted to Mottisfont, crossing two arms of the River Test to enter Mottisfont. Bear right in the village to reach the abbey.

(4) Mottisfont Abbey to Stockbridge Leave the abbey and turn right, continuing for 3½ m. along the Test Valley to Houghton. Turn left along the straggling village street, following the signs for Stockbridge. At the crossroads with the A30 turn right, crossing the River Test, to enter Stockbridge.

(5) Stockbridge to Wherwell Return along the A30 to the crossroads and there turn right on to the road signposted to Longstock. Continue on this road through Longstock and Goodworth Clatford to Upper Clatford. There, at the beginning of the village, turn right to cross the river and pass the church. Turn right at the T-junction which follows, and after ¼ m. turn right on to the A3057, following the signpost to Wherwell. After 1 m. turn left on to the B3420 and into Wherwell.

(6) Wherwell to Freefolk and Laverstoke Leave the village on the B3048 signposted to Longparish. After 2½ m. cross the A303 at the staggered crossroads, still following the Longparish signs. After about 1 m., in Middleton, turn right on to the road signposted to Barton Stacey. Cross three bridges in quick succession, and immediately turn left to follow the River Test for about 3 m. Turn left at the T-junction, go under the A34 and follow the road into Whitchurch. Turn right on to the B3400 near the White Hart Inn to Freefolk and Laverstoke.

(7) Freefolk and Laverstoke to Alresford Leave Laverstoke on the B3400 towards Overton, where the paper mills are the world's largest makers of banknote paper. About 1 m. beyond Overton is the source of the River Test. To visit the source, turn left on to the road to Ashe and soon afterwards turn left by the church. A footpath on the left leads across meadows to the spring. The route continues along the B3400 to the next crossroads by Dean Gate Inn. There turn right on the road signposted to Steventon, Jane Austen's birthplace, though the house in which she was born is no longer standing. Turn left in Steventon following the signpost to North Waltham. Bear right into North Waltham and then left on to the road signposted to Axford. At the junction with the A30, by the Wheatsheaf Hotel, turn left and immediately right on to the minor road signposted to Axford. Go under the M3 and after ½ m. turn left, following the signpost to Dummer. At the T-junction turn right and bear right at the church, on to the road signposted to Farleigh. At the junction with the B3046 turn right, signposted Preston Candover. Stay on this road to Old Alresford. At the A31 turn right and soon afterwards turn left into New Alresford.

(8) Alresford to Tichborne Leave New Alresford on the B3046 signposted to Cheriton. After 2 m. turn right on to the minor road signposted to Tichborne.

(9) Tichborne to Avington Park Continue through the village, and after ½ m. fork left. At the junction with the A31 go straight over into Ovington. Turn right opposite the church and continue parallel with the River Itchen for about 2 m., then turn right. Avington Park is on the left.

(10) Avington Park to Winchester Leave the house and turn right. At the T-junction turn right again into Avington village. Just beyond the village turn right on to the road signposted to Easton. At the T-junction by the Cricketers' Inn turn left and then immediately right, to follow the signs for Winchester. At the junction with the A33, keep ahead for Winchester city centre.

INFORMATION

Places of interest *Avington Park:* May to Sept., Sat., Sun. and Bank Hols., afternoons. *Mottisfont Abbey:* Grounds only, Apr. to Sept., Tues. to Sat., 2.30-6 p.m. Whistler Room and Cellarium, Wed. and Sat. afternoons. *Romsey Abbey:* Daily.

Events *Romsey:* Carnival, June. Agricultural show, Sept. *Tichborne:* The Tichborne Dole, Tichborne House park, 2.30 p.m., March 25.

Information City Offices, Colebrook Street, Winchester (Tel. Winchester 68166).

Towns with easy access to Winchester:

Andover	14 m.	Lymington	28 m.
Basingstoke	18 m.	Newbury	25 m.
Chichester	35 m.	Portsmouth	27 m.

The River Test near Stockbridge.

STOCKBRIDGE
The town stands on the Test, widely considered the best trout stream in England. Though the right to fish may cost several hundred pounds for a season, there is usually a waiting list. The town consists of a single straight wide street spanning the river valley. There is an 1810 town hall with its clock in a turret or cupola, and two coaching inns still survive to recall the pre-railway days. Marsh Court, 1 mile south, was designed and built by Sir Edwin Lutyens in 1901-4. It is one of the few large houses in Britain built of chalk.

Mottisfont Abbey.

MOTTISFONT ABBEY
What survives, under the protection of the National Trust, is an 18th-century reconstruction of a Tudor house built within the walls of a ruined 13th-century abbey. One side is a mixture of 12th-century wall with Tudor and Georgian windows. There is a handsome long gallery and basement dining-room in what was part of the monks' cellar.

The St Barbe monument, Romsey church.

ROMSEY
Because it did double-duty as the parish church, Romsey's 12th-century abbey escaped destruction at the Dissolution of the Monasteries in 1539. It stands on the site of a religious foundation, dated AD 907, of which King Alfred's granddaughter, Aelfleda, was first abbess. In the Civil War, Royalists barricaded themselves in the abbey and the north wall bears the marks of Roundhead cannonballs. Once a woollen town, Romsey has a long connection with brewing, and the local brewery has records going back to 1770, but is probably much older. The Mountbatten family home is near by, in Lord Palmerston's former mansion Broadlands.

SCALE
0   1   2   3   4   5 MI

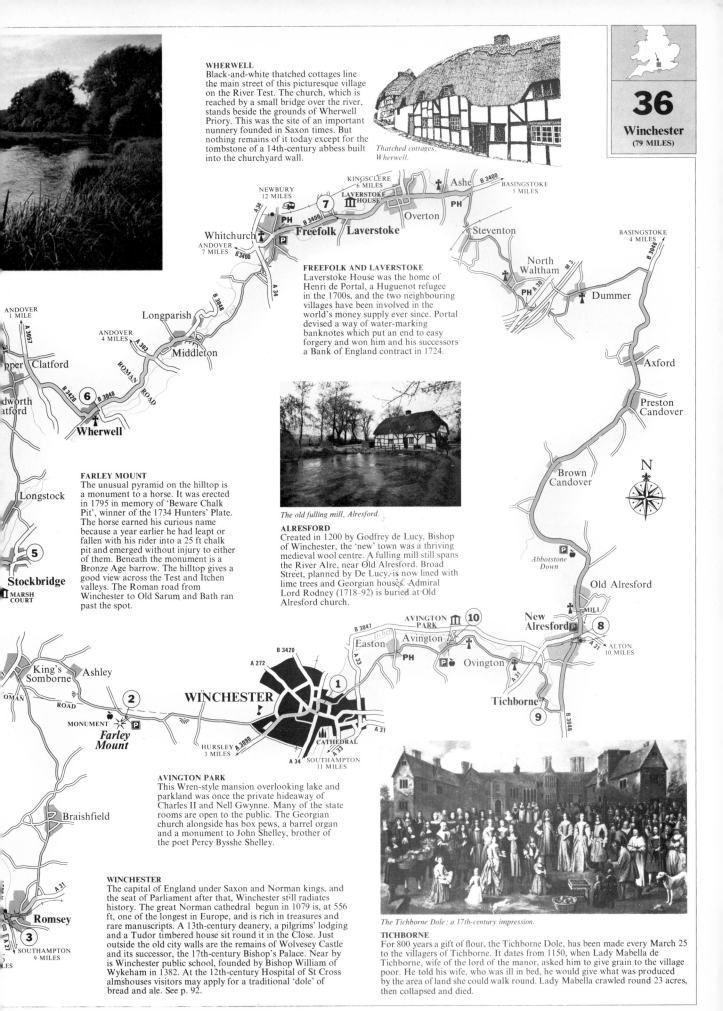

WHERWELL

Black-and-white thatched cottages line the main street of this picturesque village on the River Test. The church, which is reached by a small bridge over the river, stands beside the grounds of Wherwell Priory. This was the site of an important nunnery founded in Saxon times. But nothing remains of it today except for the tombstone of a 14th-century abbess built into the churchyard wall.

Thatched cottages, Wherwell.

FREEFOLK AND LAVERSTOKE

Laverstoke House was the home of Henri de Portal, a Huguenot refugee in the 1700s, and the two neighbouring villages have been involved in the world's money supply ever since. Portal devised a way of water-marking banknotes which put an end to easy forgery and won him and his successors a Bank of England contract in 1724.

FARLEY MOUNT

The unusual pyramid on the hilltop is a monument to a horse. It was erected in 1795 in memory of 'Beware Chalk Pit', winner of the 1734 Hunters' Plate. The horse earned his curious name because a year earlier he had leapt or fallen with his rider into a 25 ft chalk pit and emerged without injury to either of them. Beneath the monument is a Bronze Age barrow. The hilltop gives a good view across the Test and Itchen valleys. The Roman road from Winchester to Old Sarum and Bath ran past the spot.

The old fulling mill, Alresford.

ALRESFORD

Created in 1200 by Godfrey de Lucy, Bishop of Winchester, the 'new' town was a thriving medieval wool centre. A fulling mill still spans the River Alre, near Old Alresford. Broad Street, planned by De Lucy, is now lined with lime trees and Georgian houses. Admiral Lord Rodney (1718–92) is buried at Old Alresford church.

AVINGTON PARK

This Wren-style mansion overlooking lake and parkland was once the private hideaway of Charles II and Nell Gwynne. Many of the state rooms are open to the public. The Georgian church alongside has box pews, a barrel organ and a monument to John Shelley, brother of the poet Percy Bysshe Shelley.

WINCHESTER

The capital of England under Saxon and Norman kings, and the seat of Parliament after that, Winchester still radiates history. The great Norman cathedral begun in 1079 is, at 556 ft, one of the longest in Europe, and is rich in treasures and rare manuscripts. A 13th-century deanery, a pilgrims' lodging and a Tudor timbered house sit round it in the Close. Just outside the old city walls are the remains of Wolvesey Castle and its successor, the 17th-century Bishop's Palace. Near by is Winchester public school, founded by Bishop William of Wykeham in 1382. At the 12th-century Hospital of St Cross almshouses visitors may apply for a traditional 'dole' of bread and ale. See p. 92.

The Tichborne Dole; a 17th-century impression.

TICHBORNE

For 800 years a gift of flour, the Tichborne Dole, has been made every March 25 to the villagers of Tichborne. It dates from 1150, when Lady Mabella de Tichborne, wife of the lord of the manor, asked him to give grain to the village poor. He told his wife, who was ill in bed, he would give what was produced by the area of land she could walk round. Lady Mabella crawled round 23 acres, then collapsed and died.

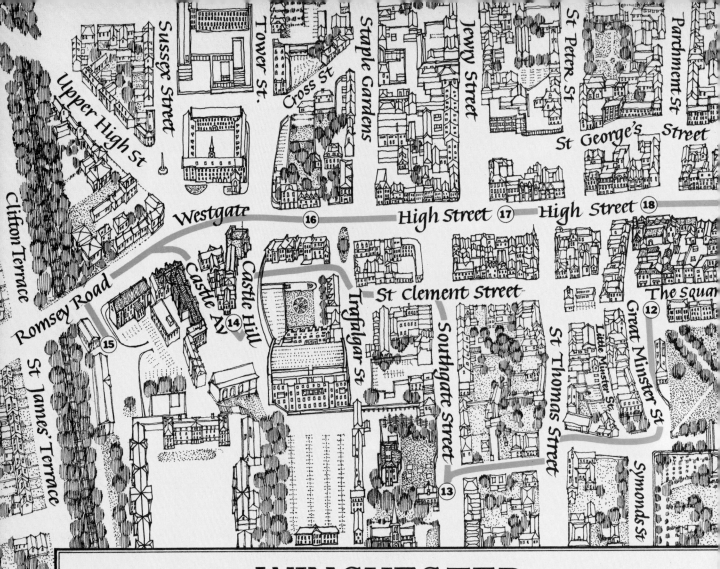

WINCHESTER

*Winchester, ancient capital of England and home of a 600-year-old public school, preserves so
many relics of its romantic past that it is seen to best advantage on foot. This city tour includes
most of its outstanding features, identified below with visiting times where appropriate.*

THINGS TO SEE IN THE CITY

1 Statue of Alfred the Great, who saved Winchester from the Danes; erected in 1901 to mark the 1000th anniversary of his death.

2 Bridge Street, start of a short walk to St Giles Hill, site of a fair and wool-trading centre in the Middle Ages.

3 City Mill, built in 1744. Open Mar. to Oct., Wed. and Sat. 2–5 p.m.; Thurs., Fri., and Bank Hol. Mon. 10 a.m.–1 p.m. Winter, by appointment with warden (Tel. Winchester 3723).

4 St Cross Hospital, 12th-century almshouse still administered as a charity.

5 The Weirs, a favourite river-bank walk alongside remains of the medieval city walls, and skirting the bishop's residence.

6 Wolvesey Castle, built in 1138. Closed to visitors since 1975, for an indefinite period for repairs.

7 College Walk, leading to St Cross Hospital. Guided tours: Apr. to Sept. weekdays, 9 a.m.–noon, 2–5 p.m.; other months, 10.30 a.m.–noon, 2–3.30 p.m.

8 Winchester College, a public school founded in 1382. Guided tours Apr. to Sept., daily, 10 a.m., 11.45 a.m., 2, 3, and 4.30 p.m. Winter, by appointment (Tel. Winchester 64242).

9 Kingsgate, entrance to old walled city, with chapel of St Swithun (open to visitors) over the arch. Many of the houses in Kingsgate Street were given new façades in the 18th century.

10 The Close. Notable buildings include the 15th-century Deanery, 13th-century Pilgrims' Cloister and Pilgrims' Hall (open daily), 16th-century Priory Stables, and houses dating from the 17th century. The four houses that make up Dome Alley were all built in 1663. Cheyney Court used to be a seat of justice for the Soke—the outer city.

11 The cathedral. The longest Gothic church in Europe (556 ft), contains Mary Tudor's wedding chair. Normally open 8 a.m.–6.30 p.m. Library, weekdays in summer, 10.30 a.m.–12.30 p.m. (except Mon.), 2.30–4.30 p.m.; winter, Wed. and Sat. only.

12 City Museum, The Square. Museum open every Sun. 2–4.30 p.m.; weekdays 10 a.m.–4 p.m. (Nov. to Feb.), 5 p.m. (Mar., Apr., Sept., Oct.), 6 p.m. (May to Aug.). Closed Christmas and Good Friday.

13 Royal Hampshire Regiment Museum in Serle's House, regimental H.Q. Open Mon. to Fri. 10 a.m.–12.30 p.m., 2–4 p.m.

14 Castle Hall, containing King Arthur's Round Table. Open (when courts not sitting) at weekends. Closed Christmas Day and Good Friday.

15 Royal Green Jackets museum, summer, Mon. to Fri. 10 a.m.–12.30 p.m., 2–4.30 p.m.; Sat. 2.30–4.30 p.m.; winter, Mon. to Fri. 10.30 a.m.–12.30 p.m., 2–4 p.m. Closed Bank Hols.

16 Westgate Museum, in medieval city gateway. Formerly a prison. Opening times as for City Museum. View of the city from the roof.

17 Old Guildhall (now Lloyds Bank). Curfew which has tolled every night since 1066 is rung from a turret on the roof.

18 City Cross, erected in the 15th century to mark the site of the produce market. It was restored in 1865.

19 New Guildhall, opened in 1873 to replace the old one. Picture gallery open Tues. to Sat. 11 a.m.–5 p.m., Sun. 2–5 p.m.

20 Abbey House, official residence of the mayor. Public gardens occupy the site of a nunnery founded by King Alfred's wife, Ethelswitha.

CAR PARKS: Broadway (near King Alfred statue), Chesil Street, Colebrook Street (cathedral end), Tower Street (near Westgate Museum), Jewry Street (behind public library), St George's Street, Worthy Lane (continuation of Sussex Street).
INFORMATION OFFICE: City Offices, Colebrook Street (Tel. Winchester 65406).

A walking tour of England's first capital
WINCHESTER

Winchester used to be England's capital: it remains one of her greatest glories. The Ancient Britons were here, and the Romans. The Danes came—to be flung out by Alfred the Great. Henry VIII and Cromwell left it a shambles. The city has survived every disaster, even to a 20th-century one which required a team of divers to avert it—there is a statue of their leader in the cathedral.

Winchester was already the most important city of the ancient kingdom of Wessex when the Romans arrived. The Normans made it their capital when they invaded in 1066, and it was not until another 100 years or so that London began to supersede it as England's principal city.

In spite of wars, fires and generations of redevelopment, many fine buildings have survived. The noblest of them all is the great cathedral, started by Bishop Walkelyn in 1079. It enshrines the ancient glory of Winchester, smaller than many county towns, which lies in a fold of the Hampshire Downs beside the River Itchen. Its former status as a seat of kings is recalled by the statue of Alfred the Great that stands, sword held high, at the foot of The Broadway.

But Winchester's roots go even deeper than the time of Alfred. About 300 years before Christ, Iron Age men fortified a site on St Catherine's Hill, a mile south of the cathedral, and their grass-covered defences can still be seen. Relics are displayed in the City Museum.

There was a cathedral on the same site at Winchester before the present one: a Saxon cathedral, built in the 7th century and known as the Old Minster. One of its bishops was St Swithun, a man so close to nature that he wanted to be buried where the rain would fall on him. He died in 862, and was laid to rest in the graveyard. But on July 15, in the year 971, his remains were removed to what was considered a worthier home inside the cathedral. According to legend the saint was so angry that he made it rain for 40 days—and the tradition grew that rain on July 15, St Swithun's Day, means that there is a long spell of wet weather ahead.

How the school began

Winchester was a wool centre in the Middle Ages, and a great trading fair on St Giles Hill attracted merchants from Europe every year. The charter authorising the fair was held by the bishops, who spent the income on the cathedral. The same funds, in 1382, enabled Bishop William of Wykeham to found Winchester College.

Winchester flourished until Henry VIII's post-Reformation fury destroyed some of its finest buildings in 1538–9. The cathedral survived, but during the Civil War in the next century, when Royalist Winchester was besieged and captured by the Parliamentarians, the cathedral narrowly escaped demolition. At the same time most of the Norman castle was destroyed.

In 1683, after the Restoration, a new royal palace was designed by Sir Christopher Wren. Winchester, however, never regained its status as a seat of the monarchy. Work on the still-

THE CATHEDRAL *Begun in 1079, it was built mainly of stone from the Isle of Wight and Normandy. The south end, seen here, houses the library, which contains priceless Bibles and old manuscripts.*

BISHOP'S TOMB *Left: 12th-century cathedral carving in black marble, depicting homage to a bishop. Right: Mortuary chest of King Canute, in the presbytery near the high altar. His wife, Emma, also buried in the cathedral, was the mother of Edward the Confessor, who was crowned at Winchester. Canute was a popular king, and both he and his wife are honoured as benefactors of the city.*

OLD WINCHESTER *Kingsgate, 14th-century entrance to the city, whose medieval walls can still be seen in places. A little church above the arch is dedicated to St Swithun, who died in 862, two years after he had built a wall to protect the city against the Danes.*

WYKEHAMIST HEROES *The War Cloister at Winchester College, commemorating old boys killed in the two world wars. Their names are engraved on plaques on the walls surrounding a cross.*

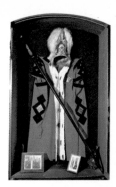

BUTTER CROSS *The City Cross, known locally as the Butter Cross because of its association with the produce market. The St John the Baptist figure is an original from the 15th century.*

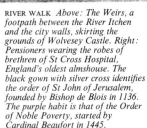

RIVER WALK *Above: The Weirs, a footpath between the River Itchen and the city walls, skirting the grounds of Wolvesey Castle. Right: Pensioners wearing the robes of brethren of St Cross Hospital, England's oldest almshouse. The black gown with silver cross identifies the order of St John of Jerusalem, founded by Bishop de Blois in 1136. The purple habit is that of the Order of Noble Poverty, started by Cardinal Beaufort in 1445.*

CITY MILL *The mill, near King Alfred's statue by the River Itchen, was originally monastic property, but was granted to the city by royal charter in 1554, after the Reformation. The present building was erected in 1744, and the bridge beside it in 1813. The bridge replaced the original one built over the Itchen by St Swithun, then Bishop of Winchester, in the 9th century. The mill, now used as a Youth Hostel, belongs to the National Trust. It is a starting point for attractive riverside walks in both directions.*

THE ROUND TABLE *The table, 18 ft across and of unknown age, was made in the Middle Ages to commemorate King Arthur and his knights. It hangs in the Great Hall of Winchester Castle.*

unfinished palace was stopped after Queen Anne's death, and it later served as a prison and barracks in the wars with France. A surviving wing is now the bishop's house.

Few cathedrals can match Winchester's links with famous figures of the past. King Canute, King William Rufus, Izaak Walton, author of the *Compleat Angler*, and the novelist Jane Austen are among those buried within its walls. In 1554 Mary Tudor married Philip of Spain in the cathedral, and her wedding chair still stands near the high altar.

The most surprising of the cathedral's many memorials is a statue to William Walker, a deep-sea diver who helped to save the cathe-dral from disaster at the beginning of this century. Immense cracks had appeared, and in 1905 a survey revealed that part of the building stood on a timber raft above a swamp. There was so much water that a diver had to be employed to strengthen the foundations. Walker laboured for five years. It has been estimated that he and his men placed 25,800 bags of concrete, 114,900 concrete blocks and almost a million bricks beneath the cathedral.

Surrounded by ancient walls, the cathedral and its close form the heart of Winchester. But the city has many other notable buildings. Westgate, at the top of High Street, dates mainly from the 13th century and has a small museum whose exhibits include a large oak chest in which the civic treasure was triple-locked at the end of the 16th century.

The Great Hall, near by, is all that remains of the castle built by William the Conqueror and demolished by Cromwell's troops in 1651. It houses a medieval representation of King Arthur's Round Table. The royal courts of justice, scene of many famous trials, sit here.

At the opposite end of the city, near the river and the public school, Wolvesey Castle is a reminder of the days when strongholds were built by bishops as well as by kings and powerful barons. A combined palace and fortress, it was built by Henry de Blois in the 12th century and was occupied by Mary Tudor before her marriage.

Elderly men in flowing robes are a familiar sight in Winchester. They are pensioners, known as 'brethren', from St Cross Hospital, founded by Henry de Blois in 1136 and the oldest almshouse in Britain. Visitors may still request the traditional Wayfarer's Dole—a piece of bread and a mug of ale.

The hospital was extended in 1445 when Cardinal Henry Beaufort founded the Order of Noble Poverty. Members wear mulberry cloaks, while those belonging to the order founded by De Blois are distinguished by black habits and silver cross.

The old Guildhall in High Street is now a bank, but from the turret on its roof the cur-few, initiated by the Normans in 1066 to signal the time when the streets had to be cleared, is still rung at eight o'clock every night. Thus, high above a temple of modern commerce, the bell tolls for a way of life long ended but always brought to mind by a visit to Winchester.

Smugglers' haunts and a spa in the Garden of England

The dignified town of Royal Tunbridge Wells came into being because a 17th-century rake found that the waters of a lonely spring helped his overburdened liver. It is set in the Garden of England, amid hopfields and orchards, where this tour wanders round a gently rolling landscape dotted with towns and villages rich in smugglers' tales and stately homes dating from Norman and Tudor times.

(1) Royal Tunbridge Wells to Bayham Abbey Leave the town on the A267, following the signposts for Eastbourne. By the Bull Inn, turn left on to the B2169, following the signpost to Lamberhurst. After 2 m. pass Frant Victorian railway station at Bells Yew Green. After another 2½ m. the entrance to Bayham Abbey ruins is on the left.

(2) Bayham Abbey to Lamberhurst Return to the B2169 and turn left. After ½ m., at the crossroads near the Elephant Head Inn on Hook Green, turn left, following the Pembury signpost. After another ½ m., at a junction where the road bears left, turn right, following the Lamberhurst signpost. The entrance to Owl House gardens is on the left. Continue for ½ m. and turn right on to the A21, entering Lamberhurst.

(3) Lamberhurst to Hawkhurst Leave the village by the A21, following the signpost to Hastings. To visit Bedgebury Pinetum, an experimental conifer nursery which forms part of the 2000 acre Bedgebury Forest, turn left after 2½ m. on to the B2079. The pinetum was planted because London air pollution seriously affected young conifers in the botanical gardens at Kew. Return to the A21, turn left into Flimwell and left on to the A268, following the signpost for Hawkhurst. Flimwell church is on the right. Continue on the road for 3 m., then enter Hawkhurst.

(4) Hawkhurst to Sissinghurst Castle In Hawkhurst, keep straight ahead on the A268 and continue for about 2 m. more to the edge of Sandhurst village. Here turn left to follow the road signposted to Benenden, where cider is still brewed. At the B2086 turn right by the old pump into the village and left by the Bull Inn. (The girls' school where Princess Anne was a pupil lies in the opposite direction and is not open to the public.) After 1¼ m. turn right at a T-junction and follow the road for 3½ m. to join the A262 into Biddenden. At the village green fork left, still on the A262, and continue for 3½ m. to Sissinghurst. The castle—which is really not a castle at all, but a former prison camp used in the Napoleonic wars—lies up a road to the right, just past the first Sissinghurst sign and before the village centre.

(5) Sissinghurst Castle to Cranbrook Return to the main road, turning right into the village centre. By the Bull Inn, turn left following the signpost for Benenden. At the crossroads turn right following the Cranbrook signpost. After 1½ m. turn left on to the B2189 and into the middle of Cranbrook, once an important centre for the cloth trade.

(6) Cranbrook to Goudhurst Leaving the town, turn left on to the A229, follow-ing the Hawkhurst signpost. After ¼ m. turn right on to a minor road and at the T-junction turn right on to the B2085. After 1½ m. turn left on to the A262 and 1 m. later enter Goudhurst, one of Kent's most attractive villages.

(7) Goudhurst to Penshurst Go through the village and after 1½ m., where the road bears sharp left, turn right, following the signpost for Horsmonden. In just under ½ m. fork right, passing Horsmonden church on the right. Go straight ahead at a small crossroads and at the T-junction turn left. After about ¾ m. go through Horsmonden and, 1½ m. later, Brenchley. After 1 m. cross the B2160 following the signs for Tonbridge. After ¾ m. pass Crittenden House, whose gardens are sometimes open to visitors. After another ½ m. go straight across the B2015, and after a further 1½ m. turn left on to the B2017, following the signpost for Tonbridge. At the A21 junction turn right and continue into Tonbridge. (The Medway bridge and castle are signposted.) In Tonbridge turn left on to the A26, following the Royal Tunbridge Wells signpost. After just over 1 m. turn right on to the B2176 and after 4 m. enter Penshurst, setting for one of the finest of England's stately homes.

(8) Penshurst to Royal Tunbridge Wells Leave the village, following the road left past Penshurst church until it becomes the B2188. After 3½ m. turn left on to the A264 and continue 3 m. into Royal Tunbridge Wells.

INFORMATION

Places of interest *Bayham Abbey:* Daily. *Bedgebury National Pinetum:* Gardens, daily. *Cranbrook:* Museum, Wed. and Sat., afternoons. *The Owl House:* Gardens only, Mon., Wed., Fri., Bank Hol. weekends, 11 a.m.-7 p.m.; Sun., 3-7 p.m. *Penshurst Place:* Easter Sat. to Oct. 2, daily (except Mon. and Fri.), 2-6 p.m. Bank Hols., 11.30 a.m.-6 p.m. *Scotney Castle:* Apr. to Oct., Wed. to Sun. and Spring and Late Summer Bank Hol. Mon., afternoons. *Sissinghurst Castle:* Gardens only, Apr. to mid-Oct., Mon. to Fri., 12 noon-6.30 p.m.; Sat., Sun., and Spring and Late Summer Bank Hol. Mon., 10 a.m.-6.30 p.m. *Tonbridge Castle:* May to Sept., daily. Grounds, all year, daily.

Craft workshops *Hawkhurst:* Harris Looms. Craftsmen-made handlooms. Mon. to Fri. *Langton Pottery:* Langton Green, Mon. to Sat.

Events *Biddenden:* Dole, Easter Mon. *Tunbridge Wells:* Antiques Fair, July; Carnival, July.

Nature trails *Bedgebury:* Pinetum. Guide available. Also a forest trail near by.

Information *Tunbridge Wells:* Assembly Hall, Crescent Road (Tel. Tunbridge Wells 26121).

Towns with easy access to Royal Tunbridge Wells:

Ashford	32 m.	Hastings	28 m.
East Grinstead	14 m.	Lewes	24 m.

Armour in the Great Hall, Penshurst Place.

PENSHURST
Penshurst Place, ancestral home of the Sidney family, dominates the village. Sir Philip Sidney, great courtier, statesman and scholar in the reign of Elizabeth I, was born here in 1554. Although the manor dates from Norman times, the present mansion was begun in 1340 by Sir John de Pulteney, a rich wool merchant and four times Mayor of London. It was greatly enlarged in the 16th century and has remained in the hands of the Sidney family until the present day. The house and its walled garden form a unit. Inside are the richly furnished state rooms as well as a toy museum.

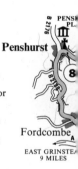

The Pantiles, Royal Tunbridge Wells, as it was in 1748.

ROYAL TUNBRIDGE WELLS
An elegant town, Royal Tunbridge Wells is still a functioning spa, with spring waters strong in iron salts. Until the springs and their reputed medicinal properties were discovered by the hard-drinking, fast-living Lord North in 1606, the area was uninhabited forest. In a very short time, as royalty and courtiers began 'taking the waters', Royal Tunbridge Wells rivalled Bath as a spa and acquired its Royal prefix. It was, in the 18th century, one of the favourite resorts of Beau Nash (1674–1762).

SCALE

0   1   2   3   4   5 MILES

GOUDHURST

On a hill, 400 ft above the Weald of Kent, Goudhurst has a 13th to 15th-century church, with marks on its walls attributed to archers sharpening their arrows before leaving to fight at Agincourt. The tower was used as a look-out position in both world wars. The church register records a raid on the village by a robber band in 1747 and the burial of George Kingsmill, leader of the robbers, who was killed by a lead bullet. The Star and Eagle Inn was once joined to the church by a tunnel and used as a base by one of the smuggling gangs which flourished in the area. Anyways, the gang's look-out house, still stands, with windows overlooking the main street in both directions. The gang was finally smashed by the villagers in 1796, and the leader's body left hanging from a gibbet on Horsmonden Heath. The abrupt bend in the main street is hazardous to traffic, but the effect of buildings at many levels on the slopes adds to the attraction of Goudhurst. There are many old houses of weatherboard and tile in the village, several of which are preserved by the National Trust.

Goudhurst under snow.

CRANBROOK

A prosperous wool town in the 14th century, Cranbrook was once bigger than nearby Maidstone. St Dunstan's Church dates from this period and is known as the Cathedral of the Weald. The 70 ft tall windmill built in 1814 is still in working order.

SISSINGHURST CASTLE

The gardens at Sissinghurst Castle are among the finest in England. They were created from a wilderness by the poet and author Vita Sackville-West and her husband Sir Harold Nicolson, who bought the property in 1930 after it had fallen into decay. There are a series of gardens, including a rose garden, a cottage garden and a white garden—laid out with white flowering and silver-leaved plants. The house is not really a castle, but a Tudor tower house built in 1535 by Sir John Baker, Speaker of the House of Commons in the reigns of Henry VIII, Edward VI and Mary. A view of the whole garden and a wide stretch of the Kentish Weald can be seen from the tower.

The white garden, Sissinghurst Castle.

HAWKHURST

William Penn, founder of the American state of Pennsylvania, owned ironworks here in the 17th century. Sir William Herschel, the astronomer (1738–1822), discovered the planet Uranus while working at Hawkhurst. In the 18th century the Hawkhurst Gang of smugglers are said to have used the Royal Oak Inn as their headquarters. The old inn is now surrounded by weatherboard houses.

Bayham Abbey.

BAYHAM ABBEY

The original abbey, now in ruins, dates from the early 13th century. It was built on an attractive stretch of the River Teise, which forms the Kent-Sussex border. On the Kent side of the river there is a Tudor-style private house which is also called Bayham Abbey.

Scotney Castle, near Lamberhurst.

LAMBERHURST

Once an important iron-producing centre, Lamberhurst was also notorious for its illicit trade with France. The 16th-century timbered Owl House was a smugglers' haunt, so named because of the owl hoot which the smugglers used as a warning signal. In a wooded valley near the town are the ruins of the 14th-century moated Scotney Castle, set in a carefully landscaped garden. The new castle was built between 1837 and 1843, and is privately owned. The 14th-century church has been twice restored, the last time in 1964.

dandy, who turned it into a gambling spot. The first shops and colonnades were built in the late 17th and early 18th centuries. The tiling, or paving stones, which gave the name 'Pantiles' to the oldest street in the town, were laid, at the request of Queen Anne, in 1700. The 17th-century church of King Charles the Martyr (named after Charles I who spent much time here) has a wooden cupola and a white marble font which came from a Wren church in London.

England's look-out point to the south

From the open plains of the Sussex Weald, the land moves up into the downlands and a land of views. Near Brightling Needle, where lookout was kept against a Napoleonic invasion, astronomers at Herstmonceux scan the skies. From the top of Gibraltar Tower, built over a military museum, it is said that 40 towers and spires can be seen. But 'Mad Jack' Fuller wanted more. He added a spire, a tower and other fantasies.

1 Pevensey to Herstmonceux Castle From Pevensey Castle take the A27 towards Bexhill. Join the A259 and turn left just beyond the traffic-lights, following the signpost to Wartling. At the Y-junction fork right for Wartling. Bear sharp left in the village and drive ¾ m. to a roadside car park on the left, signposted Isaac Newton Telescope. (For a detour through the grounds of Herstmonceux Castle, take the private road on the far side of the car park. After ¾ m. join the public road at the church. Turn right, and continue for 1¾ m. to the A271. Right again, then first left to Bodle Street Green, rejoining the main route after ¼ m.)

2 Herstmonceux Castle to Brightling Needle From the car park turn left and continue to the junction with the A271. Turn left for Windmill Hill. After ½ m. fork right and turn right at the next junction for Bodle Street Green. After 1½ m. fork left at the large-windowed inn and carry on for 2¾ m. past all left turnings to a Y-junction, signposted Dallington-Narrow Road, and turn sharp right. Follow the winding lanes to Dallington, bearing right on to the B2096. After 350 yds, take the left turn signposted Brightling/Bateman's. At the next junction go left. Over the crossroads is Brightling Needle.

3 Brightling Needle to Burwash Continue along this road and after 1 m. take a sharp left turn, signposted Burwash. Continue for 1 m., then turn left into Bateman's Lane for Bateman's, Rudyard Kipling's home. Return down Bateman's Lane and turn left to Burwash.

4 Burwash to Heathfield Park Carry on west, along the A265 and after 6 m., at the crossroads at the top of the hill, turn sharp left on to the B2203. Heathfield Park is on the left.

5 Heathfield Park to Horam Leaving the park, turn left and bear left again, following the park's stone wall. Then hairpin right at the Y-junction signposted to Vine's Cross. At the B2203, turn left for Horam.

6 Horam to Rotherfield Turn right on to the A267, following signs for Mayfield for 5¼ m., until it veers right at Butcher's Cross. Turn left, signposted to Rotherfield.

7 Rotherfield to Fletching This stage through Ashdown Forest is ideal for picnics. Leave Rotherfield on the B2100 signposted to Crowborough. After about 1¼ m., turn left on to the minor road signposted to Uckfield. After 1 m. the road forks right. Cross Crowborough Common and reach the A26. Turn left, and after 1¼ m. turn right on to the minor road signposted Duddleswell/Camp

Hill. At the B2026 turn left, then immediately right on to a minor heathland road signposted to Nutley. After 1¾ m. turn left on to the A22. After 500 yds go right, signposted Fletching.

8 Fletching to Glynde Take the first left after Fletching church, continue to the junction with the A272 and turn right. After 200 yds turn left on to the B2102 signposted Isfield. Where the B2102 veers sharply left 1 m. later, keep straight ahead on the minor road signposted to Isfield. After 2½ m. turn right at the T-junction on to the road signposted for Lewes. At the A26, 1 m. later, turn right, still following the Lewes signpost. After 1¾ m. turn left on to the road signposted to Ringmer. At the B2192 in Ringmer turn right, and ½ m. later turn left, signposted to Glynde 2 m. away.

9 Glynde to Drusillas Cross the river and the railway in Glynde, and as the road swings sharp right round the station, turn left up the steep hill. Then turn left on to the A27 signposted Eastbourne. After 4¾ m. turn right. Drusillas is on the left.

10 Drusillas to Alfriston Turn left on to the B2108 and drive 1¼ m. to Alfriston.

11 Alfriston to Pevensey Return along the B2108 towards the A27 and take the first right turn, signposted to Litlington. Turn right at the first T-junction, and left at the second, for Wilmington. After about 1¼ m. the Long Man, a giant figure cut into the chalk hill above the village, is on the right. At the A27 turn right for Polegate. After 1¾ m. turn left on to the A22, then right to rejoin the A27 for the 5 m. drive back to Pevensey.

INFORMATION

Places of interest *Alfriston Clergy House:* Apr. to Christmas Eve, daily, 11 a.m.-6 p.m. *Bateman's:* Mar. to Oct., Mon. to Thur., Sat., Sun. and Good Friday, afternoons; June to Sept., Mon. to Thur. mornings also. *Fletching:* Model village, any reasonable time. *Glynde Place:* Easter, May to beginning Oct., Thur., Sat., Sun., Spring and Late Summer Bank Hol., afternoons. *Heathfield:* Wild Life Park and Gibraltar Tower Car Museum, daily, 10 a.m.-6 p.m. *Herstmonceux Castle:* grounds, Easter to Sept., Mon. to Fri. afternoons; Sat., Sun. and Bank Hols., 10.30 a.m.-5 p.m. *Horam:* Merrydown Cider and Wine Factory, Apr. to Sept., tours at 10, 10.30 and 11 a.m., 2, 2.30 and 3 p.m. *Pevensey Castle:* All year, weekdays, Sun. afternoons.

Event *Glyndebourne:* Opera season from end May to early Aug.

Information *Eastbourne:* 3 Cornfield Terrace (Tel. Eastbourne 27474). *Lewes:* 187 High Street (Tel. Lewes 6151).

Towns with easy access to Pevensey:

Brighton	25 m.	Hastings	12 m.
Eastbourne	5 m.	Tunbridge Wells	31 m.

Ashdown Forest, near Fletching.

FLETCHING
On the approaches to Fletching lies the tree-broken heathland which forms the southern part of Ashdown Forest, a delightful picnicking spot. The village of Fletching contains a model village that incorporates, somewhat surprisingly, a miniature Stonehenge and a Chinese pagoda.

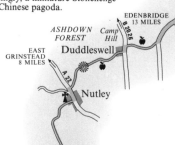

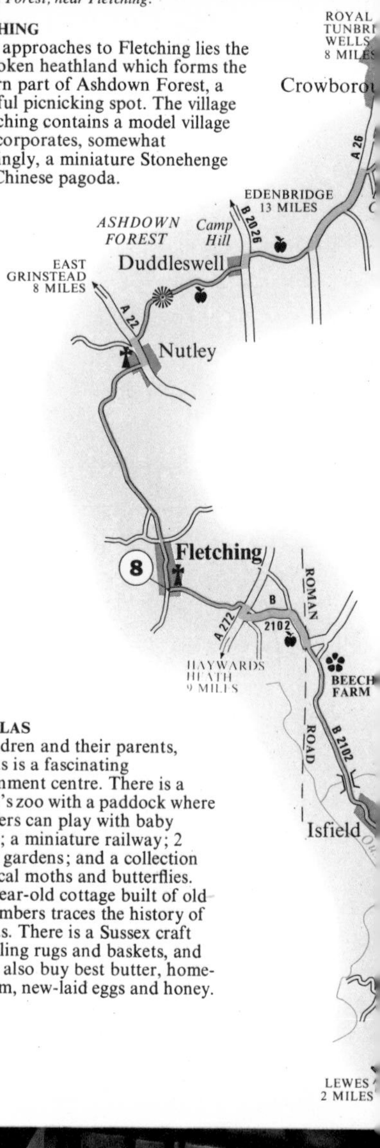

DRUSILLAS
For children and their parents, Drusillas is a fascinating entertainment centre. There is a children's zoo with a paddock where youngsters can play with baby animals; a miniature railway; 2 acres of gardens; and a collection of tropical moths and butterflies. A 300-year-old cottage built of old ship's timbers traces the history of Drusillas. There is a Sussex craft shop selling rugs and baskets, and you can also buy best butter, home-made jam, new-laid eggs and honey.

Clergy House, Alfriston.

SCALE

0   1   2   3   4   5 MILES

ROTHERFIELD

Rotherfield is a village of small shops, small inns and a big church dating from about 1200 with a 15th-century tower. Inside is a pre-Reformation fresco with a lively drawing of St Michael, a stained-glass window by the Victorian artist Sir Edward Burne-Jones, and a carved Jacobean pulpit 'begged' from York by a former rector's wife, who happened to be the daughter of the Archbishop of York.

Kipling's study, Bateman's.

BATEMAN'S

Once a neglected but beautiful Jacobean farmhouse, Bateman's was bought in 1902 by 36-year-old Rudyard Kipling, who had won fame as a storyteller and 'poet of empire'. Here he drew upon the folklore and history of Sussex to write *Puck of Pook's Hill*, his poem, 'If', and many other works. Kipling and his wife restored and improved the house, now owned by the National Trust. Kipling's study remains exactly how he left it.

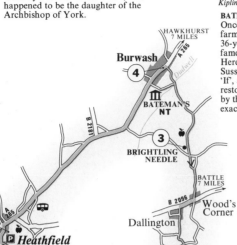

BRIGHTLING NEEDLE

'Mad Jack' Fuller, an eccentric squire of Brightling, built a series of odd buildings around his estate in the early 19th century. His 'follies' include a mock church steeple, a hermit tower and the Brightling Needle, an obelisk erected on the highest spot in the locality. Fuller, who died aged 77 in 1834, is buried under his last 'folly'— a massive pyramid in Brightling churchyard. He is reputed to be entombed sitting up, wearing a top hat and holding a bottle of claret.

Concrete sculpture, Glynde Place.

GLYNDE PLACE

The Elizabethan manor of Glynde Place, built of flint, brick and caen stone, stands on the hill over Glynde village. Among a collection of paintings, bronzes, china, needlework and historical documents is a Rubens sketch, painted on wood, of James I surrounded by angels. Glynde church was built by Bishop Trevor, who redesigned Glynde Place in 1752.

HEATHFIELD PARK

The wildlife and country park at Heathfield is a 200 acre home for animals and birds. There is a military museum in the 60 ft Gibraltar Tower, and a display of veteran cars. Cannons were made here in the 16th century, when Sussex had an iron industry.

HORAM

At Horam the old manor house, rebuilt after fire damage, is the centre of a cider and wine industry. Visitors may see the factory processes and the vineyards, but advance notice should be given. Footpaths in the district, wandering over the typical wealden countryside, are indicated by unusual milestone-type signposts.

Isaac Newton Observatory, Herstmonceux.

HERSTMONCEUX CASTLE

Herstmonceux Castle is more a fortified residence than a military strongpoint. Built during the 15th century, it provided the lady of the house with a chamber so placed that she could keep an eye on the kitchenmaids at work. It is now the home of the Royal Greenwich Observatory and has one of the world's largest optical telescopes, with a 98.2 in. reflector.

ALFRISTON

In the village of Alfriston there is a church so big that it is often called the Cathedral of the Downs. It stands on a knoll beside the Cuckmere River, away from the village centre. Near by is the timber-and-thatch 14th-century Clergy House, the first building acquired by the National Trust. They bought it in 1896—for £10. The façade of the 15th-century Star Inn includes some fine old carved woodwork. Smuggling once thrived in the town.

Elizabethan cannon, Pevensey Castle.

PEVENSEY CASTLE

The site of Pevensey Castle, once on the edge of the sea, has been fortified against invaders from Roman times. The main fortress is a massive 13th-century structure; around it still runs the Roman wall, about 1000 years older. The castle was garrisoned throughout the medieval wars of kings and barons, and guarded the Channel in the days of the Armada. King Alfred is said to have used it while fighting the Danes in the 9th century. During the Second World War it housed British and Canadian troops and the US Army Air Corps.

Map labels: WADHURST 5 MILES, Rotherfield, ROYAL TUNBRIDGE WELLS 11 MILES, Butcher's Cross, HAWKHURST 7 MILES, Burwash, BATEMAN'S NT, BRIGHTLING NEEDLE, BATTLE 7 MILES, Wood's Corner, Dallington, Heathfield, Heathfield Park, Vine's Cross, Horam VINEYARDS, HAILSHAM 5 MILES, Bodle Street Green, Windmill Hill, Herstmonceux, BATTLE 7 MILES, HERSTMONCEUX CASTLE, ISAAC NEWTON TELESCOPE, Wartling, HASTINGS 12 MILES, PEVENSEY CASTLE, EASTBOURNE 5 MILES, Ringmer, Glyndebourne, GLYNDE PLACE, Glynde, BRIGHTON 1 MILES, SOUTH DOWNS, Berwick, Wilmington, Polegate, EASTBOURNE 4 MILES, DRUSILLAS, THE LONG MAN, Alfriston, Litlington, SEAFORD 3 MILES

Castles against the French— oasthouses amid the hops

The spot where William of Normandy defeated King Harold's army to become William the Conqueror in 1066 begins a route full of colour and contrast. Old castles show how England stayed on the defensive against marauding Frenchmen for several centuries. Quaint oasthouses stand amid the fields where hops grow. Hammer ponds remain as the last traces of ironworks where local ore was smelted with oak wood and hammered into shape by water power. Traces of maritime history as far inland as Tenterden show how the receding sea has changed the shape of the countryside and the industries of its people.

1 Battle to Bodiam From Battle Abbey go up the High Street, past the George Hotel, and turn first right (signposted Car Park) into Mount Street—which eventually becomes Caldbec Hill—before running into open country. This is the hill where William of Normandy fought and defeated King Harold in 1066. Follow the road down the valley, through Whatlington, and then uphill to join the A21, turning left. After $\frac{1}{2}$ m. turn right on to the B2089, which then passes through pleasant woods and rolling hills. Cross the bridge over the A229, then turn right at the White Hart Inn and right again on to the A229, passing under the bridge. The route here is at first wooded, then flanked by hop gardens. After about $3\frac{1}{2}$ m. turn right on to a minor road signposted to Bodiam, which lies about 1 m. ahead, with the castle beyond the village.

2 Bodiam to Ewhurst Green Leave the castle car park and turn left over a narrow river bridge and a disused railway. After $\frac{1}{2}$ m., passing the big Guinness hop farms, turn left along a road signposted to Ewhurst Green and Northiam. Turn left at the T-junction and into Ewhurst Green.

3 Ewhurst Green to Northiam Continue through the village along a narrow, winding road for about $1\frac{3}{4}$ m. Turn left at the T-junction and continue for about 1 m. partly through a tunnel of trees into Northiam. Turn left at the first crossroads in Northiam following the signposts to Great Dixter, a half-timbered manor house.

4 Northiam to Newenden Return to the crossroads in the village and turn left, then left again on to the A28 signposted Tenterden. After 1 m. the road crosses a disused railway and runs into a flat, cultivated valley reclaimed from marshland. Cross the River Rother to reach Newenden and its church on the other side of the valley.

5 Newenden to Rolvenden Continue on the A28 through the village. Drive straight up the hill and turn right at the top, still following the A28 for another $2\frac{1}{2}$ m. into Rolvenden.

6 Rolvenden to Smallhythe Place Leave Rolvenden by remaining on the A28. After $1\frac{1}{2}$ m. go over a level crossing and pass the old Rolvenden station. Follow the A28 for about another 2 m. to the outskirts of Tenterden. Turn right on to the B2082, continuing for $2\frac{1}{2}$ m., following the National Trust signs to Smallhythe Place, the home of the actress Ellen Terry. There is parking in a lay-by beside a bridge just beyond the house.

7 Smallhythe Place to Rye Continue on the B2082 for about $2\frac{1}{2}$ m., through flat meadows drained by wide channels, until it climbs to Wittersham on the Isle of Oxney, so called because it was once an island in a marsh. It is still surrounded by streams and ditches. Continue through Wittersham and, after 1 m., at the crossroads where the B2082 bears right, go straight ahead. After 1 m. turn right on to a narrow road signposted to the Royal Military Canal. Continue on this road as it winds downhill to a T-junction beside the canal. Turn right and drive alongside Britain's only 'gunboat waterway', built during the Napoleonic wars to carry armed vessels across the vulnerable Kent and Sussex marshes in the event of invasion. Follow the canal for $3\frac{1}{2}$ m., then turn left on to the A268 and enter Rye.

8 Rye to Sedlescombe Street Leave Rye on the B2089, following the Battle signposts. Go over the level crossing and past the windmill on the left. As the road climbs, the sea and Winchelsea on its hill come into view on the left. After about 4 m., at Broad Oak crossroads, turn left on to the A28 signposted to Hastings. After $\frac{3}{4}$ m., at the beginning of Brede, turn right along a narrow wooded road signposted to Sedlescombe and Battle. After about 3 m. the road enters Sedlescombe Street.

9 Sedlescombe Street to Battle Leave Sedlescombe Street by turning left on to the A229. Pass the Pestalozzi Children's Village on the left, and after about $\frac{1}{2}$ m. turn right on to the A21. After $\frac{1}{2}$ m. turn left on to a minor road signposted Battle. Pass through the edge of Petley Wood, after $1\frac{1}{2}$ m. cross the railway and continue for another $\frac{1}{2}$ m. to join the A2100 near Battle Abbey, and enter the town.

INFORMATION

Places of interest *Battle:* Abbey, daily. Museum, Easter to Oct., weekdays, Sun. afternoons. *Bodiam Castle:* Apr. to Oct., daily; Nov. to Mar., weekdays. *Great Dixter:* Apr. to mid-Oct., Tues. to Sun. and Bank Hol. Mon., 2-5 p.m. *Great Maytham Hall:* May to Sept., Wed. and Thur. 2-4 p.m. *Kent and East Sussex Railway:* Weekends and Bank Hols., also daily, Aug. 20-31 and Wed. afternoons, June to Aug. *Rye:* Lamb House, Apr. to Oct., Wed. and Sat., 2-6 p.m. Museum, Ypres Tower, Easter to mid-Oct., daily. *Smallhythe Place:* Mar. to Oct., Mon., Wed., Thur., weekends and Bank Hols., 2-6 p.m. (or sunset if earlier).

Information South-East England Tourist Board, Cheviot House, 4-6 Monson Road, Tunbridge Wells (Tel. Tunbridge Wells 33066).

Towns with easy access to Battle:

Eastbourne	16 m.	Maidstone	28 m.
Hastings	7 m.	Tunbridge Wells	22 m.

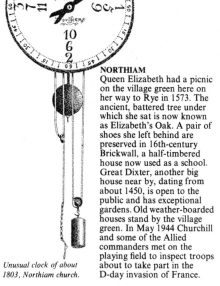

Unusual clock of about 1803, Northiam church.

NORTHIAM
Queen Elizabeth had a picnic on the village green here on her way to Rye in 1573. The ancient, battered tree under which she sat is now known as Elizabeth's Oak. A pair of shoes she left behind are preserved in 16th-century Brickwall, a half-timbered house now used as a school. Great Dixter, another big house near by, dating from about 1450, is open to the public and has exceptional gardens. Old weather-boarded houses stand by the village green. In May 1944 Churchill and some of the Allied commanders met on the playing field to inspect troops about to take part in the D-day invasion of France.

EWHURST GREEN
The church here dates back to the 12th century, with later additions. The spire leans on one side and bulges on the other, due to a slapdash repair job in 1792 after it had been struck by lightning. The church register, beginning in 1558, opens by recording the baptism and death on the same day of a local child, and the baptism of his twin brother who died two weeks later. Oasthouses (hop-drying stores) stand by the 15th-century 'preacher's house', once the shop of the local butcher and part-time Methodist pastor.

BODIAM
The castle was built between 1386 and 1388 on the orders of Richard II to secure the upper reaches of the Rother against French raids which had ravaged Rye, Hastings and Winchelsea. Although the river was then navigable as far as Bodiam, the castle garrison never had to fight. The village grew as an adjunct to the castle. Thriving local activity today centres on the Guinness hop farms, claimed to be the biggest in Britain, where modern machinery now does the work of the hop-pickers who used to flock there every year from London's East End.

Ruins of Battle Abbey on the site of William the Conqueror's victory

SCALE

| 0 | 1 | 2 | 3 | 4 | 5 MILES |

locomotives on the Kent and East Sussex line, Rolvenden.

ROLVENDEN

A prosperous village in an area where hops and apples are grown, Rolvenden is full of mellow brick-and-weather-boarded houses. The church is mainly 14th century with round and octagonal pillars. Great Maytham Hall, designed by Sir Edwin Lutyens, stands on the site of an 18th-century house destroyed by fire. In Victorian times it was the home of Frances Hodgson Burnett, who wrote _Little Lord Fauntleroy_. It was also reputed to be the setting for her children's book _The Secret Garden_. The Kent and East Sussex Railway, now in the hands of a preservation society, runs near the village.

One of Ellen Terry's stage costumes.

SMALLHYTHE PLACE

A distinctive timbered house, Smallhythe Place, built in 1480, was for 30 years the home of Ellen Terry, who lived here until her death in 1928. In memory o. her, it is now a National Trust museum, in which the actress's costumes and other relics are preserved. Beside the house is an ancient ship-repair dock, in use until the waterways silted up in the 17th century. Goods were being brought to Small Hythe by boat from Rye during this century, but drainage of the marshes has removed much of the navigable water. Improvements to the land-drainage system during the 20th century have turned the valley into rich farmland. A small stream is all that remains of the tidal creek.

NEWENDEN

Early records claim that the first community of Carmelite monks to arrive in England, in 1241, 'made their nest at Newendene which was before a wooddie and solitary place'. Now it is a picturesque hamlet on the Kent-Sussex border, where the little River Rother is spanned by a narrow 18th-century humpbacked bridge. The small medieval church has a grotesquely decorated large, square Norman font with a design of dragons and other fabulous beasts. A door to the left of the entrance leads up to a tiny prison cell. But the 'Norman' chancel was built in 1930. The White Hart, a white-painted weatherboarded inn, dates from the time of Elizabeth I.

Hops (humulus lupulus)

diam Castle.

TTLE

hill outside the town was the scene the Battle of Hastings, where the story of England was changed in 66. Here the troops of William, uke of Normandy fought those of arold, the English king, in a dispute er the rightful succession to the rone of England. By clever tactics illiam beat Harold who, according tradition, was killed by an arrow rough the eye. William, henceforth med the Conqueror, had an abbey ilt on the battlefield in thanksgiving r his victory, even though the onks complained that the site was poor one. It was consecrated in 94 and dissolved by Henry VIII 1538. Part of the abbey now uses a girls' school, but the other ildings and the grounds are open visitors. Near the abbey is a small useum devoted to the battle, though ry little material evidence of the nflict has been found. Battle is a lightful small town of tile-hung and nber-clad houses, situated on the ddle of a ridge with a steep wooded lley to the south.

SEDLESCOMBE STREET

An extension of the old village of Sedlescombe, Sedlescombe Street is the home of the Pestalozzi Children's Village, established at Oaklands Park in 1958. The objective of the settlement, named after the 18th-century Swiss educational reformer Johann Heinrich Pestalozzi, is to teach children from poorer countries practical skills to enable them to help their homelands after they go back. Visits can be made by appointment.

RYE

Surprise and delight await the visitor at almost every corner of this distinguished old town. Once a fort, almost surrounded by sea, it still has the atmosphere of an ancient port. The fact that the sea receded from the town 400 years ago has not diminished Rye's status as part of the confederation of the Cinque Ports, charged from the 13th century with the duty of providing ships in time of war. The 1120 church of St Mary has a clock with figures that strike the quarter-hours. Ypres Tower is 13th century and is now used as a museum. The medieval Mermaid Inn, where a notorious smugglers' gang used to drink, has a fireplace in the bar deep enough to sit in. Henry James, the author, lived at 18th-century Lamb House.

The Mermaid Inn, Rye.

Map labels

ASHFORD 11 MILES A 28
HYTHE 17 MILES B 2067
Tenterden
6
A 28
BENENDEN 2 MILES B 2086
Rolvenden
Small Hythe
B 2082
SMALLHYTHE PLACE
GREAT MAYTHAM HALL
7
Isle of Oxney
Wittersham
B 2082
A 268
Newenden
Rother Levels
HAWKHURST 6 MILES
5
Rother
ROYAL MILITARY CANAL
HAWKHURST 3 MILES
A 229
2
Rother
GREAT DIXTER
Northiam
B 2088
A 28
Bodiam
CASTLE NT
4
N
NEW ROMNEY 10 MILES
Ewhurst Green
3
A 268
A 259
A 268
Rye
8
PH
Broad Oak
A 28
Tillingham
A 259
HASTINGS 12 MILES
A 21
B 2089
A 229
B 2089
Brede
Sedlescombe
A 28
Sedlescombe Street
HASTINGS 7 MILES
ROYAL TUNBRIDGE WELLS 20 MILES
9
PESTALOZZI CHILDREN'S VILLAGE
A 2100
Whatlington
Petley Wood
Caldbec Hill
A 21
HASTINGS 6 MILES
BEXHILL 9 MILES A 269
ABBEY
BATTLE
HASTINGS 6 MILES
HASTINGS 1066
1
A 2100

101

CANTERBURY CATHEDRAL

The cathedral has stood at the heart of Christian worship in England since the beginning of the 7th century. From the time of the first Archbishop of Canterbury, St Augustine, to the installation of Dr Donald Coggan in 1975, Canterbury has been the seat of the Primate of All England. The succession goes on; but time has much changed—and is still changing—the great building that for more than 300 years was a place of pilgrimage to the shrine of England's martyr-saint, Thomas Becket. Here in history and picture is the Canterbury Tale.

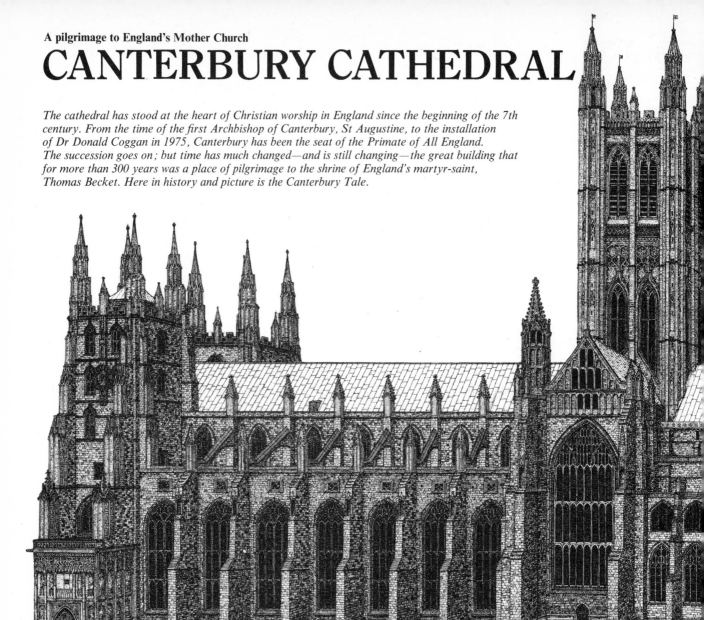

CURE SEEKERS *Pilgrims flocked to Canterbury after the murder of Archbishop Thomas Becket in 1170. He was canonised three years later. This stained-glass window panel shows a group praying at Becket's tomb in the cathedral crypt before it was moved to the shrine behind the High Altar. The 13th-century window is one of the 'miracle' series of 12 in the Trinity Chapel depicting scenes from the life of the murdered prelate and some of the cures attributed to him. The windows were removed for safety during the two World Wars.*

Canterbury has been the centre of Christian England since 603. In June that year, Augustine, the first Archbishop, an Italian monk sent by Pope Gregory six years earlier to re-convert the English, consecrated a cathedral on the site of the old Romano-British church. Here, in January 1975, the 101st Archbishop of Canterbury, Dr Donald Coggan, was enthroned on St Augustine's Chair—under television lights.

The history of the present building begins in 1070 when the first Norman Archbishop, 70-year-old Lanfranc, friend of William the Conqueror, started rebuilding the cathedral after a disastrous fire. Much of his work remains, including the extreme western portion of the crypt, the ground plan of the nave, and walling in the cloisters. Lanfranc was followed by Archbishop Anselm, who carried out a great rebuilding of the choir and eastern transepts.

It was in this Norman cathedral, just one century after its founding, that a crime took place that was to shock Christendom, and be a source of literary inspiration from Chaucer down to the present day. On December 29,

1170, the 40th Archbishop of Canterbury, Thomas Becket, was murdered in his own cathedral. He was struck down by four knights, who believed they were carrying out the wishes of Henry II. In a rage, he had asked at court, 'Who will deliver me from this turbulent priest?'

Becket was soon revered as a martyr-saint, and the great pilgrimages to Canterbury began. Geoffrey Chaucer was to immortalise them in the late 14th century. The two hallowed places were the small area of the north-west transept where the four knights rushed in from the cloisters to strike Becket down, known still as The Martyrdom; and the tomb in the crypt.

In 1174, another fire destroyed the Norman choir and the chapel beyond it to the east, beneath which Becket's tomb lay. The great fire could hardly have been more timely. Now the monks could build a cathedral-shrine worthy of the miracle-working martyr who was bringing them such wealth and prestige. After long debate they entrusted the work to a French mason, William of Sens. He not only brought the stone from Caen in Normandy,

The Reeve.

The Knight.

The Wife of Bath.

Canterbury Cathedral, the south front.

shipping it along the River Stour, but also imported an architectural revolution—the early-Gothic style.

After four years' work, William was crippled by a fall from the scaffolding and was obliged to turn the task—and probably his plans—over to William the Englishman, who went on from the east transept to complete the new Trinity Chapel that rose 16 steps from the choir, with its lofty windows of stained glass. These are often called the Poor Man's Bible. To men who could not read they presented, in living blues, reds and purple, numerous parables, miracles of Christ and suggested miracles of St Thomas. William also created the chapel's surrounding French-style ambulatory or walking area and the Corona Chapel (often known as 'Becket's Crown' from its exterior appearance).

The vision of the priests, realised by the two Williams, was complete: to turn the choir and the eastern end of the cathedral into an ever-rising vista towards what was to be the shrine of St Thomas the Martyr.

Pilgrims paid for further changes. Towards the end of the 14th century the old Norman

nave was beyond repair. It was pulled down and rebuilt by Henry Yevele, the king's master mason, architect of Westminster Hall and Westminster Abbey nave. It is his beautiful creation that is seen today. Where Lanfranc's rotund Norman pillars once bore down, many-shafted columns now soar 80 ft to branch into the vault far above. Bell Harry Tower, too, stems in part from pilgrim wealth. Towards the end of the 15th century this magnificent central tower replaced Lanfranc's square Norman tower with its angel-topped steeple.

But, by the time of the Reformation, pilgrim donations had fallen off; and in 1538, Henry VIII issued a writ which was read aloud before the shrine in Trinity Chapel. It denounced Becket for 'treason, contumacy and rebellion', and 26 cartloads of gold and jewels from the shrine were removed to the royal treasury. All traces of shrine and saint were ordered to be erased. Now nothing but a pool of light, brass letters on the floor and grooves worn in the mosaic tiling by the feet and knees of countless pilgrims mark this as a historic spot.

Despite its important role in England's history, only one king is buried in Canterbury

Cathedral—Henry IV, who died in 1413. Effigies of Henry and his wife cover the tomb.

However, about 50 of Becket's fellow archbishops lie within the walls. Henry Chichele, the 62nd Archbishop, founder of All Souls College, Oxford, has a two-level tomb, dated 1443, near the north-east transept. Above, he is shown gold-mitred, red-robed, surrounded by carvings of the great; and below, as a skeletal corpse. Down the steps from the choir, in the Warriors' Chapel, lies Archbishop Stephen Langton, who helped to compel King John to sign Magna Carta.

Near by, more steps lead down into the largest Norman crypt in the world. Here Lanfranc's architecture comes into its own. Because of the elevation of the cathedral's choir, much of the crypt is above ground level and flooded with light. This reveals every detail of the masons' lively carvings on the block capitals of the piers, including a wyvern—a two-legged winged dragon—fighting a dog, jugglers, animals playing musical instruments, and a shy doe. For 900 years visitors to Canterbury have delighted in these little jokes of the anonymous masons.

A pilgrimage to England's Mother Church

CANTERBURY CATHEDRAL

12 THE CLOISTER
Originally built about 1073, the Cloister was reconstructed in 1220. The arches in the wall belong to this period. When it was remodelled as the Great Cloister about 1400, the added vaulting displayed more than 820 family coats of arms, largely of pilgrims and other subscribers to the work. This is the greatest collection in stone of medieval heraldry in Europe. A vast Chapter House, rebuilt and heightened in the 14th century, stands on the eastern side. Its barrel-vault of Irish bog oak is the second biggest wooden roof in England after Westminster Hall.

Heraldic shields in the cloister roof.

An 11th-century crypt carving.

11 THE CRYPT
At the far western end of the great Norman crypt, begun in 1070, is the oldest part of the cathedral. On the block capitals of some of the massive piers the masons carved lively human and animal scenes. One shows a benign lion with a cross attached to its upheld tail.

Becket and his murderers.

10 THE MARTYRDOM
A vigorous 15th-century painting hangs near the place known as The Martyrdom, where Thomas Becket was killed. It shows him confronting his murderers.

13 BELL HARRY TOWER
Bell Harry (as the central tower was called for its first, single bell) was built around 1490 by John Wastell, who was also the master mason at King's College, Cambridge. The tower is open inside to a height of 153 ft and, from below, its ornate fan-vaulted ceiling looks like an exotic flower.

Bell Harry Tower, from inside the cathedral.

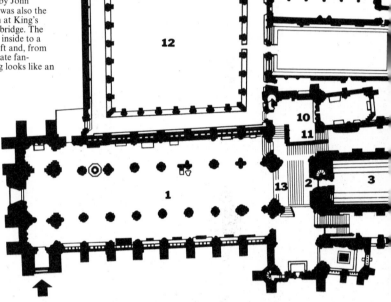

The nave, looking east.

1 THE NAVE
In the late 14th century, revenue from the pilgrims enabled the monks of Canterbury to rebuild the old Norman nave in the majestic and soaring Perpendicular style. The king's mason, Henry Yevele, who had built the nave of Westminster Abbey, completed the work in 1403. The stout old Norman pillars are encased in multiple mouldings and half-shafts and, magically transformed, now soar to the heightened roof and branch out into handsome vaulting. The windows are as tall and wide as the aisle walls and buttresses will allow. Far away, through the central doorway in the choir screen, can be seen the glow of stained glass, which once beckoned pilgrims on to the shrine of St Thomas Becket.

The three kings on the pulpitum.

2 THE PULPITUM
The stone screen or pulpitum set up in the 15th century to divide nave from choir is hea and ornate, with elabe ately vaulted niches. The Puritans destroye many of its 'graven images' in 1644, but th statues of six kings sti look out from the wes face of the screen. The are symbols rather tha portraits, but the thre on the right of the doe are believed to represe Edward the Confesso Henry V and Henry V

3 THE CHOIR
The Norman quire (still the Canterbury spelling) was burnt down in 1174. Within ten years it had been rebuilt by William of Sens and William the Englishman to a design that formed a rising 'frame' to what was to be its highest point—the Trinity Chapel in which was placed the golden shrine of St Thomas the Martyr.

THE TOMBS OF THE BLACK PRINCE AND HENRY IV

...ward, the Black Prince, who died in 1376 aged 46, asked in his will to be ...ried in Canterbury's crypt, but popular opinion decreed that the hero of ...écy and Poitiers should lie in the Trinity Chapel beside the shrine of St ...omas. The saint's shrine has gone, but the tomb of the soldier remains, ...th his effigy bright in battle armour. On the other side of the chapel is the ...mb of Henry IV, with his elaborate effigy in crown and robes. This is ...e only tomb of a king in the cathedral; the effigy of his wife, Joanna of ...avarre, lies beside him.

Effigy of Edward, the Black Prince.

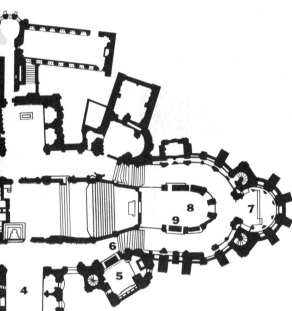

Zodiac tiles in the Trinity Chapel, polished by centuries of kneeling pilgrims.

8 TRINITY CHAPEL

In front of the place where Thomas Becket's bejewelled shrine once stood in the Trinity Chapel there is a handsome mosaic pavement, laid down early in the 13th century, possibly by Italian craftsmen. On either side of this are groups of picture tiles of yellow limestone, with designs in red. They depict the signs of the Zodiac, 'Virtues trampling on Vices' and the 'Labours of the Month'—men sowing, haymaking, reaping, pruning. They give a vivid picture of rural life in the Middle Ages. In the walking area around the chapel are the 'miracle' windows which tell of the life of St Thomas and miracles it is claimed he performed.

7 THE CORONA

St Augustine's Chair, in which every new archbishop is enthroned, stands in the centre of the small, circular easternmost chapel known as the Corona or Becket's Crown. The chair, cut from Purbeck marble, dates from the 13th century. It may be a copy of an earlier chair in the Norman cathedral that was destroyed in the fire of 1174. The central stained-glass window belongs to the so-called Poor Man's Bible series in the north choir aisle. It shows the main events from Good Friday to Pentecost, illustrated by the Old Testament episodes that foreshadowed them. Thus Jonah, disgorged by the whale, is a symbol of the Resurrection.

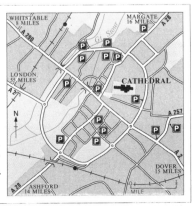

St Augustine's Chair.

6 PILGRIMS' STEPS

The Pilgrims' Steps to the Trinity Chapel were worn down by the feet of countless pilgrims who thronged to the shrine of St Thomas after his bones had been removed there from the crypt in 1220. The shrine, said a 15th-century Italian visitor, 'passes all belief—covered with plates of pure gold and studded with sapphires, diamonds, rubies, emeralds'. When it was broken down and all traces of the saint removed in 1538 by order of Henry VIII, 26 cartloads of treasure were taken away.

The worn treads of the Pilgrims' Steps.

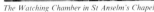

The Watching Chamber in St Anselm's Chapel.

5 ST ANSELM'S CHAPEL

From the low-vaulted Watching Chamber built high up in the chapel of St Anselm, Canterbury's second Norman archbishop, pilgrims could keep night-long vigil over the tomb of a later saint—St Thomas.

4 SOUTH-EAST TRANSEPT

The dominant blues and purples of the cathedral's ancient glass give way to fiery reds and glowing crimsons in the south-east transept. These four modern stained-glass windows were completed in 1960 by Hungarian-born Erwin Bossanyi. One of them, 'Peace', shows Christ smiling on children of many races. 'Salvation' shows the serpent of evil departing.

...ace' window, by Bossanyi.

VISITING CANTERBURY

How to get there:
Canterbury Cathedral lies at the heart of the city which stands on the main London-Dover road (A2), 56 m. from London, 15 m. from Dover. Canterbury is close to the route of Tour No. 40, based on Deal.

Opening times: Sun., 7.30 a.m.–6 p.m.; weekdays (summer), 7.30 a.m.–7 p.m.; (winter), 7.30 a.m.–6.30 p.m. (Sat., 5 p.m.). Special services can cause variations.

Information: Longmarket (Tel. Canterbury 66567).

105

Still the gateway of England after 2000 years

Bounded by the stretch of coastline closest to the continent of Europe, the pleasant countryside of east Kent reflects 2000 years of English history, from the arrival of the Romans to the evacuation from Dunkirk in the Second World War. There is evidence here of Romans, Saxons and Normans, and of St Augustine, the man who brought Christianity to England.

(1) Deal to Walmer Castle Leave Deal on the A258 signposted to Walmer. Turn left by the lifeboat on to the B2057. After 1 m. reach Walmer Castle.

(2) Walmer to Dover Continue along the B2057 to the T-junction with the A258 at Ringwould. Turn left, signposted Dover, and after 1½ m. turn left again on to the B2058 signposted to St Margaret's at Cliffe, which is reached after ¾ m. (To visit St Margaret's Bay follow the road on through the village.) Just past the church turn right into Reach Road. At the junction with the A258 turn left and go down the hill to Dover Castle. Continue into Dover

(3) Dover to Barfreston Return past the castle and keep ahead on a minor road, following the signpost to Guston. In Guston turn left on to the road signposted to Whitfield and, very shortly, left again. Keep straight ahead at two crossroads, following the Sandwich signposts, and at the junction with the A256 turn right. After 1 m. turn left on to the road signposted to Eythorne, and at the roundabout in the village follow the Barfreston signpost. By the White Horse Inn keep straight ahead and at the church turn left, following the signpost into Barfreston.

(4) Barfreston to Bishopsbourne Leave the village on the road past the church signposted to Barham. At Woolage bear left, and at the crossroads on the far side keep ahead, following the signpost to Folkestone. At the junction with the A2 turn right signposted Canterbury. After ½ m. turn left on to the road signposted to Barham and at the crossroads turn right to the village centre. At the T-junction turn right on to the B2065 signposted to Canterbury. At the junction with the A2 turn left. Shortly afterwards turn left for Bishopsbourne.

(5) Bishopsbourne to Patrixbourne Leave Bishopsbourne on the road signposted to Bossingham. After 1½ m. fork right and at the crossroads keep ahead on the road signposted to Upper Hardres Court. At the T-junction turn right and continue through Upper Hardres Court bearing right, and after ½ m. turn right, following the signpost to Pett Bottom. At the T-junction by the Duck Inn turn left, and at the next T-junction turn right on to the road signposted to Bridge. At the junction with the old A2 keep ahead on the minor road signposted to Bekesbourne, which runs into Patrixbourne.

(6) Patrixbourne to Fordwich Turn left at the church for Bekesbourne, and after the watersplash by Bekesbourne church turn left again. Go under the railway bridge and immediately left, following the signpost to

Fordwich. At the junction with the A257 turn right, and then shortly afterwards turn left down Stodmarsh Lane which is signposted to Fordwich. After 1 m. turn left into Fordwich.

(7) Fordwich to Pegwell Bay Return to Stodmarsh Lane turning left into it at the T-junction. After 1 m. turn right, following the signpost to Wickhambreaux, and at the crossroads turn left. After ½ m. turn right again, signposted Wickhambreaux, and at the T-junction turn right into the village. Beyond the village turn left, following the signpost to Ickham and, keeping left through the village, continue to the junction with the A257. Turn left into Wingham, and at the end of the village left again on to the B2046 signposted to Preston. In Preston turn left, following the signpost to Groveferry. Turn right over the bridge and right again at the junction with the A28 signposted to Sarre. In Sarre turn right on to the A253 signposted Ramsgate. After 1 m. turn right on to the B2047, following the signpost to Minster. In the town turn left at the T-junction and then right on to the B2048 signposted Sandwich. At the junction with the A256, turn left for Pegwell Bay.

(8) Pegwell Bay to Sandwich Leave on the A256 signposted Sandwich.

(9) Sandwich to Richborough Castle Leave the town on the A257 signposted to Canterbury. On the outskirts, turn right and follow Richborough Road to the castle.

(10) Richborough Castle to Deal Leave the castle on the public road through Richborough. After ½ m. turn left to Ash and at the fork turn right. At the junction with the A257 cross over into Cherry Garden Lane and then turn left at the T-junction. Continue through Woodnesborough, following the signpost to Eastry, and at the crossroads turn left signposted Deal. At the junction with the A256 turn left on to the road signposted to Sandwich, but shortly afterwards turn right to follow the signpost to Deal. At the junction with the A258 turn right again into Deal.

INFORMATION

Places of interest *Deal Castle:* Daily (except Sun. mornings Oct. to Mar.). *Dover:* Castle, daily, except Sun. mornings Oct. to Mar. Maison Dieu Hall, Mon. to Fri. 10 a.m.-4 p.m., Sat. 10 a.m.-12 noon. *Richborough Castle:* Daily, except Sun. mornings Oct. to Mar. *Sandwich:* Guildhall museum, daily. *Walmer Castle:* Tues. to Sun. and Bank Hol. Mon. except Sun. mornings Oct. to Mar.

Information *Dover:* South-East England Tourist Board, Townwall Street (Tel. Dover 205108). *Deal:* Sea Front (Tel. Deal 61161).

Towns with easy access to Deal:

Canterbury	19 m.	Margate	15 m.
Folkestone	16 m.	Ramsgate	13 m.

Town Hall, Fordwich.

FORDWICH
Fordwich was once the port for Canterbury, but its tidal river has now dwindled to a stream. The stocks still stand outside the Tudor town hall with its old gaol and courtroom. Behind it is the crane once used to lower criminals into the river for ducking or drowning. The church has traces of Saxon work and a sculptured tomb in which, it is said, the body of St Augustine once lay.

PATRIXBOURNE
The small Norman church at Patrixbourne has some fine 12th-century carving. Most notable is the arch to the south door which is decorated with birds, beasts and little men set in a scroll of leaves. There is also some old Swiss stained glass.

BISHOPSBOURNE
The church at Bishopsbourne contains much good stained glass, including a window by the Victorian artist Sir Edward Burne-Jones. The novelist Joseph Conrad lived in the rectory from 1919 until his death in 1924.

Norman carvings over church door, Barfreston.

BARFRESTON
The church at Barfreston was built in 1080 of flint and Caen stone. The stonework, both outside and in, is decorated with elaborate carving. Particularly fine is the south doorway, where a robed Christ and a mitred Becket stand wreathed in delicate mouldings. All round the building grotesque heads and faces intertwine with birds, animals and leaves, and over the altar exquisitely carved columns divide up an impressive stained-glass wheel window. The church has no tower, so worshippers are summoned by a bell suspended on a yew tree in the churchyard. The church was restored during the 19th century when much of the original carving was saved.

SCALE

0   1   2   3   4   5 MILES

...horough Castle, a Roman fort.

RICHBOROUGH CASTLE

Built at the end of the 3rd century AD, the Roman fort of Rutupiae, at Richborough, is one of the most impressive legacies of the Roman occupation. A massive stone structure, much of which survives, it stood at the end of Watling Street, the road from London to Salop, and protected a port and the sea lane between the mainland and the Isle of Thanet. The Roman invading army of AD 43 landed here, and the defensive ditches dug by the legionaries can still be seen, as can the earthworks. The collection of pottery in the museum is thought to be some of the best found on any Roman site. Also on view are weapons, coins, ornaments and other Roman remains. Wantsum Channel, which once separated Thanet from the mainland, has silted up to form fertile farmland.

Prow of Viking ship, Pegwell Bay.

PEGWELL BAY

In AD 597 St Augustine landed at Ebbsfleet, on the wide sands of Pegwell Bay, on virtually the same spot as the Saxon invaders, Hengist and Horsa, had arrived 150 years earlier. To commemorate the arrival of the Saxons, a replica of a Viking long-boat sailed from Denmark to Pegwell Bay in 1949. It now stands close to the site of the original landings and overlooks the new hovercraft terminal.

SANDWICH

Kings and armies once passed through Sandwich, for it was one of the original Cinque Ports, which supplied the men and ships to defend the south coast. Now, due to the silting up of the River Stour, it is over 2 miles from the sea, but its former importance is displayed in its wealth of old buildings. On the quayside is Fisher Gate, the only surviving medieval gate, built in 1384, and close by is the attractive Barbican, a gatehouse built by Henry VIII in 1539. The timbered guildhall dates from 1579. The interior has been little changed since then and contains relics of the Cinque Ports.

The Fisher Gate, Sandwich.

[map with the following labels:]

MARGATE 6 MILES
HERNE BAY 7 MILES
...TERBURY 7 MILES
Sarre
Groveferry
Grove
...odmarsh
...hambreaux
Preston
...Ickham
Wingham
Minster
ABBEY
CROSS
RAMSGATE 2 MILES
RAMSGATE 2 MILES
EBBSFLEET
HOVERPORT
8
Pegwell Bay
Richborough
10 RICHBOROUGH CASTLE
9
Ash
Woodnesborough
Sandwich
...ALMER CASTLE
...ne of Henry VIII's castles, ...almer became the ...sidence of the Lord Warden ...Cinque Ports in 1708. ...anding in superb gardens, it ...full of the belongings of ...rmer wardens, including ...e Duke of Wellington.
Eastry
Barfreston
4 PH
Eythorne
DEAL
SANDOWN CASTLE
1
CASTLE
Walmer
2
WALMER CASTLE
Ringwould
Kingsdown
...field
Guston
Dover
3
BLERIOT MEMORIAL
CASTLE
St Margaret's at Cliffe
St Margaret's Bay
N

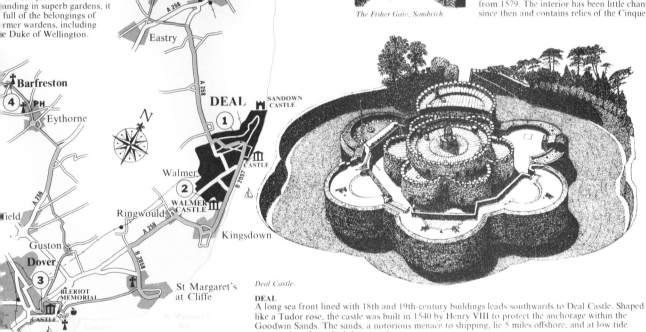
Deal Castle.

DEAL

A long sea front lined with 18th and 19th-century buildings leads southwards to Deal Castle. Shaped like a Tudor rose, the castle was built in 1540 by Henry VIII to protect the anchorage within the Goodwin Sands. The sands, a notorious menace to shipping, lie 5 miles offshore, and at low tide the remains of wrecked ships can be seen.

...e white cliffs of Dover.

DOVER

Best known for its white cliffs and its busy modern port, Dover also has the strongest castle in England. The castle was principally designed by Henry II in the 12th century, but includes much Norman architecture, notably Peverell's Tower, named after William de Peverell, Constable of Dover for William the Conqueror. Within the walls is the Roman Pharos, or lighthouse, built in AD 43 and said to be the most complete Roman building in Britain. Close to this is the church of St Mary-in-Castra which dates back to the 4th century and was later embellished by the Saxon King Eadwald. The white cliffs were first mentioned in writing by Julius Caesar, 2000 years ago. Among the many interesting buildings in the town is the 13th-century Maison Dieu Hall, which houses historic armour and paintings.

Castles high and dry above the bed of a vanished sea

For many centuries before England had a regular navy, five Channel towns—the Cinque Ports—had the duty of providing ships in a national emergency. The sea has since retreated from some of Kent's ancient coastal defences, leaving castles and harbour towns marooned inland, including Hythe, one of the original Cinque Ports.

(1) Tenterden to Biddenden Leave Tenterden on the A28 signposted to Ashford, and then after St Michaels turn left on the A262 and follow the signpost to Biddenden.

(2) Biddenden to Charing Leave the village on the A274 signposted to Maidstone, but after 1 m. turn right on to the B2077 signposted to Charing. The route passes through Smarden, a collection of weatherboard and half-timbered cottages. Cross the A20 into the centre of Charing.

(3) Charing to Chilham Keep ahead on the main road in the village, and at the junction with the A252 turn right, following the Canterbury signpost. The road travels through woodland, and at the crossroads with the A251, by the Halfway House Inn, turn right towards Ashford and then fork left on to the road signposted to Wye and the car park for King's Wood, an excellent picnic spot. Return to the A252 and continue towards Canterbury. After 4 m. turn right on to the road signposted to Chilham.

(4) Chilham to Saltwood Leave the village, passing the church on the left, and turn left on to the A28 towards Canterbury. At Chartham turn right at the crossroads for the village centre. Cross the railway by the station, and beyond the village turn right at the T-junction and, at the following crossroads, turn left on to the road signposted to Petham. Opposite St Augustine's Hospital turn right, following the signposts to Garlinge Green.

Continue along this road to the T-junction and there turn right. In a few yards, by the Dukes Head Inn, turn left and continue to the junction with the B2068, which is a Roman road. Turn right, following the Hythe signpost, and after 4 m., by the Six Miles Garage, turn left on to the road signposted to Elham. At the crossroads keep ahead, following the signpost to Elham, and at the next T-junction turn left. Soon after turn right, and at the T-junction turn left on to the road signposted to Elham. At the T-junction on the village outskirts turn left to the B2065, then right to the centre of the village. Continue on the B2065 through Lyminge. At the crossroads beyond the village, where the B2065 goes left, keep ahead on the road to Saltwood. Turn right on to the A20 towards Ashford and then left, following the signpost to Saltwood. Turn left at the green to see the castle.

(5) Saltwood to Hythe Return to the village green and go down Brockhill Road. Turn right at the T-junction, and at the next T-junction with North Road turn right again and immediately left down Barrack Hill. Turn left at the bottom for the town centre.

(6) Hythe to Lympne Leave town on the A261, following the signpost to Ashford.

After 1 m., where the road turns sharp right, bear left on to the B2067, following the signpost to Lympne.

(7) Lympne to Dymchurch Retrace the road to the junction by the memorial cross on Lympne's outskirts, and turn right on to the road signposted to Dymchurch. Cross the Royal Military Canal and at Botolph's Bridge turn right and then left on to the road signposted New Romney. Cross the railway and at the junction with the A259 turn right, following the signpost to Dymchurch alongside the sea wall.

(8) Dymchurch to Dungeness Continue through Dymchurch on the A259 signposted New Romney. After 3 m., on the outskirts of New Romney, turn left on to the B2071, signposted to Littlestone-on-Sea. New Romney station, exhibition centre of the R.H.&D. Railway, is on the left after ¼ m. Continue on the B2071 to Littlestone and turn right at the T-junction on the sea front. Follow the coast road and, when it bears inland, turn first left to visit the Ness and lighthouse. The power station is further on towards Lydd.

(9) Dungeness to New Romney Return to Littlestone-on-Sea and along the B2071 to the A259 and turn left into New Romney.

(10) New Romney to Appledore Take the A259 from New Romney. At the junction of the A259 and the B2080, continue ahead on the B2080, following the Tenterden signposts to Appledore.

(11) Appledore to Tenterden Just beyond the village turn left, still on the B2080 to Tenterden. On entering Tenterden turn left on the A28 to the town centre.

INFORMATION

Places of interest *Tenterden:* Kent and E. Sussex Railway Co. station, weekends and Bank Hols., also daily, Aug. 20-31 and Wed. afternoons, June to Aug. *Chilham Castle* and *Chilham Museum:* May to Nov., Tues. to Thur., Sat., Sun. and Bank Hols., afternoons. *Saltwood Castle:* Sun. and Bank Hol. afternoons from Whitsun; Aug., daily (except Mon. and Sat.). *Lympne Castle:* Apr. to Oct., Wed., Sun. and Bank Hol. weekends, 2.30-6 p.m.; July to Sept., daily, 10.30 a.m.-6 p.m. *Dymchurch Martello Tower:* All year, daily, Sun. afternoons. *Romney, Hythe and Dymchurch Railway:* Easter to Oct., daily. *Dungeness Lighthouse:* Summer, afternoons. *Nuclear Power Station:* All year; tours at 2 p.m. and 3 p.m., Wed.

Nature trail *Lyminge Forest:* West Wood, conifers and sweet-chestnut coppice.

Information South-East England Tourist Board, Cheviot House, 4-6 Monson Road, Tunbridge Wells (Tel. Tunbridge Wells 33066).

Towns with easy access to Tenterden:

Canterbury	27 m.	Hastings	20 m.
Dover	24 m.	Rochester	28 m.

CHARING
The village stands on the ancient highway call the Pilgrims' Way, along which Canterbury pilgrims used to travel to the shrine of Thom Becket. But even earlier it had been a pack roa for transporting Cornish tin. The remains of Manor House, once the property of the archbishops of Canterbury and a residence of Henry VIII's archbishop, Thomas Cranmer, can be visited.

BIDDENDEN
The village has many Tudor houses, built when it was a prosperous weaving centre. Many of them have communicating attics which once housed the looms. A fine medieval cloth hall has seven gables. The Biddende Maids—Siamese twins Eliza and Mary Chulkhurst—liv in the village in the 12th century. They were joined at th hips and shoulders and survived 34 years, making a bequest for an annual Easter Day gift of bread to the poor. The ceremony still takes place every Easter Monday at 10 a.m. with a distribution of special biscuits imprinted with a picture of the maids. They once gave away beer, too, but not any more.

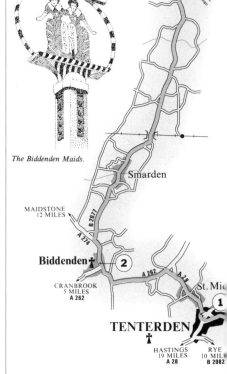

The Biddenden Maids.

View from Appledore.

SCALE
0 1 2 3 4 5 MILES

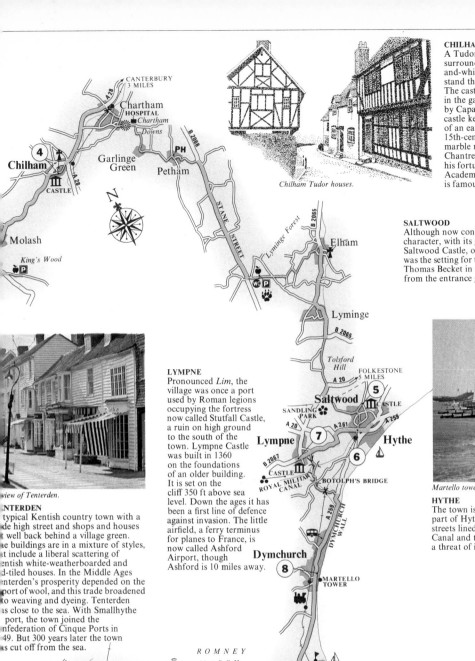

CHILHAM
A Tudor village with a main square surrounded by timbered black-and-white houses, among which stand the gates to Chilham Castle. The castle was built in 1616, and in the gardens, which were laid out by Capability Brown, is a Norman castle keep built on the foundations of an earlier Roman building. The 15th-century church has a white marble monument to Sir Francis Chantrey (1781–1841), who left his fortune to the Royal Academy in London. The Woolpack is famous as an old smuggling inn.

Chilham Tudor houses.

SALTWOOD
Although now continuous with Hythe, Saltwood retains its village character, with its green, its well-tended gardens and roadside hedges. Saltwood Castle, one of the best-preserved medieval castles in Britain, was the setting for the conspiracy by four knights to murder Archbishop Thomas Becket in Canterbury Cathedral eight centuries ago. A path from the entrance gate gives good views of the castle.

Martello towers at Hythe.

LYMPNE
Pronounced *Lim*, the village was once a port used by Roman legions occupying the fortress now called Stutfall Castle, a ruin on high ground to the south of the town. Lympne Castle was built in 1360 on the foundations of an older building. It is set on the cliff 350 ft above sea level. Down the ages it has been a first line of defence against invasion. The little airfield, a ferry terminus for planes to France, is now called Ashford Airport, though Ashford is 10 miles away.

...view of Tenterden.

...NTERDEN
...typical Kentish country town with a ...de high street and shops and houses ...t well back behind a village green. ...he buildings are in a mixture of styles, ...t include a liberal scattering of ...entish white-weatherboarded and ...d-tiled houses. In the Middle Ages ...enterden's prosperity depended on the ...port of wool, and this trade broadened ...to weaving and dyeing. Tenterden ...s close to the sea. With Smallhythe ... port, the town joined the ...nfederation of Cinque Ports in ...49. But 300 years later the town ...s cut off from the sea.

HYTHE
The town is one of the original Cinque Ports, but now the main part of Hythe is half a mile inland. It is a leafy town of narrow streets lined with 18th-century buildings. The Royal Military Canal and the Martello towers were built as defences against a threat of invasion by Napoleon.

DYMCHURCH
This small resort is strung out behind a grass-covered sea wall dating from Roman times. On either side of the town are two Martello towers built strategically to guard the sluices which control the water level on the Romney Marsh. One of the towers has been restored, complete with a cannon mounted on a rotating platform.

DUNGENESS
A collection of chalets and buildings line an isolated flat headland of shingle which the Channel tides are still extending. Fishing from the shore is excellent, but the strong tides make bathing and boating dangerous. Visitors can see over the old lighthouse, the 12,000 acre bird reserve and the observatory, which has recorded more than 200 species in ten years.

Kentish plover

APPLEDORE
This village, on a low ridge overlooking Romney Marsh, now inland from the coast, was once a flourishing port on the estuary of the River Rother. In AD 892 a Danish invasion force of 250 ships rowed up the river, built an earthworks, and used the town as a base. They abandoned it a year later to turn their attentions to London and Cheshire. The present 13th-century church was probably built on the site of the Danish encampment. It was destroyed by the French in the 13th and 14th centuries, but rebuilt. The town had declined by the start of the 19th century due to the canal to Rye harbour silting up, but the construction of the Royal Military Canal in 1805 restored its prosperity by providing a regular barge and passenger service.

R.H.&D. Railway.

NEW ROMNEY
This is the largest town of the marsh and one of the original Cinque Ports. It once stood at the mouth of the Rother, but a storm in 1287 changed the course of the river. The pillars of the church, which has a notable Norman tower, are still discoloured by the flood waters. Romney Marsh is now well-drained pasture land protected by sea walls and embankments. The Romney, Hythe and Dymchurch Railway, with its 14 mile track, is the smallest public railway in the world. It was built in 1927 by two racing drivers—Captain J. E. P. Howey and Count Louis Zborowski. Five trains run every day during the summer.

Houses of the great amid the orchards of Kent

Kent can claim more than its fair share of country houses, ranging in date from the Roman villa at Lullingstone to Chartwell, home of Sir Winston Churchill from 1922 until his death in 1965. The most lavishly furnished of these houses, and probably the largest private house in England, is Knole, home of the Sackville family for ten generations. These treasured houses are set amid the parklands and orchards that earn Kent its title 'The Garden of England', still appropriate despite the encroachment of commuters.

(1) Westerham to Chartwell Leave the town on the A25, following the signpost to Sevenoaks. Turn right opposite Quebec House on to the B2026, following the signpost to Edenbridge. After 1½ m. turn left to follow the signpost to Four Elms, shortly reaching the entrance to Chartwell on the left.

(2) Chartwell to Knole Leaving the house, continue on the road towards Four Elms, then turn left to Toys Hill. Turn left at the crossroads, following the signpost to Brasted, and almost immediately, on the left, is a car park convenient for drivers wishing to take a walk to the woods on Toys Hill. Continue on the road to Brasted, turning right on to the A25 and into the village. Follow the road through Sundridge and cross the A21 to Riverhead. At the Riverhead roundabout join the A2028, following the signpost to Sevenoaks. Keep on the A2028 through Sevenoaks to join the A225, following the signpost to Tonbridge, and almost immediately, on the left opposite the church, is Knole.

(3) Knole to Ightham Mote Return to the A225, turning left on to it, and after just over 1 m. turn left, following the signpost to Ightham. Keep straight ahead at two crossroads, following the signpost to Ivy Hatch. Turn right at the next T-junction, and on entering Ivy Hatch turn right into the village and right again at the next junction, to visit Ightham Mote, one of the few moated manor houses left in England.

(4) Ightham Mote to Old Soar Manor Return to Ivy Hatch and turn right, following the signpost to Plaxtol. After ¼ m. turn right then left to cross the A227. In Plaxtol turn left by the Rorty Crankle Inn, and at the end of the village turn right into Brooklands Road and left at the T-junction into a narrow lane which bears right to the entrance to Old Soar Manor.

(5) Old Soar Manor to West Malling Continue along the lane and turn right at the T-junction. Follow this road through West Peckham to the crossroads. Here go straight over the B2016, following the signpost to Mereworth. Just beyond Mereworth turn left on to the A228, following the signpost to West Malling. Continue along the road, passing St Leonard's Tower on the left, and into West Malling.

(6) West Malling to Farningham In the centre of the village turn left, and immediately left again into Offham Road. Turn right at the T-junction and continue into Offham. At the village green turn right at the crossroads, following the signpost to Addington, and immediately left at the next junction.

Turn left on to the B2232, following the signpost to Wrotham Heath. At the junction with the A25 bear right, and at the roundabout keep ahead on to the A20. Just beyond the Moat Hotel, turn left into Wrotham. At the junction in the village centre turn right, past the church, and then turn left, following the signpost to Farningham. Turn left on to the A20 and continue through West Kingsdown and past Brands Hatch motor-racing circuit on the right. At the foot of Death Hill turn left on to the A225 and immediately right into Farningham.

(7) Farningham to Lullingstone Villa In the village, cross the river and turn left into Sparepenny Lane. Continue to the end of the lane to visit Lullingstone Roman villa.

(8) Lullingstone Villa to Eynsford Return along Sparepenny Lane to the first junction and turn right for Eynsford.

(9) Eynsford to Westerham Leave the village on the A225, following the signpost to Sevenoaks. After 3 m. turn right to follow the signpost to Shoreham. After crossing the river into Shoreham, turn left at the T-junction. Just before the railway bridge turn left, following the signpost to Otford, and then right at a T-junction, following the signpost to Sevenoaks. Turn left on to the A21 and immediately left on to the A2028, still signposted to Sevenoaks. Turn right by the Rose and Crown and, after crossing the A21 by flyover, turn left on to the B2211, signposted to Brasted. Continue along the B2211 and, where the road turns sharp left, bear right. After 1 m. turn left on to Pilgrims' Way signposted to Westerham, and continue to the A233. Here, turn left back to Westerham.

INFORMATION

Places of interest *Chartwell:* Mar. to Nov., Sat., Sun., Bank Hols., 11 a.m.-6 p.m., Tues. (not after Bank Hol.), Wed., Thur., 2-6 p.m. Gardens, same time, Apr. to mid-Oct. *Eynsford Castle:* Daily. *Ightham Mote:* Fri., 2-5 p.m. *Knole:* Mar. and Nov., Wed., Sat., Sun. afternoons; Apr. to Oct., Wed. to Sat., Bank Hols., Sun. afternoons. Gardens, May to Sept., 1st Wed. in month. *Lullingstone Castle:* Weekend afternoons, May to Sept. *Lullingstone Villa:* Weekdays, Sun. afternoons. *Old Soar Manor:* Apr. to Sept., weekdays, Sun. afternoons. *Westerham:* Quebec House, Mar. to Oct., daily (except Wed. and Thur.), 2-6 p.m. Squerryes Court, Mar. to Oct., Wed., Sat., Sun., Bank Hols., 2-6 p.m.

Information South-East England Tourist Board Cheviot House, 4-6 Monson Road, Tunbridge Wells (Tel. Tunbridge Wells 33066).

Towns with easy access to Westerham:

Town	Distance	Town	Distance
Dartford	19 m.	Maidstone	22 m.
Gravesend	24 m.	Reigate	14 m.
London	22 m.	Uckfield	23 m.

Floor of Roman villa, Lullingstone.

LULLINGSTONE VILLA
The remains of the Roman villa contain two examples Roman mosaic floors. In the dining-room the scene depicts the abduction of Europa by the god Jupiter in the guise of a white bull. In the reception-room the mos shows Bellerophon, seated on the winged horse Pegasu killing the mythical Chimera. Excavations show that th villa was occupied from 80 BC to about AD 400, when it was burnt down—no one knows how or why.

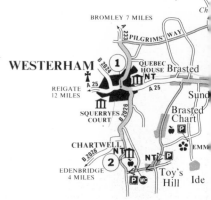

WESTERHAM
The memory of General James Wolfe, hero of the Battle of Quebec in 1759, pervades this small town. A statue of Wolfe stands in the town square. His home, Quebec House, is now a National Trust property crowded with mementoes of his career. Not far away is Squerryes Court, where he received news of his first commission in 1741 when he was 14 years old. Also in the town is Pitt's Cottage, a 13th-century house which was once the home of William Pitt, at 24 the youngest British Premier.

Painting of Wolfe, Quebec Hou

Sir Winston Churchill— photograph at Chartwell.

CHARTWELL
This country house, partl Tudor but rebuilt in Victo times, was bought by Sir Winston Churchill in 192 largely for its grounds an fine views over the Kent countryside. In 1965 Lad Churchill put the house and its contents into the hands of the National Trust, and it has been ope to the public since 1966. Visitors can see the room in which Sir Winston live and worked, including his study and his studio. The house contains many souvenirs of Churchill's long career, and 29 of his own flamboyant landscape paintings. In the grounds vis may see examples of his bricklaying skill, and the splendid bed of roses which were the family's gift to hir and his wife to mark their golden wedding in 1958. The museum room has two walls devoted to photographs of Churchill from childhood to old age.

SCALE

0   1   2   3   4   5 MILES

EYNSFORD

The Dartford Tunnel to the north-west has brought a great deal of traffic into Eynsford, destroying its peace but not its charm. A small hump-back bridge crosses the River Darent beside the 500-year-old ford. Behind this, on top of a grassy bank, can be seen a group of timbered cottages. Near the village are the ruins of Eynsford Castle, parts of which date from the Norman occupation.

FARNINGHAM

The wide main street of Farningham is a reminder of the days when it was a busy coaching centre on the London to Dover road. An 18th-century bridge carries the road over the River Darent. Facing each other near the bridge are the Lion Hotel and a white-painted weather-board mill. The manor house was once the home of Captain Bligh of the *Bounty*.

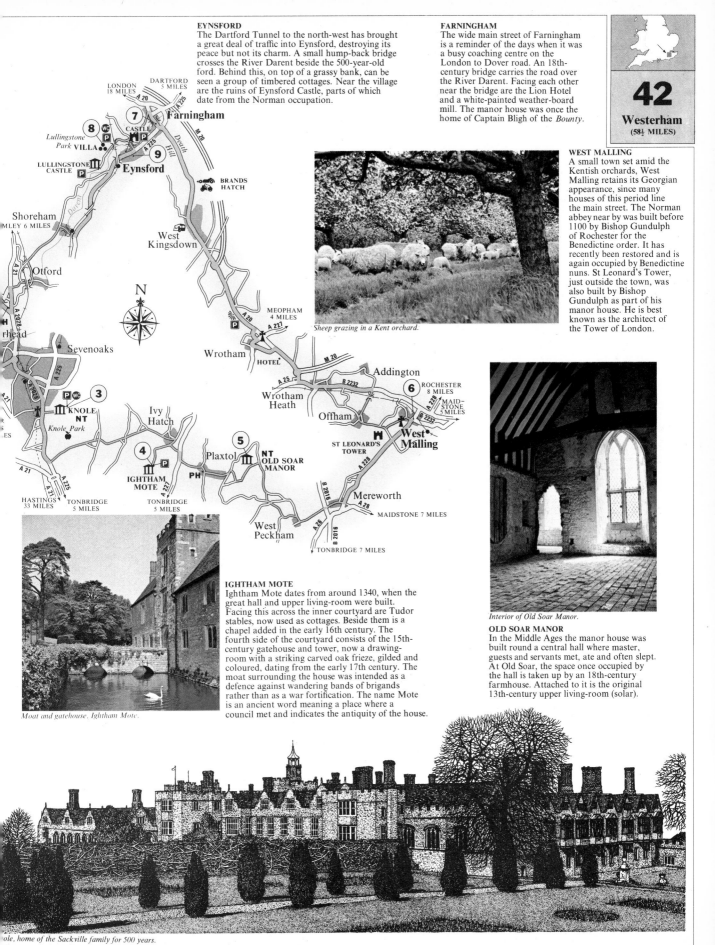

Sheep grazing in a Kent orchard.

WEST MALLING

A small town set amid the Kentish orchards, West Malling retains its Georgian appearance, since many houses of this period line the main street. The Norman abbey near by was built before 1100 by Bishop Gundulph of Rochester for the Benedictine order. It has recently been restored and is again occupied by Benedictine nuns. St Leonard's Tower, just outside the town, was also built by Bishop Gundulph as part of his manor house. He is best known as the architect of the Tower of London.

Interior of Old Soar Manor.

OLD SOAR MANOR

In the Middle Ages the manor house was built round a central hall where master, guests and servants met, ate and often slept. At Old Soar, the space once occupied by the hall is taken up by an 18th-century farmhouse. Attached to it is the original 13th-century upper living-room (solar).

IGHTHAM MOTE

Ightham Mote dates from around 1340, when the great hall and upper living-room were built. Facing this across the inner courtyard are Tudor stables, now used as cottages. Beside them is a chapel added in the early 16th century. The fourth side of the courtyard consists of the 15th-century gatehouse and tower, now a drawing-room with a striking carved oak frieze, gilded and coloured, dating from the early 17th century. The moat surrounding the house was intended as a defence against wandering bands of brigands rather than as a war fortification. The name Mote is an ancient word meaning a place where a council met and indicates the antiquity of the house.

Moat and gatehouse, Ightham Mote.

Knole, home of the Sackville family for 500 years.

KNOLE

The great hall at Knole was built in the 15th century by Archbishop Bourchier of Canterbury. The house was later given to Henry VIII, who added the wing now known as the King's Stables. Queen Elizabeth gave Knole to Thomas Sackville in 1566 and the family made numerous additions, enlarging the house into its present size—it has 365 rooms and 52 staircases. Knole is richly furnished. Its treasures include tapestries woven in the 15th and 16th centuries as well as paintings and silver of the same period.

A walking tour of Greenwich
GREENWICH

*The home of kings for centuries, Greenwich stands today as the finest collection of
17th and 18th-century buildings in Britain. A covetous king, Henry VI, probably killed
to obtain the estate for his young wife. Henry VIII and the Reformation were born
there, beside the Thames. Mary, Queen of Scots died because of an order Elizabeth I
signed in the old Tudor Palace. Charles II founded the Observatory in the spreading
parkland, and it was eventually chosen to mark the zero meridian of longitude.
Christopher Wren's Classical buildings house the Royal Naval College and, among a
mass of art treasures, the finest painted ceiling outside the Vatican. It was at
Greenwich that Nelson lay in state after his last voyage, and another famous voyager,
the tea clipper* Cutty Sark, *found a final resting place.*

CUTTY SARK *The raking bow of this great sailing clipper is
model of beauty and function. She was brought to Greenwich
in 1954. On board is a collection of ships' figureheads. The
'tween decks are the place where her most famous skipper,
Captain Woodgett, used to roller skate. The* Cutty Sark
could carry 32,000 sq. ft of sail and race at 17½ knots.

The tour begins at Greenwich Pier, a
landing place for centuries, across
which have walked some of the most
famous feet in English history. At this loop in
the River Thames there was a fishing port
before the Romans came. Kentish kings ruled
from this site. So did the Normans, the
Plantagenets, the Tudors and the Stuarts.

For more than 200 years, until 1629, English
monarchs lived at Greenwich. It remains a
magnificent monument to them, and the royal
buildings present the finest architectural vista
in England.

To the right of the pier is a monument to
another age and other men—the *Cutty Sark,*
once the fastest, most beautiful, and now most
famous of clipper ships. On one occasion she
covered 363 miles in 24 hours.

She was built in a Clyde shipyard by a
company that went bankrupt, and she was designed for the tea trade. But she was launched
in November 1869—a week after the Suez
Canal was opened—and the tea business had
already gone to the steamships.

Cutty Sark turned to the wool trade and
Australia. She traded, circumnavigating the
world and rounding Cape Horn, until 1922,
when she retired, having become a legend. She
was brought to Greenwich in 1954 and, after
restoration, opened to the public three years
later.

From *Cutty Sark* another right turn leads to
a second notable ship—*Gipsy Moth IV.* In
1966–7 Sir Francis Chichester, then aged 65,
sailed this 54 ft yacht single-handed around the
world in 226 days, following the clipper route.

From *Gipsy Moth IV,* back across Cutty
Sark Gardens and along the riverside, is the
Royal Naval College, the centrepiece of
Greenwich and site of the great royal palaces.

Home of kings
Norman kings took over Greenwich after
1066, but it was not until 1427 that the first
royal residence was built there by Duke
Humphrey of Gloucester, Regent for the boy
king, Henry VI. The palace was seized for the
king's wife, Margaret of Anjou, in 1447 after
the duke had been mysteriously found dying. It
seems most likely that he had been murdered
on the order of the king.

The palace became the main residence of the
English monarchs. Set amid green meadows,
with its great armoury, tilting grounds, orchards and gardens, and flanked by the naval
dockyards of Deptford and Woolwich, it was a
symbol of English might.

Henry VIII, Mary I and Elizabeth I were
born at Greenwich. It was there that Henry
first turned to Ann Boleyn, and started the

Reformation. And from there Elizabeth sent
the order to behead Mary, Queen of Scots.

It was ironically Mary's Scottish son, James
I, who commissioned the first of the new
buildings that survive to this day. In 1616 he
ordered Inigo Jones, the court architect, to
build the Queen's House for his wife, Anne of
Denmark. But she died in 1619 and the house
was not finished until 1637, when it was completed for Charles I's wife, Queen Henrietta
Maria.

Jones's work began the transformation of
Greenwich. For 200 years the village was to
absorb the talents of the country's major
architects.

The work of Wren
After the Civil War, Charles II ordered the
ancient palace by the river to be razed and a
new one built to match the splendour of the
Queen's House. He appointed Jones's pupil,
John Webb, as his architect, but soon became
absorbed with Hampton Court instead. In
1694 Christopher Wren was appointed by
Queen Mary to develop the site as a hospital
for retired and wounded seamen. He kept
Charles's building, the King's House, copied
it a little way downstream, and designed the
narrowing progression of courts focusing on
the Queen's House.

Admiral Byng was imprisoned there before
his court-martial and execution, in 1756, for
neglect of duty in failing to relieve the French
siege of Minorca; Captain Cook worked there
before his last fatal journey to the South Seas;
and Nelson lay in state in the beautiful Painted
Hall after Trafalgar. Then his body was transported up the river in a state barge for his
funeral at St Paul's.

Sir James Thornhill took 17 years to
decorate the hall, completing it in 1724. He
charged £3 a foot for the ceiling, £1 a foot for
the walls, and produced a masterpiece un-
matched outside the Vatican's Sistine Chapel.
In 1893 the hospital became the Royal Naval
College.

To the right of the college, and a short
distance along the river front, is the Trafalgar
Tavern. This is one of the most famous
Georgian public houses in England, haunt of
authors such as Charles Dickens and Captain
Marryat, as well as George Cruickshank, who
as 'Boz' did sketches for Dickens's novels.

Along Crane Street, beyond the tavern, is
Trinity College. This was founded in 1613 as
almshouses by the Earl of Northampton. The
chapel and courtyard are now dwarfed by the
London Transport power station.

Beyond the power station, passing Anchor
Wharf on the left, is Ballast Quay, the port's

GIPSY MOTH IV *This was home for Francis Chichester during
his epic lone voyage. Double-sided dials enabled him to chec[k]
his progress from inside the cabin. He returned a hero in 196[7]
to be knighted by Elizabeth II in the grounds of the Royal
Naval College. He had completed, single-handed and at the
age of 65, a voyage of 29,630 miles.*

ballast-loading point for all ships in days gone by. It is now flanked by a fine Georgian terrace, with the Cutty Sark Tavern and the old harbourmaster's office.

Back at the Trafalgar Tavern a left turn leads into Park Row. After 300 yds the museum, with the Queen's House at its centre, is on the right.

Inside the Great Hall, the spiral staircase, first of its kind in Britain, and the Queen's apartments have been restored to their original splendour after a noisy spell as a boys' school. The road to Woolwich once ran in a tunnel beneath the house and the tunnel entrance is still there.

The Queen's House and its wings contain one of the largest maritime collections in the world. Scale models of great warships, relics, archives, navigational aids, charts and marine paintings record a history of the sea. The collections date from Tudor to modern times.

The west wing houses a collection of English maritime paintings, and a series of portraits by Kneller, Reynolds, Romney, Hogarth and Gainsborough, as well as Turner's painting of HMS *Victory* at Trafalgar. There is also a gallery devoted to Captain Cook, and a Navigation Room telling the story of the long search for an accurate method of measuring longitude at sea.

The east wing contains models, paintings and reconstructions, representing the story of the change from sail and wood to steam and iron. The Polar gallery commemorates one of the saddest stories of British exploration—Sir John Franklin's ill-fated search for the north-west passage in 1845.

A path by the west wing of the Maritime Museum runs through the royal park to the first official observatory in Britain, founded by Charles II in 1675 and designed by Wren.

One of the first things to greet the visitor's eye is the Greenwich Time Ball, the world's first visual time signal. It has been in operation since 1833, when the Admiralty issued the following notice to mariners: 'The Lords Commissioners of the Admiralty hereby give notice, that a ball will hence forward be dropped, every day, from the top of a pole on the eastern turret of the Royal Observatory at Greenwich, at the moment of one-o'-clock p.m. solar time.' The ball is still dropped at precisely 1 p.m. G.M.T. every day.

The observatory's work was vital to Sir Isaac Newton in studying the laws of gravity. The observatory produced the world's first Nautical Almanack in 1767, and in 1884 was chosen, after discussions by the world's maritime nations, as the zero line of longitude, and demarcator of Greenwich Mean Time—on which all the world's time is based.

In the observatory courtyard you can stand astride the prime meridian, with one foot in each hemisphere, East and West. The work of the observatory was transferred to Herstmonceux in Sussex in 1950. Wren's observatory remains a record of the history of navigational instruments and astronomy. It contains the 24-hour clock, which keeps Greenwich Mean Time, and Airy's Transit Circle, by which the prime meridian was calculated.

Named after John Flamsteed, the first Astronomer Royal, Flamsteed House was built by Wren 'for the Observator's habitation and a little for Pompe'. Successive astronomers royal lived there from 1676 to 1948.

It was there, in the Octagon Room, that Flamsteed made the first accurate measurement of time. Today, the house is a museum. In the Halley Gallery—named after astronomer Sir Edmund Halley, the discoverer of Halley's Comet—there is a fine collection of

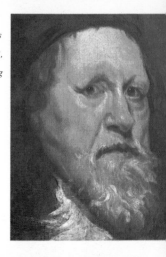

QUEEN'S HOUSE *The Great Hall of the Queen's House was designed by Inigo Jones as a perfect cube, 40ft × 40ft × 40ft. Charles I and Henrietta Maria spent their last night together in the house. On February 11, 1642, the queen left, taking nine-year-old Princess Mary to marry William of Orange. The king left on a journey that was to lead to bitter years of civil war and eventually to the scaffold seven years later.*

INIGO JONES *This expressive portrait by William Dobson hangs in the Queen's House, generally regarded as Jones's masterpiece. Jones, the first real architect in Britain, designed the house in 1616. James I ordered it for his wife, Anne of Denmark, but she died three years later. Charles I had the work completed for his wife, Henrietta Maria. There he hung many of his famous collection of pictures. But they were sold after the Civil War.*

COVERED WALK *Symmetrical colonnades flank either side of the Queen's House, which is now a museum housing treasures of British naval history.*

BATTLE OF LEPANTO *The last great sea battle (1571) fought in oared galleys as shown in one of the famous pictures in the Maritime Museum. The artist is unknown.*

GREENWICH

astrolabes and models of the solar system. In the Spencer Jones Gallery, displays tell the story of time. Sundials of many types are on show in the Maskelyne Gallery, and other fascinating reminders of Greenwich's role in the history of science can be seen in the Nathaniel Bliss Gallery.

Blackheath Avenue leads from the observatory across the royal park. Past the junction with Great Cross Avenue is another path on the right. At the end of this is the Ranger's House, once the home of the Earl of Chesterfield (1694–1773), whose letters to his son set a pattern for polite behaviour in 18th-century society. The house is now owned by the Greater London Council, and the public can enjoy the same lovely views from the three bow windows of the earl's gallery that Chesterfield himself enjoyed. Concerts are held there on Sunday evenings in the summer.

Outside the Ranger's House, a left turn along the edge of the park leads to the next building, Macartney House, where James Wolfe, conqueror of Quebec, lived. There are fine views across Blackheath, once the haunt of highwaymen and footpads.

Behind Macartney House is Crooms Hill, which descends towards the river, passing one of the finest streets of Georgian houses in London. The Manor House is on the left. It was completed in 1694, the year when Wren began his grand design for Greenwich.

Further down Crooms Hill, past King George Street, is a left turn into Gloucester Circus, a magnificent example of 18th-century architecture. Through the circus is a right turn into Royal Hill, where there are some fine early-Victorian houses.

A hero's burial place

At the bottom of Royal Hill is Greenwich High Road. To the right it leads back to the river front, passing St Alfege's Church.

This beautiful baroque church was started by Nicholas Hawksmoor in 1714. It is on the site of the parish church where Henry VIII and Elizabeth I were christened.

Major-General James Wolfe, the hero of the capture of Quebec in 1759, is buried there. Wolfe was only 32 when he died at the moment of victory. His audacity—as well as his extreme youth—had alarmed some of his older colleagues, who told George II that he was mad. The King replied: 'Mad, is he? Then I wish he would bite some others of my generals.'

The church takes its name from Alfege, Archbishop of Canterbury in 1012. Danish invaders kidnapped him and imprisoned him at Greenwich. When he refused to let his followers raise a £3000 ransom, the Danes beat Alfege to death.

During the Second World War, German bombs destroyed the inside of the church and the rare wood-sculptured pulpit and pews by Grinling Gibbons, the master carver of the 17th and 18th centuries.

The tour of Greenwich ends along Greenwich Church Walk, and back to Cutty Sark Gardens. There is a foot tunnel by the pier, with a lift at each end, that crosses under the river to Island Gardens. The reward at the end of this walk is to look back across the river for the finest view of Greenwich, barely changed since painted by Canaletto 200 years ago.

THE MANOR HOUSE *One of the many fine old buildings in Greenwich, it stands on Crooms Hill. The house was completed in 1694.*

BENEATH THE RIVER *The foot tunnel leads under the Thames to Island Gardens . . . and the best view of all of Greenwich's glories.*

GREENWICH MEAN TIME *The red time ball that tops the eastern tower of the Royal Observatory is pictured falling, as it has done every day since 1833 at 1 p.m. Once a signal for busy Victorian shipping in the Thames, it is now a reminder of the meaning of Greenwich Mean Time, adopted as a world standard for calculating longitude at sea.*

THINGS TO SEE

1 *Cutty Sark*: Daily, 11 a.m. (Sun. 2.30 p.m.)–6 p.m. (5 p.m. in winter).

2 *Gipsy Moth IV*: Daily (as *Cutty Sark*).

3 Royal Naval College: Daily except Thur., 2.30–5 p.m.

4 Trafalgar Tavern.

5 Trinity College almshouses.

6 Ballast Quay.

7 National Maritime Museum and Queen's House: Weekdays, 10 a.m.–6 p.m., Sun. 2.30–6 p.m.

8 Old Royal Observatory: Weekdays, 10 a.m.–6 p.m., Sun. 2.30–6 p.m. Caird Planetarium: Certain days only.

9 Ranger's House.

10 Macartney House.

11 Manor House.

12 St Alfege's Church.

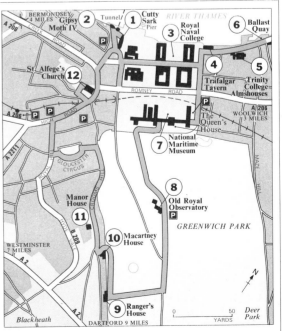

The Cotswolds: a heritage of stone founded on wool

When religious persecution drove the Huguenots from France during the 17th century, many settled in English 'wool' towns such as Witney. Their industry and skill soon made the area around Burford one of the wealthiest in the country. Masons shaped the local stone into lasting symbols of this prosperity—the mellow cottages and mansions of the Cotswolds. Even the shops lend elegance to such villages as Filkins and Langford.

1 Burford to Cotswold Wild Life Park Leave Burford on the A361, heading south, and at the roundabout junction with the A40, on the outskirts of the town, keep ahead (still on the A361), following the signpost for Swindon. After 2 m., at the crossroads just beyond the hospital, turn right. The Cotswold Wild Life Park is on the left.

2 Cotswold Wild Life Park to Filkins Return to the A361 from the park and turn right towards Swindon. After about 2 m. turn left off the A361 on the road signposted to Filkins, which has a museum of country life.

3 Filkins to Langford Turn left by The Lamb public house in Filkins, go straight over the crossroads on the outskirts of the village and carry on for 1 m. to Langford, continuing through the village to the old, towered church on the right.

4 Langford to Faringdon Return to the centre of the village and turn right by The Crown public house on to the road signposted for Broadwell. After a few hundred yards, turn right again on to the road signposted to Clanfield and follow it to its junction with the B4020. There, turn right into Clanfield. On the 14th-century tower of the church, just to the right, there is a large statue of St Stephen, whose death by stoning in AD 35 made him the first Christian martyr. Go through the village on the B4020 and at the junction with the A4095 keep straight ahead following the signpost for Faringdon. At the T-junction on the outskirts of Faringdon, turn right for the centre of the town.

5 Faringdon to Great Coxwell Leave Faringdon on the A420 signposted for Swindon. About ½ m. from the centre of the town, just past the hospital, turn right on to the B4019 signposted for Coleshill. After just over 1 m. on this road, turn left, following the signpost for Great Coxwell. The village's Great Barn is on the right of the road.

6 Great Coxwell to Stanton Harcourt From the centre of Great Coxwell take the first turning left, from the direction of the Great Barn, and follow this to the A420. There turn right and, after 150 yds, turn left for Little Coxwell. At the T-junction on the far side of Little Coxwell turn right, following the signposts to Fernham. Turn left at the B4508 in Fernham, following this road through the village and through the next village, Shellingford. At the A417 take a right-and-left turn to continue on the B4508, following the signposts to Hatford. Turn left by the church in Hatford and after just over 2 m., at the junction with the A420, turn right. After 1 m. take the second turning on the left, following the signpost for Bampton, and

after a further 2 m., very shortly after crossing the River Thames at Tadpole Bridge, turn right. After just over 1 m. go left at the T-junction, take the first turning on the right, and go left again at the next T-junction on the road signposted for Witney. Go straight over the B4449 at Cote. At the next T-junction turn right on to the road for Yelford. Follow this road through Yelford and keep straight on over the A415 for Hardwick. Continue through the village, following the signpost for Stanton Harcourt. Cross two bridges over the River Windrush, and after 2 m. enter Stanton Harcourt. There, turn right at the T-junction on to the B4449 to visit the medieval church.

7 Stanton Harcourt to Witney Go back through the village on the B4449, signposted for Eynsham and Oxford. Just over 1 m. beyond the village, turn left on to the road signposted for South Leigh and Witney. Just after this road crosses a disused railway, turn left through South Leigh and bear left out of the village. At the junction with the A40 turn left and follow the A40 into Witney.

8 Witney to Minster Lovell Leave Witney on the B4022 signposted for Charlbury, but after ½ m., at the mini-roundabout where the B4022 goes right, keep straight ahead for Crawley. At the junction in Crawley go right, then immediately left, for Minster Lovell. Turn left again at the top of the hill outside the village, and keep straight ahead for Minster Lovell, past the right fork. Cross the 500-year-old bridge to enter the village.

9 Minster Lovell to Burford At the T-junction in Minster Lovell turn right, and at the next junction fork left following the signpost for Asthall Leigh. At the T-junction in Asthall Leigh turn left, and after a further 1½ m. turn left again on the road signposted to Asthall. Follow the road through Asthall and on the far side of the village turn right, to follow signposts for Swinbrook and Burford. After ¾ m., at the crossroads, keep straight on. Bear right at the next junction and take the road back to Burford.

INFORMATION

Places of interest *Burford:* Tolsey Museum, Easter to Oct., afternoons. *Cotswold Wild Life Park:* Daily, 10 a.m.-6 p.m. (except Christmas Day). *Filkins Museum:* Daily, 10 a.m.-5 p.m. *Great Coxwell Barn:* All reasonable times, by application to Court House Farm. *Minster Lovell Hall:* All year, weekdays, Sun. afternoons.

Information Thames and Chilterns Tourist Board, 8 The Market Place, Abingdon (Tel. Abingdon 22711).

Towns with easy access to Burford:

Banbury	24 m.	Oxford	20 m.
Cheltenham	23 m.	Swindon	20 m.

Otters in Cotswold Wild Life Park.

COTSWOLD WILD LIFE PARK
Creatures from all over the world live in natural conditions in this 120 acre zoo park. They include monkeys, otters, pelicans, penguins, pumas, crocodiles, white rhinos, red pandas, leopards, pythons and vultures. Other attractions include a tropical-fish aquarium and a pets' corner, picnic areas and an adventure playground for children. Dogs are permitted in the park. Light meals and picnic lunches are obtainable at the restaurant. There is also a gift shop and a garden centre, where plants are on sale.

Saxon carving, Langford church.

LANGFORD
St Matthew's parish church at Langford displays some of the best Saxon architecture in England. The three-stage tower, with two large, arched bell-openings on each side, is almost entirely Anglo-Saxon. Some experts believe it may have been built shortly after the Norman Conquest—but certainly by Anglo-Saxon masons, using mortar greatly superior to that of the Normans. Limestone figures reset into the 13th-century porch at some later period are also Saxon work. The Crucifixion scene has been dated between 1020 and 1040. The figure of Christ in Majesty, known as the Langford Rood, is said to pre-date the Norman Conquest.

FARINGDON
This grey-limestone market town is set on a low hill. It looks northwards over the upper valley of the River Thames and southwards to the broad Vale of White Horse. Alfred the Great is believed to have had a palace at Faringdon. The oldest building left in the town, however, is the 13th-century church in the market-place. Distinctive features of the town's church include the low central tower, which lost its spire during the Civil War, and the 13th-century south door with its decorative scroll-work. Much of the rest of the town's architecture is 17th and early 18th century, including the town hall. The Folly, a 140 ft high brick tower with an arcaded look-out room, half a mile east of the town centre, was built by Lord Berner in 1935 to provide work for local people.

RFORD

any of the shops, inns and
uses in Cotswold stone that line
rford's broad main street date
m Tudor times, though most
re given new fronts towards the
d of the 17th century. The town's
tory goes back at least 1200 years.
ng Aethelbald of Mercia was
feated by the West Saxons here
AD 752. Wool brought
osperity in the Middle Ages.
e 16th-century Tolsey Museum
lects the impact of history on a
all town from the Norman
nquest to the Industrial
volution. The Tolsey, so called
cause market and other tolls were
lected there, is a distinctive
ilding supported by eight pillars.

Georgian doll's house, Tolsey Museum, Burford.

MINSTER LOVELL

A river bridge and the Old Swan Inn,
both 500 years old, lend distinction to this
lovely village on the Windrush. Near by
are the ruins of 15th-century Minster
Lovell Hall, where the first Viscount
Lovell, a supporter of Richard III, hid
after the king's defeat at Bosworth in 1485.
Lovell is said to have died of starvation
because the key of his room, locked from
the outside, was lost. His skeleton, seated
at a table with pen and paper in front
of it, was found by workmen making
alterations to the building in 1708.

Minster Lovell Hall.

KINS

llage museum is housed
in a Cotswold cottage
the adjoining lock-up.
rest in the museum was
ouraged by the late Sir
ford Cripps, the post-war
terity' Chancellor of the
hequer, who lived in
ins. Exhibits range from
nestic utensils, in common
150 years ago, to mantraps
e set to catch poachers.

WITNEY

The famous Witney blankets have been
produced in the town since at least 1277.
Witney's oldest firm has been in business
since 1669, and many blankets are still made
in 18th-century mills. The Blanket Hall, in
Bridge Street, was built in 1721 as a meeting
place for merchants in the wool trade. An
unusual feature is its one-handed clock.
In the main street is an unusual 17th-
century Butter Cross with a clock turret
and sundial. Dominating the south end of
the town is the 13th-century church of
St Mary, with its handsome central tower.

Tomb of Sir Robert Harcourt, Stanton Harcourt church.

STANTON HARCOURT

This village has been the home of the Harcourt family for
900 years. One of them, Sir Robert, was Henry VII's
standard bearer at the Battle of Bosworth in 1485, and the
remains of the banner hang above his tomb in the church.
The gardens of the Harcourt home are occasionally open.

GREAT COXWELL

When the first Cistercian monks
came to England in the 12th century,
one of their priorities was to build
storehouses for the crops which
they grew and collected as tithes.
The Great Barn in this village is an
example. From the outside it could
easily be mistaken for a church. The
monks supported the massive stone
roof on slender oak posts mounted
on stone bases. Their skilful work
is still bearing the load after 700
years, during which time not one
of the posts has been dislodged.

The Great Barn, Great Coxwell.

Blanket Hall, Witney.

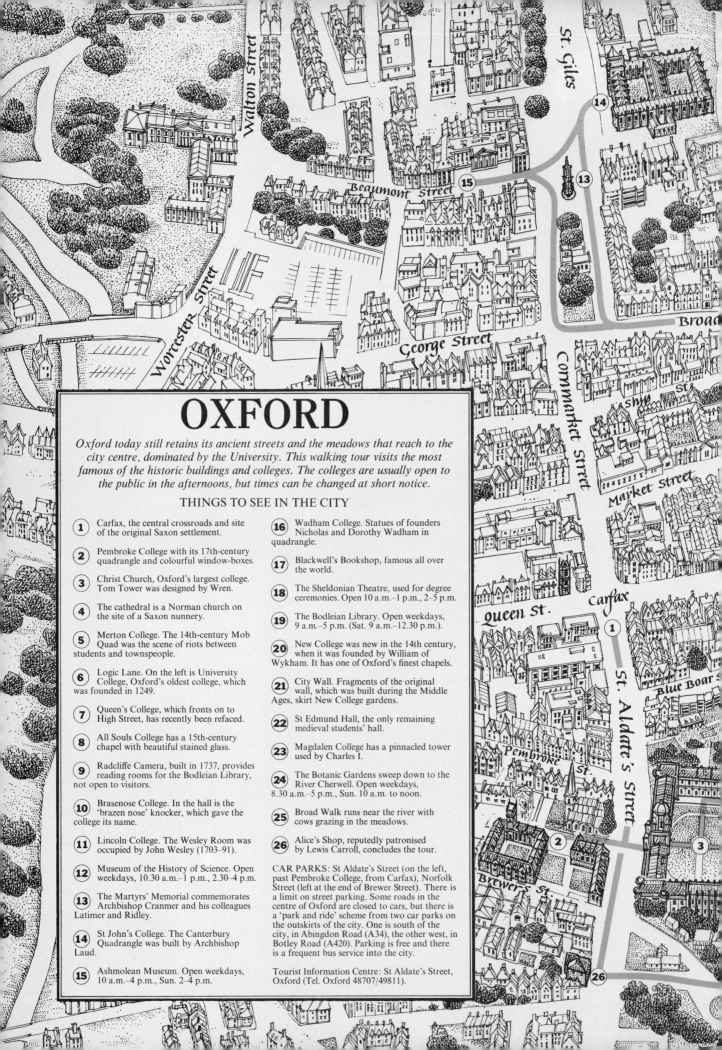

OXFORD

Oxford today still retains its ancient streets and the meadows that reach to the city centre, dominated by the University. This walking tour visits the most famous of the historic buildings and colleges. The colleges are usually open to the public in the afternoons, but times can be changed at short notice.

THINGS TO SEE IN THE CITY

(1) Carfax, the central crossroads and site of the original Saxon settlement.

(2) Pembroke College with its 17th-century quadrangle and colourful window-boxes.

(3) Christ Church, Oxford's largest college. Tom Tower was designed by Wren.

(4) The cathedral is a Norman church on the site of a Saxon nunnery.

(5) Merton College. The 14th-century Mob Quad was the scene of riots between students and townspeople.

(6) Logic Lane. On the left is University College, Oxford's oldest college, which was founded in 1249.

(7) Queen's College, which fronts on to High Street, has recently been refaced.

(8) All Souls College has a 15th-century chapel with beautiful stained glass.

(9) Radcliffe Camera, built in 1737, provides reading rooms for the Bodleian Library, not open to visitors.

(10) Brasenose College. In the hall is the 'brazen nose' knocker, which gave the college its name.

(11) Lincoln College. The Wesley Room was occupied by John Wesley (1703–91).

(12) Museum of the History of Science. Open weekdays, 10.30 a.m.–1 p.m., 2.30–4 p.m.

(13) The Martyrs' Memorial commemorates Archbishop Cranmer and his colleagues Latimer and Ridley.

(14) St John's College. The Canterbury Quadrangle was built by Archbishop Laud.

(15) Ashmolean Museum. Open weekdays, 10 a.m.–4 p.m., Sun. 2–4 p.m.

(16) Wadham College. Statues of founders Nicholas and Dorothy Wadham in quadrangle.

(17) Blackwell's Bookshop, famous all over the world.

(18) The Sheldonian Theatre, used for degree ceremonies. Open 10 a.m.–1 p.m., 2–5 p.m.

(19) The Bodleian Library. Open weekdays, 9 a.m.–5 p.m. (Sat. 9 a.m.–12.30 p.m.).

(20) New College was new in the 14th century, when it was founded by William of Wykam. It has one of Oxford's finest chapels.

(21) City Wall. Fragments of the original wall, which was built during the Middle Ages, skirt New College gardens.

(22) St Edmund Hall, the only remaining medieval students' hall.

(23) Magdalen College has a pinnacled tower used by Charles I.

(24) The Botanic Gardens sweep down to the River Cherwell. Open weekdays, 8.30 a.m.–5 p.m., Sun. 10 a.m. to noon.

(25) Broad Walk runs near the river with cows grazing in the meadows.

(26) Alice's Shop, reputedly patronised by Lewis Carroll, concludes the tour.

CAR PARKS: St Aldate's Street (on the left, past Pembroke College, from Carfax), Norfolk Street (left at the end of Brewer Street). There is a limit on street parking. Some roads in the centre of Oxford are closed to cars, but there is a 'park and ride' scheme from two car parks on the outskirts of the city. One is south of the city, in Abingdon Road (A34), the other west, in Botley Road (A420). Parking is free and there is a frequent bus service into the city.

Tourist Information Centre: St Aldate's Street, Oxford (Tel. Oxford 48707/49811).

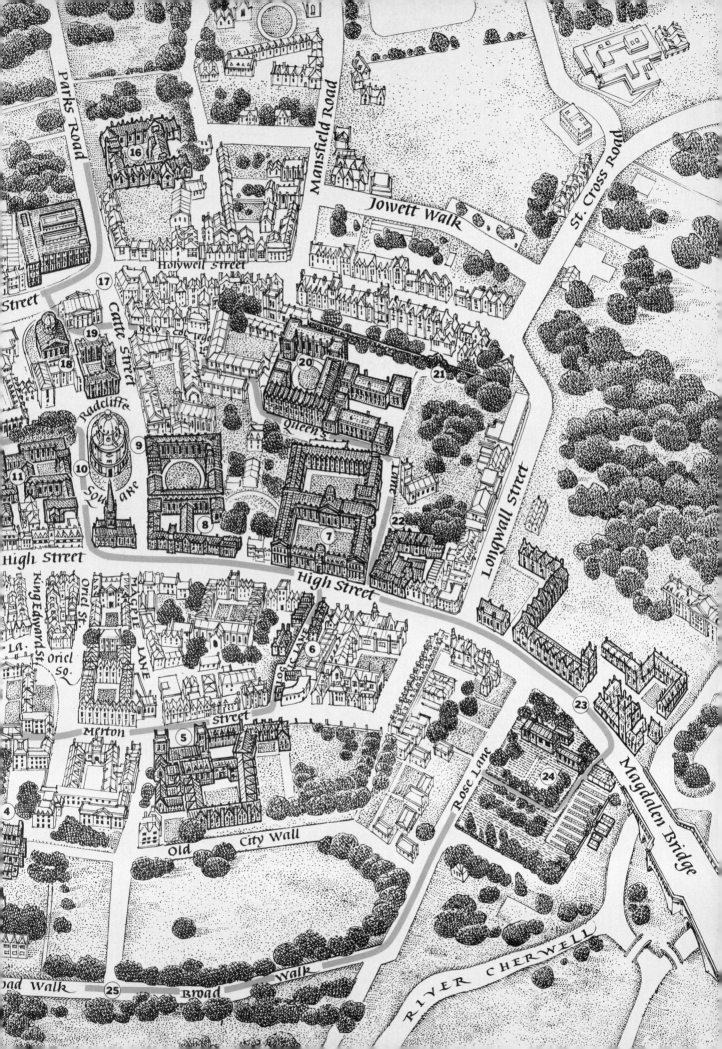

A walking tour of Oxford
OXFORD

A stained-glass detail from Christ Church Cathedral.

Romantically christened the 'city of dreaming spires' by the 19th-century poet Matthew Arnold, Oxford has grown from its Saxon beginnings to become one of Britain's chief cultural heritages. Much of its importance is due to its university—the first to be founded in England.

Oxford's origins go back to Saxon times, when a busy settlement grew up on an ox-drovers' ford across the River Thames. But at Oxford the river is called the Isis. Despite many efforts, where Thames becomes Isis and Isis becomes Thames has never been clearly defined.

The Saxons named their settlement *Oxna-forda*, and in the city the central crossroads —Carfax (from the Old French *carrefour*, four forks)—commemorates the meeting of the roads used by the ox-drovers. In the 8th century a nunnery dedicated to St Frideswide was founded there, and in 912 Oxford was mentioned in the *Anglo-Saxon Chronicle*.

But the city's real rise to prominence began in 1167, when Henry II took reprisals against France for sheltering Thomas Becket, the exiled Archbishop of Canterbury. Henry ordered all English scholars studying on the Continent to return home at once. Many of them settled at Oxford, where they tried to re-create the scholarly life they had known in Paris and other continental universities.

An uncertain beginning

Life at Oxford was precarious at first. The townspeople resented the students who gathered there. They were boisterous—and they certainly drank too much. In 1209 the townspeople hanged some students for alleged murder, and the scholars fled. Some went back to Paris, but others found refuge in a small town in the East Anglian fens—Cambridge.

In 1214 'town and gown' in Oxford reached an agreement which was ratified by the papal legate. This marked the formal founding of the university. But disputes between the two continued well into the 14th century. The biggest of these was a three-day riot which began on St Scholastica's day in February 1355. According to contemporary accounts 63 scholars were killed and hundreds injured.

Other features of Oxford life were slow to develop. Originally, there were no colleges where the students could live and study. Most of them resided in halls under the care of a Master of Arts. The last of these, St Edmund

MEDIEVAL CALM *The tower of Merton College, seen from the Grove. Founded by Walter de Merton in 1274, the coll[?] has Oxford's oldest-surviving university buildings and many rare books in its fine library.*

Hall, only became a college formally in 1956, and still keeps its old name. There were no formal entrance examinations. The courses of study that could be followed—grammar, rhetoric, logic, geometry, astronomy and music—were long and expensive.

Rich men soon realised that the best way to help Oxford's students was to found colleges where they could live and work. University, Balliol and Merton were all founded in the 13th century. Others soon followed. By Tudor times, most students were members of colleges, each of which had its own hall, chapel, library, studies and gardens.

Eventually, too, the senior members—the Fellows—began to supervise the work of the students and so the tutorial system developed. Today, most undergraduates live outside the college after their first year of study, while most Fellows have their homes elsewhere. In some colleges, only the Master retains his own 'lodgings' on the premises.

The purpose behind most of these foundations is still commemorated in a prayer used at university sermons—'that there may never be wanting a succession of persons duly qualified for the service of God in Church and State'. One man who followed this belief was William of Wykeham, Bishop of Winchester, who founded New College in 1379. Not only did he give Oxford one of its finest buildings,

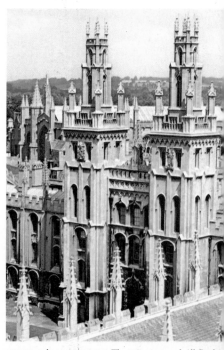

ARCHITECT'S ACHIEVEMENT *The twin towers of All Souls College were designed by Nicholas Hawksmoor, a pupil o[?] Christopher Wren. They are a prominent Oxford landmar[?]*

TEMPLE OF LEARNING *Duke Humphrey's Library, founded by Henry V's brother in 1444, is now a part of the massive Bodleian library. It contains some of Oxford's rarest manuscripts.*

CLERICAL INNOVATOR *William of Wykeham, the saintly Bishop of Winchester who founded New College in 1379, also gave Oxford one of its most distinguishing landmarks—the college quadrangle (above).*

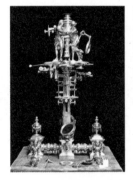

ROYAL SCIENTIST *Among the exhibits in Oxford's Museum of the History of Science are these elaborately styled microscopes, made for George III by George Adams in about 1770. The king was also a keen astronomer.*

DECORATION *A detail from a gargoyle in the main quadrangle of Magdalen College. Magdalen's beautiful buildings have changed little since they were built at the end of the 15th century.*

TREASURE HOUSE *The Italian painter Bellini's 'St Jerome in the Wilderness' is one of the many treasures in the Ashmolean Museum, based on a collection given by Elias Ashmole in 1677. Among English relics on display are the 'lanthorn' used by the Gunpowder Plotter Guy Fawkes, and the Alfred Jewel, of gold, rock crystal and enamel, made for Alfred of Wessex in the 9th century.*

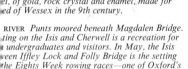

RIVER *Punts moored beneath Magdalen Bridge. Boating on the Isis and Cherwell is a recreation for many undergraduates and visitors. In May, the Isis between Iffley Lock and Folly Bridge is the setting for the Eights Week rowing races—one of Oxford's most famous summer spectacles.*

he also gave it one of its best-known landmarks—the college quadrangle.

Other benefactors gave help in different ways. One of the most important was Sir Thomas Bodley, an Elizabethan diplomat. In 1598 he offered to restore the university library, which had been founded by Humphrey, Duke of Gloucester in 1444. Bodley gave it his own valuable collection of books as well as supervising the plans for its rebuilding. But his most valuable contribution was the agreement he reached in 1610 with the Stationers' Company to give the library a copy of every book it printed. Today, the Bodleian Library houses more than 2,500,000 books, and is one of the finest libraries in the world.

Another man who left his mark on Oxford was Elias Ashmole, who gave the curiosities collected by his friend, the traveller and naturalist John Tradescant, to the university in 1677 on condition that a suitable building was erected to house them. This was the start of the Ashmolean Museum, now one of Oxford's most important treasure houses.

Centre of learning

Kings, too, played their part in making Oxford a leading centre of British learning. Henry VIII took a special interest in Cardinal College, founded by his one-time chief minister, Cardinal Wolsey, which he had renamed King Henry VIII's College. It is now Christ Church. And during the Civil War of the 17th century, Christ Church was the headquarters of the ill-fated Charles I.

Men who taught at Oxford included the medieval friar-scientist Roger Bacon, the 17th-century scientists Robert Boyle and Robert Hooke and the architect Christopher Wren, who left his own legacy in the Sheldonian Theatre, built to house the degree ceremony. It was Wren's first major commission, and he went on to build Tom Tower in Christ Church and a new quadrangle in Trinity.

Another teacher was a shy 19th-century mathematics don, C. L. Dodgson. He is better known to posterity as Lewis Carroll, the author of the immortal *Alice in Wonderland.* Alice herself was based on the little daughter of the Dean of Christ Church.

Such teachers spread the influence of Oxford throughout the world, and they took great pride in their achievements. Students have ranged from future Prime Ministers to poets. Shelley was among the latter. But he was 'sent down'—expelled—from University College for publishing *The Necessity of Atheism.*

The 20th century brought great changes to Oxford. A young engineer, William Morris, launched a revolution in the city when he founded a car factory there. Today, the British Leyland works at Cowley is one of the largest in the world.

But Oxford's glorious buildings still survive, and the heart of the city remains breathtaking in its loveliness. All the colleges are worth visiting and most of them are within an easy walk of the High Street. Christ Church, with its splendid 18th-century library and recently built picture gallery, is the largest. Magdalen, with its famous deer park, is probably the most beautiful. Others competing for this title include Trinity, St John's and Worcester.

The lake at Worcester is especially memorable. And in Christ Church's meadows, which lead on to the river, the calm of the country comes close to the heart of the city centre.

The England of St George and Alfred the Great

The Vale of White Horse, carpeted with wheatfields, stretches westwards from the old market town of Abingdon. To the south the land swells up to the Berkshire Downs, reaching its highest point where Iron Age men carved their strange white horse into the chalk at Uffington. Here also, according to legend, St George slew the dragon. It is a county of thatched villages and mansions surrounded by scented gardens.

(1) Abingdon to Dorchester Leave Abingdon on the A415 southwards, crossing the River Thames on the way out of the town. Follow the road to the junction with the A423 and turn right into Dorchester.

(2) Dorchester to Wittenham Clumps Return along the A415 towards Abingdon, but turn left in Clifton Hampden, following the signpost for Didcot. Follow the road round to the left, across the Thames and into Long Wittenham. Here bear left for Little Wittenham. (To visit the Pendon Museum of Miniature Landscape and Transport in Long Wittenham, bear right into the village off the through road. The museum is down a lane at the far side of the village. Its exhibits include models of the Vale of White Horse and railway relics from the start of the 19th century.) Follow the road to Little Wittenham and turn right on to the road signposted to Brightwell and Wallingford. This road skirts the foot of Wittenham Clumps. (To follow the footpath to the top of Wittenham Clumps, turn left at the junction in Little Wittenham. The footpath starts just before the church.)

(3) Wittenham Clumps to Didcot At the T-junction after the Clumps turn left, and at the junction with the A4130 turn right, following the signpost for Didcot. Continue along this road for 2½ m. into Didcot.

(4) Didcot to Wantage Leave Didcot on the A4130 signposted to Wantage, and turn right just over 2 m. later, at the junction with the A417 in Harwell. Follow the A417 across the A34 for another 5 m. to Wantage, birthplace of Alfred the Great.

(5) Wantage to Whitehorse Hill Leave the centre of Wantage on the A338 signposted to Hungerford. On the outskirts of the town, turn right on to the B4507. Turn left at the fourth crossroads, which follows after 6 m., and follow the road up Whitehorse Hill.

(6) Whitehorse Hill to Uffington Follow the road down the hill and go straight across the B4507 into Woolstone, a cluster of cottages among which some Roman remains have been found. The small church retains some Norman features and contains a rare lead font. Turn right at the T-junction in Woolstone, following the signpost for Uffington, and go right again after 1 m. at the next junction. On reaching the village, turn left to visit the church.

(7) Uffington to Pusey House Swing right by the church in Uffington and then turn left, following the signpost for Stanford in the Vale, on the far side of the village. Turn right after crossing the railway, and then left at the junction with the A417. After 1 m. turn right into Stanford in the Vale, an old market town. The church here has a Norman doorway, a richly carved Elizabethan pulpit, and a 14th-century brass of a rector in his robes. Follow the road through the town and turn right after 1 m. at the junction with the B4508, following the signpost to Pusey, which is reached after 1½ m. Pusey House is on the right.

(8) Pusey House to Milton Continue on the B4508 to the junction with the A420 and turn right. Follow the road for 3 m. into Kingston Bagpuize and turn right on to the A415 signposted to Abingdon. In Frilford, turn right on to the A338, following the signpost for Wantage, and follow the Roman road south-westwards for 3 m. to East Hanney. There, turn left at the crossroads on to the road signposted to Steventon, which is reached after 3½ m. Here, there is a raised path known as The Causeway leading to the 14th-century church. This was built by monks to enable people to walk dryshod in times of flood. The monks' priory has vanished, but some of the buildings attached to it, including the great hall, are now cottages owned by the National Trust. At Steventon, turn right on to the A34. After 1 m. turn left at the signpost for Milton, and follow the road for 1 m. into the village, with its fine 17th-century manor house.

(9) Milton to Sutton Courtenay At the far side of Milton turn right at the signpost for Sutton Courtenay, and follow the road into the village.

(10) Sutton Courtenay to Abingdon At the junction with the B4016 in Sutton Courtenay turn right, then left on the far side of the village, following the signpost for Culham and Abingdon. Follow the road across the Thames and keep straight ahead. At the junction with the A415 turn left on to the road signposted to Abingdon, and follow the road for 1¼ m. into the town.

INFORMATION

Places of interest *Abingdon:* Museum, all year, daily, afternoons only. Closed Bank Hols. *Didcot:* Railway museum, Easter to mid-Sept., Sun. and Bank Hols., 11 a.m.-5 p.m. *Dorchester:* Museum, Easter to Oct., weekdays, Sun. afternoons. *Milton Manor:* Easter to Oct., weekends and Bank Hols., afternoons. *Long Wittenham:* Pendon Museum, summer, Sat., Sun. and Bank Hols., 2-6 p.m., closed Christmas, Boxing and New Year's Day. *Pusey House:* July to mid-Oct., daily (except Mon. and Fri.); Apr. to July, Wed., Thur., Sun., Bank Hols., afternoons.

Information Thames and Chilterns Tourist Board, 8 The Market Place, Abingdon (Tel. Abingdon 22711).

Towns with easy access to Abingdon:

Faringdon	14 m.	Oxford	7 m.
Newbury	21 m.	Wallingford	11 m.

MILTON
William of Orange stayed at Milton Manor when he came to England in 1688 to be crowned King William III. The many treasures of the 17th-century mansion include a chapel and library, both in the Gothic style, a telescope belonging to Admiral John Benbow, who d fighting the French in 1702. Milton was known as Middletune (the middle farm) in Saxon days. Relics of nearly 2000 years ago have been found in the area, including jewelled brooches and the boss of a shield.

Pusey House.

PUSEY HOUSE
It is said that the Pusey estate was granted to William Pewse by King Canute at the beginning of the 11th cen The present house, a Georgian mansion built in 1748 surrounded by 20 acres of gardens which are open to public. The grounds contain a large variety of flowers and shrubs, and a water-garden with a fine collectio aquatic plants. There are also some beautiful trees, some as old as the house, a lake and walled gardens. From the terrace of the house are views to the south of the Berkshire Downs and Whitehorse Hill.

UFFINGTON
The author Thomas Hughes (1822–96) lived at Uffington and made the area famous as the home of the hero of his book *Tom Brown's Schooldays.* There is a memorial to Hughes in the village's 13th-century church, which also has an unusual octagonal tower. Close to the church is Uffington School, dating from 1617. Like much of the village, it is built of chalk.

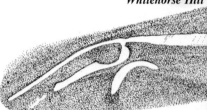

White Horse, Uffington.

WHITEHORSE HILL
The great white horse from which the hill takes its na is 360 ft long and 130 ft high. It is the oldest of all the white horses carved on the chalk downs in many parts of England. It is thought to be the work of Iron Age Celts, and may have been cut as early as 350 BC. Above the horse is Uffington Castle, an Iron Age hill-fort which crowns the 856 ft summit of the Berkshire Downs. St George is said to have killed the dragon on the little hill below the horse. The bald patch on the hilltop has, according to the legend, been devoid of gr since the beast's blood was spilt on it.

SCALE

0   1   2   3   4   5 M

ABINGDON

Situated at the point where the tiny River Ock runs into the Thames, Abingdon was founded as a monastic settlement in the 7th century. It was the county town of Berkshire until 1870 and contains many old buildings, as well as the factory where MG cars are made. The 15th-century bridge, which is broader than it is long, crosses the Thames through a cluster of boat-houses. Downstream, the fine spire of St Helen's Church rises among 15th-century almshouses. The abbey's main gateway and its church of St Nicholas have survived from the 12th century, and other remains include a building which is now an Elizabethan-style theatre. The 17th-century County Hall contains the town's museum. Exhibits include town and county archives, plate, arms and uniforms.

y Hall, Abingdon.

The abbey guest-house, Dorchester.

DORCHESTER

Built on the banks of the Thame, a major tributary of the Thames, Dorchester dates back to the Bronze Age; later it was an important Roman settlement. The Norman abbey is 200 ft long and noted for its 13th-century stained glass. The great east window was restored as a memorial to Sir Winston Churchill in 1966. It is flanked by a 14th-century Jesse window, showing the family tree of Jesus back to Jesse. The abbey's 15th-century guest-house is now a museum.

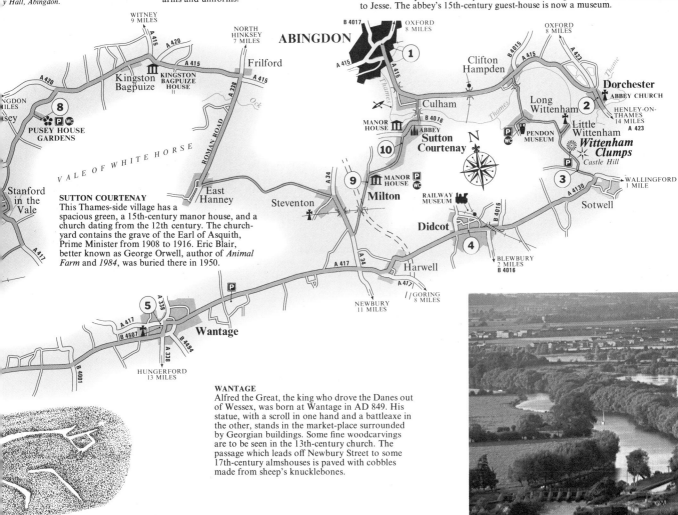

SUTTON COURTENAY

This Thames-side village has a spacious green, a 15th-century manor house, and a church dating from the 12th century. The church-yard contains the grave of the Earl of Asquith, Prime Minister from 1908 to 1916. Eric Blair, better known as George Orwell, author of *Animal Farm* and *1984*, was buried there in 1950.

WANTAGE

Alfred the Great, the king who drove the Danes out of Wessex, was born at Wantage in AD 849. His statue, with a scroll in one hand and a battleaxe in the other, stands in the market-place surrounded by Georgian buildings. Some fine woodcarvings are to be seen in the 13th-century church. The passage which leads off Newbury Street to some 17th-century almshouses is paved with cobbles made from sheep's knucklebones.

DIDCOT

Didcot was an isolated village until Isambard Brunel built the Great Western Railway through it in 1841. The old village buildings have survived among those that sprang up to serve an important railway junction, but the town's major attraction is the Great Western Society's Motive Power and Live Steam Museum. About 16 locomotives and a large amount of rolling-stock are maintained in the old Great Western Railway's Motive Power Depot. The oldest of the locomotives, *Shannon*, was built in 1857. It is believed to be the world's oldest standard-gauge locomotive in regular service when it was 'retired' in 1945. The engine has now been restored to working order and is painted in crimson.

comotive, Didcot steam museum.

View from Wittenham Clumps.

WITTENHAM CLUMPS

A half-mile walk up a path from Little Wittenham leads to the summit of Wittenham Clumps, one of the Sinodun Hills. It is only 400 ft high, but commands views over the Vale of White Horse to the west, and the plain which leads to the Chilterns in the east. Close to the south is Castle Hill, well wooded but scarred by the remains of an earth fortification. The fort has not been excavated, but Iron Age and Roman pottery has been found on the site. The slopes below the fort to the north are thickly wooded.

Racehorses on the downs, elephants in the church

The chalk steed carved on the face of the Vale of White Horse sets the scene for this tour of Berkshire. Racehorses canter on the downs around the training centre of Lambourn, and deer wander in sight of the picnickers on Snelsmore Common. Nearby Wickham has a surprise for visitors—life-size model elephants in the parish church. The route starts from the place where William the Conqueror forded the Thames on his way to claim the English crown in London; and it crosses and recrosses the prehistoric Ridge Way which runs from South Devon to The Wash.

(1) Wallingford to Goring Leave Wallingford on the A423 signposted to Henley. After ½ m. the road crosses the Thames, and another ½ m. brings it to Crowmarsh Gifford. Keep straight on at the traffic lights, but turn right on to the A4074 shortly after, following the Reading signpost. After 1 m., where the A4074 swings left for Reading, keep straight ahead on the B4009 signposted to Goring.

(2) Goring to Hermitage In the centre of Goring turn right to follow the B4009 across the Thames to Streatley. At the traffic lights where the road crosses the A329 keep straight on, following the Newbury signpost. Follow the B4009 through Aldworth and Hampstead Norris to Hermitage.

(3) Hermitage to Newbury Leave Hermitage, still on the B4009, for the 4 m. drive to Newbury.

(4) Newbury to Donnington Castle Leave Newbury on the B4494 signposted to Oxford. Cross the A4 on the outskirts of Newbury, and just after the river turn left for Donnington Castle.

(5) Donnington Castle to Snelsmore Common Return to the B4494 and turn left. Continue ahead for just under 2 m. Snelsmore Common country park is on the left.

(6) Snelsmore Common to Wickham On leaving the park, turn left along the B4494, and shortly afterwards turn left again on to the road signposted to Winterbourne. At the T-junction 1 m. later turn right for Winterbourne. In the village turn left on to the road signposted to Boxford. Follow the road across the River Lambourn into Boxford. On the far side of Boxford, just after passing under a railway bridge, turn right, then immediately left. At the next crossroads turn right on to the B4000, following the signpost to Wickham, whose hilltop Church of St Swithin is reached by a short detour to the left of the village, up the road signposted to Kintbury.

(7) Wickham to Lambourn Return to Wickham and turn left, continuing along the B4000 through the village. After 1 m. the road crosses the M4 and continues for 2 m. to join the A338. Here turn left, then after a few hundred yards turn right still on the B4000 signposted to Lambourn. The road runs parallel to the M4 on the left, and passes through Woodlands St Mary. Continue for 1 m. to the Hare and Hounds public house, turn right still on the B4000 and follow the road into Lambourn.

(8) Lambourn to the Lord Wantage monument Leave Lambourn on the B4001 signposted for Wantage. The road runs over downs and crosses the ancient Ridge Way above the Vale of White Horse. After dropping down into the vale the road meets the B4507. Here turn right, following the signpost for Wantage. After just over 1 m. turn right again on to the road signposted to Letcombe Regis. Go through the village and, after 2 m. at the top of Court Hill, turn right on to the A338. Continue for 3 m. then turn left, following the signpost for Woolley. At the next crossroads turn left, following the signpost for Farnborough. After 2 m., at the junction with the B4494, turn left and drive on for 2 m. to the edge of the downs. A short walk along the Ridge Way to the right leads to the Lord Wantage monument.

(9) The Lord Wantage monument to East Hagbourne Return to the B4494 and retrace the route southwards for just over 1 m., taking the first turn left for Farnborough. Continue through Farnborough and over the downs for about 3 m. to West Ilsley. In the village turn left on to the road signposted for Chilton. After crossing the Ridge Way again, turn left at the junction with the A34. Take the second turning on the right, about 1 m. later by an inn. After 2 m. at the A417 turn left then immediately right, following the signpost to West Hagbourne. Beyond West Hagbourne, at Coscote, turn right on to the road signposted to East Hagbourne where, in Elizabethan times, a beacon used to be kept ready on the church tower to signal an invasion.

(10) East Hagbourne to Wallingford Follow the road through the village and turn right on meeting the B4016. Just over 1 m. later turn left, go through Aston Upthorpe, then turn left following the signpost for South Moreton and Wallingford. Just before the road enters South Moreton, turn right and follow the road back to Wallingford.

INFORMATION

Places of interest *Donnington Castle:* Exterior only, any reasonable time. *Newbury:* Museum (Cloth Hall), all year, weekdays, except Wed. afternoons.

Events *Newbury:* Racing during the year. *Wallingford:* Regatta, May. Carnival, June.

Information Thames and Chilterns Tourist Board, 8 Market Place, Abingdon (Tel. Abingdon 22711).

Towns with easy access to Wallingford:

Abingdon . . . . . . 11 m.	Oxford . . . . 13 m.
Aylesbury . . . . . . 25 m.	Reading . . . . 13 m.
Henley-on-Thames . . . . . . 11 m.	Wantage . . . . 13 m.

Market cross, East Hagbourne.

LORD WANTAGE MONUMENT
The monument, erected early this century in memory of a local benefactor, stands on the Ridge Way, commanding fine views over to the Cotswolds and the Chilterns. Lord Wantage was the founder of Reading University College and the British Red Cross Society.

LAMBOURN
Racehorses can often be seen exercising in the open country around the town, for Lambourn is a leading training area. The town is a centre for exploring the downs, which are dotted with limestone burial mounds and earthworks. Just under 2 miles to the north, a short detour to the left of the B4001 leads to the Seven Barrows, a group of these old mounds. The town has some Victorian almshouses and a 12th-century church, which contains a stone carving depicting hare-coursing. Lambourn featured as Maryland in Hardy's *Jude the Obscure.*

Model elephant, Wickham church.

WICKHAM
St Swithin's Church at Wickham has the only Saxon tower still standing in Berkshire. When the body of the church was rebuilt in the middle of the last century, its interior was lavishly adorned with an odd assortment of articles. These include papier mâché angels and life-size elephants, brought from the Paris Exhibition of 1862. The font cover, carved by Maori craftsmen, also came from the exhibition.

SCALE

0   1   2   3   4   5 MILES

WALLINGFORD

Wallingford is a country town on a lovely stretch of the Thames between Reading and Oxford, with the Chilterns to the north-east and the Berkshire Downs to the south-west. William the Conqueror's army forded the Thames here in 1066 in their advance to London, and the Normans built a castle to protect this strategic point. The castle was demolished in the Civil War 600 years later. The remains are in private grounds. The town's borough status dates from 1155; a plaque on the 17th-century Town Hall commemorates the 800th anniversary of the charter. Most of the buildings date from after 1675, when Wallingford was ravaged by a great fire.

HAGBOURNE (partial, left edge)

...ewashed, thatched cottages ...mellow timber-framed ...dings adorn this village ...h was rebuilt after 1659, ...n a fire wiped out everything ...pt the 12th-century church. ...561 Charles II ordered a ...ction to ease 'the great ...overishment and deplorable ...dition of the poor ...bitants'. The king's arms ...displayed in the church, ...t of which was restored ...two or three centuries. ...e of the glass in the windows ...survived from the 14th ...ury, a good example ...hich is the Nativity and ...in in a north window. The ...r contains an attractive ...canopy. North-east of the ...ch, grouped round the ...ge cross, are some delightful ...ered houses. At the end ...e main street is another cross.

GORING

At Goring the Thames is squeezed into a narrow, wooded valley that divides the Chilterns from the Berkshire Downs. The town is a boating and fishing centre and has a lock gate. This is one of the most picturesque stretches of the Thames and is a good base for riverside walks.

Lock gate and weir, Goring.

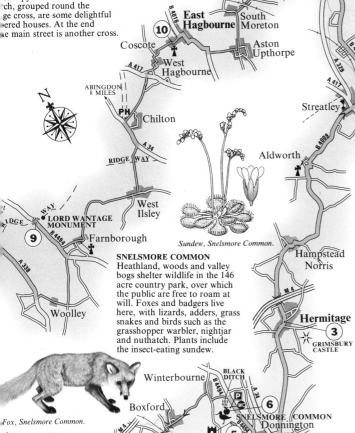

Sundew, Snelsmore Common.

Fox, Snelsmore Common.

...nington Castle.

HERMITAGE

The 'wishing well' here is fed by a spring which was once thought to cure diseases of the eyes. The church was founded by Queen Adelaide in 1835, and the altar vessels that she presented are still in use. Grimsbury Castle, a prehistoric earthwork, is among trees to the south. There are beautiful views over the commons.

SNELSMORE COMMON

Heathland, woods and valley bogs shelter wildlife in the 146 acre country park, over which the public are free to roam at will. Foxes and badgers live here, with lizards, adders, grass snakes and birds such as the grasshopper warbler, nightjar and nuthatch. Plants include the insect-eating sundew.

NEWBURY

Cloth made Newbury prosperous in the Middle Ages, as testified by the Cloth Hall in the market-place, with its wealth of Jacobean woodwork. The hall is now a museum. John Winchcombe—'Jack of Newbury'—became England's leading clothier, achieving such wealth and prominence that he entertained Henry VIII and his first wife, Catherine of Aragon, at his house in Northbrook Street. He led 100 men to fight the Scots at the Battle of Flodden, and in the early 16th century paid for the rebuilding of St Nicholas's Church. The remains of Jack's home can still be seen. The Kennet and Avon Canal runs through the town under a bridge near the market-place. There are many ancient buildings in the town, including a number of almshouses. Newbury is also well known for its race course, where there is horse-racing throughout the year.

Cloth Hall museum, Newbury.

DONNINGTON CASTLE

The castle stood where two highways met, and was badly damaged in the Civil War. The most impressive survival is the gatehouse, added about 1386 when the original manor house was fortified against a possible French invasion. When the Civil War started in the 17th century the castle was held for Charles I, whose headquarters were at Oxford, 25 miles away, and it withstood a 20 month siege before being taken by Cromwell's troops. Near the village, between two bridges on the Oxford road, is an almshouse founded in 1393 for poor inmates, who were required to attend daily Mass in the chapel of Donnington Priory. The priory was burnt down at the time of the second Battle of Newbury in 1644.

Barge on the Kennet and Avon Canal.

Map labels: OXFORD 11 MILES, THAME 12 MILES, WANTAGE 13 MILES A 4130, A 329, A 423, A 423, HENLEY 11 MILES, **WALLINGFORD**, Crowmarsh Gifford, A 4074, READING 10 MILES, B 4016, **East Hagbourne**, South Moreton, Coscote, Aston Upthorpe, B 4009, A 329, West Hagbourne, A 417, A 4527, A 417, ABINGDON 8 MILES, **Goring**, Streatley, A 329, READING 9 MILES, PH, Chilton, A 34, RIDGE WAY, Aldworth, B 4009, West Ilsey, RIDGE WAY, LORD WANTAGE MONUMENT, B 4494, Farnborough, B 4494, A 338, Hampstead Norris, M 4, Woolley, Winterbourne, B 4494, BLACK DITCH, B 4000, A 34, Boxford, P, WC, SNELSMORE COMMON, Donnington, DONNINGTON CASTLE, READING 17 MILES A 4, 1644, A 4, B 4000, **Newbury**, **Wickham**, ROMAN ROAD, M 4, odlands Mary, HUNGERFORD 3 MILES, 1643, WINCHESTER 25 MILES A 34, ANDOVER 17 MILES A 343, Kennet & Avon Canal, GRIMSBURY CASTLE

125

Cottage gardens in the sun, galloping ghosts at midnight

Overlooked by the steep, tree-clad escarpment of the Chilterns, the broad Vale of Aylesbury embraces villages, thriving market towns and mansions. The timber-framed thatched cottages with their neat gardens contrast with the splendour of Waddesdon Manor—a French-style château—or Claydon House. There are links with the Civil War that ravaged England in the 17th century, including a large monument in a tiny church to the man who died clutching the royal standard at the Battle of Edgehill. And headless cavalrymen, so it is said, ride at midnight over Quainton Hill.

(1) Aylesbury to Leighton Buzzard Leave the centre of the town on the A413, signposted to Buckingham, and 2 m. after the roundabout on the outskirts, turn right on to the road signposted to Weedon. Go through the village and follow this road as it rises towards Aston Abbotts. There are views of the Chilterns over to the right just before the village. The disused abbey to the left, near the church, was once surrounded by a moat, traces of which can be seen. In Victorian times the abbey was the home of Sir James Clark Ross, the explorer who located the North magnetic pole in 1831. His tomb is in the adjoining churchyard.

At the green in Aston Abbotts, turn right and follow the signposts for Wingrave, going straight over the A418. By the pond in Wingrave fork left off the main road on to the road signposted for Ledburn. Go through Ledburn and turn left at the junction with the B488, following the signpost for Leighton/Linslade. After just under 1 m. the road merges with the A418 in Linslade and turns right to go over the Grand Union Canal and the River Ouzel to Leighton Buzzard.

(2) Leighton Buzzard to Ascott House From the High Street return along the A418 across the river and canal. Stay on the A418 through Linslade. After about 2 m., turn left. The entrance to Ascott House is on the left.

(3) Ascott House to Winslow Return to the A418 and turn left into Wing. Fork right just inside the village on to the minor road signposted to Stewkley. Turn right on the further side of Wing and bear right. About 2 m. later, at the Carpenters' Arms on the outskirts of Stewkley, turn left on to the road signposted to Dunton. After 2 m. turn right on to the road signposted to Hoggeston, a village of whitewashed and thatched cottages. At the A413, beyond the village, turn right for Winslow.

(4) Winslow to Claydon House Follow the A413 past Winslow church and turn left almost immediately on to the road signposted to Granborough/The Claydons. About 200 yds later, at Verney Junction, fork right for The Claydons. Keep straight ahead under two railway bridges, and at the T-junction, about 3 m. from Winslow, turn right. After 200 yds turn right, following the signposts for Claydon House. The house and park are on the left, with the village church on a hillock near by. In the church is a marble monument to Sir Edmund Verney. He was the king's standard-bearer at the Battle of Edgehill in 1642. When the smoke cleared, his body was found hacked to pieces—with his severed hand still clutching the royal standard.

(5) Claydon House to Quainton Return to the road from Claydon House, bear left and turn left, and at the T-junction turn left again on to the road signposted to Botolph Claydon. In the village, where the road swings left by the Methodist church, carry straight on, and after about 500 yds turn right. About 2 m. past Botolph Claydon, the road swings left for Quainton. On the outskirts of the village take the left fork into the centre. Go past the green to the end of Church Street to see the church and windmill.

(6) Quainton to Waddesdon Manor Return to the village green, turn left and take the first turning on the right, then go left by the Sportsman Inn. After about 1 m., just after crossing the railway, turn left at the crossroads following the signpost for Waddesdon. In Waddesdon, turn right on to the A41 and shortly after the War Memorial turn left for Waddesdon Manor.

(7) Waddesdon Manor to Cuddington Return to the A41 and turn right signposted Aylesbury/London. After about 1 m. turn right on the road signposted to Winchendon. After about 4 m., at a crossroads, turn left following the signpost for Cuddington. Turn left again at the next T-junction, cross the bridge over the River Thame, and into Cuddington.

(8) Cuddington to Aylesbury Bear left on the road out of Cuddington, carry on to the junction with the A418 and turn left, following the signpost for Aylesbury. The ruins of Dinton Castle, an 18th-century folly, are on the left just past the junction.

INFORMATION

Places of interest *Ascott House:* Apr. to Sept., Wed., Sat. and Bank Hol. Mon., afternoons; also Sun. July and Aug. *Aylesbury:* Bucks County Museum, weekdays. Hartwell House, May to mid-July, Wed. afternoons. Garden only, Sept., Wed. afternoon. *Claydon House:* Apr. to Oct., daily (except Mon. and Fri.), Bank Hol. afternoons. *Leighton Buzzard:* Narrow-gauge railway, end Mar. to end Sept., Sun. 10.30 a.m.-6.30 p.m.; also Easter, Spring and Late Summer Bank Hol., weekends. *Waddesdon Manor:* Mar. to Oct., Wed. to Sun., 2-6 p.m., also Spring and Late Summer Bank Hol. Mon. 11 a.m.-6 p.m.

Events *Aylesbury:* Festival of the Arts, Spring. *Quainton Railway Society:* Gala weekends, Apr., May and Aug.

Information Thames and Chilterns Tourist Board, 8 The Market Place, Abingdon (Tel. Abingdon 22711).

Towns with easy access to Aylesbury:

Buckingham	17 m.	High Wycombe	17 m.
Dunstable	16 m.	Oxford	20 m.
Hemel Hempstead	12 m.	Watford	24 m.

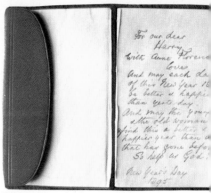

Florence Nightingale's diary, Claydon House.

CLAYDON HOUSE
Although two-thirds of Claydon was demolished in the 18th century, the remainder, with its lavishly decorated rooms, is high on the list of Buckinghamshire's most interesting stately homes. Florence Nightingale, whose sister, in 1858, married into the Verney family, owner of the estate since 1463, was a frequent visitor. A museum contains relics of the 'Lady with the lamp', as well as letters written by Charles I and Oliver Cromwell.

Chinese Room, Claydon House.

The Baron's bedroom, Waddesdon Manor.

WADDESDON MANOR
The mansion built in the French Renaissance style for Baron Ferdinand de Rothschild between 1874 and 1889 snuggles amid the trees above the village. On display inside are Sèvres and Dresden china, paintings by Gainsborough, Reynolds and Romney, and rare works by 17th-century Dutch artists. The library is noted for its 18th-century French bindings, and among the rich French period furniture is a writing table made for Queen Marie Antoinette. In the grounds there are two large deer-pens, rare trees and shrubs, a large ornate aviary, fountains and a collection of sculpture of the 17th and 18th centuries from France, Italy and the Netherlands.

SCALE

0   1   2   3 MILES

WINSLOW

The little town on the Aylesbury-Buckingham road has a 13th-century church north of the market square. It is dedicated to St Laurence, and a statue of the saint stands in a niche above the south porch. Ancient Bibles and other books, the oldest dated 1507, are displayed in a case inside. There is an elaborately carved Jacobean pulpit, traces of 15th-century wall-paintings, and brasses up to 400 years old. The Western Tower, 64 ft high, contains a clock and eight bells. The chimes play the hymn tune 'Old Saint David's' every three hours. The George Inn, at the south side of the market square, has a wrought-iron balcony which is a fine example of 18th-century workmanship.

...aurence statue, Winslow church.

Fountain sculpture, Ascott House.

ASCOTT HOUSE

This timber-framed house, dated 1606 over the front entrance, contains works by Gainsborough, Reynolds, Turner, Tiepolo and other great artists, rare French furniture, and one of the world's finest collections of oriental pottery. The house was presented to the National Trust in 1949 by Anthony de Rothschild. His father bought it in 1874, enlarged it in Jacobean style and had the 35 acre garden laid out.

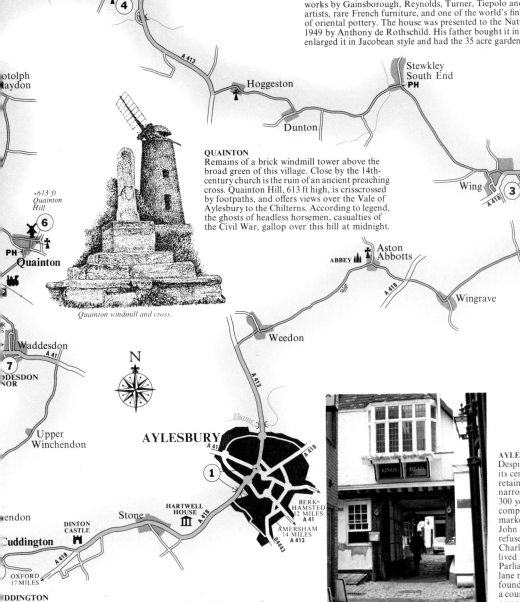

QUAINTON

Remains of a brick windmill tower above the broad green of this village. Close by the 14th-century church is the ruin of an ancient preaching cross. Quainton Hill, 613 ft high, is crisscrossed by footpaths, and offers views over the Vale of Aylesbury to the Chilterns. According to legend, the ghosts of headless horsemen, casualties of the Civil War, gallop over this hill at midnight.

Quainton windmill and cross.

LEIGHTON BUZZARD

Leighton (the 'Buzzard' is probably from an ancient family, not the bird) was a market township in Saxon days. It keeps its country atmosphere amid the industrial development which began with the arrival of the Grand Union Canal in 1805. There are half-timbered cottages in the streets leading to the 600-year-old ornate Market Cross, and lattice-windowed almshouses in North Street. The cathedral-like parish church dates from 1288.

AYLESBURY

Despite the rapid growth of the county town, its centre, by-passed by through traffic, has retained much of its old character. There are narrow alleyways and several fine houses up to 300 years old. The red-brick County Hall, completed in 1740, overlooks the cobbled market square, where statues include one to John Hampden, who became a hero when he refused to pay Ship Money, a tax levied by Charles I to build warships. Hampden, who lived near Aylesbury, died fighting for the Parliamentary cause in 1643. In a cobbled lane near the statue is King's Head Inn, founded in 1386, with a medieval gateway into a courtyard. The hall of the inn, which is now owned by the National Trust, has good 15th-century stained glass. Next to the parish church of St Mary—a 13th-century foundation much restored and rebuilt—is 18th-century Prebendal House, once the home of John Wilkes, the town's MP from 1757 to 1764.

King's Head Inn, Aylesbury.

...DDINGTON

...o village greens—one complete with pump—and a setting among the ...oad meadows beside the River Thame give a spacious old-world air ...Cuddington. There are several fine old houses and thatched and ...itewashed cottages. The 13th-century church has several unusual ...tures, including a bearded figure, dating from the 15th century, who ...oks down from the chancel arch.

Memories of the famous, and infamous, in the Chilterns

The Chiltern Hills form a barrier between London and the central plain of England. Despite the influx of London commuters, this is still a country of villages and farms. Beechwoods cover many of the hills, yielding here and there to rolling downs, as at Whipsnade, where Britain's first 'open' zoo is sited. The area is rich in associations with the famous—from John Milton, the poet, Benjamin Disraeli, Queen Victoria's favourite Prime Minister, to Sir Francis Dashwood, founder of the notorious Hell-Fire Club.

(1) Beaconsfield to Jordans Leave the centre of Beaconsfield, on the A40 signposted to London. Just after the roundabout on the outskirts of the town, take the left turn signposted to Jordans and Chalfont St Giles.

(2) Jordans to Chalfont St Giles Leave Jordans on the road signposted to Chalfont St Giles. After 1 m. turn right at the T-junction into Chalfont St Giles.

(3) Chalfont St Giles to Dudswell Go through Chalfont St Giles, and on the far side of the village cross the A413 on to the B4442 signposted to Little Chalfont. After 1 m., past the long left-hand bend, turn right on to the road signposted to Chorleywood. Keep straight on at the crossroads 1 m. later, to the junction with the A404. At the junction, turn right and then immediately left on to the road signposted to Latimer. After the steep hill, continue straight over the B485. Go through Latimer. After 1 m. take the left turn signposted to Ley Hill. Stay on this road across the next junction and, in Ley Hill, keep ahead to Chesham. Fork right on to the road signposted to Ashley Green. At the T-junction with the B4505 turn left towards Chesham. After ½ m., where the B4505 turns sharp left, keep straight ahead on the minor road signposted to Ashley Green. At the junction with the A416 turn right, following the Berkhamsted signpost, and carry on to the outskirts of the town. At the right-hand bend, keep straight ahead leaving the A416 to join the road signposted to Champneys and Hawridge. After 2 m. turn right on to the road signposted to Dudswell. Stay on this road to the junction with the A41, turn right and immediately left at the signpost to Dudswell.

(4) Dudswell to Ashridge Park Leave Dudswell on Wharf Lane. Bear sharp left over the bridge, to the junction with the A41, and turn right, following the signpost to Tring. After ½ m. turn right on to the road signposted to Aldbury. In the centre of the village, take the right turn signposted to Little Gaddesden. Follow this road to the B4506 crossroads and turn left following the Dagnall signpost into Ashridge Park.

(5) Ashridge Park to Whipsnade Zoo Stay on the B4506 through the park as far as Ringshall, and there turn right on to the road signposted to Little Gaddesden. Continue through the village, and on the far side turn left at the signpost to Whipsnade. Stay on this road through Studham and turn left on to the B4540 signposted to Whipsnade Zoo.

(6) Whipsnade Zoo to Pitstone Windmill Leave the zoo on the B4540 signposted Aylesbury and Ivinghoe. Bear right at the junction at the foot of the hill, and continue to the junction with the B489. Turn left, following the signpost to Ivinghoe. Keep straight on at the junction with the A4146. On the outskirts of Ivinghoe, turn left on to the B488 signposted to Tring. The Pitstone Windmill is in a field to the right.

(7) Pitstone Windmill to Tring Keep on the B488 signposted to Tring. After 3 m., at a T-junction turn right into Tring.

(8) Tring to Coombe Hill Leave Tring on the road signposted to Aylesbury. At the roundabout junction with the A41 turn right and after ½ m. turn left on to the A4011 signposted to Wendover. After the golf course turn left on to the road signposted to St Leonards. Go up Aston Hill and through Wendover Woods. Take the right turn, signposted to Wendover, and turn right again to stay on this road. At the foot of Boddington Hill turn left and after 500 yds turn left on to the A413. After 1 m. turn right for Coombe Hill.

(9) Coombe Hill to West Wycombe At the T-junction beyond Coombe Hill, take the left turn signposted to Great Missenden. After 1 m. turn right on to the road signposted to Princes Risborough, and at the A4010 turn left for West Wycombe.

(10) West Wycombe to Hughenden Manor Leave West Wycombe on the A40 towards London. After 1 m. turn left on to the road signposted to Downley. Bear right at the fork in the village, and turn right at the T-junction. Stay on this road to the junction with the A4128 and turn left, following the Great Missenden signpost. After 1 m. the entrance to Hughenden Manor is on the left.

(11) Hughenden Manor to Beaconsfield Leave Hughenden Manor on the A4128 signposted to Great Missenden. At the top of the hill take the right turn signposted to Widmer End. In Widmer turn left on to the road signposted Penn/Wycombe. Keep bearing right for 1½ m. through Hazlemere. Cross the A404 and join the B474 to Beaconsfield.

INFORMATION

Places of interest *Beaconsfield:* Bekonscot miniature village, daily. *Chalfont St Giles:* Milton's cottage, Feb. to Oct., weekdays (except Tues.), Sun. afternoons; Nov. to Jan., Sat., Sun. afternoons. *Pitstone Windmill:* May to Sept., Sun., Bank Hol. Mon., 2.30-6 p.m. *West Wycombe Park:* June, Mon. to Fri., July to Sept., Sun. also, 2.15-6 p.m. *Whipsnade Zoo:* Daily.

Information 8 The Market Place, Abingdon (Tel. Abingdon 22711).

Towns with easy access to Beaconsfield:
Aylesbury . . . . . 20 m.   Oxford . . . . 32 m.

TRING
The Zoological Museum in Tring Park, now part of the British Museum, has thous of exhibits of rare birds, fish and reptiles, as well as a lar insect collection. It was buil by the second Lord Rothsc who bequeathed the collect to the British Museum in 1 Tring parish church dates f the 13th century. To the no of the town, a group of reservoirs forms a bird sanctuary and nature reserv

Dodo skeleton, Tring Zoological Museum.

Permits are needed to visit the areas off the public rig of way. The reservoirs were built in the 19th century, provide water for the Grand Union Canal. They cove 49 acres on the site of ancient marshlands, which still yield the occasional fossil.

COOMBE HILL
From the chalky summit of Coombe Hill, 848 ft abov sea level, St Paul's Cathedral, more than 30 miles awa can be seen southwards across the Chilterns on an exceptionally clear day. The hill is a national nature reserve, and the site of Britain's first public nature tra At the summit stands a monument to the men of Buckinghamshire who died in the South African War Chequers, the official country home of Britain's Prime Ministers, stands in wooded grounds a mile to the south-west.

WEST WYCOMBE
The Palladian mansion of West Wycombe House, no for its art treasures and painted ceilings, stands in a landscaped park studded with Classical temples and waterways. The house was built in the 18th century fo Sir Francis Dashwood, who was also responsible for rebuilding of the church, which has a huge gilded ball top of its tower. Sir Francis founded the Hell-Fire Cl notorious for its orgies and black-magic rites. The clu met in the nearby ruins of Medmenham Abbey, in the caves beneath the hill and in the ball on the church to which has room for ten people inside. Although he is known for the activities of his club, Sir Francis was al a scholar and politician, serving as Chancellor of the Exchequer and joint Postmaster-General.

Tapestry Room, West Wycombe House.

SCALE
0   1   2   3   4   5 MILES

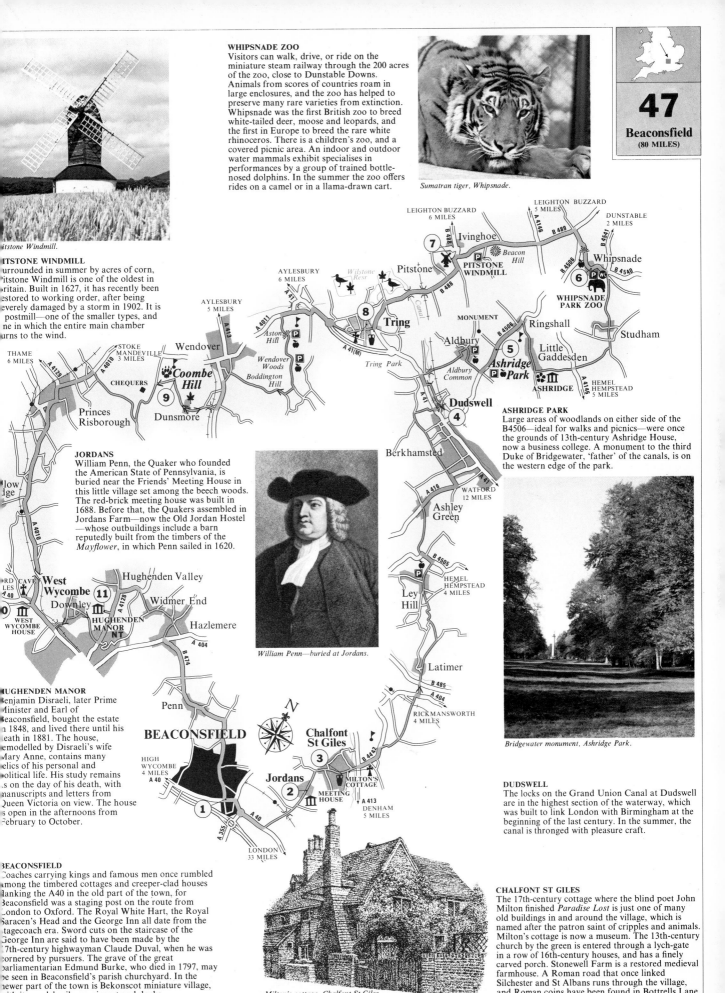

WHIPSNADE ZOO

Visitors can walk, drive, or ride on the miniature steam railway through the 200 acres of the zoo, close to Dunstable Downs. Animals from scores of countries roam in large enclosures, and the zoo has helped to preserve many rare varieties from extinction. Whipsnade was the first British zoo to breed white-tailed deer, moose and leopards, and the first in Europe to breed the rare white rhinoceros. There is a children's zoo, and a covered picnic area. An indoor and outdoor water mammals exhibit specialises in performances by a group of trained bottle-nosed dolphins. In the summer the zoo offers rides on a camel or in a llama-drawn cart.

Sumatran tiger, Whipsnade.

itstone Windmill.

ITSTONE WINDMILL

urrounded in summer by acres of corn, itstone Windmill is one of the oldest in ritain. Built in 1627, it has recently been estored to working order, after being everely damaged by a storm in 1902. It is postmill—one of the smaller types, and ne in which the entire main chamber urns to the wind.

JORDANS

William Penn, the Quaker who founded the American State of Pennsylvania, is buried near the Friends' Meeting House in this little village set among the beech woods. The red-brick meeting house was built in 1688. Before that, the Quakers assembled in Jordans Farm—now the Old Jordan Hostel —whose outbuildings include a barn reputedly built from the timbers of the *Mayflower*, in which Penn sailed in 1620.

William Penn—buried at Jordans.

HUGHENDEN MANOR

enjamin Disraeli, later Prime Minister and Earl of eaconsfield, bought the estate n 1848, and lived there until his eath in 1881. The house, emodelled by Disraeli's wife Mary Anne, contains many elics of his personal and olitical life. His study remains s on the day of his death, with manuscripts and letters from Queen Victoria on view. The house s open in the afternoons from ebruary to October.

ASHRIDGE PARK

Large areas of woodlands on either side of the B4506—ideal for walks and picnics—were once the grounds of 13th-century Ashridge House, now a business college. A monument to the third Duke of Bridgewater, 'father' of the canals, is on the western edge of the park.

Bridgewater monument, Ashridge Park.

DUDSWELL

The locks on the Grand Union Canal at Dudswell are in the highest section of the waterway, which was built to link London with Birmingham at the beginning of the last century. In the summer, the canal is thronged with pleasure craft.

BEACONSFIELD

Coaches carrying kings and famous men once rumbled among the timbered cottages and creeper-clad houses flanking the A40 in the old part of the town, for Beaconsfield was a staging post on the route from London to Oxford. The Royal White Hart, the Royal Saracen's Head and the George Inn all date from the stagecoach era. Sword cuts on the staircase of the George Inn are said to have been made by the 7th-century highwayman Claude Duval, when he was cornered by pursuers. The grave of the great arliamentary Edmund Burke, who died in 1797, may be seen in Beaconsfield's parish churchyard. In the ewer part of the town is Bekonscot miniature village, with its model railway, airport and docks.

Milton's cottage, Chalfont St Giles.

CHALFONT ST GILES

The 17th-century cottage where the blind poet John Milton finished *Paradise Lost* is just one of many old buildings in and around the village, which is named after the patron saint of cripples and animals. Milton's cottage is now a museum. The 13th-century church by the green is entered through a lych-gate in a row of 16th-century houses, and has a finely carved porch. Stonewell Farm is a restored medieval farmhouse. A Roman road that once linked Silchester and St Albans runs through the village, and Roman coins have been found in Bottrells Lane.

129

A conducted tour of the home of England's monarchs

WINDSOR CASTLE

That early tourist and 17th-century diarist Samuel Pepys described Windsor Castle as 'the most romantique castle that is in the world'. The square towers, curtain walls and great round tower of the present skyline form a symbol of the British monarchy to people all over the world. The first fort was built here by William the Conqueror in 1070, and the castle has been the home of kings and queens for over 850 years, with only one short interruption during the Commonwealth of 1649–59. Forty-one monarchs have continued the process of building, and restoration, to suit their tastes and times. Many of them have left the mark of their personalities on Windsor.

THE CLOISTERS *The 13th-century covered way known as the Dean's Cloister is reached through the east door of St George's Chapel. The wall and fine arcading, which now form one side of the memorial chapel built by Queen Victoria for her beloved Albert, was built by Henry III, fourth of the Plantagenet kings (1216–72). The stone bench running round the cloister is carved with holes used for the medieval game of nine holes, which was similar to the modern game of bowls. A passage on the north side of the cloister leads to the Canons' Cloister, built during the reign of Edward III (1327–77). It was Edward III who established the Order of the Garter, and expanded an earlier chapel for ceremonies connected with the order. The elaborately carved choir stalls include those of the 26 Knights of the Garter, each with the banner and nameplate of its owner above. The present chapel, St George's, was begun during the reign of Edward IV (1461–83) and completed by Henry VIII in the following century.*

THE NORMAN GATEWAY *Despite its popular name, the narrow gateway flanked by twin drum towers was built by Edward III. There is still a portcullis in working order which is drawn up into the walls of the room above the gate, but it is rarely used. Now the home of the governor of the castle, the gatehouse was a prison until the 17th century. James I of Scotland (1406–37) was kept there for 11 years, and it was from these windows that he first saw Lady Jane Beaufort walking in the garden below the Round Tower; he fell in love with her at once and eventually married her.*

CHANGING THE GUARD *A battalion of one of the five regiments of Foot Guards is stationed at the castle at all times, and the guard-changing is a daily ceremony. When the Queen is in residence it takes place in the quadrangle; at other times on the parade ground outside the guardroom (on left in the picture). The brick-and-timber building on the right is part of the Horseshoe Cloister, built in the 15th century in the shape of a horse's fetlock, one of Edward IV's badges. Its purpose then was to house the clergy; now it is used as living quarters for the vergers and choristers.*

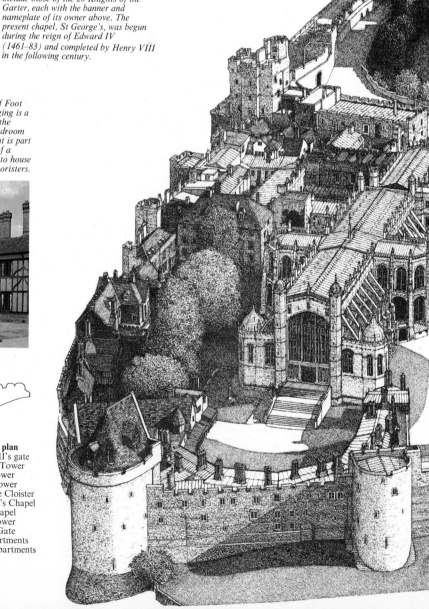

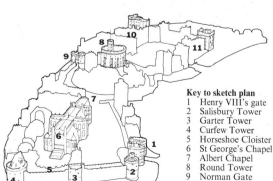

Key to sketch plan
1 Henry VIII's gate
2 Salisbury Tower
3 Garter Tower
4 Curfew Tower
5 Horseshoe Cloister
6 St George's Chapel
7 Albert Chapel
8 Round Tower
9 Norman Gate
10 State Apartments
11 Private Apartments

THE ROUND TOWER *The huge hollow crown which gives the tower (in picture below) its shape was added by George IV (1820–30). In the stairwell hangs the 17 cwt Sebastopol Bell captured from the Russians in the Crimean War. It is tolled only on the death of a monarch. The tower rises to a height of 215 ft above the River Thames, and commands views over several counties. It is topped by a 72 ft flagpole, from which the Royal Standard flies when the Queen is in residence.*

THE PRIVATE APARTMENTS *It was George IV who moved the private apartments from the chilly north wing of the upper ward to the east and south wings, though he preferred to live in the Royal Lodge. He built the Grand Corridor which connects the private and state apartments. This gained an unhappy reputation during the long reign of Queen Victoria (1837–1901), who often sat there after dinner talking to each guest in turn while the rest stood about uneasily in the draughty and unheated corridor.*

CHARLES II *On the west side of the upper quadrangle is the statue of the king by the German sculptor Josiah Ibach. It was donated by Toby Rustat, Yeoman of the Robes, in 1697 and cost him £1000.*

HENRY VIII'S GATE *Inset above the huge Tudor archway are the arms of Henry VIII, with the Tudor rose and the pomegranate of his first wife, Catherine of Aragon.*

THE LONG WALK AND SOUTH FRONT *Nearly 3 miles long and 240 ft wide, this walk was laid out for Charles II in 1685, the year in which he died. It was originally lined with 1650 elm trees, planted 30 ft apart. These had to be cut down in 1945 when attacked by disease, and were replaced with alternate chestnut and plane trees. The walk starts from the main entrance to the castle (top picture) and stretches away south to the Copper Horse, a huge statue of George III in the guise of a Roman emperor on his mount. It was erected in 1824 by George IV as a sardonic memorial to his father's bad taste in allowing a clutter of miscellaneous buildings to spoil the avenue. The son swept them away, including one which the old king himself had designed. Nothing now blocks this magnificent approach to the castle, flanked on the right by the visitors' quarters and the start of the royal apartments.*

131

WINDSOR CASTLE

It is hardly possible to walk through the magnificent Henry VIII gate and into the lower ward of Windsor Castle without being reminded of the growth of the British nation. The walls and towers of Norman kings surround the achievements of the Plantagenets, the Tudors, the Stuarts and the Hanovers, a reminder that the nation, and its monarchy, turned a host of invaders and languages into a coherent whole, solving problems from within with little force and steady progress.

The exact plan of the castle built by William the Conqueror is not known, but the upper and lower wards are substantially unchanged. The raised mound would, in William's day, have been topped by a wooden fort commanding both wards and views down the Thames and over the Thames Valley. Henry I (1100–35) was the first Norman king to make his home at Windsor; he held court there for the first time in 1110 and had by then constructed a chapel and a great hall.

Henry built the first royal lodge for his own occupation in the most secure part of the defensive stockade, and successive monarchs used it as their private apartments for the next seven centuries.

Henry II, the first of the Plantagenet kings, constructed the first solid stone defences. These included the square towers of the upper ward and the foundations of the great Round Tower, which would be better described as a rounded square with the diameter varying between 94 and 103 ft. Henry II had four sons, whose bitter rivalry caused him so much trouble that it is said he had a picture painted to symbolise his problem. In it an old eagle was surrounded by four young eagles, three of which were attacking the old bird.

Brothers at war

Not surprisingly, Windsor had its first siege when Henry's son John wrested power from his brother Richard I in 1199, by which time the castle was firmly established as the centre for the court. It was from here that King John rode out to Runnymede in 1215 to sign the Magna Carta. When he broke faith with his barons the castle was besieged a second time, and the lower ward was badly damaged. His successor, Henry III, repaired much of the damage and built the west wall with the D-shaped towers (Salisbury, Garter and Curfew) to strengthen the castle's defences.

The Curfew Tower, built in 1227, contains a clock, dated 1689, which plays a hymn tune, 'St David's', every three hours.

As the visitor enters the castle through the Henry VIII gate, St George's Chapel can be seen. This was begun by the Yorkist king Edward IV and was part of his plan to expand and embellish the Order of the Garter first founded by Edward III, a Plantagenet, in 1348. These kings, and many since, rewarded those who distinguished themselves in battle by making them Knights of the Garter. The tradition and ceremony, with less military bias, continues today. To Edward also we owe the charming group of houses in Horseshoe Cloister, which shelter the ceremonial steps to the chapel, used for Garter processions and other royal occasions.

The fine St George's Chapel was completed by the huge, gregarious and much-married Henry VIII, who also built the great gateway that bears his name. Henry was fond of Windsor; dancing and making music there as well as hunting in the surrounding parkland. Early in his life Henry expressed a wish to be buried there; he and his favourite wife Jane Seymour share the same tomb in the chapel.

By now England had forged a distinct style of its own, divorced from Norman influence, and with its own flexible and rich language. Queen Elizabeth cemented the achievement of her father, Henry VIII, in bringing greater unity and stability to England and a degree of civilisation to Windsor, which she used as a retreat when the plague threatened London. It was she who built much of the northern terrace of the upper ward, replacing the medieval wooden buildings already decaying in her father's time. She also built the picture gallery that links the royal apartments with the Norman Gateway.

The Norman gatehouse is now the home of the governor of the castle, but despite its name it is not Norman. It was built in 1359, and was a state prison for three centuries. James I of Scotland spent 11 years there. It is said that he fell in love with Lady Jane Beaufort when he saw her walking in the moat gardens; they were married when James was released in 1424.

Civil War damage

The reigns of the early Stuart kings, James I (1603–25) and Charles I (1625–49), were a time of unrest which culminated in the Civil War and the beheading of Charles I. His decapitated body was found near that of Henry VIII in St George's Chapel, when the tomb was opened by George IV during the 19th century.

The castle was badly damaged by Roundheads during the Civil War, but was still strong enough to be used as a prison during the Commonwealth. The king himself, when he was Cromwell's prisoner and awaiting trial, had spent two short periods of captivity in his own apartments.

When Charles II eventually came to the throne in 1660 he set about repairing and modernising the castle in accordance with French fashion. Little remains of his work on the outside, but many of the present state apartments owe their shape and style to him. During this period, he had nearly all the rooms painted on both ceilings and walls by the Italian artist Antonio Verrio, though only three examples of his work remain to show the grandiose quality of Charles II's mode of life.

Sad times

The first two Hanoverian kings, George I (1714–27) and George II (1727–60), disliked Windsor and neglected its upkeep, which is why many of Verrio's fine ceilings were removed. With George III, the most anglicised of the early Hanovers, Windsor became once more a real family home. He set in hand the restoration and refurnishing which gave Windsor its present shape, and took advantage of the wonderful furniture and works of art thrown on to the market by the upheavals of the French Revolution, collecting paintings and art works which still adorn the state apartments.

Although a kindly family-loving man who preferred a homely life, he had a sense of style and, like Henry VIII and Elizabeth I, a respect for books, his choice of which can now be found in the Royal Library. His son, who

QUEEN MARY'S DOLLS' HOUSE *Given to the late Queen Mary in 1923, the house was designed by Sir Edwin Lutyens (1869–1944), and built to a scale of 1:12. It is complete in every detail, down to the plumbing and electrical fittings. Even the pictures were painted by famous artists.*

REMBRANDT'S MOTHER *This remarkable portrait is one of three Rembrandts in the King's Dressing Room. Among works by Van Dyck is the famous triple portrait of Charles I, sent to Rome so that the Italian sculptor Bernini could make a bust of the king without travelling to England. The picture was brought back to England in 1802, and now hangs with works by Rubens, Holbein and others. The room was used as a bedroom by Charles II and was enlarged by George IV for use as a sitting-room. The ceiling is decorated with the arms of George's brother William IV (1830–7).*

STUDY FOR LEDA BY LEONARDO DA VINCI *Part of the huge royal collection of drawings by Old Masters (totalling 20,000) is displayed in a room adjacent to the state apartments. The exhibition is changed from time to time as drawings are brought from other parts of the castle or lent to outside exhibitions, but a number of drawings by Dürer, Rubens and Rembrandt are on show.*

THE KING'S DINING-ROOM *This is the first of the state apartments and contains one of the only three surviving ceilings painted by Verrio for Charles II in 1678–80. The subject, a banquet of the gods, is echoed in the carved panelling by Grinling Gibbons.*

GEORGE III *(Portrait in the National Gallery.) Of all the kings who lived at Windsor none did more to restore the glory lost through earlier neglect.*

THE QUEEN'S GUARD CHAMBER *The armoured figure represents the King's Champion who, until the time of George IV, defended the sovereign's authority.*

became Prince Regent during George III's last illness and lapse into senility, inherited his father's enthusiasm if not his sense of elegance.

The Regency, 1811–20, was a time of flamboyance and gaiety, but on his accession to the throne in 1820, at the age of 57, George IV embarked on the life of a country squire with eagerness. He disliked the chilly private apartments and during the Regency lived at the Royal Lodge while the apartments were transferred to the south and east wings of the upper ward. George used the services of the architect Jeffry Wyatt (1766–1840) to make extensive alterations to the castle. He restored the walls and towers, took out the rounded windows of Charles II and replaced them with the present ones, more in keeping with the Gothic style he wished to achieve. Having made the private apartments for the first time cheerful and comfortable, Wyatt was knighted for his work and allowed to call himself Wyatville—adding the 'ville' because he thought it sounded more impressive.

The wars with Napoleon had taken place in the reign of George III, but George IV felt very much part of the eventual British victory. So he had the great Waterloo Chamber created as a permanent memorial to the king's soldiers and statesmen who had helped to bring about Napoleon's downfall. It was built on the site of a herb garden. The chamber houses the paintings by Sir Thomas Lawrence (1769–1830) of the heroes of the day. The walls date from the 12th century. The carpet on the floor, 80 ft long and 40 ft wide and said to be the largest seamless carpet in the world, was made for Queen Victoria in Agra, India.

Since George IV's time the fabric of the castle has been little changed. Queen Victoria preferred the quiet domesticity of Balmoral in Scotland or Osborne House on the Isle of Wight, but she did build the Albert Memorial Chapel and kept Windsor in good repair.

VISITING WINDSOR

HOW TO GET THERE From London: west to Hammersmith, then M4 and turn left at Exit 6. From Reading: M4 and turn right at Exit 6.

OPENING TIMES *Precincts:* daily, 10 a.m.–sunset. *State Apartments* (when Queen not in residence) and *Dolls' House*:* weekdays, 11 a.m.–3, 4 or 5 p.m., depending on season; Sun., May to Sept. 1.30–5 p.m., Oct. 1–4 p.m. *Albert Chapel:* as above, but closed 1–2 p.m. and Sun. *St George's Chapel:* during services, also weekdays 11 a.m. (Fri. 1 p.m.)– 3.45 p.m., Sun. 2.30–3.45 p.m. (usually closed in Jan.). *Curfew Tower:* Oct. to Aug., Tues. to Sat., 11 a.m.–12.30 p.m., 2–4 p.m. *Round Tower:* Apr. to Sept., weekdays; times and conditions as for State Apartments.

*Dolls' House closes 15 min. earlier.

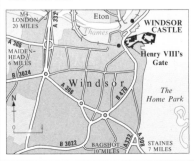

A ducal palace, rare deer and a pancake race

Proudly dominating the Bedfordshire countryside is Woburn Abbey, home of the Dukes of Bedford and one of Britain's chief treasurehouses of art and architecture. The many varieties of rare deer in the park are a legacy of the 11th Duke, who brought 18 Père David's deer from China in 1900 to save them from extinction. But the tour has other attractions too. One of them is at Olney, where a tradition dating back to the 15th century is still observed. Every Shrove Tuesday a pancake race is held there, the contestants nowadays being timed against friendly rivals in Liberal, USA.

1 **Woburn to Woburn Abbey** Leave the centre of the village on the road signposted to Woburn Abbey (the Duke of Bedford pronounces it 'Wooburn') and turn right in to the abbey grounds.

2 **Woburn Abbey to Newport Pagnell** Return to the public road and turn right. Follow the Eversholt signpost as the road bears round to the left. After 1 m. turn left for Ridgmont. In the village, at the junction with the A418, turn right and almost immediately left on to a minor road signposted to Salford. Follow the road under the M1, then over a level crossing, and after ¼ m. go straight ahead at the crossroads with the A5140. Continue for 1½ m. to Salford, and in the village turn right at the Cranfield signpost. After 2 m., at the edge of Cranfield Airfield, turn left, and about 1 m. later turn sharp right on to the road signposted to Wharley End/Cranfield Institute. After just under 1 m., at a sharp right-hand bend, turn left on to a narrow, unsignposted lane and follow this to North Crawley. At the T-junction in the village turn left, and 2½ m. later turn right on to the A5130 for Newport Pagnell.

3 **Newport Pagnell to Emberton** Leave the town on the A422, signposted to Bedford. Immediately after crossing the River Great Ouse, turn right, still on the A422. After just under 1 m. turn left on to the A509, signposted to Emberton and Olney. Go through Sherington and follow the road for 1½ m. A road to the left leads into Emberton.

4 **Emberton to Olney** Return to the A509 and turn left. Follow the road for about ½ m., cross the Great Ouse and enter Olney.

5 **Olney to Weston Underwood** Leave the town on the minor road signposted to Weston Underwood. The Flamingo Gardens are signposted on the right about 1 m. later in Weston Underwood.

6 **Weston Underwood to Gayhurst** Continue through the village, ignore all right turns, after 1½ m. fork left. At the junction with the B526 turn left to enter Gayhurst ¼ m. later.

7 **Gayhurst to Stewkley** Return along the B526 and take the first turn left, signposted to Tathall End. After 1½ m. cross the M1 and bear left into Tathall End. In the village, where the road swings right, keep ahead, following the signpost for Wolverton. Keep straight on at the next junction, and after ½ m. turn right on to the road signposted to Castlethorpe. At the junction in Castlethorpe turn right, then bear right

through the village. At the T-junction by the railway turn left, cross the railway, then the River Tove and ¼ m. later the Grand Union Canal. At the next junction turn left on to the road signposted to Cosgrove.

At the crossroads in Cosgrove turn right into Stratford Road, continue to the junction with the A508 and turn left into Old Stratford. At the crossroads turn left on to the A5, cross the Great Ouse, turn right at the Winslow signpost and enter Stony Stratford, home of the original Cock and Bull inns. Just past the traffic lights in the town centre, turn right on to the B4033 signposted to Winslow. Follow this road for just under 6 m., cross the A421 and continue into Great Horwood. In the village turn left on to the road signposted to Little Horwood. At the T-junction 1¼ m. later turn right, and in Little Horwood turn left on to the road signposted to Mursley. Follow the road across the railway bridge and through Mursley. Where the road merges with the B4032, go straight on, following the signpost for Stewkley, which is reached 2 m. later.

8 **Stewkley to Three Locks** Just beyond the church turn left, staying on the B4032 signposted to Soulbury. After 2 m., at the T-junction in Soulbury, turn left, following the signpost for Great Brickhill. Follow the road over the railway to the junction with the B488. Turn left and Three Locks appears on the right almost immediately.

9 **Three Locks to Woburn** Return along the B488 and take the first turning on the left for Great Brickhill. Cross the canal and the river to enter Great Brickhill 1 m. later. Where the road bears left, take the right-hand fork through the village leading to a winding, tree-lined road. Continue for about 1 m. to the junction with the A5 at the centre of Little Brickhill. Turn right and almost immediately left, by the church, on to a lane signposted to Woburn. Follow the lane, keeping right at a fork, for about 2 m. through woodland. At the junction with the A418 turn left and continue uphill into Woburn.

INFORMATION

Places of interest *Olney:* Cowper and Newton Museum, Tues. to Sat., 10 a.m.-12 noon, 2-5 p.m. *Weston Underwood:* Flamingo Gardens, Easter to end Sept., Wed., Thurs., Sat., Sun. and Bank Hol., 2-8 p.m. *Woburn Abbey:* Daily. Closed Nov. and Dec.

Information Thames and Chilterns Tourist Board, 8 The Market Place, Abingdon (Tel. Abingdon 22711). Woburn Abbey (Tel. Woburn 666).

Towns with easy access to Woburn:
Bedford........14 m.   Leighton Buzzard . 6 m.
Bletchley ....7 m.   London ....45 m.

GAYHURST
A hamlet in thick woodlands near the Great Ouse, Gayhurst played a big part in the Gunpowder Plot. At Gayhurst House in 1604 the owner, Sir Everard Digby, and his friends Robert Catesby and Thomas Winter hatched their plan for Guy Fawkes to blow up Parliament. The house dates from the late 16th century, but was extensively altered in 1750 and again a century later. The grounds were laid out in the 18th century by Capability Brown, famous for his landscape gardens. The church near the house dates from 1728. Near by is an old gatehouse which has been converted into an inn. The 18th-century Tyringham Hall is across the river. Gayhurst House is now used partly as a school and is not normally open to the public.

Sir Everard Digby, Gayhurst plotter.

St Michael's Church, Stewkley.

STEWKLEY
St Michael's Church, built about 1150, is claimed to be one of the few of the country's 6000 Norman churches to have survived virtually unaltered. It is decorated with carvings both inside and out, with Norman curved arches and a low, square tower. Many of the furnishings, including the font, are as old as the church itself.

SCALE
0   1   2   3   4   5 MILES

WESTON UNDERWOOD

The Flamingo Gardens in the village hold one of the finest private collections of birds and mammals in the world. The collection was made by Christopher Marler, and was opened to the public in 1968. It includes the rare Andean and James flamingos from the highlands of Peru and Bolivia. There are also bison, llamas, wallabies and other animals. The village is attractive, with houses built of honey-coloured stone, many of them thatched. The poet William Cowper (1731–1800) lived in Weston Underwood in a house that still stands.

…ingo Gardens, Weston Underwood.

EMBERTON

Canoes and small boats scud over the shallow lakes of Emberton Park, which almost surrounds the village. The park stretches towards Olney and is bounded to the west by the Great Ouse. Wildfowl live on the waterways, and a 1 mile nature trail starts from the A509 just north of the village.

Cowper and Newton Museum, Olney.

OLNEY

A pancake race from the church to the Market Square has been run in Olney on Shrove Tuesdays since 1445. The town, dominated by the spire of its 14th-century church, has a museum in the house where the poet William Cowper lived from 1767 to 1786. He wrote hymns such as 'God moves in a mysterious way' in collaboration with the Rev. John Newton, a former slave-trading sea captain.

Official starter, Olney pancake race.

NEWPORT PAGNELL

Tickford Bridge, which crosses the River Lovat here, was cast in 1810 and is one of the oldest iron bridges in the world still carrying daily traffic. There are several Georgian houses in the town. The church, described by the 17th-century diarist Samuel Pepys as 'very fair and like a cathedral', dates from the 14th century.

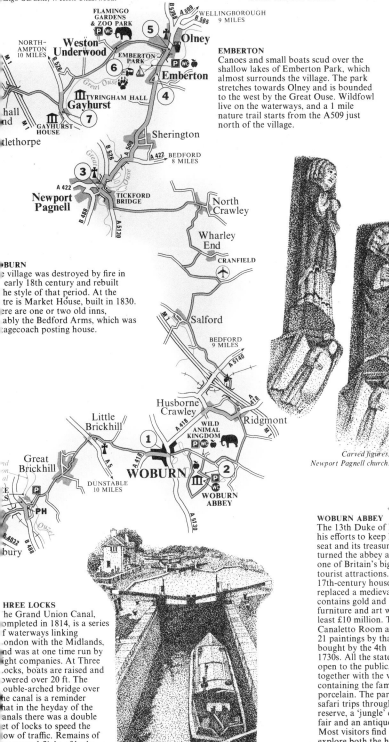

Carved figures, Newport Pagnell church.

WOBURN

…e village was destroyed by fire in … early 18th century and rebuilt … he style of that period. At the …tre is Market House, built in 1830. …re are one or two old inns, …ably the Bedford Arms, which was …agecoach posting house.

State Saloon, Woburn Abbey.

WOBURN ABBEY

The 13th Duke of Bedford, in his efforts to keep his family seat and its treasures intact, turned the abbey and park into one of Britain's biggest tourist attractions. The palatial 17th-century house, which replaced a medieval monastery, contains gold and silver, furniture and art works worth at least £10 million. The Canaletto Room alone houses 21 paintings by that artist, bought by the 4th Duke in the 1730s. All the staterooms are open to the public, together with the vaults containing the family plate and porcelain. The park provides safari trips through the game reserve, a 'jungle' chairlift, a fun fair and an antiques market. Most visitors find it difficult to explore both the house and the park in a single visit and it is sensible to make a choice between the two.

Deer in Woburn Abbey wildlife park.

THREE LOCKS

…he Grand Union Canal, …ompleted in 1814, is a series …f waterways linking …ondon with the Midlands, …nd was at one time run by …ight companies. At Three …ocks, boats are raised and …owered over 20 ft. The …ouble-arched bridge over …he canal is a reminder …hat in the heyday of the …anals there was a double …et of locks to speed the …low of traffic. Remains of …he second flight of locks …an still be seen. In summer, … steady flow of pleasure …raft can be seen passing …hrough the locks.

Three Locks, Grand Union Canal.

THE SHUTTLEWORTH COLLECTION

A conducted tour of a unique collection of historic aircraft

Close to the A1 in Bedfordshire, a tiny aerodrome houses a unique collection of historic aeroplanes, cars and horse-drawn carriages. It began as the whim of a young man in the 1920s and developed into the most famous aircraft museum in the world. Here you can see historic aircraft not only on the ground but in the air, flying as they did 50 or more years ago. The museum is run by the Shuttleworth Trust Collection. How it began and what it offers to the visitor is recorded here after discussion with the Aviation Trustee, Air Commodore Allen Wheeler.

When American astronaut Neil Armstrong, the first man to set foot on the moon, visited Britain in 1971 he asked to be taken to the Shuttleworth Collection. It was a natural request from an airman, for the collection is now the most famous aircraft museum in the world.

Once a month throughout the summer, visitors flock to the tiny Old Warden aerodrome in the heart of the Bedfordshire countryside to see aircraft dating back to the beginning of the century take to the air. In the hangars, other historic aircraft, vintage and veteran cars, fire-engines and horse-drawn carriages are displayed as a reminder of a bygone age.

How did it all start? It stemmed from the enthusiasm of a young man named Richard Shuttleworth who, in the late 1920s, began to buy up veteran cars, and in 1930 bought his first aeroplane.

The aeroplane was a de Havilland Gypsy Moth, and when in 1934 he was offered a 1909 Bleriot and a semi-wrecked 1910 Deperdussin by an Ampthill garage owner, the collection had begun. Not that Shuttleworth envisaged the splendid museum that can be seen at Old Warden today, and tragically he did not live to see his creation develop to its present fame and importance.

When war came, Richard Shuttleworth joined the Royal Air Force. He was killed in 1940. A rich man with no direct heirs, he left £1 million to his mother, and in remembrance of her son and his love for old aircraft she endowed a trust to maintain his collection.

I was appointed trustee. I had known Richard and shared his infectious enthusiasm. Together we had rescued the Bleriot and the Deperdussin from Ampthill, an operation I well remember as the Bleriot was enmeshed in the branches of an elder tree which I had to cut down with a hacksaw!

Shuttleworth's small collection, the Bleriot, Deperdussin, a Sopwith Pup, Blackburn Monoplanes, two Comper Swifts, two Desoutters, a Hanriot Biplane and the Gypsy Moth, was stored for the duration of the war. But, despite this, the Shuttleworth Trust was founded in 1944.

It was not until 1947 that we were able to get the aircraft operating again. Before the war, Richard had received invaluable assistance from Mr L. A. Jackson, a man whose knowledge, experience and technical skill were equalled only by a few, even in those days. Mr Jackson, now Squadron Leader Jackson, left the RAF and returned to Old Warden to apply his skills once more, and before long the Bleriot and Deperdussin were flying again.

Richard Shuttleworth had always been determined that every piece of historical machinery he owned should be made to work as it had done for its designer—and with the same materials. This became the policy of the Shuttleworth Trust Collection. We are an educational trust and believe that inspiration is the most important factor in education. Nothing can be more inspiring than watching an historic aeroplane take to the air again, instead of being caged in a museum and hemmed in by other lifeless exhibits.

This policy has created its own problems. In many cases rebuilding aircraft of the First World War is largely a matter of expense, but before the war aircraft were not made to drawings—they simply evolved on the workshop floor. Even with modern techniques, rebuilding some of these veterans depends

BRISTOL BOXKITE *The Bristol Boxkite was originally designed in 1910, but the Old Warden model was specially reconstructed for the film 'Those Magnificent Men in their Flying Machines'. It needs perfect weather conditions in which to fly but, despite this defect, it was the first British aircraft to be sold abroad. Eight Boxkites were exported to the Russian Imperial Army and other planes found their way to many countries, including New Zealand and Australia. The reconstruction is powered by a modern engine. The original rotary engine must have made the plane much more difficult to handle.*

DEPERDUSSIN *Built in 1910, the Deperdussin monoplane is powered by a three-cylinder Anzani engine, and was bought by Richard Shuttleworth before the Second World War. Like the Bleriot, which the collection also owns, it was of French design. Originally a single-seater, two and three-seater versions were developed from it, and in 1910 it sold for £460—ready to fly. Today, its low power and the risk of damage allow only short hops, but the hope is that one day it can make a full flight. Even these brief flights are enough to remind visitors of the courage of the pioneer aviators.*

entirely on the remaining bits, photographs and the fading memories of those who once saw them fly.

The Old Warden workshops are unique. Skilled engineers head the team, and the crafts which are traditional to aircraft building—such as wood and fabric work—are being passed on to a new generation of apprentices.

It is not uncommon for a plane to stand idle for five years or more before work can be started. An example of this is the de Havilland Comet racer. This beautiful aeroplane won the England to Australia air race in 1934 in a time of 70 hours 54 minutes. In 1938 it achieved the England to New Zealand return record by covering the 26,450 miles in ten days, 21 hours and 22 minutes.

The Comet spent the war years in the open at Gravesend, and in 1951 it made a brief appearance as a static exhibit at the Festival of Britain. It seemed its flying days were over.

In 1965 the aeroplane was handed over to the Shuttleworth Collection for preservation, and in our language that means restoration to flying condition if possible. Grants from the Transport Trust and Hawker Siddeley Aviation (successors to the de Havilland Aircraft Co.) have made this a practical proposition. Much needs to be done, and large sums of money are still required, but it is the aim of the collection to put the Comet racer back into the air before 1980.

No less a skill than rebuilding these machines is the art of flying them. I recall, with a shudder, the day that Richard Shuttleworth collected the Hanriot from Brussels. A quick examination seemed to confirm that the aeroplane was airworthy, so Richard took off and headed for Lympne in Kent, where he landed safely. Thereafter the engine refused to start, and when the aeroplane finally arrived by road at Old Warden, Mr Jackson gave it a preliminary inspection. After peering inside

AVRO TRIPLANE IV *The ungainly looking Triplane takes to the air at Old Warden, but this aeroplane is younger than it looks. Like the Bristol Boxkite, the plane is a faithful reproduction of the original. The name Avro is a contraction of A. V. Roe, one of Britain's most famous aviation pioneers. His company built one each of four versions of the Triplane in 1910, and started a long line of successful civil and military aircraft. From the Triplane sprang the very successful 504 trainer, followed by the Tutor of the 1930s and the Anson. During the Second World War Avro produced the Lancaster bomber, which in peacetime reopened the commercial routes as the Lancastrian. The collection's Triplane flies well, except for a tendency, on occasion, to resist coming out of a turn. Nevertheless, it is a regular performer on flying days. The costs of keeping machines like the Avro Triplane in working order are huge, but the trustees are against purely static displays, even though the policy brings problems.*

L.V.G. C VI *A German reconnaissance and bomber aeroplane gives a low-level view as it swoops low over the airfield (right). The L.V.G.—the initials stand for Luft-Verkehrs Gesellschaft—was built in 1917 and was powered by a 6-cylinder, 230 h.p. Benz engine. After the First World War parts from captured aircraft were cannibalised by the RAF to make a complete plane for comparison with its British rival, the Bristol Fighter. Later it appeared at the Hendon Air Pageants and took part in mock dog-fights against a Bristol Fighter. In 1966 the collection bought the plane and restored it to its original condition. It often appears in the air on flying days at Old Warden, usually repeating its battles with the collection's Bristol Fighter. The L.V.G. is slightly larger and heavier than the Bristol Fighter. The only other specimen of this plane hangs from the roof of a museum in Belgium. This was used as a model by the Shuttleworth engineers when restoring their own plane at Old Warden.*

HAWKER TOMTIT *The typical lines of a Hawker biplane are seen in the Tomtit. Designed in 1928 as a trainer to replace the Avro 504, the Tomtit had a welded steel-tube frame which set the pattern for a line of Hawker fighters. Until 1959 the collection's Tomtit was owned by the Hawker company, and their chief test pilot, Squadron Leader Neville Duke, raced it on several occasions. The Tomtit is the only surviving example of its type in the world, and was extensively restored at the Old Warden workshops.*

the engine bay for a few moments he withdrew his head and shook it sadly. 'It's just like looking into a scrap merchant's yard,' he remarked.

Nowadays, we make sure that every aeroplane is as safe as we can make it before it is flown, but some of the early models have peculiar characteristics which either endear them to the pilot or scare him to death—depending on one's point of view!

The Bristol Boxkite, for example, is tricky to fly. Its large wings and light frame make it hard to handle in gusty winds, but on a calm day it can climb to several hundred feet and fly sedately, though noisily.

The First World War aircraft are more pleasant to fly. The pilot feels part of the machine, and although it may not always do what he wants—or expects—this is a challenge to his ability. Some aircraft have to be cajoled, others forced; it is a good pilot who knows which to apply and when.

Landing these aircraft is often the trickiest part of the flight. A sudden gust of wind can flip an aeroplane on to its back if the pilot is not fully alert.

The magnificent men who fly these machines are all service-trained pilots with many hours of flying experience. Some are test pilots or flying instructors, sometimes both; others are airline pilots who are only too eager to swop their big jets for an aeroplane 50 years old or more.

The regular flying days were started in the

1960s, shortly after the collection had been opened to the public. At first only four or five of the aircraft were flown, but as more were added to the collection and others were restored it became possible to put on a very full programme.

One of the most popular days is when the military aircraft are featured. The First World War aircraft are a great attraction, with their ability to confine their display to the airspace immediately above the airfield.

One star of these occasions is the 'Brisfit', the RAF's nickname for the Bristol Fighter. Built in 1918, it is powered by a Rolls-Royce Falcon engine—the oldest working Rolls-Royce aero engine in the world.

Another popular performer is the Sopwith Pup. This single-seater fighter went into service with the Royal Flying Corps, but previously it was used by the Royal Naval Air Service and in August 1917 was the first aeroplane to land on the deck of a ship at sea. Its armament consisted of a single Vickers machine-gun mounted in front of the pilot and firing through the propeller. The Pup at Old Warden has been in the collection since 1936.

Representing the German air force is the L.V.G. c VI, a bomber reconnaissance aeroplane of 1917. It is the latest aeroplane to be restored at Old Warden, a task that took five years. When it made its first flight for over 30 years, in 1972, two rather tricky situations occurred. During a preliminary hop along the airfield it was discovered that the aeroplane

GLOSTER GLADIATOR *Last of the RAF's biplane fighters, and the first to be fitted with an enclosed cockpit, the Gladiator first flew in 1934 and served with more than 30 squadrons. Just before the outbreak of the Second World War, the faster Hurricanes and Spitfires went into service, but the Gladiator continued to distinguish itself in many fields of combat. Three Gladiators—Faith, Hope and Charity—were at one time the main air defence of Malta against German and Italian attacks. The Shuttleworth specimen (above and below) was built from two separate machines after the war. Later it was restored by the original maker. It is one of the most popular models in flying displays.*

AVRO TUTOR *The basic RAF trainer in the 1930s, the Tutor (above and right) won a government contract against its rival the Tomtit. It was bigger than its competitor, with a large tandem cockpit, adjustable seats and wheelbrakes. It was powered by the Lynx engine, made by Armstrong Siddeley, and could achieve a top speed of 122 mph. The Tutor carried on a tradition of Avro trainers for the RAF, which started with the Avro 504K biplane in the First World War. By 1936 it had superseded all other trainers in RAF schools. A team of six Tutors gave displays at the Hendon Air Pageants, and were the predecessors of the RAF's display formation team of today. The model in the collection, one of the last in service, was used by the RAF from 1933 until 1946, when it was sold to a private owner. It is another of the collection's film stars, having appeared in the film 'Reach For The Sky', which told the story of Second World War ace Douglas Bader. The Shuttleworth Trust restored it in 1972.*

was a lot livelier than it looked, and the engine had to be quickly switched off to stop the machine from over-running the airfield. When the aeroplane was at last taken into the air for the first time the flight had to be cut short, for within four minutes the radiator temperature reached near-boiling point. Luckily our engineers managed to solve this problem.

The between-war years are represented by the Gloster Gladiator, the Avro Tutor, the Hawker Tomtit and soon, it is hoped, by a Hawker Hind. The Hind, now being restored, was presented to the collection by the Royal Afghan Air Force, a squadron of which flew Hinds until 1953.

Moving on to the Second World War, what other plane could represent that period more faithfully than the Spitfire? This famous marque served throughout the war in many roles, and the collection owns two of these machines. One, the Mark Vc, took part in the film 'The Battle of Britain'. The other is a Mark XI, once used as a high-speed taxi by the American Air Attaché in Britain.

The Spitfire that appears in the displays, however, is the only genuine Mark I flying anywhere in the world—a plane which it is my pride and pleasure to own.

While the flying exhibits are obviously a big attraction, the ground displays are also full of interest. One item which we certainly never intend to fly is the reproduction of a 1942 V1 flying bomb. This is a replica made for the film 'Operation Crossbow'. We are also fortunate in having an impressive array of aero engines and propellers. The earliest engine—and they do not come any earlier—is the steam unit of 1870, designed for the Frost Ornithopter. At the other end of the scale, the 1600 h.p. Rolls-Royce Merlin represents the ultimate in piston-engine design.

Most intriguing perhaps are the rotary engines. The propeller is bolted to the radial cylinders which revolve around a stationary crankshaft. Many of the First World War aircraft used this type of engine.

Although the Shuttleworth Collection is basically an aircraft museum, we have not forgotten that Richard Shuttleworth began by collecting veteran cars. Among the cars at Old Warden is a Panhard Levassor of 1898 that was once driven to Ascot carrying Edward VII.

SUPERMARINE SPITFIRE *No enthusiast could fail to thrill to the sight and sound of a Spitfire zooming low over Old Warden airfield. The throb of the Rolls-Royce engine was a familiar sound over the fields of Kent in 1940, when Spitfires fought the Battle of Britain and gave the RAF its 'finest hour'. Over 20,000 were built, and they served in many roles throughout the war. The Mark I (above), owned by the collection's Aviation Trustee, is often put through its paces on flying display days.*

VISITING OLD WARDEN

The Shuttleworth Collection is open all year round except for Christmas. Flying days are normally the last Sunday every month in summer. The A1 passes within 2 miles of the airfield, near Biggleswade. The turn-off here, and the approaches from major roads in the area, are clearly signposted.

PROVOST *One of the more modern planes in the collection is the Percival Provost, which came into service with the RAF in 1953 as the basic trainer for pilots. It was noted for its aerobatic abilities. In 1961, however, it was replaced by a later development— the Jet Provost. The collection has a Jet Provost but will not display it until the RAF stops using this model.*

FIESELER STORCH *Used chiefly as an observation plane by the* Luftwaffe *during the Second World War, the Fieseler Storch high-winged monoplane made up in manoeuvrability what it lacked in speed. On one occasion, it played a decisive part in politics. In 1943 German paratroops used a Fieseler Storch to fly the fallen Italian dictator Mussolini to safety. It was the only plane capable of landing on the mountain-top where Mussolini was held prisoner.*

Exotic birds and ancient aircraft in rural Bedfordshire

Rare birds and even rarer aircraft are notable features of this tour from Bedford, where John Bunyan wrote The Pilgrim's Progress *and spent 13 years in gaol for his free-thinking religious views. The birds are at Stagsden and include such exotic species as the satyr tragopan from the Himalayas. The veteran flying machines preserved at Old Warden go back to 1909. Much of Bedfordshire is flat, and can be seen in panorama from the hills at Hexton and Sharpenhoe. The route includes walks along the nature trails of Maulden Wood and the park at Ampthill, where Henry VIII used to hunt.*

(1) Bedford to RAF Cardington Leave the centre of Bedford on the A6, following the signpost for Luton. Where the A6 goes off to the right, shortly after crossing the Great Ouse, keep straight ahead on the A600 signposted to Hitchin. Soon after leaving the town the road passes RAF Cardington on the left.

(2) RAF Cardington to Old Warden Continue along the A600 towards Hitchin for 5 m., then turn left at the signpost for Old Warden. Fork left soon afterwards. Just under 2 m. later turn right on to the road signposted to Old Warden, and follow the road into the village.

(3) Old Warden to Hexton Follow the road out of the village. On the right soon afterwards is Old Warden Aerodrome, where the Shuttleworth Collection of historic aircraft is housed. At the junction with the B658, turn right and follow the road through Stanford and into Shefford. There turn left at the junction with the A600. Keep straight on at the traffic lights in the town, but soon afterwards turn right, following the signpost to Meppershall. Close to the church in Meppershall is the early-17th-century manor house, a gabled building with a timber-framed façade. Turn right in the village, following the signpost for Shillington, and after 1 m. turn left at the signpost for Apsley End. Bear right at the next junction and follow the road into Shillington, where the large church of All Saints was built about 1300 and has remained little altered. At the junction on the far side of Shillington, bear left on to the road signposted to Pegsdon. After 2 m., at the junction with the B655, turn right and follow the road for ¾ m. to Hexton.

(4) Hexton to Sharpenhoe Continue along the B655 to the junction with the A6 at Barton in the Clay. There turn right and then left 50 yds later, following the signpost to Sharpenhoe, which is reached after 1 m.

(5) Sharpenhoe to Wrest Park Continue along the same road out of Sharpenhoe and through Harlington, to the junction with the A5120. There turn right and follow the road into Westoning. In the village turn right, following the signpost for Greenfield and Flitton. The entire east end of the parish church at Flitton is taken up by the De Grey Mausoleum, where the earls of Kent have been buried for six centuries. Follow the main road past the church and then turn left by the Jolly Coopers public house, following the signpost for Silsoe. Turn right at the T-junction and follow the road into Silsoe to join the A6. Here turn right again and the entrance to Wrest Park is on the left.

(6) Wrest Park to Maulden Wood Leave Silsoe on the A6 northwards. Follow it across the A507 to the top of Deadman's Hill. Maulden Wood is to the left. At the end of the wood, by the turning to Haynes West End, is the Forestry Commission office.

(7) Maulden Wood to Ampthill Take the turning to Haynes West End and turn left in the village down to Limbersey Lane, following the signpost to Maulden. In Maulden, turn right at the junction with the A507 and follow the road into Ampthill.

(8) Ampthill to Houghton House Leave Ampthill on the A418 signposted to Bedford. At the top of the hill leading out of the town, turn right at the signpost to Houghton House and follow the drive.

(9) Houghton House to Stagsden Bird Zoo Return to the A418 and turn right. After 2 m. turn left on to the road signposted to Stewartby. Keep straight ahead at the first roundabout, and then turn left, following the signpost for Marston. On meeting the A5140 turn left, then immediately right at the signpost for Wootton Green. Turn right again at the T-junction shortly afterwards, still following the Wootton signpost. Follow the road through Wootton and after 1 m. keep ahead at the staggered crossroads, following the signpost for Green End. Turn left at Kempston Church End on to the A5134, then turn left again on to the B560 to Stagsden. After 1 m. turn right by the Three Horseshoes public house, still on the B560 signposted to Stagsden. Turn left on to the A422 in Stagsden. Turn right by the church, signposted Stevington, for the Bird Zoo.

(10) Stagsden Bird Zoo to Bedford Follow the road from the zoo to the junction with the A428. Turn right and follow the road through Bromham to Bedford.

INFORMATION

Places of interest *Bedford:* Museum, Tues. to Sat., and Sun. afternoons. Bunyan Museum, all year, weekdays. Cecil Higgins Art Gallery, all year, weekdays, Sun. afternoons. *Houghton House:* All year, weekdays, Sun. afternoons. *Stagsden Bird Zoo:* All year, daily. *Wrest Park:* Grounds only, Apr. to Sept., Sat., Sun. and Bank Hols.

Nature trail *Maulden Wood:* 1–2 m. No dogs. Guide from Forestry Commission, Cambridge.

Information *Bedford:* Town Hall, St Paul's Square (Tel. Bedford 67422, ext. 263).

Towns with easy access to Bedford:

Aylesbury	30 m.	Kettering	24 m.
Cambridge	29 m.	Northampton	21 m.
Hitchin	17 m.	Peterborough	38 m.

Bunyan's signature and thumbprint.

BEDFORD
A five-arched Georgian bridge crosses the River Great Ouse and on either bank there are public gardens. Each Wednesday and Saturday a market is held in St Paul's Square, where St Paul's Church overlooks a statue of John Howard (1726-90), the penal reformer. Bunyan (1628-88), author of *The Pilgrim's Progress*, lived in the town for more than 30 years, and spent 13 of them in Bedford Gaol for his Nonconformist religious beliefs. His statue stands by the part-Saxon church of St Peter and there is a Bunyan museum in Mill Street containing, among other relics, the only specimens of his handwriting known to exist. The Cecil Higgins Art Gallery has a fine collection of paintings, sculptures and porcelain. In the Swan Hotel, a staircase with twisted balustrades is thought to have been designed by Wren. The Lion Hotel, with its Georgian balconies and pilasters, is another of Bedford's many historic inns.

NORTH
14

Bunyan statue, Bedford.

Satyr tragopan, Stagsden Bird Zoo.

STAGSDEN BIRD ZOO
Many birds threatened with extinction in the wild have flourished here since the zoo was founded in 1961. One of the most rare is the beautifully coloured satyr tragopan, 100 of which have been bred at Stagsden. These, and about 130 other species of birds from distant lands, share the zoo with old breeds of poultry, sacred ibis, black-necked swans and red-breasted geese from Siberia. In the East Garden is a display of shrubs and old-fashioned roses.

Houghton House.

HOUGHTON HOUSE
An impressive ruin set on a hill with extensive views to the west, Houghton House is thought to have been the 'House Beautiful' of John Bunyan's *The Pilgrim's Progress*. It was built in 1615 for the Countess of Pembroke, the sister of Sir Philip Sidney (1554-86), the Elizabethan soldier and poet, and altered some 25 years later, possibly by Inigo Jones. The house, a turreted Jacobean mansion, has been in ruins since it was dismantled by the Duke of Bedford in 1794, leaving only its sandstone shell.

SCALE
0   1   2   3 MILES

OLD WARDEN
The village, whose church is 800 years old, was rebuilt in the 19th century as a model settlement to house the tenants of the local landowner, Lord Ongley. Just outside the village is Old Warden Aerodrome, home of the famous Shuttleworth Collection of historic aircraft and vintage cars. (See pp. 136-9.)

Thatched cottage, Old Warden.

...hute training balloon, Cardington.

...CARDINGTON
...ips were built in the 1000 ft long hangars here during the 1920s, and in 1930 the R101 took off ...s maiden flight for India, only to crash in northern France with the loss of 46 lives. Now the ...trains parachutists at Cardington, using wartime barrage balloons, and the place is also a centre ...e fast-growing modern sport of hot-air ballooning.

AMPTHILL
In the 14th-century church there is a monument incorporating the cannonball that killed Richard Nicholls, a local man who became the first governor of Long Island, USA, and who died fighting the Dutch at the Battle of Sole Bay in 1672. Ancient oaks stand in the public park to the west of the town where Henry VIII used to hunt.

...LDEN WOOD
...ntjac deer, foxes, badgers, pheasants, ...dpeckers and tawny owls are among the ...y creatures that live in this Forestry ...mmission woodland. The wood can be ...ored along walks that take between 45 and ...minutes to complete.

...EST PARK
...est House at Silsoe, the third to ...d on the site, was built in 1834 by a ...nch architect, and with its Louis XV ...rior is a rare example in England ...he French château style. In the early ...rs of this century this was the ...ntry home of the American ...bassador: now it is used by the ...ional Institute of Agricultural ...gineering. Paths radiate from the ...ace at the back of the house through ...formal gardens, which were begun ...706 and later improved by ...pability Brown (1715-83). Buildings ...he gardens include an orangery, a ...nese bridge and the star-shaped ...her's Pavilion, which overlooks a ...d statue of William III. The estate is ...sidered a model of formal canal ...dening. It belonged to the now ...nct De Grey family, earls of Kent, ...m about 1280 to the 19th century. ...ward VII was a frequent visitor.

Wrest Park, Silsoe.

HEXTON
The wooded Barton Hills, part of the Chilterns, rise to the south of this little village, where laburnum trees line the main street and extend beyond it over what the local people call the 'golden mile'. On one of the hills is Ravensburgh Castle, an oval Iron Age hill-fort, covering 22 acres and surrounded by a deep ditch. There are views north from the village over the plains towards Bedford. Large yews encircle St Faith's Church, with its vaulted chapel.

SHARPENHOE
The village probably gained its name from the steep hill which rises above it: *ho* is Old English for a spur of land. A footpath leads to the summit, which is National Trust land and offers fine views northwards. Nearby Bury Farm has an early-Tudor timber-framed barn.

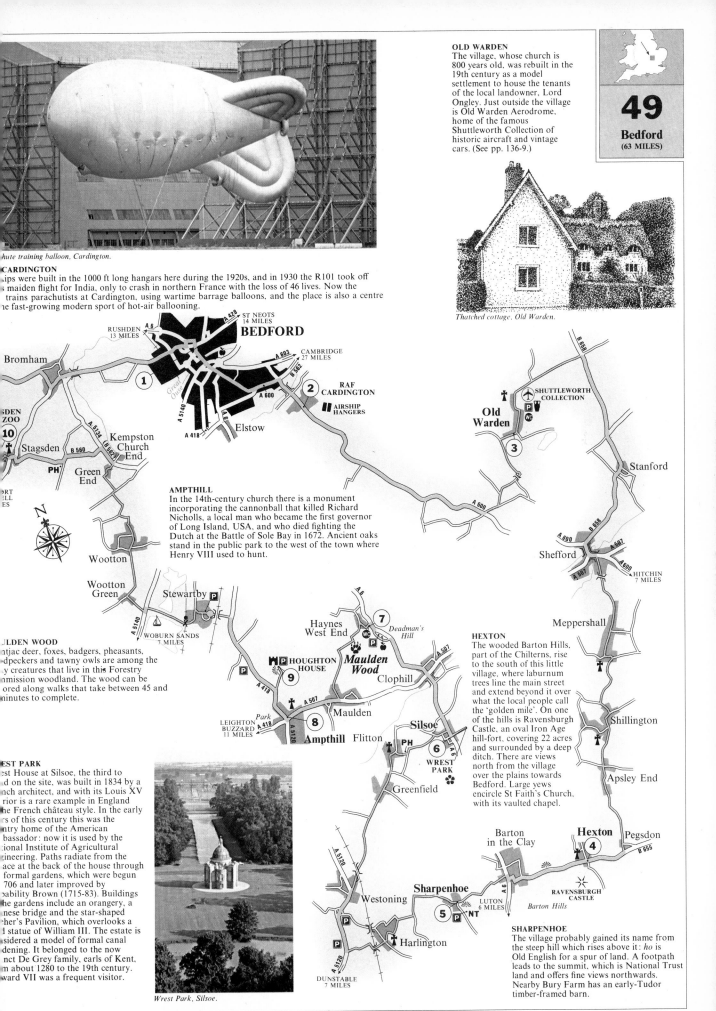

Down Hertfordshire's quiet country lanes

Britain's first garden city, the village where the Queen Mother was born, and the 'royal' silk farm that produced Princess Anne's wedding dress are all in this quiet corner on the borders of Hertfordshire and Bedfordshire. The silk-farm village of Ayot St Lawrence was also the home of the playwright George Bernard Shaw for 44 years. Country lanes lead on to two lavishly stocked country houses—Knebworth and Luton Hoo—and at the same time link a series of villages that seem to have remained unchanged for centuries.

1 Hitchin to Letchworth Leave the town on the A600 signposted for Bedford. Just beyond the outskirts of Hitchin pass the boundary sign for Ickleford and almost immediately turn right on to the road signposted to Ickleford. Follow the road through the village and under a railway bridge. At the next junction turn right, following the signpost for Letchworth. On the outskirts of Letchworth go left, immediately right, and then turn left into Wilbury Road for the town centre.

2 Letchworth to Ashwell Leave the town on Norton Road, passing through the old village of Norton. After passing Norton parish church on the right, turn right on to the road signposted to Baldock. At the T-junction on the outskirts of Baldock turn left on to the Icknield Way, and at the junction with the A507 turn left again. Go under a railway bridge, and turn right on to the road signposted to Ashwell. From here the route follows a narrow winding road through low hills, entering Ashwell 4 m. later.

3 Ashwell to Benington Leave the village on the road signposted to Baldock. At the junction on the edge of the village keep straight ahead, following the signpost for Sandon and Walkern. Just over 2 m. later go under a railway bridge and then cross the A505 on to the road signposted to Wallington, Sandon and Walkern. Just beyond the turn-off to Rushden, the road joins the A507 (coming in from the right). After a few yards, where the A507 bears left, bear right on the road signposted for Cromer, Ardsley and Walkern. In Cromer join the B1037 and continue into Walkern. On the far side of the village, where the B1037 bears right, go straight ahead, following the Benington signpost. After about 2 m., turn left and follow the road into Benington.

4 Benington to Knebworth House Leave the village on the road signposted to Aston and Stevenage. At the crossroads on the edge of the village go straight on, following the Aston signpost. Go through Aston to the outskirts of Stevenage. At the T-junction with the A602, turn right and follow the signposts for the A1(M) motorway through a series of roundabouts. At the roundabout on the A1(M) take the exit signposted to Knebworth House and follow the private road to the estate.

5 Knebworth House to Ayot St Lawrence Return to the A1(M) roundabout and go straight ahead at this and the next roundabout. At the third roundabout take the third exit, signposted to the village of Knebworth. Directly opposite the Roebuck Inn, turn right into Old Knebworth Lane and continue into the village. In Old Knebworth turn right, following the signpost to Codicote. In Codicote, turn left at the T-junction with the B656. Continue through the village and take the second turning right, opposite the George and Dragon Inn, signposted to Wheathampstead. After 1 m. turn right on to the road signposted Ayot St Lawrence, and at the next junction turn left. After 1 m. turn right and follow the winding road into the scattered village.

6 Ayot St Lawrence to Luton Hoo In the village turn right at Shaw's Corner, following the Kimpton signpost. At the next T-junction turn left on to the B651 (not signposted). Keep straight on at the next two crossroads, and after 2 m. turn left at the T-junction. Follow the road to the junction with the A6129, turn right and continue to the outskirts of Luton. Where the A6129 bends sharply right, turn left into Luton Hoo.

7 Luton Hoo to St Paul's Walden Leave the park on the A6129, going away from Luton, and where the main road swings sharp right go straight ahead on to Vauxhall Road. At the T-junction with Kimpton Road turn right and shortly afterwards keep straight ahead at the traffic lights. Follow the road signposted to Tea Green and at the far side of Luton Airport continue on the road as it bears right. After just over 1 m., turn left on to the road signposted to King's Walden. At the next crossroads turn right and, on reaching the village of Whitwell, keep straight ahead. At the end of the village turn left and follow the B651 into St Paul's Walden.

8 St Paul's Walden to Hitchin Leave the village on the B651 and after 2 m., at the junction with the B656, turn left. Follow the B656 back to Hitchin.

INFORMATION

Places of interest *Ashwell:* Museum, Sun. afternoons or by appointment with Curator. *Ayot St Lawrence:* Lullingstone Silk Farm, conducted tours Mon.-Fri., Sun. afternoons. Shaw's Corner, Feb. to Nov., Wed. to Sun., and Bank Hols. *Hitchin:* Museum, Mon. to Sat. *Knebworth House:* Apr. to Sept., Tues. to Sun.; Oct., Sun. only. House, 11.30 a.m.-5.30 p.m., gardens, 11 a.m.-6 p.m. *Luton Hoo:* Easter to Sept., Mon., Wed., Thur., Sat. and Good Friday, Sun. afternoons. Gardens, mid-Apr. to mid-July, Wed., Thur., Bank Hol. July 21 to Sept., Mon., Wed., Thur., Sat., Sun. afternoons.

Information Thames and Chiltern Tourist Board, 8 The Market Place, Abingdon (Tel. Abingdon 22711). Information Office, 37 Chequer Street, St Albans (Tel. St Albans 64511).

Towns with easy access to Hitchin:

Bedford	17 m.	Hatfield	15 m.
Biggleswade	11 m.	London	35 m.
Cambridge	27 m.	St Albans	16 m.

ST PAUL'S WALDEN
The Queen Mother, widow of George VI, w[as] christened Lady Elizabeth Bowes-Lyon in th[e] 14th-century parish church. She and her bro[thers] and sisters presented the East window in 19[ ] as a memorial to their parents, the Earl and Countess of Strathmore, whose ancestors liv[ed] in the village. Five of the six bells were cast in 1665. The newest one commemorates the coronation in 1937 of George VI and his qu[een]

The Marble Hall, Luton Hoo.

LUTON HOO
Three Rembrandts are among the art treasures of Luton Hoo. The house was designed by Robert Adam in 1766 and rebuilt after a fire in 1843. It stands in 1200 acres of grounds laid out by Capability Brown. The art collection was begun in about 1900 by the diamond millionaire Sir Julius Wernher. There is a room devoted to 18th-century English painters, including Gainsborough and Reynolds; a collection of ivory miniatures, many dating from the 14th century; and examples of the work of the Russian court jeweller, Peter Carl Fabergé. Fabergé is most famous for the small decorated boxes, ornamental animals and his intricately enamelled and jewelled objects such as parasol handles. Many of these were made as small gifts to the very rich and were in everyday use.

AYOT ST LAWRENCE
George Bernard Shaw, the Irish playwright, lived here from 1906 until his death in 1950 at the age of 94. His house 'Shaw's Corner' is filled with mementoes, including his portrait by Augustus John. His desk and study have been kept exactly as he left them. Shaw's ashes were scattered in the garden. Lady Hart Dyke moved her silk farm from Lullingstone in Kent to Ayot House in 1957. It was her[e] continuing a long royal tradition, that Princess Anne's wedding gown was spun in 1973. There is a picnic area, and visitors can make a conducted tour of the farm and see the raw silk being produced.

Moth and cocoon, Lullingstone Silk Far[m]

SCALE
0   1   2   3 MILES

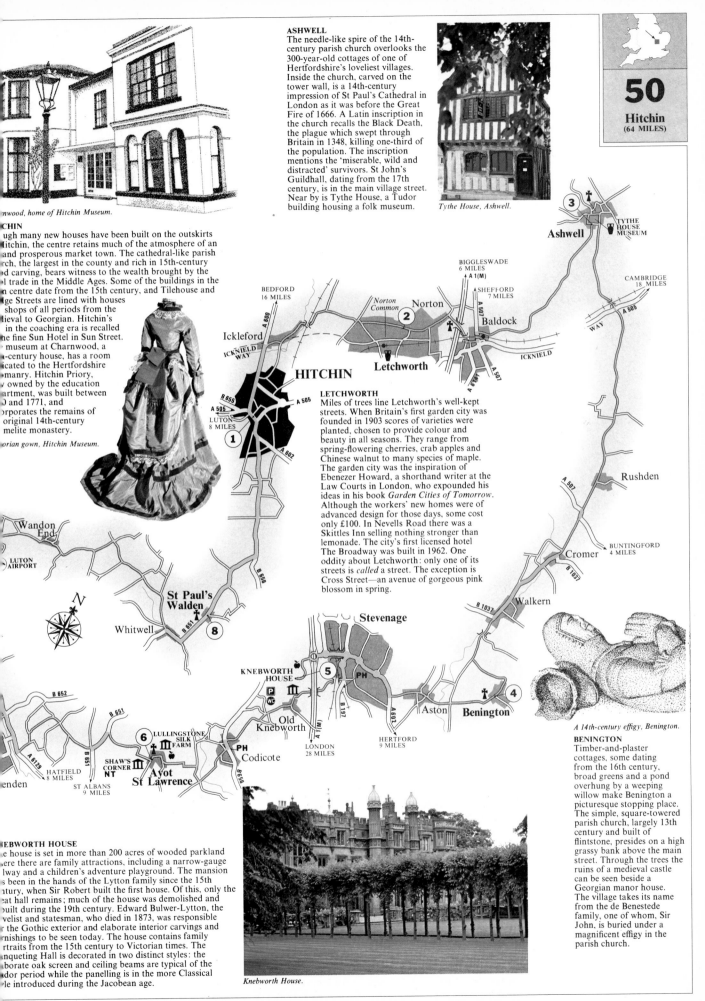

...nwood, home of Hitchin Museum.

ASHWELL

The needle-like spire of the 14th-century parish church overlooks the 300-year-old cottages of one of Hertfordshire's loveliest villages. Inside the church, carved on the tower wall, is a 14th-century impression of St Paul's Cathedral in London as it was before the Great Fire of 1666. A Latin inscription in the church recalls the Black Death, the plague which swept through Britain in 1348, killing one-third of the population. The inscription mentions the 'miserable, wild and distracted' survivors. St John's Guildhall, dating from the 17th century, is in the main village street. Near by is Tythe House, a Tudor building housing a folk museum.

Tythe House, Ashwell.

...CHIN

...ugh many new houses have been built on the outskirts ...itchin, the centre retains much of the atmosphere of an ...and prosperous market town. The cathedral-like parish ...rch, the largest in the county and rich in 15th-century ...d carving, bears witness to the wealth brought by the ...l trade in the Middle Ages. Some of the buildings in the ...n centre date from the 15th century, and Tilehouse and ...ge Streets are lined with houses ...shops of all periods from the ...ieval to Georgian. Hitchin's ...coaching era is recalled ...e fine Sun Hotel in Sun Street. ...museum at Charnwood, a ...-century house, has a room ...icated to the Hertfordshire ...manry. Hitchin Priory, ...owned by the education ...artment, was built between ...and 1771, and ...orporates the remains of ...original 14th-century ...melite monastery.

...orian gown, Hitchin Museum.

LETCHWORTH

Miles of trees line Letchworth's well-kept streets. When Britain's first garden city was founded in 1903 scores of varieties were planted, chosen to provide colour and beauty in all seasons. They range from spring-flowering cherries, crab apples and Chinese walnut to many species of maple. The garden city was the inspiration of Ebenezer Howard, a shorthand writer at the Law Courts in London, who expounded his ideas in his book *Garden Cities of Tomorrow*. Although the workers' new homes were of advanced design for those days, some cost only £100. In Nevells Road there was a Skittles Inn selling nothing stronger than lemonade. The city's first licensed hotel The Broadway was built in 1962. One oddity about Letchworth: only one of its streets is *called* a street. The exception is Cross Street—an avenue of gorgeous pink blossom in spring.

A 14th-century effigy, Benington.

BENINGTON

Timber-and-plaster cottages, some dating from the 16th century, broad greens and a pond overhung by a weeping willow make Benington a picturesque stopping place. The simple, square-towered parish church, largely 13th century and built of flintstone, presides on a high grassy bank above the main street. Through the trees the ruins of a medieval castle can be seen beside a Georgian manor house. The village takes its name from the de Benestede family, one of whom, Sir John, is buried under a magnificent effigy in the parish church.

...EBWORTH HOUSE

...e house is set in more than 200 acres of wooded parkland ...ere there are family attractions, including a narrow-gauge ...lway and a children's adventure playground. The mansion ...s been in the hands of the Lytton family since the 15th ...ntury, when Sir Robert built the first house. Of this, only the ...at hall remains; much of the house was demolished and ...built during the 19th century. Edward Bulwer-Lytton, the ...velist and statesman, who died in 1873, was responsible ...r the Gothic exterior and elaborate interior carvings and ...rnishings to be seen today. The house contains family ...rtraits from the 15th century to Victorian times. The ...nqueting Hall is decorated in two distinct styles: the ...borate oak screen and ceiling beams are typical of the ...dor period while the panelling is in the more Classical ...le introduced during the Jacobean age.

Knebworth House.

Cromwell country–with a great lake he never knew

The River Great Ouse winds through the countryside south of Huntingdon, gliding through rich soil that was once farmed by a man who became one of the most powerful rulers in British history—Oliver Cromwell. Since his day, drainage schemes have increased the farming acreage, and one of Britain's greatest man-made lakes has been added to the landscape. But Cromwell would recognise many buildings—the bridge at St Ives, Bourn post mill, his old school in Huntingdon itself, old village churches and the 15th-century inn at Fen Drayton.

(1) Huntingdon to Grafham Water Leave on the A604 signposted Kettering. Just outside Huntingdon, the fine Tudor country mansion, Hinchingbrooke House, appears on the right. About 2 m. further on, just before the roundabout at Brampton, is the gabled cottage where the parents of Samuel Pepys lived and where the famous diarist—who owned it from 1664 to 1680—is said to have once buried his money for fear of Dutch invasion. Turn left at the roundabout and almost immediately, just past the church on the left, turn right into Brampton High Street. Bear left through the town and go straight across the A1 to Grafham. At the T-junction in the village, turn left to Grafham Water.

(2) Grafham Water to Kimbolton Castle Follow the road round the man-made lake, past the dam and turn right on to the B661 signposted to Great Staughton. Follow the road through the lakeside village of Perry, and turn right at the T-junction on to the A45 to visit Kimbolton Castle.

(3) Kimbolton Castle to Bourn post mill Return along the A45, and after about 8 m. cross the A1. After a further 1 m. turn left at the T-junction, keeping on the A45, and into St Neots. At the end of the shopping area in the town turn right on to the B1043, signposted Little Barford. In Eynesbury turn left, on to the B1046 signposted to Great Gransden. After 3 m. the road passes through Abbotsley, where the brown cobble church contains an unusual 15th-century Flemish painting of the Adoration of the Magi. About 1½ m. past Abbotsley go right and left at the staggered crossroads, keeping on the B1046 into the village of Great Gransden which, as Grantsdene, was mentioned in the Domesday Book at a time (1087) when Earl Alfgar, brother of Hereward the Wake, was Lord of the Manor. On the bold west tower of the 15th-century church is the face of a working clock said by the Clockmakers Company of London to be 'one of the oldest in any parish church in England'. In the tower, too—and to be heard every three hours, day and night—is a late-17th-century six-bell carillon, worked by a heavy weight which is wound daily. It has a repertoire of five old hymns and folk tunes. Where the road bears sharp right in Great Gransden, take the second turning on the left and go uphill to the roundabout. Turn left here, on to the road signposted Caxton. At the crossroads with the A14 go straight ahead, and after ½ m. Bourn post mill is on the left.

(4) Bourn post mill to Madingley At the next T-junction turn right into Bourn. Bear left out of the village and turn left on to the B1046 signposted to Toft. In Toft, turn left off the B1046 on to the road signposted to Hardwick. Go through the village and turn right on to the A45. After about 1¼ m. there is a turn-off for Madingley, on the left. Pass it, staying on the A45, and after about 1 m. the American Cemetery and War Memorial Chapel is on the left.

(5) Madingley to Fen Drayton Return along the A45 and take the turn-off for Madingley, now on the right. Continue through Madingley and turn left on to the A604 signposted Huntingdon. After 5 m. turn right into Fen Drayton.

(6) Fen Drayton to Hemingford Grey Follow the road through the village, turn left just past the Three Tuns Inn back to the A604, and turn right following the Huntingdon signpost. After 2 m. turn right at the roundabout on to the A1096 signposted St Ives. About 1 m. down the road, turn left on to the minor road signposted to the riverside villages of Hemingford Grey and Hemingford Abbots.

(7) Hemingford Grey to St Ives Return to the A1096, turn left, over the quaint bridge with its chapel half-way across, and into St Ives.

(8) St Ives to Houghton Leave St Ives and turn left on to the A1123 towards Huntingdon. About 2 m. further on, turn left off the main road into the village of Houghton to see the watermill.

(9) Houghton to Huntingdon Rejoin the A1123, turn left and left again on to the A141 and back to Huntingdon.

INFORMATION

Places of interest *Bourn Post Mill:* All reasonable times. *Hinchingbrooke House:* Mar. to May, July to Aug., Sun., Easter, Spring and Late Summer Bank Hols. 2-5 p.m. *Huntingdon:* Cromwell Museum, Tues. to Sat., 11 a.m.-1 p.m., 2-5 p.m., Sun. 2-4 p.m. *Kimbolton Castle:* Spring Bank Hol. Sun. and Mon., Late Summer Bank Hol. Mon., mid-July-Aug., Sun. only, 2-6 p.m. *St Ives:* Norris Museum, Mon., 2-5 p.m., Tues.-Fri., 10 a.m.-1 p.m., 2-5 p.m., Sat., 10 a.m.-12 noon. Closed Bank Hol.

Events *Huntingdon:* Dicing by Sunday School children for bibles under will of Dr Robert Wilde, Spring Bank Hol. Mon., noon. *Hinchingbrooke:* Flower festival, June. *Kimbolton Castle:* Gala, July.

Information Information Centre, Wheeler Street, Cambridge (Tel. Cambridge 58977).

Towns with easy access to Huntingdon:

Bedford	21 m.	Peterborough	19 m.
Cambridge	16 m.	Royston	21 m.
Kettering	26 m.	Stamford	27 m.

Houghton watermill.

HOUGHTON
The village has a number of timber-framed yeoman farmer houses of the 16th and 17th centuries. The massive 17th-century watermill is now leased as a Youth Hostel. A bronze bust of a 19th-century miller, Potto Brown, is on the village green.

Bewick's swan.

GRAFHAM WATER
Careful planning has turned the 2½ square miles of England's largest man-made lake, opened in 1966, into a vast leisure area. As a domestic supply reservoir of the Great Ouse Water Authority, it provides drinking water for more than 1½ million people. It also provides excellent sailing and some of the finest trout fishing in Europe. It is stocked with so[me] 40,000 brown and rainbow trout every year—mainly rainbows which, a fisheries warden has said, 'jump like kangaroos'. Round its banks are surfaced car parks, pleasant picnic sites and places to buy snacks and soft drinks. Although Grafham Water is 'young' in terms of providing a completely settled habitat for birds, there i[s] wide variety of wildfowl, including Bewick's swan, a w[inter] visitor from Russia and northern Europe, which carrie[s its] neck erect instead of in the gentle curve of the mute swan. Waders and terns can be seen in spring and autum[n.]

KIMBOLTON CASTLE
This fortified Tudor mansion is where the ageing queen, Catharine of Aragon, divorced by Henry VIII, spent the last 19 months of her life. It was transformed into a late-Stuart house in the years 1690–1720; but the Queen's Room, where Catharine died in 1536, is still part of the fabric of the castle. Although it was not built in her day, she is said to haunt the fine main staircase at the castle, which is now a school.

RUSHDEN 9 MILES
CASTLE Kimbolton
BEDFORD 11 MILES B 660
Grafham
Grafham Water
Great Staughton
B 661
Perry
BEDFORD 11 MILES
A 45
Kym
St Neots
BIGGLESWADE 9 MILES
A1
Eynesbury
B 1043

SCALE
0   1   2   3   5 MILES

HEMINGFORD GREY

...th Hemingford Grey and its
...n village of Hemingford Abbots,
...t beyond, are noted for their
...erside scenery. Down a narrow
...e in Hemingford Grey, the
...urch of St James, on a bend of
...Great Ouse, has features dating
...ck to the 12th century. The upper
...tion of its truncated spire was
...own down by a hurricane in 1741,
...d is locally said to lie on the river
...d. The thick-walled and
...ated Manor House, south-west
...the church, dates back to about
...50 and still retains its original
...rman round-headed windows
...d main entrance door. It is still
...habited house in England. There
...several other fine old houses in
...e village, including Glebe Cottage,
...ilt in 1583, and the 17th-century
...emingford Grey House. In the
...rden of this house stands one of
...e largest plane trees in Britain.

St James's Church on the Great Ouse at Hemingford Grey.

ST IVES

The most striking feature of
this market town on the River
Great Ouse is the river itself,
spanned here by a narrow
stone bridge completed in
1425. The chapel at its centre
is one of only four medieval
bridge chapels surviving in
England. There is a wide
variety of 18th and
19th-century houses and
shops in the main streets of the
town, and a statue of Cromwell
in the market-place.

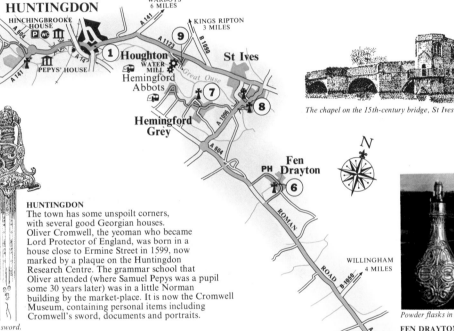

The chapel on the 15th-century bridge, St Ives.

HUNTINGDON

The town has some unspoilt corners,
with several good Georgian houses.
Oliver Cromwell, the yeoman who became
Lord Protector of England, was born in a
house close to Ermine Street in 1599, now
marked by a plaque on the Huntingdon
Research Centre. The grammar school that
Oliver attended (where Samuel Pepys was a pupil
some 30 years later) was in a little Norman
building by the market-place. It is now the Cromwell
Museum, containing personal items including
Cromwell's sword, documents and portraits.

...omwell's sword.

Powder flasks in the Three Tuns, Fen Drayton.

FEN DRAYTON

In this tiny village of 17th and 18th-century
thatched cottages, the Three Tuns Inn is
reputed to be as old as the 14th–15th-century
church of St Mary. It has a tiled, half-timbered
gable, with heavy thatch on the remainder of the
roof. Inside are many exposed beams, some of
which are richly carved.

Bourn post mill.

BOURN POST MILL

This is believed to be the oldest
windmill of its type still standing in
England. Unlike smock mills and
tower mills, which are topped by
movable caps, the entire body of
the post mill is turned round the
post on which it is internally
supported, so that the sails always
catch the wind. The miller used a
'tail pole' to turn his mill into the
wind. The base and outer
structure of the Bourn mill are
known to have been in existence
in 1636, but the working parts—
which can be viewed on most
days—have been replaced
from time to time.

MADINGLEY

The village of thatched houses
and modern bungalows is on the
edge of the well-wooded park of
Madingley Hall, an Elizabethan
red-brick house now used as a
hostel by Cambridge graduates.
Close to the handsome iron gates
of the park is the parish church,
which dates mainly from the
late 12th century. There are 15th
and 16th-century stained-glass
fragments, and six 17th-century
panels of saints. A mile to the
south-east lies the American
Cemetery. The War Memorial
Chapel, completed in 1954, is a
striking example of modern
architecture. Inside is a map 30 ft
long and 18 ft high showing
Atlantic sea and air routes used
by men of the US Air Force during
the Second World War. Many of
those who died on these routes
lie in the cemetery.

American War Memorial Chapel, Madingley.

Wildlife on the reclaimed riches of the Fens

In 1634 the Earl of Bedford began the systematic reclamation of a vast waste of marshland, 70 miles long and 30 miles wide, that lay between the North Sea coast and the inland forests. When it was finished, 170 years later, entire rivers had been moved from their courses and some of the richest farmland in Britain raised up to the plough. Provision was made for the teeming fen wildlife; pockets of marsh were preserved so that, 300 years on, they still find their former sanctuary.

(1) Peterborough to Peakirk Leave the city on the A15, which is signposted to Sleaford. Follow the road to Glinton, where 17th-century stone houses surround a fine 1630 manor house with mullioned windows and shaped gables. In the village, turn right on to the B1443 to Peakirk where, as the road turns right to Thorney, keep straight ahead to the Peakirk Wildfowl Refuge.

(2) Peakirk to Thorney Return to the B1443 and turn left. Keep straight on for 6¾ m., crossing the A1073 and, at the T-junction with the B1040, turn right into Thorney. To visit the abbey church and ruins, and the Thorney Wildlife Park, cross the A47 in the village. The entrance is off the B1040 on the right.

(3) Thorney to Wisbech Return to the crossroads and turn right on to the A47 signposted to Wisbech. Follow the road for 13½ m. to Wisbech.

(4) Wisbech to Walpole St Peter Take the A47 out of town towards King's Lynn and, in just under 5 m., turn left on the road signposted to Walpole St Peter. There are a number of rose nurseries along this road. After just under 2 m., at the junction where there is a grassy island with a tree, bear left, signposted to Walpole St Andrew. At the next junction turn right along Church Road, where the church of Walpole St Peter is on the right.

(5) Walpole St Peter to Denver Sluice Return to the junction and turn right. Turn second left to West Walton and, at the T-junction, turn left again and continue to West Walton. The church has a 13th-century bell tower standing a full 60 ft away from the main building. Follow the signposts back towards Wisbech. At the A47, on the outskirts of the town, turn right, following the Peterborough sign. This leads to Wisbech town centre. There, take the A1101, signposted to Downham Market. Continue to Outwell and bear left where the road becomes the A1122 and follows the Well Creek to Nordelph. Keep on the A1122 and into Downham Market. In the town, turn right on to the A10 signposted to Ely. Follow this road to Denver and, in the village, at the crossroads by the church, turn right on to the road signposted to Denver Sluice. The road crosses the Ouse and New Bedford rivers to reach the gates of Denver Sluice.

(6) Denver Sluice to Welney Return the same way to Downham Market and back along the A1122 to Nordelph. Turn left on to the B1094, which is signposted to Welney and, at the crossroads, turn left on to the A1101, which is signposted to Ely.

Continue for 3 m. to Welney. Go through the village and over the Old and New Bedford rivers. Turn left towards Ten Mile Bank. After 1 m., on the right, is Pintail House and the Welney Wildfowl Refuge. Return to Welney.

(7) Welney to March In the village, turn left on to the B1100, which is signposted to March. At the T-junction turn left on to the B1093, which is signposted to Manea and Wimblington. Bear right just outside Manea, where the B1093 divides, and follow the branch to Wimblington. At the T-junction with the A141, turn right for March. After 2¾ m., at the Seven Stars public house, turn left into Church Street. The church is 200 yds from the junction on the left.

(8) March to Ramsey From the church, return to the A141 and turn right, retracing the route to Wimblington. Stay on the A141 through the village to Doddington, and turn right on to the B1093, signposted to Benwick. In the village turn left on to the B1096 and continue into Ramsey.

(9) Ramsey to Peterborough Turn right on to the B1040, which is signposted to Pondersbridge. Just after crossing the river at Pondersbridge, turn left on to the B1095. At the T-junction with the A605 turn left, following the road into Peterborough.

NATURE NOTES
Black-tailed godwits and a few ruffs breed in the marshland meadows in summer. In some winters flooding creates a large lake in the Ouse Washes between the Hundred Fort and the Old Bedford river, attracting many wildfowl, especially pintail ducks.

INFORMATION

Places of interest *Peakirk*: Wildfowl Trust, Daily except Christmas Eve and Day, 9.30 a.m.-6.30 p.m. *Thorney*: Wildlife Park, Good Friday to Oct., daily, 10 a.m.-dusk. *Wisbech*: Peckover House, Tues. to Thur., Sat., Sun. and Bank Hol. Mon., 2-6 p.m.; mid-Oct. to Mar. by appointment. Wisbech and Fenland Museum, Tues. to Sat., 10 a.m.-1 p.m., 2-5 p.m. (winter, 4 p.m.). Closed Bank Hols.

Nature trail *Norwood Road Reserve*: Starts behind March station. Guidebook from Cambridgeshire & Isle of Ely Naturalists' Trust, Cambridge.

Events *Peterborough*: Carnival and Bridge Fair, Sept. East of England Agricultural Show, mid-July. Expo Steam (steam engines), Nov. *Thorney*: Gala, early June. *Wisbech*: Rose fair, early July.

Information Tourist Information Bureau, Town Hall, Bridge Street, Peterborough (Tel. Peterborough 63141).

Towns with easy access to Peterborough:

Bedford	38 m.	Leicester	41 m.
Cambridge	35 m.	Spalding	19 m.
King's Lynn	34 m.	Stamford	14 m.

Hawaiian goose

Red-breasted goose

PEAKIRK
Laid out over 15 landscaped acres, the wooded ponds of the gardens at Peakirk provide an ideal refuge for more than 100 different species of wildfowl. The birds range from the Australian black swan to the muscovy duck, from the Chilean flamingo to the Hawaiian goose. Most are allowed to roam free about the waterways and islands, where it is permitted to feed them with brown bread or biscuit. Pens contain the quarrelsome types that might attack other birds—or visitors. Run by the Wildfowl Trust, Peakirk is open to the public all year round.

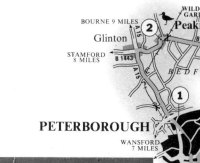

Cathedral west front, Peterborough.

PETERBOROUGH
A short history of medieval England is told within the walls of Peterborough Cathedral. It is buried in the Saxon foundations and carved into the memorial stone for the monks massacred by the Danes. It is painted upon the nave roof in grotesque Norman portraits, and it is locked in Catherine of Aragon's grave. Outside, a modern industrial city bustles around broad parks that sweep down to the River Nene.

SCALE
0   1   2   3   4   5 MILES

WALPOLE ST PETER

The 14th-century church at Walpole St Peter became unique when its builders were forced to 'lift' it over an ancient right of way, by running a vaulted passage beneath the chancel. Designed in the Perpendicular style, it is one of the most splendid churches in Norfolk. Its peal of bells includes three dated 1629, and two that were cast in 1747. The church contains a rare example of an 18th-century 'hudd', a movable shelter used for funerals in bad weather.

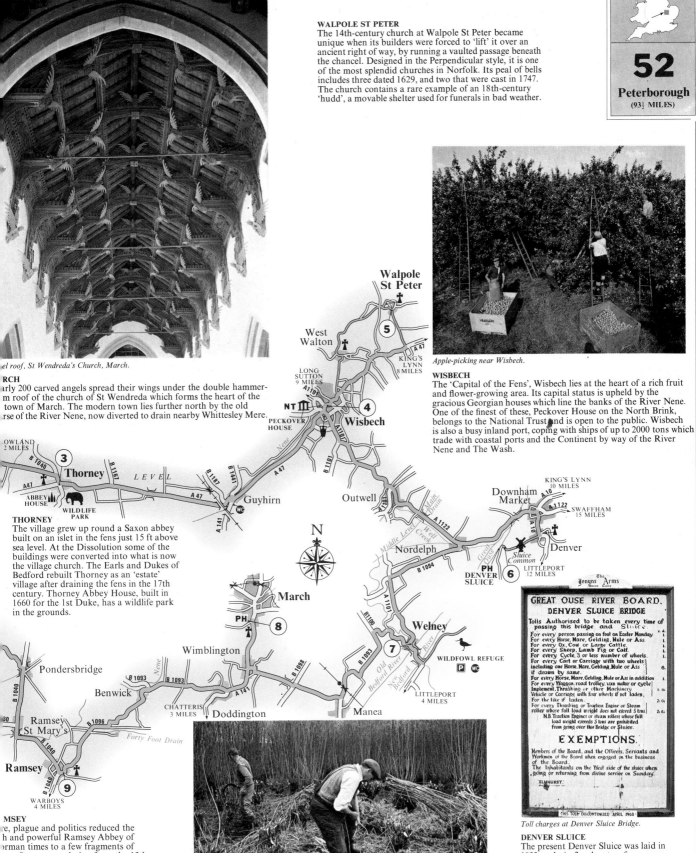

el roof, St Wendreda's Church, March.

Apple-picking near Wisbech.

RCH

arly 200 carved angels spread their wings under the double hammer-m roof of the church of St Wendreda which forms the heart of the town of March. The modern town lies further north by the old rse of the River Nene, now diverted to drain nearby Whittlesey Mere.

WISBECH

The 'Capital of the Fens', Wisbech lies at the heart of a rich fruit and flower-growing area. Its capital status is upheld by the gracious Georgian houses which line the banks of the River Nene. One of the finest of these, Peckover House on the North Brink, belongs to the National Trust and is open to the public. Wisbech is also a busy inland port, coping with ships of up to 2000 tons which trade with coastal ports and the Continent by way of the River Nene and The Wash.

THORNEY

The village grew up round a Saxon abbey built on an islet in the fens just 15 ft above sea level. At the Dissolution some of the buildings were converted into what is now the village church. The Earls and Dukes of Bedford rebuilt Thorney as an 'estate' village after draining the fens in the 17th century. Thorney Abbey House, built in 1660 for the 1st Duke, has a wildlife park in the grounds.

MSEY

re, plague and politics reduced the h and powerful Ramsey Abbey of rman times to a few fragments of ne. One corner, dating from the 13th tury, now forms part of a local ool. The town, which was threatened h a similar fate, revived to become hriving agricultural community when e surrounding fens were drained. msey parish church was built ut 1180 as the guesthouse for the bey's visitors and pilgrims.

Willow-cutting, Welney.

WELNEY

At Welney, on marshy land between the two Bedford rivers, willows are grown to be cut and woven into the protective lattice-work which defends the river banks against erosion. Here also is the Welney Wildfowl Refuge, where the free-roaming birds can be watched from an observatory and hides run by the Wildfowl Trust.

Toll charges at Denver Sluice Bridge.

DENVER SLUICE

The present Denver Sluice was laid in 1832 to drain flood waters from more than 800,000 acres of fen farmland. The first sluice here was built in 1652 by the Earl of Bedford. Near by is the Jenyns Arms, a popular pub among yachtsmen and anglers, which has an entertaining list of former toll charges displayed on one of its walls.

Hereward and a steam engine —defenders of the Fens

Through green and golden seas of wheat, or rich earth black as soot, past rolling pastures light with their chalky underlay and over gentle heathland, the route traces its way into the flat but fascinating countryside of the Fens. Here, man has won a long and cunning battle against water to gain soil for cultivation. From Newmarket, Britain's horse racing and training capital, the route goes to Ely, where a mighty cathedral towers on the island where Hereward the Wake defied the Normans, not far from a symbol of the other fight for the fenland—a great steam pump.

(1) Cambridge to Newmarket Leave on the A45 signposted Newmarket. On the outskirts of Cambridge, by the 40 mph sign, turn left to Fen Ditton. On entering the village turn left by the Blue Lion Inn and down to the river. Return to the A45 and turn left to Newmarket. Almost immediately on the right is Cambridge Airport used by gliding enthusiasts. Vantage points to watch the gliding can be reached by turning right about 1 m. along the A45 towards Teversham. If this is done, return to the A45, turn right and after about 5½ m., at the roundabout, continue straight ahead on to the A1304. At the next roundabout, turn left at the signpost marked National Stud, July Racecourse. Beyond the entrance to the stud, which is sometimes open to the public, is the footpath that runs along the northern portion of the 7½ m. long Devil's Ditch. Return to the roundabout and turn left on to the A11 for Newmarket.

(2) Newmarket to Isleham Continue on the A11 through the town, then after 4 m. keep ahead at a roundabout and 1 m. later turn left on the B1085 to Chippenham. Soon, on the left, is Chippenham Park, with an artificial lake ¾ m. long. The village itself has neat cottages behind gardens filled with fruit trees, and a red-brick schoolhouse, built in 1714, opposite the church. Just beyond the village, fork right on the B1104 to Isleham.

(3) Isleham to Ely Go through Isleham, bearing left by the church and keeping on the B1104, to the fen village of Prickwillow, where some of the houses are slightly tilted because the peat on which they were built has dried and shrunk over the years. An unusual sight in the small rural church is an elaborately carved 18th-century marble font. Turn left in the village on to the B1382 and into Ely.

(4) Ely to Stretham Join the A10, following the signposts to Cambridge. After about 4½ m., at the Stretham roundabout, turn left on to the A1123. In 200 yds turn right to visit Stretham Old Engine.

(5) Stretham to Wicken Fen Return to the A1123, turn right, and after 4 m., on entering Wicken village, turn right for Wicken Fen. A windmill has been erected by the National Trust near the entrance to the fen walks, as a reminder of the days when unpredictable winds powered the water pumps of the fenlands, before the coming of such steam engines as the one at Stretham. Before entering the fen, consult the Warden at the National Trust office, where there is a large collection of literature on the geological structure, vegetation and wildlife.

(6) Wicken Fen to Anglesey Abbey Return to the A1123, turn left and after 1 m. turn left again, on to the road signposted Upware. Go through Upware and, just after the road bears round to the left, turn right, signposted Reach. At the T-junction, turn left and continue straight over the crossroads. The narrow fen roads broaden into the village street of Reach, which stands at the north-western end of the Devil's Ditch crossed at Newmarket. Reach was the centre of quarrying for clunch, a soft white limestone used in the building of many Cambridge colleges. Follow the road out of the village to Swaffham Prior, which has two churches in the churchyard. One is disused, the other, St Mary's, has a striking Norman tower. The massive 6 ft thick clunch walls form a square at the base, then the tower becomes octagonal and is 16-sided at the top. The church is notable for the large amount and variety of its 20th-century stained glass, which includes scenes from the trenches of the First World War, the mountains of Switzerland, an eruption of Vesuvius and medieval warfare. Follow the road to the junction with the B1102 and turn right, following the signposts to Cambridge. At the crossroads on the outskirts of Swaffham Bulbeck, a short detour can be made by turning right to Commercial End at the end of a short canal running into the River Cam. It has a tiled warehouse and other buildings typical of an inland port. Return to the B1102, turn right, and just past the village of Lode is the entrance, on the right, to Anglesey Abbey.

(7) Anglesey Abbey to Cambridge Stay on the B1102, and after 1¾ m. turn right on to the A45 and back into Cambridge.

INFORMATION

Places of interest *Anglesey Abbey:* Apr. to Oct., Tues., Wed., Thur., Sat., Sun., Bank Hols. 2-6 p.m. Gardens only, Mon. to Fri., 2-6 p.m. *Newmarket:* National Stud, May to June, Sun. and Bank Hols., 2-5 p.m. *Stretham Beam Engine:* Daily, 8 a.m.-8 p.m.

Nature trail *Ely:* Roswell Pits. Guidebook from Cambridgeshire and Isle of Ely Naturalist Trust and Ely Cathedral.

Events *Cambridge:* Boat races, Feb. and June. Antique fair, Apr. Regatta, end May. Midsummer fair, June. Festivals, July. *Ely:* Three-day fair, May and Oct.

Information Information Centre, Wheeler Street, Cambridge (Tel. Cambridge 58977). 24 St Mary's Street, Ely.

Towns with easy access to Cambridge:

Bedford	30 m.	London	54 m.
Bishop's		Luton	31 m.
Stortford	26 m.	Peterborough	35 m.
Bury St Edmunds	28 m.	Saffron	
Huntingdon	16 m.	Walden	15 m.

West tower, Ely Cathedral.

ANGLESEY ABBEY
The 'abbey', an Augustinian priory in 1135, was rebuilt as a country house in the reign of Elizabeth I, and much altered and improved in this century by a patron of the arts, Lord Fairhaven, to house his collections of clocks, furniture, tapestries, paintings, rare porcelain and silver. The paintings, with works by Claude, Landseer and Gainsborough, include Constable's view of Waterloo Bridge. Lord Fairhaven also laid out the abbey grounds, in which formal gardens with statues and urns, trees and shrubs, are combined with bold landscaping over an area of 100 acres. The big herbaceous garden is framed by beech hedges.

Pagoda clock, Anglesey.

A 604
GODMANCHESTER
15 MILES
ST NEOTS
18 MILES
A 45

BARTON
3 MILES

A 603

ROY
13 M

FEN DITTON
Although it is almost part of the Cambridge suburbs, the place has retained its village character, with two old pubs—one on the River Cam—thatched cottages and yellow-brick almshouses. The spacious church of St Mary has 13th, 14th and 15th-century work, fine old timbering and a 600 year old font. Fen Ditton is at the western end of the Fleam Dyke, a defensive earthwork once crowned with a wooden palisade, which was probably raised between AD 500 and 700.

CAMBRIDGE
The town is inseparable from the university, the spires of which can be seen for miles across the Fens. A feature on Cambridge appears on pp. 150–3.

SCALE

0   1   2   3   4   5 MILES

The great cathedral of Ely, dominating the countryside for many [mil]es around, was begun by the Normans in 1083, only a few years [afte]r they had driven Hereward the Wake from his last fen-island [str]onghold here. Ely remained an island until the Fens were [dra]ined in the 17th and 18th centuries, and there are many [rem]inders of the city's 'inland port' status, including the Quay area, [litt]le changed in layout since the 15th century when grain and [go]ods came in by water. The further bank of the River Ouse is now [ter]raced and laid out as moorings for yachts and pleasure craft. [Oli]ver Cromwell lived in the half-timbered house near St Mary's [chu]rchyard for 11 years, from 1636. A nature trail with emphasis [on] Ely's history starts in Springhead Lane.

Cromwell House, Ely.

STRETHAM OLD ENGINE

[On]e of the few surviving beam [pu]mping engines that took over [the] drainage from the [win]dmills in the early 19th [cen]tury is preserved in full [wor]king order at Stretham. The [hor]izontal cast-iron beam was [rai]sed and lowered like a [see-]saw by steam power, to [dri]ve the flywheel below it. This [in] turn drove a scoop-[wh]eel—shown in the [draw]ing—which could lift [wat]er 12 ft into a dyke at the [rat]e of 124 tons a minute. A [die]sel engine replaced it in [19]25, doing in three and [thr]ee-quarter hours what the old [en]gine did in 11, but the steam [pu]mp has since been called [up]on in time of flood. [Fr]agments of bog oak and [Ro]man pottery from the Fens [ar]e shown in the engine house.

[Stre]tham Old Engine.

ISLEHAM

This is the first typical fenland village on the route, built on a low chalk spur that is part of the 'shore' of the Fens which now spread away towards Ely. Old cottages with tiled roofs stand around a basically 14th-century church (the 'candle-snuffer' tower is 19th century). The inside of the church is remarkable for the beauty of its lofty 15th-century roof and the number and variety of its monuments and brasses. One brass shows a 15th-century High Sheriff, Thomas Peyton, in armour with enormous elbow guards, flanked by his two elegant wives in fashionable dress.

WICKEN FEN

It is possible to picnic on the fen, but rubber boots and a waterproof groundsheet are advisable over most of its 700 acre area, for Wicken has been preserved by the National Trust as an example of how much of fenland looked before widespread drainage in the 17th century. The great variety of plant and animal life is under constant study by amateur and professional scientists, and pamphlets on the work are sold at the fen.

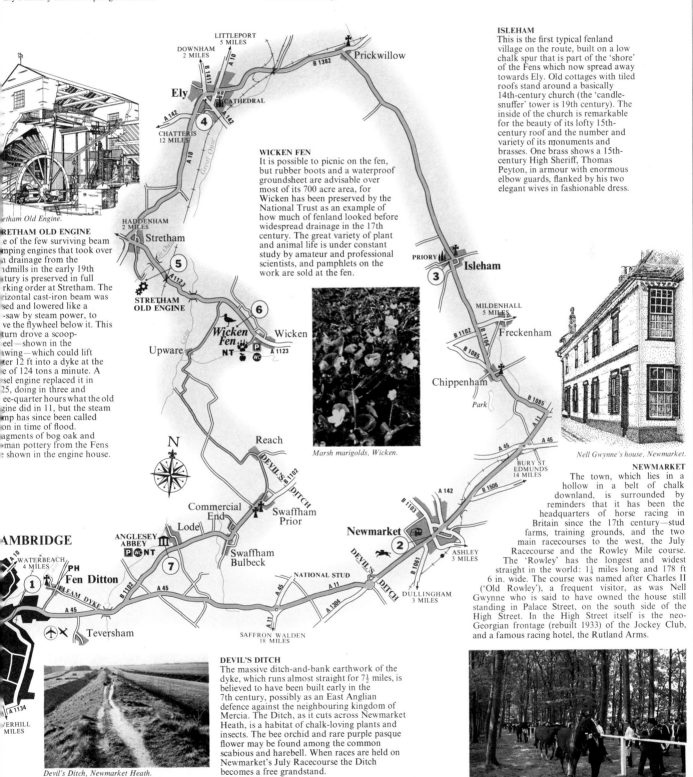

Marsh marigolds, Wicken.

Nell Gwynne's house, Newmarket.

NEWMARKET

The town, which lies in a hollow in a belt of chalk downland, is surrounded by reminders that it has been the headquarters of horse racing in Britain since the 17th century—stud farms, training grounds, and the two main racecourses to the west, the July Racecourse and the Rowley Mile course. The 'Rowley' has the longest and widest straight in the world: 1¼ miles long and 178 ft 6 in. wide. The course was named after Charles II ('Old Rowley'), a frequent visitor, as was Nell Gwynne who is said to have owned the house still standing in Palace Street, on the south side of the High Street. In the High Street itself is the neo-Georgian frontage (rebuilt 1933) of the Jockey Club, and a famous racing hotel, the Rutland Arms.

DEVIL'S DITCH

The massive ditch-and-bank earthwork of the dyke, which runs almost straight for 7½ miles, is believed to have been built early in the 7th century, possibly as an East Anglian defence against the neighbouring kingdom of Mercia. The Ditch, as it cuts across Newmarket Heath, is a habitat of chalk-loving plants and insects. The bee orchid and rare purple pasque flower may be found among the common scabious and harebell. When races are held on Newmarket's July Racecourse the Ditch becomes a free grandstand.

Devil's Ditch, Newmarket Heath.

Parade before a Newmarket race.

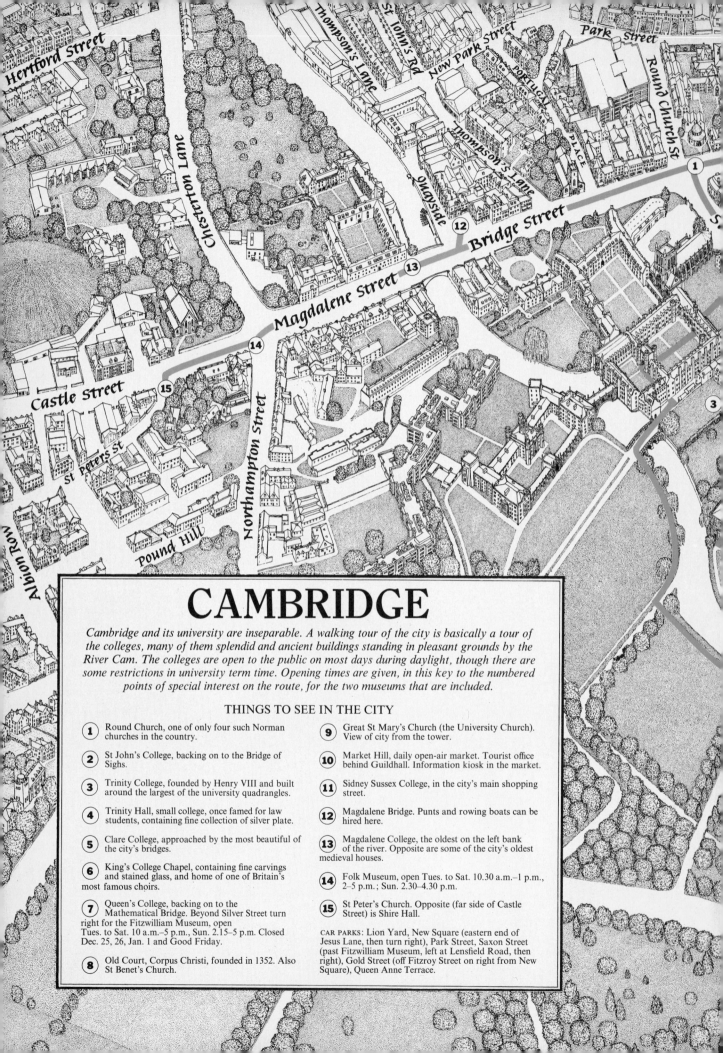

CAMBRIDGE

Cambridge and its university are inseparable. A walking tour of the city is basically a tour of the colleges, many of them splendid and ancient buildings standing in pleasant grounds by the River Cam. The colleges are open to the public on most days during daylight, though there are some restrictions in university term time. Opening times are given, in this key to the numbered points of special interest on the route, for the two museums that are included.

THINGS TO SEE IN THE CITY

(1) Round Church, one of only four such Norman churches in the country.

(2) St John's College, backing on to the Bridge of Sighs.

(3) Trinity College, founded by Henry VIII and built around the largest of the university quadrangles.

(4) Trinity Hall, small college, once famed for law students, containing fine collection of silver plate.

(5) Clare College, approached by the most beautiful of the city's bridges.

(6) King's College Chapel, containing fine carvings and stained glass, and home of one of Britain's most famous choirs.

(7) Queen's College, backing on to the Mathematical Bridge. Beyond Silver Street turn right for the Fitzwilliam Museum, open Tues. to Sat. 10 a.m.–5 p.m., Sun. 2.15–5 p.m. Closed Dec. 25, 26, Jan. 1 and Good Friday.

(8) Old Court, Corpus Christi, founded in 1352. Also St Benet's Church.

(9) Great St Mary's Church (the University Church). View of city from the tower.

(10) Market Hill, daily open-air market. Tourist office behind Guildhall. Information kiosk in the market.

(11) Sidney Sussex College, in the city's main shopping street.

(12) Magdalene Bridge. Punts and rowing boats can be hired here.

(13) Magdalene College, the oldest on the left bank of the river. Opposite are some of the city's oldest medieval houses.

(14) Folk Museum, open Tues. to Sat. 10.30 a.m.–1 p.m., 2–5 p.m.; Sun. 2.30–4.30 p.m.

(15) St Peter's Church. Opposite (far side of Castle Street) is Shire Hall.

CAR PARKS: Lion Yard, New Square (eastern end of Jesus Lane, then turn right), Park Street, Saxon Street (past Fitzwilliam Museum, left at Lensfield Road, then right), Gold Street (off Fitzroy Street on right from New Square), Queen Anne Terrace.

ROUND CHURCH *The Church of the Holy Sepulchre is one of the few round churches left in England. It was built in 1140 with a round nave and a round aisle, with probably a small chancel.*

CAMBRIDGE

The river made Cambridge a centre of commerce many centuries ago. Trade routes between London, the Midlands and Europe met at the bridge over the Cam. How—and exactly when—the university was founded here in the Fens is unknown. Students began to gather round teachers whose ideas appealed to them. Then, in the 13th and 14th centuries, the first colleges were founded.

Stand on the corner where Bridge and Round Church Streets meet St John's Street and you are within a few steps of the heart of this university city.

Ahead, to the south-west, is St John's College, followed by a succession of other famous seats of learning which lie along The Backs—in other words, the backs of the colleges—the name given to the stretch of the River Cam immediately behind some of these time-honoured buildings.

St John's was founded in 1511 by Lady Margaret Beaufort, mother of Henry VII. The buildings have been extended with a fine sense of continuity, spanning the centuries and the river, on the west side of which the glass and concrete of our own day contrast with more mellow materials of earlier times.

Famous undergraduates

The gatehouse on to St John's Street is richly decorated with heraldic carvings. The Hall (which is not generally open to the public) has a Tudor hammerbeam roof and is hung with portraits of the famous men of St John's. These include the poet Wordsworth, Elizabeth I's chief minister William Cecil (Lord Burghley), the humanitarian Wilberforce and the statesman Lord Palmerston. Beyond the Third Court, cross the river by the New Bridge, a covered bridge built in 1831 and better known as the Bridge of Sighs after the one in Venice. The best view of it is from the Old Bridge to the south, built more than a century earlier.

BRIDGE OF SIGHS *A covered bridge, inspired by the 16th-century Bridge of Sighs in Venice, spans the Cam in a single arch at St John's College. It was built in 1831. The unglazed windows were barred to prevent students sneaking in late at night. The bridge links Third Court with New Court.*

Return over The Backs by Trinity Bridge, passing the Wren Library in Nevile's Court.

Thomas Nevile, appointed Master of Trinity by Elizabeth I, was responsible for much of the college's present appearance, including the charming Nevile's Court, completed in 1614, which he built at his own expense. Sir Isaac Newton (1642–1727) worked out his theory on the speed of sound in the cloister of this court by measuring the speed at which sound produced an echo.

King Edward's Tower, dating from 1428–32, was re-erected when the Great Court of Trinity was built at the turn of the 16th century, and its 18th-century clock strikes the hour twice over.

Approach Trinity Hall down narrow Trinity Lane, with its towering array of chimney pots. On to Clare College, founded as University Hall in 1326 and rebuilt in the 17th century. It is best seen from across the river. This way, too, the walk passes the college's delightful Master's and Fellows' Garden, and through the iron gates on to the handsome bridge. Clare has one court, and from its main entrance turn right to approach the most famous of all Cambridge buildings—King's College Chapel.

Henry VI, who founded Eton, also founded King's College in 1440 to provide further education for Eton scholars. The chapel is one

TRINITY COLLEGE *Henry VIII had ambitious plans to commemorate his royal patronage of the arts when he founded Trinity in 1546. After his death it continued to grow on a grand scale. Thomas Nevile, appointed Master in 1593, created the Great Court, larger than any other court in Cambridge. At his own expense he built Nevile's Court (above) in which stands the Wren Library (below), with its ancient manuscripts and wood-carvings by Grinling Gibbons.*

TRINITY LANE *A stroll past the towering chimney stacks of Trinity Lane gives a vivid impression of the Cambridge of the Elizabethan age. The lane, which dates from 1600, backs on to the vast expanse of Trinity Great Court. Trinity is a showpiece of a college which has the most impressive architecture of any Cambridge college. Across the lane lie Gonville and Caius Colleges and the smaller Trinity Hall, which has been chiefly a lawyers' college since its foundation in 1350. The Hall has fine gardens and one of the city's most interesting features: an Elizabethan library in which books are chained to the shelves.*

KING'S COLLEGE CHAPEL *The soaring, fan-vaulted roof (left) is composed of 2 miles of stone ribs. Other major features are Rubens's 'Adoration of the Magi' (detail, above), the carving of the early-Renaissance choir stalls, and the 16th-century stained glass through which sunlight floods like a celestial vision. It is an unforgettable experience to attend the Festival of Nine Lessons and Carols on Christmas Eve, when the great Gothic building resounds with the singing of the choir.*

QUEENS' COLLEGE *Founded in 1448 by Henry VI's wife, Margaret of Anjou, and refounded in 1465 by Edward IV's wife, Elizabeth Woodville, this is the city's finest group of medieval buildings. The sun-and-moon dial (right), which dates from 1733, can be seen above the archway in the First Court. In the south-west corner of the court stands Erasmus's Tower, where the Dutch scholar, whose condemnation of Church abuses made him a controversial figure during the Reformation, occupied a room in 1511–15.*

FOLK MUSEUM *These decorated truncheons were, until 1922, the traditional present to councillors by the outgoing mayor and are on display at the Folk Museum in Northampton Street. Converted in 1936 from the old White Horse Inn, the museum preserves tools and domestic equipment used locally in Cambridgeshire in past centuries.*

in 1281. Most of the present buildings are from the 15th century onwards, but the Hall, although much altered in the 19th century, is still basically the stone structure of 1290.

Return along Trumpington Street into King's Parade, and turn off into Benet Street to see the Anglo-Saxon tower of St Benet's Church and an old coaching inn, The Eagle, with its galleried courtyard.

Back in King's Parade, the next stopping point is Great St Mary's Church on the corner of St Mary's Street. This is a fine building in Perpendicular style. The view from the top of the tower, reached by steep, winding stone stairs, takes in several major colleges and a bird's-eye view of the market. The stairway gets very congested at weekends. The clock in the tower chimes the same tune as Big Ben at the Houses of Parliament. The tune was composed for Great St Mary's in 1793.

Great St Mary's is the official university church. Degree ceremonies took place there until the 18th century, and university sermons are still preached there twice a term.

The market is held daily at Market Hill which, despite the name, is flat. Under a host of bright awnings is sold anything from locally grown fruit and vegetables to sandals and saris from India, and silver crosses from Ethiopia.

The next stage of the walk passes through the main shopping streets. On the south side of Petty Cury is the great modern complex of the new centre, housing library, shops and courts. In Sidney Street pass Sidney Sussex, one of the smaller colleges, before reaching the Round Church once more. The tour can end here, but an additional section is recommended—given time and stamina.

Home of Samuel Pepys

The view from Magdalene Bridge is well worth the extra stroll up Bridge Street. Here is another punt and boat-hiring stage, and across the Cam lies mellow Magdalene College, founded in 1542. Samuel Pepys, the diarist, took up residence at the college in 1650, and later bequeathed his library of 3000 books to Magdalene, where they can be seen in 12 tall bookcases made for Pepys. The books are bound in leather and are arranged much as they were by Pepys himself; according to size and not subject. Among them are works on naval matters—Pepys was Secretary of the Admiralty—prints, ballads, early printed books and ancient manuscripts. Also in the Pepys Library are the shorthand manuscripts of his diary, in six volumes.

On the corner of Castle Street and Northampton Street is a rewarding group of buildings. Almost next door to the well-arranged Folk Museum, in which old Cambridge comes to life, is the little church of St Peter. It has been largely rebuilt, but contains much original Norman work and a late Norman font, upon which are carved mermen with double tails.

A passage alongside the churchyard leads to Kettle's Yard, where a gracious home full of art treasures can be visited.

If it is a warm evening a further diversion can be made; a walk across Jesus Green or down Thomson Lane and along the river. Here refreshments can be taken in the open, looking out over Midsummer Common where there may be a fair in progress, or simply cows and horses placidly cropping grass. There can surely be few such rural spots so close to any city centre in Britain.

of the greatest Gothic creations in the world, and took nearly 70 years to complete. Originally it was to form part of a Great Court that was never finished.

A walk round Queens' College affords a picture of the surroundings our forefathers knew. The half-timbered President's Lodge contrasts with the stone used so much elsewhere in Cambridge. Then there is the highly decorated and well-restored Hall (entrance to the right in the passage leading through to the Cloistered Court); the pure Tudor loveliness of the Cloistered Court itself; and the Mathematical Bridge.

The bridge is so called because of the calculations used in its design in 1749, which enabled it to be constructed without the use of metal nails. Wooden pegs were used to hold it together. Some zealous Victorian pulled it to pieces to see how this was achieved. But once he had demolished it, he could not put it together again without the aid of iron bolts.

From Queens' Lane, enter Silver Street and down by the bridge join the visitors and locals milling round this embarkation point for punts and boats, or quaffing beer by one of the riverside inns. In Trumpington Street it is only a short walk to the Fitzwilliam Museum, housing one of the best art collections in the country.

The museum has fine displays of English paintings, china and porcelain, together with Egyptian, Greek and Roman collections and illuminated manuscripts. The way goes past the oldest of the colleges, Peterhouse, founded

By cottages of thatch and plaster to a palace bought by a king

The inland landscape of Essex is a gentle swell of fields, with long horizons broken by reefs of trees. Unspoilt villages with ancient churches lie down narrow, winding side roads. Place names are reminders of old industries: Saffron Walden, Cutler's Green. Not far from London's sprawl, the route leads past cottages whose thatch sheltered refugees from plague and fire in the capital 300 years ago, past a Norman castle mound, through a royal hunting forest and on to a great house fit to be a king's palace.

(1) Saffron Walden to Audley End Leave the town on the B1052. After ¼ m. fork right and right again to Audley End. The entrance to the car park is through the gates on the right, while the model railway is opposite the gates on the left.

(2) Audley End to Finchingfield Return to Saffron Walden and this time leave the town on the B1053 eastwards to Sewards End and the large village of Radwinter, where the Victorian architect who rebuilt the 14th-century church in 1870 also designed the houses and shops round about it. Go straight over the crossroads in the village, but at the next crossroads, by the Plough Inn, turn right, still on the B1053, following the road to Great Sampford, where there are some pleasant gabled houses and the 17th-century Bull Inn. Turn left at the church, following the B1053 to Finchingfield.

(3) Finchingfield to Great Bardfield At the war memorial in Finchingfield, turn right on to the B1057 signposted to Dunmow, and follow this to Great Bardfield.

(4) Great Bardfield to Pleshey Leave the village on the B1057 signposted to Dunmow. At Bran End, turn left on to the road signposted to Stebbing and soon, on the right, is Stebbing Park, where a 50 ft castle mound, believed to have been raised in the 11th century, rises out of a moat. Carry on into Stebbing, turn right at the war memorial in the village, over Stebbing Brook, and at the T-junction turn right on to the A120. After about 200 yds turn sharp left on to the road signposted to Little Dunmow. The remains of a priory established in 1104 form the major part of the present parish church. Follow the road as it winds through the village and passes a large sugar refinery on the right. Continue on to Felsted. There are some attractive groupings of old cottages in the village. In Felsted, turn right on to the B1417 and after about 3 m. bear left on to the A130 and continue to Howe Street. Just past the village, where the A130 bears sharp left, keep straight ahead on the minor road signposted to Pleshey. Turn left at the T-junction and carry on through two sharp bends into the village of Pleshey. Enclosed by its ditch, Pleshey has never sprawled in the way many other villages have, and few modern buildings interrupt the pattern of its narrow streets.

(5) Pleshey to Hatfield Forest Leave the village on the road past the church. Turn right at the first T-junction, to High Easter. Keep left through the village past the church and, after 100 yds, fork right. After ¾ m. turn left, and 1 m. further on turn right. On meeting the B184 turn left to Leaden Roding.

Just past a large post mill turn right on to the A414 signposted White Roding. In the village turn right again, just past the Whale Bone public house. Turn right at the T-junction, and in Hatfield Broad Oak turn right to join the B183. Follow this road and take the first turning left signposted to Hatfield Forest. Turn right at the next junction, keeping Hatfield Forest on the left.

(6) Hatfield Forest to Horham Hall Continue on the same road from Hatfield Forest and turn right on to the A120. In the centre of Takeley turn left at the crossroads, following the signposts to Elsenham. Bear right when Stansted airport comes into view, keeping on the road signposted to Elsenham. In Elsenham, turn right on to the B1051. On the right, on the village outskirts, is the large and beautiful Elsenham Place, a manor farm, timber-framed with two symmetrical wings. After about 1 m. turn left on the road signposted to Henham. Turn right at the junction in Henham, follow this winding road for about 1¼ m. then, where a GPO radio tower soars up on the left, turn right on to a road signposted Broxted. After 1¾ m., turn left on to the B1051, signposted Thaxted, and just within ¾ m. is the entrance on the left to Horham Hall. The house was built between 1502–20 by Sir John Cutte, treasurer to Henry VIII. The Great Hall has a beautiful oriel window with Tudor stained glass.

(7) Horham Hall to Thaxted Return to the B1051 from Horham Hall and turn left on to the road signposted to Thaxted, which is 2 m. further on.

(8) Thaxted to Saffron Walden In Thaxted, turn left on to the A130 up the hill in the middle of the town and, just past the church as the A130 bears right, turn left downhill and carry on through Cutler's Green and Debden back to Saffron Walden.

INFORMATION

Places of interest *Audley End:* Apr. to Oct., daily (except Mon.) and Bank Hols. (except Good Friday), 10 a.m.-5 p.m. *Great Bardfield:* Cottage Museum, Apr. to Oct., Sat. and Sun. 2 p.m. to dusk. *Horham Hall:* Easter to Sept., Sun. and Bank Hol. afternoons. *Pleshey Castle:* Open at all reasonable times. *Saffron Walden:* Museum, weekdays, Sun. and Bank Hol. afternoons (except Good Friday and Christmas).

Event *Saffron Walden:* Market day, Tues.

Information Information Centre, Wheeler Street, Cambridge (Tel. Cambridge 58977).

Towns with easy access to Saffron Walden:

Bishop's Stortford	14 m.	London	44 m.
Cambridge	15 m.	Newmarket	20 m.
Chelmsford	27 m.	Royston	16 m.
Hertford	26 m.	Stevenage	24 m.

Tea House Bridge by Robert Adam, at Audley End.

AUDLEY END
Before its many alterations and reductions in size, Audley End, completed and furnished in 1616 at a cost of £200,000 (more than £8 million in terms of present-day money), was as big as Hampton Court. Charles II called it the New Palace when he bought it for £50,000 in 1669—he never completed payment. Contents of the mansion, still massively beautiful, include portraits, grand furniture and a remarkable collection of stuffed birds. Just opposite the main gate to the gardens is a mile-long model railway.

Cutlers Guildhall, Thaxted.

THAXTED
Wealth from cutlery and wool went into many of Thaxted's medieval buildings, including the arcaded 15th-century Cutlers Guildhall and the cathedral-like church further up the hill. The 14th-15th-century church, one of the largest and grandest in Essex, has a striking exterior, with battlements, buttresses, pinnacles and grotesque gargoyles. This is matched by the spacious interior which has a fine early-18th-century organ. While organist here in 1916, Gustav Holst composed 'The Planets' suite. Behind the guildhall are other timber-framed, overhanging houses, and there is a double row of gabled, colour-washed cottages on the road from the church, whose spire shares the skyline with a tower windmill.

SCALE

0   1   2   3   4   5 MILES

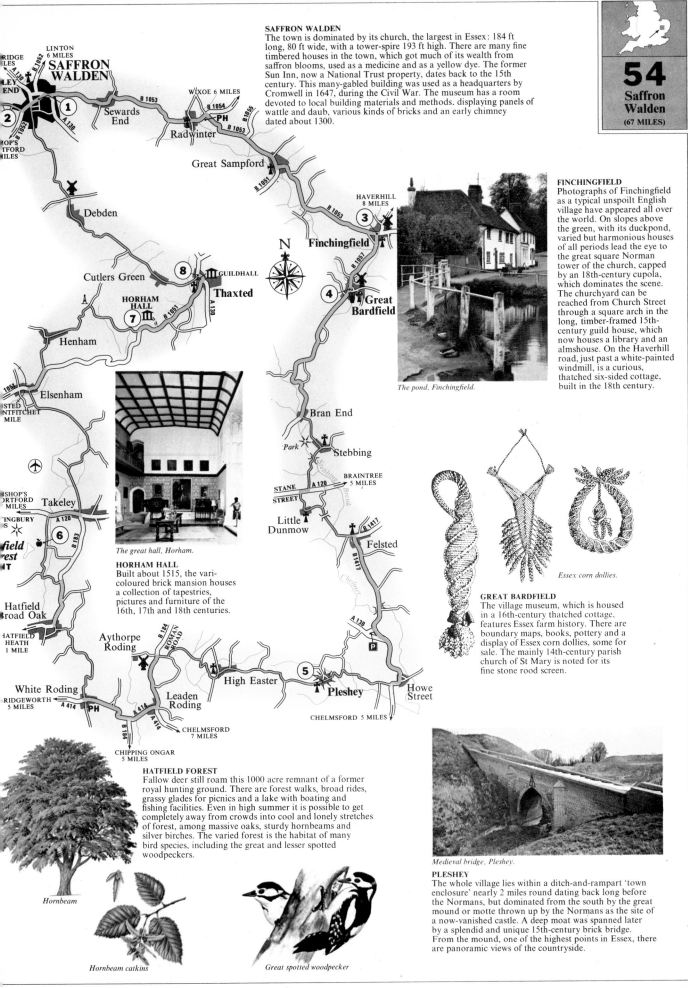

SAFFRON WALDEN

The town is dominated by its church, the largest in Essex: 184 ft long, 80 ft wide, with a tower-spire 193 ft high. There are many fine timbered houses in the town, which got much of its wealth from saffron blooms, used as a medicine and as a yellow dye. The former Sun Inn, now a National Trust property, dates back to the 15th century. This many-gabled building was used as a headquarters by Cromwell in 1647, during the Civil War. The museum has a room devoted to local building materials and methods, displaying panels of wattle and daub, various kinds of bricks and an early chimney dated about 1300.

The great hall, Horham.

HORHAM HALL

Built about 1515, the vari-coloured brick mansion houses a collection of tapestries, pictures and furniture of the 16th, 17th and 18th centuries.

The pond, Finchingfield.

FINCHINGFIELD

Photographs of Finchingfield as a typical unspoilt English village have appeared all over the world. On slopes above the green, with its duckpond, varied but harmonious houses of all periods lead the eye to the great square Norman tower of the church, capped by an 18th-century cupola, which dominates the scene. The churchyard can be reached from Church Street through a square arch in the long, timber-framed 15th-century guild house, which now houses a library and an almshouse. On the Haverhill road, just past a white-painted windmill, is a curious, thatched six-sided cottage, built in the 18th century.

Essex corn dollies.

GREAT BARDFIELD

The village museum, which is housed in a 16th-century thatched cottage, features Essex farm history. There are boundary maps, books, pottery and a display of Essex corn dollies, some for sale. The mainly 14th-century parish church of St Mary is noted for its fine stone rood screen.

Hornbeam

Hornbeam catkins

Great spotted woodpecker

HATFIELD FOREST

Fallow deer still roam this 1000 acre remnant of a former royal hunting ground. There are forest walks, broad rides, grassy glades for picnics and a lake with boating and fishing facilities. Even in high summer it is possible to get completely away from crowds into cool and lonely stretches of forest, among massive oaks, sturdy hornbeams and silver birches. The varied forest is the habitat of many bird species, including the great and lesser spotted woodpeckers.

Medieval bridge, Pleshey.

PLESHEY

The whole village lies within a ditch-and-rampart 'town enclosure' nearly 2 miles round dating back long before the Normans, but dominated from the south by the great mound or motte thrown up by the Normans as the site of a now-vanished castle. A deep moat was spanned later by a splendid and unique 15th-century brick bridge. From the mound, one of the highest points in Essex, there are panoramic views of the countryside.

The wooded landscapes that inspired a master painter

Thomas Gainsborough, when old, complained to a friend: 'I'm sick of portraits and wish very much to take my viol-da-gamba and walk off to some sweet village where I can paint landskips and enjoy the fag end of life in quietness and ease.' So, after a lifetime of travel and fame, he pined after his Sudbury home. For here, still, are the sweet villages and the quietness and ease that nurtured his genius and inspired those earliest works which, for some critics, will always be among his most powerful.

1 Sudbury to Castle Hedingham Leave the market-place on the A131 signposted to Chelmsford. The road leaves the town across Ballingdon Bridge over the River Stour, and then follows King John's ancient highway past woodlands on the right. In Bulmer Tye bear right on to the B1058, and after 5 m. enter Castle Hedingham.

2 Castle Hedingham to Halstead Continue on the B1058, across the River Colne and between the Tudor cottages to Sible Hedingham and turn left on to the A604. Turn first right on to Rectory Road, go sharp right at the first junction and left at the second. Pass Cuckoos Farm on the left and go through Almshouse Green to Wethersfield. In the village, turn left on to the B1053. Follow this road through Shalford. About 1 m. beyond Shalford, as the B1053 bears right, keep straight ahead along a winding lane. Turn left at the T-junction and, in Beazley End, turn right and follow the road past the lake to Gosfield. At the junction with the A1017, turn left then turn right for Halstead.

3 Halstead to Coggeshall Entering Halstead, turn left on to the A131 and then right on to the A604 which is signposted to Colchester. Just outside the town, where the road recrosses the River Colne, is Blue Bridge House, on the left. Follow the road down the Colne Valley and, about 2½ m. beyond the village of Earls Colne, at the roundabout, take the B1024, and follow this road into Coggeshall.

4 Coggeshall to Layer Marney Turn left on to the A120 and after ½ m., at the crossroads, turn right to Feering. Follow the road through the village. Continue under the railway arch, turn right on to the B1024 and, almost immediately, turn left on to the B1023 which is signposted to Tiptree. Go through Inworth and Tiptree and, at the crossroads, on the far side of Tiptree, just before the speed-limit sign, turn left on the road signposted to Layer Marney. Take the second road on the right, which is signposted to Layer Breton, and turn right at the crossroads to Layer Marney Tower.

5 Layer Marney to Abberton Reservoir Return to the crossroads and turn right. At the T-junction, 1½ m. later, turn right and follow this road over the reservoir causeway. Turn left on to the B1026, recrossing the Abberton Reservoir.

6 Abberton Reservoir to Colchester Zoo Continue along the B1026 into Layer-de-la-Haye. Turn left at the crossroads, following the signpost for Birch and Layer Breton. After ¾ m. turn right on to the road

signposted to Stanway, and marked 'unsuitable for heavy vehicles'. In spite of this sign, there is ample room for cars. At the T-junction 1¼ m. later, opposite the Angel Inn, turn right on to the B1022 (no signpost). Stay on the B1022 as it bears right at the top of a hill. The entrance to Colchester Zoo is on the right after ½ m.

7 Colchester Zoo to Wakes Colne Return along the B1022, and just past the Angel Inn turn right on to the road signposted to Easthope. At the next T-junction bear right, following the signpost for Copford and Marks Tey. At the fork soon afterwards keep right, still following the signpost for Copford and Marks Tey. Go through Copford and at the T-junction with the B1408 (no signpost) turn left. At the roundabout take the second exit signposted A120/Packeridge. This road bridges the A12, and at a second roundabout 300 yds later continue on the A120 towards Packeridge. After 1 m. turn right on to the road signposted to Great Tey and Wakes Colne. Go through Great Tey, following the signpost for Chappel. In Chappel the village green, overlooked by the church and flanked by old houses, is on the left of the road. At the junction with the A604 go straight across and up Station Road, signposted to Bures and Sudbury. Chappel and Wakes Colne railway station is signposted on the right after 300 yds.

8 Wakes Colne to Bures Return to the main road and turn right. Follow on this road to Mount Bures. Go over the level crossing and immediately fork left. Turn left on to the B1508 and into Bures. To reach St Stephen's Chapel, go straight on up Cuckoo Hill where the B1508 bears sharp left in the town. At the farm buildings on the right, take the second track across the fields to the chapel.

9 Bures to Sudbury Return to the B1508 and follow the road back along the Stour Valley into Sudbury.

INFORMATION

Places of interest *Castle Hedingham:* May to Sept., Tues., Thur., Sat. 2-6 p.m., Bank Hols. 10 a.m.-6 p.m. *Coggeshall:* Paycocke's House, Apr. to Sept., Wed., Thur., Sun. and Bank Hols. 2-5.30 p.m. *Colchester Zoo:* Daily, 9.30 a.m. to dusk. *Halstead:* Blue Bridge House, May to Aug., Thur., Fri., Sat. and Bank Hol. Mon., afternoons. *Gosfield Hall:* May to Oct., Wed., Thur. afternoon. *Layer Marney:* Tower, Apr. to Oct., Sun., Tues., Thur. 2-6 p.m., Bank Hols. 11 a.m.-6 p.m.

Information Tourist Information Centre, 4 Trinity Street, Colchester (Tel. Colchester 46379).

Towns with easy access to Sudbury:

Braintree	17 m.	Colchester	15 m.
Bury St Edmunds	17 m.	Ipswich	22 m.

The keep, Castle Hedingham.

CASTLE HEDINGHAM
Built around 1140 to provide a last resort against invaders, the Norman keep at Castle Hedingham has withstood the siege of centuries and is one of the best-preserved Norman buildings in England. Decorated by one superb magnolia, the village main street contains a 13th-century moot house, an old coaching inn and a Norman church.

HALSTEAD
Blue Bridge House was built in 1713 by John 'Carcase' Morley, a Halstead butcher who became one of the richest land dealers in England. The house, now a commercial art gallery, is open to the public and has a collection of animal pictures of the 18th and 19th centuries on permanent show.

Paycocke's House, Coggeshall.

COGGESHALL
Paycocke's House in Coggeshall is one of Britain's finest Tudor houses. This two-storeyed, half-timbered building, with its oriel windows and elaborate wood carving, was a typical well-to-do dwelling of the time. There are several other fine buildings of the same period in the town.

SCALE

0   1   2   3 MILES

...sborough's bedroom.

SUDBURY

Three Royal Charters had established the importance of this market town by the time wool merchant John Gainsborough and his wife began raising a family in 46 Sepulchre Street. In 1727 they produced a son who was to make the town famous: Thomas Gainsborough, master painter. He made his name with portraits, but it was here that he began to paint his enchanting landscapes. Sudbury has made his house into a public gallery and renamed Sepulchre Street after him. More importantly, it can still offer the settings for some of his famous works. The view of 'Cornard Wood', now in the National Gallery, is still there in the original. And at The Auberies, just outside the town, the setting for the portrait of Mr and Mrs Andrews remains unchanged.

Gainsborough's house.

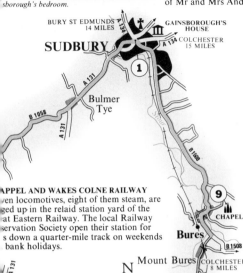

APPEL AND WAKES COLNE RAILWAY

...ven locomotives, eight of them steam, are ...ged up in the relaid station yard of the ...at Eastern Railway. The local Railway ...servation Society open their station for ...s down a quarter-mile track on weekends ...bank holidays.

Mr and Mrs Robert Andrews, by Thomas Gainsborough.

St Stephen's Chapel, Bures.

BURES

Near this river village, with its half-timbered buildings, is the restored St Stephen's Chapel. It was here, on Christmas Day AD 855, that St Edmund, then a boy of 15, was crowned King of East Anglia.

COLCHESTER ZOO

Built in the reign of Henry VIII, Stanway Hall, centrepiece of Colchester Zoo, is named after the Roman road or 'stoneway' built through here. The zoo is stocked with a wide range of beasts, birds, snakes and fish. It also has a model railway and an amusement arcade for children. Visitors can picnic in grounds where Saxon King Harold must have trodden when he was lord of the manor, before he became King of England early in 1066.

Pochard

ABBERTON RESERVOIR

Although largely man-made, with 9 miles of its 12 mile perimeter banked in concrete, Abberton Reservoir has become home to vast flocks of water fowl and a staging post for rare migrating birds of passage. Since stopping on the causeway disturbs the birds, a 40 ft hide and car park have been built about 1 mile from the end of the causeway. From here enthusiasts have clear views over the 1240 acre expanse of the reservoir, one of the largest of its kind in Britain.

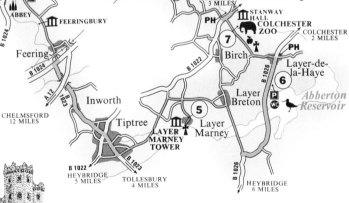

Layer Marney towers.

LAYER MARNEY

The giant towers of Layer Marney were to be the frontispiece of the mansion of the lords of Marney, but they became twin monuments to a double tragedy. For, in 1523, the first lord died and two years later his son was also dead. The building was abandoned, and the Italian artists who were imported to decorate the towers turned instead to creating a black marble effigy for the tomb of the second lord in St Mary's Church near by. Alongside it is the alabaster effigy of his ancestor, Sir William Marney.

Tomb effigy of Sir William Marney.

Buried king and living history in Suffolk

History has crossed and recrossed this ancient kingdom of East Anglia, leaving traces of its wealth on the countryside. At Bury St Edmunds are the remains of one of Christendom's most important shrines, the last resting place of a martyred king. At Lavenham stands the intact core of a medieval town. And Long Melford, with its mellowed brick and timber, still retains that air which made it Suffolk's Georgian Bath.

(1) Bury St Edmunds to Ickworth House Leave the town on the A143 signposted Haverhill, passing Great Horringer Hall on the right. In 2 m. turn right across the grounds landscaped by Britain's most famous 18th-century gardener, Capability Brown, which form the setting for Ickworth House.

(2) Ickworth House to Clare Return to the A143 and turn right, passing Adkin's Wood on the right. Continue through the picturesque village of Horringer and take first left. At the T-junction turn right on to the B1066. The road borders Long Wood, climbs over Harram Hill, and then runs direct over farming country to Whepstead. Continue through Whepstead, Brockley Green and Hartest, where the road runs for a while beside a tributary of the River Glem. Turn right 1 m. beyond Hartest to Hawkedon, where the cottages are haphazardly scattered to make a protective ring round the walled church which sits in the centre of the wide green. Bear right by the church and straight on at the next junction. Continue, ignoring minor roads, crossing hilly countryside dotted with woodland to Poslingford. Continue through the tiny village and turn left on to the B1063 and into Clare, a town which once existed only to service the mighty fortress of the Earls of Clare. All that remains of the castle is the ruined keep.

(3) Clare to Cavendish Follow the road left past the church and turn left at the Bell Hotel on to the A1092, into the Stour Valley. Keep on this Roman road, bordering the north bank of the river, to the thatched cottages of Cavendish.

(4) Cavendish to Long Melford Through Cavendish, the road runs in an almost straight line to the towers, turrets and trees of the stately town of Long Melford.

(5) Long Melford to Lavenham In the town turn right on to the A134, past Melford Hall, home of Sir William Hyde-Parker to whom Nelson turned his blind eye, across the river and then left at the Bull Hotel, signposted Lavenham. In 1 m. the road to Lavenham bears sharp left at a junction. After about 2¾ m., turn left on to the B1071 past the church into Lavenham, probably the most complete medieval town in Britain.

(6) Lavenham to Woolpit In the town turn right by the Swan Hotel on to the A1141 through Brent Eleigh, and at Monks Eleigh, where the A1141 bears right, keep straight ahead on to the B1115. Continue through Chelsworth and turn left at T-junction to Bildeston and on to Hitcham. In Hitcham turn left and follow the road right, ignoring the first right-hand turning, past Home Wood on the left and on up past Devil's Hill Wood on the right. After 2 m. turn right signposted Brettenham. In Brettenham, fork left by the church. Ignore all side turnings, but in just under 3 m., at T-junction, turn right and go through the old river port town of Rattlesden, set in a fold of the gently rolling hills, then turn left, signposted Woolpit. Continue on this road past Clopton Hall on the right and into Woolpit.

(7) Woolpit to Pakenham windmill In the town turn right at the pump and then left by the church. Stay on this road, cross over the A45 at a staggered crossroads, and uphill to the church. Here, fork left and into Elmswell over the traces of the 'Lord's Highway', once travelled by the Abbots of Bury who owned this village. At the next T-junction turn left. Continue on this road about 4 m., passing on the left the moated Hall Farm and Castle Hill. Turn right into Badwell Ash and on to Walsham le Willows. Fork left at the junction before the village and, just before the bridge, turn right then left and left again, following the main road through the town centre. Stay on this road across undulating hills to the T-junction with the A143, marked by a water tower. Turn left into the village of Ixworth. Ixworth Abbey, a private house, incorporates the cloisters of a 12th-century Augustinian priory. Beyond Ixworth, leave the A143 at the first turning on the left. Pakenham windmill is on the left at the first crossroads.

(8) Pakenham windmill to Bury St Edmunds Turn right at the crossroads and at the T-junction with the A143 turn left and continue to Bury St Edmunds.

NATURE NOTES

In areas where the boulder-clay is chalky, the woodland flora include oxlip, meadow-sweet and dog's mercury. In more sandy areas there is bracken and broom and the bird's nest orchid occurs.

INFORMATION

Places of interest *Bury St Edmunds:* Angel Corner, weekdays 10 a.m.-1 p.m., 2-5 p.m. Moyses Hall, weekdays 10 a.m.-1 p.m., 2-5 p.m. *Clare:* Priory gardens, daily 10 a.m.-1 p.m., 2 p.m. to dusk. *Ickworth House:* Apr. to Oct., Tues., Wed., Thur., Sat., Sun. and Bank Hols. 2-6 p.m. *Ixworth Abbey:* June to Aug., 2-4 p.m. *Lavenham:* Guildhall, daily, except 12.30-2 p.m. *Pakenham:* Windmill, daily, normal working hours.

Events *Bury St Edmunds:* Music festival, June. Cakes and Ale Ceremony, Thur. before St Peter's Day. *Long Melford:* Festival of music, mid-Sept.

Information Thingoe House, 118A Northgate Street, Bury St Edmunds (Tel. Bury St Edmunds 63233).

Towns with easy access to Bury St Edmunds:

Cambridge	28 m.	King's Lynn	40 m.
Colchester	32 m.	Norwich	42 m.

The Rotunda, Ickworth House.

ICKWORTH HOUSE

This was to be the crowning achievement of the wealthy, eccentric, art-loving Frederick Hervey, 4th Earl of Bristol and Bishop of Derry. But it became his folly. In 1794 he directed work to begin on the construction of the 100 ft high rotunda, linked by curved stone corridors to flanking wings across a 6[?] frontage. The whole was to house both himself and his enormous fine art collection. But four years late[r] both the bishop and his collection were captured in Rome by the soldiers of Napoleon. The bishop wa[s] thrown into prison and the collection confiscated. [He] died in 1803, with his house only half complete. His son finished the work and began to furnish it[?] with what is now considered to be a very fine collec[tion] of 18th-century French and English furniture. Sple[ndid] silverware, statuary, family portraits and miniature[s] on show. Ickworth House is now National Trust property. The Marquess of Bristol occupies a small [part.]

Priest's House, Clare.

CLARE

Much of the medieval town built up beneath the walls of the castle of Richard de Clare is still standing. Many of the buildings, including the 15th-century priest's house beside the churchyard, are decorated with the raised ornamental plasterwork known as pargeting. North of the village is an Iron Age fort enclosed by a double ditch and bank.

SCALE

0   1   2   3   4   5 MILES

BURY ST EDMUNDS

The town grew up round the shrine of St Edmund, the East Anglian king martyred by the Danes in AD 869. The abbey which housed the shrine was one of the biggest in medieval England. Now all that remains are the great gates and scattered fragments among the lawns of today's Abbey Garden. Abbot's Bridge linked the abbey to its vineyard. Moyses Hall, a 12th-century house, is now a museum. The 18th-century Angel Hotel is where Dickens had Mr Pickwick stay, and the Nutshell is the smallest pub in East Anglia. Angel Corner, a Queen Anne house, contains the Gershom-Parkington collection of clocks and watches.

Abbot's Bridge, Bury St Edmunds.

17th-century table clock.

Enamelled 19th-century watch.

PAKENHAM

The brick-built tower mill at Pakenham is one of the few in Britain which still grinds corn. It was erected in the early 19th century and has recently been fully restored. The mill is open to the public during working hours. There are two steam engines and many farm animals on the site.

WOOLPIT

Originally Wolf-pit, the town appears in the Domesday Survey of 1086 as the place where wolves were taken to be destroyed and buried. Bricks made in the now derelict brickyard were sent to America and used in the building of the White House. The waters of Lady's Well were supposed to be able to cure bad eyesight. Beneath the church's soaring hammer-beam 'Angel' roof stands a rare brass eagle lectern, the gift of Elizabeth I.

CAVENDISH

One of the most beautiful villages in Suffolk, it was the home of Richard II's Chief Justice, Sir John Cavendish, who was killed in the Peasants' Revolt of 1381. Thatched cottages surround the village green which slopes up to the church. The 14th-century church tower has a bell-ringing chamber furnished as a living-room—complete with fireplace and windows.

LAVENHAM

A medieval picture village, this town has been used by several film companies as a set for period movies. The market-place, with its 16th-century half-timbered Guildhall, was once the scene of bear-baiting contests, staged at the foot of the market cross—a 2 cwt lump of stone that has balanced on its slender column for 500 years. Lavenham's church is considered the finest of the many splendid 'wool' churches raised in East Anglia on the wealth of the medieval wool trade.

Half-timbered houses, Lavenham.

LONG MELFORD

Holy Trinity Church in Long Melford was raised upon the buried ruins of a Roman temple, where sacrifices were offered to pagan gods. The present building has dominated both town and surrounding districts for the past 500 years. The extraordinary stained-glass windows include the mysterious Rabbit Window, showing three rabbits linked by three ears. This is said to symbolise the Trinity. The Clopton Chantry contains notable monuments and brasses.

Flushwork on Long Melford church.

Fine flint-stone flushwork decorates the exterior. But even without the church, the town could make its claim as 'the stateliest in Suffolk'. The long, wide main street sweeps on past shops and houses of dignity and charm. Facing the green is the turreted Tudor Melford Hall, containing collections of porcelain, paintings and antiques. Near by is Kentwell Hall, built in 1564, and surrounded still by a moat. It is reached down a long avenue of limes. Melford Place, in the High Street, has a chapel converted to an entrance hall.

ng Melford church.

Map labels: THETFORD 10 MILES A 1088, DISS 15 MILES, A 143, MILDENHALL 10 MILES A 1101, Ixworth, B 1106, Walsham le Willows, BURY ST EDMUNDS, A 45, 8, PAKENHAM WINDMILL, NEWMARKET 15 MILES, MOYSES HALL, ABBEY CATHEDRAL, Badwell Ash, Ickworth Park, A 143, ...ORTH ...OUSE NT, 2, 1, Horringer, ...ERHILL MILES, A 143, B 1066, A 1088, Elmswell, Whepstead, Woolpit, 7, STOWMARKET 4 MILES, ...ckley ...reen, Rattlesden, Hartest, Brettenham, STOWMARKET 7 MILES, B 1115, 6, A 1141, GUILDHALL NT, Long Melford, Lavenham HOTEL, Hitcham, MELFORD HALL NT, 5, HOTEL, B 1071, ROMAN ROAD, Bildeston, B 1078, P, SUDBURY 3 MILES, Brent Eleigh, B 1115, NEEDHAM MARKET 7 MILES, Monks Eleigh, Chelsworth, A 1141, HADLEIGH 4 MILES, HADLEIGH 4 MILES

Forests bring a new look to the bare Breckland

This is an exploration of the Breckland, the once wild land that stretches for hundreds of square miles over the borders of Norfolk and Suffolk. For centuries its light, sandy soil and the dry climate defeated all attempts at cultivation. By 1900 it had become a rural wasteland. Today, although the army retains a large area for battle training, improved farming methods and new forests have changed the face of Breckland.

1 Thetford to Kilverstone Park Leave Thetford on the A11 signposted to Norwich. About 1 m. outside the town turn right on to the road signposted to Kilverstone. The wildlife park, in the grounds of Kilverstone Hall, is on the right, ½ m. later.

2 Kilverstone Park to East Wretham Return to the A11 and turn right. About ¾ m. later turn left on to the A1075, signposted to Watton. After 2¾ m. the East Wretham Nature Reserve office is on the left. To visit the reserve, first call at the office.

3 East Wretham to Santon Downham Continue along the A1075 for ½ m. then turn left on to the road signposted to East Wretham. At the crossroads ½ m. later turn left following the signpost for Croxton. Notices warn that much of the adjoining land is still an army battle-training area. After 1½ m. the road bears left, signposted to Croxton/Thetford. Continue for 1 m. then turn right on to the road signposted to Mundford. After 2¾ m. at the T-junction with the A134 (no signpost) turn right, and 1 m. later turn left down a forest lane signposted to Santon Downham.

4 Santon Downham to Brandon Leave the village on the road opposite the church signposted to Brandon. Continue for 1½ m. to the B1107 (no signpost) and there keep ahead for Brandon.

5 Brandon to Grime's Graves Leave Brandon on the A1065 signposted to Swaffham. Go over the level crossing and turn right, keeping to the A1065. About 2 m. from Brandon turn right on to the road signposted to Grime's Graves. The entrance is marked on the right after 1¼ m.

6 Grime's Graves to Lakenheath Return to the A1065 and turn right. After 1¼ m., in Mundford, turn left on to the A134 signposted to Downham Market. After 1 m., where the A134 swings right, keep straight on the minor road signposted to Methwold. At the crossroads 3½ m. later keep straight ahead, through Methwold. Stay on this road, now numbered B1112, to Methwold Hythe. Continue along the B1112 as it swings south along the low ridge flanking the fenland, and after 2½ m. reach Feltwell. On the edge of the village bear left at the church with the ruined tower, following the Brandon signpost. Turn right in front of the next church, and left again on to the main street. This is still the B1112 which passes a small airfield, then drops down to fen level, intersecting some of the drainage dykes. Cross the level-crossing at Lakenheath station, and after 2 m. reach Lakenheath village. The air base is on the left about 1 m. further on.

7 Lakenheath to Mildenhall Carry on past the base and at the roundabout take the third exit, still B1112. After 1½ m., at the junction with the A1065, turn right. Ignore the first right turn signposted to Mildenhall, but take the second. After ½ m., at the T-junction opposite the Half Moon Inn, turn left then right on to the A1101.

8 Mildenhall to West Stow Leave the town on the B1102 signposted for Worlington. On the edge of the town cross the river bridge and turn immediately left for Barton Mills. By the Bull Inn turn left on to the A11, signposted Thetford. At the roundabout stay on the A11, still signposted to Thetford. After 4 m. the tall column of the Elveden war memorial comes into view. About 2 m. beyond the memorial turn right on to the B1106 signposted to Bury St Edmunds. After 5½ m., where the B1106 goes sharp left, turn right following the signpost to West Stow. On the outskirts of West Stow turn right, following the signpost for Icklingham/Mildenhall. The King's Forest nature trail is signposted on the right after ½ m.

9 West Stow to Thetford Return to the B1106 and keep straight ahead towards Bury St Edmunds. After ½ m., where the main road swings right, bear left for Ingham. In Ingham cross the A134 on to the road signposted to Ampton/Great Livermere. At the T-junction turn right, following the signpost for Timworth/Bury St Edmunds. After 1 m. turn left on to the road signposted Great Livermere/Troston. At the next junction (no signpost) bear left and 2 m. later in Great Livermere turn right following the signpost for Troston/Honington. In Troston bear left at the Bull public house and at the give-way sign 1¼ m. later turn right for Honington. In the village turn left on to the A1088, signposted Euston/Thetford, and 7 m. later turn left on to the A1066 for Thetford.

INFORMATION

Places of interest *Grime's Graves:* Weekdays, Sun. afternoons (also Sun. mornings, Apr. to Sept.). *Kilverstone Wildlife Park:* Daily. *Thetford:* Museum, weekdays 10 a.m.-5 p.m. (closed 1-2 p.m. Mon.), Sun. 2-5 p.m.

Nature trails *East Wretham Heath Nature Reserve:* Apr. to Sept., daily except Tues. Guidebook and permission to walk the two-mile trail from the Warden's house. *King's Forest Walk:* Two-mile walk, starts near West Stow village. Guidebook from the Forestry Commission, Brooklands Avenue, Cambridge.

Information Tourist Information Centre, Town Hall, Cornhill, Ipswich (Tel. Ipswich 55851).

Towns with easy access to Thetford:
Bury St Edmunds 12 m.   King's Lynn .... 32 m.
Downham   Newmarket .... 20 m.
  Market ...... 22 m.   Norwich .... 29 m.

Ancient flint mine, Grime's Graves.

GRIME'S GRAVES
Neolithic man dug these shafts about 4000 years ago to obtain flint for his primitive tools and weapons, and to lay the foundations for what later became a busy axe-making industry. More than 700 Stone Age mines penetrate up to 40 ft under the chalk. They were dug with picks made mainly from the antlers of deer—researchers have estimated that over 50,000 of these were used. The early miners started their excavations with wooden shovels and, as the work progressed, descended to the galleries by ladders made of leather thongs. A small selection of objects found by archaeologists is on view at the custodian's hut.

Prehistoric deer picture scratched on a flint.

Phantom jet fighters, Lakenheath.

LAKENHEATH
Anglo-Saxon invaders colonised this village more than 1300 years ago. Less than 20 years ago a farm worker, ploughing the fertile, drained fenland, dug up a hoard of more than 500 early-English coins in an earthenware pot. Nowadays Lakenheath owes its place on the map more to the Phantom jets based on the American Air Force station —one of the biggest in Britain. The base is not normally open to the public. St Mary's, the Norman village church, contains a memorial to Lord Kitchener.

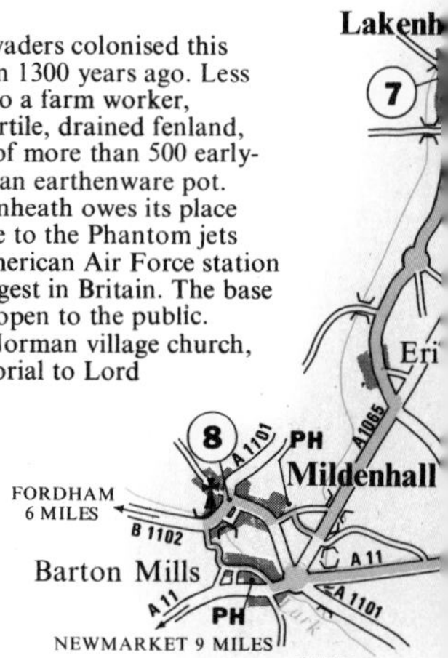

Lakenh

7

Eri

8 PH
FORDHAM
6 MILES
B 1102
Mildenhall
Barton Mills
A 11 PH A 1101
NEWMARKET 9 MILES
BURY ST EDM
12 MILES

MILDENHALL
Lord Derby and Sir Thomas Bunbury, lord of the manor of Mildenhall, tossed a coin to decide which of their names should be given to a horse race. Bunbury lost the toss, but it was his horse, Diomed, that won the first Derby in 1780. The small town has a fine old market cross and some 18th-century almshouses founded by Sir Thomas Hanmer, a Speaker of the House of Commons.

WEST STOW
This is the starting point for the 2 mile King's Forest nature trail, so named to commemorate the silver jubilee of King George V and Queen Mary. The trail has a curlew-breeding ground and is a reserve for fallow deer and badgers— good friends of the forester since they eat harmful tree insects. European hardwoods are planted in belts to stop the spread of fires among conifers.

SCALE
0   1   2   3   4   5 MILES

BRANDON

A Brandon flint-knapper.

Standing on flint and largely built of flint, Brandon is the home of Britain's oldest industry—flint-knapping. Soldiers once relied on Brandon flints to fire their muzzle-loaders. Overseas gun collectors still keep a few of the Brandon flint-knappers busy, though handling timber from the surrounding forests is now a more important part of the town's industry. There is still a public house in the town called The Flint Knappers Arms where men used to be seen working on flint in the yard. They have now moved to larger premises.

Barley and Scots pines border, Thetford Forest.

Stacked timber, Santon Downham forestry centre.

SANTON DOWNHAM

A rarity in modern England, Santon Downham owes its existence entirely to forestry. It is the 'capital' of the 52,000 acre Thetford Forest—the largest in England. The Forestry Commission headquarters is also an information centre, with parking space and toilets. It stands at the start and finish of a 2 mile forest trail through plantations of beech, pine, poplar, elm, oak, sweet chestnut, and fir. There is a splendid avenue of lime trees first planted in 1880. By felling and replanting in sections every ten years, the Commission plans to bring this avenue to a peak of splendour, even though it will probably take 180 years. Some of the banks on the trail were thrown up because of the provisions of the Land Enclosures Act of 1805. The older buildings in Santon Downham, which include the church, date from the time when the village was part of the Downham Hall estate. This was taken over by the Commission in 1923. At this time it had become difficult for farmers to earn a living from the land and many areas were deserted. The forward planning by the Commission has brought a new prosperity to Breckland, though it has also changed the previous moorland character of the countryside.

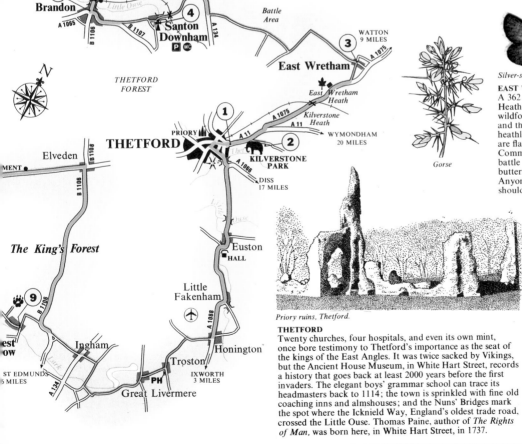

Priory ruins, Thetford.

Silver-studded blue butterfly underwings

Gorse

EAST WRETHAM

A 362 acre nature reserve on East Wretham Heath shelters roe deer, red squirrels, wildfowl, woodlarks, buzzards, sparrowhawks and the occasional rare hen-harrier. Open heathland, fens, meres and deciduous woods are flanked by the conifers of Forestry Commission plantations, and the adjoining battle area gives added sanctuary to a thriving butterfly population and many wild flowers. Anyone wishing to walk the 2 mile nature trail should first report to the Warden's house.

THETFORD

Twenty churches, four hospitals, and even its own mint, once bore testimony to Thetford's importance as the seat of the kings of the East Angles. It was twice sacked by Vikings, but the Ancient House Museum, in White Hart Street, records a history that goes back at least 2000 years before the first invaders. The elegant boys' grammar school can trace its headmasters back to 1114; the town is sprinkled with fine old coaching inns and almshouses; and the Nuns' Bridges mark the spot where the Icknield Way, England's oldest trade road, crossed the Little Ouse. Thomas Paine, author of *The Rights of Man,* was born here, in White Hart Street, in 1737.

KILVERSTONE PARK

Animals and birds rarely seen outside captivity stock the wildlife park in the grounds of this 17th-century mansion. The hall was extensively modernised in 1917 and again in 1928. Its present appearance is largely Victorian but there are pleasant outbuildings and an odd-looking water tower. The collection includes bison, skunks, chipmunks, monkeys, prairie dogs, flamingoes and a variety of birds from the Amazon Basin. A footpath leads into Thetford through open countryside.

161

The quiet country where Nelson was a boy

The low, undulating countryside of north-west Norfolk is the setting for the spectacular ruins of a medieval priory, a great royal estate and the birthplace of Lord Nelson. Elsewhere there is the bizarre reconstruction of an Iceni village, while the Romans, who exterminated the tribe, have left only a place name behind them—Brancaster, site of a long-vanished naval base, and now an unpretentious holiday village.

(1) Swaffham to Castle Acre Leave the town on the A1065 signposted to Fakenham. After 2½ m. turn left, following the signpost to Castle Acre. Continue through the old gateway and into the village. There, turn right to visit the castle mound. The priory is signposted to the left.

(2) Castle Acre to Burnham Thorpe Leave Castle Acre on the road signposted to Massingham. Cross the B1145 and enter Great Massingham. Keep straight ahead through the village and past the church, following the signposts to Harpley. Beyond Harpley, turn left on to the A148 and then immediately right. At the crossroads turn right again and bear second left at the large triangle of grass. Pass the front of Houghton Hall on the right and carry on to Great Bircham. There, turn right by the inn, and after 600 yds right again on to the B1155 signposted to Burnham Market. Keep straight ahead at the crossroads, over the B1454, and turn right at the T-junction in Stanhoe. Follow this road along a shallow valley and into Burnham Market. Opposite the church, turn right. Cross the B1355 and then turn left into Burnham Thorpe.

(3) Burnham Thorpe to Brancaster Staithe Return to Burnham Market, turning right on to the B1355 at the first crossroads. Turn sharp left to go through the village, past the church and then sharp right on to the road signposted to Hunstanton. Turn left on to the A149 and continue into Brancaster Staithe.

(4) Brancaster Staithe to Brancaster Continue on the A149 through Brancaster Staithe and on to Brancaster. To visit the beach at Brancaster, turn right at the church.

(5) Brancaster to Heacham Leave Brancaster on the B1153 (opposite the church) signposted to Docking. Follow the road into Docking and through the one-way system to turn right on to the B1454. After ¼ m. take the left turn signposted to Fring. At the T-junction in Fring turn left to visit the lavender distillery. Return to the junction, turn left and then right to go past the church and up the hill to Sedgeford. Turn left on to the B1454, following the signpost to Heacham. Just before Heacham, turn right on to the A149 and immediately right again into the lay-by in front of Caley Mill.

(6) Heacham to Sandringham Return to the A149 and turn left. Follow the road through the villages of Snettisham and Ingoldisthorpe into Dersingham. There, turn left on to the B1440, bearing right past the church and uphill, then turn right to the Sandringham Estate. There is a free car park opposite the wrought-iron gates to the estate.

(7) Sandringham to Castle Rising Leaving the car park, turn right and after ½ m. fork left. Go straight ahead at the crossroads and then turn left on to the A149. After 1½ m. turn right, to Castle Rising.

(8) Castle Rising to Oxburgh Hall From the car park, turn left and follow the one-way system through the village and back on to the A149. Turn right, and at the roundabout turn left on to the A148 and immediately right on to the road signposted to Grimston. In Grimston turn right on to the B1153. Go through Gayton and after 5 m. turn left on to the A47 signposted to Narborough. Turn right at the end of Narborough village to follow the road signposted to Marham. Ignore the first road to the right and turn right on to the A1122 and after ¼ m. turn left. Continue to the crossroads and turn left towards Beachamwell and then first right. Keep right at the next two junctions and turn left at the T-junction. Turn right at the next T-junction, signposted to Stoke Ferry. Take the first turning left and after about 2 m. the entrance to Oxburgh Hall is on the right.

(9) Oxburgh Hall to Cockley Cley Continue on the road past the hall and in Oxborough go straight on at the staggered crossroads following the sign to Cockley Cley, which is reached after 3½ m. To visit the Iceni village, turn right by the church.

(10) Cockley Cley to Swaffham Return to the village and leave on the road signposted to Swaffham. The road runs through pine woods and heath for 4 m. to Swaffham.

NATURE NOTES
The red squirrel can be seen in many parts of Norfolk where the grey squirrel is absent. Plants rarely found in the south east, such as sundew, butterwort and cranberry, grow in the areas of bog near Sandringham and Grimston.

INFORMATION
Places of interest *Castle Acre:* Castle and priory, weekdays, Sun. afternoons. *Castle Rising:* Castle, weekdays, Sun. afternoons. *Cockley Cley:* Iceni village, May to Sept., Sun. afternoons. *Heacham:* Caley Mill and Norfolk Lavender distilling, weekdays July and Aug. *Oxburgh Hall:* Apr. to Oct., Tues. to Thur., Sat., Sun., Bank Hol. afternoons. *Sandringham:* Gardens only, Apr. to Sept., Tues. to Thur.; also Fri. and Sun., June to Aug.; Easter Sun. and Mon. and Bank Hols. 11 a.m.-5 p.m.

Nature trail *Scolt Head Island:* May to Sept., regular boats from Brancaster Staithe.

Information Tourist Information Centre, Augustine Steward House, 14 Tombland, Norwich (Tel. Norwich 20679/23445).

Towns with easy access to Swaffham:
Downham

Market . . . . . . 15 m.		King's Lynn . . . . 16 m.
Fakenham . . . . . 16 m.		Norwich . . . . . . 29 m.

Old English lavender

HEACHAM
Caley Mill, on the A149 at Heacham, is the packing and dispatch centre for the lavender that is grown in the vicinity. The lavender is harvested in July and August and then taken to a small distillery at nearby Fring. Distillation produces about two gallons of lavender oil per acre. This oil is used as a base for perfumery. Visitors to the Mill and the distillery are welcome. Organised tours can be arranged.

SANDRINGHAM ESTATE
One of the queen's favourite country homes, Sandringham House was built in the 1870s by the Prince of Wales, later Edward VII. The grounds are open to the public when the royal family is not in residence. The house is to be opened to the public in 1976. The church contains many gifts from the royal family.

CASTLE RISING
Situated on the southern slope of the River Babingley, Castle Rising was a flourishing port between the 12th and 15th centuries. The church of St Lawrence was built in the 12th century by William d'Albini, who also built the castle. Though roofless and partly collapsed, the 50 ft hall keep is still impressive. The earthworks surrounding the castle are believed to be of Roman origin. Near the church by the village green is Howard Hospital, built in the early 17th century by Henry Howard. Now used as an almshouse for the elderly, the hospital still has much of the original Jacobean furniture. Residents still wear red cloaks with the Howard badge when attending church.

Oxburgh Hall.

SCALE
0   1   2   3   4   5 MILES

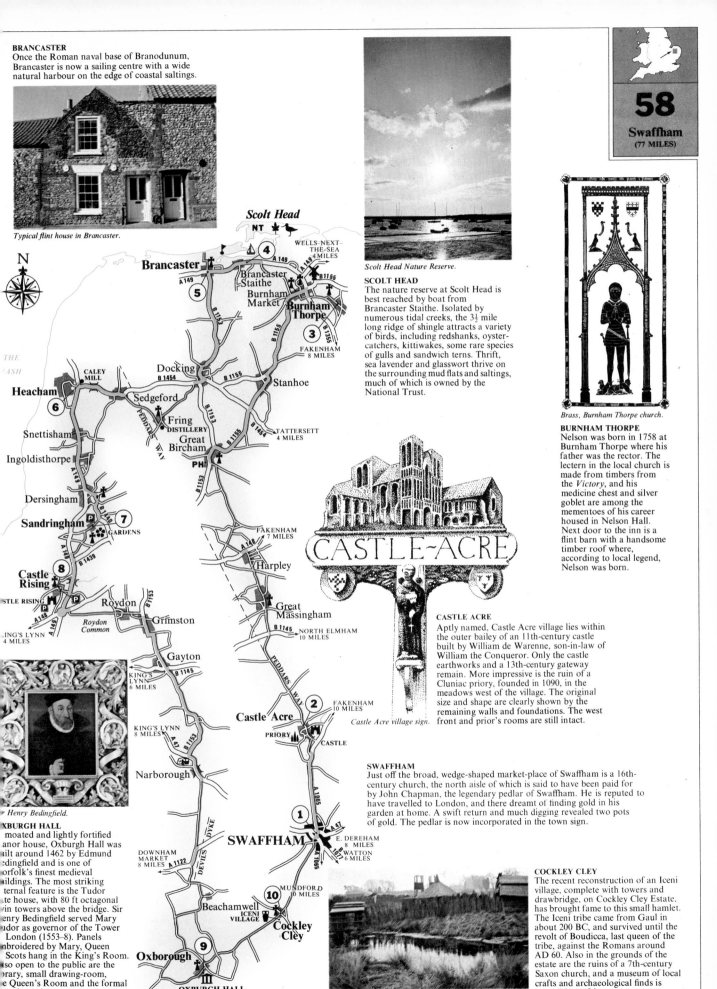

BRANCASTER
Once the Roman naval base of Branodunum, Brancaster is now a sailing centre with a wide natural harbour on the edge of coastal saltings.

Typical flint house in Brancaster.

Scolt Head Nature Reserve.

SCOLT HEAD
The nature reserve at Scolt Head is best reached by boat from Brancaster Staithe. Isolated by numerous tidal creeks, the 3½ mile long ridge of shingle attracts a variety of birds, including redshanks, oyster-catchers, kittiwakes, some rare species of gulls and sandwich terns. Thrift, sea lavender and glasswort thrive on the surrounding mud flats and saltings, much of which is owned by the National Trust.

Brass, Burnham Thorpe church.

BURNHAM THORPE
Nelson was born in 1758 at Burnham Thorpe where his father was the rector. The lectern in the local church is made from timbers from the *Victory*, and his medicine chest and silver goblet are among the mementoes of his career housed in Nelson Hall. Next door to the inn is a flint barn with a handsome timber roof where, according to local legend, Nelson was born.

Castle Acre village sign.

CASTLE ACRE
Aptly named, Castle Acre village lies within the outer bailey of an 11th-century castle built by William de Warenne, son-in-law of William the Conqueror. Only the castle earthworks and a 13th-century gateway remain. More impressive is the ruin of a Cluniac priory, founded in 1090, in the meadows west of the village. The original size and shape are clearly shown by the remaining walls and foundations. The west front and prior's rooms are still intact.

SWAFFHAM
Just off the broad, wedge-shaped market-place of Swaffham is a 16th-century church, the north aisle of which is said to have been paid for by John Chapman, the legendary pedlar of Swaffham. He is reputed to have travelled to London, and there dreamt of finding gold in his garden at home. A swift return and much digging revealed two pots of gold. The pedlar is now incorporated in the town sign.

Henry Bedingfield.

OXBURGH HALL
moated and lightly fortified manor house, Oxburgh Hall was built around 1462 by Edmund Bedingfield and is one of Norfolk's finest medieval buildings. The most striking external feature is the Tudor gate house, with 80 ft octagonal twin towers above the bridge. Sir Henry Bedingfield served Mary Tudor as governor of the Tower of London (1553–8). Panels embroidered by Mary, Queen of Scots hang in the King's Room. Also open to the public are the library, small drawing-room, the Queen's Room and the formal French garden.

Iceni village at Cockley Cley.

COCKLEY CLEY
The recent reconstruction of an Iceni village, complete with towers and drawbridge, on Cockley Cley Estate, has brought fame to this small hamlet. The Iceni tribe came from Gaul in about 200 BC, and survived until the revolt of Boudicca, last queen of the tribe, against the Romans around AD 60. Also in the grounds of the estate are the ruins of a 7th-century Saxon church, and a museum of local crafts and archaeological finds is housed in a 15th-century cottage.

163

Through Constable's unchanging country

The river banks and villages on the borders of Suffolk and Essex have been made famous by the paintings of John Constable (1776–1837), who was born at East Bergholt above Dedham Vale and spent his life recording the local scene. The extent to which the countryside remains unspoilt is the greatest surprise and charm of this peaceful area of East Anglia. The route winds through quiet roads and small hamlets like Kersey, Stoke-by-Nayland and Flatford, where many 15th and 16th-century half-timbered or thatched cottages are to be found.

(1) Dedham to Stoke-by-Nayland From the village cross, by Dedham church, leave on the B1029 and at the bottom of the hill turn right to Stratford St Mary. Cross the A12 and at the junction turn sharp right into Stratford St Mary, where there are several notable 15th-century houses, including Ravenys, the subject of Constable's painting 'House in the Water Lane'. Go through the village, and at the crossroads turn left on to the road signposted to Higham. On the outskirts of Higham turn left on to the B1068 signposted to Stoke-by-Nayland. Cross the River Brett and turn right on the road signposted to Withermarsh Green. Turn second left, by Tea Pot Cottage, and left again at the T-junction. Fork right by the pine tree following the signposts to Polstead, bear left at the minor junction and into Polstead. Made notorious in the 19th century by the Red Barn Murder, Polstead is a neat, quiet village built on hills. The Red Barn is now demolished, but a notice close to the tower of the church marks the burial place of the victim, Maria Marten. Continue through the village and turn left at the T-junction by the pond, on to the road signposted to Stoke (turn right at this junction to visit the church). Turn right at the next T-junction and in just under 1 m. turn left on to the B1068 to enter Stoke-by-Nayland.

(2) Stoke-by-Nayland to Lindsey At the crossroads turn right on to the B1087, signposted to Nayland, and follow the road into the village. Keep straight ahead through the High Street and right on to the A134, following the signpost to Sudbury (or detour left before the A134 to Nayland church in which hangs one of Constable's only two religious paintings). After 4 m. turn right on to the A1071 signposted to Boxford. Just past the church in Boxford turn left on to the road signposted to Groton. Bear right at the Fox and Hounds Inn just before Groton village, then turn left by the church. Turn right at the crossroads in Broad Street, following the signpost to Lindsey. Keep straight ahead at the crossroads by the White Rose Inn, to enter Lindsey (or turn right to visit the 13th-century St James's Chapel).

(3) Lindsey to Kersey Turn right by the church on the road signposted to Kersey. Turn left at the T-junction and at the next junction turn right into Kersey.

(4) Kersey to Hadleigh Continue down the village street, through the ford and left past the church. At the A1141 turn right into Hadleigh. Turn left at the T-junction with the A1071 for the town centre.

(5) Hadleigh to Pin Mill Leave town on the B1070 signposted Colchester. Just beyond Raydon turn left, through Great Wenham and right at the T-junction, following the signposts to Capel St Mary. Go straight across the A12 and on to the minor road signposted to Bentley. Turn left on to the A137 signposted Ipswich. After 3 m. turn right, by the Ostrich Inn, on to the B1456 signposted to Shotley. Go through Woolverstone and into Chelmondiston. At the end of the village, turn left down a lane to Pin Mill.

(6) Pin Mill to Flatford Return to Chelmondiston and turn left on the road signposted to Shotley. Just before Shotley Street, turn right to Erwarton. Turn right at the T-junction, opposite the unusual gatehouse to Erwarton Hall, and follow the road into Erwarton and on through Harkstead. Turn left on to the B1080 and continue through Holbrook, Stutton and Upper Street. At the A137 bear left and go through Brantham and Cattawade. Just before crossing the River Stour, turn right on to the B1070 signposted to East Bergholt. Where the road turns sharp right, keep ahead to East Bergholt. Opposite the parish church in East Bergholt turn left, joining the one-way system to Flatford. Turn right to Flatford Mill and the car park.

(7) Flatford to East Bergholt Return to the one-way system and turn left at the crossroads to re-enter East Bergholt.

(8) East Bergholt to Dedham On the far side of the village turn left and left again on to the A12 signposted Colchester. After 1 m. turn left on to the B1029 for Dedham.

NATURE NOTES

The clay soil of the area supports woods of oak, hazel and birch, with ash and hornbeam on the wetter sites. Many interesting flowers may be found, including herb paris and green hellebore.

INFORMATION

Places of interest *Dedham:* Sir Alfred Munnings Art Museum, Castle House, May to mid-Oct., Wed., Sun., Spring and Aug. Bank Hols. (Sat. and Thur. in Aug.). *Hadleigh:* Guildhall, all year, Thur.

Craft workshops *Nayland:* Peter Collingwood, the Old School, hand-woven rugs and wall-hangings, daily. *Kersey:* Kersey Pottery, stoneware, daily.

Event *Hadleigh:* Market day, Mon.

Information East Anglia Tourist Board, 14 Museum Street, Ipswich (Tel. Ipswich 214211).

Towns with easy access to Dedham:

Braintree	22 m.	Felixstowe	23 m.
Bury St Edmunds	27 m.	Hadleigh	9 m.
Clacton-on-Sea	18 m.	Harwich	15 m.
Colchester	7 m.	Ipswich	11 m.

LINDSEY
Houses scattered along narrow lanes are a reminder of the cottage industry, developed during the 14th and 15th centuries, which produced linsey-woolsey, a coarse woollen cloth. St James's Chapel, built in the 13th century, was restored in 1930 after years of use as a barn.

KERSEY
Once famed for kerseymere wool cloth, the village is now rated one of the loveliest in England. A variety of timbered, pastel-washed cottages line the main street, which runs down one side of a narrow valley and up the other, fording a shallow stream at the bottom.

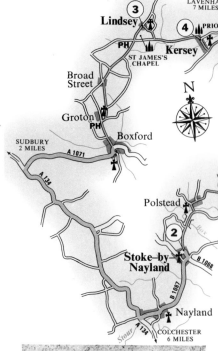

St Mary's Church, Stoke, by Constable.

STOKE-BY-NAYLAND
Parts of St Mary's Church, including the carved oak south doors, date from the 13th and 14th centuries, although the main part of the church was built in the 15th century. The 120 ft ornamented tower appears in scores of paintings by Constable. Liberal use of brick among freestone and flint gives the tower its unusual warmth of colour. Stoke also contains many half-timbered houses with overhanging second storeys, dating from the 16th century. The Guildhall and Maltings, in School Street, were built around 1620 and are now preserved by the National Trust. Thorington Hall, an oak-framed Tudor mansion 1½ miles east of Stoke, can be visited by appointment.

SCALE
0   1   2   3 MILES

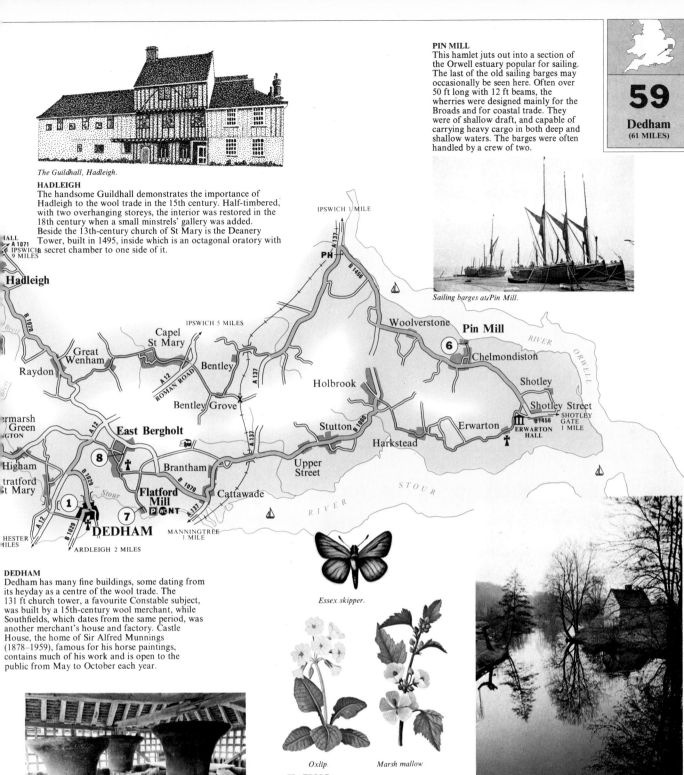

The Guildhall, Hadleigh.

HADLEIGH

The handsome Guildhall demonstrates the importance of Hadleigh to the wool trade in the 15th century. Half-timbered, with two overhanging storeys, the interior was restored in the 18th century when a small minstrels' gallery was added. Beside the 13th-century church of St Mary is the Deanery Tower, built in 1495, inside which is an octagonal oratory with a secret chamber to one side of it.

PIN MILL

This hamlet juts out into a section of the Orwell estuary popular for sailing. The last of the old sailing barges may occasionally be seen here. Often over 50 ft long with 12 ft beams, the wherries were designed mainly for the Broads and for coastal trade. They were of shallow draft, and capable of carrying heavy cargo in both deep and shallow waters. The barges were often handled by a crew of two.

Sailing barges at Pin Mill.

DEDHAM

Dedham has many fine buildings, some dating from its heyday as a centre of the wool trade. The 131 ft church tower, a favourite Constable subject, was built by a 15th-century wool merchant, while Southfields, which dates from the same period, was another merchant's house and factory. Castle House, the home of Sir Alfred Munnings (1878–1959), famous for his horse paintings, contains much of his work and is open to the public from May to October each year.

Essex skipper.

Oxlip.   *Marsh mallow.*

The bell cage, East Bergholt.

EAST BERGHOLT

The parish church of St Mary in East Bergholt was built during the early 16th century. The tower, intended to house the bells, was left unfinished after the death of Cardinal Wolsey and the bells were housed in a huge wooden cage beside the church, where they have remained ever since. The bells are unusual in that they are rung by swinging the wooden headstocks. John Constable was born in East Bergholt in 1776. Though the house owned by his father has been destroyed, many other fine old houses and cottages remain in this unspoilt village.

FLATFORD

The little hamlet of Flatford, on the Suffolk bank of the Stour, was the subject of four of Constable's most famous paintings. The buildings he depicted still stand, though only the Thatched Cottage is now open to the public—as a riverside café. The Mill, Mill House and Willy Lot's Cottage are leased by the Field Studies Council. The Field Centre offers residential courses in botany, zoology and local history to teachers, undergraduates and adult amateurs. The surrounding countryside is a network of rivers and drainage systems, which supports a variety of ducks, wading birds and flowers, such as the marsh mallow and the oxlip. The area is a stronghold of the Essex skipper butterfly, which is rare elsewhere in Britain.

The River Stour, near Dedham.

STOUR VALLEY

The River Stour rises in Cambridgeshire, and runs through chalky lowlands on the southern boundary of Suffolk and Essex to join the River Orwell in an estuary flanked by Harwich and Felixstowe. The painter John Constable made the stretch of the Stour between Flatford and Nayland familiar to many people through his landscapes, often held to be typical of the English countryside. Yet the still waters and low banks of the Stour form scenery unique to the Eastern Counties. The valley has changed very little since Constable said of it: 'Those scenes made me a painter.' And he lovingly wrote of those scenes along the winding river: 'As long as I am able to hold a brush, I shall never cease to paint them.'

The rivers, marshes and woodlands of eastern Suffolk

Despite its flatness, the eastern coastal area of Suffolk provides a surprising variety of terrain. Lush marshlands are interspersed with heath and woodlands, providing refuge for a wide range of plants and birds. The area between Dunwich and Orford encompasses a number of nature reserves and established bird sanctuaries, where rare birds such as the avocet and the marsh harrier breed in peace.

(1) Framlingham to Blythburgh From the market-place drive uphill, keeping the church on the left and, just before the castle, follow the road right. At the crossroads turn left on to the B1120 signposted to Badingham. Turn right on to the A1120 which follows the route of the old Roman road through the villages of Badingham, Peasenhall and Sibton. Continue into Yoxford and turn left by the thatched shelter on to the A12. Follow the A12 through the attractive parklands surrounding Yoxford to Blythburgh.

(2) Blythburgh to Dunwich To visit the Church of the Holy Trinity in Blythburgh, turn left at the first crossroads, just past the bus shelter. From the church, follow the lane to the right, and turn right on to the A12 back to the crossroads and there turn left. Continue to the T-junction and turn right on to the B1125 signposted to Westleton. Follow the B1125 for 1½ m., and at the first signpost to Dunwich turn left. After passing through conifer woods, fork left, signposted Beach, and left again down a track to the beach car park.

(3) Dunwich to Thorpeness Leave the beach and keep straight on uphill past the friary, and in ½ m., on the left, is the sign to the Dunwich Common car park. The road goes on through the Westleton Heath Nature Reserve, one of the few heathlands left in East Suffolk. In the village of Westleton turn left on to the B1125 and then left on to the B1122 signposted to Leiston. Go through Theberton to Leiston. The ruins of Leiston Abbey are on the right just before the village. Built in the late 14th century by Robert de Ufford, Earl of Suffolk, much of the abbey was destroyed in the 16th century, and a farmhouse and barn were built in the aisles. These buildings and the Lady Chapel have been restored and are open to the public. Still on the B1122 continue into Leiston, over the level crossing, left at the crossroads, right into the main street. Continue on the same road to Aldringham, and there turn left at the crossroads on to the B1353 and into Thorpeness.

(4) Thorpeness to Aldeburgh In Thorpeness bear right and follow the road past The Meare, and into Aldeburgh, where there is a car park at the far end of the main street.

(5) Aldeburgh to The Maltings From the car park, return along the main street and, just after the Festival Office, turn left on to the A1094 which runs through the southern part of The Warren Nature Reserve. Continue into Snape and turn left opposite the village church to go through Snape Street to The Maltings, which are ¼ m. beyond the village on the far side of the river.

(6) The Maltings to Orford After The Maltings take the left fork signposted to Orford, and in 4 m. go straight over at the crossroads on to the B1084 and into Orford.

(7) Orford to Rendlesham Forest From Orford, return to the crossroads and turn left on to the B1084. Follow the road past Tunstall Forest on the right and through Chillesford and Butley to Rendlesham Forest. There is a picnic site in the forest.

(8) Rendlesham Forest to Woodbridge From the forest, continue on the B1084 to join the A1152 at Bromeswell. Turn right at the next T-junction, keeping on the A1152 to Melton. In Melton, turn left on to the B1438 and into Woodbridge. To see the harbour and the Tide Mill, turn left at the traffic lights in the town centre, left again at the railway station and first right over a level crossing.

(9) Woodbridge to Framlingham Return by the same route going straight ahead at the traffic lights to Market Hill. Follow the road left of Shire Hall and immediately right and then left, on the road signposted to Saxmundham. Pass the windmill and fork left on to the B1079 signposted Grundisburgh. Turn right on to the A12 and 1½ m. later turn left, following the signpost to Bredfield. Take the first right at the water pump into Bredfield, through the village and right at the first junction and left at the next signposted Dallinghoo. Turn right at the next junction, through Dallinghoo, fork left, signposted Hoo Charsfield, and follow the road left. Turn right on to the B1078 and in ¾ m. turn left on to the road signposted to Letheringham. At the T-junction turn right to Easton and the 250 year old watermill. Just beyond the watermill turn right to Easton, and in the village fork left. Ignore all roads to the left until the junction with the B1116, there turn left and continue into Framlingham.

INFORMATION

Places of interest *Aldeburgh:* Moot Hall, Easter, Whitsun to end Sept., afternoons (occasional mornings). *Dunwich:* Cottage Museum, by prior appointment. *Framlingham:* Castle, daily. *Orford:* Castle, daily. *Woodbridge:* Buttrums Mill, exterior accessible at all times, interior by special arrangement with owners at Hill House or Suffolk County Council, Ipswich.

Events *Aldeburgh:* Music festival, June. *Framlingham:* Spring Bank Hol. fair.

Information Tourist Information Centre, Town Hall, Cornhill, Ipswich (Tel. Ipswich 55851).

Towns with easy access to Framlingham:

Bury St Edmunds 34 m.	Lowestoft . . . . . . 26 m.
Harleston . . . . . . 15 m.	Saxmundham . . . 7 m.
Ipswich . . . . 18 m.	Southwold . . . . . 20 m.

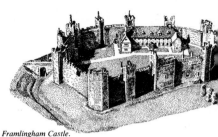

Framlingham Castle.

FRAMLINGHAM

The hilltop castle which dominates Framlingham was built by Roger Bigod, 2nd Earl of Suffolk, at the end of the 12th century. The 13 towers and linking outer walls are still in almost perfect condition since the castle was under siege only once, by King John in 1215. The ornamental chimneys on the towers are mostly dummies, added in the 16th century. The castle was turned into a home for local paupers during the 17th century, and the present Poor House was built during the 18th century against the inside of the west wall. It is now the home of the custodian of the castle. There are a number of fine old buildings of varying periods in the narrow streets of the town. St Michael's Church contains many fine tombs and monuments to members of the Mowbray and Howard families, both past owners of the castle.

Tide mill, Woodbridge.

WOODBRIDGE

A happy place for yacht-spotters, with quays and boatyards making the broad stretch of the River Deben look much like a coastal resort. An Elizabethan merchant, Thomas Seckford, built several prominent buildings which still survive, including Shire Hall and Seckford Hall, now a hotel. But the town's unique building is the recently restored watermill, powered by the tide.

SCALE
0 1 2 3 4 5 MILES

The Meare, Thorpeness.

BLYTHBURGH
Many Aldeburgh Festival concerts are held in the huge Church of the Holy Trinity, visible for miles around Blythburgh and known as the Cathedral of the Marshes. The Jack o' the clock, in the shape of a knight in armour, dates from 1682 and has recently been restored. When the rope is pulled the head turns and a hatchet strikes the bell, which used to announce the entry of the clergy at the beginning of a service.

o' the clock, Blythburgh.

THORPENESS
The quaint look of Thorpeness belies its creation as a 20th-century resort with a man-made lake—The Meare, an imported windmill and a 'house in the clouds'. This is a sham cottage built to disguise a water tower.

ALDEBURGH
Once a fishing port, now a quiet seaside resort, Aldeburgh grew up after the medieval fishing and shipbuilding centre of Slaughden was destroyed by the sea in the 19th century. It achieved international status with the June music festival, started there in 1948 by the composers Eric Crozier and Benjamin Britten. Although concerts are now also held in Snape and Blythburgh, the festival still centres on the 15th-century church of St Peter and St Paul and the Jubilee Hall. The 16th-century Moot Hall is still used for council meetings and there is a small museum on the ground floor. South of the town is the most northerly of the chain of Martello towers built in 1810–12 as a defence against invasion by Napoleon.

Moot Hall, Aldeburgh.

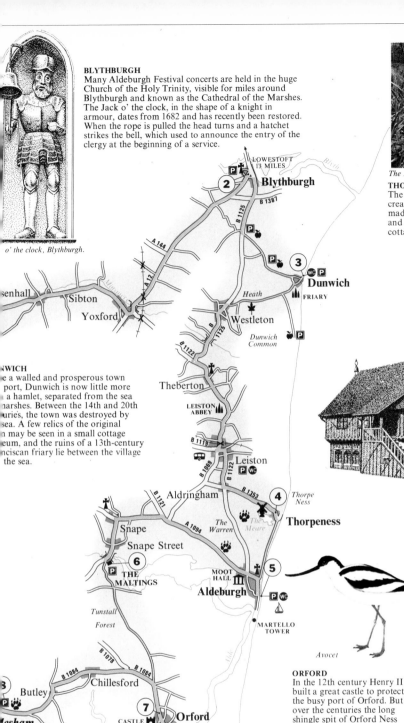

NWICH
e a walled and prosperous town port, Dunwich is now little more a hamlet, separated from the sea marshes. Between the 14th and 20th uries, the town was destroyed by sea. A few relics of the original n may be seen in a small cottage eum, and the ruins of a 13th-century nciscan friary lie between the village the sea.

RENDLESHAM FOREST
Covering an area of about 6 square miles, Rendlesham Forest is owned by the Forestry Commission and consists largely of Scots and Corsican pine trees, with a scattering of oak, birch and poplar. The forest is a stronghold of the red squirrel, which is in decline in most other parts of Britain. Fallow deer also find refuge among the trees. A picnic site is signposted about half a mile after entering the forest, and there is a well-marked walk through the trees. Seen in the forest are the crossbill and the nuthatch. The village of Rendlesham lies on the A1152 to the north of the forest.

llesham Forest.

ORFORD
In the 12th century Henry II built a great castle to protect the busy port of Orford. But over the centuries the long shingle spit of Orford Ness grew, cutting the port from the sea, and today Orford survives as a small fishing and holiday village on the River Alde. The 90 ft keep of the castle still remains and houses a collection of arms and armour. It is also used as a navigation mark by local shipping. When tides scour the shingle beaches of the Ore, beachcombers can often find the pink semi-precious stone, cornelian. Amber may also be found. Havergate Island, 2 miles south in the river channel, is a nature reserve. It is visited by many migrant birds, including avocets which breed there.

The Maltings, Snape.

THE MALTINGS
The hub of Snape village is Snape Street, an inland port on the River Alde, which still has a small trade in grain, carried by barge. The Maltings are a group of early-19th-century buildings beside the river, where barley was malted for brewing. One of the maltings was turned into a concert hall for the Aldeburgh Festival. It was rebuilt in 1970 after a fire.

167

History on the move among the settled Suffolk farmlands

Down the Waveney Valley and out over these sweeping landscapes, history is on the move. At Bressingham, it is under a full head of steam. At Saxtead Green, it is under sail. And at Debenham it is in the hands of a group of craftsmen-weavers. The river still flows beneath the bridge where St Edmund was betrayed to the pagan Danes and martyred. And the Black Dog of East Anglia turns and turns atop his weather-vane in Bungay—a reminder of the phantom dog that haunts East Anglia.

(1) Bungay to Eye Go past the church and left by the Butter Cross on to the A143. Continue on this road along the Waveney Valley to Harleston, a predominantly 18th-century town with a fine Georgian public house, the Swan Inn. Leave Harleston on the A143 and on the outskirts turn left on to the B1116. Immediately after crossing the river, turn right on the road signposted to Hoxne. Follow the signposts for Syleham then, by a telephone kiosk, turn left on to the road signposted Wingfield/Stradbroke. After 2 m. the road opens out on to a broad green with Wingfield Castle, the only inhabited castle in Suffolk, on the right. Turn left at the T-junction at the far end of the green, and after ½ m. turn sharp right on to the B1118 signposted to Hoxne. At the T-junction 2 m. later turn right, still on the B1118, and into Hoxne. This is the village where St Edmund was taken and slain by invading Danes in AD 869. Just beyond the church in the town, turn sharp left and then bear right, following the signpost to Eye. After 2 m. turn right at the T-junction on to the B1117 and continue into Eye.

(2) Eye to Diss Leave Eye on the B1077 going north to Brome and Diss. Note the curved crinkle-crankle garden wall on the left beyond the town centre. At the A140 turn right and immediately left back on to the B1077. Turn left on to the A143 then keep ahead on to the A1066. After ½ m., turn right along Mere Street into Diss town centre.

(3) Diss to Bressingham Hall Leave the town on the B1132, opposite the church, then turn right on to the A1066 and go through Roydon. The entrance to Bressingham Hall and the steam museum is on the left after about 1 m.

(4) Bressingham Hall to Thornham Parva Return along the A1066 toward Roydon. Just before the village turn right on to the road which is signposted to Wortham. Turn right at the T-junction and then take first left. Turn left at the next T-junction and, by the church with another circular tower, turn right on the road which comes out on to the common at Wortham. Turn right on to the A143 and go through the linked villages of Botesdale, Rickinghall Superior and Rickinghall Inferior, where the combined village church-cum-chapel house was once a school. Just past the church, turn left on to the B1113 signposted to Finningham. Follow this road for 4 m. to Finningham and, at the crossroads by the White Horse, turn left. Keep on this road through Wickham Street, and turn left 1 m. later to Thornham Magna. At the T-junction beyond the village, turn left for Thornham Parva. Just over ½ m. from the T-junction is Thornham Parva church.

(5) Thornham Parva to Debenham Just beyond the church turn right. At the T-junction with the A140 turn right again, and after 1 m., at a crossroads, turn left. After 2 m. the road goes through Thorndon. Bear left by the church lych-gate, turn right on to the B1077 and continue into Debenham.

(6) Debenham to Saxtead Green Continue through Debenham and, in 1½ m., turn left on to the A1120. Bear right, then left through Earl Soham. Keep on the A1120 for just under 2 m. to Saxtead Green.

(7) Saxtead Green to Laxfield Continue along the A1120 to Dennington. There, at the double bend by the church, keep left on to the B1116. After 3 m. turn right on to the road signposted to Laxfield, which is about 1 m. down this road.

(8) Laxfield to Heveningham Hall Leave the village on the B1117, going south. Stay on this road through Heveningham village and follow the signposts to Heveningham Hall, which is about 1 m. beyond the village.

(9) Heveningham Hall to Bungay Leave the hall from the main exit and turn right on to the B1117. Go through Walpole and on the outskirts of Halesworth keep ahead on to the A144. Continue through Halesworth on the A144, following the signposts to Bungay.

NATURE NOTES
In the Waveney Valley a few small areas of fen remain, dominated by reeds but with abundant meadowsweet, hemp and common valerian. Meadow saffron and green-winged orchids can be found in a few unploughed meadows.

INFORMATION

Places of interest *Bressingham Hall:* Gardens and steam museum, mid-May to end Sept., Sun.; end May to mid-Sept., Thur.; Aug., Wed.; Spring and Late Summer Bank Hols., from 1.30 p.m. *Bungay:* Castle, all reasonable times; keys from Norman's Shoe Shop, Earsham Street and Swan inn. *Heveningham Hall:* Easter Sun. to Oct., Wed., Thur., Sat., Sun. and Bank Hols.; Aug., Tues.; park 2-7 p.m. (Sun. and Bank Hols. Noon-7 p.m.); hall 2-5.30 p.m. *Laxfield:* Guildhall Museum, Spring Bank Hol. to Oct., Sat. and Sun. afternoons by previous arrangement. *Saxtead Green:* Mill, Mar., Apr. and Oct., weekdays 9 a.m.-5.30 p.m.; May to Sept., 9.30 a.m.-7 p.m.; Nov. to Feb., 9.30 a.m.-4 p.m.

Event *Bungay:* Dwile Flonking, reintroduced harvest festival celebrations, Aug.

Information Tourist Information Centre, Town Hall, Cornhill, Ipswich (Tel. Ipswich 55851).

Towns with easy access to Bungay:
Bury St Edmunds	36 m.	Lowestoft ...... 14 m.
Great Yarmouth .	20 m.	Norwich .... 15 m.
Ipswich	37 m.	Thetford .... 33 m.

Burrell steam traction engine.

The road roller, Boxer.

BRESSINGHAM HALL
Started as a side attraction at one of Europe's largest plant nurseries, the Live Steam Museum at Bressingham Gardens today claims to be the most comprehensive of its kind in Britain, with 40 wheeled locomotives of many types and sizes. Steam hauled rides are given on 4 tracks totalling over 5 miles, and in the 6-acre display gardens there are more than 5000 different kinds of plants. The locomotives range from the 1 ton, 9½ in. gauge *Princess* to the 143 ton Britannia Class *Oliver Cromwell*. Also in working order are 14 road traction engines, including the 8 ton roller *Boxer* and a 19th-century fairground roundabout—also powered by steam.

THORNHAM PARVA
Huddling in the middle of a field in the scattered parish of Thornham Parva is a little thatched church which houses a remarkable medieval retable, or altar painting. It is one of the finest medieval paintings to be produced in England. Painted around 1300 by an unknown artist, the retable consists of three panels. The centre panel depicts the crucifixion, with four saints on each of the side panels. The painting was discovered in 1927 among a job lot of bric-à-brac bought at a fa . auction in the nearby village of Stradbroke, and still carries the auctioneer's tag. But, sadly, its immense value has meant that the church is usually kept locked. The key can be obtained from the house nearest to the church.

SCALE
0 1 2 3 4 5 MILES

Black Dog weather-vane, Bungay.

...lt around a 6 acre mere, or
..e, the part-Tudor town
..es its name from the Anglo-
..on word 'dice', meaning
..nding water'. The whole is
..minated by the Norman
..er of St Mary's Church,
..ere the Company of Change
..gers still ring out the bells
..one of Norfolk's finest peals.

BUNGAY

A ruined Norman keep is one of many reminders of Bungay's long
history. Another is the title of its chief citizen—the Town Reeve. This
title goes back to Saxon times, pre-dating that of mayor, which was
introduced by the Normans. Most of the town was built after a
disastrous fire in 1688 which razed Tudor Bungay. The domed, octagonal
Butter Cross in the market dates from this period. It is surmounted by
a wide-eyed figure of Justice and is now occupied by a fishmonger. A lamp
standard in the market-place is surmounted by a weather-vane in the
shape of Old Shuck, the Black Dog of East Anglia and Devil incarnate,
who first appeared in 1577 and is still reported roaming the area.

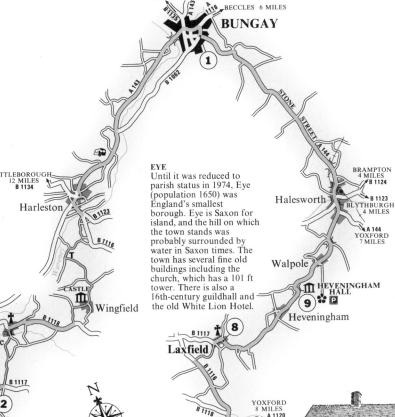

EYE

Until it was reduced to
parish status in 1974, Eye
(population 1650) was
England's smallest borough.
Eye is Saxon for
island, and the hill on which
the town stands was
probably surrounded by
water in Saxon times. The
town has several fine old
buildings including the
church, which has a 101 ft
tower. There is also a
16th-century guildhall and
the old White Lion Hotel.

Crinkle-crankle wall, Heveningham Hall.

HEVENINGHAM HALL

One of the finest Georgian mansions in Britain, Heveningham Hall
was the creation of three of the most talented men of the late 18th
century: Sir John Taylor, the architect: James Wyatt, the designer:
and Capability Brown, the gardener. Bought by the government in
1970, the house and grounds are now open to the public. A feature
of the garden is the curving crinkle-crankle wall, a type of wall used
in East Anglia to shelter tender plants. The entrance hall, Etruscan
room and library contain much original furniture. The Saloon has
magnificent walls and ceilings painted by Biago Rebecca.

Timbered houses, Laxfield.

LAXFIELD

No fewer than 48 of the thatched and
timbered houses in Laxfield have been
scheduled as being of historic or
architectural interest. They include a
guildhall, built in 1461 and now restored
to house a community centre and
museum. The church, set at the end of
the wide main street, is built around a
100 ft tower decorated with flint panels,
which dates from the 15th century.
Inside is a memorial to William Dowsing,
Puritan destroyer of church ornaments.

..sh weaving, Debenham.

DEBENHAM

The ancient craft of rush weaving still
flourishes in Debenham. The weavers
have a workshop near the river at the
southern end of the village. There they
can be seen at work and their products,
including baskets, table mats and carpets,
are on sale. At the other end of the
village is the church of St Mary, famous
among bell-ringers for its peal of eight
bells cast in 1761. The church also has a
15th-century nave with hammer-beam
roof. Parts of the tower are Saxon. The
long main street of the village is lined
with trees and a number of fine old
timbered buildings.

Post mill, Saxtead Green.

SAXTEAD GREEN

A shining white post mill in full
working order stands in the middle
of the common at Saxtead Green.
Inside, the creaking floorboards and
clanking sails give the visitor the
illusion that a lost industry still lives.
Post mills are the oldest type of
windmill. The brick base supports a
massive timber post round which the
wooden mill house turns to catch the
wind. The small fantail, or wind-vane,
fitted at right angles to the sails, turns
the mill into the wind automatically.
The superstructure dates from 1854,
but parts of the mill are 18th century.

Inland from the Broads to the Waveney Valley

The summer bustle of Oulton Broad, with its power boats and yachts, provides a striking contrast to the winding roads and quiet farmlands to be found inland. There is contrast, too, between the Victorian dignity of Somerleyton Hall, with its formal gardens, and the casual atmosphere of the Museum of Modern Transport at Carlton Colville. The most characteristic feature of the Waveney Valley, however, is the neat, round-towered church to be found in every village.

(1) Beccles to Carlton Colville Leave Beccles on the A146 signposted to Lowestoft and go into Carlton Colville, following signs to the right to visit the transport museum.

(2) Carlton Colville to Oulton Broad Return by the same route and turn right on to the A146, following the road into Oulton Broad.

(3) Oulton Broad to Somerleyton Continue on the A146 and, where it bears sharp right, keep straight ahead on to the A1117, and into the village of Oulton. There turn left at the crossroads and on to the B1074, following the signs to Somerleyton. Just before the village, turn off to the right to visit Somerleyton Hall, where there is a free car park. Return to the B1074 and continue into Somerleyton.

(4) Somerleyton to Herringfleet Keep on the B1074 as it bears right and then left past the village and on to Herringfleet.

(5) Herringfleet to Fritton Decoy Continue through Herringfleet, past the Norman church on the right and on into St Olaves, where there is an attractive picnic site. Turn right at the T-junction on to the A143. The entrance to Fritton Decoy is a short distance along this road to the right.

(6) Fritton Decoy to Loddon From the lake return to the A143 and turn left, going over the River Waveney and the county border into Norfolk. In Haddiscoe turn right on to the B1136 and follow the road to Hales. There turn right at the T-junction on to the A146. Follow the signposts into Loddon.

(7) Loddon to Wymondham From Loddon High Street, go down George Lane to the Loddon by-pass. Cross the by-pass on to the minor road to Mundham. Follow the road through Mundham and on to Brooke. In the village bear left, going over the B1332. Follow the road through Shotesham and on to Stoke Holy Cross. In the village centre turn left on to the road signposted to Swainsthorpe. Cross the mill bridge and bear right. Turn left on to the A140 following the signposts to Swainsthorpe. Just after the Swainsthorpe town boundary sign, take the right turn signposted to Mulbarton. Ignore the minor side roads and at the T-junction turn left and first right into Mulbarton, where a large village green and pond are flanked by several cottages and Mulbarton Hall, an attractive Georgian house. Turn right by the green on to the B1113 and just after Mulbarton take the first left to East Carleton. There turn left, following the signpost to Wymondham. Turn left at the first T-junction and right at the next T-junction. Go straight ahead over the A11 into Wymondham.

(8) Wymondham to Barsham Leave Wymondham on the B1135 signposted Bungay, going straight ahead at the traffic lights and crossing the A11. Continue through Ashwellthorpe to the crossroads and turn right then left, still on the B1135. Go straight ahead at the next major crossroads, over the A140 and through Hempnall and into Woodton. There turn right on to the B1332 and after 2 m., at the end of the parkland of Ditchingham Hall, turn left on to the road signposted to Thwaite St Mary. Fork left at the church, and at the T-junction, just past All Hallows Anglican Convent, turn left towards Thwaite and immediately right on to the road signposted to Loddon. Keep straight ahead at the first crossroads and right at the next crossroads. Go straight on over the A143 and across the railway bridge to turn right at the church.

Follow the road as it winds past the old watermill at Ellingham, now a private residence, and cross the River Waveney. At the next T-junction turn left, and after just over 1 m. turn left again on to the A1116 and into Barsham with its village church set in a meadow on the left.

(9) Barsham to Beccles From Barsham, continue on the A1116, past Roos Hall on the left, and into Beccles.

NATURE NOTES

To the margin of the Broads in the north, hornbeam reaches its northern limit as a native tree. Some woods still have a pure hornbeam coppice beneath a canopy of oak and birch. Disturbance caused by motor boats has reduced the bird population of Oulton Broad, but large numbers of mallard, wigeon and teal can be seen in winter on the lake at Fritton. The marshlands of the Broads produce the best reeds for thatching.

INFORMATION

Places of interest *Carlton Colville:* Transport museum, weekends only. *Fritton Decoy:* Apr. to Sept., daily. *Herringfleet:* Smock mill, exterior accessible at all times, interior by appointment only. *Somerleyton Hall:* Easter to Oct., Thur., Sun., Bank Hols 2-6 p.m., also Tues., Wed., July, Aug.

Nature trail *Somerleyton Hall:* Easter to end Sept., Thur. and Sun., July and Aug., Tues., Wed., Thur. and Sun. afternoons only. Leaflet from estate office.

Events *Beccles:* Market day, Fri. Regatta, Aug. Festival of sport, Sept. *Oulton Broad:* Regatta week, Aug.

Information Tourist Information Centre, The Esplanade, Lowestoft (Tel. Lowestoft 65989).

Towns with easy access to Beccles:

Aldeburgh	24 m.	Norwich	18 m.
Great Yarmouth	14 m.	Saxmundham	20 m.
Halesworth	11 m.	Southwold	12 m.

Wymondham market cross.

WYMONDHAM
The octagonal, half-timbered market cross in Wymondham was rebuilt in 1618 after a fire which destroyed most of the town. Beckett's Chapel, in Market Street, was one of the few 15th-century buildings to survive. A 14th-century dispute between town and abbey resulted in the building of two towers for the Abbey Church.

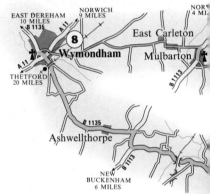

BARSHAM
The church of the Holy Trinity at Barsham has an unusual thatched nave, and is a fine example of the round-towered church which is typical of East Anglia. During the time of the Viking invasions the towers served as look-out posts on rivers like the Waveney, which offered easy access from the sea. The round form derives from the need to build with flint, since stone suitable for corners was scarce in this part of the country. There are more than 40 churches of this type in East Anglia.

Beccles from the River Waveney.

BECCLES
Standing on a low ridge above the River Waveney, Beccles is a predominantly 18th-century town, since most of the old town was destroyed by a series of fires in the 16th and early 17th centuries. The church of St Michael dates from the 14th century and is notable for its detached church tower. According to parish records, it was felt the tower, which weighs 3000 tons, would have been unsafe on the church so near the edge of a ridge. There are pleasant walks beside the river which is busy with all kinds of sailing and powerboats through the summer.

SCALE

0   1   2   3   4   5 MILES

LODDON

On the pillar facing the door of the church in Loddon is an unusual poor box, carved from a solid block of oak. It is believed to date from Saxon times. There is also a fine painted screen said to be older than the 14th-century church. The quayside, once used by sailing boats carrying coal and corn, now provides good moorings on the River Chet for pleasure craft, and attracts many holidaymakers.

The Saxon poor box in Loddon church.

Carp

Perch

FRITTON DECOY

Part of the Somerleyton Estate, Fritton Decoy is a 3 mile long lake, called a decoy because of the two round-mouthed net traps at either end, into which ducks are lured during the shooting season (August to October). The lake offers excellent fishing, being stocked with perch, roach, pike and bream, and the surrounding woodlands provide cover for many wildfowl. Between Fritton village and the lake is a thatched 14th-century church, with remnants of Roman tiles used in the base of its round tower by its Saxon builders.

The smock mill at Herringfleet.

HERRINGFLEET

The parish of Herringfleet includes the riverside village of St Olaves, named after the ruined 12th-century priory near by. Near Herringfleet is a restored 18th-century smock mill (a windmill with a revolving top to bring the sails into the wind). The mill is accessible on foot and the interior may be viewed by appointment.

SOMERLEYTON

Both the village and Somerleyton Hall were virtually rebuilt in Jacobean style by Samuel Morton Peto, a wealthy railway magnate, between 1844 and 1857. Little remains of the original Elizabethan and Jacobean house, though some of the panelling still decorates the Oak Parlour where it is overlaid by carvings attributed to Grinling Gibbons. The house contains many fine tapestries and paintings. The gardens, which have a maze and a miniature railway, are open to the public.

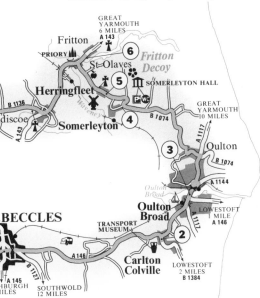

CARLTON COLVILLE

The Museum of Modern Transport at Carlton Colville houses more than 40 vehicles illustrating the history of public transport since 1900. Among the exhibits, all kept in working order, are 15 trolley buses from different parts of Great Britain. There are also five trams, an old pit engine, and a lorry used in France during the First World War. Short tracks have been laid for two of the trams, and power lines have been erected so that one of the trolley buses can be operated. Small diesel engines pull trains which give rides through the nearby woods.

Carlton Colville transport museum.

Yachts racing on Oulton Broad during Regatta Week in August.

OULTON BROAD

One of the most popular sailing centres in Norfolk, Oulton Broad provides holidaymakers with constant activity. Powerboat racing and sailing may be seen throughout the summer and there is a week-long regatta in August. Beside the Broad is the Nicholas Everitt Park, with an open-air swimming pool, bowls, tennis and a children's playground. The Broad is linked with Lowestoft by a lock and Lake Lothing. The village of Oulton is in a separate parish and connected by dyke to the River Waveney.

The rich lands behind Norfolk's lonely shore

Marshes and pebble banks, where birds and seals find refuge, lie alongside safe, sandy beaches on Norfolk's lonely northern shore. Inland a range of low hills gives an undulating quality to a well-farmed landscape which supports several splendid stately homes. All round the route are tidy villages in which the older houses, and often the churches, are built with the flint pebbles that crop up everywhere in the chalky soil.

(1) Holt to Felbrigg Leave Holt on the A148 signposted to Cromer – a long straight road that runs parallel with the sea for several miles. After 4 m. turn left, downhill through woods into Upper Sheringham. Turn right, past the church, and follow the road right to Pretty Corner. Keep straight on at the crossroads and turn left on to the A148. After 3 m. turn right on to the B1436 and ½ m. later twin gatehouses on the right mark the entrance to Felbrigg Hall.

(2) Felbrigg to Blickling Continue on the B1436 for 2 m. to Roughton. There turn right on to the A140, signposted to Ingworth, passing the round flint tower of Roughton church. At Ingworth, where the main road and the River Bure converge, go over the bridge, turn right and almost immediately left following the signposts to Blickling. Turn right on to the B1354, and after ½ m. Blickling Hall appears on the right at a dip in the road.

(3) Blickling to Cawston Continue along the B1354 for 1½ m. then turn left on to the road signposted to Cawston. After 2 m. cross the B1149 and 1 m. later go over the level crossing and enter Cawston.

(4) Cawston to Reepham Leave the village on the B1145 signposted to Reepham. After 3 m. turn left at the crossroads in the village to visit Reepham church.

(5) Reepham to North Elmham Return to the crossroads and go straight ahead on the B1145 signposted to Bawdeswell. At the T-junction with the A1067, on the far side of Bawdeswell, turn left and immediately right, on to the B1145 signposted to Billingford/King's Lynn. In Billingford, 2 m. later, there is a modern art gallery and jewellery workshop. At the crossroads 2 m. beyond Billingford turn right on to the B1110 and uphill to North Elmham. The remains of the Saxon cathedral are just beyond the church.

(6) North Elmham to Little Walsingham Continue along the B1110, cross the river and enter Guist. There turn left on to the A1067 signposted to Fakenham. After 4½ m. the A1067 turns left into Fakenham. Ignore this and keep straight ahead. Soon afterwards, at the T-junction with the A148, turn left, bearing right almost immediately following the signposts to King's Lynn. On the far side of Fakenham, keep ahead on to the A148 and shortly afterwards turn right on to the B1105 signposted to Wells/Walsingham. The road goes through East Barsham to Little Walsingham.

(7) Little Walsingham to Holkham Leave Little Walsingham on the B1105 signposted to Wells. After 4½ m., at the junction with the A149 on the outskirts of Wells, turn left and keep on the A149 for 1½ m. beyond the town to visit Holkham.

(8) Holkham to Blakeney Return to Wells. Go through the town on the A149 signposted to Sheringham/Cromer. After 4 m. the road passes through Stiffkey, a straggling village, which achieved notoriety in the 1930s when its rector, the Rev. Harold Davidson, the self-styled 'prostitutes' padre' was unfrocked by a church court for associating with 'loose women'. He subsequently took part in a sideshow on Blackpool's Golden Mile, sitting in a barrel, wearing a 'dog collar'. In 1937, while appearing in another sideshow at Skegness, he was mauled by a lion and died. He is buried in Stiffkey churchyard. Continue on the A149 to Blakeney. In the village, pass the garage then turn sharp left down to the quayside. The beacon church overlooks the marshes.

(9) Blakeney to Cley next the Sea Follow the quayside road out of Blakeney; along the marshes and uphill to the A149. There turn left and keep on downhill into Cley next the Sea where a turning left, beyond the church, leads to Cley beach, which is 1 m. from the village.

(10) Cley next the Sea to Glandford Return to the A149 and turn right, back through the village, and as the road bears sharp right keep straight ahead. Bear right by the green and turn right at the crossroads, over a narrow bridge, with a watermill near by. Wiveton church is a few yards further on. Turn left on to the B1156 and after ¾ m. enter Glandford, turning left at the telephone kiosk to park near the church with its fine stained-glass windows, and the Shell Museum.

(11) Glandford to Holt Follow the B1156 to Letheringsett. There turn left on to the A148 to return to Holt.

INFORMATION

Places of interest *Felbrigg Hall:* Apr. to mid-Oct., Tues., Wed., Thur., Sat., Sun. and Bank Hols., 2-6 p.m. *Blickling Hall:* Apr. to mid-Oct., daily (except Fri.), 2-6 p.m. May to Sept. *Glandford Shell Museum:* Weekdays; also May to Oct., Sun. afternoons. *Holkham Hall:* June to end-Sept., Thur., also July and Aug., Mon.; Spring and Late Summer Bank Hol. 11.30 a.m.-5 p.m.

Craft workshops *Holt:* Richard & Lorna Bradley, 29 Bull Street, modern jewellery in gold, silver, enamel, weekdays, except Thurs.

Information Tourist Information Centre, Augustine Steward House, 14 Tombland, Norwich (Tel. Norwich 20679/23445).

Towns with easy access to Holt:

Hunstanton	.... 30 m.	Norwich	..... 22 m.
King's Lynn	.... 33 m.	Yarmouth	..... 42 m.

THE COAST

The north Norfolk coast is one of the finest areas for wildlife in Britain. Its dunes, shingle and salt marshes provide refuge for huge numbers of birds and a wide variety of plant life. Offshore sandbanks are a breeding ground for the common seal. There are nature reserves with public access at Holkham, Blakeney Point and C[..] Marshes. The seaside resort of Wells-next-the-Sea sti[..] maintains its status as a fishing port and supplies mos[..] of the whelks eaten in Britain. The villages include Blakeney and Cley next the Sea. Blakeney stands at t[..] head of a narrow creek in which fishing boats jostle w[..] the yachts of weekend sailors. The church has a beac[..] tower which still shines every night as a mark for ship[..] at sea. Cley was once a busy port, but is now cut off from the sea by about a mile of marshland. Its church[..] one of the finest in Norfolk, is a reminder of the villa[..] former importance. On the old Quay is an early 18th-[..] windmill, restored and now a private house.

Common seal

HOLKHAM

Holkham Hall, a vast classical mansion, was built around 1735 to the design of William Kent for Thomas Coke, Earl of Leicester, whose family still live there. It has sumptuously decorated rooms, in which are housed an important art collection, including works by Rubens and Gainsborough. In the grounds are a lake with wildfowl, a garden centre and a pottery. Opposite the entrance to the hall, a road leads to a pleasant beach.

Marble Hall, Holkham.

LITTLE WALSINGHAM

This small town, where a shrine to the Virgin Mary was established in 1061, still retains a medieval atmosphere. The shrine was destroyed by Henry VIII, together with the priory which grew up beside it. The shrine was reinstated by the Church of England in 1937, and a Roman Catholic shrine is established at the Slipper Chapel 1 mile to the south. Behind a high wall in the main street the grounds of the priory are laid out as gardens, in which the empty arch of the east window rises from the lawn. *East window, Walsingham Prio[..]*

SCALE

0	1	2	3	4	5 MILES

akeney, once a busy commercial port, is now used mainly by yachtsmen.

GLANDFORD

The Glandford Shell Museum
has a unique collection of shells
from all parts of the world.
Thousands of specimens of all
colours and sizes are on show,
together with delicate figures
and models elaborately
decorated with tiny shells. The
church, next to the museum, has
a carillon that rings on the hour
at noon, three, six and nine.
Near the museum is a deep ford
across the River Glaven.

Shell figurine, Glandford.

HOLT

The Georgian houses in this neat
market town were built after a fire
in 1708 which destroyed the
medieval town. Discolouring caused
by the heat can still be seen on
pillars in the church. Sir Thomas
Gresham, financial agent to
Elizabeth I and founder of the
Royal Exchange in London, was
born here in 1519. His brother Sir
John Gresham, when he was Lord
Mayor of London, founded
Gresham's School in the town in
1555. The school moved to larger
buildings on the outskirts of the
town in 1900, but the 19th-century
schoolhouse in the town square is
still in use.

Jacobean front, Felbrigg Hall.

FELBRIGG

The motto 'Gloria Deo in excelsis' in giant stone
letters runs along a balustrade on the roof of
Felbrigg Hall. It dates from the 1620s when the
house was built. Inside, the principal rooms – the
great hall, dining-room and library together with
their splendid furnishings – date from the 18th
century. The hall stands in a wide park with fine
trees, many of which were planted in the 1680s.
The parish church is also in the park.

REEPHAM

Three churches share the village churchyard. Two of them—St Mary's, Reepham,
and St Michael's and All Angels, Whitwell
—still stand. All Saints, Hackford, was
destroyed by fire in 1543 and survives
only as a ruin. The three parishes are
now united. The Georgian market square
has some fine houses.

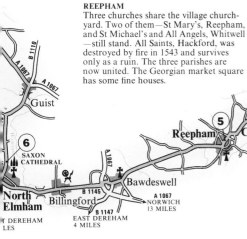

Blickling Hall in 1760.

BLICKLING

The warm brick facade of Blickling Hall,
which dates from 1620, is approached
between great 300-year-old yew hedges.
The rest of the grounds include a range
of gardens dating from the early 18th
century to the 1930s. Much of the interior
and furnishings of the house are Georgian
and a new wing was added at this time.

NORTH ELMHAM

...the hilltop stands a substantial flint church
...ting from early Norman times, but it is young
...mpared to the Saxon cathedral whose ruins
...e only 50 yds away. The cathedral was
...ginally built of wood in AD 673, but was
...uilt in flint at the beginning of the 11th
...tury. However, the bishopric moved to
...etford in 1075. Some time later a bishop tried
...convert the cathedral into a house. Eventually
...ell into decay. Today, the outline and some
...lls of the ancient building can be clearly
...en—a reminder that this was once the
...gious capital of the Saxon North Folk.

CAWSTON

Towering above the village is a massive church, built
in the 14th century by Michael de la Pole, Earl of
Suffolk, and paid for by the wool which made north
Norfolk rich in the Middle Ages. It has a hammer roof
with finely carved angels, and there are paintings of the
Apostles on a well-preserved rood screen. The 'Duel
Stone', an urn on a pedestal in woodland 100 yds south
of the Woodrow Inn, marks the spot where Sir Henry
Hobart of Blickling and Oliver le Neve of Great
Witchingham fought a duel to the death in August 1698.
Sir Henry was the loser, but the inscription
on the stone says that his opponent 'Fought Foul'.

Angel carving, Cawston church.

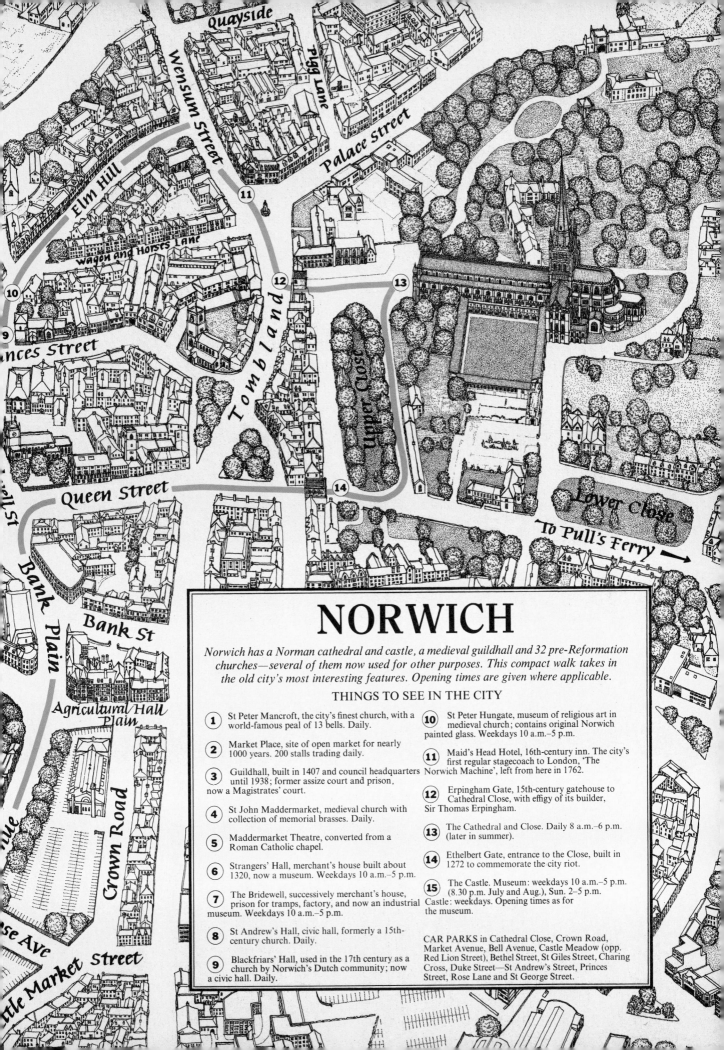

NORWICH

Norwich has a Norman cathedral and castle, a medieval guildhall and 32 pre-Reformation churches—several of them now used for other purposes. This compact walk takes in the old city's most interesting features. Opening times are given where applicable.

THINGS TO SEE IN THE CITY

(1) St Peter Mancroft, the city's finest church, with a world-famous peal of 13 bells. Daily.

(2) Market Place, site of open market for nearly 1000 years. 200 stalls trading daily.

(3) Guildhall, built in 1407 and council headquarters until 1938; former assize court and prison, now a Magistrates' court.

(4) St John Maddermarket, medieval church with collection of memorial brasses. Daily.

(5) Maddermarket Theatre, converted from a Roman Catholic chapel.

(6) Strangers' Hall, merchant's house built about 1320, now a museum. Weekdays 10 a.m.–5 p.m.

(7) The Bridewell, successively merchant's house, prison for tramps, factory, and now an industrial museum. Weekdays 10 a.m.–5 p.m.

(8) St Andrew's Hall, civic hall, formerly a 15th-century church. Daily.

(9) Blackfriars' Hall, used in the 17th century as a church by Norwich's Dutch community; now a civic hall. Daily.

(10) St Peter Hungate, museum of religious art in medieval church; contains original Norwich painted glass. Weekdays 10 a.m.–5 p.m.

(11) Maid's Head Hotel, 16th-century inn. The city's first regular stagecoach to London, 'The Norwich Machine', left from here in 1762.

(12) Erpingham Gate, 15th-century gatehouse to Cathedral Close, with effigy of its builder, Sir Thomas Erpingham.

(13) The Cathedral and Close. Daily 8 a.m.–6 p.m. (later in summer).

(14) Ethelbert Gate, entrance to the Close, built in 1272 to commemorate the city riot.

(15) The Castle. Museum: weekdays 10 a.m.–5 p.m. (8.30 p.m. July and Aug.), Sun. 2–5 p.m. Castle: weekdays. Opening times as for the museum.

CAR PARKS in Cathedral Close, Crown Road, Market Avenue, Bell Avenue, Castle Meadow (opp. Red Lion Street), Bethel Street, St Giles Street, Charing Cross, Duke Street—St Andrew's Street, Princes Street, Rose Lane and St George Street.

Norwich Snapdragon, symbol of the Guild of St George, worn as procession mask in medieval times.

NORWICH

Through all the changes of 1000 years, Norwich has remained the capital of East Anglia. A great port in Saxon times, it became a centre of the cloth trade in the Middle Ages, moving on into banking in the 18th century and engineering and shoemaking in the 19th century. Each period and each trade has contributed its share to the making of this fine city.

MUSTARD SHOP *There is a museum devoted to the manufacture of mustard in this 18th-century shop in Bridewell Alley. Mustard seed is grown locally and a thriving industry has been built around it.*

STRANGERS' HALL *This Victorian sitting-room crammed with bric-à-brac is one of more than 20 rooms at the hall furnished in different period styles.*

ST PETER MANCROFT *This stained-glass window of the Last Supper is on the east side of the south transept. It is a copy, dating from 1840, of a 15th-century original which was once in the east window of the church. The original has disappeared, but the east window still contains a magnificent display of 15th-century stained glass.*

Norwich was the first truly English city, since, unlike England's other ancient cities, including London, it owes nothing to the Romans or earlier settlers. It was founded by the Saxon North Folk some time in the 5th or 6th centuries. They were a seafaring people and chose a site where the rivers Yare and Wensum meet close to the sea in the flat lands of East Anglia.

It was not until the reign of King Athelstan (925–40) that the name Norwich first appeared—on coins struck at Athelstan's mint in the town. Before the end of the 10th century its river link with the sea had made it the chief port on the east coast and, by the time of the Norman Conquest, Norwich had about 6000 inhabitants and was the third town in England after London and York.

William the Conqueror recognised the importance of Norwich by establishing a castle there in 1067. About 100 houses were cleared to create the site, and the huge castle mound was raised by the forced labour of the townsfolk. The wooden fortress which was built on top was replaced about 60 years later by the stone castle.

For nearly 100 years the castle was a military stronghold, but with the coming of more settled times it became the county gaol and remained so from 1220 to 1887—when it was converted into a museum.

Today it houses a fine collection of paintings by the Norwich School of artists—John Crome (1768–1821), John Sell Cotman (1782–1842) and their followers. There are also specimens of local silver, glass and porcelain, natural history and archaeological collections, and a series of dramatic displays illustrating Norfolk life from prehistoric to medieval times. The dungeons and battlements can be visited, and there is a display of arms and armour.

When William the Conqueror made Norwich his administrative centre in East Anglia, the church decided to follow suit and in 1095 Herbert de Losinga, the Bishop of East Anglia, moved his headquarters from Thetford and began building the cathedral.

The building was added to by later genera-

ELM HILL *Houses and shops of all periods from the 14th to 18th centuries line this quiet, cobbled street. The elm tree, which gives it its name, stands at the top near the thatched Briton's Arms, the only house in the street to survive a disastrous fire in 1507. Other notable buildings are the 16th-century timber-framed Strangers' Club, the 17th-century Flint House and the 15th-century church of Saints Simon and Jude.*

tions and restored after various disasters, including a 13th-century fire and the collapse of the spire in the 14th century. But the basic structure has been little tampered with, and remains one of the most perfect Norman interiors in the country.

The throne on the steps behind the high altar is the oldest bishop's throne still used in England. It is constructed round fragments of stone which came from the 8th-century Saxon cathedral at North Elmham. The 315 ft spire, which was rebuilt in 1480, is the second highest in England after Salisbury.

The grave of Nurse Edith Cavell, shot by the Germans in 1915 on a charge of helping prisoners to escape from a hospital in Belgium, is just outside the cathedral, beside the east wall. In the precinct are many fine houses and the ancient grammar school where Nelson was a pupil. At the end of a lane leading from the

Lower Close to the River Wensum is Pull's Ferry, the 15th-century watergate to the cathedral.

Two fine gates lead to the cathedral from Tombland. The Erpingham Gate was built in 1420 by Sir Thomas Erpingham, commander of the English archers at Agincourt.

St Ethelbert's Gate was built after a riot in 1272, when the townsfolk rejected the cathedral monks' claim to levy tolls on the annual fair held in Tombland. The monks were issued with arms and mercenaries were called in. Between them they pillaged the city, while the townsfolk set fire to the priory—a fire that spread to the cathedral itself. As a result the pope excommunicated the whole city, a huge fine was exacted, and monks and citizens were ordered to erect the gate as a penance.

Besides the cathedral, medieval Norwich had more than 50 churches, of which 33

PULL'S FERRY *An 18th-century ferryman who plied across the River Wensum gave his name to this beauty spot. The arch beside the ferryman's house is a 15th-century watergate, built to guard a canal that carried building materials—and later the bishop—to the cathedral.*

THE CASTLE *The Norman keep is one of the largest in England—70 ft high and 100 ft along each side. It owes its unblemished look, after 850 years, to a facing of Bath stone put up in 1834–9.*

ETHELBERT GATE *Elaborate carving decorates the arch of the Ethelbert Gate, built in 1316 to replace a gate destroyed in a riot in 1272. The gate was originally the entrance to the cathedral priory.*

RESURRECTION *Christ rising from the tomb is one of the five scenes in a brilliantly painted and gilded retable, or altar painting, now in St Luke's Chapel in the cathedral. It was painted in the 14th century by an unknown East Anglian artist in a style that rivals the fine Italian work of the same period. Many retables were destroyed at the Reformation. This one survived because it was made into a table.*

CATHEDRAL APSE *A lofty vault with fine windows added in the 15th century transformed the Norman apse into the finest in England. At Norwich the bishop's chair is housed in the apse—the semi-circular extension behind the altar.*

CASTLE MUSEUM *'Silver birches' shows a Norfolk scene painted by John Sell Cotman about 1826. It is one of many fine paintings of the Norwich School displayed in the museum.*

survive. Two at least date from Saxon times—St Mary Coslany and St Julian's.

Many of the other churches were rebuilt in the 14th and 15th centuries when Norwich prospered from the wool trade. St Peter Mancroft, built between 1430–55, has a magnificent hammerbeam roof and rare 15th-century glass.

St John Maddermarket has a fine collection of brasses. St John's Alley, which runs through the church tower, leads to the Maddermarket Theatre. Once a chapel, it was converted into an Elizabethan-style theatre in the 1920s. Its resident repertory company is noted for the high standard of its productions. The Maddermarket was the place where red dye made from madder roots was sold to cloth-makers in the Middle Ages.

Norwich has a long tradition of converting churches to secular use. St Andrew's Hall and Blackfriars' Hall were respectively the nave and chancel of the priory church of the Dominican or Black Friars. At the Dissolution of the Monasteries in 1538 the church was bought by the city and made into two public halls. St Peter Hungate is preserved as a museum of church art.

The wealthy citizens who built these fine churches built with equal care for themselves, and Norwich has some of the best medieval town houses in England. In Bridewell Alley modern shopfronts camouflage ancient timber-framed houses which lead up to the Bridewell Museum. The museum is in the house of William Appleyard, who in 1404 was the first mayor of Norwich. The house was used as a bridewell, or prison, from 1583–1828. It then became a factory, and was opened as a craft museum in 1925.

Strangers' Hall, in Charing Cross, is another fine merchant's house, dating from 1320. Its name probably derives from a tradition that immigrant Flemish weavers once lived there. It is now a museum of domestic life.

There are similar ranges of style among the houses in the old city streets, such as Elm Hill, a cobbled thoroughfare lined with colour-washed shops and houses. The elm after which it is named stands at the top where the hill opens out into a 'plain'—the Norwich name for an irregular city square.

Tombland, another 'plain', has a number of Georgian façades, some of which conceal older work. The Maid's Head Hotel has had a more recent face-lift, but parts of the building date from before 1578 when Queen Elizabeth slept there. The name 'Tombland' has nothing to do with graveyards. It comes from the Anglo-Saxon word *tom*—empty—and this 'empty space' was the town market-place until the present site came into use after the Norman Conquest.

It was beside this 'new' market that the citizens built their Guildhall in 1407—four years after Henry IV gave them the right to govern themselves. It was the seat of city government until 1938, and courts still sit there.

Modern Norwich, a city of 120,000, remains a busy port, though it is more famous today for mustard, shoes and insurance. But whatever else changes, the Market Place is still the city centre. The new city hall is there, a few yards from the Guildhall, and the townsfolk still come to the Market Place to buy and sell as they have done for more than 900 years.

177

Glimpses of prehistory on the coast of south-west Wales

The coast and hills of south-west Wales are littered with relics of prehistory, and include the magnificent burial chamber at Pentre Ifan near Newport. Small villages and quiet, sandy bays are interspersed with steep cliffs and rocky headlands to provide one of the most varied coastlines in Wales. Haverfordwest makes an ideal touring centre with attractions of its own, not least of which is its situation on the Western Cleddau, which comes down from the Prescelly Hills to join the main river 2 miles below the town.

(1) Haverfordwest to Newgale Leave on the B4330 signposted to Hayscastle. After 4 m., as the B4330 bends to the right at a crossroads, go straight on, following the signpost to Roch. After 2 m. turn left at a T-junction, then first right to Roch and the junction with the A487. Turn right on to the A487 and follow the road into Newgale.

(2) Newgale to Solva Continue on the A487, passing Brawdy Royal Air Force Base on the right. On the left is St Elvis, with a population of 7, making it the smallest parish in the district. Cross the bridge over the river and into Solva.

(3) Solva to St David's Leave Solva on the A487 and continue to the centre of St David's to visit the cathedral.

(4) St David's to Whitesand Bay Return to the A487 signposted to Whitesands, and on the outskirts of St David's fork left on to the B4583 and follow the signpost to Whitesand Bay.

(5) Whitesand Bay to Abereiddy Return along the B4583 and, just before the junction with the A487, turn left. After 4 m. turn left again and follow the road into Abereiddy. Turn left along the beach road to the car park.

(6) Abereiddy to Porthgain Return along the lane from the beach and keep left, ignoring the turning to the right. After 1 m. turn left at the crossroads on to the road signposted to Llanrian. Just before the village on the left is a prehistoric standing stone. In Llanrian turn left and follow the lane to its end at Porthgain.

(7) Porthgain to Strumble Head Return to Llanrian and turn left, following the road through the villages of Trevine and Abercastle and turning inland to Mathry. Here, turn left on to the road signposted to Letterston and Fishguard. Turn left on to the A487 and left again at the second crossroads, following the signpost to St Nicholas. Pass through the village and 1½ m. beyond go right at the crossroads, ignoring the signpost to Pwllderi. After ½ m. turn left, following the signs across the Pen Caer peninsula to Strumble Head.

(8) Strumble Head to Nevern Return from the headland and turn left at the T-junction, following the road signposted to Goodwick and Fishguard. At the foot of the steep hill leading down to Goodwick turn right and go into the centre of Fishguard. Here, turn left and almost immediately right

on to the B4313 signposted to Llanychaer, Gwaun Valley and Maenclochog. The Lower Town of Fishguard is the old fishing village and is reminiscent of villages in Cornwall and Brittany. About 1 m. beyond Llanychaer, where the B4313 swings right, go straight ahead following the signpost to Gwaun Valley, where New Year is still celebrated on January 13, according to the old calendar abolished in 1752. After 2 m., at the Diffryn Arms, fork left and follow this lane for about 3½ m., turning right on to the A487. Continue on the A487 and into Newport, an attractive small town with a wide stretch of sands and a castle on the hill just above. Go through Newport and after 1½ m. turn left on to the B4582 and into Nevern, where pilgrims used to rest on their way to St David's.

(9) Nevern to Pentre Ifan Return to the A487 and go straight across it on to the road signposted to Cilgwyn, Gwaun Valley, Brynberian and Pentre Ifan. Go left at the next crossroads and first right to reach the burial chamber of Pentre Ifan.

(10) Pentre Ifan to Haverfordwest Continue along the lane from Pentre Ifan and straight on at the crossroads. Turn right on to the B4329. The route back to Haverfordwest climbs more than 1300 ft into the Prescelly Hills, and in clear conditions there are spectacular views of south-west Wales. In the hills to the left of the higher parts of the road are the quarries from which over 80 stones, weighing about 250 tons, are reputed to have been taken to Stonehenge more than 4000 years ago. Continue on the B4329 and into Haverfordwest.

INFORMATION

Places of interest *Haverfordwest:* Castle museum, weekdays (closed Christmas, Boxing Day and New Year's Day). *St David's:* Cathedral and Bishop's Palace, daily, 7 a.m.-8 p.m. (6 p.m. winter). *Strumble Head Lighthouse:* Weekdays 1 p.m. to sunset, except in fog.

Craft workshop *Fishguard:* Inskin, leather workshop, open weekdays.

Events *Haverfordwest:* May fair. *Portfield:* Fair, Oct. Admiral's River Pageant, June. *Gwaun Valley:* Old Calendar New Year Celebration, Jan. 13. *Market Days:* Haverfordwest, Sat. Fishguard, Thur.

Information Pembrokeshire Coast National Park, 40 High Street, Haverfordwest (Tel. Haverfordwest 66141). Pembrokeshire Coast National Park and Wales Tourist Board, Town Centre, Fishguard (Tel. Fishguard 873484).

Towns with easy access to Haverfordwest:

Cardigan	26 m.	New Quay	41 m.
Carmarthen	30 m.	Pembroke	20 m.
Milford Haven	7 m.	Tenby	21 m.

WHITESAND BAY
Rocks and islets known as the Bishops and Clerks stud the sea off this long and very popular sandy beach. To the right, as the beach is approached, the Pembrokeshire Coast Path leads to St David's Head, where there is an Iron Age stronghold protected by the remains of a stone rampart known as Warrior's Dyke. Near by are the remains of a 5000-year-old burial chamber. The headland and bay are overlooked by the 595 ft crag of Carnllidi. Ramsey Island, a bird sanctuary and breeding ground for seals, lies south-west of Whitesand Bay.

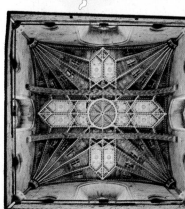

Painted oak ceiling in St David's Cathedral.

SCALE
0 1 2 3 4 5 MILES

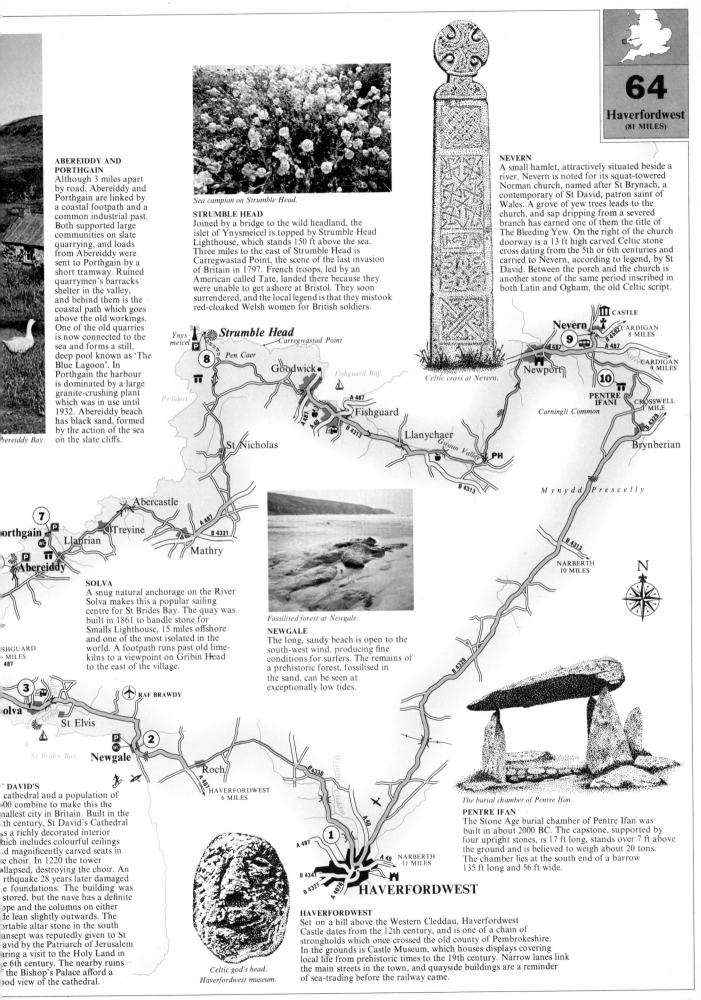

ABEREIDDY AND PORTHGAIN

Although 3 miles apart by road, Abereiddy and Porthgain are linked by a coastal footpath and a common industrial past. Both supported large communities on slate quarrying, and loads from Abereiddy were sent to Porthgain by a short tramway. Ruined quarrymen's barracks shelter in the valley, and behind them is the coastal path which goes above the old workings. One of the old quarries is now connected to the sea and forms a still, deep pool known as 'The Blue Lagoon'. In Porthgain the harbour is dominated by a large granite-crushing plant which was in use until 1932. Abereiddy beach has black sand, formed by the action of the sea on the slate cliffs.

...bereiddy Bay.

Sea campion on Strumble Head.

STRUMBLE HEAD

Joined by a bridge to the wild headland, the islet of Ynysmeicel is topped by Strumble Head Lighthouse, which stands 150 ft above the sea. Three miles to the east of Strumble Head is Carregwastad Point, the scene of the last invasion of Britain in 1797. French troops, led by an American called Tate, landed there because they were unable to get ashore at Bristol. They soon surrendered, and the local legend is that they mistook red-cloaked Welsh women for British soldiers.

NEVERN

A small hamlet, attractively situated beside a river, Nevern is noted for its squat-towered Norman church, named after St Brynach, a contemporary of St David, patron saint of Wales. A grove of yew trees leads to the church, and sap dripping from a severed branch has earned one of them the title of The Bleeding Yew. On the right of the church doorway is a 13 ft high carved Celtic stone cross dating from the 5th or 6th centuries and carried to Nevern, according to legend, by St David. Between the porch and the church is another stone of the same period inscribed in both Latin and Ogham, the old Celtic script.

Celtic cross at Nevern.

SOLVA

A snug natural anchorage on the River Solva makes this a popular sailing centre for St Brides Bay. The quay was built in 1861 to handle stone for Smalls Lighthouse, 15 miles offshore and one of the most isolated in the world. A footpath runs past old lime-kilns to a viewpoint on Gribin Head to the east of the village.

Fossilised forest at Newgale.

NEWGALE

The long, sandy beach is open to the south-west wind, producing fine conditions for surfers. The remains of a prehistoric forest, fossilised in the sand, can be seen at exceptionally low tides.

The burial chamber of Pentre Ifan.

PENTRE IFAN

The Stone Age burial chamber of Pentre Ifan was built in about 2000 BC. The capstone, supported by four upright stones, is 17 ft long, stands over 7 ft above the ground and is believed to weigh about 20 tons. The chamber lies at the south end of a barrow 135 ft long and 56 ft wide.

...DAVID'S

...cathedral and a population of ...00 combine to make this the ...mallest city in Britain. Built in the ...th century, St David's Cathedral ...s a richly decorated interior ...hich includes colourful ceilings ...d magnificently carved seats in ...e choir. In 1220 the tower ...llapsed, destroying the choir. An ...rthquake 28 years later damaged ...e foundations. The building was ...stored, but the nave has a definite ...ope and the columns on either ...e lean slightly outwards. The ...rtable altar stone in the south ...ansept was reputedly given to St ...avid by the Patriarch of Jerusalem ...ring a visit to the Holy Land in ...e 6th century. The nearby ruins ...the Bishop's Palace afford a ...od view of the cathedral.

Celtic god's head, Haverfordwest museum.

HAVERFORDWEST

Set on a hill above the Western Cleddau, Haverfordwest Castle dates from the 12th century, and is one of a chain of strongholds which once crossed the old county of Pembrokeshire. In the grounds is Castle Museum, which houses displays covering local life from prehistoric times to the 19th century. Narrow lanes link the main streets in the town, and quayside buildings are a reminder of sea-trading before the railway came.

Map labels: Strumble Head, Ynys meicel, Pen Caer, Carregwastad Point, Goodwick, Fishguard Bay, Pwllderi, Fishguard, St Nicholas, Llanychaer, Gwaun Valley, PH, Nevern, Newport, Carningli Common, CARDIGAN 8 MILES, CARDIGAN 9 MILES, CASTLE, PENTRE IFANI, CROSSWELL 1 MILE, Brynberian, Mynydd Prescelly, Abercastle, Trevine, ...orthgain, Llanrian, Mathry, Abereiddy, NARBERTH 10 MILES, ...SHGUARD ...MILES 487, RAF BRAWDY, St Elvis, St Brides Bay, Newgale, Roch, HAVERFORDWEST 6 MILES, ...olva, B 4329, NARBERTH 11 MILES, HAVERFORDWEST, A 487, A 40, A 4076, B 4341, B 4327

179

A little bit of England on the coast of Wales

Southern Pembrokeshire got its nickname of 'Little England beyond Wales' in Norman times, when English-speaking people settled there and built a line of castles cutting the region off from the rest of Wales and its language. The coastline, with its sheltered sandy beaches and deep-water harbours, has attracted seafarers for centuries, from Viking invaders in their longboats to modern oilmen in their supertankers, and from the armed hordes of Henry Tudor to the holiday tourists of today. The area is also popular with ornithologists, who come to study the great variety of sea birds on the islands.

(1) Tenby to Slebech Forest Leave the town northwards on the A478, which is signposted to Narberth. After 3 m., just after the road runs under a railway bridge, turn left. Go straight over the crossroads with the A477 and on to the B4586. Follow this road, by-passing Jeffreyston, to the A4075. Turn right on to the A4075, which is signposted to Haverfordwest. After 4 m., just before the junction with the A40, turn left and follow the road along the south bank of the Eastern Cleddau to Blackpool Mill. The history of this old power house, built in 1813, is contained in a museum room. Follow the road past the mill to the start of the Slebech Forest Trail.

(2) Slebech Forest to St Brides Return past the mill to the A4075, turn left and left again on to the A40 crossing Canaston Bridge over the Eastern Cleddau. Follow the A40 to Haverfordwest, the 12th-century garrison town of Richard de Clare. The Western Cleddau divides the town, two road bridges join it. Cross one of these and leave the town on the B4327 which is signposted to Dale. After 8 m., when the B4327 swings sharply to the left, keep straight ahead and follow the lane to St Brides. After 2 m., at the junction by the telephone kiosk, fork right for the beach, or take the left fork and then turn right down the lane to St Brides.

(3) St Brides to Marloes Return to the junction and bear right. After 1½ m. turn right on to the B4327 and just over ½ m. later turn right again. The road runs to Marloes, the most westerly village in Dyfed, formerly Pembrokeshire.

(4) Marloes to Martin's Haven In the village, turn left by the church for the car park and the pathway to Marloes Sands. Return to the village and turn left again to Martin's Haven.

(5) Martin's Haven to St Ann's Head Return to Marloes and, immediately beyond the village, fork right. At the T-junction with the B4327, turn right for Dale. Follow the one-way system through Dale. Turn left by the last houses in the village for St Ann's Head.

(6) St Ann's Head to Milford Haven Return to Dale and take the B4327. In 2 m., just after the bridge, as the B4327 swings sharp left, go straight ahead on a broad lane signposted to Milford Haven. Ignore all side turnings and stay on this lane, following the signposts into Milford Haven. The town is steeped in history. Legend says King Arthur and St Brynach landed here. Henry II left here for Ireland, and Henry Tudor arrived here to capture the throne.

(7) Milford Haven to Pembroke Leave the town on the A4076 signposted to Haverfordwest. Just outside the town turn right on to the B4325 to Neyland. Turn left and continue on the B4325 to the roundabout. Turn right on to the A477 and cross the toll bridge. At the crossroads, go straight ahead on the A4139 to Pembroke.

(8) Pembroke to Lamphey Palace Leave Pembroke on the A4139 signposted to Tenby. In Lamphey, 2 m. later, where the main road swings sharply to the right, keep straight on. Just past this junction, on the left, is the lane leading to Lamphey Palace, former seat of the bishops of St David's.

(9) Lamphey Palace to Manorbier Return down the lane from the palace and turn left. After 2¾ m. turn right, signposted to Manorbier. Go over the level crossing and straight on at the crossroads. Turn right and left through Jameston, crossing the A4139. Go straight on at the next crossroads and down to Manorbier Bay. Then follow the road up the valley and into Manorbier to visit the castle.

(10) Manorbier to Tenby In the town, join the B4585 which is signposted to Tenby. Turn right on to the A4139 and follow this road back to Tenby.

INFORMATION

Places of interest *Blackpool Mill:* Daily 11 a.m.-6 p.m., *Lamphey Palace:* Weekdays, winter; daily, summer. *Manorbier Castle:* Spring Bank Hol. to Sept., daily. *Pembroke:* Castle, weekdays 9 a.m.-dusk (also Sun. in summer). Pembrokeshire Motor Museum, Easter to Sept., daily 9 a.m.-6 p.m., except Sat. *Tenby:* Castle, daily. Museum, daily. *St Catherine's Zoo:* Accessible at low tide. *St Ann's Head:* Lighthouse, at discretion of keeper, weekdays 1 p.m. to 1 hr. before sunset, except in fog.

Craft workshop *Pembroke Dock:* Pemgems, daily.

Nature trails *Dale Peninsula:* Starts Griffin Inn, Dale. Guide from local shops, and Countryside Unit, Broad Haven. *Marloes Sands:* From car park. Guidebook from West Wales Naturalists' Trust, Haverfordwest. *Slebech Forest:* Easter to Oct., from Canaston Bridge car park. Guidebook at local office, Forestry Commission, Cardiff, and National Park Information Centres.

Events *Pembroke:* Michaelmas Fair, Oct. *Tenby:* St Margaret's Fair, July. Carnival, Aug.

Information Pembrokeshire Coast National Park Office, 40 High Street, Haverfordwest (Tel. Haverfordwest 66141). South Pembrokeshire District Council, The Norton, Tenby (Tel. Tenby 2402).

Towns with easy access to Tenby:

Cardigan	33 m.	Fishguard	35 m.
Carmarthen	27 m.	Haverfordwest	21 m.

Marloes Sands.

MARLOES
A 20 minute walk from the National Trust car park lea to the cliff-backed Marloes Sands and Gateholm (goat island). The island, down at the western end of the bea is cut off, except at low tide—an advantage which led Iron Age men to settle there.

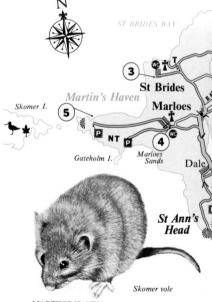

Skomer vole

MARTIN'S HAVEN
Daily through the summer, boats leave this roc inlet for the island nature reserve of Skomer. Owned jointly by the West Wales Naturalists' Trust and the Nature Conservancy, the 722 acr island that rises up 1½ miles off the coast is visited by some 30 different species of birds, an is also the sole home of the tame little Skomer vole. In spring and summer, a riot of wild flowers dresses the island.

ST ANN'S HEAD
Slowly easing their enormous bulk into the harbour, the 300,000 ton supertankers that ente Milford Haven make an impressive sight from t lighthouse on St Ann's Head. The lighthouse w built on the site of a chapel so old that it was a ruin in the time of Elizabeth I.

SCALE

0   1   2   3   4   5 MILES

...ckpool Mill.

BECH FOREST
...gfishers and woodpeckers, squirrels
...badgers flutter and scurry among
...larch, beech and towering Douglas
...trees that line the 1 mile Forestry
...mmission walk which runs through
...ech Forest. Near by, on the banks
...he Eastern Cleddau, stands in full
...ding order the stone-built, water-
...ven Blackpool Mill, with craft shop
...tea room.

BRIDES
...red-stone cove with its
...ch of red and white sand,
...church, the rectory and a
...age bear the old name of
...famous missionary of th
...century, St Brigid of
...are. The church replace
...old chapel, which was
...shed away by the sea.

Cistercian monastery, Caldy Island.

TENBY
The gentry first adopted Tenby as a health resort in the mid-18th century, and now it has become one of the most popular seaside holiday towns in Wales. The centre of the old town is a maze of narrow streets enclosed by a 14th-century towered wall. Sandy beaches with acres of rolling dunes spread out beneath high cliffs from both sides of the harbour. Pleasure boats head out to the zoo on St Catherine's Island and on to Caldy Island, where silent Cistercian monks farm the land of a 12th-century monastery.

The castle at Manorbier.

MANORBIER
High above the beach that rims the sheltered waters of Manorbier Bay stand the ruins of a moated castle which has dominated this coastline since the 12th century. It was the birthplace of Geraldus Cambrensis, the great Welsh scholar and topographer, who travelled about Wales with the Archbishop of Canterbury in 1188, preaching support for the Third Crusade.

PEMBROKE
The town of Pembroke is dominated by its mighty castle, mounted on a ridge, defended on three sides by water, and with a 75 ft high rounded keep rising on walls 20 ft thick. It was the Norman headquarters for the invasion of Wales, and the invaders' main bastion against successive Welsh rebellions. Henry Tudor was born there, and in the Civil War it was such a strong Royalist centre that the Cromwellians dismantled its defences.

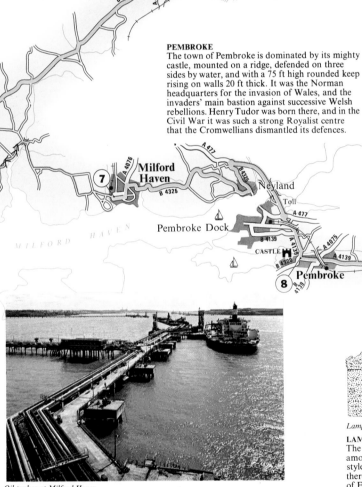

Oil tanker at Milford Haven.

MILFORD HAVEN
Lord Nelson called it one of the finest harbours he had ever seen, but the vast 'drowned valley' of Milford Haven, stretching 10 miles inland, remained just another fishing port for 150 years. Then, in 1957, Esso opened its deep-water terminal at Milford Haven, to become the first of five oil companies to set down bases for giant supertankers, turning the harbour into Britain's biggest oil port—the second largest in Europe.

Lamphey Palace.

LAMPHEY PALACE
The old Bishops of St David's lived in fine style, numbering a castle and two palaces among their estates. Lamphey Palace, built in the Early-English architectural style, dates in part from the 13th century. Henry, Earl of Richmond stopped there on his journey to Bosworth and the battle that would make him Henry VII of England. Robert Devereux, Earl of Essex and favourite of Queen Elizabeth, passed childhood years roaming around the 144 acre grounds that once contained a deer park, fishponds, orchards, watermills and windmills and a dovecot. After the death of Essex in 1601 the castle was allowed to decay.

From Cardigan Bay to the winding course of the River Teifi

The changing moods of the Teifi, one of the loveliest of Welsh rivers, give a rich variety to the country inland from Cardigan. At Cardigan the river is broad and tidal, while a few miles upstream at Cilgerran it is squeezed into a deep, narrow and thickly wooded gorge with a ruined castle perched on its rim. On the coast, small villages overlook sandy beaches and clifftop walks offer fine views over Cardigan Bay.

1 Cardigan to St Dogmaels From the city centre take the A487 southwards following the signposts to Fishguard. Immediately after crossing the River Teifi turn right on to the B4546 and into the village of St Dogmaels, with the abbey on the left. In the summer there are boat trips round the Cardigan Island Nature Reserve which lies off the headland to the east of the Teifi Estuary.

2 St Dogmaels to Cilgerran Continue along the B4546 and, where the road swings to the right at the top of the village, go straight on to the road signposted to Moylgrove. Keep straight on at the next junction and after 1 m. turn left at a T-junction. After another 1½ m. go straight over the A487 and follow the narrow lane across the A478 and into Cilgerran, turning left to view the castle.

3 Cilgerran to Manordeifi Return to the main road through Cilgerran and continue through the village. Take the first road on the left, signposted to Llechryd, and after 1 m. turn left again at a T-junction. Immediately before the bridge over the River Teifi turn right into a narrow lane. On the right are the remains of an old canal, built to carry slate barges from Cilgerran and Cenarth down to Cardigan. Follow this lane to the old church at Manordeifi.

4 Manordeifi to Cenarth Immediately after the church follow the road sharply to the left. Keep straight ahead at the next junction and on to the road signposted to Abercych and Penrhiw, which runs parallel to the River Cych. In Penrhiw turn left on to the B4332. Cross the Cych and follow the road back to the Teifi Valley and Cenarth.

5 Cenarth to Newcastle Emlyn In the village, turn right on to the A484 and follow this to the edge of Newcastle Emlyn. Turn left on to the A475 and follow it into the village, with the castle mound and picnic site on the right.

6 Newcastle Emlyn to Llangranog From the castle return to the A475, following the signpost to Lampeter. Immediately after crossing the Teifi, turn left at a junction and then right on to the B4571 which winds through lush farmlands bordering the River Ceri. After 4 m. turn left on to the B4334, and 4 m. further on turn right and immediately left to cross the A487. Continue along the B4334 into the seaside village of Llangranog.

7 Llangranog to Aberporth Leave the village on the sea-front road, which climbs sharply and steeply. Keep straight ahead at the first junction and turn right at the second junction. At the following junction swing right on to the road signposted to Penbryn. At the next junction keep straight ahead, signposted Tresaith, and after ¾ m. turn right. Follow the road to the village of Tresaith, where a small waterfall splashes down on to the shingle beach. Continue through Tresaith and turn right on to the B4333 and into Aberporth.

8 Aberporth to Traeth-y-mwnt From the village keep on the B4333 signposted to Blaenannerch and after 1½ m. turn right, following the signpost to Verwig, Gwbert-on-sea and Mwnt. After ¾ m., turn left, and 1½ m. later turn right into a narrow lane. Follow the lane, which gradually swings westwards, for 1½ m. and then turn right to the bay of Traeth-y-mwnt, where steep paths zig-zag down shale cliffs to the sandy shore. The 250 ft headland to the north is owned by the National Trust.

9 Traeth-y-mwnt to Cardigan Return to the T-junction and turn right. At the next junction turn right and immediately left. Follow this lane and turn left on to the B4548 and back into Cardigan, passing the eastern bank of the Teifi Estuary. Opposite lie Poppit Sands, a popular caravan site.

NATURE NOTES

The most interesting flowers are found near the coast; sea holly and sea rocket grow on the dunes near Gwbert-on-sea and the cliff paths are carpeted with kidney vetch and eyebright in mid-summer. Inland, many of the hedges are of laburnum and are thickly covered in yellow flowers during the summer. Columbines, spread from cottage gardens, are often found in the hedgerows near villages. Cornish moneywort reaches its northern limit in Britain in this corner of Wales.

INFORMATION

Places of interest *Cilgerran Castle:* All year, weekdays, Sun. afternoons (closed Christmas and Boxing Day). *Cenarth:* Watermill, all reasonable times, key from house next to post office. *St Dogmael's Abbey:* All year, weekdays, Sun. afternoons. *Newcastle Emlyn:* Castle ruins, accessible at all times.

Craft workshops *Cardigan:* Quixote, College Row, handthrown stoneware pottery, weekdays, early closing Wed.

Events *Cilgerran:* Annual festive week, Aug. Coracle races and aquatic sports, Aug. *Cardigan:* Hymn-singing festivals, Apr., May, June. District agricultural show, July. Civic week, July. Annual hiring and pleasure fair, Nov.

Information Wales Tourist Office, The Market Place, Cardigan (Tel. Cardigan 3230).

Towns with easy access to Cardigan:

Carmarthen	28 m.	Lampeter	30 m.
Fishguard	18 m.	New Quay	20 m.
Haverfordwest	26 m.	Tenby	33 m.

Grey seal

TRAETH-Y-MWNT
Seals can often be seen in this bay with its attractive sandy beach. At the foot of the knife-ridge hill which overlooks the bay is a whitewashed 13th-century church, built on the site of an older church used by 5th-century pilgrims on their way to Bardsey Island. Mwnt was invaded by Flemings in 1155 and their defeat was celebrated until the 18th century as 'The Bloody Sunday of Mwnt'.

CARDIGAN
The sheltered estuary of the River Teifi, famed for its salmon and trout fishing, enabled Cardigan to become a busy port during the 17th and 18th centuries. Gradual silting of the estuary, combined with the development of the railway, killed the seaborne trade during the 19th century and Cardigan became the quiet market town it is today. The 17th-century bridge over the river is overlooked by the remains of a castle which was largely destroyed by Cromwell's troops in 1645. The remains are now a private house. The Victorian Guildhall houses a covered market among the massive pillars and arches of its basement.

ST DOGMAELS
Founded in 1115, the abbey of St Dogmaels is believed to stand on the site of a Celtic monastery sacked by Vikings 150 years earlier. Building continued almost until the Dissolution of the Monasteries in 1536. In St Dogmael's Church is a 6th-century stone pillar carved with an inscription in both Latin and ogham, which enabled 19th-century scholars to decipher the ancient Celtic script.

CILGERRAN
Like many other medieval forts, the castle at Cilgerran was built at the tidal limit of a river, accessible to ships and controlling the natural crossing point. The present castle was built around 1240 with the round towers seen so often in South Wales. The view of the castle from the river has inspired many artists, including J. M. W. Turner whose painting of Cilgerran now hangs the Tate Gallery in London. The remains of the castle two large towers and parts of the gatehouse, which stand on a rocky promontory above the river gorge.

Cilgerran Castle by Turner.

SCALE
0   1   2   3 MILES

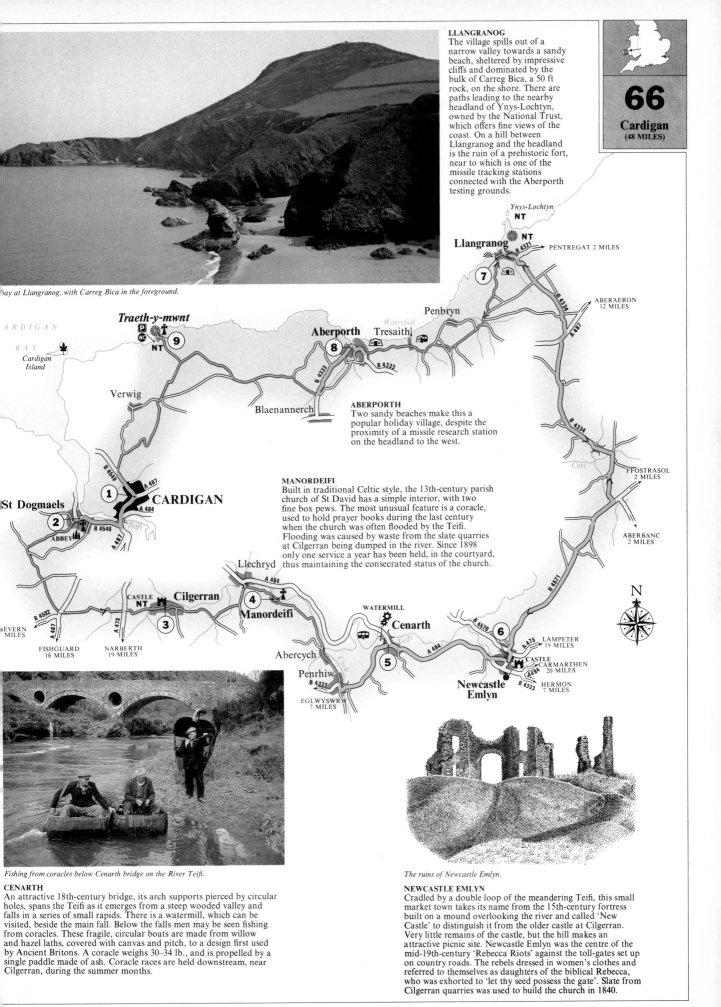

LLANGRANOG
The village spills out of a narrow valley towards a sandy beach, sheltered by impressive cliffs and dominated by the bulk of Carreg Bica, a 50 ft rock, on the shore. There are paths leading to the nearby headland of Ynys-Lochtyn, owned by the National Trust, which offers fine views of the coast. On a hill between Llangranog and the headland is the ruin of a prehistoric fort, near to which is one of the missile tracking stations connected with the Aberporth testing grounds.

...bay at Llangranog, with Carreg Bica in the foreground.

Ynys-Lochtyn
NT

Llangranog NT
7

PENTREGAT 2 MILES

ABERAERON
12 MILES

Waterfall

Penbryn

Aberporth **Tresaith**
8

A 487

B 4333

B 4334

ARDIGAN
BAY
Cardigan Island

Traeth-y-mwnt
P WC NT
9

Verwig

Blaenannerch

FFOSTRASOL
2 MILES

Ceri

ABERPORTH
Two sandy beaches make this a popular holiday village, despite the proximity of a missile research station on the headland to the west.

B 4333

B 4570

ABERBANC
2 MILES

MANORDEIFI
Built in traditional Celtic style, the 13th-century parish church of St David has a simple interior, with two fine box pews. The most unusual feature is a coracle, used to hold prayer books during the last century when the church was often flooded by the Teifi. Flooding was caused by waste from the slate quarries at Cilgerran being dumped in the river. Since 1898 only one service a year has been held, in the courtyard, thus maintaining the consecrated status of the church.

St Dogmaels
1
A 487
CARDIGAN
A 484
B 4546

2
ABBEY

B 4582
SEVERN MILES
A 487
A 478

FISHGUARD
16 MILES
NARBERTH
19 MILES

Llechryd
A 484

CASTLE NT **Cilgerran**
4
3
Manordeifi

WATERMILL
Cenarth
5
Abercych

Penrhiw
B 4332
EGLWYSWRW
7 MILES

A 484

B 4571

6
A 475
LAMPETER
19 MILES
CASTLE
A 484
CARMARTHEN
20 MILES
Newcastle Emlyn
B 4333
HERMON
7 MILES

N

Fishing from coracles below Cenarth bridge on the River Teifi.

CENARTH
An attractive 18th-century bridge, its arch supports pierced by circular holes, spans the Teifi as it emerges from a steep wooded valley and falls in a series of small rapids. There is a watermill, which can be visited, beside the main fall. Below the falls men may be seen fishing from coracles. These fragile, circular boats are made from willow and hazel laths, covered with canvas and pitch, to a design first used by Ancient Britons. A coracle weighs 30–34 lb., and is propelled by a single paddle made of ash. Coracle races are held downstream, near Cilgerran, during the summer months.

The ruins of Newcastle Emlyn.

NEWCASTLE EMLYN
Cradled by a double loop of the meandering Teifi, this small market town takes its name from the 15th-century fortress built on a mound overlooking the river and called 'New Castle' to distinguish it from the older castle at Cilgerran. Very little remains of the castle, but the hill makes an attractive picnic site. Newcastle Emlyn was the centre of the mid-19th-century 'Rebecca Riots' against the toll-gates set up on country roads. The rebels dressed in women's clothes and referred to themselves as daughters of the biblical Rebecca, who was exhorted to 'let thy seed possess the gate'. Slate from Cilgerran quarries was used to build the church in 1840.

Gold mines and castles among green hills

The River Tywi winds lazily down to Carmarthen through meadows where dairy cattle graze on some of the best pasture in Britain. Among the green hills sloping up from the valley nestle ancient farmhouses with roses climbing up whitewashed walls. The gold mines at Dolaucothi once added to the prosperity of the land, but hill-forts and strongholds—with the magnificent Carreg-Cennen Castle among them—are reminders that this wealth was once defended with sword and spear.

1 Carmarthen to Paxton's Tower Leave on the A48 for Swansea. Cross the bridge and after ¾ m. turn left on to the B4300 where it is signposted to Llandeilo. In Llanarthney village turn right by the Paxton Inn. Bear left at the first fork and turn left at the top of the hill, following the signs to Paxton's Tower, which is on the left, set in 14 acres of National Trust land.

2 Paxton's Tower to Carreg-Cennen Castle Continue along the road, which runs close to the crest of the hill, and at the T-junction (no signpost) turn left on to the B4297, down the hill and left on to the B4300 signposted to Carmarthen. Take the first turning on the right, across the river to the ruins of Dryslwyn Castle, the fortress of a 13th-century Welsh prince, on a steep, isolated hill. Return to the B4300 and turn left along the valley, turning left again on to the A476. At the next junction, with the A483, go straight over on to the road signposted Bethlehem and, immediately after crossing the bridge, take a right turning signposted Carreg-Cennen Castle. Keep straight on as the road climbs wooded hills, through the village of Trapp on the road signposted Gwynfe, and after 1 m. fork right to Carreg-Cennen Castle. To the left, as the castle is approached from the car park, a footpath runs down through the oak trees to the floor of the valley and then swings sharp right, following the stream. The path soon joins a narrow lane that runs along the foot of the cliff before climbing to meet the lane leading back to the car park. Just under 2 m. long, this pleasant walk can be completed in less than an hour.

3 Carreg-Cennen Castle to Carn Goch From the castle, return to the junction and turn right. After about 1½ m. turn left on to a road which is signposted to Llandeilo, and keep straight on to a three-road junction. Take the road to the right, which is signposted to Bethlehem. Turn right at the next T-junction, also signposted to Bethlehem. The Iron Age hill-fort is up the hill of Carn Goch to the right after about ¼ m.

4 Carn Goch to Dolaucothi Continue along the road to the next T-junction. There, turn left (no signpost) and immediately right at the signpost to Llangadog. Follow the road across a bridge and then left, joining the A4069 (no signpost) and straight through Llangadog, following the signposts to Llandeilo. Just after the town, turn right on to the A40, where the signpost is to Llandovery, and after 2 m., at Llanwrda, turn left on to the A482 signposted Lampeter. Follow the road up the tree-lined valley of the River Dulais. After 7 m. turn right on to the road which is signposted to Cwrt-y-

Cadno, and within 600 yds the site of the Roman gold mines at Dolaucothi is reached in the woods to the right of Ogofau Lodge. One of two marked archaeological trails leading through the site starts here. Just opposite Ogofau Lodge is a stone pitted with smooth hollows. According to legend, these were made by the shoulders of five saints, Gwynne, Gwynno, Gwynoro, Cilyen and Ceitho, who clustered around the stone for shelter during a blizzard. The name of a nearby village, Pumpsaint, is Welsh for five saints.

5 Dolaucothi to Talley Abbey Return to the A482 and turn left. After 1 m. turn right by the Bridge End Inn and follow the B4302 to Talley. Turn right in the village and right again at the sign to Abbey/Lakes circular road, to reach Talley Abbey.

6 Talley Abbey to Abergorlech Follow the road round the two lakes, and down an avenue of stately oaks. Turn left on to the main road (B4302) and almost immediately fork left on to the B4337 to Llansawel, then fork left by the chapel on the far side of the village, following the signposts to Abergorlech/Brechfa. The road runs over the hills to enter Abergorlech 3 m. later.

7 Abergorlech to Carmarthen Continue on the B4310 for 11 m. until its junction with the A40. Turn right and follow the A40 back along Tywi Valley, passing (on the left) the palace of the bishops of St David's at Abergwili. Carmarthen is 1½ m. beyond the palace.

NATURE NOTES

There are few areas of extensive woodland but many rocky, wooded gorges in which ferns abound. The Talley Lakes are rich in water plants and the water-lilies are particularly fine. Butterwort and sundew grow in the low-lying bog areas.

INFORMATION

Places of interest *Talley Abbey:* All year, daily. *Carreg-Cennen Castle:* All year, weekdays, Sun. afternoon. *Dolaucothi:* Roman gold mines, accessible at all times. *Paxton's Tower:* Accessible at all times. *Carmarthen:* County Museum, from July, Mon.-Fri., except Christmas, Boxing Day and New Year's Day. *Dryslwyn Castle:* Accessible at all times.

Nature trail *Dolaucothi:* From Roman gold mine; guide book from site or County Museum, Carmarthen.

Events *Carmarthen:* United Counties Agricultural Show, Aug. *Llandeilo:* Agricultural Show, Aug.

Information South Wales Tourism Council, Darkgate, Carmarthen (Tel. Carmarthen 7557).

Towns with easy access to Carmarthen:

Cardigan	28 m.	Swansea	27 m.
Lampeter	23 m.	Tenby	27 m.

Abergorlech picnic site.

Carmarthen cattle market.

CARMARTHEN
Modern buildings and the gatehouse of a ruined Norman castle dominate the skyline of this lively market town. The Romans, too, favoured this strat site on the upper tidal reaches of the River Tywi called their base here Moridunum. Roman jewellery is among the many exhibits in the County Museum Quay Street. In Welsh folklore, King Arthur's wiza Merlin. was born hereabouts in 480, and his famou oak, a withered stump at the end of Priory Street, i said to carry his spell—that if it falls down 'then sh. fall Carmarthen Town'. Something of the true past survives on the river in the shape of coracles—fishir boats made to a 2000-year-old design.

NEWCASTLE EMLYN 15 MILES — A485 LAMPETER 21 MILES

CARMARTHEN 1 — Abergwili

CASTLE — BIS PA

ST CLEARS 9 MILES

KIDWELLY 9 MILES — SWANSEA 27 MILES

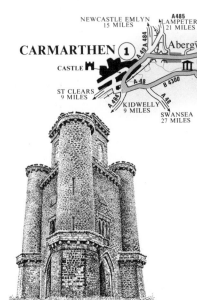

Paxton's Tower.

PAXTON'S TOWER
The tower was built in 1805 by a local banker and M Sir William Paxton, to commemorate Nelson's victo It is now a shell, but there are fine views from the si

SCALE

0 — 1 — 2 — 3 MILES

DOLAUCOTHI
Gold was probably mined at Dolaucothi more than 2000 years ago, and was still being mined on the wooded slopes above the River Cothi in the 1930s. But it was the Romans who dug most of the workings which can be seen today: remains of aqueducts and reservoirs which supplied water power for machinery. They extracted about a million ounces of gold in the 300 years from AD 70. Prospecting has started again in the area following recent increases in the price of gold.

Roman gold pendant from Dolaucothi.

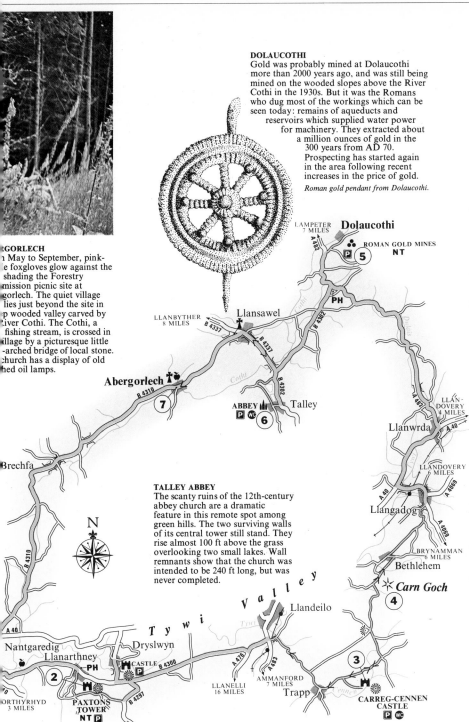

LAMPETER 7 MILES

Dolaucothi

ROMAN GOLD MINES
NT

5

PH

LLANBYTHER 8 MILES

Llansawel

B 4337

B 4337

B 4302

LLAN-DOVERY 4 MILES

A 482

Abergorlech ✝

B 4310

7

ABBEY
P WC
6

Talley

A 40

Llanwrda

LLANDOVERY 6 MILES

A 4069

Brechfa

Llangadog

A 40

BRYNAMMAN 6 MILES

Bethlehem

N

A 4310

TALLEY ABBEY
The scanty ruins of the 12th-century abbey church are a dramatic feature in this remote spot among green hills. The two surviving walls of its central tower still stand. They rise almost 100 ft above the grass overlooking two small lakes. Wall remnants show that the church was intended to be 240 ft long, but was never completed.

✳ **Carn Goch**

4

Llandeilo

Tywi Valley

Nantgaredig

Dryslwyn

Llanarthney

2 PH

CASTLE P

B 4300

A 476

A 483

3

AMMANFORD 7 MILES

ORTHYRHYD 3 MILES

PAXTONS TOWER
NT P

B 4237

LLANELLI 16 MILES

Trapp

CARREG-CENNEN CASTLE
P WC

CARREG-CENNEN CASTLE

PENYGROES 3 MILES

Carreg-Cennen Castle.

CARREG-CENNEN CASTLE
Perched on the brink of a sheer limestone cliff, 300 ft above the Cennen river, Carreg-Cennen has a setting few British castles can equal. It was built in the 13th and 14th centuries, changed hands many times, resisted a siege by Owain Glyndwr, was partially demolished in 1462 during the Wars of the Roses, and restored as a picturesque ruin in the 19th century. A 150 ft passage, leading steeply down through rock to a well, has 'windows' cut through the cliff face itself, giving bold views of the Black Mountains. Legend says that the site was originally used for a castle by Urien, one of King Arthur's Knights of the Round Table.

ORGORLECH
In May to September, pink-e foxgloves glow against the shading the Forestry mission picnic site at gorlech. The quiet village lies just beyond the site in p wooded valley carved by iver Cothi. The Cothi, a fishing stream, is crossed in illage by a picturesque little -arched bridge of local stone. church has a display of old hed oil lamps.

THE TYWI VALLEY
From Carmarthen to Carreg-Cennen, long stretches of the route run along the valley of the Tywi, at 68 miles the longest river in Wales. Large farmhouses are a feature of this dairy-farming area, a contrast with the smaller, rougher stone buildings to be seen later when the roads rise into the rough grazings of sheep country. There are frequent views of the broad, shallow Tywi winding through the fertile meadows that fill the flat valley bottom.

Tywi Valley farmhouse.

CARN GOCH
One of the largest Iron Age forts in Wales can be seen on Carn Goch (Red Cairn) 4 miles south of Llangadog. Belts of drystone walling, mainly tumbled, but still 20 ft high on the western side, show that the camp of the iron-using Celts was more than 2000 ft long and up to 500 ft wide. Traces of two smaller camps remain on the western part of Carn Goch. Such unmortared buildings date from two or three centuries before the Roman occupation.

Buzzards and oases in the deserted mountains

The hilly heart of central Wales is one of the few deserted landscapes remaining in Britain. Forestry Commission woodlands patchwork the map, and there are man-made 'oases'— the great reservoirs of the Elan Valley which supply water to Birmingham. But there is little else of man's handiwork to be seen, for this is the most sparsely populated area in England and Wales. In this mountainous land of buzzards and sheep, the time-softened ruins of Strata Florida Abbey lend a touch of beauty and romance.

(1) Aberystwyth to Devil's Bridge Leave the town on the A487 signposted to Cardigan. On the outskirts of Aberystwyth, with the white buildings of the National Library of Wales clearly visible a mile away on the other side of the valley, fork left uphill on to the A4120 for the 11 m. run to Devil's Bridge, a three-tier structure spanning the River Mynach. The road climbs to almost 1000 ft, giving fine views to the east and north over the wooded Rheidol Valley. Devil's Bridge is the terminus of the narrow-gauge railway line which runs excursion trains from Aberystwyth during the summer months.

(2) Devil's Bridge to Elan Valley In Devil's Bridge, turn right on to the B4574 for the climb up to Jubilee Arch and down to the remote village of Cwmystwyth. Three marked woodland trails wend their way from the car park at Jubilee Arch, a landmark built by a local landowner to commemorate the Golden Jubilee of George III in 1810. About 1 m. beyond Cwmystwyth, on the left of the road as it runs parallel with the Ystwyth river, is a disused mine, a reminder that this valley, like others in central Wales, was once rich in lead ore. Continue on the mountain road for about 10 m. and, just after the first of a series of reservoirs comes into view, turn right and over a bridge across the Elan river (Pont ar Elan).

(3) Elan Valley to Rhayader Continue down the valley past three of the reservoirs and round the top of the fourth, past the Caban dam on the right. Beyond the dam the road becomes the B4518 to Rhayader. The reservoirs—now well-matured lakes which add to the natural beauty of the valley—are Craig Goch, Pen-y-garreg, Garreg Ddu and Caban Coch. They were built between 1892 and 1952 and now pipe water to Birmingham. The Pen-y-garreg dam, 184 ft high, is the highest gravity dam in Britain. On the right of the road, at the start of the B4518, is Elan village, built for employees of the Birmingham Waterworks. This unromantic name refers to the complex of beautiful lakes and dams which was opened by the Queen in 1952. Pass the village and continue on the B4518 to Rhayader.

(4) Rhayader to Abergwesyn From Rhayader take the A470, signposted for Builth Wells, and follow it down the Wye Valley to Newbridge on Wye. In Newbridge. turn right on to the B4358 signposted Beulah. About 8 m. further on, just before Beulah, turn right for Abergwesyn. After 1 m. bear right at the T-junction by the chapel, and after another 5 m., on the outskirts of Abergwesyn, turn right on to the road signposted for Tregaron—the Mountain Road.

(5) Abergwesyn to Tregaron The road continues over the hills, and about 2 m. after the Abergwesyn junction it crosses and recrosses the Irfon river. The road then climbs steeply round acute bends known as the Devil's Staircase. From a high point of nearly 1600 ft, the road descends into the valley of the River Tywi. From the river, the road climbs steeply again, and for the next 8 m. to Tregaron it follows an up-and-down course across the hills and valleys.

(6) Tregaron to Strata Florida At Tregaron, turn right on to the B4343 to Pontrhydfendigaid and on the outskirts of this village, turn right on the road signposted to Strata Florida Abbey, where the preserved ruins of the 12th-13th century Cistercian monastic settlement stand in a sheltered valley.

(7) Strata Florida to Nanteos Return to Pontrhydfendigaid, turn right at the T-junction and then, at the end of the village, bear left on to the B4340 for Trawscoed. This road gives a good view southwards over the Cors Tregaron, one of the largest peat bogs in Britain and the main wintering area in England and Wales of the Greenland white-fronted goose. It is a National Nature Reserve and visitors need a permit. Past the Cors Tregaron, the road drops down into the valley of the Ystwyth river. About 3 m. after climbing out of the valley, the mansion of Nanteos comes into view down on the right, and the sharp right turn back to the house is 1 m. further along the road. Nanteos, an unspoilt early-18th-century mansion is a treasure house of antique furniture, works of art and kitchenware.

(8) Nanteos to Aberystwyth Return to the B4340 and turn right and continue back to Aberystwyth.

INFORMATION

Places of interest *Aberystwyth:* Castle, daily. National Library of Wales, weekdays. *Nanteos:* June to Sept., daily, afternoons. *Strata Florida:* Daily. *Vale of Rheidol Light Railway:* Regular service, Apr. to Oct.

Craft workshop *Pontrhydfendigaid:* Abaty Pottery, weekdays.

Events *Aberystwyth:* Agricultural show, June. Yacht club regattas, most summer months. Boat festival, Aug.

Information Wales Tourist Office, Information Bureau, Promenade, Aberystwyth (Tel. Aberystwyth 7111).

Towns with easy access to Aberystwyth:

Cardigan	. . . . . .38 m.	Lampeter	. . . . . .29 m.
Carmarthen	. . . .45 m.	Newcastle Emlyn	34 m.
Dolgellau	. . . . . .34 m.	Newtown	. . . . . .43 m.

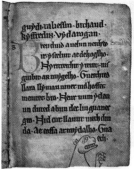

A page from the Black Book.

ABERYSTWYTH
This pleasant mixture of resort and university town is the home of the National Library of Wales. The library contains 2 million books and more than 2½ million documents, including the 12th-century Black Book of Carmarthen, the oldest manuscript in the Welsh language in existence.

NANTEOS
Rhododendrons grow in exotic profusion beside the drive leading to this handsome mansion, built between 1739 and 1757. The house contains a fine collection of period furniture and paintings, together with a healing cup that is claimed to be the original Holy Grail. Antiques are sold in the old stables courtyard at the back of the house.

Strata Florida Abbey.

STRATA FLORIDA
Most of the ruins of the once rich and influential abbey at Strata Florida date from the late 12th and early 13th centuries. The western doorway is a particularly eye-catching example of Norman architecture. The adjacent church was built in 1700, and stands on the foundations of the abbey's infirmary. In the north transept there is a memorial to Dafydd ap Gwilym, who began a new, lyrical tradition in Welsh poetry. He was buried here about the year 1370.

TREGARON
George Borrow, the Victorian traveller and author of *The Bible in Spain,* compared Tregaron with a Spanish town set against the dark mountains of Andalusia when he tramped through Wales in the 1850s. He stayed at the early-19th-century Talbot Inn in the central square of the little town. The church, which has a 14th-century tower, stands in an oval churchyard.

SCALE

0   1   2   3   4   5 MILES

DEVIL'S BRIDGE

Three bridges, each built on top of the other, span the deep, rocky and thickly wooded gorge of the River Mynach near its meeting place with the Rheidol. According to local legend, the lowest, which dates from the 12th century, was built by the Devil. The second was built at the start of the 18th century and the third 200 years later.

ELAN VALLEY

The great dams in this deep, flooded valley were built between 1892 and 1904 of stone rather than concrete, and do not look out of place among the mountains. The lakes they formed hold a total of 21,780 million gallons of water for Birmingham.

68
Aberystwyth
(94 MILES)

... of Rheidol Railway.

...IDOL VALLEY
...bing up to 600 ft, along what many ...called the most beautiful valley in Wales, ...e Vale of Rheidol Railway. The 12 mile ...ow-gauge stretch between Aberystwyth ...Devil's Bridge is operated by ...sh Rail's last steam locomotives.

Three-tiered Devil's Bridge.

Pen-y-garreg dam.

Kite

RED KITE

The mountains of central Wales are the last British breeding area for the red kite, a striking and colourful bird of prey which is easily recognised by its deeply forked tail. Despite protection, a bare score of pairs nest here.

...ntain Road near Abergwesyn.

ABERGWESYN

One of the most beautiful and spectacular roads in Britain runs from Abergwesyn to Tregaron. Called the Mountain Road, it is an ancient route over the hills originally trodden out by cattle drovers, on their way to London and the Midlands in the 18th and early 19th centuries. The Mountain Road climbs to almost 1600 ft above sea level, with gradients of 1-in-4 where it descends into and climbs out of the valleys of the Irfon, Tywi and Camddwr rivers before following the valley of the Berwyn down to Tregaron. The view across deserted open moors, from the rocky gap at the top of the Berwyn Valley, makes it easy to understand why this part of the country was commonly called 'The Great Desert' of Wales. It provides a strong contrast to the sheltered valleys and winding streams surrounding the earlier part of the road.

RHAYADER

This little market town has grown in importance this century as a holiday centre. Beside the man-made lakes that are Birmingham's reservoirs, the River Wye and dozens of subsidiary streams provide excellent fishing. The hills that surround the town are covered with a maze of lanes, bridleways and footpaths, popular with walkers and pony-trekkers. Near the town bridge is the church of Llansantffraid Cwmdauddwr, 'the church of St Bride in the valley of the two waters'. It has a carved Norman font. The town centre retains its charm. A mixture of brick, stone and whitewashed buildings, all well kept and solid, give the market square great character. Rhayader is Welsh for waterfall, but the falls for which the town is named were destroyed when the River Wye was bridged in 1780.

187

The heights and depths of Brecon Beacons National Park

The distinctive shapes of the Brecon Beacons have been likened to immense waves frozen on the point of breaking. The steep north-facing scarps were carved out by glacial action during the Ice Age. Below these massive ramparts the mountains slope gently into green valleys where turbulent rivers have carved deep underground caves, the most spectacular being at Dan-yr-Ogof, which extend for 20 miles under Black Mountain. The tour also offers reminders of early Welsh history, including the Roman fort at Brecon Y Gaer, just outside the ancient town of Brecon itself.

1 **Brecon to the Mountain Centre** From the town centre take the A40 signposted to Llandovery as far as the roundabout on the outskirts of Brecon, and here turn left on the A470 (signposted Merthyr Tydfil). After about 4 m. at Libanus turn right where a minor road is signposted to the Mountain Centre. Take right fork at junction of lanes and continue until cattle grid has been crossed. The Mountain Centre is to the right.

2 **Mountain Centre to Porth yr ogof** Leave the centre and turn left over a cattle grid. Continue along the lane to join the A470 at Libanus. There turn right and follow the A470 to Storey Arms—which is an Adventure Centre from which walkers can climb Pen y Fan, 2907 ft above sea level and the highest of the Brecon Beacons. Continue on the A470 past Storey Arms, and about 1½ m. later fork right on to the A4059, following the signpost to Neath. After 6½ m. turn sharp right, following the signs to Ystradfellte. After 1¼ m. bear left at a junction, and after a further ½ m. turn left again into a narrow lane which leads to the car park at Porth yr ogof. Scwd-yr-Eira waterfall can be reached by a footpath along the River Mellte from the caves of Porth yr ogof.

3 **Porth yr ogof to Henrhyd Falls** Return to the lane and at the top of the hill turn left. After 2½ m. turn right where the road is crossed by telephone wires (there is no signpost here). Follow the lane down into a thickly wooded valley and cross the bridge over the River Neath. There is a picnic site to the left of the bridge. After ½ m. turn right on to the track which runs through the Forestry Commission plantation of Coed y Rhaiadr. After ¾ m. keep right at a junction, beyond which the track changes to a properly surfaced road which affords glimpses of the industrial fringe of South Wales to the left. About 2 m. after emerging from the forest, turn right at a T-junction and almost immediately go straight ahead over a bridge. At the top of the hill is the car park from which a footpath leads to the beautiful Henrhyd Falls on the River Llech.

4 **Henrhyd Falls to Dan-yr-Ogof** Leave the car park and continue on the road to Pen-y-cae. There turn right on to the A4067 which shortly passes Craig-y-nos Castle on the left. Now a hospital, this 19th-century Gothic mansion was the home, from 1879 to 1919, of the famous coloratura soprano Adelina Patti. In the village she opened her own private theatre, which is still used by local amateur groups. Follow the road past the castle to the car park for the Dan-yr-Ogof caves on the left of the road.

5 **Dan-yr-Ogof to Brecon Y Gaer** Return to the road and after 1 m. turn left on to the road signposted for Trecastle. Follow the road for 7 m. with Black Mountain towering almost vertically on the left. At the T-junction turn right and continue into Trecastle, where the old coaching inns, with impressive coachyard entrances, are a reminder of the town's previous importance as a stage on the Fishguard road. In Trecastle turn right on to the A40, following the signs to Brecon. Continue on the road to Sennybridge and, just before the A40 is crossed by a bridge, turn left on to the road signposted Pentre'r-felin. After 900 yds bear right and follow the road for about 2 m. to the T-junction. Turn right towards Trallong and, after a further 4½ m., shortly after crossing the second bridge, turn sharp right (no signpost) on to a lane which leads to the Roman remains of Brecon Y Gaer.

6 **Brecon Y Gaer to Brecon** Return to the lane and turn right, continuing to Cradoc. In the village go right and then immediately left by the telephone kiosk. This road leads to the B4520, passing a path on the right which goes uphill to Pen-y-crug. This Iron Age hill-fort has a circumference of over 550 yds, with five ramparts, three of which are 18 ft high. A walk to the top of the hill is rewarded by fine views of the Usk Valley and Brecon Beacons. On reaching the B4520, turn right and follow the road past the cathedral, which was once a 13th-century priory church, and into Brecon.

NATURE NOTES

The high crags on the north side of Brecon Beacons support many arctic and alpine plants, such as purple saxifrage and roseroot. On the high moors may be seen buzzards and ravens and an occasional peregrine or merlin; dippers and grey wagtails are to be found by the mountain streams.

INFORMATION

Places of interest *Brecon:* Brecknock Museum, weekdays. 24th Regiment Museum, daily (closed Christmas Day). *Dan-yr-Ogof:* Daily, Easter to Nov. *Pen-y-crug:* Iron Age fort, accessible at all times. *Brecon Y Gaer:* Roman remains, accessible at all times. *Mountain Centre:* Daily, except Christmas Day.

Events *Brecon:* Town fairs, May and Nov. Market days: Fri. produce, 1st and 3rd Tues. and last Fri., cattle. Brecknock Agricultural Show, autumn.

Information Brecon Beacons National Park Office, Glamorgan Street, Brecon (Tel. Brecon 2763). Wales Tourist Board, Market car park, Brecon (Tel. Brecon 2485).

Towns with easy access to Brecon:

Abergavenny	20 m.	Llandovery	21 m.
Builth Wells	17 m.	Merthyr Tydfil	19 m.
Hereford	36 m.	Neath	35 m.

The lower slopes of Black Mountain.

BLACK MOUNTAIN
Like the Brecon Beacons, the steep face of Black Mountain faces north-west, where the valleys get little sun and Ice Age glaciers remained longest. During the glacial period, the action of ice upon sandstone and grit gave the mountains of the park their distinctive swooping faces and lakes. The highest point of Black Mountain, Bannau Brycheiniog (2632 ft above sea level) can be seen clearly from the road.

Flitch of Bacon stalactite in Dan-yr-Ogof caves.

DAN-YR-OGOF
Over 7000 ft of these extraordinary caves have been explored since 1912, when two Welsh brothers navigated some of the underground lakes in a coracle. Visitors can walk through over a mile of caverns to see the many strange and beautiful stalagmites and stalactites with fanciful but often apt names such as The Elephant Head, The Nuns, Trojan Waterfall and Flitch of Bacon.

HENRHYD FALLS
The coalfields and tips of industrial Wales are barely 2 miles away from this magnificent waterfall where the River Llech drops 90 ft before joining the River Tawe. To the north and west the countryside is still wild and almost untouched, but from nearby Coelbren can be seen the last of the tips in the Tawe Valley to the south. The gleaming dark rocks behind the falls are a reminder of the proximity of coal faces.

SCALE

0   1   2   3   4   5 MI

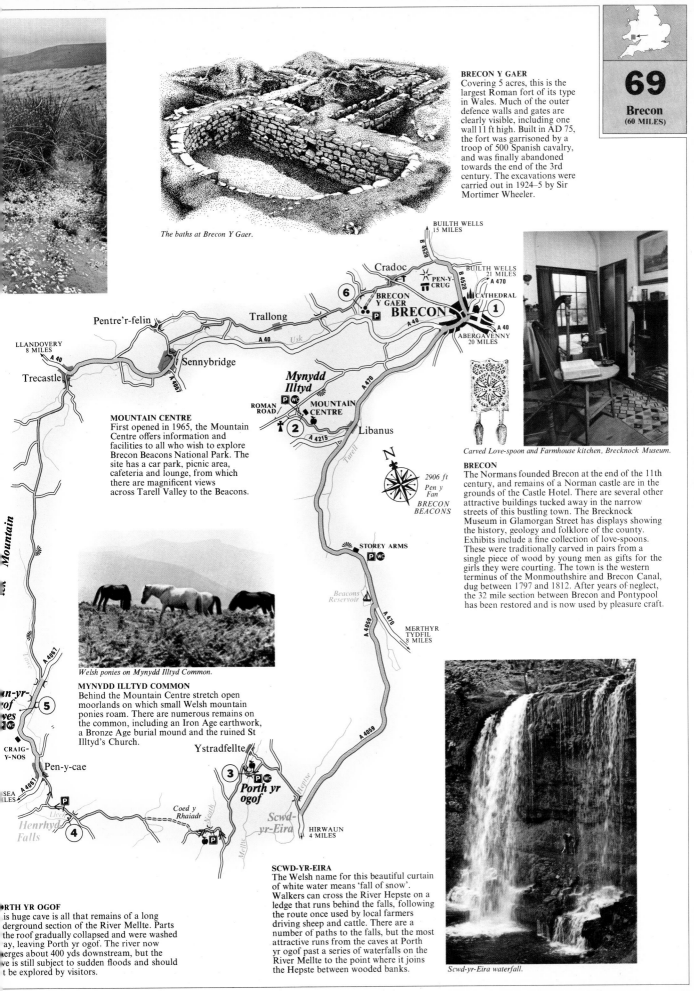

BRECON Y GAER
Covering 5 acres, this is the largest Roman fort of its type in Wales. Much of the outer defence walls and gates are clearly visible, including one wall 11 ft high. Built in AD 75, the fort was garrisoned by a troop of 500 Spanish cavalry, and was finally abandoned towards the end of the 3rd century. The excavations were carried out in 1924–5 by Sir Mortimer Wheeler.

The baths at Brecon Y Gaer.

Carved Love-spoon and Farmhouse kitchen, Brecknock Museum.

BRECON
The Normans founded Brecon at the end of the 11th century, and remains of a Norman castle are in the grounds of the Castle Hotel. There are several other attractive buildings tucked away in the narrow streets of this bustling town. The Brecknock Museum in Glamorgan Street has displays showing the history, geology and folklore of the county. Exhibits include a fine collection of love-spoons. These were traditionally carved in pairs from a single piece of wood by young men as gifts for the girls they were courting. The town is the western terminus of the Monmouthshire and Brecon Canal, dug between 1797 and 1812. After years of neglect, the 32 mile section between Brecon and Pontypool has been restored and is now used by pleasure craft.

MOUNTAIN CENTRE
First opened in 1965, the Mountain Centre offers information and facilities to all who wish to explore Brecon Beacons National Park. The site has a car park, picnic area, cafeteria and lounge, from which there are magnificent views across Tarell Valley to the Beacons.

Welsh ponies on Mynydd Illtyd Common.

MYNYDD ILLTYD COMMON
Behind the Mountain Centre stretch open moorlands on which small Welsh mountain ponies roam. There are numerous remains on the common, including an Iron Age earthwork, a Bronze Age burial mound and the ruined St Illtyd's Church.

ORTH YR OGOF
is huge cave is all that remains of a long derground section of the River Mellte. Parts the roof gradually collapsed and were washed ay, leaving Porth yr ogof. The river now erges about 400 yds downstream, but the ve is still subject to sudden floods and should t be explored by visitors.

SCWD-YR-EIRA
The Welsh name for this beautiful curtain of white water means 'fall of snow'. Walkers can cross the River Hepste on a ledge that runs behind the falls, following the route once used by local farmers driving sheep and cattle. There are a number of paths to the falls, but the most attractive runs from the caves at Porth yr ogof past a series of waterfalls on the River Mellte to the point where it joins the Hepste between wooded banks.

Scwd-yr-Eira waterfall.

189

A conducted tour of old Wales

WELSH FOLK MUSEUM, ST FAGANS

The life and culture of the Welsh nation—its arts and crafts, its language and music—are brought together in the busy atmosphere of the Welsh Folk Museum. The curator, Trefor M. Owen, here takes the visitor round the 100 acre grounds from the Elizabethan grandeur of St Fagans Castle to the cottages, farmhouses and workshops which have been brought to the site from all parts of Wales to show how ordinary people lived and worked in the past. In the workshops weavers and other craftsmen still work to traditional methods.

Warriors and politicians have determined the course of Welsh history, but the real character of this essentially rural country has been moulded by ordinary people. This grassroots aspect of Welsh life is portrayed in the Welsh Folk Museum at St Fagans on the western outskirts of Cardiff, the national capital since 1955.

The 100 acres of gardens and wooded parkland adjoining St Fagans Castle are a setting for buildings from many parts of Wales, but the museum also includes exhibits that range from an early potato-peeling machine to an 18th-century fire engine. All the buildings given to the museum—some because they were threatened by road-widening or other developments—reflect the architectural and social history of Wales. The aim has been to collect structures typical of their period and region rather than more spectacular works by well-known architects.

Plans for such an open-air folk museum along lines pioneered in Scandinavia were discussed by the National Museum of Wales before the Second World War, but it was not until 1946 that an ideal site close to Cardiff became available. The 16th-century St Fagans Castle, with its grounds and gardens, was a gift from the Earl of Plymouth, whose family had owned it since 1730; and when he learnt that more land would be needed to expand the museum, he made 80 acres of adjacent St Fagans Park available at a nominal price.

The castle is now considered as an exhibit in the folk museum, depicting the life associated with such a mansion from the 16th century onwards. Broadly speaking, the time-span covered by the museum starts in 1536, the year of the Act of Union with England, and goes right up to the present day to include wedding dresses worn by members of the staff.

Most of the exhibits have been presented by the people of Wales—some of them a good time ago. Much collecting went on around the turn of the century, when the National Museum of Wales was established by Royal Charter. These gifts have been waiting for an appropriate setting. The agricultural gallery at St Fagans was not opened until 1974, but many of the exhibits had been available since

about 1910. We would never have been able to make the gallery what it is had we been forced to start from scratch in the early 1970s.

The agricultural implements share the museum's main building with the Gallery of Material Culture, where hundreds of items illustrate domestic, social and cultural life in Wales. They come from the homes of peers and peasants alike. Furniture from great houses, such as a table from the home of the Vaughans, of Nannau, Llanfachreth, contrasts with kitchen utensils used for making the oatcakes that once formed an important part of the country-dweller's diet. Rapiers, duelling pistols and an elaborate piano made for a member of the Crawshay family, leading South Wales industrialists in the 19th century, share the gallery with reminders of the 'friendly societies' that provided working people with a measure of security.

Sport has not been forgotten as part of the social scene. Equipment used over the years in games such as bando, quoits and rugby is on show. Bando is a rough-and-tumble game that rivalled rugby in the last century, particularly in Glamorgan. Teams of 20 or 30 players fought it out between goals that were often miles apart.

Exhibits in the medical section of the gallery recall the bizarre career of Dr William Price of Llantrisant, the schizophrenic pioneer of cremation in Britain. In 1884 he cremated the body of his son whom he had named Jesus Christ Price. When he died in 1893, aged 93, tickets were issued for the spectacle of his own

ST FAGANS HOUSE *A castle was first built at St Fagans in Norman times, and remains of its medieval successor are incorporated in the present house. This was built between 1560 and 1580 and is a characteristic Elizabethan mansion of many gables containing high-ceilinged, well-lit rooms. St Fagans passed to the Windsor family in 1730 and remained in their possession until 1947 when their descendant, the Earl of Plymouth, gave it to the National Museum of Wales as a centre for a folk museum. The arms of the Windsor family are displayed on the finely carved overmantel (above) in the main hall of the castle. The hall and first floor parlour (left) are both set out with 17th-century furniture collected from all parts of Wales.*

WELSH NOTES *In the music section, the museum displays examples of the best-known of all Welsh musical instruments, the harp. The Welsh version, or 'triple harp', was a forerunner of the modern pedal harp. In the 'triple harp', semi-tones are struck by fingering through two outer rows.*

FARMHOUSE KITCHEN *The museum likes to give a lived-in look to its old dwellings, as with this kitchen in the 16th-century Cilewent farmhouse, which is equipped with the simple furnishings it had in the 18th century. Cilewent, built from a shaly stone quarried locally—and roofed with the same material—is a long-house, a building in which the family lived at one end and their cattle at the other. The family section, stone-floored, is 1ft higher.*

cremation. The gallery also has a display of love spoons, carved by young men for their sweethearts, with the accent on elaboration. The earliest is dated 1667.

There is a pleasant walk from this part of the museum, in the modern buildings, to St Fagans Castle itself. The westward path descends into a little valley where carp, bream and tench—typical species of the time—swim in 18th-century pools. The castle's furnishings are varied. One of the oldest pieces, an oak chair from Pembrokeshire which stands in the main hall, was made around 1530. The kitchen features several types of spit. One that was fitted to the main fireplace in the 18th century was driven by a 'smoke-jack' worked by hot air rising from the hearth. Another spit was turned by a dog, like one of the butter churns in the Gallery of Material Culture.

The withdrawing-room at the opposite end of the ground floor is hung with Flemish tapestries. In this place of family relaxation there is a 1654 virginal and a triple harp from Powis Castle, Welshpool. This type of harp, with three rows of strings, became popular during the 18th century, when the Eisteddfod—originally a session for licensing bards—was developing into its present-day form.

All the contents of the dining-room on the first floor were given to us by sisters from Pontypool. The gift has enabled us to re-create their family dining-room as it was in the 1860s. There are examples here of the japanned lacquer ware for which Pontypool was famous. Most of the contents of the library also came

from a single source, a house in Abergele, Clwyd, and date from the start of the 19th century. The exceptions include a family woven carpet from Powis Castle and a clock from Cardiff Castle.

In the buildings adjoining the castle there are workshops, where demonstrations are given by a wood-turner using a pole-lathe. Spoons and ladles are made, like dairy equipment, from sycamore—one of the few woods that does not taint foodstuffs. One of the last coopers in Wales can also be seen at work.

Re-erected buildings form the most typical aspect of an open-air museum. The first of these, the woollen factory and the barn, went up at St Fagans in 1951.

The water-powered woollen factory was originally built in 1760 at Esgair Moel, near the village of Llanwrtyd, in Powys. It contains an 1830 spinning jack, probably the only one in working order. One can watch the old but efficient machinery of the mill still operating.

Across the pool from the factory are a boathouse and net house with gaffs, nets and other implements used to catch salmon in the rivers and gather shellfish from inshore waters. Stryt Lydan, near Penley, Clwyd, was the site of the barn. The oldest part dates from about 1550 and the most recent from some 50 years later. Before re-erection in 1951 it had a slate roof but this was replaced by a thatch of wheaten straw, the original covering.

One of the museum's most recently re-erected buildings is also one of the rarest:

Capel Pen-rhiw. The Rev. William Thomas, a great-uncle of Dylan Thomas, the Swansea-born poet, was one of the ministers of this Unitarian chapel from Carmarthenshire. It almost certainly started life as a barn and did not become a place of worship until 1777. It was used as a meeting house when nonconformism became a mass movement in the early 19th century. Many early nonconformist chapels were later Victorianised, but Capel Pen-rhiw was left in its original condition.

At one time it was used as a school, and when it was dismantled a 'Welsh Not' was discovered. This rectangular board (now in the Gallery of Material Culture) is a relic of the days when the Welsh language was actively discouraged. It was hung round the neck of any child who spoke Welsh in class. As the hours went by—and Welsh words slipped out—it passed from pupil to pupil, and the last one to be wearing it at the end of lessons was beaten by the teacher.

The Abernodwydd farmhouse, from Llangadfan, Powys, was one of the westernmost timber-framed buildings of a style that stretched from Wales through the heart of Shakespeare's England to East Anglia and, on the other side of the North Sea, to Germany, southern Sweden, Poland and Russia. It was built in the 16th century and altered in the 17th, when social and living conditions improved. A loft, windows and a chimney were added.

The Cilewent farmhouse, moved from near the Claerwen reservoir in Powys, is a typical

SALMON PUTCHERS *These conical wicker traps were used to catch salmon on Welsh rivers. The fish entered at the wide end and once it had pushed itself down to the narrow end it could not get out.*

WORKING LOOMS *An 18th-century, water-powered woollen factory is still at work in the grounds of the folk museum, and products from the looms are on sale. The factory was originally built at Esgair Moel, near Llanwrtyd, Powys, in 1760 and the interior was altered in the 19th century to cope with increased trade. When it was re-erected at St Fagans in 1951, a special source of water power had to be laid on. Water is electrically pumped from a pool to the top of the bank behind the mill, and from there runs down to turn the millwheel before returning to the pool.*

CRAFTSMAN AT WORK *A cooper—one of the last to practise his craft in Wales—works in a room off the stableyard of St Fagans Castle. His products, such as decorative casks, are on sale. A wood turner has a neighbouring workshop. He makes bowls, ladles and spoons for sale.*

TANNERY WORKSHOP *Knives used for fleshing and unhairing hides hang from the walls of the tannery 'beam-house'. The tannery made leather for boots and harnesses. Unlike the woollen factory, the tannery, although complete in every respect, is not kept working—the process is too smelly.*

MOVING IN *An 18th-century corn-mill from Dyfed waits for its roof after re-erection at St Fagans. As with the other old buildings at the museum, the mill was carefully taken apart and removed piecemeal from its original site and re-assembled at St Fagans by specially trained craftsmen.*

'long-house' of the moorlands of mid-Wales. The farmer and his family lived in one end of the building and livestock occupied the other. The single entrance was made wide enough to admit long-horned cattle.

Hendre'r-ywydd Uchaf is a farmhouse from Llangynhafal in Denbighshire's Vale of Clwyd. It was built at the end of the 15th century. This posed problems. Inventories do not go back that far and there is no way of knowing what the interior would have looked like in the 1490s. However, furniture would have been sparse, and it was decided to include a period type of chest. This would have been used for storing clothes and food and also as a bed and a seat. Hendre'r-ywydd Uchaf was an open-hearth house. There was no chimney and smoke had to find its own way out through the doors and windows.

Craftsmen who dismantle a building try to re-erect it at the museum as quickly as possible, while they retain a mental picture of how it looked on its original site. Drawings and photographs are used, but a good memory helps. This applied strongly in the case of Llainfadyn, the 18th-century cottage from Rhostryfan, Caernarvonshire, built of large and irregularly shaped boulders. It was not enough for the men who re-erected the cottage to place a boulder in the right place on the right

wall. They had to fit it at the proper angle and in correct relationship to its neighbours.

This cottage illustrates the way in which homes had to be built of local materials—in this case bulky boulders that could not conveniently be trimmed or dressed. Some of the bigger ones must have been difficult even to lift and place in position.

An 18th-century corn-mill from Cardiganshire, the museum's most recent acquisition, stands close to Kennixton, a farmhouse from the Gower village of Llangennydd that illustrates the way some houses developed. The farmhouse was built around 1630, but the kitchen was added later and the whole house was altered in the early 18th century.

Among the other re-erected buildings on museum sites are a circular cockpit, a late-18th-century tollhouse from near Aberystwyth, and the last oak-bark tannery in Wales, operated by generations of tanners at Rhayader.

Smaller items should not be overlooked. The gipsy caravan is typical of those which were once common in South Wales. The milestones and iron tollgate from Thomas Telford's London-Holyhead road all paint a picture of Welsh life down the centuries.

An important part of the museum's research and preservation work is carried out by its Department of Oral Traditions and Dialects.

ABERNODWYDD FARMHOUSE *The original timber-framed house was built in the 16th century, and gained its loft, chimney and windows later.*

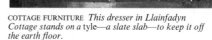

COTTAGE FURNITURE *This dresser in Llainfadyn Cottage stands on a* tyle—*a slate slab—to keep it off the earth floor.*

There is a small display devoted to this work in the entrance to the Gallery of Material Culture. Since 1957 the staff have travelled throughout Wales to interview people about agriculture, crafts, domestic life, folklore, folk-songs and local dialects.

More than 3000 tapes have been recorded and together with films and photographs they provide detailed background information about the Welsh way of life which helps us to make the museum's general exhibits more accurate and 'alive'.

Farmers talk about their methods of cultivation, crop-growing, harvesting, threshing and the rearing of animals. Wheelwrights, blacksmiths, millers and other craftsmen describe the complete processes of their crafts and their early training in them. Housewives have recorded their ideas on preparing and cooking local dishes—and give tips on domestic washing and home crafts like sewing, knitting and quilting.

Folk-music recordings include triple-harp music, folk-songs, ballads and congregational chanting. Discs have been made from tapes for general release, including one of Welsh Christmas carols.

Recordings have preserved examples of the Welsh language in areas where it is falling into disuse, particularly along the border with England. Some of the voices are of the last native speakers of local dialects who have since died. Without the museum, their speech patterns would have been lost to students of the language.

KENNIXTON FARMHOUSE *This house was built at Llangennydd in the Gower peninsula in about 1630 and enlarged over the next 100 years. There are no rafters in the roof—the thatch is supported on straw matting that extends from the ridge to the eaves.*

DENBIGH COCKPIT *Only the walls and roof of this 18th-century cockpit remained when it was removed from the yard of the Hawk and Buckle Inn, Denbigh. Museum craftsmen reconstructed the fighting stage and seating accommodation.*

NEW BEDROOM *A four-poster bed stands in a bedroom added to Kennixton farmhouse in the 18th century. The quilt is made to a traditional Welsh design.*

WHEN TO VISIT ST FAGANS

Apr. 1 to Sept. 30, Mon. to Sat., 10 a.m.–6 p.m., Sun., 2.30–6 p.m.; Oct. 1 to Mar. 31, Mon. to Sat., 10 a.m.–5 p.m., Sun., 2.30–5 p.m. The museum closes Dec. 24–26 and Jan. 1.

HOW TO GET THERE The Welsh Folk Museum at St Fagans Castle is 4 m. west of Cardiff. From the A48 Cardiff-Swansea road, it is signposted north on Green Farm Road. From the A4119 Cardiff-Llantrisant road, it is signposted south on Crofft-y-cenau road. From Cardiff, leave on the A48 signposted to Swansea. After 2 m. turn right, keeping on the A48, and after another ¾ m. turn left on to St Fagans Road, which is signposted to the Folk Museum.

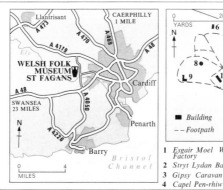

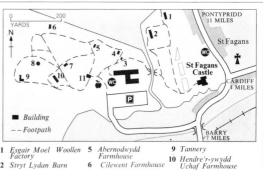

■ *Building*
-- *Footpath*

1 *Esgair Moel Woollen Factory*
2 *Stryt Lydan Barn*
3 *Gipsy Caravan*
4 *Capel Pen-rhiw*
5 *Abernodwydd Farmhouse*
6 *Cilewent Farmhouse*
7 *Llainfadyn Cottage*
8 *Cockpit*
9 *Tannery*
10 *Hendre'r-ywydd Uchaf Farmhouse*
11 *Kennixton Farmhouse*

Through the black and beautiful mountains

Mountains well over 2000 ft high look down on the broad and fertile valleys of the Usk and Wye on a tour that visits some of the least-explored corners of Wales. The impressive ruins of a 12th-century priory are sheltered in a beautiful fold in the Black Mountains. Sheep crop the rough pastures, cattle graze in the valleys, and both are taken to market in such character-filled old towns as Abergavenny and Hay-on-Wye. Ruined castles are reminders of past wars, and a great stone marks the place where the last native Prince of Wales, Llewelyn, was killed in 1282.

(1) Abergavenny to Llanthony Priory Leave the town on the northbound A465 which is signposted to Hereford, and after 2 m. turn left at the by-pass just after the railway bridge. Continue for about 2½ m. and turn left in Llanfihangel Crucorney on to the B4423. Follow this road up the Vale of Ewyas, with a river (Afon Honddu) on the right and the Black Mountains towering to the left. After about 6 m. there is a signpost indicating Llanthony Priory on the right. The priory lies at the end of a short cul-de-sac.

(2) Llanthony Priory to Capel-y-ffin Leaving the priory, turn right and follow the narrow mountain road up the valley to Capel-y-ffin. Some 300 yds west of the hamlet is a 'modern' monastery built in 1870 by the Rev. Joseph Leycester Lyne, an Anglican clergyman who became known as Father Ignatius, self-styled Evangelist Monk of the British Church. Monastic life ceased there soon after his death in 1908, and the building is now in private occupation. There is a car park near by.

(3) Capel-y-ffin to Hay-on-Wye Beyond Capel-y-ffin the road runs over the top of Gospel Pass and reaches a grassy plateau above Hay-on-Wye. From this point there are superb views of the Wye Valley, the highlands of central Wales, the escarpment of the Black Mountains and, in the distance, the peaks of the Brecon Beacons. On a clear day, the view to the north-east includes the tops of the Clee Hills, more than 30 miles away in Salop. On the outskirts of Hay-on-Wye, turn right (the road is signposted to Hereford) and this leads into the centre of the town.

(4) Hay-on-Wye to Builth Wells Leave Hay by turning left on the B4351 just past the Crown Hotel, signposted to Clyro/Hereford/Leominster. Cross the river and in Clyro go straight across the A438 on to a road signposted to Painscastle. Keep left by the church and, after about ¾ m., turn left and bear right at the next junction. At the junction in Painscastle, where there is an early-Norman castle mound to the left, go straight ahead on to the B4594, which is unmarked at this point but signposted to Erwood. About 6 m. from Painscastle, after descending a steep, winding road into the valley of the River Wye, turn right on to the B4567 signposted to Aberedw. Follow this road to the junction with the A481 and turn left. Bear left at the next junction, joining the A483, and turn left again at the roundabout, following the A483 over the River Wye and into Builth Wells.

(5) Builth Wells to Brecon Take the A483 westwards out of Builth Wells. The road is signposted to Llandovery/Llandeilo/Carmarthen. After about 2½ m. the route passes through the village of Cilmery. On the left, on the far side of the village, a huge stone marks the place where the last native Prince of Wales, Llewelyn ap Gruffydd, was trapped in 1282 by a party of Englishmen and killed. His head was cut off and sent to Edward I. The body was buried at Abbey Cwm Mir, north of Llandrindod Wells.

Keep on the A483 and, after about 3½ m., at Garth, turn left on to the B4519 signposted to Upper Chapel. After crossing open moorland, with danger signs indicating artillery ranges on either side of the road, turn right on to the B4520 and follow the signposts for about 9 m. to Brecon.

(6) Brecon to Crickhowell Leave Brecon on the A40 signposted to Abergavenny passing, on the left, the Regimental Museum of the South Wales Borderers; and after 2 m. turn right on to the B4558 signposted to Talybont. The road soon runs parallel with the Monmouthshire and Brecon Canal, on the left. Go through Talybont and in just under 8 m. turn left, crossing the 13-arched 17th-century bridge over the River Usk into Crickhowell.

(7) Crickhowell to Abergavenny Return from Crickhowell over the bridge and turn left on to the A4077 signposted to Gilwern and Abergavenny. The broad valley of the River Usk is on the left of the road, with the Black Mountains, including the 1955 ft Sugar Loaf, rising beyond it. Go through Gilwern and at the T-junction turn left on to the A465. Follow the signposts into Abergavenny.

INFORMATION

Places of interest *Brecon:* Castle ruins not safe to enter. Brecknock Museum, weekdays (except Christmas, Boxing Day and Good Friday). 24th Regiment Museum, daily (except Christmas). *Crickhowell:* Castle grounds, open all year. *Abergavenny:* Museum, Apr. to Sept., weekdays, Sun. afternoons, Nov. to Mar., Mon., Tues., Thur., Fri., Sat. Castle, daily. *Llanthony Priory:* Accessible at all times.

Nature trail *Brecon:* Priory groves. Starts near the junction of A438 and B4520. Leaflet obtainable from the National Park Information Centre, 6 Glamorgan Street, Brecon.

Event *Builth Wells:* Royal Welsh Show, July.

Information Brecon Beacons National Park and Wales Tourist Board Centre, Monk Street, Abergavenny (Tel. Abergavenny 3254).

Towns with easy access to Abergavenny:

Bristol	38 m.	Gloucester	40 m.
Cardiff	31 m.	Merthyr Tydfil	19 m.
Chepstow	25 m.	Newport	19 m.

Sheep-shearing at the Royal Welsh Show.

BUILTH WELLS
This small market town, with the remains of a Norman castle just off its long main street, is a good centre for exploring a lovely stretch of the Wye Valley. There is a weekly sheep market, and the Royal Welsh Show is held near by every July.

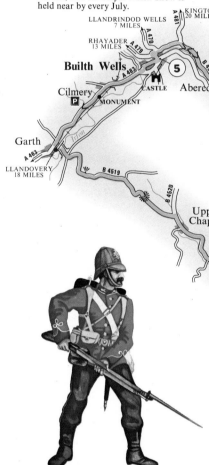

Private soldier, 24th Regiment Foot, 1879.

BRECON
Exhibits at the 24th Regiment Museum (South Wales Borderers) in Brecon span the regiment's history, from its formation in 1689 to post-1945 service against terrorists in Malaya, Borneo and Aden. There are relics of the Battle of Isandhlwana and the Defence of Rorke's Drift during the 1879 Zulu War, when men of the regiment won nine Victoria Crosses in 24 hours. Some of the crosses are on display.

SCALE
0   1   2   3   4   5   MILES

...cky bed of the River Wye, near Hay.

The Capel-y-ffin chapel of ease.

CAPEL-Y-FFIN
The tiny chapel of ease at
Capel-y-ffin has a pulpit dated
1780, wooden benches, a gallery
on the north side and a turret
with one bell. The porch was
added in 1817.

...AY-ON-WYE
...ellow buildings line the narrow streets of this small market town high above the southern bank of the
...ver Wye. Hay is the rather unlikely home of the world's largest second-hand bookshop, which was
...rted in 1963 and has spread into seven different premises, including the old fire station and a disused
...ema. In the centre of the town are the remains of a 12th-century castle, the gate and keep of which
...rm a picturesque part of a Jacobean house now in private hands. The English border is almost
...thin a stone's throw.

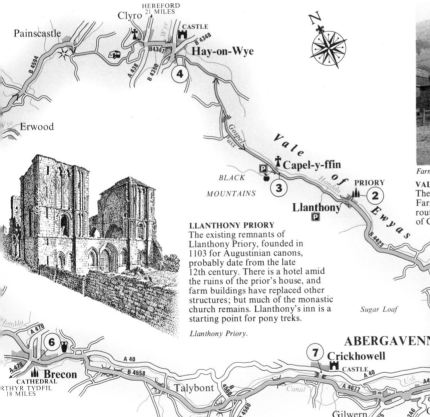

Farmhouse south of Llanthony, Vale of Ewyas.

VALE OF EWYAS
The Vale of Ewyas is in an eastern fold of the Black Mountains.
Farmhouses lie on either side of its river, the Honddu, which the
route parallels most of the way to the source some 3 miles north
of Capel-y-ffin. There is rich birdlife in the area.

LLANTHONY PRIORY
The existing remnants of
Llanthony Priory, founded in
1103 for Augustinian canons,
probably date from the late
12th century. There is a hotel amid
the ruins of the prior's house, and
farm buildings have replaced other
structures; but much of the monastic
church remains. Llanthony's inn is a
starting point for pony treks.

Llanthony Priory.

Rudolf Hess's signature, Abergavenny Museum.
30.5.43

ABERGAVENNY
The town is the eastern gateway to the
Brecon Beacons National Park. An
exhibition in Lower Monk Street illustrates
many aspects of the area. Among items of
local interest in the museum, set amid the
ruins of an 11th-century castle, is the
beer-mat signed by Rudolf Hess, Hitler's
deputy, who flew to Britain to plead for
peace in 1941 and was in a services hospital
at Abergavenny from 1942 to 1945.

...recon and Monmouthshire Canal, near Crickhowell.

CRICKHOWELL
The road to Crickhowell from Brecon crosses
and recrosses the Brecon and Monmouthshire
Canal, which in the 19th century ran to
Newport on the Bristol Channel. A 32 mile
stretch to Pontypool was restored in the 1960s,
mainly for pleasure-craft use, and is
increasingly popular. The attractive little
market town of Crickhowell grew up around a
Norman castle. It was captured and destroyed
by the last great Welsh rebel against the
English, Owain Glyndwr, in 1403. The
remains include the mound and a ruined keep.
The crumbling gate in the town belonged to a
manor house which has disappeared. There are
some good Georgian houses.

The gentle land where Roman legionaries strode

Those who hurry into wilder Wales on fast main roads miss the many charms of the ancient kingdom of Gwent, as Monmouthshire is now renamed. This tour shows what they miss: broad valleys, gentle hills darkened with trees, a great salmon river, magnificent limestone scenery, and views from Gray Hill and Wyndcliffe of the Bristol Channel and the distant slopes of the Cotswolds. Blending into the natural scene are the unique Roman amphitheatre at Caerleon and castles at Chepstow, Raglan and St Briavels.

1 **Chepstow to Caerwent** Leave Chepstow on the A48 signposted to Newport. About 4 m. after the roundabout fork left on to part of a Roman road that cuts through the centre of Caerwent. A map showing the boundaries of the Roman settlement is on the roadside by the church.

2 **Caerwent to Wentwood Reservoir** Turn right at the church in Caerwent, left on to the A48 and, after about ½ m., right to Llanvair-Discoed. In the village, turn right on to the road signposted to Wentwood and carry on uphill past the reservoir to the picnic area and the countryside trail.

3 **Wentwood Reservoir to Caerleon** Keep on the road signposted to Wentwood, but just before reaching a cluster of buildings, turn left on to a narrow, unsignposted road. Follow this downhill, keeping right at the first junction, straight ahead at the next. Keep bearing left until the junction with the A48, then turn right. After about 2¼ m. turn right at the crossroads in Langstone, take the first turning left (about 500 yds) and almost immediately turn left again. About 1½ m. from the bridge over the dual carriageway, turn right for Caerleon. At the bottom of the hill turn right on to the B4236 and cross the river to Caerleon. A lane signposted to Isca Roman Fortress is on the left after about 600 yds.

4 **Caerleon to Usk** Leave the town on the road signposted to Llangybi. Go through Llangybi and on the outskirts of Usk turn right and over a bridge into the little town.

5 **Usk to Raglan** Take the A471 north out of Usk, with the river on the left. The road is signposted to Abergavenny. After about 2 m., where a ruined windmill can be seen on the left, fork right on to the road signposted to Clytha/Bettws Newydd and carry on for about 1¾ m. Go straight over the crossroads in Bettws Newydd. After 1¾ m., at the junction with the A40, turn right to Raglan. Carry on for about 3 m., and at the roundabout in the northern part of the town keep on the A40. After ¼ m. turn left up a lane to Raglan Castle.

6 **Raglan to Monmouth** Returning to the A40 from Raglan Castle, turn left and after 1 m. fork left to join the dual-carriageway section of the road to Monmouth. Just after this road goes through twin tunnels, fork left and take the first right into Monmouth, over the ancient Monnow Bridge with its 13th-century gateway—the only Norman fortified bridge surviving in Britain.

7 **Monmouth to The Kymin** Leave the town on the A466, heading for Chepstow, but immediately after crossing the River Wye keep straight ahead on to the A4136 signposted to Mitcheldean and, after just over ½ m., turn sharp right on to the lane that climbs up the Kymin hill to the Naval Temple.

8 **The Kymin to St Briavels** Return to the A4136, turn right and follow the road to Staunton. In the village turn right, and follow the road round to the left and turn right again on to the road signposted to Newland/Redbrook. After ½ m. take the left fork, and at the next junction turn right and immediately left on to the B4231. Go through Newland and Clearwell, and 1 m. later turn right on to the B4228 for St Briavels.

9 **St Briavels to Tintern** Follow the road right and then left through the village, passing the partly restored remains of the castle, and after about 1½ m. turn right for Brockweir and Tintern. Keep left at the next junction. After crossing the Wye at Brockweir, turn left on the A466 to Tintern.

10 **Tintern to Wyndcliffe** From Tintern, follow the A466 down the valley for about 3 m. and take a sharp right turn signposted to Wyndcliffe. There is a car park 800 yds up this lane.

11 **Wyndcliffe to Chepstow** Return down the lane from Wyndcliffe and turn right on to the A466. Pass Chepstow Racecourse and turn left at the roundabout for Chepstow.

INFORMATION

Places of interest *Caerleon:* Isca Roman fort and amphitheatre, weekdays, Sun. afternoons. Legionary Museum, weekdays, Sun. afternoons. *Raglan:* Castle, May to Sept., daily, Mar. to Apr., Sun. afternoons. *Monmouth:* Castle, daily. Nelson Museum, Apr. to Oct., weekdays, also Sun. afternoons, Easter, Whitsun, July, Aug. *Tintern Abbey:* Weekdays, Sun. afternoons. *The Kymin:* Tower accessible at all times. *Chepstow:* Castle, weekdays, Sun. afternoons.

Nature trails *Tintern Forest Trail:* Starts from car park at old Tintern Saw Mills. Guide from Forestry Commission, Cardiff, and Forest Office. *Gray Hill Countryside Trail:* Starts from the car park, Wentwood Reservoir. Leaflets at start of trail. *Wyndcliffe Nature Trail:* Starts from the car park, leaflets at the start.

Events *Chepstow:* Agricultural show, Sept. *Monmouth:* Regatta, May. Agricultural show, Aug.

Information Wales Tourist Office, High Street, Chepstow (Tel. Chepstow 3772). Wales Tourist Office, Town Centre, Monmouth (Tel. Monmouth 3899).

Towns with easy access to Chepstow:

Bristol	17 m.	Hereford	34 m.
Cardiff	28 m.	Newport	16 m.
Gloucester	28 m.	Ross	25 m.

Raglan Castle.

RAGLAN
Because it was built more as a luxurious fortified manor than a military stronghold, 15th-century Raglan Castle is among Britain's most picturesque ruins. The massive keep was of little use to the Royalists when Parliamentary forces attacked the castle in 1646. It is outside the main structure—and the Parliamentary troops approached from the opposite side and overcame the defenders. Features still to be seen include the banqueting hall, grand staircase, the state apartments in which Charles I stayed, and the keep, called the 'Yellow Tower of Gwent'.

Rood screen, Usk parish church.

USK
Excavations in recent years suggest that the Roman fort of Burrium was sited at Usk even before the legionaries started to build at Isca (Caerleon). But the present fame of the little market town is based on the River Usk—from which it takes its ancient Celtic name—a river that ran through the broad meadowlands long before the Romans came, and now provides anglers with some of the finest salmon fishing in Britain. Usk is an important livestock market as well as a fishing centre. The 12th and 13th-century parish church has an unusually tall, finely carved rood screen.

SCALE

0   1   2   3   4   5 MILES

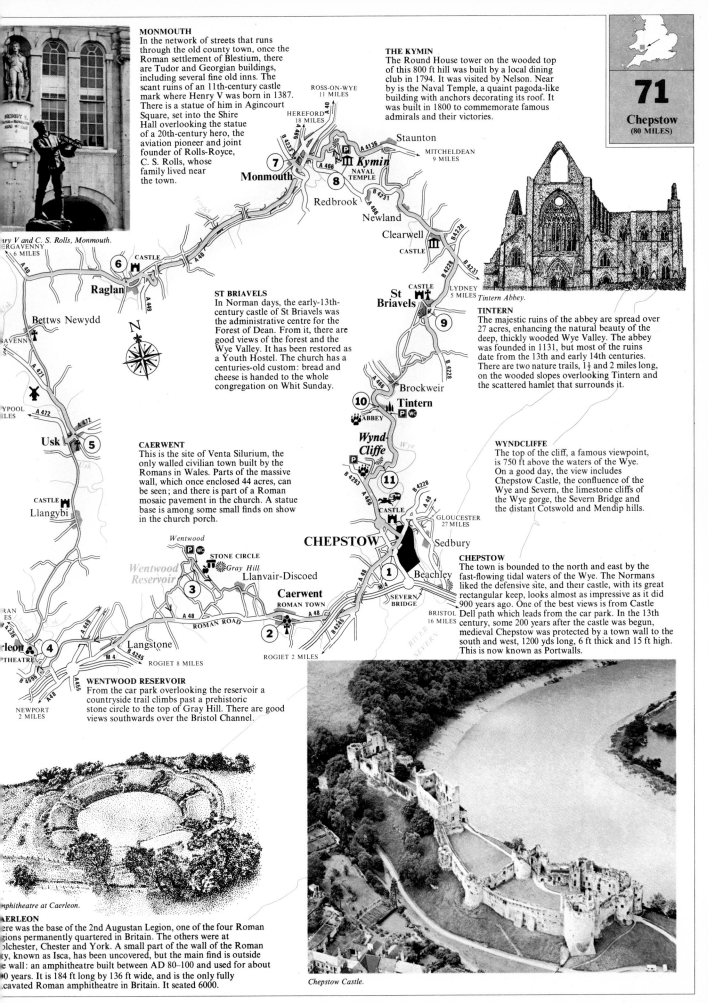

MONMOUTH

In the network of streets that runs through the old county town, once the Roman settlement of Blestium, there are Tudor and Georgian buildings, including several fine old inns. The scant ruins of an 11th-century castle mark where Henry V was born in 1387. There is a statue of him in Agincourt Square, set into the Shire Hall overlooking the statue of a 20th-century hero, the aviation pioneer and joint founder of Rolls-Royce, C. S. Rolls, whose family lived near the town.

Henry V and C. S. Rolls, Monmouth.

THE KYMIN

The Round House tower on the wooded top of this 800 ft hill was built by a local dining club in 1794. It was visited by Nelson. Near by is the Naval Temple, a quaint pagoda-like building with anchors decorating its roof. It was built in 1800 to commemorate famous admirals and their victories.

Tintern Abbey.

ST BRIAVELS

In Norman days, the early-13th-century castle of St Briavels was the administrative centre for the Forest of Dean. From it, there are good views of the forest and the Wye Valley. It has been restored as a Youth Hostel. The church has a centuries-old custom: bread and cheese is handed to the whole congregation on Whit Sunday.

TINTERN

The majestic ruins of the abbey are spread over 27 acres, enhancing the natural beauty of the deep, thickly wooded Wye Valley. The abbey was founded in 1131, but most of the ruins date from the 13th and early 14th centuries. There are two nature trails, 1½ and 2 miles long, on the wooded slopes overlooking Tintern and the scattered hamlet that surrounds it.

CAERWENT

This is the site of Venta Silurium, the only walled civilian town built by the Romans in Wales. Parts of the massive wall, which once enclosed 44 acres, can be seen; and there is part of a Roman mosaic pavement in the church. A statue base is among some small finds on show in the church porch.

WYNDCLIFFE

The top of the cliff, a famous viewpoint, is 750 ft above the waters of the Wye. On a good day, the view includes Chepstow Castle, the confluence of the Wye and Severn, the limestone cliffs of the Wye gorge, the Severn Bridge and the distant Cotswold and Mendip hills.

CHEPSTOW

The town is bounded to the north and east by the fast-flowing tidal waters of the Wye. The Normans liked the defensive site, and their castle, with its great rectangular keep, looks almost as impressive as it did 900 years ago. One of the best views is from Castle Dell path which leads from the car park. In the 13th century, some 200 years after the castle was begun, medieval Chepstow was protected by a town wall to the south and west, 1200 yds long, 6 ft thick and 15 ft high. This is now known as Portwalls.

WENTWOOD RESERVOIR

From the car park overlooking the reservoir a countryside trail climbs past a prehistoric stone circle to the top of Gray Hill. There are good views southwards over the Bristol Channel.

Amphitheatre at Caerleon.

CAERLEON

Here was the base of the 2nd Augustan Legion, one of the four Roman legions permanently quartered in Britain. The others were at Colchester, Chester and York. A small part of the wall of the Roman city, known as Isca, has been uncovered, but the main find is outside the wall: an amphitheatre built between AD 80–100 and used for about 300 years. It is 184 ft long by 136 ft wide, and is the only fully excavated Roman amphitheatre in Britain. It seated 6000.

Chepstow Castle.

A journey through time around ancient Anglesey

A trip around Anglesey is a short tour in a time machine: from silent megalithic burial sites to a bustling Royal Air Force base, and from the seat of 7th-century Welsh princes to the source of power in the 20th century—one of the world's biggest nuclear reactors. And all of it runs through timeless landscapes where hamlets still sleep beside long and unspoilt stretches of sandy beach.

(1) Llangefni to Llangadwaladr Leave the town westwards on the B5109. After ¾ m. turn left on to the B4422 signposted A5. Turn right on to the A5 and immediately left on to the road signposted to Aberffraw. Go through Bethel and straight on where the B4422 swings left, and then left over the railway bridge, signposted Aberffraw, and in to Llangadwaladr.

(2) Llangadwaladr to Aberffraw In the village turn right on to the A4080 and continue to Aberffraw.

(3) Aberffraw to Porth Trecastell Continue on the A4080 through the village and on to Porth Trecastell.

(4) Porth Trecastell to RAF Valley Continue on the A4080 keeping straight on at the next junction signposted A5/Treban crossroads. Cross the railway bridge and turn second left signposted Bryngwran, and after 800 yds a path on the right leads to the Ty Newydd burial chamber. Keep on this road for another 2 m. and turn left at the crossroads. After 1½ m. turn left at the T-junction. Keep on this road past RAF Valley.

(5) RAF Valley to South Stack Turn right at the T-junction beyond the airfield and after 1 m. turn left on to the A5. After ¾ m. turn left on to the B4545 at the traffic lights, across the creek to Holy Island. Follow the road in to Treaddur Bay and turn left, signposted South Stack. Continue for 2½ m. past the sandy bay, with car park and toilets, and turn right to Penrhosfeilw standing stones, which are in a field on the left, 500 yds from the junction. Return to South Stack Lane, turn right and after 1 m. turn left, passing the so-called Irishmen's huts on the right to the South Stack lighthouse car park.

(6) South Stack to Cemlyn Bay Return down the lane and turn left at the T-junction signposted Holyhead. The harbour in Holyhead is protected by the largest breakwater in Britain—9860 ft long—and is a major departure point for Irish ferries. Leave the town on the A5. Immediately before the A5 crosses the Stanley Embankment, turn sharp left for the Penrhos Nature Trail. To continue the route stay on the A5, and at the traffic lights in Valley turn left on to the A5025. After 1¾ m., in Llanynghenedl, turn right on to the B5109 and immediately fork right. After ¾ m. turn left, signposted Llanddeusant. Follow the road for 3¼ m. and just before the village turn left, signposted Llanfaethlu/Llanrhyddlad, passing the ruined Llynon Windmill on the right. Turn right at the T-junction and continue for 2 m. to the A5025. Turn right and after 2 m., where the A5025 swings right, turn left on to the road sign-posted to Cemlyn Bay. After 1½ m. keep right by the telephone kiosk and almost immediately fork left, signposted Traeth Cemlyn, and down the lane to the car park overlooking Cemlyn Bay.

(7) Cemlyn Bay to Wylfa Nuclear Power Station Return to the fork and turn left. At the A5025 turn left and, almost immediately, left again and down to the car park to the right of Wylfa Nuclear Power Station.

(8) Wylfa Nuclear Power Station to Amlwch Return to the A5025, turn left and follow the road past Cemaes Bay and Bull Bay to Amlwch.

(9) Amlwch to Din Lligwy In the village turn left to the old harbour and, after about 1½ m., take the lane left to Llaneilian. Just past Llaneilian turn left, signposted to Porth Eilean, and follow the road to the bay. Return along the road to the junction and go left on the road signposted to Penysarn. At the T-junction in Penysarn turn right and almost immediately left on to the A5025. After 4 m., just past the Pilot Boat Inn, fork left and turn right at the crossroads which leads uphill to Capel Lligwy and Din Lligwy. A few hundred yards further down the lane is the prehistoric Lligwy burial chamber.

(10) Din Lligwy to Llangefni Keep on the lane, straight on at the crossroads rejoining the A5025. Turn right after 1 m. on to the B5110 to return to Llangefni.

NATURE NOTES
The cliffs of South Stack are a blaze of colour in spring and summer with vernal squill, thrift, and kidney vetch. Several species of orchids and other lime-loving plants grow round the many shallow-water lakes and wet fens of Anglesey. The open water is rich in animal life and attracts many birds, including greylag and Canadian geese. Brown and rainbow trout live in Cefni Reservoir near Llangefni.

INFORMATION
Places of interest *Wylfa:* Nuclear power station, open by appointment to organised parties. Observation tower exhibition open to all visitors. *Din Lligwy:* Burial chamber accessible at all times. *South Stack lighthouse:* Open Mon. to Sat., 1 p.m. to sunset, except in fog.

Nature trails *South Stack:* Open Apr. to July, leaflets from South Stack café and Anglesey Tourist Association Centre, Menai Bridge. *Penrhos:* Leaflets from Anglesey Aluminium Ltd, Caegan, Holyhead. *Wylfa:* Leaflets from observation tower.

Information Isle of Anglesey Tourist Association and Wales Tourist Information Centre, Coed Cyrnol, Menai Bridge (Tel. Menai Bridge 712626).

Towns with easy access to Llangefni:

Town	Distance	Town	Distance
Bangor	10 m.	Caernarfon	17 m.
Betws-y-coed	31 m.	Holyhead	17 m.
Caergeiliog	12 m.	Llandudno	30 m.

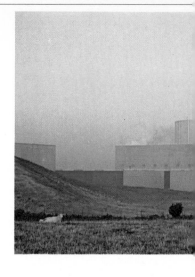

South Stack cliffs.

SOUTH STACK
The 360 steps that lead down the cliffs to the South Stack lighthouse are a favourite haunt for bird watchers and nature lovers. The cliffs provide ideal breeding grounds for thousands of razorbills, herring gulls, puffins, fulmars, guillemots and auks. The pathway winds through a profusion of wild flowers, including wild thyme, stonecrop, sea campion, vernal squill and many others. At the bottom, a narrow suspension bridge reaches across to the 200 ft tall lighthouse. Built in 1809, it is now one of the best-known landmarks in Britain.

RAF VALLEY
Gnats, Hunters, Whirlwind helicopters, Chipmunks and visiting Lightning and Phantom jet fighters operate from this busy RAF base daily. The Gnats and Hunters are the modern pilot's main training craft. The helicopters are kept constantly on standby for air, sea and mountain rescue operations in the area.

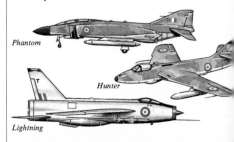

Phantom

Hunter

Lightning

SCALE

0   1   2   3   4   5 MILES

a nuclear power station.

Copper workings, Parys Mountain.

Amlwch old harbour.

AMLWCH

Large copper deposits discovered on nearby Parys Mountain turned Amlwch hamlet into an 18th-century boom town. Today's boating harbour was, in 1828, the world's biggest copper port, and the town an explosive mixture of 5000 people and 30 public houses. Fifty years later the boom broke and Amlwch became a quiet little port. But now there is a new boom under way: a major oil terminal is being developed here.

...FA

...n commissioned, Wylfa had the highest capacity of ...nuclear power plant in the world, producing 1000 ...awatts, enough for a city of 1 million people. It is ... on solid rock and needs 55 million gallons of sea ...r every hour to keep its nuclear core cool. The ...tor is housed inside the main building, which is ...ft high. There is a well-equipped observation tower, ...guided tours are possible through the power ...on by arrangement with the warden.

CEMLYN BAY

The car park which overlooks the sweeping bay and its pebble beaches also provides views of the large National Trust nature reserve. Near by, the privately owned Cemlyn Bird Observatory gives guided tours through the natural habitat of both rare and migratory birds like bitterns, herons, kittiwakes, fulmars and choughs. On the west side of the bay a cliff path leads to the wild headland of Trwyn Cemlyn with views out to sea.

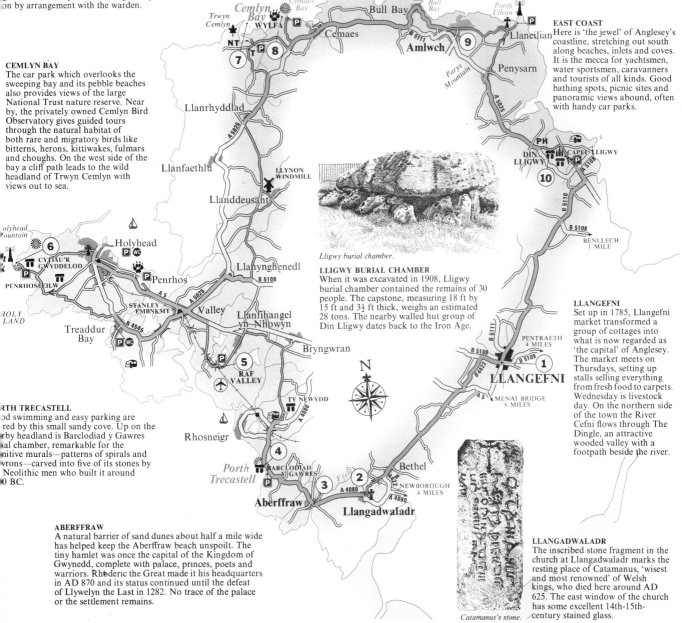

Lligwy burial chamber.

LLIGWY BURIAL CHAMBER

When it was excavated in 1908, Lligwy burial chamber contained the remains of 30 people. The capstone, measuring 18 ft by 15 ft and 3½ ft thick, weighs an estimated 28 tons. The nearby walled hut group of Din Lligwy dates back to the Iron Age.

EAST COAST

Here is 'the jewel' of Anglesey's coastline, stretching out south along beaches, inlets and coves. It is the mecca for yachtsmen, water sportsmen, caravanners and tourists of all kinds. Good bathing spots, picnic sites and panoramic views abound, often with handy car parks.

LLANGEFNI

Set up in 1785, Llangefni market transformed a group of cottages into what is now regarded as 'the capital' of Anglesey. The market meets on Thursdays, setting up stalls selling everything from fresh food to carpets. Wednesday is livestock day. On the northern side of the town the River Cefni flows through The Dingle, an attractive wooded valley with a footpath beside the river.

...RTH TRECASTELL

...od swimming and easy parking are ...red by this small sandy cove. Up on the ...rby headland is Barclodiad y Gawres ...al chamber, remarkable for the ...nitive murals—patterns of spirals and ...vrons—carved into five of its stones by ...Neolithic men who built it around ...0 BC.

ABERFFRAW

A natural barrier of sand dunes about half a mile wide has helped keep the Aberffraw beach unspoilt. The tiny hamlet was once the capital of the Kingdom of Gwynedd, complete with palace, princes, poets and warriors. Rhoderic the Great made it his headquarters in AD 870 and its status continued until the defeat of Llywelyn the Last in 1282. No trace of the palace or the settlement remains.

Catamanus's stone.

LLANGADWALADR

The inscribed stone fragment in the church at Llangadwaladr marks the resting place of Catamanus, 'wisest and most renowned' of Welsh kings, who died here around AD 625. The east window of the church has some excellent 14th-15th-century stained glass.

Bridges to the past, in a land of green pastures

Surging tidal waters are spanned by two masterpieces of 19th-century civil engineering at the start of this route, which takes in sandy beaches, marshes, countryside of green pastures, a Bronze Age burial chamber and one of the best-preserved 13th-century castles in Britain. Few points are more than 500 ft above the sea, but these offer fine seascapes and spectacular views of the coast of North Wales, and the ramparts of Snowdonia.

(1) Menai Bridge to Bryncelli Ddu Leave on the A5 towards Holyhead. After about 1¼ m., at the approach to Llanfairpwllgwyngyll, turn left down the lane to the church. Continue on foot to the water's edge to see the Nelson statue, which has the immortal message 'England Expects . . .' from the Battle of Trafalgar inscribed on its base. Return to the A5, turn left, and in 300 yds on the right is the car park for the Marquis of Anglesey's Column, built in honour of the first marquis, who was Wellington's aide at Waterloo. A flight of 115 steps leads up the inside of the 112 ft high column which stands on a hillock 250 ft above sea level. Continue into Llanfairpwllgwyngyll, turn left on to the A4080 and after 2 m. turn right at the crossroads for a detour to the Bronze Age burial chamber at Bryncelli Ddu, about ½ m. from the road.

(2) Bryncelli Ddu to Llanddwyn Bay Return to the A4080, turn right and follow the road through Brynsiencyn to Newborough. Turn left by the White Lion Hotel for the beach and the track to the car park on the dune-lined shore of Llanddwyn Bay, from which there are walks to Llanddwyn Island, Newborough Warren and Forest.

(3) Llanddwyn Bay to Capel Coch Return to Newborough and turn left on to the A4080. The embankment carrying the A4080 over the River Cefni, known as Malltraeth Cob, was built by the famous Scottish civil engineer Thomas Telford in the mid-19th century as part of a land reclamation scheme. Cross the Cob and after 1 m. bear left to stay on the A4080. After about ½ m., where the road bends right, go straight ahead down the lane which leads to Aberffraw through grass-covered dunes.

From Aberffraw, a short detour can be made to St Cwyfan's Church, on an islet that is completely cut off at high tide. Return to Aberffraw, and cross the A4080 on to the road signposted Gwalchmai. Go through Gwalchmai, turn right on to the A5 and immediately left. After 1¾ m., at the T-junction (no signpost), turn left and bear right along the road signposted Llanerchymedd, then after 200 yds fork right. Turn left at the next T-junction, then right on to the B5111 (no signpost). After 800 yds turn left on to the road signposted Maenaddwyn, and after about 2½ m., at Capel Coch, there is a disused windmill and, 1 m. further on, a standing stone set in a wall on the right.

(4) Capel Coch to Pentraeth Carry on to the village of Maenaddwyn and turn right on to the road signposted to Benllech, and after 2½ m. go straight over the crossroads by the California public house. Take the second road on the right, pass through Llanbedrgoch, and ¾ m. beyond the village, at the junction with the A5025, turn right for Pentraeth.

(5) Pentraeth to Penmon At the crossroads in Pentraeth, turn left on to the B5109, which is here signposted to Beaumaris, and after about 4½ m. there is an archway on the left leading to a courtyard of Jacobean almshouses. Just past the almshouses, turn left for Llanddona. Go through Llanddona, keeping straight ahead by the post office. Soon after the road swings right, turn left and take the narrow, twisting lane downhill to Red Wharf Bay. At the beach, turn right along a rough track, soon rejoining a surfaced lane, and turn left by the telephone kiosk and church. At the T-junction by the radio mast, turn left downhill to Llangoed and turn left at the T-junction in the village. Cross the bridge and go right, on the road signposted to Penmon. At the T-junction turn right and at the next junction keep straight ahead following the Penmon signpost.

(6) Penmon to Black Point Just beyond Penmon, a toll road leads to the rocky coast of Black Point, the easternmost tip of Anglesey, a favourite stretch for anglers.

(7) Black Point to Beaumaris Retrace the route beside the shore, bear first left following the lane to the B5109, and turn left to Beaumaris.

(8) Beaumaris to Menai Bridge Leave Beaumaris on the A545, which hugs the coast, with the Menai Strait on the left, to Menai Bridge.

INFORMATION

Places of interest *Bryncelli Ddu:* Burial chamber, all year, weekdays, Sun. afternoon. *Penmon:* Dovecote, open at all reasonable times. *Beaumaris:* Castle, all year, weekdays, Sun. afternoons.

Nature trails *Hendai Forest Trail:* Starts from Newborough Forest Car Park. Guidebook from Forest Information Centre in car park and from Forestry Commission, Gwydyr Uchaf, Llanrwst. *Newborough Forest Trail:* Guidebook from Forest Warden, Llanrwst (¾ m.).

Craft workshop *Beaumaris:* F. L. J. Products, craftsmen working in local stone, viewing, Easter to Oct., weekdays, Sat. morning, late night Tues., Thurs.; winter by appointment.

Events *Menai Bridge:* Straits Regatta Fortnight, late July to early Aug. Ffair Borth (Annual Fair) Oct. *Beaumaris:* Town Regatta, Aug.

Information Isle of Anglesey Tourist Association and Wales Tourist Information Centre, Coed Cyrnol, Menai Bridge (Tel. Menai Bridge 712626).

Towns with easy access to Menai Bridge:
Betws-y-coed . . . . 24 m.   Holyhead . . . . . . 21 m.
Caernarfon . . . . 11 m.   Llandudno . . . . . . 23 m.

Standing stone near Capel Coch.

CAPEL COCH
There are remains or records of 39 standing stones in Anglesey, all probably erected between 1900 BC and 150 BC, some as grave markers. This fine specimen is now part of a wall 1 mile beyond Capel Coch windmill.

LLANDDWYN BAY
From the parking place near the gently shelving sandy bay, Llanddwyn Island can be reached on foot. Near the lighthouse are the ruins of a 15th-century church, a holy well and a rock that is said to have split to form a chair, from which the dying St Dwynwen could watch what was to be her last sunset 1500 years ago.

The lighthouse, Llanddwyn Island.

SCALE
0   1   2   3   4   5 MI

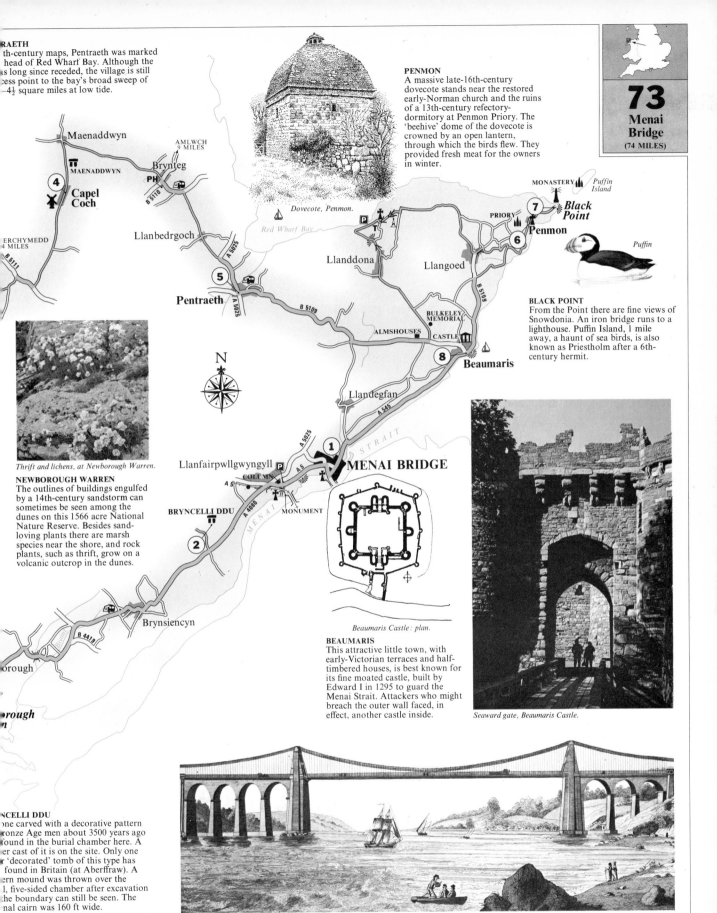

RAETH
th-century maps, Pentraeth was marked
head of Red Wharf Bay. Although the
s long since receded, the village is still
cess point to the bay's broad sweep of
—4½ square miles at low tide.

PENMON
A massive late-16th-century
dovecote stands near the restored
early-Norman church and the ruins
of a 13th-century refectory-
dormitory at Penmon Priory. The
'beehive' dome of the dovecote is
crowned by an open lantern,
through which the birds flew. They
provided fresh meat for the owners
in winter.

Dovecote, Penmon.

BLACK POINT
From the Point there are fine views of
Snowdonia. An iron bridge runs to a
lighthouse. Puffin Island, 1 mile
away, a haunt of sea birds, is also
known as Priestholm after a 6th-
century hermit.

Thrift and lichens, at Newborough Warren.

NEWBOROUGH WARREN
The outlines of buildings engulfed
by a 14th-century sandstorm can
sometimes be seen among the
dunes on this 1566 acre National
Nature Reserve. Besides sand-
loving plants there are marsh
species near the shore, and rock
plants, such as thrift, grow on a
volcanic outcrop in the dunes.

Beaumaris Castle : plan.

BEAUMARIS
This attractive little town, with
early-Victorian terraces and half-
timbered houses, is best known for
its fine moated castle, built by
Edward I in 1295 to guard the
Menai Strait. Attackers who might
breach the outer wall faced, in
effect, another castle inside.

Seaward gate, Beaumaris Castle.

NCELLI DDU
one carved with a decorative pattern
ronze Age men about 3500 years ago
found in the burial chamber here. A
er cast of it is on the site. Only one
r 'decorated' tomb of this type has
found in Britain (at Aberffraw). A
ern mound was thrown over the
l, five-sided chamber after excavation
he boundary can still be seen. The
nal cairn was 160 ft wide.

The Menai Bridge, soon after it was opened.

MENAI BRIDGE
The suspension bridge, from which the lively little town of Menai Bridge takes its name, was designed by Thomas Telford
and opened in 1826 to carry Anglesey's only road to the mainland (now the A5). It was the world's longest bridge at that
time, with a main span of 579 ft, and it continues to cope with modern traffic. Telford's wrought-iron chains were replaced
with steel as late as 1938–40. The best views of the bridge can be enjoyed by parking at the information centre beside the A5,
walking down the path towards the shore and turning left along Belgian Walk, built by Belgian refugees in the First World War.

Lleyn—a land guarded by mountains and the sea

Thrusting out into the Irish Sea like an arm outstretched from the mountainous shoulder of Snowdonia, the Lleyn peninsula is an area of outstanding natural beauty described by a Welsh poet as 'the place where the spirit finds peace'. Bounded by the sea on three sides, and by the mountains to the east, this wild and lovely part of Wales has much of the unblemished atmosphere usually found only on small islands. Matching the grandeur of its surroundings is Caernarfon Castle, standing guard over the Menai Strait. It was in this splendid setting that the Prince of Wales was invested in 1969.

(1) Caernarfon to Pont-y-Cim Leave the town on the A487 signposted Porthmadog. After 3 m. keep right on to the A499, following the signposts to Pwllheli. After about 3½ m., just beyond the turning on the left to Penygroes, fork left into a narrow lane (no signpost) which twists and turns southwards to Pont-y-Cim.

(2) Pont-y-Cim to Tre'r Ceiri Cross the bridge and follow the road round to the left. After 1 m., at the next junction, turn right then first left, signposted Tai'n-Lôn. After 1 m. turn right, then immediately left (no signpost) and up the hill to a T-junction. At the T-junction turn left and after 2½ m. turn right, following the signpost to Pencaenewydd and Pwllheli. After just over ½ m. turn right (no signpost) and follow the road for 3 m. to the A499 at Llanaelhaearn. Turn right, then first left and almost immediately join the B4417, following the signpost for Llithfaen and Pistyll. Just over 1 m. from Llanaelhaearn village a wicket gate on the right leads uphill to Tre'r Ceiri, an Iron Age hill-fort.

(3) Tre'r Ceiri to Porth-y-Nant Continue on the B4417 to Llithfaen and turn right at the crossroads by the village post office. In just under 1 m. fork left to the car park and continue along the steep footpath to the deserted village of Porth-y-Nant.

(4) Porth-y-Nant to Cefnamwlch Return to the Llithfaen crossroads and turn right on to the B4417. Continue through Pistyll to Nefyn and bear right to Morfa Nefyn. Here fork right, following the sign for Porth Dinllaen, to the car park above the beach. From there a track leads past the coastguard station and over the golf course to the hamlet itself. Return to Morfa Nefyn and turn right on to the B4417 through Tudweiliog and after 1½ m., following a left and right twist of the road, turn off to the left. After about ¼ m. the stones of the Cefnamwlch come into sight.

(5) Cefnamwlch to Porth Oer Return to the B4417, turn left and continue to its junction with the B4413. Turn right, following the signpost to Aberdaron. After about ½ m. go right again, following the signpost to Porth Oer. After 2 m. turn right into the car park and take the footpath to Porth Oer.

(6) Porth Oer to Mynydd Mawr Turn right out of the car park, and after 1½ m. right again at the T-junction. Follow the lane for 2 m. and turn right at the next T-junction. After another 2 m. a gate leads to a steep, but well surfaced, track to the top of Mynydd Mawr, a viewpoint 524 ft above the sea.

(7) Mynydd Mawr to Aberdaron Return to the road, and after 1½ m. turn right and downhill into Aberdaron.

(8) Aberdaron to Penarth Fawr Leave the village on the road for Y Rhiw, which is reached after 3½ m. Pass through Y Rhiw, heading downhill towards Porth Neigwl. After 3 m. cross a small bridge and turn right on the road signposted for Abersoch and Pwllheli. A mile further on fork left, uphill, and turn right on to the B4413. Almost immediately, where the road swings right, keep straight on to Rhŷd-y-clafdy, turning right in the village on to the B4415 signposted Pwllheli. At Efailnewydd turn left on to the A497 and almost immediately right for Llannor. Just past the village turn right, and after ½ m. right again. Keep on this road and turn right on to the B4354. Keep straight on through Fourcrosses, and 1½ m. later turn right, and right again at the T-junction ¾ m. further on. Follow the lane to Penarth Fawr Hall, a 15th-century gentleman's mansion.

(9) Penarth Fawr to Llanystumdwy Continue down the lane to the A497. There turn left, and Llanystumdwy is reached after 3½ m. In the village, cross the bridge and turn left. On the right, after 50 yds, is the entrance to the Lloyd George Museum.

(10) Llanystumdwy to Criccieth Return to the A497 and turn left for Criccieth. The castle is on the right, on the outskirts of the town.

(11) Criccieth to Caernarfon Leave Criccieth on the B4411, following the signposts for Caernarfon. After 4 m. turn left on to the A487, and remain on the A487 for 10 m. to the junction with the A499. Turn right, still on the A487, and 2 m. after passing through Bontnewydd, reach Caernarfon.

INFORMATION

Places of interest *Caernarfon:* Castle, weekdays, Sun. afternoons. Segontium Roman fort and museum, weekdays, Sun. afternoons (closed Christmas, Boxing Day and Good Friday). *Penarth Fawr Hall:* Daily. *Criccieth:* Castle, weekdays, Sun. afternoons. *Llanystumdwy:* Lloyd George Museum, Easter week, Spring Bank Hol. to Sept., weekdays.

Craft workshops *Criccieth:* Promenade Car Park, Welsh love-spoons, daily. Slate Centre, Criccieth, sculpture in Welsh slate, open Mon. to Fri. and Sat. mornings.

Information Wales Tourist Office, Slate Quay, Caernarfon (Tel. Caernarfon 2232).

Towns with easy access to Caernarfon:
Bangor	9 m.	Dolgellau	41 m.
Betws-y-coed	24 m.	Llandudno	28 m.

CAERNARFON
The castle and town were founded by Edward 1283 after his armies had conquered the native princes of North Wales. As the centre of English rule, the castle was partly burnt during a Welsh uprising in 1294, and attacked twice by Owain Glyndwr in 1401–4. During the Civil War it changed hands three times. The first Prince of Wales, later Edward II, was born in the castle 1284. In 1911 and 1969 his most recent successors were invested there. Standing where the River Seiont joins the Menai Strait, Caernarfon is close to the site of the Roman garrison town of Segontium, which dates back to AD 78. The remains of the Roman settlement and a museum of relics can be seen on the outskirts of the city. According to legend, the Emperor Maximus met Helen, then the world's most beautiful woman, here in Caernarfon and took her as his bride.

Bronze Age burial place at Cefnamwlch.

CEFNAMWLCH
Also called 'Arthur's Quoit', this Bronze Age burial place was originally covered by a mound of earth which the centuries have gradually eroded. The massive capstone, which is perched on three uprights, is 11 ft long, 8 ft wide and almost 3 ft thick. The communal burial places, known as cromlechs or dolmens, are found all over this area, but this is one of the largest and most complete.

'Whistling Sands' of Porth Oer.

PORTH OER
The pale sand of this sheltered little bay, also known as Whistling Sands Bay, makes a strange singing sound when it is walked on in dry, sunny weather. The Porth Oer sand is very fine, and the individual grains have weathered into uneven shapes. The whistling is caused by the oddly shaped grains rubbing together.

MYNYDD MAWR
Crowned by a coastguard look-out post, this windswept hilltop, 524 ft above the sea, overlooks the westernmost tip of North Wales and the holy island of Bardsey. Separated from the mainland by 2 miles of water, where dangerous currents swirl, Bardsey became a Christian refuge and place of pilgrimage in the 7th century.

SCALE

0   1   2   3   4   5 MILES

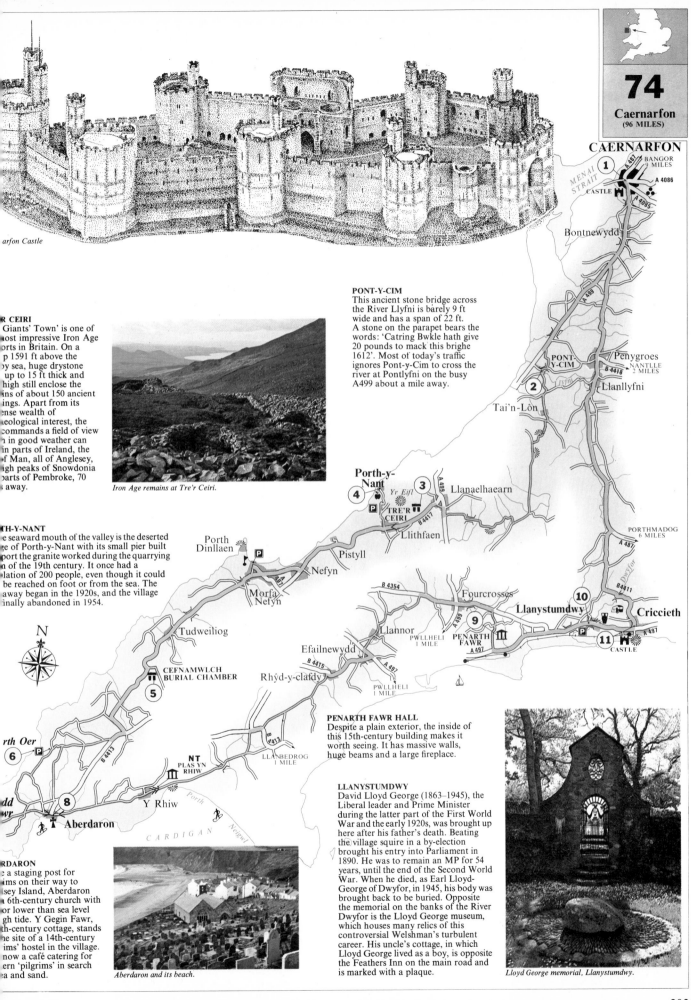

...arfon Castle

CAERNARFON

BANGOR 9 MILES

CASTLE

Bontnewydd

PONT-Y-CIM
This ancient stone bridge across the River Llyfni is barely 9 ft wide and has a span of 22 ft. A stone on the parapet bears the words: 'Catring Bwkle hath give 20 pounds to mack this brighe 1612'. Most of today's traffic ignores Pont-y-Cim to cross the river at Pontlyfni on the busy A499 about a mile away.

Penygroes
NANTLLE 2 MILES
Llanllyfni

PONT-Y-CIM

Tai'n-Lôn

...R CEIRI
...e Giants' Town' is one of ...ost impressive Iron Age ...orts in Britain. On a ...p 1591 ft above the ...y sea, huge drystone ... up to 15 ft thick and ... high still enclose the ...ins of about 150 ancient ...ings. Apart from its ...nse wealth of ...eological interest, the ...commands a field of view ...h in good weather can ...n parts of Ireland, the ...f Man, all of Anglesey, ...gh peaks of Snowdonia ...arts of Pembroke, 70 ...away.

Iron Age remains at Tre'r Ceiri.

Porth-y-Nant

Yr Eifl

TRE'R CEIRI

Llanaelhaearn

PORTHMADOG 6 MILES

...TH-Y-NANT
...e seaward mouth of the valley is the deserted ...e of Porth-y-Nant with its small pier built ...port the granite worked during the quarrying ...n of the 19th century. It once had a ...lation of 200 people, even though it could ... be reached on foot or from the sea. The ...away began in the 1920s, and the village ...inally abandoned in 1954.

Porth Dinllaen

Pistyll

Nefyn

Llithfaen

Morfa Nefyn

Fourcrosses

Llanystumdwy

Criccieth

Tudweiliog

Llannor

PENARTH FAWR

PWLLHELI 1 MILE

CASTLE

Efailnewydd

CEFNAMWLCH BURIAL CHAMBER

Rhŷd-y-clafdy

PWLLHELI 1 MILE

PENARTH FAWR HALL
Despite a plain exterior, the inside of this 15th-century building makes it worth seeing. It has massive walls, huge beams and a large fireplace.

...rth Oer

NT PLAS YN RHIW

LLANBEDROG 1 MILE

Y Rhiw

...dd ...wr

Aberdaron

CARDIGAN

LLANYSTUMDWY
David Lloyd George (1863–1945), the Liberal leader and Prime Minister during the latter part of the First World War and the early 1920s, was brought up here after his father's death. Beating the village squire in a by-election brought his entry into Parliament in 1890. He was to remain an MP for 54 years, until the end of the Second World War. When he died, as Earl Lloyd-George of Dwyfor, in 1945, his body was brought back to be buried. Opposite the memorial on the banks of the River Dwyfor is the Lloyd George museum, which houses many relics of this controversial Welshman's turbulent career. His uncle's cottage, in which Lloyd George lived as a boy, is opposite the Feathers Inn on the main road and is marked with a plaque.

...RDARON
...e a staging post for ...ims on their way to ...sey Island, Aberdaron ...a 6th-century church with ...or lower than sea level ...gh tide. Y Gegin Fawr, ...h-century cottage, stands ...e site of a 14th-century ...ims' hostel in the village. ...now a café catering for ...ern 'pilgrims' in search ...a and sand.

Aberdaron and its beach.

Lloyd George memorial, Llanystumdwy.

Snowdonia—a wilderness only partly tamed by man

From the Menai Strait the land swoops up to the mountains of Snowdonia where there are 14 peaks more than 3000 ft high. Two glacial valleys cut deep into the mountains. They form paths now followed by the main roads which offer views over some of the wildest scenery in Britain. But even in this untamed landscape man has made his mark: a railway climbs the bulk of Snowdon itself and the road over the Nant Ffrancon Pass is a monument to one of the most remarkable engineers of the 19th century, Thomas Telford.

(1) Bangor to Penrhyn Castle Leave the town on the A5, which is signposted to Betws-y-coed. Port Penrhyn, shipping outlet for the slate quarried at Bethesda, can be seen on the left. After 2 m., just before the traffic lights and the junction with the A55, turn left on to a 1½ m. drive through the beautiful woods and parklands surrounding the marble neo-Gothic façade of Penrhyn Castle.

(2) Penrhyn Castle to Bethesda Return along the drive and at the traffic lights bear right to keep on the A5 signposted to Betws-y-coed. The road follows the valley to a small mining village surrounded by dwarf mountains of slate-rubble—Bethesda.

(3) Bethesda to Nant Ffrancon Pass Leave the village, still on the A5. The mountains that towered over Bethesda now crowd in upon the road: Carnedd y Filiast, the 'Cairn of the Greyhound Bitch', rising to 2695 ft; Glyder Fawr and Fach, which are also known as 'The Slippery Ones', reaching 3279 ft and 3262 ft; and the peaks of Carnedd Dafydd (3427 ft) and Carnedd Llywelyn (3485 ft), named after two Welsh patriots who fought Edward I. Between these giants, Telford constructed this road over the Nant Ffrancon Pass.

(4) Nant Ffrancon Pass to Capel Curig The pass climbs to its head at the spectacular Llyn Ogwen. The lake is more than a mile long, but never more than 10 ft deep. The road meets it at Pen-y-benglog bridge where the waters of the lake spill down into the cataracts of Benglog Falls before forming the Ogwen River. A 1½ m. nature trail begins over on the other side of the lake, and skirts it to open out on good views of the great glacial valley of Nant Ffrancon. Behind Ogwen Cottage Mountain School another pathway over rougher ground leads, in ½ m., to Cwm Idwal Nature Reserve. Here also is Llyn Idwal, the haunted lake. It is named after a prince called Idwal who, according to legend, was drowned there by his foster father. From Llyn Ogwen the road runs through wild mountain grandeur to Capel Curig.

(5) Capel Curig to Llanberis In the village, turn right on to the A4086, which is signposted to Caernarvon. The road passes Plas-y-Brenin, the National Mountaineering Residential Centre, and then runs out into Nantygwryd valley. To the left of the valley is the trout stream and beyond it the 2860 ft Moel Siabod. To the right stand The Glyders and up ahead the four-pointed crown of majestic Snowdon. The road climbs towards it and, after 4 m., reaches the Pen-y-Gwryd

Hotel. Here fork right, signposted to Llanberis. The road runs steeply up to Pen-y-Pass. At the crest is Gorphwysfa (resting place) Y.H., a climbing centre and starting point for the ascent of Snowdon by the Pyg Track. Here the road pauses before plunging into the Pass of Llanberis. Halfway down is Pont y Gromlech over the Afon Nant Peris, with its surrealistic group of gigantic boulders. After this, the pass gradually widens, the road skirts Llyn Peris and enters Llanberis, which is an important climbing centre and departure point of the Snowdon Mountain Railway and Llanberis Lake Railway.

(6) Llanberis to Bryn Bras Castle Leave the town, still on the A4086, and at Cwm-y-glo, just after the post office, turn left and follow the steep and narrow lane which leads, in just under 1 m., to Bryn Bras Castle.

(7) Bryn Bras Castle to Llanddeiniolen Keep on this lane and, just past the castle at the crossroads, turn right on to the road which is signposted to Llanberis. Continue straight ahead at the next crossroads, over the A4086, straight on at the next junction and keep ahead at the crossroads on the hill. After ½ m. bear left to Llanddeiniolen.

(8) Llanddeiniolen to Bangor At the crossroads in the village turn right on to the B4366. After 1½ m. go straight ahead at the roundabout, and 3½ m. further on turn left and go through Glasinfryn. After 1½ m. fork right and follow the lane back to Bangor.

INFORMATION

Places of interest *Bangor:* Museum of Welsh Antiquities, weekdays. Bible Garden, daily. *Bryn Bras Castle:* Easter to Oct., daily. *Llanberis Lake Railway:* Mid-Apr. to Oct., daily. *Llanberis:* North Wales Quarrying Museum, Easter to Sept., daily. *Snowdon Mountain Railway:* Apr. to Sept., daily. *Penrhyn Castle:* Apr. to end Oct., daily; Apr., May, Oct., all Sats. and Suns., 2-5 p.m.; June to end Sept., Mon. to Fri., 11 a.m.-5 p.m. *Bethesda:* Slate mines, Apr. to Sept., Mon. to Fri.

Craft workshop Penrhyn Castle Pottery, daily.

Nature trails *Cwm Idwal Nature Reserve Trail:* Starts from A5 behind Ogwen Cottage Mountain School. Guide from The Nature Conservancy, Penrhos Road, Bangor. *The Miners' Track:* Starts from Pen-y-Pass car park near Llanberis. Guidebook from Nature Conservancy, Bangor. *Gwerngof Uchaf:* Starts from A5 near Capel Curig.

Information Wales Tourist Office, Waterloo Complex. Betws-y-coed (Tel. Betws-y-coed 426). Wales Tourist Board/Snowdonia National Park Centre, Llanberis (Tel. Llanberis 765).

Towns with easy access to Bangor:

Betws-y-coed	20 m.	Holyhead	24 m.
Caernarfon	9 m.	Conwy	15 m.

Dolls from Penrhyn Castle collection.

PENRHYN CASTLE
Penrhyn Castle, massive, tall-towered and embattled, looks like one of Edward I's mighty fortresses. In fact, it is the 19th-century home of a family that made a fortune quarrying the slate hereabouts. A collection of dolls from around the world and a 4 ton slate bed are on show.

BANGOR
Nestling in a valley that runs parallel to the Menai Strait, Bangor traces its history to a 6th-century monastic settlement. The monks founded a cathedral which, in the centuries that followed, was repeatedly destroyed and rebuilt. Today's cathedral was last restored in 1880. Laid out beside it is Bishop's Garden, with an enclosure called the Bible Garden. It contains examples of every flower, shrub and tree mentioned in the Bible that can exist in our climate—planted in the order they appear in the text.

Flowers in Bangor Bible Garden.

Slate gravestones at Llanddeiniolen.

LLANDDEINIOLEN
Inside the Llanddeiniolen village church, left of the doorway, hangs a picture of Christ with his eyes closed. But if the eyes are studied closely, they appear to open. The optical illusion was achieved by cleverly blending 14 different colours. The picture is a copy of a work by the Austrian artist, Gabriel Max.

SCALE
0   1   2   3 MILES

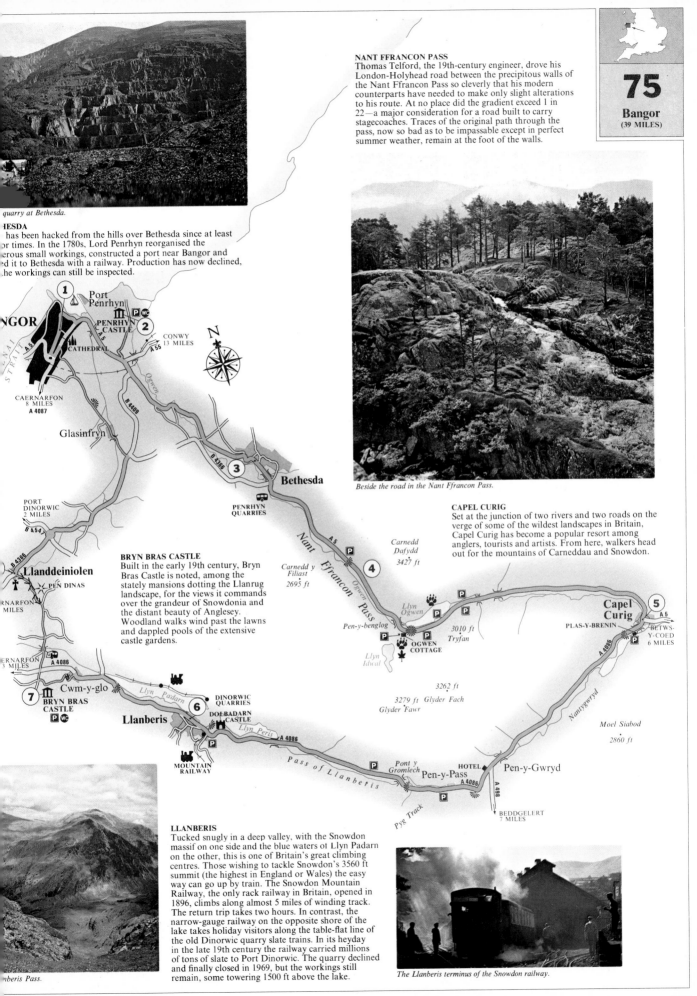

...quarry at Bethesda.

NANT FFRANCON PASS

Thomas Telford, the 19th-century engineer, drove his London-Holyhead road between the precipitous walls of the Nant Ffrancon Pass so cleverly that his modern counterparts have needed to make only slight alterations to his route. At no place did the gradient exceed 1 in 22—a major consideration for a road built to carry stagecoaches. Traces of the original path through the pass, now so bad as to be impassable except in perfect summer weather, remain at the foot of the walls.

...HESDA

...has been hacked from the hills over Bethesda since at least ...or times. In the 1780s, Lord Penrhyn reorganised the ...erous small workings, constructed a port near Bangor and ...d it to Bethesda with a railway. Production has now declined, ...the workings can still be inspected.

Beside the road in the Nant Ffrancon Pass.

CAPEL CURIG

Set at the junction of two rivers and two roads on the verge of some of the wildest landscapes in Britain, Capel Curig has become a popular resort among anglers, tourists and artists. From here, walkers head out for the mountains of Carneddau and Snowdon.

BRYN BRAS CASTLE

Built in the early 19th century, Bryn Bras Castle is noted, among the stately mansions dotting the Llanrug landscape, for the views it commands over the grandeur of Snowdonia and the distant beauty of Anglesey. Woodland walks wind past the lawns and dappled pools of the extensive castle gardens.

LLANBERIS

Tucked snugly in a deep valley, with the Snowdon massif on one side and the blue waters of Llyn Padarn on the other, this is one of Britain's great climbing centres. Those wishing to tackle Snowdon's 3560 ft summit (the highest in England or Wales) the easy way can go up by train. The Snowdon Mountain Railway, the only rack railway in Britain, opened in 1896, climbs along almost 5 miles of winding track. The return trip takes two hours. In contrast, the narrow-gauge railway on the opposite shore of the lake takes holiday visitors along the table-flat line of the old Dinorwic quarry slate trains. In its heyday in the late 19th century the railway carried millions of tons of slate to Port Dinorwic. The quarry declined and finally closed in 1969, but the workings still remain, some towering 1500 ft above the lake.

The Llanberis terminus of the Snowdon railway.

...nberis Pass.

205

A conducted tour of a great garden

BODNANT GARDEN

One of the finest gardens in Britain, Bodnant is laid out on a slope of the Conwy Valley in North Wales. It has been created to blend with the natural lie of the land and with trees that have been there for up to 100 years. How it has been achieved is explained here by Charles Puddle, the head gardener.

THE MAUSOLEUM *Seen through an avenue of flowering tree and shrubs is the tomb that Henry Pochin built for himself and his family about 100 years ago.*

THE PIN MILL *Originally a garden house in Gloucestershire the mill was derelict when the 2nd Lord Aberconway boug it and rebuilt it at Bodnant in 1939.*

The story of Bodnant starts in 1875, the year the estate was bought by Henry Pochin, the present Lord Aberconway's great-grandfather. At that time there was a fairly modest house here, in a small garden surrounded by fields. The gardens now extend over 120 acres and 70 of them have been open to the public since the 2nd Lord Aberconway handed them over to the National Trust in 1949. More than 100,000 people now visit Bodnant every year and I think most of them are pleasantly surprised when they realise how much there is to see.

Mr Pochin was particularly interested in trees. Those he planted are now in their prime and 100 ft high or more. The tallest, down in The Dell, is about 158 ft. The original trees form a marvellous background to the many other features developed in the gardens. For instance, the cedars at either end of the Lily Terrace, planted in 1875, played a very big part when the terraces were built between 1905 and 1918. They were used to frame this formal part of the garden. That is why the terraces are offset in relation to the house and do not run straight down from it.

Mr Pochin's daughter, the 1st Lady Aberconway, loved the garden, but it was her son, the 2nd Lord Aberconway, who created Bodnant as we know it today. He devoted nearly all his spare time to it from about 1897, when he was 18, until his death in 1953. He designed the terraces and developed what had previously been fields. During his lifetime he watched it all grow from almost nothing to near maturity.

That sort of steady growth has really been the making of Bodnant. We believe that if a garden stands still it deteriorates, so we have improved and added over the years. Plants grow and get crowded. What was a nice area 20 or so years ago may not be quite so attractive now, so we are constantly doing our utmost to keep each part looking at its best. We have also added more than 20 acres to the garden in the past five years.

The old mills

The present Lord Aberconway is every bit as interested in the gardens as his father was, and we have made many advances since he succeeded to the title in 1953. My father came here in 1920 and stayed until the end of the Second World War, when I took over. I was brought up here and grew up with the gardens.

Their features include some buildings that considerably enhance the overall appearance. One, the Pin Mill, stands at the southern end of the Canal Terrace and looks out over a long, narrow pool, with lilies at either end, to an

THE OLD MILL *Built in the Classical Italian style of the 18th century, the mill, which used to grind corn, once stood at edge of open fields. Now magnolias, cherries and many other trees grow round it.*

open-air stage fashioned from clipped yew. The Pin Mill was built in the first half of the 18th century as a garden house in the grounds of a Gloucestershire mansion. It was later used for making pins (hence the name) and as a tannery, and was purchased and rebuilt at Bodnant in 1939. It now shelters French tapestries woven in the 16th century. It may seem strange to see them almost out in the open, but the Victoria and Albert Museum in London has assured us that plenty of fresh air will do a lot more good than harm.

Down in The Dell, where there are some very fine rhododendrons from the Himalayas, an old mill stands by a little bridge over the River Hiraethlyn, one of the tributaries of the Conwy. The machinery of this handsome mill, built in 1837, was driven by water power, and the old millpond is now a feature of the gardens. I wonder what the men who worked in the mill would think if they could see the area now? In their day, the whole slope above the mill race was open fields. Since 1898 it has been planted with Douglas fir, cypress, wild cherry and many other trees.

The gardens drop gently down to the

west towards the River Conwy, and there are magnificent views down the terraces, over the trees and across the valley to the mountains of Snowdonia. The terraces are flanked by the informal gardens, but they are so carefully merged you do not notice the transition. We create vistas and viewpoints, making use of the fact that the lowest parts of the gardens are 200 ft below the level of the house. We have done a lot of this kind of alteration during the last few years or so. Things planted 50 years ago had grown out of proportion, so we removed some to create visual surprises.

There is a good example of this as you leave the Canal Terrace on the narrow, tree-lined path behind the Pin Mill. You come to a left turn, walk a few yards—and there, straight ahead, is a lovely view down to the old flour mill and the bridge over the Hiraethlyn.

Another fine viewpoint, with a seat, is high

THE TERRACES *A gap was cut in the trees to open up this view of Snowdonia from one of the upper terraces. The terraces, which replaced a sloping lawn, were built by the 2nd Lord Aberconway to take advantage of the natural landscape.*

CANAL TERRACE *Mirrored in the water of the canal is a Classical seat, a copy of one designed by William Kent, set in the centre of an open-air stage framed by clipped yews in the 18th-century Italian style.*

STRAWBERRY TREE *A specimen of* Arbutus andrachnoides, *a native of the Middle East, flourishes on the Rose Terrace.*

FLOWER BORDER *Crocosmia forms a bac[k] ground for lilies, lamb's tongue and the re[d] Himalayan euphorbia.*

FRAGRANT STEPS *The stonework of this linking staircase between terraces is ideal for growing wistarias; and in June, when this picture was taken, the bloom is at its best. This variety is* Floribunda rosea, *producing fragrant rosy flowers with purple wings.*

HIMALAYAN POPPIES *The blue poppy,* Meconopsis grandis, *is a native of Nepal and Tibet. Its flowers often have a reddish tinge near the centre.*

CHILEAN FIREBUSH *Bodnant has many sp[eci]mens of this tree, seen at its best in May[. It] was introduced in Britain in 1846 by Wil[liam] Lobb, and does well in sun on acid soil.*

BODNANT GARDEN

above The Dell and just beyond the mausoleum (built by Mr Pochin). The slope behind the viewpoint is planted with arbutus, magnolias and embothriums—the aptly named Chilean fire trees—and in the spring has a golden carpet of daffodils.

We believe in planting for effect throughout the year, studying shapes, foliage, the combination of deciduous and evergreen plants and so on. We do not mind if shrubs grow into one another, because that is natural and beautiful. However, we do site particularly spectacular plants in places where you come upon them suddenly. The embothriums are fine examples and are seen at their best in May and June.

My favourite plants and views vary with the time of year. In April, for instance, there are huge numbers of camellias, magnolias and rhododendrons.

The bank behind the Pin Mill is one of the best places for camellias, and there is a fine magnolia with cup-shaped flowers of pure white in the North Garden. Towards the end of May, you are coming into azalea time; and you will also see *Pieris forestii*, notably in the

Round Garden—a very popular shrub with beautiful red growths. The Dell area is particularly fine in late May and June, when there are many shades of green, but the contrasts are a delight at all times. In autumn, the colours are softly spectacular when the reds, browns and oranges of the deciduous plants mingle with the multi-hued evergreens.

The Laburnum Arch near the entrance is a famous sight when it blooms in late May and June. It was one of the first features of the garden to be created, at the turn of the century. The arch is just the right height and the path is slightly curved, so you get the impression of walking through a hanging forest of gold. The arch is in a constant state of renewal, but a few of the original trees are still there.

As the summer goes on there are many thousands of water lilies on the terrace ponds, the herbaceous borders look beautiful and the roses are in bloom. In August the terraces are a splendid sight and the hydrangeas look superb. In autumn, the beauty of foliage mingles with the lovely bark on such trees as the witch hazel, particularly attractive after rain.

Bodnant is renowned for its rhododendrons. The 2nd Lord Aberconway was a member of a syndicate that financed expedi-

tions to areas of the Himalayas that had never before been explored for plants and may never be explored again. Some of our Chinese rhododendrons have grown from seeds sent here between 1900 and 1906 by Dr E. H. Wilson, the first man to introduce large numbers of the shrubs from China. Some of these plants grow to 80 ft. Many visitors are fascinated by the way we have rhododendrons in bloom throughout the year. This is the result of years of hybridisation aimed at extending the blooming period. Other noted collectors followed in the footsteps of Dr Wilson, and between them over the years they introduced thousands of plants that had never been seen before in Europe. Fortunately we were able to establish and grow most of them here at Bodnant.

Bodnant first won fame for blood-red and scarlet rhododendrons, but since then we have gone off on many different tracks. We produce plants that are suitable for smaller gardens, rather than huge specimens. They are no more than 4–6 ft high—some are only 2 ft—but they are very bushy, free-spreading and free-flowering shrubs. Good leaf is important; it is there for 10 or 11 months while the flowers last for only one. Incidentally, every single rhododendron flower-head is picked off by hand after it has died. It is a considerable job, but if it is not done the strength of the plant goes into the production of unwanted seeds.

We have also managed to produce differently shaped flowers; to increase their hardiness and improve their scent. Fragrance is the easiest thing to lose in hybridisation, so we are trying to bring it back as much as possible.

An outstanding feature of Bodnant is its trees, 99 per cent of which come from abroad. There are many from Chile—the monkey-puzzle tree is the best-known—and other parts of South America. We have some from New Zealand and Tasmania and even a few from Australia, including the eucalyptus, but these are liable to be hit in a severe winter. Hundreds of plants were lost in the winter of 1962–3, and later in the 1960s a terrific gale brought down 53 trees in a single night, leaving the gardens like a battlefield. These losses were replaced from propagation stocks and no sign of the damage is visible today. We propagate our own plants on a very large scale, so that we always have new stocks ready to replace trees and shrubs that are damaged by exceptionally severe weather.

Despite our location in North Wales we are considered a 'mild' garden. Between 15 and 20 degrees of winter frost is normal, but we are sheltered from the east wind and helped by the moderating influence of the Gulf Stream—the open sea is only about 3 miles away. Winds from the north-west can be a nuisance, and those from the south tend to funnel down the Conwy Valley.

We have a very good staff to cope with our problems. There are 25 altogether and many have worked at Bodnant since they left school—some more than 40 years ago. The estate is self-sufficient, with its own carpenters, electricians and other skilled workers. Even the water for the gardens comes from a specially built reservoir higher up the hill.

Planning for the future

We are now facing the fact that many of the trees planted here at the turn of the century have reached maturity and will now be declining; a few have already started to do so. The life of a tree outside its native land is relatively short; generally, the faster it grows the sooner it will die. So we must always be thinking four or five years in advance. We have to bear in mind also that what may seem a good idea for a summer display is unlikely to be as pleasing in the winter.

Lord Aberconway and I have a close working relationship. Alterations and additions to the gardens are planned a long time ahead, but nothing is ever put down on paper. We grow plants only if they have garden value and not just for the sake of having a fine specimen of this or that. We occasionally make mistakes and have to remove plants, but not very often. If you are designing a formal garden, such as those created by Capability Brown, you have to get everything down on paper. We specialise in the natural and informal. We 'paint' the garden just like an artist paints a picture. That is the closest parallel I have been able to think of, and it is what we try to do at Bodnant.

How many plants do we have? I must admit we really have no idea. I once tried to count our magnolias and decided there were 720 mature specimens. But that was ten years ago, and I did not include anything under about 12 ft high, so there are probably many more.

LABURNUM ARCH *This is a fine sight in early summer, when the clusters of golden flowers, drooping from hidden frames, form a tunnel fringed by flowering shrubs. The arch is just a few yards from the public entrance to the gardens. Visitors with children should take care when the laburnums drop their seed pods later in the season; they are highly poisonous.*

WHEN TO VISIT BODNANT

Apr. 1 or Easter Sat. (whichever is the earlier) to Oct. 31, Mon. to Thur., Sat. and some Sun., 1.30–4.45 p.m.

HOW TO GET THERE The entrance is ½ m. along the Eglwysbach road off the A470/A496, halfway (7 m.) between Llandudno and Llanrwst. From Colwyn Bay, leave on the A55 and take the Llanrwst road after 3 m.

1 Croquet Terrace   4 Mausoleum
2 Lily Terrace   5 Laburnum Arch
3 Pin Mill   6 Canal Terrace

LLANDUDNO 7 MILES

North Garden

HALL Entrance

Front Lawn

East Garden

Rock Garden

The Old Mill

Round Garden

BETWS-Y-COED 11 MILES

River Hiraethlyn

The Dell

Yew Garden

Bodnant Old Park

☐ National Trust
— Wall
- - Selected Footpath

0 100
YARDS

Mill Pond

Great Ormes Head

0 2
MILES
N

Llandudno

A 546

A 546

Colwyn Bay

A 55

B 5383

Llandudno Junction

RHYL 10 MILES

Conwy

BANGOR 12 MILES

A 55

B 5381

B 5016

BODNANT GARDEN

A 470

B 5113

BETWS-Y-COED 13 MILES

N

The mountains whose wealth is water

Gold and copper have been mined in North Wales, but the true and enduring wealth of the mountains is plain and beautiful to see—water. Of the three big lakes on the route, two were made by man. From Llyn Trawsfynydd, whose water cools the great Trawsfynydd nuclear power station, the route passes one of Britain's most famous castles, stark on a crag at Harlech. From there it goes to a 'cathedral' in the heart of a mountain, once seen only by the slate miners who carved it, and on to the beautiful Mawddach Estuary. Here steep wooded bluffs dip into the water with mountains towering above.

(1) Dolgellau to Bala From the town centre leave on the A470 signposted to Barmouth, but immediately after crossing the bridge over the River Wnion turn right at the T-junction on to the A494, which is signposted to Bala. Follow the Wnion Valley for about 13 m. to Llanuwchllyn. Turn right at the village on to the B4403. After about ½ m. the terminus of the Bala Lake Railway is on the left. This narrow-gauge line, opened in 1972, gives trips along part of the lake shore and back, a round journey of about 30 minutes. To the left of the road there are now sweeping views of Bala Lake. Llyn Tegid, as it is known in Welsh, is the biggest natural lake in Wales: just over 3½ m. long and nearly 150 ft deep in places. At the end of the B4403, turn left for Bala.

(2) Bala to Llyn Celyn Leave Bala on the A4212 signposted to Trawsfynydd. The road climbs gently to the shores of another lake—the man-made Tryweryn holding reservoir, also known as Llyn Celyn.

(3) Llyn Celyn to Trawsfynydd Stay on the A4212. The road runs round the western end of the reservoir, then roughly follows the course of the lake's feeder river, the Tryweryn, to its source at Llyn Tryweryn. It then follows the valley made by the Prysor, feeder river of the next big man-made lake on the route, Llyn Trawsfynydd. At the T-junction with the A470 turn left, over a bridge, then immediately right into Trawsfynydd.

(4) Trawsfynydd to Maentwrog Rejoin the A470, turning left. Follow the road northwards, with the lake on the left, passing the entrance to Trawsfynydd Nuclear Power Station. Bear left on to the A487 down into the beautiful Vale of Ffestiniog. The narrow-gauge track of the Festiniog Railway runs along the slopes on the further side of the valley. At the foot of the hill turn left on to the A496 into Maentwrog.

(5) Maentwrog to Harlech Leave Maentwrog on the A496 westwards. The road runs through trees, then skirts along steep slopes above the tidal waters of the Dwyryd Estuary. About 1 m. beyond the hamlet of Talsarnau, the A496 swings right for Harlech. The road crosses the billiard-table flatness of Morfa Harlech, and there are splendid views of the castle on its rocky crag. Immediately after going over the level crossing at the foot of the crag, turn left on to the winding 1-in-4 hill that climbs up to the centre of Harlech.

(6) Harlech to Llandanwg Leave the town on the A496 signposted for Barmouth. Just over 2 m. beyond Harlech, the first turning on the right leads down to the sandy, boulder-strewn beach at Llandanwg.

(7) Llandanwg to Llanfair From Llandanwg, return to the main road and turn right into Llanfair. The entrance to the slate-mine caverns is at the further end of the village. In the church is a memorial window to Ellis Wyn, the poet, born at Llanfair in 1671.

(8) Llanfair to Shell Island Continue down the A496 for 1½ m. to Llanbedr. A right turn in the village leads down to Mochras, the 'official' name for the long spit of land known as Shell Island.

(9) Shell Island to Barmouth Return to Llanbedr and turn right, heading southwards on the A496 to Barmouth with its long, sandy beach.

(10) Barmouth to Bontddu Beyond Barmouth, keep on the A496 as it follows the northern bank of the Mawddach Estuary, to Bontddu. A track on the left leads to the old gold-mine workings of St David, which may be viewed from the path.

(11) Bontddu to Dolgellau Continue on the A496 to Llanelltyd. Turn right in the village and cross the bridge over the River Mawddach. A short detour up a farm road on the left, just past the bridge, leads to the sparse but romantic ruins of Cymer Abbey, founded by supporters of Llewelyn the Great in 1198. Return to the main road and turn left to return to Dolgellau.

INFORMATION

Places of interest *Bala Lake Railway:* Easter to Oct., daily. *Cymer Abbey:* Daily. *Harlech Castle:* Apr. to Sept., daily, Oct. to Mar., afternoons. *Llanfair Quarry:* Easter to Oct., daily. *Trawsfynydd Nuclear Power Station:* Visits by appointment only.

Craft workshops *Harlech:* Harlech Pottery, weekdays. *Bala:* The Seren Centre, stoneware, jewellery, hand-woven rugs, open daily (except Sun. in winter).

Nature trails *The Precipice Walk:* Starting point near Cymer Abbey, signposted. *Llanbedr:* Cefn Isaf Farm Trail, working of traditional Welsh hill farm, guided by signs.

Events *Bala:* Eisteddfod Talybont, Easter. Carnival week, July. *Dolgellau:* Spring fair, Apr. *Barmouth:* Carnival week, May. *Harlech:* Horticultural show, sheepdog trials, Aug.

Information Snowdonia National Park and Wales Tourist Offices: The Bridge, Dolgellau (Tel. Dolgellau 42288). High Street, Bala (Tel. Bala 367). High St., Harlech (Tel. Harlech 658).

Towns with easy access to Dolgellau:

Aberystwyth	....34 m.	Llangollen	......40 m.
Betws-y-coed	....34 m.	Welshpool	......38 m.

Harlech Castle.

HARLECH
The well-preserved castle that towers over this pleasant little town was one of the great string of fortresses built by Edward I after his conquest of North Wales in 1283. It then had a watergate and the sea lapped the foot of the crag on which the massive walls and towers still stand. At the start of the 15th century the castle was captured by the Welsh and became the headquarters of Owain Glyndwr, leader of the last great campaign for independence. In 1647 it was the last Royalist castle to surrender to Cromwell. Morfa Harlech, the plain at the foot of the cliff, was largely formed by 19th-century land reclamation.

LLANDANWG
Nearly buried in the dunes that back the sandy but boulder-strewn beach is a small, disused church, parts of which date from the 6th century. On a clear day, there are good views of the entire length of the Lleyn peninsula from the beach.

LLANFAIR
Chwarel Hen Llanfair—Old Llanfair Quarry—is actually a mine where slate was worked from 1874 to 1906. The miners hacked and blasted huge, cathedral-like caverns from the heart of the hill. These are lit by shafts of light from openings high above. After being derelict for more than 50 years, the workings were opened to the public in 1973. The small church of St Mary near by has a well-preserved 15th-century roof. The churchyard has many slate tombstones.

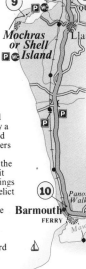

On the beach at Shell Island.

SHELL ISLAND
The 'island', reached by a rough causeway that skirts tidal sands, was formed in the 19th century when the River Artro was diverted in a land-reclamation scheme. The old channel silted up. Over 200 different kinds of shells are found on the beach.

SCALE

0   1   2   3   4   5 MILES

TRAWSFYNYDD

In the centre of the hillside village is a statue of the Welsh shepherd poet, Hedd Wyn, gaitered and with rolled shirt-sleeves. He wrote much about the mountains, streams, marshes and wild creatures of this stark countryside, but not of the tranquil lake that now lies below. He was killed in Flanders in the First World War, and 3 mile long Llyn Trawsfynydd was not created until 1930—to supply water to the Maentwrog hydro-electric power scheme. Today it also provides 35 million gallons of cooling water an hour to the futuristic nuclear power station at its head, completed in 1964. The recirculating water has raised the lake's temperature slightly, improving the fishing. Boats can be hired, and there is also pony trekking from the village.

MAENTWROG

The pretty village, all of local stone, was built below a wooded cliff early in the 19th century by a local pioneer of the slate industry. There are some fine old yew trees in the churchyard and a great stone (maen) from which the village took its name. It is said to have been placed there by the 6th-century Celtic St Twrog. Another legend says it was hurled there by a giant.

Trawsfynydd nuclear power station.

LLYN CELYN

This is a Liverpool Corporation reservoir, landscaped to harmonise with the scene; 16,400 million gallons of water cover the site of the village of Capel Celyn. A small stone chapel, seatless and floored with slate, is a memorial to the drowned valley.

BARMOUTH

Barmouth overlooks a long, sandy beach that has made it one of the most popular summer resorts in Wales. There are fine views of Cader Idris from the little harbour, where the sturdy hulls of lobster boats contrast with the sleek shapes of colourful private craft. Ty Gwyn, a house near the harbour, is said to have been built in the 15th century for Henry Tudor, later to become Henry VII. The cliffs behind the town were the first property acquired, in 1895, by the newly formed National Trust. To the east of Barmouth, the Panorama Walk above the Mawddach Estuary offers superb views.

Barmouth harbour.

BALA

The little town, which centres on a wide main street lined with Victorian-style buildings, was a centre of the Welsh Methodist revival in the 18th and 19th centuries, when great revivalist meetings were held on The Green. This open space now features a Bardic stone circle, erected in 1967 when the Royal National Eisteddfod was held in the town. Nearby Bala Lake, which can be viewed from a tiny promenade, is the main attraction for visitors, offering good sailing and fishing. It is the only known home of the gwyniad, a kind of white-scaled salmon, which lives in its depths and is rarely caught. Specimens have been cast up by storms.

Gwyniad

BONTDDU

A short walk up the path beside the racing, tree-lined river—the Cym-llechen—leads to the remains of the St David's mine, where gold was extracted in the 19th and early 20th centuries. It is the best-known of a number of small mines around Dolgellau and at one stage produced £60,000 worth of gold in a year. Gold from the district has been used in royal wedding rings and in the regalia of the Prince of Wales. Copper has also been mined in this area; and in the Rhinog range to the north, shale deposits of manganese, used in steel-making, have been mined in recent years.

Cader Idris, from Dolgellau.

DOLGELLAU

From this grey, granite-and-slate market town and tourist centre, gentle foothills rise to the rugged precipices of Cader Idris, the 2927 ft mountain whose fame in Wales is second only to that of Snowdon. There are two walks to the top from Dolgellau: the Foxes' Path (4½ miles) and the Pony Track (6 miles). From the north side of the town's graceful, seven-arched bridge, built in 1638, a gentler walk climbs to the golf course near Hengwrt. There is a good view from here of the long granite ridge and the five peaks that make up Cader Idris.

Mountains which a barefoot girl crossed to make history

Wave upon wave of mountains make the landscape from Snowdonia to the Plynlimon range a tumultuous green sea. The small and scattered population is outnumbered by the sheep which graze beneath the watchful eyes of birds of prey. The valleys contain impressive modern works of man—great dams and reservoirs to tame the mountain streams and harness power for faraway towns. To the west, the mountains sweep down to the sandy crescent of Cardigan Bay with its tall cliffs and pounding waves.

(1) Machynlleth to Nant-y-môch Reservoir Leave the town, heading south along the A487 towards Aberystwyth. After 10½ m. turn left by the White Lion in Talybont and almost immediately left again by the Black Lion, then bear right on to a mountain road signposted to Nant-y-môch and Ponterwyd. Carry on between steep slopes, through a forest, and finally alongside the huge Nant-y-môch lake before reaching the Nant-y-môch dam.

(2) Nant-y-môch Reservoir to Llanidloes Past the dam, carry on for another 4 m. to Ponterwyd and turn left on to the A44. Beyond Ponterwyd the road climbs the southern flank of Plynlimon (shortest footpath to the top starts on this road from a car park at Eisteddfa Gurig). Continue for 8 m. to Llangurig, following the infant Wye part of the way. In Llangurig turn left and follow the A470 for 5 m. into Llanidloes.

(3) Llanidloes to Llyn Clywedog Go through the centre of the town and turn left just past the old market hall on to the B4518 signposted to Llyn Clywedog and Staylittle. After 2 m. fork left and 1 m. later reach the car park, café and viewpoint above the dam at Llyn Clywedog. The 237 ft high dam is the tallest in Britain. To enjoy Llyn Clywedog on foot, take the 2½ m. scenic trail by turning right from the parking area on to the narrow road edging the lake. The trail leaves the road between the first and second cattle grids. Another track, a short way back on the route, gives access to an old lead mine at the foot of the dam.

(4) Llyn Clywedog to Castell y Bere Leave the car park and turn right on the lakeside road. Turn right at the T-junction at the end of the lake, following the signposts for Llanbrynmair and Llanidloes. At the B4518, turn left and remain on this road to Llanbrynmair, 15 m. from the dam. In Llanbrynmair, turn left on to the A470 (formerly A489, which may still be seen on some signposts) and almost immediately right again, on to a narrow road up the valley. After 7 m., at the junction with the A458, turn left and after another 2½ m., at Mallwyd, turn right on to the A470, following the signposts to Dolgellau. After 8 m., by the Cross Foxes Hotel, turn left on to the A487. After 4 m., where the A487 curves left, keep straight on, joining the B4405 signposted Tywyn (Towyn). After 4 m., having passed Tal-y-llyn lake, fork right on the road signposted to Llanegryn. After 1¼ m. keep right at the junction, and 1 m. further on turn right on the road signposted Tyn-y-ddol and Castell y Bere. The remains of the castle, last stronghold of the Welsh princes, are on the left. Beyond the castle is St Michael's 12th-century church,

where the window nearest the vestry door allowed lepers, who were banned from mixing with the congregation, to follow the services. About 1 m. further on, where the road ends, is the monument to Mary Jones, the girl who crossed the mountains barefoot to obtain a Bible.

(5) Castell y Bere to Tywyn Return down the valley, beneath 1000 ft crags, ignoring turns, and follow the signs for 6 m. to Bryncrug. At the T-junction in Bryncrug, turn right and immediately left over the bridge and on to the A493, towards Tywyn (Towyn), which is reached 2½ m. later.

(6) Tywyn to Aberdyfi (Aberdovey) In Tywyn, ignore the first sign to Aberdyfi and remain on the A493 to pass the terminus of the Talyllyn Railway at Wharf Station. Now one of the best known of enthusiasts' lines, the little narrow-gauge track, with its antique stock, goes back up the valley for 6½ m. to Abergynolwyn below Tal-y-llyn lake, through splendid rocky country. Aberdyfi is 4 m. beyond the station on the A493.

(7) Aberdyfi to Machynlleth Pass through Aberdyfi and follow the A493 as it skirts the northern shore of the sandy estuary of the River Dyfi, before turning inland to reach Machynlleth after a total of about 10 m.

NATURE NOTES

Between Talybont and the sea lies Borth Bog, one of the largest raised bogs in Wales. Several varieties of heather and sphagnum grow here. Buzzards, merlin and many woodland birds can be seen along the banks of the River Dyfi.

INFORMATION

Places of interest *Aberdyfi:* National Park Centre, Easter to Oct., daily. Nautical Museum, daily, mornings. *Castell y Bere:* Daily. *Llanidloes:* Old Market Hall, Easter week, Spring Bank Hol. to Sept., weekdays. *Machynlleth:* Owain Glyndwr Senate House, The Plas, Mon. to Fri.

Craft workshop *Llangurig:* Wye Garage, woodcraft, Welsh love-spoons, pepper-mills, stools, daily, except Sun. in winter.

Nature trail *Llyn Clywedog:* Leaflets at start in car park. Old lead mine viewed from alternate track. Lakeside walk.

Events *Machynlleth:* Town fairs, May and Sept. Sheep-dog trials, Aug. *Llanidloes:* Pleasure and hiring fair, Apr. Town fair, July. *Llangurig:* Agricultural show, Aug. *Tywyn:* Merioneth and District County Show, Aug.

Information Wales Tourist Offices: Owain Glyndwr Centre, Machynlleth (Tel. Machynlleth 2401), and Llanidloes (Tel. Llanidloes 2605).

Towns with easy access to Machynlleth:

Aberystwyth	18 m.	Barmouth	26 m.
Bala	26 m.	Dolgellau	16 m.

Dolgoch Falls, near the Talyllyn line.

TYWYN

Beside the sea below the Cader Idris hills, Tywyn hou the oldest known example of written Welsh—St Cadfan's Stone, in the parish church. The inscription is believed to date from about the 7th century, but so far no satisfactory translation has ever been made. T picturesque narrow-gauge Talyllyn Railway from Tywyn to Abergynolwyn was built in 1865 to bring slate down from the mountain quarries. Later it provided a passenger service. Although it was one of world's first narrow-gauge lines to use steam power i place of horses, the railway never carried heavy traffi so that many of the original locomotives and wagons did not wear out and are still in existence. Now that railway is operated by a preservation society, more rolling stock has been acquired, and a narrow-gauge museum opened at the Tywyn terminus. Among the displays is the last wood-sided slate wagon.

MACHYNLLETH

This old market town is on a site inhabited since the early Iron Age. Its position in the enchanting Dyfi Valley, a great natural feature of mid-Wales, makes it an agreeable little town. It was made, for a short while, capital of Wales by Owain Glyndwr, the Welsh patriot who was proclaimed king there in 1404. The Senate House, a 16th-century stone building, is said to stand on the site of Glyndwr's first assembly and is part of the Owain Glyndwr Institute. Its position at the junction of several roads gave it importance as a sheep-trading centre and explains the many old inns.

Aberdyfi harbou

SCALE

| 0 | 1 | 2 | 3 | 4 | 5 MILES |

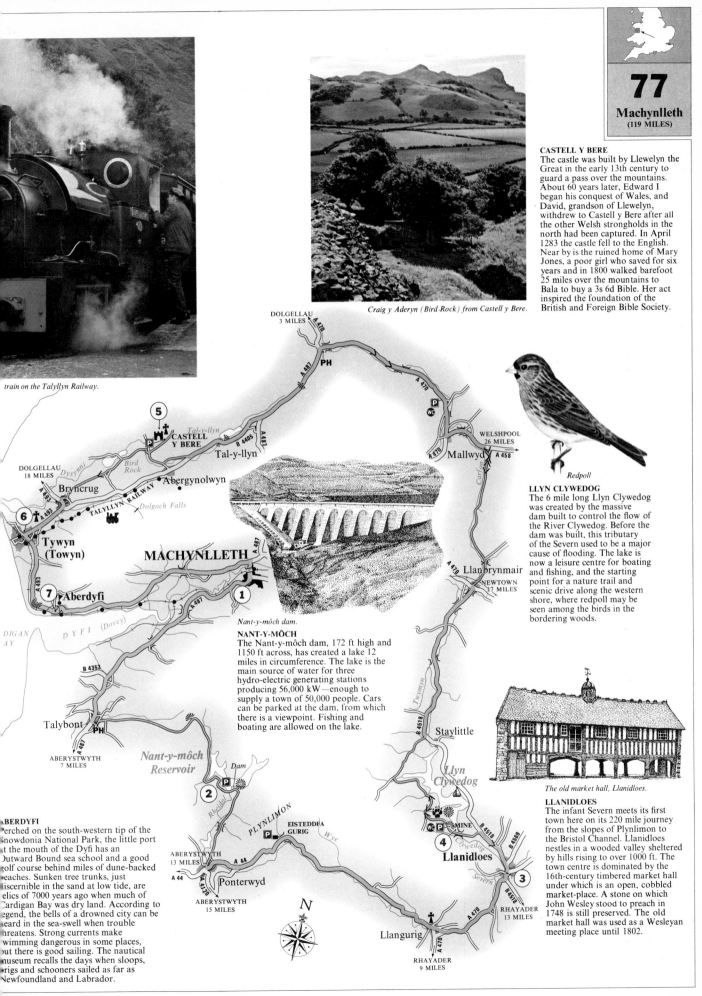

train on the Talyllyn Railway.

CASTELL Y BERE
The castle was built by Llewelyn the Great in the early 13th century to guard a pass over the mountains. About 60 years later, Edward I began his conquest of Wales, and David, grandson of Llewelyn, withdrew to Castell y Bere after all the other Welsh strongholds in the north had been captured. In April 1283 the castle fell to the English. Near by is the ruined home of Mary Jones, a poor girl who saved for six years and in 1800 walked barefoot 25 miles over the mountains to Bala to buy a 3s 6d Bible. Her act inspired the foundation of the British and Foreign Bible Society.

Craig y Aderyn (Bird Rock) from Castell y Bere.

Redpoll

LLYN CLYWEDOG
The 6 mile long Llyn Clywedog was created by the massive dam built to control the flow of the River Clywedog. Before the dam was built, this tributary of the Severn used to be a major cause of flooding. The lake is now a leisure centre for boating and fishing, and the starting point for a nature trail and scenic drive along the western shore, where redpoll may be seen among the birds in the bordering woods.

Nant-y-môch dam.

NANT-Y-MÔCH
The Nant-y-môch dam, 172 ft high and 1150 ft across, has created a lake 12 miles in circumference. The lake is the main source of water for three hydro-electric generating stations producing 56,000 kW—enough to supply a town of 50,000 people. Cars can be parked at the dam, from which there is a viewpoint. Fishing and boating are allowed on the lake.

The old market hall, Llanidloes.

LLANIDLOES
The infant Severn meets its first town here on its 220 mile journey from the slopes of Plynlimon to the Bristol Channel. Llanidloes nestles in a wooded valley sheltered by hills rising to over 1000 ft. The town centre is dominated by the 16th-century timbered market hall under which is an open, cobbled market-place. A stone on which John Wesley stood to preach in 1748 is still preserved. The old market hall was used as a Wesleyan meeting place until 1802.

ABERDYFI
Perched on the south-western tip of the Snowdonia National Park, the little port at the mouth of the Dyfi has an Outward Bound sea school and a good golf course behind miles of dune-backed beaches. Sunken tree trunks, just discernible in the sand at low tide, are relics of 7000 years ago when much of Cardigan Bay was dry land. According to legend, the bells of a drowned city can be heard in the sea-swell when trouble threatens. Strong currents make swimming dangerous in some places, but there is good sailing. The nautical museum recalls the days when sloops, brigs and schooners sailed as far as Newfoundland and Labrador.

213

From grandeur to folly in northern Wales

This tour is dominated by the peaks of Snowdonia. Their bleak grandeur is enhanced by a view of the Llechwedd slate mines, whose huge caverns were hewn from the depths of the mountains. Out in the open, and down near the sea, is the lighter world of Portmeirion. The place is one of the great 20th-century follies—an Italianate coastal village perched on the shores of North Wales.

(1) Betws-y-coed to Ugly House Leave the town on the A5, heading towards Capel Curig and following closely the course of the River Llugwy. After 2 m. pass the entrance to Swallow Falls on the right. The name Llugwy means 'light' or 'bright' in Welsh, and refers to the large number of waterfalls on this river. Just beyond the falls on the left is a Forestry Commission car park and picnic site, giving access to several walks in the Llugwy Gorge and Gwydyr Forest. Continue on the A5 until it swings right and then left over the bridge beside Ugly House.

(2) Ugly House to Pen-y-Gwryd Keeping on the A5, now with the river winding back and forth to the left of the road, enter the village of Capel Curig and turn left on to the A4086. The road passes Llynnau Mymbyr, two large stretches of water linked by a channel and usually called the Capel Curig lakes. Continue to the next fork in the road, with the Pen-y-Gwryd Hotel on the right.

(3) Pen-y-Gwryd to Nantgwynant Keep on the A498. After 1 m. there is a stopping point on the road from which there are excellent views of the Snowdon range on the right and the beginning of Nantgwynant ahead. Continue downhill past Llyn Gwynant on the right and into Nantgwynant.

(4) Nantgwynant to Beddgelert Follow the A498 over Bethania Bridge, past Llyn Dinas and on to the village of Beddgelert.

(5) Beddgelert to Tremadog In the village turn left over the bridge and follow the A498 signposted to Porthmadog. The road passes through the Pass of Aberglaslyn, with 700 ft cliffs rising sharply on either side. Before the reclamation of land in the Glaslyn Estuary, early in the 19th century, this was the river mouth, and the Glaslyn was navigable up to this point. Near the end of the pass, where the road swings left over a bridge, keep straight on for 5 m. into Tremadog.

(6) Tremadog to Porthmadog In the town, turn left on to the A487 and continue into Porthmadog.

(7) Porthmadog to Portmeirion Leave the town on the A487 signposted to Dolgellau. Cross the Cob alongside the Festiniog Railway, and after passing the toll gate follow the signs and turn right in Minffordd for the car park at Portmeirion.

(8) Portmeirion to Llechwedd Quarries From the car park return to the main road and turn right, following the A487 to Penrhyndeudraeth. The village name means Head of the Hill-slope over the Two Reaches

of Sand, and aptly describes its situation. Here, keep straight ahead at the crossroads and into the Vale of Ffestiniog, thought by many to be the most beautiful valley in North Wales. Here the road runs close to the Festiniog Railway, though the track is often 500 ft above the road. At Tan-y-bwlch follow the road round to the right and then left, skirting Maentwrog and signposted to Dolgellau. Then take the first left turn on to the A496 signposted to Blaenau Ffestiniog and Betws-y-coed. Keep straight on at the next junction, and after about 1 m., still on the A496, head up the hill towards Tanygrisiau and turn left on to the A470 at the edge of Blaenau Ffestiniog. Continue along the road, passing through hills of slate waste, and in less than 1 m. turn in to the entrance to the Llechwedd slate caverns on the right. Opposite, left, is Gloddfa Ganol Mountain Centre.

(9) Llechwedd Quarries to Dolwyddelan Castle Return to the A470 and keep on the road towards Betws-y-coed. After 4 m. reach Dolwyddelan Castle on the left.

(10) Dolwyddelan Castle to Betws-y-coed Still on the A470, continue through the village of Dolwyddelan. After 6 m., where the A470 swings to the right, keep straight on, avoiding the busy A5 and following a small lane back to Betws-y-coed.

INFORMATION

Places of interest *Dolwyddelan Castle:* Daily. *Llechwedd slate caverns* and *Gloddfa Ganol:* Mar. to Oct., daily (winter weekends). *Porthmadog:* Festiniog Railway and Museum, Feb. to Oct. Maritime Museum, daily, Apr. to Sept. *Portmeirion:* Village, accessible at all times.

Craft workshops *Betws-y-coed:* Pennant Crafts, The Pottery, weekdays. *Porthmadog:* Snowdon Mill, Welsh tapestry, daily. Porthmadog Pottery, weekdays, and weekends in summer. *Penrhyndeudraeth:* Beddgelert Pottery. Easter to end Aug., daily.

Nature trails *Beddgelert Forest Trail:* Starts from A4085, 2 m. from village. Guide from wardens at Gwydyr Uchaf, Llanrwst, and from Forestry Commission, Cardiff. *Gwydyr Forest Trail:* Starts above the Ugly House, off the A5. Guide from wardens, Gwydyr Uchaf, Llanrwst. *Gwydyr Forest:* Ten different walks. Guidebook from wardens, Gwydyr Uchaf, Llanrwst, or from local shops.

Information Wales Tourist Office, Waterloo Complex, Betws-y-coed (Tel. Betws-y-coed 426). Wales Tourist Office, Porthmadog (Tel. Porthmadog 2981). Wales Tourist Board, Snowdonia Nat. Park Centre, Blaenau Ffestiniog (Tel. 360).

Towns with easy access to Betws-y-coed:

Bala	23 m.	Colwyn Bay	20 m.
Bangor	20 m.	Dolgellau	34 m.
Caernarfon	15 m.	Llangollen	33 m.

Nantgwynant.

NANTGWYNANT
The road between Pen-y-Gwryd and Llyn Gwynant affords some of the finest views of the Snowdon range. The valley itself is softer and more pastoral than those of the other six Snowdon lakes. Where the River Glaslyn joins Llyn Gwynant and Llyn Dinas is Bethania Bridge and the start of a nature trail which covers just over 2 miles. The first part follows the Watkin Path, another route to the summit of Snowdon. Feral goats, descendants of domestic goats that have reverted to the wild, are among animals to be seen on the trail. The trail passes Gladstone Rock, named after the Victorian Prime Minister, W. E. Gladstone. A plaque records that he 'addressed a multitude' here in 1892. Further along is the 'Gladstone Slab', a 100 ft rock used for climbing practice. *Feral goat*

BEDDGELERT
Situated at the meeting point of three valleys, Beddgelert crowds on to the banks of the River Glaslyn between the hills of Hebog and Craig y Llan. The name, 'Grave of Gelert', refers to a legend that Llewelyn the Great, returning home to find his son savaged to death and his hound, Gelert, covered in blood, killed the hound, only to find that it had rescued his son from a wolf. The story dates no further back than the 18th century, though a 'grave' may be reached by a footpath from the bridge. It is more likely that the village was named Bethkelert after an Augustinian priory founded by Llewelyn the Great. Relics of the priory may be seen in St Mary's Church.

TREMADOG
An almost unaltered example of early-19th century town planning, Tremadog was the brainchild of W. A. Madocks, the MP who also engineered the Cob at Porthmadog and was largely responsible for the land reclaimed in the Glaslyn Estuary. Shelley admired the town and wrote much of his epic poem 'Queen Mab' while staying there. T. E. Lawrence (Lawrence of Arabia) was born there in 1888.

SCALE

| 1 | 2 | 3 | 4 | 5 M |

Ty Hyl—Ugly House.

UGLY HOUSE
Ty Hyl or Ugly House is so named because it is made from huge boulders, instead of the neat grey stones common to this area. It dates from the 15th century and is said to have been a thieves' hideout and a camp for cattle drovers.

PEN-Y-GWRYD
Famous among mountaineers as the training headquarters of the first team to climb Mount Everest, this remote mountain inn lies at the fork of the roads to Llanberis and Beddgelert. The signatures of Hunt and Hillary, leaders of the expedition, are among those on the ceiling of the Everest Room. One of the most popular paths to the summit of Snowdon, the Pyg (or Pig) Track, is said to be named after the initials of the inn, though it starts from a spot on the Llanberis Pass, 11½ miles away.

BETWS-Y-COED
One of the most beautifully situated villages in Snowdonia, Betws-y-coed nestles in a narrow, wooded valley near the meeting place of three rivers, the Conwy, Llugwy and Lledr. An iron bridge, built by Thomas Telford in 1815, spans the Conwy to the south of the village, and an attractive 15th-century stone bridge crosses the Llugwy. Made famous as a beauty spot in the early 19th century by the painter David Cox, Betws is now a popular touring centre. Cox painted the original sign for the Royal Oak, now inside the hotel. In the disused church behind the station is an effigy in studded armour, dated 1380, of Dafydd Goch, grandson of a leader of the 13th-century Welsh rebellion.

Betws-y-coed from the River Llugwy.

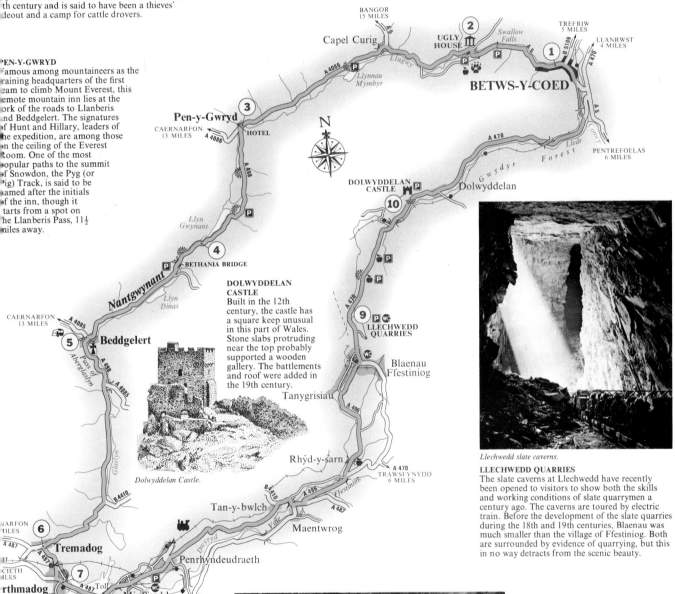

DOLWYDDELAN CASTLE
Built in the 12th century, the castle has a square keep unusual in this part of Wales. Stone slabs protruding near the top probably supported a wooden gallery. The battlements and roof were added in the 19th century.

Dolwyddelan Castle.

Llechwedd slate caverns.

LLECHWEDD QUARRIES
The slate caverns at Llechwedd have recently been opened to visitors to show both the skills and working conditions of slate quarrymen a century ago. The caverns are toured by electric train. Before the development of the slate quarries during the 18th and 19th centuries, Blaenau was much smaller than the village of Ffestiniog. Both are surrounded by evidence of quarrying, but this in no way detracts from the scenic beauty.

PORTHMADOG
The harbour which turned Porthmadog into a large slate port was also the work of W. A. Madocks. Today, Porthmadog is more famous as the headquarters of the Festiniog Railway, opened in 1836 to carry slate from Blaenau Ffestiniog. It was allowed to fall into disrepair during the 1930s and was rescued from ruin by volunteers. Restoration work, begun in 1954, still continues. The line as far as Tanygrisiau now carries much holiday traffic over one of the finest scenic routes in Wales.

The village of Portmeirion.

PORTMEIRION
Designed and built in the 1920s by the Welsh architect Sir Clough William-Ellis, Portmeirion is an extravagant fantasy imposed on a quiet corner of the Welsh coast. The village includes palaces and colour-washed cottages in Italianate style, set amid gardens full of sub-tropical plants and ornate pools and follies. Run as a large hotel, the village is open to day-visitors on payment of a toll. There are antique and souvenir shops and a restaurant.

The gentle valleys where Wales and England meet

Embracing the valleys of Llangollen and Clwyd, this corner of Wales has an altogether gentler beauty than the wild crags and moorlands of neighbouring Snowdonia. Much of it is near the border with England, an area rich in both history and legend, the dividing line between the two being blurred by the Celtic talent for embroidering the facts. A king who died over 1000 years ago is remembered in Valle Crucis, while folk-memories of Owain Glyndwr surround Corwen. Denbigh honours a more recent hero, Sir Henry Morton Stanley, the African explorer.

(1) Llangollen to Valle Crucis Abbey Cross the River Dee by the famous Llangollen bridge and turn left on to the A542 signposted to Ruthin. After 1¾ m. turn off the road on the right to see Valle Crucis Abbey. Eliseg's Pillar is 300 yds further along the A542, also on the right of the road.

(2) Valle Crucis Abbey to Moel Fammau Stay on the A542 as it winds up Horseshoe Pass, which reaches a height of 1367 ft and affords views of both Llangollen and Valle Crucis Abbey. After descending the pass, cross the A5104 at a roundabout and after ½ m. turn left on to the A525. Almost immediately fork right and keep right on the B5431 signposted to Llanarmonyn-Ial. In the village, follow the road round to the right by the church, and then turn left on to the B5430 signposted for Ruthin. After 1½ m. keep straight on where the B5430 swings to the left and then bear right on to the A494.

Pass through the village of Llanferres and turn left at the crossroads. After 1 m. turn left at a T-junction and continue for ¼ m. to the car park on the right and the start of the nature trail leading to the summit of Moel Fammau.

(3) Moel Fammau to Ruthin Return to the road and continue up the pass, then steeply down towards Ruthin. At the bottom of the hill bear right, then right again on to the A494 and on into Ruthin.

(4) Ruthin to Denbigh Leave Ruthin on the B5105 signposted to Cerrigydrudion. After ½ m., just past the Roman Catholic church, turn right for Bontuchel and Cyffylliog. In Bontuchel bear left, following the signposts to Cyffylliog, and after ¼ m. turn right over the bridge crossing the River Clywedog. On the approach to Cyffylliog, turn second right on to the road signposted to Prion. After 1 m., just past the second cattle grid, bear right past a farm into a narrow lane; after another 1½ m. turn right at the first junction and left at the next, signposted Prion. Follow the road round a sharp right bend, and after climbing out of the wooded valley go straight on at the crossroads. After ¾ m. turn right at the T-junction, then bear right again at the next junction. Follow the road to the A525 and turn left, then left again at the traffic lights and into the centre of Denbigh.

(5) Denbigh to Clocaenog Forest Leave Denbigh on the B4501 signposted to Cerrigydrudion. After 4 m. turn left at the first crossroads and almost immediately go straight on at the next crossroads, following the signpost to Llanfihangel Glyn Myfyr. Turn right at the next junction to cross open moorland into the Clocaenog Forest. After just over 3 m. of forest road, turn left at the crossroads, signposted Cyffylliog, and after a further 1½ m. there is a picnic site and car park at the heart of the Clocaenog Forest.

(6) Clocaenog Forest to Corwen Return to the road and after 1 m. turn right, following the sign to Cerrig. Cross the B5105 and go down into Melin-y-wig, where turn right then right again at the far side of the village. Continue to Bettws Gwerfil Goch. Here turn left on to the road for Corwen, which climbs steeply before dropping into the valley of the River Alwen. At the bottom of the hill turn left and almost immediately left again on to the A5 and into Corwen.

(7) Corwen to Horseshoe Falls In the town, turn left just past the Owain Glyndwr Hotel and right at the T-junction on the far side of the valley. After 1½ m. keep right, and at Carrog keep straight ahead—do not cross the river. The lane is narrow in places and follows the course of the River Dee, avoiding the busy A5. After approximately 7 m. there is an excellent view of Horseshoe Falls in the valley on the right.

(8) Horseshoe Falls to Llangollen Continue on the road, bearing left where it joins the B5103. After ½ m., at the T-junction with the A542, turn right to return to the centre of Llangollen.

NATURE NOTES

Much of the tour runs over the Denbigh Moors, an area rich in moorland birds. Species to be seen include merlins, red grouse, whinchats and ravens. The moorland south of Denbigh runs over a band of limestone rock. This rock can be traced by the lime-loving plants that grow above. These include limestone woundwort and the rare blue gromwell.

INFORMATION

Places of interest *Llangollen:* Plas Newydd, May to Sept., daily; winter, weekdays by appointment. Dinas Bran, daily. Valle Crucis Abbey and Eliseg's Pillar, daily. *Denbigh:* Castle and museum, weekdays, Sun. afternoons (all Sun. in summer).

Craft workshops *Llangollen:* Abbey Crafts, tapestry, stools, benches, table-mats, daily. Llangollen Pottery, Regent Street, weekdays. *Denbigh:* David Frith Pottery, weekdays.

Nature trail *Moel Fammau:* Starts from car park, leaflets available. Detailed guidebook from Forestry Commission Office, Ruthin.

Events *Llangollen:* International Musical Eisteddfod, early July. Sheep-dog trials, Aug.

Information Wales Tourist Office, Town Hall, Llangollen (Tel. Llangollen 860828).

Towns with easy access to Llangollen:

Bala	22 m.	Oswestry	13 m.
Betws-y-coed	33 m.	Shrewsbury	29 m.
Chester	23 m.	Wrexham	11 m.

CLOCAENOG FOREST
Once barren moorland, the rolling highlands between the A5 and the Vale of Clwyd are now covered by Forestry Commission conifers. Through gaps in the woodlands there are dramatic views eastwards to the mountains behind Ruthin. There is a picnic site near Nilig, in the heart of the forest.

CORWEN
Situated at the junction of the rivers Alwen and Dee, Corwen is closely associated with the hero of the 14th-century Welsh uprising, Owain Glyndwr. He took his name from the Glyndyfrdwy estate, 4 miles east of Corwen. Glyndwr's dagger is said to have made the cross-like mark above the door of Corwen's 13th-century parish church, dedicated to Mael and Sulien, 6th-century saints. The stretch of the Dee which flows past Corwen is noted for salmon and trout, and there are fine walks in the Berwyn Mountains above the town. On market days Corwen is crowded with farmers, and thousands of sheep and cattle change hands here every year.

HORSESHOE FALLS
The horseshoe-shaped falls across the River are actually a weir, designed and built in 179[.] by Thomas Telford, the canal and road engineer, to trap water for the nearby Llangollen Canal. It is now a quiet beauty spot within easy reach of Llangollen. In summ[.] horse-drawn barges ply the waterway betwee[.] the falls and the town.

SCALE

0   1   2   3   4   5 MILE

DENBIGH

The broad pastures of the Vale of Clwyd, which spread out below Denbigh, are now the basis of a peaceful prosperity. But the town originally grew up around the castle built to hold the district after Edward I had overcome the Welsh in 1282. The castle is now a ruin, but there is an impressive gatehouse. The remains of several towers and parts of the old town walls still stand. The castle museum contains relics excavated in the town and mementoes of Sir Henry Morton Stanley, the explorer who found Dr Livingstone in Africa. Stanley was born in 1841, in a cottage that stood by the castle entrance.

Sir Henry Morton Stanley, African explorer (1841–1904).

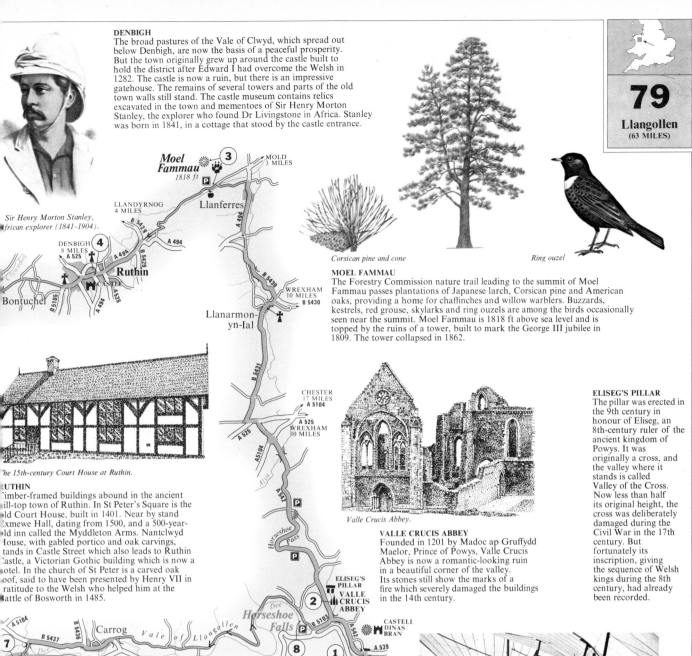

Corsican pine and cone

Ring ouzel

MOEL FAMMAU

The Forestry Commission nature trail leading to the summit of Moel Fammau passes plantations of Japanese larch, Corsican pine and American oaks, providing a home for chaffinches and willow warblers. Buzzards, kestrels, red grouse, skylarks and ring ouzels are among the birds occasionally seen near the summit. Moel Fammau is 1818 ft above sea level and is topped by the ruins of a tower, built to mark the George III jubilee in 1809. The tower collapsed in 1862.

The 15th-century Court House at Ruthin.

RUTHIN

Timber-framed buildings abound in the ancient hill-top town of Ruthin. In St Peter's Square is the Old Court House, built in 1401. Near by stand Exmewe Hall, dating from 1500, and a 500-year-old inn called the Myddleton Arms. Nantclwyd House, with gabled portico and oak carvings, stands in Castle Street which also leads to Ruthin Castle, a Victorian Gothic building which is now a hotel. In the church of St Peter is a carved oak roof, said to have been presented by Henry VII in gratitude to the Welsh who helped him at the Battle of Bosworth in 1485.

Valle Crucis Abbey.

VALLE CRUCIS ABBEY

Founded in 1201 by Madoc ap Gruffydd Maelor, Prince of Powys, Valle Crucis Abbey is now a romantic-looking ruin in a beautiful corner of the valley. Its stones still show the marks of a fire which severely damaged the buildings in the 14th century.

ELISEG'S PILLAR

The pillar was erected in the 9th century in honour of Eliseg, an 8th-century ruler of the ancient kingdom of Powys. It was originally a cross, and the valley where it stands is called Valley of the Cross. Now less than half its original height, the cross was deliberately damaged during the Civil War in the 17th century. But fortunately its inscription, giving the sequence of Welsh kings during the 8th century, had already been recorded.

Llangollen International Eisteddfod.

LLANGOLLEN

Set astride the River Dee at the head of a beautiful valley, Llangollen is internationally famous for the Eisteddfod held there each July since 1947. Musicians, singers and folk dancers compete in marquees erected near the river. Not far from the Eisteddfod ground, the four arches of St Asaph's Bridge span the Dee above a salmon leap. Held locally to be one of the seven wonders of Wales, the bridge is believed to date from the 12th century, though it has been altered over the centuries. Five minutes' walk from the town centre is Plas Newydd, a magnificent timbered house in formal gardens, which was the home of the 'Ladies of Llangollen', Lady Eleanor Butler and Miss Ponsonby. They refused society marriages and moved to Llangollen, where they lived from 1779 to 1831. They entertained many famous people, including the Duke of Wellington and William Wordsworth. To the north-east the town is overlooked by Dinas Bran, the ruins of an 8th-century castle on a hill. In the background are the limestone cliffs of Eglwyseg Mountain.

Horseshoe Falls on the River Dee.

Plas Newydd, home of the 'Ladies of Llangollen'.

Powys: an unspoilt 'Paradise' above the Severn

Gently at first, and then in leaps, the land rises out of the flatness of the Severn Valley. The rivers, formed in the mountains, respond to the terrain, at one point flowing to fill a man-made lake between wooded hills, and at another flying over a precipice to form Britain's highest waterfall south of Scotland. The land, once the ancient kingdom of Powys, was described by a 9th-century Welsh bard as 'The Paradise of Wales'.

(1) Welshpool to Powis Castle Leave on the A483 which is signposted to Newtown. After 1 m. turn right down the lane which passes the entrance to Powis Castle.

(2) Powis Castle to Llanfair Caereinion Continue along the lane for 3½ m. and turn right at the junction on to the B4385 signposted to Castle Caereinion. Go through Castle Caereinion, and turn left just before the A458, still on the B4385, continuing over the level crossing and on to Llanfair Caereinion. At the junction in the middle of the village, turn right on to the road crossing the swift-flowing waters of the River Banwy. Turn right again on to the A458; the main terminus of the Welshpool and Llanfair Light Railway is on the right after a few hundred yards.

(3) Llanfair Caereinion to Lake Vyrnwy Return to the A458 and turn left, following the signpost for Dolgellau. After swinging left and right to cross the River Banwy, the road passes near the impressive 1107 ft high Moel Bentyrch before going through the villages of Llanerfyl and Llangadfan. After Llangadfan, turn right on to the B4395 which is signposted to Llanfyllin. Follow the B4395 northwards over wooded hills. At the junction with the B4393 turn left. After 3 m. there is a steep descent into Llanwddyn, where the road swings left towards Lake Vyrnwy.

(4) Lake Vyrnwy to Pistyll Rhaeadr Go back to Llanwddyn and bear left on to the B4396, through Hirnant and into Penybontfawr. Turn right on to the B4391 and, almost immediately, turn left on the road which is signposted to Llanrhaeadr-ym-Mochnant. Keep right after crossing the River Tanat and enter Llanrhaeadr-ym-Mochnant. In the village, turn left just beyond the bridge and follow the lane to the Pistyll Rhaeadr waterfall.

(5) Pistyll Rhaeadr to Llanarmon Dyffryn Ceiriog Return down the lane for 2¾ m. and turn left for Maengwynedd. After 1 m. turn left at the T-junction (no signpost), and 3 m. later turn right on to the road for Llanarmon Dyffryn Ceiriog. Go straight ahead at the next junction and down into the village of Llanarmon Dyffryn Ceiriog.

(6) Llanarmon Dyffryn Ceiriog to Glyn Ceiriog Join the B4500, crossing the River Ceiriog, and stay on this road into Glyn Ceiriog.

(7) Glyn Ceiriog to Offa's Dyke In the village turn right on to the B4579, which is signposted to Selattyn and Oswestry. Immediately after crossing the bridge turn right and steeply uphill. At the top of the hill, fork left. After 1¼ m. turn right at the T-junction and, ¾ m. later, turn left on to the road signposted to Oswestry. The road now travels through Forestry Commission woodland, past the picnic area on the right and then downhill to a T-junction. On the left, still clearly visible, is a section of Offa's Dyke, the 8th-century border with Mercia over which an armed Welshman strayed only at the peril of having his right arm cut off.

(8) Offa's Dyke to Llanyblodwel From the T-junction turn right and then immediately turn left. Continue on this road to the staggered crossroads at the old racecourse. Although little more than 1000 ft high, this expanse of gorse, bracken and springy turf commands an immense view over the plain of Salop and the mountains of Wales. The land was used as a racecourse from the 18th century until 1848, and fragments of the old grandstand can still be seen. From these ruins, a footpath runs into the beautiful Candy Woods. At the crossroads by the racecourse, go left then right on the road which is signposted to Trefonen. After 2 m. turn right at the T-junction, go through Trefonen and turn left on the road signposted to Porth y waen. Turn right at the bottom of the hill on to the A495, and ½ m. later, where the A495 swings left, go straight ahead on to the B4396. After ½ m. turn left into Llanyblodwel.

(9) Llanyblodwel to Welshpool Turn first left across the bridge and swing left around the end of the Horseshoe public house. Keep on this lane, which climbs steeply, eventually turning right on to the A495. Follow the A495 to Llansantffraid-ym-Mechain, where the church, dedicated to St Bridget, has an unusual vault, used exclusively for burials by gipsy families. There is also a fine Jacobean window dating from about 1619. Beyond the village keep left on the A495, and after 3 m. turn left on to the A490, which crosses the River Vyrnwy and continues for 7 m. before entering Welshpool.

INFORMATION

Places of interest *Glyn Ceiriog*: Memorial Institute and museum, all year, afternoons. *Llanfair Caereinion*: Welshpool and Llanfair Light Railway, Easter to Oct., weekends; mid-July to Sept., daily. *Powis Castle*: May to Sept., Wed. to Sun., 2-6 p.m., Bank Hol. Mon., 11.30 a.m.-6 p.m. Gardens, July and Aug., Wed. and Sun., otherwise as for castle. *Welshpool*: Powysland Museum, weekdays, Sat. afternoons (not Wed. in winter).

Information *Welshpool*: Vicarage Garden Car Park (Tel. Welshpool 2043).

Towns with easy access to Welshpool:

Dolgellau	38 m.	Oswestry	16 m.
Ludlow	32 m.	Shrewsbury	19 m.

Pistyll Rhaeadr waterfall.

PISTYLL RHAEADR FALLS
George Borrow, the 19th-century author, described the waterfall of Pistyll Rhaeadr as 'like an immense skein of silk, agitated and disturbed by tempestuous blasts'. Others, more simply, have called it 'the finest in Wales'. The first leap of the Disgynfa River is down an unbroken cataract of 100 ft to a rock pool from which it cascades again, in a series of smaller leaps, down a further 140 ft. There is a small footbridge over the bottom of the cascade. The top is reached by a path climbing the slope to the right from the car park. In nearby Llanrhaeadr-ym-Mochnant a tablet in the church commemorates the Rev. William Morgan who, in 1588, first translated the Bible into Welsh.

The tower on Lake Vyrnwy.

LAKE VYRNWY
One of the largest man-made lakes in Wales, Vyrnwy was formed between 1880 and 1890 to provide a water supply to Liverpool. The 'Gothic' tower rising on the northern shore marks the start of the 75 mile long aqueduct that carries the water to the city. The stone dam, 144 ft high and stretching 390 yds across the valley, holds back 13,000 million gallons of water. A road runs across the dam, allowing a complete circuit of the lake to be made.

SCALE
0   1   2   3   4   5 MILES

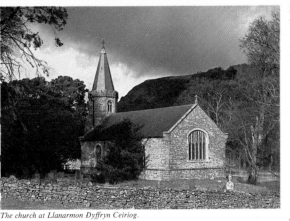

The church at Llanarmon Dyffryn Ceiriog.

LLANARMON DYFFRYN CEIRIOG

A popular centre for walking on the Berwyns, Llanarmon is set near the headwaters of the River Ceiriog. The village is also noted for the fishing and shooting to be had in the surrounding countryside. It has two handsome inns: the 16th-century West Arms, and The Hand. On the left of the gateway that opens on to the village churchyard is a mound said to be the burial place of St Garmon. The church is dedicated to him—and so the tongue-twisting village name translates into English as 'Garmon's Church in the Valley of Ceiriog'. The church, which was restored in 1846, is approached by an avenue of ancient yews.

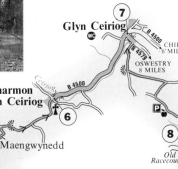

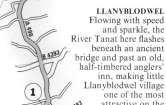

GLYN CEIRIOG

The slate quarries that were once the source of prosperity in these parts have now closed, allowing Glyn Ceiriog to revert into a sleepy little village. But it does have the Ceiriog Memorial Institute, which houses a collection of objects of local interest.

WELSHPOOL

A market town since 1263, Welshpool has become one of the most important Welsh agricultural centres. The market meets on Mondays, dealing in livestock from the border counties of England and Wales. A great deal of the architecture is Georgian, mixed in with earlier timbered buildings.

A section of Offa's Dyke.

OFFA'S DYKE

In 784, Offa, King of Mercia, ordered a dyke—a ditch and rampart—to be constructed to define the boundary between his kingdom and the Welsh. A long-distance footpath now runs the 168 mile length of the dyke from the north coast of Wales to the estuary of the River Severn.

LLANYBLODWEL

Flowing with speed and sparkle, the River Tanat here flashes beneath an ancient bridge and past an old, half-timbered anglers' inn, making little Llanyblodwel village one of the most attractive on the border between Salop and Wales. Rebuilt in the 19th century, the church has a detached spire.

The inn at Llanyblodwel.

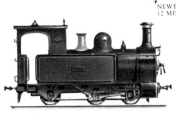

Engines of the Welshpool and Llanfair Light Railway.

LLANFAIR CAEREINION

Sturdy, colourful little steam locomotives from Austria, the West Indies and Britain still work upon the narrow-gauge tracks of the Welshpool and Llanfair Light Railway. Opened in 1903 and closed by British Rail in 1956, the line is now run by volunteers and is open to visitors throughout the summer.

POWIS CASTLE

Powis Castle has stood on a hill overlooking the Severn since the 13th century. Reconstruction and modernisation have kept it one of the finest in Britain. The interior, decorated in plasterwork and wood panels, contains a selection of mementoes of Clive of India. The gardens were laid in the formal Dutch manner in about 1690 and have survived intact through three centuries of changing fashions in gardening. Stone balustrades and lead statuary line terraces descending to the park containing a Douglas fir, nearly 200 ft tall, which is the tallest tree in Britain.

Powis Castle.

A conducted tour of the castle that has been the Berkeleys' home for 900 years

BERKELEY CASTLE

The West Country barons assembled at Berkeley Castle, overlooking the River Severn, in 1215 before riding on to Runnymede to witness the signing of Magna Carta by King John. The present castle was built in 1153. A rugged place of narrow doorways and winding passages, it could be defended by a few resolute men against a small army. A king was murdered here. A queen came to stay, and was made to feel that she was not a welcome guest. Berkeley is hardly a stately home—more a fortress, a living symbol of 900 years of English history. Mr Robert John Berkeley writes about the place and some of the strange characters who have lived in it before him.

Not every home can claim that a king was murdered within its walls. Edward II was barbarously put to death when he was a prisoner here in 1327. I like to think that my family was not instrumental but, although the Lord Berkeley of the day had an alibi and was cleared of complicity, he obviously knew what was going on. It is not a nice thing to have happened in your home—but the story helps to interest the tourists.

In the guardroom, where the deed was done, we used to have a small ivory skull, and I was showing a party round once when a woman asked if it was the skull of the murdered king. I said: 'Yes, as a small boy.' The king, of course, was buried in Gloucester Cathedral—but the lady swallowed my joke.

Despite the royal murder, there are no ghosts that I know of, although the late Lord Berkeley, who died in 1942, had a certain amount of trouble between the wars. Servants will not stay in a haunted house, and he got so fed up with guests talking in front of the staff about ghosts in one particular bedroom that he had it pulled down.

My wife and I have no servants living in, but rely on dailies. We divide our time between Berkeley Castle and Spetchley Hall, our other home near Worcester.

I was brought up at Spetchley, but I have grown to love Berkeley Castle just as much. I am a tremendous traditionalist, and I am very proud to feel that my family have been here for nine centuries. The title died out with the 8th Earl, in 1942. My father, who inherited the place, was a very distant relative of the earl, something like a 13th cousin.

The succession had ceased to be direct from father to son in 1810 when William Fitzhardinge, first of the four illegitimate sons of the 5th Earl, inherited the castle, but not the Berkeley title. Eventually he was created the 1st Earl Fitzhardinge in 1841.

The wicked earl

This son must have been no less fond of his amours than his father, for he became known as the 'Wicked Earl'. My father, who died in 1969, used to say that the earl practised the *droit de seigneur* here, and that his many illegitimate children were shipped off to various parts of the world, particularly Australia. I am always getting letters from Australians and Americans saying: 'My name is Berkeley Fitzhardinge. How am I related?'

The Chamberlain's Worcester China in the China Room is interesting because it was made to commemorate William's birth. It was designed by his mother, Mary Cole, the daughter of a Gloucester butcher. She eventually married William's father, the earl, in 1796—though he protested, without success,

that they had married secretly nine years earlier. If only he could have convinced the courts, this would have made William his legitimate son and heir.

Mary Cole was a very remarkable woman. After her husband died, she was proposed to by the Duke of Clarence, who later became William IV. She turned him down; otherwise she would have become Queen of England.

The 8th and last Earl of Berkeley—the one who died in 1942—was another quite remarkable character. He had the chapel converted into a morning room, and put up an angel with the Berkeley coat of arms.

This Lord Berkeley was also a scientist and Fellow of the Royal Society, and one of his self-imposed tasks was to try to disprove Einstein's theory of relativity. He lived in terrific style. My father used to say that he got the gardeners to bring in to him fruit trees growing in pots so that he could pick the fruit direct, untouched by any other hand.

Digging up the past

Another interest of the 8th Earl was digging up the foundations to try to find out what the castle looked like before it was attacked during the Civil War in the 17th century.

A great deal had been destroyed during a three-day siege: the outer enclosure was destroyed and the walls were flattened; the drawbridge was done away with and the Gate House wrecked. Fortunately the garrison surrendered before more damage could be done. I think there was a certain amount of string-pulling to spare the rest of the castle.

As well as digging up the foundations, the last Lord Berkeley did a great deal to improve the castle. The Fitzhardinges had spent nothing on it and it was very uncomfortable. The draughts were terrific: my father could remember sitting with his overcoat on in front of a roaring fire when he first visited the castle. This Lord Berkeley, who married an American, did much to make the castle more comfortable, installing central heating, double-glazing and more bathrooms, many of which were built into the walls.

He sold the Berkeley property in London—buildings in and around Berkeley Square—to raise some ready cash for the changes he and his wife made in the castle. Among other things, he built the main entrance—the little octagonal clock-tower in the Inner Courtyard.

I came to live here in 1955. My father decided to open the castle to the public, one of the reasons being that he needed a grant from the Historic Houses Council for re-wiring and for roof repairs. He also felt that it was a place that ought to be seen. Lord Berkeley had not allowed visitors. When anyone asked to see around, the answer was often 'No'.

WHERE IT ALL BEGAN *A view of the oldest part of Berkeley Castle, the keep, built between 1153 and 1156 by permission of Henry II. The design is of the unusual 'shell' type, with keep built around a mound instead of on top of it.*

THE GREAT HALL *This room, 62 ft long and more than half high, was built in the 14th century just within the castle wall into which two windows were knocked. The screen seen in the picture retains its 16th-century decoration.*

SILVER TUREEN *A piece from the 18th-century service on the dining-room table. This English silver replaced a Louis XV set sold in 1961 for £210,000, which made it the world's most valuable silver dinner-service.*

ROOFTOP VIEW *Looking down from the battlements on the Inner Courtyard to the main entrance (centre of picture) of the castle. The Norman doorway opens on to a flight of steps leading to the room where Edward II was murdered. The effect of restoration work is seen beyond the wall.*

BERKELEY CASTLE

A certain number of alterations had to be made to let visitors through, and the old laundry was converted into a tea room. Three bachelor quarters were knocked into one to make the picture gallery. I went to Arundel and Chatsworth to get ideas.

When we opened, on Easter Sunday in 1956, there was a queue all the way down to the car park; we have only beaten the number of visitors on two days since. By Monday night, we were all on our knees. We ran out of guidebooks and the tea room ran out of food.

From then until 1960, when we got a custodian, I ran the castle myself, organising the staff and taking people round. They didn't always appreciate my jokes. For instance, when I was showing some Russian officials round, and we were looking at the cannons, I told them that we were re-arming. They were not amused.

There is very little literature about the castle. There are one or two scandalous books about the family, but there is very little authenticated history except for the work of John Smyth, a steward in the 16th and 17th centuries, who wrote a very detailed history of the family, giving them names like William the Waste-all, Maurice the Make-peace and Maurice the Magnanimous—early ancestors of mine between the 12th and 16th centuries.

£210,000 dinner-service

The family were not great collectors. They were always much keener on sport and enjoyment than on being patrons of the arts. But there is a lot of very early timber work about the castle. Drake's chest in the King's Gallery comes from his ship *Golden Hind*.

Many of the smaller things which used to be on show are now locked up because they are too valuable to leave around. This applies to most of the jade collection, though one or two pieces are still on show in the Small Drawing Room—I love the white and green piece with butterflies on flowers.

It is an awful waste to lock things away, but we don't have a guard in every room, and we once had a tip-off that there was to be an attempt to steal a valuable miniature painting and substitute a copy.

We used to have a Louis XV dinner-service by Jacques Roettiers, but it was sold at Sotheby's in 1961. It made £210,000, which still stands as a record for a silver dinner-service. The service on the dining-room table now is mostly 18th-century English.

There is a tradition that the Godwin Cup, in the Housekeeper's Room, belonged to Earl Godwin, father of King Harold, who owned the Saxon manor of Berkeley in the 10th century. The story is that one morning he forgot to have communion out of the cup, as was his practice, and a storm swallowed up all his lands off the Kent coast. I don't know how the cup came to be in the castle, but it has been here from time immemorial. Unfortunately there is no evidence of its being actually Saxon—but why spoil a good story?

The collection of family portraits is quite large, going back to the 16th century. There are some good ones among them, and it is interesting to see what one's ancestors looked like.

The ones I like best are the Gainsborough, in the Great Hall, of Admiral Sir George Cranfield Berkeley; and, on the Grand Staircase, a painting of Sir George when he was a

KING EDWARD'S ROOM *A shaft leads to a pit into which rotting animals used to be dropped, with the idea that the stench would slowly asphyxiate prisoners in the room. Edward II survived this treatment but was murdered much more violently.*

DRAKE'S CHEST *It sailed round the world with Sir Francis in the Golden Hind. More of his furniture is displayed in various parts of the castle.*

HMS TYGER *The warship (on the right of this painting by the Dutch master Van der Velde) was commanded by Charles, Lord Berkeley, one of the first captains of England's infant Navy. He died at sea in 1681.*

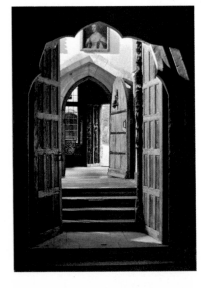

SIEGE GUN *The gun seems to suggest a stormy history, but the Berkeleys, unlike many of their contemporaries, generally had a reputation as men of peace. Even the castle's role in the Civil War was relatively bloodless.*

THE BERKELEY ARCH *The massive doors lead from the Great Hall to the Grand Staircase beneath the arch that dates back to around 1340. The hall was built then on the site of an earlier one. The wooden staircase is the work of 17th-century craftsmen.*

midshipman, by Francis Cotes—the figure is far less stilted than most of the others. Mary Cole by Hoppner, in the Long Drawing Room, is interesting, and on the Grand Staircase there is a good Reynolds of the 4th Earl's wife, Elizabeth Drax, who embroidered the suite of furniture in the Long Drawing Room.

In the Dining Room, which used to be the billiards-room, there are portraits of the Bruton Berkeleys, saviours of the family fortune, who started the London property investment. When they died out, they left everything to Berkeley Castle, including the collection of Van der Veldes which they had commissioned. One of the sons, Charles, Lord Berkeley, went into the Navy and there is a fine painting by Van der Velde of the ship he commanded, HMS *Tyger*.

Unfortunately there is no portrait of William the Waste-all. I would love to have known what he looked like. He gave everything away to Henry VII—land, castle, the whole bag of tricks—as the price for being made Earl Marshal, after the Norfolks, who were on the wrong side at the Battle of Bosworth, lost the hereditary title. But he died without marrying, so the title reverted to the Norfolk family.

Quarrels with a queen

Henry VII, Henry VIII and Edward VI owned the castle in turn. When Edward VI died without a son in 1553 and first Mary, then Elizabeth, came to the throne, the entail was broken and all the property came back to the Berkeley family.

That was always a sore point with Queen Elizabeth. She tried to give the property to the Earl of Leicester, her favourite courtier. But it was not hers to give away, and she was very bitter about it. The first time she came here, Lord Berkeley rode out as she rode in—an awful slight to the monarch. She stayed for ten days or so, making herself a bit of a nuisance in the neighbourhood. So she was no friend.

The castle gardens are very simple, but I love gardening, especially planning and trying to blend colour schemes. We have some unusual shrubs—two very fine *Carpenteria californica*; two very big *Magnolia delavayi*, which have enormous yellow flowers that come out in August; a large number of *Ceanothus*, *Olearia* and very fine *Actinidia kolomikta*. And there is a very good double pomegranate, with rosy-pink flowers.

I enjoy weeding. I find it is the best tonic when you are feeling overwrought and everything is getting on top of you. I weed for four or five hours and forget all my worries. Through sheer necessity one works quite hard because of the problem of getting gardeners—and anyway I love just being among plants.

I also love hunting, and I am Master of the Berkeley Hunt, whose servants still wear the distinctive yellow livery instead of the red used by all other hunts. I think this is the best hunting country in England, though the motorways have messed it up a bit. We have a lot of grass and not much ploughed land, so we can start earlier because there is not too much corn to worry about. I was born 100 years too late for the golden age of fox hunting. As I said, I am a great traditionalist.

GODWIN CUP *Legend says that King Harold's father took daily communion from this 10th-century silver chalice—until one day he forgot, and disaster followed.*

MORNING ROOM *The candles and Bible recall the room's earlier role as the castle chapel, ended by the last Lord Berkeley, a scientist.*

MARY COLE *(right), the butcher's daughter who became a countess, and (above) a plate from the china service which she designed to celebrate the birth of her illegitimate son, William.*

MEDIEVAL KITCHEN *Roasting spits hang over the iron grate. The ovens, solid-lead sinks and old chopping block are in the buttery, through the archway.*

TERRACE WALK *A corner of the gardens just outside the castle walls. The gardens are unpretentious, but they contain some fine shrubs.*

WHEN TO VISIT BERKELEY CASTLE

OPENING TIMES: Mar. 28 to Apr. 30 and Sept., daily (except Mon.) 2–5 p.m.; May to Aug., Tues. to Sat. and Bank Hol. Mon., 11 a.m.– 5 p.m., Sun. 2–5 p.m.; Oct., Sun. 2–4.30 p.m.

HOW TO GET THERE: Berkeley Castle is halfway between Bristol and Gloucester, ½ m. west of the A38 at the junction of the B4066 and the B4509. The nearest access point on the M5 is junction 14. Leave the motorway by the B4509, following the signpost for Thornbury.

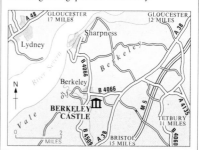

White-faced bulls, cider and reminders of a battle-torn past

Castles, cattle and cider are the dominant features of this border countryside. Red-and-white Herefordshire cattle, renowned throughout the world for the quality of their beef, crop the long, lush grass in meadows overlooked by orchards, where thousands of tons of cider apples are gathered in the autumn. Most of the apples go to Hereford, the home of the world's largest cider factory. Through this lush countryside runs the Wye, one of the loveliest rivers in Britain. Gaunt ruined castles serve as a reminder of a sterner past—that this peaceful land was once a battleground for rival rulers of England and Wales.

(1) Hereford to Mordiford Leave Hereford on the A438 signposted to Worcester and Tewkesbury, but on the outskirts of the city, where this road turns left, keep straight ahead on to the B4224, signposted for Mordiford. After 4 m., in Mordiford, turn left by The Moon public house and follow the lane to Haugh Wood.

(2) Mordiford to Ross-on-Wye Return to Mordiford and turn left on to the B4224 signposted to Ross and Fownhope. Continue for 2 m. into Fownhope, and turn right by the church on to a minor road. After 1 m. the road runs between a wood and the River Wye. Carry straight on over two sets of crossroads, and 2 m. later bear left uphill away from the Wye. Continue for another 2½ m. towards Ross-on-Wye, but on the outskirts of the town turn right at the Hereford and Monmouth signpost and follow the road into the town centre.

(3) Ross-on-Wye to Goodrich Castle From the market hall in the centre of Ross, take the B4228 signposted to Coleford. After 4 m. turn right on to the B4229, signposted to Goodrich and Monmouth. Cross the Wye and follow the road up the hill and under a bridge. Just beyond the bridge, turn right and follow the signpost for the path to the castle.

(4) Goodrich Castle to Symonds Yat Return to the B4229 and turn right. After 1 m. turn left on to the road signposted Symonds Yat East and Yat Rock. The road almost immediately crosses the river and then climbs the hill to a Forestry Commission car park, starting point for forest walks.

(5) Symonds Yat to Skenfrith Return down the hill from the car park, recross the river and turn left on to the B4229. After 1 m., where the road joins the A40, turn left again, following the Monmouth signpost. Go on for 1 m., cross the main road by the bridge to Whitchurch and turn left on to the road signposted to Llangarron. After 3 m., at the T-junction beyond Llangrove, turn left, following the signpost to Welsh Newton, and in the village turn right on to the A466, following the Hereford signpost. After 500 yds turn left on to the road signposted to Broad Oak. After 3 m., at Broad Oak, turn left along the B4521 into Skenfrith.

(6) Skenfrith to Kilpeck Rejoin the B4521 opposite the castle and church, turning right towards Abergavenny. After 1 m. turn right on to the B4347 and follow this road for 4½ m. to Grosmont. A short walk is signposted to the castle. Follow the B4347 out of the village, but 1 m. later, after a steep descent to the River Monnow, turn right into a lane signposted to Garway and Monmouth. Take the first (unsignposted) turn on the left, just before the church, and 2 m. later go left again at the T-junction, also unsignposted. After a further ½ m. turn right and follow the signposts to Kilpeck. To visit the church, turn left by the Red Lion Inn.

(7) Kilpeck to Abbey Dore Continue on the road past the church, turn left at the first crossroads and, after just over ½ m., fork left immediately after the railway bridge, following the signpost for Wormbridge and Pontrilas. After ½ m. turn left on to the A465 and right after a further ½ m., following the signpost for Abbey Dore. Follow the road for 3 m. to Abbey Dore, keep ahead, ignoring side roads, and then left at a T-junction. At the junction with the B4347 in Abbey Dore turn left, signposted to Ewyas Harold and Pontrilas, in order to see the abbey church.

(8) Abbey Dore to Arthur's Stone Return to the village by the B4347 and keep on it, along the valley of the River Dore. After 4½ m., at the junction with the B4348, turn left, following the signpost for Hay-on-Wye. After 5 m., on the approach to Dorstone where the B4348 bends sharply left, turn right up the hill, following the signpost for Bredwardine and Arthur's Stone. After 1 m. turn left on to the lane for Arthur's Stone.

(9) Arthur's Stone to Hereford Continue on along the lane into the village of Bredwardine and turn right on to the B4352, following the Hereford signpost. After 9 m. bear left where the road merges with the B4349, and 2 m. later go left again at the junction with the A465, and follow the road back to Hereford.

INFORMATION

Places of interest *Goodrich Castle:* Weekdays and Sun. afternoons. *Grosmont Castle:* Daily. *Hereford:* Bulmer's Railway Centre, Easter, Spring and Late Summer Bank Hol. Mon. 11 a.m.-5 p.m., April to Sept., Sat. and Sun. afternoons. *Monmouth:* Castle, daily. Nelson Museum, April to Oct., weekdays; July and Aug., weekdays and Sun. afternoons; Easter and Spring Bank Hol. afternoons. *Skenfrith Castle:* Daily.

Events *Hereford:* The May Fair, May. Hereford Show and Sale of Bulls, Jan., Mar. and April. Carnival, July. Antiques Fair, Oct.

Information *Hereford:* Town Hall (Tel. Hereford 68430). *Ross-on-Wye:* 20 Broad Street (Tel. Ross-on-Wye'2768).

Towns with easy access to Hereford:

Abergavenny	24 m.	Ludlow	24 m.
Gloucester	28 m.	Monmouth	18 m.
Hay-on-Wye	21 m.	Worcester	26 m.

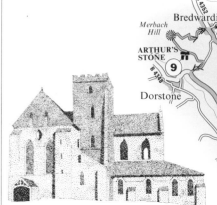

Arthur's Stone, near Bredwardine.

Bredwardi
Merbach Hill
ARTHUR'S STONE 9
Dorstone

Church of Abbey Dore.

ABBEY DORE
Founded by the Cistercians in 1174, the abbey fell into decay after the Dissolution of the Monasteries in 1538. The buildings were being used as a cowshed when the 1st Viscount Scudamore began restoration work in 1632. The magnificent oak screen was designed by John Abel, carpenter to Charles I.

SKENFRITH
Early in the 13th century a triangular defensive system, known as The Three Cas was built by the kings of England to guard Welsh Marches. One of the castles was Skenfrith; the others were Grosmont and White Castle. John Morgan, last governor of the castles, was buried in Skenfrith in 15

Symonds Yat, from the rock.

SYMONDS YAT
The 400 ft high spur of Yat Rock commands the finest view in the Wye Valley. Steep cliffs fall awa on each side, and the river forms a 4 mile loop before returning to within 400 yds of its original course through the 'yat', or gate, in the hills.

SCALE

0 1 2 3 4 5 MILES

ARTHUR'S STONE

There are three legends about this arrangement of enormous stones—that they mark the burial place of King Arthur, of a giant whom he slew, and of a king who started a fight with Arthur. What is certain is that the stones are the entrance to a long barrow, or grave, dating from around 2000 BC. They stand on Merbach Hill, 1045 ft up, from which there are views over the Golden Valley to the Black Mountains. It is claimed that in clear weather 11 counties can be seen from the hilltop. The village of Bredwardine, near the stones, is a fishing centre where a fine Norman bridge spans the Wye. There are some attractive houses, including the 17th-century Old Court Farm, and a Norman church containing effigies of medieval knights.

Chained library, Hereford Cathedral.

HEREFORD

Treasures of Hereford's 12th-century cathedral include the world's finest chained library, a collection of nearly 1500 volumes, each chained to its bookcase. The bookcases were made in 1611, but the books go back almost 12 centuries to the Anglo-Saxon Gospels, written in Latin about AD 800. Another cathedral curio is the Mappa Mundi, a 'flat earth' map of the world drawn around 1290 by one of the clergy. Hereford is the home of the world's biggest cider factory—Bulmer's—founded in 1887 by a son of the rector of Credenhill, who made cider from the apples in the rectory orchard. The city's fine old buildings include several inns. A plaque on a house in Gwynne Street marks the birthplace of Nell Gwynne.

MORDIFORD

Wooded hills overlook this village near the junction of the rivers Lugg and Wye. Siskins, small yellow-green finches uncommon in England, can be seen among the conifers along the Haugh Wood nature trails in winter and spring. The male is distinguished by its black bib and crown.

Siskins

Norman doorway, Kilpeck church.

KILPECK

The masons who worked on Kilpeck's little Norman church carved dozens of figures—some amusing, some grotesque and some that offended Victorian worshippers so much that they were destroyed. But there is still a wealth of sculpture left.

Kyrle memorial gate, Ross-on-Wye.

ROSS-ON-WYE

Local benefactor John Kyrle (1637–1724) was praised by the poet Alexander Pope in an ode to this 'Man of Ross'. One of the town's many Kyrle monuments is the gateway to The Prospect public garden, which Kyrle gave to the town. His house is in the marketplace. Near by is the 14th-century church, from which there are views of the valley and hills. Many attractive old buildings line the streets that radiate from the 17th-century market hall, which dominates the market-place.

John Kyrle, 'Man of Ross'.

GOODRICH CASTLE

The red-sandstone fortress was seized by Cromwell's troops at the outbreak of the Civil War, but passed to the Royalists. Finally, in 1646, it was battered into submission by Cromwell's men using a mortar which fired 200 lb. shots. The mortar, called Roaring Meg, now stands on Castle Green in Hereford. The castle was built in the 12th century as a defence against Welsh raiders, commanding the river crossing of the old Roman road from Monmouth to Gloucester. It stands on a wooded hill above the Wye Valley, surrounded by a deep dry moat, excavated from the solid rock. A steep and narrow stairway leads to the top of the Norman keep, and a climb to the top is rewarded with spectacular views. In the courtyard is a 168 ft deep well. The castle became government property in 1920, since when much has been done to preserve it.

Goodrich Castle.

Map labels

Tyberton
Madley
Wormbridge
Abbey Dore
Grosmont
Skenfrith
Broad Oak
Welsh Newton
Whitchurch
Llangrove
Goodrich
Symonds Yat
Fownhope
Mordiford
Kilpeck

HEREFORD
CASTLE

LUDLOW 24 MILES
HAY-ON-WYE 21 MILES
BROMYARD 14 MILES
TEWKESBURY 29 MILES

ABBEY CHURCH
ABERGAVENNY 11 MILES

CASTLE
Haugh Wood
NT

LEDBURY 12 MILES
WORCESTER 35 MILES
GLOUCESTER 16 MILES

Ross-on-Wye

GOODRICH CASTLE

MONMOUTH 4 MILES
Yat Rock

225

Soaring up on Wenlock Edge, puffing down in the valley

A motorist hurrying through Salop by the main roads could easily by-pass three of its most interesting old towns—Ludlow, fortress in the Welsh border battles and seat of the Lord President of the Marches until the office was abolished in 1689; Much Wenlock, featured in history since St Milburga, grand-daughter of the pagan king, Penda the Terrible, founded her nunnery in 680; Bridgnorth, so precipitous that a cliff railway climbs to the 17th-century town centre. The route traverses Wenlock Edge, commanding splendid views of mountains and valleys. Tourists with an hour or so to spare can enjoy the scenery from a different angle by taking a steam-train ride on the Severn Valley Railway, which runs down beside the river from Bridgnorth.

(1) Ludlow to Stanton Lacy Leave Ludlow on the A49 signposted for Shrewsbury, and after 1½ m. turn right on to the B4365 signposted to Much Wenlock. Just over 1 m. later, turn right on to the minor road for Stanton Lacy.

(2) Stanton Lacy to Aston Munslow Return to the B4365 and turn right towards Much Wenlock. Continue through Culmington to the junction with the B4368, 2 m. beyond the village. Turn right, signposted for Much Wenlock/Bridgnorth, and follow the road up Corve Dale through Diddlebury. Aston Munslow is 1 m. further on. Turn left in the village to visit the museum of country life at The White House.

(3) Aston Munslow to Wilderhope Manor After visiting the museum, return to the B4368, turn left and continue about 3 m. Then, just after passing the Seven Stars public house, turn left on to the road signposted to Longville in the Dale. Follow the valley for about 1½ m. along the flank of Wenlock Edge with a tributary of the River Corve to the right, and then turn right into a long drive which leads to the National Trust property of Wilderhope Manor.

(4) Wilderhope Manor to Wenlock Edge Return to the road and turn right to continue up the valley, crossing a strip of woodland and a disused railway, before running into Longville in the Dale. There turn right on to the B4371, following the signpost to Much Wenlock, and climb to the steep wooded crest of Wenlock Edge. There are roadside lay-bys offering fine viewpoints just beyond the Plough Inn at Hilltop, a little under 3 m. from the turning in Longville.

(5) Wenlock Edge to Much Wenlock Continue along the B4371, through Presthope and Stretton Westwood, beyond which the road starts to descend towards Much Wenlock. At the junction with the A458 turn right, keeping straight on at the next junction on to the B4376 for the centre of Much Wenlock.

(6) Much Wenlock to Bridgnorth Return to the A458 and turn left, following the signposts for Bridgnorth. After 5 m. the road runs into Morville, an attractive village spaced between the gilded domes of the 18th-century Morville Hall and the Norman tower of the church. Continue along the A458 and after 3 m., where the road swings right on the outskirts of Bridgnorth, go straight on uphill into the centre of the town.

(7) Bridgnorth to Cleobury Mortimer From the town centre, rejoin the A458 signposted to Kidderminster, and follow it down the hill past the Severn Valley Railway headquarters. Then turn right on to the B4363, following the signpost to Cleobury Mortimer. For the 13 m. to Cleobury Mortimer, the road runs through open countryside, dropping now and then into wooded valleys cut by tributaries of the Severn. There are no settlements of any size along the way. At Kinlet, after 9 m., there is a small group of houses opposite the entrance to Kinlet Hall. There was once a village here, but all that remains is the large parish church standing in the hall grounds about ¾ m. from the road to the right. Beyond Kinlet the road skirts the western borders of Wyre Forest before going sharp left to join the A4117. Turn right here to cross the River Rea and enter Cleobury Mortimer.

(8) Cleobury Mortimer to Titterstone Clee Hill Leave the town on the A4117 signposted to Ludlow. Go through Hopton Wafers, where the road starts to climb steeply, to Foxwood and Doddington. Just beyond Doddington there is a view indicator on the left of the road, 1047 ft above sea level. From here there are wide views south and west to the Malvern Hills, and over much of Herefordshire. Just over 2 m. later, beyond Cleehill village, turn right along a lane signposted to Dhustone. This leads almost to the top of Titterstone Clee Hill, a fine vantage point.

(9) Titterstone Clee Hill to Ludlow Return from the hilltop to the A4117, turn right and continue 7 m. back to Ludlow.

INFORMATION

Places of interest *Aston Munslow:* The White House, house and museum, Good Friday afternoon; Bank Hol. weeks Mon. to Thur. and Sat., 11 a.m.-5.30 p.m.; for June to Aug. see local information. Museum only, Apr. to Oct., Wed. 2-6 p.m., Sat. 11 a.m.-6 p.m. *Bridgnorth:* Castle, all year, daily. Severn Valley Railway, Mar. to Oct., Sat., Sun., Bank Hols., afternoons. Daily in Aug. *Ludlow:* Castle, Apr. to Sept., Sundays. Museum, Easter to Sept., weekdays. Oct. to Easter, Mon. to Fri. afternoons, Sat. all day. *Much Wenlock:* Guildhall, Apr. to Sept., Tues. to Sat., Sun. and Mon. afternoons. Museum, Tues. to Sat. 11 a.m.-5 p.m., Mon. and Sun. afternoons. Priory, weekdays and Sun. afternoons. *Wilderhope Manor:* Apr. to Sept., Wed. afternoons.

Information Heart of England Tourist Board, Castle Square, Ludlow (Tel. Ludlow 3857).

Towns with easy access to Ludlow:

Hereford	24 m.	Shrewsbury	28 m.
Kidderminster	23 m.	Welshpool	32 m.
Leominster	11 m.	Worcester	30 m.

Early seed drill, White House museum.

ASTON MUNSLOW
The White House, in the heart of Corve Dale, is a country-life museum of agricultural implements and domestic utensils covering eight centuries. Exhibits include ancient carts and ploughs, a 19th-century granary and cider mill and 1910 General Election posters.

Norman carving in choir stalls, St Lawrence's Church, Ludlow.

LUDLOW
The town is noted for its two-week summer festival, when Shakespeare dramas are performed in the Norman castle and orchestras play in the 12th-century parish church. The ashes of A. E. Housman, the poet who wrote 'A Shropshire Lad', are buried in the shadow of the 135 ft high church tower, which dominates the town. The young princes Edward and Richard, sons of Edward IV, lived at the castle before their murder in the Tower of London in the 15th century. One of the most spectacular buildings in the town, the Feathers Hotel, in the Bull Ring, has been an inn since 1521: a plaque records an ancient boast of meals 'served by comelye and complyante wenches'.

Feathers Hotel, Ludlow.

SCALE
0   1   2   3   4   5 MILES

WENLOCK EDGE

This wooded limestone ridge runs from Craven Arms to the Severn Valley at Buildwas, with views across the Shropshire Plain. It was here, at Major's Leap, that Major Thomas Smallman jumped his horse over a cliff to elude Roundhead pursuers during the Civil War. The horse was killed, but the major clung to a tree and escaped.

Wenlock Priory.

82
Ludlow
(60 MILES)

Wilderhope Manor.

WILDERHOPE MANOR

Major Thomas Smallman, a Civil War hero, was imprisoned in his own house here but escaped to carry important Royalist dispatches to Shrewsbury. The 1586 building, now a youth hostel, is notable for its ceilings.

MUCH WENLOCK

Narrow streets of black-and-white buildings offset the ruins of St Milburga's Priory, rising from spacious, well-kept lawns. The priory, established in 680, was destroyed by the Danes in the 9th century and was followed by another religious house, endowed by Lady Godiva and her husband, the Saxon Earl Leofric. The present remains date from just after the Norman Conquest in 1066. The eastern block, which was built in 1500, is still used as a private house. A 16th-century Guildhall, standing on oak pillars, houses the whipping post and mobile stocks, last used in 1852.

STANTON LACY

One of the few recognisable examples of Saxon sculpture can be seen in the doorway of the church in this little Corve Dale village. Near by is the 1564 Langley Chapel, containing 17th-century furnishings. The chapel, scheduled as an ancient monument, is open at certain times.

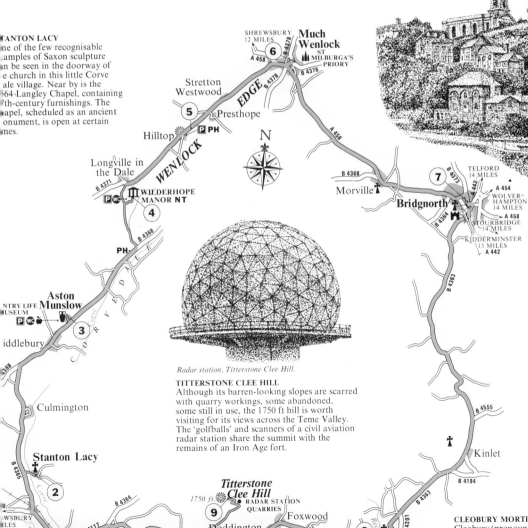

Bridgnorth High Town, from the Severn.

TITTERSTONE CLEE HILL

Although its barren-looking slopes are scarred with quarry workings, some abandoned, some still in use, the 1750 ft hill is worth visiting for its views across the Teme Valley. The 'golfballs' and scanners of a civil aviation radar station share the summit with the remains of an Iron Age fort.

Radar station, Titterstone Clee Hill.

BRIDGNORTH

Cromwell's troops blew up the Norman castle and burnt most of the town in 1646. The ruined castle keep now has a tilt three times that of the Leaning Tower of Pisa. The grounds are a public park with what Charles I, who often stayed at the castle, described as 'the finest walk in my domain'. Adjoining the park is St Mary Magdalene's Church, built in 1792 by Thomas Telford, the engineer better known for his canals and bridges. The castle and church are in Bridgnorth High Town, standing on a sandstone bluff 120 ft above the Severn. A cliff railway drops almost vertically to the Low Town on the river bank. Bridgnorth is the headquarters of the privately owned Severn Valley Railway. Steam trains run a service to Bewdley, 12¾ miles downstream, throughout the summer.

CLEOBURY MORTIMER

Cleobury (pronounced *Clibbery*) was a parish before the Norman family of Mortimer, later the Earls of March, founded the church around 1300. The church is notable for its twisted spire—due to warping of the timber—and outward-bulging walls, repaired by the engineer Thomas Telford in 1793 when he was Shropshire's county surveyor.

Map labels

SHREWSBURY 12 MILES — Much Wenlock — ST MILBURGA'S PRIORY — A 458 — B 4378 — **6** — B 4376 — Stretton Westwood — B 4378 — WENLOCK EDGE — **5** — Presthope — Hilltop — Longville in the Dale — B 4371 — WILDERHOPE MANOR NT — **4** — B 4368 — PH — Aston Munslow — COUNTRY LIFE MUSEUM — **3** — Diddlebury — B 4368 — Culmington — Stanton Lacy — B 4365 — **2** — SHREWSBURY MILES — A 4117 — B 4364 — **1** — LUDLOW — A 49 — HEREFORD 24 MILES — B 4214 — Cleehill — Doddington — Hopton Wafers — **9** — Titterstone Clee Hill 1750 ft. — RADAR STATION QUARRIES — Foxwood — **8** — Cleobury Mortimer — KIDDERMINSTER 11 MILES — B 4201 — A 4117 — B 4363 — Kinlet — B 4194 — B 4555 — B 4363 — **7** — Morville — A 458 — B 4368 — Bridgnorth — A 442 — A 454 — WOLVERHAMPTON 14 MILES — TELFORD 14 MILES — B 4373 — A 458 — A 364 — STOURBRIDGE 15 MILES — KIDDERMINSTER 13 MILES — A 442

227

Cider, hops and pure water in the Malverns

Travellers pausing to refresh themselves at St Ann's Well in Great Malvern will drink the pure water that is bottled for the Queen as well as customers all over the world. It comes from the streams of the Malvern Hills, which rise to 1394 ft at Worcestershire Beacon. Between the hills, in the valleys of the Teme and Severn, the road winds through hop gardens and cider-apple orchards, linking drowsy villages, medieval castles and moated Elizabethan mansions.

(1) Great Malvern to Ledbury Leave Great Malvern on the A449, signposted to Ledbury, with the Malvern Hills on the right. The road passes the Herefordshire Beacon before running down into Ledbury.

(2) Ledbury to Bromyard Leave Ledbury on the A438 signposted Hereford, but where the road turns left on the outskirts of the town, by the railway bridge, go straight ahead on the B4214. At the staggered crossroads with the A4103 keep ahead on the B4214 for Bromyard, turning right at the junction with the A465, 5 m. later. Turn right on to the A44 to enter Bromyard.

(3) Bromyard to Lower Brockhampton Leave Bromyard on the A44 signposted to Lower Brockhampton. Lower Brockhampton, a 15th-century manor, is approached through a National Trust park, the entrance to which is on the left about 2 m. beyond Bromyard.

(4) Lower Brockhampton to Great Witley Return to the A44, turn left and continue towards Worcester, descending into the Teme Valley. Immediately after crossing the river, turn left on to the B4197 and continue for 3½ m. to Martley. Here turn left on to the B4204 signposted Tenbury. Recross the Teme after 1½ m. and immediately turn right, following the signpost for The Shelsleys. The road now runs for 4 m. along the Teme Valley to Stanford Bridge, with the river on the right and wooded hills on the left. Normally quiet, it can be busy when car and motor-cycle hill climbs are staged at Shelsley Walsh. At Stanford Bridge, turn right on to the B4203 and, after 2½ m., right again on to the A443. About 1 m. further on, shortly after passing the B4197, turn right for Great Witley parish church.

(5) Great Witley to Hartlebury Return to the main road, go straight across it and turn right for Stourport-on-Severn at the junction with the A451. In Stourport, after 6 m., follow the signposts for Worcester, and at the roundabout on the far side of the town centre join the B4193 for Hartlebury.

(6) Hartlebury to Harvington Hall Rejoin the B4193 and continue to the junction with the A449. Turn left here then, soon after, right on to the A450. After 2 m., at the Mustow Green roundabout, take the Stourbridge exit, still on the A450. In Harvington, after about ½ m., turn right and follow the lane to Harvington Hall.

(7) Harvington Hall to Avoncroft Museum From the hall, continue straight on along the lane, which joins the A448. Turn left for Bromsgrove, passing under the M5, and after a further 1 m. turn right on to the A38 signposted Worcester. On the outskirts of Bromsgrove, fork left on to the B4091 signposted Hanbury. At the traffic lights just after the fork, turn left on to the B4024. Continue for ½ m. then turn right and follow the signposts for the museum.

(8) Avoncroft Museum to Hanbury Hall Return to the traffic lights and turn left, following the B4091 to Hanbury. In Hanbury, turn right into School Road and follow the signposts to Hanbury Hall.

(9) Hanbury Hall to Droitwich Beyond the hall fork right, and after 1 m. turn right at the junction with the B4090 for the 3 m. drive to Droitwich.

(10) Droitwich to Holt In Droitwich, turn left on to the A38. Then, after 600 yds, turn right on to the A4133 signposted Tenbury. Keep following the Ombersley and Tenbury signposts and, still on the A4133, go straight through Ombersley. After 1½ m. cross the River Severn. In ¼ m., where the main road swings sharply right, turn left into a minor road for Holt village church.

(11) Holt to Great Malvern Follow the lane round to the right beyond the church, and turn left on to the A443 at the T-junction, heading towards Worcester. On the outskirts of Worcester fork right into Renwick Road, turn left at the T-junction just beyond the railway, and leave the roundabout by the exit signposted Ross-on-Wye, on the A449, for the 8 m. drive back to Great Malvern.

INFORMATION

Places of interest *Avoncroft Museum of Buildings:* Apr. to Oct., daily (except Mon.) but open Bank Hol. Mon., 11 a.m.–6 p.m. *Hanbury Hall:* Ceiling and staircase shown only. Apr. to Sept., Wed., Sat., 2–6 p.m. *Hartlebury:* Castle, State rooms. Feb. to Nov., daily except Fri. Hereford and Worcester County Museum. Feb. to Nov., Mon. to Thur., 10 a.m.–6 p.m., Sat., Sun., 2–6 p.m. *Harvington Hall:* All year, afternoons daily (except Mon., Good Friday and Fri. after Bank Hols.) 2–6 p.m.; also 11.30 a.m.–1 p.m. from Easter to Sept.

Event *Malvern:* Three Counties Agricultural Show, June.

Nature trail *Brockhampton Woodland Walk:* Leaflet from Bringsty Post Office and at start of walk near by, off A44.

Information *Droitwich:* St Andrew's Brine Baths, Victoria Square (Tel. Droitwich 2352). *Malvern:* Wintergarden (Tel. Malvern 2700).

Towns with easy access to Great Malvern:

Cheltenham Spa . 23 m.	Gloucester . . . . . 25 m.
Evesham . . . . . . 22 m.	Hereford . . . . . . 21 m.

Gipsy caravan, Hartlebury Castle museum.

HARTLEBURY
The 15th-century castle is the home of the Bishop of Worcester, and also houses the county museum. Exhibits include a cider mill almost 300 years old, gipsy caravans and showmen's wagons. There is a nature reserve and picnic area in the grounds.

Moated manor, Lower Brockhampton.

LOWER BROCKHAMPTON
The moated manor, timber-framed and with a tiled roof, was built for a local squire around 1400. The range of buildings includes a well-preserved gatehouse added later in the 15th century, and a ruined 12th-century chapel. Brockhampton Park, which contains a church built in 1790 in the Gothic revival style, is National Trust property, where Herefordshire cattle graze in the pastures between the woods. Two woodland walks start from Bringsty Post Office, back on the A44.

BROMYARD
Notable buildings include Tower Hill House, built in 1630, and two old inns—the Falcon and the Bay Horse. The town, originally called Broomsgeard—an Anglo-Saxon word meaning 'broom enclosure'—looks out across Bringsty Common to the Midland Plain. Bromyard Downs provide views of the whole range of the Malverns to the mountains of Wales.

LEDBURY
The Poet Laureate John Masefield (1878–1967), who was born at Ledbury, described the Norman church as having 'a golden vane surveying half the shire'. There are several historic inns, and St Katherine's Hospital is still an almshouse after seven centuries.

SCALE

0   1   2   3   4   5 MILES

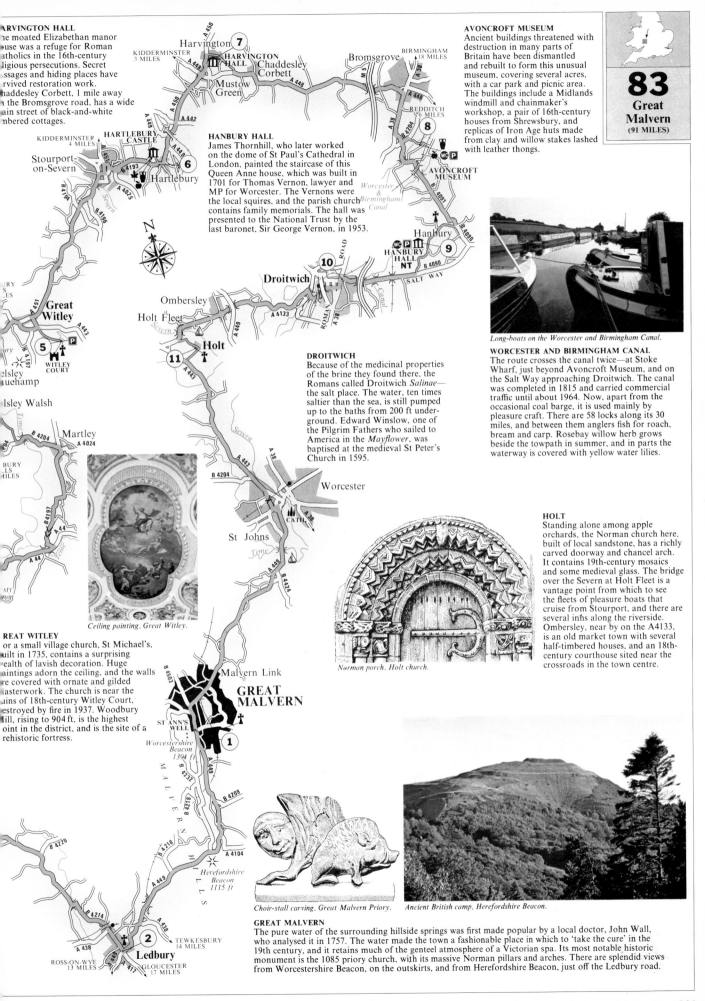

HARVINGTON HALL
The moated Elizabethan manor house was a refuge for Roman Catholics in the 16th-century religious persecutions. Secret passages and hiding places have survived restoration work. Chaddesley Corbett, 1 mile away on the Bromsgrove road, has a wide main street of black-and-white timbered cottages.

HANBURY HALL
James Thornhill, who later worked on the dome of St Paul's Cathedral in London, painted the staircase of this Queen Anne house, which was built in 1701 for Thomas Vernon, lawyer and MP for Worcester. The Vernons were the local squires, and the parish church contains family memorials. The hall was presented to the National Trust by the last baronet, Sir George Vernon, in 1953.

AVONCROFT MUSEUM
Ancient buildings threatened with destruction in many parts of Britain have been dismantled and rebuilt to form this unusual museum, covering several acres, with a car park and picnic area. The buildings include a Midlands windmill and chainmaker's workshop, a pair of 16th-century houses from Shrewsbury, and replicas of Iron Age huts made from clay and willow stakes lashed with leather thongs.

Long-boats on the Worcester and Birmingham Canal.

DROITWICH
Because of the medicinal properties of the brine they found there, the Romans called Droitwich *Salinae*—the salt place. The water, ten times saltier than the sea, is still pumped up to the baths from 200 ft underground. Edward Winslow, one of the Pilgrim Fathers who sailed to America in the *Mayflower*, was baptised at the medieval St Peter's Church in 1595.

WORCESTER AND BIRMINGHAM CANAL
The route crosses the canal twice—at Stoke Wharf, just beyond Avoncroft Museum, and on the Salt Way approaching Droitwich. The canal was completed in 1815 and carried commercial traffic until about 1964. Now, apart from the occasional coal barge, it is used mainly by pleasure craft. There are 58 locks along its 30 miles, and between them anglers fish for roach, bream and carp. Rosebay willow herb grows beside the towpath in summer, and in parts the waterway is covered with yellow water lilies.

HOLT
Standing alone among apple orchards, the Norman church here, built of local sandstone, has a richly carved doorway and chancel arch. It contains 19th-century mosaics and some medieval glass. The bridge over the Severn at Holt Fleet is a vantage point from which to see the fleets of pleasure boats that cruise from Stourport, and there are several inns along the riverside. Ombersley, near by on the A4133, is an old market town with several half-timbered houses, and an 18th-century courthouse sited near the crossroads in the town centre.

Ceiling painting, Great Witley.

GREAT WITLEY
For a small village church, St Michael's, built in 1735, contains a surprising wealth of lavish decoration. Huge paintings adorn the ceiling, and the walls are covered with ornate and gilded plasterwork. The church is near the ruins of 18th-century Witley Court, destroyed by fire in 1937. Woodbury Hill, rising to 904 ft, is the highest point in the district, and is the site of a prehistoric fortress.

Norman porch, Holt church.

Choir-stall carving, Great Malvern Priory.

Ancient British camp, Herefordshire Beacon.

GREAT MALVERN
The pure water of the surrounding hillside springs was first made popular by a local doctor, John Wall, who analysed it in 1757. The water made the town a fashionable place in which to 'take the cure' in the 19th century, and it retains much of the genteel atmosphere of a Victorian spa. Its most notable historic monument is the 1085 priory church, with its massive Norman pillars and arches. There are splendid views from Worcestershire Beacon, on the outskirts, and from Herefordshire Beacon, just off the Ledbury road.

229

The Vale of Evesham— England's other garden

Watered and drained by the Severn and Avon rivers, this part of the Midlands rivals Kent for the title of 'The Garden of England'. Visitors flock to the Vale of Evesham in spring to see the fruit trees in blossom; but there are attractions all the year round in this area sheltered by the Malvern Hills and the Cotswolds, of which Bredon Hill, an isolated mass of limestone 961 ft high, is an outlying part. Today's peaceful atmosphere in the ancient towns and villages, with their many fine old buildings, belies an often bloody past. Great battles were fought at Evesham in 1265 and at Tewkesbury in 1471.

(1) Evesham to Elmley Castle Leave Evesham on the A435 signposted to Cheltenham. After crossing the River Avon on the outskirts of the town keep straight ahead, and 2 m. later turn right at the crossroads, following the signpost to Elmley Castle. At the T-junction on the edge of Elmley Castle turn left, and head for the church at the top of the wide village street.

(2) Elmley Castle to Bredon After visiting the church, leave the village on the road signposted to Ashton under Hill. Go straight through the village, where the half-timbered Old Manor Farm dates from 1638, and on for 1½ m. to Beckford. In the village, turn right at the signpost to Overbury. Follow the road along the lower slopes of Bredon Hill through the villages of Overbury and Kemerton. When the road meets the B4079 keep straight ahead, following the signpost to Bredon, with its fine views over the Avon Valley.

(3) Bredon to Tewkesbury Leave Bredon on the B4080 signposted to Tewkesbury. Pass under the M5 just outside Bredon and 2½ m. later enter Tewkesbury, where the Severn and Avon meet.

(4) Tewkesbury to Longdon Take the A38, signposted Worcester, out of Tewkesbury. After crossing the River Avon on the edge of the town, turn left on to the A438. Three miles later turn right on to the B4211, passing Longdon Hall on the left after about 1 m. This long, black building used to be a coaching inn. Follow the road under the M50 into Longdon. Just before the village on the left is the half-timbered Moat House.

(5) Longdon to Upton upon Severn From Longdon, follow the B4211 for 2 m. to the junction with the A4104. Turn right at this junction, taking the road signposted to the old market town of Upton upon Severn.

(6) Upton upon Severn to Pershore Go into the town centre and turn right to follow the A4104 over the River Severn. A mile further on, where the road meets the A38, turn left and immediately right, back on to the A4104, signposted to Pershore. Follow the road past the village of Defford, where the pastureland begins to give way to market gardens, and on into Pershore.

(7) Pershore to Ragley Hall After exploring the centre of the Georgian town, still remarkably intact, leave Pershore on the A44 signposted to Worcester. On the outskirts of Pershore turn right on to the B4082, taking the road signposted to Upton Snodsbury. Continue on the B4082, which forks left at the junction with the B4083, going over the railway line, with Pershore station on the right. Keep ahead at the crossroads with the B4084, and turn right just before Upton Snodsbury on the road signposted to Inkberrow and Alcester. Turn right again on meeting the A422 and continue to the village of Inkberrow, with its half-timbered houses. Go through the village, still on the A422, and continue for 2 m. before turning left and immediately right at the junction with the A441. Two miles further on, turn right on to the A435. The entrance to Ragley Hall is on the right after 200 yds.

(8) Ragley Hall to Bretforton From Ragley Hall, continue on the A435 but 1 m. later, where the main road swings right, keep straight on, taking the B4085 signposted to Wixford. Follow the road through the village, which has a church with a 15th-century brass and a very rare, formerly thatched, shelter originally used for the vicar's horse. Continue on the B4085 out of the village and straight on for just over 1 m. to Bidford-on-Avon, with its 15th-century bridge. Turn right at the junction with the A439 then left at the traffic lights, taking the B4085 over the river. After ½ m., at the crossroads where the B4085 goes right, keep straight ahead. Continue for 4½ m. to a crossroads after crossing the railway. Here turn right, following the signpost for Honeybourne and Evesham. Follow the road round by the church in Cow Honeybourne and turn left along Gloster Ades. Then go right at the next crossroads on to the B4035 and follow this road to Bretforton. On the approach to the village, turn left up Main Street to visit the 14th-century Fleece Inn.

(9) Bretforton to Evesham Follow Main Street out through the village back to the B4035. At the junction turn left and keep on the B4035 back into Evesham.

INFORMATION

Places of interest *Bredon:* Tithe barn, all year, daily. *Evesham:* The Almonry, Mar. to Sept., afternoons (except Mon. and Wed.). *Ragley Hall:* Easter Weekend and Apr., Sun. only; May to end Sept., daily (except Mon. and Fri.) but open Bank Hols., 2-6 p.m.

Events *Evesham:* Regatta, May. *Tewkesbury:* Steam Fair and Organ Festival, July. Pram Race, Late Summer Bank Hol. Fair, Oct.

Information *Tewkesbury:* Town Hall, High Street (Tel. Tewkesbury 294639). *Worcester:* Heart of England Tourist Board, Bank Street (Tel. Worcester 29511).

Towns with easy access to Evesham:

Cheltenham . . . . 16 m.		Great Malvern . . 22 m.
Chipping		Stratford-upon-
Norton . . . . . . 22 m.		Avon . . . . 14 m.

Pershore Abbey church.

UPTON UPON SEVERN
Pleasure craft now glide past this old town with its wh In the 17th century nearly half Britain's river-borne tra was carried on the Severn, and until the 1900s cargo boats went upstream to Pool Quay near Welshpool. Near the river is a fine tower, the remains of a 13th-century church.

LONGDON
The village, set among willows and ditches, overlooks Longdon Marsh. The area was once part of the tidal estuary of the River Severn, and maritime plants can still be found growing there. The church is mainly 18th century, but it has a 14th-century spire.

TEWKESBURY
The town was the scene of a great Yorkist victory during the Wars of the Roses, and the site of the battle is still called Bloody Meadow. The Avon is navigable for many miles upstream and has made the town a popular centre for waterborne holidays. Tewkesbury Abbey, founded in 1092 by a kinsman of William the Conqueror, was closed by Henry VIII in 1541. The townspeople paid the king £453 to retain the abbey church. This superb building, with its 14th-century stained glass, has a Norman tower 132 ft high.

A 14th-century window.

SCALE

0   1   2   3   4   5 MILES

230

PERSHORE

...mous for its plums, Pershore grew ...around a religious community ...nded by King Oswald in AD 689. ...e Avon is spanned by a 14th-...tury bridge which incorporates ...nes taken from Elmley Castle on the ...rby slopes of Bredon Hill. Pershore ...bey, one of England's greatest ...gious houses, was closed in the 16th ...tury, but the abbey church was ...ed and is still in regular use. It is ...ninated by a 14th-century tower. ...ts of the building have remained ...ct for 800 years.

The east front, Ragley Hall.

RAGLEY HALL

Chippendale furniture, Minton, Sèvres and Meissen china, carvings by Grinling Gibbons and a gold brooch made by a Saxon craftsman are among the treasures at Ragley Hall. Set in parkland laid out by Capability Brown, Ragley was built in 1680 and has remained unchanged externally since the 18th century. The home of Lord and Lady Hertford, it has a great hall 70 ft long with a decorated plaster ceiling 40 ft high.

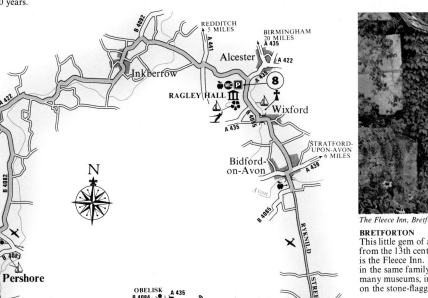

The Fleece Inn, Bretforton.

BRETFORTON

This little gem of a village is often missed by passers-by. The church dates from the 13th century and has some fine carvings, but the main attraction is the Fleece Inn. Built in the 14th century as a farmhouse, it has been in the same family ever since. It has a better collection of antiques than many museums, including a 48-piece set of Stuart pewter. Marks painted on the stone-flagged floor were to keep out witches and evil spirits.

EVESHAM

Evesham, set in a loop of the River Avon, dates from the foundation of the abbey in AD 708. Abbot Reginald's Gateway, at the end of a passage from the market-place, and dating from 1135, leads to the abbey remains. A 16th-century bell tower overlooks the riverside park, formerly the abbey grounds. A plaque near by marks the burial place of Simon de Montfort, father of the English parliament, who was killed fighting the army of Henry III at the Battle of Evesham in 1265.

Abbot Reginald's Gateway, Evesham.

BREDON

The slender spire of Bredon church stands 161 ft above the level of the Avon Valley, and is a landmark for miles around this village with its thatched black-and-white cottages. No traces remain of a monastery founded in the 8th century, but near the river is a 14th-century tithe barn which is now carefully preserved. It belongs to the National Trust and is reputed to be one of the finest in England.

River Avon and Bredon Hill from Eckington Bridge.

The Savage Memorial, Elmley Castle church.

ELMLEY CASTLE

This old village is notable for the memorials in its 11th-century church. One commemorates the 1st Earl of Coventry (1639–1705) and another, in alabaster, depicts seven members of the Savage family and dates from the 17th century. The castle from which the village took its name was a ruin in 1316. Behind the village, an ideal starting point for walks, Bredon Hill rises to 961 ft. Badgers are frequently seen on its slopes.

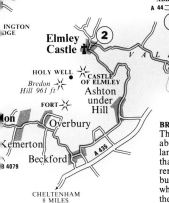

231

Where the Thames begins and history is woven in wool

Starting in Cirencester, source of the Thames and once the second largest town in Britain, this tour runs through beautiful countryside and delves back more than 4000 years into the past. Hetty Pegler's Tump, a prehistoric burial chamber near Uley, was perhaps 2500 years old before the Romans founded the city and built the great, straight roads that still run over the Cotswolds. In later years this country became a land of sheep, and wool merchants built the churches that are gems of English architecture.

(1) Cirencester to Fairford Leave Cirencester on the A417 signposted for Lechlade, and continue for 9 m. to Fairford.

(2) Fairford to Bibury Continue through Fairford on the A417 and, on the far side of the town, turn left and go straight ahead at the next crossroads on to the road signposted for Hatherop. In Hatherop turn left for Coln St Aldwyns. In Coln St Aldwyns turn right then first left, signposted to Bibury. At the A433, turn left into Bibury.

(3) Bibury to Northleach In Bibury, where the A433 swings left to cross the River Coln, keep straight ahead on the road signposted to Ablington and Northleach. Bear right through Ablington and after 3 m., at the second of two closely spaced crossroads, turn right for Northleach.

(4) Northleach to Chedworth Roman Villa Leave Northleach on the A40 signposted to Cheltenham and, at the crossroads just outside the village, turn left on to the A429. Take the first right, signposted to Yanworth. Continue through Yanworth and keep straight ahead past a junction in the valley of the River Coln. Chedworth Roman Villa is on the right, beyond the junction.

(5) Chedworth Roman Villa to Prinknash Abbey Return to the junction by the river and turn left for Withington. At the T-junction on the edge of the village, turn left and follow the road, signposted Andoversford, to its junction with the A436. Turn left on to the A436, signposted for Gloucester, and after about 3½ m., at the junction with the A435, go left, then immediately right, still on the A436 for Gloucester. After 2 m., at the roundabout, take the A417 exit for Cirencester. At the T-junction in Birdlip turn right, then immediately left on to the B4070 signposted for Stroud. After 1 m. fork right for Painswick, and at the junction with the A46 turn right. After ½ m. fork left for Prinknash Park and the abbey.

(6) Prinknash Abbey to Painswick Follow the one-way system through the abbey grounds. At the public road turn left, and at the T-junction with the A46 turn right for the 2½ m. run into Painswick.

(7) Painswick to Minchinhampton Follow the A46 from Painswick to Stroud. Before the road reaches Stroud town centre, turn left to follow the A46 signposted for Bath. Keep straight on at the next crossroads, then turn left for Minchinhampton opposite The Anchor public house. Go right at the Give Way sign on Rodborough Common, then keep straight ahead at Tom Long's Post, and after 1 m. turn right down Butt's Street into the middle of Minchinhampton.

(8) Minchinhampton to Uley Long Barrow Leave Minchinhampton on the road signposted for Stroud and Nailsworth, then shortly afterwards fork left, following the signpost for Nailsworth. After 1 m., at the T-junction with the A434, turn right, still following the signpost for Nailsworth. At the junction with the A46 in the village turn right, then immediately left, on to the road signposted for Nympsfield. On the outskirts of Nympsfield, turn left then immediately right for Uley. Turn right at the next junction, then left on to the B4066. Uley Long Barrow is on the right after about 400 yds.

(9) Uley Long Barrow to Westonbirt Follow the B4066 downhill, and at the crossroads beyond Uley turn left for Kingscote and Tetbury. After 1½ m., at the A4135, bear left, and 1¼ m. later fork right for Westonbirt. Cross the A46 and 3 m. later turn right on to the A433. Westonbirt Arboretum is on the right ¼ m. later.

(10) Westonbirt to Sapperton Follow the A433 to Tetbury. In the town centre turn left, still on the A433, signposted here for Cirencester. Then, when the A433 swings right after about 200 yds, carry straight on to the B4014 signposted for Avening. At the T-junction in Avening turn right, following the signpost for Minchinhampton. At the top of the hill, bear right on the road signposted for Stroud. At the next T-junction turn right, then bear right on to the A419. Pass Aston Down airfield, then turn left for Frampton Mansell. Go through the village to Sapperton.

(11) Sapperton to Cirencester At the T-junction on the far side of Sapperton, turn left. After 1 m. turn right for Daglingworth. Bear right through Daglingworth and turn right on to the A417 for Cirencester.

INFORMATION

Places of interest *Cirencester:* Corinium Museum, weekdays, Sun. afternoons; closed Mon. in winter. *Arlington Mill:* Daily, Mar. to Oct. and weekends in winter. *Chedworth Roman Villa:* Mar. to Sept., Tues. to Sun. and mid-Oct. to Feb., Wed. to Sun. *Bibury Trout Farm:* Apr. to end Oct. afternoons. *Prinknash Abbey:* All year, daily. *Westonbirt Arboretum:* All year, daily.

Events *Cirencester:* Mop Fair, Oct. Sheep Fair, 1st Mon. in Sept. *Painswick:* Feast and yew-clipping ceremony, Sept. 19 or 1st. Sun. after.

Information Car Park, The Forum, Cirencester (Tel. Cirencester 4180).

Towns with easy access to Cirencester:

Bath	34 m.	Gloucester	17 m.
Faringdon	19 m.	Swindon	24 m.

Market House, Minchinhampton.

MINCHINHAMPTON
The approach to the old cloth-making village and market centre is over Minchinhampton Common, a popular leisure area. An 1800-year-old earthwork called The Bulwarks provides an unusual hazard on the local golf course. One end of the 3 mile long earthwork is at Woeful Dane Bottom—so named after a Danish defeat there. Among some fine houses and cottages in the village, the Market House is outstanding. Built in 1698, it is supported on stone columns with a row of wooden columns in the centre. It was the scene of dramatic stage triumphs by the great tragic actress of the late 18th and early 19th centuries, Sarah Siddons. Tom Long's Post, where six roads converge on the common, marks a highwayman's grave.

ULEY LONG BARROW
This prehistoric burial mound, also known as Hetty Pegler's Tump, is about 180 ft long. It contains a stone-built central passage with two chambers on either side and another at the end. When it was excavated in 1854, the remains of about 28 people were found. From the top of the mound, the Malvern Hills can be seen nearly 30 miles away to the north.

WESTONBIRT
The 116 acres of Westonbirt Arboretum, together with the 45 acres of nearby Silk Wood, contain one of the finest collections of trees in Britain. The Forestry Commission now owns this area. The first trees were planted in 1829. At least seven are the tallest of their kind in the country, including a 100 ft high silver maple and a 79 ft Caucasian oak. The rarest trees include a Japanese horse chestnut, two Japanese birches and an ebony tree. A walk right round the arboretum takes about two hours. A tour of Silk Wood can be completed in 90 minutes or so. It begins near the car park, and passes a 154 ft fir.

Westonbirt Arboretum in the autumn.

SCALE

0 1 2 3 4 5 MILES

PRINKNASH ABBEY

The modern part of this monastery, famous for its pottery, was built at a cost of £400,000 by Benedictine monks who moved to Prinknash from Caldy Island, off the Pembrokeshire coast, in 1928. The abbey and its pottery are open to visitors, and in the grounds is a bird park where 70 species from all over the world can be seen.

PAINSWICK

This delightful little town, at the head of one of the many valleys radiating from Stroud, is famous for its churchyard yews and tombs. Local tradition says there are 99 yews and that all attempts to grow the 100th have failed. The Cotswold stone tombs, carved by local craftsmen between the 17th and 19th centuries, are of such interest that each one of the 75 tombs is mentioned in 'tomb trail' guides obtainable in the church porch.

CHEDWORTH ROMAN VILLA

The villa is one of the best preserved in Britain. Many of the original walls stand several feet high, complete with their 'central-heating' ducts. These walls have been built up and roofed so that the buildings may be entered. The villa, occupied between the 2nd and 4th centuries AD, had two bath suites—one for damp heat, like a Turkish bath, the other for dry heat, like a sauna. There is a small museum on the site.

Some of the 99 yews in Painswick churchyard.

Stone carvings, Northleach parish church.

NORTHLEACH

One of the finest of the Cotswold 'wool' churches, paid for by the wealth of wool merchants in the Middle Ages, is the pride of Northleach. In the 15th century the place was as important in the wool trade as Cirencester; but it has remained a village, with narrow, winding streets and some fine old buildings, including Tudor almshouses.

SAPPERTON

The wooded Golden Valley—said to have been so called by Queen Victoria—ends here. A footpath leads to the overgrown mouth of the 2 mile Sapperton Tunnel. Along this, between 1789 and 1911, bargees propelled their craft by pushing with their feet against the walls and roof. The canal is now disused.

Arlington Row, Bibury.

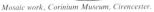

Mosaic work, Corinium Museum, Cirencester.

CIRENCESTER

In Roman times, Cirencester was Britain's second largest town after London. It stands at the crossing point of the Foss Way and the Ermin Way. In the Park Street museum there are many relics of the ancient town, then called Corinium, including coins, pottery and mosaics. Old buildings of Cotswold stone blend with modern work in the town's centre, which is dominated by the 15th-century parish church, containing one of Britain's few remaining pre-Reformation pulpits. The church's peal of 12 bells is the oldest in the country. The Weavers' Hall in Thomas Street is still maintained by the Weavers' Guild, as it has been for over 500 years. Visitors can dismiss the controversy about how the town's name is pronounced; the local people pronounce it just as it is spelt.

Medieval stained glass, Fairford.

FAIRFORD

The little town of stone houses has a late 15th-century church famous for its stained glass. The 28 windows by artists of the 15th and 16th centuries tell the Bible story from the Garden of Eden to the Last Judgment. These priceless works were removed for safe keeping during the Civil War and again in the Second World War.

BIBURY

This tiny village, which has a population of less than 800, was hailed by the Victorian artist and social reformer William Morris as 'the most beautiful in England'. The attractions include Arlington Row, a terrace of 16th to 17th-century stone cottages with stone-tiled roofs. The cottages, now owned by the National Trust, were once occupied by weavers whose products were finished at nearby Arlington Mill, a 17th-century building restored in the 1960s and now a folk museum and art gallery. Bibury also has a trout farm where fish are reared in a series of 40 ponds surrounded by footpaths. The church was rebuilt and altered in the 12th and 13th centuries, but parts of the original Saxon church can still be seen, including carving on the chancel arch and a circular window. There are notable 17th-century Spanish needlework pictures of saints. Adjoining the church is Bibury Court, a Tudor mansion with a wing attributed to Inigo Jones.

A conducted tour of a Cotswold farm
DENFURLONG FARM

Farmers and townsfolk have not always understood each other. To promote a better understanding of the industry that provides half the nation's food, and of how it is planned and managed, several farms now welcome visitors. One of them is Denfurlong Farm in the Cotswolds. Nigel Finch, who runs it, has prepared this commentary.

Agriculture is not only one of the most traditional parts of British life but it is also one of the most vital. Britain's farmers today produce more than half of the nation's food. But the vast majority of people, living as they do in towns and cities, have little idea of how a farm is run and the problems that a farmer has to face.

At Denfurlong I have tried to bridge this gap. Visitors are always welcome; we show them what goes on and explain how, for example, their milk and butter ends up on the breakfast table. Two trails have also been established. One goes round the farm buildings, while the other explores the fields. The field trail is about 2 miles long—but there is an optional short cut!

It was my father who bought Denfurlong Farm in 1937 and established a dairy herd. We sold our milk from door to door in the village, like thousands of other farmers. I can remember taking the milk round in a horse-drawn trap, dipping into a churn with a measure to fill the customers' jugs.

Times have changed since then. We started sending our milk to the dairy in Cirencester, then to Cheltenham and later to Droitwich, slowly moving out to the bigger centres.

The really big change has come since the middle 1960s, when the bulk tanker was introduced. The milk now goes to Cricklade, where it is transferred to a bigger tanker and whisked along the M4 to London, then across the city to Woolwich for bottling.

The difference between selling milk from door to door in Chedworth and sending it to a dairy on the other side of the country illustrates the revolution in farming. Since the Second World War the country has been convinced of the need for greatly increased food production. A lot more capital has been injected into new buildings and machinery. Fields have tended to get bigger, more suitable for machines and much easier to manage with fewer men. In 1953 it took three men to work Denfurlong; now only one is needed.

The buildings, too, reflect the changing appearance that comes with increasing mechanisation. There is a quarry very near the farm, and the older buildings are of stone and slate. But some of them have outlived their purpose and it is cheaper and more efficient, when they

OLD WAYS *Crumbling stone walls mark field boundaries in part of the farm where the soil is poor and the land is used rough pasturage for animals.*

NEW WAYS *Mechanisation is changing the face of the countryside. Huge combine harvesters, which reap and thre the corn in one operation, need room to work. This means bigger fields with fewer walls and hedges.*

have to be replaced, to go in for more functional concrete blocks and asbestos sheets. They may not look so attractive, but a careful eye to their design and colour, and where they are sited, can go a long way towards minimising any clash with the beauties of the surrounding countryside.

Food for the winter
The buildings and yards account for about five of the farm's 289 acres—an acre is about half the size of a football pitch. A walk over the fields will reveal the uses to which the rest of the land is put. Thirty acres on the steep slopes of the valley are used for rough grazing. Fifty acres provide the cattle with special grass mixtures. Hay is grown on 30 acres; silage is produced on 55 and cereals on the remaining 119. On average, 1 acre will produce 34 cwt of wheat or 4800 pints of milk each year.

Some of the good-quality grazing land can be seen from the car park. The cattle are kept within an electric fence to make sure that they do not waste too much grass by trampling on it. The fence is moved at least once a day, so there is always a supply of fresh grass.

Grass is also used to make silage in a pit alongside the car park. Many people think silage is some sort of manure, but this smelly stuff is an important food in winter, when a cow will eat up to 10 tons of it.

A small exhibition area with wall charts and models is the first stop on the tour of the farm buildings. It gives background material about farming as well as an overall picture of the way Denfurlong works.

The food store next to the exhibition area underlines the fact that cattle do not live on grass alone. A balanced diet is essential for the production of milk, and also of good lean beef. Oats, barley and other foods are given to the cows just before their afternoon milking. Calves are fed twice a day on oats, barley, molasses, meal and concentrates. All the barley and oats are grown on the farm.

Calves are penned in the next section of the building and represent a big part of the farmer's investment in the future. Cows have a nine-month gestation period—just like humans—and each one should produce a calf every year between February and May.

The bull calves are reared for beef on one of the estate's other farms, and sold as steers when they are between one year and 18 months old. The other calves—about half of the total—remain at Denfurlong, eventually joining the herd and having calves of their own when they are about three years old or slightly younger.

Before going into the milking parlour, the cows gather in the circular collecting yard. The yard is overlooked by a big Dutch barn, almost 100 ft by 50 ft, where hay is stored. Like silage, hay is needed for the winter diet: a full-grown cow can eat up to 30 lb. every day from October to April.

Push-button control
Dairy-farm techniques have changed a lot since the days of the traditional milkmaid with her milking stool and pail. I designed my milking parlour in 1965. It is fully automated, and is still one of the most modern in the country; one man can milk 65 cows in an hour.

A recorded commentary explaining how it all works is operated by a push-button control on the viewing platform.

The cows are milked twice a day, with as near as possible a 12-hour interval. Milking rules the dairy farmworker's life. It is a seven-days-a-week, 52-weeks-a-year job. You cannot persuade the cows to stop producing milk to give you a weekend rest. The day's work is from 6 a.m. to about 6 p.m. with an hour off for breakfast and another for lunch.

Milk for a million
There are 80 milking cows on the farm, and between them they produce about 78,000 gallons a year—an average of more than $2\frac{1}{2}$ gallons daily from each cow. The average person uses just over half a pint of milk a day, excluding what goes into butter and cheese, so Denfurlong's annual production would keep 1 million people—a city, say, almost the size of Birmingham—going for a day.

Milk from the parlour is automatically pumped to a tank in the dairy. The viewing platform is built over part of the cowhouse that is the milking herd's home from October until the middle of March, the period when the weather is likely to be at its worst. The cows are free to roam out into the yard and to the silage pit. Manure is cleared from the cowhouse regularly with a tractor and scraper, then spread over the grassland as a fine natural fertiliser. The idea of recycling materials is now considered modish, but farmers all over the world have been doing it for centuries.

The Denfurlong field trail is liable to be muddy in places, so stout boots should be

MEMORY IN STONE *Farm architecture, too, is changing. This barn was built to house a threshing machine. The combine harvester has made the thresher redundant, and the barn is to be converted into a house.*

THE YOUNG GENERATION *Calves spend six to eight weeks with their mother. Most calves at Denfurlong are produced by artificial insemination, the offspring of a bull chosen for the required qualities.*

A conducted tour of a Cotswold farm
DENFURLONG FARM

worn. Unfortunately, fields are not suited to pushchairs or wheelchairs.

The trail crosses a field of grass that is used for grazing, haymaking or silage. Haymaking is no longer the colourful, extremely laborious task it used to be, but its importance is as great as ever. Tractor-machines cut, turn and bale the grass and clover, but no amount of mechanisation can ensure the right weather at the right time. In June the farmers pray for a few good days because, apart from anything else, sunshine helps to make the hay more digestible. Granted good conditions, each acre will produce about 2 tons.

From the grassland the trail drops into a valley where the soil is too thin and poor for cultivation. There are plenty of trees and bushes, but the elms have been ravaged by Dutch elm disease in recent years.

Planting conifers might not be a bad investment, but there is a fair chance that half of them would 'walk' at Christmas time; and anyway I prefer the look of the valley as it is, with its fine view.

Around the fields
The stream at the lower side of the farm carries a lot of sediment, causing waterlogging in the fields alongside. We tried to remedy this by digging a pool where the silt now accumulates. One answer may be to clear out the pool regularly and use the silt to build up the fields. Looking on the bright side, I realise that another person's land is being transported down to me by the running water.

The stream is slowed down by the many plants that flourish along its course—wild mint, watercress, great willow-herb and others—and this adds to the drainage problem we have to tackle.

Beyond the stream, the trail climbs back to the flatter, more fertile fields on the farm's higher ground. These are used for growing grass and cereals. We work on a four-year rotation system—one year of grass and three years of cereals. The main cereal crops are winter wheat, winter oats and spring barley. About two-thirds of the harvest is used to feed our animals. The remainder is sold, so the surplus oats may end up on your breakfast table as porridge. The wheat is used for seeding.

Wheat and oats are sown in September and October, and grow for up to 11 months. The barley, sown in March or April, is ready for harvesting from August onwards, so late summer and autumn is a busy time. Sowing is done with a seed drill—invented by Jethro Tull in the 18th century—which deposits seeds and fertiliser at the same time.

Why stubble is burnt
Visitors to the country often wonder why fields of stubble are set on fire after the harvest. The reason is that the cost of baling straw is higher than the market price. So for farms which, like Denfurlong, have a surplus, it is cheaper to burn it than to sell it. Besides, the ash is a useful fertiliser. Most farmers follow a set of rules prepared by the National Farmers' Union to ensure that burning does not harm wildlife or cause a nuisance to the public. Visitors to Denfurlong after the harvest can see for themselves that we try to follow the code of peaceful coexistence between town and country.

THEIR ALLOTTED PATCH *Grass is valuable: it means milk. Once, cows were allowed to wander all over a pasturage, spoiling much of it by trampling. The electric fence, cheap and efficient, has altered all that. The single strand of wire carries a high voltage and low amperage. A shock from it is harmless, but the cows do not like it and soon learn to avoid it. By moving the fence regularly the farmer 'folds' his herd over a field, strip by strip, so that the diet is always fresh and clean. At present there are 80 milking cows on the farm. Between them, they produce 78,000 gallons of milk a year.*

IN THE QUEUE *Cows wait outside to take their turn in the milking parlour, a twice-daily routine every day of the year. Just before going in for the afternoon milking the cows are given a supplementary feed which is measured out individually, each one's ration depending on her recorded milk production.*

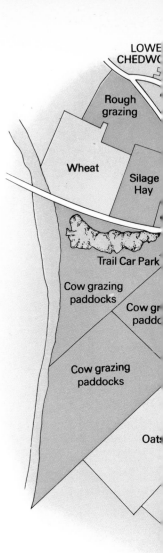

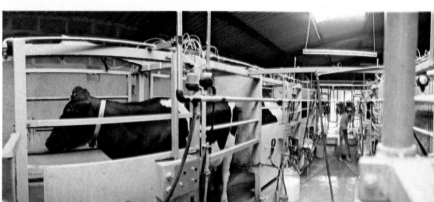

AUTOMATION *No milkmaids, no pails or three-legged stools . . . this dairy, designed by Nigel Finch in 1965, enables one man to milk 65 cows in an hour. Visitors can watch it all happening from a special viewing platform. Modern farmers scoff at the notion that cows prefer the old-fashioned method of being milked—Denfurlong's production record proves them right.*

LOADING UP *It takes only a few minutes to pipe the milk from the bulk storage tank into the waiting tanker, which will take it to Cricklade on the first stage of its journey to the bottling dairy at Woolwich. Like the milking parlour itself, there are no days off for the tanker fleet. From Denfurlong alone it distributes an average of 1600 pints a day, winter and summer.*

236

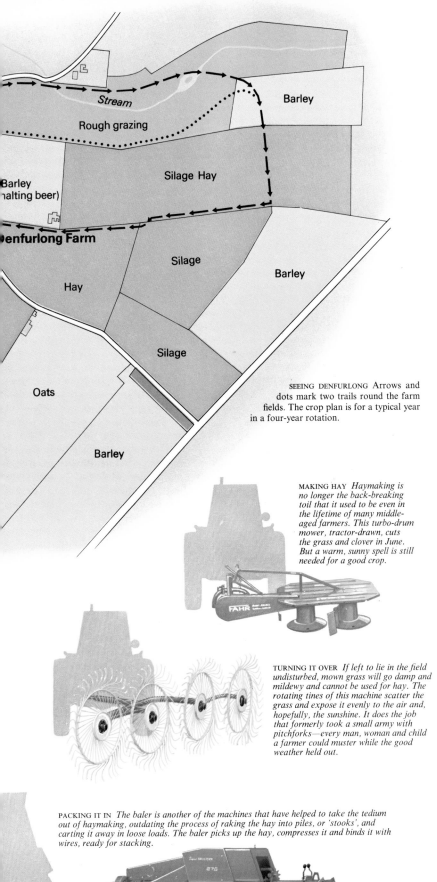

Stream

Rough grazing

Barley

Barley
(malting beer)

Silage Hay

Denfurlong Farm

Silage

Hay

Barley

Silage

SEEING DENFURLONG Arrows and
dots mark two trails round the farm
fields. The crop plan is for a typical year
in a four-year rotation.

Oats

Barley

Great willow-herb   *Water mint*

TRESPASSERS *Things that attract the nature-lover are
not always welcome on a well-run farm, and here are
two examples. The great willow-herb and the water
mint are among Denfurlong's problems. With other
weeds growing by the stream they tend to check the
free flow of water, adding to the drainage difficulties.*

Wheat   *Oats*   *Barley*

HARVEST FRUITS *Wheat and oats are sown in the
autumn, barley in spring. All three crops should be
ready for harvesting from August onwards. Severe
storms sometimes batter down the ripening corn,
making it difficult to cut. Plant biologists have been
trying for years to develop strains that will stand up
to the worst weather, so far without complete success.*

MAKING HAY *Haymaking is
no longer the back-breaking
toil that it used to be even in
the lifetime of many middle-
aged farmers. This turbo-drum
mower, tractor-drawn, cuts
the grass and clover in June.
But a warm, sunny spell is still
needed for a good crop.*

TURNING IT OVER *If left to lie in the field
undisturbed, mown grass will go damp and
mildewy and cannot be used for hay. The
rotating tines of this machine scatter the
grass and expose it evenly to the air and,
hopefully, the sunshine. It does the job
that formerly took a small army with
pitchforks—every man, woman and child
a farmer could muster while the good
weather held out.*

PACKING IT IN *The baler is another of the machines that have helped to take the tedium
out of haymaking, outdating the process of raking the hay into piles, or 'stooks', and
carting it away in loose loads. The baler picks up the hay, compresses it and binds it with
wires, ready for stacking.*

WHEN TO VISIT DENFURLONG

The farm is open to visitors
every day of the year from
daylight to dusk.
Milking time in the afternoon
starts between 4–5 p.m.

HOW TO GET THERE *The farm is approached by a
turning, signposted Chedworth, off the A429
between Cirencester and Stow-in-the-Wold.
From Northleach, heading south, turn right
after 4 m.; from Cirencester turn left after 6 m. The
farm is half a mile along the Chedworth road, on
the left by the first junction.*

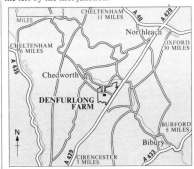

Picture villages framed in Cotswold stone

No area of comparable size in Britain has more enchanting small towns and villages than the Cotswolds. This tour links such gems as Chipping Campden, Stow-on-the-Wold, Lower Slaughter and Snowshill. Broadway, from which it starts, has probably topped more 'prettiest village' polls than any other in the country. Bourton-on-the-Water is distinguished by its chain of low stone river bridges, all reproduced in a model of the village. The breed of cows whose milk first produced Double Gloucester cheese can be seen, with other rare farm animals, at the Cotswold Farm Park; and the surprising collection of curios at Snowshill Manor includes a Japanese 'war council' of Samurai chiefs in armour.

(1) Broadway to Dover's Hill Leave the village on the A46, signposted to Stratford, and after about 1 m. go through Willersey. About 1¼ m. further on, in Weston Subedge, turn right on to the road signposted to Dover's Hill and reach the highest point, 754 ft, after about 1½ m.

(2) Dover's Hill to Chipping Campden Continue on the road over the hill and go straight across at the next crossroads. On the outskirts of Chipping Campden, bear left into the centre of the town.

(3) Chipping Campden to Stow-on-the-Wold Leave the town on the B4081 signposted to Broadway. On the outskirts, turn left on to the road signposted Broad Campden. In Broad Campden turn right, following the signpost for Blockley. In Blockley village turn left on to the road signposted to Moreton-in-Marsh, and then right at the next junction on to the B4479. After just over 1 m. turn left on to the A44 and go through the village of Bourton-on-the-Hill. After 1½ m. enter Moreton-in-Marsh. At the junction with the A429 turn right. After 4 m. turn left on to the A424 for Stow-on-the-Wold town centre.

(4) Stow-on-the-Wold to Bourton-on-the-Water Leave Stow on the A429 signposted to Cirencester. After just under 3 m. turn left into Bourton-on-the-Water.

(5) Bourton-on-the-Water to Cotswold Farm Park Return to the A429 and turn right towards Stow-on-the-Wold. After about ½ m. turn left on to the road signposted to The Slaughters. At the T-junction in Lower Slaughter turn left, and at the next T-junction turn right, following the signpost for Upper Slaughter. Keep ahead past Upper Slaughter to the junction with the A436, and turn left. At the next crossroads, turn right and follow the road for just over 2 m. to the entrance to Cotswold Farm Park on the left.

(6) Cotswold Farm Park to Winchcombe Continue on the road past the farm to the junction with the B4077. Turn left, following the Tewkesbury signpost. Continue through Ford, keeping on the B4077, and at the second crossroads, outside the village, turn left. After just over 3 m., at a T-junction, turn right and follow the signpost into Winchcombe. To visit Sudeley Castle, turn left on to the A46 in the town, then left again, following the signpost to the castle. Follow the one-way system through the castle grounds. Turn left to return to Winchcombe, whose church has an altar cloth worked by Henry VIII's first wife, Catherine of Aragon.

(7) Winchcombe to Hailes Abbey Leave the town on the A46 signposted to Stratford-upon-Avon. After about 2 m. turn right on to the road signposted to Hailes Abbey, which is reached after crossing the railway.

(8) Hailes Abbey to Snowshill Return to the A46 and turn right, then immediately right again, following the signpost to Didbrook. Continue past Didbrook church to the junction with the B4077 and turn right. Follow the road up a wooded hillside, and at the top turn left on to the road signposted to Snowshill. After 1 m. follow the road round to the right, and at the T-junction turn left. Turn left again about 1 m. later and follow the road to Snowshill.

(9) Snowshill to Broadway Tower Country Park Leave the village on the road that goes up past the church, keeping straight ahead at the crossroads. At the next crossroads turn left, following the signpost for Chipping Campden. After about 1 m. fork left, following the Broadway signpost, and continue for ½ m. to the entrance to the country park on the left.

(10) Broadway Tower Country Park to Broadway Continue along the road from the park to the junction with the A44 and turn left. Descend Fish Hill and return to Broadway.

INFORMATION

Places of interest *Bourton-on-the-Water:* Model Village, all year, daily. Birdland Zoo Gardens and Wildlife Art Gallery, all year, daily. *Broadway Tower Country Park:* Apr. to Sept., 11 a.m.-6 p.m. (3 p.m., Oct. to Mar.). *Chipping Campden:* Market Hall, daily. Woolstaplers Hall, Apr. to Sept., daily. *Cotswold Farm Park:* Mid-May to Oct., daily. *Hailes Abbey Museum:* Weekdays, Sun. afternoons. *Snowshill Manor:* Apr., Oct., Sat., Sun.; May to end Sept., Wed. to Sun. (except Fri. mornings) and Bank Hol. Mon. *Sudeley Castle and Gardens:* Mar. to mid-Oct., daily (except Mon.), 12-5.30 p.m. Grounds, 11 a.m.-7 p.m. (5.30 p.m., Bank Hol. Sun. and Mon.).

Craft workshops *Bourton-on-the-Water:* The Pottery, Clapton Row. Most days except Sun. *Stow-on-the-Wold:* Sheep Street Studio. Porcelain and terracotta jewellery and panels. Open most days, or telephone first (Tel. Stow 30120).

Events *Stow-on-the-Wold:* Agricultural shows, May and July. Agricultural Fair, Oct.

Information Heart of England Tourist Board, Bank Street, Worcester (Tel. Worcester 29511).

Towns with easy access to Broadway:

Cheltenham Spa	16 m.	Stratford-upon-Avon	15 m.
Chipping Norton	16 m.	Tewkesbury	13 m.
Evesham	6 m.	Worcester	22 m.

Broadway Tower.

BROADWAY TOWER COUNTRY PARK
Nature trails, that take between 30 and 90 minutes to walk, cover the country park on Broadway Hill, 1024 ft above sea level. In a 150-year-old barn is a display showing the geology of the hill, and there are exhibitions and demonstrations of local crafts, including furniture-making. The park is overlooked by Broadway Tower, a late-18th-century sham castle built by the 6th Earl of Coventry as a landmark to be seen from his home at Croome Court, near Worcester. Thirteen counties are visible from the rooftop viewing gallery. The lower floors house displays of artistic and historic interest.

View from Broadway Tow...

Winchcon...

CHELTEN-HAM
6 MILES

SUDE...
CAS...

Hailes Abbey.

HAILES ABBEY
The abbey was founded in 1242 by Richard, Earl of Cornwall and brother of Henry III. Twenty-eight year... later a phial said to contain the blood of Christ was g... to the abbey by Richard's son Edmund. It was declare... a fake in the 16th century, but not before it had broug... the abbey fame as a pilgrimage centre. Little remains ... the abbey above ground, but the site is being excavate...

WINCHCOMBE
This little market town is overlooked by Sudeley Cast... once the home of Catherine Parr, the last of Henry VI... six wives. Built in the early 15th century and restored ... the 19th, the castle stands in parkland adorned by and... yew hedges. The George Hotel dates from the 13th century and was built by the Prior of Hailes to lodge pilgrims to the abbey. It is much altered, but still has ... open gallery in the courtyard.

SCALE

0   1   2   3 MILES

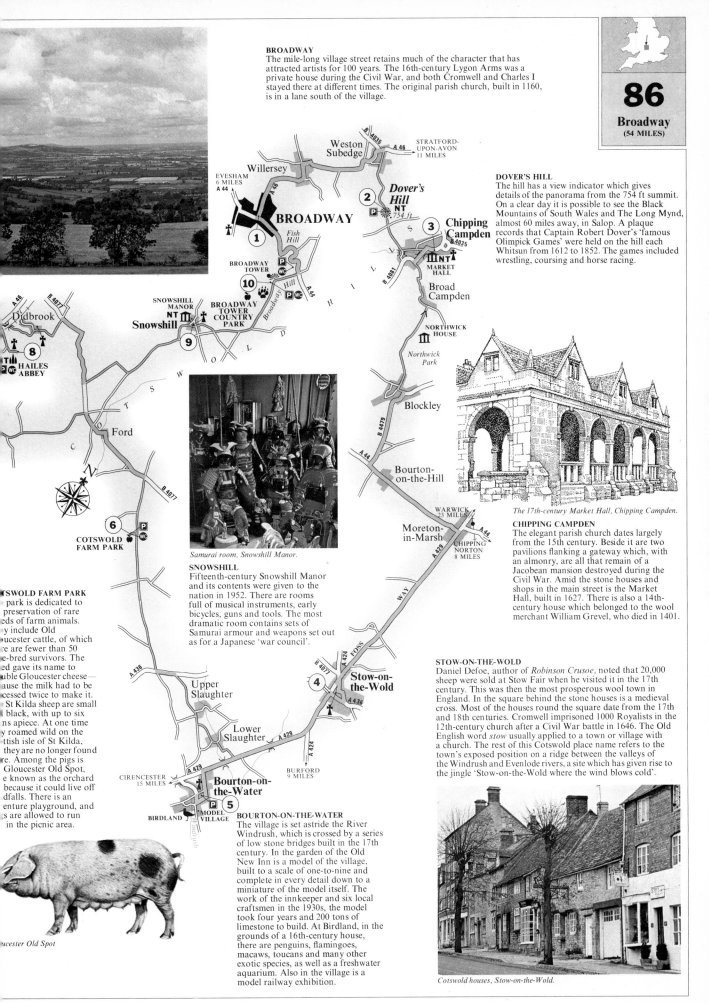

BROADWAY

The mile-long village street retains much of the character that has attracted artists for 100 years. The 16th-century Lygon Arms was a private house during the Civil War, and both Cromwell and Charles I stayed there at different times. The original parish church, built in 1160, is in a lane south of the village.

DOVER'S HILL

The hill has a view indicator which gives details of the panorama from the 754 ft summit. On a clear day it is possible to see the Black Mountains of South Wales and The Long Mynd, almost 60 miles away, in Salop. A plaque records that Captain Robert Dover's 'famous Olimpick Games' were held on the hill each Whitsun from 1612 to 1852. The games included wrestling, coursing and horse racing.

The 17th-century Market Hall, Chipping Campden.

Samurai room, Snowshill Manor.

SNOWSHILL

Fifteenth-century Snowshill Manor and its contents were given to the nation in 1952. There are rooms full of musical instruments, early bicycles, guns and tools. The most dramatic room contains sets of Samurai armour and weapons set out as for a Japanese 'war council'.

CHIPPING CAMPDEN

The elegant parish church dates largely from the 15th century. Beside it are two pavilions flanking a gateway which, with an almonry, are all that remain of a Jacobean mansion destroyed during the Civil War. Amid the stone houses and shops in the main street is the Market Hall, built in 1627. There is also a 14th-century house which belonged to the wool merchant William Grevel, who died in 1401.

...TSWOLD FARM PARK

...park is dedicated to ...preservation of rare ...eds of farm animals. ...y include Old ...oucester cattle, of which ...e are fewer than 50 ...e-bred survivors. The ...ed gave its name to ...uble Gloucester cheese — ...ause the milk had to be ...cessed twice to make it. ...St Kilda sheep are small ...l black, with up to six ...ns apiece. At one time ...y roamed wild on the ...ttish isle of St Kilda, ...they are no longer found ...re. Among the pigs is ...Gloucester Old Spot, ...e known as the orchard ...because it could live off ...dfalls. There is an ...enture playground, and ...s are allowed to run ...in the picnic area.

...ucester Old Spot

STOW-ON-THE-WOLD

Daniel Defoe, author of *Robinson Crusoe,* noted that 20,000 sheep were sold at Stow Fair when he visited it in the 17th century. This was then the most prosperous wool town in England. In the square behind the stone houses is a medieval cross. Most of the houses round the square date from the 17th and 18th centuries. Cromwell imprisoned 1000 Royalists in the 12th-century church after a Civil War battle in 1646. The Old English word *stow* usually applied to a town or village with a church. The rest of this Cotswold place name refers to the town's exposed position on a ridge between the valleys of the Windrush and Evenlode rivers, a site which has given rise to the jingle 'Stow-on-the-Wold where the wind blows cold'.

BOURTON-ON-THE-WATER

The village is set astride the River Windrush, which is crossed by a series of low stone bridges built in the 17th century. In the garden of the Old New Inn is a model of the village, built to a scale of one-to-nine and complete in every detail down to a miniature of the model itself. The work of the innkeeper and six local craftsmen in the 1930s, the model took four years and 200 tons of limestone to build. At Birdland, in the grounds of a 16th-century house, there are penguins, flamingoes, macaws, toucans and many other exotic species, as well as a freshwater aquarium. Also in the village is a model railway exhibition.

Cotswold houses, Stow-on-the-Wold.

239

A sturdy land of oak at the heart of England

The heart of England is dominated by the great industrial cities of Birmingham and Coventry, but between them is a corridor of countryside crossed by quiet lanes. Once it was not so peaceful—arrows flew in anger at the siege of Kenilworth Castle in the 13th century. Now the local bowmen hold friendly contests at Meriden. Like Kenilworth, Henley-in-Arden has strong links with English history and literature. The Forest of Arden is no longer the great sea of oak that Shakespeare immortalised in As You Like It. *Some of its trees at least can still be seen in the timber frames of the ancient black-and-white houses that still stand in the old forest villages. Hatton Locks, on the Grand Union Canal, are an illustration of the skill and ingenuity of the 18th-century engineers.*

1 Henley-in-Arden to Packwood House Leave the town on the A34 signposted to Birmingham, and after just over 3 m. take the right turn signposted for Lapworth. Keep right at the next junction, go through the village, and after ¼ m. turn right at the crossroads on to the B4439, following the Warwick signpost. Take the first turning on the left, and at the next junction bear left for Packwood House, a Tudor building with an unusual yew garden which represents the Sermon on the Mount.

2 Packwood House to Knowle Continue along the road past Packwood House, ignoring side turnings, for 2½ m. Then, at Rotten Row, keep straight ahead at the crossroads, joining the A41 for the 1 m. drive to Knowle, which has a 15th-century church and guildhall.

3 Knowle to Maxstoke Continue towards Solihull and Birmingham on the A41 but, still in the town, turn right on to the road signposted to Hampton in Arden. After 3 m. turn right at the T-junction with the B4102, and follow the road into Hampton in Arden. On the far side of the village turn left on to the road signposted to Stonebridge, then go left again on meeting the dual-carriageway A452 just before the Stonebridge roundabout. Leave the roundabout on the A45 signposted Coventry. After 1 m. take the first turn left, following the signpost for Maxstoke. The road passes under the M6 motorway about 2 m. later, just before entering the village.

4 Maxstoke to Arbury Hall Turn left by the church at the T-junction in Maxstoke, and keep straight on for 1 m. to a second T-junction. Here turn left, and then almost immediately right for Shustoke. At the T-junction in the village turn right on to the A47, following the Nuneaton signpost. Turn right again at the Furnace End crossroads, 1½ m. later, to stay on the A47. Continue on this road for 4 m. to Church End and there fork right on to the B4112. Follow the road through Ansley and over the roundabout towards Nuneaton. About 2 m. beyond the roundabout, just after passing the junction with the B4102 on the right, a turning to the right leads to Arbury Hall, which has associations with the writer George Eliot.

5 Arbury Hall to Meriden Rejoin the B4112 and turn left, back towards Ansley, and after 150 yds turn left on to the B4102 signposted to Meriden. Keep straight on at the crossroads in Astley and Fillongley, and follow the road all the way to Meriden.

6 Meriden to Kenilworth Leave Meriden village green on the road signposted to Coventry. After ½ m. turn right on to the road signposted to Berkswell. Keep straight ahead at the crossroads in Four Oaks and Berkswell. At the junction with the B4105, 1 m. beyond Berkswell, turn right then immediately left, following the Kenilworth signpost. Cross the A4023, and at the T-junction ¾ m. later turn right, then take the first turn left after 350 yds. Turn left again on meeting the A452 and, after ¼ m., where the A452 bears left, keep straight ahead on to the B4103 which leads to Kenilworth Castle.

7 Kenilworth to Hatton Locks From the castle, continue along the B4103 into the centre of Kenilworth, and at the roundabout by the De Montfort Hotel take the road signposted to Warwick and Leamington. On the outskirts of Kenilworth turn right, then immediately left, following the signpost for Leek Wootton. Shortly after, turn right on to the road signposted to Beausale. After 4 m. the road bears left to skirt Beausale, and 2 m. later joins the A41. Turn right on to the A41 and 200 yds later a very short detour to the left leads to Hatton Locks on the Grand Union Canal.

8 Hatton Locks to Henley-in-Arden Leaving the locks, continue along the A41 towards Solihull and Birmingham, but soon afterwards turn left on to the B4439, following the signpost for Hockley Heath. After 2 m. turn left on to the road signposted to Claverdon, which is reached 2 m. later. In the village turn right on to the B4095 and follow the road back to Henley-in-Arden.

INFORMATION

Places of interest *Arbury Hall:* Sun. afternoons from Easter Sun. to first Sun. in Oct., also Bank Hol. Mon. and Tues. following. *Henley-in-Arden:* Guildhall, open on application to caretaker at Guild Cottage (Tel. Henley-in-Arden 3504). *Kenilworth Castle:* Daily, but not Sun. morning in winter. *Packwood House:* Apr. to Sept., afternoons except Mon. and Tues. (open Bank Hol. Mon.); Oct. to Mar., Wed., Sat. and Sun. afternoon.

Craft workshop *Kenilworth:* 186 Warwick Road, weekdays, except Thur. afternoon.

Event *Meriden:* Archery contests in grounds of Forest Hall, late July to early Aug.

Information Heart of England Tourist Board, Bank Street, Worcester (Tel. Worcester 29511).

Towns with easy access to Henley-in-Arden:

Birmingham . . . . 15 m.	Stratford-upon-Avon . . . . 9 m.
Coventry. . . . . . 21 m.	Warwick . . . . 10 m.
Evesham . . . . . . 18 m.	Worcester . . . . . . 25 m.

KNOWLE
The early-15th-century parish church and guildhall stand together, and half a mile away is Grimshaw Hall, built in the shape of the letter E as a compliment to the first Queen Elizabeth. The sandstone church has a memorial window quoting the official account of the bravery of the Warwickshire Regiment in 1916.

Medieval church and guildhall, Knowle.

Trimming the yews, Packwood House.

PACKWOOD HOUSE
Fine Jacobean panelling and period furniture can be seen in the mansion, but Packwood is better known for its immaculately clipped yews, its 17th-century painted sundials, and the 30 niches for beehives in the 400-year-old walls around the gardens. The yews, planted about 1660, are grouped to represent Christ preaching to his followers in the Sermon on the Mount. The yews are clipped in August by the head gardener and seven men

George House, Henley-in-Arden.

SCALE
0   1   2   3   4   5 MILES

MAXSTOKE

Richard III slept here in 1460 on his way to defend his throne against Henry Tudor's Lancastrian army at Bosworth, in Leicestershire. A few nights later a king again rested at Maxstoke, but this time it was Henry VII, newly crowned on the battlefield where Richard lay dead. The bedroom of the two kings is in Maxstoke Castle, built a century earlier by William de Clinton, later the Earl of Huntingdon, at the same time as the priory and church. The castle and priory are both privately owned; but the castle can be seen from Castle Lane, and the priory gatehouse from the churchyard.

ARBURY HALL

Mary Ann Evans was born in 1819 at South Farm, where her father was land agent to the Newdegates of Arbury Hall. Years later, under the pen name of George Eliot, she brought to life the countryside which she loved, in books like *The Mill on the Floss*, *Silas Marner* and *Adam Bede*. The 18th-century hall, which Mary often visited with her father, is set in a park dappled with lakes. The hall, decorated with ornate plaster-work, contains fine furniture, paintings and glass. One of its paintings is thought by some to be of Shakespeare's mysterious 'dark lady of the sonnets'.

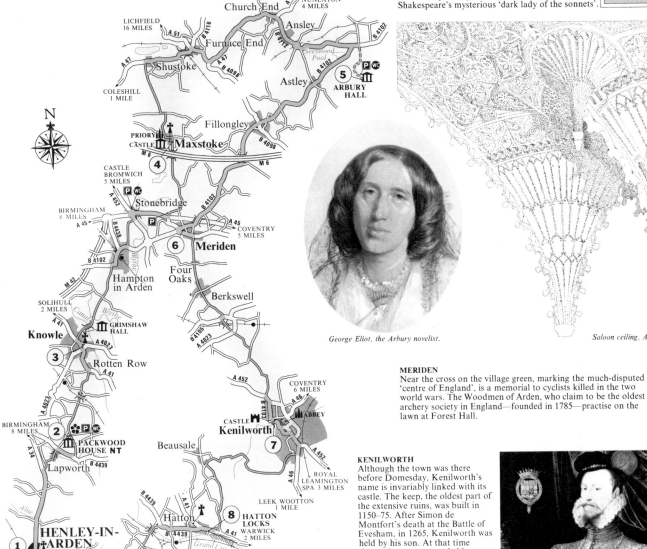

George Eliot, the Arbury novelist.

Saloon ceiling, Arbury Hall.

MERIDEN

Near the cross on the village green, marking the much-disputed 'centre of England', is a memorial to cyclists killed in the two world wars. The Woodmen of Arden, who claim to be the oldest archery society in England—founded in 1785—practise on the lawn at Forest Hall.

KENILWORTH

Although the town was there before Domesday, Kenilworth's name is invariably linked with its castle. The keep, the oldest part of the extensive ruins, was built in 1150–75. After Simon de Montfort's death at the Battle of Evesham, in 1265, Kenilworth was held by his son. At that time the castle was surrounded by Kenilworth Great Pool—a lake covering about 120 acres—and Henry III's army brought in barges to try to cross this huge moat and take the castle. They failed, and De Montfort held out for six months until starvation forced his surrender. About 300 years later Elizabeth I visited Kenilworth, then held by her favourite, the Earl of Leicester. He laid on celebrations that cost £60,000, in which the Queen was welcomed by the 'Lady of the Lake' floating on an artificial island.

Robert Dudley, Earl of Leicester.

The 16th-century barn, Kenilworth Castle.

HATTON LOCKS

A flight of 15 locks in 2 miles raises the London-Birmingham Grand Union Canal 150 ft over what are sometimes called 'The Golden Steps to Heaven'. This stretch of the canal, originally the Warwick and Birmingham, was authorised by Parliament in 1793: it can take a boat between one and two hours to get through. From the bridge near the top of the 'staircase' there is a view down the hill to the 174 ft high tower of Warwick's parish church, 3 miles away. Hatton's own village church, built mainly in 1880, contains some 17th-century plate and a Portuguese alms dish of the same period.

HENLEY-IN-ARDEN

Little remains today of the ancient Forest of Arden, setting for Shakespeare's *As You Like It*, but the town, once a commercial centre for the forest, still has many fine old timber-framed houses built of Arden oak. Many buildings in the town date from the 15th and 16th centuries. Typical of them is George House, formerly an inn and now used as offices. Henley was destroyed after Simon de Montfort's defeat at the Battle of Evesham in 1265, but was rebuilt. The timber-framed Guildhall, built in 1448, contains relics and records of medieval Henley. Across the River Alne, in the neighbouring parish of Beaudesert, the outline of the De Montforts' castle can be seen on a grassy hill, though the fortress has long since disappeared.

241

Poetry in stone along the Cotswold by-ways

Lovers of Shakespeare and of fine art, students of history and architecture will find their interests well satisfied on this tour, which links the counties of Oxford, Warwick and Gloucester. Shakespeare's mother lived at Wilmcote, where her cottage is a museum of Tudor times. From the wooded ridge of Edge Hill can be seen the arena of the first major battle of the Civil War in 1642.

(1) Chipping Norton to Rollright Stones Leave Chipping Norton on the B4026, signposted to Over Norton. After ½ m. turn left just beyond a sharp right-hand bend. Bear left at the next junction, and at the crossroads 1½ m. later turn right, signposted to Great Rollright. Rollright Stones are on the right.

(2) Rollright Stones to Compton Wynyates Continue along the lane towards Great Rollright. At the junction with the A34 turn right, then immediately left for Great Rollright. Continue ahead, keeping the village on the right, and bear left at the second junction. At the crossroads keep ahead, signposted for Brailes. Continue for 2 m., fording the River Stour, and another 2 m. to the B4035. Here turn left, signposted for Lower Brailes, but on the outskirts go right for Winderton. In Winderton turn right, and ¾ m. later turn left at the T-junction for Compton Wynyates. The entrance to the mansion is on the right.

(3) Compton Wynyates to Upton House Continue along the lane for 1 m. to the T-junction, and turn right following the signpost for Tysoe. After 1 m., in Upper Tysoe, turn left, for Oxhill and Kineton, then right on to the road signposted Shenington and Banbury. At the top of Tysoe Hill turn left at the crossroads and drive 2 m. to the junction with the A422. Turn right towards Banbury. Upton House is ½ m. on the right.

(4) Upton House to Edge Hill Return to the A422 and turn left, then right into a lane at the T-junction where the main road goes left. After 1 m., on the left, is Edge Hill Tower, overlooking Edgehill battlefield.

(5) Edge Hill to Farnborough Hall Continue along the crest of the hill for 1 m., when the lane becomes the B4086. Keep straight on downhill. Just before the foot of the hill, turn right on to the road signposted to Arlescote and Avon Dassett. After 1½ m. cross the A41; then, on the outskirts of Avon Dassett, go first right to Farnborough Hall.

(6) Farnborough Hall to Burton Dassett Turn left from the hall, keep ahead and follow the road straight on over the crossroads 2 m. later. Continue over the hills to Burton Dassett.

(7) Burton Dassett to Charlecote Park Follow the lane round to the left, past Chapel Beacon, to the A41, and turn right for Gaydon. In Gaydon turn left on to the B4451 signposted to Kineton. After 3 m., in Kineton, turn right on to the B4086, following the signpost for Wellesbourne which is reached 5 m. later. Keep on the B4086, following the signpost for Stratford. After 1 m. turn right on to the B4088 for Charlecote Park.

(8) Charlecote Park to Wilmcote Beyond the entrance to the park, take the first turn left, skirting the park, and go on for 1 m. into Hampton Lucy. Turn left, following the Stratford signpost. After 2½ m., at the junction with the A46, turn left, then first right on to the road signposted Snitterfield. At the next junction, after just under 2 m., turn left and after ½ m. fork right, following the Wilmcote signpost. After 2 m., at the A34, turn right and then first left, signposted for Wilmcote.

(9) Wilmcote to Hidcote Bartrim Leave Wilmcote by turning left at the T-junction near Mary Arden's house, and continue 2 m. to the T-junction just south of Billesley. Turn left here, following the signpost for Temple Grafton. Go straight across the A422 and after 1 m. turn left at the crossroads by a public house. Go through Binton, and at the junction with the A439 go straight ahead for Welford. Follow the road through to Long Marston. After just under 3 m., where the road becomes the A46, keep straight on to Mickleton. Here turn left on to the road signposted Ilmington. After 1½ m. turn right at the T-junction. Just over 1 m. later by Kiftsgate Court, turn left to Hidcote Bartrim.

(10) Hidcote Bartrim to Chastleton Return to the main road, turn left and continue for 3 m. to Ebrington. Join the B4035, follow it through the village, and after 4 m. turn right on to the A429. After 2 m., turn left for Todenham. Turn right, then left, in Todenham, continue through Great Wolford, and Barton-on-the-Heath, to the A44. Here turn right, then immediately left for Chastleton.

(11) Chastleton to Chipping Norton Just over 1 m. beyond Chastleton, turn left at the junction with the A436. After 1 m. turn right on to the A44 for Chipping Norton.

INFORMATION

Places of interest *Charlecote Park:* Apr. to Oct., weekends. Daily in Easter week and from May to Sept. (except Mon.). Spring and Late Summer Bank Hol. Mon. *Chastleton House:* Weekdays (except Wed.) and Sun. afternoons. *Compton Wynyates:* Apr. to Sept., daily (except Mon. and Fri.), Spring and Late Summer Bank Hol., 2-5.30 p.m. *Farnborough Hall:* Grounds only, Apr. to Sept., Wed. and Sat. afternoons. *Hidcote Manor:* Gardens only, Apr. to Oct., daily, except Tues. and Fri. *Wilmcote:* Mary Arden's house, weekdays and Apr. to Oct., Sun. afternoons also. *Upton House:* May to Sept., Wed. and Sat. afternoons. Wed. afternoons only in winter.

Information *Worcester:* Heart of England Tourist Board, Bank Street, Worcester (Tel. Worcester 29511).

Towns with easy access to Chipping Norton:

Banbury	13 m.	Evesham	22 m.
Cheltenham Spa	27 m.	Oxford	20 m.
Cirencester	27 m.	Warwick	28 m.

Inside Mary Arden's house, Wilmcote.

WILMCOTE
Shakespeare's mother, Mary Arden, was born in Wilmcote, and the house where she lived until she married in 1557 is still there. A typical Tudor farmhouse, it was taken over by the Shakespeare Birthplace Trust in 1930 and preserved as a museum. It is furnished and equipped as it was in Mary Arden's day. The outbuildings contain an old cider mill, firearms and mantraps formerly set to catch poachers.

HIDCOTE BARTRIM
Overlooking the single-street village is Hidcote Manor, surrounded by gardens protected by tall hedges. Each hedged garden is devoted to a particular group of flowers. The name Hidcote has been given to several varieties developed here.

CHASTLETON
Robert Catesby, one of the conspirators in the 1605 Gunpowder Plot, sold the land on which Chastleton House was built in 1603. One of the house's treasured exhibits is the Bible which Charles I gave to Bishop Juxon, who prayed with him before his execution. The bishop lived near Chastleton and the Bible was presented to the owner of the house when the last of the Juxons died in the 18th century.

Victorian tweed mill, Chipping Norton.

SCALE
0   1   2   3   4   5 MILES

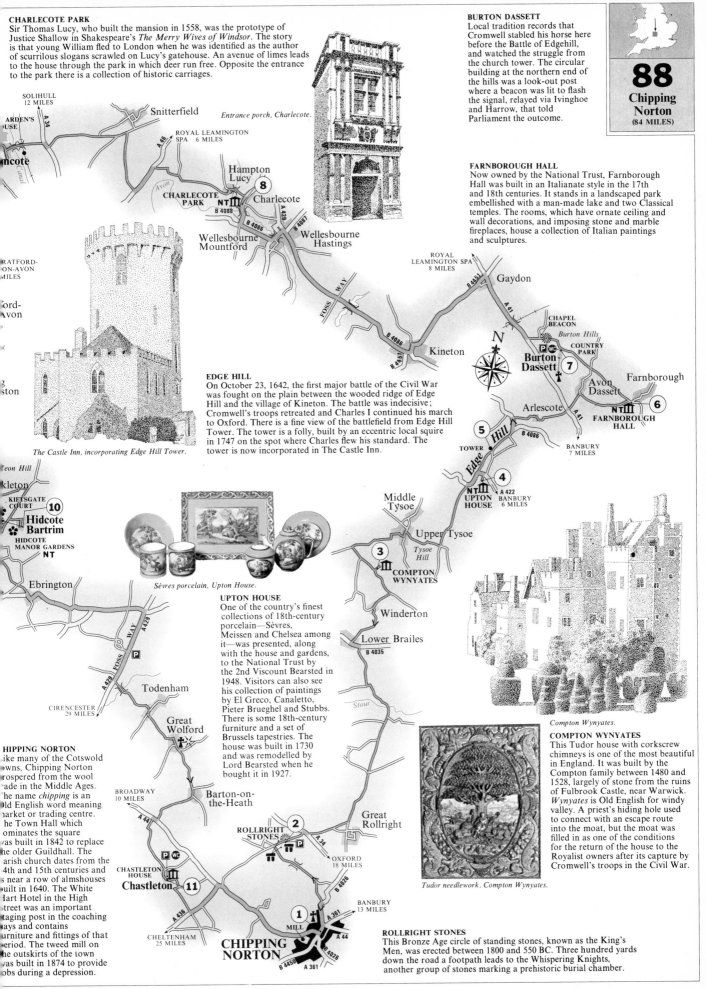

CHARLECOTE PARK
Sir Thomas Lucy, who built the mansion in 1558, was the prototype of Justice Shallow in Shakespeare's *The Merry Wives of Windsor*. The story is that young William fled to London when he was identified as the author of scurrilous slogans scrawled on Lucy's gatehouse. An avenue of limes leads to the house through the park in which deer run free. Opposite the entrance to the park there is a collection of historic carriages.

Entrance porch, Charlecote.

BURTON DASSETT
Local tradition records that Cromwell stabled his horse here before the Battle of Edgehill, and watched the struggle from the church tower. The circular building at the northern end of the hills was a look-out post where a beacon was lit to flash the signal, relayed via Ivinghoe and Harrow, that told Parliament the outcome.

FARNBOROUGH HALL
Now owned by the National Trust, Farnborough Hall was built in an Italianate style in the 17th and 18th centuries. It stands in a landscaped park embellished with a man-made lake and two Classical temples. The rooms, which have ornate ceiling and wall decorations, and imposing stone and marble fireplaces, house a collection of Italian paintings and sculptures.

The Castle Inn, incorporating Edge Hill Tower.

EDGE HILL
On October 23, 1642, the first major battle of the Civil War was fought on the plain between the wooded ridge of Edge Hill and the village of Kineton. The battle was indecisive; Cromwell's troops retreated and Charles I continued his march to Oxford. There is a fine view of the battlefield from Edge Hill Tower. The tower is a folly, built by an eccentric local squire in 1747 on the spot where Charles flew his standard. The tower is now incorporated in The Castle Inn.

Sèvres porcelain, Upton House.

UPTON HOUSE
One of the country's finest collections of 18th-century porcelain—Sèvres, Meissen and Chelsea among it—was presented, along with the house and gardens, to the National Trust by the 2nd Viscount Bearsted in 1948. Visitors can also see his collection of paintings by El Greco, Canaletto, Pieter Brueghel and Stubbs. There is some 18th-century furniture and a set of Brussels tapestries. The house was built in 1730 and was remodelled by Lord Bearsted when he bought it in 1927.

CHIPPING NORTON
Like many of the Cotswold towns, Chipping Norton prospered from the wool trade in the Middle Ages. The name *chipping* is an Old English word meaning market or trading centre. The Town Hall which dominates the square was built in 1842 to replace the older Guildhall. The parish church dates from the 14th and 15th centuries and is near a row of almshouses built in 1640. The White Hart Hotel in the High Street was an important staging post in the coaching days and contains furniture and fittings of that period. The tweed mill on the outskirts of the town was built in 1874 to provide jobs during a depression.

Compton Wynyates.

COMPTON WYNYATES
This Tudor house with corkscrew chimneys is one of the most beautiful in England. It was built by the Compton family between 1480 and 1528, largely of stone from the ruins of Fulbrook Castle, near Warwick. *Wynyates* is Old English for windy valley. A priest's hiding hole used to connect with an escape route into the moat, but the moat was filled in as one of the conditions for the return of the house to the Royalist owners after its capture by Cromwell's troops in the Civil War.

Tudor needlework, Compton Wynyates.

ROLLRIGHT STONES
This Bronze Age circle of standing stones, known as the King's Men, was erected between 1800 and 550 BC. Three hundred yards down the road a footpath leads to the Whispering Knights, another group of stones marking a prehistoric burial chamber.

Ancient strongholds on the Welsh marches

Red sandstone, English oak and Welsh slate are the basic materials of the black-and-white box-framed buildings which are characteristic of Salop. They are seen everywhere: in cottages, old town houses, even the church at Melverley. The district retains much of its Welsh character, despite the fact that it became officially English in 1535 after centuries of bloody dispute. The route sweeps over the farmlands of the Salop plain and touches the borderland's own 'Lake District', centred on Ellesmere.

(1) Oswestry to St Winifred's Well Leave Oswestry on the A4083 signposted for Shrewsbury. Immediately after crossing the bridge on the outskirts, fork right on to an unclassified road signposted to Maesbury. Continue for 3½ m. through Maesbury and over the Shropshire Union Canal to a T-junction. Turn left, and almost immediately left again on to a track which ends at a gate. A short path on the right leads to the well.

(2) St Winifred's Well to Melverley Return to the road and turn right to return to the T-junction near the river. Keep straight ahead, following the signposts to Knockin. After 1½ m. bear left on to the B4396 and go on into Knockin. There turn right on to the road signposted to Kinnerley. Turn right at the T-junction past Kinnerley's sandstone church, and first right on to the road signposted to Melverley. Bear left at the next junction, and almost immediately left again. Turn left at the next T-junction and follow the signposts into Melverley.

(3) Melverley to Nesscliffe On leaving the church, turn left at the Tontine public house and then take the first turning to the right signposted to Pentre/Shrewsbury. Turn right at the T-junction, follow the road into Pentre and turn right. After 1½ m. turn left at the crossroads into Nesscliffe. Turn left on to the A5 and almost immediately right into a lane opposite The Old Three Pigeons Inn. At the start of the lane, a track to the right leads to Nesscliffe Hill.

(4) Nesscliffe to Ruyton-XI-Towns Return to the A5 and turn right, following the signpost for Whittington. After 2½ m., at Shotatton, turn right at the crossroads on to the B4397 for Ruyton-XI-Towns.

(5) Ruyton-XI-Towns to Hodnet Leave the town on the B4397 which is signposted to Baschurch. Pass through Baschurch, and after 1½ m., where the B4397 swings left, continue straight ahead on the road signposted to Myddle. At the junction with the A528 in Myddle turn right, but go left almost immediately on to the road signposted to Clive. Go straight ahead, across the B5476. Go under the bridge and immediately turn left and continue into Clive. About 1 m. beyond the village a road to the right leads to the Corbet Woods picnic area. Return to the road from Clive and turn right, and right again on meeting the A49. After 1 m. turn right, following the signpost for Moreton Corbet. Pass RAF Shawbury's runways on the right, and at the T-junction soon after, turn right. Go left almost immediately, and after a few yards turn right to Moreton Corbet Castle. Continue down the lane past the castle to

the T-junction with the A53. Turn left and on into Hodnet to visit Hodnet Hall gardens.

(6) Hodnet to Ellesmere Leave Hodnet on the A442 signposted to Whitchurch. After ½ m. turn left on to the road signposted to Wem. In Weston bear right, still following the Wem signpost, and continue ahead, crossing the A49. At the junction with the B5065 turn left and continue into Wem. Leave Wem on the B5063 signposted to Ellesmere and continue on this road to its junction with the A495 at Welshampton. There turn left. Newton Mere is on the left and a little further on Blake Mere comes into view, also on the left, beside the T-junction with the A528. Turn right for Ellesmere, passing The Mere on the right.

(7) Ellesmere to Chirk Leave the town on the B5068 signposted to St Martin's. At the T-junction in St Martin's, turn right on to the road signposted to Overton, and almost immediately left by a garage. Keep left at the next junction, entering a valley. Cross the river and, keeping left, continue into Chirk. In Chirk turn left on to the A5 and then first right for Chirk Castle park.

(8) Chirk to Whittington From Chirk Castle return towards Chirk but, immediately after crossing the railway bridge, turn right and right again on to the B4500, following the signpost for Glyn Ceiriog. Take the first turning on the left, signposted to Weston Rhyn, and bear left after crossing the bridge. In Weston Rhyn, turn left opposite the Lodge public house. Near the end of the village turn right, following the signpost for Gobowen. At the roundabout in Gobowen, turn on to the A5 signposted to Shrewsbury and continue into Whittington.

(9) Whittington to Old Oswestry Leave the village on the A495 signposted to Oswestry. At the junction with the A483 turn left and take the fourth turning on the right to visit Old Oswestry's Iron Age fort.

(10) Old Oswestry to Oswestry Return to the A483 and turn right for Oswestry.

INFORMATION

Places of interest *Chirk Castle:* Easter weekend to Oct., Tues., Thur., Sat. and Sun. afternoons and Bank Hols. *Hodnet Hall gardens:* Apr. to end Sept., afternoons. *Moreton Corbet Castle:* All year, weekdays, Sun. afternoons.

Information The Square, Shrewsbury (Tel. Shrewsbury 52019).

Towns with easy access to Oswestry:

Chester	28 m.	Shrewsbury	18 m.
Llangollen	13 m.	Wrexham	16 m.

Iron Age fort, Old Oswestry.

OLD OSWESTRY

Iron Age man left few more impressive examples of military engineering than the 40 acre hill-fort here. The hill was originally protected by two massive earth banks. A third rampart was added later. Then all three were surrounded by two more enormous banks. The main period of occupation was from about 300 BC to AD 75, when the Romans completed their conquest of the area, and there is also some evidence of reoccupation during the Middle Ages.

OSWESTRY

English or Welsh? For centuries both armies fought for Oswestry, and in the 13th century it was burnt twice in years. The 1535 Act of Union finally made it English, but many of the townsfolk still speak Welsh. In 1559 a plague killed one-third of the population. The Croeswylan, or Weeping Stone, in Morda Road is a memorial to the disaster. The 13th-century parish church is dedicated to St Oswald, King of Northumbria, who was killed in 642 in battle with the army of Penda, the pagan King of Mercia. Llwyd Mansion, a 17th-century building in the town, bears a double-headed eagle. The insignia was granted to the Lloyd family by the Holy Roman Emperor for outstanding service in the Crusades. Little remains of Oswestry Castle, but there are fine views from the grassy mound where it stood until the Civil War.

Double-headed eagle, Oswestry.

St Winifred's Well.

ST WINIFRED'S WELL

According to legend, St Winifred was beheaded in the 7th century by Prince Caradoc, whose advances she had spurned. She was restored to life, became a nun and died a natural death. The well marks the spot where a spring is said to have gushed forth when her body rested there on its way from Holywell, in North Wales, for burial at Shrewsbury. The village of Knockin (pronounced 'Nuckin') close by, has a medieval dog pound, a 12th-century church, and a single street of black-and-white timbered houses. Hardly anything remains of Knockin's Norman castle, and the site has been laid out as a garden.

SCALE

0   1   2   3   4   5 MILES

CHIRK

The River Ceiriog marks the English border, with the town just on the Welsh side. Chirk Castle, 2 miles west, is set in a park rising from the valley. The castle was built in 1310 by Roger Mortimer. Since 1595 it has been the home of the Myddleton family, but is open for visits on certain days. The rectangular castle has round 'drum' towers at each of its four corners and a fifth tower built over the gateway.

Chirk Castle gates.

ELLESMERE

Nine lakes lie around the centre of Salop's 'Lake District'. The town gets its name from the haunt of the merehen, or lake bird, now called moorhen, though it has no connection with moors. The lakes are also the home of herons, kingfishers, mallard, tufted ducks and great crested grebes. Cormorants, wigeons, teals and pomarine skuas may be seen in winter. The lakes were formed when the last Ice Age ended about 10,000 years ago. The lake at Ellesmere covers 116 acres and is a popular spot for boating and fishing. On the lakeside are the Cremorne gardens. The parish church dates from the 13th century and contains a medieval parish chest 9 ft long made from a solid block of oak. The south chapel was extended in the 15th century and has carved beams and panelwork. The church was partly rebuilt in 1849.

Moorhen

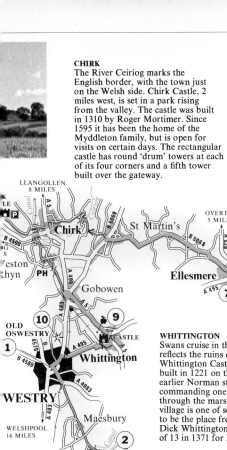

WHITTINGTON

Swans cruise in the moat that reflects the ruins of Whittington Castle, which was built in 1221 on the site of an earlier Norman stronghold commanding one of the few routes through the marshes. The village is one of several that claim to be the place from where Dick Whittington set out as a boy of 13 in 1371 for London.

RUYTON-XI-TOWNS

This mellow sandstone village gained its name in 1301 when 11 local townships were merged to form a single borough, with a combined high street more than a mile long. Near the road are the three walls of a castle keep built by Edmund, Earl of Arundel, who created the borough. The Norman church of St John the Baptist stands near the castle, and contains the mace given to the newly created borough.

Hodnet Hall gardens.

HODNET

This is a small hill town of typical Salop black-and-white houses. St Luke's Church, mainly 14th century, has a Nuremberg Bible, printed in 1479. A tile in the chancel commemorates a 19th-century rector, Reginald Heber, who wrote 'From Greenland's Icy Mountains' and other hymns. Hodnet Hall, a 19th-century mansion built in the Tudor style, stands in grounds which are open to the public. The layout of the gardens and ornamental pools was started in 1921 by Brigadier A. G. W. Heber-Percy, who spent 30 years transforming them out of a marshy valley. Brigadier Heber-Percy's son still lives at the hall. Near the house is a half-timbered building, containing big-game trophies, and a 17th-century barn.

Melverley church.

MELVERLEY

Perched above the River Vyrnwy, the black-and-white church of Melverley dates from the 15th or early 16th century. It is one of only two timber-framed churches in Salop. The interior suggests a barn rather than a church. From the church the monument to Admiral Rodney, the 18th-century naval hero, can be seen on Breidden Hill.

NESSCLIFFE

The wooded sandstone hill that overlooks the village is criss-crossed with public footpaths and crowned with the remains of an Iron Age fort. From the top of the hill, there are views northwards over the Salop plain to the hills of North Wales. In the cliff face is Kynaston's Cave, which is reached by steps carved from the solid sandstone. This is said to have been the hideaway of Humphrey Kynaston, a highwayman known as the 'Robin Hood of Shropshire'.

Highwayman's cave, Nesscliffe.

The frontierland where Offa built his dyke

England and Wales blend together in the valleys and hills of this borderland tour. The landscape is dotted with quiet villages and townships such as Clun, Montgomery and Bishop's Castle; and rises 1695 ft to The Long Mynd, beauty spot and launching site for gliders. A highlight of the tour is a visit to Stokesay Castle, a medieval fortified manor house. It is marvellously preserved, since it was surrendered to Cromwell's forces in the Civil War without a fight. Memories of more ancient wars are evoked by the 8th-century rampart of Offa's Dyke, built to defend the kingdom of Mercia from the Welsh.

(1) Shrewsbury to Montgomery Leave Shrewsbury town centre on the A458 signposted to Welshpool, but after crossing the River Severn join the B4386 signposted to Montgomery at the roundabout in Frankwell. Follow the road through Yockleton and Westbury to Worthen, and about 4 m. beyond Worthen turn left, still on the B4386, following the signpost for Montgomery and Chirbury. In Chirbury turn right at the junction with the A490, then take the first left, again the B4386, and follow the road for 2½ m. into Montgomery.

(2) Montgomery to Bishop's Castle Leave Montgomery on the B4385, signposted to Bishop's Castle. The road runs through hilly, wooded country, and crosses the A489 after 3 m. Bishop's Castle is 6 m. further on.

(3) Bishop's Castle to Offa's Dyke In Bishop's Castle, turn right down Bull Street and continue downhill to the parish church. Here turn right, following the signpost for Bishopsmoat. (At this point the tour can be shortened by 9 m. by turning left, following the signpost to Clun, and then turning right on to the A488 and following it to Clun.) Follow the road, which soon becomes a narrow lane, up out of Bishop's Castle. At the T-junction, after 1½ m., turn left, following the signpost to Bishopsmoat. Continue along the road for ¾ m. to a three-way junction and take the middle road signposted to Pantglas and Hopton. Take the first turning left (no signpost) just before a telephone kiosk, and at the next junction turn right up the hill. Shortly afterwards follow the road round to the right, and ¾ m. later reach Offa's Dyke, which is marked by an acorn symbol on a post on the right-hand side of the road.

(4) Offa's Dyke to Clun Follow the road to the crossroads 1¾ m. beyond the dyke and turn right, following the signpost to Newcastle. Bear left at the next junction, by Brook House, and continue into Newcastle. Turn left at the junction with the B4368, following the signpost to Clun, which is reached after 4 m.

(5) Clun to Aston on Clun In Clun, turn left by the bridge on to the A488 signposted Shrewsbury. Then turn right, rejoining the B4368 signposted to Craven Arms. Follow the road for 6 m. through Clunton and Little Brampton, and on into Aston on Clun.

(6) Aston on Clun to Stokesay Castle On the far side of Aston on Clun turn right, following the signpost for Clungunford. Keep straight on at two crossroads, the second of which is signposted to Onibury. Climb the hill to View Edge and then go on down to Onibury.

At the approach to the village, turn left at the crossroads and then left again a few yards later, joining the A49 signposted to Craven Arms. After 2 m. turn left at the signpost to Stokesay Castle.

(7) Stokesay Castle to The Long Mynd Return to the A49, turn left and follow the road through Craven Arms. About 1 m. beyond the town, turn left on to the A489 signposted to Newtown. After 4 m. fork right at the signpost for Asterton, and follow the narrow lane for 2½ m. before turning right, following the signpost to Gliding Field. A steep climb leads to the top of The Long Mynd.

(8) The Long Mynd to the Stiperstones Follow the road along the crest of The Long Mynd and take the first turning left, signposted to Ratlinghope. Turn left at the next T-junction, signposted to Bishop's Castle, and soon afterwards bear right, following the signpost for Bridges. At the junction just beyond the Horseshoe Inn, turn left and then right after 75 yds. Keep straight on at the next junction and follow the road to the Stiperstones. The Devil's Chair is 1 m. to the right.

(9) The Stiperstones to Pontesbury Continue on the same road and turn right at the next T-junction. Follow the road along the foot of the Stiperstones through Snailbeach to the junction with the A488. Turn right, following the Shrewsbury signpost, and go through Minsterley and on into Pontesbury.

(10) Pontesbury to Shrewsbury Follow the A488 for 8 m. to Shrewsbury.

INFORMATION

Places of interest *Clun:* Museum, by appointment (Tel. Clun 284). *Shrewsbury:* Castle, Easter to Oct., daily; Nov. to Easter, weekdays. Clive House museum, weekdays (Mon., afternoons only). Queen's Dragoon Guards regimental museum, Tues. to Sat. all day, Mon. afternoons. Bear Steps (14th-century shops and cottages), weekdays. Longden Coleham Pumping Station, Wed. and Fri. afternoons. Rowley's House (Roman remains), weekdays. *Stokesay Castle:* Daily (except Tues.).

Events *Shrewsbury:* Flower Show, Aug.; Regatta, June. National Tractor and Horse Ploughing Championships, Oct. West Midlands Agricultural Show, May.

Nature trails *Frankwell Riverside Trail:* 1 m. from public car park near Welsh Bridge.

Information The Square, Shrewsbury (Tel. Shrewsbury 52019).

Towns with easy access to Shrewsbury:

Chester	40 m.	Stafford	31 m.
Kidderminster	34 m.	Stoke-on-Trent	34 m.
Ludlow	28 m.	Wolverhampton	30 m.

Tomb in Montgomery church.

MONTGOMERY
Nestling in a fold of the hills and overlooked by the rui of its 13th-century castle, Montgomery has many old buildings and a street pattern that has hardly changed s Tudor times. In the churchyard a patch of earth marks the 'Robber's Grave', where John Davies was buried after being hanged in public for highway robbery in 1821. Davies vowed that, in proof of his innocence, no grass would grow on his grave for a generation—and n did. The church itself was founded in the 13th century.

House on Crutches, Bishop's Castle.

BISHOP'S CASTLE
A bowling green now stands on the site of the castle which was built here for the Bishop of Hereford in 1127. The Three Tuns Inn in Salop Street dates back to 1642, and is one of the few public houses in England that still brews its own beer. At the top of the High Street is the House on Crutches, a Tudor building with an overhanging upper storey supported on two wooden posts.

BROOK
HOUSE

Clun Forest sheep

CLUN
This was described by the poet A. E. Housman (1859-19 as 'one of the quietest places under the sun'. The words still apply to this town where a medieval bridge crosses the River Clun beneath the ruins of a Norman castle. In the centre of the main street is the Court House, built in 1780. The Clun Forest, the hilly area to the west of th town, gives its name to a breed of hardy sheep, which h been kept there since medieval times.

ASTON ON CLUN
On May 29, Royal Oak Day, a huge and ancient oak tree in the middle of this village is draped with flags, many of which then remain there throughout the year. tree was first decorated in this way to celebrate the marriage of a local landowner on May 29th, 1786. The village has a picturesque Gothic inn, the Kangaroo.

SCALE

0   1   2   3   4   5 MILES

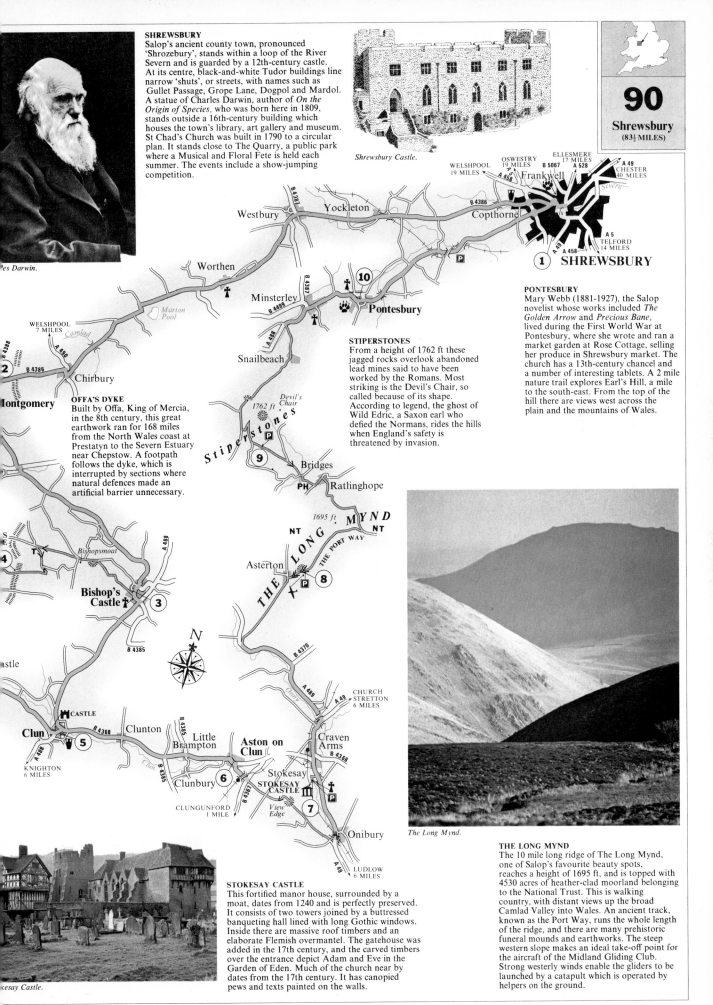

SHREWSBURY

Salop's ancient county town, pronounced 'Shrozebury', stands within a loop of the River Severn and is guarded by a 12th-century castle. At its centre, black-and-white Tudor buildings line narrow 'shuts', or streets, with names such as Gullet Passage, Grope Lane, Dogpol and Mardol. A statue of Charles Darwin, author of *On the Origin of Species*, who was born here in 1809, stands outside a 16th-century building which houses the town's library, art gallery and museum. St Chad's Church was built in 1790 to a circular plan. It stands close to The Quarry, a public park where a Musical and Floral Fete is held each summer. The events include a show-jumping competition.

es Darwin.

Shrewsbury Castle.

PONTESBURY

Mary Webb (1881-1927), the Salop novelist whose works included *The Golden Arrow* and *Precious Bane,* lived during the First World War at Pontesbury, where she wrote and ran a market garden at Rose Cottage, selling her produce in Shrewsbury market. The church has a 13th-century chancel and a number of interesting tablets. A 2 mile nature trail explores Earl's Hill, a mile to the south-east. From the top of the hill there are views west across the plain and the mountains of Wales.

STIPERSTONES

From a height of 1762 ft these jagged rocks overlook abandoned lead mines said to have been worked by the Romans. Most striking is the Devil's Chair, so called because of its shape. According to legend, the ghost of Wild Edric, a Saxon earl who defied the Normans, rides the hills when England's safety is threatened by invasion.

OFFA'S DYKE

Built by Offa, King of Mercia, in the 8th century, this great earthwork ran for 168 miles from the North Wales coast at Prestatyn to the Severn Estuary near Chepstow. A footpath follows the dyke, which is interrupted by sections where natural defences made an artificial barrier unnecessary.

The Long Mynd.

THE LONG MYND

The 10 mile long ridge of The Long Mynd, one of Salop's favourite beauty spots, reaches a height of 1695 ft, and is topped with 4530 acres of heather-clad moorland belonging to the National Trust. This is walking country, with distant views up the broad Camlad Valley into Wales. An ancient track, known as the Port Way, runs the whole length of the ridge, and there are many prehistoric funeral mounds and earthworks. The steep western slope makes an ideal take-off point for the aircraft of the Midland Gliding Club. Strong westerly winds enable the gliders to be launched by a catapult which is operated by helpers on the ground.

STOKESAY CASTLE

This fortified manor house, surrounded by a moat, dates from 1240 and is perfectly preserved. It consists of two towers joined by a buttressed banqueting hall lined with long Gothic windows. Inside there are massive roof timbers and an elaborate Flemish overmantel. The gatehouse was added in the 17th century, and the carved timbers over the entrance depict Adam and Eve in the Garden of Eden. Much of the church near by dates from the 17th century. It has canopied pews and texts painted on the walls.

kesay Castle.

Roman stone, royal oak and drama wrought in iron

The machine age was forged in the Iron-Bridge Gorge, nursery of the Industrial Revolution that changed the face of Britain. From an area full of survivals of this great pioneering workshop, it is an easy drive through the Severn Valley into a more peaceful part of Salop, a countryside adorned with mansions and the ruins of monasteries. Boscobel House and White Ladies Priory bring to mind the romantic escape story of Charles II and the oak. And at Viroconium are important Roman remains, which give the visitor a vivid impression of what life there was like 1900 years ago.

1 **Iron-Bridge to Buildwas Abbey** Leave Iron-Bridge on the B4380 signposted to Shrewsbury. After 2 m. turn left, on to the B4378, which immediately crosses the River Severn. The entrance to Buildwas Abbey is on the right.

2 **Buildwas Abbey to Viroconium** Return to the B4378 and turn left, retrace the route over the river and turn left on to the B4380 towards Shrewsbury. Drive on through Buildwas village to Leighton and there bear left, keeping on the B4380. After 5½ m. the B4380 leads to the Roman town of Viroconium, near Wroxeter.

3 **Viroconium to Atcham** Continue along the B4380 for ¾ m. to the junction with the A5. Turn left, cross the River Tern, with a large deer park to the right, and drive a further 1 m. into Atcham.

4 **Atcham to Haughmond Abbey** In Atcham, turn right for Uffington immediately before the A5 crosses the River Severn. The road runs alongside the boundary of Attingham Park. Keep left at the fork after 1 m. and stay on this road through Uffington then turn right on to the B5062 at the T-junction beyond the village. The entrance to the remains of the Augustinian abbey is on the left after just over 1 m.

5 **Haughmond Abbey to Longdon upon Tern** Return to the B5062 and turn left. The road crosses the end of Haughmond Hill and a short strip of woodland, then continues over flat, open country to cross the River Roden and reach High Ercall. At the T-junction in the village turn right, remaining on the B5062, and take the next turning to the right, joining the B5063 signposted to Wellington. A drive of 2 m. leads to Longdon upon Tern, where Thomas Telford built the first iron aqueduct.

6 **Longdon upon Tern to Weston Park** Continue on the B5063, going over the crossroads with the A442 and following the signpost towards Hadley. Just over 1½ m. later, turn left on to the road signposted for Horton. On reaching the village, follow the road round to the left. At the roundabout, just over 2 m. later, take the second exit, signposted for Lilleshall. Follow this road to the junction with the A518 and turn right. Take the first turning left, passing Lilleshall village and abbey 1 m. later. About 2 m. past the abbey, at the junction with the B4379, turn left, then immediately right on to the road signposted for London. On meeting the A41, after 1 m., keep straight ahead, joining the B5314. Follow this road for 2 m. to the A5 and turn left towards Weston-under-Lizard. Almost immediately, fork right off the A5 to enter Weston Park.

7 **Weston Park to Boscobel House** Rejoin the A5 and turn right, and continue for about 2½ m. to Ivetsey Bank. Here, at the inn, turn right on to the road signposted for Bishop's Wood. Go through the village and about ¾ m. later turn right for Boscobel House.

8 **Boscobel House to White Ladies Priory** Return to the lane and turn left. The ruins of the 12th-century White Ladies Priory are on the right 1 m. later.

9 **White Ladies Priory to Tong** Continue, still on the same lane, for a further 2½ m., and turn right on meeting the A41. After 1 m., turn right into Tong.

10 **Tong to Coalport** Follow the road through the village and back to the A41. Here turn right and after ¼ m. turn left, on to the road signposted to Shifnal. In Shifnal turn left, then immediately right, leaving the town on the A464 signposted for Shrewsbury; but at the roundabout on the outskirts take the A4169 exit signposted to Bridgnorth. At the next roundabout, soon afterwards, stay on the A4169 following the Iron-Bridge signpost. After 2½ m., where the main road swings right for Telford and Iron-Bridge, fork left on to the B4379. 1 m. later turn right for Coalport and continue straight on over the crossroads at the junction with the A442. At the foot of the hill turn right for Coalport.

11 **Coalport to Iron-Bridge** Follow the same road along the Severn Valley back to Iron-Bridge.

INFORMATION

Places of interest *Attingham Park:* Easter Mon. to end Sept., Tues., Wed., Thur., Sun., and Bank Hol. Mon., 2-5.30 p.m. *Boscobel House:* All year, weekdays, Sun. afternoons. *Buildwas Abbey:* All year, weekdays, Sun. afternoons. *Haughmond Abbey:* All year, weekdays, Sun. afternoons. *Ironbridge Gorge Museum:* Daily. *Lilleshall Abbey:* All year, weekdays, Sun. afternoons. *Weston Park:* Apr. to Sept. 25, daily (except Mon. and Fri., but open Bank Hol.). Park, 11 a.m.-7.30 p.m. House, 2-6 p.m. *White Ladies Priory:* All year. *Wroxeter:* Viroconium Museum, all year (except Sun. mornings from Oct. to Mar.).

Event *Iron-Bridge Regatta:* June.

Information *Iron-Bridge:* The Toll House, The Iron Bridge (Tel. Telford 882753). *Shrewsbury:* The Square (Tel. Shrewsbury 52019).

Towns with easy access to Iron-Bridge:

Bridgnorth	10 m.	Wellington	6 m.
Shrewsbury	14 m.	Wolverhampton	24 m.
Stourbridge	21 m.	Stafford	24 m.

LONGDON UPON TERN
Soon after his appointment as joint engineer to the Shrewsbury Canal Company, Thomas Telford wrote to a friend in 1795 that he was working on an entirely new 'application of iron'. The result was the world's first iron aqueduct, carrying the canal over the River Tern in this little village. It became the prototype for the much more ambitious aqueduct at Pont-Cysyllte, on the Llangollen Canal. The aqueduct remains, though the canal has vanished.

The picture gallery, Attingham.

ATCHAM
The Severn bends sharply through the village and is spanned by two bridges, the older of which was completed in 1771. The 12th-century church has a window dedicated to St Eata, 7th-century Abbot of Lindisfarne, and a stained-glass memorial to Blanche Parry, Queen Elizabeth's chief lady-in-waiting until her own death in 1589. The memorial was installed by a vicar's wife who was descended from the Parry family. Across the A5, Attingham Park surrounds an 18th-century house, where the picture gallery is illuminated by ceiling windows made up of the world's first curved cast-iron frames.

Entrance to the Roman baths, Viroconium.

VIROCONIUM
About AD 58 the Romans built a military base here, and it soon grew into a town of 4000 people, protected by more than 2 miles of ditches and ramparts. The massive entrance to the baths is through the highest Roman wall remaining in Britain. It stands 20 ft above the rest of the site. The museum contains a plan of the original town.

SCALE

0   1   2   3 MILES

...nteenth-century pouch for the ...t Seal of England—Weston Park.

...STON PARK
...s is the ancestral home of the
...s of Bradford. Benjamin
...raeli, the 19th-century
...esman, was a frequent guest
...re and some of his letters can be
... in the library. Other treasures
...he 17th-century house include
...ntings by Holbein, Constable,
... Dyck, Gainsborough and
...nolds. Outside, there are nature
...s, an aquarium, a pets' corner
... a pottery. The formal gardens
... dominated by the biggest
...ntal plane tree in the country,
...ch is over 300 years old.

Boscobel House—an engraving of 1660.

The Royal Oak, Boscobel.

BOSCOBEL HOUSE
One of the most romantic tales about the runaway Charles II, after his defeat at Worcester in 1651, is that he hid in an oak tree. Generations of souvenir-hunters hacked it down, but what is now called the Royal Oak is thought to have been grown from one of its acorns. Scenes depicting the oak-tree escapade are carved in marble over the fireplace in the parlour of Boscobel House.

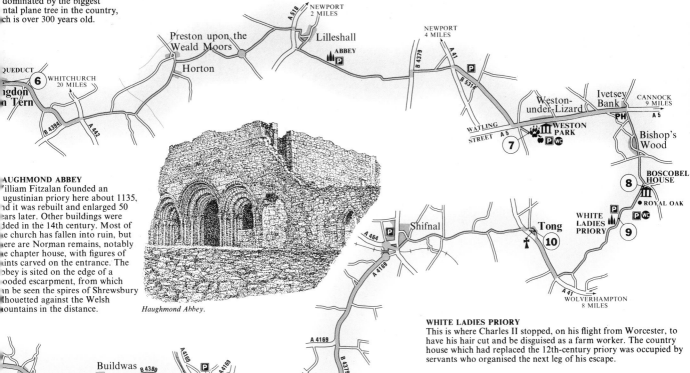

Haughmond Abbey.

...AUGHMOND ABBEY
...illiam Fitzalan founded an
...ugustinian priory here about 1135,
...d it was rebuilt and enlarged 50
...ears later. Other buildings were
...dded in the 14th century. Most of
...e church has fallen into ruin, but
...ere are Norman remains, notably
...e chapter house, with figures of
...ints carved on the entrance. The
...bbey is sited on the edge of a
...ooded escarpment, from which
...n be seen the spires of Shrewsbury
...ilhouetted against the Welsh
...ountains in the distance.

WHITE LADIES PRIORY
This is where Charles II stopped, on his flight from Worcester, to have his hair cut and be disguised as a farm worker. The country house which had replaced the 12th-century priory was occupied by servants who organised the next leg of his escape.

Effigy of Lady Elizabeth Pembruge, Tong church.

TONG
The 15th-century church at Tong is so stocked with tombs and effigies that it is sometimes called 'the village Westminster'. Many of the monuments are to the Vernons of Haddon Hall, including Sir Harry, who was guardian to Prince Arthur, brother of the future Henry VIII. Charles Dickens mentioned the church in *The Old Curiosity Shop*. Little Nell, the heroine, was buried there.

IRON-BRIDGE
This small town saw the birth of Britain's 18th-century Industrial Revolution (see special feature, p. 250). The town, rising in tiers above the River Severn, takes its name from the world's first iron bridge, built in 1779 but used only by pedestrians since 1934. The builders used wooden joints; bolts and rivets were a thing of the future. The bridge is 196 ft long and has three arches, the central one with a span of 100 ft.

...LDWAS ABBEY
... abbey was founded by Roger de Clinton, Bishop of Coventry
... Lichfield, in 1135. Its Norman arches, surrounded by lawns and
...s, make a pleasant contrast to the neighbouring power stations.
... life at the abbey was not always peaceful. In the 14th and 15th
...turies an abbot was murdered, another was taken prisoner by
...sh raiders, and the abbey's possessions were plundered by Owen
...ndower's troops from over the border.

COALPORT
Formerly a great industrial centre, Coalport is now part of the area administered by the Ironbridge Gorge Museum. Its visible links with the birth of the Industrial Revolution include the old china works and an 1818 iron bridge.

A conducted tour round the birthplace of the Industrial Revolution

IRONBRIDGE

The Industrial Revolution was born in the Ironbridge Gorge in Salop. There stands the world's first iron bridge, built between 1777 and 1781 to span the River Severn. Today, the bridge is preserved and the Ironbridge Gorge Museum Trust, founded in 1968, is caring for a wide range of industrial archaeological sites. The director, Neil Cossons, explains below why this quiet corner of Salop saw the start of a revolution that was to make Britain the 'workshop of the world'.

Natural resources and the genius of a single family provide the key to why this part of Britain became the cradle of the Industrial Revolution in the 18th century. It had an immense wealth of raw materials—coal, iron ore, water for both power and transport, sand ideal for moulding cast iron, limestone to flux the slag in the blast-furnaces, and clay for bricks and tiles.

It was this abundance that helped to attract Abraham Darby to Coalbrookdale in 1708—the first of three generations whose achievements were to win them the title of founding fathers of the Industrial Revolution.

Darby was a Quaker ironmaster who came from Bristol to take over a blast-furnace at Coalbrookdale. In 1709 he became the first man to smelt iron by using coke as a fuel instead of the traditional charcoal.

This was a breakthrough of great importance. At that time, Britain was in the grip of a fuel crisis. Charcoal, made from timber, was the sole source of fuel for the iron industry, whose demands were rapidly stripping the countryside of its woodlands. A single blast-furnace producing only a few tons of iron a week devoured several tons of timber a day.

A new fuel was urgently needed. Darby found it in the coal of the gorge. Having perfected the technique of converting it to coke, by separating out the gases, he launched the entire industry on a process of breakneck expansion. High-quality iron now became available in quantities undreamt of in the days of charcoal smelting.

Teaching the world

Darby's iron, together with the new techniques that evolved around it, provided the basis for the Industrial Revolution that transformed Britain in the 18th and 19th centuries. Among the customers who came to his works was Richard Trevithick, the pioneer of the steam-engine. The Ironbridge Gorge became a centre of innovation and new-found knowledge that attracted people from all over the civilised world. Engineers and industrialists from Sweden, Germany, France, North America and many other countries flocked there to look, learn and marvel.

But the greatest memorial to the Darby family—and the first priority on the museum's preservation list—is the iron bridge upstream on the Severn from Blists Hill. Now perhaps the best-known industrial monument in Britain, the bridge was the first in the world to be built of metal.

The idea came about in 1775, when a group of local businessmen met to discuss improving communications between the industries established on both sides of the river. They included Abraham Darby III, who became the project's treasurer; John Wilkinson, a fellow iron-

master; and Thomas Farnolls Pritchard, an architect from Shrewsbury. Up to that time, the nearest bridges were at Buildwas and Bridgnorth.

Because of the great number of trading vessels using the Severn, a bridge with a single arch was essential. Pritchard proposed a revolutionary iron structure spanning 120 ft at an estimated cost of £3200, and Darby agreed to build it.

Darby and his craftsmen needed all their hard-won experience, for they were entering a totally new field. They had no idea of the structural properties of cast iron. Casting and transporting the main ribs of the bridge must also have posed formidable problems, for each of the ribs weighed 5 tons 15 cwt. The bridge's actual span is 100 ft 6 in. and its total weight is 378 tons 10 cwt.

The builders obviously opted for wide safety margins, and the graceful arch has stood the test of time remarkably well. It was not closed to traffic until 1931, and pedestrians continued to use it for another 19 years on payment of a penny toll.

One of the bridge's sternest tests came in the 1790s, when catastrophic floods swept away many of the Severn's bridges. But over the years, the greatest threat has come not from the river but from the stone abutments that

ARTISTIC TESTAMENT *This 19th-century iron plaque, showing the Last Supper, is a testament to the skill and delicacy of Coalbrookdale's craftsmen.*

ANOTHER FIELD *A hand-painted tile from the display at Coalport shows another facet of Coalbrookdale's thriving 19th-century industry.*

IRON DECORATION *The Great Warehouse's striking clock-tower is made of cast iron and was added to the Coalbrookdale Company's building in 1843.*

One of the most famous of Britain's industrial monuments, the iron bridge at Coalbrookdale, still stands as evidence of the courage and skill of the 18th-century founders of the Industrial Revolution. It was the first bridge in the world to be built of iron and its origins go back to 1775, when a group of leading citizens met to discuss improving communications between the industries which had developed on both banks of the Severn. Abraham Darby III, the leading local ironmaster, was entrusted with the scheme and casting began in 1779; it was eventually completed in 1781. In recent years, however, the bridge has been seriously threatened by bank movements and restoration, sponsored by the Ironbridge Gorge Museum Trust, began in 1972.

WORLD SHOWPIECE
The craftsmen at Coal-brookdale contributed this elaborate casting of a fountain to the exhibits at the Great Exhibition of 1851. Held in London under the auspices of Queen Victoria's husband, Prince Albert, the exhibition was de-signed to show to the world the best of British craftsmanship.

...RNACE SITE *This is the place where Abraham Darby I developed his coke-smelting process in 1709. ...e centre of the site is Darby's furnace, round which are displayed examples of the ironwork it ...oduced. The cast-iron columns were made in the early 19th century to support the foundry roof. ...ey were erected with the cross-members uppermost to carry the roof timbers. Similar columns can ...seen still in use in the Great Warehouse near by. In the background stands the chassis of a wagon, ...ich ran on one of the early railways laid down at Coalbrookdale in the late 18th century.*

STEAM POWER *Two double-beam steam-engines—*David *and* Sampson—*stand at the entrance to Blists Hill (left), while a rocking beam from one of the engines is seen above. They were built in 1851 to provide the air supply for the blast-furnaces of the Lilleshall Company and were finally retired in 1952. According to tradition, they were given these distinctive names by Thomas Smith, one of their first mechanics.*

DEEP UNDERGROUND *Tar drips from the walls of the 1000 yd long Tar Tunnel, the first 300 ft of which is open to visitors. The tunnel was started to improve the local collieries, but its purpose changed when the miners struck a natural tar spring in 1787. The tar was soon being collected and sold by the enterprising Coalbrookdale businessmen.*

INDUSTRIAL PIONEER *The ironmaster William Reynolds (1758–1803), a grandson of Abraham Darby II and a partner in the Coalbrookdale Company, was one of the leading pioneers of the Industrial Revolution. Not only did he plan the Tar Tunnel under Blists Hill, but he was also the driving force behind the construction of the Shropshire Canal. As part of this, he supervised the building of the Hay Inclined Plane, which carried barges up and down the 207 ft slope which separated the two levels of the canal.*

FIRST FUEL *A carefully restored charcoal-burning site. Abraham Darby I began the Industrial Revolution when he replaced charcoal with coke.*

IRONBRIDGE

flank the arch. Ever since the bridge was built they have been moving inwards, and eventually the pressure started to crush the arch.

Preservation work started in 1972 and about £170,000 has been spent on making the bridge safe. The rescue work included putting an inverted arch of reinforced concrete on the bed of the river to keep a constant distance between the abutments.

This was the first major project the museum undertook, and it was the starting point for many others.

As industry expanded elsewhere in the 19th century, the Ironbridge Gorge went into decline. But, unlike other areas, no new industries sprang up to replace the old ones. Thus, many of the earliest relics of the Industrial Revolution survive there today.

Darby's original furnaces still stand in the grounds of the Coalbrookdale Company, where iron castings of one sort or another have been made since the 1630s. The site is dominated by the Great Warehouse, built in the 1830s, which has window lintels, frames and sills all made of cast iron. Iron was also used for the arch over the loading bay and for the ornate clock-tower that was added in 1843.

A change in policy

The Coalbrookdale site shows that there was a major change in policy during the first half of the 19th century. In the 1760s, the Darbys were making the world's first iron rails for wagons to run on. Later, the works made the cylinders and the boiler for Trevithick's first steam locomotive.

In the 1780s, the world's first iron boat was launched into the Severn. At about the same time, iron from Coalbrookdale was used by Thomas Telford to build the first iron aqueduct at Longdon upon Tern.

Even after the raw materials that had made such achievements possible had been exhaus-

ted, the successors to Abraham Darby I still had a priceless human asset—craftsmen who were probably the finest pattern and mould-makers in the world.

What would now be called an industrial designer was employed as early as the 1840s, and the company produced an astonishingly wide range of highly specialised castings. A catalogue reveals that customers could choose from 46 patterns of cast-iron tables and more than 100 different gas lamps. Many products from this era are displayed in the museum beside the Great Warehouse. They make a vivid contrast to the huge cauldrons that were Abraham Darby I's stock-in-trade.

The exhibits at Coalbrookdale are part of the museum's policy of preserving industrial monuments on their original sites whenever possible. But Blists Hill has become an 'orphanage' for important buildings and machines that would otherwise have been destroyed. Fortunately, the 42 acre site has an industrial history of its own.

Blast-furnaces operated there from the 1830s until 1912; brickworks, tileworks and a coalmine were in use until 1941. The site also has the track of a railway, opened in 1861, and the remains of a tramway—including an iron bridge—that was used by horses hauling trucks laden with coal.

There is also another legacy from the past. Part of the Shropshire Canal—inspired by William Reynolds, Abraham Darby II's grandson, and opened in 1793—runs across Blists Hill. It ends at the top of the Hay Inclined Plane. This provided a very efficient means of moving tub boats to and from the Severn more than 200 ft below.

Secured to cradles that ran on rails, the boats went up or down the incline in three and a half minutes. The alternative method, involving a long staircase of conventional locks, would have taken three or four hours.

At the foot of the slope, the boats were floated off into the short final section of canal that runs parallel to, but slightly above, the

REVIVING TRADITIONS *The pottery at Blists Hill is part of the museum's plan to re-create the working methods that won the Coalbrookdale potters and china makers world fame. Among satisfied customers was Queen Victoria, who ordered a presentation dinner service for Nicholas I of Russia. A full-time potter is now employed to make wheel-thrown pottery, and coal mining, iron smelting, puddling and rolling are all part of the plans for the future.*

river. It ends at the wharf by Coalport Bridge. This section passes the old Coalport china works, with its distinctive bottle ovens. The works have also been acquired by the museum and will eventually house displays telling the story of the local brick and china industry.

The incline, the blast-furnaces and the other legacies of Blists Hill's industrial past make an ideal background for the exhibits brought in from elsewhere.

These include *David* and *Sampson,* a pair of double-beam steam-engines built in 1851; a tollhouse, designed by the great 18th-century engineer Thomas Telford, that previously stood on the A5 near Shrewsbury; a Victorian printing shop; and an iron tub boat.

The Tar Tunnel

Another remarkable feature is the Tar Tunnel, which starts near the foot of the Hay Inclined Plane and runs under the hill for at least 1000 yds. It was driven into the hillside in 1787—probably in connection with the nearby coal workings—but the miners struck a source of thick, black, treacle-like bitumen that still oozes from the walls. It was mainly used for treating ropes and caulking ships, but small amounts were processed, bottled and sold as 'Betton's British Oil', a remedy for 'rheumatic and scorbutic affections'.

It is only over the last 20 years or so that we have become aware of the significance of the relics of our industrial past. The work at Ironbridge Gorge shows what can be done to preserve it—even if it is still not complete.

The long-term plan at Blists Hill, for example, is to create an area in which the industry and the industrial techniques of the 18th century can be seen within their general social and economic context. This means adding shops, cottages and other buildings, and it may be as long as 50 years before the site is fully developed. But Ironbridge as it exists today is enough to take the visitor back to the days when a revolution that was to transform the world was being forged.

SOURCE OF ENERGY *Easy access to coal made the development of Ironbridge possible. The museum has rebuilt one of the shafts of the Blists Hill mine, which originally supplied coal and iron ore for the blast-furnaces on the site. Later the mine provided clay for the brick and tile works on the other side of the canal. It was closed down in 1941.*

VICTORIAN SURVIVAL *One of the chief exhibits brought to the museum at Blists Hill to save it from destruction is this 19th-century printing press, which was among the first to be made of iron. Among the other exhibits in the printing shop is a rotary press, a guillotine for trimming and a small jobbing press.*

BEGINNINGS *Primitive bellows were originally used to supply air to the blast-furnaces. They were driven by water from the gorge's streams but were eventually replaced by steam-engines.*

FURNACE SITE *The three blast-furnaces at Blists Hill were built in the 19th century and produced pig iron until 1912. They are in the process of being restored.*

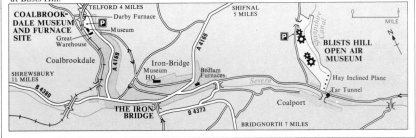

WHEN TO VISIT IRONBRIDGE

Ironbridge is the starting point for Tour No. 91 on p. 248. It stands beside the River Severn in Salop, south of the A5, west of the A442 and 30 minutes drive from the M6. The Coalbrookdale Museum is off the A4169 four miles from Telford; the iron bridge itself is on the B4380 at Ironbridge and the Blists Hill Open Air Museum is near Coalport. All are open daily, 10 a.m.–6 p.m. There is parking at Coalbrookdale and at Blists Hill.

Ivanhoe's castle, steam locos, and jungle giants in the park

Although never far from towns of the industrial Midlands, this is a pleasant country drive. It links the stately home of Lord Melbourne, the Victorian Prime Minister; a castle where the hero of Sir Walter Scott's Ivanhoe *jousted; and the birthplace of the tragic girl-queen, Lady Jane Grey. Another royal tragedy is recalled at Bosworth Field, at which Richard III lost his horse, his throne and his life.*

(1) Ashby-de-la-Zouch to Shackerstone Leave Ashby on the A50 signposted to Leicester. After 1 m. turn right on to the B5396, following the signpost to Packington. In Packington bear left on to the B5326 and go through Normanton le Heath to Heather. At the junction by the Queen's Head Inn, turn right on to the B591. After passing the church, keep ahead on the minor road signposted to Shackerstone. Keep ahead at the crossroads and, just after crossing the railway and canal, turn left to Shackerstone Railway.

(2) Shackerstone to Twycross Zoo Go through Shackerstone, and after 1 m. turn right and follow the signpost into Bilstone. Turn right at the T-junction, following the signpost to Twycross. At the junction with the B4116 turn left, and then right at the A444. Twycross Zoo is reached after 1½ m.

(3) Twycross Zoo to Bosworth Field Return along the A444. After 3½ m. turn left on to the B585 signposted to Market Bosworth. At the market square in the town turn right to follow the signpost to Sutton Cheney. On the outskirts of the village turn right for Shenton, and drive ½ m. to Bosworth Field.

(4) Bosworth Field to Sutton Cheney Return down the minor road and turn right into Sutton Cheney.

(5) Sutton Cheney to Kirkby Mallory At the T-junction in the village, turn left on to the road signposted to Kirkby Mallory. Bear right at the fork beyond the village, reaching the A447 soon after. Turn right, then left, on to the road signposted to Kirkby Mallory.

(6) Kirkby Mallory to Kirby Muxloe At the crossroads in Kirkby Mallory, turn left to Peckleton. After 1 m., in Peckleton, turn left on to the road signposted to Desford, and at the T-junction turn left to the village. At the junction with the B582 in Desford turn right. Fork left on to the B5380 signposted to Kirby Muxloe, which is 2½ m. further on.

(7) Kirby Muxloe to Bradgate Park Continue past the castle, and at the roundabout turn left, following the signpost to Ratby. Go through the village and over the M1 to Groby. At the T-junction turn right and immediately left, following the signpost for Newtown Linford. At the B5327 junction turn right. Bradgate Park is on the left.

(8) Bradgate Park to Beacon Hill Leaving the park, turn right on to the B5327, following the park border. In Newtown Linford bear right for Woodhouse Eaves. After 1½ m. cross the B5330, following the signpost to Woodhouse Eaves, and at the T-junction turn left. Turn left again, still signposted to Woodhouse Eaves, and go into the village. At the T-junction with the B591 turn left for Coalville. Beacon Hill is on the right.

(9) Beacon Hill to Breedon on the Hill Continue along the B591, cross the B5330 and take the first right, signposted to The Oaks. Cross the B5350 and go under the M1 and in ½ m. go left to Mount St Bernard Abbey. About 1 m. beyond the abbey, turn sharp right at the rocky outcrop. Just over 1 m. later turn left for Belton. Cross the A512 and after 1¼ m., at the crossroads with the B5324, turn right then first left into Belton. Go past the church to a T-junction and turn right, following the Castle Donington signpost. After 1 m., where the road bears sharp right, keep ahead on the road signposted to Tonge. At the T-junction turn left, and at the A447 junction turn right, signposted Tonge. Turn left off the A447 into Tonge. There turn left for Breedon on the Hill. At the junction with the A453, turn left into Breedon.

(10) Breedon on the Hill to Melbourne At the war memorial on the village green turn right, and drive up Breedon Hill, bearing right at the fork to the church. Return towards the village, but at the junction halfway down the hill turn right and, at the T-junction, left. Follow this road to Melbourne.

(11) Melbourne to Staunton Harold Leave on the B587, signposted to Ashby-de-la-Zouch, and continue to Staunton Harold.

(12) Staunton Harold to Ashby-de-la-Zouch Return to the B587 and turn right. At the junction with the A453, turn right and follow the signposts to Ashby-de-la-Zouch.

INFORMATION

Places of interest *Bradgate Park:* Grounds, daily. House, Apr. to Oct., Wed., Thur., Sat. afternoons, Sun., 10 a.m.-12.30 p.m. *Kirby Muxloe Castle:* Daily. *Melbourne Hall:* Easter weekend; mid-Apr. to Oct., Sun. and Spring Bank Hol., mid-June to mid-Sept., afternoons, except Mon. and Fri. *Mount St Bernard Abbey:* Grounds, daily. Tours of the abbey, Mon. to Sat. (men only, by appointment). *Shackerstone Railway Society:* Easter to Nov., Sat. and Sun., 11 a.m.-6 p.m.

Events *Ashby-de-la-Zouch:* Annual Statues Fair, Sept. *Bosworth Field:* Commemorative service at the well, Aug.

Nature trail *Bradgate Park:* Apr. to Oct. Starts at car park. Newtown Linford. Leaflet from Department of Education, Leicester Museum.

Information Tourist Information Office, 12 Bishop Street, Leicester (Tel. Leicester 20644).

Towns with easy access to Ashby-de-la-Zouch:
Birmingham . . . . 28 m.   Leicester . . . . 17 m.
Derby . . . . 15 m.   Nottingham . . . . 22 m.

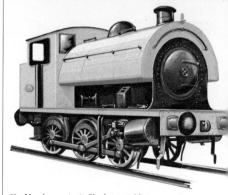

No. 21, a locomotive in Shackerstone Museum.

SHACKERSTONE
As the steam engine passed into history, groups of enthusiasts joined together to save some specimens from the scrapyard. At Shackerstone, a railway society was formed in 1969 to preserve not only the locomotives but also a stretch of line on which to run them. The seven engines maintained here were all used on private industrial railways. The society also has several steamrollers and a museum of railway exhibits.

TWYCROSS ZOO
Apes and monkeys are the speciality of Twycross Zoo, but there are many other animals in its 50 acre park, including chimpanzees which have appeared on television. Most visitors want to see the giant gorillas and orang-utans.

Gorilla, Twycross Zoo.

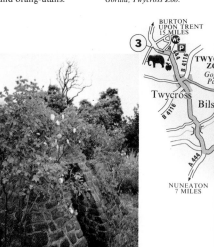

King Dick's Well, Bosworth Field.

BOSWORTH FIELD
This battleground is known to every schoolboy, if only as the scene where Richard III, defeated and without a mount, is said to have cried despairingly: 'A horse, a horse—my kingdom for a horse!' On August 22, 1485, the king died fighting in the last and decisive battle of the Wars of the Roses. His crown was found on a thorn bush.

SCALE
0   1   2   3   4   5 MILES

ASHBY-DE-LA-ZOUCH

This pleasant and busy little town acquired its name 900 years ago, with the arrival of the Norman, Alan de Zouch, who became lord of the manor. Elizabethan half-timbered houses stand alongside bow-fronted Georgian shops in the wide main street. Behind lies the ruined, but still impressive, castle dating from the 15th century. Ashby was the scene of the tournament in Sir Walter Scott's novel *Ivanhoe*.

Fireplace in the Hastings Tower, Ashby Castle.

The Commonwealth church, Staunton Harold.

STAUNTON HAROLD

Oliver Cromwell is reputed to have been angry when Sir Robert Shirley, a staunch Royalist, built a church here about 1650 instead of using the money to raise a regiment. For his error he was sent to the Tower of London, where he died aged 32. Church services still follow the 17th-century custom of segregation of the congregation, the men sitting on the right of the aisle, the women on the left. The organ was built in the 18th century, and is one of the oldest-surviving examples of English work of this kind. The hall, home of the Shirleys from 1423, is now one of the Cheshire Homes for handicapped people, run by Group Captain Leonard Cheshire, VC.

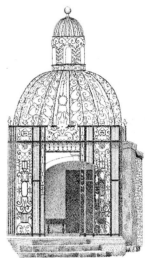

Birdcage pergola, Melbourne Hall.

MELBOURNE

Lord Melbourne, first Prime Minister to the young Queen Victoria, took his title from this place. The name means mill-stream. The church, built on the site of a Saxon chapel, is basically Norman, and the nave contains good Norman pillars and arches. Opposite the church is Melbourne Hall, once Lord Melbourne's home. It is well known for its gardens, patterned on those at Versailles, with long avenues, a tunnel of yew, fountains, statuary and a shell grotto. There is a locally made pergola of wrought iron, known as the birdcage. The hall and gardens are open most days in summer.

BEACON HILL

A large car park near the summit reduces the walk to the top of Beacon Hill, from which there is a fine view of Charnwood Forest. Although still wooded in parts, Charnwood is no longer a true forest. But in the Middle Ages thick woodlands sheltered game for the royal hunts and provided the raw material for a charcoal-burning industry. Beacon Hill is the site of a Bronze Age fortress.

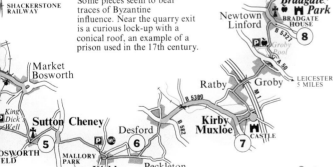

BREEDON ON THE HILL

Perched on a quarry edge high above the village, Breedon church looks out over a wide expanse of the Trent Valley. Examples of Saxon sculpture, mainly in the sanctuary and south aisle, were saved from a monastery which was destroyed by the Danes in the 9th century. Some pieces seem to bear traces of Byzantine influence. Near the quarry exit is a curious lock-up with a conical roof, an example of a prison used in the 17th century.

Old John's Tower, Bradgate Park.

KIRBY MUXLOE

In 1480, towards the end of the Wars of the Roses, Lord Hastings began to build Kirby Muxloe Castle to consolidate his power. Although his masons worked with a will, he never saw the stronghold completed, for he was executed for treason in 1483. The castle was one of the first to have gun-ports for firing cannon.

The castle, Kirby Muxloe.

BRADGATE PARK

This stretch of heath and woodland with a deer park surrounds the ruins of Bradgate House, birthplace in 1537 of the ill-fated Lady Jane Grey. In 1553, during the turbulent days after Henry VIII's death, she was offered the throne of England. But she was queen for only nine days and was beheaded in February 1554, not yet 17 years old. Old John's Tower, built in 1786, marks the spot where a flagpole fell out of a bonfire, killing an old servant called John. The park is now publicly owned.

A quiet journey by turnpike and towpath

Lovers of the canals and the traditions of the families who lived and worked on them will find a special fascination on this tour. Elegant mansions surrounded by wild-life parks, and colourful waterside inns make varied stopping points. By contrast, the drive halts near Naseby, at the battlefield where Cromwell's army defeated Charles I more than 300 years ago and established the authority of Parliament once and for all.

(1) Market Harborough to Lamport Leave Market Harborough on the A508 signposted to Northampton. After 8½ m., in Lamport, turn left on to the B576 to visit Lamport Hall.

(2) Lamport to Brixworth Return to the A508, and turn left towards Brixworth. To visit the Saxon church turn right in Brixworth on to the road signposted to Creaton.

(3) Brixworth to Althorp Return to the A508, turn right and at the crossroads in the village turn left on the road signposted to Holcot. At the crossroads in Holcot turn right to follow the signpost for Moulton. After 1½ m. turn right at the signpost to Pitsford. On the far side of Pitsford, at the T-junction with the A508, turn left and then right on to the road signposted to the Bramptons. In Chapel Brampton cross the A50 on to the road signposted to Church Brampton. About 1 m. beyond the village, at the junction with the A428 in Harlestone, turn right—Althorp is on the left after 1 m.

(4) Althorp to Stoke Bruerne Return south down the A428 through Harlestone, and about 1 m. later turn right on to the road signposted to Kislingbury. Go through a pinewood and at the T-junction turn left and immediately right, following signposts to Kislingbury. Cross the A45 into Kislingbury. As the B4525 bears right keep ahead on the road signposted to Gayton. After crossing the M1 fork right, and after ¾ m. keep ahead at the crossroads. At the T-junction on the outskirts of Gayton turn right and left by the church for Blisworth. In Blisworth cross the A43, following the signposts to Stoke Bruerne.

(5) Stoke Bruerne to Towcester Return across the canal and keep straight ahead at the crossroads. Follow the signs through Shutlanger to Heathencote. At the A5, turn right for Towcester.

(6) Towcester to Coton Leave Towcester on the A43 signposted to Silverstone. (The motor-racing circuit is beyond the village.) Turn right for the village centre then right again on to the road signposted to Blakesley. Bucknell Wood is on the left, about 1 m. beyond. Keep ahead at the crossroads, and at the T-junction turn right, following the Blakesley signpost. In Blakesley turn left on to the road signposted to Maidford and after 2 m., at the junction with the B4525, turn right, following the Northampton signpost. After 4 m., at the junction with the A5, turn left, following the Weedon signpost, but after 2 m., at the Narrow Boat Inn, turn right on to the road signposted to Flore. Shortly afterwards turn left, still signposted to Flore, crossing the canal. On the outskirts of Flore turn right into Nether Lane, and then left into Sutton Street. At the junction with the A45 turn right and then almost immediately left on to the road signposted to the Bringtons. Keep ahead at the crossroads. In Little Brington, at the T-junction, turn left, following the signpost to East Haddon. Cross the A428, and at the T-junction by East Haddon church turn left and then right on to the road signposted to Ravensthorpe. Go straight through the village to Coton. The Manor car park is on the right.

(7) Coton to Guilsborough Turn right out of the car park and follow the road to Guilsborough. At the T-junction turn left, following the signpost to West Haddon through Guilsborough. Grange Bird Park is on the left past the modern school.

(8) Guilsborough to Naseby Return to Guilsborough and turn left on to the road signposted to Naseby. Cross the A50 at the staggered crossroads and after 2½ m., on the outskirts of Naseby, turn right to the village centre. At the T-junction with the B4036 turn left, following the Welford signpost. At the church turn right, and shortly afterwards turn right again to Sibbertoft. On the left is Naseby Field.

(9) Naseby to Foxton Continue along the road and at the T-junction turn left, following the signpost to Sibbertoft. In the village turn right on to the road signposted to Theddingworth. At the junction with the A427 turn right, following the Lubenham signpost, but after about ¾ m. turn left on to the road signposted to Gumley. Keep ahead at the crossroads, and at the T-junction turn right for Foxton Locks.

(10) Foxton to Market Harborough Continue towards Foxton. Outside the village turn right, following the signpost to Market Harborough. At the A6 turn right, and return to Market Harborough.

INFORMATION

Places of interest *Althorp:* May, Sun. afternoons; June to Sept., Sun., Tues., Thur., afternoons; Easter Sun. and Mon., Spring and Late Summer Bank Hols., afternoons. *Coton Manor:* Apr. to Oct., Thur., Sun. and Bank Hols., afternoons. *Guilsborough Grange Bird Park:* Mar. to Nov., daily, 11 a.m.-6 p.m. *Lamport Hall:* May to end Sept., Thur., Sun. and Bank Hols., afternoons. *Stoke Park Pavilions:* July and Aug., Sat. and Sun. afternoons. *Stoke Bruerne:* Waterways Museum, daily, except Mon. in winter and Christmas and Boxing Day.

Information East Midlands Tourist Office, Bailgate, Lincoln (Tel. Lincoln 31521).

Towns with easy access to Market Harborough:
Leicester . . . . . . 15 m.   Northampton . . 18 m.
Melton Mowbray 21 m.   Rugby . . . . 17 m.

FOXTON LOCKS
Just before the village, the road meets the Grand Union Canal, where there is a remarkable series of locks built in 1808 and arranged in two 'staircases' of five locks each. A narrow boat in experienced hands could navigate the lock in under 30 minutes. Nowadays a pleasure boat arriving there takes up to an hour to get through. At the locks the remains of an ingenious inclined lift can still be seen. This was designed to winch boat up the canal in one movement.

Foxton Locks.

NASEBY
This quiet village owes its fame to the crucial battle fought on June 14, 1645, in which the Civil War was decided by the victory of Cromwell's forces over those of Charles I. A monument put up in 1823 just outside the village commemorates the battle, and a more modest memorial records the position of Cromwell's cavalry before their decisive charge. The church of All Saints, in the village, contains 'Cromwell's Table', at which some of the soldiers had a meal the night before the battle. There are also some relics of the three-hour struggle, including two rusted swords and a stirrup iron. The church was built in the 13th century. Ironically a bell hangs in the belfry with Charles I's cipher and the inscription 'God Save the King'. In the churchyard is a huge metal ball retrieved from a building destroyed in the siege of Boulogne, 1544.

Naseby monument

GUILSBOROUGH
Birds and wild life are the main attraction of Guilsborough Grange Bird Park. The birds include exotic parrots and penguins and some unusual waders. For children there is a play area with a pets' corner containing lambs, ponies, rabbits and a friendly pig. The acres of grassland and wooded hills, dotted with ponds and streams, provide plenty of pleasant picnic spots. In the town is a fine 17th-century gabled house built of ironstone.

Coton Manor.

COTON
A wide variety of bird life—flamingoes, several species of ducks and cranes—populate the ornamental lake overlooked by Coton Manor. The gardens also have pheasants, geese and parrots—about 50 species in all—and two Californian sea lions provide fun for children. The manor was built in 1662 from the remains of Holdenby Hall, destroyed by Cromwell after the Civil War.

SCALE

0   1   2   3   4   5 MILES

MARKET HARBOROUGH
One of the most attractive features of this picturesque small town is its wide main square. Its most notable building is the former grammar school, built in 1614. It stands above the street on carved wooden pillars; pedestrians can walk under it. The parish church of St Dionysius, built between the 13th and 15th centuries, is topped by a steeple which is a landmark for miles around. The interior of the church has galleries, added since 1683 to accommodate an overflow of the congregation. The town was a trading centre as early as 1203, and markets are still held there on Tuesdays and Saturdays. Industrial development has not destroyed the town's wealth of fine Georgian buildings. The inn sign that swings outside the Three Swans is a worthy example of 18th-century ironwork. Charles I made his headquarters in the town before the Battle of Naseby. When he was routed Cromwell occupied Market Harborough and from here wrote to Parliament telling of victory.

Grammar school on 'stilts', Market Harborough.

LAMPORT
Inigo Jones's son-in-law John Webb began the building of Lamport Hall in the 17th century. The wings were added later. A feature of the interior is the Music Hall, with plasterwork by John Woolston. The lawn in front of the house is laid out around a 17th-century cockpit, centre for the village sport at that time. All Hallow's Church, opposite the hall, is a chapel and vault used by the Isham family, who have owned the hall since 1673.

BRIXWORTH
The Saxon church of All Saints which dominates Brixworth from a hill is all that remains of a monastery built by Saxons in the 7th century. It is made partly of Roman tiles and brickwork taken from a demolished building in the area. The church has remained almost unchanged, with the exception of a Norman south door and a 13th-century Lady Chapel and 14th-century spire. Inside are several interesting features, including a relic reputed to be the larynx bone of the 8th-century St Boniface. The village is the home of the Pytchley Hunt kennels.

All Saints' Church, Brixworth.

ALTHORP
It was here that Queen Anne stayed on her way to London to join her husband James VI of Scotland when he became James I of England in 1603. The mansion, which is of medieval origin, was altered in 1573. It had been the home of the Spencer family since 1508. The architect Henry Holland also had a hand in its reconstruction in 1787. Visitors can see in its 115 ft picture gallery a fine collection of Dutch and Italian masters and portraits by Gainsborough and Reynolds.

STOKE BRUERNE
Nostalgic memories of the golden days of the canals are aroused by a stop at the lock in Stoke Bruerne village. In the first half of the last century, until the coming of the railways, this was a busy link in the first great transport system developed in Britain since the Romans built their roads. Nowadays, working barges carrying commercial cargo are rare; but replicas of the gaily painted boats make a visit to the Waterways Museum a memorable experience. Among the exhibits is an enormous padlock and key used to secure lock gates around 1770—but which failed to shackle the famous 'escapologist' Houdini 160 years later.

Bargees' water can, Stoke Bruerne.

TOWCESTER
St Lawrence's Church has one of the 'treacle' Bibles, printed in 1568 and full of errors. The name 'treacle' comes from the passage in the Book of Jeremiah 'Is there no balm in Gilead?' with the word 'balm' changed to 'treacle'. Towcester (pronounced *Toaster*) lies across the Roman Watling Street, and a section of the original fortifications of the Roman town of Lactodorum can still be seen near the police station.

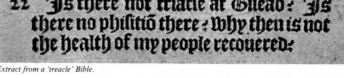

Extract from a 'treacle' Bible.

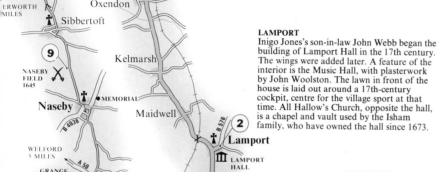

England's lost county whose past still lives

Why did Elizabeth II, like her 16th-century namesake, contribute to a castle's collection of horseshoes? How were medieval sinners told to 'get lost'? Why do two girls appear on the badge of a famous boys' school? The answers to these questions, and a host of other fascinating scraps of knowledge, are provided along this trail from the heart of Rutland, once England's smallest county, now swallowed up by Leicestershire.

1 Oakham to Wing Leave Oakham on the A6003 signposted to Kettering. After 2½ m., soon after going under a railway bridge, turn left for Manton and then immediately right for Wing. Follow the road for 1 m. and bear left into Wing.

2 Wing to Rockingham Leave Wing, following the signpost to Morcott. Drive through Morcott and turn right at the junction with the A6121 by the White Horse Inn (no signpost). Turn right again at the junction with the A47, and immediately left on to the B672 signposted to Caldecott. Follow this road to the Harringworth Railway Viaduct. Drive under the viaduct and turn left back under it into Harringworth. In the village turn right for Gretton, going under the viaduct for the third time. In Gretton bear right, following the signpost to Rockingham. Immediately after the railway bridge at the far side of the village turn left, still following the signpost to Rockingham. At the junction with the A6003 turn left into the village.

3 Rockingham to Kirby Hall Return from Rockingham to Gretton and turn right just after the church, on to the road signposted to Weldon. Then turn left at the T-junction, following the signpost for Kirby Hall. After ¾ m. turn left, again following the signpost for Kirby Hall, the entrance to which follows on the left after ¾ m.

4 Kirby Hall to Fotheringhay Return to the road and turn left towards Deene. Turn right at the first T-junction and go through the village. At the junction with the A43 turn left, following the signpost to Bulwick. After 1 m. turn right in Bulwick, on to the road signposted to King's Cliffe and Blatherwycke. Follow the road through Blatherwycke, King's Cliffe and Apethorpe, and turn left after the bridge just beyond Woodnewton. Fotheringhay is reached after 1½ m. Where the road bears sharp right after the church, the castle mound is on the left.

5 Fotheringhay to Oundle In Fotheringhay follow the road right, cross the bridge and continue to Tansor. Here, turn right by the church at the signpost for Cotterstock. After ½ m. turn right into Cotterstock. At the crossroads beyond the village turn left, following the Oundle signpost, and at the T-junction turn left into the town.

6 Oundle to Lilford Park Leave Oundle on the A605 signposted to Thrapston. Barnwell Picnic Park is on the right just after the bridge. After another 1½ m. turn left beside a small disused railway station, and then first right to the village of Barnwell. Return to the A605 and turn left towards Thrapston. After 1½ m. turn right at the crossroads, following the Pilton signpost. The entrance to Lilford Park is on the right.

7 Lilford Park to Geddington Continue into Pilton and turn left on to the road signposted to Wadenhoe. Go through Wadenhoe, following the signposts to Aldwincle, and at the T-junction after the village turn left and follow the road into Aldwincle. Here turn right, following the signpost for Lowick. Turn right again where the road bears left. At the junction with the A6116, turn right into Lowick. Follow the road past Sudborough to Brigstock, and turn left at the signpost to Grafton Underwood. Just before the village, turn right for Geddington, which is reached after 2 m.

8 Geddington to Rushton Leave Geddington on the road past the Eleanor Cross, and at the junction with the A43 cross over, following the signpost to Great Oakley. Where the road turns right to Great Oakley keep straight ahead, following the signpost to Rushton. At the junction with the A6003, turn right under the railway bridge and then left for Rushton, which is reached after ¾ m. To visit the Triangular Lodge, turn right at the T-junction on the far side of the village and follow the road round to the left.

9 Rushton to Uppingham Return towards Rushton, but take the first turning left over the railway and follow the road to Pipewell. Immediately after the Pipewell sign, take the left turn signposted to East Carlton and Wilbarston, and at the T-junction, after 1½ m., turn left for Wilbarston. At the junction with the A427 turn left, and follow this road through Brampton Ash to Dingley. Just after Dingley turn right on to the road signposted to Sutton Bassett. After 1¼ m. bear right on the B664 and follow the road for 8 m. to Uppingham.

10 Uppingham to Oakham Leave Uppingham on the A6003 signposted to Oakham, which is reached after 6 m.

INFORMATION

Places of interest *Cotterstock Hall:* Gardens Apr. to Oct.; House by appointment. *Kirby Hall:* Daily, Sun. afternoons. *Lilford Park:* Daily. *Oakham:* Castle, daily. County museum, weekdays (except Mon.). *Rockingham Castle:* Easter to Sept. 30, Sun., Thur., Bank Hol. Mon. and following Tues., afternoons. *Rushton:* Triangular Lodge, weekdays and Sun. afternoons.

Events *Oakham:* Autumn horticultural show. Sept. Rutland County Show, Aug.

Information East Midlands Tourist Board, Bailgate, Lincoln (Tel. Lincoln 31521).

Towns with easy access to Oakham:
Grantham . . . . . 21 m.   Leicester . . . . 19 m.
Kettering . . . . . . 20 m.   Stamford . . . . . . 11 m.

Horseshoe collection, Oakham Castle.

UPPINGHAM
A school, founded in 1584 by Archdeacon Johnson, i a feature of this market town. Johnson appears on the school badge alongside a group of pupils, two of whom are wearing skirts. It is said that Elizabeth I wished the school to be for boys and girls; and thou the governors disagreed, they placated the queen by including girls on the badge. T north side of the church ope on to the ancient market-place, and on the south side there are views of the open countryside.

MARKET HARBOROUGH 1 MILE — Sutt Bass
Dingley
Brampton Ash
B 664   A 427   TRIAN

Uppingham School badge.

The Triangular Lodge, Rushton.

RUSHTON
In the grounds of Rushton Hall is the curious Triang Lodge which was built by the eccentric Sir Thomas Tresham in 1597. It is a religious allegory symbolising Trinity with the number three as its architectural then It has three sides, three floors, three trefoil windows o each floor, even three smokeholes in the chimney. The church has some interesting monuments, including a 13th-century effigy of a crusader.

GEDDINGTON
When Eleanor of Castile, the wife of Edward I, d at Harby in Nottinghamshire in 1290, the king erected a cross on each of the 12 places at which her coffin rested on its journey to London. The b of the three that remain forms the centre-piece o the square at Geddington. It is flanked by some well-preserved stone cottages and the recently restored 14th-century church.

SCALE
0   1   2   3   4   5 MILES

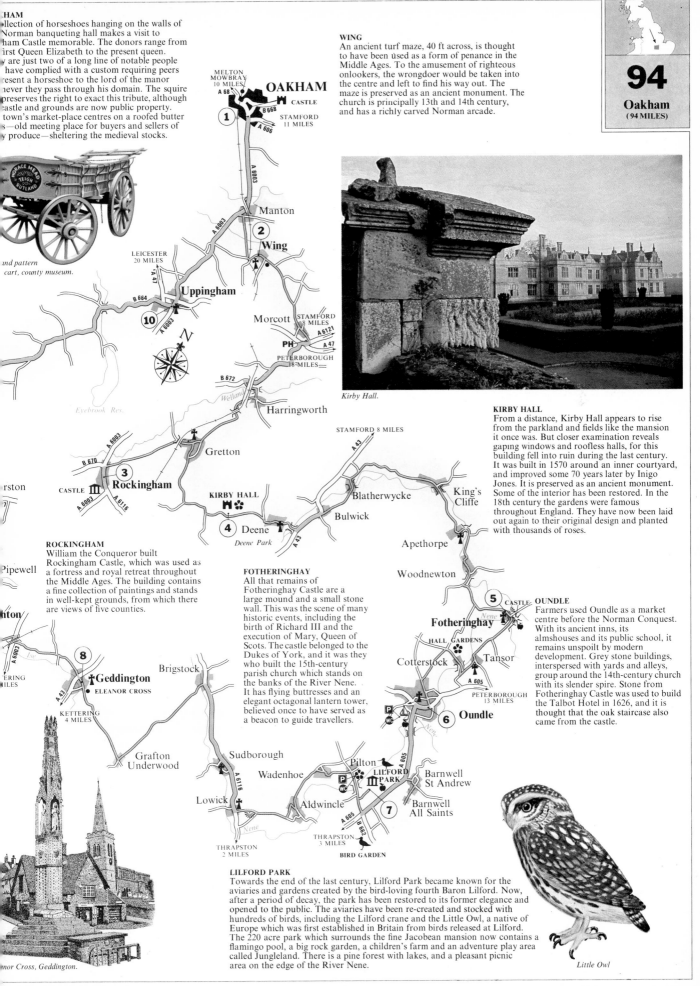

HAM

llection of horseshoes hanging on the walls of
Norman banqueting hall makes a visit to
ham Castle memorable. The donors range from
irst Queen Elizabeth to the present queen.
y are just two of a long line of notable people
have complied with a custom requiring peers
esent a horseshoe to the lord of the manor
never they pass through his domain. The squire
preserves the right to exact this tribute, although
castle and grounds are now public property.
town's market-place centres on a roofed butter
s—old meeting place for buyers and sellers of
y produce—sheltering the medieval stocks.

*nd pattern
cart, county museum.*

WING
An ancient turf maze, 40 ft across, is thought
to have been used as a form of penance in the
Middle Ages. To the amusement of righteous
onlookers, the wrongdoer would be taken into
the centre and left to find his way out. The
maze is preserved as an ancient monument. The
church is principally 13th and 14th century,
and has a richly carved Norman arcade.

Kirby Hall.

KIRBY HALL
From a distance, Kirby Hall appears to rise
from the parkland and fields like the mansion
it once was. But closer examination reveals
gaping windows and roofless halls, for this
building fell into ruin during the last century.
It was built in 1570 around an inner courtyard,
and improved some 70 years later by Inigo
Jones. It is preserved as an ancient monument.
Some of the interior has been restored. In the
18th century the gardens were famous
throughout England. They have now been laid
out again to their original design and planted
with thousands of roses.

ROCKINGHAM
William the Conqueror built
Rockingham Castle, which was used as
a fortress and royal retreat throughout
the Middle Ages. The building contains
a fine collection of paintings and stands
in well-kept grounds, from which there
are views of five counties.

FOTHERINGHAY
All that remains of
Fotheringhay Castle are a
large mound and a small stone
wall. This was the scene of many
historic events, including the
birth of Richard III and the
execution of Mary, Queen of
Scots. The castle belonged to the
Dukes of York, and it was they
who built the 15th-century
parish church which stands on
the banks of the River Nene.
It has flying buttresses and an
elegant octagonal lantern tower,
believed once to have served as
a beacon to guide travellers.

OUNDLE
Farmers used Oundle as a market
centre before the Norman Conquest.
With its ancient inns, its
almshouses and its public school, it
remains unspoilt by modern
development. Grey stone buildings,
interspersed with yards and alleys,
group around the 14th-century church
with its slender spire. Stone from
Fotheringhay Castle was used to build
the Talbot Hotel in 1626, and it is
thought that the oak staircase also
came from the castle.

nor Cross, Geddington.

LILFORD PARK
Towards the end of the last century, Lilford Park became known for the
aviaries and gardens created by the bird-loving fourth Baron Lilford. Now,
after a period of decay, the park has been restored to its former elegance and
opened to the public. The aviaries have been re-created and stocked with
hundreds of birds, including the Lilford crane and the Little Owl, a native of
Europe which was first established in Britain from birds released at Lilford.
The 220 acre park which surrounds the fine Jacobean mansion now contains a
flamingo pool, a big rock garden, a children's farm and an adventure play area
called Jungleland. There is a pine forest with lakes, and a pleasant picnic
area on the edge of the River Nene.

Little Owl

259

Bulbs and bird-cries in the steps of Hereward the Wake

Centuries of heartbreak and backache have gone into the draining of the Lincolnshire marshes where the bulbs grow, acre upon acre of blazing colour in the spring. Hereward the Wake rallied his followers here, and the fearless Queen Boudicca routed a Roman army way back in history when today's rich farmland was desolate fen, echoing to the cry of wildfowl. The tour wanders over a course dotted with silent reminders of battles fought and of outlandish punishments inflicted on the defeated.

1 **Stamford to Burghley House** Leave Stamford by the B1081 signposted A1 South. After 1 m. an imposing gatehouse on the left marks the entrance to Burghley Park.

2 **Burghley House to Folkingham** Return to Stamford and follow the A43(T) to the junction with the A6121 where turn right then fork left, leaving the town on the A6121 signposted to Bourne/Sleaford. Follow the road for about 7 m. and go through Toft. Cross pleasant farmland and woods, and after just under 2 m. turn left on to the A151, signposted to Colsterworth. After 1¾ m., past Bourne Wood, turn right just before the Five Bells Inn at Edenham on to the road signposted to Elsthorpe and Bulby. In Bulby take the right turn signposted to Kirkby Underwood/ Rippingale. Keep left at the next junction, following the Irnham/Corby signpost. After about ½ m. follow the road left signposted Corby, then almost immediately turn right to Keisby. Beyond Keisby keep bearing right, following the signposts to Folkingham, and after just 4 m. drive into the old market town of Folkingham.

3 **Folkingham to Sleaford** Keep straight ahead, joining the A15 signposted to Sleaford. Keep on the A15, and after just over 8 m. turn right at the T-junction and almost immediately left over the level-crossing into Sleaford.

4 **Sleaford to Heckington** At the Handley Memorial in Sleaford turn right, joining the road signposted to King's Lynn. After 5 m. enter Heckington. Turn right on to the B1177 signposted to Helpringham. The windmill is a short way down this road on the right.

5 **Heckington to Spalding** Return to the A17 in Heckington, turn right and drive across Holland Fen and after 4 m. cross the South Forty Foot Drain, an important part of the system which turned Hereward the Wake's fens into productive farmland. The drain heads straight for Boston, 6 m. on the left, and discharges into the sea. Pass through Swineshead, where King John stopped after losing his baggage in the Wash. Drive straight ahead at the crossing with the A52 and then 4 m. further to Sutterton, with its circular house. After 3½ m. cross the River Welland and 4 m. later, just beyond the Saracen's Head, turn right on the B1168 to Holbeach and into the bulb fields. In the centre of Holbeach turn right on to the A151 for the 7 m. drive through Whaplode and Moulton to Spalding. Follow the A151 along the near bank of the River Welland opposite central Spalding. For a visit to the town, turn right where the A151 crosses the river. (Otherwise drive straight ahead along the A1073 signposted to Crowland.)

6 **Spalding to Crowland** Return to the east bank of the Welland, and immediately after the bridge turn right on to the A1073 signposted to Crowland. Follow the road for 3 m., with the New River on the right, and go through Cowbit. After a further 4 m. turn right. On the outskirts of Crowland turn right on to the B1166 or go left on the A1073 to the town centre to see the ruined abbey and 14th-century bridge.

7 **Crowland to Northborough** Leave on the B1166 following the signpost to Deeping St James. Cross the bridge and turn left, following the course of the River Welland, reaching a level-crossing after 3½ m. Take the right turn here, still on the B1166, and turn left at the next crossroads. A right turn at the next junction leads into Deeping St James, with its village cross containing a prison. Keep left in the village along the river bank, then turn left across the bridge at Deeping Gate and on to the B1162 signposted to the Peakirk Wildfowl Trust. After ¾ m. turn left on to the A15 and into Northborough to visit Manor House. As the A15 bears right, away from the village, the house, known locally as 'the castle', is on the right.

8 **Northborough to Market Deeping** Go back along the A15, which goes through Northborough, and at the junction with the B1162 keep ahead on the A15 and after 1 m. enter Market Deeping, which has the oldest inhabited rectory in the country.

9 **Market Deeping to Stamford** In the village, turn left at the roundabout on the road signposted to Stamford. Follow the road for 7 m. to return to Stamford.

INFORMATION

Places of interest *Burghley House:* Apr. to beginning Oct., Tues. to Thur., Sat., Spring and Late Summer Bank Hols., 11 a.m.-5 p.m. Sun. and Good Friday, 2–5 p.m. *Heckington windmill:* Mon. to Fri., all day. Sat., mornings only. *Northborough Castle:* May to Oct., Sun. only 2–6 p.m. *Spalding:* Ayscoughfee Hall Museum, grounds and aviary, weekdays. *Springfield Gardens:* Apr. to Sept., daily.

Events *Burghley:* Horse Trials, Aug./Sept. *Heckington:* District Agricultural Show, July. *Spalding:* Flower Parade, May. Festival of the Arts, Oct. *Stamford:* Arts Festival, June.

Craft Workshop *Toft:* Old World Lamps, open at any reasonable time.

Information *Lincoln:* East Midland Tourist Office, Bailgate (Tel. Lincoln 31521). *Spalding:* Ayscoughfee Hall, Churchgate (Tel. Spalding 5468). South Lincolnshire Travel Association, Springfield (Tel. Spalding 4843).

Towns with easy access to Stamford:

Leicester	31 m.	Nottingham	40 m.
Northampton	36 m.	Peterborough	14 m.

FOLKINGHAM
A thousand years ago, and again in medieval times, Folkingham was the home of great lords. The 14th-century nave of the church, once resplendent with wall paintings and stained glass, was robbed and defaced in the 16th and 17th centuries. In the church are the stocks and whipping post, installed in 1600 for the correction of erring villagers. And one of the buildings the market place was a Correction House, where vagrants of the same period were rounded up by the constable and made to work. It has a 'dark room' for solitary confinement.

The Heaven Room, Burghley House.

BURGHLEY HOUSE
William Cecil, the first Lord Burghley, who was Lord High Treasurer to Elizabeth I, built Burghley House on the site of a monastery. Completed in 1589, it lies in a walled park south of Stamford. It is the home of the Marquis of Exeter, better known as Lord Burghley. The original Great Hall has a magnificent roof. Also remarkable is the painted Heaven Room, completed by Verrio in 1694. The gardens were laid out by the ubiquitous Capability Brown.

Stamford, seen from the River Welland.

SCALE
0 1 2 3 4 5 MILES

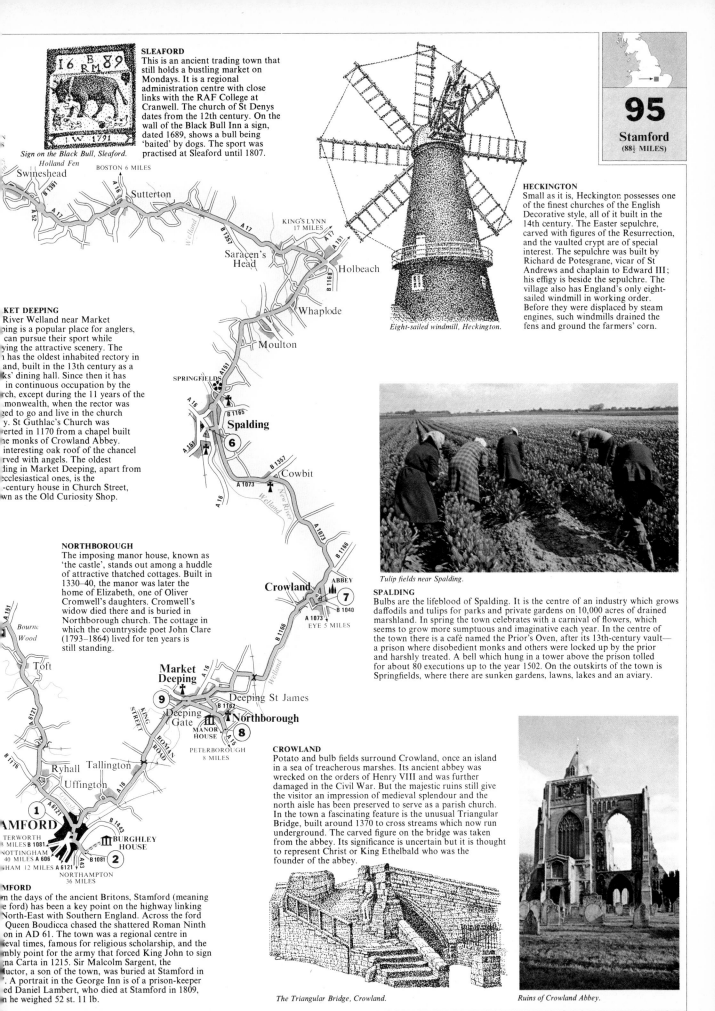

SLEAFORD

This is an ancient trading town that still holds a bustling market on Mondays. It is a regional administration centre with close links with the RAF College at Cranwell. The church of St Denys dates from the 12th century. On the wall of the Black Bull Inn a sign, dated 1689, shows a bull being 'baited' by dogs. The sport was practised at Sleaford until 1807.

Sign on the Black Bull, Sleaford.

HECKINGTON

Small as it is, Heckington possesses one of the finest churches of the English Decorative style, all of it built in the 14th century. The Easter sepulchre, carved with figures of the Resurrection, and the vaulted crypt are of special interest. The sepulchre was built by Richard de Potesgrane, vicar of St Andrews and chaplain to Edward III; his effigy is beside the sepulchre. The village also has England's only eight-sailed windmill in working order. Before they were displaced by steam engines, such windmills drained the fens and ground the farmers' corn.

Eight-sailed windmill, Heckington.

...KET DEEPING

...River Welland near Market ...ing is a popular place for anglers, ... can pursue their sport while ...ying the attractive scenery. The ...n has the oldest inhabited rectory in ...and, built in the 13th century as a ...ks' dining hall. Since then it has ...in continuous occupation by the ...rch, except during the 11 years of the ...monwealth, when the rector was ...ed to go and live in the church ...y. St Guthlac's Church was ...erted in 1170 from a chapel built ...he monks of Crowland Abbey. ...interesting oak roof of the chancel ...rved with angels. The oldest ...ding in Market Deeping, apart from ...ecclesiastical ones, is the ...-century house in Church Street, ...wn as the Old Curiosity Shop.

NORTHBOROUGH

The imposing manor house, known as 'the castle', stands out among a huddle of attractive thatched cottages. Built in 1330–40, the manor was later the home of Elizabeth, one of Oliver Cromwell's daughters. Cromwell's widow died there and is buried in Northborough church. The cottage in which the countryside poet John Clare (1793–1864) lived for ten years is still standing.

SPALDING

Bulbs are the lifeblood of Spalding. It is the centre of an industry which grows daffodils and tulips for parks and private gardens on 10,000 acres of drained marshland. In spring the town celebrates with a carnival of flowers, which seems to grow more sumptuous and imaginative each year. In the centre of the town there is a café named the Prior's Oven, after its 13th-century vault—a prison where disobedient monks and others were locked up by the prior and harshly treated. A bell which hung in a tower above the prison tolled for about 80 executions up to the year 1502. On the outskirts of the town is Springfields, where there are sunken gardens, lawns, lakes and an aviary.

Tulip fields near Spalding.

CROWLAND

Potato and bulb fields surround Crowland, once an island in a sea of treacherous marshes. Its ancient abbey was wrecked on the orders of Henry VIII and was further damaged in the Civil War. But the majestic ruins still give the visitor an impression of medieval splendour and the north aisle has been preserved to serve as a parish church. In the town a fascinating feature is the unusual Triangular Bridge, built around 1370 to cross streams which now run underground. The carved figure on the bridge was taken from the abbey. Its significance is uncertain but it is thought to represent Christ or King Ethelbald who was the founder of the abbey.

The Triangular Bridge, Crowland.

Ruins of Crowland Abbey.

...MFORD

...m the days of the ancient Britons, Stamford (meaning ...e ford) has been a key point on the highway linking ...North-East with Southern England. Across the ford ...Queen Boudicca chased the shattered Roman Ninth ...on in AD 61. The town was a regional centre in ...eval times, famous for religious scholarship, and the ...mbly point for the army that forced King John to sign ...na Carta in 1215. Sir Malcolm Sargent, the ...ductor, a son of the town, was buried at Stamford in ... A portrait in the George Inn is of a prison-keeper ...ed Daniel Lambert, who died at Stamford in 1809, ...n he weighed 52 st. 11 lb.

Nature's refuge above the industrial heartlands

From vantage points on the 1000 ft hills of the Peak, Lancashire's industry can be seen sprawling towards a smudged horizon. Then the road descends into the valleys and a different world. Here wildfowl flourish around wooded rivers, reservoirs and canals. The towns, like Georgian Buxton, are full of proud reminders of their founders. The country around is adorned with grand houses preserved by the National Trust and set in deer parks and gardens that remain untouched by the industrial upheaval that surrounds them.

1 **Buxton to Chapel-en-le-Frith** Leave the town on the A6, heading northwards and passing Black Edge and Hob Tor hills on the left. After 4 m. keep left to stay on the A6 and continue into Chapel-en-le-Frith.

2 **Chapel-en-le-Frith to Abbot's Chair** As the A6 bears left in the town, fork right on to the A624. Follow the road under a railway bridge and continue to Hayfield, passing the moorland of High Peak on the right. Keep on the A624, and 2 m. beyond Hayfield turn left on to Monk's Road, following the sign to Charlesworth. On the left, 400 yds past the turning, Abbot's Chair is set back about 70 ft from the road.

3 **Abbot's Chair to Melandra Castle** Continue on Monk's Road over the hills to Charlesworth. Turn left into the village, and then turn right by the George and Dragon Inn on to the A626. After just over 1 m. turn left on to the A57, and after 1 m. turn left again. Immediately after crossing the bridge, follow the path to the left to visit Melandra Castle, the remains of a Roman fort.

4 **Melandra Castle to Etherow Country Park** Return to the A57 and turn left, on the road signposted to Hyde. Keep on the A57 to Mottram in Longdendale, and turn left at the traffic lights on the B6174 signposted to Broadbottom. After 200 yds. keep straight ahead at the junction on the road signposted to Charlesworth. After about 2½ m., turn right on to the A626 and take the first left on to New Mills Road. Follow the lane over the hills to the junction with the A626 and turn left. By the Windsor Castle public house turn right on to the B6104 and follow it into Compstall. Here turn right by the post office to visit Etherow Country Park with its abundance of wildlife.

5 **Etherow Country Park to Marple** On leaving the park, return to the A626 and turn right, following the signpost to Stockport. Continue across the railway and into Marple.

6 **Marple to Lyme Hall** At the next major junction in Marple, take the second turning on the left into Church Lane. Turn right and follow the signs to High Lane. In the village, at the junction with the A6, turn left, following the signpost to Buxton. After 1 m. turn right into Lyme Park and follow the road to Lyme Hall.

7 **Lyme Hall to Adlington Hall** Return through Lyme Park to the A6 and turn left into High Lane. After 2 m. turn left into Norbury Hollow Road. Follow the lane out of the valley and keep bearing right. At the

Poynton crossroads turn left on to the A523, following the signpost to Macclesfield. After 2 m. turn right to visit Adlington Hall.

8 **Adlington Hall to Bollington** Continue on the lane past the hall, and at the junction with the B5358 turn left, following the signpost for Prestbury. Continue for about 2 m. to the junction with the A523 and turn right. After 1 m. fork left on to the B5091, signposted to Bollington, and follow the road into the town.

9 **Bollington to Jenkin Chapel** Continue through the town to the junction beside the Turner's Arms, bearing right on to the road signposted to Pott Shrigley and Whaley Bridge. At the next junction keep straight ahead, and after just over 1 m. turn sharp right and left to cross the A5002 at the top of the hill. After 2 m. the road drops sharply to a junction. Here turn left and continue to the next junction to see Jenkin Chapel.

10 **Jenkin Chapel to Goyt Valley** If the Goyt Valley road is open, turn right by Jenkin Chapel and follow the road over the hill and down into the valley. (If the Goyt Valley Road is closed, return from Jenkin Chapel to the junction but keep straight ahead. After 2 m. turn left on to the A537. The road climbs steadily up to the Cat and Fiddle Inn, which is a good viewpoint. Cross the moor and turn left on to the A53 and return to Buxton.)

11 **Goyt Valley to Buxton** Keep straight ahead on the one-way road through the valley to the Derbyshire Bridge car park, and follow the road right. Turn first left, and almost immediately left again, on to the A537. After 2 m. turn left on to the A53 and follow the road back to Buxton.

INFORMATION

Places of interest *Adlington Hall:* Good Friday to Oct., Sun., Spring and Late Summer Bank Hols., Sat. also July and Aug., 2.30-6 p.m. *Lyme Hall:* Mar. to Oct. (except Mon.), afternoons. Gardens open all year, daily.

Events *Buxton:* Antiques Fair, Apr./May. Well-dressing Festival, July. *Chapel-en-le-Frith:* Morris dancing, last week in June.

Craft workshop *Dove Holes, Nr. Buxton:* The Forge, wrought ironwork, Mon. to Fri., all day.

Information *Buxton:* Tourist Information Centre, The Crescent (Tel. Buxton 5106). Goyt Valley operates a park and ride scheme (in the zones that are closed to traffic) on Sun. and Bank Hols. from the last Sun. in May to the last Sun. in Sept.

Towns with easy access to Buxton:

Ashbourne ..... 21 m.	Macclesfield .... 12 m.
Bakewell .... 12 m.	Manchester .... 25 m.
Chesterfield .... 24 m.	Matlock .... 20 m.

ETHEROW COUNTRY PARK

Yellow loosestrife

The centrepiece of this 160 acre country park, opened in 1966, is the reservoir. This was built in 1815 by the Andrews family, local mill owners, to supply power to the cotton mills. One of the old mills still stands on the edge of the park, but the water wheel and turbine engines have long since been removed. Now the quiet waterways attract mallards, herons and kingfishers, and are used by both sailing and fishing enthusiasts. There is a 1¼ mile nature trail which starts at Compstall. Most of the trees in the park are native Britain and include ash, elm, elder, beech and oak.

MARPLE

Although only a few miles from the heart of Manchester, Marple has retained its small-town character. The River Goyt flows through a deep wooded valley on the edge of the town, and the Peak Forest Canal adds to the placid atmosphere. The canal crosses the River Goyt by a 308 ft aqueduct a mile from Marple. A series of 16 locks reduce the level by 200 ft.

The Great Hall in Adlington Hall.

ADLINGTON HALL

A branch of the Legh family, who owned Lyme Hall, built Adlington, an attractive mixture of timber, plaster and Classical stonework. The black-and-white wing of the house was completed in 1581 and includes the Great Hall, where there is an organ dating from 1670 and built by Bernard Smith. It is believed that Handel played this organ when a guest at the hall and that 'The Harmonious Blacksmith' was composed here. The south wing, with its Palladian portico, was not built until the 18th century, when the hall was enlarged. The house is surrounded by wooded parkland where there is a magnificent avenue of chestnut trees. The remains of a moat and an 18th-century rotunda complete the setting.

BOLLINGTON

Three churches and two chapels were all built in the second half of the last century, when Bollington's prosperity, based on cotton milling, was at its peak. Stone houses and cottages alongside a small river and canal give the town a character of its own. Two of the cotton mills still stand: one of them is now a nylon factory. To the south of the town is Kerridge Hill, crowned by a monument known as White Nancy. This folly, in the shape of an artillery shell, was erected by a local landowner to commemorate the Battle of Waterloo.

SCALE

0   1   2   3 MILES

MELANDRA CASTLE
Excavations are being carried out on this square hill-fort, the most extensive Roman relic in Derbyshire. Foundations of walls, corner towers and gateways are now visible. The fort, measuring 398 ft by 368 ft, was built in the 1st century AD to guard the western end of two passes over the Pennines. The hill provides views over the village of Dinting and the industrial town of Glossop.

ABBOT'S CHAIR
Set back from the road is a large square stone with a deep recess similar in shape to an armchair. It is thought to be the socket for a cross from which one side has been broken. Local tradition links the stone with the monks of the 14th century who used to drive sheep along Monk's Road from Charlesworth to the Peak.

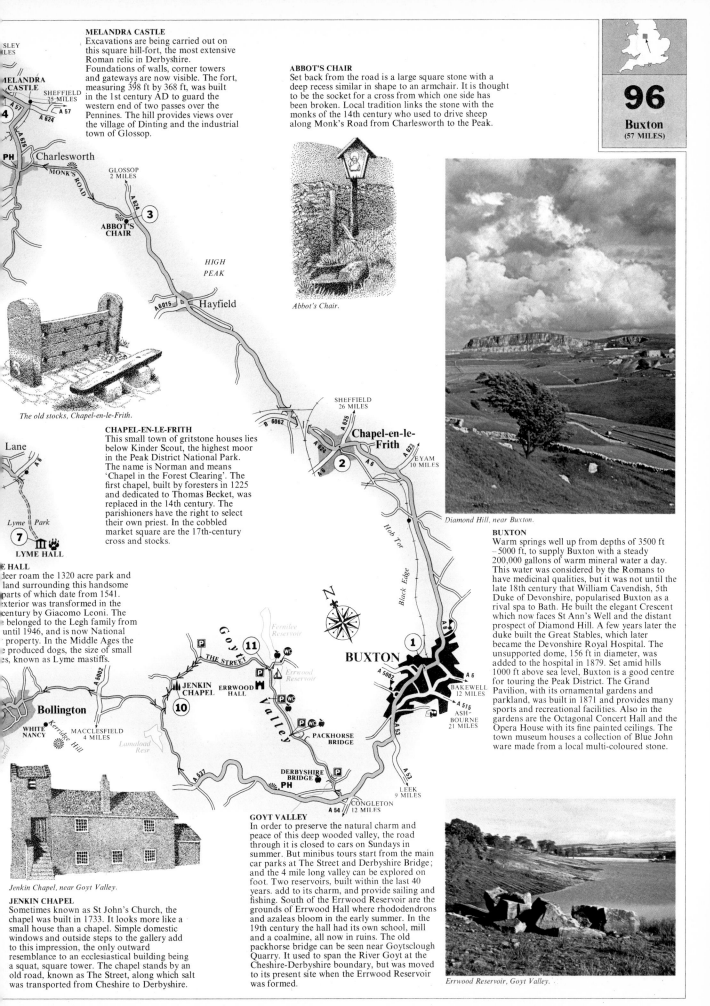

Abbot's Chair.

The old stocks, Chapel-en-le-Frith.

Diamond Hill, near Buxton.

CHAPEL-EN-LE-FRITH
This small town of gritstone houses lies below Kinder Scout, the highest moor in the Peak District National Park. The name is Norman and means 'Chapel in the Forest Clearing'. The first chapel, built by foresters in 1225 and dedicated to Thomas Becket, was replaced in the 14th century. The parishioners have the right to select their own priest. In the cobbled market square are the 17th-century cross and stocks.

HALL
deer roam the 1320 acre park and land surrounding this handsome parts of which date from 1541. exterior was transformed in the century by Giacomo Leoni. The belonged to the Legh family from until 1946, and is now National property. In the Middle Ages the produced dogs, the size of small es, known as Lyme mastiffs.

BUXTON
Warm springs well up from depths of 3500 ft – 5000 ft, to supply Buxton with a steady 200,000 gallons of warm mineral water a day. This water was considered by the Romans to have medicinal qualities, but it was not until the late 18th century that William Cavendish, 5th Duke of Devonshire, popularised Buxton as a rival spa to Bath. He built the elegant Crescent which now faces St Ann's Well and the distant prospect of Diamond Hill. A few years later the duke built the Great Stables, which later became the Devonshire Royal Hospital. The unsupported dome, 156 ft in diameter, was added to the hospital in 1879. Set amid hills 1000 ft above sea level, Buxton is a good centre for touring the Peak District. The Grand Pavilion, with its ornamental gardens and parkland, was built in 1871 and provides many sports and recreational facilities. Also in the gardens are the Octagonal Concert Hall and the Opera House with its fine painted ceilings. The town museum houses a collection of Blue John ware made from a local multi-coloured stone.

Jenkin Chapel, near Goyt Valley.

JENKIN CHAPEL
Sometimes known as St John's Church, the chapel was built in 1733. It looks more like a small house than a chapel. Simple domestic windows and outside steps to the gallery add to this impression, the only outward resemblance to an ecclesiastical building being a squat, square tower. The chapel stands by an old road, known as The Street, along which salt was transported from Cheshire to Derbyshire.

GOYT VALLEY
In order to preserve the natural charm and peace of this deep wooded valley, the road through it is closed to cars on Sundays in summer. But minibus tours start from the main car parks at The Street and Derbyshire Bridge; and the 4 mile long valley can be explored on foot. Two reservoirs, built within the last 40 years, add to its charm, and provide sailing and fishing. South of the Errwood Reservoir are the grounds of Errwood Hall where rhododendrons and azaleas bloom in the early summer. In the 19th century the hall had its own school, mill and a coalmine, all now in ruins. The old packhorse bridge can be seen near Goytsclough Quarry. It used to span the River Goyt at the Cheshire-Derbyshire boundary, but was moved to its present site when the Errwood Reservoir was formed.

Errwood Reservoir, Goyt Valley.

The hills and dales below Derbyshire's Peak

The Peak is an area where bare windswept hills, scored with endless drystone walls, contrast with the wooded slopes of green dales that shelter snug farms and villages. From the hills there are dramatic views of the surrounding lowlands to which brief descents are made to see a masterpiece of black-and-white architecture, Little Moreton Hall, and the medieval magnificence of Haddon Hall. The moors around Meerbrook harbour a naturalised colony of up to 30 wallabies.

(1) Bakewell to Haddon Hall Leave Bakewell on the A6 signposted to Matlock, and drive for 2 m. to Haddon Hall.

(2) Haddon Hall to Youlgreave Continue along the A6 towards Matlock, but after ½ m. turn right on to the B5056. After 1 m. fork right on to the A524 and climb the wooded valley to Youlgreave.

(3) Youlgreave to Arbor Low Continue beyond the village for 1½ m. then fork right on to the road signposted to Parsley Hay/Buxton. Go straight on at the crossroads and bear left at the next junction. This road, known as the Long Rake, runs for 2 m. to Arbor Low, which is signposted on the left.

(4) Arbor Low to Hartington Leave Arbor Low and rejoin the Long Rake, turning left at the next junction, then left again on to the A515. After 1½ m. turn right on to the B5054 into the valley of Hand Dale, which runs down to Hartington and the Dove Valley.

(5) Hartington to Rudyard Continue on the B5054 to the junction with the B5053 and turn left, following the signposts to Warslow and Onecote. In Onecote turn right, following the signpost to Bradnop. Follow the lane up to where it crosses the Morridge. Go over the crossroads and downhill to Bradnop. At the A523 turn right, and go into Leek. Leave the town, noted for textiles, on the A523 signposted to Macclesfield. After 1½ m. turn left on to the B5331. Bear right by the Station Hotel, at the signpost to Biddulph and Congleton, and immediately fork right for the lake.

(6) Rudyard to Mow Cop Castle Returning from the lakeside turn right, then left, following the signpost to Horton. Beyond Horton, turn right at the T-junction and in 400 yds turn left. Bear right at the fork on the road signposted to Lask Edge. Go straight on at two crossroads, then at a T-junction just past a large outcrop of rock turn left, following the signpost to Knypersley. In Knypersley, cross the A527 and turn right on to the road signposted to Mow Cop. Turn left at the T-junction at the top of the hill, fork right by the Mow Cop Inn. A rough track on the left leads to Mow Cop Castle.

(7) Mow Cop Castle to Little Moreton Hall Return to the road and turn left. At the T-junction by the Cheshire View Inn, turn right and go down the hill. Go over the level-crossing and immediately left at the T-junction. Bear right at the next junction, following the signpost for Rode Heath, then take the first right on to Stone Chair Lane. At the A34 turn right, signposted to Congleton. Little Moreton Hall is 1 m. on the right.

(8) Little Moreton Hall to Meerbrook Rejoin the A34 going towards Congleton and after 2 m., in Astbury, turn right on to the road signposted to Congleton Station and Biddulph, and take the left fork beyond the village. After crossing the Macclesfield Canal and the railway the road swings left, parallel to the railway. At the T-junction by the second railway bridge turn right. Cross the A527 and start climbing. Just over the crest of the hill, turn left on to the road signposted to Cloud Side. After 400 yds, fork right, and keep right at the junction with a telephone kiosk. Turn right on to the A523 and after 400 yds fork left, off the main road, up a hill signposted to Meerbrook. At the top of the hill turn left, go over a crossroads and take the second right to Meerbrook, a village among the moors and crags which make it a centre for hill-climbers exploring the Peak District.

(9) Meerbrook to Bakewell Continue through Meerbrook on the same road, which is signposted to Blackshaw Moor. Turn right on to the A53, and after 100 yds turn left, following the signposts to Thorncliff. Turn left in the village and start climbing steeply. At the Mermaid Inn turn right, and follow the road over moorland for just over 2 m. to a crossroads. Turn left, signposted to Longnor. At the B5053 turn left, and after 2 m. go through Longnor. At the A515 turn right and immediately left on to the A5270 signposted to Chelmorton and Bakewell. Just after Chelmorton village sign, turn left to the church. Turn round at the church and take the first left and left again at the T-junction. After 3 m. turn left on to the road signposted to Sheldon. At the T-junction beyond the village turn left, and immediately fork right. After 2 m., at the B5055, turn left for Bakewell.

INFORMATION

Places of interest *Arbor Low:* Weekdays, Sun. afternoons. *Bakewell:* Old House Museum, Easter to Sept., afternoons. *Haddon Hall:* Apr. to Sept., Tues. to Sat. and Bank Hols. 11 a.m.-6 p.m. Bank Hol. Sun. afternoons. *Leek:* Local History Museum, daily except Thurs. *Little Moreton Hall:* Apr. to Oct., afternoons, except Tues. and Good Friday. Mar., weekends 2-6 p.m.

Nature trail *Lathkill Dale:* Starts from Lathkill Dale Hotel, over Haddon. Leaflet from Peak National Park Office and Information Centre.

Events *Bakewell:* Well-dressing and carnival, July. Show, Aug. *Leek:* Festival of Sunday Schools, second Sat. in July. *Longnor:* Wakes Festival, Sept. *Youlgreave:* Well-dressing, June.

Information Peak District National Park Office, Market Hall, Bakewell (Tel. Bakewell 3227).

Towns with easy access to Bakewell:

Ashbourne . . . . . 18 m.	Derby . . . . 30 m.
Buxton . . . . 12 m.	Sheffield . . . . 17 m.

Little Moreton Hall.

LITTLE MORETON HALL
The oldest parts of this superb example of Tudor architecture date from the start of the 16th century. Various alterations were made in later years but the house, which is surrounded by a moat, has remained virtually unchanged since 1580.

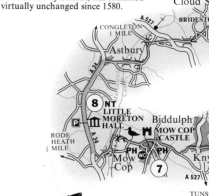

Mow Cop Castle.

MOW COP CASTLE
This is really not a castle at all, but a 'folly' erected in 1750 to gratify some whim of its builder, Randle Wilbraham. It crowns a ragged outcrop of rock.

RUDYARD RESERVOIR
Rudyard Kipling was named after the lake and village where his parents had courted. The reservoir is a man-made lake formed in 1793 to supply water for the Trent Mersey Canal. A 5 mile footpath, part of it an abandon railway, circles the shore, passing woods and caverns a the remains of Roman copper workings.

SCALE

0   1   2   3   4   5 MILES

...n Cloud, near Meerbrook.

BAKEWELL

Nestling in the valley of the Wye, with wooded slopes rising steeply to the east, the largest town in the Peak District National Park is dominated by its attractive church. Parts of it are Norman, but the remains of earlier Saxon crosses are in the churchyard. The five-arched bridge over the river is one of the oldest in Britain. Bakewell tart originated at the Rutland Arms Hotel, in the centre of the town. A customer ordered strawberry tart, but there was a slip-up in the kitchen: the egg mixture intended for the pastry was accidentally poured over the jam instead. A variety of buildings in mellow brownstone, including the market and town halls, gives the town an air of warmth unusual in the Peak District. Notable among these are Holme Hall and Bath House, both built in the 17th century. The town's name derives from the Saxon *bad-quell*, or 'bath well', and refers to the warm springs first discovered in Roman times. The water maintains a constant 15°C all the year.

...EERBROOK

...e wild upland country around this tiny moorland village ...pports one of the most unusual animal communities in ...tain—a naturalised colony of red-necked wallabies. These ...ngaroo-like animals, natives of Australia, are descended ...m wallabies which escaped from a private estate about ... years ago. In spite of the climate, the colony numbers up ... 30 in a good year, and individuals can sometimes be seen ... the road as well as the open moorland where they live. ...rth of the tip of Tittesworth Reservoir is Hen Cloud, ...e of a series of bare, rocky outcrops stretching ...t along the skyline for 2 miles called the ...paches from *Les Roches* (The Rocks), the ...me given to them by French prisoners in ...e Napoleonic wars. This is popular climbing ...untry, among the moors and crags ...at mark the southern end of the Pennines. ...e border of the Peak District National ...rk.

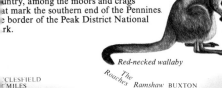

Red-necked wallaby

HADDON HALL

Most of the mansion, which belongs to the Duke of Rutland, dates from the 16th and 17th centuries, though some of it is 400 years older. The house was empty from the early 18th century until a 20 year restoration programme was completed not long before the Second World War. The many notable features include the magnificent Long Gallery, 110 ft long, with a richly decorated ceiling. The terraced garden is outstanding for its fine display of roses.

ARBOR LOW

Derbyshire's version of Stonehenge, which crowns a 1231 ft hill, was built by Bronze Age men between 2000 and 1600 BC. It is the county's most notable stone circle, formed of 40 stones up to 10 tons in weight. The stones originally stood upright: now they lie in a circle 160 ft across, surrounded by a ditch and a 12 ft high bank. Near the circle is a large tumulus on Gib Hill, where some bones were found in 1845.

The stone circle, Arbor Low.

Well-dressing, Youlgreave.

YOULGREAVE

The name (pronounced *Yoolgrave*) means 'yellow grove'. The massive tower of the Norman church of All Saints dominates the stone-built hilltop village. The ancient custom of well-dressing, with its origins in pagan water-worship, is followed in June, when the ceremony starts with a procession through the village. The Christian custom is a form of thanksgiving for water, and it is common for taps, not only wells, to be 'dressed' with pictures formed of flower petals and pebbles pressed into moist clay.

HARTINGTON

Drystone walls are a feature of this area. Those dividing fields are generally about 4 ft 6 in. high, walls defining farm boundaries about 1 ft higher. It has been estimated that on average there are 24 miles of drystone walls to the square mile of farmland in the district. Hartington, on the Staffordshire border, is a good centre for exploring the surrounding dales. The village centres round a wide market place, and has a row of cottages dated 1777. The name of the Charles Cotton Hotel commemorates the landowner-poet who introduced Izaak Walton to the fishing potential of the River Dove.

...stone walls near Hartington.

265

Down from the Pennines into stately Derbyshire

The Pennine mountain spine drops down to low hills and valleys, then flattens out into rich brown plains. The quick rivers slow, widen and begin to wander across fertile farmlands. This rich land supports many grand houses, like 17th-century Sudbury Hall, and Alton Towers, with its 600 acre garden park. A simpler way of life survives in the quiet villages where ancient rituals like the Horn Dance are still performed.

(1) Ashbourne to Church Broughton Leave Ashbourne on the A52 signposted to Derby. After 1 m. turn right, following the signpost to Osmaston. Follow the road through the village and bear right, following the signpost to Wyaston opposite the entrance to Osmaston Park. Go through Wyaston and ¼ m. later turn left on to the road signposted to Rodsley. At the T-junction beyond the village turn left, following the signpost to Longford. Opposite Longford Hall turn right, signposted for Tutbury. After 3 m. turn right at the crossroads and into Church Broughton.

(2) Church Broughton to Sudbury Turn left opposite the church in Church Broughton, and almost immediately right. At the T-junction turn left, following the signpost to Foston, and after just under 1 m. turn right. Follow this lane to the A50 and turn right. After 1 m. turn left at the Sudbury signpost.

(3) Sudbury to Tutbury Go through Sudbury and right on to the A515. Turn left almost at once along the valley of the Dove to Scropton. After 1¼ m. turn right on to the A50 and then cross the river into Tutbury. On the way into the town fork right on the road signposted to Draycott in the Clay and Tutbury Castle.

(4) Tutbury to Abbots Bromley Leave Tutbury on the road signposted to Draycott in the Clay. After 3 m. turn left on to the road signposted to Hanbury. Follow the road into Hanbury and bear right, following the road signposted to Newborough. After 2 m. go straight across the junction with the A515, still following the signposts for Newborough. In Newborough turn right on to the B5234 signposted Abbots Bromley. After 3½ m. turn right on to the B5014 signposted to Uttoxeter, and follow the road into Abbots Bromley.

(5) Abbots Bromley to Blithfield Hall Leave Abbots Bromley on the B5014 signposted to Uttoxeter. Soon afterwards, turn left on to the B5013, following the Rugeley signpost. Cross the causeway over Blithfield Reservoir and follow the road into Admaston. The entrance to Blithfield Hall is on the right.

(6) Blithfield Hall to Draycott in the Moors Leaving the hall turn right and continue along the road towards Rugeley, but very soon turn right on to the road signposted to Newton and Hixon. Bear left at the next junction, following the signpost for Drointon and Hixon, and after 1 m. fork right on to the road signposted to Drointon. After ½ m. turn right again, following the Kingstone signpost. Keep straight on through Drointon and bear left at the next junction which is signposted to Uttoxeter and Stafford. After ½ m. turn left again and follow the road

to the junction with the A518. Here turn left, following the Stafford signpost. After 1¼ m. turn right on to the road signposted to Gayton. Turn first right and go through Gayton, following the signposts for Milwich. At the junction with the B5027, by The Wheatsheaf, turn left and follow the road through Milwich to the crossroads with the B5066. Here turn right, following the signpost to Hilderstone. Turn right in Hilderstone, following the signpost to Cresswell. Follow the road for 4 m. through Cresswell to Draycott in the Moors.

(7) Draycott in the Moors to Croxden Leave Draycott in the Moors on the A50 signposted to Upper Tean. At Upper Tean cross the river and, as the A50 bends sharply right, go left on to the road signposted to Hollington. At the T-junction turn right, following the signpost to Hollington. At the T-junction in the village turn left at the Rocester signpost. After 1 m. take the lane, left, to Croxden.

(8) Croxden to Alton Continue along the lane, and at the T-junction turn right, following the signpost to Alton. After 1½ m. at the junction with the B5032 turn right, and soon afterwards turn left by The Blacksmith's Arms, following the signpost to Alton.

(9) Alton to Alton Towers Continue through Alton and down into the wooded Churnet Valley. Cross the river and climb the hill on the far side. Alton Towers is on the right.

(10) Alton Towers to Ashbourne Continue up the hill and turn right on to the road signposted to Ellastone. At the next T-junction turn right, following the signpost for Prestwood and Denstone. Follow the road down the hill over the crossroads, and turn right at the junction with the B5032. Almost immediately, turn left on to the B5033 signposted to Norbury. In Norbury go under a bridge and turn left at the Clifton signpost. In Clifton turn left on to the A515 for Ashbourne.

INFORMATION

Places of interest *Alton Towers:* Daily, Good Friday to early Oct. *Blithfield Hall:* Good Friday to mid-Sept., Wed., Thur., Sat., Sun. and Bank Hols., Mon. and Tues. afternoons. *Sudbury Hall:* Apr. to Oct., Wed. to Sun., and Bank Hol. Mon. 1-5.30 p.m. *Tutbury:* Castle, daily, 10 a.m.-dusk. Webb and Corbett glass factory, telephone to book tours for Mon. afternoons.

Events *Abbots Bromley:* Horn Dance, Sept. *Ashbourne:* Shrovetide football, Feb. Carnival, July. Sheep-dog trials, Aug. Market days, Thur. and Sat.

Information Tourist Information Centre, 13 Market Place, Ashbourne (Tel. Ashbourne 3666).

Towns with easy access to Ashbourne:

Derby	13 m.	Nottingham	29 m.
Lichfield	26 m.	Sheffield	34 m.
Macclesfield	28 m.	Stoke-on-Trent	22 m.

CROXDEN
At Croxden the road crosses what was o the nave of Croxden Abbey. Now a pile ruins, the abbey was founded by Bertrar de Verdun for Cistercian monks from Normandy in 1179. The building was completed in 1360 and fell into decay in 16th century. Substantial fragments of th church, the chapterhouse and the abbot house have survived, and some of them h been incorporated into a Georgian farmhouse.

DRAYCOTT IN THE MOORS
Set near the River Blithe, Draycott in the Moors is quiet and unspoilt. The 13th-century church of St Margaret contains many monuments to the Draycott family, including a cross-legged knight dating from about 1300, and a tomb chest against which stand a number of stone figures of children. In the churchyard there is an ancient hollow yew tree which has a trunk 18 ft in diameter. Painsley Hall, the old family seat of the Draycotts, is now a farmhouse.

BLITHFIELD HALL
The hall has been in the Bagot family for almost 900 years, but the present house is mainly Elizabethan, with a Gothic façade added in the 1820s. There are a collection of relics from the Stuart period, a toy museum, a display of Georgian costumes and, in the stables, the old family coaches. The landscaped gardens are set in wooded parkland roamed by the black-necked Bagot goats, whose ancestors were presented to the family by Richard II.

Abbots Bromley Horn dancers at Blithfield Hall.

SCALE

0   1   2   3   4   5 MILES

The conservatories, Alton Towers.

ALTON TOWERS

The 600 acre parkland at Alton Towers was originally the design of the imaginative 15th Earl of Shrewsbury, who created it from barren hillside in the early years of the last century. Thousands of tons of earth and rock were shifted, and water was piped down from a spring 2 miles away to feed the ornamental lakes and fountains. A Chinese temple, a Roman bath and colonnade, a Swiss cottage and many other features were added to enliven the garden. In 1831 the Gothic-style house, with its turrets and castellations, was added. Since 1926 Alton Towers has been open to the public, who can enjoy the full extent of the well-kept gardens, lawns and woodland walks. The attractions also include pony and donkey rides, a scenic railway, boating pools, a sea-lion pool, a funfair, a planetarium and aerial cable cars.

ASHBOURNE

This red-brick Midlands market town, because of its situation at the southern end of the Pennines, has been dubbed 'the gateway to the Peaks'. The 13th-century parish church is crowned with a 212 ft steeple which the Victorian novelist George Eliot described as 'the finest single spire in England'. Inside is Thomas Banks's white marble sculpture of Penelope Boothby, the daughter of a local family, who died at the age of five in 1791.

Penelope Boothby memorial, Ashbourne church.

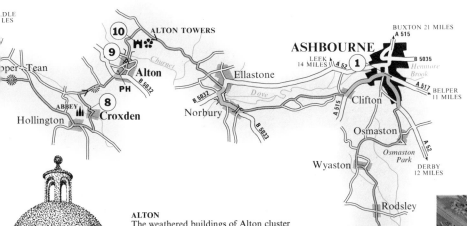

CHURCH BROUGHTON

Surrounded by farmland, Church Broughton retains the tranquil charm of a traditional Midlands village. An avenue of limes leads to the 14th-century church with its large tower topped by a diminutive spire. The spacious interior contains a Norman font, richly carved with zigzag decorations, and at the back of the church is an enormous royal arms of George IV dating from 1827. To the north, the 18th-century mansion of Barton Hall and its tiny medieval chapel can be seen.

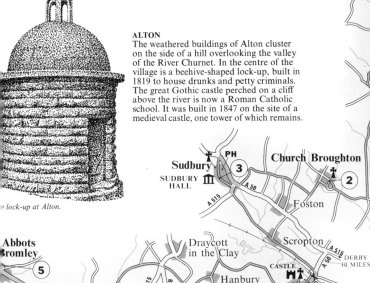
lock-up at Alton.

ALTON

The weathered buildings of Alton cluster on the side of a hill overlooking the valley of the River Churnet. In the centre of the village is a beehive-shaped lock-up, built in 1819 to house drunks and petty criminals. The great Gothic castle perched on a cliff above the river is now a Roman Catholic school. It was built in 1847 on the site of a medieval castle, one tower of which remains.

The staircase, Sudbury Hall.

SUDBURY

Brick cottages line Sudbury's long main street, and at one end is the Vernon Arms, dating from 1671. In full view from the road is Sudbury Hall, built between 1613 and 1695. It belonged to the Vernon family until 1967, and is an excellent example of a Stuart country house. Its treasures include a collection of English paintings, carvings by Grinling Gibbons (1648–1720) and ceilings by Laguerre, the 17th-century French painter who specialised in murals. Particularly noteworthy are the carved staircase, an exceptional example of its period, and the Long Gallery which fills the whole south front and which is hung with family portraits. Queen Adelaide, William IV's consort, lived in the hall for three years in the 1840s. The church which stands close by is 14th century, and contains many memorials to the Vernons as well as some Victorian stained glass.

ABBOTS BROMLEY

...got Street and the Market Place ... Abbots Bromley are full of ...ellowed old buildings which include ...e 16th-century Church House and ...e Bagot Almshouses, which were ...ilt in 1705. The town is famous ...r its annual Horn Dance on the ...st Monday after September 4. ...e celebration commemorates the ...anting to the villagers of hunting ...hts in the now vanished ...eedwood Forest. The dancers and ...usicians wear Tudor dress. One of ...em rides a hobby horse, another ...ays a 'fool', and six carry reindeer ...tlers which have belonged to the ...lage since Saxon times.

Tutbury crystal glass.

TUTBURY

Perched on a hill above the River Dove, Tutbury's castle stands on a site that was a military stronghold from prehistoric times until the 17th century. The present building is predominantly 15th century, but there is a 12th-century chapel within the walls. Mary, Queen of Scots was twice imprisoned at Tutbury, and Charles I rested here after his defeat at Naseby in 1646. Tutbury cut crystal glass is hand-made by craftsmen at the Webb and Corbett factory in the town.

Where cotton took over from Derbyshire's wolves

This was for centuries a wild and remote area on the edge of the Peak District. Wolves roamed here until the 17th century—and can still be seen at Riber Castle Zoo. The real taming of the countryside started with the harnessing of its water in the mill-races of cotton pioneer Sir Richard Arkwright, who built Britain's first factory at Cromford in 1771. The works of man are shown, too, in gracious Matlock Spa, the ruins of a great manor and a tramway museum. But the tour ends where it began, with a glimpse of nature's poetry in the cliffs of the Derwent Valley.

(1) Matlock to Riber Castle Leave Matlock Bridge on The Causeway, and at the roundabout by the Crown Hotel take the A615 signposted to Alfreton. After 800 yds turn right, following the signpost to Starkholmes. In the village of Starkholmes, fork left up a steep hill. At the crossroads turn left to visit Riber Castle Zoo and nature reserve.

(2) Riber Castle to Ogston Reservoir Leave the castle on the road opposite the entrance to the park, and continue into Tansley. In the village turn right on to the A615 and after ½ m. turn left on to the B6014, following the signpost to Clay Cross. After 2½ m. turn right to follow the Brackenfield signpost. On the left is Ogston Reservoir.

(3) Ogston Reservoir to Wingfield Manor From the car park follow the road into Brackenfield. In the village turn left by the church on to the road signposted to Shirland. Bear left at the next fork and turn right at the T-junction, following the signpost to Wessington. In Wessington turn left on to the A615. After ½ m., where the A615 forks left, bear right to follow the signpost to South Wingfield. In the village turn right on to the road signposted to Crich, and at the next junction go straight ahead on to the B5035, still following the Crich signpost. On the outskirts of South Wingfield, a track on the left leads to Wingfield Manor.

(4) Wingfield Manor to Crich Continue along the B5035 into Crich. (To visit the unusual Sherwood Foresters' war memorial, turn right at the T-junction by the church. For the tramway museum, bear right by the village cross and follow the signpost.)

(5) Crich to Cromford At the T-junction by the tramway museum turn left and follow the road to Holloway. For a short diversion, to enjoy some good views, turn sharp right just before the yew tree in the village, and continue up a steep hill. Just before the de-limit sign, turn left along a road which ends at a rhododendron nursery. Return by the same route to Holloway, turning right and following the road through the village. Bear left by the post office, and left again. Follow the road along the Cromford Canal, to the left, and into Cromford. At the crossroads with the A6 turn right, then immediately left on to the A5012 for the centre of the village.

(6) Cromford to Robin Hood's Stride Leave Cromford on the A5012, passing through Middleton Wood and Griffe Grange Valley. This section of road is known locally as the Via Gellia, after a textile family who built the road in the last century. At the Grange-mill crossroads, turn left on to the B5056 and first right on to the road signposted to Aldwark. At the junction before the village, turn right to follow the signpost for Elton. At the next crossroads go straight ahead over the A5012. Keep ahead again at the next crossroads and continue into Elton, a village with several 18th-century stone houses. At the T-junction by the church turn right on to the road signposted to Winster, but after ¾ m. turn left on to the B5056. After 1¼ m. a footpath on the left leads up to Robin Hood's Stride.

(7) Robin Hood's Stride to Bonsall Continue along the B5056, and after 1½ m. turn right on to the road signposted to Stanton in Peak. Keep on through the village on the road signposted to Birchover, passing Stanton Moor Plantation on the left. There are footpaths leading from the car park here to the prehistoric Nine Ladies Stone Circle, the King's Stone and Cork Stone. Continue along this road and at the T-junction turn right into Birchover. At the centre of the village turn left into a lane marked 'Unsuitable for Motors' (though it is no worse than many others in the district). Follow the narrow lane downhill, and at the T-junction with the B5057 turn left and continue into Winster. Turn first right by a traffic mirror in the village, and ¼ m. later go left again on to the B5056. Soon afterwards turn left on to the road signposted to Bonsall and continue across moorland, ignoring side roads, into Bonsall.

(8) Bonsall to Matlock In the village, bear right at the cross and left at the next T-junction. Follow the lane back to the A5012 and turn left. Continue into Cromford and turn left on to the A6. Follow the road past Masson Mills, on the right, and back to Matlock by way of Matlock Bath, the town's spa and entertainments centre.

INFORMATION

Places of interest *Crich Tramway Museum:* Apr. to Oct., weekends and Bank Hols.; June to Aug., also Tues. to Thur. *Cromford Mill:* Repairs in progress, parties by arrangement. *Riber Castle Fauna Reserve:* Daily. *Wingfield Manor:* Undergoing renovation. *Winster Market House:* Easter Sat. to Oct., Wed., weekends and Bank Hol. Mon., afternoons.

History trails Conducted tours around Cromford organised by the Arkwright Society. Local history trails round Matlock and Bonsall.

Information Tourist Information Centre, Town Hall, Matlock (Tel. Matlock 2994).

Towns with easy access to Matlock:

Ashbourne	14 m.	Derby	18 m.
Buxton	20 m.	Mansfield	17 m.
Chesterfield	10 m.	Nottingham	26 m.

Cratcliff Tor and hermit's cave, from Robin Hood's Stride.

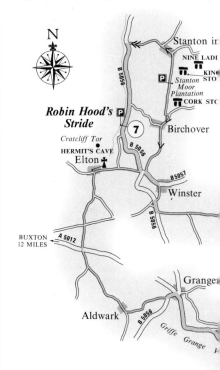

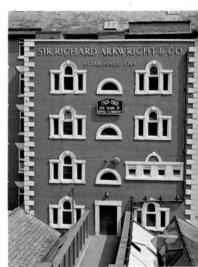

Masson Mills near Cromford.

CROMFORD
Plenty of water that could be harnessed for power attracted the inventor Sir Richard Arkwright to Cromford, where he set up the world's first mechanical textile mill in 1771. It still stands, close to the canal which Arkwright built.

SCALE

0   1   2   3 MILES

MATLOCK

A deep wooded gorge carved by the River Derwent provides a lush setting for Matlock, with its public gardens, varied walks and spectacular views. The original village, from which the town grew into a 19th-century holiday centre, stands high on a hill, grouped around the church of St Giles. Round a bend in the river, which is spanned by the 15th-century Matlock Bridge, High Tor cliffs rise 389 ft. Across the valley are the Heights of Abraham.

Ascension Day collecting boxes, Bonsall.

BONSALL

Lead was the main source of livelihood for the people of Bonsall until the late 1770s, and disused mines surround the village. A 17th-century market cross stands in the square. The 13th-century church has an unusual set of decorated collecting boxes which are used only on Ascension Day. The custom of well-dressing—decorating wells with flowers—takes place in late August.

Matlock Bath from the River Derwent.

Eagle owl, Riber Castle Zoo.

RIBER CASTLE

John Smedley, a textile manufacturer who popularised Matlock Bath as a spa, built this now-derelict castle as his home in 1862. The 800 acres of parkland have been turned into a nature reserve and zoo. From the neighbouring Riber village an attractive walk leads to Lea Hurst, the home of Florence Nightingale.

IN HOOD'S STRIDE

stacks of gritstone rock, known ly as Inaccessible and Weasel, are rated by about 20 paces, and are to represent the giant stride of in Hood. Near by is the craggy mass wn as Cratcliff Tor, often used for tice by rock climbers. At the foot e Tor is a shelf below an hanging rock, where a 4 ft high cross rved in the stone. It is believed to he work of a medieval hermit.

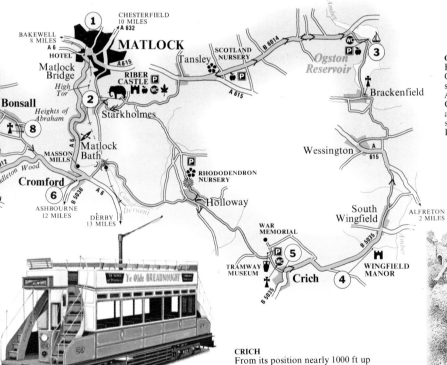

OGSTON RESERVOIR

Fitting into the landscape like any natural lake, the Ogston Reservoir has become a haven for waterfowl since it was created by flooding the valley of the River Amber in the 1960s. It has also become a sailing centre. Car parks run almost to the water's edge. Ogston Hall, a private residence which overlooks the reservoir to the south, stands on a site occupied since the time of the Domesday Book.

Open-top Dreadnought, tramway museum, Crich.

CRICH

From its position nearly 1000 ft up in the hills above Crich, one of the most unusual war memorials in Britain commands views over the Derwent Valley. It is a 63 ft high tower which could be mistaken for a lighthouse. It was built in 1922 as a memorial to the 11,409 men of the Sherwood Foresters Regiment who were killed in the First World War. It stands, a landmark for miles around, on the site of a centuries-old signal station. Tablets have been added to honour the regiment's Second World War dead. At the bottom of the hill is the tramway museum, opened in 1959 by a group of enthusiasts in an old quarry. The quarry has been realistically set out with street lamps and tram stops, and visitors can take a ride on clanking tramcars.

The Leicester 76 tramcar.

Wingfield Manor.

WINGFIELD MANOR

A Cromwell built it, and a Cromwell pulled it down. That in a few words is the history of Wingfield Manor. It was started in 1441 by wealthy Lord Cromwell, Henry VI's treasurer. Two hundred years later Oliver Cromwell, determined to wipe out every possible rallying place for Royalist forces, had it destroyed by parliamentary decree. In between the two events, Mary, Queen of Scots spent part of her imprisonment here before her execution in 1587. The Roundhead demolition squad of 1646 made a fairly thorough job of their work, but the vaulted crypt survived undamaged. The tower and two well-proportioned gateways also are still intact. But crumbling walls and fallen stone trace the outline of a once-magnificent building that measured 416 ft by 256 ft.

Up to the Peak District and down the caverns

The landscape rises into the Peak District, leaving all that is ordinary behind. Here, even a church spire has a twist to it. There are villages like Eyam, which died to save its neighbours, and Edensor, which died to preserve a view. There are Winnats Pass, where boats glide into a mountain, and the crystal chambers of the Blue John Caverns. At Hathersage, Robin Hood's lieutenant, Little John, lies buried in a giant's grave.

① Chesterfield to Old Brampton Leave Chesterfield on the minor road signposted to Ashgate Hospital and Old Brampton. After 3 m. the road runs into Old Brampton.

② Old Brampton to Edensor Continue through Old Brampton and after 1½ m. turn left at the crossroads, following the signpost to Eastmoor and Beeley. Go straight across the A619, and after 1½ m. turn right at the T-junction. After 1½ m., at the crossroads in the middle of Beeley Moor, turn right following the signpost for Beeley. Go right again at the next junction and follow the road as it winds down the hill to Beeley. Bear left in the village, and then turn right on to the B6012 signposted Chatsworth Park. Edensor is reached after 2 m. (To visit Chatsworth House, turn right just over 1 m. after the bridge with the traffic lights.)

③ Edensor to Curbar Gap Leave Edensor on the B6012 signposted to Baslow. On the edge of Baslow, join the A619 signposted to Chesterfield and Sheffield, follow it through the town, and at the roundabout take the A621 signposted to Sheffield. After 1½ m., at the crossroads at the top of the hill, turn left across the moorland to Curbar Gap, the rocky cleft that divides Baslow Edge on the left from Curbar Edge on the right.

④ Curbar Gap to Eyam Follow the road into Curbar and turn right at the crossroads, following the signpost for Froggatt. Go straight across the junction with the B6054, and at the approach to Froggatt turn left over the bridge. Turn right at the T-junction with the B6001 and after 1 m. turn left on to the B6251, following the signpost to Eyam, which is reached after 2 m.

⑤ Eyam to Great Hucklow Leave the village on the minor road signposted to Foolow and Bradwell. Bear left through Foolow and after 1 m. turn right. Follow the lane through the hamlet of Grindlow to the T-junction on the outskirts of Great Hucklow and turn right. After ½ m. turn sharp left, following the signpost for Hathersage. The Derbyshire and Lancashire Gliding Club airfield is a little way down this road.

⑥ Great Hucklow to Castleton Return to the outskirts of Great Hucklow and bear right through the village. After ½ m., at the crossroads, turn right following the signpost to Bradwell Hope, and almost immediately turn right again on to the B6049. After just under 1 m. turn left on to the road signposted to Little Hucklow. Go through the village and at the unmarked T-junction on the far side turn right. Follow this lane across the hills into Castleton.

⑦ Castleton to Winnats Pass In Castleton, turn left on to the A625 signposted to Chapel-en-le-Frith, and after ¾ m. turn left again. Follow this road to Speedwell Cavern and Winnats Pass.

⑧ Winnats Pass to Blue John Caverns At the top of Winnats Pass turn right on to the B6061 and right again on to the A625. Follow this past Mam Tor to the Blue John Caverns.

⑨ Blue John Caverns to Treak Cliff Cavern Follow the A625 round for about ½ m. to Treak Cliff Cavern.

⑩ Treak Cliff Cavern to Hathersage Return along the A625 through Castleton and on for 5½ m., down Hope Valley to Hathersage, of Charlotte Brontë associations.

⑪ Hathersage to Ringinglow Turn left at the far side of the village where the main road swings right. (To visit Hathersage church and the grave of Little John, take the first turning on the left.) Keep right at the first junction and left at the next, crossing the moorland towards Sheffield. Ringinglow is reached soon after the city comes into view.

⑫ Ringinglow to Chesterfield Turn right by the old toll house at Ringinglow. After 1 m. turn left and follow Long Line. Cross the A625 and follow the road into Dore. Here turn right into the High Street and keep straight ahead. After 1½ m. turn right at the T-junction with the A621, by the Fleur de Lys. After 2 m. turn left just before the roundabout on to the B6051; follow the road for 4 m. to Barlow. Keep on the B6051. It is 3 m. to Chesterfield.

INFORMATION

Places of interest *Castleton:* Blue John Caverns, Speedwell Cavern, Treak Cliff Cavern, daily except Christmas Day. Peak Cavern, Good Friday to Sept., daily. Peveril Castle, weekdays, Sun. afternoons. Douglas Museum, afternoons except Fri., Easter to Sept. *Chatsworth House:* Apr. to beginning Oct., Wed., Thur., Fri., 11.30 a.m.-4 p.m.; Sat. and Sun., 1.30-5 p.m.; Good Friday and Bank Hol. Mon. and Tues., 11.30 a.m.-5 p.m.

Events *Barlow:* Well-dressing, Aug. *Baslow:* Festival, July. *Castleton:* Festival of Music, Art and Craftwork, Aug. *Chesterfield:* Music and Drama Festival, June. District Show, Aug. *Eyam:* Well-dressing, Aug.; Plague Commemoration Service, last Sun. in Aug.

Information *Castleton:* National Park Information Centre, Castle Street (Tel. Hope Valley 20679). *Chesterfield:* Public Library, Corporation Street (Tel. Chesterfield 32047/32661).

Towns with easy access to Chesterfield:

Buxton	24 m.	Nottingham	26 m.
Derby	26 m.	Rotherham	17 m.

BLUE JOHN CAVERNS
The Blue John Caverns are the world's only source of the mineral Blue John, a translucent variety of the stone fluorspar banded in red, blue, purple and yellow. It has been highly prized for making ornaments

Polished section of Blue John sto

since the Romans discovered it nearly 2000 years ago. The caverns were rediscovered by accident 3 years ago by local miners following up a seam which the Romans worked. The full sequence of caves and mine workings is 3 miles long, and includes such features as the Crystallised Cavern the Waterfall Cavern, the Variegated Cavern and the Mirror Lake. The biggest cavern is called Lo Mulgrave's dining-room, after a local peer who u the room to entertain a party of miners to dinner The limestone walls and roofs of the caves displa marine fossils as evidence of long-receded oceans

Winnats Pass.

WINNATS PASS
The wild and craggy Winnats Pass used to be a haunt bandits and highwaymen, and it is said that in 1748 tw runaway lovers were murdered here. Below the pass is Speedwell Cavern, an old lead mine which has 3 ft of water in its tunnels, allowing visitors to tour it by boat It is the deepest cave open to the public in Britain, and includes a vast natural cavern known as the Bottomless Pit.

Peveril Castle, Castleton.

CASTLETON
Towering over Castleton are the ruins of Peveril Castle, which was built in the 11th century and later immortalised by Sir Walter Scott in his novel *Peveril of the Peak.* The keep was added in 1176 by Henry II. Beneath the castle is the Peak Cavern, or Devil's Hole, which extends more than 2000 ft into the earth. There are 1 mile long guided tours around the underground maze.

SCALE

0   1   2   3   4   5 M

Variegated Cavern, Blue John Caverns.

Millstones at Hathersage.

The toll house, Ringinglow.

TREAK CLIFF CAVERN
Some of these caves at the foot of Treak Cliff were not discovered until 1926. They have been floodlit to create fairytale grottoes, including Aladdin's Cave and Fairyland.

HATHERSAGE
Hathersage was the home of Robin Hood's huge lieutenant, Little John. The head and foot stones of his grave in the churchyard are 7 ft apart. The village is also rich in associations with Charlotte Brontë, who immortalised it as 'Morton' in *Jane Eyre*. The old house of Moorseats, a mile north-east of the village, was the 'Moor House' of the novel. Just outside the village, at Millstone Edge, millstones were quarried until the end of the last century. The ground is still littered with unwanted millstones. To the east of Hathersage is the Iron Age hill-fort of Carl Wark and the 1500 ft high Neb, which is well known to rock climbers.

RINGINGLOW
The octagonal house on the right by the crossroads was built in 1795 as a toll house, where people paid dues to travel on the Hathersage to Eccleshall turnpike road. It is now a private house.

100
Chesterfield
(67 MILES)

Church of the Crooked Spire, Chesterfield.

CHESTERFIELD
Now a neat industrial town, Chesterfield owes much of its prosperity to George Stephenson, the railway pioneer, who lived near by and promoted local industry until his death in 1848. But it is the 13th-century church of the Crooked Spire that never fails to catch the eye of visitors. Its curious shape is probably due to the inexpertise of early builders who were trying to erect a wooden spiral sheathed in lead.

CURBAR GAP
A break in the ramparts of gritstone which overlook the Derwent Valley, the Curbar Gap affords views over distant hills as far as Matlock and Buxton.

AT HUCKLOW
...bers of the Derbyshire ...Lancashire Gliding Club ...ch their gliders from ...phill Farm. Writer L. du ...de Peach founded the village ...trical company.

The Riley graves, Eyam.

EYAM
...hen the plague reached Eyam in 1665 the villagers, led by the rector ...illiam Mompesson, decided to stay rather than flee and risk spreading ...e infection. Eventually five out of every six died, leaving many grim ...minders of their suffering. Among these are the Riley graves, where ...l six members of one family are buried; Plague Cottage, home of the ...rst victim; and Mompesson's Well at the edge of the village. Here ...llagers came to collect food brought from outside, leaving in payment ...oins which they first washed in the spring water.

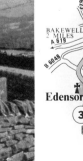

EDENSOR
Because it obstructed the view from Chatsworth, home of the Dukes of Devonshire, the old village of Edensor was demolished and a new village built in 1839. Standing at the north-west entrance to Chatsworth, the houses are of strikingly different designs. (See also p. 272.)

OLD BRAMPTON
The partly Norman church at Old Brampton contains a curious monument to Matilda le Claus, who died in 1224. She is portrayed in stone, holding her heart in her hands. Outside there are 14th-century figures of Saints Peter and Paul in the south wall. Behind the church, a footpath leads across a field to the woods surrounding Linacre reservoir, 500 yds away.

271

A conducted tour of the Derbyshire seat of the Duke of Devonshire

CHATSWORTH

Chatsworth, aptly called 'The Palace of the Peak', is one of the greatest of the stately homes of England. Seat of the Dukes of Devonshire and their ancestors for more than 400 years, its history begins in 1549, when Elizabeth Cavendish—'Bess of Hardwick'—persuaded her fourth husband, the Earl of Shrewsbury, to build the original mansion. This was pulled down and replaced by the present building by the 4th Earl, later the 1st Duke, who inherited the estate in 1684. In this article the 11th Duke describes his home and some of its treasures for the visitors whom he never tires of showing round the magnificent house that is his pride.

The first thing that springs to mind when I think of Chatsworth is surprise that I am living here at all. I came here as a child, always at Christmas, when my grandfather was alive and, being a younger son, I never expected that Chatsworth would one day become my home. But my brother William was killed in Belgium in 1944. When my grandfather died in 1938, my father moved in until war broke out, and the house became a girls' school until about a year after the war. My parents were planning to return to Chatsworth when my father died in 1950. My wife and I were then faced with the problems of raising the money for death duties, and any idea of living in Chatsworth was quite out of the question for several years. The fact that we moved back here in 1959 is entirely thanks to my wife. In the end I listened to her advice rather than that of my financial advisers.

My Christmases here as a child were always times of great excitement. My father had one brother and five sisters, and all the sisters had quite large families. By the mid-thirties there were about 20 grandchildren here all at the same time. When I got a bit older and was allowed to come down to dinner, we always met in the library, where my grandfather had his own wing chair by the fireplace. We all used to gather in the centre of the room and walk through the ante-library into the big dining-room, where 30 or 40 people sat down to dinner. There would be about 100 people, all told, sleeping in the house.

The weather book

When I returned, I discovered that one rather nice tradition had been kept up during the 21 years the house was not lived in by the family. When my grandfather came down for breakfast in the dining-room (the one open to the public now) the first thing he used to do was to consult a book on a side table and tell us how much frost or rain there had been during the night. When we moved back I told Dennis Fisher, who runs the house, that I remembered my grandfather's weather book and would very much like to start it again. He said there was no need: it had been kept up all the time.

What fascinates me about the inside of the house is the astonishing variety of objects in it. In the Chapel Passage, for example, I remember as a child being fascinated by the Turkish barge, or caique, and the huge carved foot next to it. Both these were collected by the 6th Duke and show his catholic taste. He collected every kind of thing, from fine illustrated books to curiosities. He bought the wood panelling in the Oak Room one day when he happened to go into an auction room. In his own words: 'They were knocking down a wealth of old oak; I bought it all.' The

two Egyptian *stelae* (commemorative tablets) in the west sub-corridor, which again the 6th Duke bought, are very interesting and very early. Two experts came over from America to see them a few years ago, but they were too well screwed into the wall to be removed.

We also owe a lot of the statuary here to the 6th Duke. The Statue Gallery is where the Christmas tree was put, and whenever I go into the room I am reminded of it. I think Canova's statue of Napoleon's mother has great human interest: she had it done to give to Napoleon, and hoped he would put it in the throne room of the Tuileries. But he seemed to like it as little as Churchill liked the Graham Sutherland portrait of himself. The statue vanished to some basement, to be bought later by the 6th Duke. It is a very fine example of Canova's work and, in the present fashion for neo-classicism, it is very much admired. It shows how fashions change.

Changing fashion

During my youth, and until quite recently, neo-classicism was not considered the thing at all. Nowadays everyone thinks it is simply marvellous.

The same thing also applies to the whole of the North wing. I was brought up to think what a tragedy it was that this 19th-century wing had been added on to the marvellous Classical square block of the house, and there was a time when my father was toying with the idea of having it pulled down. Now it is the height of fashion, and if one suggested pulling it down there would be a terrible outcry.

The Library is a marvellous room. It was very much changed by the 6th Duke, who put in the brass gallery and made it into a delightful room. Prior to that it had marble columns along the inside wall, which made it rather austere.

The ante-library contains a copy of Audubon's *Birds of America*, the greatest of all illustrated books. I am very fond of it because illustrated books are a great interest of mine.

The Sabine Room, which has been described as one of the great baroque interiors of Europe, is extraordinary. It is the only part of the house—apart from the ceiling of the West stairs—painted by Sir James Thornhill, who did all the work at Blenheim. I slept alone in this room on a camp bed under the great white horse when I was six.

The carvings at Chatsworth are of great interest: they are by Samuel Watson, who came from Eyam, about 6 miles away, and they are of immensely high standard, particularly in the State Dining Room. Sachevarell Sitwell, the art critic, made the point that the Chatsworth carvings show the craftsmanship in

RIVER VIEW *This is the grandest view of Chatsworth—the face it presents to the west, across the River Derwent. The bridge in the foreground was designed by James Paine and completed in 1762. It replaced a pack-horse track over the moors.*

THE FIRST CHATSWORTH *The west front of the original Chatsworth House as depicted in a tapestry attributed to Bess of Hardwick. The building was begun by her and her husband, Sir William Cavendish, in 1552. It was their second son who became the 1st Earl of Devonshire in 1618. The house remained intact until 1686, when the 4th Earl—later the 1st Duke—began to pull it down and rebuild it. The house finally assumed its present form about 20 years later.*

THE SOUTH FRONT *In the foreground is the Emperor Fountain seen across the canal pond. The fountain was installed by the 6th Duke in 1843 to impress his friend Tsar Nicholas I of Russia—who, as it turned out, never saw it. The fountain throws its jet 290 ft up, making it the highest in Britain: the pressure comes from a specially built hillside lake which has a circumference of almost three-quarters of a mile.*

PAXTON'S PRIDE *Part of what Joseph Paxton called the Conservative Wall, a range of glass cases which he built in 1848 to grow camellias. Paxton, later knighted for his work in designing the Crystal Palace, was only 23 when the 6th Duke brought him from the Horticultural Society Gardens at Chiswick, in 1826, to be his head gardener at Chatsworth.*

A conducted tour of the Derbyshire seat of the Duke of Devonshire

CHATSWORTH

England at the end of the 18th century, when a local craftsman could be found to do work of that quality. We have got a marvellous piece by Grinling Gibbons, the lace cravat and dead bird, but that is the only piece by him.

The State rooms were never really lived in except for the State Bedroom, which was my parents' bedroom before my grandfather died. There is no water on that side of the house, so it is difficult for the rooms to be lived in. The State Music Room has the violin painting on the door which is the trademark of Chatsworth. If you ask visitors about their first reaction to Chatsworth, the vast majority will mention this painting by Van der Vaart which is so vivid that a real violin appears to hang on the door. I remember being fascinated by it as a child.

My family did very well by William and Mary. The 4th Earl of Devonshire backed them and he was made Duke as a reward. He then wanted to have a portrait painted but, like other members of his family, he was rather careful of his money; so what he did was to buy an equestrian portrait of a French field-marshal, have the face painted out and his own put in. Below this portrait on the Oak Stairs is a painting of Newmarket, to which the 1st Duke, like myself, was no stranger.

There has been a curious tradition of collecting minerals in my family. Georgiana, the famous 18th-century Duchess, was a collector, as well as a great beauty and a tremendous gambler. Her son, the 6th Duke, also collected minerals, and I have added to the collection in the Orangery. The Blue John is from the Castleton mines 12 miles away—the only place in the world Blue John comes from—and we have some very fine examples of it. There are two lovely urns standing on a showcase at the northern end of the big dining-room, to the right of the doors.

In the showcase itself there are some pieces of Berlin china, part of a 240-piece set which I bought from my father-in-law, Lord Redesdale, for very little money. Today I have a rather uncomfortable feeling that I 'did' him.

No Man's Land

There are problems in adding to the collections: it is difficult to find things that will fit in with the grandeur of the house. My wife has done a great deal. She brought back the carved marble figures in the dining-room. They had been taken out by my grandmother, who did not like the 6th Duke's taste at all. The Mary, Queen of Scots Rooms are entirely my wife's creation. When we first came here there was our part of the house and there was the part open to the public. The third area of about 15 rooms was a kind of No Man's Land. It is not good for rooms to be neglected. So my wife did them up, most of them as bedrooms in the late Regency style, as they would be if we lived in them. It was a very good way of showing things of beauty—such as the shell flowers in the Wellington Bedroom, which we bought from Sir Osbert Sitwell, a member of the famous literary family.

The gardens have always been of tremendous interest to me, and we have made some major alterations. The twin rows of pleached limes enclosing the statues on the South Lawn were the inspiration of my wife. She was also responsible for the box garden on the west front, and the serpentine beech hedge leading

THE SABINE ROOM *The chandelier here was restored by estate workmen when the house was reoccupied by the Devonshire family after the Second World War. The room is an outstanding example of baroque painting by Sir James Thornhill, who began it in 1706.*

CEILING BY VERRIO *According to a Chatsworth legend, the figure of the Fury Atropos cutting the thread of life with her 'abhorred shears' represents the housekeeper in Verrio's time, a Mrs Hacket, whom he disliked. This ceiling is in the State Dining Room.*

WELLINGTON BEDROOM *Chinese wallpaper in one of the 'No Man's Land' rooms which were decorated by the Duchess in the 1960s to reproduce the late-Regency style and to give them a 'lived in' appearance. Under the glass dome is a collection of shell flowers bought by the Duke from Sir Osbert Sitwell.*

STATE DINING ROOM *One of the richly carved gilt side tables that were designed by William Kent, around 1735, for the 4th Duke's father-in-law, Lord Burlington.*

NAPOLEON'S MOTHER *Canova's work in the Statue Gallery. This is the room which, the Duke says, reminds him of the Christmas tree and the big family gatherings in his childhood.*

'S GIFT *The silver chandelier in the State Dressing Room made by Dutch craftsmen in 1694. It was given by iam III to his friend the 1st Duke, who helped in the essful plot to make him King of England. A portrait of 1st Duke can be seen in the State Dining Room.*

AMAZON LILY *This specimen was grown from seeds from the Edinburgh Botanical Gardens. The original plant was discovered and brought to Britain by a 19th-century expedition sponsored by the 6th Duke, who built a special lily house for it.*

LIBRARY *One of the views which the Duke recommends isitors—looking through the Library towards the family's ate dining-room. The Library was remodelled by the 6th ke and his architect, Wyatville, in 1815.*

WHEN TO VISIT CHATSWORTH

Chatsworth is near the Derbyshire village of Edensor on the B6012. It is visited on Hand-Picked Tour No. 100, from Chesterfield.

The house is open from the first Sun. before Easter or the first Sun. in Apr. (whichever is earlier) until first Sun. in Oct. Hours: Wed., Thur., Fri. 11.30 a.m.–4 p.m.; Sat. and Sun. and Mon. and Tues. at Bank Hols. 2–5 p.m. The gardens are open every day.

up to the bust of the 6th Duke. It was all overgrown until she saw a photograph of a curly wall in a kitchen garden in Yorkshire, and it gave her the idea of copying it.

Gardening is one of my great hobbies; but the only active thing I do is bulb planting. I like spring bulbs—narcissi, crocuses and tulips. There is a lot of scope here, and I try to plant about 5000 a year. I have planted some 16,000 bulbs under the large willow in the courtyard at the north-west (public) entrance. We have built a new greenhouse, and that is a great source of joy. It is in three parts—cool, temperate and stove, so that we can grow things that need different temperatures. The public are not allowed in because the paths are narrow and there is not enough room, but any gardener who is really interested has only to write to me or the head gardener and he will be shown round. We put labels on the plants so that the visitor looking in can read them from the outside.

The water view

Walking in the gardens is what I enjoy best. We have a lovely walk which curves round the garden, twists and turns through the rhododendrons, the azalea dell, the pinetum and the arboretum. If you start at the west front door and walk right round it, ending up by the stables, it is 2 miles round. Every quarter-mile was marked by the 6th Duke with a carved stone and, if you like walking, as I do, you can walk as many miles as you want and know exactly how far you have been. If you do not mind a bit of a walk up to the hunting tower and then along, there is a really lovely view of the whole house and the park. Somewhat nearer, if you walk to the end of the canal and look back, the view is marvellous—as though the house were floating on the water. This was no accident: the canal pond was laid out with very great skill by the 4th Duke.

The Emperor Fountain was a very clever idea of the 6th Duke. He was a great friend of the Russian Tsar Nicholas I, and went to his coronation. He invited the Tsar back here, and he agreed. The Duke was hard put to it because obviously anything he could do the Tsar could do better. In the end the Tsar never came. But the fountain still throws its water higher than any other in this country, and is one of the highest in the world.

My pride and joy

Our gimmick at Chatsworth is to have no gimmicks—no frills or showmanship. This has one very good effect. People treat the house, and the gardens especially, with great respect. There is incredibly little litter, even on Bank Holidays when up to 10,000 people walk about the gardens. There has always been a tradition that people can walk in the park anywhere they like. At the southern end there is a free car park, which is used even in the winter. It is a source of great satisfaction to me that people love to come and walk in the park.

People do not always believe me when I say that I never tire of showing them round Chatsworth. But it is true. It is my pride and joy. It really is . . . because I am still surprised, even after all these years, that I am actually living here.

Grand estates hidden in Robin Hood's forest

From Southwell, the plain rolls eastwards into Sherwood Forest and Robin Hood country. Here are The Dukeries. This name was given to a group of neighbouring estates and mansions because they were all owned by dukes—the Dukes of Portland, Kingston and Newcastle. Grandest of the surviving houses is Thoresby Hall, set in a deer park. A different way of life can be seen in Laxton—the only village in England where the land is still farmed on the Saxon open-field system.

(1) Southwell to Newark-on-Trent Leave Southwell on the A612 signposted to Newark, and after about 3½ m. turn right on to the A617. Stay on this road to Newark.

(2) Newark-on-Trent to Laxton Leave Newark on the A6065 signposted to Doncaster. Keep on this road as far as the village of South Muskham and turn left on to the A616 signposted to Doncaster. Just over 6 m. beyond South Muskham, shortly after passing a small wood on the left, turn right at a hilltop crossroads, following the signpost to Laxton. Continue on this road, straight over another set of crossroads, to Laxton.

(3) Laxton to Clumber Park Turn left in the village on to the road signposted to Boughton, and after about 2½ m., at the junction with the A6075, turn right. Just by the church in Kirton village, turn left on to a minor road. At the T-junction turn left, following the signpost to Walesby, and at the next T-junction turn left and go through Walesby. Beyond the village, at the junction with the B6387, turn right. Stay on this road through Haughton and over two rivers, the Maun and the Meden. After crossing the Meden turn left into Bothamsall. About ½ m. beyond the village turn right on to the road signposted to Clumber. There are oil workings on both sides of the road. At the junction with the A614 turn right, and after about 300 yds turn left into Clumber Park. The road goes through woodland and bears right over Clumber Bridge.

(4) Clumber Park to Worksop To leave the park, keep straight on after the bridge and go over the crossroads. Turn left at the T-junction, through one of the park's five gateways, to the junction with the B6005. Turn right at the signpost to Worksop.

(5) Worksop to Cresswell Crags Leave Worksop on the A60 signposted to Mansfield Woodhouse. After 3½ m. turn right on to the B6042 signposted to Cresswell.

(6) Cresswell Crags to Thoresby Hall Return to the A60 and turn right. Follow this road to Cuckney. At the crossroads turn left on to the A616 signposted to Ollerton. After 3 m., on the left just before a crossroads, there is a picnic area known as Fanny's Grove. Turn left at the crossroads, and after about 2 m. Thoresby Hall is on the right.

(7) Thoresby Hall to Rufford Park Return to the A616 and turn left. After 1½ m. turn right on to the B6034 signposted to Edwinstowe. About ½ m. later, paths to the right of the road lead to the Major Oak in Sherwood Forest. Continue into Edwinstowe, whose church of St Mary is by tradition the place where Robin Hood and Maid Marian were married. Continue over the crossroads and 2 m. beyond the village, at the T-junction with the A614, turn right, following the Nottingham signpost. Rufford Park is on the left.

(8) Rufford Park to Newstead Abbey Continue along the A614 towards Nottingham for about 4 m. At the roundabout turn right on to the A617 signposted to Mansfield. Go through Rainworth, bearing right at the T-junction, and at the far side of the town turn left on to the road signposted to Blidworth. After just over 1 m. turn right, then right again at the T-junction. At the junction with the A60 turn left, go over the traffic lights, and Newstead Abbey is on the right at the next crossroads.

(9) Newstead Abbey to Papplewick Pumping Station Return to the A60, turn right towards Nottingham, and after about 2 m. turn left on to the road signposted Calverton. Bear left when this road veers to the right. The chimney of the pumping station should now be visible ahead. Follow the road as it bears left through a pine forest. The entrance to the pumphouse is on the left.

(10) Papplewick Pumping Station to Southwell Continue along the forest road and turn right at the crossroads. At the crossroads with the A614, keep straight ahead on the road signposted to Oxton. Turn right at the T-junction and take the next turning on the left. Leave the woodland by turning left at the roundabout on to the B6386, which leads back to Southwell.

INFORMATION

Places of interest *Clumber Park:* Apr. to Sept., weekdays 2-7 p.m., weekends and Bank Hol. 12 noon-7 p.m.; winter, daily 1-4 p.m. *Kelham:* Kelham Hall, Mon. to Fri. during office hours. *Newark-on-Trent:* Castle, all year on application to Curator of Newark Museum and Art Gallery. Museum and Art Gallery, weekdays 10 a.m.-1 p.m., 2-5 p.m., also Sun. afternoons, Apr. to Sept. *Newstead Abbey:* Good Friday to Sept., daily 2-6 p.m. Garden, daily. *Papplewick Pumping Station:* Sun. afternoons, Apr. to mid-Oct. when engines are not in steam. *Thoresby Hall:* Good Friday to Sept., Wed., Thurs., Sat., Sun., and Tues. after Bank Hols., 2.30-6 p.m., Bank Hol. Sun. and Mon., 12.30-6 p.m. *Queen's Sconce:* Daily.

Nature Trail *Major Oak, Sherwood Country Park:* May to Sept. Starts north of Edwinstowe on the B6034. Guides available in country park car parks.

Information *Newark-on-Trent:* The Palace, Appletongate (Tel. Newark-on-Trent 71156).

Towns with easy access to Southwell:

Grantham	12 m.	Nottingham	12 m.
Lincoln	20 m.	Sheffield	36 m.

Robin Hood mantelpiece, Thoresby Hall.

THORESBY HALL
England's biggest Victorian house, and the youngest o the 'stately homes', this is the claim made for Thoresb Hall, which was completed only in 1871. An intricatel carved mantelpiece in the library—the product of thre years' work—depicts Robin Hood and Little John bes the hollow Major Oak in Sherwood Forest. The magnificently proportioned Great Hall, 64 ft long, rise 50 ft to an open hammerbeam roof. The panelling is o white and red Sherwood Forest oak. Outside, there is wooded deer park, and a 65 acre lake, formed by damming the River Meden, is the home of a growing number of Canada geese. The first pairs of these hand birds were introduced by the naturalist Sir Peter Scott

The Major Oak, Sherwood Forest.

NEWSTEAD ABBEY
Remorse for the murder of Thomas Becket is thought to have inspired Henry II to build Newstead Abbey in 1170 as an Augustinian priory. Only the west front of the church survives, but it is an almost perfect fragment, even to the undamaged figures of the Madonna and Child in the central gable. The large adjoining mansion, adapted from the monastic buildings after the Dissolution, became the home of the Byron family in 1540. Lord *Portrait of Byron, Newstea* Byron, the poet, lived there from 1808 to 1814; but in seven years before he died in Greece, he was forced to sell the place to pay his debts. The abbey, now owned Nottingham Corporation, contains many reminders of Byron family, including one that visitors are unlikely t see—the ghost that is said to have warned the poet of his impending death. There are 9 acres of gardens.

SCALE

0   1   2   3   4   5 MILES

WORKSOP

Because of its situation at the foot of wooded hills, which once formed great ducal estates, Worksop has been called 'the gateway to The Dukeries'. The priory church, founded in 1103, displays on the south door some iron scroll work reputed to be the oldest in England. It dates from the 12th and 13th centuries. Original beams of Sherwood Forest oak are in the gatehouse.

Clumber Bridge, Clumber Park.

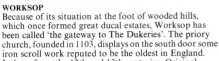

CLUMBER PARK

This Midlands playground, a 3800 acre landscaped estate sold by the Duke of Newcastle to the National Trust in 1946, has around 1 million visitors a year. Lime Tree Avenue, 2 miles long, contains about 3000 trees—a double row on each side. There are walks winding among ornamental trees and shrubs by the lakeside, woodland paths with many picnic glades, a great variety of wild plants, fine lawns, and a huge, spired Victorian church. This was built as a private chapel to Clumber House, which was pulled down in 1937, leaving only a small portion now used as a restaurant. Herons feed on the fish in the lake, which is a wintering ground for many waterfowl, including the great crested grebe.

Comfrey

Great crested grebe

CRESSWELL CRAGS

Relics of prehistoric man—some of which are now in the British Museum—have been found in the limestone caves of this ravine. They include flint and bone instruments, and fragments of decorated bone, 10,000 years old, which are among the best specimens of Stone Age art to have been found in England.

LAXTON

This village's open-field system of agriculture has survived for more than 1000 years, and is claimed to be unique in Britain today. Three fields of more than 250 acres—West Field, Mill Field and South Field—are each divided into strips averaging about 3 acres, and distributed among various tenants. In yearly rotation, one field is sown with wheat, one carries other crops and the other lies fallow. An annual Court Leet appoints a jury which checks boundaries and sees that ditches are cleared. The farmhouses in the two village streets also present an ancient pattern: they are built on narrow strips end-on to the road. The church contains the only wooden medieval effigy in Nottinghamshire, the subject being the wife of a 14th-century lord of the manor.

RUFFORD PARK

Only a vaulted crypt with round pillars remains of the medieval Rufford Abbey. The grounds and the lake became a country park in 1970, and are being developed as a recreation area. There is fishing in the lake.

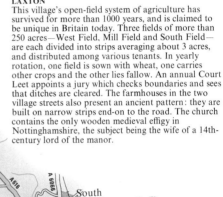

Newark Castle.

NEWARK-ON-TRENT

A stretch of the River Trent, which has been turned into a canal, carries barge traffic below the ruined walls of the 12th-century castle. The castle withstood three sieges in the Civil War between 1642 and 1646, but after the king's surrender the undefeated Royalist townsfolk were ordered to destroy the castle themselves. Most of the river wall and the gatehouse, however, still survive. The town's market-place, one of Britain's largest cobblestoned squares, has a post to which bears were tethered for the 'sport' of bear-baiting. There are some good timber-framed houses. From the balcony of the Clinton Arms Hotel, Gladstone made his first election speech. The church of St Mary Magdalen is 222 ft long and has a 252 ft spire.

PAPPLEWICK PUMPING STATION

Plans were being made in 1975 to enable the public to visit Papplewick Pumping Station, interesting because it combines engineering skill with Victorian architecture. The station, standing alone in wooded countryside, was built in 1884 to supply Nottingham, 7 miles away, with water from a 220 ft deep well. The columns which support the beams in the engine-house are ornamented with pictures of fishes, reeds, water flowers, bulrushes and other water motifs. The steam engines, which used to pump 1½ million gallons every 24 hours, are maintained in perfect condition. They are believed to be the last beam engines built by James Watt and Co.

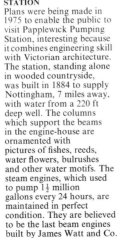

Decorated pillars, Papplewick Pumping Station.

Carving on Southwell minster.

SOUTHWELL

If Southwell were not overshadowed by its minster, the town might be better known for the red soil in the fields around. The Norman minster, raised to cathedral status in 1884, is famous for its 13th-century stone carvings. The Saracen's Head Inn, where Charles I stayed, has 500-year-old wooden doors to its courtyard.

Lions and a liner trip among the foxes' lairs

From the 'pork pie' town of Melton Mowbray, this tour runs through the heart of England's fox-hunting country. It is a rolling landscape of neatly hedged fields marked here and there by patches of woodland which are preserved as homes for the foxes. But there are more than foxes here. The tour takes in a water sports centre by the River Trent; a park where lions and rare birds breed; gardens where new varieties of roses may be seen growing; a lake on which passengers sail in model ocean-going liners; and a military museum with souvenirs of the epic charge of the Lancers at Omdurman in 1898 in which the young Winston Churchill took part.

(1) Melton Mowbray to Bunny Follow the signposts for the A6006 past the market-place in Melton Mowbray. Turn right at the traffic-lights and left at the roundabout. Follow the A6006 through Asfordby, go under the A46 flyover and turn immediately right to join the A46 towards Nottingham. Take the next turn-off to the left, and at the T-junction go right towards Willoughby-on-the-Wolds. After 1 m., at the crossroads beyond the village, turn right, following the signpost for Wysall. Turn left at the T-junction and into Wysall, where the wooden belfry ladder of the ancient church is believed to be almost as old as the 13th-century tower itself. At the T-junction in Wysall turn right, following the signpost to Keyworth, but on the outskirts of the village, turn left for Bunny. After 1¼ m. turn left at the bottom of Windmill Hill, and, on joining the A60, turn right into Bunny.

(2) Bunny to Edwalton Continue on the A60 towards Nottingham, but after 1 m., on the outskirts of Bradmore, turn right on to the road signposted to Plumtree. Turn left at the crossroads in Plumtree and left again on to the A606. At the roundabout, turn right, still on the A606, following the West Bridgford signpost. Turn immediately left to visit the rose nurseries at Edwalton.

(3) Edwalton to Cotgrave Return to the A606 and turn right. After just under ½ m., past the right-hand turn-off for Plumtree, turn left on to the road signposted to Cotgrave. Soon afterwards fork left, still following the signposts for Cotgrave.

(4) Cotgrave to Holme Pierrepont Just past the church in Cotgrave, turn left on to the road signposted to Nottingham. After 1½ m. turn left at the T-junction and left again on to the A52, following the Nottingham signpost, but 2 m. later turn right and follow the signposts to the National Water Sports Centre at Holme Pierrepont.

(5) Holme Pierrepont to Bingham Return from the National Water Sports Centre to the A52, turn left and follow the road through Radcliffe on Trent to Bingham.

(6) Bingham to Langar Leave the market-place on the A52. Turn right at the traffic-lights and then left, following the signpost to Langar. After 3 m. the 17th-century Wiverton Hall is on the left. In Langar, turn right at the crossroads to visit the church.

(7) Langar to Belvoir Return to the crossroads, turn right and continue for 3 m. to Harby. In the village fork left and ½ m. later turn left on to the road signposted to Plungar. After about 1 m. turn left again on to the road signposted to Plungar and Barkestone le-Vale. After about ¾ m. the road bears right just before the Grantham Canal. Go through Plungar and Barkestone le-Vale, following the signpost to Redmile. Cross the canal and at the T-junction, turn right and go through Redmile. Go over the crossroad to Belvoir.

(8) Belvoir to Stapleford Turn right at the T-junction in front of the castle grounds, on the road signposted to Knipton. Turn left at the next T-junction and go through Knipton. Just past the war memorial turn right, following the signpost to Croxton Kerrial. Carry on past the church and at the next T-junction turn left on to the A607. Almost immediately, at the crossroads, turn right on to the road signposted to Saltby. Go through Saltby and Sproxton, and on the outskirts of Sproxton bear right on to the road signposted to Coston. In Coston turn right on to the B676, following the signpost to Melton Mowbray, and stay on this road through Garthorpe and Saxby. Here is a landscape of narrow roads and low hedges round large, undulating fields interspersed with little woods—the 'coverts' of fox-hunting country. About ¾ m. beyond Saxby turn left, following the signpost for Stapleford. Stapleford Park is on the left, after ¾ m.

(9) Stapleford to Burton Lazars Continue along the same road. After about ¾ m. turn right on to the road signposted to Burton Lazars. The road is straight for just over 2 m. before veering left into the village.

(10) Burton Lazars to Melton Mowbray At the T-junction with the A606 in the village, turn right to follow the signpost back to Melton Mowbray.

INFORMATION

Places of interest *Belvoir Castle:* Apr. to Sept., Wed., Thur., Fri., Bank Hol. Tues., 12-6 p.m.; Bank Hol. Mon., 11 a.m.-7 p.m., Sun., 2-7 p.m. Oct., Sun., 2-6 p.m. *Edwalton:* Rose Garden, daily. *Holme Pierrepont Hall:* Apr. to Sept., Sun., 2-6 p.m., also Bank Hol. Mon. afternoons. *Stapleford Park:* Easter Sun. and Mon., May to Sept., Wed., Thur., Sun., Spring and Late Summer Bank Hol. Mon. and Tues., 2.30-6.30 p.m. Lion Reserve, end Mar. to Sept., daily (except Good Friday).

Information Tourist Information Centre, 12 Bishop Street, Leicester (Tel. Leicester 20644). East Midlands Tourist Board, Bailgate, Lincoln (Tel. Lincoln 31521).

Towns with easy access to Melton Mowbray:
Grantham . . . . . 16 m. Nottingham . . . . 19 m.
Leicester . . . . 15 m. Stamford . . . . . . 21 m.

HOLME PIERREPONT
A country park and the National Water Sports Centre, opened in 1973, have been created here on derelict land. There are walks between grassy hillocks, woodland plantations, picnic sites and coarse-fishing areas, and points from which to watch rowing, canoeing, sailing, water-skiing and powerboat racing on a specially prepared course. Just beyond is Holme Pierrepont Hall, brick-built around 1500, with a 19th-century walled garden.

COTGRAVE
In the 1960s, with the opening of a new pit, pretty little Cotgrave had a colliery village tacked on to it. But it somehow keeps its rural charm—with a village green and the tall, thin 15th-century spire of All Saints' rising above limes and elms. To the south and east, the wooded slopes of the Wolds provide excellent country for short walks.

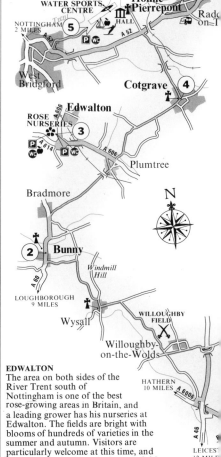

EDWALTON
The area on both sides of the River Trent south of Nottingham is one of the best rose-growing areas in Britain, and a leading grower has his nurseries at Edwalton. The fields are bright with blooms of hundreds of varieties in the summer and autumn. Visitors are particularly welcome at this time, and can stroll freely through the rose fields. There are car parks, and a picnic area has been laid out. Apart from the roses, there is a garden centre, with displays of container-grown shrubs, trees and herbaceous plants.

Rose fields, Edwalton.

SCALE
0   1   2   3   4   5 MILE

BELVOIR CASTLE
In mock-medieval grandeur, this seat of the Dukes of Rutland rises above the countryside from its site on a wooded hill. The 11th-century Norman fortress was in ruins when a series of rebuildings was begun in the 16th century. The present castle dates from 1801. Its enormous rooms house many art treasures, including paintings by Holbein and Gainsborough. Silver tableware, snuffboxes and miniatures are among the many exhibits, and there is a military museum tracing the history and traditions of the 17th/21st Lancers. Much of the castle's 19th-century 'downstairs' servants' quarters are open to view, including the vast kitchen. In one period of 18 weeks, from December 1839, Belvoir inhabitants and visitors consumed 70 hogsheads of ale (about 28,000 pints).

Entrance hall, Belvoir Castle.

NGHAM
though this little town no longer holds the markets for ich it was granted a charter by Edward II in the 14th tury, its large paved market-place still spreads around steeple-roofed butter cross, once the focal point for ying and selling dairy produce. Modern street works, signed to preserve the charm of Bingham's centre, n a Civic Trust Award in the 1960s. There are windows the spire of the parish church, which rises from an battled tower, above the surrounding trees. On the st side of the tower the battlements have, instead of nacles, two figures of bishops. There is some good rly-19th-century stained glass in the church and onument of around 1310, believed to mmemorate Sir Richard de Bingham.

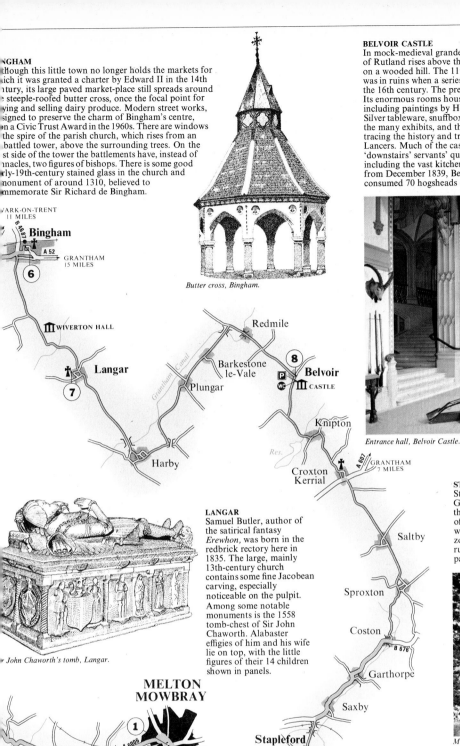

Butter cross, Bingham.

LANGAR
Samuel Butler, author of the satirical fantasy *Erewhon,* was born in the redbrick rectory here in 1835. The large, mainly 13th-century church contains some fine Jacobean carving, especially noticeable on the pulpit. Among some notable monuments is the 1558 tomb-chest of Sir John Chaworth. Alabaster effigies of him and his wife lie on top, with the little figures of their 14 children shown in panels.

John Chaworth's tomb, Langar.

STAPLEFORD
Stapleford Park, the home of Lord and Lady Gretton, has many attractions. These include the mansion itself, with tapestries and a collection of Staffordshire pottery figures; a 50 acre reserve with three prides, or families, of lions; a miniature zoo; and a 10¼ in. gauge model railway which runs 'boat trains' to the lake, where there are passenger-carrying models of ocean-going liners.

Miniature liner, Stapleford Park.

BURTON LAZARS
Only earthworks, outlining a moat and some fishponds, remain of the lazar (leper) hospital which gave the village its name. From about 1145 to its dissolution in 1544 the hospital, which lay about 450 yds west of the church, was the largest of its kind in England. The church, founded at the same time as the hospital, has Norman arcading. The 15th-century wooden roof is supported by carvings of ten minstrels. In the churchyard is the ostentatious 20 ft high tomb of William Squires, a local weaver. He left money for it in his will when he died in 1722. The carved figures represent Life, Death, Time, Faith, Hope and Charity.

UNNY
life-size carving of eicestershire's famous Vrestling Baronet', Sir homas Parkyns 663–1741), adorns the 4th-century village urch. He was the builder Bunny Hall, with its assive castellated wer; the big school with ullioned windows, near e church; and other village uildings. Parkyns, a wyer, wrote a Latin ammar and as a hobby ollected stone coffins. ut wrestling was his reatest interest.

MELTON MOWBRAY
The old town—it was granted the right to hold a market in 1077—is internationally known for its fox hunts, cheese and pies. Every hotel here prints and table-mats to remind visitors that it is the centre of a hunting district where the Quorn, the Cottesmore and the Belvoir hunts meet. The other specialities can be seen in many food shops—Stilton cheeses and pork pies, made in factories in the town. There are many good 18th-century and early-19th-century houses in Melton, and the stately medieval parish church was considered as a possible cathedral in the 1920s.

Stilton cheese in a Melton Mowbray factory.

Simple villages and a majestic cathedral

The huge but delicately fashioned cathedral presides over the countryside around Lincoln. Northwards a limestone ridge runs to the Humber. To the east the land slides down into flat, rich farmland, then climbs to the Wolds before falling again to the coastal plain. Along the way, the villages present their contrasts: from the modern RAF V-bomber base at Scampton, where the Dam Busters took off to earn their place in history, to Thornton Abbey, ruined remains of one of England's finest religious houses.

1 **Lincoln to Scampton** Leave Lincoln on the B1398 to Burton. Go through Burton and continue for 2½ m., with views to the left over the Trent Valley, into the village of Scampton, which gave its name to the famous RAF station.

2 **Scampton to Brigg** Continue on the B1398 out of Scampton. After 5 m. Fillingham Castle is seen on the right. Cross the A631 at Harpswell and continue past the wartime Spitfire base, on the right, and into Kirton in Lindsey. At the crossroads by the Queen's Head, turn right and drive to the junction with the A15. Turn left in front of the gatehouse to Redbourne Hall. In Redbourne, the building surmounted by a white horse, just past the church, contains the remains of a smithy with stocks outside. Turn right at the junction with the A18, following the signpost into Brigg.

3 **Brigg to Wrawby Mill** Take the A15 out of the town, following the road signposted to Grimsby. Fork right along the A18 through Wrawby. The windmill is on the right, about ¼ m. past the church.

4 **Wrawby Mill to Elsham Hall** Return through Wrawby to the junction with the A15 and turn right, following the Grimsby signpost. After 2½ m. the entrance to Elsham Hall is on the right.

5 **Elsham Hall to Thornton Abbey** Continue towards Grimsby on the A15 past two minor crossroads, and after 2 m. turn right on to the minor road signposted to Burnham. Go through Burnham to Thornton Curtis. At the junction with the A1077 in the village turn right, then almost immediately left on the minor road signposted to Thornton Abbey. Follow the road left at Thornton Abbey station, then turn right over the level-crossing and straight ahead to Thornton Abbey which is on the right. Founded in 1139, the abbey is among the best-preserved ruins to survive the Dissolution.

6 **Thornton Abbey to Tealby** Leave the abbey and turn left on to the road signposted to Ulceby. At the T-junction 1 m. later turn right, cross the railway, turn left and follow the narrow road to Ulceby Skitter. At the junction with the A160, turn right and after 1 m. enter Ulceby. In Ulceby, turn left on to the B1211 signposted to Brocklesby. The turreted gatehouse, soon after the railway bridge, is one of the entrances to Brocklesby Park, the Earl of Yarborough's estate (not open to the public). Drive through Brocklesby to Keelby and where the B1211 joins the A18 turn left, following the signpost to Grimsby. Views of Humberside can be seen

to the left. After 4 m., at the roundabout, take the B1431 (the second exit) signposted to Louth. After another 4 m., at the crossroads with the B1203, turn right. At Binbrook, 5 m. further on, is an RAF airfield from which Lightnings can sometimes be seen flying. Continue through Binbrook, still on the B1203, to Tealby.

7 **Tealby to Market Rasen** Continue out of the village on the B1203, down the hill across the flat expanse of Tealby Moor. After 1 m. the road turns right and left to skirt the edge of Willingham Forest before running into Market Rasen.

8 **Market Rasen to Glentham** Leave the town on the A631, following the signpost to Gainsborough. After 2½ m., in West Rasen, note the 14th-century packhorse bridge to the right of the road bridge. Go through Bishopbridge, 3 m. beyond West Rasen, and continue on the A631 to the small, pretty village of Glentham.

9 **Glentham to Lincoln** Leave Glentham, continuing on the A631 for 2½ m. to Caenby Corner and the roundabout. Turn left at the roundabout on to the A15 signposted to Lincoln. This road is the Roman Ermine Street, heading south straight as an arrow as it has done for nearly 2000 years. About 4 m. from Caenby Corner, the A15 makes a great loop off the old Ermine Street and back on to it again. This loop accommodates the RAF airfield at Scampton from which the Dam Buster raid was launched during the Second World War. The A15 leads straight back to Lincoln.

INFORMATION

Places of interest *Elsham Hall:* Daily, closed Christmas Day and Good Friday. *Lincoln:* Castle, weekdays (also Sun. afternoons Apr. to Oct.). Greyfriars City and County Museum, daily, Sun. afternoons. Museum of Lincolnshire Life, Tues. to Sun., 11 a.m.-5 p.m. Usher Gallery, daily, Sun. afternoons. *Thornton Abbey:* daily, Sun. afternoons. *Wrawby Mill:* (Tel. Brigg 2066).

Crafts *Elsham Hall:* Craft workshops, resident potters.

Nature trail Elsham Hall.

Events *Brigg:* Horse fair, Aug. *Lincoln:* Music festival, Feb./Mar. Lincolnshire Show, June. Antiques fair, July. Autumn Pleasure Fair, Sept. *Market Rasen:* Festival and carnival, Sept. Music and drama festival, Nov. Racing at various times of the year.

Information Tourist Information Centre, 90 Bailgate, Lincoln (Tel. Lincoln 29828). Assembly Rooms, Boston (Tel. Boston 64601).

Towns with easy access to Lincoln:
Doncaster ..... 39 m.   Grimsby .... 36 m.
Grantham ..... 25 m.   Nottingham ... 36 m.

Golden pheasant at Elsham Hall.

ELSHAM HALL
A country park has been created in the grounds of Elsham Hall. There are several nature trails, a bird sanctuary, domesticated animals and lakes where car. eat from the hand. There is also an art gallery in the gr and resident artists and potters at the craft workshop

Wrawby post mill.

WRAWBY MILL
Hundreds of post mills once ground corn in Lincolnshire. They were called post mills because the whole top, including sails and machinery, revolved on a central post to face the wind. Wrawby Mill, restored in 1961–5, is the only survivor of the Lincolnshire post mills which is in full working order today.

BRIGG
Founded on an island in the fens around the old river Ancholme, Brigg was originally a fishing village whos people lived on the fish and wildfowl caught in the mars This way of life ended with the draining of the fens bu Brigg grew into a prosperous centre for the farms whi were created on the former fishing grounds. There are weekly fatstock sales and a horse and sheep fair in Aug

Lancaster bomber.

RAF SCAMPTON
It was from Scampton air base that RAF Lancaster bombers of 617 Squadron took off on the Dam Buste raid that breached the great dams of the Ruhr in 1943 Today it is a V-bomber base, and Vulcans can be seer flying low as they take off and land over the A15. A fleet of Hastings transport planes also operates from the base, part of the support strength of the RAF.

SCALE
0   1   2   3   4   5 MILES

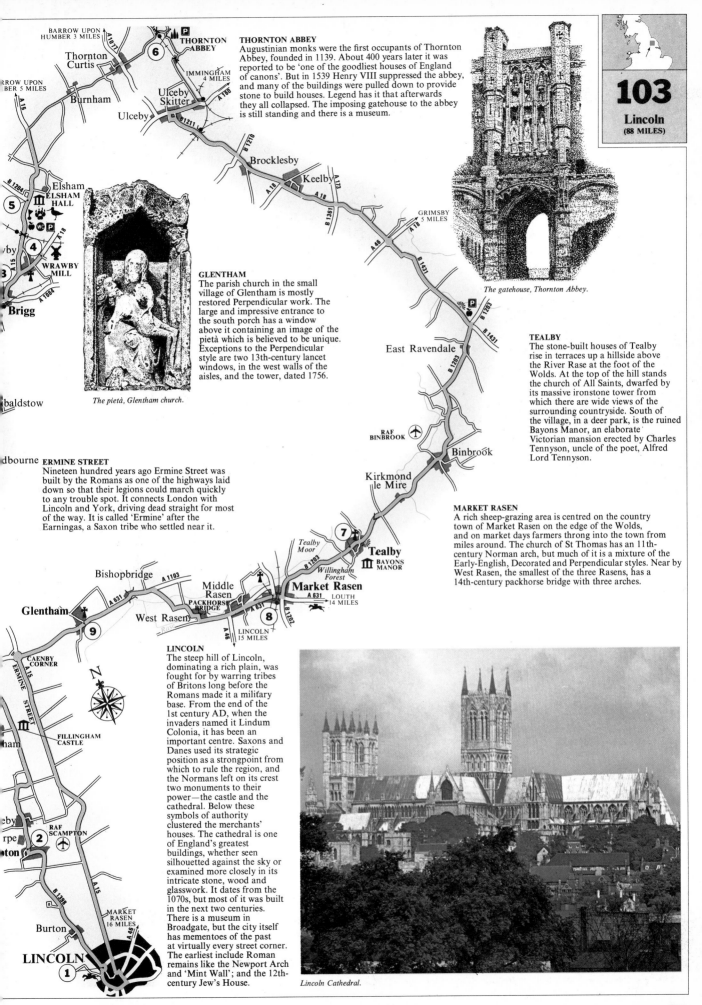

THORNTON ABBEY

Augustinian monks were the first occupants of Thornton Abbey, founded in 1139. About 400 years later it was reported to be 'one of the goodliest houses of England of canons'. But in 1539 Henry VIII suppressed the abbey, and many of the buildings were pulled down to provide stone to build houses. Legend has it that afterwards they all collapsed. The imposing gatehouse to the abbey is still standing and there is a museum.

The gatehouse, Thornton Abbey.

GLENTHAM

The parish church in the small village of Glentham is mostly restored Perpendicular work. The large and impressive entrance to the south porch has a window above it containing an image of the pietà which is believed to be unique. Exceptions to the Perpendicular style are two 13th-century lancet windows, in the west walls of the aisles, and the tower, dated 1756.

The pietà, Glentham church.

TEALBY

The stone-built houses of Tealby rise in terraces up a hillside above the River Rase at the foot of the Wolds. At the top of the hill stands the church of All Saints, dwarfed by its massive ironstone tower from which there are wide views of the surrounding countryside. South of the village, in a deer park, is the ruined Bayons Manor, an elaborate Victorian mansion erected by Charles Tennyson, uncle of the poet, Alfred Lord Tennyson.

ERMINE STREET

Nineteen hundred years ago Ermine Street was built by the Romans as one of the highways laid down so that their legions could march quickly to any trouble spot. It connects London with Lincoln and York, driving dead straight for most of the way. It is called 'Ermine' after the Earningas, a Saxon tribe who settled near it.

MARKET RASEN

A rich sheep-grazing area is centred on the country town of Market Rasen on the edge of the Wolds, and on market days farmers throng into the town from miles around. The church of St Thomas has an 11th-century Norman arch, but much of it is a mixture of the Early-English, Decorated and Perpendicular styles. Near by West Rasen, the smallest of the three Rasens, has a 14th-century packhorse bridge with three arches.

LINCOLN

The steep hill of Lincoln, dominating a rich plain, was fought for by warring tribes of Britons long before the Romans made it a military base. From the end of the 1st century AD, when the invaders named it Lindum Colonia, it has been an important centre. Saxons and Danes used its strategic position as a strongpoint from which to rule the region, and the Normans left on its crest two monuments to their power—the castle and the cathedral. Below these symbols of authority clustered the merchants' houses. The cathedral is one of England's greatest buildings, whether seen silhouetted against the sky or examined more closely in its intricate stone, wood and glasswork. It dates from the 1070s, but most of it was built in the next two centuries. There is a museum in Broadgate, but the city itself has mementoes of the past at virtually every street corner. The earliest include Roman remains like the Newport Arch and 'Mint Wall'; and the 12th-century Jew's House.

Lincoln Cathedral.

Where pilgrims sailed out and Arctic birds fly in

Birds rarely seen anywhere else in England fly down from the Arctic to make their winter home among the sea dykes and salt marshes of this part of Lincolnshire, aptly named Holland. It is a place for bird-watching, where for centuries the frontier between land and sea has swung back and forth over a no-man's-land of creeks and swamps. From the once great seaport of Boston, the successors of the Pilgrim Fathers set out for the New World. The poet Tennyson found inspiration in the gentler villages and gardens where the route winds inland.

(1) Louth to Horncastle Leave Louth on the A153 signposted to Horncastle. The road passes through the rolling chalk downlands of the Wolds, great sheep-rearing country. Continue through Scamblesby past the Dutch gabled house, an example of the influence of Holland on this part of England. Here the road turns sharp left at the summit of a hill. Continue into Horncastle, which is on the site of the Roman town of Banovallum.

(2) Horncastle to Scrivelsby Leave the town on the A153 signposted to Sleaford. After 1 m. turn left on to the B1183, signposted to Boston. After a further 1 m. the road runs past the deer park of Scrivelsby estate. The 'Lion Gateway' is the entrance to the manor.

(3) Scrivelsby to Revesby Continue on the B1183 as it twists and turns across country for 4 m. to the junction with the A155. There turn left and immediately right to keep on the B1183 into Revesby. This village is the gateway to the level expanse of the Lincolnshire fen country, some of the richest farming land in the world.

(4) Revesby to Boston Continue out of Revesby on the B1183 on a long straight stretch, passing through New Bolingbroke, Medlam, Carrington and Short's Corner to Boston. On the outskirts of the town, turn right on to the A16 for the town centre, with its busy harbourside, and the Boston Stump, the tower of the 14th-century St Botolph's Church, which is one of the largest parish churches in England. Tidemarks on the walls of the tower date from the fenland floods which contributed to the decline of Boston as a seaport.

(5) Boston to Freiston Shore Return along the A16 through the centre of Boston, and at Burton Corner turn right on to the A52 signposted to Skegness. After 1½ m. turn right at the crossroads following the signpost to Freiston. After 2 m., at the T-junction, turn left following the signposts to Freiston Shore. There is a car park near Plummers Hotel, an inn tucked on the landward side of a sea wall originally built by the Romans.

(6) Freiston Shore to Old Bolingbroke Return through Freiston to the A52. Cross the A52 at the staggered crossroads on to the minor road signposted to Sibsey. Soon afterwards the road bears right to run alongside Hobhole Drain, one of the canals that drains the fens. Continue for 3 m. to the junction with the B1184 and turn left following the signpost to Sibsey. After 1 m. go over a level crossing into Sibsey. There, at the junction with the A16, turn right. Follow the road through Stickney and Stickford, where Cromwell billeted his troops before the siege of Old Bolingbroke and the Battle of Winceby in 1643. Just beyond East Keal, with its view south over the fenlands, turn left on to the road signposted to Old Bolingbroke. At the T-junction turn left, then almost immediately right. Turn right at the next T-junction and follow the road into Old Bolingbroke village centre. The remains of the castle are in a field close to the church.

(7) Old Bolingbroke to Harrington Leaving the village, turn right at the T-junction in the centre on to the road signposted to Mavis Enderby. In Mavis Enderby turn left on to the A1115 and follow the road into the village of Lusby. At the crossroads in Lusby, turn right and follow the road signposted Hagworthingham. The road crosses a ford, and in the village is the junction with the A158. Turn right and, soon after, left on to the road signposted to Harrington. The 17th-century Harrington Hall, immortalised by Tennyson's 'Come into the garden, Maud', is on the right of the road. A row of thatched cottages adds to the charm of the village. In the church there is an effigy of a knight in chain armour, dating from about 1300.

(8) Harrington to Louth The road rises out of Harrington, and after ½ m. fork left downhill on the road signposted Brinkhill. In Brinkhill, keep right at the junction and follow the road into South Ormsby. At the crossroads, just beyond the village, turn left. This is the Bluestone Heath Road which runs for 12 m. along the crest of the Wolds. There are no villages and few houses along the whole length of the road which has wide views over the surrounding countryside. After 7 m. cross the A153, and 5 m. later Bluestone Heath Road ends at a T-junction with the A157. There turn right following the signpost to Louth, which is reached 4 m. later.

INFORMATION

Places of interest *Boston:* Guildhall, weekdays (not Sat. afternoons, Oct. to Apr.). Fydell House, weekdays. *Louth:* Museum, Sat., Sun., afternoons; Wed. in Aug., 10 a.m.-4 p.m. or by arrangement.

Events *Boston:* Cattle market, Wed. General market, Wed. and Sat. *Cadwell Park,* near Louth: Motorsports in summer. *Horncastle:* Market days, Thur. and Sat. *Louth:* Market days, Wed., Fri. and Sat. Auction of food, flowers, books and antiques. Wed. Cattle Market, Fri.

Information East Midlands Tourist Board, Bailgate, Lincoln (Tel. Lincoln 31521).

Towns with easy access to Louth:

Grimsby	15 m.	Mablethorpe	16 m.
Lincoln	26 m.	Skegness	22 m.

Market cross, Horncastle.

HORNCASTLE
The Romans built a fortified town on the site where Horncastle now stands, and part of a 13 ft thick wall with its original facing stones still remains. St Mary's Church has a library of old chained books and a collection of ancient scythes which, according to legend, were used as weapons at the Civil War Battle of Winceby. There are more than 50 pubs in the town and surrounding district, a reminder of the days when farmers met there for the great horse fairs.

SCRIVELSBY
The manor was given to Roger Marmion during the r of Henry III on condition he accepted the office of King's Champion. The duty of the champion was to ᵣ armed into the coronation banquet at Westminster H and challenge to fight to the death anyone who doubt the new monarch's right to the throne. The custom wᵢ abandoned after the 1821 coronation of George IV, bᵢ the title still goes with ownership of the estate.

REVESBY
Church, vicarage, almshouses and cottages cluster around the green at Revesby, one of the most attractive small villages in the district. It marks the beginning of the fenland called Holland. Sir Joseph Banks, the naturalist who sailed with Captain Cook, lived at Revesby Abbey

Fishing boats, Boston harbour.

SCALE
0 1 2 3 4 5 MILES

LOUTH

A needle-like spire looks down on Louth, one of the best-preserved market towns in England. The spire soars to 300 ft above the pinnacles and flying buttresses of the 15th-century parish church. Louth has many other fine buildings of all periods from the 16th century. The imposing Georgian and Victorian façades of the main street, Mercer Row, conceal a maze of curious alleyways. Alfred, Lord Tennyson, who was educated at the grammar school, had his first poems published by a Louth bookseller in 1827 when he was 18. For bargain-hunters there is an auction every Wednesday trading in furniture, books, antiques—even food and flowers.

Pulpit of St James's, Louth.

BLUESTONE HEATH ROAD

This lonely road runs along the top of the north Lincolnshire Wolds, commanding wide views in all directions. Its line was laid down by prehistoric men, who kept their tracks on high ground to avoid the perils of forest and marsh. There are no villages on the road—its heights are too bleak in winter. But in spring and summer the fields around come to life with hares, pheasants, butterflies and flowers.

HARRINGTON

'Come into the garden, Maud,' wrote Tennyson. Visitors, too, may stroll on certain days in the garden at Harrington Hall, the home of his friend Vincent Amcotts, which Tennyson had in mind when he wrote the poem 100 years ago. The red-brick mansion stands on a high point of the Wolds, 300 ft above sea level. The village church, St Mary's, contains medieval monuments.

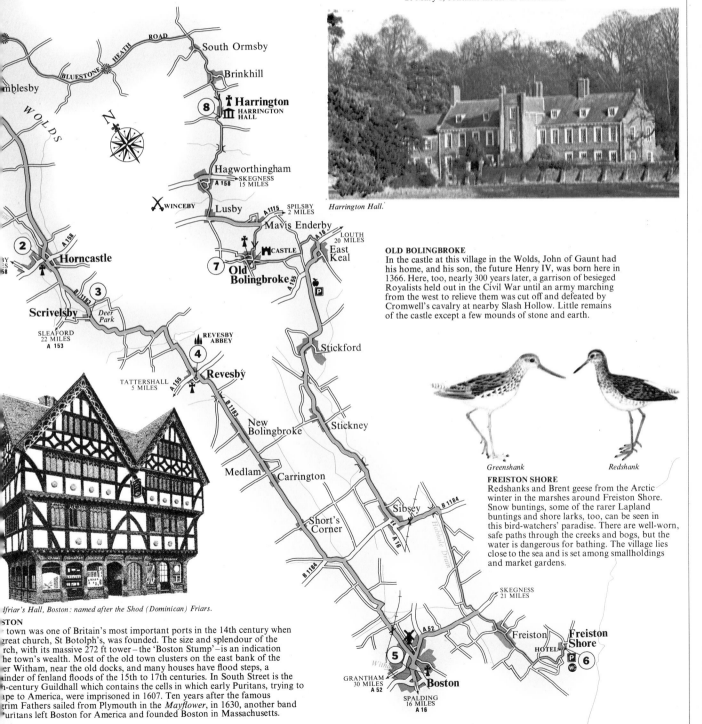

Harrington Hall.

OLD BOLINGBROKE

In the castle at this village in the Wolds, John of Gaunt had his home, and his son, the future Henry IV, was born here in 1366. Here, too, nearly 300 years later, a garrison of besieged Royalists held out in the Civil War until an army marching from the west to relieve them was cut off and defeated by Cromwell's cavalry at nearby Slash Hollow. Little remains of the castle except a few mounds of stone and earth.

Greenshank   *Redshank*

FREISTON SHORE

Redshanks and Brent geese from the Arctic winter in the marshes around Freiston Shore. Snow buntings, some of the rarer Lapland buntings and shore larks, too, can be seen in this bird-watchers' paradise. There are well-worn, safe paths through the creeks and bogs, but the water is dangerous for bathing. The village lies close to the sea and is set among smallholdings and market gardens.

...friar's Hall, Boston: named after the Shod (Dominican) Friars.

...STON

...town was one of Britain's most important ports in the 14th century when ...great church, St Botolph's, was founded. The size and splendour of the ...rch, with its massive 272 ft tower – the 'Boston Stump' – is an indication ...he town's wealth. Most of the old town clusters on the east bank of the ...r Witham, near the old docks, and many houses have flood steps, a ...inder of fenland floods of the 15th to 17th centuries. In South Street is the ...h-century Guildhall which contains the cells in which early Puritans, trying to ...ape to America, were imprisoned in 1607. Ten years after the famous ...rim Fathers sailed from Plymouth in the *Mayflower*, in 1630, another band ...uritans left Boston for America and founded Boston in Massachusetts.

Along the Wirral, by the sands of Dee

In the poem that many will remember from their school days, a farmer's daughter called Mary was bidden to 'call the cattle home ... across the sands of Dee'. Charles Kingsley wrote the poem more than 100 years ago, but the 'sands of Dee', with their sea birds and red sunsets, are eternal. With the riverside meadows and the villages hewn out of the native sandstone, they are seldom out of mind and view on this tour from the dignified old city of Chester.

1 Chester to Shotwick Leave the city on the A41 signposted Birkenhead, and almost immediately after the roundabout on the inner ring road, bear left on to the A540 signposted to Hoylake. After 3 m., just past the Wheatsheaf public house, turn left. Carry on over staggered crossroads and turn left at the junction with the A5117. Turn right at the traffic lights on to the A550, and after ¼ m. turn left into Shotwick.

2 Shotwick to Burton Return to the A550, turn left and after 1¼ m. turn left again, on to the A540. About ¼ m. later turn left on to the road signposted to Puddington. Go straight through Puddington to Burton. Just before the village on the left is Barn Farm. This is the reputed home of Charles Kingsley's character Mary from his poem 'Sands of Dee'.

3 Burton to Ness Gardens Turn left at the T-junction in Burton, and continue on this road for about 1 m. to Ness Gardens. The car park is on the left at Mickwell Brow.

4 Ness Gardens to Parkgate Turn left out of the car park and continue on the road towards Neston. Just after the Wheatsheaf public house, where there is an S-bend in the road, the three-storey Swann Cottage on the right was the birthplace in 1765 of Emma Lyon, later to become Lady Hamilton, Nelson's mistress. Drive on into Neston, and in the centre of the village turn left on to the B5135 signposted to Parkgate. Carry on to where the road becomes the promenade.

5 Parkgate to Thurstaston From the promenade at Parkgate, follow the road inland to the junction with the A540. Turn left and follow the A540 through Heswall and on to Thurstaston, where the main centre of Wirral Country Park is signposted on the left.

6 Thurstaston to Caldy Return to the A540, turn left, and after about 1 m. turn left at the crossroads on to the B5141 signposted to Caldy. To get to the coast, the northern part of the Wirral Country Park railway walk and Caldy picnic area, keep ahead by the church in Caldy and take the first right.

7 Caldy to West Kirby Return to the B5141 and turn left. The National Trust property, Caldy Hill, is on the right after ¼ m. Where the B5141 turns sharp left, continue straight ahead on the minor road into West Kirby.

8 West Kirby to Thornton Hough Leave the town by going up Black Horse Hill, the B5139 signposted to Frankby. Just before the road enters Frankby, turn right down Hillbark Road. Bear left by the Farmer's Arms to a crossroads and there turn right on to the road signposted to Irby. At the T-junction in Irby turn left along Thingwall Road. After about 1¼ m. bear left as this road meets the B5138, and almost immediately turn right on to the A551. Follow this road through wooded Barnston Dale and on into the village of Barnston. About ½ m. beyond the church, turn left into Whitehouse Lane, following the signpost to Brimstage. At the junction with the B5137, turn left, still following the signpost to Brimstage. Near the village green, Brimstage Hall Farm has part of a 1398 tower which was used as a warning beacon at the time of the Spanish Armada. At the roundabout 1 m. later, take the third exit on to the B5136 signposted to Willaston/Neston. Pass the hospital and bear right into Thornton Hough.

9 Thornton Hough to Chester Turn left at the crossroads in Thornton Hough and carry on to the village of Raby. Go straight over the crossroads in Raby, turn left at the T-junction and continue to the junction with the B5151. Turn right on to the B5151, and at the next T-junction turn left into Willaston. On Willaston Green, which is overlooked by old houses and a coaching inn, turn right, still on the B5151, to the junction with the A540. Turn left on the A540, and after 1 m. turn left again, following the signpost for Ledsham. Turn right at the S-bend, down Ledsham Hall Road, cross the A550 and go through Ledsham village. At the T-junction turn left through Capenhurst, and just before the railway bridge fork right. After ¾ m. cross the railway, turn right on to the A5117 and then first left. After 1 m., by the thatched cottage, turn left into Townfield Lane and continue through Mollington. Turn left on to the A540 back to Chester.

INFORMATION

Places of interest *Chester:* Castle, daily. City Wall Tower, May to Sept., weekdays, Sun. afternoon. Guildhall Museum, June to Sept., weekdays, except Wed. Grosvenor Museum, weekdays, Sun. afternoon. Heritage Centre, weekdays except Mon. Stanley Palace, weekdays. Zoo and gardens, daily. *Ness Gardens:* Daily.

Events *Chester:* North of England Head of the River (boat race), Mar. Sailing regattas, spring and autumn. Horse-racing, May, July, Sept.

Nature trails Neston Rock Cutting, ¾ m. Thurstaston, 1½ m. Guides from Head Ranger, Wirral Country Park, Thurstaston.

Information Chester Town Hall (Tel. Chester 40144). Wirral Country Park, Station Road, Thurstaston (Tel. Thurstaston 4371).

Towns with easy access to Chester:

Knutsford	24 m.	Rhyl	30 m.
Liverpool	18 m.	Stoke-on-Trent	37 m.
Llangollen	23 m.	Warrington	20 m.

Turnstones: winter and summer plumage

WEST KIRBY
A 32 acre marine lake runs the length of the promenade, unaffected by tides. It is used for boating and sailing, and the northern end is enclosed to make a safe paddling pool.
The resort is the main access point for Hilbre Islands bird sanctuary, about a mile offshore. The islands can be reached on foot at low tide. From the West Kirby promenade, between September and April, huge flocks of waders—knots, turnstones, sanderlings, purple sandpipers and others—can be seen wheeling above the islands. They are taking refuge there as the rising tide covers their feeding grounds. In the summer they return to the Arctic.

Marine lake, West Kirby.

CALDY
Local sandstone has been used to build most of the cottages here. The 14 mile Wirral Walk, which hugs the saltmarsh coast, can be joined at the disused railway bridge. Caldy Hill is a good vantage point from which to get a panoramic view of the Dee.

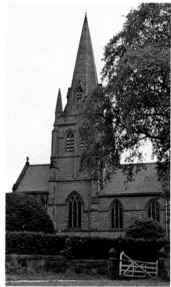
Thurstaston church.

THURSTASTON
Old cottages, a small red-sandstone church, and a 15th-century mansion are cosily grouped here. The village is the headquarters of Wirral Country Park, the backbone of which is the disused railway to the west. The park offers walking, riding, camping and fishing. There are views across the Dee Estuary to the Welsh mountains.

SCALE

0   1   2   3 MILES

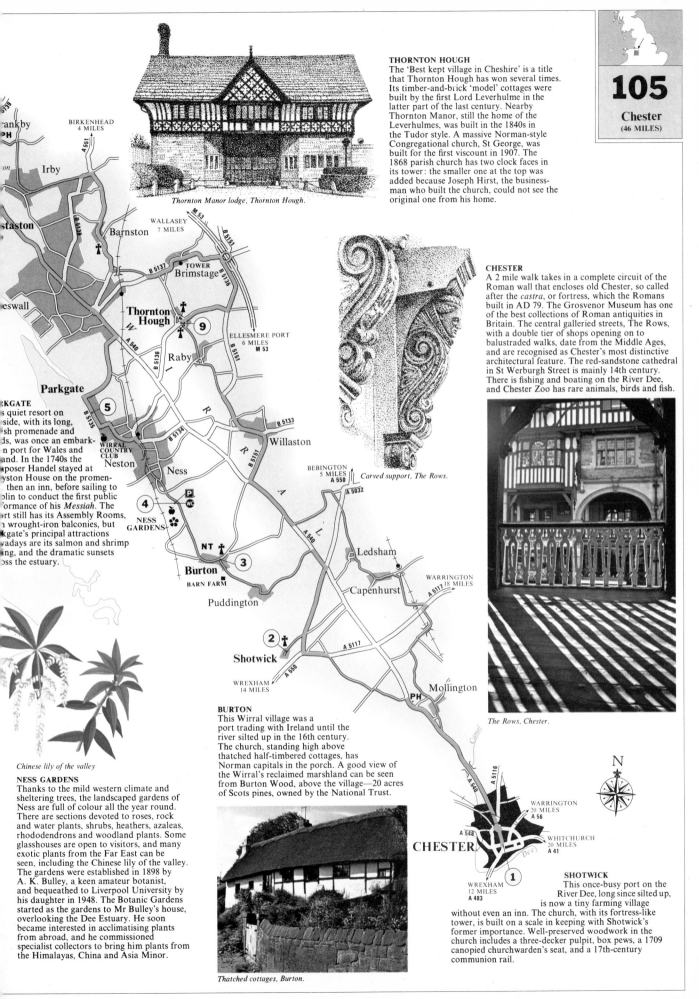

THORNTON HOUGH

The 'Best kept village in Cheshire' is a title that Thornton Hough has won several times. Its timber-and-brick 'model' cottages were built by the first Lord Leverhulme in the latter part of the last century. Nearby Thornton Manor, still the home of the Leverhulmes, was built in the 1840s in the Tudor style. A massive Norman-style Congregational church, St George, was built for the first viscount in 1907. The 1868 parish church has two clock faces in its tower: the smaller one at the top was added because Joseph Hirst, the business-man who built the church, could not see the original one from his home.

Thornton Manor lodge, Thornton Hough.

CHESTER

A 2 mile walk takes in a complete circuit of the Roman wall that encloses old Chester, so called after the *castra*, or fortress, which the Romans built in AD 79. The Grosvenor Museum has one of the best collections of Roman antiquities in Britain. The central galleried streets, The Rows, with a double tier of shops opening on to balustraded walks, date from the Middle Ages, and are recognised as Chester's most distinctive architectural feature. The red-sandstone cathedral in St Werburgh Street is mainly 14th century. There is fishing and boating on the River Dee, and Chester Zoo has rare animals, birds and fish.

Carved support, The Rows.

The Rows, Chester.

Chinese lily of the valley

NESS GARDENS

Thanks to the mild western climate and sheltering trees, the landscaped gardens of Ness are full of colour all the year round. There are sections devoted to roses, rock and water plants, shrubs, heathers, azaleas, rhododendrons and woodland plants. Some glasshouses are open to visitors, and many exotic plants from the Far East can be seen, including the Chinese lily of the valley. The gardens were established in 1898 by A. K. Bulley, a keen amateur botanist, and bequeathed to Liverpool University by his daughter in 1948. The Botanic Gardens started as the gardens to Mr Bulley's house, overlooking the Dee Estuary. He soon became interested in acclimatising plants from abroad, and he commissioned specialist collectors to bring him plants from the Himalayas, China and Asia Minor.

PARKGATE

[...]s quiet resort on [...]side, with its long, [...]sh promenade and [...]ds, was once an embark-[...]n port for Wales and [...]and. In the 1740s the [...]poser Handel stayed at [...]yston House on the promen-[...] then an inn, before sailing to [...]olin to conduct the first public [...]ormance of his *Messiah*. The [...]rt still has its Assembly Rooms, [...] wrought-iron balconies, but [...]kgate's principal attractions [...]adays are its salmon and shrimp [...]ng, and the dramatic sunsets [...]ss the estuary.

BURTON

This Wirral village was a port trading with Ireland until the river silted up in the 16th century. The church, standing high above thatched half-timbered cottages, has Norman capitals in the porch. A good view of the Wirral's reclaimed marshland can be seen from Burton Wood, above the village—20 acres of Scots pines, owned by the National Trust.

Thatched cottages, Burton.

SHOTWICK

This once-busy port on the River Dee, long since silted up, is now a tiny farming village without even an inn. The church, with its fortress-like tower, is built on a scale in keeping with Shotwick's former importance. Well-preserved woodwork in the church includes a three-decker pulpit, box pews, a 1709 canopied churchwarden's seat, and a 17th-century communion rail.

285

Among the canals where the barges ride high

The rich pastures of Cheshire produce enough milk to supply about 4 million people with a pint a day. A substantial number of the 140,000 dairy cows that make this possible will be seen peacefully grazing in the meadows along the route of this tour. Other roads wander between the meadows, and the canals are banked high above the flat countryside so that the colourful craft that use them seem to glide over the fields.

1 Northwich to Anderton From the centre of Northwich, cross the River Weaver by the Town Bridge and immediately turn right on to the A533. After 1 m. cross another bridge and turn right into Anderton. To see the Anderton barge lift, continue to the far side of the village and bear right over the canal by Bridge Farm.

2 Anderton to Arley Continue along the road from Anderton, and bear right in Comberbach to the junction with the A559. Turn right on to the A559, then immediately left into Pole Lane. After about ½ m. turn left again on to the road signposted to Warrington. Take the next turn right, after about 150 yds, signposted to Crowley/Arley, and right again at the junction just after a sharp left-hand bend by Hollies Farm. At the next junction, turn right to Arley.

3 Arley to Lymm Return from Arley to the junction and go straight ahead on the road signposted to Appleton. In Appleton, at the junction with the B5356, turn right. Turn right again at the junction with the A50, cross the M6 and turn immediately left on to the B5158 signposted to Lymm. At the T-junction on the outskirts of Lymm turn left on to the A56, then right on to the A6144 and into the centre.

4 Lymm to Dunham Park Leave Lymm on the A6144 and keep straight ahead on the road signposted to Partington. Shortly after a sharp right-hand bend, fork right on to the B5160 signposted to Dunham Massey. Continue into Dunham for Dunham Park.

5 Dunham Park to Great Budworth Just beyond the car park for Dunham Park, turn right on to the road signposted to Altrincham. At the A56 turn right again and after 1 m., at the roundabout, stay on the A56 (the third exit) signposted to Lymm. After 2½ m. turn left at the crossroads, on to the B5159. In High Legh fork left, turn left on to the A50 and immediately right on to the road signposted to Great Budworth. Turn right at the T-junction 1¼ m. after crossing the M6 and take the third turning on the right, after about 1½ m., following the signpost to Great Budworth.

6 Great Budworth to Bunbury At the far side of the village, turn left on to the A559. After 2 m., at the crossroads in Lostock Gralam, go straight ahead past the railway station and turn right on to the dual-carriageway (A556). After about 3 m., at the second roundabout, take the first exit on to the A533 signposted to Winsford. After 1 m., beyond Davenham, turn right on to the B5336, follow it round to the left in Moulton, then at the junction with the A5018 turn right, following the signpost to Winsford. Go through the town, and at the roundabout on the far side turn left on to the B5074. Keep straight on at the next crossroads and soon afterwards turn right down School Lane. After about ½ m., immediately after a sharp left-hand bend, turn right. After just over 3 m. turn right by the Boot and Slipper Inn on to the road signposted to Tarporley. At the A51 turn right, and after ½ m. turn left for Bunbury.

7 Bunbury to Peckforton Take the Spurstow road opposite the church in Bunbury and follow it as it curves left and down to a T-junction. Turn right, and in Spurstow go over the A49 at staggered crossroads and on to Peckforton.

8 Peckforton to Beeston Castle Take the Beeston road northwards from Peckforton. For 1½ m. it runs alongside the wooded Peckforton Hills on the left. At the junction in Beeston, turn left then immediately right for Beeston Castle.

9 Beeston Castle to Delamere Forest From the castle entrance, continue along the lane for 100 yds, then turn right. Keep straight on at the next junction and at the junction with the A49 turn left. After about 1 m., at the crossroads, go straight ahead on to the B5152. Go through Eaton and rejoin the A49 at Cotebrook. Turn right at this junction, then fork left on to the B5152 signposted to Delamere. Stay on the road, which crosses the A54 and the A556, through the village of Delamere to Delamere Forest.

10 Delamere Forest to Northwich At the crossroads on the far side of the forest, turn right on to the road signposted to Crowton. Keep straight ahead at the next junction, then turn right and left near the church, still following the signposts for Crowton. Turn left at the next junction, and in Crowton turn right on to the B5153. In Weaverham, turn left on to the A49 and immediately right, back on to the B5153, which leads into Northwich.

INFORMATION

Places of interest *Arley Hall Gardens:* Apr. to mid-Oct., Tues. to Sun., Spring and Late Summer Bank Hol. afternoons. *Beeston Castle:* weekdays, Sun. afternoons. *Dunham Park:* Daily. *Northwich Salt Museum:* Mon. to Sat., all day, except Wed. (mornings only).

Information North-West Tourist Board, Town Hall, Manchester (Tel. 061-236 3377). Delamere Forest Centre, Forestry Commission, Linmere (Tel. Sandiway 882167).

Towns with easy access to Northwich:

Chester	18 m.	Stoke-on-Trent	25 m.
Manchester	21 m.	Warrington	12 m.
Runcorn	9 m.	Wrexham	26 m.

ARLEY
Timber-framed cottages of mellow brick overlook lane that leads to Arley Hall, owned by Viscount Ashbrook's family since the early 16th century. Th present building is mainly early Victorian, and is c brick with decorative motifs in blue brick. There a Jacobean-style windows and gables. Next to the h is a survival of the earlier house—a 16th-century b with seven great curved beams supporting the wall and roof. Teas are served here, and the grounds a gardens of the hall, with their fine displays of rose and rhododendrons, are open to the public.

Notice in the grounds of Arley Hall.

ANDERTON
The village looks over the valley of the River Weaver to the industrial outskirts of Northwich. Its name has been ensured a plac in history by the Anderton barge lift, an impressive piece of engineering, completed in 1875, which raises and lowers 100 ton barges and smaller pleasure craft 50 ft between the Weaver and the Trent and Mersey Canal in two and a half minutes. Originally hydraulic, it is now electrically driven.

Subsidence in Castle Street, Northwich; photograph in Salt Mus

NORTHWICH
Huge underground deposits of salt, left when a sea evaporated 200 million years ago, have made Northw a busy trading centre since prehistoric times. Salt provided raw material for the alkali works founded in the last century, which grew into the vast ICI combin At the ICI Winnington works, which can be seen fron the hill, a multitude of chemical products are extracte from brine, including the plastic PVC and anti-knock chemicals for petrol. A museum housed in the public library in Witton Street is devoted to the salt industry and is well worth a visit. It shows methods of salt mining from the earliest days of the industry. It also preserves a photographic record of subsidence caused by uncontrolled pumping in the 19th century. Buildin were tilted at crazy angles, and the operations created many of the little lakes or 'flashes' seen in the district. The River Weaver, canalised in the early 18th century to help with the transport of salt, flows near the town's new shopping and pedestrian-precinct centre. Cheshire is in no danger of running short of salt. The ICI estimate that there are still 400,000 million tons le The large salt mine at Marston, north of the town, wa visited in 1844 by Tsar Nicholas I of Russia and a brilliantly lit banquet was served underground amid t salt. The church of St Helen at Witton has a richly decorated tie-beam roof with over 400 painted bosses.

SCALE
0 1 2 3 MILES

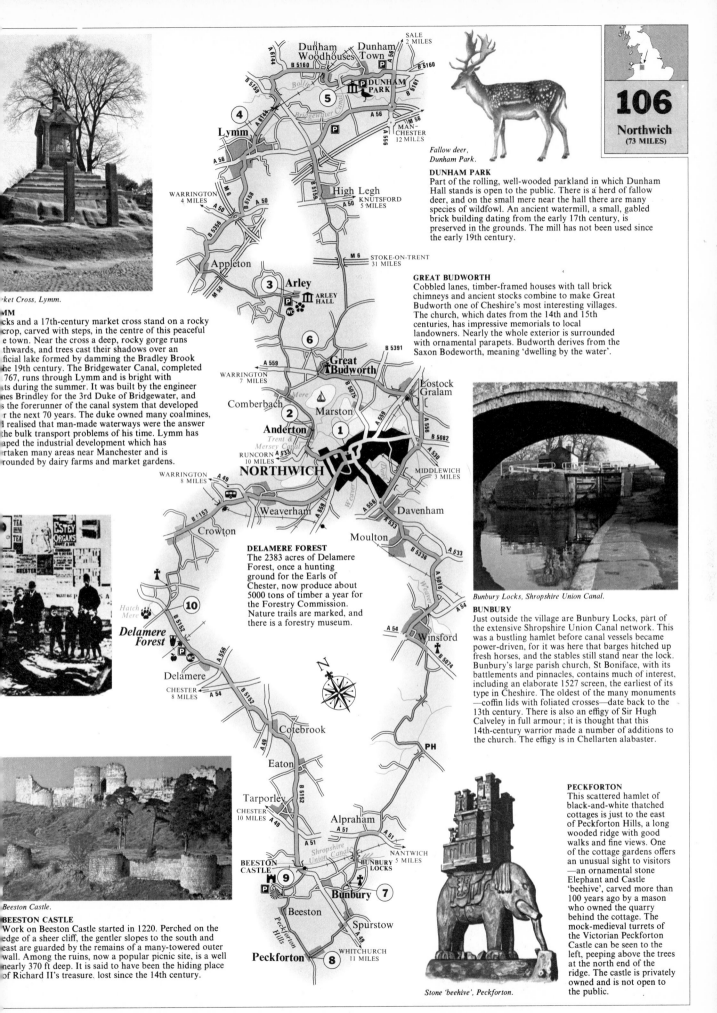

Market Cross, Lymm.

LYMM
Stocks and a 17th-century market cross stand on a rocky outcrop, carved with steps, in the centre of this peaceful little town. Near the cross a deep, rocky gorge runs northwards, and trees cast their shadows over an artificial lake formed by damming the Bradley Brook in the 19th century. The Bridgewater Canal, completed in 1767, runs through Lymm and is bright with boats during the summer. It was built by the engineer James Brindley for the 3rd Duke of Bridgewater, and was the forerunner of the canal system that developed over the next 70 years. The duke owned many coalmines, and realised that man-made waterways were the answer to the bulk transport problems of his time. Lymm has escaped the industrial development which has overtaken many areas near Manchester and is surrounded by dairy farms and market gardens.

DUNHAM PARK
Part of the rolling, well-wooded parkland in which Dunham Hall stands is open to the public. There is a herd of fallow deer, and on the small mere near the hall there are many species of wildfowl. An ancient watermill, a small, gabled brick building dating from the early 17th century, is preserved in the grounds. The mill has not been used since the early 19th century.

Fallow deer, Dunham Park.

106
Northwich
(73 MILES)

GREAT BUDWORTH
Cobbled lanes, timber-framed houses with tall brick chimneys and ancient stocks combine to make Great Budworth one of Cheshire's most interesting villages. The church, which dates from the 14th and 15th centuries, has impressive memorials to local landowners. Nearly the whole exterior is surrounded with ornamental parapets. Budworth derives from the Saxon Bodeworth, meaning 'dwelling by the water'.

Bunbury Locks, Shropshire Union Canal.

BUNBURY
Just outside the village are Bunbury Locks, part of the extensive Shropshire Union Canal network. This was a bustling hamlet before canal vessels became power-driven, for it was here that barges hitched up fresh horses, and the stables still stand near the lock. Bunbury's large parish church, St Boniface, with its battlements and pinnacles, contains much of interest, including an elaborate 1527 screen, the earliest of its type in Cheshire. The oldest of the many monuments —coffin lids with foliated crosses—date back to the 13th century. There is also an effigy of Sir Hugh Calveley in full armour; it is thought that this 14th-century warrior made a number of additions to the church. The effigy is in Chellarten alabaster.

DELAMERE FOREST
The 2383 acres of Delamere Forest, once a hunting ground for the Earls of Chester, now produce about 5000 tons of timber a year for the Forestry Commission. Nature trails are marked, and there is a forestry museum.

PECKFORTON
This scattered hamlet of black-and-white thatched cottages is just to the east of Peckforton Hills, a long wooded ridge with good walks and fine views. One of the cottage gardens offers an unusual sight to visitors —an ornamental stone Elephant and Castle 'beehive', carved more than 100 years ago by a mason who owned the quarry behind the cottage. The mock-medieval turrets of the Victorian Peckforton Castle can be seen to the left, peeping above the trees at the north end of the ridge. The castle is privately owned and is not open to the public.

Stone 'beehive', Peckforton.

Beeston Castle.

BEESTON CASTLE
Work on Beeston Castle started in 1220. Perched on the edge of a sheer cliff, the gentler slopes to the south and east are guarded by the remains of a many-towered outer wall. Among the ruins, now a popular picnic site, is a well nearly 370 ft deep. It is said to have been the hiding place of Richard II's treasure, lost since the 14th century.

A visit to Merrie England and a peep into outer space

Time might have stopped in the little village of Nether Alderley, where the wooden waterwheel of a 16th-century mill still turns. Time marches on at Jodrell Bank, where visitors can pick up signals from the sun on a miniature of the vast, space-probing radio telescope. In between these extremes, the countryside covered by this tour in mid-Cheshire is like a great park dotted with grand and ancient houses such as Capesthorne Hall, longer than Buckingham Palace, and Gawsworth Hall, with its collection of coaches that once rumbled over 18th-century turnpikes.

1 Wilmslow to Alderley Edge From Wilmslow railway station, drive towards the town, and at the junction with the A34 turn left. Follow the signposts to Alderley Edge, a large village nestling at the foot of a 2 m. long ridge. Cross the railway bridge and drive down the main street. At the junction just beyond the shops, turn left on to the road signposted to The Edge/Over Alderley. After 1 m. enter the car park just beyond The Wizard restaurant. From here the woodlands can be explored on foot and the Wizard's Well visited.

2 Alderley Edge to Nether Alderley Turn right out of the car park and then immediately left down Artist's Lane, opposite The Wizard restaurant. At the junction with the A34 turn left, following the signpost to Nether Alderley. The village is off the main road, on the right just past the mill.

3 Nether Alderley to Capesthorne Hall Return to the A34 and turn right. After 1½ m. cross the A537. In 1 m. Capesthorne Hall, one of Cheshire's finest stately homes, is signposted to the right.

4 Capesthorne Hall to Gawsworth Hall Continue along the A34, and after 1½ m. turn left on to the B5392 signposted to Gawsworth. After 2 m. turn right on to a minor road signposted to Gawsworth. At the junction with the A536 go straight ahead into Gawsworth. On the far side of the village is the hall, fought over in 1712 in the most famous duel in British history. Both duellists, Lord Mohun and the Duke of Hamilton, were killed.

5 Gawsworth Hall to Jodrell Bank Return across the A536 to the B5392, turn left and go back to the A34. Cross the A34, keeping to the B5392 and following the signposts to Withington as the great white disc of the radio telescope comes into view. Bear right at the large village green in Withington, and at the junction with the A535 turn right. After 1 m., where the A535 bears sharply right, turn left on to a road signposted to Jodrell Bank Visitors' Entrance. The entrance is on the left. As well as the radio telescope, the astronomical research centre has a planetarium, an exhibition hall and an arboretum.

6 Jodrell Bank to Knutsford Leaving the entrance, turn left along the minor road. After crossing the railway bridge, bear right on the road signposted to Knutsford. Turn right at the T-junction, just after the private road leading to the church at Over Peover (pronounced 'Peever') which has among its relics a flag presented by General 'Blood and Guts' Patton. Patton lived in nearby Peover Hall while preparing the US Third Army for the Normandy landings in 1944. Turn left at the crossroads and left at the T-junction. At the A50, by the Whipping Stocks Inn, turn right, following the signpost to Knutsford, an attractive town of old half-timbered houses. At the traffic-lights on the outskirts, turn right into the town centre. At the foot of the hill turn left into King Street, and follow the road until the shops end. The tall white tower is a memorial to the novelist Mrs Gaskell. Knutsford got its name from King Canute (or Knut), who is reputed to have forded a small stream near the town on one of the many journeys he made to consolidate his position after he became King of England in 1017.

7 Knutsford to Tatton Park Leave the town by continuing along King Street, and as the road bears left keep ahead and drive round the boundary of Tatton Park. At the junction with the A5034 turn right and immediately right again. The entrance to Tatton Park and its beautiful gardens is on the right.

8 Tatton Park to Mobberley Leaving the park, turn right and continue along the same road to Ashley. Beyond Ashley station, turn right at the crossroads by the Greyhound Inn. Follow the winding road for 2 m. Then, by a group of houses at a junction, bear left and follow the signpost to Mobberley church. Go under the railway bridge. The church is on the right after 1¼ m.

9 Mobberley to Wilmslow Continue on past the church, and in Mobberley turn left on to the B5085 signposted to Alderley Edge. After 3 m. fork left on to the B5086, left again on to the A34, and drive back into Wilmslow.

INFORMATION

Places of interest *Capesthorne Hall:* Apr. Sun., May to Sept., Wed., Sat., Sun., Good Friday, Bank Hol. Mon. afternoons. *Gawsworth Hall:* end Mar. to Oct., afternoons. *Jodrell Bank:* Mid-Mar. to Oct. 31, afternoons. *Nether Alderley Old Mill:* Apr. to Oct., Wed., Sun., Bank Hol. afternoons. *Tatton Park:* Apr. to mid-Oct., daily (except Mon., but open Bank Hol. Mon.). House and gardens afternoon, parkland 11 a.m.-6 p.m.

Events *Knutsford:* May Festival, May Day. Antique. Fair, May.

Information Manchester: North-West Tourist Board, Town Hall, Manchester (Tel. 061-236 3377).

Towns with easy access to Wilmslow:

Altrincham	8 m.	Manchester	12 m.
Cheadle	5 m.	Stockport	8 m.
Macclesfield	8 m.	Stoke-on-Trent	25 m.

TATTON PARK
It would take a 9 mile walk to go all round the beauti[ful] Tatton Park, stocked with deer, and a haunt of wildfo[wl]. The house, completed early in the 19th century, conta[ins] a spectacular array of treasures, including many paintings and travel and hunting trophies of the last Lord Egerton, who bequeathed the estate to the Nati[onal] Trust in 1958. One of the features of the grounds is a Japanese garden with a Shinto temple built by Japanes[e] craftsmen. A straight avenue of beech trees that leads towards Knutsford is the sole survivor of the formal gardens laid out in the 17th century. The house is one of the finest examples of Regency architecture still standing in England.

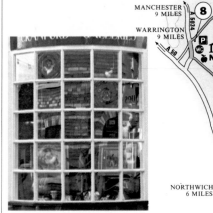

Bow-window shop front, Knutsford.

KNUTSFORD
The black-and-white houses and narrow streets of Knutsford were the model for *Cranford*—Mrs Gaskell[s] novel. Mrs Gaskell (born Elizabeth Cleghorn Stevens[on]) lived in a house overlooking the heath in what is now Gaskell Avenue, and she is buried in the Unitarian churchyard. King Street, with its bow-windowed shop[s] retains much of the atmosphere of *Cranford*, and Mrs Gaskell's readers can easily imagine one of the novelis[t's] bonneted old ladies bobbing out of a doorway after ordering a length of bombasine. Knutsford is linked b[y] name and tradition with King Canute, who is said to h[ave] forded a local stream on one of his journeys. During [the] Civil War, Prince Rupert's army lodged in the town in 1644, and seven years later the Ironsides camped on Knutsford Heath ready to do battle with Charles II. Several of the old inns were stage-coach posting house[s].

Radio telescope, Jodrell Bank.

SCALE

0   1   2 MILES

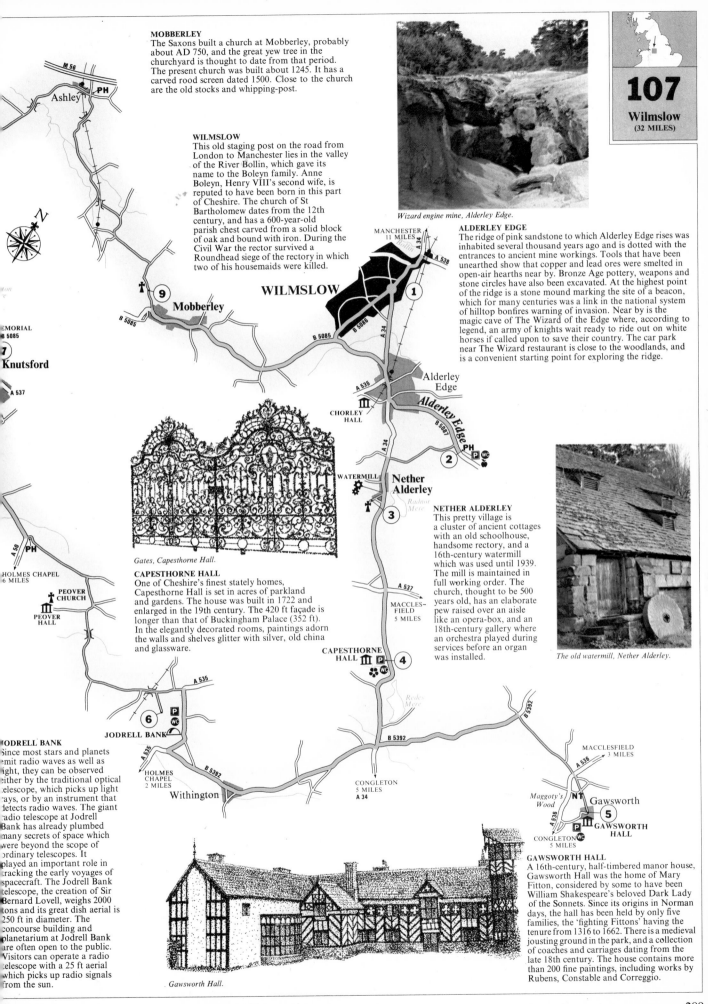

MOBBERLEY

The Saxons built a church at Mobberley, probably about AD 750, and the great yew tree in the churchyard is thought to date from that period. The present church was built about 1245. It has a carved rood screen dated 1500. Close to the church are the old stocks and whipping-post.

WILMSLOW

This old staging post on the road from London to Manchester lies in the valley of the River Bollin, which gave its name to the Boleyn family. Anne Boleyn, Henry VIII's second wife, is reputed to have been born in this part of Cheshire. The church of St Bartholomew dates from the 12th century, and has a 600-year-old parish chest carved from a solid block of oak and bound with iron. During the Civil War the rector survived a Roundhead siege of the rectory in which two of his housemaids were killed.

WILMSLOW

Wizard engine mine, Alderley Edge.

ALDERLEY EDGE

The ridge of pink sandstone to which Alderley Edge rises was inhabited several thousand years ago and is dotted with the entrances to ancient mine workings. Tools that have been unearthed show that copper and lead ores were smelted in open-air hearths near by. Bronze Age pottery, weapons and stone circles have also been excavated. At the highest point of the ridge is a stone mound marking the site of a beacon, which for many centuries was a link in the national system of hilltop bonfires warning of invasion. Near by is the magic cave of The Wizard of the Edge where, according to legend, an army of knights wait ready to ride out on white horses if called upon to save their country. The car park near The Wizard restaurant is close to the woodlands, and is a convenient starting point for exploring the ridge.

Gates, Capesthorne Hall.

CAPESTHORNE HALL

One of Cheshire's finest stately homes, Capesthorne Hall is set in acres of parkland and gardens. The house was built in 1722 and enlarged in the 19th century. The 420 ft façade is longer than that of Buckingham Palace (352 ft). In the elegantly decorated rooms, paintings adorn the walls and shelves glitter with silver, old china and glassware.

NETHER ALDERLEY

This pretty village is a cluster of ancient cottages with an old schoolhouse, handsome rectory, and a 16th-century watermill which was used until 1939. The mill is maintained in full working order. The church, thought to be 500 years old, has an elaborate pew raised over an aisle like an opera-box, and an 18th-century gallery where an orchestra played during services before an organ was installed.

The old watermill, Nether Alderley.

JODRELL BANK

Since most stars and planets emit radio waves as well as light, they can be observed either by the traditional optical telescope, which picks up light rays, or by an instrument that detects radio waves. The giant radio telescope at Jodrell Bank has already plumbed many secrets of space which were beyond the scope of ordinary telescopes. It played an important role in tracking the early voyages of spacecraft. The Jodrell Bank telescope, the creation of Sir Bernard Lovell, weighs 2000 tons and its great dish aerial is 250 ft in diameter. The concourse building and planetarium at Jodrell Bank are often open to the public. Visitors can operate a radio telescope with a 25 ft aerial which picks up radio signals from the sun.

Gawsworth Hall.

GAWSWORTH HALL

A 16th-century, half-timbered manor house, Gawsworth Hall was the home of Mary Fitton, considered by some to have been William Shakespeare's beloved Dark Lady of the Sonnets. Since its origins in Norman days, the hall has been held by only five families, the 'fighting Fittons' having the tenure from 1316 to 1662. There is a medieval jousting ground in the park, and a collection of coaches and carriages dating from the late 18th century. The house contains more than 200 fine paintings, including works by Rubens, Constable and Correggio.

A spellbinding visit to the world of the witches

Romans, monks and witches have all left memories here. The legions built a great cavalry base at Ribchester, to guard their network of strategic roads. Cistercian monks founded monasteries at Whalley and Sawley. At Newchurch the village church has a carving which was regarded as a talisman against the witches of Pendle Hill, ten of whom were hanged at Lancaster in 1612. A different past is recalled in the Tudor magnificence of Browsholme Hall, which houses the accumulated treasures of the family who have lived there for 600 years. Beacon Hill Country Park and villages such as Waddington and Bolton by Bowland tempt the tourist to park the car and walk.

1 Preston to Ribchester Leave Preston on the B6243 signposted to Longridge, and follow the road round to the right on the outskirts of the town. On the far side of Longridge, turn right on to the B6245 signposted to Ribchester, which is reached 3½ m. later. To see the remains of the Roman fortress, go straight ahead where the B6245 turns sharp left and drive to the church near the river.

2 Ribchester to Whalley Return to the centre of the village and turn right on to the B6245 by the Black Bull. After 1 m. the road crosses the river, and 1½ m. later, at the crossroads with the A59, turn left, following the Clitheroe signpost. At the roundabout 2½ m. later take the exit signposted for Whalley, where there is a ruined abbey.

3 Whalley to Newchurch From the traffic lights in Whalley, turn right on to the A671 signposted for Burnley. At the next traffic lights turn right, then almost immediately fork left, following the signpost for Sabden, which is 3 m. ahead. At the T-junction in Sabden turn right on to the road signposted to Padiham. On the outskirts of Padiham turn left, climbing steeply for ½ m. to Padiham Heights. At the crossroads at the top of the hill, turn left on to the road signposted to Newchurch. After 2 m., at the T-junction, turn left on to a narrow lane which runs down steeply to Sabden Brook Valley. From the brook the road climbs sharply for 1½ m. to Newchurch.

4 Newchurch to Bolton by Bowland Leave the village on the road signposted for Barley beside the village church. Go through Barley, with the 1831 ft high mass of Pendle Hill towering on the left, to a crossroads 2½ m. beyond Barley. Turn left here, following the signpost to Downham, 3 m. downhill. On the far side of the village, just past the church, turn right on to the road signposted to Gisburn. Follow the road through Rimington and at the A682 turn left, still following the signpost for Gisburn. In Gisburn turn left on to the A59, then almost immediately right on to the road signposted to Bolton by Bowland. The road crosses a railway, then the River Ribble, after which there is a 3 m. drive to Bolton village.

5 Bolton by Bowland to Sawley Continue through Bolton, crossing Tosside Beck on the far side of the village. Take the first turning left, at the T-junction by an inn, and continue along the Ribble Valley. After 2 m. turn left across the river towards Sawley, then go sharp right to see the abbey ruins.

6 Sawley to Waddington Recross the river and keep left to Grindleton. About ¼ m. past Grindleton church, bear left downhill. Keep right at the fork in West Bradford and drive just over 1 m. to Waddington village.

7 Waddington to Browsholme Hall Leave Waddington on the B6478 towards Newton and Slaidburn, but take the first turn left into a narrow lane. Keep right by the farm, 1 m. later, and after another 2 m. go right, following the signposts for Whitewell. At the T-junction turn right. Browsholme Hall is on the right.

8 Browsholme Hall to Beacon Fell Continue along the lane and at the first junction, 1 m. later, keep straight ahead. At the next junction turn left, following the road signposted for Chipping. After 1½ m. turn right and follow the road into Chipping. In the village turn right by the church and at the junction, ¼ m. later, bear left. After 1 m., at the next junction, follow the lane round to the left in the direction signposted for Bleasdale, and ½ m. later turn right. After 3 m., where the road swings sharp right for Inglewhite, keep straight on for Beacon Fell to join the one-way road.

9 Beacon Fell to Preston Continue circling Beacon Fell on the one-way road, and leave it by the first junction signposted for Inglewhite. After 3 m. turn left down Button Street, signposted for Preston, which leads into Inglewhite. In the village bear left on to the road signposted for Preston. After 1 m. turn right at the T-junction, and after a further 3 m., where the road meets the B5269, go right. Soon afterwards the road reaches the A6. Turn left here for Preston.

INFORMATION

Places of interest *Browsholme Hall:* Closed to visitors during 1977. *Preston:* Harris Museum and Art Gallery, all year, weekdays. *Ribchester Museum:* Weekday afternoons (except Fri.); Dec. and Jan., Sat. afternoons only. *Sawley Abbey:* All year, daily. *Whalley Abbey:* All year, weekdays, Sun. afternoons.

Events *Longridge:* Carnival, June. *Preston:* Agricultural Show, July.

Nature trail *Beacon Fell:* 8 m. north of Preston. Starts at picnic site car park. Information from Lancashire County Council.

Information North-West Tourist Board, Town Hall, Manchester (Tel. 061-236 3377).

Towns with easy access to Preston:

Blackpool ......17 m.	Manchester ....30 m.
Chorley .... 9 m.	Ormskirk ......18 m.
Lancaster ......21 m.	Southport ......17 m.

BROWSHOLME HALL (Closed during 1977.) Since 1380 this sandstone mansion has been the home of the Parkers, hereditary bow-bearers to the kings who hunted deer in Bowland Forest. The present building, which dates from 1507, contains relics ranging from Stone Age weapons to part of the first Zeppelin shot down in England in the First World War. Among the relics is a gauge which was used in the days of the hunting kings to measure the feet of dogs before they were allowed into the royal forest. Dogs whose feet passed through the gauge were judged too small enough not to menace the deer, and allowed in.

Edward II jug, Browsholme Hall.

BEACON FELL
Although only 873 ft above sea level, this tree-clad hummock commands wide views of the Lancashire moors to the north, and as far as Blackpool and the sea to the west. The fell has been turned into a country park, with car parks, picnic areas and a nature trail. In all, it covers 273 acres. Among the birds that may be seen is the treecreeper, which crawls up the trunks, sometimes in a spiral, looking for insects in the bark. The plants include arrowhead, a water species that grows around the small pond on the fringe of the fell. Most of the trees are conifers but there are also oak, mountain ash, silver birch, alder and Japanese cherry. Crowberries and cranberries, as well as blackberries, flourish in the undergrowth.

Arrowhead

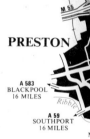

Treecreeper

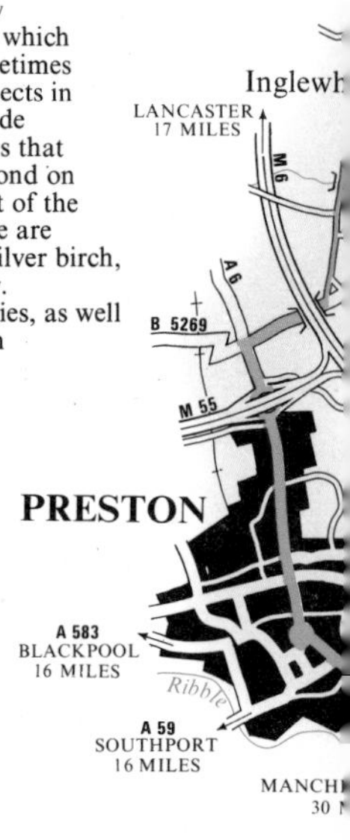

PRESTON
Despite its cotton mills, factories and inland docks, Preston has fine parks and open spaces, and one can stroll along the banks of the Ribble. Since Norman times it has been a trading centre on one of the main London-Edinburgh highways. Royal charters from as early as 1100 are preserved in the borough archives; Preston had an MP as long ago as 1295; Robert Bruce burnt the town in 1323; the Royalists lost a Civil War battle there in 1648; and Bonnie Prince Charlie visited the town during the 1745 uprising. Preston has lost its oldest buildings, but the market-place has good 19th-century architecture in the pinnacled Town Hall, the stone Sessions House, and the library, museum and art gallery where paintings by Sir Alfred Munnings, Graham Sutherland and Augustus John can be seen. Preston is the chief market for produce from the agricultural areas of the Fylde and south of the Ribble. The market is open daily and there is a large cattle market four days a week, attracting trade from all over the North and Scotland.

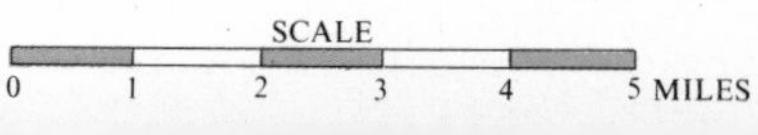

Map labels: Inglewhite, LANCASTER 17 MILES, B 5269, M 55, PRESTON, A 583 BLACKPOOL 16 MILES, Ribble, A 59 SOUTHPORT 16 MILES, MANCHESTER 30, A6

SCALE
0 1 2 3 4 5 MILES

The Tudor hall, Browsholme Hall.

Sawley Abbey ruins.

WADDINGTON

A stream spanned by footbridges flows down the street to join the Ribble, passing a garden laid out to commemorate Queen Elizabeth's coronation in 1953. By the side of the road from Sawley is the Widows' Hospital, a group of almshouses built around a green in 1700 for dalesmen's widows. The village is named after a family who sheltered Henry VI after his defeat in the Wars of the Roses. Their descendants became engineers, built bridges and made axles for the first steam engines.

SAWLEY

The last abbot of Sawley shared the fate of his fellow-priest at nearby Whalley: both were hanged for resisting the Dissolution of the Monasteries under Henry VIII. The remains of the abbey, which was founded in 1147, stand in a loop of the meandering River Ribble. The original plan of the building can be worked out from the stones which rise from the grassy site.

BOLTON BY BOWLAND

Henry VI, who took refuge with Sir Ralph Pudsay, the lord of the manor, after the Battle of Hexham in 1464, is said to have designed the tower of the parish church. Sir Ralph had three wives and 25 children: a memorial to the whole family is in the church. The number of children each mother bore is engraved on the hem of her stone gown. Another feature of the church is its massive oak door, protected by 560 iron studs. The village is built around two greens, with a medieval market cross and stocks. The attractive stone house on the edge of the upper green was built in the 17th century as a courthouse. Bolton is on a corner of the Forest of Bowland, an area of high moors which in the Middle Ages were a royal hunting ground roamed by thousands of deer. The forest is crossed by the route of an old Roman road which connected Ribchester to Carlisle and Hadrian's Wall.

WHALLEY

Sheltered by low, wooded hills, Whalley stands in the valley of the River Calder. The Nab, a popular beauty spot, is to the south; to the east is a car park and picnic site. The river flows past the ruins of an abbey founded by the Cistercians in 1296. At the peak of its power the community numbered about 120. The last abbot was hanged at the foot of Whalley Nab for taking part in the Pilgrimage of Grace, the ill-fated protest against Henry VIII's Dissolution of the Monasteries. The most prominent landmark is 'the Whalley arches', a 49 arch viaduct, 2037 ft long, which carries the railway across the valley. The church at Whalley contains fine woodwork, including 15th-century choir stalls from the abbey.

NEWCHURCH

Souvenir hunters in this district will find that the shops specialise in 'witch' mementoes, for Newchurch and the 1831 ft high Pendle Hill were the home of 19 of the 'Pendle Witches' of the 16th and 17th centuries. They were tried at Lancaster Castle in 1612, and ten of them were hanged. Alice Nutter, whose tomb is outside the village church, was, according to tradition, one of the witches who escaped the gallows. The 'all-seeing eye of God' carving on the 1544 church tower was believed to protect worshippers from the witches' wiles. Footpaths lead to the summit of Pendle Hill, where in 1652 George Fox said he had the vision that led him to found the Society of Friends, who became known as the Quakers.

'Eye of God' carving, Newchurch.

Roman helmet, Ribchester.

RIBCHESTER

For at least three centuries Ribchester was the greatest Roman fortress in Lancashire. A cavalry regiment was stationed at the base, which the legions called Bremtonacum. Excavations have revealed pottery, lamps and gold coins; but the most highly prized find is a decorated parade helmet, a replica of which is in the museum opposite the village church. The pillars at the entrance to the 18th-century White Bull Inn are fragments of a Roman temple. The Roman bath-house was partially excavated in 1927.

Pendle Hill, haunt of witches.

A view of broad beaches from the 'Taj Mahal'

A bird's-eye view of much of this route can be seen from the top of Lancaster's Ashton Memorial, sometimes called the Taj Mahal of the North. It looks across to the Lakeland peaks and Morecambe Bay, where low spring tides sometimes expose 10 miles of beaches and salt marshes. Leighton Moss, in this area, is a bird reserve. Nearby Leighton Hall is a repository of many fine examples of 18th-century furniture. The tour visits the treeless 'Forest' of Bowland; Warton church, which commemorates local links with George Washington, first President of the USA; and Steamtown, at Carnforth, where on certain days children can enjoy the thrill of a ride on the footplate of a steam locomotive.

(1) Lancaster to Jubilee Tower Leave Dalton Square in the centre of Lancaster on the road signposted to Clitheroe via Trough of Bowland. After 800 yds, fork right up Wyresdale Road, and after another 800 yds turn left, still following the Clitheroe signpost. Drop down the hill and follow the road under the M6 and on for 5 m. as it climbs steadily to the Jubilee Tower.

(2) Jubilee Tower to Trough of Bowland Continue along the same road, which drops down to meet the infant River Wyre before climbing again to the impressive 1000 ft high Trough of Bowland pass.

(3) Trough of Bowland to Slaidburn At the first junction beyond the pass turn left, following the signpost to Dunsop Bridge. Follow the road through Dunsop Bridge into Newton and turn left on to the B6478, which reaches Slaidburn after 1 m.

(4) Slaidburn to Hornby In Slaidburn, follow the road round to the right past the Hark to Bounty Inn and turn left by the war memorial, following the signpost to Bentham. The road climbs for 11 m. past lonely farms, through a spectacular pass and across wild moorland to High Bentham. There turn left on to the B6480 signposted to Lancaster, and follow it down the peaceful valley of the River Wenning through Lower Bentham and Wennington to Wray. A number of cottages in the village were carried away by a flood in 1967. A paved garden now covers the site, and a stone shelter has been erected on which a line marks the flood level. About 1 m. beyond Wray, turn right on to the minor road signposted to Hornby. After ¼ m. keep straight ahead where the road joins the A683. and continue over the bridge into Hornby.

(5) Hornby to Warton Leave Hornby on the A683 signposted to Kirkby Lonsdale, and fork left soon after the village on to the minor road signposted to Gressingham. The road crosses a pleasing stretch of the River Lune and shortly afterwards bears right to enter Gressingham. Follow the road through the village, and after 1 m. turn left at the junction with the B6254. Go right almost immediately, and climb past Lord's Lot Wood to the beautiful little village of Borwick, where Borwick Hall is an impressive Tudor building incorporating a 14th-century tower. Turn left in the village, following the signpost for Carnforth. Cross the Lancaster Canal and the M6, and then follow the road straight over the A6 and into Warton. Turn left at the crossroads to visit the church.

(6) Warton to Leighton Hall Return to the crossroads and turn left up Coach Lane, following the signpost to Leighton. The entrance to Leighton Hall follows soon afterwards on the left.

(7) Leighton Hall to Leighton Moss Return to the lane from the hall. Turn left, and follow the road into Yealand Conyers. This is an exceptionally pleasant village with a number of grand houses. The Quaker meeting house was built in 1692, and Yealand Manor House is an imposing Regency mansion dating from 1805. Turn left at the T-junction in the village and follow the road into Yealand Redmayne, an attractive village built largely of the local limestone. Keep left at the junction after the village and follow the road round the edge of Storrs Moss, which is to the left. The entrance to the Leighton Moss bird sanctuary is on the left just before the railway bridge.

(8) Leighton Moss to Carnforth Return to the road. Turn left, and then left again at the T-junction just after the railway bridge. Turn left again at the next junction, follow the road for 2 m. to the edge of Warton and turn right. After 1 m. the road reaches Carnforth, which has a museum of working steam locomotives.

(9) Carnforth to Lancaster Leave Carnforth on the A6 signposted to Lancaster. The road runs beside the Lancaster Canal as far as Bolton-le-Sands, an expanding village from which there are excellent views across Morecambe Bay to the Lakeland mountains. Follow the road on through the old village of Slyne and into Lancaster.

INFORMATION

Places of interest *Carnforth:* Steamtown museum, daily all year. Saloon rides on Bank Hol. weekends and most Sundays, Easter to Sept. *Lancaster:* Museum, Mon. to Sat. Castle, in summer, Mon. to Sat. Ashton Memorial, daily in summer. *Leighton Hall:* May to Sept., Wed., Sun., Spring and Late Summer Bank Hol. Mon., afternoons. *Leighton Moss:* Bird sanctuary, daily.

Events *Carnforth:* Festival, July. *Lancaster:* Agricultural Show, Aug. Riding the Bounds, every seven years from May 1977. Covered market, daily except Wed. and Sun.

Information 7 Dalton Square, Lancaster (Tel. Lancaster 2878).

Towns with easy access to Lancaster:

Blackpool	26 m.	Grange-over-Sands	25 m.
Burnley	36 m.	Kendal	22 m.
Fleetwood	29 m.	Preston	21 m.

Hadrian's Tower, Lancaster Castle.

LANCASTER
Above this city of grey streets and elegant Georgian architecture is a Norman castle built on the site of a Roman encampment. Now the home of a prison and county court, it also houses a museum in the 13th-century Hadrian's Tower. To the east is the Ashton Memorial, an elaborate edifice built by the linoleum tycoon Lord Ashton in 1909 to commemorate his first wife. From it there are splendid views over Morecambe Bay and the Lake District. St George's Quay, a pleasant tree-lined promenade on the banks of the Lune, is now used by private craft, but the 18th-century Custom House is a reminder that Lancaster was once a prosperous port. Two hundred years ago it claimed a greater tonnage of registered shipping than Liverpool. The old Town Hall overlooks Market Square and contains the museum of the King's Own Royal (Lancaster) Regiment.

Ashton Memorial, Lancaster.

JUBILEE TOWER
This small memorial was built in 1887 to commemorate the 50th year of Queen Victoria's reign. Steps lead to the top, from which on a clear day there is a view for 75 miles to the peaks of Snowdonia across the sea to the south-west. To the north are the mountains of the Lake District and to the west the Isle of Man.

SCALE
0   1   2   3   4   5 MILES

...eamtown, Carnforth.

CARNFORTH

...he shore of Morecambe Bay has
...adually crept away from Carnforth,
...hich was a port and shipbuilding
...ntre until the end of the 18th
...ntury. It grew rapidly in the 19th
...ntury when blast furnaces,
...stined to close in 1931, were
...tablished to process iron ore from
...e Furness peninsula on the far side
... the bay. The Carnforth Live
...eam Museum, known as
...eamtown, is a depot where about
... locomotives, including some
...usual industrial machines, can
...e seen—sometimes in action.

Great grey shrike

LEIGHTON MOSS

Marshy Leighton Moss is maintained as a nature reserve by
the Royal Society for the Protection of Birds. Among the
birds to be seen are bitterns, reed warblers, teals, shrikes,
kestrels and ospreys. The marsh was converted into farmland
in the 1840s, when a steam pump was installed to drain the
land. But coal for the pump became scarce during the First
World War and the 400 acres reverted to their natural state.

LEIGHTON HALL

This Neo-Gothic mansion has been
the home of the Gillow family for
many generations, and contains
several examples of the furniture
with which their name is linked.
The pale local limestone of which
the house is built lends a graceful
air to the pinnacles, turrets and
battlements which were added to the
Georgian façade about 1810. These
additions were suggested to
Richard Gillow by his friend Sir
Walter Scott, the author of the
Waverly novels. Richard Gillow
made billiard tables, and it was to
provide natural light for one of
these that the billiard-room, now the
dining-room, was given an oval
skylight. The house is set in
extensive grounds with fine
gardens and parkland crossed by
public paths. The home and grounds
are open on Wednesdays, Sundays
and Bank Holidays in summer.

Gillow furniture, Leighton Hall.

HORNBY

The turreted outline of Hornby
Castle, now a private residence,
stands above a grassy, tree-lined
slope, and is best viewed from
the bridge in the village. The
keep was built by Sir Edward
Stanley (1460–1523), a hero of
England's victory over the Scots
at the Battle of Flodden. The
castle became a Royalist
stronghold when the Civil War
broke out, and it was thought
to be impregnable. But
Cromwell's troops scaled the
walls and succeeded in
overpowering the garrison.

George Washington.

WARTON

George Washington, the first President of the
USA, was descended from a family who lived here,
and to commemorate the fact the Stars and
Stripes is flown from the tower of the church
on American Independence Day, July 4.
  Inside the tower the family's coat of arms
can be seen on a weathered stone plaque,
alongside family trees showing distant
links between the Washingtons and the
Churchills. Old houses line the main
street, and the town is overlooked by
the rocky Warton Crag, on top of which
are remains of a prehistoric fortress.

The Hark to Bounty Inn, Slaidburn.

...rough of Bowland.

TROUGH OF BOWLAND

One of the few roads over
the lonely and treeless
Forest of Bowland runs through this
pass and climbs to more than 1000 ft above
sea level. Highwaymen used to wait in
ambush for travellers on the pass, and
smugglers from Yorkshire passed through to
trade with the Isle of Man. Nowadays
the place is haunted mainly by walkers and
moorland birds. The wild scenery is seen at
its best in the late summer and autumn,
when the heather of the fells turns purple.

SLAIDBURN

The Hark to Bounty Inn at Slaidburn was once the seat of the Bowland Forest
Court, and the jury box is still part of the furniture. The inn gained its name
in the last century from the squire, who was a keen huntsman. When his
favourite hound, Bounty, howled up at the manor house, he would leave the
inn exclaiming 'Hark to Bounty!'

From the highest mountain to the deepest lake

'There is no other piece of wild country in all England like it', wrote the novelist Hugh Walpole of the vista from Hardknott Castle, where Roman soldiers stood guard over one of the last outposts of their empire. They are followed by today's rock-climbers, who pit their skill against Scafell Pike, at 3210 ft England's highest peak. The route of this tour varies the harsh beauty of mountain crags with green and wooded valleys, one of which plunges to England's deepest lake, Wast Water.

1 Broughton in Furness to Dunnerdale Forest Leave the town on the A595, following the signposts for Workington. After 1 m., just before Duddon Bridge, turn right and enter the wooded valley of the River Duddon. William Wordsworth, who spent most of his life in the Lake District, described this valley in some of his best-known sonnets. In spring it is transformed by wild blossom and glades of daffodils and bluebells. Now, large parts of it are owned and protected by the National Trust. Follow the road up the valley to Ulpha, with its stone bridge and tiny church bearing the arms of Queen Anne. In Ulpha, keep right to Hall Dunnerdale. Turn left at the T-junction in Hall Dunnerdale. After 3 m. the road reaches a car park and picnic area which mark the starting point for walks into Dunnerdale Forest.

2 Dunnerdale Forest to Hardknott Castle Continue along the road and 2 m. on from the forest car park, turn left across the river and up the steep and twisting Hard Knott Pass. It is a difficult climb, with gradients up to 1 in 3. (To avoid it, turn left in Ulpha by the Traveller's Rest public house. This road climbs through woods to the open moorland of Birker Fell, before descending towards Eskdale. After crossing the River Esk, bear left to rejoin the route down from Hard Knott Pass.) From the pass the road descends through Eskdale to Hardknott Castle, a dramatically sited Roman fortress of the Emperor Hadrian's day.

3 Hardknott Castle to Dalegarth Three miles beyond the fort is Dalegarth, terminus of an old railway, supported by a preservation society. The car park at the station also marks the starting point for the Stanley Ghyll Nature Trail, which ends at a gorge where a 60 ft waterfall cascades into a valley of almost tropical lushness.

4 Dalegarth to Wast Water Continue down the valley from the car park and after 2 m. turn right at the T-junction, following the signposts for Holmrook/Whitehaven. After another 1 m., follow the road right by the Bower House Inn, and just under 2 m. further on turn right, following the signposts for Wasdale. After 2 m., immediately after crossing the River Irt, turn right, following the signposts for Wasdale Head. The road soon reaches the shores of Wast Water. The Nether Wasdale Nature Trail starts just beyond the cattle grid. There are several small parking areas beside the lake, which is 3 m. long and overshadowed by Scafell Pike.

5 Wast Water to Wasdale Head Follow the lakeside road towards Wasdale Head. The lake is fringed with many colourful wild flowers, including bog asphodel. Peregrines, which come to the district to breed, can be seen swooping after their prey. Continue on the lakeside road and into Wasdale Head, where British rock-climbing began.

6 Wasdale Head to Gosforth Return along the lakeside road and, 4 m. beyond Wasdale Head, take the first turning on the right and continue into Gosforth, crossing the River Bleng, which winds eastwards to join first the Irt and then the Esk, away to the south.

7 Gosforth to Ravenglass Turn right at the junction just past the church, following the signposts to Seascale/Whitehaven. Soon afterwards turn left on to the road signposted to Seascale/Millom, and then turn left again on to the A595 signposted to Millom. After just under 5 m., turn right on to the road signposted to Ravenglass, which the Romans used as a port.

8 Ravenglass to Muncaster Castle Return to the A595 and turn right, following the signpost for Barrow in Furness. From here it is a short run to Muncaster Castle, seat of the Pennington family for 700 years, with its deer park and tropical bird garden.

9 Muncaster Castle to Broughton in Furness Continue along the A595 for 3 m., and then fork left for a scenic route which is signposted to Broughton in Furness. The road drops down into the Duddon valley. Here, turn left to rejoin the A595 for the drive back to Broughton in Furness.

INFORMATION

Places of interest *Hardknott Castle:* Accessible at all reasonable times. *Muncaster Castle:* Sun. before Easter to end Sept., Sun., Tues. to Thur. and Sun. in Oct., afternoons. Gardens, Sun. before Easter to end Sept., Sat. to Thur. afternoons. *Ravenglass and Eskdale Railway:* End Mar. to Nov., daily; Dec. to Feb. limited services.

Nature trails *Nether Wasdale, Wast Water:* Two circular routes, each 1½ m. Woodlands, fells, lake and bog. *Stanley Ghyll:* Dalegarth terminus of Ravenglass and Eskdale Railway, 2 m. Woodland, flowers. Leaflets from National Trust and National Park Information Centres.

Events *Broughton in Furness:* Charter Day, early Aug. Agricultural Show, Aug. *Ravenglass:* Folk Festival, last Sat. in May. *Gosforth:* Agricultural Show, Aug. *Hard Knott Pass:* Puppy Show, Sept.

Information North-West Tourist Board, Town Hall, Manchester (Tel. 061-236 3377).

Towns with easy access to Broughton in Furness:
Barrow in Furness 15 m.	Millom	8 m.
Kendal	31 m.	Ulverston	10 m.

Sheep pens, Wasdale Head.

WASDALE HEAD
The little village here, in the shadow of Scafell Pike, is England's chief centre for rock-climbers. Several of them, killed among the surrounding peaks, are buried in the tiny churchyard under the shelter of gnarled old yew trees. In the church, just about the size of a large garage, a tall man has to stoop to avoid bumping his head on the roof beams. One of the smallest in England, it is 40 ft long and 17 ft wide. It has Victorian iron brackets for oil lamps.

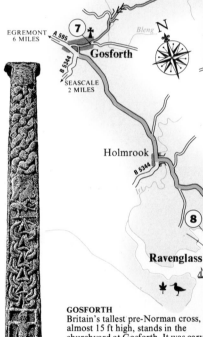
Norse cross, Gosforth.

GOSFORTH
Britain's tallest pre-Norman cross, almost 15 ft high, stands in the churchyard at Gosforth. It was carved by a Norseman around the year 1000 with a mixture of Christian and pagan symbols. Experts say the symbols depict the triumph of the Christian faith over the pagan gods. The churchyard also contains a fragment of an old Saxon cross and two Saxon tombstones. The church was largely rebuilt in the 19th century, but there is a Norman doorway and the chancel arch is probably 14th century.

Harbourside houses, Ravenglass.

SCALE
0   1   2   3 MILES

WAST WATER

Flanked by slopes of scree that tower to almost 2000 ft, and overlooked by the peaks of Scafell Pike and Great Gable, Wast Water is the deepest lake in England—258 ft. Its bed lies 58 ft below sea level. At the southern end of the lake, a nature trail winds through woodland to the pumphouse that daily feeds four million gallons of water to the nuclear power station at Calder Hall. At the foot of the lake is Wasdale Hall, set among pine trees.

Peregrine

Bog asphodel

Train on the Ravenglass and Eskdale Railway.

HARDKNOTT CASTLE

Perched on a precipice and overlooked by saw-toothed mountains, the Roman fort here was built in the 2nd century AD. It was garrisoned by 500 infantrymen whose job was to protect the route inland from the port of Ravenglass. The stone-walled stronghold has the remains of watchtowers at each corner, and the ruins of a bath-house near the main entrance. The parade ground, said to be the best example left in Britain, is 250 yards uphill from the fort. Here, as the novelist Hugh Walpole wrote in 1944, 'under the clouds the Romans move and you hear the clang of their harness...' The fort was built in the reign of the Emperor Hadrian, whose name and titles can be seen on a gateway inscription.

View from Hardknott Castle.

DALEGARTH

The little station at Dalegarth is the inland terminus of the 7 mile Ravenglass and Eskdale Railway, opened in 1875 to carry iron ore down to the coast. The line was converted from 3 ft to 15 in. gauge in 1915 by W. J. Bassett-Lowke, the model engineer. Miniature steam and diesel locomotives, operated by a group of enthusiasts, now make the run for tourist passengers.

BROUGHTON IN FURNESS

DUNNERDALE FOREST

From the riverside car park and picnic area, marked paths run through the Forestry Commission woodlands to vantage points such as Harter Fell. Rising to 2129 ft, the Fell offers views over the Duddon Valley, Hard Knott Pass and Eskdale. Below Birks Bridge, where the paths enter the forest, the River Duddon flows through a gorge.

BROUGHTON IN FURNESS

Towering horse-chestnut trees spread a canopy above the square of this old market town, built on a low hill overlooking the Duddon Estuary. Farmers from the surrounding fells crowd in for the autumn sheep fairs. Charter Day, commemorating the market, is observed with a traditional shower of new pennies for the children, and a free glass of sherry for hotel guests. The town is a collection of Georgian houses and cottages. Just beyond them, down a sloping lane, stands the parish church, basically Norman but it was much restored in the 16th and 19th centuries.

VENGLASS

ree rivers—the Esk, the Irt d the Mite—flow into the tural harbour at Ravenglass. has been a port since Roman nes, and the remains of the a or bath-house they built at alls Castle are still standing. the 18th century, smugglers de the harbour a base for ir trade in contraband from e Isle of Man. The port has ce declined, but it is still a pular sailing centre. From re boats take visitors to the ture reserve on the northern nes, which are inhabited by e largest breeding colony of ck-headed gulls in Europe— out 11,000 nests were counted 1970. To the south lies the kmeals gunnery range.

MUNCASTER CASTLE

A simple gold-and-white enamelled glass bowl has symbolised the fortunes of the Pennington family of Muncaster Castle for 500 years. Called Muncaster's Luck, the bowl was given to Sir John Pennington, the castle's owner, by Henry VI, in gratitude for sheltering him after his defeat at the Battle of Towton in 1461. Henry blessed the bowl and prophesied that so long as it remained unbroken the Penningtons would flourish. The castle, set high above the River Esk, is surrounded by gardens of exotic trees and flowering shrubs.

The Luck of Muncaster.

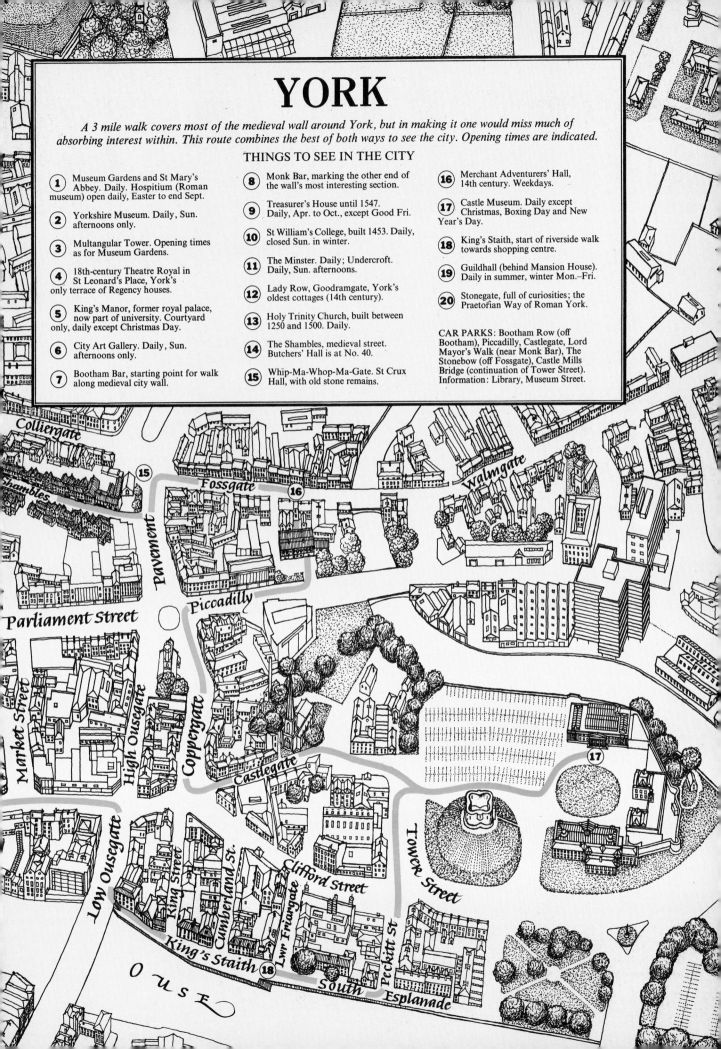

YORK

A 3 mile walk covers most of the medieval wall around York, but in making it one would miss much of absorbing interest within. This route combines the best of both ways to see the city. Opening times are indicated.

THINGS TO SEE IN THE CITY

(1) Museum Gardens and St Mary's Abbey. Daily. Hospitium (Roman museum) open daily, Easter to end Sept.

(2) Yorkshire Museum. Daily, Sun. afternoons only.

(3) Multangular Tower. Opening times as for Museum Gardens.

(4) 18th-century Theatre Royal in St Leonard's Place, York's only terrace of Regency houses.

(5) King's Manor, former royal palace, now part of university. Courtyard only, daily except Christmas Day.

(6) City Art Gallery. Daily, Sun. afternoons only.

(7) Bootham Bar, starting point for walk along medieval city wall.

(8) Monk Bar, marking the other end of the wall's most interesting section.

(9) Treasurer's House until 1547. Daily, Apr. to Oct., except Good Fri.

(10) St William's College, built 1453. Daily, closed Sun. in winter.

(11) The Minster. Daily; Undercroft. Daily, Sun. afternoons.

(12) Lady Row, Goodramgate, York's oldest cottages (14th century).

(13) Holy Trinity Church, built between 1250 and 1500. Daily.

(14) The Shambles, medieval street. Butchers' Hall is at No. 40.

(15) Whip-Ma-Whop-Ma-Gate. St Crux Hall, with old stone remains.

(16) Merchant Adventurers' Hall, 14th century. Weekdays.

(17) Castle Museum. Daily except Christmas, Boxing Day and New Year's Day.

(18) King's Staith, start of riverside walk towards shopping centre.

(19) Guildhall (behind Mansion House). Daily in summer, winter Mon.–Fri.

(20) Stonegate, full of curiosities; the Praetorian Way of Roman York.

CAR PARKS: Bootham Row (off Bootham), Piccadilly, Castlegate, Lord Mayor's Walk (near Monk Bar), The Stonebow (off Fossgate), Castle Mills Bridge (continuation of Tower Street). Information: Library, Museum Street.

A walking tour of the City of York
YORK

York is a stage on which history has been played for 2000 years. Roman emperors have walked its streets; kings have been made, and broken, there. But perhaps its special charm is the insight it preserves of the everyday life of the people of centuries gone by.

The Romans recognised the importance of the junction of the rivers Ouse and Foss as a base from which to launch their conquest of the north. In AD 71 they built a fort here and called it Eboracum. Since then every era of history has left its mark on York, and the city still has a great deal to show for it, not only in impressive monuments but in its many quaint streets, where the shopfronts have hardly changed for centuries. Overshadowing it all is England's largest Gothic cathedral, York Minster, completed in 1472 after taking more than 250 years to build. The fourth cathedral to stand on the site, it has kept the Anglo-Saxon name Minster, meaning a large church run as a mission centre.

A recent five-year restoration has left the Minster with an unusual bonus for visitors. This is the newly dug Undercroft, created so that experts could examine the suspect foundations. The cavern not only shows the new concrete foundations which support the tower, but also an architectural exhibition and display of precious plate.

The Five Sisters
There are 130 stained-glass windows in the Minster. About half of them, the most valuable, were taken out in 1939 as a precaution against bomb damage; the task of replacing all the pieces after the war was a jigsaw puzzle that took 20 years to complete. The window that possibly appeals most to visitors is the 13th-century Five Sisters, each of whose lancets is over 50 ft tall by 5 ft wide. Charles Dickens made a story of this window in his novel *Nicholas Nickleby,* ascribing it to five sisters who were supposed to have made a tapestry, then had it copied on to glass, as a family memorial.

There is a story, too—this one true—about Big Peter, the 11 ton bell that was brought by train from London in 1845 amid much excitement and flag-waving. When it was mounted in position it took 30 men to set it swinging, so a hammer was installed to strike it. Then it was found that the bell was out of tune with the rest of the peal. Ever since, Big Peter has been rung on its own, only at noon; its boom, the deepest in Europe, is heard daily over the city.

Among the many monuments to past clergy, the Minster has an astronomical clock recording the orbits of the planets. It was unveiled in 1956 as a memorial to 18,000 men of the allied air forces who were killed flying from the north-east in the Second World War.

The Minster is close to a network of narrow streets with their age-old inns and curiosity shops, starting from Minstergate and Stonegate. Guy Fawkes, the York man who tried to blow up Parliament, is thought to have been born in Stonegate in 1570.

Some of the houses and shops in the ancient streets still display the 'firemarks' or plaques

ROMAN YORK *The remains of the Multangular Tower, which the Romans built about the year 300 at one corner of their fortress square. More than 1300 years later, in 1644, it was still part of the city defences, taking a battering during the Civil War siege by Cromwell's Parliamentary forces. The work of the Roman masons still shows up to a height of 19 ft, beyond which the medieval structure was superimposed. Roman coffins inside the tower have been excavated in York, whose Roman garrison once numbered 6000 men.*

SOLDIER *Lead bust in City Art Gallery: Sir Thomas Fairfax, the Parliamentary general who accepted the surrender of York after the siege of 1644, ordering his troops not to loot.*

BUILDER *Portrait in City Art Gallery: Michael Taylor (1760–1846), who worked as a stone carver at the Minster. Some of York's earlier buildings are of wood, because plague killed so many masons.*

ROSES FOR PEACE *The south end of the Minster, looking across Petergate, which was the Romans' via principalis, or High Street. The famous rose window high above the doorway is mainly of 16th-century glass, its red and white roses (red for Lancaster, white for York) commemorating the peaceful end of the bloody rivalry between the two factions. In 1486 Henry VII of Lancaster married Elizabeth of York; the war was over. The 'sunflower' in the centre of the window is by an 18th-century craftsman. So too is the glass in the two lower windows just to the right of the door*

S WORK *Chair made by an apprentice* *t 1620. It is seen in the Merchant* *enturers' Hall, headquarters of the* *thiest and most influential of the craft* *ls which flourished in medieval York.* *sioners lived there until the 19th century.*

ES FOR PRAYER *The 18th-century wooden* *pews—each with its own door and just big* *gh to hold an average family—of Holy* *ity Church, Goodramgate. The church is* *erved as a historic monument.*

THE AGE OF ROMANCE *Collection of Victorian Valentine cards in the Castle Museum, claimed to be one of the most interesting folk museums in the world. It was founded in 1935 by John L. Kirk, a country doctor in the Yorkshire market town of Pickering, who spent years collecting objects connected with rural life.*

F-TOP FACELIFT *Under the graceful flying buttresses on the roof of the Minster nave,* *e gargoyles—ornamental figures—have been dismantled and collected to await* *oration by the masons. This was a second stage in the rescue programme launched in* *7, the more urgent task being to renew the foundations supporting the 20,000 tons of* *ain's most massive cathedral tower.*

BLITZ SURVIVOR *One of the ceiling bosses in the Inner Chamber, or committee room, of the 15th-century Guildhall, the only part to escape damage in a fire-bomb raid in 1942.*

RED DEVIL *This carving in Coffee Yard, off Stonegate, is the trade sign of York's oldest printing shop. Apprentices to the craft are still nicknamed 'printers' devils'.*

mounted in Georgian days before there was a municipal fire brigade. The insurance companies ran their own fire engines, and a customer in need could not rely on their services unless the appropriate company plaque was displayed.

Bootscrapers will be seen beside doorways in many parts of the city—a reminder that even cobbled streets were once a rare amenity. And in Low Ousegate, opposite a church, some of the shops display stone-carved cats; nobody knows for certain why, but one theory is that they were intended to scare rats away.

The 1714 Red House in Duncombe Place, by the Minster, has a torch-snuffer at the front door. It was used by linkmen, or torch-bearers, who used to escort people through the streets after dark. In adjoining Petergate, No. 76, formerly a tobacconist's shop, has a gilded horse's head in the doorway; its mouth used to spurt a gas flame for smokers wanting a light. The 12th-century Holy Trinity Church, almost hidden behind York's oldest row of cottages in Goodramgate, still has its ancient box pews. Near by is the city's best-known medieval street of overhanging timbered gables, The Shambles, or butchers' street. Wooden slabs on which the meat was displayed can still be seen, and No. 10, opposite Butchers' Hall, has its ancient swinging half-doors.

The walk leads on to York's shortest street and the one with the longest name—Whip-Ma-Whop-Ma-Gate—where petty law-breakers used to be flogged—passing the home of Margaret Clitherow, who was tortured to death in 1586 for hiding Jesuit priests in her house. She was recently proclaimed a saint.

The Merchant Adventurers' Hall in Piccadilly was built about 1361, when York was an important wool-exporting town. Samples were weighed here before shipment to Europe; the original scales are preserved.

Shopping in the past

York is well served with imaginative museums. The Castle Museum is housed in a former prison which was built in the 18th century, opposite the assize courts. Visitors can go window-shopping in a reconstruction of a Victorian cobbled street, perfect in every detail down to the hansom cab waiting by the kerb. The inventor of the cab, Joseph Hansom, was born in Micklegate; there is a plaque at No. 114. The museum has a re-created candlemaker's shop, an Edwardian tavern and the condemned cell where the highwayman Dick Turpin spent three months before being hanged in 1739. Behind the museum, by the River Foss, a watermill can be seen grinding corn in the summer.

Another museum, the Yorkshire, is devoted to the geology, archaeology and natural history of the county; it houses a notable collection of fossils discovered in Kirkdale Cave, near Kirbymoorside. In the basement the huge fireplace of the St Mary's Abbey warming room, where guests were made comfortable, is retained just as it was found when the museum was being built.

The original 15th-century Guildhall was almost burnt down in the Second World War, but the panelled committee room escaped destruction. Here Cromwell's £200,000 reward money was counted out in 1649, to be paid to the Scots who had helped him to gain victory in the Civil War.

By the entrance to the Yorkshire Museum in Museum Street can be seen a section of the city wall which the Romans built in the 2nd century. This stretch leads to the Multangular Tower, the most substantial Roman relic in the city. It was built in AD 300 to form the western corner tower of the fortress of Eboracum. The contrast between the medieval upper structure and the lower Roman section with its smaller stones is clearly visible. The City Art Gallery was built in the Italian style, in 1878, as part of the Great York Exhibition. The local artist William Etty is well represented in its collection of paintings.

Near by is Bootham Bar, from which the English armies rode out in the wars against the Scots; its Norman portcullis is still in position. Here visitors can climb to the top of the Roman wall and walk right round it to Monk Bar, where carvings of men holding stones to drop on the enemy recall the city sieges.

Water from the hills, and thunder in the valleys

Much of the finest scenery in the North is to be found in the Yorkshire Dales National Park. This tour circles the western half of the park where the action of wind and water over millions of years has carved and gouged the limestone into dramatic shapes. The landscape has been fashioned into such designs as the huge cliff of Malham Cove, the awe-inspiring ravine of Gordale Scar and, on the slopes of Ingleborough Hill, the entrance to a cavern big enough to accommodate a cathedral. Mountain streams leap and thunder over crags to hurry through mellow stone villages. The Pennine railway climbs to a great viaduct whose 24 arches stand as a monument to the age of steam.

(1) Skipton to Kirkby Malham Leave Skipton on the A65 signposted to Settle and Kendal, following the valley of the River Aire. After 7 m., at Coniston Cold, take the right turn signposted to Bell Busk and Malham. After 1 m., at Bell Busk, turn right and then left over the bridge and continue on this road through Airton to the village of Kirkby Malham, home of a pioneer of the National Parks.

(2) Kirkby Malham to Malham Follow the road through the village, bear right at the junction on the outskirts and continue to Malham. The road descends steeply for 1 m. into the village of 18th-century farmhouses and cottages, close to Gordale Scar and Malham Cove.

(3) Malham to Stainforth Leave Malham on the road that bears left. It climbs steeply and offers views of Malham Cove on the right, and Ewe Moor on the left. At the top of the climb turn left at the crossroads. Keep straight on at the next junction, following the signpost to Stainforth. The limestone bulk of Pen-y-ghent begins to dominate the view to the right. After 1½ m. turn left at the junction and follow the road down to Stainforth. The road drops steeply into the village, which stands at the junction with the B6479.

(4) Stainforth to Horton in Ribblesdale Turn right on to the B6479 and follow the course of the River Ribble for about 4 m. into Horton in Ribblesdale, near the foot of Pen-y-ghent.

(5) Horton in Ribblesdale to Ribblehead Viaduct Leave Horton on the B6479 towards Selside. On the outskirts of Horton, the road bears sharply to the left and crosses the Ribble. After 3 m. it reaches Selside, where there is a path to the Alum Pot Cave on the left. Continue through Selside to the junction with the B6255 and turn left, following the signpost to Ingleton. Ribblehead Viaduct is immediately on the right. It can be reached by a path which begins just before the railway bridge.

(6) Ribblehead Viaduct to Ingleton Stay on the B6255, which is a Roman road, through Chapel le Dale towards Ingleton. After Chapel le Dale, Raven Scar and Ingleborough Hill, 2373 ft high, can be seen on the left. On the right, across the River Doe, are Scales Moor and the craggy slopes of Twisleton Scars and Whernside, 2419 ft. Continue past White Scar Cave, on the left, to Ingleton, where the road bears right before entering the town.

(7) Ingleton to Clapham Return along the B6255 signposted to Hawes. At the bend on the outskirts of Ingleton, take the right turn. The road runs beside Ingleborough Common and Ingleborough Hill for 4 m. to the village of Clapham at the junction with the A65, one of the prettiest of the Pennine villages and a centre for visits to several caves. There are five bridges over Clapham Beck, the most picturesque being 'Brokken Bridge'.

(8) Clapham to Settle Leave Clapham on the A65 signposted to Settle and Skipton. The road crosses Harden Bridge over Austwick Beck before climbing past Cave Hole on the left. In one of the caves in this system, bones have been found suggesting that the cave was a bears' den thousands of years ago. Prehistoric remains have also been discovered in the caves closer to Settle. Also on the left is the hamlet of Feizor, which stands on a track used by the monks of Fountains Abbey travelling to their estates in the Lake District. Descending steeply, the A65 passes to the right of the long and dramatic rock formation of Giggleswick Scar and drops down into the valley of the River Ribble. Cross the bridge into the town of Settle, whose houses are overshadowed by the 300 ft mass of Castleberg Crag, a limestone knoll which was once quarried by lime-burners.

(9) Settle to Skipton Leave Settle on the A65 signposted to Skipton, and follow the road for 16 m. down the broad valley of the Ribble to Long Preston, through Hellifield and Gargrave in the Aire Valley, to Skipton.

INFORMATION

Places of interest *Skipton:* Castle, weekdays, Sun. afternoons. Craven Museum, Apr. to Sept., weekdays except Tues., Sun. afternoons; Oct. to Mar., afternoons except Tues., all day Sat. George Leatt Industrial and Folk Museum (High Corn Mill), Sun. and Bank Hols., 12 noon-6 p.m.

Events *Settle:* Carnival day, June or July. Drama Festival, early summer. *Skipton:* Agricultural Show and Exhibition, Aug. Gala, June. Craven Drama Festival, Nov. Music Festival, Mar. Livestock market, Mon. and alternate Wed. *Ingleton:* Start of the Fellsman Hike (mountain walk), May.

Nature trail *Clapham:* Reginald Farrer Trail, 3–5 m., Easter to Oct., Trees, flora, limestone scenery, show cave. Leaflet available from National Park Information Centre, Clapham.

Information *Tourist Information:* Royal Baths Assembly Rooms, Harrogate (Harrogate 65912). Yorkshire Dales National Park Information Centres: *Clapham* (Tel. Clapham 419). *Malham:* Car park.

Towns with easy access to Skipton:

Bradford	19 m.	Leeds	25 m.
Harrogate	24 m.	Ripon	36 m.

RIBBLEHEAD VIADUCT
A 24-arch viaduct, opened in 1876, carries the Settle-Carlisle railway line across a section of the Pennines known as the 'Long Drag', because of its steep gradients. Just to the north of the viaduct, which rises to 165 ft, the line vanishes into a 2629 yd tunnel under Blea Moor, emerging at the head of the River Dee.

INGLETON
Deep, wooded dales, pitted with potholes and loud with the thunder of waterfalls, run northwards between the high moors overlooking Ingleton. The walk up Kingsdale, the western valley, gives views of Pecca Falls and Thornton Force, a 50 ft waterfall which sometimes freezes in winter. Ingleton is set in a valley at the foot of Ingleborough Hill, 2373 ft and topped by an Iron Age fort. Two miles beyond Ingleton is the White Scar Cave, whose attractions include two underground waterfalls. The cave extends for half a mile under Ingleborough Hill. The town itself was until quite recently an industrial community, and its houses reflect this.

Thornton Force
Pecca Falls
KIRKBY LONSDALE 6 MILES
Ingleton

Thornton Force, frozen in winter.

CLAPHAM
Grey stone houses stand in colourful gardens beside the stream in Clapham. A nature trail from the village leads to Ingleborough Cave with its massive stalactites and stalagmites, and then on to Gaping Gill, where a 365 ft waterfall plunges into a cavern as big as York Minster. Visitors can be winched down in spring and autumn, but exploring is dangerous without expert help.

Cottages by the stream, Clapham.

SCALE

0   1   2   3   4 MILES

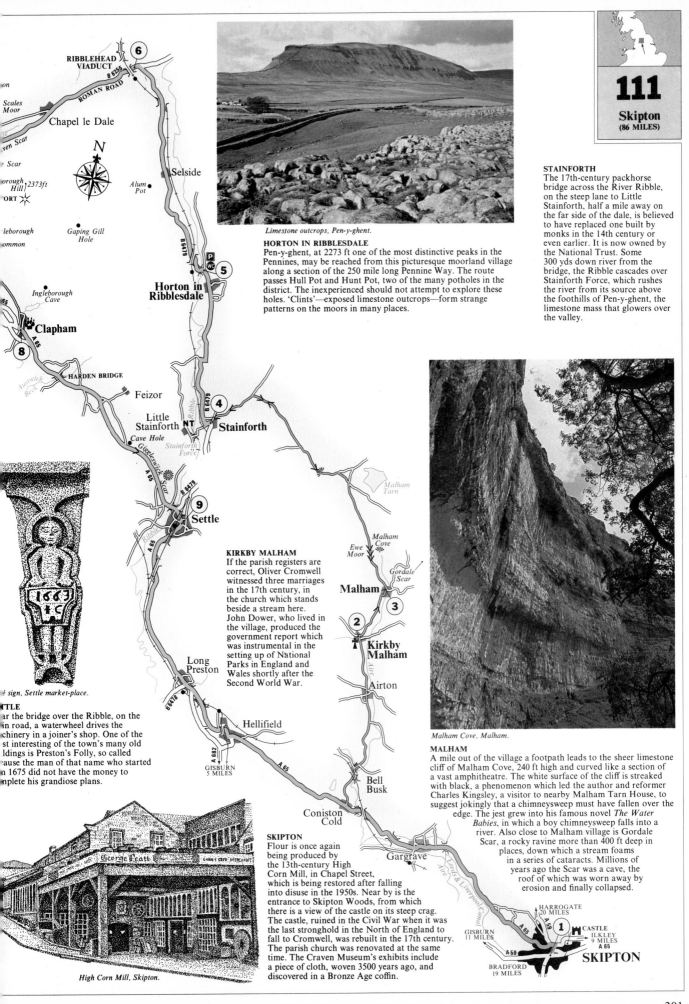

RIBBLEHEAD
VIADUCT
6

ROMAN ROAD

Scales
Moor

Chapel le Dale

ven Scar

Scar

orough 2373ft
Hill
ORT

leborough
ommon

Selside

Alum
Pot

Gaping Gill
Hole

B 6479

P
WC
5

Ingleborough
Cave

Clapham

8

HARDEN BRIDGE

Austwick
Beck

Feizor

Little
Stainforth
NT

Cave Hole

Giggleswick Scar

A 65

B 6479

4

Stainforth

Stainforth
Force

9

Settle

**Horton in
Ribblesdale**

Ribble

Malham
Tarn

Malham
Cove

Ewe
Moor

Gordale
Scar

Malham

3

KIRKBY MALHAM
If the parish registers are
correct, Oliver Cromwell
witnessed three marriages
in the 17th century, in
the church which stands
beside a stream here.
John Dower, who lived in
the village, produced the
government report which
was instrumental in the
setting up of National
Parks in England and
Wales shortly after the
Second World War.

Long
Preston

2

**Kirkby
Malham**

Airton

Aire

sign, Settle market-place.

TTLE
ar the bridge over the Ribble, on the
n road, a waterwheel drives the
chinery in a joiner's shop. One of the
st interesting of the town's many old
ldings is Preston's Folly, so called
ause the man of that name who started
n 1675 did not have the money to
nplete his grandiose plans.

B 6478

Hellifield

A 682

GISBURN
5 MILES

A 65

Bell
Busk

Coniston
Cold

SKIPTON
Flour is once again
being produced by
the 13th-century High
Corn Mill, in Chapel Street,
which is being restored after falling
into disuse in the 1950s. Near by is the
entrance to Skipton Woods, from which
there is a view of the castle on its steep crag.
The castle, ruined in the Civil War when it was
the last stronghold in the North of England to
fall to Cromwell, was rebuilt in the 17th century.
The parish church was renovated at the same
time. The Craven Museum's exhibits include
a piece of cloth, woven 3500 years ago, and
discovered in a Bronze Age coffin.

Gargrave

Leeds & Liverpool Canal

Aire

George Leatt

High Corn Mill, Skipton.

HARROGATE
20 MILES

GISBURN
11 MILES

A 65

A 59

1

CASTLE

ILKLEY
9 MILES

A 65

A 59

SKIPTON

BRADFORD
19 MILES

Limestone outcrops, Pen-y-ghent.

HORTON IN RIBBLESDALE
Pen-y-ghent, at 2273 ft one of the most distinctive peaks in the
Pennines, may be reached from this picturesque moorland village
along a section of the 250 mile long Pennine Way. The route
passes Hull Pot and Hunt Pot, two of the many potholes in the
district. The inexperienced should not attempt to explore these
holes. 'Clints'—exposed limestone outcrops—form strange
patterns on the moors in many places.

STAINFORTH
The 17th-century packhorse
bridge across the River Ribble,
on the steep lane to Little
Stainforth, half a mile away on
the far side of the dale, is believed
to have replaced one built by
monks in the 14th century or
even earlier. It is now owned by
the National Trust. Some
300 yds down river from the
bridge, the Ribble cascades over
Stainforth Force, which rushes
the river from its source above
the foothills of Pen-y-ghent, the
limestone mass that glowers over
the valley.

Malham Cove, Malham.

MALHAM
A mile out of the village a footpath leads to the sheer limestone
cliff of Malham Cove, 240 ft high and curved like a section of
a vast amphitheatre. The white surface of the cliff is streaked
with black, a phenomenon which led the author and reformer
Charles Kingsley, a visitor to nearby Malham Tarn House, to
suggest jokingly that a chimneysweep must have fallen over the
edge. The jest grew into his famous novel *The Water
Babies*, in which a boy chimneysweep falls into a
river. Also close to Malham village is Gordale
Scar, a rocky ravine more than 400 ft deep in
places, down which a stream foams
in a series of cataracts. Millions of
years ago the Scar was a cave, the
roof of which was worn away by
erosion and finally collapsed.

301

From Cromwell's war to the peace of Fountains Abbey

Included in this tour is the cave of a notorious witch who prophesied that the world would end in 1981. But first it starts out across the broad Vale of York and heads westwards beside the Civil War battlefield of Marston Moor. The village where Cromwell rested after the battle has been reconstructed to simulate a small French township, even to the inscription 'Hôtel de Ville' over the Town Hall. One of Britain's most majestic monastic ruins dozes in a peaceful wooded valley. And the traveller is invited to linger in an ancient market square where the official night watchman still blows his horn every evening.

(1) York to Knaresborough Leave the city on the A59 signposted Harrogate/ Knaresborough. After about 5 m. the road begins to skirt the northern fringe of Marston Moor, scene of one of the bloodiest battles in the Civil War. After the battlefield, the route continues through Green Hammerton and 4 m. later the road crosses the A1. Keep straight ahead on the A59, and after 3 m. enter Knaresborough.

(2) Knaresborough to Ripley Leave the town on the B6165 signposted to Pateley Bridge. After 5 m., at a roundabout, turn right on the A61 to enter Ripley.

(3) Ripley to Brimham Rocks Leave Ripley on the B6165 signposted to Pateley Bridge, with Ripley Park on the left. After 3 m., just beyond the village of Burnt Yates, take the right fork, signposted to Brimham Rocks. About 3 m. later there is a crossroads with wooded country ahead. Turn right and drive straight on for 1 m. to Brimham Rocks.

(4) Brimham Rocks to Fountains Abbey Keep ahead on the road, past the rocks, which after 1 m. drops down to meet the B6265 at Crossgates. Turn right here, following the signpost for Ripon. After just over 1 m. turn right again. A 1½ m. drive leads into Sawley. Turn right again at the T-junction in the village, following the signpost to Fountains Abbey. After 1 m. turn left at the T-junction, and left again at the next T-junction, still following the signposts to Fountains Abbey.

(5) Fountains Abbey to Ripon Follow the road over the river until it meets the B6265. Turn right here following the signpost to Ripon, which is reached after just under 3 m.

(6) Ripon to Newby Hall Leave the town on the B6265, following the signpost to Boroughbridge. After 1 m., just after crossing the River Ure, fork right on to the minor road signposted to Newby Hall/Skelton. In Skelton, where the through road turns left for Boroughbridge, keep straight on and almost immediately turn right. A 1 m. long drive leads through rolling parkland to Newby Hall, one of the masterpieces of Robert Adam.

(7) Newby Hall to Aldborough Return to Skelton and rejoin the through road, turning right towards Boroughbridge. After 1½ m. the road goes under the A1 and rejoins the B6265 at a T-junction. Turn right into Boroughbridge, an old market town which used to be an important staging post for the express coaches between London and Edinburgh. Between the town and the A1 on the right stand the Devil's Arrows, three enor-mous rocks erected in the Bronze Age—for what purpose is a mystery. Continue through Boroughbridge on the B6265, but on the edge of the town fork left following the signpost for Aldborough. After 1 m. fork right by Aldborough green for the Roman town.

(8) Aldborough to Beningbrough Hall Continue along the road from the Roman site until it rejoins the B6265 and turn left. After 3 m. turn left again following the signpost to Great Ouseburn. Drive through the village, and just beyond it turn left on to the road signposted to Aldwark. After 1 m., in Aldwark, cross the River Ure by the toll bridge and turn right almost immediately on to the road signposted to Linton-on-Ouse. Continue on to Newton-on-Ouse, and follow the road round to the left, signposted York, but almost immediately turn right on to the road signposted to Beningbrough Park.

(9) Beningbrough Hall to York Return through the park to the public road and turn right following the Shipton signposts. After 1½ m. turn right at the T-junction towards Shipton. Turn right again just after the road crosses a railway bridge on the approach to Shipton. At the A19 turn right again, following the signposts to York.

NATURE NOTES
There are several pools in the Vale of York which attract large numbers of wigeon, teal, pochard, tufted duck and swans. Many varieties of orchid, including the dark-red helleborine, flourish in the limestone areas south of Knaresborough, and pinks grow wild among the ruins of Fountains Abbey.

INFORMATION

Places of interest *Aldborough:* Roman town and museum, daily except Sun. mornings Oct. to Mar. *Beningbrough Hall:* Apr. to Oct., Wed. to Sun., Bank Hol. afternoons. Grounds 11 a.m.-6 p.m. *Fountains Abbey:* Daily. *Knaresborough Castle:* Easter to Sept., daily. Zoo, daily. *Newby Hall:* Easter to second Sun. in Oct., Wed., Thur., Sat., Sun. and Bank Hol. Mon., afternoons. Gardens only, Mon., Tues. and Fri., 11 a.m.-6 p.m. *Ripley Castle:* Easter Sun. and Mon., then May to Sept., Sun. and Bank Hols. (also gardens only, Sat.) afternoons. *Ripon:* Wakeman's House museum, daily except Wed.

Crafts *Ripon:* Littlethorpe Potteries, weekdays, appointments preferred for parties.

Events *Knaresborough:* Bed race, June. *Ripon:* Children's Festival, July. Fair, first week in Aug. St Wildrid's Feast, Aug.

Information Ripon Market Square (Tel. Ripon 4625). Dr Grey House, Exhibition Square, York (Tel. York 21756).

Towns with easy access to York:

Bridlington	41 m.	Hull	38 m.
Doncaster	34 m.	Leeds	24 m.

RIPON
An inscription on the town hall of this ancient city reminds the reader: 'Except ye Lord keep ye cittie, ye Wakeman waketh in vain.' The 13th-century Wakeman's House, official residence of the holder of the office, is in a corner of the market-place. It contains a small museum which records the history of centuries of Wakemen, who were appointed to guard the citizens' security. An official 'hornblower' perpetuates the custom of 'setting the watch' every evening by sounding a horn at 9 o'clock. The 90 ft high obelisk in the square, built in 1781, is a memorial to William Aislabie from nearby Studley Royal, who was Ripon's MP for 60 years in the 18th century. The cathedral, a short walk from the square, dates from the 12th century.

Wakeman's House, Ripon

Fountains Abbey.

FOUNTAINS ABBEY
Probably the loveliest of all ecclesiastical ruins in this country, the once-great Cistercian abbey is set in the wooded valley of the River Skell. With its guesthouses and infirmary, cellars and workshops—apart from the magnificent chapels and cloisters—it presents an exceptional opportunity to study the life of the monks who brought improved agricultural science and expertise in the wool industry to England in 1132. Fountains suffered the fate of the other abbeys under Henry VIII, but it is still well preserved.

SCALE

| 0 | 1 | 2 | 3 | 4 | 5 MILES |

NEWBY HALL
The lavishly decorated and furnished Newby Hall was built in the 18th century for Sir Edward Blackett, a mine-owner. It is approached by a drive through parkland and gardens sloping down to the River Ure. The statue near the end of the drive, commemorating Charles II's restoration, has a curious history. It came from Italy in 1675, was altered to its present form and mounted in London. Then it stood at Gautby, Lincs., before finally coming to rest at Newby in 1883. The statue on the right may be seen among the collection in the art gallery of the Hall.

Statue, Newby Hall.

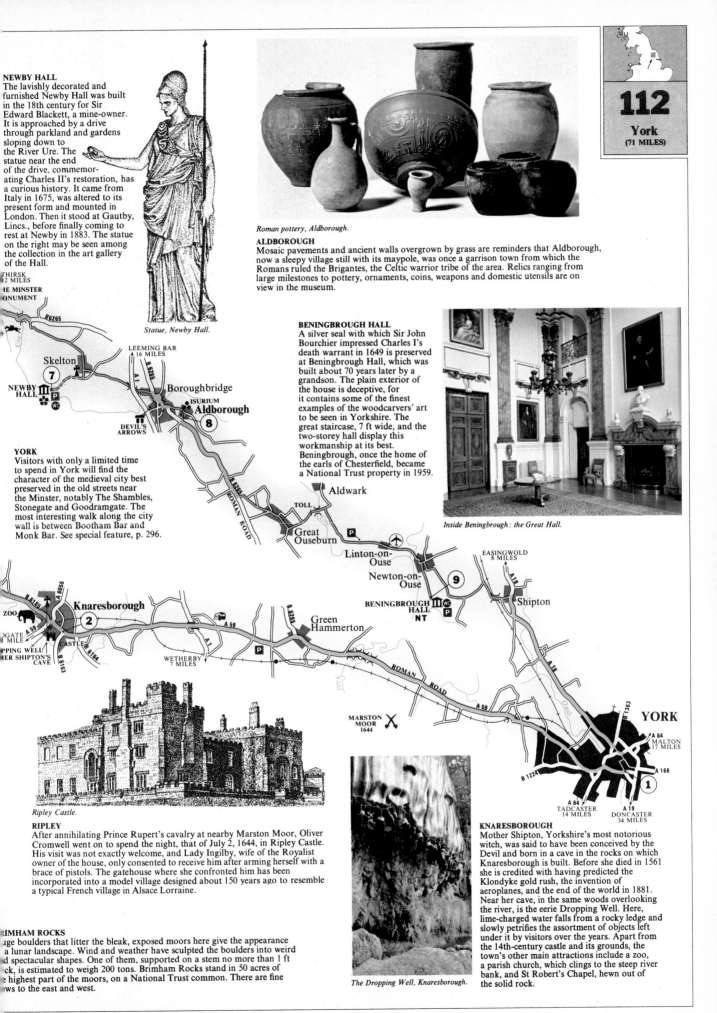

Roman pottery, Aldborough.

ALDBOROUGH
Mosaic pavements and ancient walls overgrown by grass are reminders that Aldborough, now a sleepy village still with its maypole, was once a garrison town from which the Romans ruled the Brigantes, the Celtic warrior tribe of the area. Relics ranging from large milestones to pottery, ornaments, coins, weapons and domestic utensils are on view in the museum.

BENINGBROUGH HALL
A silver seal with which Sir John Bourchier impressed Charles I's death warrant in 1649 is preserved at Beningbrough Hall, which was built about 70 years later by a grandson. The plain exterior of the house is deceptive, for it contains some of the finest examples of the woodcarvers' art to be seen in Yorkshire. The great staircase, 7 ft wide, and the two-storey hall display this workmanship at its best. Beningbrough, once the home of the earls of Chesterfield, became a National Trust property in 1959.

Inside Beningbrough: the Great Hall.

YORK
Visitors with only a limited time to spend in York will find the character of the medieval city best preserved in the old streets near the Minster, notably The Shambles, Stonegate and Goodramgate. The most interesting walk along the city wall is between Bootham Bar and Monk Bar. See special feature, p. 296.

Ripley Castle.

RIPLEY
After annihilating Prince Rupert's cavalry at nearby Marston Moor, Oliver Cromwell went on to spend the night, that of July 2, 1644, in Ripley Castle. His visit was not exactly welcome, and Lady Ingilby, wife of the Royalist owner of the house, only consented to receive him after arming herself with a brace of pistols. The gatehouse where she confronted him has been incorporated into a model village designed about 150 years ago to resemble a typical French village in Alsace Lorraine.

BRIMHAM ROCKS
Huge boulders that litter the bleak, exposed moors here give the appearance of a lunar landscape. Wind and weather have sculpted the boulders into weird and spectacular shapes. One of them, supported on a stem no more than 1 ft thick, is estimated to weigh 200 tons. Brimham Rocks stand in 50 acres of the highest part of the moors, on a National Trust common. There are fine views to the east and west.

The Dropping Well, Knaresborough.

KNARESBOROUGH
Mother Shipton, Yorkshire's most notorious witch, was said to have been conceived by the Devil and born in a cave in the rocks on which Knaresborough is built. Before she died in 1561 she is credited with having predicted the Klondyke gold rush, the invention of aeroplanes, and the end of the world in 1881. Near her cave, in the same woods overlooking the river, is the eerie Dropping Well. Here, lime-charged water falls from a rocky ledge and slowly petrifies the assortment of objects left under it by visitors over the years. Apart from the 14th-century castle and its grounds, the town's other main attractions include a zoo, a parish church, which clings to the steep river bank, and St Robert's Chapel, hewn out of the solid rock.

Over sheeplands of the wolds, where wolf packs hunted

Few areas of rural England have changed more in the past 200 years than the wolds of East Yorkshire. Wolf packs roamed the wolds until well into the 17th century, preying on the sheep that were virtually the farmers' only source of livelihood. In the next century the big landowners, led by Sir Christopher Sykes, began the task of taming the countryside and disciplining it into the orderly system of fertile fields and grazing lands that the tourist sees today. Highlights of this tour are visits to Sledmere, still the seat of the Sykes family, and nearby Burton Agnes Hall. After the 12th-century Kirkham Priory and a sprinkling of sheep-farming villages, the route meets the sea at Bridlington.

(1) Malton to Kirkham Priory Leave Malton on the A64 signposted to York. On the outskirts of the town fork right on to the Castle Howard Road. After nearly 5 m., just beyond Coneysthorpe, turn left at the crossroads. The entrance to Castle Howard is on the left, by an obelisk, 1 m. further on. (See p. 314.) At the crossroads, about 1 m. past the mansion, turn left. Go through Welburn, and at the A64 turn right. After 1 m. turn left on to the road signposted to Kirkham Abbey. Go straight over a crossroads, cross the River Derwent, and the ruins are on the right.

(2) Kirkham Priory to Sledmere Continue along the road to Westow. There turn right on to the road signposted to Leavening, but after just over 1 m. turn right at the T-junction on to the road signposted to Howsham. Go straight ahead at the crossroads immediately afterwards, and after ½ m. turn left, following the Leppington signpost. At the T-junction 1 m. later turn right. After ¾ m., and on the far side of Leppington, turn right, following the signpost to Bugthorpe. After 1 m. turn right on to the road signposted to Scrayingham and almost immediately turn left to follow the Bugthorpe signpost. In Bugthorpe, turn left and follow the signposts to Kirby Underdale. Follow the road to the left. At the T-junction turn right, and at the junction with the A166 turn left. After 4 m., just beyond Fridaythorpe, fork left on to the B1251 signposted to Sledmere, which is reached 5 m. later.

(3) Sledmere to Burton Agnes Leave the village on the B1253 signposted Bridlington. After 3 m. turn right, following the Langtoft signpost, and 400 yds later turn left, still following the Langtoft signpost. At the crossroads in Langtoft turn right on to the B1249, and on the far side of the village turn left, following the signpost to Kilham. After 2½ m. turn left into Kilham. Leave Kilham on the road signposted Rudston, but just beyond Kilham bear right, following the Bridlington signpost. At the A166 turn left, still towards Bridlington, to Burton Agnes.

(4) Burton Agnes to Rudston Leave the village on the minor road signposted to Rudston, which is reached after 2½ m.

(5) Rudston to Bridlington Leave the village on the B1253 signposted to Bridlington. After 4 m., on the outskirts of the town, turn right on to the A1038 for the harbour.

(6) Bridlington to Flamborough Head Leave the town on the B1255 signposted for Flamborough. After 3½ m., in the town, turn right on to Lighthouse Road (the B1259) which leads to Flamborough Head car park. The lighthouse on the headland is open to the public, except on Sundays.

(7) Flamborough Head to Weaverthorpe Return to Flamborough, turn left past the church and right on the B1229 signposted to Bempton. Carry on through Bempton to Buckton. There turn left into Pump Lane. At the T-junction soon afterwards turn left, go over the level crossing, then immediately turn right on to the road signposted to Grindale. Keep ahead, crossing the A165. At the T-junction turn right and stay on this road for 5 m., going through Grindale and Burton Fleming to the round barrow called Willy Howe. There the road turns sharp right. At the T-junction 400 yds later, turn left for Wold Newton. Go through the village, and 2 m. later at the crossroads with the B1249 keep straight ahead for 3 m. to Weaverthorpe.

(8) Weaverthorpe to Wharram Percy Continue through the village on the road for Helperthorpe and West Lutton. In West Lutton keep straight ahead on the road to Kirby Grindalythe and Duggleby. About 1 m. beyond Kirby, and just before Duggleby, fork left and go straight across the B1253 to Wharram le Street. At the junction with the B1248 turn left, following the Fimber signpost. Soon afterwards take the first right. About 1 m. later a footpath leads to Wharram Percy.

(9) Wharram Percy to Malton Return to the B1248, turn left and follow this road back through Wharram le Street and North Grimston to Malton.

INFORMATION

Places of interest *Bridlington:* The Bayle Museum, by appointment with Mrs K. J. Mellor, 35 St Johns Ave. (Tel. 77523). Sewerby Hall: Art Gallery, Easter to Sept. 29, daily, except Sat.; grounds, all year. *Burton Agnes Hall:* Easter Sun. and Mon.; May to mid-Oct., daily, except Sat. afternoons. *Kirkham Priory:* Weekdays, Sun. afternoons. *Malton:* Roman museum, Spring Bank Hol. to Sept., weekdays, Sun. afternoons; rest of year, afternoons. *Sledmere House:* Easter Sun. and Mon., Sun. only until mid-May; mid-May to Oct. 2, Tues. to Thur., Sat., Sun. and Bank Hol. Mon., 1.30-5.30 p.m.

Events *Bridlington:* International Dance Festival, June. *Malton:* Agricultural Show, July. Waterways Rally, Aug.

Information Information Centre, Garrison Street, Bridlington (Tel. Bridlington 3474).

Towns with easy access to Malton:

Hull	36 m.	Scarborough	24 m.
Pickering	8 m.	York	18 m.

Racehorses training near Malton.

MALTON
The twin towns of Malton and Norton, separated by the River Derwent, have long been associated with horseracing, and strings of thoroughbreds are often seen on the roads in the open countryside. The market town of Malton, on the southern edge of the Vale of Pickering, makes a good base from which to explore the Yorkshire wolds which roll down to the east coast. The Romans built a fort near the river towards the end of the 1st century. Relics of their occupation are displayed in the museum in the market square, which is built around a Norman church. The livestock pens, busy on market days, are behind the square. The Cross Keys Inn in Wheelgate has a medieval crypt.

Kirkham Priory.

KIRKHAM PRIORY
According to legend, the abbey was founded around 11__ by a judge, Walter l'Espee, as a memorial to his only so_ who was killed in a riding accident in this lovely part of the wooded Derwent Valley. The most striking featu__ of the ruins is the great gatehouse, emblazoned with carvings depicting St George and the Dragon and Davi_ and Goliath, which dates from the early 14th century. Flowering cherries blossom inside the walls in spring.

SCALE

0   1   2   3   4   5 MILES

HARRAM PERCY

roofless church is all that remains above ground
the 'lost' village of Wharram Percy, but recent
cavations have laid bare traces of other
ildings. This is the site of one of the hundreds
villages throughout the country that were
andoned in the Middle Ages and left to fall into
in. Just why this particular one suffered such a
te is not known for certain: the excavations
ve so far not yielded any decisive clue,
t they have revealed a short Anglo-Saxon nave
side the Norman church.

WEAVERTHORPE

The 12th-century parish church
of St Andrew is believed to
stand on the site of a Saxon
place of worship. A sundial
over the porch records that it
was built by Herbert of
Winchester. The church was
restored by G. E. Street in 1872
and has an iron pulpit. The
font is Norman, with an all-
over pattern of circles and
octagons. The remains of a
manor house were uncovered
when the churchyard was being
extended in 1960.

Flamborough Head.

FLAMBOROUGH HEAD

Riddled with caves and crowned by a lighthouse that stands 214 ft above the sea,
Flamborough Head is a sea-birds' paradise and one of the commanding clifftops of the east
coast. About 3000 years ago the headland was fortified by the building of a huge earthen
rampart which is still visible west of Flamborough village. Although it is known as the
Danes' Dyke, the Viking settlers did not land in the breakers below the cliffs until the
9th century. Then came the Normans, who have left their mark in the village church of
St Oswald, which is mainly 15th century but has a Norman font.

*Razorbill,
Flamborough cliffs.*

Library, Sledmere House.

RUDSTON

Britain's tallest prehistoric
standing stone—it is 25 ft 4 in.
high—towers above the graves
in the village churchyard. The
Rudston Monolith, as it is
known, is thought to have
stood there for at least 3000
years, and to have been
dragged from Cayton Bay which
is 10 miles away.

BRIDLINGTON

Miles of sands, sheltered from the north
winds by Flamborough Head, have
made Bridlington a popular holiday
resort. Just a few minutes' walk from
the harbour, the old town is sprinkled
with 17th-century buildings and
curiosity shops.

SLEDMERE

he Yorkshire wolds were almost a wasteland until
00 years ago. Then came Sir Christopher Sykes, a
an of vision and restless energy, who used his
ealth and organising ability not only to build his
ne home but also to transform the area around it
to the fertile farmland it is today. Generations of
he family have carried on the work: a grandson
ent £2 million on rebuilding and restoring local
hurches. The present Sledmere House replaces the
riginal, which was burnt down in 1911. The great
brary, 100 ft long, runs the length of the house,
hich is stocked with splendid furniture and relics
f bygone wars. The exotic decorations of the
urkish Room were copied from one of the sultan's
partments in Istanbul.

BURTON AGNES

A girl's skull, bricked up in a wall off the
staircase, is said to have laid the ghost of Anne
Griffiths which for years haunted Burton Agnes
Hall. Anne had expressed the dying wish that
her head should remain in her beloved home,
but she was buried outside. Her ghost is said
to have departed when the skull was exhumed
and taken indoors. Other features of the house
are the bow windows, the first of their kind in
England, and a collection of paintings by
Gauguin, Cézanne and Matisse. The village has
the remains of a Norman manor which preceded
the Elizabethan hall.

Gardens, Burton Agnes Hall.

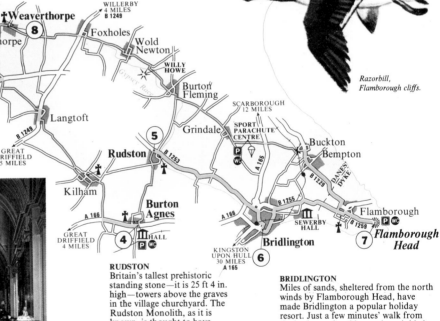

305

Swaledale, carved by ice and polished by water

Millions of years ago glaciers began grinding out the valleys that run westwards from the Vale of York. The ice melted and turned into cataracts and rivers, eternally scouring and polishing. This is how nature has created Swaledale, one of the loveliest of the Yorkshire dales. The tour begins in Richmond, where the Swale begins to slow down after its dash from the Pennines. The route then rises to Tan Hill, 1732 ft above sea level and site of the highest public house in England. The village of Bowes is the setting for Dickens's notorious Dotheboys Hall in Nicholas Nickleby. *Tourists will also see a 'coffin stone', where funeral bearers rested on their journey along Corpse Way.*

(1) Richmond to Hudswell Leave the centre of the town down steep New Road and Bridge Street, crossing the River Swale and climbing the hill on the far side. Turn first right on to the road signposted to Hudswell. The village is reached in just over 1 m.

(2) Hudswell to Grinton Continue through the village and follow the road across the moorland that is used as a training ground for soldiers from Catterick Camp. Go through Downholme, and on the far side of the village turn right on to the A6108 which drops into Swaledale. After 1 m. turn left on to the B6270, signposted to Reeth. The road winds through trees near the river to Grinton.

(3) Grinton to Gunnerside In Grinton turn left, then right, leaving the village by the lane that runs beside the church. The road shortly reaches moorlands and passes, on the left, a prehistoric earthwork, Maiden Castle, a rough hilltop circle. After 1 m. turn right and cross the River Swale. Turn left on to the B6270, signposted for Gunnerside. The road follows a straighter course than the Swale between Brownsey Moor to the north and Crackpot Moor to the south. After 3 m., enter the village of Gunnerside.

(4) Gunnerside to Ivelet Bridge In the village, follow the B6270 round to the left and cross the Swale. After 1 m. turn right on to an unsignposted lane leading to Ivelet Bridge—haunted, according to legend, by a headless dog.

(5) Ivelet Bridge to Muker Return to the B6270, turn right, and continue along the road as it follows the Swale between steeply rising moors for 1½ m., where the road does a sharp right and left turn to cross Muker Beck and enter Muker.

(6) Muker to Keld Leave Muker by continuing along the B6270, and after 1 m. pass through Thwaite. Follow the road as it skirts Kisdon hill, and after 2 m. turn right into the village of Keld, from which two waterfalls are within walking distance.

(7) Keld to Tan Hill Return to the B6270 and turn right, continuing up the valley for ¼ m. Take the first turn on the right and cross the River Swale again beside a series of small waterfalls. From here the road climbs quickly, twisting along the course of Stonesdale Beck. The road rapidly reaches the heights of Stonesdale Moor, running parallel with the Pennine Way long-distance footpath. After just over 3 m. it reaches Tan Hill.

(8) Tan Hill to Bowes At the T-junction by the Tan Hill Inn turn left, following the signpost for Kaber. After 4½ m. take the first turning on the right, following the signpost for Bowes. At the T-junction 1 m. further on, turn right again. Fork right after just under 1 m., then turn right again on to the A66 signposted to Scotch Corner. The road from here follows the road built between Penrith and Scotch Corner by the Romans, who found a direct way over difficult country which also avoided most of the streams feeding the River Greta. On the treeless slopes of Stainmore Forest, traces of Roman signal stations have been found near Bowes Moor Hotel and some 2 m. further on near Spital Park. Continue on the A66 into Bowes.

(9) Bowes to Richmond Leave the village on the A66 towards Scotch Corner, and after 3 m. turn right on to the road signposted Scargill/Reeth. After 1½ m. the road crosses the River Greta, and at the junction ¾ m. later keep right as the road starts to climb towards The Stang Forest. Beyond the forest the road re-enters the National Park on Hope Moor, before descending to a T-junction in Arkengarthdale. There turn left, following the signpost for Reeth. The road now runs beside Arkle Beck, flanked by steep slopes capped by 'battlements' of rock. In Reeth, turn left on to the B6270 and cross the river to Fremington. Here turn left on to the road signposted to Marske, which is reached after 4 m. This attractive village, with its handsome 17th-century church, is at the start of some of the richest scenery in Swaledale. Bear right at the village post office and follow the road back to Richmond.

INFORMATION

Places of interest *Bowes Castle:* All year, weekdays, Sun. afternoons. *Richmond:* Castle, all year, weekdays, Sun. afternoons (all day Sun. from Apr. to Sept.). Georgian Theatre, Easter weekend, May to end Sept., afternoons. The Green Howards museum, daily (except Sun., Nov. to end Mar.).

Events *Bowes:* Agricultural show, Sept. *Richmond:* Weekend of dancing, Apr. Biennial Festival, plays, concerts, art exhibitions, early summer in odd-numbered years. Harvest 'first fruits' ceremony, Sat. in Sept.

Information Friary Gardens, Queens Road, Richmond (Tel. Richmond 3525), or District Council Offices, Swale House, Frenchgate, Richmond (Tel. Richmond 4221).

Towns with easy access to Richmond:

Barnard Castle	15 m.	Middlesbrough	26 m.
Bishop Auckland	20 m.	Northallerton	15 m.
Darlington	12 m.	Ripon	27 m.

The May sheep market, Tan Hill.

TAN HILL
England's highest public house, the 18th-century Tan Hill Inn, stands 1732 ft up on Stonesdale Moor, with walls 3 ft thick to withstand the bitter winter winds that sweep across the moors. There is neither a village nor a house in sight, but the hill has been for centuries a crossing point of drovers' roads over the moors. Coal was mined in this area as early as the 13th century, and open-cast pits were worked late into the 1800s. Every May an important sheep sale is held beside the inn. The hardy breed of Swaledale sheep, tough enough to live and breed on the bleak Yorkshire moors in all weathers, is distinguished by black faces, grey mottled legs and horns well laid back. The thick, shaggy fleece is surprisingly soft to the touch.

MUKER
The village has lost five-sixths of its population since the decline of the lead mines about a century ago. The church was built in 1580, but was enlarged when the lead boom was at its peak in the early 19th century. Low stone cottages huddle together at the foot of Buttertubs Pass, rising to 1726 ft and linking Swaledale with Wensleydale. The buttertubs are vertical limestone potholes 60 ft to 80 ft in depth and fluted, rather like old-fashioned wooden buttertubs. There are almost 80 of these holes, scoured out by nature, near the pass. To the north, crossed by the Pennine Way long-distance footpath, Kisdon hill rises steeply to 1636 ft. At the foot of its eastern slopes a footpath, which leads to Keld, offers beautiful scenery beside the Swale. Muker village school has a memorial to two distinguished pupils—the brothers Cherry and Richard Kearton, who were born in Swaledale during the 1870s and made their name as naturalists and wildlife photographers.

Ivelet Bridge—haunted by a headless dog.

IVELET BRIDGE
Access to the hamlet of Ivelet is by a single-span, high-arched bridge beside a stream splashing down small waterfalls to the Swale. The 'coffin stone' at the northern end of the bridge is where the wicker coffins of people who had died up in the hills were placed, while the bearers rested on their long and exhausting journey.

SCALE

0   1   2   3   4   5 MILES

BOWES

A school run at Bowes by William Shaw in the 19th century was the model for the notorious Dotheboys Hall in *Nicholas Nickleby* by Charles Dickens. The school was closed shortly after the novel was published, and the building in which it was housed is now a café. In the local churchyard are the graves of both Shaw and 19-year-old George Taylor, a pupil at the school, and inspiration for Smike, the bullied cripple in the book, who was befriended by Nicholas. Stones from an old Roman fort were used in the building of both the church and the castle at Bowes. The 1187 castle keep, still standing, provides a view to the north-west of Mickle Fell which at 2591 ft is the highest peak in Yorkshire.

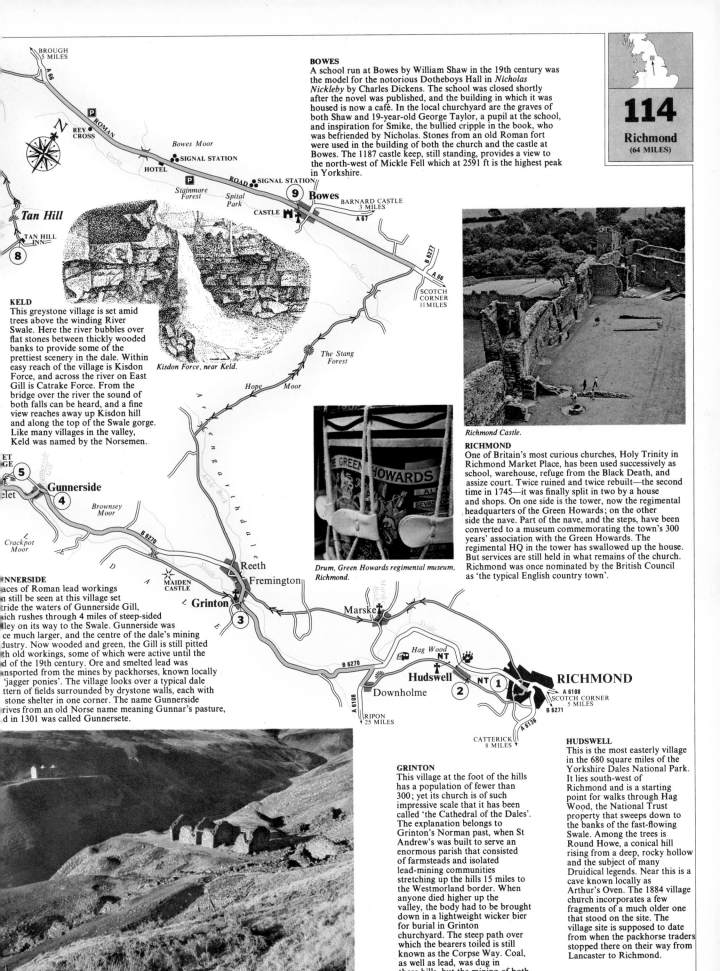

Kisdon Force, near Keld.

KELD

This greystone village is set amid trees above the winding River Swale. Here the river bubbles over flat stones between thickly wooded banks to provide some of the prettiest scenery in the dale. Within easy reach of the village is Kisdon Force, and across the river on East Gill is Catrake Force. From the bridge over the river the sound of both falls can be heard, and a fine view reaches away up Kisdon hill and along the top of the Swale gorge. Like many villages in the valley, Keld was named by the Norsemen.

Richmond Castle.

RICHMOND

One of Britain's most curious churches, Holy Trinity in Richmond Market Place, has been used successively as school, warehouse, refuge from the Black Death, and assize court. Twice ruined and twice rebuilt—the second time in 1745—it was finally split in two by a house and shops. On one side is the tower, now the regimental headquarters of the Green Howards; on the other side the nave. Part of the nave, and the steps, have been converted to a museum commemorating the town's 300 years' association with the Green Howards. The regimental HQ in the tower has swallowed up the house. But services are still held in what remains of the church. Richmond was once nominated by the British Council as 'the typical English country town'.

Drum, Green Howards regimental museum, Richmond.

GUNNERSIDE

Traces of Roman lead workings can still be seen at this village set astride the waters of Gunnerside Gill, which rushes through 4 miles of steep-sided valley on its way to the Swale. Gunnerside was once much larger, and the centre of the dale's mining industry. Now wooded and green, the Gill is still pitted with old workings, some of which were active until the end of the 19th century. Ore and smelted lead was transported from the mines by packhorses, known locally as 'jagger ponies'. The village looks over a typical dale pattern of fields surrounded by drystone walls, each with a stone shelter in one corner. The name Gunnerside derives from an old Norse name meaning Gunnar's pasture, and in 1301 was called Gunnersete.

...ined lead mines, Gunnerside Gill.

GRINTON

This village at the foot of the hills has a population of fewer than 300; yet its church is of such impressive scale that it has been called 'the Cathedral of the Dales'. The explanation belongs to Grinton's Norman past, when St Andrew's was built to serve an enormous parish that consisted of farmsteads and isolated lead-mining communities stretching up the hills 15 miles to the Westmorland border. When anyone died higher up the valley, the body had to be brought down in a lightweight wicker bier for burial in Grinton churchyard. The steep path over which the bearers toiled is still known as the Corpse Way. Coal, as well as lead, was dug in these hills, but the mining of both became uneconomic a century or so ago, and the area is littered with disused workings.

HUDSWELL

This is the most easterly village in the 680 square miles of the Yorkshire Dales National Park. It lies south-west of Richmond and is a starting point for walks through Hag Wood, the National Trust property that sweeps down to the banks of the fast-flowing Swale. Among the trees is Round Howe, a conical hill rising from a deep, rocky hollow and the subject of many Druidical legends. Near this is a cave known locally as Arthur's Oven. The 1884 village church incorporates a few fragments of a much older one that stood on the site. The village site is supposed to date from when the packhorse traders stopped there on their way from Lancaster to Richmond.

Waterfalls and cheese— the charms of Wensleydale

Old inhabitants of the scattered cottages and farmsteads between Bedale and Hawes still remember the doctor who, between the two world wars, used to do his daily rounds first on horseback and then on an ancient motor-bike. 'Will Pickles of Wensleydale' saw the isolation of his valley as an opportunity to study sickness and health from the viewpoint of a tightly knit community, and his discoveries about epidemic diseases made him one of the few family doctors ever to achieve worldwide acclaim. Though the motor-car has penetrated the remoteness of Wensleydale, it has not destroyed its charm, which is enhanced by roaring waterfalls and the ruins of once-mighty abbeys. Cheese fanciers will also appreciate the incomparable local product.

(1) Bedale to Wensley Leave Bedale on the A684 signposted to Leyburn, passing through the villages of Great Crakehall and Little Crakehall. Continue on the A684 for about 10 m. through Leyburn to Wensley.

(2) Wensley to Castle Bolton Turn right in Wensley from the A684 on to the road signposted to Preston, Redmire, Castle Bolton and Aysgarth Falls. After just under 4 m. in Redmire—a lead and coalmining village from the 17th to the 19th centuries—turn right on to the road signposted to Grinton. After ½ m. turn left at the signpost to Castle Bolton.

(3) Castle Bolton to Aysgarth Falls Follow the road through the village and round to the left. At the T-junction at the foot of the hill, turn right on to the road to Carperby and Askrigg. After 2¼ m., having passed through Carperby, turn left on to the road signposted to Aysgarth Falls. After 1 m., immediately after passing under a bridge, there is a car park for the falls. To reach the lower falls, walk along the road for a few yards to the signposted footpath. A single-arch bridge crosses the river just below the upper falls.

(4) Aysgarth Falls to Hardraw Force Continue down the road to its junction with the A684, turn right and go through Aysgarth village. Follow the A684 through Wensleydale, with its rock-rimmed hills and mellow farmhouses, for just under 5 m. to Bainbridge, dominated by Brough Hill, which has traces of a Roman fort on its summit. Bainbridge was once the centre of the Forest of Wensleydale. A hunting horn, kept at the Rose and Crown Inn, is still blown each winter evening from the village green—a ceremony which originated as a guide for travellers through the forest. From Bainbridge, continue on the A684 signposted to Hawes. After about 4 m., in Hawes, turn right on to the road signposted to Hardraw. After crossing the river turn left at the T-junction, and follow the signpost into Hardraw village. The path to the falls starts at the Green Dragon Inn.

(5) Hardraw Force to Hawes Return by the same route to Hawes. At the junction on the outskirts of the village turn right on to the A684 to the village centre.

(6) Hawes to Hubberholme Stay on the A684 and on the outskirts of the village before the junction with the B6255 turn left on to the road signposted to Gayle and Kettlewell. After 5 m. the road passes through Oughtershaw village in Upper Wharfedale

and follows the course of the Oughtershaw Beck, which plunges over a series of rocky ledges. After a further 4 m., turn left by the George Inn for Hubberholme church.

(7) Hubberholme to Kettlewell Bear right at the junction just beyond the church, and then turn right where the road joins the B6160. Continue down Wharfedale through Buckden and Starbotton to Kettlewell.

(8) Kettlewell to Middleham Turn left off the B6160 in Kettlewell and go straight ahead at the crossroads by the post office. Soon afterwards, turn left on to the road signposted to Leyburn. After climbing to 1652 ft, the road drops down to Coverdale and into the village of Carlton, where there is a Saxon burial mound beside the Foresters' Arms Inn. Continue beside the River Cover through Coverham to Middleham which, with its ruined castle, stands at the junction with the A6108.

(9) Middleham to Jervaulx Abbey Leave Middleham on the A6108 signposted to Masham. About 4 m. later, beyond East Witton, lie the ruins of Jervaulx Abbey.

(10) Jervaulx Abbey to Masham Return to the A6108 and turn left, following the signpost to Masham, 5 m. further on.

(11) Masham to Bedale Cross the River Ure on the way out of Masham, and immediately after the bridge turn left on to the road signposted to Bedale. Continue for 1 m., take the first right turn and continue for another ½ m. to the junction with the B6268. Turn left on to this road and follow it for 4 m. back to Bedale.

INFORMATION

Places of interest *Aysgarth:* Museum of horsedrawn transport, Easter to Nov., daily. *Bedale Hall:* Mar. to Sept., Tues., or by appointment. *Castle Bolton:* Tues. to Sun., including Bank Hol. weekends. *Jervaulx Abbey:* Daily. *Middleham Castle:* Weekdays, Sun. afternoons.

Event *Masham:* Traction Engine Rally, July.

Information Yorkshire Dales National Park Information Centre, Aysgarth (Tel. Aysgarth 424). *York:* Information Centre, De Grey House, Exhibition Square (Tel. York 21756).

Towns with easy access to Bedale:

Barnard Castle	. .28 m.	Richmond	. . . . . .12 m.
Darlington	. . . . .24 m.	Ripon	. . . . .12 m.
Durham	. . . . . . .39 m.	Stockton-on-Tees	30 m.
Northallerton	. . . 8 m.	Thirsk	. . . . .17 m.

Hardraw Force.

HARDRAW FORCE
Just as spectacular as the Aysgarth Falls, but in a different way, is Hardraw Force. A sheer drop of 98 ft makes it one of the highest unbroken waterfalls in England. Even so, in very severe winters it sometimes freezes to form a single, gigantic icicle. Buttertubs Pass, which gets its name from a series of deep limestone shafts, begins near the head of the falls, and links Wensleydale and Swaledale.

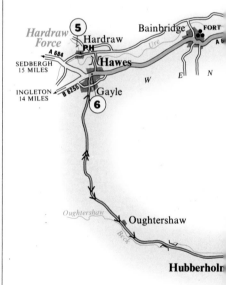

HAWES
Situated 800 ft above sea level, near several passes through the fells, the town has been a busy market centre for nearly 300 years. Each year more than 100,000 sheep, mostly of the local Swaledale breed, are sold there. Hawes is the main centre for making Wensleydale cheese; the local factory uses 7000 gallons of milk every day to produce 3 tons of pale, distinctive cheese, Yorkshire's contribution to the tables of the world.

HUBBERHOLME
The isolation of the little 12th-century church that stands 800 ft above sea level was underlined by a parson who wrote 200 years ago: 'In winter it is with great difficulty and danger that I pass over very high mountains and large drifts of snow to the chapel.' Winter hazards apart, the journey is an easy one for the modern tourist, who can take refreshment at an inn which used to be the vicarage.

SCALE
0 1 2 3 4 5 MILES

le Bolton.

CASTLE BOLTON
Perched high above Wensleydale, the 14th-century castle commands the valley which rises to the flat-topped mass of Pen Hill. The walls and towers have crumbled, but a section of the castle houses a public restaurant and a folk museum in which a Dales kitchen of 100 years ago has been reassembled. The castle was built by Richard Scrope, Lord Chancellor of England in the 14th century.

A lonely hill farm in Wensleydale.

WENSLEY
This village was once the most important town in the broad dale of that name. The size of the 13th-century church gives a hint of Wensley's importance up to 1563, when the plague struck and many survivors fled. The famous cheese is also named after the village.

three falls, Aysgarth.

SGARTH FALLS
e three sets of falls over which the River Ure bles at Aysgarth make a spectacle that has impressed erations of travellers. The church that stands within nd of the falls once served the whole of this part of nsleydale, and has a churchyard covering 5 acres.

BEDALE
The broad main street, flanked by cobblestone pavements and whitewashed houses, is packed each Tuesday with shoppers seeking bargains at the market stalls. Bedale has had its weekly market since 1251, and the street has been widened several times to cope with its growth. At the head of Market Place is St Gregory's Church, mentioned in the Domesday Book of 1085, and showing traces of even earlier architecture. The tower, built during the 14th century, had a portcullis and weapon store and served as a look-out post and stronghold against attacks by Scots raiders. Inside the church, a 13th-century fresco on the wall of the north aisle shows St George slaying the dragon. Opposite the church is Bedale Hall, a Georgian mansion which contains a small museum of domestic equipment and local craft exhibits.

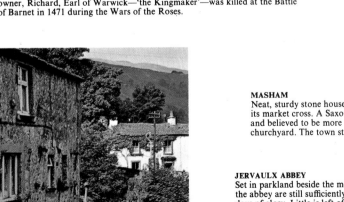
Middleham Castle.

MIDDLEHAM
Strings of racehorses can often be seen training in the rolling countryside around Middleham. The town is overlooked by the ruins of a massive 12th-century castle whose walls are up to 12 ft thick. The castle, once known as the Windsor of the North, became crown property after its owner, Richard, Earl of Warwick—'the Kingmaker'—was killed at the Battle of Barnet in 1471 during the Wars of the Roses.

Saxon pillar, Masham churchyard.

MASHAM
Neat, sturdy stone houses and shops flank the large square with its market cross. A Saxon pillar depicting Christ and His disciples, and believed to be more than 1000 years old, can be seen in the churchyard. The town stages a traction-engine rally in July.

River Wharfe, Kettlewell.

TTLEWELL
stling on the banks of the Upper harfe at the foot of 2300 ft Great ernside, the village is a popular base exploring Wharfedale, Littondale d the surrounding hills. Kettlewell s an Anglian settlement the 8th century; and after the rman Conquest formed part of the ates of the Percy family, ancestors of Dukes of Northumberland. e 12th-century font bears the rcy family crest.

JERVAULX ABBEY
Set in parkland beside the meandering River Ure, the remains of the abbey are still sufficiently well preserved to give an idea of its days of glory. Little is left of the abbey church, but much still exists of the adjacent monastery. Jervaulx was founded in 1168 by a group of Cistercian monks, who were said to have been guided to the site by a vision of the Virgin Mary. It was destroyed in 1538 during Henry VIII's Dissolution of the Monasteries.

Moors, wooden mice and doomwatch golfballs

This part of Yorkshire is a patchwork of appealing villages set in wooded valleys or on heather-clad moors. One of them is the birthplace of the church mouse that is the signature of craftsmen whose carved furniture still graces mansions and abbeys all over Britain. Moorland roads plunge steeply down to grassy valleys, zooming again to spectacular views over the heather. On the skyline across to the sea, drivers will see the huge 'golfballs' of the four-minute warning system on the Whitby Moors.

(1) Helmsley to Coxwold Leave Helmsley on the A170 signposted to Thirsk and after 4 m. turn left at the signpost for Wass, Byland Abbey and Coxwold. Follow the road through Wass to the ruins of the 12th-century Byland Abbey. Coxwold is reached 1¼ m. later.

(2) Coxwold to Kilburn Turn right in Coxwold on to the road signposted to Kilburn and then right again ½ m. after the church. Bear left soon afterwards and follow the road into the village of Kilburn.

(3) Kilburn to Sutton Bank Keep straight ahead through Kilburn and fork left at the first junction, following the signpost to White Horse Bank. Follow the zig-zagging lane steeply upwards to the car park and viewpoint near Sutton Bank.

(4) Sutton Bank to Rievaulx Abbey Follow the road on to the junction with the A170 and turn right. After ¾ m. turn left at the signpost for Rievaulx Abbey, and follow the road for 4 m. to the bridge over the River Rye. Immediately after the bridge, turn left along the wooded valley to Rievaulx Abbey.

(5) Rievaulx Abbey to Hasty Bank Continue along the same road, climbing steeply to the junction with the B1257. Turn left and follow the road through the beautiful valley of Bilsdale for 12 m. to Hasty Bank.

(6) Hasty Bank to Guisborough Follow the B1257 on through Great Broughton to a roundabout and turn right on to the A173 signposted to Guisborough. Follow the road into Great Ayton where the explorer, Captain Cook, spent much of his childhood. To visit Cook's old school, which is now a museum devoted to his memory, turn right just after the bridge. From the school follow the road on round to the junction with the A173 and turn right to continue on the route. The A173 passes the strangely shaped hill and splendid viewpoint known as Roseberry Topping before approaching Guisborough. On the outskirts, turn right along the broad cobbled street to the church and priory.

(7) Guisborough to Lastingham Leave Guisborough on the A171 signposted to Whitby. Follow the road up on to Stanghow Moor, and immediately after Lockwood Beck Reservoir turn right on to the road signposted Castleton. In Castleton, turn left and follow the valley road to Danby. Here turn right, following the signpost for Ainthorpe. Recross the river and at the fork go left, following the signpost for Fryup. After 3 m. turn left at the junction shaded by trees, and then take the first turning right, dropping into Great Fryup Dale. At the T-junction on the

other side of the valley turn right, following the signpost to Dale Head only, but after 200 yds turn sharp left uphill. This steep climb soon flattens out on to moors, where there is another T-junction. Turn right here, following the signpost for Rosedale. Follow the moorland road past shooting butts, old mine workings and, far away to the left, the huge white 'golfballs' of the Fylingdales BMEWS (Ballistic Missile Early Warning System) station. After 4 m., turn right at the T-junction, and follow the road for 3 m. down to Rosedale Abbey, a village named after a 12th-century nunnery, fragments of which remain near the church. Turn left in the village and follow the wooded valley of the River Seven for 5 m. before turning right at the signpost for Lastingham. After ½ m. cross the river and turn right again for Lastingham.

(8) Lastingham to Hutton-le-Hole Leave Lastingham on the road signposted to Hutton-le-Hole. Turn right soon after leaving the village and follow the road round into Hutton-le-Hole.

(9) Hutton-le-Hole to St Gregory's Minster Turn left in Hutton-le-Hole and follow the road for 2½ m. to the junction with the A170. Turn right and follow the road past Kirkbymoorside. About 1 m. after the Kirkbymoorside roundabout, turn right on to the road signposted to St Gregory's Minster. Go straight on at the crossroads. Just after the ford turn right into the lane leading to St Gregory's Minster.

(10) St Gregory's Minster to Helmsley Return down the lane and turn right. At the junction with the A170 keep straight ahead, following the signpost for Helmsley.

INFORMATION

Places of interest *Byland Abbey:* Daily, Sun. afternoons. *Great Ayton:* Capt. Cook Schoolroom Museum, Tues., Sat.; also Sun., Apr. to Oct. *Helmsley:* Castle, daily, Sun. afternoons. *Hutton-le-Hole:* Ryedale Folk Museum, Easter to end of Sept., afternoons; mid-July to end of Aug., 11 a.m.-6 p.m. *Rievaulx Terrace:* Apr. to Oct., Tues. to Sat., Spring and Summer Bank Hol. Mon., 10 a.m.-6 p.m., Sun., 1-6 p.m. *Shandy Hall:* June to Sept., Wed. afternoons.

Crafts *Coxwold Pottery:* Weekdays, some weekends. *Kilburn:* Robert Thompson's Craftsmen Ltd, furniture, carved figures, etc., Mon. to Sat., mornings.

Events *Kilburn Feast:* Sat. after July 6. *Stokesly:* Agricultural show, Sept.

Information Yorkshire Tourist Board, 312 Tadcaster Road, York (Tel. York 67961).

Towns with easy access to Helmsley:

Malton	16 m.	Thirsk	14 m.
Pickering	13 m.	York	24 m.

Rievaulx Abbey.

RIEVAULX
Yorkshire's first Cistercian abbey was built in the wooded Rye Valley in 1131 by 12 monks sent from France by St Bernard of Clairvaux. Rievaulx grew quickly, and by 1170 housed 140 monks and more than 500 lay brothers. From 1300 onwards it declined, and when the monasteries were dissolved in 1539 there were only 22 monks. The most striking ruin is the 13th-century choir, an exceptional example of English Gothic architecture. Behind the abbey is the National Trust preserve of Rievaulx Terrace, which was landscaped in the 18th century to provide views from Duncombe Park, then the home of the Earl of Feversham. The ends of the terrace are marked by 18th-century replicas of Greek temples, and the walk in between has many good vantage points. The temples are at either end of a stretch of greensward nearly half a mile long. The north temple, in the Ionic style, has a deep portico above a flight of stairs and a room with a coved ceiling. The other temple, which is round and Doric, has a floor of 13th-century tiling.

Glider over Sutton Bank and Kilburn White Horse.

SUTTON BANK
The White Horse at Sutton Bank, a spectacular escarpment of the Hambleton Hills, was carved by Kilburn's schoolmaster and his pupils in 1857. It is 228 ft high, 314 ft long and can be seen from Leeds, 40 miles away, on a clear day. From the car park beneath it there are views over the Vale of York. Gliders launched from the top of the slope soar over the fields below.

SCALE

0   1   2   3   4   5 MILES

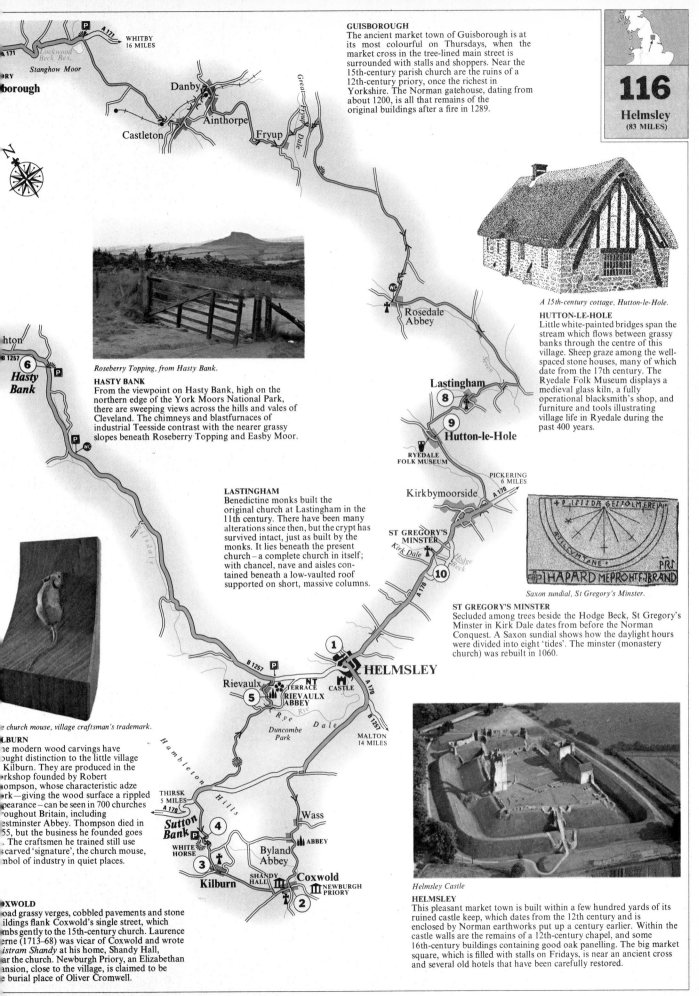

GUISBOROUGH

The ancient market town of Guisborough is at its most colourful on Thursdays, when the market cross in the tree-lined main street is surrounded with stalls and shoppers. Near the 15th-century parish church are the ruins of a 12th-century priory, once the richest in Yorkshire. The Norman gatehouse, dating from about 1200, is all that remains of the original buildings after a fire in 1289.

A 15th-century cottage, Hutton-le-Hole.

HUTTON-LE-HOLE

Little white-painted bridges span the stream which flows between grassy banks through the centre of this village. Sheep graze among the well-spaced stone houses, many of which date from the 17th century. The Ryedale Folk Museum displays a medieval glass kiln, a fully operational blacksmith's shop, and furniture and tools illustrating village life in Ryedale during the past 400 years.

Roseberry Topping, from Hasty Bank.

HASTY BANK

From the viewpoint on Hasty Bank, high on the northern edge of the York Moors National Park, there are sweeping views across the hills and vales of Cleveland. The chimneys and blastfurnaces of industrial Teesside contrast with the nearer grassy slopes beneath Roseberry Topping and Easby Moor.

LASTINGHAM

Benedictine monks built the original church at Lastingham in the 11th century. There have been many alterations since then, but the crypt has survived intact, just as built by the monks. It lies beneath the present church – a complete church in itself; with chancel, nave and aisles contained beneath a low-vaulted roof supported on short, massive columns.

Saxon sundial, St Gregory's Minster.

ST GREGORY'S MINSTER

Secluded among trees beside the Hodge Beck, St Gregory's Minster in Kirk Dale dates from before the Norman Conquest. A Saxon sundial shows how the daylight hours were divided into eight 'tides'. The minster (monastery church) was rebuilt in 1060.

e church mouse, village craftsman's trademark.

ILBURN

he modern wood carvings have ought distinction to the little village Kilburn. They are produced in the rkshop founded by Robert ompson, whose characteristic adze rk – giving the wood surface a rippled pearance – can be seen in 700 churches roughout Britain, including estminster Abbey. Thompson died in 55, but the business he founded goes . The craftsmen he trained still use carved 'signature', the church mouse, mbol of industry in quiet places.

Helmsley Castle

HELMSLEY

This pleasant market town is built within a few hundred yards of its ruined castle keep, which dates from the 12th century and is enclosed by Norman earthworks put up a century earlier. Within the castle walls are the remains of a 12th-century chapel, and some 16th-century buildings containing good oak panelling. The big market square, which is filled with stalls on Fridays, is near an ancient cross and several old hotels that have been carefully restored.

OXWOLD

oad grassy verges, cobbled pavements and stone ildings flank Coxwold's single street, which mbs gently to the 15th-century church. Laurence erne (1713–68) was vicar of Coxwold and wrote istram Shandy at his home, Shandy Hall, ar the church. Newburgh Priory, an Elizabethan ansion, close to the village, is claimed to be e burial place of Oliver Cromwell.

Captain Cook's coast and the North Yorkshire Moors

The tour plunges immediately into the North Yorkshire Moors, where villages lie tucked between the folds of heather-covered hills. At Staithes, the route pivots to follow the coastline south. Cliffs shelter Whitby, where a grocer's boy ran away to sea to win fame as the world navigator and explorer Captain Cook. Robin Hood's Bay huddles so close to the sea that a storm once tossed a ship into a harbourside inn. At Hackness the tour turns back towards the moors and returns to Pickering by way of a forest drive.

(1) Pickering to Mauley Cross Leave Pickering northwards on the road signposted to Newton-on-Rawcliffe. Follow the road up the valley through Newton and Stape to the Forestry Commission woodlands on Pickering Moor. Mauley Cross is on the right, ¾ m. after Stape.

(2) Mauley Cross to Wade's Causeway Follow the road on over the moors. It ceases to be tar-sealed for 2 m., but the surface is reasonable. Where the tarmac begins again just after a bridge, Wade's Causeway, part of a particularly well-preserved Roman highway, crosses the road.

(3) Wade's Causeway to Grosmont Continue along the same road. (To visit some old burial mounds, turn left after 3 m. by a stone with a square hole carved in it, and follow a rough track for a short distance. Return to the road and turn left.) Bear right at the junction after 1½ m., and go right again at the crossroads after another ½ m. Follow the road for 3 m. to Goathland, where moorland sheep crop the village green, and bear left by the Mallyan Hotel. Soon afterwards turn left and follow the signs to Beck Hole in its wooded valley. After the village, the road climbs steeply back on to the moors. Turn left at the T-junction and left again at the junction with the A169, following the Whitby signpost. Soon afterwards turn left again at the signpost to Grosmont.

(4) Grosmont to Staithes Leave Grosmont on the same road and follow it to Egton. Here fork left, following the signpost for Guisborough. After 2 m. turn left at the junction with the A171, and follow the road for 4 m. Turn right at the signpost to Roxby and Staithes, shortly after the B1266 comes in from the right. Follow the road through Roxby to the junction with the A174. Here, turn right and then immediately left and into Staithes. The cobbled streets are so steep and narrow that it is best to park at the top of the hill and walk down to the sea front.

(5) Staithes to Runswick Bay Return to the A174 and turn left, following the signpost for Whitby. After 1½ m., in Hinderwell, fork left through Runswick to Runswick Bay.

(6) Runswick Bay to Whitby After climbing the steep hill from the bay, turn left in the village on to the road signposted to Ellerby. Turn left on to the A174 and follow it through Lythe and Sandsend to Whitby.

(7) Whitby to Robin Hood's Bay Leave Whitby on the A171 signposted to Scarborough. After 3 m. turn left, in High Hawsker, on to the B1447 signposted to Robin Hood's Bay. As at Staithes, it is best to leave the car at the top of the hill, where there is a car park and toilets, and walk about a quarter of a mile to the little harbour.

(8) Robin Hood's Bay to Hackness Turn left on leaving the village, following the road through Fyling Thorpe to the junction with the A171, and turn left. After 5 m., just after the start of the extensive woodland on the right, turn right at the signpost for Harwood Dale. Keep straight ahead at the next junction, signposted to Silpho and Hackness, and climb steeply to more woodlands and the start of the Silpho Forest Nature Trail. After 1 m. turn right and right again shortly afterwards. Follow the road through Silpho to Hackness.

(9) Hackness to Thornton Dale Turn right at the T-junction in Hackness and follow the road out of the village. After 2 m. fork left at the sign for Bickley, and after another 3 m. turn left by a red-brick bungalow, following the signpost marked to Forest Drive. Soon afterwards there is a toll gate. Follow the road through the woods to High Staindale, where a path leads off to the Bride Stones—huge rocks carved into odd shapes by erosion. Continue through the foresters' village of High Dalby and on to Low Dalby. Here, turn right on to the road signposted to Thornton Dale. Turn left at the next junction and follow the road into Thornton Dale.

(10) Thornton Dale to Pickering Leave Thornton Dale on the A170 signposted to Pickering, which is reached after 2 m.

INFORMATION

Places of interest *Grosmont:* North York Moors Railway, most days, Easter to Oct. *Pickering:* Beck Isle Museum, May to Oct., afternoons. Castle, daily, Sun. afternoons. Museum and Arts Centre, Sat., Sun., Mon., Thur. in summer, afternoons. *Whitby:* Abbey, May to Sept., daily, Oct. to Apr., weekdays, Sun. afternoons. Museum, May to Sept., weekdays, Sun. afternoons; Oct. to Apr., Mon., Tues., Thurs., Fri. mornings, all Wed. and Sat., Sun. afternoons.

Nature trails *Newton Dale Forest Trail:* 3 m. Managed woodland, historical interest, wildlife. *Silpho:* Pickering Forest, 1¾–3 m. Guides from Forestry Commission, Pickering.

Events *Egton:* Gooseberry Show, Aug. *Sneaton and Hawsker:* Agricultural Show, July. *Thornton Dale:* Agricultural Show, Aug. *Whitby:* Folk Festival, Flower Show, Agricultural Show, Regatta, Aug.

Information Information Kiosk, New Quay Road, Whitby (Tel. Whitby 2674). Tourist Information Centre, St Nicholas Cliff, Scarborough (Tel. Scarborough 72261).

Towns with easy access to Pickering:

Helmsley . . . . 13 m.	Whitby . . . . 21 m.
Scarborough . . . . 17 m.	York . . . . 26 m.

Steam locomotive, North York Moors Railway.

GROSMONT
The North York Moors Railway, which runs from Pickering to Grosmont (pronounced 'Gro-mont'), was opened in 1836. Carriages were horse-drawn until steam engines were introduced 11 years later. The line was closed by British Railways in 1965, and reopened eight years later. The 18 mile ride is a good way to enjoy some of the finest moors scenery.

MAULEY CROSS
The many medieval stone crosses on the North Yorkshire Moors are thought to have been boundary stones or landmarks. This one probably marked the boundary of the estates owned by the De Mauley family of Mulgrave Castle. It is now the starting point of a forest drive and nature trail which run east to Newton Dale.

Mural, Pickering church.

PICKERING
Gateway to the moors and one of the oldest market towns in Britain, Pickering was founded by the Celtic King Peredurus about 270 BC. At its centre is the large 12th-century church decorated with 500-year-old wall paintings. Scenes depicted include St George and the dragon, Salome dancing for King Herod, and the murder of St Thomas Becket. The castle, now a ruin, dates from the 12th century and was frequently used as a hunting lodge by medieval kings. The town's many old inns include the Black Swan, which used to stage plays and cockfights in its yard. Beyond the river is Pickering Vale Museum and Arts Centre, a voluntary venture opened in 1967.

Pickering Castle from the air.

SCALE
0   1   2   3   4   5 MILES

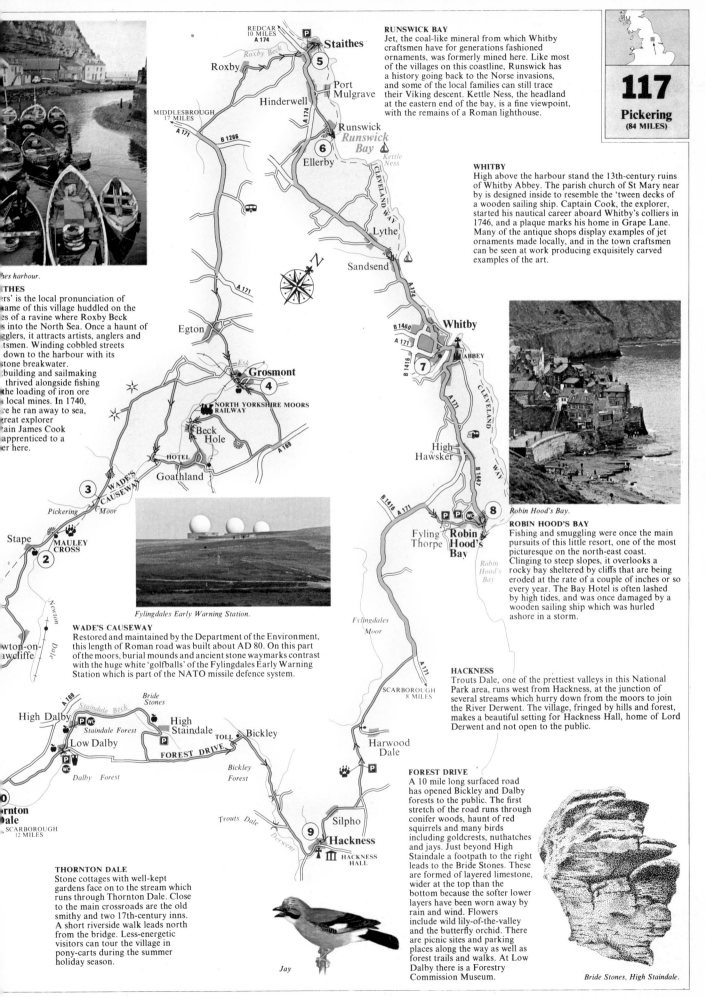

RUNSWICK BAY
Jet, the coal-like mineral from which Whitby craftsmen have for generations fashioned ornaments, was formerly mined here. Like most of the villages on this coastline, Runswick has a history going back to the Norse invasions, and some of the local families can still trace their Viking descent. Kettle Ness, the headland at the eastern end of the bay, is a fine viewpoint, with the remains of a Roman lighthouse.

WHITBY
High above the harbour stand the 13th-century ruins of Whitby Abbey. The parish church of St Mary near by is designed inside to resemble the 'tween decks of a wooden sailing ship. Captain Cook, the explorer, started his nautical career aboard Whitby's colliers in 1746, and a plaque marks his home in Grape Lane. Many of the antique shops display examples of jet ornaments made locally, and in the town craftsmen can be seen at work producing exquisitely carved examples of the art.

Robin Hood's Bay.

ROBIN HOOD'S BAY
Fishing and smuggling were once the main pursuits of this little resort, one of the most picturesque on the north-east coast. Clinging to steep slopes, it overlooks a rocky bay sheltered by cliffs that are being eroded at the rate of a couple of inches or so every year. The Bay Hotel is often lashed by high tides, and was once damaged by a wooden sailing ship which was hurled ashore in a storm.

HACKNESS
Trouts Dale, one of the prettiest valleys in this National Park area, runs west from Hackness, at the junction of several streams which hurry down from the moors to join the River Derwent. The village, fringed by hills and forest, makes a beautiful setting for Hackness Hall, home of Lord Derwent and not open to the public.

Fylingdales Early Warning Station.

WADE'S CAUSEWAY
Restored and maintained by the Department of the Environment, this length of Roman road was built about AD 80. On this part of the moors, burial mounds and ancient stone waymarks contrast with the huge white 'golfballs' of the Fylingdales Early Warning Station which is part of the NATO missile defence system.

FOREST DRIVE
A 10 mile long surfaced road has opened Bickley and Dalby forests to the public. The first stretch of the road runs through conifer woods, haunt of red squirrels and many birds including goldcrests, nuthatches and jays. Just beyond High Staindale a footpath to the right leads to the Bride Stones. These are formed of layered limestone, wider at the top than the bottom because the softer lower layers have been worn away by rain and wind. Flowers include wild lily-of-the-valley and the butterfly orchid. There are picnic sites and parking places along the way as well as forest trails and walks. At Low Dalby there is a Forestry Commission Museum.

THORNTON DALE
Stone cottages with well-kept gardens face on to the stream which runs through Thornton Dale. Close to the main crossroads are the old smithy and two 17th-century inns. A short riverside walk leads north from the bridge. Less-energetic visitors can tour the village in pony-carts during the summer holiday season.

Jay

Bride Stones, High Staindale.

...hes harbour.

...ITHES
...rs' is the local pronunciation of ...ame of this village huddled on the ...es of a ravine where Roxby Beck ...s into the North Sea. Once a haunt of ...gglers, it attracts artists, anglers and ...tsmen. Winding cobbled streets ...down to the harbour with its ...stone breakwater. ...building and sailmaking ...thrived alongside fishing ...the loading of iron ore ...local mines. In 1740, ...e he ran away to sea, ...great explorer ...ain James Cook ...apprenticed to a ...er here.

Map labels: REDCAR 10 MILES, A 174, Roxby Beck, Staithes, Roxby, Port Mulgrave, Hinderwell, MIDDLESBROUGH 17 MILES, A 171, B 1266, A 174, Runswick, Runswick Bay, Ellerby, Kettle Ness, CLEVELAND WAY, Lythe, Sandsend, A 171, Egton, Esk, Grosmont, NORTH YORKSHIRE MOORS RAILWAY, Beck Hole, HOTEL, Goathland, WADE'S CAUSEWAY, Pickering Moor, Stape, MAULEY CROSS, Newton Dale, ...wton-on-...awcliffe, A 169, Staindale Beck, Bride Stones, High Dalby, Staindale Forest, High Staindale, Low Dalby, Dalby Forest, TOLL, Bickley, FOREST DRIVE, Bickley Forest, ...rnton ...ale, SCARBOROUGH 12 MILES, Trouts Dale, Derwent, Silpho, Hackness, HACKNESS HALL, Harwood Dale, SCARBOROUGH 8 MILES, Fylingdales Moor, A 171, Fyling Thorpe, Robin Hood's Bay, Robin Hood's Bay, WC, B 1416, A 171, High Hawsker, B 1447, CLEVELAND WAY, B 1416, A 171, ABBEY, Whitby, A 171, B 1460, B 1416

CASTLE HOWARD

The work of Sir John Vanbrugh, an inspired amateur, and of Nicholas Hawksmoor, an assistant of Wren, Castle Howard near Malton in Yorkshire has been the palatial home of the Howard family since the 18th century. Then, the young Earl of Carlisle determined to create a home for his family that would rival any in the land. George Howard, the present owner, tells in this interview of his struggle to preserve his inheritance in all its splendour—a struggle against age, nature and a disastrous fire.

It is curious being brought up in a vast house like Castle Howard. If you grow up in a place like this, you do not think of it as enormous and historic. It is just home. I can remember the actual moment when, as a boy of 14, I became aware that the house was something more than this. From then on, I was determined to preserve it in all its beauty.

At one time, this looked like being impossible. At the start of the Second World War a girls' school was evacuated here from Scarborough, and while it was in occupation there was a disastrous fire. The chief victim was the beautiful High Saloon. It had walls decorated by Pellegrini and rococo plaster. Its destruction was a tragic loss.

I was at Richmond—the regimental depot of the Green Howards—at the time and raced over at once. What I remember most was the smell—that acrid burning that gets right into your lungs. It was an awful sight. Later during the war, the trustees of the estate would have sold Castle Howard and the estate to the school if the price had been right. Thank goodness it was not!

The school did not leave until 1949—the year of my marriage. I was determined to move back. Everyone believed we were mad. It was a disheartening prospect—an empty house, part of which had been destroyed by fire and the remainder not redecorated for years. Things were very difficult at first, but we gradually managed to make the rooms habitable. Then we started the detailed work of restoration.

Over the years I have tackled this work at two levels. Features such as the dome, which had been destroyed in the fire, were expensive but gratifying to rebuild. However, it is even more expensive and time-consuming to deal with less obvious tasks, which most people never notice.

Searching for stone

Chief among them was repair of the stonework. Castle Howard was built according to the very best 18th-century practice when every stone was 'cramped'—squeezed to fit tightly against its neighbours with an iron cramp.

The stone used is curious. It is sandy limestone, soft enough to be able to scratch with a thumbnail. But after it has been in position for about six months it grows a protective skin as its salts crystallise on the outside. Unless it is damaged by frost or hit sharply, it retains its great clarity and sharpness of outline.

But once the surface skin is destroyed, the stone starts to crumble away. When I examine a façade today, I find that one stone in six has usually to be repaired. Even after years of work, we have managed to replace only a third of the damaged stone. One of the chief problems is finding suitable stone for the refacing. We have tried getting stone from the

quarry which was originally used but, for some reason, it has not been satisfactory. We have a quarry on the estate, but the stone from there is not suitable either. So we ended up getting stone from 100 miles away.

What strikes me most about the house is its originality. This is not surprising when you think that it was the first building to be designed by Sir John Vanbrugh. He was a soldier and playwright, who 'hugely turned to architecture' largely for the fun of it. But, of course, he had the help of Nicholas Hawksmoor, Wren's chief assistant. Between them they created Castle Howard.

The way the commission came about was in itself curious. My ancestor, Charles Howard, the 3rd Earl of Carlisle, had originally commissioned William Talman, the designer of Chatsworth, to build his house. But the two men quarrelled about money and the scheme fell through. Instead of looking for another established architect, Carlisle turned to Vanbrugh, whom he had met at meetings of the Kit Cat Club. On the strength of a few rough drawings, he was given his great opportunity.

A masterpiece of originality

Take the Hall, for example. It is a large room, 70 ft high and 52 ft square. But despite its size, it is a very light-hearted conception. Nobody had ever put a dome on an English house before. Nobody had ever painted walls and ceilings in this way, or had an entrance to a garden front like this. Nobody had ever thought of putting staircases at either side of the main hall with pierced walls rather like the transepts in a cathedral. Scagliola—a mixture of hard plaster and marble chips—was also used here for the first time.

Apart from the Hall and the Long Gallery in the West Wing, most of the rooms are relatively small. The house is not in the least oppressive. Most people, I think, find there is a pleasant atmosphere. No one has ever suggested there are any ghosts about!

When I came to reorganise the house after we reopened it, one of the first rooms I restored was the Long Gallery. In fact, this was not designed by Vanbrugh, but by Charles Heathcote Tatham between 1805 and 1810. The room had been much altered by my grandfather, who had built bookcases along both walls to house a library he had been left by a friend.

The result was that all the pictures were too high. So I took the bookcases on the fireplace wall down. The walls were covered with William Morris wallpaper, which I generally like, but the one used here was quite wrong for the room. It was a sombre orange-red, so I had that stripped off. Eventually, we achieved what I think was the right colour, by comparing it with a painting of the room done in 1810.

But two things went wrong. First of all,

ALL ITS GLORY *Sir John Vanbrugh's bold design for the Earl of Carlisle's Castle Howard stands virtually unchanged, even though the dome and part of the front had to be restored after a disastrous fire swept the house in 1940. The gardens were restyled in the 1850s by William Nesfield, the artist and landscape gardener, who described his plans as producing 'a stability of character in accordance with that splendid fellow Vanbrugh'. The fountain, with its elaborately styled tritons spouting water, came from the Great Exhibition held in London in 1851. It forms the centrepiece of a parterre of lawns, paths and neatly trimmed hedges, uncluttered by flower beds.*

FERTILE GENIUS *The architects of the 18th century were not confined to designing houses. Vanbrugh's depth of imagination can be seen in the buildings he created to ornament Castle Howard's grounds. The pyramid-topped gatehouse (left) is the visitor's first sight of his work. Through it can be seen a 100 ft high obelisk carved with tributes to the Earl of Carlisle, who chose Vanbrugh to design Castle Howard for him, and the Duke of Marlborough, who was winning his greatest victories over Louis XIV's France while the building operations were taking place. The mock fortifications (above), with turrets and towers, repeat the deliberately chosen martial theme.*

ANOTHER HAND *Nicholas Hawksmoor, Vanbrugh's collaborator at Castle Howard, designed the mausoleum in 1728, but did not live to see the work finished. It is now to be extensively restored. In the crypt below are the tombs of the Earl of Carlisle and his family.*

315

CASTLE HOWARD

there was snow on the ground when we did the work. The result was that the light was reflected too intensely, so the final effect of the redecoration is paler than it should have been. The other thing which I did not realise, until I looked at engravings from the 1810 picture, was that the skirting board should have been painted to resemble marble.

In the Castle Howard dressing-room, I kept the original paper which was put up when the room was first decorated in 1810. It was impossible to restore its original colour, but what I did was to have all the coloured parts varnished. I wanted to replace the wallpaper in the dressing-room, named after an 18th-century ancestor, Lady Georgiana, with the identical pattern, but unfortunately the blocks had been destroyed in 1937. Luckily, the makers were able to find a very similar paper and to copy the colour exactly.

I am always trying to find out more about the collections, too. For instance, the bronze birds in the Long Gallery have always been attributed to the Italian sculptor Bernini, but I did not know where they came from. Then, when I was in Florence a few years ago, I saw the Villa Medici and its marvellous grotto, with its own birds. I suddenly realised this was where mine must have come from.

An American scholar did a great deal of work to show that the bust of the Archbishop of Pisa in the Antique Passage was also the work of Bernini. There, as in other parts of the house, I still have not got everything arranged the way it ought to be. The splendid Egyptian figure of a king should be in a more prominent place, or else have a spotlight on him, because he really is an important figure. He dates from about 1500 BC, a little before Tutankhamun.

Years of research

Paintings too, have always been one of my special interests. Among the collection, I am particularly fond of the picture of 'Omai—the Gentle Savage' by Reynolds, in the Tapestry Room, and Gainsborough's 'The Girl with Pigs', in the Music Room. I bought the Hendrik de Cort painting of Castle Howard, reproduced on the frontispiece of our guide book, very cheaply in 1950.

Sometimes the ascriptions of paintings are one's own, and sometimes they are the distilled results of other people's suggestions over the years. For example, it is only recently that I have suggested that the painting of 'The Music Master' by Domenico Feti, in the Orleans Room, could possibly be of Monteverdi. After someone put this theory forward to me, I compared my painting with the only two known portraits of Monteverdi—one as a very old man and the other in his youth. The dates are right and the place it was painted is right. But this is the sort of thing that a scholar can spend years researching.

Sometimes one can be more certain. The picture of 'The Drawing Academy' was originally thought to be by Poussin and then by Stella. But after I saw a room full of Bourdons in Russia I had no doubts whatever. Nobody has challenged it since.

Curiosities find a place here as well. The fragments of Coptic tunics worn by priests in ancient Egypt, which are now displayed in the entrance lobby, have always fascinated me. I know my grandfather collected them. When I

ELABORATE INTERIOR *The domed hall was one of Vanbrugh's most daring features. Nothing like it had ever been built in England before. The frescoes on the walls are the work of the Italian artist Giovanni Antonio Pellegrini.*

MUSIC ROOM *The elaborate furniture includes a 1796 Broadwood piano of a type used by Beethoven.*

CASTLE TREASURE *One of Castle Howard's most prized paintings is Thomas Gainsborough's 'The Girl with Pigs', which he originally sold for 100 guineas. It hangs in the Music Room.*

FROM A KING *This silver and gilt tankard, now [on di]splay on the dining-table of the Tapestry Room, [is] a gift from King Carl XI of Sweden to the 1st [Earl] of Carlisle in 1668.*

[BLUE JOHN] STONE *Among the exhibits in the Museum [Room], designed by C. H. Tatham between 1805 and [1810], is this fine French table. Its top is patterned [with] Blue John stone from Derbyshire.*

[VICT]ORIAN CHANGE *The chapel's stained-glass [win]dows were designed by Edward Burne-Jones and [mad]e by William Morris as part of an extensive [rebu]ilding scheme started in the 19th century by [Adm]iral Edward Howard. Services are still held [ther]e each year. Behind the font is a coloured plaster [bas-]relief of the Madonna and Child by Sansovino [14]60–1529).*

CLASSICAL LEGACY *Among the many statues and busts that line the length of Vanbrugh's Antique Passage are examples from Greece, Rome and Egypt. The marble-topped tables were made in the 18th century, and their designers included William Kent and Batty Langley. There is also some Flemish stained glass, dating from the 16th century, forming part of the passage windows.*

MODERN ADDITION *Among the more recent additions to Castle Howard's collections are the costume galleries housed in the stables. The galleries have on show the largest private collection of costumes in Britain, with thousands of examples dating from the 17th century to the present day. The costumes are often shown in their appropriate settings, such as this reconstruction of a York draper's shop. There are plans to build a theatre in which to display theatrical costumes.*

was in Leningrad, the Coptic section of the Hermitage Museum was closed, but the authorities very kindly opened it and showed me their own large collection. It is marvellous how fresh and bright they look, considering they are around 1500 years old.

One of our most important possessions is Sansovino's bas-relief of the Madonna and Child, which is now in the chapel. Originally it was hanging in a corridor in an appalling condition.

Eventually, I managed to get hold of Kenneth Hempel, the head of sculpture restoration at the Victoria and Albert Museum. He came, did some temporary repairs, then took the bas-relief to London, where he worked on it for four years. It could not be cleaned chemically, because of the delicacy of the painting, so he had to clean it by hand, using a tiny knife and a magnifying glass. The trouble was it would take him an evening to do a thumbnail, but in the end it came up marvellously.

The chapel itself is always very popular. In style, it is a curious mixture of Georgian and Victorian. The capitals and ceiling are all part of the original 1810 scheme. But my great-uncle later lowered the floor, made a new entrance and put Burne-Jones windows in. We still hold services there on occasions, such as the annual visit of the 1st Hartlepool Company of the Boys' Brigade. They have been camping here every summer for nearly 90 years.

The costume collection

Among the new features I have added are the costume galleries which are housed in the stables. The collection started when I was introduced to an ex-headmistress, who had a collection of costumes from pageants she had organised. We now have about 13,000 items— some 3500 of them women's dresses.

The displays consist of costumes people have given us—there is a wonderful dress which used to belong to the actress Vivien Leigh—things people have lent us and costumes I have bought myself. These included many Diaghilev ballet costumes, including all the 'Chant de Rossignol' costumes by Matisse and some for the 'Rite of Spring'.

But the scope is not limited to museum pieces. Every year, Peter Robinson are now going to give us two examples of the most typical clothes they have sold. So we shall build up an historical picture of the clothes worn by ordinary people. So far as possible, we will try to exhibit these in their appropriate setting.

I want to enlarge the displays further when the roof of one range is repaired. And I hope to make a small theatre on the site of the racquets court, where I can display all the theatrical clothes.

Running a house of this size is a tremendous responsibility. I feel myself part of a long-standing tradition. Castle Howard has been open to the public ever since it was built. And, even if the things in it are personal possessions, they are held in trust for the future.

There are problems as well. My major one at the moment is Hawksmoor's wonderful mausoleum in the grounds. Frost has got into the stonework and all the columns and the cornice will have to be replaced.

But I live much more in the present and the future than in the past. It is always exciting to make plans and, sometimes, to see what have been pipe-dreams come to fruition.

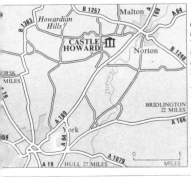

WHEN TO VISIT CASTLE HOWARD

Castle Howard is 3 miles off the A64, 6 miles west of Malton. It is on the route of Tour No. 113 from Malton.
Castle Howard is on view to the public daily from Easter Sun. to the first Sun. in Oct.

The grounds, which include a fountain, lakes and Vanbrugh's Temple of the Four Winds, are open from noon. Hawksmoor's mausoleum is closed for restoration. The house itself opens at 1 p.m. and guides operate conducted tours. The Costume Galleries in the stable court open at the same time. They house the largest private collection of costumes in Britain. Closing time is at 5 p.m.— except for Bank Hol. Mon., when Castle Howard is open from 11.30 a.m.–5.30 p.m.

Lakes and peaks—a land of living poetry

John Ruskin, the Victorian writer and social reformer, claimed to enjoy 'the finest view of Cumberland or Lancashire' from his lakeside home at Brantwood, and drivers following this tour will understand his enthusiasm. Wooded uplands and jagged peaks are mirrored in placid lakes, and spectacular waterfalls like Dungeon Ghyll Force thunder among the mountain crags. The route visits Hawkshead, where the Lakeland poet Wordsworth went to school; and the home at Near Sawrey which Beatrix Potter, author of Peter Rabbit *and other children's stories, left to the nation. Lake Side, on the shore of Windermere, provides both lake steamers and a steam railway.*

(1) Grange-over-Sands to Lindale Leave the town on the B5277 signposted to Lindale, passing the broad expanse of Meathop marsh and heathland on the right. After 2 m. enter Lindale, home of John Wilkinson, a pioneer of the Industrial Revolution.

(2) Lindale to Lake Side Leave the village on the A590 signposted for Barrow. The road follows the contours of Newton Fell, rising to 700 ft on the right. After 5 m. enter Newby Bridge, an attractive village on the River Leven with a 17th-century slate bridge. In the village, just beyond the junction with the A592, turn right to follow the signpost for Lake Side and Hawkshead. After just under 1 m. enter the village of Lake Side.

(3) Lake Side to Graythwaite Hall Continue through the village and follow the woodland road along the western shore of Lake Windermere. This affords glimpses of the lake to the right and of Furness Fells to the left. After 3 m., on the left, is Graythwaite Hall.

(4) Graythwaite Hall to Near Sawrey On leaving the Hall, turn left on to the road and then fork right just beyond the gates, following the signpost for Cunsey and Sawrey. After crossing Cunsey Beck, 2 m. later, bear left and continue into Far Sawrey. In the village, bear left on to the B5285, following the signpost for Hawkshead. After just under 1 m. on the left is the entrance to Beatrix Potter's home, Hill Top Farm, Near Sawrey.

(5) Near Sawrey to Hawkshead Leave the village on the B5285. This hugs the shore of Esthwaite Water, affording glimpses of Hawkshead Moor and Grizedale Forest to the west. After about 2 m., enter the village of Hawkshead. To visit the Court House Lakeland Museum, follow the road through the village to the junction with the B5286.

(6) Hawkshead to Dungeon Ghyll Force Leave by the B5286 signposted to Ambleside. After 3½ m., in the village of Clappergate, turn left on to the A593 and follow the road to Skelwith Bridge. Fork right on to the B5343 signposted to Langdale. After 5 m., at Dungeon Ghyll, there is a car park from which a stiff walk leads up to Dungeon Ghyll Force.

(7) Dungeon Ghyll Force to Coniston Continue along the valley, then swing left on to a minor road which climbs steeply to the pass between Lingmoor Fell and Blake Rigg. On the far side of the pass the road drops steeply. After 5 m., at the T-junction, turn right, following the signpost to Coniston.

Shortly after this, at the junction with the A593, turn right and continue along Yewdale and into Coniston village.

(8) Coniston to Brantwood Leave the village on the B5285 signposted to Hawkshead. After 1 m. turn right on to the minor road which runs by the lakeside to Brantwood. Just beyond the houses there are parking places under the trees with fine views of The Old Man of Coniston, a peak 2631 ft high.

(9) Brantwood to Holker Continue along the shore road through woods which belong largely to the National Trust, shortly reaching the end of Coniston Water. From here the road closely follows the River Crake. After 2 m., at a T-junction beside the river, turn left, following the signpost for Spark Bridge. At the T-junction in Spark Bridge turn left, and at the next crossroads go straight ahead on to the road signposted to Newby Bridge. At the next junction, turn left on to the A590. After just over 1 m. turn right on to the B5278 signposted to Holker.

(10) Holker to Cartmel Leave the village, still on the B5278, and shortly reach Cark. Here turn left on to the road signposted to Cartmel, and continue into the village to visit the Priory church.

(11) Cartmel to Grange-over-Sands Leave the village on the road signposted to Grange-over-Sands. After just under 2 m., turn left on to Grange Fell Road and continue into Grange-over-Sands.

INFORMATION

Places of interest *Brantwood:* Apr. to Oct., daily, except Sat. *Cartmel Priory Gatehouse:* Mon. to Sat., all reasonable times. *Coniston:* Ruskin museum, Easter to Oct. 31, daily. *Graythwaite Hall:* Gardens, Apr. to June, daily. *Hawkshead:* Court House, Easter to Oct., afternoons except Mon. and Thur. *Hill Top Farm:* Apr. to Oct. 31, weekdays, Sun. afternoons. *Holker Hall:* Easter to end Sept., daily, except Sat. *Lakeside and Haverthwaite Steam Railway:* May to Oct.

Crafts *Hawkshead:* The Institute, pottery, Whitsun to Sept., daily. *Esthwaite Pottery:* Most days, except Sat. in summer.

Events *Grange-over-Sands:* Lakeland Rose Show, July. *Hawkshead:* Whitsun Folk Festival, May. Agricultural show, Sept.

Information Council Offices, Victoria Hall, Main Street, Grange-over-Sands (Tel. Grange-over-Sands 2375).

Towns with easy access to Grange-over-Sands:

Barrow-in-Furness	24 m.	Keswick 38 m.
Kendal	14 m.	Lancaster 25 m.
		Windermere 16 m.

Dungeon Ghyll Force.

DUNGEON GHYLL FORCE
This waterfall is overlooked by the peaks of Langdale Pikes and Harrison Stickle. It plunges in several streams to a basin formed by sheer cliffs nearly 100 ft high. At one point the fall drops 60 ft without a break.

CONISTON
To the west, both Coniston village and the lake are dominated by The Old Man of Coniston, which rises to a majestic 2631 ft. The 5½ mile long lake, with its tree-lined bays and views to the east over Grizewood Forest, was the setting for Donald Campbell's water-speed record of 260.33 mph in 1959. He was killed eight years later on the same lake when his jet-powered *Bluebird* crashed at 300 mph. The village itself is typically Lakeland in character, with old hotels and whitewashed stone cottages. Coniston attracted the essayist, artist and social reformer John Ruskin (1819–1900), who is buried in the churchyard. There is Ruskin museum in the village. The artist himself found the collection in 1884 and the exhibits give a comprehensive picture of his life.

John Ruskin memorial, Coni

View from Brantwood, John Ruskin's home.

BRANTWOOD
Ruskin bought Brantwood, originally an 18th-century cottage, in 1871, and added the studio and dining-room as well as the whole of the second floor. Exhibits that can be seen there include much of his furniture, his boat and his coach, as well as works of art.

SCALE

0   1   2   3   4   5 MILES

HAWKSHEAD

The poet Wordsworth knew every nook and cranny of this village of narrow streets and picturesque cottages. He attended the local grammar school, founded in the 16th century, and lodged at Anne Tyson's cottage in Red Lion Square. North of the village is the folk museum in Court House, which provides a portrait of traditional life and work in the Lake District.

Anne Tyson's cottage, Hawkshead.

Hill Top Farm, home of Beatrix Potter.

NEAR SAWREY

Beatrix Potter (1866–1944), creator of charming and imaginative children's books, loved the villages of Near and Far Sawrey since she discovered them on childhood holidays. Out of the royalties from *Peter Rabbit* she bought Hill Top Farm, where she wrote about such characters as Jemima Puddleduck, Pigling Bland and Cousin Ribby. An early convert to the ideals of the National Trust, she left the farm to the Trust.

Cousin Ribby, from The Tale of Samuel Whisker.

LAKE SIDE

A hotel, station and pier mark here the southern end of Windermere, the largest of England's lakes (10½ miles long). From a quayside on the wooded banks, steamers ply to Ambleside and Bowness. More recently, Lake Side has become the northern terminus of the Lakeside and Haverthwaite Railway, a 3 mile branch line abandoned by British Railways and rescued, in 1970, by enthusiasts. Steam engines run daily in the summer on the route by the River Leven to Newby Bridge and Haverthwaite.

GRAYTHWAITE HALL

The gardens of this Tudor house are open to the public and are particularly beautiful in late spring. The house, extensively rebuilt in the last century, overlooks the wooded shores of Windermere.

LINDALE

This pretty village was the home of John Wilkinson (1728–1808), a pioneer of the Industrial Revolution. He built the world's first iron boat and the first iron bridge—at Ironbridge, in Salop. The memorial obelisk in the village is appropriately cast in iron. His body, in an iron coffin, was buried in the grounds of the house, Castle Head, which he built south of Lindale.

Oyster-catcher

Red-breasted merganser

GRANGE-OVER-SANDS

The low fells that shelter this small Victorian town are in bold contrast to the gold-grey sweep of sand exposed when the tide runs out of Morecambe Bay. Among the birds to be seen here are oyster-catchers, herons, redshanks and many species of gull.

Cartmel Priory church.

HOLKER

The massive sandstone pile of Holker Hall was the favourite home of the 7th Duke of Devonshire (1808–91) and still reflects the way of life of a 19th-century nobleman. There are sumptuously furnished rooms embellished with paintings, porcelain and silver. A particular treasure is a screen embroidered by Mary, Queen of Scots. Outside there are 22 acres of gardens with many fine plants and trees, a children's farm and a deer park.

Mary, Queen of Scots' screen.

CARTMEL

Nearly all traces of Cartmel Priory have disappeared, except the gatehouse in the village square, but the church survived the 1537 Dissolution. It contains two prized possessions—a 250 year old ornate umbrella, which generations of vergers have used to shelter the vicars at rainy burial services, and a 1596 first edition of Spenser's *Faerie Queene*. The book was stolen in 1929 and smuggled to New York; but the thief found it impossible to sell, and it was eventually allowed to fall into the hands of the police.

Over hill and dale in the weavers' country

A wooded hill that rises to more than 500 ft behind the little seaside town of Arnside gives the best idea of the variety of countryside between the tidal flats of Morecambe Bay and the distant peaks of the Lake District. Running inland through a series of picturesque villages, the tour winds through the lonely Lune Valley. Stone cottages, where craftsmen wove hard-wearing moorland cloth, and women knitted stockings sitting on galleries overlooking the streets, are interspersed with stately homes. At Levens Hall, in the Lyth Valley, visitors can stroll through gardens virtually unchanged since they were laid out by a French master gardener 300 years ago.

(1) Arnside to Beetham Leave Arnside on the B5282, following the road left at the railway station. After 1 m. turn right on to the road signposted to Hazelslack/Carr Bank, and almost immediately bear left up a hill. Carry straight on at the crossroads on the road signposted to Beetham. At the next junction turn right, carry on into Beetham and turn left to the centre of the village.

(2) Beetham to Whittington Go straight through the village and turn left on to the A6. Cross the river, and soon after turn right on to the road signposted Farleton. At the junction with the B6384, turn right. After just over 1 m. the road goes through the village of Holme, crosses the Lancaster Canal and the M6. Immediately afterwards, at the junction with the A6070, turn right and follow the road into Burton. On the far side of the village turn left on to the road signposted to Hutton Roof and Kirkby Lonsdale. Follow the road for 4 m. over low hills, ignoring all turns, into the village of Whittington.

(3) Whittington to Kirkby Lonsdale Leave the village by turning left at the junction with the B6254. After just under 2 m. turn left on to the A65 and then immediately right, returning to the B6254 to reach the centre of Kirkby Lonsdale.

(4) Kirkby Lonsdale to Dent Continue on the B6254, and after 1 m. fork right on to the road signposted to Rigmaden/Killington. The road follows the River Lune for about 4 m. After Rigmaden Park, turn right on to the road signposted to Sedbergh. Turn right again on to the A683, which here runs along the course of a Roman road on the far side of the Lune Valley. Follow the A683 towards Kirkby Lonsdale for 2 m. and immediately after crossing a small bridge turn left to the road signposted to Barbon. Follow the road signposted for Dent, through Barbon, and climb the beautiful pass of Barbondale, which reaches a height of 1025 ft and enters the Yorkshire Dales National Park before dropping down to Gawthrop. Turn right to Gawthrop on to the road signposted to Dent, and continue into the village.

(5) Dent to Sedbergh Return to the junction outside Gawthrop and bear right following the signpost to Sedbergh. The road follows the beautiful valley of the River Dee for about 6 m. into Sedbergh.

(6) Sedbergh to Sizergh Castle Leave Sedbergh, heading westwards on the main road through the town, and then fork right on to the A684 signposted to Kendal.

After 4 m., just before the M6, turn left, keeping the Killington Reservoir to the right, and follow the road signposted to Old Hutton and New Hutton. Cars may be parked at the side of the road near the reservoir, but there is no official car park. Turn right to follow the road by the reservoir and keep straight ahead at the junction 1½ m. later. Go straight ahead at the next junction and a few yards later keep left, slightly uphill and away from the M6. After 1½ m. follow the road right signposted to Kendal. Go right again at the next junction, across the M6, then turn right on to the B6254 in Old Hutton. After 3 m. turn left, just before Oxenholme railway station. The road drops down a hill until it meets the A65. Turn right here, and after 250 yds turn left on to the road signposted to Natland. Bear left (signposted 'Single-track Road') at the junction on the far side of Natland, and cross the Lancaster border and the River Kent. Turn left on meeting the dual-carriageway A591. Sizergh Castle is on the right after 1 m.

(7) Sizergh Castle to Levens Leave Sizergh by turning right on to the A591. After ¾ m. at the roundabout, join the A6 towards Milnthorpe. After 2 m., the entrance to Levens Hall is on the right.

(8) Levens Hall to Milnthorpe Leave Levens Hall again by turning right on to the A6 travelling south. After 2 m. enter Milnthorpe.

(9) Milnthorpe to Arnside Leave the town by turning right at the traffic lights on to the B5282, and follow the road for about 4 m. back to Arnside.

NATURE NOTES
This is one of the most botanically exciting areas in Britain with extensive exposures of carboniferous limestone pavement. The crevices have an abundance of ferns, including rigid buckler-fern. In ungrazed areas, lime-loving shrubs such as dogwood and buckthorn abound. The River Kent estuary is the winter headquarters of a flock of greylag geese.

INFORMATION
Places of interest *Levens Hall:* Easter to end Sept., house, Tues., Wed., Thur., Sun. and Bank Hol. afternoons, gardens daily. *Sizergh Castle:* Apr. to Sept., Wed., Sun., afternoons; also Thur. afternoons June to Aug. Gardens, Thur. afternoons, Apr., May, Sept.

Events *Sedbergh:* Market days, Wed. and Fri.

Nature trail *Arnside Knott:* 1 m. south-west of Arnside. Guide from local retailers.

Information Tourist and Information Office, Town Hall, Kendal (Tel. Kendal 23649).

Towns with easy access to Arnside:
Barrow-in-Furness . 40 m. Lancaster . . . . . 20 m.
Kendal . . . . 16 m. Windermere . . . 17 m.

LEVENS HALL
This is the biggest Elizabethan house in Cumbria, tho much of the building dates from an earlier period. Th beauty of the house is set off by gardens laid out by Guillaume Beaumont, a Frenchman, in 1690. They ar believed to be the only gardens in England which have remained unchanged since that period. The hall conta many relics of the Napoleonic wars, 15th-century paintings and rooms hung with ornate 17th-century leatherwork. One of the hall's many attractions is a collection of steam-engines, one of which was built in 1820. There is a free car park.

The gardens at Levens Hall.

MILNTHORPE
The most attractive feature of this town is its square, a hive of activity on market days. It is dominated to the north by the modern St Thomas's Church. Dallam Tower, not quite a mile from the town in a deer park crossed by footpaths, was built in the early 18th century. It is a substantial house, typical of its period, with some fine interior decoration and panelling.

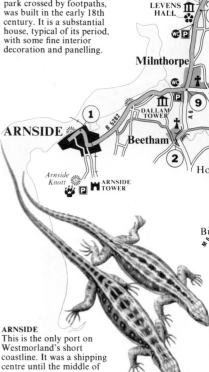

ARNSIDE
This is the only port on Westmorland's short coastline. It was a shipping centre until the middle of the 18th century, but nowadays it is mainly a haven for yachtsmen. A walk leads southwards to Arnside Knott, from the top of which there is a fine view of the surrounding countryside. A little to the south is the ruined 13th-century Arnside Tower, which was largely destroyed by fire in 1602. It seems to have been one of the chain of pele towers built during the Middle Ages in an attempt to contain the never-ending raids from across the Border. The Knott, which rises 522 ft, has an interesting variety of plants, fossils, red squirrels, lizards, birds and butterflies.

Male and female lizards.

SCALE
0   1   2   3   4   5 MILES

SIZERGH CASTLE

This handsome fortress-home has belonged to the Strickland family since 1239, and is one of the most impressive ancient houses in Westmorland. It was constructed around a pele tower, built against Scottish raiders in 1340. Other parts, including a Tudor Great Hall, were added in the 15th, 16th and 18th centuries. The pele tower itself is one of the largest ever built—60 ft high by 40 ft across—and has an unusual tunnel-vaulted basement. The walls of the tower are nearly 10 ft thick at the bottom, tapering to 5½ ft at the top. In contrast to this grim keep, the house also possesses a wealth of early Elizabethan woodwork and five elaborately decorated chimneypieces, built in the 16th century.

Sizergh Castle.

DENTDALE

Lower Dentdale is a broad, beautiful and well-wooded landscape, with Rise Hill to the north and the dramatic precipice of Combe Scar to the south. Beyond Dent village, the valley narrows until it ends in a mountain pass with a gorge. Further up the valley is Stone House marble works, where black marble used to be cut and polished.

Dentdale.

SEDBERGH

The public school which bears Sedbergh's name was founded in 1523. The town's narrow main street, flanked by shops and ancient coaching inns, is particularly picturesque on market days— Wednesdays and Fridays. Behind the King's Arms is the Weavers' Yard, where weavers and knitters used to sell their wares. The church of St Andrew was originally Norman, but later additions have not detracted from its beauty.

DENT

The manufacture of worsted stockings was once the principal industry of Dent, which lies in the secluded valley of the Dee. The women who knitted them used to sit working on first-floor galleries overlooking the streets, but the galleries were an obstruction to modern traffic and have now been removed. Even so, the town retains its cobbled streets and greystone houses. One of Dent's sons was Adam Sedgwick, a pioneer of the science of geology. Born in 1785, he was Professor of Geology at Cambridge for 55 years. A memorial to him, hewn out of solid Shap granite, stands at the gate of St Andrew's Church.

Sedgwick memorial, Dent.

BEETHAM

Set on the western bank of the River Bela, overlooked by tree-covered hills and by-passed by the A6, Beetham has retained its old-world atmosphere. A pergola entwined with roses leads to the 12th-century church of St Michael. Beetham Hall, built in 1693 and now a farmhouse, stands on the site of a 14th-century fortified manor house, parts of which still survive.

Market stalls, Kirkby Lonsdale.

The Devil's Bridge, Kirkby Lonsdale.

WHITTINGTON

Rocky peaks that rise to almost 900 ft form a backdrop to Whittington, which looks out over the broad valley of the River Lune. The village was recorded as 'Whitetune' in the Domesday Book. Its church, built in the 15th century, stands on a hillock where a sundial marks the site of a former look-out post. The churchyard is particularly beautiful in spring, when daffodils sprinkle the grass. The clock tower of Whittington Hall can be seen across the fields looming above the trees.

KIRKBY LONSDALE

John Ruskin, the 19th-century artist and social reformer, described the view of the Lune Valley from Kirkby Lonsdale as 'one of the loveliest in England—therefore in the world'. Spanning the River Lune is the 13th-century Devil's Bridge, which local legend claims was built by the Devil in one night. Much remains of the original Norman church, St Mary the Virgin, and the interior is impressive, with massive pillars alternating with piers of clustered shafts. Among the town's many fine buildings are the 17th-century Manor House and the 18th-century Fountain House. Casterton Girls' School, 1¼ miles north of the town, was formerly at Cowan Bridge, where the Brontë sisters were pupils.

A pilgrimage through Wordsworth's homeland

Dacre Castle.

William Wordsworth, greatest of the Lakeland poets, lived, worked and died among the mountains and meres traversed by this spectacular route. The tour is a Wordsworth pilgrimage steeped in memories of the poet who lies buried in Grasmere village. Some of the larger lakes have sadder associations. On them Sir Henry Seagrave and later Donald Campbell set new water-speed records—and died trying to better them.

(1) Windermere to Troutbeck Leave Windermere on the A591 signposted for Keswick. After just under 2 m. turn right on to the road signposted to Troutbeck. After 1¼ m. the National Trust property of Town End is on the left on the outskirts of Troutbeck. Carry on beyond Town End to the centre of the village.

(2) Troutbeck to Glenridding Go through Troutbeck and bear left on to the A592. This climbs to the head of the Kirkstone Pass, at 1489 ft the highest road in the Lake District, with its lonely inn and views of mountains on either side. Beyond the summit the road drops steeply, passing Brothers Water, one of the district's smallest lakes, before entering the village of Patterdale. The small 19th-century church of St Patrick on the left has some panels of modern tapestry. Continue across the bridges over Grisedale Beck and Red Tarn Beck into Glenridding, a tiny 'port' at the southern end of Ullswater.

(3) Glenridding to Aira Force Stay on the A592 as it winds along the shore of Ullswater. After 2 m., near the junction with the A5091, there is a car park from which a footpath leads through a wooded glen to the Aira Force waterfall.

(4) Aira Force to Dacre Continue along the A592 as it hugs the lakeside. After 5 m., at the head of the lake, bear left, still on the A592, which is here signposted to Penrith. After 1 m., turn left on to a minor road for the village of Dacre.

(5) Dacre to Thirlmere Continue through Dacre and 1 m. later, at the junction with the A66, turn left. Follow this mountain road westwards for 10 m. For the first 3 m. the road marks part of the north-eastern boundary of the Lake District National Park as it runs through the village of Penruddock, with Little Mell Fell (1657 ft) and Great Mell Fell (1760 ft) to the left. Beyond the Sportsman Inn the road runs into the park. Ahead lies the great bulk of Blencathra, 2847 ft high, and beyond that the rising mass of Skiddaw Forest. At Threlkeld there is a memorial in the churchyard to more than 40 parishioners who were 'noted veterans of the chase'. The district is the home of the Blencathra pack of foxhounds. As with other Lakeland packs, the hunters follow the hounds on foot.

In Threlkeld turn left on to the B5322, following the signpost for Thirlmere. The road runs down the beautiful valley called St John's in the Vale, which narrows down into a steep-sided gorge with the road parallel to St John's Beck on the right. On the left is Castle Rock, a massive crag said to be the place where Sir Gawain of the Round Table defeated the Green Knight. After 4 m., at the junction with the A591, turn left, following the signpost for Ambleside/Windermere/Kendal. Just over 1 m. later there is a car park on the right, overlooking Thirlmere. The starting point for The Swirls Forest Trail is a little further along the road, on the left.

(6) Thirlmere to Grasmere Continue towards Ambleside on the A591 and after 2 m., near the southern end of Thirlmere, stands the low, whitewashed 17th-century chapel of Wythburn. A footpath beside the church leads to the top of Helvellyn. At 3118 ft Helvellyn is one of the four Lake District peaks over 3000 ft, and the one most frequently climbed. After another 4 m. turn right on to the B5287 into Grasmere. The village is the centre for the Dale Sports.

(7) Grasmere to Rydal Continue through the village on the B5287, and where it rejoins the A591 at Town End turn right, following the Ambleside signpost. The road runs alongside the waters of Grasmere and on past Rydal Water before entering Rydal.

(8) Rydal to Ambleside Continue along the A591, which runs through the grassy vale of the River Rothay, into Ambleside.

(9) Ambleside to Brockhole On the outskirts of the town rejoin the A591, which runs due south along the eastern side of Windermere to Brockhole. The National Park Centre is signposted on the right.

(10) Brockhole to Windermere Rejoin the A591 and turn right for the 2 m. drive back to Windermere.

INFORMATION

Places of interest *Brockhole National Park Centre:* Daily from 10 a.m., mid-Mar. to mid-Nov. For current events telephone Windermere 2231. *Grasmere:* Dove Cottage, Mar. to mid-Jan., weekdays. Wordsworth Museum, Easter to Oct., weekdays. *Rydal Mount:* Mar. to Jan. daily. *Troutbeck:* Town End, Apr. to Oct., daily (except Mon. and Sat.). Bank Hol. afternoons. Mar., Wed. afternoons only.

Craft workshops *Ambleside:* Sidney Beddall, Sussex House, Lake Road, gold and silver jewellery, open weekdays.

Events *Ambleside:* Festival, July. Rushbearing, July. Vale of Rydal Sheepdog Trials, second Thur. in Aug. *Grasmere:* Sports, Aug.

Information *Windermere:* Tourist Information Centre, Victoria Street (Tel. Windermere 4561). Lake District National Park, Bank House, High Street (Tel. Windermere 2498).

Towns with easy access to Windermere:

Barrow-in-Furness	24 m.	Penrith	22 m.
Kendal	9 m.	Sedbergh	17 m.
Keswick	20 m.	Ulverston	17 m.

DACRE
Unusually well-preserved battlements distinguish Dacre Castle, which was built early in the 14th century. Tradition says it is on the site where Constantine of Scotland, Eugenius, overlord of Cumberland and Athelstan of England met in the 10th century to sign a treaty. The castle is now a farmhouse. The four corners of the original churchyard are marked by stone bears.

THIRLMERE
Until the end of the last century, Thirlmere consisted of two small lakes. When the northern one was dammed in 1879 a reservoir for Manchester (to which water travels through a 96 mile long aqueduct), the resulting public outcry was one of the reasons for the formation of the National Trust. The lake is 3 miles long, flanked by Forestry Commission plantations. The Swirls Forest Trail, just under a mile long, starts near a lakeside car park. A ¾ mile path, the shortest route to the 3118 ft high summit of Helvellyn, starts from the southern end of the lake, near Wythburn's tiny white church, mentioned in Wordsworth's verse. At top a tablet identifies the other peaks within view; observers are shielded from the buffeting winds by an x-shaped stone wall.

Douglas fir

GRASMERE
Wordsworth described the village and its little lake, set in an amphitheatre of mountains, as 'the loveliest spot that man hath ever found'. The poet lived at Dove Cottage in Grasmere from 1799 to 1808, and was buried in the churchyard 42 years later. A museum near by displays some of his belongings, including a snuffbox and shaving mug.

RYDAL
Wordsworth lived in Rydal Mount from 1813 to his death in 1850. The 16th-century house, which is open to the public, contains many Wordsworth relics, including family portraits and first editions. It overlooks 4½ acres of gardens.

AMBLESIDE
This stone-built tourist town is ringed by wooded hills, backed by mountains to the north, east and west. Two nature trails lead to Loughrigg Fell and Skelghyll Woods. Bridge House, a tiny two-roomed 17th-century structure which spans Stock Ghyll, is now a National Trust information centre.

Bridge House, Ambleside.

SCALE

| 0 | 1 | 2 | 3 | 4 | 5 MILES |

BLENCATHRA
• *2847 ft*

Glenderamackin

B 5288

PH

Penruddock

A 66

PENRITH
4 MILES

PENRITH
4 MILES

A 592

Dacre

CASTLE

5

Eamont

A 5091

Great Mell Fell
•*1760 ft*

Threlkeld

WICKE

B 5322

Little Mell Fell
• *1657 ft*

B 5320

Pooley Bridge

N

4

Aira Force

A 592

A 5091

P **WC** *Ullswater*

Castle Rock

KESWICK
3 MILES

A 591

P

P **6**
The Swirls

Glenridding

3

Red Tarn Beck

Patterdale

Griesdale Beck

Helvellyn
3118 ft •

P
WYTHBURN CHURCH

A 592

Brothers Water

A 591

AIRA FORCE
From the car park a footpath leads through a deep, rocky glen to the Aira Force waterfall, which tumbles almost 70 ft in two stages. It was near here that William Wordsworth, wandering 'lonely as a cloud', paused to confer immortality upon 'A host of golden daffodils'.

Aira Force waterfall.

Snow-capped peaks look down on Ullswater, near Glenridding.

GLENRIDDING
From the pier on the lakeside at Glenridding, launches take passengers to the northernmost point of Ullswater at Pooley Bridge. The 9 mile long lake is second to Windermere in size, but its long, twisting outline provides a variety of scenery unsurpassed by any other lake. Several fine estates were laid out on the lake shores during the 19th century, and imposing stands of timber now enhance the landscape. In 1955 Donald Campbell, in his jet-powered speed-boat *Bluebird*, became the first man to break the 200 mph water-speed barrier when he set the then world record of 202.32 mph on Ullswater. Glenridding, at the southern end of the lake, nestles between woodlands at the foot of the Red Tarn Beck, which rushes down from the Red Tarn itself—a small mountain lake 2400 ft high among the crags of Helvellyn. The tarn is, in fact, the highest body of water in the Lake District.

1489 ft

P

P

Kirkstone Pass

PH

Grasmere

P **DOVE COTTAGE**

7

A 591

Town End

RYDAL MOUNT

Rydal

8

Rydal Water

Stockghyll Force

Loughrigg Fell

9

Ambleside

A 593

Skelghyll Woods

PH

2

TOWN END

Troutbeck

Windermere

P **WC**

10

BROCKHOLE

A 592

1

Orrest Head

WINDERMERE

A 591

KENDAL
8 MILES

NEWBY BRIDGE
9 MILES

A 592

A 5074

LEVENS
12 MILES

BROCKHOLE
A wealthy Manchester man built Brockhole in 1900 as his country home. It was opened in 1969 as Britain's first National Park Centre. An exhibition here illustrates Lakeland's story from prehistoric times, and visitors can attend daily talks and film shows. The house is set in 32 acres of gardens and lawns that sweep down to the wooded edge of Lake Windermere, where there are shore walks and picnic places. From the terrace of Brockhole there are views of Scafell Pikes, England's highest mountain (3120 ft), and the rocky crest of Langdale Pikes.

Char from Windermere.

WINDERMERE
The small tourist town of Windermere is a convenient point from which to explore England's biggest lake. Windermere is 10½ miles long and 1¼ miles across at its widest. It has been the scene of many water-speed record attempts, in one of which Sir Henry Seagrave died in 1930. Boat trips are available from Bowness, the original lakeside village from which Windermere grew. The best views of the lake and the Lakeland peaks beyond are from Orrest Head, a low hill overlooking the town. A path to the summit starts opposite Windermere station. Windermere's deeper waters support char—members of the salmon family.

TROUTBECK
A feature of this hillside village is Town End, a yeoman farmer's house that has survived unaltered since it was built in 1623. It was occupied by the same family, the Brownes, for almost 300 years. The house, now owned by the National Trust, still contains the family's original oak furniture, some of it home-made, and their books and papers. There are also domestic utensils of the same period, works by local painters, and fabrics which were woven on Troutbeck looms in the late 18th century.

Town End: 17th-century house, Troutbeck.

Along the raiders' roads, with mountain sheep for company

Lowther Castle.

Tourists exploring the country that lies beyond Kendal, in the wild heights of the northern Pennines, will see more sheep than people—certainly up in the fells where the road climbs to nearly 1400 ft. This is a landscape of windswept moorland, rocky crags and distant views of lofty peaks. But down in the valleys, carved by such rivers as the Eden, Lune and Kent, there are sheltered villages and thriving little towns. Quiet today, most of them have a castle, or its ruins—a reminder that this was once a harsher land; the land of the border raids. But today, car travellers picnic peacefully near old battle sites where deer now graze and peacocks strut.

(1) Kendal to Orton Leave Kendal by the northbound A6 signposted to Penrith and, just beyond the station, fork right on to the A685 signposted to Brough. The road climbs steeply, then runs across the hills through the tiny village of Grayrigg, before descending into the Lune Valley to run alongside the M6. About 2 m. further on, the road crosses the M6 and the river before entering Tebay 1½ m. later. Keep on the A685 through the village to a roundabout, and there take the B6260 signposted to Appleby. After just over 2 m. the road leads into the attractive village of Orton, which lies in a hollow overlooked by the high fells.

(2) Orton to Appleby-in-Westmorland Leave Orton on the B6260 signposted to Appleby. The road climbs on to open moorland ribbed with limestone outcrops until, after 6 m., it reaches Hoff Lunn Wood. After running alongside the wood for a mile, the road descends to Hoff Beck, a tributary of the River Eden. On the outskirts of Appleby, 1½ m. later, pass the hilltop castle, now a private residence, and drive on to Boroughgate, the main street of what used to be England's smallest county town until Westmorland was absorbed into the new county of Cumbria under the 1974 local-government reorganisation.

(3) Appleby-in-Westmorland to Brougham Castle Continue to the end of Boroughgate and turn right, crossing the River Eden to meet the A66. At the junction turn left, following the signpost for Penrith. To the right the Pennines rise to over 2000 ft, and provide some of the wildest walking country in England. Stay on the A66 for 3 m. as it follows the Eden Valley, then turn left on to the minor road signposted Bolton and Cliburn. After ½ m., just off to the right of the road, is the site of a Roman camp. Shortly afterwards the road crosses the River Eden and enters the village of Bolton. Continue through Bolton to Cliburn, ignoring junctions to left and right. About 4 m. beyond Cliburn turn right on to the minor road signposted to Brougham. Follow this road for 1½ m. to the junction with the B6262. Go straight over the B6262; the moated ruins of Brougham Castle are on the left above the River Eamont.

(4) Brougham Castle to Lowther Turn left from the castle and continue along the lane, crossing the River Eamont and joining the A66. Here turn left towards Penrith. At the roundabout 1 m. further on, turn left on to the A6 heading southwards towards Kendal. Since the opening of the M6 motor-way, the A6 has become a pleasant traffic-free road. After 4 m., just before reaching the village of Hackthorpe, Lowther Castle and wildlife park are signposted along a road to the right.

(5) Lowther to Shap Return to the A6 and turn right through Hackthorpe towards Kendal. The road crosses over, and then under, the M6 during the run of about 7 m. to Shap. To visit Shap Abbey ruins, turn right on to the road signposted to Bampton and Haweswater, which is reached just after the A6 crosses the railway on the approach to the village. After ½ m. keep right at the first junction, and ¼ m. later go straight ahead where the lane swings right. The ruins look over to a beautiful stretch of the River Lowther.

(6) Shap to Kendal Retrace the route to the A6 and turn right through Shap village, heading south for Kendal. On the fells, 6 m. south of Shap, the road climbs to within a yard of 1400 ft, and forms the eastern boundary of the Lake District National Park before descending gently to Kendal. It is often blocked with snow in winter.

NATURE NOTES

The low fields around Orton are a mosaic of lime-rich habitats: pavement, hill grassland, streams and small fens. The cracks in the pavement are rich in ferns whilst the grassland, mainly of blue moor-grass, has such rare species as dwarf milkwort and hutchinsia.

INFORMATION

Places of interest *Brougham Castle:* All year, weekdays, Sun. afternoons. *Kendal:* Abbot Hall Art Gallery, all year, Mon. to Fri., Sat. and Sun. afternoons. Abbot Hall Museum, all year, Mon. to Fri., Sat. and Sun. afternoons. Borough Museum weekdays. Castle Dairy (old Tudor house), weekdays, 2-4 p.m. *Lowther Wildlife Park:* Apr. to mid-Oct., daily. *Shap Abbey:* All year, daily.

Events *Appleby-in-Westmorland:* Gipsy Fair, June. *Kendal:* Mary Wakefield Music Festival, May (odd-numbered years); Lake District Music Festival, May (even-numbered years); Poetry Festival, July; Folk Festival, Aug.; Westmorland Horticultural Show, Sept.; Carnival, Aug. to Sept.; Kendal Gathering, first fortnight in Sept.

Nature trail *Serpentine Wood, Kendal:* 1 m. trees, flowers, birds, geology. About 600 yds west of Kendal Town Hall.

Information Tel. Kendal 23649; Penrith 4671.

Towns with easy access to Kendal:

Grange-over-Sands	14 m.	Penrith	27 m.
Keswick	30 m.	Settle	30 m.
Lancaster	22 m.	Windermere	9 m.

LOWTHER

The wooded parkland to the south of the old village of Lowther is a sanctuary for animals and birds that are rare in Britain: five species of deer, longhorn cattle, St Kilda and Manx sheep, wild goats, and a host of exotic birds. The wildlife park, which has many beguiling picnic spots and a free car park, is overlooked by the stately ruins of Lowther Castle, where Mary, Queen of Scots once stayed.

Herdwick sheep, Shap Fell.

HERDWICK SHEEP

The rugged, rocky fells that rise to the peaks around this tour are the home of the hardy Herdwick sheep. Herdwicks, which are believed to be descended from a Scandinavian breed, can live all the year round on these wild mountains. Every Herdwick spends its entire life close to where it was born. Herdwick wool is exceptionally strong and is used in the manufacture of carpets and hard-wearing tweeds.

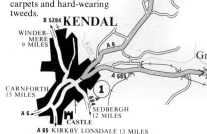

Farmhouse bedroom, Abbot Hall Museum, Kendal.

SCALE
0 1 2 3 4 5 MILES

BROUGHAM CASTLE

The Roman General Agricola built a fort by the River Eamont when he commanded the Roman forces in England in the 1st century AD. The outlines can be seen south of the ruins of the 12th-century castle. The castle was derelict by the 17th century, but restored to much of its former strength by Lady Anne Clifford in the years leading up to the Civil War. It was abandoned again after her death and once more became derelict.

Brougham Castle ruins.

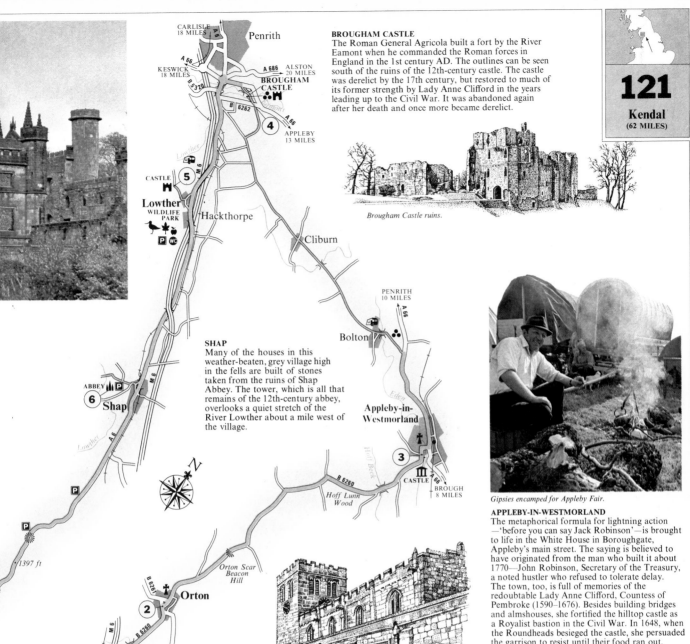

SHAP

Many of the houses in this weather-beaten, grey village high in the fells are built of stones taken from the ruins of Shap Abbey. The tower, which is all that remains of the 12th-century abbey, overlooks a quiet stretch of the River Lowther about a mile west of the village.

Gipsies encamped for Appleby Fair.

APPLEBY-IN-WESTMORLAND

The metaphorical formula for lightning action —'before you can say Jack Robinson'—is brought to life in the White House in Boroughgate, Appleby's main street. The saying is believed to have originated from the man who built it about 1770—John Robinson, Secretary of the Treasury, a noted hustler who refused to tolerate delay. The town, too, is full of memories of the redoubtable Lady Anne Clifford, Countess of Pembroke (1590–1676). Besides building bridges and almshouses, she fortified the hilltop castle as a Royalist bastion in the Civil War. In 1648, when the Roundheads besieged the castle, she persuaded the garrison to resist until their food ran out. An arched gateway to a cobbled square of picturesque cottages—known collectively as the Hospital of St Anne—makes a less sombre memorial than her tomb in St Lawrence's Church. The 12th-century church was burnt down by the Scots in 1174 and again in 1388. Appleby never fully recovered from this last raid. Today it has a population of 2000, half what it was 600 years ago. Appleby Fair, held in June, is the occasion for a colourful assembly of gipsies from all parts of the North.

St Lawrence's Church, Appleby-in-Westmorland.

KENDAL

Because of the colour of its sturdy stone buildings Kendal, one of the main gateways to the Lake District, has been called 'the auld grey town'. Old it certainly is. There was a stronghold on Castle How in prehistoric times, the Romans built a camp by the River Kent, south of the modern town centre, and a weekly market has been held since 1189. The Norman castle, now in ruins, was the birthplace of Catharine Parr, Henry VIII's sixth and last wife. Her prayer book is preserved in the Town Hall, which also houses a collection of paintings by George Romney, who was born in Kendal in 1734. The Abbot Hall art gallery and museum has paintings by Romney and Turner, a collection of 18th-century furniture, and an exhibition of Lakeland life and industry. The narrow lanes connecting the main streets with the river are said to have been built that way to make them more easily defensible against marauding Scots.

Catharine Parr's prayer book.

ORTON

This pretty little village lies below Shap Fell and Orton Scar, where a beacon used to blaze to warn of the approach of Scots raiders. The village hall was built in the days of Elizabeth I, and the church dates from roughly the same period. Its treasured possessions include a medieval chest hollowed out from a tree that once grew in Lowther Park. George Whitehead, one of the most influential of the early Quakers, was born in the village in 1636. Surrounded by a picturesque jigsaw of stone-walled fields, Orton is a fine walking centre, overlooked by rocky scars that rise to well over 1200 ft. One popular walk is over the fell of Orton Scar, 1½ m. north of the village, to the summit of Beacon Hill.

Majestic fells and peaks mirrored in lakes

Some of the most spectacular scenery in England is to be found in the north-western corner of the Lake District. High, windswept fells grazed by hardy sheep rise to majestic peaks with huge walls of naked rock that test the skill of climbers. Crags stand out against the sky like ruined castle ramparts, particularly in the Honister Pass where the road from Buttermere climbs to almost 1200 ft. The grandeur of the mountains is mirrored in such lovely lakes as Ennerdale Water, Crummock Water, Buttermere and Derwent Water—perhaps the most beautiful of them all. The tour offers many opportunities to park and explore lakeside paths and woodland walks.

(1) Cockermouth to Dean Leave the town on the road signed for Workington, then turn right 1 m. later on meeting the A66. After 2 m., at Broughton Cross, turn left on to the road signposted to Greysouthen. In the village, by the Punchbowl Inn, keep straight ahead on the road signposted to Dean. Follow the road for about 2 m. into Dean.

(2) Dean to Ennerdale Water Leave the village on the road signposted to Mockerkin/Loweswater. After just under 1 m. bear right and continue into Ullock. At the T-junction in the village turn right, following the signpost for Branthwaite, then fork left on to the road signposted to Dean Cross. At the crossroads turn left and follow the road south, forking right, right again and then left, and on to Rowrah. Go straight ahead on to the A5086 signposted to Cockermouth. After 400 yds turn right, following the signpost to Kirkland which is reached after just under 1 m. Kirkland village is overlooked by the mountains which lie between the lakes of Loweswater and Ennerdale. In the village turn right, following the signpost to Ennerdale Bridge, which is reached after about 2 m. Bear left through the village and after about 1 m., on the right, a lane leads down to Ennerdale Water.

(3) Ennerdale Water to Buttermere Return along the lane to the road and turn right, following the signpost to Croasdale/Lamplugh. After almost 1 m., at a T-junction, turn left, still following the Lamplugh signpost. Continue for 3 m., passing Murton Fell, which towers 1462 ft high on the right. Just before the village turn right, following the signpost for Loweswater and Buttermere, and continue through Lamplugh. After 1½ m. turn right and follow the road along the northern side of Loweswater, a small lake only about 1¼ m. long with an attractively wooded south shore. Continue through the village of Loweswater, and after just under 2 m. turn right on to the B5289. The road here passes below Grasmoor, 2791 ft high on the left, with Crummock Water lying below the road to the right. Crummock Water is in the same valley as Buttermere, and it is thought likely that the two were once joined together. After about 4 m. enter the village of Buttermere. To visit Scale Force, the highest waterfall (125 ft) in the Lake District, follow the path from the village through Burtness Wood on the south shore of Buttermere.

(4) Buttermere to Seatoller Leave the village on the B5289. The road follows the north-east shore of the lake, then along the bank of Gatesgarthdale Beck and up into Honister Pass. Here the road climbs steeply between huge boulders, almost vertical screes and saw-toothed crags to a height of 1176 ft. Green slates are quarried from the upper slopes of Honister Crag. From the top of the pass the road drops fairly steeply into Seatoller, the starting point for the Johnny Wood Walk.

(5) Seatoller to the Bowder Stone Continue through the village on the B5289 to enter Borrowdale, crossing the River Derwent and passing through thickly wooded slopes. After just over 2 m., on the right side of the road, is the Bowder Stone.

(6) The Bowder Stone to Lingholm Gardens Follow the road for about 1 m., and at Grange turn left over the Derwent, through the village and along the wooded western shores of Derwent Water with the vast bulk of Skiddaw (3054 ft high) rising behind Keswick at the northern end of the lake. After 4 m. turn sharp right on to a private road signposted to Lingholm Gardens, from which there are fine views of Derwent Water.

(7) Lingholm Gardens to Whinlatter Pass Return to the public road and turn right, going through the village of Portinscale to the junction with the A66. Turn left, following the signpost for Cockermouth. After 1 m. fork left on to the B5292 and go through Braithwaite. Follow the road up through steep wooded slopes on to the Whinlatter Pass.

(8) Whinlatter Pass to Cockermouth Follow the road through the pass and down into Lorton Vale. Continue through the village of High Lorton and follow the road for about 5 m. to Cockermouth.

NATURE NOTES
On the steep slopes of the Borrowdale Valley are some of the finest woodlands in the Lake District. Here rare herbs such as touch-me-not balsam and alpine enchanter's nightshade may flourish amidst the thick stands of sessile oak or ash.

INFORMATION

Places of interest *Cockermouth:* Castle, Mon., Wed., Fri. afternoons, mid-Apr. to end July, and first half Oct. Wordsworth's House, Apr. to Oct., weekdays, except Thur. afternoons. *Lingholm Gardens:* Apr. to Oct., weekdays.

Nature trail *Johnny Wood Walk, Seatoller:* 2½ m.

Information Riverside Car Park, Cockermouth (Tel. Cockermouth 2634).

Towns with easy access to Cockermouth:
Carlisle . . . . 26 m.   Penrith . . . . 30 m.
Keswick . . . . 12 m.   Whitehaven . . . . 14 m.

Gargoyle, Dean church.

DEAN
This moorland village of sto and-slate cottages has an unusually handsome parish church. Dating mainl from the 12th and 13th centuries, it is one of the few churches in the coun to be decorated with gargoy three dating from the 13th century. There is also a 12th-century raised preaching cross in the churchyar

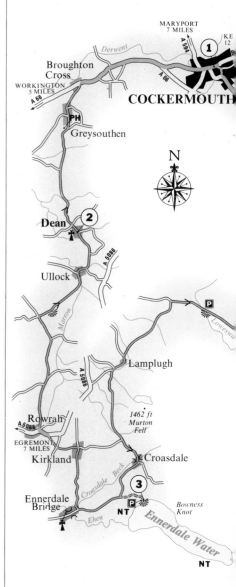

ENNERDALE WATER
The most westerly of the lakes, Ennerdale Water is also one of the quietest, since its 2½ mile length can be explored only on foot. Climbers, however, relish the challenge of the Pillar, 2927 ft high. This and another peak, called the Steeple, tower above the valley of the River Liza at the eastern end of the lake. The land along the river valley belongs to the Forestry Commission and is thickly wooded. The western shore of the lake is National Trust property occupied only by the Anglers' Hotel and How Hall Farm, a notable manor house. The nearby village of Ennerdale Bridge lies at the meeting point of the River Ehen and Croasdale Beck. The village churchyard was the setting of the poem 'The Brothers' by William Wordsworth (1770–1850).

SCALE
0   1   2   3 MILES

COCKERMOUTH

Rising above the place where the waters of the Derwent River join those of the River Cocker are the battlements of Cockermouth Castle, first built in the 12th century and later sacked by Robert Bruce. The structure that remains dates largely from the 14th century, but it was much damaged in the Civil War. The town has a pleasant main street with a double row of trees, and makes a good centre for touring the western Lake District. Among the most attractive houses is that in which William Wordsworth, the poet, was born in 1770.

...rdsworth's childhood home, Cockermouth.

Formal avenue, Lingholm Gardens.

LINGHOLM GARDENS

Up on the wooded western shore of Derwent Water lies Lingholm, home of Lord Rochdale. The gardens, with their magnificent rhododendrons and azaleas, are open to the public in spring and summer. A variety of other trees and plants flourish, and the woodland is a mass of daffodils in spring.

WHINLATTER PASS

From the village of Braithwaite, Whinlatter Pass climbs between Grisedale Pike and Lorton Fells to a height of 1043 ft. The section above Braithwaite commands fine views of Bassenthwaite Lake and 3054 ft high Skiddaw. On the far side, the road descends into Lorton Vale, which follows the River Cocker down to Cockermouth. At the beginning of the valley are High and Low Lorton, picturesque villages sharing a parish church.

...ale Force, near Buttermere.

BUTTERMERE

Huddled between the peaks surrounding Grasmoor and Buttermere Fell is the small village of Buttermere, an ideal centre from which to explore both Crummock Water and the lake of Buttermere. Buttermere, only 1¼ miles long, has a pretty, wooded south shore backed by Chapel Crags. It is joined to Crummock Water by a river which tumbles down to the magnificent falls of Scale Force. The surrounding mountains were formed of Skiddaw slate 500 million years ago and are said to be some of the oldest in the world. There are green pastures on either side of the lake and the waters provide excellent opportunities for fishing. The entire lake and plantations on the south shore are owned by the National Trust.

BOWDER STONE

Beyond Seatoller the road enters Borrowdale and passes the huge boulder, estimated to weigh 2000 tons, which appears to be balanced precariously on edge. In fact the Bowder Stone is quite stable, and a ladder leads to the top. From it there are fine views down 'The Jaws of Borrowdale' where the valley narrows before opening on to Derwent Water. A stone bridge crosses the River Derwent to the tiny stone-built village of Grange, nestling below Derwent Fells. Beyond lies Derwent Water, one of the broadest of the lakes. Wooded islands dot the surface of the lake, whose shores are a mixture of steep fells, ravines and woodland.

Borrowdale, from Seatoller.

Wellingtonia, Johnny Wood Walk.

SEATOLLER

The village of Seatoller lies at the eastern end of the magnificent Honister Pass, at the point where Hause Gill stream joins the River Derwent. The neighbouring village of Seathwaite, about a mile up the river, is said to be the wettest inhabited place in England, with an average annual rainfall of 131 in. During the 17th and 18th centuries, graphite was mined at Seathwaite for the manufacture of Keswick pencils. The Johnny Wood Walk, which starts from Seatoller, leads through a wealth of trees and shrubs to High Doat, a fine vantage point from which to see Borrowdale and the surrounding fells. The walk is laid out by the Lake District Naturalists' Trust, which is dedicated to preserving the natural habitats of a variety of animals and plants. Among the trees to be seen on the route are sycamore, ash and a Wellingtonia which is 125 ft high. At one point the path follows an old sheep trod—a feeding path of sheep which follows the contours of the land. Johnny Wood itself is a lakeland oak forest, parts of which have existed for centuries. Quick-growing conifers have also been introduced.

327

The great park that was John Peel's hunting ground

Starting from the old market town of Penrith, this tour heads towards the fells that once echoed to the calls of John Peel and his hounds. Peel, the most famous of all huntsmen, is buried in Caldbeck churchyard. Much of the tour runs through the Lake District National Park, where placid lakes nestle between towering peaks from whose summits beacons used to blaze to warn of national danger. The high peaks are the preserve of properly equipped climbers and hardy fell walkers, but beside the lakes and through the forests on the valley sides are marked trails where anyone can enjoy the splendour of this spectacular country.

(1) Penrith to Hesket Newmarket Leave Penrith on the B5288 signposted for Greystoke, but immediately after crossing the M6 turn right on to the minor road signposted to Newton Reigny. At the crossroads 2 m. beyond Newton Reigny, keep straight on and follow the road to Skelton, a close-knit village huddled round a 14th-century church. The surrounding landscape is still marked by the field strips in which medieval farmers worked the land. At the junction with the B5305, 1 m. beyond Skelton, turn left, following the signpost for Sebergham, and turn left again after 2 m., following the signpost for Hesket Newmarket. After 2 m. the road descends into the valley of the River Caldew. The road crosses the river, which it then follows for 2 m. before bearing left to enter Hesket Newmarket.

(2) Hesket Newmarket to Caldbeck Carry on along the same road for the short drive to Caldbeck across the foothills—known as 'Back o' Skiddaw'. The Skiddaw group of mountains is on the left of the road, rising beyond Caldbeck Fells to Skiddaw itself. John Peel, the huntsman, is buried in Caldbeck churchyard. Overlooked by a holly bush, the white headstone, with its carved portrait of a hound and a pair of hunting horns, lies to the left of the path to the porch.

(3) Caldbeck to Dodd Wood In Caldbeck bear left, joining the B5299. But just over 3 m. later, where the B5299 swings right for Aspatria, keep straight ahead on the moorland road signposted for Keswick. A mile along this road, turn left on to the road signposted for Orthwaite and Mirkholme. After another 2 m. there is a right turn signposted to Keswick. Ignore this and keep straight ahead on the road that skirts the western flank of Skiddaw, passing the small lakes of Over Water and Little Tarn on the right. On reaching the A591, turn left for Keswick and, with Bassenthwaite Lake on the right, reach Dodd Wood, stretching along the left of the road. Dodd Wood has three walks ranging in length from a few hundred yards to 3 m. Roe deer and red squirrels live among the trees.

(4) Dodd Wood to Keswick Return to the A591 and turn left for the drive to Keswick, alongside the River Derwent, which flows out of Bassenthwaite Lake and into Derwent Water. The two lakes were once joined, but sediment brought down by the River Greta built up on a shallow rock bar and gradually extended until a 3 m. land barrier now separates the lakes. This is the lowlying ground to the right through which the

Derwent flows. In Keswick drive through to the far side of the town and along Lake Road for a stroll by the shore of Derwent Water, with its tree-clad islands. In summer there is a regular boat service around the lake. The trip lasts about an hour.

(5) Keswick to Castlerigg stone circle Leave Keswick on the A591 signposted for Penrith. Almost immediately after the A591 turns sharp right to Kendal, fork left and then turn right up a minor road which climbs steeply for ¾ m. to the Castlerigg stone circle, the most important prehistoric site in the Lake District. The stones are in a field on the right, just past a turning to the right. There is no car park, but cars can be left at the roadside and the stones are only 100 yds away across the field.

(6) Castlerigg stone circle to Greystoke From the stone circle continue along the lane, turning left at the first T-junction, then right almost immediately after to rejoin the A66 going towards Penrith. Continue up the valley of the River Greta—with the Skiddaw range on the left and the Helvellyn peaks on the right—for a further 8 m. Then, almost 1 m. past the junction where the A5091 comes in on the right, turn left along a minor road signposted for Hutton Roof. After ¾ m. take the first turning right and follow this road for 3 m. to Greystoke.

(7) Greystoke to Penrith Leave the village on the B5288, signposted to Penrith, for the 5 m. drive to the end of the tour.

NATURE NOTES
The northern part of Skiddaw Forest is covered with grouse moors, which also provide a hunting ground for merlins, rare in most parts of Britain. The merlin will pursue birds as big as itself and the male, having caught its prey, sometimes passes it to its mate in flight.

INFORMATION

Places of interest *Keswick:* Fitz Park Museum, Apr. to Oct., weekdays. *Penrith Castle:* All year, daily.

Events *Keswick:* Agricultural show, Aug. *Skelton:* Horticultural show, Aug.

Nature trail *Friars Crag, Keswick:* 1½ m. mixed woodland, lakeshore walk. Guide from National Trust or National Park Information Centres.

Information *Keswick:* Moot Hall, Market Square (Tel. Keswick 72645). Lake District National Park Office, Moot Hall, Keswick (Tel. Keswick 72803).

Towns with easy access to Penrith:

Alston	20 m.	Hexham	44 m.
Carlisle	18 m.	Kendal	27 m.
Cockermouth	30 m.	Windermere	27 m.

DODD WOOD
The pine marten, Britain's rarest mammal, lives in Dodd Wood. Other animals found there include roe deer and red squirrels. Dodd Wood is part of the Forestry Commission's Thornthwaite Forest, the oldest national forest in the Lake District, on which planting began in 1919. There are, in addition, some fine trees planted by a local landowner in 1790. To enjoy the woods, take one of the three signposted walks, the longest of which climbs to 1612 ft at Dodd Summit. From there, looking north-west along the length of Bassenthwaite Lake, it is possible to see the hump of Criffell across the Solway in Scotland. At the car park is an old sawmill.

Raven

Over Water

Orthwaite

Little Tarn

Mirkholme

BOTHEL 5 MILES

3054 Skid

N

Bassenthwaite Lake

Thornthwaite Forest

(4) Dodd Wood •16

Derwent Water at Keswick.

DERWENT WATER
Studded with tree-clad islands and overlooked by rocky-crested mountains, this is perhaps the most beautiful of all the Cumbrian lakes. Much of the lake and its wooded shoreline belong to the National Trust, founded in 1895 by three men who included Canon H. D. Rawnsley, vicar of Keswick's Crosthwaite church. Friar's Crag, just south of Keswick, is a viewpoint from which most of the lakes can be seen. A 2 mile nature trail along the lakeside starts near by.

SCALE

0   1   2   3 MILES

CALDBECK
John Peel was born in Caldbeck in 1777, and at the age of 20 eloped to Gretna Green to marry Mary White. They had 13 children—and all but two survived to attend their father's funeral in 1854. Although Peel often rode a pony, he used to follow hounds on foot in traditional Lakeland style. The rousing 'John Peel' song was written by his friend J. W. Groves, and was first sung by Peel himself.

John Peel's grave, Caldbeck churchyard.

HESKET NEWMARKET
This tiny village near the River Caldew lies on the northern flanks of Skiddaw. There is an 18th-century market cross on the village green— a reminder of the time when the market still existed. The surrounding moorlands are managed for grouse shooting. Heather and bilberry grow among the grass tufts, providing a habitat for such day-flying moths as the northern eggar and the yellow underwing. Above 2000 ft there are wide areas of peat bog where golden plover nest.

IDDAW
3054 ft, Skiddaw soars higher than y Lakeland peak except Scafell Pike d Helvellyn. Although the climb n be gruelling, it calls for no great ountaineering skill; in Victorian es women tourists rode to the summit ponies. The bare, shale-covered mmit, called High Man, was the e of a medieval look-out post and rning beacon. It provides magnificent ws over Derwent Water and Keswick, lvellyn and Borrowdale. On an ceptionally clear day it is possible see the Cheviot Hills to the north, gleborough in Yorkshire, the Isle of an and even Ireland to the west. ere are two main approaches to ddaw, one by Mallen Dodd on the rth-eastern outskirts of Keswick, d a much steeper route beginning Dodd Wood, a haunt of ravens.

PENRITH
Sited between the Pennines and the Lake District mountains, Penrith was for centuries a strategic point on the main western route between England and Scotland. In the 10th century it was probably the capital of Owen Caesarius, King of Cumbria, said to be buried under a monument known as the Giant's Grave, outside the Norman parish church. Scottish raiders plagued the town until the 17th century, sacking it twice. Overlooking Penrith from the north-east is The Pike, an 18th-century watchtower which formed part of a national warning system. It last blazed in 1804 when Napoleon's army seemed about to invade England.

Giant's Grave, Penrith.

GREYSTOKE
The great church in the village dates from the 13th century, and has some fine, old stained glass. A railed-off stone near the entrance marks the point where a fugitive could claim sanctuary, safe from his enemies or justice for 40 days. Greystoke Castle, built in the 1350s, can be seen from the road but is not open to the public. It stands in a park of 6000 acres.

Moot Hall, Keswick.

SWICK
in a green valley, with magnificent heights all und, Keswick was transformed into a holiday town the Victorians. Earlier it had been a market town d mining centre. The Moot Hall (town hall), on an nd site in the main street, dates from 1813. Keswick links with many famous writers and there are nuscripts by Southey, Wordsworth and others in the n museum, which also has some fine paintings luding works by Turner and Steer.

Castlerigg stone circle.

CASTLERIGG STONE CIRCLE
This ancient circle, probably constructed for religious purposes about 3500 years ago, stands in a field 706 ft above sea level between the mountain massifs of Skiddaw and Helvellyn. It consists of 38 great boulders enclosing an area 107 ft by 96 ft. There is also a rectangular enclosure on the eastern side. According to Cumbrian folklore, the boulders are men turned to stone by witchcraft. It has also been suggested that the circle was a temple of the Druids, the priesthood of the pre-Roman Celts.

329

Along the wild frontier of a lost empire

Eighteen hundred years ago the Roman legions built Hadrian's Wall, a 73 mile long chain of fortresses and look-out towers, to seal off their empire against the unconquered tribes of the North. Part of this tour, between Banks and Gilsland, runs right alongside the wall, and the drive is studded with turrets and 'mile castles'. The biggest of them all can be seen at Birdoswald, a stronghold which housed a garrison of 1000. The route passes along the valley of the South Tyne, and winds among the fells and lowlands of the Cumbrian-Northumberland border.

(1) Brampton to Lanercost Priory Leave Brampton on the A69, following the signposts for Hexham and Newcastle. On the outskirts, fork left on to the minor road signposted to Lanercost. The road crosses the River Irthing at Lanercost Bridge. The priory is on the right, just before the road enters the village of Lanercost.

(2) Lanercost Priory to Banks East Turret Continue into the village and turn right on to the road signposted to Banks and Gilsland. Follow the road for 1 m. into Banks and keep right through the village to Banks East Turret.

(3) Banks East Turret to Birdoswald Continue on this road. The remains of Roman turrets, signal towers and the wall itself rise beside the road as it runs almost straight for 3 m. to the fort at Birdoswald.

(4) Birdoswald to Gilsland Continue along the same road to the T-junction with the B6318 and turn right, following the signposts to Gilsland. After 1½ m., near another Roman mile castle, is the village of Gilsland.

(5) Gilsland to Whitley Castle Leave Gilsland along the B6318, following the signpost for Greenhead and Newcastle. The road passes through Runner Foot Gap, with Hadrian's Wall on the right. After 2 m., just before Greenhead, there is a Roman camp on the right. Continue to the T-junction with the A69 in Greenhead and turn left, following the Hexham/Newcastle signpost. About 1 m. past the village, just beyond Blenkinsopp Castle, turn right on to the minor road, signposted to Featherstone Castle. Follow the road for 2 m., after which it turns left and almost immediately right to cross the bridge over the River South Tyne. Across the bridge, the road meets a T-junction. Turn right here, following the signpost to Featherstone Park station. Continue over the level crossing at the station to the T-junction with another minor road. Turn right, following the signposts for Alston. The road now follows the course of the River South Tyne. Keep straight on at the crossroads, following the signpost for Slaggyford. The road recrosses the South Tyne and, soon after, one of its tributaries, Thinhope Burn. It then runs on to meet the A689 at Knarsdale. Turn left on to the A689, following the signposts for Alston. Continue through Slaggyford on the same road. After just under 2 m. the road crosses the Pennine Way, the long-distance footpath that runs from Edale in Derbyshire to Kirk Yetholme over the Scottish border. A five-minute walk down the path, across a field on the right, leads to the remains of the Roman fort, Whitley Castle.

(6) Whitley Castle to Gamblesby Fell Take the A689 towards Alston. After 2½ m., at the T-junction with the A686, turn right following the signpost for Penrith. The road climbs steadily, and the mountains of the Lake District and the valley of the River Eden come into view. Rare plants grow on the fells alongside the road, which reaches its highest point, 1903 ft., at Gamblesby Fell.

(7) Gamblesby Fell to Armathwaite The A686 now plunges sharply down the western slopes of the Pennines. Continue through the village of Melmerby and, after 2 m., turn right on to the road signposted to Robberby and Glassonby. In Glassonby, bear left on to the road signposted to Kirkoswald. In Kirkoswald, turn right on to the B6413, following the signpost for Brampton, but on the far side of the village, where the B6413 swings to the right, go straight ahead on to the minor road signposted to Armathwaite. The road runs along the valley of the River Eden, then turns left into Armathwaite.

(8) Armathwaite to Wetheral Turn right at the T-junction in the centre of Armathwaite on to the road signposted to Wetheral. The road continues up the Eden Valley, running parallel to the railway. After 7 m. it meets the B6263. Turn right on to the B6263 for the 1 m. run to Wetheral.

(9) Wetheral to Brampton Go straight on through Wetheral on the B6263. After just over 1 m. at the T-junction with the A69, turn right and follow the road into Warwick Bridge. In the village, turn left on to the road signposted for Little Corby. At the T-junction, 1 m. later, turn right for Brampton. After another 1 m., at the T-junction with the B6264, turn right again for Brampton.

NATURE NOTES
This area contains some fine moorland and bogland. Bog asphodel, white beak-sedge and lesser butterfly orchid grow here. Cowberry, creeping lady's tresses orchid and common wintergreen may be found in pine and birch woods.

INFORMATION
Places of interest *Banks:* LYC (Li Yuan Chia) Museum, daily. *Lanercost Priory:* Weekdays and Sun. afternoons. *Birdoswald:* Roman fort, daily (apply at farmhouse).

Event *Lanercost Priory:* Dialect service, June.

Craft workshop *Brampton:* Allison Pottery and Studio, 32-34 Main Street, weekdays, Mar. to Oct.

Information 32-34 Main Street, Brampton (Tel. Brampton 2685).

Towns with easy access to Brampton:

Alston	19 m.	Hexham	29 m.
Carlisle	9 m.	Longtown	11 m.

BRAMPTON
Brampton has a cobble-flanked main street that leads up to a quaint, octagonal moot (meeting) hall. The parish church, built by the Earl of Carlisle in 1874, has stained-glass windows designed by the Victorian artist Sir Edward Burne-Jones. Bonnie Prince Charlie stayed in the town in 1745, the year of the abortive rising aimed at restoring him to the throne. The house in which he received the surrender of Carlisle is now a shoeshop in a street off the square. Hadrian's Wall is 2 miles to the north.

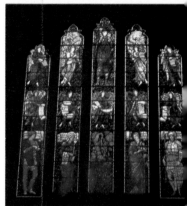

Stained-glass windows, Brampton parish church.

WETHERAL
The 17th-century Corby Castle dominates Wetheral, which is set in one of the loveliest stretches of the Eden Valley. The stone lions on the roof of the house are part of the arms of the Howard family, owners of the castle since 1611. A Benedictine priory once flourished just south of Wetheral, but its 15th-century gatehouse is all that is left. Also in the village are three caves, said to have been occupied in the 7th century by St Cuthbert.

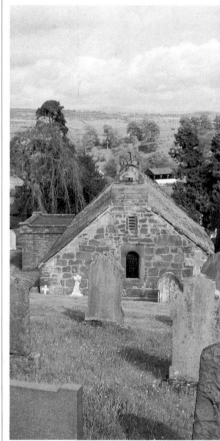

The 12th-century chapel, Armathwaite.

SCALE

0	1	2	3	4	5 MILES

Moot Hall, Brampton.

BANKS EAST TURRET
This turret is one of a series of turrets, mile castles and forts along Hadrian's Wall. It originally had two storeys and was used as a look-out post and signalling station. The Roman mile was 1620 yds long and there were two turrets between each pair of mile castles. Each turret was manned by troops from the nearest mile castle, which had a garrison of anything from a score or so to over 1000. The Pike Hill signal tower, reached by a short footpath to the east of Banks East Turret, was built before the wall itself and was later incorporated into it.

Banks East Turret, on Hadrian's Wall.

BIRDOSWALD
The outer defences of this fort, called Camboglanna by the Romans, are the largest and most impressive on Hadrian's Wall. Well-preserved lengths of the wall stretch east and west of the fort, which was built to house either 500 cavalry or 1000 infantrymen, and covered an area of about 5¼ acres. There is evidence that the fort was rebuilt four times, proof of its strategic importance.

Roman sandal found near Birdoswald Fort.

GILSLAND
To the north of Gilsland the upper reaches of the River Irthing flow through a wooded valley on the border of the Northumberland National Park. It was here that Sir Walter Scott proposed to Charlotte Carpenter beside a rock called the Popping Stone. Hadrian's Wall runs through the village, and the Poltross Burn mile castle can be visited.

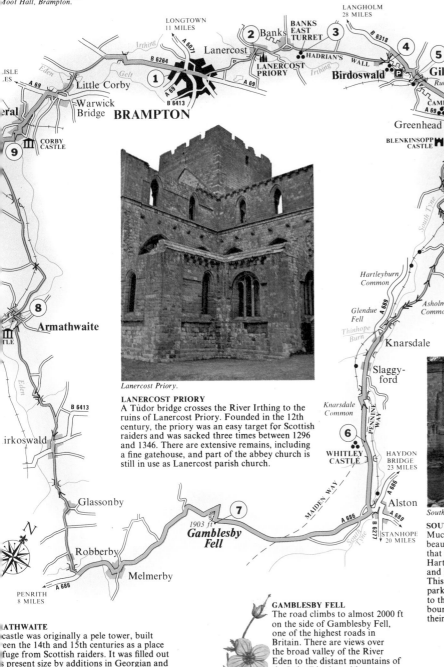

Lanercost Priory.

LANERCOST PRIORY
A Tudor bridge crosses the River Irthing to the ruins of Lanercost Priory. Founded in the 12th century, the priory was an easy target for Scottish raiders and was sacked three times between 1296 and 1346. There are extensive remains, including a fine gatehouse, and part of the abbey church is still in use as Lanercost parish church.

South Tyne river scene.

SOUTH TYNE VALLEY
Much of the southward part of the route lies along the beautiful valley of the South Tyne, one of the two streams that feed the River Tyne. On either side of the valley, the Hartleyburn Commons, Ashholme Common, Glendue Fell and Knarsdale Common, rise between 1500 and 2000 ft. This is the heart of rural Northumberland, where wooded parks shelter the houses of big landowners, and fields reach to the horizon, often unbroken by hedges or visible boundaries. Solid, greystone farmhouses and cottages lend their own charm to the scenery.

WHITLEY CASTLE
Three miles south of Slaggyford, the route crosses the Pennine Way—Britain's longest footpath—on its 250 mile course along the backbone of England. A five-minute walk to the right leads to Whitley Castle, a Roman fort built to control rebellious British tribesmen south of Hadrian's Wall.

GAMBLESBY FELL
The road climbs to almost 2000 ft on the side of Gamblesby Fell, one of the highest roads in Britain. There are views over the broad valley of the River Eden to the distant mountains of the Lake District, with Ullswater gleaming between them, 15 miles away beyond Penrith. The country round about is rich in wild flowers, including wild orchid, melancholy thistle, water avens and wood cranesbill.

Wood cranesbill

...ATHWAITE
...castle was originally a pele tower, built ...een the 14th and 15th centuries as a place ...fuge from Scottish raiders. It was filled out ...s present size by additions in Georgian and ...orian times. Now it is a private residence. ...chapel of Christ and St Mary dates back to ...2th century, but after 500 years it was ...ced to a cowshed. Then a 17th-century lord ...e manor, Richard Skelton, had it rebuilt into ...resent form.

Map labels: LONGTOWN 11 MILES, LANGHOLM 28 MILES, BANKS, BANKS EAST TURRET, HADRIAN'S WALL, Lanercost, LANERCOST PRIORY, Birdoswald, Gilsland, Runner Foot Gap, CAMP, Greenhead, BLENKINSOPP CASTLE, HEXHAM 18 MILES, NEWCASTLE UPON TYNE 38 MILES, Little Corby, Warwick Bridge, BRAMPTON, CORBY CASTLE, Armathwaite, Hartleyburn Common, Glendue Fell, Thinhope Burn, Asholme Common, Knarsdale, Slaggyford, Knarsdale Common, WHITLEY CASTLE, HAYDON BRIDGE 23 MILES, PENNINE WAY, Alston, MAIDEN WAY, 1903 ft Gamblesby Fell, STANHOPE 20 MILES, Glassonby, ...irkoswald, Robberby, Melmerby, PENRITH 8 MILES

DURHAM

This map shows the route of a suggested walking tour of Durham, indicating some of the most interesting places. Numbered features are listed below, together with opening times and other information.

THINGS TO SEE IN THE CITY

(1) Multi-storey car park, convenient for start of the walk from Market Place.

(2) Town Hall and Burlison Art Gallery, open Mon. to Fri. For Durham Light Infantry Museum (Tues. to Sat., Sun. afternoon and Bank Hol. Mon.), cross Framwelgate Bridge, turn right into Milburngate, pass station and turn right after 200 yds.

(3) Street of Georgian houses, mostly used as university colleges. Wall map at junction of Saddler Street and Owengate.

(4) Bishop Cosin's Almshouses, dating from 1838. No. 5 is a Tudor house.

(5) Castle, housing the university. Open weekdays during vacations; Mon., Wed. and Sat. afternoons in term.

(6) Palace Green. Bishop Cosin's Hall, University Library and Union building.

(7) Broken Walls, skirting extension of University Library. Views over river.

(8) Cathedral, entering by north door. Open daily until dusk.

(9) College Green. Private, cloistered garden, giving access to the river.

(10) Monastery walls, part of fortifications built by Benedictine monks.

(11) To Gulbenkian Museum. Christmas to Easter, Mon. to Fri., then daily.

(12) Church of St Mary the Less (1846) and St John's College (1730).

(13) College gatehouse, leading to College Green. Access to cathedral and river.

(14) Church of St Mary-le-Bow, rebuilt in 1685. Dramatic view of cathedral.

(15) Modern university buildings, approached by footbridge over the river.

(16) Fearon Walk. Pleasant riverside path leading behind Hatfield College.

(17) Elvet Bridge. Built by Bishop Hugh Pudsey (1153–95).

OTHER CAR PARKS: Station and Milburngate (beyond Framwelgate Bridge), Palace Green, Old Elvet, Leazes Road, South Street.
INFORMATION: 13 Claypath (Tel. Durham 3720).

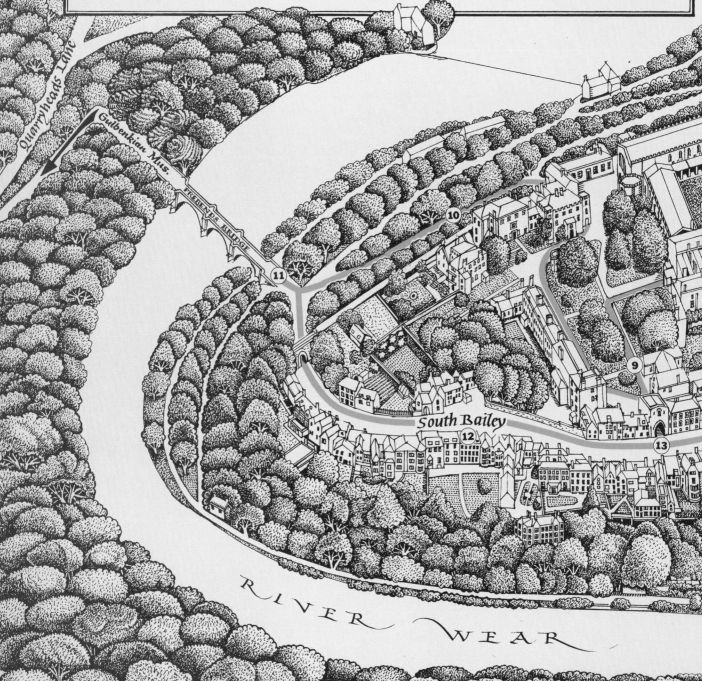

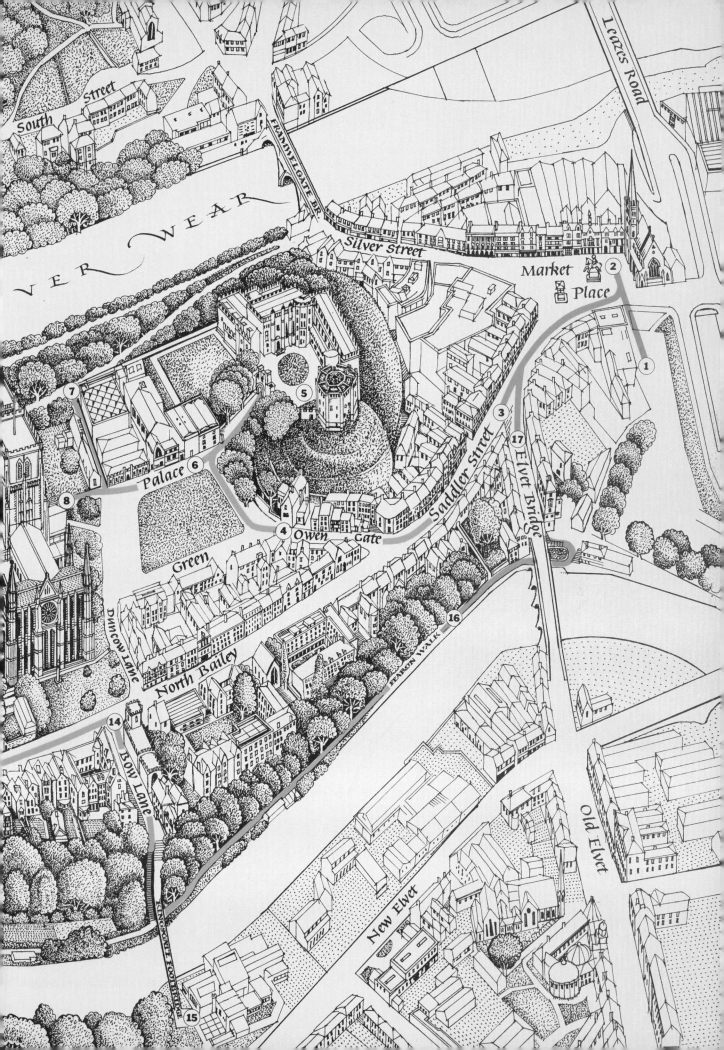

DURHAM

For 800 years the bishops of Durham were also princes—the independent rulers of County Durham. The city's ancient dual role—bastion of Christianity and seat of temporal power—is epitomised by Scott's description of its cathedral: 'Half church . . . half castle.'

Durham owes both its name and its setting—on a loop of the River Wear—not to the tastes of its founders, but to military strategy. The Saxons called it Dunholme, referring to its protected position: *dun*, meaning hill, and *holm*, or *helme*, indicating a plain surrounded by water. Later the name became Duresme, and finally Durham. It is thanks largely to this strategic siting that Durham remains a blend of ancient and modern: it is the only city near the Border that was never taken by invading Scots. The early Saxons built a castle, whose successor still dominates the city, and the Normans put up the nearby cathedral, said to be the finest building of its period in the world.

The rest of the architecture also supplements the city's colourful history of distinguished architects, skilled stonemasons, saints and scholars and prince-bishops. The rank of prince-bishop dates from about 1072, when William the Conqueror made the first Norman bishop, Walcher of Lorraine, custodian of the castle. For centuries afterwards Walcher's successors exercised the delegated authority of the king in addition to their ecclesiastical duties, and the title survived until 1836.

The narrow streets and alleys, whose buildings mark the centuries that followed the Norman Conquest, the ancient bridges and leafy riverside walks, all help to make Durham a mirror of history.

In the Market Place—the best place to begin a walking tour, as there is a multi-storey car park near by—a network of ancient winding streets spreads out from near a glass-panelled box where a policeman controls the present-day traffic with the aid of closed-circuit TV.

The Market Place is dominated by a statue of the 3rd Marquis of Londonderry (1779–1854) on horseback, by the sculptor Raffaele Monte of Milan. On the west side are the municipal buildings.

Built by public subscription in 1850, the Town Hall has a hammerbeam roof similar to that in London's Westminster Hall. Its interior is festooned with the arms of the county's leading families and city livery companies. Panels, each dedicated to a former mayor, decorate the walls.

Tom Thumb's violin

In an ante-room is the Burlison Art Gallery, named after the artist Clement Burlison, who spent most of his life in Durham and specialised in copying famous paintings from European galleries. He died in 1899. In the lobby of the art gallery are a portrait and statue of one of Durham's most remarkable characters, Joseph Boruwlaski, a Pole who, because he was only 3 ft 3 in. tall, became known as Lord Tom Thumb. After wandering through Europe, and even becoming well known in the royal circle in London, 'Count' Boruwlaski, as he called himself, made Durham his home in

1800 and became one of its most popular citizens. His charm and wit, and especially his musical talent, made him a favourite party guest; his violin is preserved with other relics in the gallery.

Boruwlaski was 98 when he died in 1837. His tomb, marked simply 'J.B.', is in the cathedral, and his epitaph, in the Church of St Mary the Less, in South Bailey, reads:

> *Poland was my cradle,*
> *England my nest.*
> *Durham is my quiet Place*
> *Where my bones shall rest.*

The Guildhall, the oldest of the municipal buildings, was founded in 1356, but was twice rebuilt, in 1535 and 1665. It is used for meetings by the eight surviving trade guilds, and on special occasions the corporation and guild plate is on display. In the lower lobby is an oak chest made in 1610 and a facsimile of the city's first charter, granted by Bishop Hugh Pudsey in 1179 and confirmed by Pope Alexander III.

Leaving the Market Place by Saddler Street, the walk leads to what was once the city's theatreland. Drury Lane is a narrow alley—known locally as a 'vennel'—leading from the lower part of the street to the river. Behind 61 Saddler Street a theatre managed by Stephen Kemble, a leading Shakespearian authority, existed from 1792 to 1850. Off Saddler Street to the right is Owengate, which leads to the castle and cathedral and contains a Tudor-style house with timbered façade and overhanging upper storeys, and a number of almshouses dating from 1838.

Bishop William van Mildert, last of Durham's prince-bishops, founded the uni-

LORD TOM THUMB *'Count' Joseph Boruwlaski, 3 ft 3 in. tall, a Polish exile, was an accomplished violinist much in demand in 19th-century Durham society. His statue (left) is in the Burlison Art Gallery. He died in 1837, aged 98, and his tomb is in the cathedral.*

OWENGATE *Originally a gateway to Palace Green, this narrow street contains a good example of a Tudor-style timber-fronted façade with overhanging upper storeys, and a number of old almshouses.*

CAPITAL CARVINGS *The stone columns of the castle's Norman Chapel are decorated with carved animals, foliage and grotesque masks, dating back to 1080. The chapel is said to be the oldest building in the city of Durham.*

COLLEGE CASTLE *Established in 1832, Durham became the third university founded in England. The castle was handed over to it in 1837.*

DISBANDED *Drums of the Durham Light Infantry, who were raised in 1758 and disappeared as a separate regiment in 1968 when the Army was reorganised.*

...versity in 1832 and five years later handed over the castle, which had been used as the bishop's palace, to house it. Durham was the first university to be founded in England after Oxford and Cambridge.

Among the castle's outstanding features are its 11th-century chapel, with elaborate and often grotesque carvings on its stone columns, Bishop John Cosin's Black Staircase, built of oak in the 1660s, and Gothic-style walls and gatehouse rebuilt in the 18th century by the architect James Wyatt.

Opposite the castle, across Palace Green, is the cathedral with its lofty turrets which inspired Sir Walter Scott to compose a verse, now recorded on a plaque on Prebends Bridge:

Grey towers of Durham
Yet well I love thy mixed and massive piles,
Half church of God, half castle 'gainst the Scot,
And long to roam these venerable aisles
With records stored of deeds long since forgot.

Visitors usually enter the cathedral by the great North Door, on which is the 12th-century sanctuary knocker. In the Middle Ages it was a custom that any hunted criminal could gain sanctuary from his pursuers by grasping the ring of the knocker. Monks, who kept watch from a room above the porch, would admit the fugitives, hear their confessions and enter the details in the Sanctuary Book. Between 1464 and 1525, 331 criminals—283 of them murderers—gained sanctuary in this way.

The cathedral's gilded Bishop's Throne—it is the highest in Christendom—contains the shrine of St Cuthbert, who died in 687 on Holy Island (Lindisfarne). His body was removed by monks fleeing from invading Danes in 875, and was finally laid to rest in Durham in 1070.

Bede's burial place

Also entombed here in the 12th-century Galilee Chapel are the remains of the Venerable Bede, the monk and historian who wrote an ecclesiastical history of the English people, and died at the monastery of St Paul, Jarrow, in 735. The remains were stolen and taken to Durham by a monk called Aelfred in 1022.

Leaving the cathedral across College Green and turning into Prebends Walk, the visitor can see the thick, fortified walls of the 10th-century Benedictine monastery on the site of which the cathedral is built. From Prebends Bridge, looking back up the river, the bustling city is almost concealed by the trees lining the riverbank. Beyond the bridge, in the outer university complex of Elvet Hill, is the Gulbenkian Museum of Oriental Art, the only museum devoted to Eastern art in Britain.

Back over the bridge, the South Bailey leads into one of the city's oldest thoroughfares, its Georgian houses taken over as college residences but retaining their character.

At the junction with Bow Lane on the right is the Church of St Mary-le-Bow, a 17th-century building believed to stand on the site of a wattle church in which St Cuthbert's body was first received when it was taken to Durham for burial.

The Kingsgate footbridge at the foot of Bow Lane gives views of the newer university buildings across the river in New Elvet. Passing under the footbridge along Fearon Walk, a riverside stroll winds up the tour and brings the visitor back into Saddler Street and the Market Place in the city centre.

SANCTUARY AND SHRINE *Durham Cathedral, the world's finest Norman building, was a sanctuary for fugitives and St Cuthbert's final resting place.*

REFUGE *By grasping this knocker, criminals and debtors gained sanctuary in the Middle Ages.*

PATTERNED *The graceful sweeps of the cathedral's distinctive Norman arches are offset by their columns patterned in chevrons and spirals. Four arches like these, 68 ft 6 in. high, support the cathedral tower.*

INSPIRATIONAL *A view from Prebends Bridge inspired Sir Walter Scott to pen the lines, now inscribed on the bridge, of 'Grey towers of Durham . . .' The bridge was built in 1772 by George Nicholson, one of the cathedral masons.*

ORIENTAL ART *A garment from the Gulbenkian Museum which has one of the world's finest collections of oriental art.*

A switchback journey over the backbone of England

Deep valleys carved by rushing rivers accentuate the height of the northern Pennines along the boundary between Northumberland and Cumbria. Cross Fell, near Alston, is almost 3000 ft above sea level and the highest point of the mountain chain that forms the backbone of England. The fells have a lonely grandeur and contrast sharply with delightful villages of mellow stone cottages. Set amid the wild beauty of the area, a reservoir is the home of many water fowl. Tourists stopping for a picnic among the hills can see a giant water wheel which used to drive machinery for the now defunct lead-mining industry.

(1) Alston to River Allen Gorge Leave Alston on the A686, following the signposts for Hexham. After 12½ m. the road crosses the 5 m. long River Allen Gorge.

(2) River Allen Gorge to Allendale Town Continue along the A686 and after 1 m. turn right on to the B6305 signposted to Hexham. At the crossroads after 1 m. turn right again on to the B6295, and keep straight ahead at the junction soon afterwards where the B6304 comes in from the left. Go through Catton and beyond the village, where the B6295 bears right, keep straight ahead on to the B6303 into Allendale Town.

(3) Allendale Town to Blanchland Leave Allendale Town southwards on the B6295, and follow the road for 6 m. up the lovely East Allen river valley to Allenheads, a tiny village surrounded by conifer woods. At the crossroads in the village turn left, following the signpost for Rookhope. Follow the road across the high moorland of Wolfcleugh Common and Redburn Common for 6 m. Turn left, just before a cattle grid, on to the road signposted for Blanchland. After 4 m. the road reaches Hunstanworth. The church here, rebuilt in 1862, still has some features recognisably 13th century. Turn left at the T-junction just after the village, and follow the road into Blanchland.

(4) Blanchland to Pow Hill Country Park Leave Blanchland on the B6306, following the signpost for Shotley Bridge. After 2 m. the road reaches the Derwent Reservoir. The Pow Hill Country Park and picnic area are on the left between the road and the reservoir.

(5) Pow Hill Country Park to Stanhope Continue along the B6306 to Edmondbyers, where the parish church of St Edmund dates from 1150. (To visit the Derwent Reservoir dam keep straight ahead in the village along the B6278, following the signpost for Shotley Bridge. The entrance to the grounds surrounding the dam follows on the left after 1 m., just after the road crosses the River Derwent.) Turn right in Edmundbyers on to the B6278 signposted to Stanhope. The road runs southwards for 6½ m. across the moorland of Muggleswick Common, reaching more than 1500 ft before it drops steeply down to Stanhope, where Iron Age implements have been found in a 500 ft deep cave.

(6) Stanhope to Killhope Picnic Area Leave Stanhope on the A689 signposted to Alston and head up the valley of the River Wear. After 2½ m. the old stone-built village of Eastgate is reached. Here there are views south across the River Wear, and there is a

camping and walking centre. Eastgate marks the eastern end of Weardale Park; 2 m. further along the road, Westgate stands at the western end, and was at one time the site of the Bishop of Durham's castle. Ruins of the castle survive, and there is an old mill with a water wheel. From Westgate, follow the road across the bridge into Daddry Shield, once notable for its cockfights, and from there into St John's Chapel. The ancient market town takes its name from the church which is dedicated to St John the Baptist. After ¾ m. the road runs into Ireshopeburn, where there is a thorn tree beside which John Wesley preached in 1749. Soon after Ireshopeburn comes Wearhead. The town stands at the head of the River Wear under the shadow of Burnhope Seat, which rises to 2452 ft and is the highest point in County Durham. From Wearhead the road climbs through Cowshill to Lanehead, around which there are many pleasant walks. The landscape, once bare and wild, is becoming less severe because of recent afforestation. After another 1½ m. the road reaches Killhope Picnic Area.

(7) Killhope Picnic Area to Nenthead Continue along the A689 towards Alston. The road soon climbs to 2056 ft, the highest point reached by a major road anywhere in England. Nenthead lies ¾ m. further on.

(8) Nenthead to Alston Follow the A689 as it drops gradually down the valley of the River Nent to Alston, which is reached after 5 m.

NATURE NOTES
The high moors of the North Pennines are dotted with bogs. Heather, cotton grass, bog asphodel and sundew grow abundantly. In the sheltered valleys are stands of oak, ash, sycamore and elm, often wearing thick coats of lichen. The new Derwent Reservoir attracts flocks of mallard and tufted duck, with regular visits from whooper swans in winter. Except for insects, animal life is not usually abundant in boglands. Lizards, short-tailed voles and the occasional adder are native to the region, and bird-watchers can expect to see curlews, skylarks, wheatears and meadow pipits among the few resident species. Many of the Pennine boglands are of the type known as blanket bog. The term describes a thick covering of bog moss covering large areas, as opposed to the raised (hummocky) bog and the treacherous quaking bog.

INFORMATION

Events *Allendale Town:* Fire Ceremony, New Year's Eve. *Stanhope:* Agricultural Show and Fair, Sept., Carnival, July.

Information City Information Service, Princess Square, Newcastle (Tel. Newcastle 610691).

Towns with easy access to Alston:

Brampton	19 m.	Hexham	24 m.
Carlisle	29 m.	Penrith	20 m.

River Allen Gorge.

RIVER ALLEN GORGE
For 5 miles the River Allen tumbles through a wooded gorge which in places is 250 ft deep. Sheltered tree-lined paths alongside provide walkers with an ever-changing spectacle. Opposite the disused railway station at High Staward, a path leads off into thickly wooded hills. After 1 mile it reaches the Staward Pele Tower, a 14th-century ruin commanding panoramic views of the surrounding countryside over which it once stood guard. The views are particularly impressive after a fall of snow.

ALSTON
At almost 1000 ft, Alston is the highest market town in England. It is also the nearest town to Cross Fell, which at 2930 ft is the highest peak in the Pennines. The town, a great favourite with experienced hikers, is built on a hillside commanding views of the South Tyne Valley and the highest fells in Pennine Chain. From Roman times until the early 19th century Alston was an important mining centre; silver, lead, copper, iron and other ores were extracted from h whose economic yield now is only a small amount of anthracite. Side streets lined with stone houses lead off cobbled main street, which climbs steeply from the market square. A stone-pillared market house covering an old cross stands in the square. The Friends' Meeting House, near by, dates from 1732.

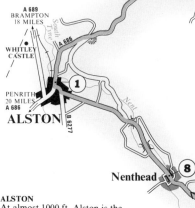
Market-place, Alston.

NENTHEAD
Surrounded by bleak moorland, Nenthead is a model village built in the 19th century to house lead miners. It is claimed to have the highest church, chapel and vicarage in England, 2000 ft up in the Pennines. An underground canal, now sealed, once linked the village with Alston.

SCALE

0 1 2 3 4 5 MILES

ALLENDALE TOWN

Perched on a cliff 1400 ft above sea level over the River East Allen, Allendale Town was once a lead-mining town, but is now a popular skiing centre. The broad main street is lined with trees, and the grey-stone market square has scarcely changed in 200 years. The town is well known for its December 31 fire festival, a survival of an old Norse custom. Accompanied by brass bands, men with blackened faces carry tubs of blazing tar on their heads and march to a bonfire in the market-place, where the turn of the year is celebrated. The festival is similar to the famous 'Up-helly-Aa' of the Shetland Islands.

EAST ALLENDALE

The fine valley of the East Allen river, broadening as it descends to the north, was a major source of lead until the mines ceased to be economic about a century ago. The old workings are now almost all overgrown by the moorland vegetation. Agriculturally the land is poor—so poor that by the middle of the 19th century it formed the only large area in Northumberland to be left unaffected by the trend towards fencing off private estates. On Allendale Common and Hexhamshire Common there are thousands of acres where local farmers still share the right to graze livestock. A number of attractive local walks follow the old lead-miners' packhorse trails to Tyneside.

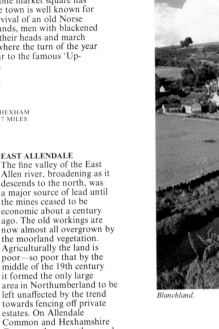

Blanchland.

BLANCHLAND

An order of monks known as the White (or Blancs) Canons, who built an abbey here in the 12th century, gave its name to this place. The present village was built around 1800, amid the remains of the abbey. The village, probably built to house lead miners, was superbly laid out by some long-forgotten pioneer of town planning. The simple stone houses are arranged in low terraces around a broad L-shaped enclave, one of whose entrances was the gateway to the old monastery. Part of the 13th-century guest house has been converted into a village inn, and the church, with its L-shaped nave, was constructed out of the ruined abbey itself. In the churchyard, John Wesley preached to a congregation of lead miners in 1747. Shrouded in trees and lapped by the moors, the village preserves its air of seclusion at the foot of Dukesfield Fell.

Rainbow trout

Brown trout

DERWENT RESERVOIR

The 1000 acre Derwent Reservoir did not exist until 1967, when a 1000 yd long dam was completed across the River Derwent, creating a popular resort for trout fishing and sailing.

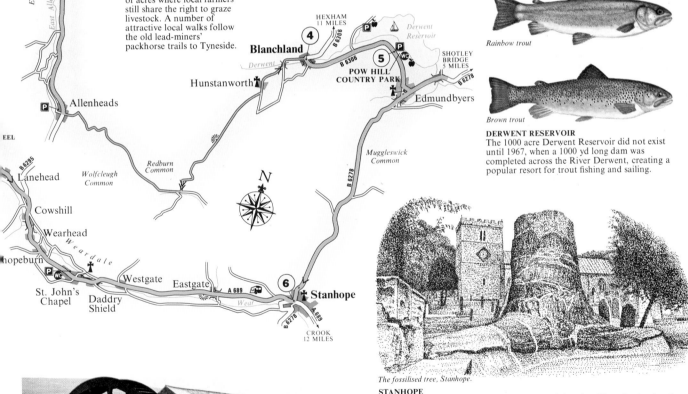

The fossilised tree, Stanhope.

STANHOPE

This moorland market town lies in the valley of the River Wear. In the churchyard is a fossilised tree stump, 250 million years old, which was discovered in a quarry near by in 1964. Some Iron Age implements were found in 1843 in Heathery Burn Cave, at the west side of the town. These finds, now in the British Museum in London, include parts of a wheel and harness, evidence that horse-drawn transport was being used in England more than 3500 years ago.

KILLHOPE PICNIC AREA

The old lead workings that overlook Killhope Picnic Area date from the 1860s. The water wheel, almost 40 ft in diameter, drove the machines that crushed the ore before it was taken by horse to the smelter at Allenheads. A stream was carried down the moors by a viaduct to power the big wheel, and the same water was then used to wash the ore. By the end of the last century most Weardale mines had been abandoned because cheaper ore was being imported from abroad.

Water wheel, Killhope Picnic Area.

The rugged land where Rome's empire ended

When the Roman legions invaded Britain 2000 years ago they not only came, saw and conquered; they also planned, organised and built, leaving on the land the imprint of their civilisation. Perhaps the grandest of their concepts to be seen in this country is Hadrian's Wall, the 73 mile long northern bastion of the Roman Empire built in the 2nd century as a defence against the fierce marauders from over the Scottish border. Drivers who like to get out and stretch their legs will get the best out of this tour, which visits several of the forts linked by the wall. But even with very little walking, the outing is a memorable experience, a flashback to England's Roman history against a background of some of the finest scenery in the country.

(1) Corbridge to Hexham Leave Corbridge on the A68 signposted Jedburgh. After 100 yds, turn left into Corchester Lane at the signpost Beaufront/Hexham. Corstopitum, the Roman military base, is ½ m. further along the road on the left. Continue along the winding Corchester Lane through undulating farmland. On the right, in beautiful grounds, is Beaufront Castle. Just under 2 m. later, turn left on to the A6079, and ½ m. later enter Hexham over the stone bridge which crosses the River Tyne.

(2) Hexham to Haydon Bridge Leave the town on the road signposted to Carlisle. It is an excellent fast road through undulating grassland, with fine views to the north over the Tyne Valley and wooded hillsides to the south. After 7 m., enter the riverside village of Haydon Bridge.

(3) Haydon Bridge to Steel Rigg Continue through Haydon Bridge on the A69 towards Carlisle. The road now skirts the bank of the River South Tyne and passes many picturesque cottages. Just over 4 m. out of Haydon Bridge, beyond Bardon Mill, take the first turning to the right signposted Once Brewed/Borcovicium (Vindolanda). Bear left at the first fork, and right at the signpost to Twice Brewed. There is now a steep climb with views of Hadrian's Wall in the distance on the right and Winshields Crag to the north. After 1 m. there is a T-junction with the B6318. Turn right and then sharp left to Steel Rigg, from which there are good views of the Roman wall.

(4) Steel Rigg to Vindolanda Return to the B6318, which was the main Roman supply road to the forts and look-out posts along the wall. The road now travels through undulating country, with fine views of the wall to the north and unexpected dips which could trouble unwary drivers. After nearly 2 m. take the unclassified road to the right, signposted Vindolanda, and follow the signposts for 1¼ m. to the car park.

(5) Vindolanda to Housesteads Return to the B6318 and turn right. The Housesteads Roman fort is 1 m. further along the road on the left. A tarmac path over two fields leads to the fort from a car park beside the B6318.

(6) Housesteads to Chesters Leave Housesteads, continuing east along the B6318. After 3 m. the road runs alongside The Vallum, the ditch which the Romans dug on the south side of the wall. Soon afterwards, on the right, is the fort of Brocolitia beside which are the remains of a temple to the god Mithras. Just over 3 m. later is Chesters, one of the largest and best-preserved forts along the Roman Wall. The car park is on the right off the main road.

(7) Chesters to Bellingham From Chesters continue along the B6318 to Chollerford. At the roundabout turn left on to the B6320 signposted to Simonburn. The road now leaves Hadrian's Wall and climbs through pleasant undulating farmland broken up by woods. After 3½ m. the road passes through Simonburn, where St Mungo's 13th-century church is signposted ½ m. to the left of the road. After 3 m. go through Wark, and 1 m. later the road runs through an avenue of woods beside the River North Tyne. Beyond the woods the road climbs into more open scenery before descending 3 m. later to cross the river by a narrow stone bridge to enter Bellingham.

(8) Bellingham to Corbridge Continue through Bellingham on the B6320 and after 7 m., at the T-junction with the A68, turn right. After 7 m. more, at Fourlaws, the modern road joins the Roman Dere Street. The road drives straight in a series of steep and narrow switchbacks, keeping to high ground for the 16 m. return run over the hills to Corbridge.

NATURE NOTES
Bean geese, the rarest species of geese to visit Britain regularly in winter, settle in the lake areas. So, too, do whooper swans, flying high in V-formation when they arrive from the Arctic in October and leave in April. Plants rarely seen south of the Scottish Highlands include dwarf cornel and coral-root orchid. Natural woodland is mainly birch, with some rowan and ash.

INFORMATION

Places of interest *Chesters:* Fort and museum, weekdays, Sun. afternoons. *Corbridge:* Corstopitum fort and museum, daily except Sun. morn., winter. *Housesteads:* Vercovicium fort and museum, daily except Sun. morn., winter. *Vindolanda:* Fort, daily.

Events *Once Brewed (Vindolanda):* Roman wall sheep-dog trials, June. *Bellingham:* Agricultural Show, Aug.

Information City Information Service, Princess Square, Newcastle upon Tyne (Tel. Newcastle 610691). Kielder Forest Centre, Kielder Castle (Tel. Kielder 209).

Towns with easy access to Corbridge:

Brampton	33 m.	Jedburgh	46 m.
Durham	27 m.	Newcastle	17 m.

VINDOLANDA
Excavations have been going on for some years at the Roman fort of Vindolanda, 2 miles south of Hadrian's Wall, but much work remains to be done before the true significance of the fort can be appreciated. The fort was built before the wall, apparently as part of the defensive system established by Agricola (AD 40–93) after he completed the conquest of Britain. Sections have been restored to demonstrate the workmanship of the Roman military builders and engineers.

Steel Rigg, from Housesteads.

STEEL RIGG
From the car park at Steel Rigg there are dramatic views in all directions. Most impressive of all, however, is the dark bulk of Hadrian's Wall marching across moorland and crag to the skyline, a monument to the ingenuity of the Roman engineers. Every fold in the ground, every natural bastion is taken advantage of and incorporated into the defence. To the east the broad ditch called The Vallum, crossed by easily patrolled causeways, can be clearly seen. This was an important part of the defence system, preventing Britons from crossing or attacking the wall from the south.

Old church, Haydon Bridge.

HAYDON BRIDGE
An arched bridge built in 1773 marks the approach to the village. The main attraction here is the old church, which stands on a hillside to the north where an earlier medieval village was sited. The church is part Norman, part 14th century. Stones from a nearby Roman camp were used in the rebuilding of the nave, and a Roman altar was salvaged to serve as a baptismal font. Attractive stone cottages and prim terraced houses line the South Tyne to form the town where 'Mad John' Martin (1789–1854), painter of melodramatic historical pictures, was born.

SCALE

0	1	2	3 MILES

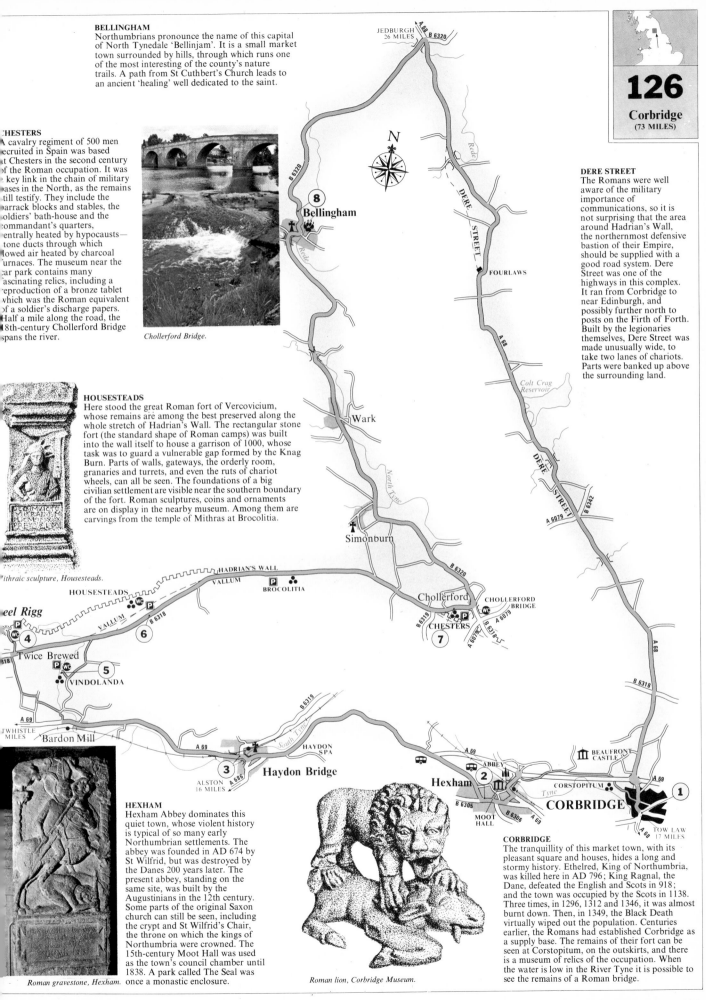

BELLINGHAM

Northumbrians pronounce the name of this capital of North Tynedale 'Bellinjam'. It is a small market town surrounded by hills, through which runs one of the most interesting of the county's nature trails. A path from St Cuthbert's Church leads to an ancient 'healing' well dedicated to the saint.

CHESTERS

A cavalry regiment of 500 men recruited in Spain was based at Chesters in the second century of the Roman occupation. It was a key link in the chain of military bases in the North, as the remains still testify. They include the barrack blocks and stables, the soldiers' bath-house and the commandant's quarters, centrally heated by hypocausts—stone ducts through which flowed air heated by charcoal furnaces. The museum near the car park contains many fascinating relics, including a reproduction of a bronze tablet which was the Roman equivalent of a soldier's discharge papers. Half a mile along the road, the 18th-century Chollerford Bridge spans the river.

Chollerford Bridge.

HOUSESTEADS

Here stood the great Roman fort of Vercovicium, whose remains are among the best preserved along the whole stretch of Hadrian's Wall. The rectangular stone fort (the standard shape of Roman camps) was built into the wall itself to house a garrison of 1000, whose task was to guard a vulnerable gap formed by the Knag Burn. Parts of walls, gateways, the orderly room, granaries and turrets, and even the ruts of chariot wheels, can all be seen. The foundations of a big civilian settlement are visible near the southern boundary of the fort. Roman sculptures, coins and ornaments are on display in the nearby museum. Among them are carvings from the temple of Mithras at Brocolitia.

Mithraic sculpture, Housesteads.

HEXHAM

Hexham Abbey dominates this quiet town, whose violent history is typical of so many early Northumbrian settlements. The abbey was founded in AD 674 by St Wilfrid, but was destroyed by the Danes 200 years later. The present abbey, standing on the same site, was built by the Augustinians in the 12th century. Some parts of the original Saxon church can still be seen, including the crypt and St Wilfrid's Chair, the throne on which the kings of Northumbria were crowned. The 15th-century Moot Hall was used as the town's council chamber until 1838. A park called The Seal was once a monastic enclosure.

Roman gravestone, Hexham.

Roman lion, Corbridge Museum.

DERE STREET

The Romans were well aware of the military importance of communications, so it is not surprising that the area around Hadrian's Wall, the northernmost defensive bastion of their Empire, should be supplied with a good road system. Dere Street was one of the highways in this complex. It ran from Corbridge to near Edinburgh, and possibly further north to posts on the Firth of Forth. Built by the legionaries themselves, Dere Street was made unusually wide, to take two lanes of chariots. Parts were banked up above the surrounding land.

CORBRIDGE

The tranquillity of this market town, with its pleasant square and houses, hides a long and stormy history. Ethelred, King of Northumbria, was killed here in AD 796; King Ragnal, the Dane, defeated the English and Scots in 918; and the town was occupied by the Scots in 1138. Three times, in 1296, 1312 and 1346, it was almost burnt down. Then, in 1349, the Black Death virtually wiped out the population. Centuries earlier, the Romans had established Corbridge as a supply base. The remains of their fort can be seen at Corstopitum, on the outskirts, and there is a museum of relics of the occupation. When the water is low in the River Tyne it is possible to see the remains of a Roman bridge.

Map labels

JEDBURGH 26 MILES
B 6320
N
Rede
B 6320
Bellingham **8**
Rede
DERE STREET
FOURLAWS
A 68
Colt Crag Reservoir
Wark
North Tyne
DERE STREET
A 6079
B 6342
Simonburn
B 6320
HADRIAN'S WALL
VALLUM
BROCOLITIA
Chollerford
CHOLLERFORD BRIDGE
HOUSESTEADS
VALLUM
B 6318
CHESTERS **7**
B 6318
A 6079
Peel Rigg **4**
6
Twice Brewed
5
VINDOLANDA
A 69
B 6318
B 6318
HALTWHISTLE MILES
Bardon Mill
A 69
B 6319
South Tyne
HAYDON SPA
Haydon Bridge **3**
ALSTON 16 MILES
A 686
ABBEY
BEAUFRONT CASTLE
A 69
Hexham **2**
CORSTOPITUM
Tyne
1
CORBRIDGE
MOOT HALL
B 6305
B 6306
A 69
A 68
TOW LAW 17 MILES
A 69

Round the country where railways first ran

From Darlington, where the first steam locomotive ever to pull a passenger train stands on the station platform, the tour follows the valley of the River Tees up to the Durham-Yorkshire border at High Force. This waterfall, where the Tees crashes over a 70 ft precipice in its dash from the Pennines, is at its best after heavy rain, but it is an impressive sight at any time. Barnard Castle, named after its ruined 12th-century fortress, is better known nowadays for the Bowes Museum, home of one of Britain's finest art collections. Tourists can wander in the great hall of Raby Castle, built to accommodate up to 700 warriors, and among the ruins of Stanwick Camp, Britain's biggest Iron Age fort.

(1) Darlington to Stanwick Camp Leave the town on the A67, following the signpost for Barnard Castle. On the outskirts of Darlington the road crosses the A1(M). After 3 m., at Piercebridge, turn left on to the B6275. After a sharp bend to cross the river, the road runs straight south, following the line of the Roman Dere Street. Continue on the road for 1½ m., then turn right on to the road signposted to Eppleby and Caldwell, and about 600 yds later take the first turning to the left. After 1 m. turn right, following the signpost for Forcett. Just after crossing Aldbrough Beck, at the T-junction, turn right. At the next junction keep straight on, still following the Forcett signpost. The fortifications of Stanwick Camp are on either side of the road.

(2) Stanwick Camp to Barnard Castle Leaving the camp, continue through Forcett, going straight ahead at the first junction. A few yards on, turn right on the B6274 signposted to Caldwell and Winston. The road continues through open country and crosses the River Tees before reaching Winston, which stands on a windy hilltop. The church is a little apart from the village and is mainly 13th century. It has an intricately carved stone font which appears to be Celtic. In Winston, at the T-junction, turn left and almost immediately left again on to the A67 signposted to Barnard Castle. Follow the road for about 4 m. to Barnard Castle, at the eastern end of the Stainmore gap across the Pennines.

(3) Barnard Castle to Middleton in Teesdale Follow the A67 through the town and over the River Tees. There is an attractive walk along the river below the castle. Just after crossing the river, swing right and at the next junction keep straight ahead to join the B6277 as the A67 goes off to the left. After about 1 m. the road passes Lartington Hall, set in grounds sloping down to the Tees, which meanders northwards between wooded banks. The hall is not open to the public. After 1 m. the road passes through Cotherstone village where a ruined, 12th-century castle overlooks the junction of the rivers Balder and Tees. The next village, Romaldkirk, contains solid stone houses and cottages on an irregular main street interspersed with grass and trees. The church, named after the infant saint, Rumwald, son of a Northumbrian king, is a mixture of styles from the 12th to 15th centuries. Almshouses, old stocks and a pound for stray cattle add to the character of the village. Two miles beyond Romaldkirk pass through Mickleton and, still on the B6277, cross the Tees and enter Middleton in Teesdale with

its fine bridge, which was rebuilt in 1811. The moors stretch away to the south-west, while to the north lie the rolling farmlands of western Durham.

(4) Middleton in Teesdale to High Force At the T-junction in the village turn left and follow the B6277, signposted to Alston. The road runs along the Tees Valley between steep fells, following the fast-flowing river for 5 m. to the High Force Hotel. There is a public car park here and a short walk leads to the spectacular High Force waterfall and the expanse of wild country above it.

(5) High Force to Staindrop Return by the B6277 to Middleton in Teesdale, and in the village go straight ahead on to the B6282, following the signpost for Barnard Castle. The road goes for 4 m. through riverside scenery to the village of Eggleston. On the far side of the village, follow the signpost for Barnard Castle. After 1 m. fork left on to the B6279, signposted to Staindrop, bearing left, 7 miles later, on to the A688 to enter the village.

(6) Staindrop to Raby Castle Leave Staindrop on the A688 signposted to Bishop Auckland. At the far side of the village, just after the road turns sharp left, there is an entrance to Raby Castle on the left, the home of Lord Barnard, lord of the manor of Barnard Castle and owner of the estates that formerly comprised the lordships of Balliol and Neville.

(7) Raby Castle to Darlington From the castle, return to Staindrop and, just before the A688 turns sharp right by the church, turn left on to the B6279 signposted for Darlington. Follow the road for 8 m., passing through the villages of Ingleton and Summerhouse. Go under the A1(M) and continue on the B6279 into Darlington.

INFORMATION

Places of interest *Barnard Castle :* Castle, weekdays, Sun. afternoons. Bowes Museum, weekdays, Sun. afternoons. *Darlington :* Museum, all year, weekdays, except Thur., mornings. *Raby Castle :* 2-5 p.m. only. Easter weekend, then Sun. only to end of May; Spring Bank Hol. week (except Fri.); Wed., Sat., Sun. in June, July, Sept.; Aug., Sun. to Thur.

Information Edward Pease Public Library, Crown Street, Darlington (Tel. Darlington 2034).

Towns with easy access to Darlington:

Bishop Auckland 12 m.		Richmond	12 m.
Durham	19 m.	Ripon	33 m.
Northallerton	16 m.	Stockton-on-Tees	11 m.

HIGH FORCE
Both Durham and Yorkshire claim the spectacular double fall of water, which boils down a sheer drop of 70 ft. The larger fall is, in fact, on the Yorkshire side of the river. The gorge through which the river plunges is slashed with cracks and crannies in which ferns and flowers grow. In a hard winter the fall has been known to freeze, providing a spectacle just as impressive as the foaming cascade.

High Force.

Drinking fountain, Middleton in Teesdale.

MIDDLETON IN TEESDALE
The stone houses of this village are set in walking country but the presence of the Teesdale and Weardale Fell Rescue Association headquarters is a reminder that the hills can be dangerous as well as beautiful. Middleton was once a lead-mining centre, and the cast-iron drinking fountain in the square commemorates the mining company. It was run by Quakers who provided good housing, and many of the miners' homes are still occupied

SCALE

0   1   2   3   4   5 MILES

RABY CASTLE

This medieval stronghold stands in 250 acres of wooded deer park. The fortress has nine towers surrounding a courtyard. It dates mainly from the 14th century, but was first mentioned in the reign of King Canute. In 1131 it was sold to a Saxon noble. The Barons' Hall, 136 ft long and overlooked by a minstrels' gallery, could accommodate 700 knights. Much history was made here, including the plot to put Mary, Queen of Scots on the throne of England in place of Elizabeth I. The abortive rising that followed, in which the Neville family played an important role, cost the family Raby Castle. The castle contains English, Dutch and Spanish paintings and a perfectly preserved Victorian drawing-room. The castle, surrounded by a moat, was renovated in the 18th and 19th centuries.

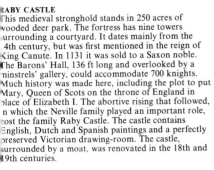
Raby Castle from the deer park.

STAINDROP

Attractive stone houses, many dating from the 18th century, surround the large, rectangular village green. At the far end is St Mary's church, with its Norman west tower and 12th-century aisle and nave. Further additions have given the architecture the characteristics of six centuries. Inside are many monuments to the Neville and Vane families, successive owners of Raby Castle, to whose domain the village belonged. In the churchyard is a large mausoleum belonging to the Neville family.

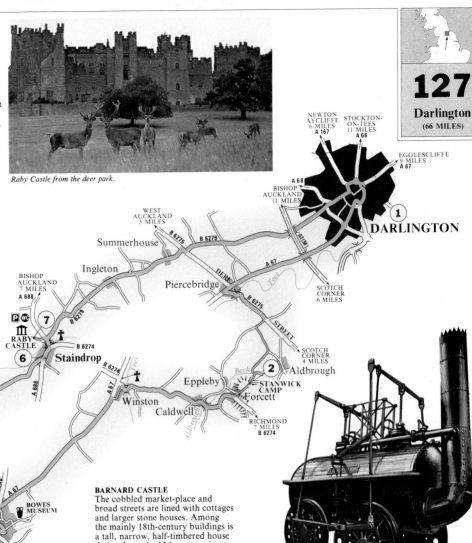

Locomotion No. 1.
Darlington station.

BARNARD CASTLE

The cobbled market-place and broad streets are lined with cottages and larger stone houses. Among the mainly 18th-century buildings is a tall, narrow, half-timbered house dating from the 15th century in which Oliver Cromwell is reputed to have stayed. It is now a café and antique shop. The streets run steeply down to the banks of the Tees. From the bridge over the river there is a view of the castle from which the town takes its name. It was built in 1112 by Bernard Baliol, ancestor of the founder of Balliol College, Oxford. It later became the property of Richard Neville, Earl of Warwick, remembered in history as the 'king-maker'. The ruins tower almost 100 ft on a rocky cliff above the fast-flowing river.

DARLINGTON

It was the railways that changed Darlington from a small market town into an industrial centre. George Stephenson's *Locomotion No. 1* drew the world's first passenger train, which opened a regular service between Darlington and Stockton-on-Tees on September 27, 1825. The engine, together with another, the *Derwent*, built in 1845, is on show at Bank Top station. Stephenson was backed by Edward Pease, a local businessman who also built the clock tower which dominates the main street and the market-place. St Cuthbert's, a 12th-century church in Perpendicular style, stands just off the market and has remained virtually unchanged for the last 700 years.

Barnard Castle.

BOWES MUSEUM

On the eastern fringe of Barnard Castle is the Bowes Museum, founded in 1869 by John Bowes, son of the 10th Earl of Strathmore. Designed on the lines of a French château, the building was completed in 1892 and is set in pleasant grounds. Inside is a remarkable art collection which includes paintings by El Greco, Goya, Canaletto and Tiepolo. There are also rooms set out with furniture of the 17th and 18th centuries, a large number of local antiquities, and a children's exhibition of dolls, dolls' houses and toys. In the entrance hall is a silver swan swimming on a 'lake' of twisted glass rods which create an illusion of running water, probably made in the mid-18th century.

Second Empire Room, Bowes Museum.

STANWICK CAMP

The largest Iron Age fort in Britain covers 850 acres with more than 4 miles of ditches and ramparts, the outlines of which can still be seen. The fort was built by King Venutius, ruler of the Brigante tribe, who defied the Romans for 25 years during the second half of the 1st century. Stanwick became the last major centre of resistance against the Romans in the North. Venutius's downfall came about through the defection of his wife, Cartimandua. She led a breakaway faction of the tribe in support of the Romans, and the camp was captured by the Ninth Legion before it could be completed. Pottery and implements found on the site are relics of the Brigantes' occupation.

The pleasant face of rural County Durham

County Durham is traditionally associated with coal mining, but much of it has remained unspoilt, particularly where the valleys to the west rise towards the Pennines. At beautiful Finchale Priory or in the Bishop's Park at Bishop Auckland, one can imagine oneself 1000 miles away from pitheads and slagheaps. The route takes in the county's biggest area of woodland, Hamsterley Forest; a lion park at Lambton Castle; and, at Escomb, what is believed to be the oldest intact Saxon church in England. Beamish Hall open-air museum is a fascinating re-creation of life in the early part of this century.

(1) Durham to Finchale Priory Leave the city on the A690 signposted to Sunderland. After 4 m. turn left, then left again almost immediately following the signposts for Leamside and Finchale. After about ¾ m. there is a sharp right-hand bend. Take the next turning left, crossing the A1(M). The footpath to Finchale Priory is on the left after 1 m.

(2) Finchale Priory to Lambton Lion Park About 100 yds beyond the footpath to the priory, turn right on the road signposted to Great Lumley. In the village turn right, then immediately left. After ½ m., at the junction with the B1284, turn right and immediately left following the signposts for Houghton Gate. Go under the A1(M) and at Houghton Gate turn left (signposted Sunderland) then immediately right on to the A183. After 1 m., Lambton Lion Park is on the left.

(3) Lambton Lion Park to Beamish Museum Leave the park beyond Lambton Castle and turn left at the first T-junction on to the road signposted for Houghton-le-Spring. Turn left again on meeting the A182, and at the roundabout 1½ m. later take the A183 for Chester-le-Street. At the big roundabout just before Chester-le-Street, take the A183 signposted for Birtley. After ½ m., at the next roundabout, turn left on to the A693 following the signposts for Stanley. After another ½ m., turn right still following the signposts for Stanley on the A693. After 4 m., in Beamish, turn right for Beamish Hall and the open-air museum.

(4) Beamish Museum to Lanchester Return from the museum to the A693 and turn right for Stanley. On the far side of Stanley, just beyond the end of the dual carriageway, turn left on to the B6313 into South Moor. After ½ m., where the B6313 swings left on the edge of the town, keep straight on following the signpost for Burnhope. After 2 m. turn right on the road signposted to Burnhope. At the crossroads on the far side of Burnhope, go straight over and follow the road into Lanchester.

(5) Lanchester to Hamsterley Forest Leave the village on the B6296 signposted to Wolsingham. After 6 m., at the junction with the A68, turn right, then immediately left, still on the B6296, into Wolsingham. In Wolsingham, turn right on to the A689 and after 200 yds turn left on to the road signposted to Bedburn. After 4 m., just after crossing Bedburn Beck, turn right on to the road signposted to Woodland. Go right at the next junction and fork right after about ½ m. to enter Hamsterley Forest. The road runs downhill through the forest to a T-junction near the river. A right turn here leads to a pleasant waterside picnic area. From this area, return to the T-junction and carry straight on along the forest drive.

(6) Hamsterley Forest to Witton le Wear Shortly after the road emerges from the trees turn right. At the junction with the B6282 turn right again following the signpost to Eggleston. After 4 m. turn right on to the B6278 (signposted for Middleton in Teesdale), go through Eggleston and stay on the B6278. Just before the bridge over Bollihope Burn, turn right on to the road signposted to Frosterley. In Frosterley, turn right on to the A689. Follow this road for 8 m. through Wolsingham to the junction with the A68. Turn right on to the A68 which arrives at Witton le Wear after 3 m. The village is off the A68, to the left.

(7) Witton le Wear to Escomb Return to the A68 south of the village, cross the river, and after 1 m. turn left on to the road signposted for Woodside. After 2½ m., at the T-junction beyond Woodside, turn left following the signpost for Escomb.

(8) Escomb to Bishop Auckland Return up the road but carry straight on past the turning to Woodside to the junction with the B6282. Turn left on to the B6282 and after 1 m. fork left on to the B6284. At the junction with the A689, turn right following the Durham signpost. After ¼ m. the entrance to Bishop's Park, with its castle and golf course, is on the left.

(9) Bishop Auckland to Durham Continue along the A689, and at the junction with the A688 fork left. At Spennymoor, follow the bypass road signposted for Durham and at the junction with the A167 turn left, still following the signpost for Durham. Stay on this road as it crosses the River Wear and climbs to a roundabout. The A1050 for Durham branches off right.

INFORMATION

Places of interest *Beamish:* Open-air museum, all year, Tues. to Sun. and Bank Hols. *Durham Castle:* First three weeks of Apr. and July to Oct., Mon. to Sat.; rest of year, Mon., Wed., Sat. afternoons. *Finchale Priory:* Apr. to Sept., daily; Oct. to Mar., weekdays, Sun. afternoons. *Lambton Lion Park:* Mar. to end Oct., daily, 10 a.m.-6 p.m.

Information Town Hall, Market Place, Durham (Tel. Durham 3720).

Towns with easy access to Durham:

Darlington	.... 20 m.	Sunderland	.... 12 m.
Hartlepool	.... 17 m.	Whitley Bay	.... 21 m.

LAMBTON LION PARK
Lions, elephants, bears, giraffes, rhinos and many other exotic animals live in the 212 acre of parkland to the south of 19th-century Lambton Castle. Hard-top cars can be driven through the animals' compounds where baboo are likely to appoint themselves as mascots o car bonnets. A safari bus is available for visitors who prefer to leave their cars in the car park. There are picnic areas in the park an near the castle, a pets' corner and an amusement park. The castle itself is now a residential college.

The 100 ton steam 'navvy' at Beamish.

BEAMISH MUSEUM
Visitors can take a half-mile ride in a clattering electric tramcar through the fast-growing open-air museum at Beamish Hall, opened in 1970 to re-create a picture of life in the north-east as it was around 1900. Other fascinating exhibits include a complete steam-railway station, a steam 'navvy', or excavator, and a 'gin gan'—a threshing shed containing machinery which used to be driven by a horse-wheel. In the hall itself there are workshops a tea room, and a period public house.

Roman altar, Lanchester church.

LANCHESTER
The Roman road that linked Hadrian's Wall and the great military base at York was guarded by a fort, Longovicium, which stood close to this attractive village. The fort was deserted after the Romans withdrew from Britain, and stones from it were used to build the Norman church. A Roman altar in the porch is thought to have come from the fort, and some of the 13th-century stained glass survives.

STANHOPE 3 MILES — A 689 — Frosterl

B 6278

B 6278

Bollihope Burn

MIDDLETO IN TEESDALE 3 MILES

BRO 16 M B 62

SCALE

0   1   2   3   4   5 MILES

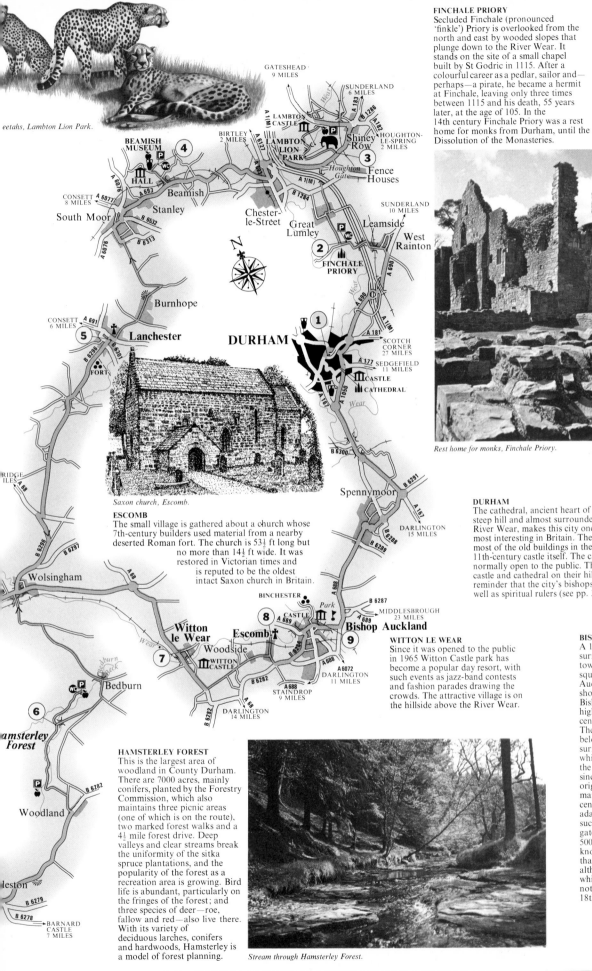

Cheetahs, Lambton Lion Park.

FINCHALE PRIORY

Secluded Finchale (pronounced 'finkle') Priory is overlooked from the north and east by wooded slopes that plunge down to the River Wear. It stands on the site of a small chapel built by St Godric in 1115. After a colourful career as a pedlar, sailor and—perhaps—a pirate, he became a hermit at Finchale, leaving only three times between 1115 and his death, 55 years later, at the age of 105. In the 14th century Finchale Priory was a rest home for monks from Durham, until the Dissolution of the Monasteries.

Rest home for monks, Finchale Priory.

GATESHEAD 9 MILES

SUNDERLAND 6 MILES

LAMBTON CASTLE

BIRTLEY 2 MILES

LAMBTON LION PARK

Shiney Row

HOUGHTON-LE-SPRING 2 MILES

3 Fence Houses

BEAMISH MUSEUM **4**

HALL

CONSETT 8 MILES

Beamish

Stanley

South Moor

Chester-le-Street

Great Lumley

SUNDERLAND 10 MILES

Leamside

West Rainton

2 FINCHALE PRIORY

Burnhope

CONSETT 6 MILES

5 Lanchester

FORT

1

DURHAM

SCOTCH CORNER 27 MILES

SEDGEFIELD 11 MILES

CASTLE

CATHEDRAL

Wear

RIDGE ILES

Wolsingham

ESCOMB

The small village is gathered about a church whose 7th-century builders used material from a nearby deserted Roman fort. The church is $53\frac{1}{2}$ ft long but no more than $14\frac{1}{2}$ ft wide. It was restored in Victorian times and is reputed to be the oldest intact Saxon church in Britain.

Saxon church, Escomb.

Spennymoor

DARLINGTON 15 MILES

BINCHESTER

CASTLE

Park

8 Witton le Wear

Escomb

Bishop Auckland

9

MIDDLESBROUGH 23 MILES

WITTON CASTLE

7 Woodside

Woodland

A6072 DARLINGTON 11 MILES

A688 STAINDROP 9 MILES

DARLINGTON 14 MILES

6

amsterley Forest

Bedburn

DURHAM

The cathedral, ancient heart of Durham, set on a steep hill and almost surrounded by a loop of the River Wear, makes this city one of the loveliest and most interesting in Britain. The university occupies most of the old buildings in the city including the 11th-century castle itself. The castle is, however, normally open to the public. The proximity of castle and cathedral on their hilltop site is a reminder that the city's bishops were once civil as well as spiritual rulers (see pp. 332–5).

WITTON LE WEAR

Since it was opened to the public in 1965 Witton Castle park has become a popular day resort, with such events as jazz-band contests and fashion parades drawing the crowds. The attractive village is on the hillside above the River Wear.

BISHOP AUCKLAND

A 15th-century gatehouse, surmounted by a clock tower, leads off the market square to Bishop Auckland's principal showpiece—the 800 acre Bishop's Park which won high praise from the 17th-century diarist John Evelyn. The park, which now belongs to the town, surrounds Auckland Castle, which has been the seat of the Bishops of Durham since the 14th century. The original building was a manor house in the 12th century, and it has been adapted and extended by successive bishops. The gatehouse was built about 500 years ago. The clock is known to be much older than the gatehouse, although the tower in which it is mounted was not added until the late 18th century.

HAMSTERLEY FOREST

This is the largest area of woodland in County Durham. There are 7000 acres, mainly conifers, planted by the Forestry Commission, which also maintains three picnic areas (one of which is on the route), two marked forest walks and a $4\frac{1}{2}$ mile forest drive. Deep valleys and clear streams break the uniformity of the sitka spruce plantations, and the popularity of the forest as a recreation area is growing. Bird life is abundant, particularly on the fringes of the forest; and three species of deer—roe, fallow and red—also live there. With its variety of deciduous larches, conifers and hardwoods, Hamsterley is a model of forest planning.

Stream through Hamsterley Forest.

BARNARD CASTLE 7 MILES

Northumberland's untouched coast and countryside

Country and coastline, remote and still largely undiscovered, are the essence of Northumberland. From Alnmouth northwards the dune-sheltered shore is officially designated as an Area of Outstanding Natural Beauty. Long sweeps of clean sand are dotted with tiny harbours and secret bays. Here and there the skyline is broken by reminders of Northumbria's fiery past—castles such as Dunstanburgh and Bamburgh. Inland is the kingdom of the untamed white cattle of Chillingham, descendants of the wild oxen that roamed Britain's forests in prehistoric times.

(1) Alnwick to Alnmouth Leave the market-place on the A1, passing through Hotspur Tower, and after almost ½ m. turn left on to the A1068 signposted to Alnmouth. Pass over a flyover, cross the River Aln, and in Lesbury bear right. Cross the Aln again, following the signpost to Alnmouth. After ½ m. bear left at a roundabout on to the B1338. Soon afterwards cross the Aln again and enter Alnmouth, turning right at the roundabout.

(2) Alnmouth to Craster Return to the last roundabout and go straight ahead on the road signposted to Foxton. At the next T-junction turn left to follow the signpost for Lesbury. In the village, turn right on to the B1339 signposted to Longhoughton. After 2 m., pass through Longhoughton keeping on the B1339. After ½ m. follow the B1339 round to the right, but where it bends left go ahead on the minor road signposted Howick/Craster. After 1 m. pass Howick Hall, an 18th-century house whose gardens are open to the public. Follow the road round to the left and after 2 m., at a crossroads, turn right on to the road signposted to Craster. Shortly turn right again to enter the village.

(3) Craster to Beadnell Leave the village by the same route, and at the first junction bear right on the road signposted to Embleton. Go sharp right at the next junction and right again at the T-junction on to the road signposted to Embleton/Seahouses. After just over 1¼ m. enter Embleton, where there is a pele tower, a relic of centuries of border strife. In Embleton, by the Blue Bell Inn, turn right at the T-junction on to the B1339 signposted to Beadnell/Seahouses. About 1 m. later the road becomes the B1340. After 3 m., at a crossroads, turn right keeping on the B1340 into Beadnell.

(4) Beadnell to Seahouses Leave the village on the B1340 signposted to Seahouses/Bamburgh. The road follows the coast before entering Seahouses. For the car park, bear right at the Farne Hotel and left at the roundabout.

(5) Seahouses to Bamburgh Leave the village on the B1340, again following the magnificent coastline. Out to sea lie the Farne Islands, home of thousands of seabirds. After 2 m. enter Bamburgh, where there is a car park just below the castle. Continue into the village and bear right at the green to visit the Grace Darling Museum.

(6) Bamburgh to Chillingham Leave on the B1342. After 1½ m. the road skirts Budle Bay, which is part of Lindisfarne Nature Reserve. At the junction at the head of the bay turn left, keeping on the B1342 signposted to Belford. After a level crossing, continue to the T-junction with the A1 and turn right, following the signpost to the North. Enter Belford and in the market square turn sharp left into West Street signposted Wooler/B6349. After almost 1 m. turn left on to a minor road signposted to the B6348 and Wooler. At the next T-junction turn right on to the B6348 signposted Chatton/Wooler. After 1½ m. cross a stone bridge into Chatton. Just beyond the village, turn sharp left on to the road signposted to Chillingham. After just over 1¼ m. enter the village and turn left, signposted to Chillingham Cattle.

(7) Chillingham to Wooler Return to the village and at the post office turn right and go back to Chatton. Here turn left on to the B6348. Soon after the B6349 comes in on the right, the road turns sharp left and descends to Wooler town centre.

(8) Wooler to Rothbury Leave the town on the A697 going south. The road passes several small villages and affords views of the Cheviot Hills to the west. After 6 m. pass, on the left, Percy's Cross, a memorial to the Lancastrian leader, Sir Ralph Percy, killed at the Battle of Hedgeley Moor in 1464. After a further 8½ m. turn right on to the B6341, and 3 m. later turn left into the Pethfoot entrance to the Cragside estate. Follow the estate road past the house to the exit. There turn right on to the B6344, and after ½ m. join the B6341 and enter Rothbury.

(9) Rothbury to Alnwick Leave the town on the B6341 signposted to Alnwick, but after ½ m. fork right to rejoin the B6344. After 5 m., at Weldon Bridge, turn left on to the A697 signposted Coldstream. At Longframlington, turn right on to the B6345 and continue to Felton. Here turn left on to the A1 and follow the road for 8 m. back to Alnwick.

INFORMATION

Places of interest *Alnwick Castle:* May to Sept., afternoons, except Fri. *Bamburgh Castle:* Easter to Sept., afternoons. *Chillingham Wild Cattle:* Apr. to Oct., weekdays (except Tues.), Bank Hols., Sun. afternoons. *Dunstanburgh Castle:* Oct. to Mar., weekdays, Sun. afternoons; Apr. to Sept., daily. *Grace Darling Museum:* Apr. to mid-Oct., daily. *Howick Hall:* Gardens only, Apr. to Sept., afternoons. *Rothbury:* Cragside, grounds only, Easter to Oct., daily.

Events *Alnwick:* 7-day fair, end June. Horse Show, June. Shrovetide football, Shrove Tues. *Wooler:* Sheep sales, July to Nov., Wed.

Information City Information Service, Princess Square, Newcastle-upon-Tyne (Tel. Newcastle 610691).

Towns with easy access to Alnwick:

Berwick	29 m.	Morpeth	19 m.
Hexham	44 m.	Newcastle	34 m.

CHILLINGHAM
For over 700 years the herd of Chillingham wild cattle have roamed without interference from man over a 600 acre park amid some of Northumberland's richest countryside. The estate was enclosed in 1220, trapping the ancestors of the herd and keeping the breed pure through subsequent centuries. The cattle are creamy-whi with curving, black-tipped horns, and are believed by experts to be descendants of the wild oxen which once roamed the length and breadth of Britain. The herd is ruled by a 'king' bull, the only one allowed to sire calve until he is successfully challenged by a younger bull. Th he has to endure months of banishment to the hills before the herd will let him rejoin them. These cattle are both agile and strong, and it is claimed by the Chilling Wild Cattle Association that the Chillingham bulls wou be a better match for any Spanish bull-fighter than mos of the specially bred Spanish bulls. Since the cattle are completely free within the estate, the time it might take to see them depends entirely upon the distance they have wandered from the park entrance.

WOOLER
A hillside market town, Wooler is backed by the 2674 ft high Cheviot. It is a natural centre for exploring the Cheviot Hills on foot. North-west of the town a stone marks the site of the Battle of Homildon Hill, at which, in 1402, an English army, led by Henry Percy (Hotspur) and his father, the Earl of Northumberland, defeated a huge Scottish army which was led by the Earl of Douglas.

ROTHBURY
'Capital' of Coquetdale, one of Northumberland's gentler valleys, Rothbury is a town of wide streets and pleasant walks, with many delightful picnic areas near the River Coquet. Approaching Rothbury from the north, the scene is dominated by Cragside estate. The gardens were created out of open moorland at the instigation of the industrialist William George Armstrong, the first Lord Armstrong (1810–1900), inventor of the Armstrong gun, a rifled, breech-loading cannon. The house is not open to the public, but visitors can make the 5 mile drive through the estate and walk through the gardens.

Cragside, Rothbury, built in 1863.

SCALE

0   1   2   3   4   5 MILES

of the Chillingham wild cattle.

BAMBURGH

A huddle of low stone cottages lies below the impressive fortress of Bamburgh Castle. Parts of the castle have been restored and converted into flats, creating homes for more people than any other castle in England with the exception of Windsor. The castle also contains armour, engravings, portraits and a Gobelin tapestry. The small village was the birthplace of Grace Darling, who rowed out in a small fishing boat with her father, keeper of the Longstone lighthouse, to rescue five people from the wreck of the *Forfarshire* in 1838. A monument and museum are dedicated to her memory. The museum, opened on the centenary of the rescue, contains the original coble used in the rescue and many other mementos of the Darling family. A few doors away is a plaque on the house where Grace was born, and in the churchyard opposite is the family grave and her memorial. A souvenir shop by the village green is the house where Grace Darling died, at the age of 26, only a few years after the heroic rescue.

Grace Darling Memorial, Bamburgh.

Bamburgh Castle.

SEAHOUSES

Brightly painted cobles—traditional square-sterned Northumbrian fishing boats—are a reminder of the historical importance of the fishing industry to Seahouses and its inland village, North Sunderland. Seahouses harbour was rebuilt with a pier in 1889. From here it is possible to visit the bird and seal sanctuaries in the Farne Islands. The sandy beaches and cliffs to the north, which are under the protection of the National Trust, have ample parking and picnic facilities.

BEADNELL

Lying on a sweeping bay, the sheltered harbour at Beadnell is frequented by both fishermen and yachting enthusiasts. The drystone harbour walls were built, like the lime-kilns, in the late 18th century. The older part of the village clusters round a 15th-century watch tower, now an inn.

...nell harbour and lime-kilns.

CRASTER

In the herring season, when the fishing cobles are bringing in their catch, the pungent smell of kippers smoked over oakwood fires lures epicures to the harbourside sheds where this breakfast delicacy is still cured in the traditional way. On the skyline to the north of the old-world village is Dunstanburgh Castle. Built during the early 14th century by the Earl of Lancaster to defend the harbour, it was captured and recaptured four times during the Wars of the Roses 100 years later. During one of the sieges Queen Margaret, wife of Henry VI, is said to have escaped by being lowered from the tower named after her into a boat waiting in the sea below. Other remains include John of Gaunt's gatehouse, built in 1380, and the Lilburn Tower, built about 1325. The rocky outcrop on which the castle is built is known as the Great Whin Sill. The castle, at the sea's edge, is reached by a 1½ mile walk along the shoreline.

Dunstanburgh Castle.

Craster kippers.

ALNWICK

For more than 600 years the Percys, earls and dukes of Northumberland, have been the most influential family in Northumberland, and they have left their mark on Alnwick. From the north, the castle, which first came into the family in 1309, dominates the skyline. Outwardly, it has changed little since the 14th century. Lion Bridge, designed by John Adam in 1773, is guarded by the heraldic lion of the Percy family with its straight, poker-like tail. The lion is seen again on 'Farmer's Folly'—the usual local name for the Percy Tenantry Column. It was built by tenants of the Duke of Northumberland in 1816 as a token of their gratitude to him for reducing their rents. A further reminder of the Percys is Hotspur Tower, named after Henry Percy (Hotspur) who died at the Battle of Shrewsbury in 1403.

ALNMOUTH

This small port, founded in 1150, was Alnwick's outlet to the sea for almost 600 years. A disastrous storm in the winter of 1806 destroyed the river's north-east bank, changing its course and cutting off the harbour from the town. The old harbour has since been allowed to silt up, but the estuary still provides a haven for small fishing and pleasure boats. Wide beaches and sand dunes attract summer holidaymakers to the peaceful huddle of red-roofed houses in the riverbank town.

345

From Flodden Field to Holy Island

A walled frontier town and ruined castles are reminders of centuries of fighting along the Border, which culminated in the bloodiest battle ever fought on English soil. At Flodden Field a cross marks the spot where 12,000 Scots and 3000 English died in 1513. But it is a gentle country, in spite of its battle-scarred past. A landscape of green, rounded hills rises to the 2676 ft mass of The Cheviot. On the coast there is the great nature reserve of Holy Island, a refuge for many rare birds and a breeding ground for seals.

(1) Berwick-upon-Tweed to Holy Island Leave the town on the A1 to the south, crossing the River Tweed. Go through the village of Scremerston, staying on the A1. After 5 m. there is a large lay-by for visitors to Haggerston Castle, on the left. About 1½ m. past this point, go left on to a minor road signposted to Beal and Holy Island. The road crosses the main north/south railway at Beal, and after about 1 m. joins the Causeway to Holy Island. Tides and safe crossing times are indicated on a board to the left of the Causeway. Follow the Causeway to the island. A signpost to, and information about, the island's nature reserve can be seen on the road to the left shortly before it turns right to the village. There is a road to the castle, signposted in the village.

(2) Holy Island to Ford Go back across the Causeway to the mainland, return to the A1 and turn left, travelling south. After about 1½ m. turn right on to the B6353. Go through Fenwick and stay on this undulating road for about 3¾ m. to Lowick. About ½ m. beyond the village, at the junction with the B6525, bear left and after 350 yds turn right, rejoining the B6353 signposted to Ford. The road crosses moorland, passes the Red Lion Inn at Ford Common—just beyond here there are good views of the Cheviot Hills ahead—and descends to the village of Ford. Turn right at the signpost in the village marked 'Lady Waterford's Pictures and Pottery'.

(3) Ford to Flodden Field Stay on the B6353, and after about ½ m. turn left over the bridge across the River Till on to the road signposted to Coldstream. Keep straight ahead, joining the B6354, and after 1 m. turn right on to the A697, heading north. After just under ½ m. turn left. There are good views in all directions. Continue on it for about 1½ m., turning right at the signpost for Flodden Field/Branxton. This sharply twisting road gives spectacular views to the north before running downhill to Branxton after 1 m. In the village, turn left at the junction on to the road signposted to Cornhill. After less than 200 yds there is a signpost on the left to Flodden Field. Branxton church is on the right and Flodden Memorial Cross can be seen high on the hill ahead. Continue on the road for about 350 yds. There is limited parking below the cross, which is reached by a short walk across the field.

(4) Flodden Field to Coldstream Return to the junction by the church and turn left on to the road signposted Cornhill/Berwick. After 1 m. this narrow, winding road meets the A697. Turn left, and after about 1½ m. go through the last village in England on this road—Cornhill on Tweed. In the village centre turn left at the roundabout on to the A698 signposted to Coldstream/Kelso, and after about 1 m. cross the River Tweed into Scotland over the five-arched Coldstream Bridge, built in 1763. Go past the tall column on the left—a memorial to the 19th-century Border MP, Charles Marjoribanks—into the main street of Coldstream. There are car parks along here from which to explore the town. For a picnic, follow the road across the river (Leet Water); there is a picnic area on the left. On the right of this road is the Hirsel Estate, family seat of Lord Home. Dundock Wood, on the western side of the estate, is a bird sanctuary.

(5) Coldstream to Twizel Retrace the route back to Coldstream Bridge and recross the Tweed into England. At the roundabout, just over 1 m. from the Border, bear left on to the A698 and follow it to Twizel.

(6) Twizel to Norham Continue on the A698, and about 3 m. after crossing Twizel Bridge turn left on to the B6470 to Norham. In the village, bear right on to the road signposted to the castle.

(7) Norham to Berwick-upon-Tweed Retrace the route back to the A698, rejoining this road by the Salutation Inn. Take the left turn here for Berwick, passing through the village of East Ord after 4½ m. About ½ m. beyond the village, the road passes through Tweedmouth and joins the A1. Turn left for Berwick town centre.

NATURE NOTES

The tidal estuary of the Tweed is notable for its large flock of mute swans in late summer. But the outstanding area for birds is around Holy Island. The intertidal sands are covered in eelgrass, which provides food for wigeon and Brent geese, which flock there in large numbers.

INFORMATION

Places of interest *Berwick-upon-Tweed:* Museum, June to Sept., weekday afternoons. Art Gallery, all year, weekdays (except Thur., but Thur. afternoons June to Sept.). Old Barracks, Mon. to Fri., Sat. mornings. *Coldstream:* Museum, daily, 2-5 p.m. *Ford:* Lady Waterford's Pictures and Pottery. *Holy Island:* Castle, Apr. to Oct., daily. Priory Ruins and Museum, weekdays, Sun. afternoons. *Norham:* Castle, weekdays, Sun. afternoons.

Events *Berwick-upon-Tweed:* The Riding of the Bounds, May 1. May Fair, last Fri. of May. *Coldstream:* Festival, 1st week in Aug. *Norham:* Blessing of the Nets, Feb. 13.

Information *Newcastle upon Tyne:* Central Library, Princess Square (Tel. Newcastle upon Tyne 610691).

Towns with easy access to Berwick-upon-Tweed:

Alnwick	29 m.	Kelso	23 m.
Dunbar	30 m.	Selkirk	42 m.

NORHAM

The solid houses of this stone village face on to two triangular greens, on one of which stands the 19th-century village cross. At the east end of the main street the 12th-century castle is perched on the rocks above the Tweed, its massive Norman keep towering 90 ft higher. The castle withstood many sieges by Scottish troops. One, by Robert Bruce in 1318, lasted nearly a year. Twelve months later came the siege immortalised by Sir Walter Scott in his 'Marmion'. The hero of the poem, Sir William Marmion, was an English knight who accepted a lady's challenge to take command of 'the most dangerous place in Great Britain' as proof of his love. The castle contains an unusual collection of stonemasons' marks, or signatures. The Blessing of the Nets, at midnight on February 13, marks the opening of the salmon season.

Norham Castle.

TWIZEL

The road rises and falls as it crosses the high, single 90 ft span of the 15th-century Twizel Bridge, giving views over the deep, wooded glen of the River Till. On a nearby ridge is Twizel Castle, the ivy-covered ruins of a 'folly' begun about 1770 and never completed.

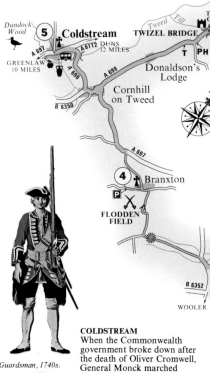

Guardsman, 1740s.

Guardsman, 1970s.

COLDSTREAM

When the Commonwealth government broke down after the death of Oliver Cromwell, General Monck marched members of his regiment of foot from their Coldstream headquarters to London in 1660. They were already known as 'Coldstreamers' and after the Restoration officially became the Coldstream Guards. The Guards' House, a 19th-century building on the site of Monck's headquarters, stands in the market square and houses the Coldstream Museum. Like Gretna Green, Coldstream was once a venue for over-the-Border weddings of eloping minors, forbidden under English law. They took place at the Marriage House at the Scottish end of Coldstream Bridge, which was built in 1766, or in a nearby inn.

SCALE
0   1   2   3 MILES

The 17th-century 15-arch bridge, Berwick-upon-Tweed.

...age cross, Norham.

BERWICK-UPON-TWEED

England's northernmost town, founded late in the 9th century with the Anglo-Saxon name of Berwick ('Barley Farm'), changed hands 13 times during the Border wars before it was finally surrendered to the English Crown in 1482. There are modern shops, a busy market, a salmon-fishing industry and a good seaport; but the town's glory is its ramparts. It is possible to walk 2 miles right round the heart of Berwick without leaving these walls and fortifications. They were planned in 1558 and built at vast cost, but never used for their purpose—as a defence against feared Scottish and French attacks. From them there are views of the winding Tweed and the 15-arch stone bridge which still carries traffic after 350 years. From these walls, too, can be seen the quayside, shipyards and salmon fisheries, and the harbour mouth opening into the North Sea. Little remains of Berwick Castle, which was swept away by the Victorians to clear the site for the railway station.

HOLY ISLAND

The sea that swirls around this 'cradle of Christianity'—historically known as Lindisfarne—makes it an island only at high tide. Missionaries from Iona, led by St Aidan, founded a monastery here in 634. It was destroyed by the Danes about 160 years later, but the gaunt Norman ruins of a Benedictine priory founded in 1082 still attract visitors. The island's restored 16th-century castle, now owned by the National Trust, contains antique oak furniture among other treasures. Examples of the islanders' needlework are displayed in the parish church. Near by is the Petting Stone, over which brides are supposed to jump to ensure a happy marriage. A modern mead brewery welcomes visitors.

St Aidan.

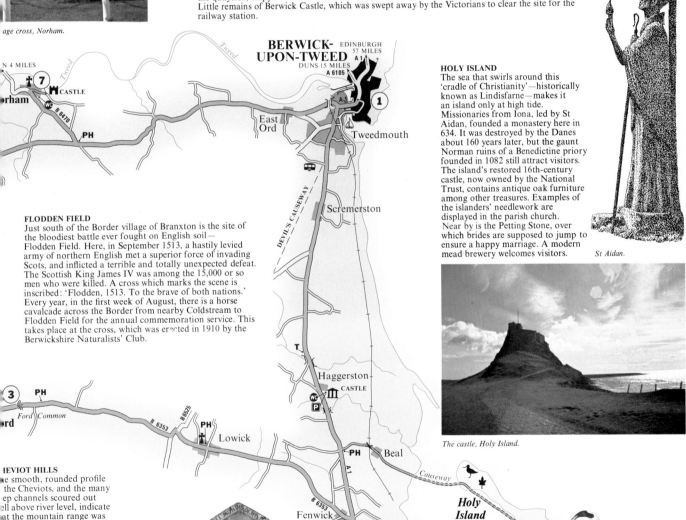

FLODDEN FIELD

Just south of the Border village of Branxton is the site of the bloodiest battle ever fought on English soil— Flodden Field. Here, in September 1513, a hastily levied army of northern English met a superior force of invading Scots, and inflicted a terrible and totally unexpected defeat. The Scottish King James IV was among the 15,000 or so men who were killed. A cross which marks the scene is inscribed: 'Flodden, 1513. To the brave of both nations.' Every year, in the first week of August, there is a horse cavalcade across the Border from nearby Coldstream to Flodden Field for the annual commemoration service. This takes place at the cross, which was erected in 1910 by the Berwickshire Naturalists' Club.

The castle, Holy Island.

CHEVIOT HILLS

...e smooth, rounded profile ...the Cheviots, and the many ...ep channels scoured out ...ll above river level, indicate ...at the mountain range was ...aped by glacial action. ...eddish chips used for road ...rfacing in the area are likely ...have come from the ...heviots' pink granite. The ...ountains, rising to 2676 ft, ...oduce the hardy Cheviot ...eep, the main support of the ...ll farms that are sited as ...gh as 1000 ft up in the hills.

Eider duck

FORD

A series of highly detailed water-colour murals by Lady Louisa Waterford, a Victorian widow who lived in Ford Castle, attracts visitors to the village school. The castle, which is not open to the public, is where James IV stayed on the eve of his death at Flodden Field in 1513. The neat and well-kept village has a 13th-century church with a massive bell turret of a type rarely seen.

NATURE RESERVE

Holy Island's nature reserve is a haven for wildfowl and wading birds, particularly wigeon and mallard. Eider ducks (known locally as 'Cudda's ducks' after St Cuthbert) are seen there, and flocks of pale-breasted Brent geese visit the island during the winter months.

Watercolour mural, Ford school.

A conducted tour of the Border Forest Park

BORDER FOREST PARK

Glorious scenery, a vast range of wildlife and a forest drive created for visitors, help to make the Border Forest Park one of the finest inland recreation areas in Britain. It covers country that for centuries was torn by strife, and grim towers are a reminder of the past.

Wilderness and beauty sum up this sparsely populated border area. Forests of birch and pine covered the land in prehistoric times, but gradual changes in climate produced smaller woodlands where birch was joined by hazel, alder and oak. Man's demands for timber, together with the need to pasture livestock, removed the original trees. Woodland birds and mammals vanished as their homes were destroyed; wolves, polecats and other predators were hunted down. Hardy sheep grazed on the poor upland pastures, while red grouse and other game provided sport for wealthy marksmen. Much of the land was owned by the Dukes of Northumberland, who built Kielder Castle as an elaborate and eye-catching shooting lodge in 1775.

The castle today is the centre of a dramatic transformation that has changed the face of this part of Britain. It started in 1926 when the Forestry Commission began a programme that called for the planting of millions of trees—and now the park is part of the largest man-made forest in Britain. The forest's total weight of timber increases by about 1000 tons every day. By 1970 it was producing 80,000 tons of timber a year and its output is expected to reach 110,000 tons by 1980. If the trees now felled every working week were laid end to end they would stretch for 100 miles.

FLOWING RIVER *The River North Tyne wends its way along the valley between Kielder and Lewisburn bridge. The trees include Scots pines, oaks and sycamores, and the river also has some fine trout fishing. Waterfowl include herons, dippers and mallards.*

Trees from Canada

Fifty per cent of the trees are sitka spruce, a native of the north-western seaboard of North America. Most of them were grown from seeds collected on the Queen Charlotte Islands of British Columbia. After a period in a nursery, the young trees are planted in the forest. About 1000 of them are needed for every acre, to allow for natural failures, thinnings and damage caused by deer, sheep, birds, frost and other hazards.

Sitka spruce are generally felled when they are between 40 and 50 years old. By that time, the tallest trees will have reached heights of up to 75 ft. In countries with harder climates, such as Finland, trees have to be left for 80 to 90 years before felling. At the other extreme, foresters in New Zealand work on growth periods of 20 years or less.

Norway spruce—the traditional Christmas tree—cover almost half of the area not planted with sitka spruce, while other trees include the native Scots pine, lodgepole pine from north-west America, Lawson cypress, Douglas fir and hemlock. Japanese larch, which is more resistant to burning, is used

to provide firebreaks. Fire is the forest's most deadly foe. A carelessly discarded match or cigarette end can destroy years of work and cause damage costing many thousands of pounds. Driven by a stiff breeze a blaze in the tops of the trees can cover a mile of forest in less than five minutes.

A magic beauty

A tree's rate of growth depends on the climate and the height of the land on which it is planted. The number of growing days a year drops as the height increases. Trees do not grow well above 1500 ft, and the open ground in the park above this height contrasts with the dense stands of growing timber lower down the slopes. Thick layers of peat and glacial clays, deposited during the Ice Ages, carpet the unplanted fells, broken here and there by outcrops of rock. Heather, purple moor grass, nodding acres of white, feathery cotton grass and clumps of bracken colour the landscape. Winters are often hard, but the beauty of the area becomes almost magical when the sun shines down from a clear blue sky on to trees covered with fresh snow.

Kielder Castle is the main centre for visitors to the Border Forest Park. It nestles in the valley of the River North Tyne, 18 miles from the little Northumbrian market town of Bellingham. There are walks, an adventure playground for children, a picnic place, parking, toilets and an exhibition about forestry and wildlife.

The car park at the entrance to the castle is the starting point for the Duchess Drive Forest Trail. This crosses Kielder Burn—a tributary of the North Tyne—and involves a pleasant walk of 2½ miles through Scots pines and other trees. The trail takes its name from a drive created by a 19th-century Duchess of Northumberland, who preferred driving in a pony and trap to the more taxing sport of fox-hunting. A short cut can reduce the walk to 1½ miles.

The park's greatest attraction is the forest drive that runs eastwards from Kielder Castle and climbs to over 1500 ft before descending to meet the A68 in Redesdale, near the village of Byrness. The drive is 12 miles long and crosses some of the most spectacular hill-country in England. Along the route are picnic places—many of them beside crystal-clear

FROM THE AIR *An unusual view of some of the park's magnificent scenery at Whickhop Burn, near Falstone. Part of this area is to be flooded to form a reservoir due for completion around 1980.*

CAMOUFLAGE *One of the park's shy roe deer stands almost totally concealed by bracken in the forest. The horns of the buck (male) are small—but are capable of inflicting serious wounds on its rivals during the rutting (mating) season, which takes place from mid-July to mid-August. The buck sheds his horns in winter.*

ANCIENT MEMORIALS *High on the slopes of Redesdale, three standing stones—the Three Kings—are part of a Bronze Age burial site. The moors are dotted with memorials of times past, including many fortress towers.*

MOORLAND VIEW *Hardy fell sheep graze peacefully on the moors, with the trees of the forest in the background. Sheep farming was the staple industry of the area for hundreds of years and there are still several farms active in the park.*

streams—viewpoints and short waymarked walks that explore little valleys or climb to vantage points. There is also access to some of the remoter fells—but walkers are warned that conditions can change quickly and it is unwise to go too far without a compass, warm clothes, and a large-scale map.

Wildlife is a prominent feature of the route. On the walk from the Blakehope Nick car park to Oh Me Edge, near the middle of the drive, wild goats from the herds that roam the moors can be seen. The herds vary between five and 20 animals, many of which grow huge pairs of horns that curve into semi-circles.

Above the tree line

Goats are by no means the only inhabitants of the moors above the tree line. Insects are plentiful throughout the summer and into the autumn. They provide food for the young grouse and other birds, as well as for lizards that can sometimes be spotted basking on sun-warmed rocks. Voles, shrews and rabbits scurry through the grass, often falling victim to the fox, stoat, weasel, carrion crow and short-eared owl. One handsome predator, the hen

harrier, has become re-established in the area after virtually disappearing.

Other rare birds sometimes observed in the forest or swooping over the moorland include the long-eared owl, osprey and goshawk. A few kingfishers have been spotted in recent years, but heron, dipper, mallard and goosander are much more likely to be seen.

The drive—and the other trails in the forest—also provide the opportunity to see the roe deer that have become established there since the 1920s. Their local name is *rae*, just as a snake is an *esk*, a blackbird a *merle*, a thrush a *mavis* and a hedgehog a *hurcheon*. About 2000 of these shy, soft-eyed deer live in the forest and their numbers are controlled to prevent them from doing too much damage to the trees. When a deer grows its new antlers, they have a covering of velvet— a thin layer of skin and fur. This is removed by scraping the horns against trees. This process, known as fraying, can damage the bark to such an extent that the tree will die.

Forest Rangers and other marksmen kill a strictly limited number of the deer each year. Experienced shots come to the park from as far

Main Habitats

MOORLAND

View across the moor from Blakehope Nick.

The moorland of the Border Forest Park, ranging in height from 1300 to nearly 2000 ft, is dominated by a rolling expanse of heather and purple moor grass. Bracken, too, flourishes where there is drier soil. Grouse are the most common birds, but rarer species include the osprey and hen harrier, recently re-established in the area. Animals range in size from voles and shrews—themselves a prey for the short-eared owl and carrion crow—to the herds of wild goats, with their rough coats.

FOREST

Kielder Forest from the hills above.

ROE DEER *About . live in the park. T numbers are care controlled.*

BILBERRY *Edible purple berries of the bilberry—one of the moor's most common plants—appear in July. They are delicious cooked as jam or in pies.*

HEN HARRIER *Only recently re-established, the hen harrier is one of the park's rarest birds.*

FOREST FLOOR *The canopy of growing trees means that flowers disappear.*

WILD GOATS *The wild goats of the moor, with their spectacularly curved horns, live in herds ranging from five to 20 in number.*

MOUNTAIN HARE *The rock-dwelling mountain hare's coat turns white in winter to blend with snow.*

GOLDEN PLOVER *Nesting plovers distract their enemies by squatting on the ground and feigning injury.*

HEATHERS *The young shoots of both the common heather and bell heather (right) are a favourite food for grouse.*

LARGE HEATH *It relies on its camouflage to escape enemies.*

FOREST TREES *Lawson cypress (left), Norway spruce (cent and Douglas fir (right) are three of the forest's trees.*

BORDER FOREST PARK

afield as France and Germany, and day permits for deer stalking are issued by the Forestry Commission. Day permits are available to anglers and to sportsmen in pursuit of grouse and pheasant which inhabit the moors and open woodland.

The roe deer is a fairly small animal that rarely exceeds a height of 2½ ft or a weight of 60 lb. Unlike many other species, it tends to live in family groups rather than herds; a typical group consists of a buck (male), a doe (female), and two fawns (youngsters).

July and August is the rutting (mating) season, when the buck uses his horns to mark out a rutting stand. This is a roughly circular area in which the male courts his chosen partner. He becomes very aggressive, pawing the ground and attacking any other bucks that dare to invade his territory. The roe deer's horns are not spectacular—they rarely consist of more than two short branches—but they are very sharp and dagger-like. Thus, the

buck is capable of inflicting serious wounds on a rival.

Britain's biggest native animal, the magnificent red deer, does not live in the forest, but individual deer may sometimes be seen passing through, possibly in search of a mate.

Natural history can be combined with archaeology at the eastern end of the forest drive. There, a walk from Rede Bridge climbs up to the Three Kings, a Bronze Age burial site almost 1000 ft up on the flank of Redesdale. Rede Bridge itself is crossed by the Pennine Way Long-distance Footpath that runs for 250 miles from Edale, in the Peak District, to Kirk Yetholm in Borders, as well as by one of the bridle paths that run for miles through the forests and over the fells.

Riding is now a leisure activity, but at one time horses were the only means of transport here until the Border Counties section of the North British Railway was opened in the mid-19th century. Its most striking memorial in the forest is the viaduct near Kielder Castle. This was completed in 1862. Even though the line is now closed to traffic, the viaduct is still a landmark in a landscape where man-made

architectural features are few and far between. Moving away from Kielder down the North Tyne Valley, there is a forest walk at Lewisburn. It is a mile in length and explores the level ground between the river and one of its many tributaries, the Lewis Burn. The trees include Scots pine and there are also oaks, sycamores and hazels. Lewisburn is also the home of the Border Forest Museum, which illustrates the area's natural and social history.

Like much of the valley below Kielder, Lewisburn is destined to vanish beneath the waters of the largest man-made reservoir in Britain. Work started in 1974 and is due to be completed in 1980. The main dam at Yarrow will be 3750 ft long and 170 ft high; the 44 million gallon reservoir behind it will flood 2680 acres. There will be facilities for sailing, fishing and canoeing—as well as holiday cabins, camping and caravan sites.

Well away from the land destined for flooding is the Warksburn forest trail, which starts from the parking area at Stonehaugh 5 miles south-west of Bellingham off the B6230. Lofty totem poles, carved by local forest workers, overlook the start of the 2 mile walk.

Below the tree line stretches the 300 square miles of woodland planted by the Forestry Commission since 1926. Despite its apparently uniform appearance, even the lowest level—the forest floor—conceals a great variety of life. Grasshoppers, mice, beetles, spiders, moths and ants, for example, all make their homes there. Larger inhabitants, such as the badger and fox, return to cover in their setts and earths after hunting in the open spaces outside the wooded area.

COMMON SORREL *The distinctive arrow-shaped leaves of the sorrel make identification easy.*

ROSSBILL *The bird is unique in Britain for its crossed bill-tips, used to extract pine seeds.*

TAWNY OWL *A night hunter, it feeds off small mammals such as mice and shrews. It attacks if its nest is disturbed.*

STARRY FEATURE *The star-shaped patterns of* Polytrichum commune, *a moss usually found in bogs.*

WATER

River North Tyne near Kielder.

YELLOW IRIS *Flowering in May, the yellow iris grows up to 2 ft high. Its leaves produce an unpleasant smell if crushed.*

DIPPER *Nature has shaped the dipper carefully to allow it to walk underwater searching for food.*

ALDER *The tree reproduces when the long male catkins scatter pollen on the small female catkins. These then develop into cones which burst to scatter seeds.*

Ponds, burns, rivers and bogs make up the water habitat of the park. Unlike forest and moor it has no separate identity of its own, being found throughout the park. But it has the most varied life of the three. Birds include heron and goosander which prey off the brown trout fighting their way upstream to spawn. Toads and frogs are found in quiet corners. There is even the chance of spotting a kingfisher, a rare bird since the hard frosts of 1963 and only now slowly recovering its numbers.

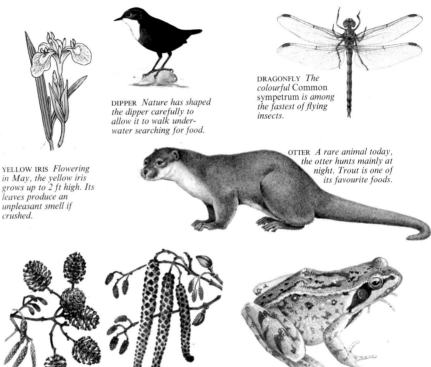

DRAGONFLY *The colourful* Common sympetrum *is among the fastest of flying insects.*

OTTER *A rare animal today, the otter hunts mainly at night. Trout is one of its favourite foods.*

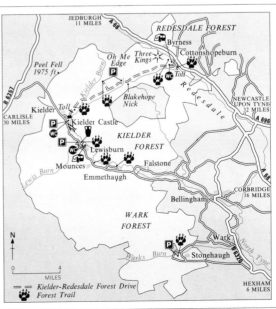

COMMON FROG *Frequently seen near the moorland burns, the frog has many enemies, including otters and grass snakes.*

It continues along a grassy track beside the stream and through young plantations with a rich variety of trees and plants.

Leaflets about the forest and its wildlife are available for the trails at Warksburn, Lewisburn and Kielder. But the walks at Emmethaugh, Mounces, Cottonshopeburn and Rede Bridge are simply waymarked routes that can be covered in one or two hours. A fifth route starts from Stonehaugh. Emmethaugh and Mounces are in the North Tyne Valley, while Cottonshopeburn and Rede Bridge are to the east in Redesdale.

The magnificent woodlands now extend outside the park's boundaries and cover more than 300 square miles, stretching across an area that was for centuries synonymous with strife. Hadrian's Wall lies a few miles to the south and from Roman times until the 17th century the hills and valleys were prowled by raiders. These grim-faced men swooped down to slay, kidnap, plunder and burn. Ancient earthworks, ruined fortress towers and once-fortified farms are reminders of this turbulent past. Even though the borderland is peaceful today, it preserves a wildness all its own.

VISITING THE PARK

The Border Forest Park is near Tour No. 126 from Corbridge and Tour No. 135 from Jedburgh. The main information centre for the park is at Kielder Castle, and there are also centres at Stonehaugh and Byrness. One of the principal attractions for motorists is the 12 mile forest drive linking Kielder and Byrness. For walkers there are forest trails at Lewisburn—also the park's main camping site—Kielder and Stonehaugh. There are also waymarked walks at Cottonshopeburn and Rede Bridge, on the A68 near Byrness; at Mounces and Emmethaugh in the North Tyne Valley; and again at Stonehaugh in Wark Forest. Walkers should carry a detailed map and compass and wear warm clothing.

JEDBURGH 11 MILES
REDESDALE FOREST
Byrness
Cottonshopeburn
Three Kings
Oh Me Edge
Toll
Peel Fell 1975 ft
Blakehope Nick
NEWCASTLE UPON TYNE 32 MILES
A 696
CARLISLE 30 MILES
Kielder Toll
Kielder Castle
KIELDER FOREST
Lewisburn
Falstone
Mounces
Emmethaugh
CORBRIDGE 16 MILES
Bellingham
WARK FOREST
Wark
Stonehaugh
North Tyne
HEXHAM 6 MILES

Kielder-Redesdale Forest Drive
Forest Trail

A Scottish garden warmed by the Gulf Stream

Logan Botanic Garden, on this route, is within 50 miles of Moscow's latitude, yet palm trees and other subtropical plants flourish there. The reason why this sheltered corner of Scotland enjoys such a mild climate is the Gulf Stream, the wide, warm current that flows from the Caribbean across the Atlantic, then laps the shores of Britain. The sea has been less kind to Portpatrick, whose battered harbour was finally abandoned in 1848, leaving runaway Irish couples without the quick marriage facilities that made the place a sort of seaside Gretna Green. Two lighthouses mark the extremities of the tour— Corsewall Point, from which, on a clear day, the Irish coast can be seen; and Mull of Galloway, meeting point of seven tidal currents.

(1) Stranraer to Corsewall Point Leave Stranraer on the A718 signposted to Kirkcolm, and stay on the same road beyond the roundabout 3 m. later. Drive alongside Loch Ryan and through Kirkcolm, still on the A718, but just under 1¼ m. beyond Kirkcolm, where the main road bears left, keep straight ahead on to a minor road. Follow the road round to the left at the next junction and keep straight ahead for Corsewall Point lighthouse, which is 2 m. beyond the junction.

(2) Corsewall Point to Portpatrick Return from the lighthouse towards Kirkcolm but take the first turning on the right. After 1 m. take the first road on the left and at the T-junction with the B738 soon afterwards turn right, following the signpost for Portpatrick. After 1½ m. go right again to stay on the B738. Keep on the B738 for about 5 m. and follow it round to the right at its junction with the B7043. Continue on the B738 for 3 m. until it joins the A764, and follow this road for 4 m. to the junction with the A77. Turn right here for Portpatrick.

(3) Portpatrick to Kirkmadrine Church Return along the A77 for 2 m., then fork right on to the B7042, following the signpost for Sandhead. Continue for 2 m. and then take the third turning on the right, signposted for Ardwell and Meoul. Just over 5 m. later, immediately past Mid Ringuinea Farm, turn left. Shortly after, turn left again along the track leading to Kirkmadrine Church. This contains some inscribed stones which are among Scotland's oldest Christian relics.

(4) Kirkmadrine Church to Logan Botanic Garden Go back along the lane, turn left into the road, then right at the T-junction after 1 m. Turn left at the first crossroads, then right on to the A716 on the shore of Luce Bay. Follow the road for just under 2 m. and then turn right on to the B7065 for Port Logan. To visit the Garden, turn right up the drive 1 m. after joining the B7065.

(5) Logan Botanic Garden to Logan Fish Pond From the Garden rejoin the B7065 and turn right to continue towards Port Logan Bay. Where the road meets the coast, a short walk to the right leads to the Logan Fish Pond.

(6) Logan Fish Pond to Mull of Galloway Continue round the bay on the B7065, skirting the fishing village of Port Logan, following the signposts for Mull of Galloway as the road turns inland. About 3 m. beyond Port Logan the road runs through Kirkmaiden. About 1 m. later, keep straight ahead where the B7065 meets the B7041. Ignore a minor turning to the left, which leads to Maryport, but ½ m. later take the left-hand fork and follow the road right down to the Mull of Galloway lighthouse.

(7) Mull of Galloway to Glenluce Abbey Retrace the route back to the junction with the B7065 and keep right on the B7041. At the T-junction 1 m. later turn left, then almost immediately right into Drummore. Turn left again shortly afterwards to join the A716 and follow it northwards along the coast. After 9 m. turn right, still on the A716, following the signpost for Sandhead. Keep right at the junction on the far side of the village, and ½ m. later, where the A716 goes left, keep right, joining the A715 signposted to Newton Stewart. After 3½ m., at the junction with the A757, turn right to remain on the A715, and 2 m. later, where the road meets the A75, turn right. Continue ahead for 2 m. then, immediately after crossing the Water of Luce, turn left, following the signpost for Glenluce Abbey.

(8) Glenluce Abbey to Lochinch and Castle Kennedy Gardens Continue from the abbey on the road up the valley of the Water of Luce for 4 m. to New Luce. There turn left and cross the river, following the signpost for Stranraer. After 6 m., at the T-junction with the A75, turn right and then immediately right again into Castle Kennedy Gardens.

(9) Lochinch and Castle Kennedy Gardens to Stranraer Return to the A75 and turn right for the 3 m. drive back to Stranraer.

NATURE NOTES
As well as the wildlife of the Mull of Galloway, there are many plants to be seen at Luce Bay, including wild pansy and English stonecrop. The freshwater lochs around Stranraer are a major centre for wildfowl, with flocks of greylag geese in winter.

INFORMATION
Places of interest *Glenluce Abbey:* All year, weekdays, Sun. afternoons. *Logan Botanic Garden:* Apr. to Oct., daily. *Lochinch and Castle Kennedy Gardens:* Daily. *Logan Fish Pond:* Daily (except Sat.), 10-12 noon, 2-5.30 p.m. *Mull of Galloway lighthouse:* At keeper's discretion, from 2 p.m.

Events *Stranraer:* Pipe Band Contest, June. Scottish Week, June.

Information *Stranraer:* Market Street (Tel. Stranraer 2595).

Towns with easy access to Stranraer:
Girvan . . . . 30 m.   Newton Stewart . 25 m.

CORSEWALL POINT
This rocky headland is a good vantage-point for ship-spotters. There are fine views of the Kintyre peninsula, Arran, the Firth of Clyde, Ailsa Craig and even the coast of Ireland. The 86 ft high lighthouse, usually open in the afternoons, was built by the father of the 19th-century novelist Robert Louis Stevenson. The ruins of Corsewall Castle are near by.

The lighthouse, Corsewall Point.

PORTPATRICK
Until the middle of the last century, the Irish ferries using Portpatrick's exposed harbour faced a constant battle against winter gales. The town was then known as the 'Gretna Green of the West'. Couples eloping from Ireland could arrive on a Saturday, have their banns called on Sunday and be married on the Monday. But in 1848 the ships moved to the more sheltered Stranraer. The harbour gradually silted up, and now the town is chiefly a holiday resort. It is one of the warmest places in south-west Scotland, and sub-tropical plants flourish in the open in summer. On a clifftop walk to the south of the harbour are the ruins of Dunksey Castle, built about 1510.

Australian tree ferns, Logan Botanic Garden.

LOGAN BOTANIC GARDEN
This remarkable garden was laid out by the McDouall family in the mid-19th century and is now an important annex of the Royal Botanic Garden, Edinburgh. The Gulf Stream gives this corner of Scotland an exceptionally mild and almost frost-free climate in which many exotic plants from the warm regions of the world flourish.

LOGAN FISH POND
Cod, saithe, wrasse and other sea fish are fed by hand in the Logan Fish Pond. The pond, in a natural basin carved by the sea, was created between 1788 and 1800 by Colonel Andrew McDouall of Logan House.

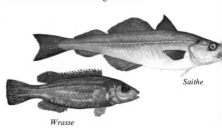

Saithe

Wrasse

SCALE
0   1   2   3   4   5 MILES

Stranraer harbour.

LOCHINCH AND CASTLE KENNEDY GARDENS
Inspired by the grounds of Louis XIV's Versailles, the castle gardens, covering about 70 acres, were created by the 2nd Earl of Stair in the first half of the 18th century. The earl was both a diplomat and a soldier, and much of the work was done by troops from the Royal Scots Greys and the Inniskilling Fusiliers. Such features as Mount Marlborough and Dettingen Avenue commemorate some of the campaigns in which the earl fought. After Stair's death in 1747 the gardens slowly fell into decay, but since the mid-19th century they have been carefully looked after. Restoration work was begun by the 8th Earl in 1840. Among the prominent features is a fine pinetum and an avenue of 70 ft high monkey-puzzle trees, more than a century old. There are also many varieties of rhododendron—some of the seeds for which were brought back from the Himalayas in India by the 19th-century botanist Sir Joseph Hooker. Among the varieties are many hybrids created in the gardens. There is a garden centre where cuttings from some of the castle's plants are on sale.

STRANRAER
Parts of a 16th-century castle, formerly used as a prison, survive in the centre of the town, which is a ferry port for Ireland. The North West Castle, now a hotel, was built in the shape of a ship by Sir John Ross, the 19th-century Arctic explorer. Loch Ryan is a good sailing centre.

Glenluce Abbey ruins.

GLENLUCE ABBEY
Burial place of Sir Walter Scott's hero Young Lochinvar, Glenluce Abbey was founded by Fergus, Lord of Galloway, in 1190. The chapterhouse, built in 1470, survives almost intact. According to local superstition a plague that was ravishing Galloway in the 13th century was diverted from the community by a wizard who lured it into a vault and locked the door. To the north-east is the ruined 17th-century Carscreugh Castle.

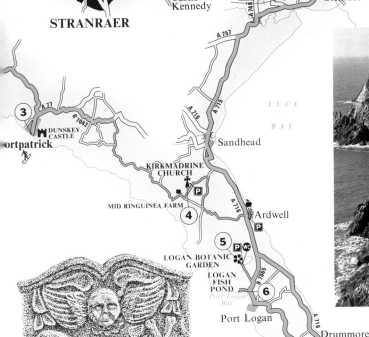

Mull (promontory) of Galloway. The lighthouse is just visible on the skyline.

Early Christian stone, Kirkmadrine Church.

KIRKMADRINE CHURCH
In this remote little church at the end of a leafy track are preserved eight Latin-inscribed stones that rank among the earliest relics of Christianity in Scotland. Some of them date from the 5th century and commemorate 'holy and excellent' priests and bishops. The others were carved between the 8th and 12th centuries. The stones were found in the churchyard; there are also some early Northumbrian crosses on display in the church.

Cormorant

MULL OF GALLOWAY
Traces of earthwork defences built by the Picts in pre-Roman times can still be seen at the Mull of Galloway, on the south-western tip of Scotland. Seven tides meet in the sea beneath its high cliffs. The cliffs are the nesting sites for many birds, including guillemots, razorbills, kittiwakes, cormorants and fulmars. Several plants reach their northern limits in Britain here. They include golden samphire, rock sea spurrey and rock sea lavender. There is a legend that the last of the Picts jumped to his death from the Mull four or five centuries ago, clutching his tribe's secret recipe for heather ale. Robert Louis Stevenson used the story in his poem 'Heather Ale, a Galloway Legend'. Near the Mull is St Medan's Cave, which was used as a chapel in the Middle Ages. The rubble was excavated by the Catholic Marquis of Bute in the 19th century, but an anti-Catholic mob from Stranraer threw his finds, which included a statue and pilgrims' badges, into the sea. There is a lighthouse on the headland which may be visited in fine weather.

True love and black deeds in Peter Pan's green valleys

West of Dumfries lies a land of green valleys and rolling hills, threaded by rivers and streams winding to the sea. Here Robert Burns wrote 'Auld Lang Syne', James Barrie was inspired to create 'Peter Pan' and Captain John Paul Jones sailed before crossing the Atlantic to found the American Navy. Sweetheart Abbey enshrines the memory of a wife's undying love, and Threave Castle the evil of the 'Black' earls of Douglas. It is a land full of recollections of odd characters—including a gipsy 'king' who fathered four children when he was over 100 years old. His memorial is at Kirkcudbright, where a 15th-century abbot's unhappy experiment in aviation is still remembered.

(1) Dumfries to New Abbey Leave the town on the A75 signposted to Stranraer and cross the River Nith, heading south-west. Still in Dumfries, bear left on to the A710 signposted New Abbey/Solway Coast. After 3 m. there is a signpost to Solway Forest, which has picnic spots and forest walks. Continue along the A710 for a further 3 m., cross a bridge, and enter New Abbey. About ¼ m. further along the road, on the left, is the car park for Sweetheart Abbey.

(2) New Abbey to Kirkbean Continue on the A710. The sea comes into view on the left after 2½ m. and the village of Kirkbean is reached 2½ m. further on.

(3) Kirkbean to Rockcliffe Continue on the A710. After 3½ m. pass through Caulkerbush. About 2½ m. later there is a car park on the left for the attractive bay of Sandyhills. Just over 1½ m. beyond this car park, at Lochend, turn left on to the road signposted to Rockcliffe. Descend a steep hill and enter Rockcliffe. At the far end of the village is a car park close to footpaths leading to Mote Hills and Mote of Mark National Trust site.

(4) Rockcliffe to Orchardton Tower Return to the A710 and turn left, following the signpost for Dalbeattie. On the outskirts of Dalbeattie, turn left on to the by-pass signposted Castle Douglas/A711. After passing over a bridge, turn left at a T-junction, following the A711, signposted now to Auchencairn. After 2½ m. pass through Palnackie, and just past the village turn sharp left on to a narrow road immediately past a school sign. This road has frequent passing places. After 1 m. turn right to Orchardton Tower, which is on the right after about ¼ m. The key to the tower can be obtained from Redliggat Cottage, which is signposted at the tower.

(5) Orchardton Tower to Dundrennan Abbey Follow the road past the tower, and after ¾ m., at the T-junction with the A711, turn left. After 2½ m. there is a lay-by with views of the coast. Go through Auchencairn, remaining on the A711, following the signpost for Kirkcudbright. Dundrennan is a further 4½ m. Just beyond the village on the left is a signpost to Dundrennan Abbey car park.

(6) Dundrennan Abbey to Kirkcudbright. Continue along the A711 towards Kirkcudbright. After 4 m. the road descends a winding hill, with views over Kirkcudbright Bay, and enters the town 1½ m. later. At the Royal Hotel turn left into Harbour Square for the car park.

(7) Kirkcudbright to Threave Castle Leave Kirkcudbright by continuing on the A711 past the Arden House Hotel. After ½ m. cross the Tongland Bridge and pass the Tongland power station. After 2½ m. there is a lay-by with views back towards Kirkcudbright. A T-junction with the A75 is reached after a further 1 m. There turn right, following the signpost for Castle Douglas. After 1½ m. the road crosses the River Dee. Here turn sharp left. After 1 m. turn on to a road signposted Threave Castle. The road continues for 1 m. to a car park near a farm. Take a well-marked path through farmland for ½ m. to the riverside, where the castle custodian will ferry visitors across the river to the castle.

(8) Threave Castle to Threave Garden Return to the A75 and turn left at the signpost for Castle Douglas. After about 400 yds turn right on to a minor road signposted Threave Garden. A further few hundred yards leads to a car park and information centre.

(9) Threave Garden to Haugh of Urr Return to the A75 and turn right to Castle Douglas. Pass through Castle Douglas and, just beyond the town, leave the A75 by forking right on to an unclassified road signposted to Haugh of Urr, which is about 3 m. on.

(10) Haugh of Urr to Dumfries Go straight over the crossroads with the B794 on to the minor road signposted to Hardgate/Milton. Continue through Milton and Lochfoot and about 3 m. beyond Lochfoot turn left on to the A711 into Dumfries.

INFORMATION

Places of interest *Dumfries:* Burgh Museum, weekdays (except Tues.) Sun. afternoons; winter, daily (except Tues., Sat., and Sun.). Old Bridge House, Apr. to Sept., weekdays (except Tues.), Sun. afternoons. Burns House, weekdays (and Sun. afternoons in summer). *Dundrennan Abbey:* Weekdays, Sun. afternoons. *Kirkcudbright:* Broughton House, Apr. to Oct., Mon. to Fri.; Nov. to Mar., Tues. and Thur. afternoons. Maclellan's Castle, weekdays, Sun. afternoons. Stewartry Museum, daily. *Orchardton Tower:* Weekdays, Sun. afternoons. *Sweetheart Abbey:* Weekdays, Sun. afternoons. *Threave Castle:* Apr. to Sept., weekdays, Sun. afternoons. *Threave Garden:* Daily.

Events *Dumfries:* Good Neighbours Festival, first Sat. in June. Agricultural Show, Aug. Burns ceremony, Jan. 25.

Information *Dumfries:* Whitesands (Tel. Dumfries 3862). *Kirkcudbright:* (Tel. Kirkcudbright 30494).

Towns with easy access to Dumfries:

Carlisle	33 m.	Lanark	55 m.
Cumnock	44 m.	Moffat	22 m.
Dalbeattie	13 m.	New Galloway	25 m.

Threave Castle.

THREAVE CASTLE
A large bell by the riverside is tolled to summon the boatman to ferry visitors across the Dee to the castle, built on a grassy islet where the river forks into two branches. There is hardly a more beautifully sited castle in Scotland, nor one with a more sinister history. Built by the 3rd Earl of Douglas—'Archibald the Grim'—in the 14th century, it became the stronghold of the 'Black Douglases', so called because of their savagery. On the front of the castle is the granite 'gallows knob' from which the Douglases hanged their foes. Archibald used to boast that the knob 'never lacked a tassel'. The Douglases were overthrown in 1455, and the castle was last inhabited during the Napoleonic wars, when it was used to guard French prisoners.

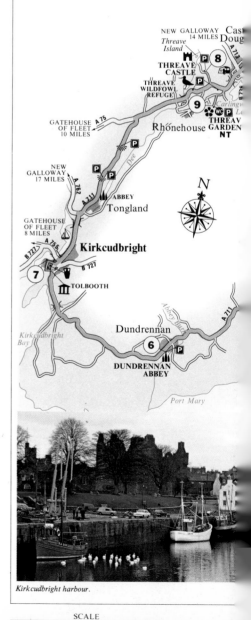

Kirkcudbright harbour.

SCALE
0   1   2   3   4   5 MILES

THREAVE GARDEN
Whatever time of the year a visit is made to Threave Garden, there is always interest and beauty. The estate incorporates a School of Gardening, and there is much evidence of the trainees' skill—formal gardens, tree-lined pathways and shaded, scent-filled bowers. Of particular interest in late May and June is the Woodland Garden, with its brilliant rhododendrons. As their colours fade, the Rose Garden comes into full maturity. At all times of the year the Walled Garden, Heath and Peat Gardens, Rock Gardens and herbaceous beds provide a riot of colour. The estate was given to the National Trust by Major Alan Gordon, an Irish Guardsman and amateur horticulturist, who died in 1957.

Threave Garden.

HAUGH OF URR
The village lies on a small plain where Spottes Burn emerges from a wooden glen to join Urr Water. Haugh is a lowland Scottish word meaning a meadow beside a stream. Just south of the village, beside Urr Water, is the Mote of Urr, a huge castle mound dating from around 1100.

Robert Burns.

DUMFRIES
Called 'The Queen of the South', the town is best known for its connections with Robert Bruce and two great literary figures. It was here in 1306 that Bruce stabbed to death a laird known as Comyn—an event which was followed by the War of Independence. Robert Burns, the ploughman-poet, spent his last years in Dumfries and his house in Mill Street is a museum. The playwright James Barrie gained inspiration for *Peter Pan* in a riverside garden. A plaque marks his house in Victoria Street.

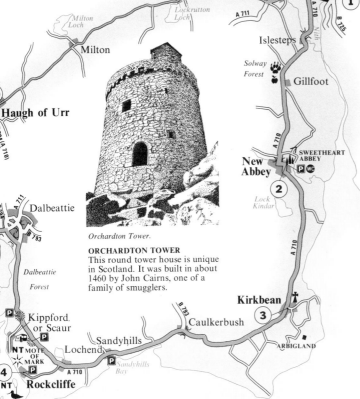

Orchardton Tower.

ORCHARDTON TOWER
This round tower house is unique in Scotland. It was built in about 1460 by John Cairns, one of a family of smugglers.

The remains of Sweetheart Abbey.

NEW ABBEY
Devorgilla, the Lady of Galloway, founded the Cistercian monastery here in 1273 in memory of her husband, John Baliol, founder of Balliol College, Oxford. When he died she had his heart embalmed, and it was buried with her own body, 21 years later, before the high altar of the church. Her devotion gave the word 'sweetheart' to the English language, and the popular name Sweetheart Abbey to her burial place. The long, low church and the central tower still stand. Three women who ferried stone for the abbey are depicted in a carving on one of the village houses.

DUNDRENNAN ABBEY
Mary, Queen of Scots spent her last night in Scotland in the abbey, after her followers were defeated at the Battle of Langside. From here she fled down the Abbey Burn to Port Mary, to make her escape to England. The abbey was founded by Cistercians in 1142.

Effigy, Dundrennan Abbey.

KIRKCUDBRIGHT
In his novel *Guy Mannering* Sir Walter Scott refers to an extraordinary character called Billy Marshall, a gipsy 'king' who married 17 times and was reputed to have fathered four children after the age of 100. Marshall died in 1792, aged 120. A stone to his memory stands in the Old Churchyard among graves dating back to the 16th century. *Guy Mannering* also contains a graphic description of the condemned cell in the 17th-century Tolbooth. Maclellan's Castle is a 16th-century mansion with vast underground kitchens. North of the town is Tongland Abbey, one of whose abbots, John Damian, tried to fly from the battlements of Stirling Castle in about 1500—and landed in a manure heap.

ROCKCLIFFE
A sheltered bay lies beneath this village of houses rising steeply up the banks of the Rough Firth Estuary. There are plenty of good picnic spots, sandy beaches and rock pools for safe bathing. At low water it is easy to reach Rough Island, which is a bird sanctuary. From Rockcliffe there are a number of country walks. One leads to the Mote of Mark, the 20 acre site of a prehistoric hill-fort. From the summit of the Mote there are views of the wooded hills surrounding the estuary. A number of other attractive walks, both gentle and strenuous, start from the village.

Lesser black-backed gull

KIRKBEAN
A memorial font in the parish church of this tiny, attractive village is dedicated to John Paul Jones, the 18th-century sailor who is credited with having founded the American Navy. He lived in a cottage at Arbigland on the coast of the Solway Firth, 2 miles from Kirkbean. The cottage is reached through a maze of lanes, and tourists wishing to drive there should seek local directions. Alternatively, they could park in Kirkbean; the walk is rewarded with views across the Solway Firth to the mountains of the Lake District.

The beautiful battleground of the Border country

For centuries the warring English and Scots turned the borderland into a battlefield. The novels of Sir Walter Scott brought its tempestuous history, and the men who made it, back to life. It is Scott's own country: the tour visits the splendid Abbotsford House which he built for himself, and Dryburgh Abbey, where he is buried. The River Tweed and its tributaries, stocked with salmon and trout, intersect this landscape of wooded valleys and hills, broken up by farm cottages and the grander homes of the lowland lairds.

The view that Scott loved.

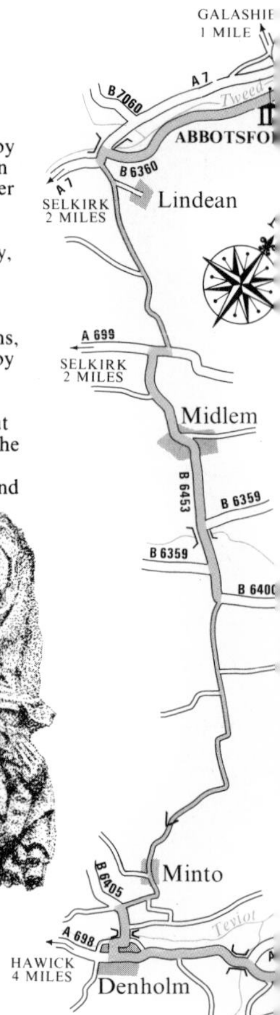

1 Jedburgh to Abbotsford From Jedburgh market-place leave on the B6358 signposted to Hawick. After 2½ m. there is a small lay-by with a viewpoint. About 1 m. beyond the lay-by keep straight ahead on to the A698 signposted to Hawick. In Denholm turn right on to the B6405, signposted to Minto/Hassendean, and cross the River Teviot. After ¾ m. turn right at the crossroads, following the signpost for Minto. Drive through Minto and continue on, ignoring side turnings, for 4 m., and then bear left on to the B6400. Keep ahead on to the B6359, signposted to Melrose. After ½ m. cross a narrow bridge, leaving the B6359, and keep straight ahead on to the B6453, signposted to Selkirk/Midlem. Drive straight through Midlem and 1½ m. further on, at the T-junction with the A699, turn right. After 200 yds turn left on to the minor road signposted to Lindean and 2¾ m. later, at the T-junction with the A7, turn right. Almost immediately turn sharp right again on to the B6360, signposted to Melrose. Abbotsford, home of Sir Walter Scott, is 2¼ m. on.

2 Abbotsford to Melrose Abbey From the car park turn right on to the B6360, and after ¼ m. turn right at the roundabout on to the A6091 signposted to Jedburgh. Follow the road into Melrose and, about 200 yds beyond the caravan site on the right, branch left on to the B6361, signposted to Newstead. Melrose Abbey car park is 200 yds ahead.

3 Melrose Abbey to Scott's View Leaving the car park, continue along the B6361 through Newstead. After ¾ m. there is a small lay-by with a view towards the viaduct over the Tweed. Drive on ¼ m. to the road junction, turn right and after 150 yds left on to the fly-over, signposted A68 Edinburgh. Cross the Tweed, then follow the signpost marked B6360 to Gattonside, Bemersyde and Smailholm. After ¼ m. bear left at the signpost Bemersyde/Smailholm/Dryburgh Abbey, and 600 yds on turn right, following the signpost for Dryburgh Abbey. About 1 m. further on bear right on to the B6356, following the signpost for Scott's View, which is ½ m. ahead.

4 Scott's View to Dryburgh Abbey Return from the car park to the B6356, and continue towards Dryburgh. Go through Bemersyde and at the T-junction 1 m. later turn right. The abbey car park is ½ m. on.

5 Dryburgh Abbey to Smailholm Tower Return along the B6356, continuing straight ahead for 1½ m. to Clintmains. Bear right at the houses, and after ¼ m. turn left at the T-junction on to the B6404. After 2¾ m. turn left on to·a minor road, noting Smailholm Tower in the distance to the left.

Special care is needed on this road as it is single-tracked in places. After just over ½ m. turn left at a T-junction by a line of trees, and ½ m. along is Sandyknowe Farm, where visitors can collect the key to Smailholm Tower. The car park is 200 yds further on.

6 Smailholm Tower to Mellerstain House Return to the minor road and at the first junction, by the line of trees, keep ahead, taking care on the winding road. After ¾ m. turn right into Smailholm village, then left along the B6397, signposted to Earlston. After 1½ m. turn right on to a minor road signposted to Mellerstain. Drive almost 1 m. and turn right for Mellerstain House.

7 Mellerstain House to Kelso Turn right on leaving the grounds of Mellerstain House. Continue for 1¼ m. to a Y-junction with the A6089, and turn right again for Kelso.

8 Kelso to Cessford Leave Kelso on the A698 signposted to Yetholm by crossing the Tweed bridge. After ½ m. join the B6352, ignoring the right turn to Jedburgh, and ½ m. later, at the Kelso Tractors corner, turn right on to the B6436, signposted to Morebattle. At the junction 4 m. ahead bear right to stay on the B6436. After 2 m., at the junction with the B6401, turn right through Morebattle. After a further 1½ m. turn left on to a minor road signposted to Crailinghall/Cessford. Cessford village is 1½ m. ahead.

9 Cessford to Jedburgh At the crossroads 3¾ m. past Cessford, drive straight ahead, following the signpost to Jedburgh. After 2¼ m., at the T-junction, bear right towards the outskirts of Jedburgh. Turn right on to the A68 at another T-junction and return to Jedburgh.

INFORMATION

Places of interest *Abbotsford House:* Mar. 21 to Oct., weekdays, Sun. afternoons. *Dryburgh Abbey:* All year, weekdays, Sun. afternoons. *Floors Castle:* Grounds, summer, Wed. 10 a.m.–4 p.m. *Jedburgh:* Castle, Apr. to Sept., weekdays, Sun. afternoons; Mary Queen of Scots' House, Apr. to Oct., weekdays, Sun. afternoons; Abbey, all year, weekdays, Sun. afternoons. *Kelso Abbey:* All year, weekdays, Sun. afternoons. *Mellerstain House:* May to Sept., every afternoon except Sat. *Melrose Abbey:* All year, weekdays, Sun. afternoons.

Event *Jedburgh:* Summer Festival, July.

Information *Jedburgh:* 3 Exchange Street (all year) (Tel. Jedburgh 2227). *Melrose:* Prior Wood Gardens.

Towns with easy access to Jedburgh:

Berwick	35 m.	Lauder	21 m.
Coldstream	20 m.	Otterburn	26 m.
Galashiels	17 m.	Peebles	40 m.
Hawick	12 m.	Selkirk	18 m.

MELROSE ABBEY
A shepherd named Cuthbert was received by the monks of Melrose in the 7th century, and later became their prior and Northumbria's greatest saint. The present abbey, founded in 1136, was plundered by invading English armies in 1322, 1385 and 1545. The ruins, however, are regarded by many as the best preserved in Scotland. Almost the whole layout can still be seen—from the dramatic arches of the church to the cloisters and kitchens.

Gargoyle, Melrose Abbey.

ABBOTSFORD
Sir Walter Scott was already a celebrated author when in 1811 he bought a farmhouse on the Tweed. There he began work on his romantic *Waverley* novels, which brought him such fame and wealth that in 1820 he decided to pull down the farmhouse and build Abbotsford House. The sumptuous mansion is stocked with Scott relics, as well as weapons used in the border wars. The beautiful grounds and gardens look across to the Tweed.

JEDBURGH
For many centuries a pivot of the Border warfare with English kings and barons, Jedburgh fought so gallantly that on several occasions its garrison was acknowledged to have saved Scotland from conquest. Its castle was once a favourite residence of Scottish kings; Malcolm IV died there in 1195. Mary, Queen of Scots, stayed for a month in a house in the town in 1566, when she was near to death from a fever. Today Jedburgh's most impressive memento of those historic days is the ruined Jedburgh Abbey, founded in 1118 and wrecked by English troops in 1523. The Border Games in July attract athletes of world repute. Jedburgh is a good centre for anglers, and some of the fishing is free.

GALASHIE
1 MILE

ABBOTSFOR

SELKIRK
2 MILES
Lindean

A 699

SELKIRK
2 MILES

Midlem

B 6453

B 6359

B 6359

B 6400

Minto

HAWICK
4 MILES
Denholm

SCALE

0   1   2   3   4   5 MILES

SCOTT'S VIEW

...is hilltop near Dryburgh offers ... unforgettable view over the ...weed to the Three Sisters peaks ... the Eildon Hills rising to 1385 ft. ...can stand on the Eildon Hills ...d point out 43 places famous in ...r and verse,' Sir Walter Scott ...ce said. The same can be said ... the hilltop view named after ...mself. An AA guide-plate at the ...mmit indicates the directions and ...stances of places within the ...norama, many of them steeped in ...gend. King Arthur and his ...ights are said to lie in a vault ...eneath the Three Sisters awaiting a ...umpet call to action.

SMAILHOLM TOWER

Standing 60 ft high on the rocky outcrop of Sandyknowe Crag, this 16th-century castle tower is such a prominent landmark that it was once used as a navigation aid by ships making for Berwick-upon-Tweed. Sir Walter Scott describes the tower in his epic poem 'Marmion'. As a child, the author had lived with his grandfather at the nearby farmhouse of Sandyknowe. The keys to the tower can be obtained from a box in Sandyknowe farmyard. Visitors are advised to take a torch if they propose to climb the tortuous spiral staircase.

Library, Mellerstain House.

MELLERSTAIN HOUSE

This is one of the great country houses of Scotland, an epitome of 18th-century elegance in architecture and furnishing. The building was begun in 1725 by William Adam, and also bears the stamp of his famous son, Robert. An outstanding work by Robert Adam is the library with its coloured plasterwork, described by Sacheverell Sitwell as 'fine drawn as a spider's web on a frosty morning'. The mansion is the home of Lord Binning.

KELSO

When the Scots Covenanters made common cause with the English Presbyterians in the 17th-century Civil War, Kelso became a transit camp for troops marching south to join Cromwell's armies. The whole Scottish army was disbanded here in 1647 after the defeat of the Royalists. Kelso Abbey, founded in 1128, was once the richest and most powerful in Scotland. It suffered the fate of most of the others in the Reformation, and little remains of it. The town's 1803 Rennie Bridge, however, used as a prototype for London's old Waterloo Bridge, still carries traffic over the Tweed. From it can be seen the gardens of Floors Castle, where a holly bush marks the spot where James II of Scotland was killed when a cannon exploded in 1460.

Town Hall, Kelso.

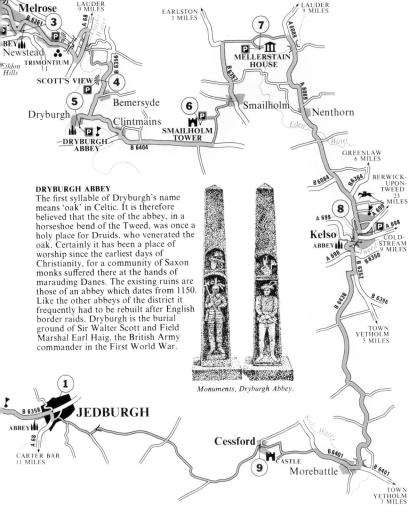

DRYBURGH ABBEY

The first syllable of Dryburgh's name means 'oak' in Celtic. It is therefore believed that the site of the abbey, in a horseshoe bend of the Tweed, was once a holy place for Druids, who venerated the oak. Certainly it has been a place of worship since the earliest days of Christianity, for a community of Saxon monks suffered there at the hands of marauding Danes. The existing ruins are those of an abbey which dates from 1150. Like the other abbeys of the district it frequently had to be rebuilt after English border raids. Dryburgh is the burial ground of Sir Walter Scott and Field Marshal Earl Haig, the British Army commander in the First World War.

Monuments, Dryburgh Abbey.

CESSFORD

The ruin of a 'barmkyn' at Cessford is a reminder of a military lesson the Scots learnt from their defeat at Flodden in 1513—the need for more fortifications. Border landowners were ordered to build, for the protection of their families and workers, 60 ft square towers and 'barmkyns', or stone enclosures, for cattle. These pocket-sized castles were scenes of many a bloody siege.

Remains of Kelso Abbey.

Jedburgh Abbey.

EDINBURGH

Capital city of Scotland since about 1450, Edinburgh's turbulent history still lives on in the medieval streets of the Royal Mile. But there is another legacy—the 18th-century elegance of the new town that won the city the title of the 'Athens of the North'.

THINGS TO SEE IN THE CITY

(1) *The Castle:* Open daily, 9.30 a.m.–6 p.m. (5.15 p.m., winter), Sun. 11 a.m.–6 p.m. (12.30–4.30 p.m., winter).

(2) *Outlook Tower:* June to Sept., weekdays 10 a.m.–6 p.m.

(3) *Riddle's Court:* Home of the murdered Bailie John Macmorran.

(4) *Lady Stair's House:* Weekdays 10 a.m.–5 p.m., June to Sept. until 6 p.m.

(5) *Old Tolbooth:* Cobblestone heart set in road marks the old prison site.

(6) *St Giles's Cathedral:* Knox's church. Weekdays 10 a.m.–5 p.m.

(7) *Parliament House:* Mon. to Fri. 10 a.m.–4.30 p.m., Sat. until 12.30 p.m.

(8) *Mercat Cross:* Centre of Old Edinburgh. Place of execution.

(9) *Tron Kirk:* Built 1637. Named after an old weighing beam.

(10) *Childhood Museum:* Weekdays 10 a.m.–5 p.m., June to Sept. until 6 p.m.

(11) *John Knox House:* House of the great preacher and reformer. Weekdays 10 a.m.–5 p.m.

(12) *Moray House:* Historic 17th-century house associated with Charles I and Oliver Cromwell.

(13) *Huntly House:* Weekdays 10 a.m.–5 p.m., June to Sept. until 6 p.m.

(14) *White Horse Close:* Site of the coaching terminus to London.

(15) *Holyrood House:* May to Oct., weekdays 9.30 a.m.–6 p.m., Sun. 11 a.m.–6 p.m., Nov. to Apr. 9.30 a.m.–5.15 p.m., Sun. 12.30–4.30 p.m.

ROYAL REGALIA *The Sword of State, part of the ancient regalia of the Scottish kings, was presented by Pope Julius II to James IV in 1507. The pope's arms are enamelled on a plate on the scabbard. It is now in the Crown Chamber of Edinburgh Castle, together with the sceptre and crown of Scotland. From the 17th century onwards, many attempts were made to take the regalia to London. All were foiled. Oliver Cromwell came closest to capturing the regalia when he seized Dunottar Castle in Angus, where it had been hidden for safety. But a local minister's wife managed to smuggle it away. She buried it under the floor of the church at Kinneff, where it remained until the Restoration.*

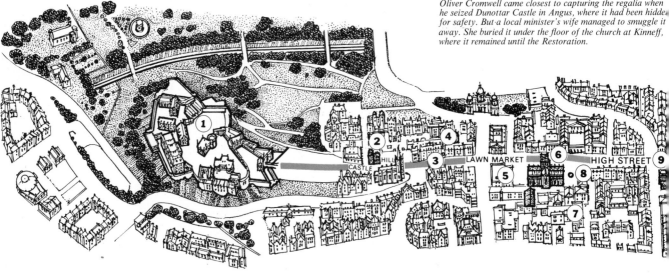

The history of Edinburgh goes back to Iron Age times, but the visible legacy of the past begins at the castle that still dominates the city today. It was from there that Edinburgh, ringed by craggy hills, slowly grew along the winding ridge that now makes up the Royal Mile.

The earliest references to a castle go back to the 6th century, and the oldest-surviving building is the Norman chapel, associated with Queen Margaret, wife of Malcolm III. Another royal benefactor was David I, who founded Holyrood Abbey in 1128. But it was not until James IV set up permanent court in the city in 1488 that Edinburgh became the seat of royal authority in Scotland.

James began building Holyrood House, the palace of the Stuart dynasty, in 1501. Twelve years later, the dismayed citizens crowded around the Mercat Cross near St Giles's to hear how he had died with 13 earls, two bishops and 10,000 young Scots in battle with the English at Flodden Field.

Overlooking Palace Yard in the castle is a tiny bedroom where another tragic Stuart, Mary, Queen of Scots, gave birth to a son who became James VI of Scotland and James I of England. The Crown Chamber houses the historic sword and regalia of Scotland.

Beyond the castle esplanade, Castlehill leads to the Lawnmarket, the first part of the Royal Mile. On the left of Castlehill is the Outlook Tower. It has a camera obscura that reflects a fascinating image of Edinburgh.

About halfway down the Lawnmarket, a fine 17th-century tenement called Gladstone's Land stands on the left. The word *land* is Scottish for tenement, and each unit in the six-storey building is called a house. Gladstone's Land, which belongs to the National Trust for Scotland, has an outside stairway, crow-stepped gables and remarkable painted ceilings. It is open in the afternoons from Monday to Friday.

Near by is Lady Stair's House, where manuscripts and relics can be seen of Scotland's three most famous men of letters—Robert Burns, Sir Walter Scott and Robert Louis Stevenson.

In the High Street outside St Giles's Cathedral, cobbles form the shape of a heart in the roadway. It marks the site of the Old Tolbooth, or prison. Its storming in the Porteous Riot in 1736 was immortalised by Scott in his novel *The Heart of Midlothian*.

Captain Porteous, an officer of the city guard, had ordered his troops to fire on an unruly Edinburgh crowd protesting at the execution of a popular smuggler. Six of the mob were killed and Porteous was condemned to death for murder but later granted a stay of execution. On hearing of this, a crowd broke into the gaol and lynched him in Grassmarket.

This was the scene of many executions. It is reached by crossing George IV bridge and walking down Candlemakers' Row. A cross in the cobblestones marks the spot where 100 Covenanters died in the 17th century for the right to worship as Presbyterians.

WRITER'S RELICS *A riding crop, hat and stirrups which belonged to Robert Louis Stevenson (bust centre) are kept in Lady Stair's House. It was originally the home of Lady Eleanor Stair, a famous 18th-century Edinburgh hostess.*

LOCAL HISTORY *These Holyrood glass jugs, designed by John Ford in 1865, are among the many historic objects on display in Huntly House, the city's museum in the Canongate. Among other items in the museum is a copy of the National Covenant. This was signed at Greyfriars' Church in February 1638.*

CHILD'S TOY *A musical Puss-in-Boots, made in France in 1875, is one of many toys in the Museum of Childhood.*

...RMOIL AND PEACE *This house in Riddle's Court, once the ...ne of Bailie (magistrate) Macmorran, has been superbly ...tored, like many historic places along the Royal Mile. The ...lie was shot dead by a schoolboy in 1595 when he ...ervened at the old High School to break up a strike by the ...dents over a refusal to let them have a holiday. But near ...there is a more peaceful memory. In a house in the outer ...rt, the 18th-century philosopher David Hume began his ...story of England.*

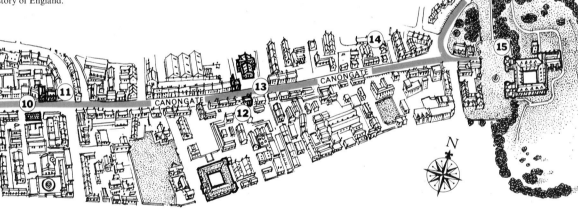

The bridge itself is a memorial to a royal visitor to the city—George IV. He went there in 1822 for the first official state visit for nearly two centuries, and made his mark by wearing a very short kilt and pink tights. One Edinburgh lady commented: 'As he is to be with us for such a short time, the more we see of him the better!'

A church has stood on the site of St Giles's Cathedral since 1120, but only four octagonal pillars remain of the original building. The cathedral's quiet Gothic walls have, in the centuries, echoed with dissension and angry dispute. St Giles's was a towering background to the Reformation, for John Knox was its minister from 1561 until his death in 1572. From its pulpit Knox hurled his attacks on 'idolatry', which played a large part in the overthrow of the Catholic Mary, Queen of Scots in 1567.

Behind the cathedral is Parliament House, meeting place of the Scottish Parliament from 1639 until the Act of Union with England in 1707. Now it is the home of Scotland's most important courts—the Court of Session and the High Court. Sir Walter Scott was the clerk there for 25 years. Visitors can mingle with be-wigged lawyers in the Parliament, which has a superb 17th-century hammerbeam roof. The great south window depicts the inauguration of the Court of Session by James V in 1532.

Beyond St Giles's along the High Street is the Mercat Cross, the centre of old Edinburgh. There, 300 years ago, traders crowded their stalls around the cross and against the cathedral walls. Fishwives pushed through the throng selling oysters, mussels and herrings from Newhaven. Kings, queens and provosts made their proclamations from the cross and many nobles fell to the executioner. Among them was Kirkcaldy of Grange, who held the castle for Mary, Queen of Scots at the time of her overthrow, and the Royalist Marquis of Montrose, who died in 1646.

Tron Kirk, further along the High Street, was built in 1637. It takes its name from a

THE ROUTE
The outward route runs west-east from the castle to the Palace of Holyrood House. It follows the Royal Mile, the most famous sequence of streets in Scotland, composed of Castle Hill, the Lawnmarket, High Street and Canongate. The return route, on pp. 360–1, runs west-east from the palace to Charlotte Square by way of Abbey Hill, Regent Road, Calton Hill, Waterloo Place, Princes Street, Hanover Street and George Street.

CAR PARKS: Andrew Square, Castle Terrace, Charlotte Square, George Street, Greenside Row, Jamaica Street, Lothian Road.

THINGS TO SEE IN EDINBURGH

(16) *Royal High School:* Now the home of the Scottish Assembly. Not open to the public.

(17) *Calton Hill:* Site of the Parthenon and Nelson's Monument.

(18) *Observatory:* Open to the public by special arrangement.

(19) *Register House:* Exhibition open Mon. to Fri. 10 a.m.–4.30 p.m.

(20) *Scott Monument:* Apr. to Sept., weekdays 10 a.m.–6.40 p.m., Sun. 1–6.40 p.m.. Oct. to Mar., weekdays only, 10 a.m.–2.45 p.m.

(21) *Scottish National Gallery:* Weekdays 10 a.m.–5 p.m., Sun. 2–5 p.m.

(22) *Charlotte Square:* Designed by Robert Adam. Part of Craig's New Town plan.

AGE-OLD PALACE *Holyrood House, home of the Stuarts, is still the official royal residence in Scotland. Although the twin towers look alike, 150 years separate their building. James IV started the west tower before being killed at Flodden in 1513. Much of the palace is the work of Charles II, who began rebuilding it in 1671.*

SEEKING SANCTUARY *An 'S' in the road marks Holyrood Abbey's sanctuary line. Until 1880 debtors could find safety by crossing it.*

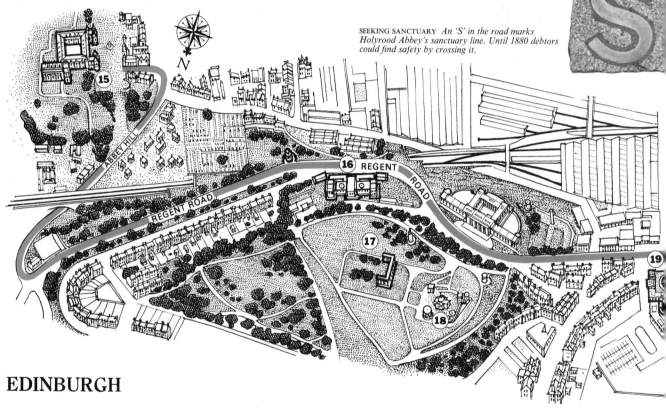

EDINBURGH

'tron' or weighing beam, which stood outside the church. This was used to check merchants' weights and it is said that if the weights were wrong, the culprit was nailed to the beam by the ears.

Farther down, on the left, is the manse reputed to have been the home of John Knox from 1561 to 1572. The house, built in 1490, is the most picturesque of Edinburgh's historic monuments. It has a fine oak room and a collection of Knox relics. The fiery preacher is said to have frequently harangued passers-by from the stone steps.

Almost opposite is the fascinating Museum of Childhood, with its large collection of historic toys, books and dolls.

Old Edinburgh ended a few yards away, where the great Netherbow Gate once straddled the Royal Mile—a name given to the streets linking the castle and Holyrood because of their royal associations. After the English victory at Flodden in 1513, the terrified townspeople threw up the Flodden Wall,

starting at the gate and rounding Cowgate and Grassmarket to the back of the castle. Over the next century, towering 'lands' or tenements, some ten storeys high, were built within the walls. Traders, artisans, gentry and vagabonds crowded in them for safety. Some of the tenements stand to this day.

Canongate is the last stretch of the Royal Mile to Holyrood. Moray House, on the left, was built in 1628 and is one of the city's most famous buildings. Charles I was a frequent visitor and Oliver Cromwell made it his headquarters.

From its balcony in 1646 the Duke and Duchess of Argyll and their wedding guests watched as their defeated enemy, the Royalist Marquis of Montrose, was dragged past on a cart to be hanged at Mercat Cross.

Only a short distance away from Moray House is Huntly House, a reconstructed dwelling of 1517. It is now the city's main museum of local history. On the same side of the street is Acheson House, built in 1633, and

now the headquarters of the Scottish Craft Centre.

Near the end of Canongate on the left is White Horse Close, a unique survival from the 17th century. At the far side of the close is a house once known as the White Horse Inn, from which coaches left for London.

Across the Canongate the letter 'S' is set at intervals in the roadway. It marks the sanctuary line of Holyrood Abbey. Any debtor who crossed the line was safe from his pursuers. Ahead stands Holyrood House with its backcloth of Salisbury Crags and Arthur's Seat.

The abbey was established by David I in 1128. According to legend, the king founded it in gratitude for an escape from death when he was chased through the forest by a stag. Knocked to the ground, he grasped the animal's antlers. The stag vanished and the antlers turned to a cross in his hands.

For 400 years Scottish kings and queens were associated with the abbey. But in 1544 it was destroyed by Henry VIII during the

SCOTTISH ATHENS *The National Monument on Calton Hill stands like a Grecian ruin above the city. The architect William Playfair modelled it on the Parthenon in Athens, as a monument to the Scots killed in the Napoleonic Wars, but it was never finished because the money ran out. Nelson's Monument, in the form of a telescope 108 ft high, stands near by. It is surmounted by a time ball in an open shaft which descends at 1 p.m., acting as a time check for ships lying in the Firth of Forth. The top of Nelson's Monument commands fine views over both the old and new city, separated by the elegant Princes Street.*

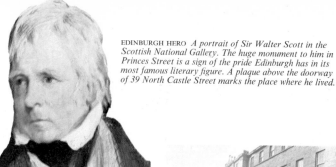

EDINBURGH HERO *A portrait of Sir Walter Scott in the Scottish National Gallery. The huge monument to him in Princes Street is a sign of the pride Edinburgh has in its most famous literary figure. A plaque above the doorway of 39 North Castle Street marks the place where he lived.*

FOREIGN MASTER *A portrait by Degas of Diego Martelli is one of many works by continental masters on display in the Scottish National Gallery in Princes Street.*

AGE OF ELEGANCE *A carriage recaptures the elegance of a past age in Charlotte Square, part of James Craig's new town. Although Craig's plan was altered, the city never lost his bold idea of a grid system, which still exists behind Princes Street. Charlotte Square itself is noted for the fine Georgian terrace, on the north side, designed by Robert Adam in 1791. He died in 1792, before completing the other sides of the square.*

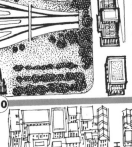

so-called 'rough wooing', when the Scots refused to fall in with his plans to marry the young Mary, Queen of Scots to Prince Edward.

The story of Holyrood House itself is dominated by Mary's career. She arrived at the palace in 1565 as Queen of Scots when she was only 18 years old. And tragedy soon struck. Mary married Lord Darnley, but the couple soon quarrelled. Darnley became jealous of his wife's friendship with her Italian secretary, David Riccio, and turned a willing ear to the conspirators who stabbed Riccio to death in the presence of the queen in March 1566. A brass plate in the supper room in the James IV tower marks the spot where he fell.

Mary's career became even more clouded when Darnley himself was murdered a year later. Popular rumour blamed the Earl of Bothwell, who Mary promptly married. The outraged nobles stepped in and Mary was overthrown and forced to flee to England. She languished there for 19 years in prison before

her cousin, Elizabeth I, had her beheaded at Fotheringhay.

The last Stuart to hold court at Holyrood was Bonnie Prince Charlie, who gave a ball there during his abortive attempt to win back the throne for his father. But it was the anti-Jacobites, holding out in the castle, who had the last word. The brave prince and his army were totally defeated at Culloden.

Historic Holyrood is still used by the British monarch as an official residence in Scotland. Investitures are held in the throne room; the state apartments contain French and Flemish tapestries and fine 18th-century furniture.

North-west of the palace stands Calton Hill, crowned by the National Monument which earned Edinburgh the nickname the 'Athens of the North'. The monument, a copy of the Parthenon, was intended to be a memorial to the dead of the Napoleonic Wars. But the money ran out before it was finished.

Calton Hill looks straight down Princes Street, which runs along the south side of the

Georgian New Town, built in the 18th and 19th centuries. The street opens spectacularly to the gardens and the castle.

Edinburgh New Town was the brainchild of a 23-year-old architect, James Craig, who in 1767 won a competition organised by the Town Council for a plan to develop the newly drained Nor' Loch. Craig's plan is based on three wide thoroughfares—Queen Street, George Street and Princes Street, which run east-west and parallel to one another. They are linked by intersecting streets to form a gridiron pattern with a square at each end.

Charlotte Square, at the west end, was designed in part by Robert Adam. He laid out the houses on the north side of the square as a unit with a Classical façade, so creating one of the greatest street fronts in the world. Other fine buildings in the New Town include the Register House, also by Adam, which houses Scotland's public records, and the Scottish National Gallery by William Playfair, architect of the Calton Hill monuments.

The gentle beauty of the Tweed Valley

For centuries, man and nature have lived in harmony in the valley of the Tweed. In a landscape of green hills rolling gently to forest glens, of moors that blaze with purple in the autumn and lowland forests with their changing tints, mellow stone mansions and castles seem to fit naturally. Traquair House, which brews its own brand of beer, has been lived in for 1000 years. Neidpath Castle has evolved into a country house from its medieval role as a fortified dwelling. A museum at Biggar takes visitors round a 19th-century village, and in Skirling an odd display of cartoons in wrought iron brings a touch of humour to the village green.

(1) Peebles to Innerleithen Leave Peebles on the A72 signposted for Galashiels, passing Peebles Hydro on the left. After 2¼ m. the starting point for Glentress Forest Trails is on the left. About 4 m. later the road enters Innerleithen. At the crossroads where the B709 goes off to the right, turn left for St Ronan's Well. Caerlee Mill is off the main street in Innerleithen.

(2) Innerleithen to Traquair House Return to the crossroads and turn left on to the B709 signposted to Yarrow. Cross the River Tweed and pass the pedestrian entrance to Traquair House. Carry on to Traquair village and turn right on to the B7062 signposted to Peebles. The entrance to Traquair House is on the right, ½ m. later.

(3) Traquair House to Neidpath Castle Leave the house and turn right on to the B7062 towards Peebles. After 3 m. the road runs through Cardrona, and about 4 m. later re-enters the outskirts of Peebles. Continue on the B7062 over the River Tweed into the town. At the junction with High Street bear left on to the A72 signposted to Biggar. About ½ m. beyond the town turn sharp left for Neidpath Castle.

(4) Neidpath Castle to Dawyck House Return to the A72 and turn left. After 2½ m. turn left on to the road signposted to Lyne Station and, at the give-way sign ¾ m. later, bear left on to the B712. Carry on through Stobo and about 2 m. later cross the River Tweed and turn left, following the signpost into Dawyck House gardens.

(5) Dawyck House to Biggar Return to the B712 and turn left. After 2 m. the road goes through Drumelzier, recrosses the River Tweed, and 1 m. later meets the A701. Here turn right, following the signpost for Edinburgh. After 1 m., just beyond Calzeat, turn left at the War Memorial on to the road signposted to Coulter/Hartree. At the Y-junction about 1 m. later bear left on the road signposted to Coulter. About 3 m. later, there are lay-bys with spectacular views in all directions. Continue down to Coulter, pass Coulter parish church and the church at Birthwood Road. At the T-junction soon afterwards turn right, and bear right to follow the A702 into Biggar.

(6) Biggar to Skirling Leave the town on the A702 signposted to Edinburgh. After ¾ m. turn right on to the A72, following the Peebles signpost. Skirling Mill is on the left just over 1 m. later and Skirling village green is ½ m. beyond the mill.

(7) Skirling to Romannobridge Continue towards Peebles on the A72. After 3½ m., where the A72 bears right by an AA telephone box, keep straight ahead on to the A701. After 3½ m. the road crosses Lyne Water to enter Romannobridge.

(8) Romannobridge to Eddleston Leave the village on the B7059, by the hotel, following the Peebles signpost. After 1 m. there is a lay-by below the 'Roman Terraces' on the hills to the left. Newlands church, with a large car park, is about 200 yds further on. The road runs beside Lyne Water for 2½ m. to the T-junction with the A72. Here turn left. After 2 m. the road crosses Lyne Water. About ¾ m. beyond the bridge turn left on to the minor road signposted to Eddleston via Meldons. The road begins to climb, and after ½ m. crosses a cattle grid. There are two car parks beyond the grid—one after ¾ m. and the other about ½ m. further on. Each offers wide views over the surrounding hills. About 3½ m. beyond the second car park, pass the Black Barony Hotel and turn right into Station Road, Eddleston. The miniature railway can be seen beyond the post office on the right.

(9) Eddleston to Peebles Leave the village on the A703 signposted to Peebles. The road follows the course of Eddleston Water for 4½ m. back to Peebles town centre.

INFORMATION

Places of interest *Biggar:* Gladstone Court, Easter to Oct., daily except Wed. afternoons and Sun. mornings. *Dawyck House gardens:* Good Friday to end Oct., daily. *Eddleston Railway:* Open two or three days a year. Contact Peebles 20138. *Neidpath Castle:* Daily. *Peebles:* The Chambers Institution Museum, all year, weekdays. Key for Art Gallery from Library in same building. *Traquair House:* Easter Sun., Mon., May to end Sept., daily (except Fri.), 1.30-5.30 p.m.

Events *Biggar:* Agricultural Show, Aug. Horticultural Show, Aug. Crowning of the Fleming Queen, July. Hogmanay Bonfire, Dec. 31. *Innerleithen:* St Ronan's Border Games, July. Cleikum Ceremony, July. *Peebles:* Beltane Festival, June. Agricultural Show, Aug. Open golf tournament, July.

Nature trails *Glentress Forest Trails:* 2 m. east of Peebles on A72. Booklet from dispenser at car park.

Information *Peebles:* High Street (Tel. Peebles 20138).

Towns with easy access to Peebles:

Edinburgh	23 m.	Moffat	33 m.
Jedburgh	40 m.	Penicuik	14 m.
Lanark	28 m.	Selkirk	21 m.

EDDLESTON
Scotland's 'dry' Sundays are mainly attributable to an Eddleston man, William Forbes Mackenzie, a lawyer-MP. In 1852 it was his Forbes Mackenzie Act, as it became known, that banned public-house opening on the Sabbath. The 17th-century Black Barony Hotel was formerly a home of the Murrays, an influential Border clan. There are traces of prehistoric hill-forts on the outskirts of the village.

ROMANNOBRIDGE
A Roman road which crossed the Lyne Water gave the hamlet its name nearly 2000 years ago. Near Newlands church are the so-called Roman Terraces, 14 wide steps built up on a hillside. They have puzzled historians for centuries, but the most widely held view is that they are 'strip lynchets', medieval cultivation terraces resembling some modern continental vineyards.

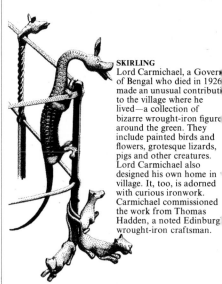

SKIRLING
Lord Carmichael, a Governor of Bengal who died in 1926, made an unusual contribution to the village where he lived—a collection of bizarre wrought-iron figures around the green. They include painted birds and flowers, grotesque lizards, pigs and other creatures. Lord Carmichael also designed his own home in village. It, too, is adorned with curious ironwork. Carmichael commissioned the work from Thomas Hadden, a noted Edinburgh wrought-iron craftsman.

Wrought-iron figures, Skirling village green.

BIGGAR
Old shops, a bank and a schoolroom have been reconstructed to form the Gladstone Court Museum, where visitors can see how small-town tradesmen lived and worked in the 19th century. Hanging on the school wall is an illustration of 'the road to damnation', warning children of various evils, especially Sunday train journeys. The ancient Cadger's Bridge is named after the Scottish independence hero William Wallace, who is said to have crossed it disguised as a hawker, or cadger, on his way to spy out the disposition of Edward I's army in 1297. He found his own force heavily outnumbered, but inflicted a resounding defeat on the English at the Battle of Biggar. The 16th-century St Mary's Church tower affords good views of the countryside.

CARNWATH
8 MILES

Biggar
6

LANARK
10 MILE

Coulte

ABINGDON
9 MILES

A 19th-century general store, Gladstone Court Museum, Biggar.

SCALE
0   1   2   3   4   5 MILES

...d grouse

Purple heather

THE MOORFOOT HILLS
...ackhope Scar, 2137 ft high, tops this range of hills
...hich rise from the valley of the Eddleston Water.
...e heather on the moorland areas is burnt in rotation
...ch year to promote the growth of the tender young
...oots on which the red grouse feed.

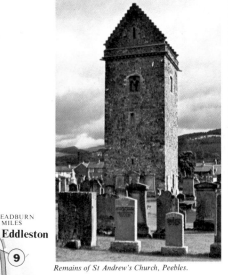
Remains of St Andrew's Church, Peebles.

PEEBLES
In ancient Britain the word *pebyll,*
the origin of Peebles, meant a good
site for pitching the skin tents in
which wandering tribes lived. The
town's oldest enduring relic is a cross
marking the burial place of the
martyred Bishop Nicholas in 296. It
was found in 1261, when Cross Kirk
was built as a shrine. Over the
centuries, the church became derelict,
and around 1800 permission was
given for it to be used as a coal
depot. It was restored after the First
World War. One of the most notable
buildings in the town centre is the
Chambers Institution—library,
museum and art gallery—named after
one of the founders of the Edinburgh
publishing house, William Chambers.
At his own expense he converted it
in 1859 from a 17th-century house
in which the 4th Duke of Queensberry,
known as 'Old Q', was born in 1725.

INNERLEITHEN
Every July at Innerleithen a
week-long celebration comes to
a climax when a schoolboy is
installed as St Ronan and handed
a pastoral staff with which he
'cleiks the De'il'—expels the Devil.
The ceremony keeps alive a legend
that St Ronan came to the valley
in 737 and drove out Satan. The
17th-century Cross Keys Hotel
is said to be the Cleikum Inn of
Sir Walter Scott's *St Ronan's Well.*
Tweed is manufactured at Caerlee
Mill, founded in 1790 and thought
to be the oldest mill in the Borders
which is still in use.

TRAQUAIR HOUSE
Scotland's oldest inhabited house,
Traquair dates from 950. It is occupied
by a direct descendant of James Stuart,
1st Laird of Traquair, who was killed
at the Battle of Flodden in 1513. The
house has sheltered 27 kings as well as
Mary, Queen of Scots, whose rosary
and crucifix are among its many
historic relics. Visitors can buy the
strong ale which is still brewed on the
premises to the recipe that has been
used since the 16th century.

The King's Room, Traquair House.

NEIDPATH CASTLE
The L-shaped castle, property of the Earl
of Wemyss and March, has been continuously
occupied since it was built by the Hays of
Yester in the 14th century. The carved crest
of the Yesters, a goat's head above a crown,
can be seen above the doorway in the courtyard.
The castle, with walls up to 12 ft thick, was
the last stronghold south of the Forth to be
held for Charles I. It was surrendered to
Cromwell after the Battle of Dunbar in 1650.
A bedroom used by Mary, Queen of Scots in
1563 is on the second of the four floors.

View of the Tweed Valley from Neidpath Castle.

...e glen in the gardens of Dawyck House.

...WYCK HOUSE GARDENS
...e grounds of privately occupied Dawyck House are noted for
...ir trees and shrubs. The horse chestnut was first planted in
...otland here in 1650, and the larch in 1725. There is a fine avenue
...imes, and a wooded glen.

Map labels
LEADBURN 5 MILES
Eddleston
HOTEL
MINIATURE RAILWAY
PENICUIK 10 MILES
...nannobridge
HOTEL
TERRACES
Mountain Cross
MOORFOOT HILLS
PEEBLES
Black Meldon
White Meldon
NEIDPATH CASTLE
CAERLEE MILL
ST RONAN'S WELL
GALASHIELS 12 MILES
Innerleithen
Cardrona
TRAQUAIR HOUSE
Traquair
Quair Water
YARROW 10 MILES
FORT
Stobo
DAWYCK HOUSE GARDENS
Skirling
Broughton
Calzeat
Drumelzier
MOFFAT 2 MILES

Birds and battlements in the 'Garden of Scotland'

The gentle countryside between the Lammermuir Hills and the Firth of Forth is sometimes called the 'Garden of Scotland', though castle ruins from Dunbar to Tantallon bear witness to a grimmer past. In North Berwick's 12th-century Auld Kirk, witches are said to have met the Devil in 1591 to plot the overthrow of James VI of Scotland. There is so much to see in Haddington that the council has signposted a walk through the old town. Other features along this route include a veteran-car museum, a visit to a 400-year-old working water mill, and a view of the sea-bird sanctuary on Bass Rock.

(1) Dunbar to Haddington Leave the town on the A1087, following the signposts for Edinburgh. After almost 1 m. from the outskirts of Dunbar, in West Barns, turn left on to the B6370 signposted to Stenton. On meeting the A1, go right and immediately left, staying on the B6370. From here the route passes through gentle hills and farmland before entering Stenton. Here, red-roofed stone cottages line the village green on which lies the Wool Stone, where wool was weighed in the 13th century before being sold at the fair. Near by is a 14th-century stone well with a conical top. (To visit the Pressmennan Forest Trail, take the left fork on the far side of Stenton on to a minor road signposted for the trail, and after 1 m. turn down the track to the car park.)

Continue through Stenton on the B6370, following signposts for Gifford. After 6 m., at the junction with the B6355, turn right and continue into Gifford, a large village built mainly in the 18th century and surrounded by woodlands. Keep on the B6355 through the village, and 3 m. from Gifford fork right on to the minor road signposted to Bolton. At the junction with the A6137, go straight ahead and then go right to follow the A6137 through Bolton, a small village where the mother, sister and brother of the poet Robert Burns are buried in the churchyard. Continue on the road to Haddington, crossing the bridge over the River Tyne and bearing left on to the A6093 to reach the town centre of Haddington, packed with scores of carefully restored historic buildings which can be seen in a short walk through the town. This is carefully signposted and takes about half an hour.

(2) Haddington to Myreton Motor Museum Return along the A6093 to the junction with the A6137 and turn left. Where this road goes sharp right on the outskirts of Haddington, keep straight ahead, following the signpost for North Berwick. Almost immediately, keep straight ahead again to cross the A1. Follow the road over the Garleton Hills and 1½ m. beyond the A1 cross the B1343. After a further 2 m., at the bottom of a hill, turn left on to the B1377. Turn right after ½ m. on to a minor road which is signposted to the Myreton Motor Museum.

(3) Myreton Motor Museum to Dirleton Continue along the road from the museum and turn right. Soon afterwards take the first turning on the right, following the signpost for Gullane. Continue along this road, ignoring lanes to the left and right, and after 2½ m. keep straight ahead on to the A198. Follow the road into Gullane, which has five of East Lothian's 12 golf courses, including the championship course of Muirfield. About 2 m. beyond Gullane, the road runs into the village of Dirleton. The castle is on the right. At the far side of the village, a signposted turning to the left leads to the Yellowcraig Nature Trail. This runs for ¾ m. through woodland and sand dunes.

(4) Dirleton to North Berwick Leave the village on the A198 and continue past a golf course for the 3 m. drive to North Berwick.

(5) North Berwick to Tantallon Castle Leave the town on the A198 signposted to Dunbar, and follow it for 3 m. Just after the main road bears sharp right, there is a lane on the left leading to Tantallon Castle, once a Douglas stronghold.

(6) Tantallon Castle to East Linton Return to the main road and turn left, following the A198 through the village of Whitekirk, with its pre-Reformation church. In the next village, Tyninghame, turn right on to the B1407. Follow the road for 2 m., and just outside East Linton turn left to visit the Preston Water Mill. Return to the B1407 and turn left to enter East Linton.

(7) East Linton to Dunbar Continue through the village to the junction by the railway bridge, and turn left on to the road signposted to Dunbar. Keep straight ahead shortly after where the road joins the A1. The stone Phantassie dovecote is to the left of the road behind Phantassie Farm. Continue on the A1, and after 3 m., at the roundabout, turn on to the A1087 to enter Dunbar.

INFORMATION

Places of interest *Dirleton Castle:* All year, daily. *Myreton Motor Museum:* Easter to Oct., daily, weekends in winter. *East Linton:* Preston Mill and Phantassie dovecote, weekdays, Sun. afternoons. *Tantallon Castle:* All year, weekdays, Sun. afternoons.

Events *Dunbar:* 'Round the Streets' cycle race, Aug. Vintage vehicle rally, last weekend in Aug. Golf Week, first week in Oct. *Haddington:* Festival, June.

Nature Trails *Dunbar:* Starts at Barns Ness, 3 miles south of Dunbar. Geology and shore life. Further details: District Clerk, Town House, Dunbar. *Pressmennan:* 1½ m. south of Stenton village. Starts at Woodend, signposted, leaflets available there. *Yellowcraig:* At Dirleton. Dunes, geology and plants. Guide from Information Office, North Berwick, or County Buildings, Haddington.

Information *Dunbar:* Town House, High Street (Tel. Dunbar 63353). *North Berwick:* 18 Quality Street (Tel. North Berwick 2197).

Towns with easy access to Dunbar:
Dalkeith . . . . 25 m. Eyemouth . . . . . . 22 m.
Edinburgh . . . . . 28 m. Kelso . . . . 39 m.

Dirleton Castle.

Citröen Kegresse, Myreton Motor Museum

MYRETON MOTOR MUSEUM
The museum, which is open daily in summer, houses 57 cars and commercial vehicles, 34 motor cycles and 17 bicycles, together with old garage signs and a pump which used to dispense petrol at 1s 6d (7½p) a gallon. Most of the motors have been restored to working order. Among them is a 1935 Citröen Kegresse, with half tracks, which was used as an estate car in the North, a 1925 'Bullnose' Morris and a Beeston-Humber motor cycle, built in 1903. The oldest car is an 1897 Arnold-Benz.

HADDINGTON
Numbered boards map out a walk round an 11-point itinerary through this medieval town. The trail starts at the Town House, built in 1748, and lasts for approximately half an hour. The Council of British Archaeology lists 129 buildings of special interest, and they are interspersed with green spaces, courtyards and alleyways. The most notable is the 14th-century St Mary's Church, which was known as the 'Lamp of the Lothians'. The town is the birthplace of the reformer John Knox (1505-72), founder of the Presbyterian Church.

The Town House, Haddington

SCALE
0   1   2   3   4   5 MI

Tantallon Castle.

...RLETON

...ely trees, a fine 17th-century
...rch and carefully preserved
...tages make Dirleton one of the
...st attractive villages in this part of
...tland. Perched high above on a
...k is a 13th-century castle, built to
...minate what was once the main
...asion route between England and
...tland. It was captured by
...ward I's troops in 1298, and
...nged hands on several occasions
...ter years. From the 16th century
...wards, it was a stronghold
...he Ruthven family, one of the
...st important in Scotland at that
...e. Patrick, the 3rd Lord Ruthven,
...s a leader of the conspirators who
...rdered David Riccio, favourite of
...ry, Queen of Scots. The castle was
...ally destroyed in the 1650s after
... Civil War. Within the ruined walls
...a flower garden and a 17th-century
...wling green, which is still in use.
...e Yellowcraig Nature Trail, off the
...98 at Dirleton, has a great variety
...rock plants and shore life.

TANTALLON CASTLE

For more than 300 years, Tantallon was
considered to be almost impregnable. Built
in 1375 by the earls of Angus, the chiefs of the
'Black' Douglas clan, it was protected on three
sides by 100 ft cliffs rising straight out of the
sea, and on the fourth side by ditches and
ramparts. But a 12 day bombardment by
Cromwell's artillery in 1651 battered it into
submission. The ruins are still impressive,
and from them there is a view over the Firth
of Forth to the bird sanctuary on Bass Rock.

EAST LINTON

Beside the River Tyne, on the outskirts of East Linton, is
Preston Mill, whose water-driven grinding machinery still
turns after 400 years. It is open daily all the year round.
A few hundred yards south, reached by a footpath, is the
massive 16th-century stone dovecote in the grounds at
Phantassie, the house where John Rennie, famous
engineer and bridge builder, was born in 1761. The
village is dominated by Hailes Castle, where Mary, Queen
of Scots and her lover, Bothwell, stayed when fleeing
after the murder of Mary's husband in 1567.

Preston Watermill, East Linton.

The Phantassie dovecote, East Linton.

NORTH BERWICK

A conical volcanic hill, 613 ft
high, called North Berwick
Law, is a permanent
landmark at this popular
seaside resort. It is topped
by a ruined look-out tower
and an arch formed from the
jawbone of a whale. The
tower was built in 1803
when Britain was threatened
with invasion by Napoleon.
In the Firth of Forth, 3
miles offshore, lies the 350 ft
Bass Rock, which gave its
name to the gannet (Sula
bassana) which breeds
here as a protected species.
Before it became a bird
sanctuary the rock was used
as a fortress and prison. It
was the last place in Britain
to recognise the sovereignty
of William III in 1694.

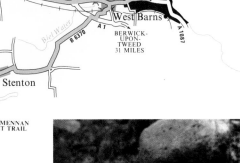

...RESSMENNAN FOREST TRAIL

...rthur's Seat, in Edinburgh, and Bass
...ock, off the coast by Tantallon Castle,
...e just two of the many landmarks
...ible from the highest point of this
...mile walk. The trail passes through
...odland roamed by roe deer. Swans,
...ted ducks and several other species of
...ter birds can be seen on the lake at
...ferent times of the year.

DUNBAR

Kittiwakes mingle with fishing boats and
pleasure craft in the harbour overlooked by
Dunbar Castle, which was wrecked during
Cromwell's campaign to subdue the Scots in
1650. The old town is full of architectural
interest. The 17th-century Town House in the
High Street, which has a hexagonal tower, is still
used for council meetings. John Muir
(1838-1914), one of the first naturalists to stress
the importance of conserving natural resources,
was born at 128 High Street.

Kittiwakes, Dunbar harbour.

365

Clyde's bonny banks, and where to buy a bonnet

All the dramatic beauty of the Clyde estuary is summed up at Largs, a sailing resort that nestles among hills. And some of the secrets of life beneath the estuary's waters are revealed at the marine station just across the ferry from the town. The tour strikes inland, winding between mountains and moors untouched by the industrial hand that has shaped the shipbuilding towns further down the Clyde. Linn Park and Pollok House, with its remarkable art collection, show the more pleasant face of Glasgow; and for a picnic, the recreation area up the glen of the River Calder would be hard to surpass. Dunlop cheese is made at the little town of Dunlop, which is just off the route. It can be bought at Stewarton—which is also the place to go shopping for a Tam o' Shanter.

(1) Largs to Great Cumbrae Island Take the car ferry to the island—there is a fast shuttle service—and turn left from the landing stage at Tattie Pier. After driving ½ m. along the coast road take the first turn on the right, and go right again at the next junction, climbing to the Glaid Stone, the highest point—415 ft—on Great Cumbrae. Continue on from the hilltop, turn right at the first junction and keep straight ahead immediately after. The road passes the little Cathedral of the Isles before reaching the A860 at Millport. Turn left at the A860 and follow it back to the ferry.

(2) Great Cumbrae Island to Stewarton Turn right on landing at Largs and follow the A78 south along the coast. After 4 m. turn left by the Hunterston ore terminal, following the signpost for Dalry. After 6 m. turn left at the junction with the B780, on the approach to Dalry. At the next T-junction, go right following the Kilwinning signpost. Shortly afterwards go left on to the A737 signposted to Beith, and follow the road out of the town. Beyond Dalry, take the first turn right, joining the B707 signposted to Stewarton. Follow this road for 5 m. until it meets the A736. Turn right here, then left after 1 m. on to the B778, and follow the signpost to Stewarton.

(3) Stewarton to Eaglesham Leave the town on the B778, signposted to Fenwick. Immediately after crossing Annick Water on the outskirts of Stewarton, bear left, and about 2 m. later turn right. Continue to the A77 and turn left, and about 3 m. later turn right on to the B764, signposted to Eaglesham. A straightforward drive of 6 m. or so through lonely mountain country leads to Eaglesham, where Hitler's deputy, Rudolf Hess, landed in 1941 after his sensational flight from Germany with peace proposals.

(4) Eaglesham to Linn Park Leave Eaglesham on the B767 signposted to Glasgow. Continue for just under 4 m. to the roundabout in the built-up area of Clarkston. There join the A726, signposted to Paisley. At the next roundabout, after ½ m., join the A727 signposted for Glasgow. Just over 1 m. later, turn right into Netherlee Road, which leads to Linn Park.

(5) Linn Park to Pollok House Continue along Netherlee Road to the traffic lights at Cathcart station, and go straight on over the junction, bearing slightly left into Newland Road. Continue on this road over two sets of traffic lights and over the crossroads beyond the A77. After swinging sharply left and right, the road meets the A736 outside the grounds of Pollok House, which has one of Britain's finest art collections.

(6) Pollok House to Muirshiel Country Park Return down the drive and turn right on to the A736. Stay on this road at two roundabouts, following the signposts for Barrhead. At the traffic lights, follow the road right then left for Barrhead. Stay on the A736 at the roundabout in Barrhead. After a further 6 m. cross the railway near Uplawmoor and immediately turn right on to the B776, signposted to Howwood, which is reached 5 m. later. In Howwood bear half right over the A737, then cross the railway and the river and continue for 3 m., ignoring side turnings, until the road meets the B786. Here turn right, following the Kilmacolm signpost. Just under ½ m. later, where the main road bends right, keep straight ahead for Muirshiel Country Park, which is 3 m. further on, in the Calder Valley.

(7) Muirshiel Country Park to Loch Thom Return from the park down the valley to the B786 and turn left. At the crossroads, after 6 m., turn left on to the B788 signposted to Greenock. The road now climbs to almost 700 ft, commanding fine views of the Firth of Clyde to the right. Follow the B788 into Greenock and turn left at the first T-junction. At the next T-junction—with Baker Street (B7054)—turn left again, following the Largs signpost. Almost 1 m. later, fork left, and follow the signposted road to Loch Thom.

(8) Loch Thom to Largs Follow the road on past the loch, climbing steeply to more than 800 ft and then dropping down the wooded Brisbane Glen for the 8 m. run back to Largs.

INFORMATION

Places of interest *Millport:* Marine Biology Station, Mon. to Fri., also Sat. in summer. Cathedral of the Isles, daily. *Pollok House:* Weekdays and Sun. afternoons.

Events *Largs:* Regattas in May, July and Aug.

Information *Largs:* The Esplanade (Tel. Largs 673765). *Glasgow:* George Square (Tel. 041 221-6136).

Ferry services Car ferry from Largs to Tattie Pier, Great Cumbrae Island, every 30 min. in summer, every hour in winter. Crossing takes 10 min.

Towns with easy access to Largs:

Ayr	29 m.	Greenock	14 m.
Glasgow	39 m.	Kilmarnock	25 m.

Waterfall, Muirshiel Country Park.

LOCH THOM
The loch is named after Robert Thom, the engineer who used it 150 years ago as a reservoir to supply the industrial towns of Greenock and Port Glasgow. The high points of the plateau provide views of the Western Highlands and of the harbours at Greenock on the Clyde estuary. The estuary is one of the best landlocked anchorages in the world and is usually busy with shipping.

The Pencil, Largs.

LARGS
The monument overlooking the sea, known as The Pencil, commemorates the Battle of Largs in 1263, when Alexander III of Scotland defeated an army of invaders from Norway, and broke the Vikings' power over western Scotland. Tucked away in an old churchyard off Main Street is the Skelmorlie Aisle, built as a mausoleum for St Columba's Church in 1636, and considered to be one of Scotland's best examples of Italian Renaissance architecture. Largs (meaning hillside) is a lively holiday resort and a springboard for pleasure cruises to the Western Isles and the Highland lochs.

GREAT CUMBRAE ISLAND
Millport is a cruising port and the only town on the island: its population outside the holiday season is fewer than 1300. It has sandy beaches, good bathing facilities and children's attractions. The Episcopal Church in College Street was built by the Earl of Glasgow in 1851, and later became the Cathedral of Argyll and the Isles. From the high point of the Glaid Stone (or Gleadstane) the lighthouse of Little Cumbrae Island can be seen to the south. To the east is the tiny Castle Island, with the ruins of a fortress destroyed by Cromwell's Parliamentary forces in 1653.

SCALE
0 1 2 3 4 5 MILES

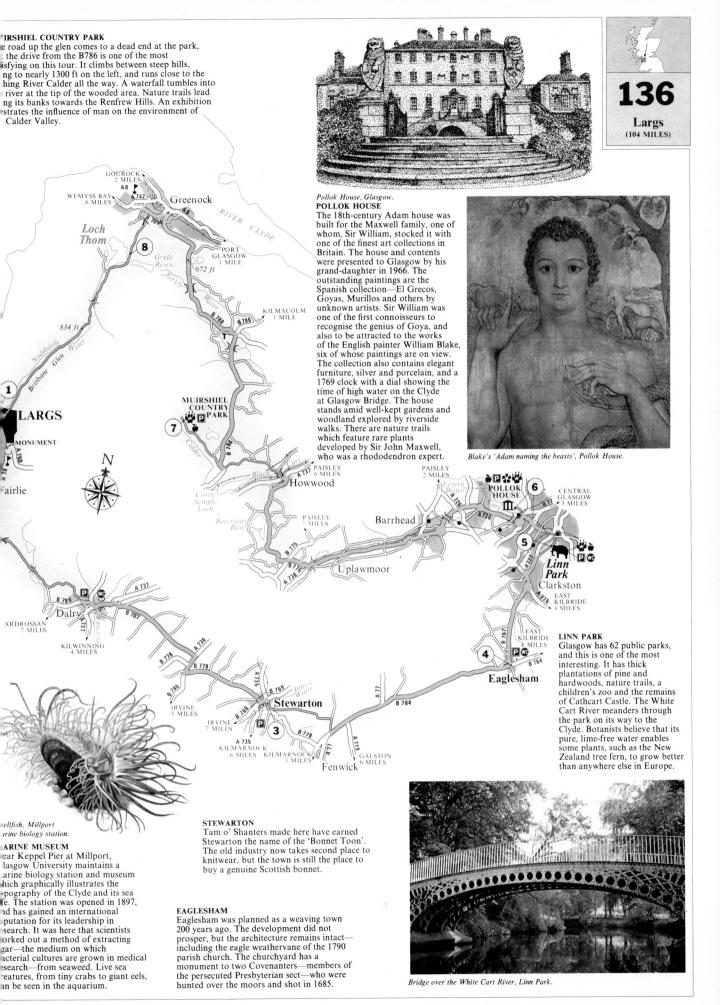

...IRSHIEL COUNTRY PARK

...e road up the glen comes to a dead end at the park, ... the drive from the B786 is one of the most ...isfying on this tour. It climbs between steep hills, ...ng to nearly 1300 ft on the left, and runs close to the ...hing River Calder all the way. A waterfall tumbles into ... river at the tip of the wooded area. Nature trails lead ...ng its banks towards the Renfrew Hills. An exhibition ...strates the influence of man on the environment of ... Calder Valley.

Pollok House, Glasgow.

POLLOK HOUSE

The 18th-century Adam house was built for the Maxwell family, one of whom, Sir William, stocked it with one of the finest art collections in Britain. The house and contents were presented to Glasgow by his grand-daughter in 1966. The outstanding paintings are the Spanish collection—El Grecos, Goyas, Murillos and others by unknown artists. Sir William was one of the first connoisseurs to recognise the genius of Goya, and also to be attracted to the works of the English painter William Blake, six of whose paintings are on view. The collection also contains elegant furniture, silver and porcelain, and a 1769 clock with a dial showing the time of high water on the Clyde at Glasgow Bridge. The house stands amid well-kept gardens and woodland explored by riverside walks. There are nature trails which feature rare plants developed by Sir John Maxwell, who was a rhododendron expert.

Blake's 'Adam naming the beasts', Pollok House.

LINN PARK

Glasgow has 62 public parks, and this is one of the most interesting. It has thick plantations of pine and hardwoods, nature trails, a children's zoo and the remains of Cathcart Castle. The White Cart River meanders through the park on its way to the Clyde. Botanists believe that its pure, lime-free water enables some plants, such as the New Zealand tree fern, to grow better than anywhere else in Europe.

...ellfish, Millport ...arine biology station.

...ARINE MUSEUM

...ear Keppel Pier at Millport, ...lasgow University maintains a ...arine biology station and museum ...hich graphically illustrates the ...pography of the Clyde and its sea ...fe. The station was opened in 1897, ...d has gained an international ...putation for its leadership in ...search. It was here that scientists ...orked out a method of extracting ...gar—the medium on which ...acterial cultures are grown in medical ...esearch—from seaweed. Live sea ...reatures, from tiny crabs to giant eels, ...n be seen in the aquarium.

STEWARTON

Tam o' Shanters made here have earned Stewarton the name of the 'Bonnet Toon'. The old industry now takes second place to knitwear, but the town is still the place to buy a genuine Scottish bonnet.

EAGLESHAM

Eaglesham was planned as a weaving town 200 years ago. The development did not prosper, but the architecture remains intact—including the eagle weathervane of the 1790 parish church. The churchyard has a monument to two Covenanters—members of the persecuted Presbyterian sect—who were hunted over the moors and shot in 1685.

Bridge over the White Cart River, Linn Park.

A journey through the heart of Burns country

From the Tam o' Shanter Inn at Ayr to Alloway's Brig o' Doon and Souter Johnnie's cottage at Kirkoswald, the country is full of reminders of the people and places immortalised in the poems of Robert Burns. Culzean Castle, in contrast, is the height of 18th-century elegance and sophistication, standing in a fine country park beside the Firth of Clyde. Inland, the route covers some of the loveliest scenery in southern Scotland as it climbs into the Galloway Hills, home of wild goats and of the rare golden eagle.

(1) Ayr to Alloway Leave Ayr on the A79, signposted to Girvan. On the outskirts, fork right on to the B7024 for the drive of just over 1½ m. to Alloway.

(2) Alloway to Straiton Continue along the B7024. After 3 m., just after zigzagging over a bridge, turn left at the staggered crossroads. Follow the road to the junction with the A77 and turn right. Take the first left turn, joining the B7045 for Straiton, a run of about 8 m. along the wooded valley of the Water of Girvan.

(3) Straiton to Rowantree Toll Leave the village on the road signposted to Newton Stewart. After driving 3 m. along the valley, with the river to the right, the road climbs into the Carrick Forest, eventually reaching a height of 1421 ft. Rowantree Toll, an 8 m. drive through the forest, is a road junction in a natural park, with car park and picnic area in the forest.

(4) Rowantree Toll to Barr Turn right on to the road signposted for Barr. Follow the road down the steep Nick of the Balloch, and 4 m. from Rowantree Toll turn left, still following the signpost for Barr, which is reached after a drive of 4 m.

(5) Barr to Old Dailly Continue through Barr until the road meets the B734 on the far side of the village. Here turn right, following the Girvan signpost. At the T-junction 4 m. later turn right, still on the B734, and follow the road into Old Dailly.

(6) Old Dailly to Kirkoswald Keep straight ahead at the crossroads in Old Dailly, and immediately afterwards follow the road round to the right. After ½ m. turn left at the first T-junction. At the junction with the B741, turn right, then take the first turn left, by the quarry. After 2 m., at the next T-junction, turn left to follow the Kirkoswald signpost. Shortly afterwards, where a road to the right leads to South Threave, bear left and ¾ m. later turn left on to the road signposted to Turnberry. Follow the road round to the right at the foot of the hill, and keep straight on at the fork immediately after. Just over 1 m. later, at the next T-junction, turn left then almost immediately right on to the A77 for the 1 m. drive into Kirkoswald.

(7) Kirkoswald to Culzean Castle Leave Kirkoswald on the A77, and on the far side of the village turn left, following the signpost for the Culzean Country Park. After 1 m., at the T-junction with the A719, turn right. About 1 m. later, turn left into the country park and follow the road to Culzean Castle.

(8) Culzean Castle to Electric Brae Return to the A719 and turn left. After 1½ m. follow the A719 sharp left at the junction. Electric (or Croy) Brae, where the gradient creates a strange optical illusion, is 2 m. along on the main road close to the sea, with waterfalls in the hills to the right.

(9) Electric Brae to Dunure Continue on the A719 for the 2½ m. drive, close to the sea, into the fishing village of Dunure, which is approached by a turning to the left which runs down from the main road. The village stands by a sandy beach at the foot of rocky cliffs.

(10) Dunure to Ayr Continue through the village and rejoin the A719, turning left to follow the Ayr signpost. The road runs along the coast, passing Bracken Bay and the cape known as the Heads of Ayr. About 2½ m. along the road from Dunure a road to the right leads to a notable view from a point 913 ft up on Brown Carrick Hill. Ayr is a further 3 m. on, along the A719.

NATURE NOTES
Bird-watchers have spotted up to 128 species in the western Lowlands. The young conifer plantations harbour migrant warblers such as the chiffchaff, willow warbler and blackcap. The goldcrest sings high up in the tree-tops, and the greater spotted woodpecker can sometimes be heard—but seldom seen—drumming on dead trees for insects. Wild hyacinth, garlic and red campion flourish in spring along the cliffs between Culzean and the Heads of Ayr. Below the cliffs, the seashore teems with marine life, supporting colonies of red-breasted merganser, shag, shelduck and other species which fly out from Ailsa Craig.

INFORMATION

Places of interest *Ayr*: Loudoun Hall, outside viewing only, daily. Tam o'Shanter Museum, all year, weekdays, also Sat. and Sun. in summer. *Alloway*: Burns Cottage, Monument and Gardens, all year (except Oct.), weekdays, Sun. afternoons in summer (all day June to Aug.). *Culzean Castle*: Mar. to Oct., daily.

Events *Ayr*: Burns Anniversary Ride, Tam o' Shanter Inn to Brig o' Doon. Music Festival, March. Highland Gathering, July. Sea-angling contest, July.

Nature trails *Culzean Country Park*: Mar. to Oct. ¾–1½ hrs. Guide at Country Park Information Centre. *Rozelle*: 500 yds from Burns Cottage. ½ m. Booklet from Director of Parks, 30 Miller Road, Ayr.

Information *Ayr*: 30 Miller Road (Tel. Ayr 68077). *Culzean Castle* (Tel. Kirkoswald 274).

Towns with easy access to Ayr:

Cumnock	16 m.	Kilmarnock	12 m.
Girvan	21 m.	Lanark	44 m.
Glasgow	32 m.	New Galloway	37 m.

Culzean Castle and country park.

CULZEAN CASTLE
The sham castle, a clifftop mansion overlooking the Firth of Clyde, is one of Robert Adam's masterpieces. Adam designed it for the 10th Earl of Cassillis around 1780. Its most notable features are the oval staircase and the round drawing-room. The top floor contains the flat which was Scotland's gift to General Dwight D. Eisenhower in recognition of his services as Allied Supreme Commander in the Second World War. The wooded grounds and gardens are a country park, with daily conducted walks, and frequent nature lectures and film shows. The grounds include an 18th-century walled garden, an aviary and a camellia house. There is access to the beach below the castle, and semi-precious stones, such as agate, occur in the shingle.

Fountain, Culzean Castle gardens.

'Tam o' Shanter' characters in stone, Kirkoswald.

KIRKOSWALD
Douglas Graham and John Davidson, the Tam o' Shanter and Souter Johnnie of Burn's greatest poem, are buried in Kirkoswald churchyard. Shanter was Graham's farm. Davidson was the village souter, or cobbler: his thatched cottage is open to the public, and life-size statues of characters from 'Tam o' Shanter' stand in the garden.

SCALE

0   1   2   3   4   5 MILES

DUNURE

The harbour of this fishing village on a rocky coast is overlooked by the ruins of a 15th-century castle built by the powerful Kennedy clan. Here in 1570 the Earl of Cassillis, head of the clan, had the Abbot of Crossraguel roasted alive to make him surrender abbey lands.

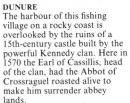

ELECTRIC BRAE

What appears to be the top of this hill is 286 ft above sea level, but the 'bottom' is 17 ft higher. It is an optical illusion created by the configuration of the land. When the phenomenon was first noticed by early travellers, the apparent defiance of the law of gravity was attributed to magnetism or electricity. The gradient is equally deceptive whether going up or down.

Dunure Castle.

AYR

A royal burgh since 1203, Ayr is the most popular holiday resort on Scotland's west coast, with sandy beaches and first-class golf courses. The Tam o' Shanter Inn in the High Street, with a sign showing Tam mounting his grey mare, Meg, is a Burns museum. The River Ayr is still spanned by the 13th-century Auld Brig, one of the 'Twa Brigs'—the other being a 1788 bridge, later replaced. The town's oldest building, Loudoun Hall, dates from the 16th century and is filled with furniture of the period. The Auld Kirk of Ayr was built in 1654, with money given by Oliver Cromwell, to replace the 12th-century church of St John.

Poet's razor, shaving mirror and mug, Burns Cottage, Alloway.

ALLOWAY

This was the birthplace of Robert Burns, Scotland's national poet. Visitors from all over the world go to see the humble thatched cottage where he was born in 1759, two years after his parents moved there from Kincardine. The cottage is now a Burns museum, open all the year round. Burns's father is buried in the churchyard of the ruined Auld Kirk of Alloway, where Tam o' Shanter had a vision of Auld Nick and fled on his horse to the Brig o' Doon, knowing that the witches chasing him would not dare to cross the running water. A Burns monument, completed in 1823, overlooks the bridge. Alloway Mote, formerly a court-house, is on the bank of the River Doon.

STRAITON

Here, before the route plunges into Carrick Forest, is a pleasant stopping place from which to admire the hills around, cut by burns that feed the Water of Girvan. The village was laid out about 1760, and has a 14th-century parish church.

BARR

This secluded village in the valley of the River Stinchar is the 'Starr' of John Buchan's novels. It marks a fine stretch of the coastline between Ballantrae and Girvan. The woods and hills around are the home of wild goats and red deer, buzzards and peregrines.

View from Rowantree Toll.

OLD DAILLY

During the religious persecutions of the 17th century the hills around here were used for secret religious services by the Covenanters—diehard Presbyterians. Many were hunted down and killed by troops, and their graves surround the ruins of Old Dailly's 14th-century church.

ROWANTREE TOLL

There is no longer a tollhouse at this lonely road junction in the Carrick Forest Park within sight of 2770 ft Merrick, southern Scotland's highest peak. The Highwayman memorial commemorates David Bell, a modern cycling enthusiast who wrote under that pen-name.

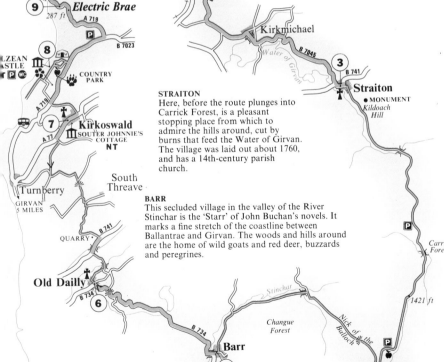

Map labels:
KILMARNOCK 12 MILES — A 79
A 758 — MAUCHLINE 11 MILES
AYR — ①
CUMNOCK 16 MILES — A 70
DALMELLINGTON 13 MILES — A 713
A 70 — A 79
BURNS COTTAGE MUSEUM
Heads of Ayr — Bracken Bay — A 719
AULD KIRK — ② — MONUMENT — Alloway — Doon
913 ft — Brown Carrick Hill
⑩ Dunure CASTLE
Waterfalls
⑨ Electric Brae — 287 ft — A 719 — B 7023
⑧ LZEAN ASTLE — COUNTRY PARK
⑦ Kirkoswald — SOUTER JOHNNIE'S COTTAGE NT — A 77
Turnberry — South Threave
GIRVAN 5 MILES
QUARRY — B 741
Old Dailly — ⑥ — B 734
Barr — ⑤ — B 734
Changue Forest — Stinchar
Nick of the Balloch
Kirkmichael — B 7045 — Water of Girvan
③ B 741 — Straiton — MONUMENT Kildoach Hill — B 742 — B 7045
Carrick Forest
1421 ft
Rowantree Toll — ④

369

Bloody Bannockburn and a battle to reclaim a desert

William Wallace defeated the English at Stirling, and Robert Bruce rubbed home the lesson at Bannockburn. Monuments to these two mighty men stand over battlefields where thousands died in the old wars of independence. History of a very different kind is enshrined in the museum of early motor-cars at Doune Park. There are links with the past, too, on Blairdrummond Moss, where crops grow on what was once desolate peat bog, thanks to an ingenious piece of engineering 200 years ago. Few parts of Scotland are untouched by associations with the country's tragic queen, Mary. This tour visits the garden where she played as a child—on a tiny island in the only 'lake' in Scotland.

(1) Stirling to Bannockburn Leave Stirling on the southbound A9. At the roundabout, at the end of the dual carriageway near the outskirts, take the A80 exit, and after ½ m. turn right into the car park for the monument and exhibition commemorating the Battle of Bannockburn in 1314.

(2) Bannockburn to Blair Drummond Safari Park From the car park, turn right on to the A80. After 100 yds turn right on to a minor road, and immediately turn left on to the road signposted to Carron Bridge. Keep straight ahead at the next two crossroads and follow the road round to the right at the next two junctions. Continue past the North Third Reservoir and at the T-junction turn right. After 3 m. the road passes through Cambusbarron. Continue for another 3 m. and turn left on to the A811. After 2 m. turn right on to the B8075 signposted to Doune. After crossing the River Forth the road runs over the rich reclaimed farmlands of Blairdrummond Moss. Follow the B8075, until it ends at the T-junction with the A84, and turn right, following the Stirling signpost. The safari park is reached by turning left at the crossroads ½ m. later.

(3) Blair Drummond Safari Park to Kippen Return to the crossroads and turn right along the A84. Pass the junction with the B8075 and ¼ m. later fork left on to the A873. After 1 m. turn left on to the B8031, signposted for Kippen, and go left again, still following the Kippen signpost on meeting the A822. Keep straight on over the crossroads with the A811, following the Fintry signpost. Kippen is reached after 1 m.

(4) Kippen to Port of Menteith From the crossroads in the village centre, take the B8037 and go left as it joins the A811. The road now begins to skirt Flanders Moss, which lies off to the right beyond the River Forth. After 2 m. turn right on to the B8034 and continue for 4½ m. to Port of Menteith.

(5) Port of Menteith to Doune Park Leave Port of Menteith on the A81 signposted for Callander. Just over 1 m. later turn left, still following the Callander signpost on the A81. Continue past Loch Rusky, through and then on the fringe of Torrie Forest, to the T-junction at the edge of the woods. Turn right here on to the B822 signposted for Thornhill and Kippen, but almost immediately go left on to the B8032 signposted for Doune. After about 6 m., at the junction beside the River Teith, turn left on to the A84 and follow the road round to the left through Doune. Just over 1 m. beyond the village, turn right

off the A84 into Doune Park to visit the museum of motoring history.

(6) Doune Park to Doune Castle Return along the A84 to Doune, taking the left fork on the approach and keeping straight ahead on the A820 signposted for Dunblane. On the far side of Doune a short detour to the right leads to the castle.

(7) Doune Castle to Dunblane Rejoin the A820 and turn right, following the Dunblane signpost. At the junction with the A9 on the edge of Dunblane turn left, then left again at the roundabout shortly afterwards. This road leads to the cathedral of this pocket-sized city founded by the Celtic missionary St Blane in the 7th century.

(8) Dunblane to the Wallace Monument From the cathedral return to the A9 and turn right, following the Stirling signpost. About 1 m. beyond the city, at the roundabout junction with the M9, keep on the A9, taking the exit signposted Bridge of Allan. Continue through Bridge of Allan, passing Stirling University on the left. Just beyond the university turn left on to the A997, signposted to Alva. The Wallace Monument is on the right.

(9) Wallace Monument to Stirling Return along the A997 turning left downhill to a roundabout on the A9. Keep ahead, taking the exit signposted to Stirling.

INFORMATION

Places of interest *Bannockburn Battlefield:* Information centre, Apr. to Sept., daily. *Blair Drummond House:* Safari Park, daily. *Doune Castle:* (closed for repair). *Doune Park:* Gardens, Apr. to Nov., daily; Motor Museum, Apr. to Oct., daily (park closed some days during hill-climbing trials). *Dunblane Cathedral Museum:* End May to Oct., daily. *Inchmahome Priory:* Apr. to end Sept., weekdays, Sun. afternoons. (Winter depends on availability of boat service. Contact Mr Armstrong, Stirling Castle.) *Stirling:* Castle, weekdays, 10 a.m.-6.45 p.m., Sun., 11 a.m.-6 p.m. (June to Aug. 9 p.m., Oct. to Mar. 4 p.m.). Wallace Monument and Mar's Wark (16th-century mansion), daily, all year round.

Event *Stirling:* Festival fortnight, May.

Nature trail *Abbey Craig:* Off A997, 1½ m. north of Stirling. Access route to Wallace Monument. Guide from Tourist Centre, Stirling.

Information *Dunblane:* Burgh Chambers (Tel. Dunblane 3300). *Stirling:* 41 Dumbarton Road (Tel. Stirling 5019).

Towns with easy access to Stirling:
Callander	16 m.	Falkirk	11 m.
Crieff	23 m.	Glasgow	27 m.
Edinburgh	37 m.	Perth	35 m.

Port of Menteith, village by the lake.

PORT OF MENTEITH
The Lake of Menteith, beside which the village stands, is the only lake in Scotland that is not called a loch. A small boat ferries visitors across to the wooded island of Inchmahome, where a priory, now in ruins, was built in 1238. Robert Bruce visited it three times, and Mary, Queen of Scots was sent there as a child of five after the Scottish defeat at the Battle of Pinkie in 1547. This was during Henry VIII's 'rough wooing', an attempt to force the Scots to betroth the queen to his son, Prince Edward. Her garden, known as Queen Mary's Bower, can still be seen. On the smaller island of Inch Tulla there is a ruined castle, once the home of the earls of Menteith. Pike have bred in the lake for at least 600 years. The medieval monks of Inchmahome fished for them. The Scottish sport of curling is practised on the lake when it is frozen.

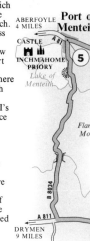

KIPPEN
The village stands on a hillside above the Forth Valley, with views northwards to the 3000 ft peaks of the Gargunnock and Fintry hills. The thick peat of Flanders Moss, across the Perthshire border, is thought to be the accumulation of millions of years of decomposition from a long-extinct forest. The artist Sir David Cameron (1865–1945) lived at Kippen, where he painted many of his landscapes. Jean Key, who was abducted by Robin Oig, the youngest son of Rob Roy MacGregor (1671–1734), is buried in the churchyard.

BLAIR DRUMMOND SAFARI PARK
Baboons settled down happily at the safari park— the first of its kind in Scotland when it was opened in 1970—and bred for two or three years. But they did so much damage to visitors' cars that they had to be replaced by rhesus monkeys. The park, in the grounds of stately Blair Drummond House, features the wildlife of Africa—lions, elephants, giraffes, zebras and eland. There are also performing dolphins from Miami Beach, Florida, a pets' corner and boat trips to 'chimpanzee island'.

Giraffes, Blair Drummond Safari Park.

SCALE
0   1   2   3   4   5 MILES

DOUNE PARK

A museum of cars, dating back to a 1923 Citroën 5CV, has been built up by Lord Doune in the grounds. Most of the cars, which include a 1938 Alfa Romeo, several Bentleys and two Grand Prix Maseratis, are maintained in running order. Some are brought out for the hill trials which are held in the park three times a year in summer, when drivers compete on the twisting 1550 yd long hill. The gardens were laid out by the Earl of Moray in the early 19th century. Among the features are some rare conifers, rhododendrons and azaleas, rose borders and woodland walks.

Alfa Romeo built for the 1938 Le Mans race, Doune Motor Museum.

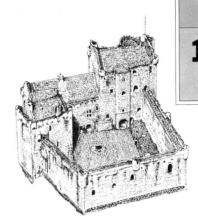
Doune Castle, from the air.

DUNBLANE

The city's main feature is its cathedral, built about the middle of the 13th century on the bank of the Allan Water. It has traces of an earlier building, believed to date from around 1100. The cathedral has a museum in what is now known as The Dean's House. The single-arch river bridge was originally the work of a 15th-century bishop.

DOUNE CASTLE

Sir Walter Scott ensured Doune Castle a lasting place in literature in his novel *Waverley* and his poem 'The Lady of the Lake'. Robert Stewart, Duke of Albany and Regent of Scotland during the reigns of Robert III and James I, was the most powerful man in the country when he built the castle at the end of the 14th century. Prince Charles Edward Stuart used it to house English prisoners after the Battle of Falkirk in 1746. After falling into decay in the 18th century, the building was restored in the 1880s and is one of the best-preserved of Scotland's medieval castles.

WALLACE MONUMENT

This 220 ft high tower, crowned with pinnacles, was erected just over 100 years ago to commemorate one of the great heroes of Scotland's long struggle against the English. It looks across to Stirling, scene of Sir William Wallace's great victory in 1297. He was later captured, taken to London and executed. The armour displayed in the tower hall includes what is claimed to be Wallace's sword.

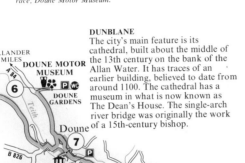

BLAIRDRUMMOND MOSS

The fertile farms in this area bear witness to the success of a remarkable land reclamation project 200 years ago. Large tracts of the upper Forth Valley were then covered by peat up to 12 ft deep. The work of digging away the peat, to expose the rich soil underneath, was slow and tedious. Then Lord Kames, a local landowner, had the idea of washing the peat away into the River Forth. A great wheel was set up on the River Teith at Mill of Tor, to carry the water by bucket chain and wooden pipes and feed it into channels cut into the peat. The work took nearly a century to complete. A good idea of the success of the scheme can be gained by contrasting the fertile fields with parts of the unreclaimed Flanders Moss to the north of Kippen.

Gatehouse, Stirling Castle.

STIRLING

For at least 800 years a castle has topped the great crag that overlooks the city. The present castle, built in the 15th century, was attacked for the last time in 1746. Prince Charles's Highlanders failed to take it, although they held the city against the English army. The castle now houses the regimental museum of the Argyll and Sutherland Highlanders. The infant Mary was crowned Queen of Scots in 1542 in the 15th-century Church of the Holy Rude, whose tower bears shot marks of the siege by General Monk in 1651. The Mercat Cross in Broad Street marks the spot where, in 1571, Archbishop Hamilton was tried and hanged, on the same day, for being concerned in the murder of Lord Darnley, husband of Mary, Queen of Scots.

BANNOCKBURN

Crowds still gather on the battlefield every year to celebrate the anniversary of Bannockburn, the decisive battle in 1314 which made Scotland an independent nation. An impressive statue of Robert Bruce, mounted and armoured, looks out over the field where, on June 24, his 8800 strong Scottish army barred the way of Edward II and his force of 29,000, marching from Falkirk to raise the siege of Stirling Castle. A quarter of Bruce's men were irregular infantry known as 'the small folk'. But they handled their spears with such deadly effect that they threw the English cavalry into confusion. The result was a rout, and eventually Edward's army was almost destroyed. The English king fled to the coast, where he took ship for safety. Much of the battlefield is now built over, but the area around the Borestone, the site of Bruce's headquarters, has been protected. The story of Bannockburn is told in sound and pictures in the exhibition centre at the entrance to the site.

Bruce, victor of Bannockburn.

Mercat Cross, Stirling.

371

Memories of the Stuarts round their ancient capital

Ancient St Andrews, home of golf, stands on the Fife coast not far from those two monuments of engineering, the road and rail bridges over the Tay. Near Perth, the hapless Stuarts left their happiest home, Falkland, a royal palace, set in a pleasant landscape. In the city itself, the historic capital of Scotland, the church still stands where John Knox preached the sermon that launched the nation's wrath on the monasteries.

(1) Perth to Kinnoull Hill Leave Perth on the A85, signposted for Dundee, and follow the road to the right after crossing the River Tay. Soon afterwards, turn left up Manse Road, and go right at the crossroads ¼ m. later. The footpaths to Kinnoull Hill, and one of the most spectacular views in Scotland, are on the right.

(2) Kinnoull Hill to Tay Bridge Carry on along the road, turning right at the first T-junction, and right again 3 m. further on, following the signpost for Perth and Dundee. At the A85 turn left for Dundee and after 2 m. fork left on to the B958, signposted for St Madoes and Errol. Turn right to cross the bridge over the A85. Drive through the flat farmlands of the Carse of Gowrie until 3 m. beyond Errol, where the road turns sharply left and crosses a railway. Beyond the level-crossing turn right, still on the B958, and carry on to Invergowrie on the outskirts of Dundee. At the junction with the A85 turn right to the shore of the Firth of Tay. At the big roundabout near the road bridge, join the A92 signposted for Aberdeen, to cross the Tay by the longest road bridge in Britain.

(3) Tay Bridge to Balmerino At the roundabout on the far side of the bridge take the first exit to join the B946, and turn left at a T-junction shortly afterwards. Keep on the B946 through Newport-on-Tay and Wormit, then turn right following the signpost for Balmerino on the far side of the village. Turn right at the next junction, and right again just over 1 m. later to reach Balmerino. Keep turning left in Balmerino to reach the abbey which is on the left, just after the road bears inland from the Tay.

(4) Balmerino to Leuchars From the abbey continue along the road, turning left at the first junction and right immediately afterwards. Keep straight on at the hilltop crossroads, then turn left at the junction with the A914. At the roundabout 4 m. later take the road signposted for St Andrews. After 1½ m. turn right on to the A92. Shortly afterwards, where the A92 bears right, keep straight on the A919 for Leuchars.

(5) Leuchars to St Andrews Bear right at the eastern end of Leuchars church then turn left, following the signpost for St Andrews, and go left soon afterwards to rejoin the A919. On the far side of Guardbridge turn left at the A91 and follow it to St Andrews.

(6) St Andrews to Ceres Leave the town on the southbound A915, signposted for Leven and Kirkcaldy. At the roundabout leave on the exit signposted to Craigtoun Park, and turn right shortly afterwards. About ¼ m. ahead, where the B939 swings right,

keep straight ahead. After 2 m. the entrance to Craigtoun Park, a large wooded recreation area, is on the left. About 3½ m. beyond the park, turn left on to the B939 and follow the road to Ceres.

(7) Ceres to Hill of Tarvit In Ceres turn right on to the road signposted for Cupar. About ½ m. later turn left and leave the village on Wemyshall Road. After 1 m. turn right along the drive to Hill of Tarvit mansion house.

(8) Hill of Tarvit to Falkland To see Scotstarvit Tower continue down the main drive to the A916. A footpath opposite the drive exit leads to the tower. From the tower take the A916 towards Cupar, but turn left almost immediately and go left again at the crossroads on to the A92. After 5 m. turn right on to the road signposted to Freuchie and Falkland Palace. Keep straight ahead at the crossroads over the A914 into Freuchie. There turn right on to the B936. After 2 m. turn right again on to the A912 in Falkland for the palace.

(9) Falkland to Perth Leave Falkland on the A912, signposted for Strathmiglo. After 4 m., in Strathmiglo, turn left on to the A91. Turn right soon after on to the road signposted to Glentarkie and Abernethy. After 5½ m. turn left on to the A913 and 1 m. later, at the junction with the A90, turn right for Perth.

INFORMATION

Places of interest *Ceres:* Fife Folk Museum, every afternoon (except Tuesday). *Falkland Palace:* Apr. to mid-Oct., weekdays, Sun. afternoons. *Hill of Tarvit:* May to end Sept., Wed. and Sun. afternoons. *Perth:* Branklyn Garden, Mar. to Oct., daily. Fair Maid's House, weekdays, but closed Wed. afternoons except in July, Aug., Sept. Balhousie Castle, Mon. to Fri. *St Andrews Castle:* All year, weekdays, Sun. afternoons. *Scotstarvit Tower:* All year, weekdays, Sun. afternoons.

Craft workshop *St Andrews Woollen Mill:* The Golf Links. All stages of manufacture of Shetland and Fair Isle knitwear, weekdays.

Events *Ceres:* Highland Games, June. *Perth:* Festival of the Arts, May. Sheep-dog Trials, July. Agricultural Show, Aug. *St Andrews:* Kate Kennedy Procession, Apr. Lammas Fair, Aug. Golf tournaments, monthly, May to Sept.

Nature trails *Ceres:* Craighall Den, ¼ m. west of Ceres. Geographical and botanical interest. Leaflet from Ceres Post Office or Folk Museum. *Kinnoull Hill:* Starts at Lodge in Hatton Road. 1 m. Guide from Director of Parks and Recreation, Marshall Place, Perth.

Information *Perth:* The Round House, Marshall Place (Tel. Perth 27108). *St Andrews:* South Street (Tel. St Andrews 2021).

Towns with easy access to Perth:

Blairgowrie	15 m.	Dunfermline	30 m.
Dundee	22 m.	Stirling	35 m.

View from Kinnoull Hill.

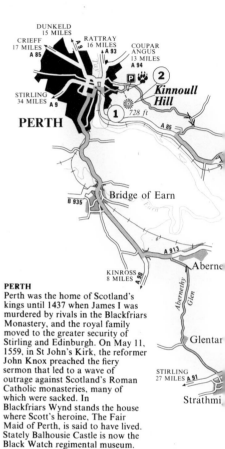

PERTH
Perth was the home of Scotland's kings until 1437 when James I was murdered by rivals in the Blackfriars Monastery, and the royal family moved to the greater security of Stirling and Edinburgh. On May 11, 1559, in St John's Kirk, the reformer John Knox preached the fiery sermon that led to a wave of outrage against Scotland's Roman Catholic monasteries, many of which were sacked. In Blackfriars Wynd stands the house where Scott's heroine, The Fair Maid of Perth, is said to have lived. Stately Balhousie Castle is now the Black Watch regimental museum.

The King's Bedchamber, Falkland Palace.

SCALE
0   1   2   3   4   5 MILES

KINNOULL HILL

The wooded slopes of Kinnoull Hill climb only 728 ft above sea level, but from the top is one of the most breathtaking views in all Scotland. To the south and east the River Tay winds towards the sea against a background of the Ochil Hills. On a clear day Cairn Toul, 4,241 ft high, can be seen 50 miles away to the north. In the west is the summit of Ben More, 3,843 ft high and 44 miles away. An ornamental tower, built in the 18th century, perches on the very edge of the cliffs, which plunge dramatically to the floor of the valley below. The nature trail on the hill covers moorland and wooded areas which are the breeding ground of a variety of wildlife, including red squirrels.

TAY BRIDGE

The Tay rail bridge, opened in 1887, stands beside the ruins of the old one which crashed in 1879, hurling the Edinburgh express into the Tay and killing more than 75 people. The longest rail bridge in Britain, it is more than 2 miles long. It stands downstream from Britain's longest road bridge, completed in 1966. Before then, motorists had to cross the Tay by ferry, or make a 60 mile detour through Perth.

Tay rail bridge, beside the remnants of the one that fell.

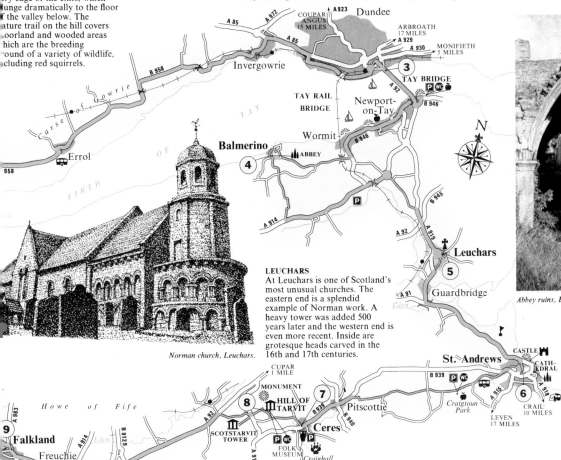

Norman church, Leuchars.

Abbey ruins, Balmerino.

LEUCHARS

At Leuchars is one of Scotland's most unusual churches. The eastern end is a splendid example of Norman work. A heavy tower was added 500 years later and the western end is even more recent. Inside are grotesque heads carved in the 16th and 17th centuries.

BALMERINO

Sleepy Balmerino, tucked behind a tangle of lanes, was chosen as the site for an abbey built by King Alexander III for his mother, Ermengarde, widow of King William the Lion. She is buried under the high altar of the abbey, which has been in ruins since reformers smashed it in the 16th century. Beyond the battered walls stands a huge, carefully supported tree, said to have been planted by Mary, Queen of Scots.

FALKLAND

The splendidly restored King's Bedchamber is a feature of the old Stuart palace at Falkland. The ornate golden bed in the room dates from the time of James VI, who died in 1625. Falkland was the favourite home of the Stuarts for more than 300 years from the 14th century. They went there to hawk and hunt in the nearby hills, and played real tennis on a court built in 1539, and still in use. Charles II was the last monarch to stay at Falkland, leaving in 1651, but the palace remains a possession of the royal family. Much of the palace has been restored, and guides can trace the family history of the ill-fated Stuarts through its ancient stones. The walled garden also has recently been restored to the original Stuarts' plan.

CERES

Mellow, pantiled roofs and old cottages make Ceres one of the most attractive villages in Scotland. The picturesque old weigh-house is the county's folk museum. A 1½ m. nature trail explores Craighall Den.

HILL OF TARVIT

The mansion house, Hill of Tarvit, stands in spacious grounds overlooking the Howe of Fife. It was built in 1696 and remodelled 210 years later for the owner to house his splendid collection of paintings, tapestries, furniture and porcelains, which can still be viewed. The house was bequeathed to the National Trust for Scotland in 1949. Near by is Scotstarvit Tower, home of Sir John Scot, the famous map-maker.

Making golf clubs, St Andrews.

ST ANDREWS

For more than 500 years, golf has been played beside the sea at St Andrews, and the Old Course is the most famous in the world, with its origins in the days when the townsfolk played a kind of golf among bunkers created entirely by nature. St Andrews is also the seat of Scotland's oldest university, founded in 1410. The cathedral, once the largest in Scotland, was razed after John Knox's sermon at Perth, but its ruins are impressive. Townsfolk used the stones to build the harbour. In the remains of the castle can be seen the grim bottle-shaped dungeon from which few prisoners emerged alive.

Garden statue, Hill of Tarvit.

Eighth-century stone tomb, St Andrews Cathedral.

Loch Tay and the glens where Arctic flowers bloom

It was through Dunkeld that Malcolm, in Shakespeare's Macbeth, *led his army from Birnam Wood to Dunsinane to avenge his murdered father, King Duncan. The Picts, whom Macbeth ruled for 17 years, have left their relics and the clans their castles, but the glens are places for nature-lovers rather than hunters of ancient monuments.*
The Tay valley is where the salmon leap on their autumn migration upstream. Douglas firs grow 2 ft a year, flowers native to the Arctic carpet the slopes of Ben Lawers, and deer and black grouse can be seen from the car. The roads are often steep and narrow, but they are the gateway to some of the finest scenery in Britain.

(1) Dunkeld to Aberfeldy Leave Dunkeld on the A9, signposted for Perth. Shortly after crossing the River Tay, while still in the town, turn right on to the A822 and follow the road round to the left 200 yds later. After following the valley of the River Braan for 7 m., cross Cochill Burn and turn right on to the A826, signposted to Aberfeldy. The 9 m. drive to the town runs up Glen Cochill through the mountains, with no side turnings to worry about. The A826 roughly follows the course of General Wade's Military Road, built as part of the English campaign to subdue the Highlands after the Jacobite rising of 1715. Just before Aberfeldy is reached, there is a car park for a nature trail on the far side of the bridge over Urlar Burn.

(2) Aberfeldy to Kenmore From the cross-roads in the centre of Aberfeldy go straight ahead on to the B846, signposted to Kinloch Rannoch. Follow the road towards the River Tay, but just before the road crosses the bridge, turn left, and then right to join the A827. Follow this road for 6 m. alongside the river to its union with Loch Tay at Kenmore.

(3) Kenmore to Ben Lawers Continue ahead on the A827, which turns sharply left between the loch and a forest: nature trails start near this corner. The road follows the shore for about 8 m. to the village of Lawers, where a footpath to the left leads to the re-mains of the old village by the lochside. Continue along the A827, with the 3984 ft peak of Ben Lawers on the right. About 4 m. from Lawers a road leads off to the right up into the mountains. Turn off here and climb the steep, narrow road to the National Trust for Scotland centre on the slopes of Ben Lawers.

(4) Ben Lawers to Fortingall Continue up the road, following the pass through the mountains. For just over 1 m. it hugs the shore of Lochan na Lairige, and there are small parking areas in which to stop and admire the grandeur of the scenery. The road descends and bears right to Bridge of Balgie, where the pass opens out into Glen Lyon. Keep right, on crossing the bridge, and cross a tributary of the Lyon at Innerwick, and drive along Glen Lyon, above which the mountains rise steeply on either side. At the T-junction at the end of the glen, 12 m. from Innerwick, turn left, following the signpost for Fortingall. According to local legend Pontius Pilate, the Roman governor who condemned Christ to death, was born here to a girl of the Menzies or MacLaren clan, when his father was a legionary stationed in the district.

(5) Fortingall to Weem Drive on through Fortingall, still close to the River Lyon, and 3 m. later, just after crossing a bridge, turn right at the T-junction on to the B846, following the signpost for Aberfeldy. Continue for just over 5 m. to Weem. The castle just off the road to the left before entering the village was the 16th-century seat of the Menzies clan.

(6) Weem to Grandtully Where the B846 bears right in the village for Aberfeldy, keep straight on to the road signposted Strath Tay. Follow the road along the valley, and after 6 m. turn right. Keep ahead on to the A827, and cross the river to Grandtully, where national canoeing championships are held over the Tay rapids twice a year during summer.

(7) Grandtully to Hermitage From the village take the B898 signposted to Dunkeld. After 11 m., just before the Inver boundary sign, turn sharp right into the lane signposted for Hermitage, a beauty spot in Craigvinean Forest.

(8) Hermitage to Dunkeld Return to the B898 and turn right. Drive through Inver and turn left on crossing the bridge just beyond the village. After driving alongside the railway for just over ½ m. turn left on meeting the A9 and cross the Tay back to Dunkeld.

INFORMATION

Places of interest *Dunkeld:* National Trust for Scotland centre, Easter to Oct., weekdays, Sun. afternoons. *Weem:* Castle Menzies, during restoration, open as shown at Castle.

Craft Workshop *Aberfeldy:* McKerchar & MacNaughton Ltd., Mill Street. Water mill, complete process from raw grain to finished oatmeal, Mon. to Fri.

Events *Aberfeldy:* Agricultural Show and Games, Aug. Folk Music Festival, June. Sheep-dog Trials, July.

Nature trails *Birks of Aberfeldy:* 2¼ m. of birch and mixed woodland. Booklet from Town Council. *Drummond Hill, Kenmore:* 3 m. walk amongst hardwoods and European larch. Views overlooking Loch Tay. Details from Chief Forester, Loch Tay, Aberfeldy. *Ben Lawers:* 1½–2 m. and 7 m. Mountain plants on burnside, grassland, bog and a pine zone. *Hermitage:* 1½ m. woodland trail by River Braan. Guide from National Trust for Scotland centre at car park.

Information *Dunkeld:* The Cross (Tel. Dunkeld 460). *Aberfeldy:* The Square (Tel. Aberfeldy 276).

Towns with easy access to Dunkeld:

Blairgowrie	11 m.	Perth	15 m.
Crieff	22 m.	Pitlochry	13 m.

Stag in Glen Lyon, near Bridge of Balgie.

GLEN LYON
Mountain peaks that tower on all sides above woods, waterfalls and scattered hill farms make this one of Scotland's most spectacular glens. The route joins the 30 mile long glen at Bridge of Balgie, where deer are a commonplace sight and black grouse can be seen 'lekking', or performing their courtship rites. Wayside picnic sites enable visitors to enjoy the beauty of the glen to the full.

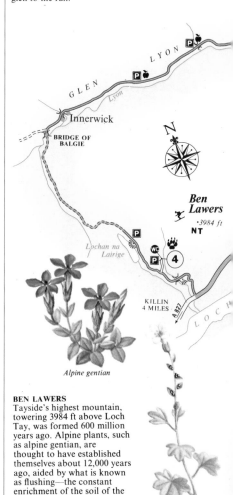

Alpine gentian

BEN LAWERS
Tayside's highest mountain, towering 3984 ft above Loch Tay, was formed 600 million years ago. Alpine plants, such as alpine gentian, are thought to have established themselves about 12,000 years ago, aided by what is known as flushing—the constant enrichment of the soil of the lower slopes by water-borne nutrients from higher up. Examples which grow near the burns include lady's mantle, purple saxifrage, golden rod and various hawkweeds. The National Trust centre by the roadside provides information about the unusual botany of the mountain area.

Drooping saxifrage

SCALE
0   1   2   3   4   5 MILES

WEEM

General George Wade, who built 235 miles of roads in Scotland after the 1715 rising, is remembered at Weem by an inn sign. His portrait, inscribed 'Soldier and Engineer', hangs outside the inn where he stayed during the building of his bridge at Aberfeldy. Castle Menzies, just outside the village, was built in 1570 by the chief of the Clan Menzies, who shared the domination of Glen Lyon with the Robertsons and MacGregors. Weem's 16th-century church has been a Menzies mausoleum for 150 years. On the almost sheer face of Weem Rock is the legendary St David's Cave, which is said to have a secret tunnel leading to Loch Glassie, 2 miles to the north.

Castle Menzies, 16th-century seat of the Clan Menzies, Weem.

FORTINGALL

A protective wall surrounds Britain's oldest tree, a great yew, said to be at least 1500 years old, in the village churchyard. The Cairn of the Dead, opposite the hotel, marks the burial spot of victims of the 14th-century plague. There are several relics of prehistoric forts and burial grounds in the area. The Praetorium, a rectangular site surrounded by ditches, is thought to have been a fortified homestead in the early Middle Ages.

HERMITAGE

A small summerhouse built in 1758 for the son of Lord George Murray, Prince Charles's commander in the abortive uprising of 1745, gives the name Hermitage to this area of woodland walks and nature trails. One of the Douglas firs in the bridge area (numbered 57) was 173 ft high when it was last measured in 1968.

GRANDTULLY

Vividly coloured, painted wood medallions adorn the ceiling of the 16th-century St Mary's Church, which is preserved as an ancient monument. Grandtully Castle, built in the same period, is the Tullyveolan Castle of Scott's novel *Waverley*.

Houses restored by the National Trust for Scotland, Dunkeld.

ABERFELDY

In 1667 some of the clan chiefs formed a force 'to secure peace in the Highlands and to watch upon the braes'. It was known as The Watch, later the Black Watch because of the colour of the tartan. The imposing monument near the bridge was put up in 1887 to mark the enrolment of the regiment into the British Army in 1740. The bridge was built in 1733 by General Wade as part of his system of military communications for disciplining the rebellious Scots. It was then the only bridge over the Tay, and later helped the town to develop its industries.

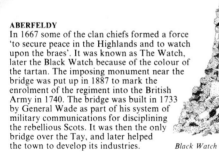

Black Watch memorial, Aberfeldy.

Wade's bridge over the Tay at Aberfeldy, built in 1733.

DUNKELD

The town was attacked by the Danes three times up to 1027 and was reduced to little more than rubble in 1689 by the Scottish army of James II marching from their victory over the English at the Battle of Killiecrankie. Birnam Wood, just outside Dunkeld, played its role in the downfall of Macbeth, who had murdered Duncan at Dunsinane and seized the kingdom of the Picts and Scots. Duncan's son, Malcolm, gathered an army in England, and defeated and killed Macbeth, having camouflaged his advance with branches from Birnam Wood. Some of the oldest houses in the town have been preserved, and parts of the 13th-century cathedral have been incorporated into the parish church.

KENMORE

Robert Burns visited Kenmore around 1787, and was so captivated by the view from the bridge that he wrote a few lines of praise. They can be seen in the parlour of the Kenmore Hotel, where he stayed. Just off the shore of Loch Tay is a tiny island with the ruins of a 12th-century priory. Forest walks and nature trails radiate from the village along the shores of the loch.

Ruins of medieval cathedral, Dunkeld.

Loch Tay, with snowcapped mountains in the background.

375

A conducted tour of Blair Castle

BLAIR CASTLE

The proud centre of a 135,000 acre estate, Blair Castle in Tayside has been the fortress home of the earls and dukes of Atholl since the 13th century. In its 700 years of history the castle has known the misery of siege and capture. It has also known the splendour of many royal occasions. Here, the colourful story of his ancestral home is told by George Iain Murray, 10th Duke of Atholl.

DETAIL *from a suit of tilting armour.*

ACROSS THE PARK *Blair Castle has been the home of the Atholls since the 1400s, but the present building dates largely from the 18th century. The family paid for the rebuilding with the cash they had received from the British Government for selling it the sovereignty of the Isle of Man. The estates around the castle cover 135,000 acres.*

We opened the main part of Blair Castle to visitors in 1937, but its history dates back to the 13th century. Then, the castle at Blair was basically four towers with linking walls, but little of this building survives today. The castle's present appearance dates largely from the 18th century, when my family had some ready cash after selling the sovereignty of the Isle of Man to the Government.

My tour begins in the Entrance Hall, which was added by the 7th Duke in 1872. Here the dominant features are the muskets, swords, rifles and crossbows which cover the panelled walls. These are part of one of the largest collections of its kind in the country—started by the 6th Duke, a great enthusiast for old weapons. Some of the weapons are not authentic. Almost all the round targes (shields), for example, were made in 1839. But two of them are originals and at least one of the two was used at Culloden.

The stuffed stag near the fireplace is 'Tilt', one of five tame deer which were kept last century in a park near the castle to see how well their antlers would develop if they were carefully looked after and specially fed. But the antlers on 'Tilt's' head are not the ones he grew in the year that he died. They were selected from the ones he had shed from the age of three onwards and screwed into place.

Away from the Entrance Hall, and in one of the oldest parts of the castle, the first of the rooms on show to the public is the Stewart Room. The name comes from the fact that the Atholl title was held by the Stewarts until it passed by marriage to the Murrays in 1629.

So in this room we have several Stewart portraits, including James V and his wife, Mary of Lorraine, Mary, Queen of Scots and the young James VI. My favourite piece of furniture is the Regal Organ, dating from 1630. It seems to be unique.

Heroic ancestors

Earl John's Room next door is again furnished in 17th-century style, with original bed, hangings and chairs. We always point out the breastplate and helmet of 'Bonnie Dundee', who was fatally wounded at the Battle of Killiecrankie in 1689. There is a wicked-looking hole in the centre of the breastplate, but I fear that it was put there some time in the last century by one of the estate workers who was trying to produce a more dramatic effect!

Passing through the Old Guard Room, now a museum, we go up the Picture Staircase which leads to the first floor. Over the last 15 to 20 years I have managed to have every painting

in the castle cleaned or restored, and this part of the collection includes many famous members of my family.

John, the 1st Duke, is shown in a full-length portrait by Thomas Murray. His first son was killed at the Battle of Malplaquet in 1709, and he had an Act of Parliament passed to disinherit his second son, who was a Jacobite.

The 1st Marquis of Atholl—the title was first an earldom, then a marquisate and finally a dukedom—is seen in a curious painting by Jacob de Witt, which has him dressed as Julius Caesar with the Battle of Bothwell Brig going on in the background.

Upstairs is the first of the 'grand' rooms—the Small Drawing Room. This suite was totally redecorated in the 18th century, when most of the castle was remodelled. There are eight mahogany chairs, with fish-scale decorations which are very rare. The bill for them is dated 1756—though I notice it wasn't paid until 1757!

A family hobby

In the Tea Room, the chairs are part of a huge set of Chinese Chippendale furniture, scattered about the castle, which was made by William Masters. The Tea Room also has cabinets in the style of Chippendale and Sheraton, with a fine collection of Sèvres china.

But the castle's most valuable china is housed in its own room near the end of the tour. China-collecting has been a family hobby for generations and I keep up the interest. Although I am no authority, I like the yellow Derby and the Sèvres dessert-service, ornamented with fruit and flowers.

One oddity is the 18th-century Chinese armorial service, unusual and very valuable, with the Atholl coat of arms on each piece. It was hand-painted by a variety of artists and there are clear differences in the interpretations of the coat of arms.

The next stop after the Tea Room is the Dining Room, with its ornate overmantel and elaborate ceiling decorations. To me it is one of the handsomest rooms in the castle. The paintings are landscapes of the Atholl estates by Charles Stewart, a local artist. The large glasses on the table are said to be the 2nd Duke's whisky glasses, and there is a 42 quart whisky bottle near by. In his time—the mid-18th century—the family owned the distillery at Edradour, which may explain the scale of the bottle!

On one wall are the colours of the Atholl Highlanders, as far as I know the only officially

FAMILY COLLECTION *The top landing of the Entrance Hall gives a fine view of some of the round targes (shields) that the Atholls have collected, together with a great variety of other weapons. Most of the targes were made in 1839—but one of them, at least, was used in battle at Culloden in 1746. A portrait of the 7th Duke, by Guthrie, hangs on the south wall.*

COLLECTOR'S ITEM *The prominent feature of the Derby Dressing Room is the unique furniture made of broom wood. This cabinet is one of the finest examples; it was made by Sandeman of Perth for the 3rd Duke in 1758. It holds part of the china collection.*

ELEGANT CHAIR *This lyre-backed chair stands in the Derby Room. The name of the room dates from the 17th century when the 1st Marquis of Atholl married Lady Amelia Stanley, a daughter of the Earl of Derby.*

SIMPLE BEAUTY *Another legacy from the past is this Charles I rose-water bowl and ewer in the Derby Room. The ewer is veneered with mother-of-pearl. Other furniture includes a fine 18th-century bed and portraits of the 2nd Duke's two daughters. Lady Jean, the elder, eloped with the Earl of Crawford in 1747—only to die of plague during her honeymoon at Aix-la-Chapelle. Her sister, Lady Charlotte, obeyed her father by marrying her cousin, John Murray.*

DRAWING ROOM *The cultured elegance of the 18th century is the dominant feature of the magnificent main Drawing Room. The furniture includes fine cabinets on either side of the fireplace. They are made of larch wood from the estate, which was the first to grow the trees in Britain. Among the pictures is Johann Zoffany's view of the '3rd Duke and Duchess with their seven children'. Lord George, the boy on the right, is the direct ancestor of the present Duke.*

A conducted tour of Blair Castle
BLAIR CASTLE

recognised private army to survive in Europe. It was organised into more or less its present form during the time of the 6th Duke. At the moment, we have about 20 officers and 75 other ranks, including pipers and drummers.

In the Ante-Room to the Blue Bedroom is one of my favourite family portraits, a sketch by Landseer of the Hon. James Charles Plantagenet Murray.

More of the Chinese Chippendale furniture appears in the bedroom itself. The 18th-century four-poster bed is a legacy from the days when my family owned Castle Mona in the Isle of Man. Next door to the bedroom is the Blue Dressing Room, with Christmas presents from Queen Victoria—pictures of herself, Prince Albert and their many children.

Along the gallery of the main Entrance Hall more of our weapons are on show. The circular staircase beyond is in one of the older towers of the castle, and the simple plaster decoration of the ceiling is much earlier than the ornate 18th-century plasterwork elsewhere. In the 4th Duke's Corridor there is a rather attractive David Allen portrait of that duke and his family, as well as a smaller picture of the duke himself.

The Book Room includes the library that Lord George Murray, the 2nd Duke's brother and the Jacobite general of the '15 and '45 rebellions, had with him in exile in Holland. In the Derby Dressing Room there are some examples of furniture made of broom wood in the 18th century by Sandeman of Perth. As far as I know, there is no other broom-wood veneer furniture in existence.

Reminders of the past
The pictures here are mostly watercolours of Castle Mona, but one recalls an old royal custom. When there was a coronation, the Duke of Atholl had to present a pair of falcons to the king. The picture is of John Anderson, who acted as falconer at the coronation of George IV. I think the idea was to borrow a neighbour's falcons, which were ceremoniously presented and then the king handed them back with relief afterwards. Anyway, the custom came to an end at the coronation of William IV.

There is rather a sad story behind the portrait of the 2nd Duke's two daughters, Lady Jean and Lady Charlotte, in the Derby Room. Since their father had no sons, it was arranged that Lady Jean should marry her cousin John, son of Lord George Murray, and keep the title within the Murray family. But she eloped with the Earl of Crawford—only to die of the plague on her honeymoon at Aix-la-Chapelle. This was taken as a warning and her sister, Charlotte, obeyed the family's wishes.

The Red Bedroom, with its portraits of the 2nd Duke's political friends, leads on to the main Drawing Room. Here is my favourite of all our portraits—the 18th-century artist Zoffany's painting above the fireplace of the 3rd Duke and his family. Lord George, the boy on the right, is my own direct ancestor. The cabinets by the fireplace are of larch wood. This came from the estate, which, we claim, was the first to introduce the trees into Britain.

The Tullibardine Room is a place of Jacobite memories—not only of the Murrays but also of Prince Charles Edward himself. Beyond it is the Tapestry Room, where the

ELABORATE DECORATION *The exquisitely worked mantel clock (above) is on show in the Tapestry Room. Some of the ornaments used to decorate it are believed to have belonged to Cardinal Richelieu, principal minister of France in the 17 century. The room takes its name from the fine set of Brussels tapestries (see background) displayed there, which were made for Charles I and later sold by order of Cromwell. They tell the story of the Classical Greek myth of Atalanta and Meleager. Atalanta was a famous huntress who was raised by a she-wolf. Meleager fell in love with her and, as a result, slew one of his uncles, whereupon his mother brought about his death. Luxurious Spitalfields silk hangings (left) form part of the elaborate decoration of the William and Mary period bed. This was part of the furnishings of the 1st Duke's suite at Holyrood in Edinburgh. Four ornate knobs crowned by plumes of ostrich feathers, top the canopy of the bed and almost reach the ceiling.*

CHINA ROOM *China-collecting has been a favourite hobby of the Atholls for generations, and the impressive displays in the China Room bear witness to their taste. This plate comes from an 18th-century dessert-service made by the Sèvres factory in France. The decoration is hand-painted.*

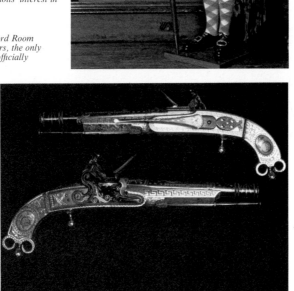

HUNTER'S CHAIR *Purchased in Germany in 1841 by the — Duke, this chair, positioned halfway up the main — staircase, is a constant reminder of the Atholls' interest in — deer-stalking.*

ATHOLL HIGHLANDERS *A figure in the Sword Room — wears the uniform of the Atholl Highlanders, the only — private army to survive in Europe. It was officially — recognised by Queen Victoria in 1844.*

FIDDLER *Raeburn's portrait of Neil — Gow, official musician to three — dukes, in the Ballroom.*

THE ORIENT *A heron decorates this — detail from the Chinese wallpaper in — the Transvaal Room. Round the walls — are displays of Jacobite relics.*

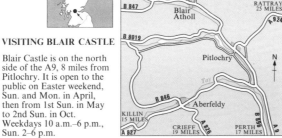

A BRACE OF PISTOLS *The best part of the castle's vast weapon collection is — kept in the Terrace Room, where there are many rare specimens. The most — prized exhibit is this pair of pistols, ornamented with the royal coat of arms. — They were made in 1810, and it is believed that they were a present from the — Prince Regent to the 1st Lord Glenlyon, the 5th Duke's younger brother — and father of the 6th Duke.*

VISITING BLAIR CASTLE

Blair Castle is on the north — side of the A9, 8 miles from — Pitlochry. It is open to the — public on Easter weekend, — Sun. and Mon. in April, — then from 1st Sun. in May — to 2nd Sun. in Oct. — Weekdays 10 a.m.–6 p.m., — Sun. 2–6 p.m.

wall coverings were made for Charles I, sold by Cromwell's orders and bought by my family. The bed here was made for the 1st Duke's apartments at Holyrood Palace. As the Marquis of Atholl, he was the equivalent of the Chancellor of the Exchequer in the last Scottish Parliament, and his oak despatch-box is preserved here. He opposed the Act of Union with England, and I think he might have been made a duke to keep him quiet!

The Glenlyon Lobby leads to the Banvie Room, which takes its name from the burn which flows through the grounds. The furniture was made by Webb and bought for the visit of Queen Victoria and Prince Albert in 1844. It was then that the queen officially recognised the private-army status of the Atholl Highlanders in return for the 'loyalty and devotion' of the estate staff. There are also several presents from the queen to the family and, in the Banvie Turret, more modern pictures and papers.

Downstairs in the Terrace Room we keep the most valuable part of the arms collection. There are some very rare weapons here, such as the Ferguson rifle of 1777. The best pair of the pistols are ornamented with the royal arms. They were made by Watson in 1810 and we believe they were given to the 1st Lord Glenlyon (the 5th Duke's younger brother) by his friend 'Prinny', later George IV.

In the Sword Room we have on display the uniforms various members of the family have enjoyed wearing. The 1854 version of the Atholl Highlanders' uniform, with its silver work, is grander than that of today.

Perhaps the most unusual exhibit is the head-dress and insignia of a 'rich and rare' regiment, the Royal Dunkeld Volunteers. It was founded in 1789, disbanded in 1803, and no military museum in the country seems to have anything to prove it ever existed.

Antlers and arms

There follow the Old Scots Room, the Natural History Museum and the China Room. Then there is the Costume Room and the Transvaal Room, with its Chinese wallpaper and tremendous variety of family bits and pieces. Finally, we reach the Ballroom, which was built in the time of the 7th Duke. Yet another part of the arms collection is kept here, and there are rows of antlers around the walls. The military colours hanging from the ceiling include several of the Atholl Highlanders— from the time when they were a regular regiment of the British Army as well as from their later days as the Duke of Atholl's personal bodyguard.

Other flags were brought back as trophies from the Sudan by the 8th Duke, who was Lord Kitchener's ADC. Raeburn's portrait of Neil Gow—the famous fiddler who was official musician to three dukes—is also in the room.

Tucked away in a corner is a model of the vast palace which one of my ancestors planned to build at Dunkeld. He was convinced that it would be the answer to his housing problems, but it was only 5 ft up from the foundations when he died. Fortunately for later members of the family, such as myself, who have had to look after Blair, this vast Gothic pile at Dunkeld was never completed.

Argyll–where Scotland's first kings ruled

Although less than 50 miles from Glasgow, Argyll has a sense of limitless space equal to that of the remotest Highlands. Mountains tower to more than 3000 ft, rivers race down wooded glens and golden eagles soar above wide forests roamed by deer. This has for centuries been the domain of the Clan Campbell, whose chiefs have lived at Inveraray since the 15th century. A thousand years before the Campbells came, this same land was the heart of the first Scottish kingdom—Dalriada—whose kings led their people over from Ireland to found a new nation which they ruled from the great hill-top fort of Dunadd.

1 **Inveraray to Kilchurn Castle** Leave Inveraray on the A819, signposted to Oban, and follow the road up the wooded valley of the River Aray, flanked by mountains on either side. After 4 m. the road emerges from the woodland and continues through the valley, hugging the river most of the way. About 5 m. further on, the road crosses the River Cladich, just outside the village of Cladich, and bears right to run close to the southern shore of Loch Awe. Continue for 5 m. to the T-junction with the A85 and turn left. The road runs alongside Kilchurn Castle, standing on a promontory in the loch on the left. Cars can be parked at a lay-by. It is possible to walk across to the castle at any time, except after heavy rain.

2 **Kilchurn Castle to Inverliever Forest** Continue along the A85 following the northern shore of Loch Awe, with the loch on the left and, to the right, the peaks of Monadh Driseig (2104 ft), Beinn a Bhuiridh (2941 ft) and Meall Cuanail (3004 ft). Beyond the tiny village of Lochawe there is a visitors' reception centre for Cruachan Power Station, which is built in a cavern deep under the twin summits of 3689 ft high Ben Cruachan. The road shortly pierces the dark Pass of Brander. Beyond the pass, approaching the village of Taynuilt, turn left on to the B845, signposted to Kilchrenan. After 7 m. follow the road round to the right, through Kilchrenan, and beyond the village turn right at the next junction, following the signpost to Dalavich. An 8 m. drive along the wooded shore of the loch leads to Dalavich, main centre for exploring Inverliever Forest.

3 **Inverliever Forest to Carnasserie Castle** Follow the road on through the forest for about 9 m. to Ford. Just beyond the southern end of Loch Awe, at the junction by the Ford Hotel, keep straight ahead on to the B840. After 3 m., as the road joins the A816, bear left, following the Lochgilphead signpost. Very shortly, a footpath on the right leads to Carnasserie Castle.

4 **Carnasserie Castle to Kilmartin** Continue along the A816 for 1¼ m. into the village of Kilmartin, where the churchyard is noted for its collection of ancient carved stones and crosses.

5 **Kilmartin to Dunadd Fort** Still continue towards Lochgilphead on the A816. The country here is rich in prehistoric relics. There are cairns, standing stones, burial chambers and hill-forts on either side of the road for the 3½ m. run to Dunadd, the largest and most dramatic of all the remains. Dunadd is signposted to the right up a short track, where

it stands in the otherwise flat landscape between Kilmichael Forest and the Sound of Jura.

6 **Dunadd Fort to Crinan** Rejoin the A816 and turn left back towards Kilmartin, but take the first turn left, signposted to Crinan Ferry. The road crosses two river bridges and after 1½ m. meets the B8025 at a crossroads. Here turn left and go straight on for about 1½ m. to cross the Crinan Canal and meet the B841. Turn right here following the signpost to Crinan. At the T-junction just over 1 m. later turn left, still following the Crinan signpost. At the fork shortly after, keep right for the yacht basin where the canal runs into Loch Crinan.

7 **Crinan to Crarae Gardens** Retrace the route back to the B841 and follow it to the junction with the A816 just beyond the Cairnbaan Hotel. Bear right on to the A816 for Lochgilphead with the canal now on the right. After 2 m. turn left on to the A83, signposted to Glasgow. At the far side of Lochgilphead the road turns sharp right to run beside Loch Gilp. There are views across the loch to Ardrishaig, the eastern terminus of the Crinan Canal, which is marked by a small lighthouse. The road then bears inland before joining the shore of Loch Fyne for the 9 m. run to Crarae Gardens.

8 **Crarae Gardens to Auchindrain** Follow the A83 along the side of the loch to Furnace, where it swings inland to the left. The Auchindrain Farming Township Museum is on the right, 2 m. beyond Furnace.

9 **Auchindrain to Inveraray** Rejoin the A83 and turn right for the 6 m. drive back to Inveraray.

INFORMATION

Places of interest *Auchindrain Farming Township Museum:* Apr. to Oct., weekdays, Sun. afternoons. *Carnasserie Castle:* Daily. *Crarae Gardens:* Daily. *Crarae Lodge:* Mar. to Nov., daily. *Inveraray Castle:* Fire Damage Exhibition, May 28 to Oct. 10, 1977, daily. *Kilchurn Castle:* Undergoing renovation.

Event *Inveraray:* Highland Games, July.

Nature trails *Inverliever Forest Trails,* Loch Awe, 1½, 2, 2¼, 4½, 5 m. Managed woodland. Booklet from Forestry Commission, 20 Renfrew Street, Glasgow. Forest information centre, Dalavich.

Information *Inveraray:* Front Street (Tel. Inveraray 2063). *Lochgilphead:* Near Main Car Park (Tel. Lochgilphead 2344).

Towns with easy access to Inveraray:

Arrochar	22 m.	Oban	39 m.
Crianlarich	34 m.	Tarbert	38 m.
Dunoon	39 m.	Tyndrum	28 m.

Buzzard and bilberry, Inverliever Forest.

INVERLIEVER FOREST
Tree planting on the hills here began in 1908, and the Forestry Commission now have about 80 square miles around Loch Awe. The forest trails teem with wildlife, including protected birds of prey such as the kestrel, buzzard and hen harrier.

CARNASSERIE CASTLE
The remains of the castle, wrecked in 1685, include a fine tower and a wall pierced for guns.

KILMARTIN
This was the centre of the kingdom of Dalriada, which the Scots established when the landed from Ireland in the 6th century. Stones and circles nea the village testify to a Bronze Age occupation 25 centuries earlier. Ancient gravestones ar carvings of knights in armour are preserved in the 19th-centu churchyard.

Stone carving, Kilmartin.

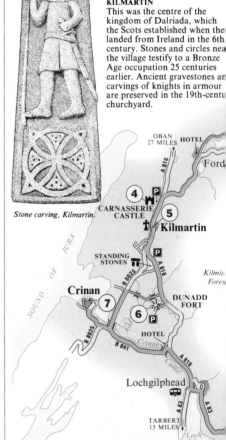

Sunset over Crinan harbour.

CRINAN
The tiny harbour here is sometimes known as the Atla Gate because the end of the Crinan Canal gives access the open sea. The canal, 9 miles long, was built betwee 1793 and 1801 to enable ships to reach the Atlantic fro Loch Fyne, by-passing the rough voyage of 130 miles round the Mull of Kintyre.

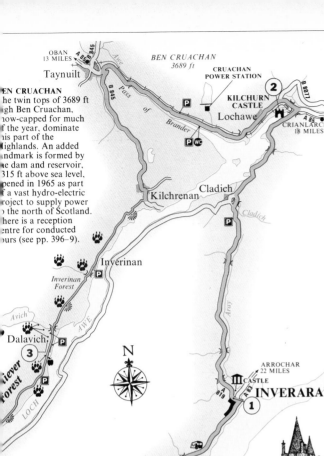

KILCHURN CASTLE

Kilchurn Castle is romantically sited on a spit of land jutting into the loch and overlooked by the glowering mass of Ben Cruachan. In 1879 the great gale which smashed the newly opened Tay Bridge also wrecked most of the castle, founded by Sir Colin Campbell, whose prowess in battle earned for him, and for all hereditary chiefs of his clan, the surname Mor (Great). Sir Colin, killed in battle in 1294, is buried at Kilchrenan, on the far side of the Pass of Brander. Dotted around the loch are some of the most fascinating nature walks in Britain, haunts of wildcats and badgers, crossbills, sparrowhawks and golden eagles. Fishing is free.

Kilchurn Castle, Loch Awe, with Ben Cruachan in the background.

Inveraray Castle.

INVERARAY

For nearly six centuries Inveraray has been the headquarters of the Clan Campbell. The present town of white Georgian buildings, beside the blue waters of Loch Fyne, dates from the 18th century. It was built after 1743 when the old town was destroyed to make way for the rebuilding of Inveraray Castle, seat of the Dukes of Argyll, chiefs of Clan Campbell. The castle houses a large collection of Highland weapons, as well as fine furniture and paintings. The drawing-room is lined with 18th-century French tapestries, and the gilded chairs are covered in Aubusson tapestry.

Inside the armoury, Inveraray Castle.

Spinning-wheel, Auchindrain museum.

AUCHINDRAIN

This might have become a derelict township when the last of the tenant-farmers left in 1963, but since then it has been re-created as a museum of the Highland crofters' life in the 18th and 19th centuries. The museum is spread over a number of buildings, including the former school, the registrar's house and a barn stocked with early farm implements. The whole set-up recalls the days when the crofters paid a communal rent and drew lots for their plots of land.

DUNADD FORT

This was once the capital of ancient Dalriada, which was ruled by the first Scottish king, Fergus, who landed from Ireland in the 6th century. The fort was occupied for 300 years. Near the top of the hill are the imprint of a human foot and a small basin hollowed out of the rock. The local legend is that the print is King Fergus's, and that the basin was used for the ceremonial washing of feet. Near by is a rock-carving depicting a wild boar.

Crarae Gardens.

CRARAE GARDENS

Nearly 60 years ago Sir George Campbell, a local landowner, began to lay out his loch-side glen as a forest garden. It was given to the nation in 1955, and has become one of the tourist attractions of Loch Fyne, especially noted for its rhododendrons. But many other interesting shrubs and trees, some of them rare specimens raised by Sir George from seed, grow in the gardens. They include Cunninghamia, *Clethra delavayi*, many different eucryphias, and 75 ft tall eucalyptuses planted by Sir George half a century ago. Species seen in the picture include *Disanthus cercidifolia* and the red-leaved *Acer palmatum*. Dense thickets of bamboo are a feature of the more formal area of the gardens, which follow the course of a mountain stream to Crarae Lodge overlooking the loch. The shrubs are at their best in May and June.

Westward to the isles across the Sound of Mull

Westminster Bridge and several London monuments are built of the red granite that forms the southern peninsula of the Isle of Mull, cast up from the sea by volcanic activity perhaps 2000 million years ago. The island is only 26 miles across at its widest point, but its deep creeks and fissures give it a coastline of 300 miles, with rock formations sometimes resembling boiling porridge that has suddenly become petrified. Storm petrels, fulmars and occasionally Iceland gulls wheel around caves where pipers have been known to practise in secret, fearful that rivals would steal their tunes. Here and there on the island, whose shrinking population of about 2000 is mainly concentrated in Tobermory and two or three villages, are derelict schools whose pupils each used to take a block of peat to keep the winter's fire burning. Mull, 45 minutes by ferry from the mainland, is itself a stepping-off place for a shorter trip to the island of Iona.

Tobermory harbour.

(1) Craignure to Duart Castle On leaving the car ferry from Oban at Craignure, turn left on to the A849 signposted for Bunessan and Fionnphort. After 2 m. turn left to Duart Castle.

(2) Duart Castle to Iona (via Fionnphort) Return to the main road from Duart Castle and turn left. The A849 soon heads westwards through the spectacular Glen More, which is dominated to the north-west by the 3171 ft high bulk of Ben More, the island's highest mountain. It was through Glen More that David Balfour tramped in R. L. Stevenson's great adventure novel *Kidnapped*, after he had been cast ashore on the tidal island of Erraid, near Iona. He came through the glen to Craignure, from which he was ferried to Lochaline on the mainland. The road descends from the bleak glen to run along the southern shores of Loch Scridain, giving fine views over the loch to the Ardmeanach peninsula. The 20 m. stretch of the Ross of Mull, the 'leg' of the island to the left of the road, is mainly hilly moorland; some of Mull's richest soil lies to the south, around Carsaig Bay.

Stay on the A849 through Bunessan. This is the chief village in the south of Mull, with good shops, hotels and a sheltered harbour. On the left of the road, 5 m. from Bunessan, is Loch Poit na h'I, where the monks from Iona used to fish. Nowadays the fishing is mainly by otters. Geese, wildfowl and water birds can be seen throughout the year. About 1 m. further on, the A849 ends at Fionnphort (pronounced Finnafort). This is the embarkation point for the Iona passenger ferry.

(3) Iona to Gribun Return to Fionnphort and retrace the route along the A849 through Bunessan to the head of Loch Scridain. At the junction with the B8035, turn left following the signpost for Salen. After about 8 m. the waterfall-streaked cliffs of Gribun tower on the right. Between two cottages on the right of the road, which runs between cliffs and sea, is a boulder weighing thousands of tons. It fell from the cliffs during a storm in the last century, crushing a cottage and its occupants, a newly married couple, on their wedding night. The old garden wall still stands.

(4) Gribun to Calgary Follow the spectacular cliff road round the shores of Loch na Keal. At the head of the loch, where the B8035 cuts across the island to Salen, turn left on to the B8073 for the run along the coast—with views of the island of Ulva to the west—and over a short stretch of inland road to the sandy bay of Calgary.

(5) Calgary to Dervaig From Calgary, the road rises steeply giving fine views to the north. The Ardnamurchan peninsula can be seen on the mainland, and beyond are the mountainous islands of Rhum and Skye. Then the road descends to the wooded head of the narrow Loch a' Chumhainn, and what has been described as Mull's most beautiful village, Dervaig.

(6) Dervaig to Tobermory The road from Dervaig twists and turns, rises and falls. After skirting the man-made Lochan Torr, it runs downhill and then up a steep rise to run close beside the shores of the Mishnish Lochs—three together—then dips until it reaches the upper parts of Tobermory.

(7) Tobermory to Aros Park Leave Tobermory on the A848, signposted for Salen. After 1 m. turn left for Aros Park.

(8) Aros Park to Aros Castle Return to the main road and turn left. After 7 m., just before the bridge across the Aros River and the point where the A848 is joined by a road from Dervaig, a short walk to the left leads to the ruins of Aros Castle.

(9) Aros Castle to Craignure From the castle continue along the coast road to Salen, where it is believed St Columba landed on his way to Iona in the 6th century. Carry straight on through the village, to join the A849 for the 11 m. coastal run back to Craignure.

INFORMATION

Places of interest *Duart Castle:* May to Sept., Mon. to Fri., also Sun. afternoons July and Aug.

Events *Tobermory:* Finish of Clyde yacht race, 3rd Mon. in July. Highland Games, 3rd Thur. in July. *Salen:* Mull Agricultural Show, Thur. nearest to Aug. 20. Flower Show, Sat. in mid-Aug. *Dervaig:* Little Theatre season, end May to end Sept.

Craft workshop The Gallery, Tobermory, in old church with fine rose window, hand-loom weaving. Normal shop-opening hours.

Information *Tobermory:* 48 Main Street (Tel. Tobermory 2182). *Oban:* Boswell House, Argyll Square (Tel. Oban 3122 or 3551).

Ferry services to Mull
Oban–Craignure. Tel. Gourock 33755.
8 departures daily, Mon. to Sat.; 5 Sun. (45 min.)

DERVAIG
A church tower shaped like a sharpened pencil is the most prominent feature of Dervaig, which has a single street of neat cottages and shops. The 1755 tower, typical of early-Christian architecture in Celtic and Gaelic areas, was retained when the church was rebuilt in 1905. When the original church was built the parish had a population of 2590. Little more than 2000 now live on the whole of Mull. About half a mile from Dervaig, on the road to Salen, is the Mull Little Theatre, which claims to be the world's smallest professional theatre. During the summer modern plays are presented in a converted cowshed, with seats for 36 people. The village hall is recommended for a visit when there is a Ceilidh—a Gaelic party-style entertainment which usually develops into an impromptu sing-song in which all join.

Pencil point church tower.

IONA
On this enchanting island St Columba, an Irish nobleman, brought Christianity to Scotland in 563. Close to St Mary's Abbey, built by his followers, is the cemetery where from the 6th century onwards 59 kings were buried—48 from Scotland, four from Ireland and seven from Norway. Excavation has uncovered a section of the old 'Street of the Dead', along which bodies were conveyed from the shore to the 11th-century St Oran's Chapel for the funeral service.

Celtic cross, Iona.

St Mary's Abbey, Iona.

SCALE
0 1 2 3 4 5 MILES

TOBERMORY

Mull's 'capital' was founded as a fishing port in 1788. Now it flourishes as a tourist centre, an ideal base for exploring the Hebrides and the spectacular mainland coast by sea. Brightly painted buildings look out over a natural harbour where yachts and cabin cruisers call during the summer. One of the stormbound ships of the Spanish Armada, the *Florencia*, took refuge in Tobermory Bay in 1588, and was later blown up by a prisoner aboard. The galleon was said to have been carrying 3 million gold doubloons. Numerous relics have been recovered by diving expeditions, but the treasure has never been found. Tobermory has a 'drive-in' forest park with plenty of picnic areas. The entrance is on the Tobermory—Salen road.

AROS PARK

Waterfalls, woodlands, picnic places and a little loch make this one of the most attractive stopping places on Mull. The park has 5 miles of footpaths winding among rhododendrons and azaleas, seen at their best in early summer.

AROS CASTLE

The castle, once the seat of the Lords of the Isles, was built in the 14th century on the site of an earlier fortress. Now in ruins, it was last used in 1608 when warring Hebridean chiefs were summoned there by Lord Ochiltree, acting for James VI of Scotland. They were kidnapped and conducted to Edinburgh to make promises of peace in the islands. From the ruins there are fine views across the Sound of Mull to the mountains of Morvern, on the mainland of Argyll.

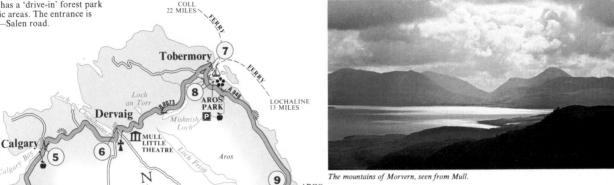

The mountains of Morvern, seen from Mull.

CALGARY

Motorists can drive almost to the water's edge on the firm white sands of Calgary Bay, a good spot for safe bathing and for a picnic—there is no hotel or restaurant. Geology-minded visitors find interest in the natural wall of rock that runs up from the old jetty. Calgary, Alberta, was named in 1876 by Col. J. F. MacLeod, a Highlander and chief of Canada's Mounted Police, in honour of his happy memories of Mull.

GRIBUN

Sheer cliffs streaked with narrow waterfalls make this one of the most dramatic parts of Mull. Visitors tempted to climb around the cliffs are warned that the rock is soft and crumbly. From the road at the foot of the cliffs can be seen the uninhabited island of Staffa, where Fingal's Cave inspired Mendelssohn (who visited Mull in 1829) to write his *Hebrides* overture.

CRAIGNURE

A sheltered deep-water bay has made Craignure Mull's chief link with the mainland and the principal port for cruise steamers. The pier, opened in 1964, also handles timber shipments from Forestry Commission plantations on the island. From the jetty can be seen Java Point, where the former islanders of Soay, near Skye, were housed in flats in 1953. They had petitioned the government for a new home where they could make a better living, as the population of their island had shrunk almost to vanishing point. Most of them have now left Mull.

DUART CASTLE

Ancient home of the chiefs of the Clan Maclean, the castle is perched on a crag overlooking the Sound of Mull. The foundations are believed to date from the middle of the 13th century, and the castle was enlarged by the addition of new living quarters in 1633. Following the abortive Highland uprisings of 1715 and 1745, Duart was garrisoned by English soldiers. It became a ruin after they left, and was uninhabited until restoration was completed by Sir Fitzroy Maclean in 1912. Duart is now the home of the present chief, his grandson, Lord Maclean of Duart and Morvern. In the dungeons are models of Spanish prisoners from the galleon *Florencia*, which was blown up and later sunk in Tobermory Bay in 1588. Other relics on display include guns salvaged from the wreck. The castle also has an exhibition on the 70 year history of the Boy Scout movement, in which the Macleans have played a leading role. From the Sea Room, Ben Nevis, more than 30 miles away, can be seen on a clear day. Lochdonhead, a small hamlet near the castle, has a restored barn used as a showroom for craft work made on the island.

Model of prisoner, Duart.

Duart Castle.

The lochs and glens under Ben Nevis

Ben Nevis, Britain's highest mountain with its head three-quarters of a mile up in the clouds, glowers over this land soaked in the blood of centuries of strife. Here, in the glens of the Western Highlands, clan fought against clan, and castles bring back memories of the ill-fated Jacobite risings of 1715 and 1745. Gleaming lochs are linked by trout streams and, at Neptune's Staircase, by a spectacular example of 19th-century canal engineering. The tour provides an almost unbroken panorama of majestic views, with opportunities for sailing and fishing.

(1) Fort William to Corran Narrows Leave the town on the A82, signposted to Crianlarich. The road runs along the shore of Loch Linnhe, overlooking the water and the mountains beyond. After 8 m. turn right and take the ferry over Corran Narrows to the hamlet of Corran.

(2) Corran Narrows to Strontian From the ferry turn left on to the A861, signposted to Strontian. For the first 3 m. or so the road is wide and fast, crossing flat moorland, and there are fine views down the loch towards the sea. At the hamlet of Inversanda, keep on the A861 as it veers right to run through Glen Tarbert. The 6 m. long glen has open moorland to the south, and to the north steep hills backed by the 2903 ft peak of Garbh Bheinn. After about 3 m. the hills become gentler as the road runs down to the head of Loch Sunart. Keep straight ahead on the A861 along the north shore of the loch and continue into Strontian.

(3) Strontian to Salen Continue out of Strontian on the A861 and follow it as it hugs the loch shore. From here the scenery increases in richness, taking in woodland and rocky outcrops overhung with heather and gorse. To the north lies Beinn Resipol, rising to 2775 ft. After 10 m. the road swings inland to the head of Salen Bay. Fork left at the junction here to visit Salen village.

(4) Salen to Castle Tioram Return to the junction at the head of Salen Bay and turn left on to the A861. The road runs across the narrow stretch of hills and woodlands that separates Loch Sunart and Loch Shiel. After 3 m. cross Shiel Bridge, and at the next junction leave the A861 and keep straight ahead on a narrow lane signposted to Dorlin. From the end of the road there is a view of Castle Tioram, which is on an island and can be reached on foot at low tide.

(5) Castle Tioram to Kinlochmoidart Return to the A861 and turn left, following the signpost for Kinlochmoidart. After just over 3 m. the road bears north, and after a further 2 m. reaches the scattered village of Kinlochmoidart. About ½ m. beyond the village sign the trees commemorating the Seven Men of Moidart stand in a field on the left beside Loch Moidart.

(6) Kinlochmoidart to Glenfinnan Leave the village, still on the A861, and follow the road round the wooded north shore of Loch Moidart. As the road rises into the hills there are views of the Isle of Skye to the north. At Glenuig Bay, where the road meets the shore of Loch Ailort, the islands of

Eigg and Rhum can be seen to the west. About 8 m. on from the bay, at the head of Loch Ailort, turn right on to the A830, following the Fort William signpost. The road runs along the northern shore of Loch Eilt to Glenfinnan, where one of the most impressive monuments in Britain stands at the head of Loch Shiel where Bonnie Prince Charlie raised his father's standard in 1745.

(7) Glenfinnan to Neptune's Staircase Follow the A830 towards Fort William and after 14 m., just before Banavie, turn left on to the B8004, signposted to Gairlochy, to see the canal locks at Neptune's Staircase.

(8) Neptune's Staircase to Inverlochy Castle Return to the A830 and turn left. Continue through Banavie—notable for its view of Ben Nevis—and at the T-junction beyond the second bridge turn right on the A82, signposted for Fort William. After ½ m. turn right, following the signpost to the railway goods depot. Bear right and cross a small bridge to see the ruin of Inverlochy Castle.

(9) Inverlochy Castle to Fort William Return to the main road and turn right, continuing into Fort William. New Town Park at Claggan in Fort William is the start of the annual Ben Nevis Race, first held in 1895. The race up the mountain path attracts runners from all over the world and the record, set up in 1964 by Peter Hall from a Barrow athletic club, is 1 hr. 38 mins. 50 secs.

NATURE NOTES

More than 100 species of birds have been identified in the Western Highlands, and many of them can be seen in the forests and lochs around Fort William. The Strontian area is noteworthy for its variety of lichens, some of which can survive only where the atmosphere is completely free from pollution. Loch Sunart brings the sea 25 miles inland, and seaweed and shellfish occur around the tidal limit.

INFORMATION

Places of interest *Castle Tioram:* Daily, but accessible only at low tide. *Fort William:* West Highland Museum, weekdays. *Glenfinnan:* Stuart monument, historical display, daily. *Inverlochy Castle:* Daily.

Events *Fort William:* Ben Nevis Race, 1st Sat. in Sept. Highland Games, 1st Sat. in Aug. Agricultural Show, 4th Sat. in Aug. Six-day motor-cycle trials, 1st week in May. *Glenfinnan:* Highland Games, 3rd Sat. in Aug. *Salen:* Agricultural Show, Aug.

Information *Fort William:* Travel Centre (Tel. Fort William 2232).

Towns with easy access to Fort William:

Ballachulish . . . . 14 m.	Kinlochleven . . . 22 m.	
Kingussie . . . . . . 49 m.	Oban . . . . 49 m.	

GLENFINNAN

A tall castellated tower marks the spot where the Stuart standard, red on white, was firs unfurled when more than 1000 clansmen mustered here at the start of the '45 uprising. An inr staircase leads to the top of the tower, where visitors can stand the stone Highlander erected in 1815 as a memorial to those wh fought and died for Bonnie Prin Charlie. Each year, in August, Highland Games are held at Glenfinnan to recall the last gre Scottish uprising, which ended barely a year later in crushing defeat for the Stuarts at Cullode The view down Loch Shiel, narrow and glittering, with mis mountains rising on either side, magnificent.

Glenfinnan memorial.

KINLOCHMOIDART

The glen at the head of Loch Moidart opens out into meadows running down to a sparsely wooded shore. The village is a scattering of houses and crofters' cottages with the hills of Moidart rising behind. Near by stand seven birch trees planted in memory of the Seven Men of Moidart, the followers that Bonnie Prince Charlie brought with him when he returned from exile in France. After landing at Loch nan Uamh the party rested at Kinlochmoidart. There they were welcomed by the Macdonalds, who remained staunch Stuart supporters.

Castle Tioram.

CASTLE TIORAM

Perched on a spit of land that becomes an island with the rising tide, this 13th-century castle is one of the mo romantic and beautifully situated ruins in the Western Highlands. It was built by the Macdonalds of Clanrana as a stronghold in their feud with the Campbells. Wher Allan Dearg, then leader of the Macdonalds, led out hi followers to fight for the Stuart cause in 1715, he foresa the failure of the rising and set fire to Tioram rather tha let it fall intact into the hands of the Campbells. The turreted keep and gloomy dungeons remain. The island may be reached on foot at low tide.

SCALE

0   1   2   3   4   5 MILES

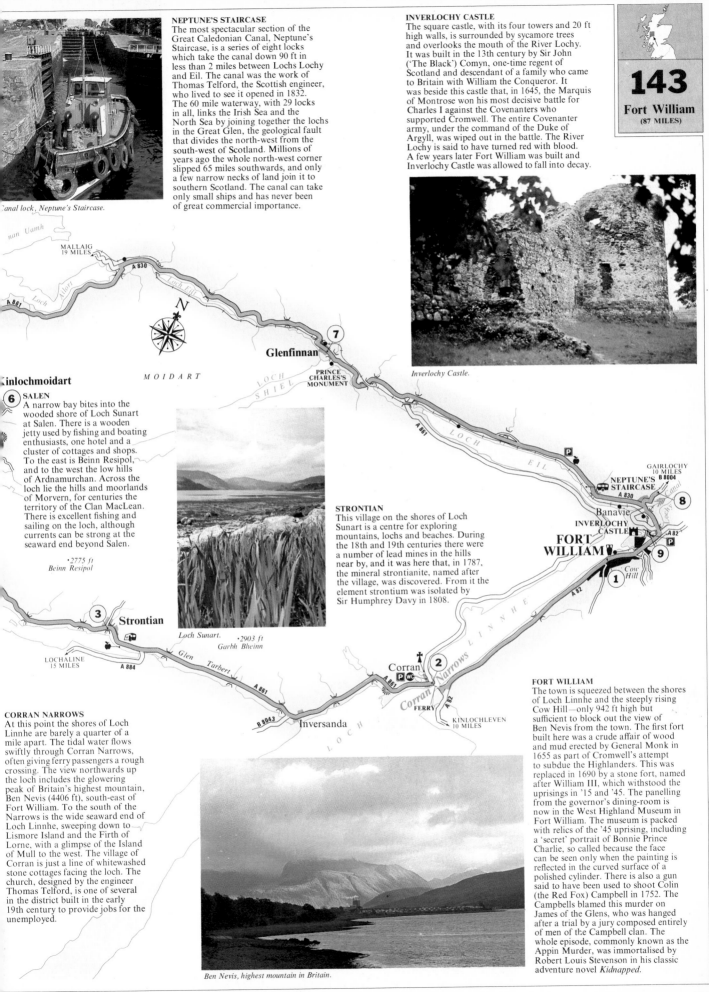

NEPTUNE'S STAIRCASE
The most spectacular section of the Great Caledonian Canal, Neptune's Staircase, is a series of eight locks which take the canal down 90 ft in less than 2 miles between Lochs Lochy and Eil. The canal was the work of Thomas Telford, the Scottish engineer, who lived to see it opened from 1832. The 60 mile waterway, with 29 locks in all, links the Irish Sea and the North Sea by joining together the lochs in the Great Glen, the geological fault that divides the north-west from the south-west of Scotland. Millions of years ago the whole north-west corner slipped 65 miles southwards, and only a few narrow necks of land join it to southern Scotland. The canal can take only small ships and has never been of great commercial importance.

Canal lock, Neptune's Staircase.

INVERLOCHY CASTLE
The square castle, with its four towers and 20 ft high walls, is surrounded by sycamore trees and overlooks the mouth of the River Lochy. It was built in the 13th century by Sir John ('The Black') Comyn, one-time regent of Scotland and descendant of a family who came to Britain with William the Conqueror. It was beside this castle that, in 1645, the Marquis of Montrose won his most decisive battle for Charles I against the Covenanters who supported Cromwell. The entire Covenanter army, under the command of the Duke of Argyll, was wiped out in the battle. The River Lochy is said to have turned red with blood. A few years later Fort William was built and Inverlochy Castle was allowed to fall into decay.

Inverlochy Castle.

SALEN
A narrow bay bites into the wooded shore of Loch Sunart at Salen. There is a wooden jetty used by fishing and boating enthusiasts, one hotel and a cluster of cottages and shops. To the east is Beinn Resipol, and to the west the low hills of Ardnamurchan. Across the loch lie the hills and moorlands of Morvern, for centuries the territory of the Clan MacLean. There is excellent fishing and sailing on the loch, although currents can be strong at the seaward end beyond Salen.

Loch Sunart.

STRONTIAN
This village on the shores of Loch Sunart is a centre for exploring mountains, lochs and beaches. During the 18th and 19th centuries there were a number of lead mines in the hills near by, and it was here that, in 1787, the mineral strontianite, named after the village, was discovered. From it the element strontium was isolated by Sir Humphrey Davy in 1808.

CORRAN NARROWS
At this point the shores of Loch Linnhe are barely a quarter of a mile apart. The tidal water flows swiftly through Corran Narrows, often giving ferry passengers a rough crossing. The view northwards up the loch includes the glowering peak of Britain's highest mountain, Ben Nevis (4406 ft), south-east of Fort William. To the south of the Narrows is the wide seaward end of Loch Linnhe, sweeping down to Lismore Island and the Firth of Lorne, with a glimpse of the Island of Mull to the west. The village of Corran is just a line of whitewashed stone cottages facing the loch. The church, designed by the engineer Thomas Telford, is one of several in the district built in the early 19th century to provide jobs for the unemployed.

FORT WILLIAM
The town is squeezed between the shores of Loch Linnhe and the steeply rising Cow Hill—only 942 ft high but sufficient to block out the view of Ben Nevis from the town. The first fort built here was a crude affair of wood and mud erected by General Monk in 1655 as part of Cromwell's attempt to subdue the Highlanders. This was replaced in 1690 by a stone fort, named after William III, which withstood the uprisings in '15 and '45. The panelling from the governor's dining-room is now in the West Highland Museum in Fort William. The museum is packed with relics of the '45 uprising, including a 'secret' portrait of Bonnie Prince Charlie, so called because the face can be seen only when the painting is reflected in the curved surface of a polished cylinder. There is also a gun said to have been used to shoot Colin (the Red Fox) Campbell in 1752. The Campbells blamed this murder on James of the Glens, who was hanged after a trial by a jury composed entirely of men of the Campbell clan. The whole episode, commonly known as the Appin Murder, was immortalised by Robert Louis Stevenson in his classic adventure novel *Kidnapped*.

Ben Nevis, highest mountain in Britain.

Skye–the island of mists and legends

The Gaelic name for Skye means 'The Isle of Mist', and refers to the clouds that often envelop the stark peaks of its Cuillin Hills. The island's history is misty, too, with colourful legend and romantic fact mingled together. There is, for example, the legend of the Fairy Flag which brings victory to the Clan MacLeod in battle. The flag is still preserved in the clan's stronghold of Dunvegan Castle, where it has been for more than 600 years. There is, too, the true story of Bonnie Prince Charlie and Flora Macdonald, the girl who saved him in his flight over the sea—which is more romantic than most legends. The landscape is every bit as memorable as the island's history. Immense terraces of volcanic rock, carved into weird shapes by 70 million years of natural sculpting, look out over sheltered bays to a bright sea studded with smaller islands.

1 Portree to Dun Beag Leave the centre of Portree on the road signposted for Kyleakin, but just after crossing the bridge on the outskirts of the town turn right on to the A850 signposted for Uig and Dunvegan. After ¼ m., turn left on to the B885 and follow it over the island's low central hills. The road rises to 500 ft before dropping down to Bracadale where it meets the A863. Turn right on to the A863, signposted for Dunvegan. Just under 1½ m. from this junction, after passing through the village of Struan and just past a left turn signposted for Ullinish, there is a gate on the right of the road. A short walk through here leads to the Dun Beag broch, a ruined Pictish tower.

2 Dun Beag to Dunvegan Castle Returning from the broch, continue northwards on the A863. There are numerous lay-bys on the road, with views of the Duirinish peninsula to the west. The twin flat-topped mountains that stand out on the peninsula, each about 1600 ft high, are known as Macleod's Tables. Bear left in the village of Dunvegan on to the A850 for Dunvegan Castle, which is on the left after about 1 m.

3 Dunvegan Castle to Uig Return to Dunvegan village and follow the A850, signposted for Portree, round to the left. After 3½ m. the road, rising steadily through green moors, reaches Fairy Bridge, where it swings sharply right, to the east; and after reaching a height of 542 ft descends to the head of Loch Greshornish. Stay on the road, the A850, to Skeabost. A few hundred yards after crossing Skeabost Bridge, over the River Snizort, turn left on to the B8036, signposted for Uig, and bear left where this road meets the A856. Stay on the A856 as it runs northwards, passing through the scattered hamlets of Kensaleyre and Romesdal, where there is a bridge over the river of that name. Just over 1 m. from the bridge, on the left of the road, is a track that leads to Kingsburgh House, successor to the house where Prince Charlie found refuge in 1746 and had 'a good night's rest'. In 1773 Dr Johnson and Boswell were entertained there by the laird and his wife—Flora Macdonald. Dr Johnson slept in what had been the prince's bed but 'had no ambitious thoughts about it'. From this point, the road descends into Glen Hinnisdal, well-wooded on the right, then rises again after crossing the River Hinnisdal. After about ¾ m., on the left by the shore of Loch Snizort, is the ruin of Caisteal Uisdean, fortress of a 17th-century pirate, Hugh Gillespie. The road soon runs down to Uig Bay and on to Uig.

4 Uig to Kilmuir Take the A855 from Uig, signposted for Staffin, but ignore the 'Staffin via Quirang' turn at the top of the hill outside Uig and bear left to stay on the A855 as it heads northwards. After 6 m., on the far side of the scattered village of Kilmuir, turn right for the short detour to Flora Macdonald's Memorial. The road passes the thatched Skye Cottage Museum.

5 Kilmuir to Duntulm Castle Return to the A855 and continue northwards. After 2 m. the ruins of Duntulm Castle are on the left, on cliffs overlooking bays of shingle and seaweed-draped rocks.

6 Duntulm Castle to Quirang The A855 now cuts across the tip of the Trotternish peninsula and runs southwards. Within 4 miles, the scenery on the right is dominated by the spectacular and massive inland cliffs of Quirang.

7 Quirang to The Storr The road winds west by Staffin Bay then heads southwards again, skirting inland Loch Mealt and gradually rising with the coast until it is over the 500 ft mark, giving wide views of the mainland. After about 10 m., The Storr (2358 ft), North Skye's highest peak, is on the right.

8 The Storr to Portree From The Storr the road leads further inland, skirting the western shores of Loch Leathan and Loch Fada then continuing south to Portree.

INFORMATION

Places of interest *Dunvegan*: Colbost Folk Museum, Easter to Oct., daily. Castle, end Mar. to mid-Oct., weekday afternoons. *Kilmuir*: Skye Cottage Museum, Easter to Oct., daily.

Craft workshops *Portree*: Marine Handweavers, daily. Skye Wool Mill Ltd (spinning, dyeing, blending, weaving and finishing of wool), daily.

Events *Dunvegan Castle*: Silver Chanter Piping Competitions, Aug. *Portree*: Highland Games, Aug.; Gaelic Mod (festival), June; Agricultural Show, July; Horticultural Show, Aug.

Information *Portree*: Meall House (Tel. Portree 2137).

Ferry services to the Island of Skye
Kyle of Lochalsh–Kyleakin. Tel. Kyleakin 282. Daily until 11 p.m. No booking. 5 min. crossing.
Mallaig–Armadale. Tel. Gourock 33755. Frequent departures daily. 30 min. crossing. No winter or Sunday service.
Glenelg–Kylerhea. Tel. Glenelg 224. Frequent service. 4 min. crossing. No Sunday or winter service.

Carting peat, near Uig.

UIG
Loamy soil, formed by the breakdown of basaltic rock, makes the west coast of the Trotternish peninsula the richest in Skye, with croft crowding on croft. It was on this coast, about 1½ miles north-west of Uig, that Bonnie Prince Charlie landed on June 29, 1746, after escaping 'over the sea to Skye'—in the words of one of Scotland's best-known songs. He had been on the run since the defeat of his army at Culloden, two months earlier. After more months in hiding on Skye, Raasay and the mainland, the prince finally escaped to France on September 29.

DUNVEGAN CASTLE
The oldest parts of Dunvegan Castle, the outer walls, were built towards the end of the 13th century, and the stronghold has been the seat of the chiefs of Clan MacLeod ever since. No other castle in Scotland can boast a longer record of continuous occupation by the same family. The castle stands on a rock high above an inlet of Loch Dunvegan and, until the 18th century, could be entered only from the sea. Drinking water came from a well in the gun courtyard until 1812, when it was closed after a guest fell in during christening celebrations for the 25th chief and was drowned. Johnson and Boswell visited the castle in 1773 and a portrait of Johnson, by Sir Joshua Reynolds, hangs in the drawing-room. Among many clan treasures in the castle is the Fairy Flag. This silken banner, said to have been given to a 14th-century chief by a fairy, reputedly has powers to protect the MacLeods.

Dunvegan Castle.

DUN BEAG
This is the most substantial ruin of a broch on Skye. These massive, round stone towers were built by the Picts some 2000 years ago, possibly as combined look-out points and refuges from invaders. Remains of the stone staircase that originally ran inside the broch's 12 ft thick walls can still be seen, together with several ruined rooms. The walls, which are now about 12 ft tall, originally rose to 40 ft. They were entered through a single tunnel-like entrance.

SCALE
0   1   2   3   4   5 MILES

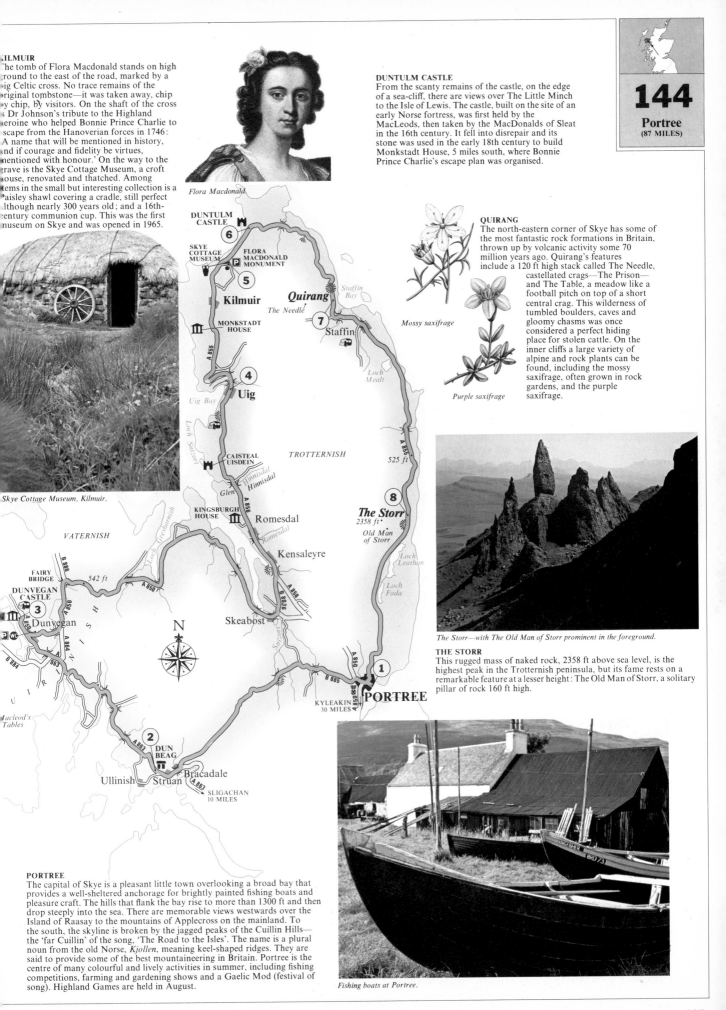

KILMUIR

The tomb of Flora Macdonald stands on high ground to the east of the road, marked by a big Celtic cross. No trace remains of the original tombstone—it was taken away, chip by chip, by visitors. On the shaft of the cross is Dr Johnson's tribute to the Highland heroine who helped Bonnie Prince Charlie to escape from the Hanoverian forces in 1746: 'A name that will be mentioned in history, and if courage and fidelity be virtues, mentioned with honour.' On the way to the grave is the Skye Cottage Museum, a croft house, renovated and thatched. Among items in the small but interesting collection is a Paisley shawl covering a cradle, still perfect although nearly 300 years old; and a 16th-century communion cup. This was the first museum on Skye and was opened in 1965.

Flora Macdonald

Skye Cottage Museum, Kilmuir.

DUNTULM CASTLE

From the scanty remains of the castle, on the edge of a sea-cliff, there are views over The Little Minch to the Isle of Lewis. The castle, built on the site of an early Norse fortress, was first held by the MacLeods, then taken by the MacDonalds of Sleat in the 16th century. It fell into disrepair and its stone was used in the early 18th century to build Monkstadt House, 5 miles south, where Bonnie Prince Charlie's escape plan was organised.

QUIRANG

The north-eastern corner of Skye has some of the most fantastic rock formations in Britain, thrown up by volcanic activity some 70 million years ago. Quirang's features include a 120 ft high stack called The Needle, castellated crags—The Prison—and The Table, a meadow like a football pitch on top of a short central crag. This wilderness of tumbled boulders, caves and gloomy chasms was once considered a perfect hiding place for stolen cattle. On the inner cliffs a large variety of alpine and rock plants can be found, including the mossy saxifrage, often grown in rock gardens, and the purple saxifrage.

Mossy saxifrage

Purple saxifrage

The Storr—with The Old Man of Storr prominent in the foreground.

THE STORR

This rugged mass of naked rock, 2358 ft above sea level, is the highest peak in the Trotternish peninsula, but its fame rests on a remarkable feature at a lesser height: The Old Man of Storr, a solitary pillar of rock 160 ft high.

PORTREE

The capital of Skye is a pleasant little town overlooking a broad bay that provides a well-sheltered anchorage for brightly painted fishing boats and pleasure craft. The hills that flank the bay rise to more than 1300 ft and then drop steeply into the sea. There are memorable views westwards over the Island of Raasay to the mountains of Applecross on the mainland. To the south, the skyline is broken by the jagged peaks of the Cuillin Hills—the 'far Cuillin' of the song, 'The Road to the Isles'. The name is a plural noun from the old Norse, *Kjollen*, meaning keel-shaped ridges. They are said to provide some of the best mountaineering in Britain. Portree is the centre of many colourful and lively activities in summer, including fishing competitions, farming and gardening shows and a Gaelic Mod (festival of song). Highland Games are held in August.

Fishing boats at Portree.

Thrums and the castle of the nine ghosts

From the tidal basin of Montrose, teeming with birds, to the fertile Vale of Strathmore, this is a land of small lochs and salmon streams, fields and forest parks. History is up on the hills near Kirriemuir, where the Picts in their two primitive forts probably harassed the Romans 18 centuries ago; and down at the Angus Folk Museum, which re-creates everyday life as it was in Victorian times. The tour visits 'Thrums', the weaving town of the J. M. Barrie novels, and a couple of very different castles—Edzell, notable mainly for its garden; and Glamis, reputed to be the home of nine ghosts and the bones of a monster.

1 Montrose to Forfar Leave Montrose on the A92, signposted for Dundee. Cross the bridges over the channel that links Montrose Basin to the sea, and 1 m. beyond the second bridge turn right on to the A934, following the signpost for Forfar. After 7 m., at the A933, turn left and immediately right on to the B9113, signposted for Forfar. Just past Rescobie Loch, 8 m. from the junction, a short detour to the right leads to the mellow ruins of Restenneth Priory. The B9113 continues into Forfar.

2 Forfar to Glamis Castle Leave on the A94, signposted for Perth. After 5 m. turn right on to the minor road signposted to Glamis village, where the Angus Folk Museum can be visited. Drive through the village, turn right at the A928 and right again, just after a sharp bend into the long drive of Glamis Castle.

3 Glamis Castle to Kirriemuir From the castle return to the A928 and turn right. Keep straight on for Kirriemuir, a centre of the jute-weaving trade and birthplace of James Barrie, creator of Peter Pan. His house is kept by the National Trust for Scotland.

4 Kirriemuir to the Caterthuns Leave Kirriemuir on the A926, signposted for Blairgowrie. On the far side of the town fork right on to the B955, following the signpost for Clova. At the next crossroads turn right. Turn left at the next T-junction, to keep on the B955. About 1 m. beyond Prosen Bridge, turn right on to the road signposted to Memus. Go through Memus and just beyond the village take the road signposted to Glenogil and Menmuir. After 10 m. just beyond Kirkton of Menmuir, fork left, following the signpost for Edzell, and 2 m. on, turn left again for the Caterthuns. These two impressive prehistoric strongholds are on either side of the road 1½ m. from the junction.

5 The Caterthuns to Edzell Castle Keep on the road and turn right at the T-junction at the foot of the hill. After 7 m. turn left on to the lane leading to Edzell Castle, a 16th-century fortress built of red sandstone, with an unusual walled garden, The Pleasance. Carved wall panels depict the seven cardinal virtues, and immaculate shrubs are trimmed to spell out Latin mottoes.

6 Edzell Castle to Fettercairn Turn left on to the road to Edzell village. There go left on to the B966, signposted for Fettercairn which is 5 m. further on. Queen Victoria and Prince Albert once stayed secretly overnight here as 'wedding guests from Aberdeen'. An arch commemorates the visit.

7 Fettercairn to Drumtochty Forest Leave Fettercairn on the B974, signposted for Strachan and Banchory. After 4 m. turn right at Clatterin Brig on the road signposted to Drumtochty and Auchenblae. The road runs up Strath Finella through Drumtochty Forest. The forest, planted only in 1926, has transformed this lovely glen. A forest walk starts near Drumtochty Castle.

8 Drumtochty Forest to Johnshaven Continue on through the glen to Auchenblae. In Auchenblae turn right at the first T-junction, and right again at the one soon after, following the signposts for Laurencekirk. On the far side of the village, where the road swings right, keep straight ahead, following the signposts for Fordoun and Johnshaven. Cross the B966 about 1 m. later. After a further 2 m., at the A94, go right and immediately left, following the signpost for Johnshaven. After 6 m. at the junction with the A92 turn right, then almost immediately left for Johnshaven, a picturesque fishing village.

9 Johnshaven to St Cyrus Return to the A92 and turn left, following the signpost for Montrose. After 3 m. turn left for St Cyrus. This salmon-fishing village, nestling in a nature reserve, was once destroyed by a tidal wave.

10 St Cyrus to Montrose Return to the A92, turn left and continue southwards for 5 m. to return to Montrose.

NATURE NOTES
The steeply sloping cliffs of red sandstone at St Cyrus have over 150 species of flowering plants growing on them. Many of these are at the northern limit of their range in Britain, including wild liquorice, knotted clover and rough clover. In winter the lochs around Forfar attract goosander and goldeneye ducks.

INFORMATION

Places of interest *Edzell Castle:* All year, daily. *Glamis:* Castle, May to Sept., Sun., Mon., Tues., Wed., Thur., Bank Hols., 2-5.30 p.m. Angus Folk Museum, Easter to Sept., afternoons. *Kirriemuir:* Barrie museum, Apr. to Sept., weekdays, Sun. afternoons. *Montrose Museum:* All year, daily.

Event *Montrose:* Festival of Music, Drama and Art, June.

Nature trail *St Cyrus National Nature Reserve:* 2½ m. of cliff, dunes and salt marsh. Guide from Tourist Information Centre, Montrose or Nature Conservancy, Edinburgh.

Information *Montrose:* 212 High Street (Tel. Montrose 2000).

Towns with easy access to Montrose:
Arbroath . . . . . . 13 m.   Dundee . . . . 30 m.
Brechin . . . . 19 m.   Stonehaven . . . . . 23 m.

Glamis Castle, reputed to have nine ghosts.

GLAMIS CASTLE
No other house in Scotland can match the castle's nine legendary ghosts, which include that of Macbeth, the 11th-century King of Scotland, and subject of a play by Shakespeare. In Shakespeare's play Macbeth is Lord of Glamis, but he was killed at Lumphanan in Aberdeen. As well as its ghosts, Glamis also has a traditional monster, said to have been bricked up in a secret room 200 years ago. Queen Elizabeth, the Queen Mother is descended from the Earls of Strathmore, lairds of Glamis for 500 years, and Princess Margaret was born in the castle in 1930.

GLAMIS
Glamis village houses the fascinating Angus Folk Museum in a row of single-storey cottages about 200 years old. The museum includes a traditional Victorian kitchen and an elegant manse parlour of the same period.

SCALE
0   1   2   3   4   5 MILES

The Pleasance, Edzell Castle.

EDZELL CASTLE
A remarkable walled garden, created in 1604, still remains at the ruined 16th-century Edzell Castle. The carved wall panels portray religious symbols, and shrubs have been planted and trimmed to spell out mottoes. The crumbled red-sandstone fortress was once the most splendid in Angus. Mary, Queen of Scots stayed there, and so did Cromwell's men. The Argyll Highlanders did much damage to it in the Jacobite rising of 1745, but repairs have been made during the last 50 years.

FETTERCAIRN
A great arch commemorates a visit by Queen Victoria in 1861. In the square is a stone shaft marked with the Scottish ell—37 in.

DRUMTOCHTY FOREST
The slopes of Drumtochty Forest climb for 1000 ft on either side of Strath Finella. The trees planted by the Forestry Commission in 1926 are now mature and enhance the beauty of the glen.

JOHNSHAVEN
Set in the rocky coast, Johnshaven is typical of the many little fishing villages that punctuate the shores of Angus. Nets are spread out to dry beside the tiny harbour, where crabs, lobsters and salmon are landed. Seals can sometimes be seen basking on the nearby rocks. Stone cottages cluster along a ledge between the road and the beach.

Hairy violet and viper's bugloss, St Cyrus

ST CYRUS
The village has been completely rebuilt since 1795, when a gale-driven tide swept in and destroyed it. A 2½ mile nature trail rambles across the nearby cliffs, dunes and saltings. There are more than 300 varieties of wild flowers, including the viper's bugloss, which was once thought to be a cure for snake bites. Nets staked out to catch salmon can be seen near the shore. Sands run south to the site of the old village near the River North Esk.

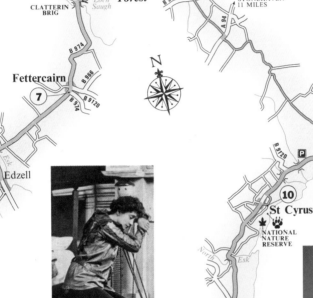

'Peter Pan', 1904.

KIRRIEMUIR
Sir James Barrie, the creator of Peter Pan, made Kirriemuir the model for Thrums, the weaving town of his novels. He was born in 1860 in a cottage, 9 Brechin Road, which is now a Barrie museum. One of the exhibits is a letter written to him by his friend Captain Scott, the Arctic explorer. At the back of the cottage is the wash-house which Barrie used as a theatre for his earliest plays.
Peter Pan was written for the five orphans Barrie adopted.

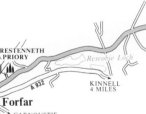

FORFAR
County town of Angus, Forfar was once a seat of the Kings of Scotland. A turret marks the spot in Castlehill where the palace stood. The town is also famed for its witches—nine were burnt to death here in the 1650s. Near by are the ruins of Restenneth Priory, which was destroyed by Edward I. A tall square tower and a 13th-century chancel remain.

Restenneth Priory, Forfar.

Victorian parlour, Angus Folk Museum.

Sunset over Montrose Basin.

MONTROSE
Montrose sits in an enviable position with the sea on one side, the River South Esk on another and the 4 square miles of Montrose Basin on a third. The basin, an incomparable sight as the sun sets behind the hills, is the home of ducks, swans, terns and oystercatchers. Thousands of geese winter along its muddy shores. Montrose has remained relatively untouched by Scotland's violent history. Yet it produced one of the country's most famous soldiers, John Graham, Marquis of Montrose, who played a major role on the Royalist side in the Civil War, but was later captured and hanged at Edinburgh. James Stuart, father of Bonnie Prince Charlie, sailed back to France from the town after the 1715 uprising.

The hills and castles of Royal Deeside

Ever since Queen Victoria fell under the spell of Bonnie Scotland, and her husband Prince Albert bought Balmoral in 1852, the valley of the Dee has been known as Royal Deeside. The people of Aberdeen also call it the Castle Country; for its banks, and the hills and forests between the Don and the Dee, are dotted with history in stone, from the romantic ruins of Kildrummy to the graceful elegance of Craigievar. From the woods came the oaks out of which earlier fortresses were hewn, and the stone circle near Tarland is a reminder that men lived there nearly 4000 years ago.

(1) Banchory to Blackhall Forest Leave Banchory on the B974 signposted to Aberdeen, cross the River Dee on the outskirts of the town and shortly after, where the Aberdeen road swings left over the Bridge of Feugh, go straight ahead, still on the B974, to Strachan. Keep straight ahead in Strachan, now on the B976 signposted to Aboyne. After 2 m. turn right on to the road signposted to Potarch at the T-junction by an inn. The forest trail begins just over 1 m. along on the right.

(2) Blackhall Forest to Aboyne Continue ahead to Potarch and there turn left on to the B993. At the junction after 2½ m. bear right on to the B976, continue for 3½ m. and turn right on to the B968 for Aboyne.

(3) Aboyne to Tomnaverie Leave Aboyne on the B9094 signposted for Tarland. The road skirts woodland backed by hills rising to over 1000 ft. About 4 m. beyond Aboyne fork left on to a short track signposted to Tomnaverie prehistoric stone circle.

(4) Tomnaverie to Tarland Rejoin the B9094, turn right at the junction with the B9119 and continue for ½ m. into Tarland.

(5) Tarland to Kildrummy Castle Retracing the route from the centre of Tarland, just beyond the bridge over Tarland Burn turn right on to the road signposted to Coldstone. After 3½ m., at the junction with the A97, turn right. At the next T-junction 7 m. later turn right, still on the A97, which crosses two river bridges, and follow the road along the Don Valley. After about 5 m. the road swings left away from the river and leads, after 2 m., to the ruins of Kildrummy Castle. The entrance to the gardens of the 'new' castle, and hotel, is 300 yds further on.

(6) Kildrummy Castle to Leith Hall Continue ahead on the A97 through Kildrummy village to the junction with the A944, and turn right. For just over 6 m. the road follows the Don Valley again to Bridge of Alford. There turn left on to the road signposted for Montgarrie. After ½ m. turn left on to the road signposted to Tullynessle and continue ahead, through Tullynessle, along the steep valley of Suie Burn over Suie Hill to the village of Clatt. Here turn right, following the signpost to Kennethmont. At Kennethmont, turn left on to the B9002, and shortly afterwards, just round a corner, turn right for the entrance to Leith Hall.

(7) Leith Hall to Craigievar Castle Turn left on to the B9002 and go back through Kennethmont. After 6 m. pass the hilltop ruin of Dunnideer Castle, and just before the road enters the village of Insch, turn right on to the B992 signposted for Alford. Continue on this road for 6 m., and at the crossroads where the B992 goes left, turn right into Montgarrie. At the crossroads in Montgarrie, turn left for Alford. In Alford turn left along the A944, then shortly after turn right up Kingsford Road. After 1 m., opposite the entrance to Kingsford House, turn left on to the road signposted for Deeside. Bear right at the next junction, and then turn left on meeting the A980. The entrance to Craigievar Castle is on the right, just under 2 m. later.

(8) Craigievar Castle to Crathes Castle Return to the A980 and turn right. Keep straight on over the B9119 and follow the road towards Lumphanan. Just over 2 m. along, on the left, is Macbeth's Cairn, marking his flight in 1056, when Malcolm Canmore's men overtook and killed him and took his head to the king. Go through Lumphanan and turn left at the T-junction, still on the A980. Keep straight on through Torphins, a village thought to be named after Thorfinn, a Norse ally of Macbeth. About 5 m. beyond Torphins, where the A980 swings sharply to the right, keep straight on to join the B977. After 2 m., ignoring narrow tracks on either side, turn right at the junction, and 1 m. further on, at the T-junction, turn left. Shortly after, swing right to follow the Crathes signpost. Go straight on at the next junction, and after 1 m. turn right then immediately left down the drive to the castle.

(9) Crathes Castle to Banchory Leave the castle by the front drive, which leads through the wooded park to the A93. Bear right here for the 2 m. drive back to Banchory.

INFORMATION

Places of interest *Craigievar Castle:* May to mid-Oct., Wed., Thur., Sun., afternoons, also Tues., July, Aug. and Sat., July to Sept. *Crathes Castle:* May to Sept., weekdays, Sun. afternoons; Apr. and Oct., all day Wed., weekend afternoons. Gardens: Daily. *Kildrummy Castle:* Daily. *Leith Hall:* May to Sept., weekdays, Sun. afternoons. Gardens: Daily.

Craft workshop *Banchory:* Ingasetter Ltd, North Deeside Road. Conducted tours of perfumery and distillery, Mon. to Fri.

Events *Aboyne:* Highland Games, 1st Wed. in Sept. Sheep-dog Trials, Aug. *Banchory:* Festival of Scottish Music, May. Agricultural Show, last Sat. in July. Flower Show, Aug. *Tarland:* Agricultural Show, Aug.

Information *Banchory:* Dee Street car park (Tel. Banchory 2000).

Towns with easy access to Banchory:

Aberdeen	18 m.	Brechin	28 m.
Ballater	24 m.	Stonehaven	17 m.

KILDRUMMY CASTLE
In 1306, after the defeat of his army at Methven, Robert Bruce sent his wife and the ladies of his court to Kildrummy. The women escaped during a siege of the castle by the Prince of Wales—the future Edward II—but the Scots were betrayed by one of the defenders, who set fire to the fortress. The English, who had promised him as much gold as he could carry, are said to have settled the debt by pouring the molten metal down his throat. The castle played its part in later campaigns, but slowly fell into decay after the abortive Jacobite rising of 1715. The ruins can be seen from the open gardens of the 'new' castle, now a hotel, which was built in 1901 by a local laird.

Kildrummy Castle.

TARLAND
The fertile country round Tarland is a noted breeding area for the shaggy Highland cattle. Alastrean House, on the outskirts of the village, was presented to the RAF by Lady MacRobert of Douneside in memory of her three sons. One died in an air accident in 1933; the other two were killed in action while flying during the Second World War. The village is a centre for pony-trekking. Short walks provide striking views of the Dee Valley.

Highland cattle

Bronze Age remains, Tomnaverie.

TOMNAVERIE
Tomnaverie stone circle is a relic of primitive tribes who lived in the Highlands long before Christianity. The circle is of a type found only in north-eastern Scotland—stones surrounding a burial cairn. It dates from the Bronze Age, 3500 to 3700 years ago.

SCALE

0   1   2   3   4   5 MILES

LEITH HALL

he hall, dating from 1650, was
ven to the nation after the last
the Leith-Hays was killed in the
cond World War. Exhibits
clude a sash which belonged to
apoleon, and a writing-case given
the then owner, Andrew Hay,
y Bonnie Prince Charlie on the eve
the Battle of Culloden in 1746.
ay was exiled after the prince's
feat, but was pardoned by George
I in 1780. The pardon, believed
be the only such document in
xistence, is on display in the hall.
he grounds contain a rock
rden and a Chinese moon-gate.

Leith Hall.

CRAIGIEVAR CASTLE

The castle, with its conical 'candle-snuffer' turrets, was built in
1626 for William Forbes, a wealthy merchant known as Danzig
Willie because of his lucrative speculations in the Baltic trade.
The heavily studded outer door and iron grille, or 'yett', lead
to the great hall by a stairway above which is the Forbes crest,
with the motto 'Doe not Vaiken Sleiping Dogs'. The Barony
Court, for trying petty law-breakers, used to sit in the great
hall, and its records are preserved. Among the crimes noted is
that of 'abusing the minister and calling him a liar', for which
the offender was put in the stocks. The interior of the great hall
has been little altered since the decorations were completed,
shortly before the death of William Forbes.

Craigievar Castle.

CRATHES CASTLE

An Aberdeenshire family of masons
called the Bells were the master castle-
builders of their time, and they have left
the imprint of their craftsmanship on this
L-plan tower house, finished in 1596 after
40 years' work. An ancestor of the first
owner had been the King's Forester, and
the symbol of his office, a 14th-century
ivory horn, hangs over the fireplace in the
hall. The painted ceilings of the upper
bedrooms had been concealed by lath and
plaster for over a century, when they were
uncovered in 1877. The house contains fine
period furniture, and some of the paintings
are by George Jamesone, an Aberdeen
artist who was a pupil of Rubens. The
yew hedges around the gardens are nearly
300 years old.

Painted ceiling, Crathes Castle.

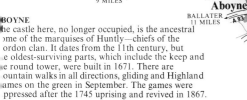

BOYNE

he castle here, no longer occupied, is the ancestral
ome of the marquises of Huntly—chiefs of the
ordon clan. It dates from the 11th century, but
e oldest-surviving parts, which include the keep and
e round tower, were built in 1671. There are
ountain walks in all directions, gliding and Highland
ames on the green in September. The games were
ppressed after the 1745 uprising and revived in 1867.

LACKHALL FOREST

rom the roadside car park a trail, 3 miles long,
mbs the 815 ft Hill of Tillylair, with views of the
rampians beyond the Dee Valley reaching up to the
t. The armies of Edward I, Robert Bruce and the
arquis of Montrose marched here during the
nglish-Scottish wars and rebellions up to the 17th
ntury. They often forded the Dee a little below
otarch, where now there is a bridge over the river.

BANCHORY

Chief town of Lower Deeside, Banchory is a
holiday and health resort sheltered by forests
and heather-clad hills. Its chief attraction is the
Bridge of Feugh, where the Water of Feugh
tumbles over a corridor of crags and rapids
into the River Dee. The bridge carries the date
1799, but could be older. From it one can
watch the salmon leap on their way upstream
to the spawning grounds. The Watch Tower
(or Mort House) in Banchory churchyard was
built as a look-out against body-snatchers in the
18th century. A distillery in the town, which
welcomes visitors, makes perfume from the
lavender, which can be seen from the main
Deeside road just west of the town. The lavender
is at its best in July and August, when it is in full
bloom and at the peak of its fragrance.

Bridge of Feugh, Banchory.

Mountains and lochs in Scotland's wildest corner

Few rivers come close to equalling the magnificent setting of the Spey, as it threads its way through the ancient province of Badenoch. Woodlands flank its course for many miles and its valley is overlooked by range upon range of majestic mountains, including some of the highest peaks to be found in Britain. Their slopes are speckled with hundreds of brightly clad skiers in winter. In sharp but appealing contrast are the sandy pine-fringed shores of Loch Morlich on hot summer days.

(1) Grantown-on-Spey to Carrbridge Leave the town on the A95 signposted for Perth. After 3 m. at Dulnain Bridge, where the A95 goes off to the left, keep straight ahead on the A938, following the signpost for Carrbridge. After 6½ m. at Carrbridge bear left on to the A9. The Landmark Visitors Centre is on the right on the far side of the village.

(2) Carrbridge to Aviemore Continue southwards on the A9 for 6½ m. to Aviemore.

(3) Aviemore to Highland Wildlife Park Leave Aviemore on the A9, heading south. After 3 m. the road skirts Loch Alvie, with the peaks of the Monadhliath Mountains beyond. The Highland Wildlife Park is on the right, 5 m. beyond the loch.

(4) Highland Wildlife Park to Kingussie Leaving the park turn right on to the A9 for Kingussie. After 3 m. take the second turning on the left in Kingussie to visit the Highland Folk Museum.

(5) Kingussie to Newtonmore Return to the A9 and continue southwards to Newtonmore which is reached after 2½ m. The Macpherson Museum is at the junction of the A9 and the A86.

(6) Newtonmore to Ruthven Barracks Continue southwards from the village on the A9 but just over 1 m. later, shortly after crossing the River Spey, turn sharp left on to the B970 signposted to Insh. After 4 m. just beyond a road on the left that leads back to Kingussie, the ruins of Ruthven Barracks are on the left.

(7) Ruthven Barracks to Loch an Eilein Continue towards Insh on the B970. After 2 m. cross Tromie Bridge and immediately turn sharp left to continue on the B970. About 5 m. later turn left on to the road signposted to Kincraig for a short detour to the eastern shore of Loch Insh. There is a car park and picnic site near the boat club on the loch side. From the loch return to the B970 and turn left, and continue along the Spey Valley. The Inshriach Nursery, on the left 4 m. later, is open to visitors. About 2 m. beyond the nursery turn right by a Celtic-style memorial on to the road signposted to Loch an Eilein, which is just under 1 m. further on.

(8) Loch an Eilein to Cairn Gorm Bear left out of the car park and return to the B970. There turn right and after 1 m., where the road joins the A951 at Inverdruie, turn right again. After 1 m., at Coylumbridge, bear right off the A951 on to the minor road signposted for Cairn Gorm. The road passes several parking places along the sandy shores of Loch Morlich. Just past the loch end the Glen More Forest Park information centre is on the left. The road climbs for 3 m. more to a car park half way up Cairn Gorm.

(9) Cairn Gorm to Loch Garten Return down the mountain and past the loch to Coylumbridge and there turn right on to the B970, following the signpost for Nethy Bridge. About 7 m. from Coylumbridge turn left for Boat of Garten and the Strathspey Railway. At the T-junction after crossing the River Spey turn left for the railway station. From the station return to the B970 and turn left. After ¾ m. turn right on to the road signposted to Tulloch. After 1½ m. this road leads to Loch Garten, where a short walk through the woods on the left leads to a building belonging to the Royal Society for the Protection of Birds, from which ospreys can be seen nesting during the breeding season.

(10) Loch Garten to Grantown-on-Spey Return to the B970 and turn right. After 3 m. go through Nethy Bridge and 4 m. later at the junction with the A95 turn left, following the signpost for Grantown-on-Spey. The road crosses the River Spey before entering the town ½ m. later.

NATURE NOTES
The woods on the hills above the Spey Valley are mainly of birch with rowan, aspen, bird cherry and juniper. On the slopes of the Cairngorms are the extensive remnants of the native Scots pine forest that once covered the hills. Besides the ospreys at Loch Garten, birds of prey that breed in the area include golden eagles, peregrines and buzzards. Red deer, roe deer and wildcats all roam in the Cairngorms National Nature Reserve.

INFORMATION

Places of interest *Boat of Garten:* Strathspey Railway, viewable May to Oct. (further information at station). *Kincraig:* Highland Wildlife Park, daily. *Kingussie:* Highland Folk Museum, Apr. to Oct., weekdays and Sun. afternoons. *Carrbridge:* Landmark Visitors Centre, daily. *Newtonmore:* Clan Macpherson House and Museum, Easter to Sept., weekdays.

Events *Aviemore:* Midsummer Curling Bonspiel, June. *Kingussie, Newtonmore:* Clan Macpherson Rally, Aug.

Nature trails *Craigellachie:* Easter to Sept. Starts near Aviemore Centre. Natural birchwood, variety of plants, mammals, birds and insects. Guide from Centre. *Loch an Eilein:* Easter to Sept. Starts north of car park. Guide from shed at lime-kiln.

Information *Aviemore:* Main Street (Tel. Aviemore 363); *Kingussie:* 26 Duke Street (Tel. Kingussie 228).

Towns with easy access to Grantown-on-Spey:

Ballater	41 m.	Inverness	34 m.
Elgin	33 m.	Keith	36 m.

Wildcat

HIGHLAND WILDLIFE PARK
Animals that vanished from Scotland centuries ago were reintroduced to the Highlands when this 260 acre park was opened in 1972. Brown bears, bison, antelope, beaver, reindeer and other species share the park with creatures that still live in the Scottish wilds, but are rarely seen. These include wildcats, pine martens, Soay sheep from the island of St Kilda and birds such as the golden eagle, ptarmigan and capercaillie. Many of these birds and animals can be seen without leaving the car.

Ptarmigan   *Capercaillie*

KINGUSSIE
The 'capital of Badenoch', Kingussie is a neat little 18th-century town that looks across the Spey Valley to the grandeur of the Cairngorm mountains. The Highland Folk Museum in Duke Street houses a fascinating collection of objects from the past. In the grounds is a typical Hebridean 'black house'. These dwellings got their name because, as they had no chimneys, but only a hole in their thatched roofs, a thick layer of soot built up on the ceiling.

Nursery furniture at Kingussie.

NEWTONMORE
This village, now noted as a pony-trekking centre, was for centuries the heart of the lands held by the powerful Clan Macpherson. Among the clan relics in the Macpherson Museum is an elaborate 4 ft high silver candelabrum. On it is depicted an incident in the life of Cluny Macpherson, one of Bonnie Prince Charlie's supporters in the 1745 Rebellion. He is described in Stevenson's novel *Kidnapped*.

RUTHVEN BARRACKS
Built after the 1715 Jacobite rebellion, the barracks saw a Stuart victory and a Stuart defeat. In 1745 they were captured by Bonnie Prince Charlie. But a year later, it was there that the shattered remains of the clans gathered after their defeat at Culloden. They expected the prince to join them, but instead they received a message of farewell.

SCALE
0   1   2   3   4   5 MILES

GRANTOWN-ON-SPEY

A fashionable resort since Victorian times, Grantown dates from 1765 and is now a popular centre for salmon fishermen and skiing enthusiasts. Its broad streets are typical of the many Scottish 'new towns' of the 18th and 19th centuries. Most of the buildings are of granite. The oldest piece of building to survive is the Old Spey Bridge, erected in the 1750s as part of the military road-building programme which was designed to pacify the Highlands. It is now closed to traffic.

CARRBRIDGE

At the south end of the village, standing on a wooded site overlooking the A9, is Landmark, a permanent environmental museum opened in 1970. A short nature trail runs through the woods behind. A vivid panorama of the Highlands during the last 20,000 years is painted in the multi-screen theatre. Three pairs of projectors tell the story of Strathspey and the Cairngorms from the Ice Age to the present day. The theatre is surrounded by an exhibition area where relics, paintings and photographs develop the story told in the theatre.

Mill for hand-grinding, Landmark.

Speyside Railway symbol.

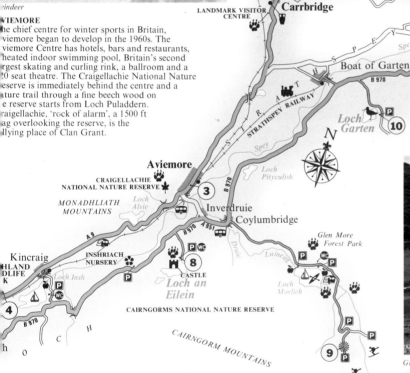

reindeer

AVIEMORE

The chief centre for winter sports in Britain, Aviemore began to develop in the 1960s. The Aviemore Centre has hotels, bars and restaurants, a heated indoor swimming pool, Britain's second largest skating and curling rink, a ballroom and a 720 seat theatre. The Craigellachie National Nature Reserve is immediately behind the centre and a nature trail through a fine beech wood on the reserve starts from Loch Puladdern. Craigellachie, 'rock of alarm', a 1500 ft crag overlooking the reserve, is the rallying place of Clan Grant.

BOAT OF GARTEN

A short drive away from this pleasant village is Loch Garten. Up to 100,000 people a year visit the loch to see the rare ospreys, which have been breeding there since the return of the species to Britain. Ospreys had not bred in Britain since early in the century, having been hunted for many years. The village itself is now the headquarters of the Strathspey Railway, the only standard-gauge steam railway in the Highlands.

GLEN MORE

The Glen More Forest Park, in the Cairngorms, was established by the Forestry Commission in 1948. It has way-marked nature trails, picnic sites and a camping ground. There is also small-boat sailing on Loch Morlich.

Glen More across the mountains.

LOCH AN EILEIN

On the northern boundary of the Cairngorm National Nature Reserve, the wooded shores of the loch are best explored by the nature trail that starts from the car park. The castle on the little island in the centre of the loch is traditionally associated with the 'Wolf of Badenoch', the outlawed son of Robert II of Scotland. But it was built about 100 years after his death in 1405.

CAIRNGORMS

A cluster of peaks more than 4000 ft high makes this the greatest mountain range in Britain. Among the granite, the crystals of smoky quartz known as 'cairngorms' can be found. The wild beauty of the mountains can be treacherous—even in summer, cloud can descend and temperatures fall rapidly. Walkers must be properly prepared: a map, warm clothes, stout boots, food and a compass are essential. The Cairngorms National Nature Reserve, the largest in Britain, covers 100 square miles of mountains, glens and forests. This is the haunt of deer, golden eagles, wildcats, otters, foxes, badgers and many other creatures.

Fairy-tale castle in Loch an Eilein.

A day's outing in the whisky country

The peat streams from the Grampian Hills that feed the River Spey account for the many whisky distilleries along the river valley. Dufftown is the centre of the industry and visitors can see round working distilleries. The land between Elgin and the fishing grounds of the Moray Firth is fertile farming country. In ancient times the combined harvest of land and sea produced wealth which has left its evidence in planned villages and small towns, and such notable buildings as Elgin Cathedral and Pluscarden Abbey, now being restored by its community of monks. The coastline has some fine sandy beaches, and fishing harbours at Burghead and Lossiemouth.

(1) Elgin to Monaughty Forest Leave the town on the A96 signposted to Inverness, but at the roundabout on the outskirts take the B9010 signposted to Dallas. Keep ahead on the B9010 at the next roundabout but 1 m. later, where this road swings to the left, go straight on. After 3 m. the Monaughty Forest walks are reached. They are marked on both sides of the road.

(2) Monaughty Forest to Pluscarden Abbey Continue ahead on the road, which shortly swings left away from the forest and leads, in 1¼ m., to the abbey on the right.

(3) Pluscarden Abbey to Burghead Continue along the same road, and 3 m. beyond the abbey turn right and climb through woodland. At the T-junction on the far side of the hill, turn right again. Follow the road to the A96 and turn right, then take the first left turn, signposted to East Grange. After ½ m., immediately past a sharp left-hand bend, turn right, cross the railway and continue for 1½ m. to the junction with the B9089. Turn right here and, at the crossroads just under 3 m. later, follow the B9089 round to the left, drive straight on through Roseisle Forest, and then turn left on to the road signposted to Burghead.

(4) Burghead to Duffus Leave Burghead harbour, cross the railway and take the second turning on the left (St Aethan's Place). Shortly afterwards go left again on to the B9012. On the far side of Newtown and Hopeman turn right, still on the B9012, following the signpost for Elgin. A short drive leads to Duffus. To see St Peter's Kirk and cross, keep ahead where the road goes round to the right by the post office. To see Duffus Castle, continue on the B9012 for 1 m. beyond the village and turn left. After ¾ m. turn right down a short lane which leads to the castle.

(5) Duffus to Lossiemouth Return down the lane from the castle and turn right. After ½ m. turn left. The road now runs close to the runways of the RAF's Lossiemouth airfield. After 1¾ m., at the T-junction with the B9040, turn right and follow the road into Lossiemouth.

(6) Lossiemouth to Fochabers Leave the town on the A941, signposted to Elgin, but on the outskirts fork left on to the B9103 signposted for Fochabers. The road runs into Lossie Forest, crosses the River Lossie at Arthur's Bridge and passes Milltown airfield. Just beyond the airfield, turn left by the entrance to Leuchars House and keep straight ahead on the road to Urquhart. Turn left at the first T-junction in Urquhart, then right at the next and keep straight on at the crossroads soon after. At the T-junction with the A96, turn left and continue for 4 m. to Fochabers.

(7) Fochabers to Dufftown To visit Speymouth Forest, leave the town on the A96 but on the outskirts bear left on to the A98 signposted to Fraserburgh. The starting point for walks is on the right, about ½ m. along from the A96. From the forest return to the A96 and turn left towards Keith and Aberdeen. At the crossroads, about 3 m. later, turn right on to the road signposted Mulben. On meeting the A95 keep straight ahead, following the Craigellachie signpost. After 5 m., in Maggieknockater, fork left on to the road signposted for Dufftown. After running parallel to the River Fiddich for 4 m., the road meets the B9014. Turn right and follow it into Dufftown.

(8) Dufftown to Craigellachie Leave the town on the A941 signposted to Elgin. After 1 m. a short detour to the right along the B975 leads to Grant's distillery and Balvenie Castle. Return to the A941 and turn right. Craigellachie is 3½ m. further on beside the River Spey.

(9) Craigellachie to Elgin Continue ahead from Craigellachie on the A941, which immediately crosses the railway, then the river. The A941 here is carried over the River Spey by a new bridge. Telford's bridge is on the left. After 3 m., in Rothes, where the A941 veers off to the left keep straight ahead on to the B9015, following the signpost for Orton. After 5 m. turn left under the railway on to the B9103, following the signpost for Elgin, and 6 m. later, just beyond another stretch of the railway, go left on to the A96 and follow the road back to Elgin.

INFORMATION

Places of interest *Dufftown:* Balvenie Castle, all year, weekdays, Sun. afternoons. *Duffus Castle:* All reasonable times. *Grant's Glenfiddich Distillery:* Tours weekdays. *Pluscarden Abbey:* All year, daily.

Events *Dufftown:* Gala Week, last week in July. *Elgin:* Fiddle Festival, June. Highland Games, July. *Fochabers:* Gala Week, July.

Nature trails *Monaughty Forest:* 1 m. and 2 m. On road to Pluscarden, all year.

Information *Elgin:* High Street (Tel. Elgin 2666).

Towns with easy access to Elgin:

Banff	33 m.	Huntly	28 m.
Grantown-on-Spey	33 m.	Inverness	38 m.

Duffus Castle.

DUFFUS
Gordonstoun School, where the Duke of Edinburgh and the Prince of Wales were pupils, is on the outskirts of the village. The 15th-century castle replaced an earlier, mainly wooden, fortress which was destroyed during the Scottish revolt against the English at the end of the 13th century. Closer to the village centre are the ruins of the parish church of 1226, containing medieval tombs, and facing it the old 14 ft high churchyard cross. The church was burnt during the rebellion of 1298, and Edward I gave the rector 20 oaks to repair it.

BURGHEAD
A fishing village on a rocky headland, Burghead overlooks 7 miles of sandy beaches sweeping south and west round Burghead Bay. The headland is known to have been occupied by the Romans, but all traces of their settlements have disappeared. The so-called Roman Well, believed to have been used for baptisms, is attributed to 6th-century followers of St Columba. The village is the base for the Outward Bound Moray Sea School, where boys from all over Britain are trained in seamanship.

Pluscarden Abbey.

PLUSCARDEN ABBEY
Alexander Stewart, son of Robert II of Scotland, known as the Wolf of Badenoch, went on a rampage of destruction in the 14th century in revenge for being excommunicated by the Bishop of Moray. In 1390 he destroyed Elgin Cathedral and Pluscarden Priory, which had been founded in 1230. It was later restored, but was destroyed during the Reformation, and remained derelict until a small community of Benedictine monks began to rebuild it in 1948. It was made an abbey in 1974.

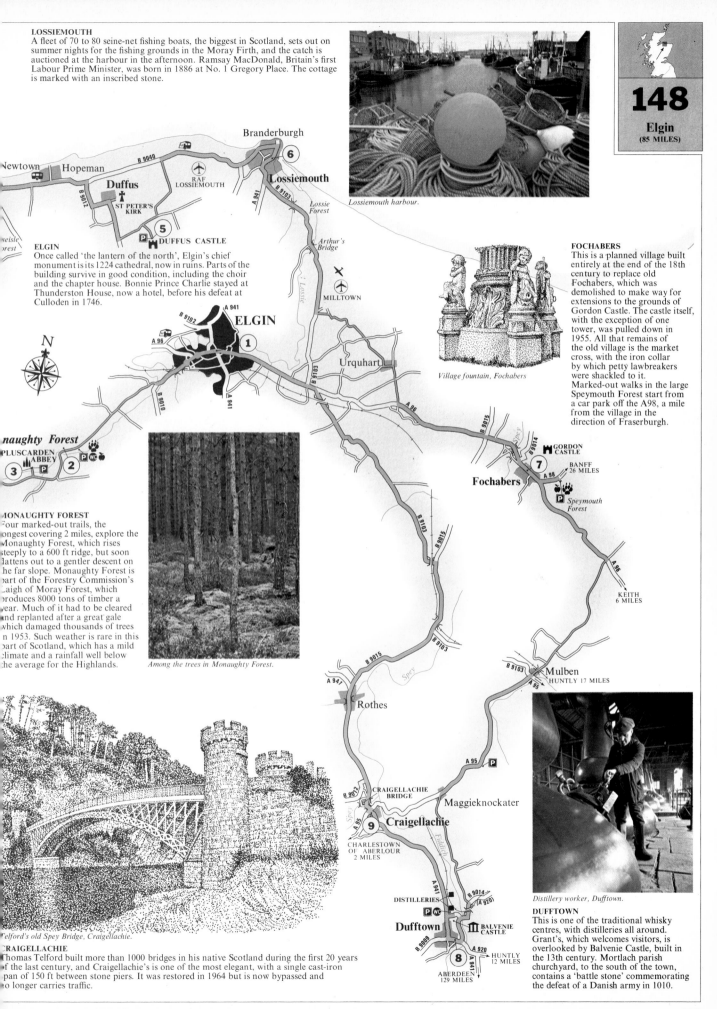

LOSSIEMOUTH
A fleet of 70 to 80 seine-net fishing boats, the biggest in Scotland, sets out on summer nights for the fishing grounds in the Moray Firth, and the catch is auctioned at the harbour in the afternoon. Ramsay MacDonald, Britain's first Labour Prime Minister, was born in 1886 at No. 1 Gregory Place. The cottage is marked with an inscribed stone.

Lossiemouth harbour.

ELGIN
Once called 'the lantern of the north', Elgin's chief monument is its 1224 cathedral, now in ruins. Parts of the building survive in good condition, including the choir and the chapter house. Bonnie Prince Charlie stayed at Thunderston House, now a hotel, before his defeat at Culloden in 1746.

FOCHABERS
This is a planned village built entirely at the end of the 18th century to replace old Fochabers, which was demolished to make way for extensions to the grounds of Gordon Castle. The castle itself, with the exception of one tower, was pulled down in 1955. All that remains of the old village is the market cross, with the iron collar by which petty lawbreakers were shackled to it. Marked-out walks in the large Speymouth Forest start from a car park off the A98, a mile from the village in the direction of Fraserburgh.

Village fountain, Fochabers.

MONAUGHTY FOREST
Four marked-out trails, the longest covering 2 miles, explore the Monaughty Forest, which rises steeply to a 600 ft ridge, but soon flattens out to a gentler descent on the far slope. Monaughty Forest is part of the Forestry Commission's Laigh of Moray Forest, which produces 8000 tons of timber a year. Much of it had to be cleared and replanted after a great gale which damaged thousands of trees in 1953. Such weather is rare in this part of Scotland, which has a mild climate and a rainfall well below the average for the Highlands.

Among the trees in Monaughty Forest.

Distillery worker, Dufftown.

DUFFTOWN
This is one of the traditional whisky centres, with distilleries all around. Grant's, which welcomes visitors, is overlooked by Balvenie Castle, built in the 13th century. Mortlach parish churchyard, to the south of the town, contains a 'battle stone' commemorating the defeat of a Danish army in 1010.

Telford's old Spey Bridge, Craigellachie.

CRAIGELLACHIE
Thomas Telford built more than 1000 bridges in his native Scotland during the first 20 years of the last century, and Craigellachie's is one of the most elegant, with a single cast-iron span of 150 ft between stone piers. It was restored in 1964 but is now bypassed and no longer carries traffic.

395

A tour to the heart of a mountain
CRUACHAN POWER STATION

Deep in the heart of 3689 ft high Ben Cruachan is a great cavern, as big as Coventry Cathedral, hewn by man out of the solid granite. It is the power-house of an ingenious engineering project that turns surplus energy into precious electricity. A tour of this wonderful world of the 20th-century cavemen begins with a bus ride into the mountain.

Cruachan Dam and reservoir nestle in the hollowed-out shoulder of Ben Cruachan, in Argyll. The setting provides a breath-taking panorama: to the south, Loch Awe stretches away for 30 miles, to the west is the rugged Pass of Brander and all around are the dark humps of mountains and ranges of conical hills. But the true marvels of Cruachan lie underground.

A visitor to this West Highland hydro-electric power complex can take a mini-bus two-thirds of a mile through a granite-hewn tunnel into the heart of the mountain.

Four pump-turbine machines are housed there, 120 ft below the level of Loch Awe and 1000 ft beneath the mountain. These machines boost Scotland's electricity by about 577 million units a year—enough to keep 443,000 domestic cookers going for 12 months.

The principle of the power station—known as the Cruachan Pumped-Storage Development—is simple. At night-time and at week-ends, when demand for electricity in Scotland is low, surplus energy from steam and nuclear stations in Southern Scotland is directed to Cruachan. This drives the 134,000 h.p. reversible machines which pump water from Loch Awe up through inclined shafts inside the mountain into the reservoir, high on Ben Cruachan. At peak-demand times this water is released through the same shafts, which are 1000 ft long, 16½ ft in diameter and lined with concrete. This drives the dual-purpose pump-turbines, generating electricity that is then fed back into Scotland's central power grid via 65 miles of overhead high-voltage cable.

The project involves two other conventional power stations linked to Loch Nant and Loch Awe. It was inaugurated by the Queen in 1965, having been proposed eight years earlier.

The idea of pumped storage is not new, but the Cruachan method of combining pump and turbine in one machine is cheaper than earlier schemes in Britain and on the Continent, which used separate units.

Visitors park their cars at the foot of the mountain and are driven by mini-bus down the largely unlined tunnel, its roof lights stretching to a pinpoint ahead. Running parallel to this access tunnel is the tailrace that carries the water to and from Loch Awe, between the pump-turbines and the lower reservoir.

At the end of the access tunnel is the immense underground machine hall: 300 ft long, 77 ft wide and 127 ft high, hewn from solid granite. Its 70,000 cu. yds could contain

MOUNTAIN RESERVOIR *This hydro-electric project on Ben Cruachan gives a massive annual boost to Scotland's power system; enough to keep 443,000 domestic cookers going for a year.*

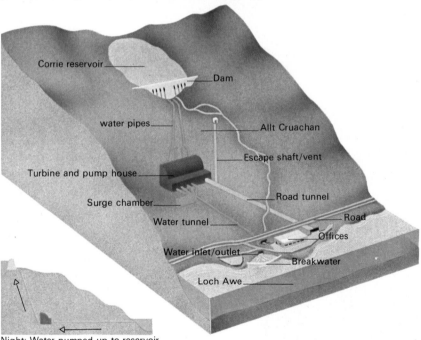

Corrie reservoir

Dam

water pipes

Allt Cruachan

Escape shaft/vent

Turbine and pump house

Surge chamber

Road tunnel

Water tunnel

Road

Offices

Water inlet/outlet

Breakwater

Loch Awe

Night: Water pumped up to reservoir

Day: Water released to turn turbines

ALTERNATING CURRENT *By night, when electricity demand is lowest, water is pumped up from Loch Awe to the mountainside reservoir. Then, during the day, the water is released to drive four giant turbines. Each year these machines feed the equivalent of 577 million units of electricity back into Scotland's power grid. The project was inaugurated in 1965. Underground chambers for pumped-storage schemes have technical advantages. They also avoid the necessity for large surface buildings and pipelines, which can be unsightly.*

In contrast to its modern engineering marvels, the Loch Awe area is steeped in history and legend. ...e loch itself was said to have formed when a hag who was 'guardian of the ridges' neglected to replace a rock that ...ugged a spring welling up from Ben Cruachan. Here also, in the Pass of Brander, Robert Bruce routed the ...acDougalls in fierce Highland warfare.

...ALL OF POWER Cruachan reservoir was created by damming the mouth of a corrie—or bowl—on a shoulder of the ...ountain. Before work could begin on the 1037 ft long, 153 ft high wall, some 31,700 cu. yds of rock had to be ...xcavated to form the foundations. Control gates beneath the central section of the dam lead to the two tunnels which carry ...ater to the turbines 1000 ft below. It is on excursions up the mountain to the dam itself that the best panoramic views ...f the surrounding area emerge.

Coventry Cathedral, or a seven-storey building on the site of a soccer pitch. From a viewing gallery high up on the eastern wall, visitors look down on the four, 100 megawatt pump-turbines, each weighing 650 tons, which dominate the hall like props in a science-fiction film. Each machine can attain full output as a generator within two minutes and, in reverse as pumps, reach peak performance in seven minutes. The four machines force through 120 tons of water a second.

The weight of the four machines is so great that each had to be taken apart to be brought to the site but, even so, many bridges on the route had to be strengthened beforehand. This was the first time that machines of this size had ever been transported in sections, and special arrangements had to be made to assemble them under controlled conditions at the site.

From a control room overlooking the machine hall, only three men are needed to operate the whole of the Loch Awe scheme, including the other two power stations at Nant and Inverawe, and switching stations at Dalmally and Taynuilt. Two large cranes, each of 110 tons capacity, can traverse the length of the hall. In places, where the walls are not covered with banks of monitoring dials and pressure gauges, the bare rock retains marks of drills made by the men who carved out the cavern.

Two transformers, through which Cruachan's power is fed into the national system, are housed in two other large chambers near the machine hall. A combined cable and ventilation shaft rising 1000 ft to the mountain

JOURNEY INTO A MOUNTAIN *Visitors to the Cruachan complex are taken by mini-bus through a tunnel hewn from solid granite, reaching two-thirds of a mile into Ben Cruachan. Overhead lights in the tunnel seem to recede to a pinpoint in the distance as the bus begins its journey.*

CRUACHAN POWER STATION

surface is the link with the terminal tower of the transmission line which connects with Scotland's power grid. Energy for pumping is fed back along the same line.

The shaft also has a network of ladders and platforms for maintenance access, or as an escape route in the event of an accident.

Above ground, excursions are also organised to the dam itself, 1300 ft above sea level up Ben Cruachan. A 3½ mile access road rises from a point near Lochawe village, 2 miles east of the visitors' reception centre. At the junction of this access road with the A85 is a group of stone-built houses, where the men who operate the station live with their families.

As the access road climbs the mountain, magnificent views emerge. Before the road was built, only shepherds and a few hikers ever saw them.

The dam itself, 1037 ft long and reaching a maximum height of 153 ft, is composed of 116,000 cu. yds of concrete. Its crest is 1315 ft above sea level. Before building could be started, 31,700 cu. yds of rock had to be excavated to form the foundations.

In addition to the water that drains down naturally from the upper slopes of Ben Cruachan into the reservoir, a 10 mile system of piped aqueducts and tunnels diverts water which originally flowed into Loch Etive and

Loch Awe. This added water alone contributes 50 million units of electricity a year to the power station's output.

Below the dam on the shore of Loch Awe is an area built by dumping excavated rock from the tunnel and machine hall. On this area are the dam's administration building, behind which is the entrance to the 22 ft wide access tunnel, and a semi-circular lagoon known as the forebay. It is through this that the water passes in and out of the loch. Screens and mobile-cleaning apparatus remove any debris, and prevent fish and floating timber from entering the tailrace tunnel and jamming up the shafts and mechanism. Because the surface area of Loch Awe is 15 sq. m., the operation of the station has little effect on the water level. However, if all the machines were kept pumping for 24 hours, the level of water in the loch would fall by 9 in.

Cruachan is the third largest power station of its kind in Europe, the largest being in Spain. Its setting is also steeped in local history and folklore.

In the Pass of Brander, for example, Robert Bruce and Sir James Douglas routed the MacDougalls in 1308. After foiling a MacDougall ambush in the pass, aided by Douglas and a team of archers up on the mountain, Bruce went on to take Dunstaffnage Castle at Loch Etive, leaving a heavy toll of MacDougall dead, and turning over much of their property to Campbell of Loch Awe.

Through the pass, at the village of Taynuilt,

on a small hill behind the church of Muckairn, stands a memorial to Lord Nelson which predates Nelson's Column in Trafalgar Square by 37 years. It is a large standing stone, raised by Lancashire men employed in local iron-smelting furnaces. Smelters had been ordered to Scotland in Elizabethan times to save English woodlands from further deforestation. England needed all her home-grown oak for shipbuilding—Scotland would provide timber for smelting. Two hundred years later, when the workmen at Taynuilt heard of Nelson's death at Trafalgar, they put up the monument.

There is also a legend about Cruachan itself, fittingly depicted in a relief carved in wood, 60 ft long by 8 ft deep, which occupies the wall of the underground machine hall. The carving tells the story of the Cailleach Bheur, or Bera, the hag of the ridges. It was her duty, the story goes, to guard a spring that welled up from the peak of Ben Cruachan. At sundown each day she would cover the spring with a slab of stone, then remove it at sunrise. But one night she fell asleep and forgot to cover the spring. It overflowed and its waters, rushing down the mountain, flooded the valley below, drowning all its people and cattle and forging a new outlet to the sea through the Pass of Brander.

It was in this way that the River Awe and Loch Awe were formed, according to folklore. For her neglect, the Cailleach was turned to stone and somewhere high on the mountain her petrified form, it is said, still sits overlooking the pass.

MAMMOTH CAVERN *The site of Cruachan's great machine hall was hewn from solid granite. Its 70,000 cu. yd capacity is large enough to contain Coventry Cathedral. Here the hall is seen under construction as the massive job of excavation proceeded. Total cost of the entire Loch Awe scheme was some £24 million.*

DUAL PURPOSE *From a viewing gallery in the machine hall, visitors can see the four reversible pump-turbines, nerve centre of the project. Each machine weighs 650 tons and reaches maximum output in minutes. The rotating parts, which weigh 250 tons, operate at 500 rpm.*

SPACE-AGE POWER HOUSE *Looking like something from a science-fiction drama, the four 100 megawatt pump-turbines dominate the huge machine hall. They can force through the water at a rate of 120 tons a second. Cruachan is the third largest power station of its kind in Europe, the largest being in Spain. Before the advent of reversible, dual-purpose machines like these, both pumps and turbines had to be used, making such projects much more costly. The control room, which overlooks the entire machine hall, can be seen above, on the right, level with the top of the pump-turbine housing. It also acts as the control centre for the whole Loch Awe scheme, including the power stations at Inverawe and Nant. Three men only operate all three power stations and the switching stations at Dalmally and Taynuilt. VHF radio links the control room to Taynuilt and, in addition to providing speech communication, carries the control channels.*

OVERALL CONTROL *From these banks of gauges, dials and switches only three men are needed to operate the entire Loch Awe hydro-electric scheme.*

WHEN TO VISIT CRUACHAN

Cruachan Power Station stands beside Loch Awe on the A85 about halfway between Dalmally and Taynuilt. It is on the route of Hand-picked tour No. 141 based on Inveraray.

VISITING ARRANGEMENTS The underground power station is open to visitors from late April to late Sept., 9.30 a.m.–5 p.m. Diesel-powered vehicles are allowed into the access tunnel, but petrol-engined cars are forbidden. Motorists must leave their cars at the reception centre, where they can catch a special mini-bus which operates a frequent service to and from the machine hall.

The enchanted Highlands of Bonnie Prince Charlie

Memories of Bonnie Prince Charlie and his devoted but doomed followers are brought vividly to life on this tour through the Highlands. It visits Culloden Moor where, in 1746, the young prince's Jacobite army was cut to pieces in the last battle fought on the soil of Britain. The uprising prompted the building of Fort George, which looks over the Moray Firth to the hills of the Black Isle. Loch Ness abounds in beauty and interest, even without a glimpse of the monster! Inverness, gateway to the Highlands, is a good place to start this tour in the morning and to return to in the evening, when there is every chance that a pipe band will be playing under the lights by the waterside.

(1) Inverness to Smithtown Leave Inverness on the A9 signposted for Perth, and follow this road as it swings southwards from the roundabout on the outskirts of the city. About 2 m. from the roundabout, turn left on to the B9006 signposted for Croy. After ½ m. turn left for Cradlehall, and after a further ½ m. turn right at the T-junction. About halfway through Smithtown, just past the old corrugated-iron village hall, turn right at the crossroads. Continue to the sawmill and car park, start of the Forestry Commission's Culloden Forest Walk.

(2) Smithtown to Fort George Return from the car park to the crossroads and turn right. Carry straight on for just over 1 m. and turn right on to the A96. Just over 1½ m. later, turn left on to the B9039 for Ardersier. The fine turreted house to be seen on the left is Castle Stuart, built early in the 17th century, despoiled in a clan battle, but repaired since. At the T-junction in the fishing village of Ardersier, turn left and follow the shore road for 1¾ m. to Fort George. Here, bear right into the visitors' car park.

(3) Fort George to Culloden Returning from the fort, go straight through Ardersier and follow the straight line of the Old Military Road for about 2 m. to the A96. Go ahead over the crossroads, and after about ½ m. turn right on to the B9006 for Culloden Moor. Keep straight on in Croy, where the road is joined from the left by the B9091, and carry on for just under 5 m. to the site of the Battle of Culloden. Documents and plans of the battle can be obtained in Old Leanach cottage on the left, round which the fighting raged in 1746. It is now a museum of the National Trust for Scotland. The NTS Information Centre on the site stages exhibitions and illustrated talks about the battle.

(4) Culloden to Clava Cairns From the battlefield, retrace the route back along the B9006 and turn right at the first crossroads, signposted to Clava Cairns. Keep straight ahead at the next crossroads, go over the bridge across the River Nairn and follow the road round to the right. The prehistoric cairns are on the right.

(5) Clava Cairns to Foyers Carry on past the cairns, and follow the narrow, twisting road under a railway viaduct. At the junction just past the railway, turn right on to the road signposted as the C9 for Daviot. After about ½ m. the road veers right to cross the railway, and immediately after this another road cuts off to the right. Ignore this and carry straight on along the valley of the River Nairn. Turn right on meeting the A9, then after about ½ m. bear left on to the B851 signposted to Fort Augustus.

Stay on this road for 14 m. For much of this distance the road runs south-west through the Nairn Valley—Strathnairn—with the river on the right. Just before the junction where the B851 runs into the A862 for Fort Augustus, Loch Mhór can be seen to the left. Bear left on to the A862 as it runs down to Loch Mhór and 2 m. later, in Errogie, bear left to stay on the A862 which runs parallel to the loch. After another 5 m., beyond the end of Loch Mhór, turn right on to the B852 for Foyers which is reached after 3 m.

(6) Foyers to Inverfarigaig Continue on the B852, which runs parallel to the wooded shore of Loch Ness, to Inverfarigaig, starting point for a forest walk.

(7) Inverfarigaig to Knocknagael Boar's Stone Just past the Forestry Commission offices in Inverfarigaig, which are on the left beside the B852, turn right and up the narrow, steep, unsignposted lane known as Corkscrew Hill. After a series of hairpin bends it straightens out to run over gentle countryside for just over 4 m. to join the A862. Go left on to the A862, and after 3 m. fork right on to the road signposted for Essich and Inverness. Stay on this road, going straight over the crossroads, for 7 m., to the Boar's Stone, which is on the right.

(8) Knocknagael Boar's Stone to Inverness Carry on along the same road to Inverness, running into the outskirts after 1½ m.

INFORMATION

Places of interest *Culloden:* Site, all year; visitor centre and museum, Apr. to Oct., weekdays, Sun. afternoons. *Fort George:* All year, weekdays, Sun. afternoons. *Inverness:* Museum, all year, weekdays.

Craft workshops *Culloden Pottery:* Weekdays, also Sun. in summer. *Inverness:* Holm Woollen Mills, Dores Road, spinning and weaving, Mon. to Fri. Isle of Skye Handloom Co. Ltd., Tomnahurich Street, weaving, Mon. to Fri., shop, open Mon. to Sat.

Events *Inverness:* Highland Games, 2nd. Sat. in July. Market and livestock sales, every Tues. Ceilidhs (Highland concerts), two or three times weekly.

Information *Inverness:* 23 Church Street (Tel. Inverness 34353).

Towns with easy access to Inverness:

Aviemore	32 m.	Elgin	37 m.
Dingwall	24 m.	Fort Augustus	34 m.
Dingwall (by ferry)	14 m.	Grantown-on-Spey	34 m.

Loch Ness.

INVERFARIGAIG
This cluster of houses overlooking Loch Ness is the starting point for the 3 mile Farigaig Forest Walk. Beside the car park a Forestry Commission exhibition of photographs and models illustrates forestry and wildlife conservation. From the top of Corkscrew Hill, leaving the village, the view northwards includes Urquhart Bay, on Loch Ness, where a photograph claimed to be that of the Loch Ness monster was taken in 1955. Though narrow, the loch is over 700 ft deep in places and has never been known to freeze over, even in the coldest Highland winter. The loch is 24 miles long and, in 1952, it was used by the racing driver John Cobb in his fatal attempt on the world water-speed record. He was killed when his jet-powered speedboat capsized and sank.

FOYERS
The village was the site of Britain's first hydro-electric scheme in 1896, but its greatest attraction is a magnificent waterfall. It is reached by a footpath that starts opposite the post office and zig-zags downwards. The fall is in two stages, with a main drop of 90 ft. At the top of the fall, the River Foyers is squeezed into a narrow channel from which it shoots dramatically into a spreading white cataract. From a rocky pool at the foot of the fall, the river races towards Loch Ness through a wooded gorge. The village looks out across Loch Ness to Mealfuarvonie looming 2284 ft above the forest which stretches along the western shore of the loch.

The 90 ft fall, Foyers.

SCALE
0   1   2   3   4   5 MILES

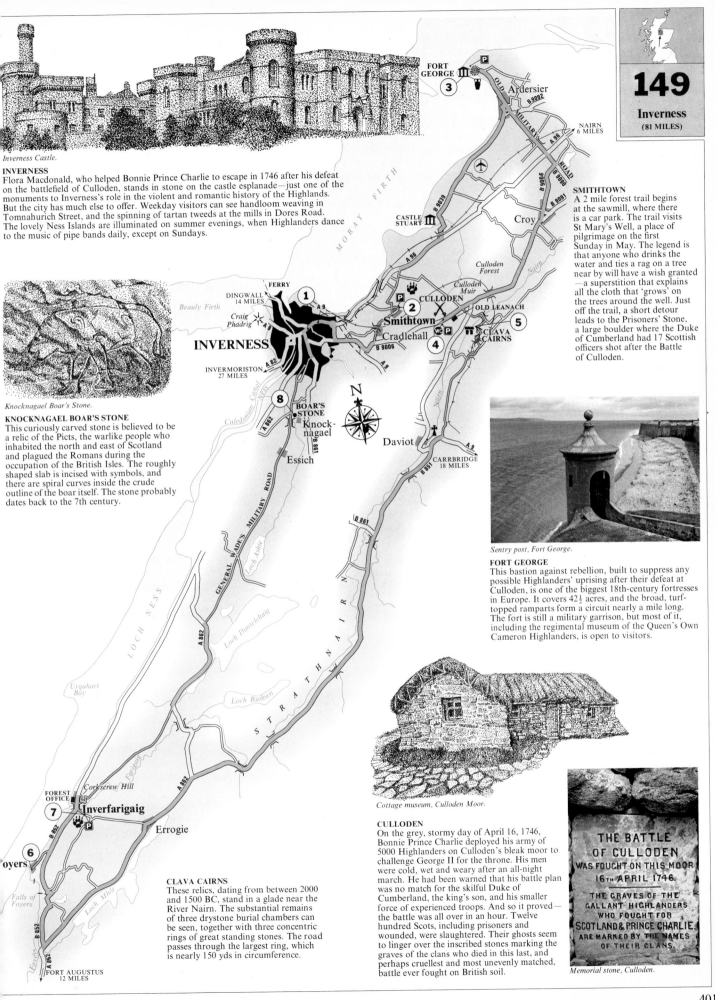

Inverness Castle.

INVERNESS

Flora Macdonald, who helped Bonnie Prince Charlie to escape in 1746 after his defeat on the battlefield of Culloden, stands in stone on the castle esplanade—just one of the monuments to Inverness's role in the violent and romantic history of the Highlands. But the city has much else to offer. Weekday visitors can see handloom weaving in Tomnahurich Street, and the spinning of tartan tweeds at the mills in Dores Road. The lovely Ness Islands are illuminated on summer evenings, when Highlanders dance to the music of pipe bands daily, except on Sundays.

Knocknagael Boar's Stone.

KNOCKNAGAEL BOAR'S STONE

This curiously carved stone is believed to be a relic of the Picts, the warlike people who inhabited the north and east of Scotland and plagued the Romans during the occupation of the British Isles. The roughly shaped slab is incised with symbols, and there are spiral curves inside the crude outline of the boar itself. The stone probably dates back to the 7th century.

FORT GEORGE

Ardersier

NAIRN 6 MILES

CASTLE STUART

Croy

SMITHTOWN

MORAY FIRTH

Culloden Forest

SMITHTOWN

A 2 mile forest trail begins at the sawmill, where there is a car park. The trail visits St Mary's Well, a place of pilgrimage on the first Sunday in May. The legend is that anyone who drinks the water and ties a rag on a tree near by will have a wish granted — a superstition that explains all the cloth that 'grows' on the trees around the well. Just off the trail, a short detour leads to the Prisoners' Stone, a large boulder where the Duke of Cumberland had 17 Scottish officers shot after the Battle of Culloden.

FERRY

DINGWALL 14 MILES

Craig Phadrig

Beauly Firth

INVERNESS

INVERMORISTON 27 MILES

Culloden Muir

CULLODEN

Smithtown

Cradlehall

OLD LEANACH

CLAVA CAIRNS

Caledonian Canal

BOAR'S STONE

Knock-nagael

Essich

N

Daviot

CARRBRIDGE 18 MILES

Sentry post, Fort George.

FORT GEORGE

This bastion against rebellion, built to suppress any possible Highlanders' uprising after their defeat at Culloden, is one of the biggest 18th-century fortresses in Europe. It covers 42¼ acres, and the broad, turf-topped ramparts form a circuit nearly a mile long. The fort is still a military garrison, but most of it, including the regimental museum of the Queen's Own Cameron Highlanders, is open to visitors.

LOCH NESS

GENERAL WADE'S MILITARY ROAD

Loch Ashie

STRATHNAIRN

Loch Duntelchaig

Urquhart Bay

Loch Ruthven

Loch Mhor

FOREST OFFICE

Inverfarigaig

Errogie

Foyers

Falls of Foyers

Corkscrew Hill

FORT AUGUSTUS 12 MILES

Cottage museum, Culloden Moor.

CLAVA CAIRNS

These relics, dating from between 2000 and 1500 BC, stand in a glade near the River Nairn. The substantial remains of three drystone burial chambers can be seen, together with three concentric rings of great standing stones. The road passes through the largest ring, which is nearly 150 yds in circumference.

CULLODEN

On the grey, stormy day of April 16, 1746, Bonnie Prince Charlie deployed his army of 5000 Highlanders on Culloden's bleak moor to challenge George II for the throne. His men were cold, wet and weary after an all-night march. He had been warned that his battle plan was no match for the skilful Duke of Cumberland, the king's son, and his smaller force of experienced troops. And so it proved— the battle was all over in an hour. Twelve hundred Scots, including prisoners and wounded, were slaughtered. Their ghosts seem to linger over the inscribed stones marking the graves of the clans who died in this last, and perhaps cruellest and most unevenly matched, battle ever fought on British soil.

THE BATTLE OF CULLODEN WAS FOUGHT ON THIS MOOR 16TH APRIL 1746.

THE GRAVES OF THE GALLANT HIGHLANDERS WHO FOUGHT FOR SCOTLAND & PRINCE CHARLIE ARE MARKED BY THE NAMES OF THEIR CLANS.

Memorial stone, Culloden.

A magic wasteland where man is the intruder

Nature, as naked and untamed as anywhere in Britain, rules this part of lonely Sutherland. There are no towns, and fewer villages than mountain peaks. But water is everywhere: from the sea to the 6 mile long Loch Assynt, and in between so many lochans, or tiny lochs, that they gleam like gems sprinkled in the glens. It is hardly surprising to find at Inchnadamph that bears and reindeer lived here in the wild thousands of years ago. About half the tour is in and around the vast nature reserve of Inverpolly, where char swim in the deep lochs and wildcats can be seen in the forests.

1 Lochinver to Inverkirkaig From the bridge near the harbour take the road signposted to Ullapool. This is the start of what has been called 'the mad little road of Sutherland'—winding, hilly and full of pitfalls for the unwary driver. The run to Inverkirkaig is only 2½ m., but is a curtain-raiser to the grand scenery encountered throughout this tour. The road enters the Inverpolly National Nature Reserve just after swinging right beyond Inverkirkaig and crossing the River Kirkaig.

2 Inverkirkaig to Knockan Visitor Centre Keep on ahead: there are no side turnings to worry about—just 'the mad little road', which becomes narrower after the Kirkaig bridge, swinging through wooded valleys and between mountains, with a sprinkling of lochs on either side. After about 8 m. it comes to a T-junction near the end of the large Loch Bad a'Ghaill. Turn left here, following the Ullapool signpost, and drive 4 m. along the loch shore. Just beyond the loch there is a car park overlooking the deep waters of Loch Lurgainn, which offers a close-up view of the 2009 ft peak of Stac Pollaidh. Continue for another 5 m., mostly along the shore of Loch Lurgainn, to the junction with the A835. Turn left here, following the Ledmore signpost. After 3 m. turn right into the car park for Knockan Visitor Centre, which marks the eastern end of the Inverpolly National Nature Reserve.

3 Knockan Visitor Centre to Inchnadamph From the car park turn right on to the A835, and keep ahead through Knockan village and Elphin. This is a good place to stop for spectacular views of 2786 ft high Cul Mor, to the west in Drumrunie Forest, and of the twin peaks of Suilven beyond. About 3 m. past Elphin the road joins the A837. Turn left here for the 7 m. run to Inchnadamph, where hill caves have been found to contain bones of wild animals long extinct in Scotland.

4 Inchnadamph to Ardvreck Castle Continue along the A837. There are several lay-bys along the shore of Loch Assynt on the way to Ardvreck Castle, which stands beside the loch about 2 m. from Inchnadamph.

5 Ardvreck Castle to Stoer Head This is the longest leg of the tour. It runs for 26 m., first between steep mountains, then skirting the large Loch a'Chairn Bhain and the deeply indented coastline. From the castle continue north on the A837, but after 1 m. turn right on to the A894, following the signpost for Kylesku Ferry. About 3 m. beyond the junction, at the southern end of Loch na Gainmhich, an unsignposted footpath strikes off to the right to Britain's highest waterfall, Eas coul Aulin. Follow the road on down the

pass, with the formidable bulk of Quinag on the left, then turn left on to the B869 following the signpost for Drumbeg. Immediately after turning, the view to the left is dominated by the 2000 ft cliffs on the north face of Quinag. After 8 m. the road runs through Drumbeg, and 5 m. later passes Clashnessie Bay, which has a beach of red sand and good sea bathing. About 2 m. beyond Clashnessie turn right on to the road signposted to Stoer Point and at the T-junction, just under 2 m. later, turn left and follow the road to Stoer Head lighthouse.

6 Stoer Head to Clachtoll Return to the B869 and turn right. The broch at Clachtoll is on the right, 2 m. further on.

7 Clachtoll to Achmelvich Keep ahead on the B869, with the sea to the right. After almost 5 m. turn right on to the road signposted to Achmelvich.

8 Achmelvich to Lochinver Return to the B869 and turn right. After 2 m., at the junction with the A837, turn right again and follow the signpost into Lochinver.

NATURE NOTES
The route circles Inverpolly National Nature Reserve, with its wide range of habitats. On the loch shores there are bottle sedge, shoreweed and water lobelia. Divers, herring gulls and occasionally greenshank can be seen feeding. There are over 80 lochs on the reserve, the richest in bird life being those with islands to provide shelter for nesting birds such as wigeon and black-throated diver. The moorland is covered with heather, and on the grasslands there are milkwort, foxglove and bugle. Red grouse, meadow pipit and golden plover inhabit the moors and red deer can be seen. In the mountains there are snow bunting and ptarmigan. Fir clubmoss, rare on lower ground, grows here.

INFORMATION

Places of interest *Ardvreck Castle:* Daily. *Inchnadamph National Nature Reserve:* Permission must be obtained to visit between July 15 and Oct. 15. *Knockan Visitor Centre:* Inverpolly National Nature Reserve, Mon. to Fri. in summer.

Events *Lochinver:* Assynt Games and Flower Show, Aug.

Nature trail *Knockan Cliff:* circular route. 1½ m., open all year. Of geological interest; plant life on lime soil. Guide from Knockan Visitor Centre.

Ferry *Kylesku Ferry:* Between Kylesku and Kylestrome, mid-April to end Aug., 9 a.m.–9 p.m. Sept. to mid-April, 9 a.m.–dusk. Free of charge (Tel. Kylestrome 202).

Information *Dornoch:* Information Centre, The Square, Castle Street (Tel. Dornoch 400). *Lochinver:* May to Sept. (Tel. Lochinver 330).

Highland centres near to this tour:
Lairg . . . . 45 m.   Ullapool . . . . . . 36 m.
Scourie (ferry) . . 28 m.

Agate, found at Achmelvich.

ACHMELVICH
A gem-cutter's shop on the road to Achmelvich Bay displays a variety of the semi-precious stones, curious rocks and fossils which make the Sutherland coastline of special interest to geologists. Agates, beryl and chalcedony have been picked up on the white-sand beaches here; and pebbles polished into intriguing designs by the sea are not hard to find. Achmelvich has one of the best sandy bays on the Assynt coast and is a popular spot for caravan and camping holidays.

Fishing boats, Lochinver harbour.

LOCHINVER
This is one of the loveliest villages on the wild, rocky coast of what is called the Assynt district—after Loch Assynt, which empties into the sea here by way of the River Inver. Though it has a population of little more than 300, it is a popular centre in the Western Highlands for holidays and fishing. The harbour is busy when the boats return with their catch; and it was from here that many of the Highlanders, who were expelled from their crofts by harsh landowners in the last century, sailed for Australia and New Zealand.

INVERKIRKAIG
This tiny village at the mouth of the Kirkaig (*inver* meaning estuary) marks one of the entrances to the huge Inverpolly National Nature Reserve. The reserve is the biggest in the country after the Cairngorms, and the haunt of wildcats and pine martens as well as deer, foxes and badgers. Birds that may be seen include the golden eagle, buzzard, ptarmigan and ring ouzel. The Nature Conservancy warns tourists of the dangers of walking into the hills without leaving word and taking proper equipment.

Pine marten

SCALE
0   1   2   3   4   5 MILES

STOER HEAD
Stoer peninsula is a place of sandy beaches, sea birds and dwindling population. The lighthouse is perched on a 100 ft clifftop, from which visitors can look across to the Outer Hebrides. A 2 mile walk leads to the Point of Stoer, the headland, and passes the 200 ft high pillar of rock called the Old Man of Stoer, which rises sheer from the sea.

QUINAG
Between Loch Assynt and the turn-off for Drumbeg, the A894 climbs to 849 ft and is overlooked by the massive cliffs of Quinag, a many-peaked mountain which rises to 2653 ft. Little streams spurt into life all round and rush down the glens to feed the lochs. Near the highest point of the road, a track leads off to the right through wild country to Eas coul Aulin, whose vertical drop of 658 ft makes it Britain's highest waterfall. The walk is 3 miles each way over difficult country; but this can be cut to a return trip of about 1½ miles by taking a boat from Kylesku Ferry along Loch Glencoul to Loch Beag.

The view from Clachtoll (left to right): Canisp, Suilven, Cul Beag and Stac Pollaidh.

CLACHTOLL
The broch, or Pictish tower, at Clachtoll is of the type found only in Scotland, mainly in the Highlands. Relics indicate that the brochs were occupied by farmers and weavers between 100 BC and AD 50.

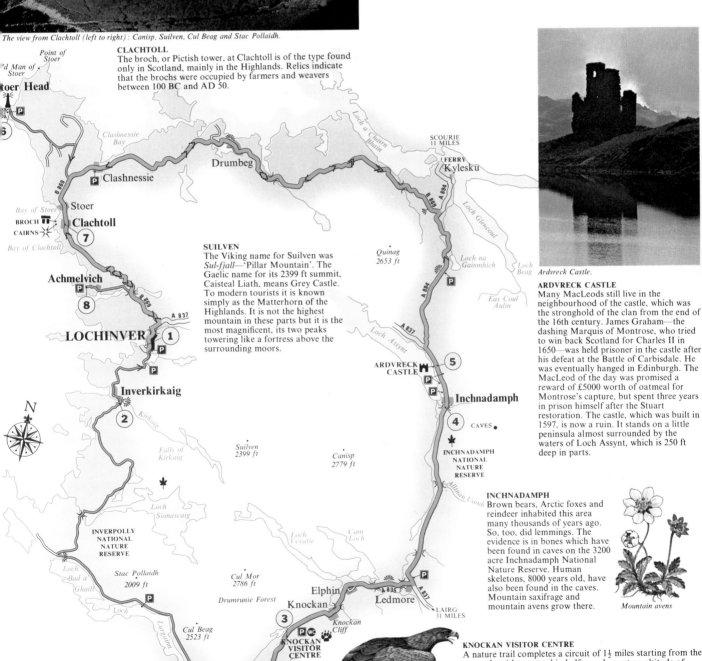

Ardvreck Castle.

SUILVEN
The Viking name for Suilven was *Sul-fjall*—'Pillar Mountain'. The Gaelic name for its 2399 ft summit, Caisteal Liath, means Grey Castle. To modern tourists it is known simply as the Matterhorn of the Highlands. It is not the highest mountain in these parts but it is the most magnificent, its two peaks towering like a fortress above the surrounding moors.

ARDVRECK CASTLE
Many MacLeods still live in the neighbourhood of the castle, which was the stronghold of the clan from the end of the 16th century. James Graham—the dashing Marquis of Montrose, who tried to win back Scotland for Charles II in 1650—was held prisoner in the castle after his defeat at the Battle of Carbisdale. He was eventually hanged in Edinburgh. The MacLeod of the day was promised a reward of £5000 worth of oatmeal for Montrose's capture, but spent three years in prison himself after the Stuart restoration. The castle, which was built in 1597, is now a ruin. It stands on a little peninsula almost surrounded by the waters of Loch Assynt, which is 250 ft deep in parts.

INCHNADAMPH
Brown bears, Arctic foxes and reindeer inhabited this area many thousands of years ago. So, too, did lemmings. The evidence is in bones which have been found in caves on the 3200 acre Inchnadamph National Nature Reserve. Human skeletons, 8000 years old, have also been found in the caves. Mountain saxifrage and mountain avens grow there.

Mountain avens

STAC POLLAIDH
The stac, meaning steep rock or conical hill, towers to 2009 ft less than a mile from the road that skirts Loch Lurgainn. The mountain's long narrow crest of weather-beaten sandstone looks like the ruined ramparts of an immense fortress.

Golden eagle

KNOCKAN VISITOR CENTRE
A nature trail completes a circuit of 1½ miles starting from the car park, with a rest cabin halfway along at an altitude of 970 ft. Visitors are advised to wear stout shoes and thick socks, and to be prepared to turn back in bad weather. Birds to be seen range from the tiny wren to the golden eagle. Knockan Cliff has attracted world attention by geologists because of its unusual formation—the older of the horizontal rock layers are at the top, due to cataclysmic earth movements 400 million years ago.

Glorious Sutherland, where a handful of people is a crowd

Sheep outnumber people by more than 1000 to one in Sutherland. Dornoch, the chief town, would be regarded as a small village in England. It is an area of dwindling population, but the beauty of its scenery is eternal—a primeval panorama of heather-clad hills and dark forests where fast-flowing rivers feed quiet lochs. Between the scattered townships, great buildings, like people, are thin on the ground. But what this tour lacks in man-made monuments it makes up in the incomparable beauty of nature and the wealth of wildlife. Golden eagles soar over the hills, salmon leap in the rivers, and near the coast the eerie wail of the great northern diver can sometimes be heard.

(1) Dornoch to Bonar Bridge Leave the town on the A949, but fork left just past the cathedral on to Sutherland Road. After 3 m., where the road runs close to a seashore golf links, follow the road round to the right. Almost immediately cross the River Evelix and continue for about 1 m. to the junction with the A9 at Clashmore. Here turn left and follow the A9 for 4½ m. to Spinningdale, where the ruins of an old cotton mill overlook the north shore of Dornoch Firth, a favourite winter resort for wild geese, and much frequented by waders in the autumn. Turn right for Migdale by the post office and, at the fork after nearly 3 m., bear left. After 1 m. turn left at the junction just beyond Migdale church and follow the road to Bonar Bridge.

(2) Bonar Bridge to the Falls of Shin Turn right on to the A836 signposted to Lairg. After 1 m. the road passes the start of the Balblair Wood Forest Trail. Continue along the shore of the Kyle of Sutherland. The road passes under the railway at Invershin, and just across the water can be seen the modern Carbisdale Castle, close to the spot where Montrose lost his last battle in 1650. The ruins of Invershin Castle are less than 1 m. further on, to the left of the road. Just beyond this point, fork left on to the A837. After 1 m., approaching Shin Forest, turn right on to the B864 signposted to Lairg and Shin Falls, and drive just over 1 m. through the forest to a short footpath on the right which leads to the falls.

(3) The Falls of Shin to Lairg Continue ahead on the B864, which hugs the bank of the River Shin, with forest and mountains on either side. Keep straight ahead at the junction where the A839 comes in from the left, cross the river bridge and follow the road left into Lairg.

(4) Lairg to Rovie Lodge Leave by the A839 signposted to Mound and Rogart. The road runs through the town from the waterfront and narrows as it passes through steep gorges alongside the railway and the River Fleet. After 9 m. Rovie Lodge gardens are on the left.

(5) Rovie Lodge to Brora Continue ahead on the A839, with the river on the right, and after 2 m., opposite Rogart post office, turn left on to the road signposted to Balnacoil Lodge. Follow the road for about 6 m. over the hills, ignoring all side turnings, to Strath Brora. The strath, or broad mountain valley, is entered where the road crosses a bridge over the River Brora. Follow the road all the way into the little coast town of Brora, a drive of

about 14 m. alongside the river and then Loch Brora, with mountains rising on either side to more than 1700 ft.

(6) Brora to Dunrobin Castle Leave Brora by the A9, turning right on the coast road towards Dornoch. The road crosses the railway and leads, 4 m. beyond Brora, to a turning on the left signposted to Dunrobin Castle.

(7) Dunrobin Castle to Golspie Rejoin the A9, turn left and follow the road for 2 m. into Golspie.

(8) Golspie to The Mound Keep ahead on the A9. After 4 m. the road passes over the railway to Loch Fleet, which is crossed by the man-made embankment known as The Mound.

(9) The Mound to Dornoch Follow the road over The Mound and, by the disused railway station, turn left on to the lochside road signposted to Embo. Drive on past the ruins of the 14th-century Skelbo Castle, originally built of wood in 1259. The name is Norse, meaning 'the place of the mussels'. Ignore the first junction and follow the road round to the right, past another disused railway station, for the 4 m. drive back to Dornoch.

NATURE NOTES
The wild country of Sutherland is a haven for many rare species of birds and animals. Birds which may be seen—especially on the shores of Loch Fleet and on The Mound—include black and red-throated divers, waders (knot, curlew, godwit, turnstone and oystercatcher), and geese in winter. Further inland there are golden eagles, buzzards, kestrels, grouse and hen harriers. There is also the chance of seeing—and hearing—the great northern diver, which sometimes spends the summer off the coast.

INFORMATION

Places of interest *Dunrobin Castle:* May to Sept., weekdays. *Rovie Lodge:* Closed until further notice due to change of ownership.

Events *Bonar Bridge:* Salmon Queen Gala Week, Aug. *Dornoch:* Highland Gathering, Aug. *Golspie:* Gala Week, Aug. Sutherland Sheep-dog Trials, Aug. Agricultural Show, Aug. Golf tournaments at Brora and Dunrobin.

Craft workshop *Brora:* Sutherland Wool Mills. Manufacture of wool from raw material to finished articles. Open weekdays, Fri. mornings only.

Forest trail *Falls of Shin:* Starts opposite footpath to Falls.

Information *Brora* (Tel. Brora 465). *Dornoch:* The Square, Castle Street (Tel. Dornoch 400).

Towns with easy access to Dornoch:
Dingwall ...... 40 m.   Tain .... 28 m.

Waterfall in Strath Brora.

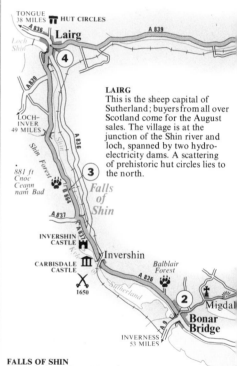

LAIRG
This is the sheep capital of Sutherland; buyers from all over Scotland come for the August sales. The village is at the junction of the Shin river and loch, spanned by two hydro-electricity dams. A scattering of prehistoric hut circles lies to the north.

FALLS OF SHIN
The turbulent River Shin races through a deep, thickly wooded gorge on its way from Loch Shin to the Kyle of Sutherland. The falls here form a staircase which salmon leap on their way to breeding waters upstream. There is a viewing platform for visitors. On the other side of the B864, opposite the footpath to the falls, is the start of a forest trail in the foothills of 881 ft high Cnoc Ceann nam Bad.

BONAR BRIDGE
The only way of crossing Dornoch Firth used to be by a ferry. In 1809 the ferry sank and more than 100 people were drowned. Then the first bridge here, since replaced, was built to cross the water where it narrows into the Kyle of Sutherland. Salmon are netted for the market just upstream. This is interesting to watch—but tourists should remember that fishing rights are totally preserved. Visitors can also watch hand weaving in a local shop.

SCALE
0   1   2   3   4   5 MILES

STRATH BRORA

The River Brora, which rises near the 1000 ft peak of Sron Leathad Chleansaid, among the wild mountains to the north-west, tumbles down scores of little waterfalls on its way to the sea. Surrounded by peaks with romantic sounding Gaelic names, the valley descends to Loch Brora, 4 miles long but less than 100 yds wide at one point. The Loch is an angler's paradise, with salmon, sea and brown trout. From the road about 3 miles round the loch, Carrol Rock can be seen across the water, towering over 500 ft high.

Carrol Rock, seen across Loch Brora.

BRORA

Its population is less than 1200, but it is the largest community in Sutherland. Brora makes whisky and cloth. It has the oldest coal mine in Scotland, which has been in operation since 1598. The fuel from here was originally used for evaporating seawater into salt. Its bridge was the only one in the whole county until Thomas Telford started building roads in the 19th century, carrying them over the rivers on iron bridges. Traffic in the harbour has dwindled almost to nothing since the first settlers from northern Scotland sailed from it in 1839 to start a new life in New Zealand. This was when the Highland clearances were going on.

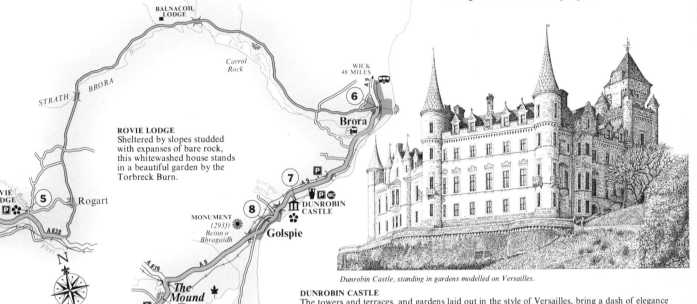

ROVIE LODGE

Sheltered by slopes studded with expanses of bare rock, this whitewashed house stands in a beautiful garden by the Torbreck Burn.

THE MOUND

This embankment, which carries the road and the railway for 1000 yds across Loch Fleet, was built in 1815 to reclaim land and replace a ferry. It sealed off the upper estuary from the sea. The area around is a nature reserve where swans, geese in winter, oystercatchers and many other birds can be seen.

Dunrobin Castle, standing in gardens modelled on Versailles.

DUNROBIN CASTLE

The towers and terraces, and gardens laid out in the style of Versailles, bring a dash of elegance to the wild coast. The oldest parts are possibly 11th century, though most of the present castle was built between 1835 and 1850, when Sir Charles Barry, the architect of the Houses of Parliament, was called in to remodel the castle. Barry's work itself had to be restored after a fire in 1915. Dunrobin is the ancient seat of the chiefs of the Sutherland clan. The staircase is hung with hunting trophies and the colours of the 93rd Sutherland Highlanders—the regiment that formed the 'thin red line' at the Battle of Balaclava in 1854. Paintings by Canaletto and Sir Joshua Reynolds share the drawing-room with 18th-century tapestries and Louis XV furniture. There is a museum in the grounds.

GOLSPIE

A statue of the 1st Duke of Sutherland (1758–1833), designed by Sir Francis Chantrey and erected in 1834, overshadows the village from the 1293 ft summit of Beinn a' Bhragaidh. A track about 3 miles long leads up to the monument from the village, and from it there are views over a wide area of north-eastern Scotland.
Golspie Burn, which runs down to the sea from Dunrobin Glen, is spanned by an old bridge. A stone inscribed in Gaelic marks the spot where Sutherland clansmen used to rally in times of trouble.

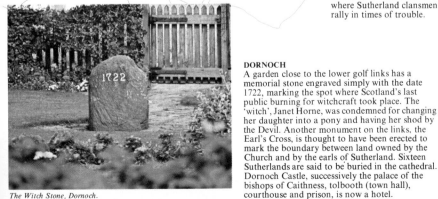
The Witch Stone, Dornoch.

DORNOCH

A garden close to the lower golf links has a memorial stone engraved simply with the date 1722, marking the spot where Scotland's last public burning for witchcraft took place. The 'witch', Janet Horne, was condemned for changing her daughter into a pony and having her shod by the Devil. Another monument on the links, the Earl's Cross, is thought to have been erected to mark the boundary between land owned by the Church and by the earls of Sutherland. Sixteen Sutherlands are said to be buried in the cathedral. Dornoch Castle, successively the palace of the bishops of Caithness, tolbooth (town hall), courthouse and prison, is now a hotel.

The bridge over Golspie Burn.

North to the land of the midnight sun

There is no need to go to the Arctic to see the phenomenon of nature's floodlighting, caused by the tilt of the North Pole towards the sun in summer. Night in the far north of Scotland is so short, especially in late June and early July, that in places such as Thurso and John o' Groats it is possible to read a newspaper out of doors at midnight, and the sky is so light that stars are seldom seen. In this area, 'the Lowlands beyond the Highlands', the land flattens out towards the coast, but the Pentland Firth and the North Sea have carved the horizontal rock layers into cliffs and chasms that give Caithness a drama of its own—by day or night.

(1) Thurso to Dunnet Head Leave the town on the A836, signposted to Castletown and John o' Groats. Beyond the town the road runs straight for 3 m. across a gently undulating plateau to Castletown, a village built to house workers in the nearby stone quarries. Caithness stone was used to pave cities all over the world during the 19th century. The industry declined severely with the advent of cement. Continue through Castletown, staying on the A836 and skirting Dunnet Bay. In the hamlet of Dunnet turn left on to the B855. Follow the road to Brough and there turn left to stay on the B855. Continue for almost 3 m. to the lighthouse at Dunnet Head.

(2) Dunnet Head to Gills Bay Return along the B855 to Brough and turn left on to a minor road. After 2 m., beside the school, turn left and continue through the scattered village of Scarfskerry. Follow the road as it swings round to the right. The Castle of Mey can be seen across the fields to the left of this road. Continue to the junction with the A836 and turn left through the hamlet of Mey. Follow the road for about 3 m., after which it skirts Gills Bay. The Island of Stroma can be seen north of the bay.

(3) Gills Bay to John o' Groats Continue on the road past the bay and after 1 m. reach Kirkstyle, with Canisbay Kirk, where one of the De Groot family is buried. Keep to the A836 for 3 m., and at the junction with the A9 take the left turn, signposted to John o' Groats. Follow the A9 to the hotel and the clifftop.

(4) John o' Groats to Duncansby Head Return along the A9, passing the junction with the A836. About 200 yds beyond the junction turn left on to a minor road, and follow this for about 2 m. to the magnificent cliff scenery at Duncansby Head.

(5) Duncansby Head to Wick Return by the same route to the A9 and turn left. Follow the A9 across low hills and moorland for about 4 m. After this, the road follows the almost deserted coast for a further 14 m. into Wick. The few fishing and crofting communities that dot this stretch of road are witness to the rugged nature of this coast.

(6) Wick to Dounreay Leave the town on the A882, following the Thurso signpost. The road runs inland across rich farmland dotted with trees and grazing cattle, a complete contrast to the rugged coastline. After 8 m., at the crossroads in the village of Watten, turn left on to the B870, following the signpost for Mybster. Beyond Watten the landscape reverts to rough moorlands. After 7 m., at the junction with the A895, keep straight ahead to stay on the B870. After 3 m. cross the River Thurso, then turn right, still on the B870, and cross the railway near Scotscalder station. Continue for 2 m., then turn left off the B870 on to a minor road that passes the end of Loch Calder. Follow the road round to the right, signposted to Broubster, and after 3 m., at the T-junction, turn right to follow the signpost to Shebster. In Shebster turn left at the junction and continue for about 2½ m. to the junction with the A836 just east of Reay. Turn right on to the A836. After 1 m. the Experimental Reactor Station at Dounreay is on the left.

(7) Dounreay to Crosskirk Continue on the A836 for 4 m., then just after Bridge of Forss turn left on to the minor road leading to the village of Crosskirk. A short walk along the cliffs to the west leads to the ruined chapel of St Mary.

(8) Crosskirk to Thurso Return to the A836 and turn left for Thurso. Follow the road past low hills, and after about 3 m. a detour to the left on to the A882 leads to Scrabster, a sheltered fishing harbour and lifeboat station. It was from this harbour that HMS *Hampshire* sailed in 1916, with Lord Kitchener, the War Secretary, on board. The cruiser sank off the Orkneys and Kitchener was drowned. Thurso is ½ m. beyond the A882 junction on the A836.

NATURE NOTES
The high coastal cliffs abound in guillemots, black guillemots, puffins, kittiwakes and fulmars. These birds are seen at their best in spring and early summer. Round Dunnet Bay two rare coastal plants grow: Baltic rush and curved sedge. Inland, ducks, including pochard and goldeneye, inhabit the lochs, many of which are fringed with yellow iris, bogbean and amphibious bistort.

INFORMATION

Places of interest *Castle of Mey:* Gardens only, summer (dates from local Tourist Office). *Dounreay:* Atomic station exhibition May to Sept., weekdays. *Thurso:* Folk Museum, May to Oct., weekdays. Town Museum and Library, weekdays. *Wick:* Carnegie Library and Museum, weekdays. Castle of Old Wick, closed when adjoining rifle range is in use. Noss Head lighthouse, afternoons.

Craft workshop Caithness glass, Harrowhill, Wick. Conducted tours, weekdays. Showroom, Sat.

Events *Thurso:* Highland Games, July. *Wick:* Gala week, July. *Mey:* Sheep-dog trials, Aug. *Thurso or Wick* (alternate years): Agricultural Show, July.

Information *Thurso:* Car park. Riverside (Tel. Thurso 2371). *Wick:* Whitechapel Road (Tel. Wick 2596 or 2145).

Towns with easy access to Thurso:
Helmsdale . . . . . 44 m.   Tongue . . . . 44 m.

DUNNET HEAD
Sand yachting is a popular sport in Dunnet Bay, under the shadow of cliffs topped by a lighthouse from which there are views of the Orkneys. Most prominent of the islands that can be seen from the promontory is Hoy, with cliffs at some points 1000 ft high, and the rock known as the Old Man of Hoy dominating the horizon. It is also possible on a clear day to see Cape Wrath, almost 60 miles away to the west. Thousands of sea birds nest on the cliffs below the headland. These include guillemots, razorbills and parrot-billed puffins.

THURSO
The old town near the narrow harbour is made up of pleasant 18th-century stone houses and owes much to Sir John Sinclair, MP for Caithness from 1790 to 1811, and one of the more enlightened landowners during the Highland Clearances. Another famous son of Thurso was Robert Dick, a baker who became a leading 19th-century botanist and geologist. He discovered several plants new to Britain including holy grass, a scented grass used in Poland to flavour vodka. His collection is housed in the town museum. Also on show there are two early Christian symbol stones and a cross inscribed with Scandinavian lettering of a style dating from the 2nd century, which was found in a ruined church near the harbour. There is a folk museum in the Town Hall. A circular building with a conical roof houses the Meadow Well, for centuries the town's only source of water.

Holy grass

CROSSKIRK
Reached by a footpath, the ruined chapel of St Mary's at Crosskirk Bay overlooks a quiet rocky cove at the point where Forss Water joins the sea. The chapel dates from the 12th century and is said to be the oldest in Caithness. To the east of the bay lies Brims Ness headland, topped by the remains of a 16th-century castle.

Dounreay Experimental Reactor Station.

SCALE

0   1   2   3   4   5 MILES

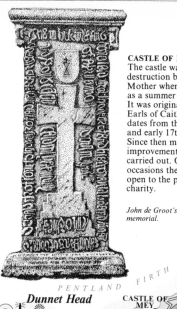

John de Groot's memorial.

CASTLE OF MEY
The castle was rescued from destruction by the Queen Mother when she bought it as a summer home in 1952. It was originally built for the Earls of Caithness and dates from the late 16th and early 17th centuries. Since then many improvements have been carried out. On very rare occasions the grounds are open to the public in aid of charity.

JOHN O' GROATS
Although Dunnet Head is 2 miles closer to the Arctic Circle, John o' Groats, 876 miles from Land's End, is commonly regarded as the last point on the mainland of Britain. The name dates from 1496 when James IV of Scotland, anxious to establish closer links with the Orkneys, gave three Dutchmen, the De Groot brothers, permission to run a ferry from Caithness to the islands. The service ran for 250 years. John de Groot chose an elaborate way to settle a dispute about who should sit at the head of the table when the family, who by then numbered eight, met to celebrate their arrival in Scotland. He built an eight-sided house in which he put eight doors and an octagonal table. A flagged mound marks the spot where the house once stood. One of the family, another John de Groot, died in 1568 and is buried at Canisbay Kirk, 3 m. west of John o' Groats, just off the A836. His ornately carved memorial stone stands against the church wall. A type of small cowrie shell, unique to this part of Britain, and known as the Groatie Buckie, is found on the sands below the cliffs. From the top of the cliffs there are views across the Pentland Firth to the Orkney Islands.

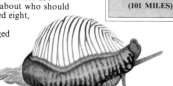

Groatie Buckie, shellfish found at John o' Groats.

DUNCANSBY HEAD
Horizontal rock strata of almost mathematical precision make the cliffs among the most striking in Britain. From the Head, the cliffs plunge to deep seas, 300 ft below. A short walk to the south reveals caves, chasms and stacks carved by the sea like the Thirl Door, a natural arch, the 218 ft Little Stack and the more massive Muckle Stack, 297 ft above the sea—higher than some of the cliffs. To the north the horizon is broken by the Orkneys and the Pentland Skerries, a cluster of small islands on which stands the second oldest lighthouse in Britain, built in 1794 with twin towers. To the south of Duncansby Head lighthouse, marking the gateway between the North Sea and the Atlantic, is Humlie's Hole, a natural arch joining the cliff to a stack of rock in the sea. Large colonies of sea birds nest in the cliffs in May and June.

Muckle Stack, Duncansby Head.

GILLS BAY
Low grassy dunes conceal the beach from the road, and it is possible, by approaching cautiously, to watch seals basking in the sun or splashing in the deep pools left by the tide. From St John's Point, to the east of the bay, a vicious tide-race known as 'The Merry Men of Mey' runs out towards Hoy. The *North Sea Pilot*, a guide to mariners produced by the Admiralty, warns that the violence of this race, particularly in gales, 'can hardly be exaggerated'. At low tide there are patches of sand on the shingle beach.

WICK
This town of sturdy greystone houses has been a royal burgh since 1589. To the south of the River Wick lies the newer part, built by the British Fishery Society as a model fishing village in the 19th century and laid out by the engineer Thomas Telford. Though the fishing trade has declined in this century, fishing boats still throng the harbour in the early morning. In Harrowhill is the Caithness glass factory, established in 1960, where craftsmen can be seen producing high-quality ware by hand. South of the town are the ruined castle of Old Wick and the 300 ft high Brig o' Trams, a natural arch. To the north, at Noss Head, is a small lighthouse and, near by, the ruins of Girnigoe and Sinclair castles, built by the Earls of Caithness in the 16th and 17th centuries.

Glass engraving, Wick.

DOUNREAY
The spherical atomic reactor and chimneys of the Experimental Reactor Station bring an air of science fiction to the Caithness coast. Built in the 1950s at a cost of almost £30 million, the station houses an experimental 'fast' reactor. It uses plutonium fuel, 1 ton of which produces 18,000 million units of electricity for the National Grid system. In a conventional power station 1 ton of coal produces 2400 units of electricity. The reactor was the first of its kind to generate electricity for public use. It also acts as a testing station for new processes and materials used in nuclear engineering. From May to September there is an exhibition which explains the project in simple terms.

A wall of Caithness stone.

CAITHNESS WALLS
In western Caithness, where stone is plentiful, the fields are divided by 'fences' or walls of upright slabs of Caithness stone—the stone that used to be exported in the 19th century from Thurso. These slender slabs give Caithness much of its distinctive, austere character. The stone is also used for building local houses and garden walls, and for making roof tiles. The mason's craft is still very much alive here.

The harbour at Wick.

INDEX

Tour centres and special features are shown in **bold type**; places fully described on the tours are shown in roman type; all other places are shown in *italic type*.

L

Lacock 60-61
Lairg 404-5
Lake Side 318-19
Lake Vyrnwy 218-19
Lakenheath 160-1
Lakeside and Haverthwaite Railway 318-19
Lamberhurst 96-97
Lambert's Castle 38-39
Lambourn 124-5
Lambton Lion Park 342-3
Lammermuir Hills 364-5
Lamphey 180-1
Lamphey Palace 180-1
Lamplugh 326-7
Lamport 256-7
Lancaster (Tour 109) 292-3
Lanchester 342-3
Landewednack 10-11
Landmark Visitor Centre 392-3
Land's End 8-9
Lanehead 336-7
Lanercost Priory 330-1
Langar 278-9
Langdale Pikes 318-19, 322-3
Langford 116-17
Langstone, Gwent 196-7
Langstone, Hants. 74-75
Langtoft 304-5
Langton Matravers 48-49
Lanherne House 12-13
Lanhydrock House 14-15
Lansallos 14-15
Lapworth 240-1
Largs (Tour 136) 366-7
Lastingham 311-12
Latimer 128-9
Latteridge 52-53
Lavenham 158-9
Laverstoke 90-91
Lawers 374-5
Laxfield 168-9
Laxton, Notts. 276-7
Layer Marney 156-7
Layer-de-la-Haye 156-7
Ledburn 126-7
Ledbury 228-9
Ledsham 284-5
Lee Bay 20-21
Lee Moor 18-19
Leeford 28-29
Leek 264-5
Leigh 42-43
Leighton 248-9
Leighton Buzzard 126-7
Leighton Hall 292-3
Leighton Moss 292-3
Leiston 166-7
Leiston Abbey 166-7
Leith Hall 390-1
Leith Hill 86-87
Lelant Model Village 8-9
Lepe 68-69
Leppington 304-5
Lesbury 344-5
Letchworth 142-3
Letcombe Regis 124-5
Letheringham 166-7
Letheringsett 172-3
Leuchars 372-3
Leuchars House 394-5
Levens Hall 320-1
Ley Mill 128-9
Leyburn 308-9
Leys, The 22-23
Libanus 88-89
Liddington Castle 66-67

Lilford Park 258-9
Lilleshall Abbey 248-9
Linacre Reservoir 270-1
Lincoln (Tour 103) 280-1
Lindale 318-19
Lindisfarne Castle 346-7
Lindisfarne Nature Reserve 344-5
Lindsey 164-5
Lingholm Gardens 326-7
Linn Park 366-7
Linslade 126-7
Linton-on-Ouse 302-3
Liscombe 34-35
Little Badminton 52-53
Little Brampton 246-7
Little Brickhill 134-5
Little Brington 256-7
Little Cheverell 62-63
Little Coxwell 116-17
Little Dunmow 154-5
Little Gaddesden 128-9
Little Horwood 134-5
Little Hucklow 270-1
Little Mell Fell 322-3
Little Moreton Hall 264-5
Little Sodbury 52-53
Little Somerford 60-61
Little Walsingham 172-3
Little Wittenham 122-3
Littlebredy 38-39
Littlestone-on-Sea 108-9
Litton Cheney 38-39
Liverton 26-27
Lizard Point 10-11
Llanaelhaearn 202-3
Llanarmon Dyffryn Ceiriog 218-19
Llanarmon-yn-Ial 216-17
Llanarthney 184-5
Llanbedrgoch 200-1
Llanberis 205-6
Llanberis Railway 204-5
Llanbrynmair 212-13
Llandanwg 210-11
Llanddeiniolen 204-5
Llanddwyn Bay 200-1
Llanddwyn Island 200-1
Llandeilo 184-5
Llandeusant 198-9
Llandona 200-1
Llaneilian 198-9
Llanelltyd 210-11
Llanerfyl 218-19
Llanfair 210-11
Llanfair Caereinion 218-19
Llanfair-Discoed 196-7
Llanfairpwllgwyngyll 200-1
Llanferres 216-17
Llanfihangel Crucorney 194-5
Llanfihangel Glyn Myfr 216-17
Llangadfan 218-19
Llangadog 184-5
Llangadwaladr 198-9
Llangefni (Tour 72) 198-9
Llangoed 200-1
Llangollen (Tour 79) 216-17
Llangranog 183-4
Llangrove 224-5
Llangurig 212-13
Llangybi 196-7
Llanidloes 212-13
Llanmor 202-3
Llanrhaeadr Waterfall 218-19
Llanrhaeadr-ym-Mochnant 218-19
Llanrian 178-9
Llansantffraid-ym-Mechain 226-7
Llansawel 184-5
Llanthony Priory 194-5
Llanuwchllyn 210-11
Llanwddyn 218-19

Llanwrda 184-5
Llanyblodwel 218-19
Llanychaer 178-9
Llanynghenedl 198-9
Llanystumdwy 202-3
Llechwedd Slate Cavern 214-15
Llithfaen 202-3
Lloyd George Museum 202-3
Llugwy Gorge 214-15
Llyn Celyn 210-11
Llyn Clywedog 221-2
Llyn Dinas 214-15
Llyn Gwynant 214-15
Llyn Idwal 204-5
Llyn Ogwen 204-5
Llyn Padarn 204-5
Llyn Tegid 210-11
Llyn Trawsfynydd 200-1
Llyn Tryweryn 200-1
Loch a' Chairn Bhain 402-3
Loch Ailort 384-5
Loch an Eilein 392-3
Loch Assynt 402-3
Loch Awe 380-1
Loch Bad a' Ghaill 402-3
Loch Beag 402-3
Loch Calder 406-7
Loch Eil 384-5
Loch Fadn 386-7
Loch Fyne 380-1
Loch Garten 392-3
Loch Gilp 380-1
Loch Greshornish 386-7
Loch Insh 392-3
Loch Leathan 386-7
Loch Linnhe 384-5
Loch Lochy 384-5
Loch Lurgainn 402-3
Loch Mealt 386-7
Loch Mhor 400-1
Loch Moidart 384-5
Loch Morlich 392-3
Loch na Ghainmhich 402-3
Loch na Keal 374-5
Loch Ness 400-1
Loch Puladdern 392-3
Loch Rusky 370-1
Loch Ryan 352-3
Loch Scridain 374-5
Loch Shiel 384-5
Loch Snizort 386-7
Loch Sunart 384-5
Loch Tay 374-5
Loch Thom 366-7
Lochan na Lairige 374-5
Lochawe 380-1
Lochend 354-5
Lochfoot 354-5
Lochinver (Tour 150) 402-3
Lockeridge 66-67
Lockwood Reservoir 310-11
Loddon 170-1
Lode 148-9
Logan Bay 352-3
Logan Gardens 352-3
Lomeswater 326-7
Long Bredy 38-39
Long Marston 242-3
Long Melford 159-60
Long Mynd 246-7
Long Preston 300-1
Long Sutton, Hants. 76-77
Long Sutton, Som. 40-41
Long Wittenham 122-3
Longdon 230-1
Longdon upon Tern 248-9
Longford 166-7
Longframlington 344-5
Longhoughton 344-5
Longleat House 58-59
Longnor 264-5
Longridge, Lancs. 290-1
Longstock 90-91

Looe 14-15
Lord Wantage Memorial 124-5
Lorton Fells 326-7
Lorton, High and Low 326-7
Lossie Forest 394-5
Lossiemouth 394-5
Lostock Gralam 286-7
Lostwithiel 14-15
Louth (Tour 104) 282-3
Low Dalby 312-13
Lower Bentham 292-3
Lower Brailes 242-3
Lower Brockhampton 228-9
Lower Chicksgrove 64-65
Lower Slaughter 238-9
Loweswater 326-7
Lowick, Northants. 258-9
Lowick, Northld 346-7
Lowther 324-5
Loxhore Cott 20-21
Luce Bay 352
Ludlow (Tour 82) 226-7
Ludwell 64-65
Lullingstone Villa 110-11
Lulworth Cove 48-49
Lune Valley 320-1, 324-5
Lusby 282-3
Luton Hoo 142-3
Luxborough 34-35
Lydford 18-19
Lydlinch 42-43
Lyme Hall 262-3
Lyme Regis (Tour 14) 38-39
Lymebridge 16-17
Lyminge 116-17
Lyminge Forest 108-9
Lymington 68-69
Lymm 286-7
Lympne 108-9
Lyndhurst (Tour 27) 68-69
Lyne Water 362-3
Lyneham 60-61
Lynmouth 20-21
Lynon Windmill 198-9
Lynton 20-21
Lytes Cary 40-41
Lythe 312-13

M

Macclesfield Canal 264-5
Machynlleth (Tour 77) 212-13
Macleod's Tables 386-7
Madingley 144-5
Madingley Hall 144-5
Maenaddwyn 200-1
Maentwrog 210-11
Maesbury 244-5
Maggieknockater 244-5
Maiden Bradley 64-65
Maiden Castle, Dors. 44-45
Maiden Castle, N. Yorks. 306-7
Maiden Newton 42-43
Maidwell 256-7
Malham 300-1
Malham Cove 300-1
Malham Tarn 300-1
Mallory Park 254-5
Malltraeth Cob 200-1
Mallwyd 212-13
Malmesbury (Tour 23) 60-61
Malmsead 34-35
Malton (Tour 113) 304-5
Malvern, Great (Tour 83) 228-9

Mam Tor 270-1
Man o' War Beach 48-49
Manaton 26-27
Manorbier 180-1
Manordeifi 182-3
Manton 26-27
Mappowder 42-43
Marazion 8-9
March 146-7
Marhamchurch 16-17
Market Bosworth 254-5
Market Deeping 260-1
Market Harborough (Tour 93) 256-7
Market Lavington 62-63
Market Rasen 280-1
Marks Tey 156-7
Marlborough (Tour 26) 66-67
Marldon 26-27
Marloes Sands 180-1
Marple 262-3
Marquis of Anglesey's Column 200-1
Marshwood 38-39
Marske 306-7
Marston Magna 40-41
Marston Moor 302-3
Martinhoe 20-21
Martin's Haven 180-1
Martinshoe 44-45
Martley 228-9
Martock 40-41
Masham 308-9
Mathry 178-9
Matlock (Tour 99) 268-9
Maulden Wood 140-1
Mauley Cross 312-13
Maumbury Rings 44-45
Mavis Enderby 282-3
Mawgan Porth 12-13
Mawnan Smith 10-11
Maxstoke 240-1
Meall Cuanail 380-1
Meare 36-37
Meavy 18-19
Medina Valley 70-71
Medlam 282-3
Medmenham Abbey 128-9
Meerbrook 264-5
Melandra Castle 262-3
Melbourne 254-5
Melbourne Hall 254-5
Melbury Abbas 46-47
Meldons 362-3
Melford Hall 158-9
Melin-y-wig 216-17
Melksham 60-61
Mellerstain House 356-7
Melmerby 330-1
Melrose Abbey 356-7
Melton 166-7
Melton Mowbray (Tour 102) 278-9
Melverley 244-5
Membury 28-29
Memus 388-9
Menai Bridge (Tour 73) 200-1
Men-an-Tol 8-9
Mendip Hills 36-37, 50-51
Meppershall 140-1
Mere 64-65
Mereworth 110-11
Meriden 240-1
Merrick 368-9
Merriott 40-41
Merrivale 24-25
Merrow 88-89
Methwold 160-1
Methwold Hythe 160-1
Mey 406-7
Mickle Fell 306-7
Mickleton, Glos. 242-3
Mickleton, N. Yorks. 340-1
Mid Lavant 84-85

Subject Index

People

The Country Code

GUARD AGAINST FIRE Carelessness may cost hundreds of thousands of pounds, and disrupt the natural life of a large area. Do not throw away lighted matches or cigarettes. Do not leave bottles or jars to focus the sun's rays and start fires.

FASTEN ALL GATES A farm animal on a road may cause a serious accident or, if it gets into the wrong field, gorge itself to death. A cow is worth about £200.

KEEP DOGS UNDER PROPER CONTROL The friendly household pet may prove a killer in the open countryside. Almost 5000 sheep – worth £100,000 – are killed by visiting dogs each year. Remember that a farmer can shoot a dog worrying his animals, and claim for losses.

KEEP TO THE PATHS ACROSS FARM LAND The law obliges all walkers in the countryside to keep to public footpaths. Even grass is a valuable crop. Remember that what seems to be grass may be more costly wheat, oats, barley or hay.

AVOID DAMAGING FENCES, HEDGES AND WALLS Fencing can cost £1 a yard, and drystone walls £8 a yard.

LEAVE NO LITTER Take home litter after a picnic. It is unsightly, and it can kill farm animals.

SAFEGUARD WATER SUPPLIES Most of the water used in Britain comes from country streams and reservoirs. Do not pollute them with rubbish and waste food, or allow them to be used as lavatories.

PROTECT WILD LIFE, WILD PLANTS AND TREES The countryside is a closely knit community of animals, plants and trees – all of them depending on the others for survival. Do not pick or root up flowers or break off branches.

GO CAREFULLY ON COUNTRY ROADS The unsuspected tractor or a milling flock of sheep, hidden by a corner, can cause a serious and expensive accident. When walking, keep to the right in single file, facing oncoming traffic, if there is no footpath.

RESPECT THE LIFE OF THE COUNTRYSIDE Country people are often suspicious of summer visitors from the towns, with good reason. Do not harm animals, farm machinery or property. Obey the Country Code.

Useful addresses

Ancient Monuments Society
33 Ladbroke Square, London W11 3NB
01-221 6178

Association for the Preservation of Rural
Scotland
1 Thistle Court, Edinburgh EH2 1DE
031-225 6744

Automobile Association
Fanum House, Basing View, Basingstoke,
Hants. RG21 2EA
Basingstoke 20123

British Caravanners' Club
383 Harehills Lane, Leeds LS9 6AP
Leeds 453284

British Federation of Hotel & Guest House
Associations
23 Abingdon Street, Blackpool FY1 1DG
Blackpool 24241

British Federation of Music Festivals
106 Gloucester Place, London W1H 3DB
01-935 6371

British Hotels & Restaurants Association
20 Upper Brook Street, London W1Y 2BH
01-499 6641

British Naturalists' Association
Willowfield, Boyneswood Road, Four Marks,
Alton, Hants. GU34 5EA
Medstead 3659

British Ornithologists' Union
Zoological Society of London,
Regent's Park, London NW1 4RY
01-586 4443

British Tourist Authority
64 St James's Street, London SW1A 1NF
01-629 9191

British Waterways Board
Melbury House, Melbury Terrace,
London NW1 6JX
01-262 6711

Camping Club of Great Britain & Ireland Ltd
11 Lower Grosvenor Place, London SW1 0EY
01-828 1012

Caravan Club
65 South Molton Street, London W1Y 2AB
01-629 6441

Civic Trust
17 Carlton House Terrace, London SW1Y 5AW
01-930 0914

Commons, Open Spaces and Footpaths
Preservation Society
166 Shaftesbury Avenue, London WC2H 8JH
01-836 7220

Council for British Archaeology
7 Marylebone Road, London NW1 5HA
01-486 1527

Council for the Protection of Rural England
4 Hobart Place, London SW1W 0HY
01-235 4771

Council for the Protection of Rural Wales
14 Broad Street, Welshpool, Powys SY21 7SD
Meifod 383

Council for Small Industries in Rural Areas
35 Camp Road, Wimbledon Common,
London SW19 4UP
01-947 6761

Countryside Commission
1 Cambridge Gate, Regent's Park,
London NW1 4JY
01-935 5533

Countryside Commission for Scotland
Battleby House, Redgorton, Perth PH1 3EW
Perth 27921

Craftsmen Potters Association of Great
Britain Ltd
William Blake House, Marshall Street,
London W1V 1LP
01-437 7605

Department of the Environment
2 Marsham Street, London SW1P 3EB
01-212 3434

Forestry Commission
231 Corstorphine Road, Edinburgh EH12 7AT
031-334 0303

HMSO
PO Box 569, London SE1 9NH or
49 High Holborn, London WC1V 6HB
01-928 6977

HMSO (Scotland)
13a Castle Street, Edinburgh 2
031-225 6333

HMSO (Wales)
41 The Hayes, Cardiff
Cardiff 23654

Museums Association
87 Charlotte Street, London W1P 2BX
01-636 4600

National Gardens Scheme
57 Lower Belgrave Street, London SW1W 0LR
01-730 0355

National Trust for Places of Historic Interest
or Natural Beauty
42 Queen Anne's Gate, London SW1H 9AS
01-930 0211

National Trust for Scotland
5 Charlotte Square, Edinburgh EH2 4DU
031-226 5922

Nature Conservancy
19-20 Belgrave Square, London SW1X 8PY
01-235 3241

Ordnance Survey
Romsey Road, Maybush,
Southampton SO9 4DH
Southampton 775555

Royal Society for the Protection of Birds
The Lodge, Sandy, Beds. SG19 2DL
Sandy 80551

Scottish Canals
Caledonian Canal Office,
Clachnaharry, Inverness IV3 6RA
Inverness 33140

Scottish Wildlife Trust
8 Dublin Street, Edinburgh EH1 3PP
031-556 4199

Society for the Promotion of Nature Reserves
The Green, Nettleham, Lincoln LN2 2NR
Lincoln 52326

Society for the Protection of Ancient Buildings
55 Great Ormond Street, London WC1N 3JA
01-405 2646

Youth Hostels Association
Trevelyan House, 8 St Stevens Hill,
St Albans, Herts. AL1 2DY
St Albans 55215

TOURIST BOARDS

English Tourist Board
4 Grosvenor Gardens, London SW1W 0DU
01-730 3400

Cumbria Tourist Board
Ellerthwaite, Windermere, Cumbria
Windermere 4444

East Anglia Tourist Board
14 Museum Street, Ipswich, Suffolk IP1 1HU
Ipswich 214211

East Midlands Tourist Board
Bailgate, Lincoln LN1 3AR
Lincoln 31521

Heart of England Tourist Board
65 High Street, Worcester WR1 2EW
Worcester 29511

North West Tourist Board
119 The Piazza, Piccadilly Plaza,
Manchester M1 4AN
061-236 0393

Northumbria Tourist Board
Prudential Building, 140-50 Pilgrim Street,
Newcastle upon Tyne NE1 6TQ
Newcastle upon Tyne 28795

South East England Tourist Board
Cheviot House, 4-6 Monson Road,
Tunbridge Wells, Kent TN1 1NH
Tunbridge Wells 33066

Thames & Chilterns Tourist Board
8 The Market Place, Abingdon, Oxon
Abingdon 4344

West Country Tourist Board
Trinity Court, Southernhay East,
Exeter, Devon EX1 1QS
Exeter 76351

Yorkshire, Cleveland & Humberside Tourist
Board
312 Tadcaster Road, York YO2 2HF
York 97961

Scottish Tourist Board
23 Ravelston Terrace, Edinburgh EH4 3EU
031-332 2433

Wales Tourist Board
Welcome House, Llandaff, Cardiff CF5 2YZ
Cardiff 566133

Acknowledgments

The photographs in this book are by the following photographers:

THE NUMBER IN BRACKETS REFERS TO THE NUMBER ON THE TOUR MAP

8-9 (1) Patrick Thurston (2) Martyn Chillmaid (9) West Cornwall Museum of Mechanical Music (10) Spectrum Colour Library

10-11 (2) & (4) Patrick Thurston (5) Mary Evans Picture Library (6) Homer Sykes (7) Martyn Chillmaid

12-13 (3) Michael St Maur Sheil (5) Patrick Thurston (7) & (10) Martyn Chillmaid

14-15 (2) & (5) Michael St Maur Sheil (9) & (11) Martyn Chillmaid

16-17 (5) Patrick Thurston (6) Penny Tweedie (7) Mike Newton

18-19 (3) & (5) Martyn Chillmaid (7) Morwellham Quay Centre for Recreation & Education (9) Robert Harding Associates

20-21 (1) & (5) Penny Tweedie (4) Martyn Chillmaid

22-23 (2) Penny Tweedie (3) Martyn Chillmaid (5) both Malcolm Aird

24-25 (1) Martyn Chillmaid (4) Mary Evans Picture Library (6) & (8) British Tourist Authority. Dartmoor ponies—Penny Tweedie

26-27 (1) & (2) Martyn Chillmaid (5) Penny Tweedie

28-29 (1) Martyn Chillmaid (5) & (8) Patrick Thurston

30-33 Gorgon's Head—British Tourist Authority. 'Comforts of Bath'—Mansell Collection. Roman Baths and Door of Bath Abbey—Gordon Moore. Costume— Museum of Costume, Assembly Rooms, Pulteney Bridge and Royal Crescent— John Vigurs. No. 1 Royal Crescent and Sampler—Michael Holford. Dr Oliver and Beau Nash—Bowell Studio. Queen Charlotte—National Portrait Gallery

34-35 (1) Penny Tweedie (3) Spectrum Colour Library (5) and Exmoor—Patrick Thurston

36-37 (1) Admiral Blake Museum (3) Martyn Chillmaid. Sedgemoor and withy harvesting—Gordon Moore

38-39 (1) Michael St Maur Shiel (2) British Tourist Authority (4) Patrick Thurston (5) Martyn Chillmaid

40-41 (2) & (8) Martyn Chillmaid (9) Robert Harding Associates (3) Penny Tweedie

42-43 (4) Robert Harding Associates (5) Patrick Thurston (6) & (9) Martyn Chillmaid

44-45 (1) Mary Evans Picture Library (2) & (7) Martyn Chillmaid (3) Robert Harding Associates (5) Mansell Collection (8) Penny Tweedie

46-47 (2) Robert Harding Associates (4) & (7) Martyn Chillmaid (5) Malcolm Aird

48-49 (5) C. M. Dixon (6) & (7) Martyn Chillmaid

50-51 (1) Susan Griggs Picture Agency (2) British Tourist Authority (3) Robert Harding Associates (6) Gordon Moore

52-53 (3) & (6) Spectrum Colour Library (7) Martyn Chillmaid

54-55 Victoria and Albert Museum

56-57 Malcolm Aird

58-59 (2) Penny Tweedie (5) Robert Harding Associates (6) Anthony Miles, William Pitt—Mary Evans Picture Library (7) Sunset—Spectrum Colour Library. Merlin —British Museum

60-61 (1) Penny Tweedie (2) Spectrum Colour Library (4) Mansell Collection. Lacock Abbey—Jonathan Moore (8) Malcolm Aird

62-63 (1) & (3) Malcolm Aird (6) E. S. Risdon (8) Martyn Chillmaid

64-65 (3) Malcolm Aird. Chevy Chase—Martyn Chillmaid (4) National Trust (5) Martyn Chillmaid (8) Robert Harding Associates

66-67 (4) & (10) Malcolm Aird (6) & (8) Robert Harding Associates

68-69 (1) & (4) Martyn Chillmaid (6) George Rodger. New Forest pony—Robert Harding Associates

70-71 (2) & (4) Tony Evans (6) Martyn Chillmaid (10) Angelo Hornak

72-73 (1) Osborne House—Ian Yeomans. Castle Point—Angelo Hornak (4) Osborn-Smith's Wax Museum

74-75 (1) Spectrum Colour Library (2) Mary Evans Picture Library (3) & (5) Martyn Chillmaid (7) Vineyard—Spectrum Colour Library. Inn sign—Michael St Maur Sheil

76-77 (1) Robert Harding Associates (4) Birds & (7) Martyn Chillmaid. Selbourne— Birds & Country Magazine (5) Patrick Thurston

78-79 (3) British Tourist Authority (5) Bridget Morley (6) Eric Meacher (10) Martyn Chillmaid

80-83 Philip Dowell: except Turrets of Pavilion and rock shop—Peter Keen; Posset pots—Eric Meacher

84-85 (2) & (10) Ian Yeomans (4) Peter Phillips (8) A. F. Kersting (9) Victoria and Albert Museum

86-87 (2) Malcolm Aird (3) Mary Evans Picture Library (6) Victoria and Albert Museum (8) Spectrum Colour Library. Nymans Gardens—National Trust

88-89 (1) A. F. Kersting (2) National Trust (5) Spectrum Colour Library (8) Eric Meacher

90-91 (3) Martyn Chillmaid (5) Chris Morris (8) Michael St Maur Sheil (9) British Publishing Corporation

92-95 Malcolm Aird: except King Arthur's Round Table—Michael Holford

96-97 (1) Victoria and Albert Museum—R. B. Fleming (2) Martyn Chillmaid (5) British Tourist Authority (7) Penny Tweedie (8) Malcolm Aird

98-99 (2) & (8) Malcolm Aird (4) National Trust (11) Peter Phillips

100-1 (1) British Tourist Authority (6) Bridget Morley (7) National Trust (8) Martyn Chillmaid

102-3 Mike Wells

104-5 Mike Wells: except The lantern—Penny Tweedie

106-7 (3) Michael Holford (4) Martyn Chillmaid (8) Malcolm Aird (10) Martin Weaver

108-9 (1) & (11) Malcolm Aird (6) Ian Yeomans (10) Martyn Chillmaid

110-11 (1) National Trust (2) Martyn Chillmaid (4) Spectrum Colour Library (5) & (8) Martyn Chillmaid (6) A. Blake The Picture Library

112-13 Malcolm Aird: except Naval College from the Isle of Dogs by Canaletto—National Maritime Museum, London

114-15 Malcolm Aird: except The Battle of Lepanto; Portrait of Inigo Jones by Dobson; The Time Ball O.R.O.—National Maritime Museum, London

116-17 (1) Michael Hardy (2) Patrick Thurston (7) Rev. Fletcher Campbell (9) Martin Weaver
118-21 Merton, All Souls, punts and gargoyle—Adam Woolfit. Window at Christ Church—Sonia Halliday. Duke Humphrey's Library—Thomas Photos. 'St Jerome in the Wilderness'—Ashmolean Library. Microscope—Tony Evans. New College—Peter Keen.
122-3 (2) Michael Hardy (3) Chris Morris (4) Great Western Railway Society (8) Philip Llewellin
124-5 (2) Brian Shuel Expression (4) John Perkins (7) & (9) Michael Hardy
126-7 (1) Philip Llewellin (3) & (7) National Trust (5) both Ian Yeomans
128-9 (2) Mansell Collection (5) & (10) National Trust (6) The Zoological Society of London (7) Philip Llewellin
130-1 Malcolm Aird: except Horseshoe Cloister—Picturepoint Ltd. Quadrangle—Pitkin Pictorials Ltd
132-3 All copyright reserved
134-5 (2) Deer—Michael Taylor. 'The Salon'—By kind permission of the Marquess of Tavistock and the Trustees of the Bedford Estates (5) & (6) Philip Llewellin (7) Mansell Collection
136-9 Philip Dowell
140-1 (1) Bunyan Museum. Statue & (2) Philip Llewellin (6) The Institute of Agricultural Engineers
142-3 (1) Hitchin Museum and Art Gallery (3) & (5) Philip Llewellin (7) Woodmansterne Ltd
144-5 (5) & (7) Malcolm Aird (6) Martyn Chillmaid
146-7 (1) Malcolm Aird (4) Patrick Thurston (6) & (7) Trevor Wood (8) Michael Holford
148-9 (2) Adam Woolfit/Susan Griggs Picture Agency (4) Patrick Thurston (6) Trevor Wood. Devil's Ditch—Malcolm Aird
150-1 Trevor Wood: except Trinity Lane—Penny Tweedie
154-5 (2) Michael Holford (3) & (5) Malcolm Aird (7) Transglobe
156-7 (1) Gainsborough House—Trevor Wood. Gainsborough Painting—National Gallery (4) & (9) Malcolm Aird (5) Ian Yeomans
158-9 (1) Eric Meacher (3) Michael Taylor (5) Church—Trevor Wood. Flushwork—Homer Sykes (6) Adam Woolfit/Susan Griggs Picture Agency
160-1 (1) Both & (5) Trevor Wood (6) Penny Tweedie
162-3 (3) Victoria and Albert Museum (4) Portrait—Picturepoint (8) Oxburgh Hall (10) and Scolt Head—Trevor Wood
164-5 (2) Victoria and Albert Museum (6) Trevor Wood. River Stour—Malcolm Aird (8) Martyn Chillmaid
166-7 (4) & (9) Philip Dowell (6) Patrick Thurston (8) Malcolm Aird
168-9 (6) & (9) Trevor Wood
170-1 (1) & (2) Malcolm Aird (3) Adam Woolfit/Susan Griggs Picture Agency (5) Patrick Thurston
172-3 (2) Trevor Wood (8) Transglobe (9) & (11) Malcolm Aird
174-7 Trevor Wood: except Elm Street and Altar Screen—Malcolm Aird; 'Silver Birches'—Norfolk Museums Service (Norwich Castle Museum)
178-9 (1) Haverfordwest Museum (2) Studio Jon (4) Spectrum Colour Library (6) Welsh Tourist Board (8) Tony Evans
180-1 (2) Roger Worsley (4) Malcolm Aird (7) Esso Petroleum (10) Robert Harding Associates
182-3 (1) British Museum (Michael Holford) (5) Aspect Picture Library/Larry Burrows (7) Spectrum Colour Library
184-5 (1) British Tourist Authority. Tywi Valley—Philip Evans (3) Adam Woolfit (7) Forestry Commission
186-7 (1) National Library of Wales. Rheidol Valley—Malcolm Aird (3) Philip Llewellin (5) Philip Evans
188-9 (1) Museum—British Tourist Authority. (3) Philip Llewellin (5) Adam Woolfit. Wild ponies—British Tourist Authority. Black Mountain—Philip Evans
190-3 Philip Evans
194-5 (1) Abergavenny Museum. Vale of Ewyas & (3) Malcolm Aird (4) Penny Tweedie (5) T. LeGoubin/Colorific (7) Philip Llewellin
196-7 (1) Crown copyright reproduced with permission of the Controller of HMSO (6) Malcolm Aird (7) British Tourist Authority
198-9 (6) E. Herbert Natural Science Photos (8) Robert Harding Associates (9) Copper mine—Philip Evans. Amlwch—Penny Tweedie
200-1 (1) Radio Times Hulton Picture Library (3) Edna Knowles (4) Philip Llewellin (8) Adam Woolfit. Newborough Warren—Edna Knowles
202-3 (3) & (8) Philip Llewellin (5) Homer Sykes (10) Alan Clifton/Aspect
204-5 (3) Penny Tweedie (4) British Tourist Association (6) Station—Penny Tweedie. Llanberis Pass—Bridget Morley (8) Philip Llewellin
206-9 Philip Dowell
210-11 (1) Adam Woolfit (3) Central Electricity Board (6) Penny Tweedie (9) Philip Evans (10) Spectrum Colour Library
212-13 (4) Wales Tourist Board (6) & (7) Adam Woolfit. Dolgoch Falls—Spectrum Colour Library
214-15 (1) Bridget Morley (4) Philip Evans (8) Adam Woolfit (10) Llechwedd Slate Caverns
216-17 (1) Plas Newydd—Philip Evans. Eisteddfod—Spectrum Colour Library (5) Mary Evans Picture Library (8) Adam Woolfit
218-19 (2) Adam Woolfit (5) British Tourist Association (6) & (8) Robert Harding Associates
220-3 Philip Dowell: except 'Seascape with "The Tyger" ' by William Van de Velde—English Life Publications Ltd
224-5 (1) Penny Tweedie (3) both J. Perkins (5) Malcolm Aird
226-7 (1) (3) & (6) Philip Llewellin (4) National Trust
228-9 (1) Windsor-Fox Photos (4) Philip Llewellin. Canal—Patrick Thurston
230-1 (2) & (9) Philip Llewellin (3) Picturepoint Ltd (4) Sonia Halliday
232-3 (2) (3) & (7) Philip Llewellin (10) Illustrated London News
234-7 Tony Evans
238-9 (4) Brian Shuel (8) & (10) Philip Llewellin (9) Patrick Thurston
240-1 (1) & (2) Philip Llewellin (5) National Portrait Gallery/Woodmansterne Ltd (7) National Gallery/Woodmansterne Ltd
242-3 (1) Philip Llewellin (3) Transglobe (4) National Trust (9) British Tourist Authority
244-5 (2) (4) (7) & (11) Philip Llewellin
246-7 (1) Shrewsbury Library (2) & (5) Philip Llewellin (8) Robert Harding Associates
248-9 (3) (8) (10) Philip Llewellin (4) National Trust (8) Crown Copyright reproduced with permission of the Controller of HMSO
250-3 Philip Evans
254-5 (3) East Midlands Zoological Society (5) & (8) Michael St Maur Sheil (12) Martyn Chillmaid
256-7 (3) Rev. N. Chubb (5) Adrianus Van Helfteren, Art & Antiques Weekly (6) & (10) Martyn Chillmaid (7) Cmdr Pasley-Tyler
258-9 (1) Martyn Chillmaid (4) Malcolm Aird
260-1 (1) J. Butcher (2) Transglobe (6) Adam Woolfit/Susan Griggs Picture Agency (7) Martyn Chillmaid

262-3 (1) & (11) W. H. Brighouse (8) Charles Legh
264-5 (3) Brian Shuel (5) Roxby Press (8) British Tourist Authority (9) W. H. Brighouse
266-7 (3) National Trust (5) Brian Shuel (10) Michael Hardy
268-9 (1) Penny Tweedie (3) (6) & (7) W. H. Brighouse
270-1 (5) & (11) W. H. Brighouse (8) R. Wilsher (9) Crown Copyright Geological Survey. Reproduced with permission of the Controller of HMSO. The Proprietor, Blue John Caverns
272-5 Philip Dowell
276-7 (7) Adam Woolfit/Susan Griggs Picture Agency (9) The Trustees of Newstead Abbey (M. Dixon) (10) Martyn Chillmaid
278-9 (1) United Dairies (3) Harry Wheatcroft Gardening Ltd (8) English Life Publications (9) Michael St Maur Sheil
280-1 (1) Malcolm Aird (3) & (4) W. H. Brighouse (5) Philip Llewellin
282-3 (1) D. Dunn (3) Trevor Wood (8) Martyn Chillmaid
284-5 (1) Penny Tweedie (3) & (6) W. H. Brighouse (7) Robert Estall
286-7 (1) Northwich Salt Museum (3) Robert Estall (4) & (7) Philip Llewellin (9) Martyn Chillmaid
288-9 (2) Spectrum Colour Library (3) (6) & (7) Martyn Chillmaid
290-1 (2) Tony Howarth (4) John Perkins (6) Philip Llewellin (8) both Brian Shuel
292-3 (1) British Tourist Authority (3) John Perkins (6) Mansell Collection (7) & (9) Brian Shuel
294-5 (3) Philip Llewellin (4) & (8) Patrick Thurston (6) Spectrum Colour Library
296-9 Trevor Wood: except Multangular Tower and Minster Buttresses—Susan Elwes
300-1 (3) Patrick Thurston (5) & (7) Tom Parker (8) Trevor Wood
302-3 (2) Patrick Thurston (5) C. M. Dixon (8) Crown Copyright reproduced with permission of the Controller of HMSO (10) National Trust
304-5 (1) Alec Russel (3) Photo Precision Ltd (4) Patrick Thurston (7) Penny Tweedie
306-7 (1) Castle—Patrick Thurston. Green Howards Museum—Trevor Wood (4) & (8) Geoffrey Wright
308-9 (2) & (3) Jack Wetherby (5) Philip Llewellin (8) Patrick Thurston
310-11 (1) Crown Copyright reproduced with permission of the Controller of HMSO (3) Patrick Thurston (4) Warren Jepson (9) W. H. Brighouse
312-13 (1) C. M. Dixon (3) W. H. Brighouse (5) Trevor Wood (8) Patrick Thurston
314-15 Trevor Wood: except Carrmire Gate—Angelo Hornak
316-17 Trevor Wood: except Archway in Great Hall—Angelo Hornak
318-19 (5) The National Trust (6) & (7) Philip Llewellin (8) Patrick Thurston (10) British Tourist Authority
320-1 (4) Philip Llewellin (5) Patrick Thurston (7) Cheze-Brown (8) Robert Harding Associates
322-3 (1) & (3) Patrick Thurston (4) Philip Llewellin
324-5 (1) Abbot Hall Museum. Catherine Parr's Prayer Book—Gordon Wood (3) Penny Tweedie/The Picture Library (5) Michael Hardy
326-7 (1) Ian Yeomans/Susan Griggs Picture Agency (4) Robert Harding Associates (5) Robin Crane (7) Philip Llewellin
328-9 Derwentwater & (3) Philip Llewellin (6) Partick Thurston
330-1 (1) W. F. Davidson (2) (3) (8) & South Tyne Valley—Philip Llewellin
332-5 Trevor Wood: except Norman Chapel—Jarrolds; Exterior of Durham Cathedral—M. Breese; Tunic in Gulbenkian Museum—Tony Howarth
336-7 (1) Patrick Thurston (2) & (7) Philip Llewellin (4) Robin Crane
338-9 (2) John Marmaras (4) Spectrum Picture Library (7) Trevor Wood
340-1 Bowes Museum T. Scott (5) & (7) Penny Tweedie
342-3 (2) & (6) Philip Llewellin (4) Beamish Museum
344-5 (3) Kippers—Patrick Thurston. Castle & (6) Spectrum Colour Library (4) Trevor Wood
346-7 (1) (3) & (7) Spectrum Colour Library (2) Trevor Wood
348-51 Tony Evans: except Golden plover, and roebuck—K. H. C. Taylor; Feral goats—V. Blakenburgs
352-3 (1) & (5) Philip Llewellin (6) Tom Weir (7) W. H. Brighouse
354-5 (2) Philip Llewellin (7) & (8) Penny Tweedie (9) Brian Shuel
356-7 (1) Brian Shuel (4) & (8) Penny Tweedie (7) Philip Llewellin
358-9 Tony Evans: except The Scottish Sword of State—Crown Copyright reproduced with the permission of the Controller of HMSO
360-1 Holyrood House—Anthony Howarth/Susan Griggs Picture Agency. Sanctuary Stone and Parthenon—Tony Evans. Sir Walter Scott—National Portrait Gallery. Diego Martelli—National Gallery of Scotland. George Street—Malcolm Aird
362-3 (1) Brian Shuel (3) Jarrolds (4) Philip Llewellin (6) Gladstone Court Museum
364-5 (1) (4) & (7) Mike Taylor
366-7 (5) & (7) Philip Llewellin (6) Pollok House
368-9 (2) John Marmaras (4) & (8) Philip Llewellin (10) Penny Tweedie
370-1 (1) John Perkins (3) Scottish Tourist Board (5) Philip Llewellin (6) Brian Shuel
372-3 (2) & (4) Brian Shuel (6) Adam Woolfit/Susan Griggs Picture Agency (9) National Trust for Scotland
374-5 (1) National Trust houses—D. H. A. Barrett; Dunkeld Cathedral—Philip Llewellin (3) Chris Bonnington. Glen Lyon—Tom Weir
376-9 Tony Evans: except the Small drawing-room—Anthony Howarth/Susan Griggs Picture Agency; and exterior—Robert Harding Associates
380-1 (1) Philip Llewellin (2) British Tourist Authority (7) Scottish Tourist Board (8) Sir Ilay Campbell
382-3 (2) Duart Castle & (7) Philip Llewellin (2) Lord Maclean—Duart Castle (9) British Tourist Authority
384-5 (1) Malcolm Aird (8) (9) & Loch Sunart—Philip Llewellin
386-7 (1) Adam Woolfit/Susan Griggs Picture Agency (4) Spectrum Colour Library (5) The Folk Museum—Philip Llewellin. Flora Macdonald—Mary Evans Picture Library (8) Tom Parker
388-9 (1) (3) & (6) Philip Llewellin. Glamis Castle—Mike Shiel
390-1 (4) Brian Shuel (5) Sonia Halliday (8) Julian Plowright (9) National Trust for Scotland
392-3 (3) Mike Taylor (5) Brian Shuel (8) Patrick Thurston. Glen More—Robert Harding Associates
394-5 (2) & (3) Brian Shuel (6) Philip Llewellin (8) Robert Harding Associates
396-7 Tony Evans: except dam—North of Scotland Hydro-Electric Board
398-9 Tony Evans: except chamber under construction and reversible pumps—North of Scotland Hydro-Electric Board
400-1 (3) & (4) Philip Llewellin (6) Homer Sykes (8) & Inverfarigaig—Brian Shuel
402-3 (1) & (7) G. W. Wright (5) D. Paterson/Aspect
404-5 (1) (6) & (8) Brian Shuel. Stratha Brora—Philip Llewellin
406-7 (5) Highlands & Islands Development Board (6) both and Caithness walls—Brian Shuel

423

Acknowledgments

The illustrations throughout the book are the work of the following artists:

S. R. Badmin
David Baird
Norman Barber
David Baxter
Leonora Box
Terry Callcut
David Carl-Forbes
Helen Cowcher
Patrick Cox
Michael Craig
Royston Edwards
Helen Fisher
Ian Garrard
Terry Hadler
Vana Haggerty
Nick Hall
Hargrave Hands
Hermann Heinzel
Gillian Kenny
Richard Lewington
John Vernon Lord
Dorothy Mahoney
Robert Micklewright
Sean Milne
Peter Morter
Linda Nash
John Norris-Wood
Patrick Oxenham
Stanley Paine
Josephine Rankin
John Rignall
Jim Robbins
Ann Savage
Kathleen Smith
Michael Woods

Many people and organisations assisted in the preparation of this book. The publishers wish to thank all of them, particularly:

Aerofilms
American Museum, Bath
Barnaby's Picture Library
Francesca Barron (National Trust)
Bath Preservation Trust
Bill Bawden
British Tourist Authority
Cameo Books, Huddersfield
Dean and Chapter of Canterbury Cathedral
J. Allan Cash
Corinium Museum, Cirencester
Peter Clayton
Clement Marten Advertising
The Clinton Devon Estates

R. E. J. Compton, Newby Hall
Countryside Commission
County and local council offices
Crich Tramway Museum
The Dalesman Publishing Co.
Ministry of Defence
The Bursar, Durham Castle
Dean and Chapter of Durham Cathedral
East Midlands Tourist Board
English Tourist Board
Department of the Environment
Derek Evans
Fairey Surveys
F. H. FitzRoy-Newdegate, Arbury Hall
Forestry Commission
Institute of Geological Sciences
Charles C. Greenwood
Anthony Hall
J. P. Harding
Heart of England Tourist Board
Horsham District Council
A. F. Kersting
Librarians throughout Britain who have helped with local information
Dr P. Morris
National Trust
National Trust for Scotland
Nature Conservancy
Norfolk Museums Service, Norwich
Dean and Chapter of Norwich Cathedral
Ordnance Survey
Christ Church, Oxford
City Museum and Art Gallery, Plymouth
Royal Doulton Tableware Ltd
The Royal Pavilion, Brighton
Rutland County Museum
Ryedale Folk Museum
The Master, St Cross Hospital, Winchester
Dean and Chapter of Salisbury Cathedral
Scottish Tourist Board
Regimental Museum of the South Wales Borderers & Monmouthshire Regiment
Dr Henry Teed
Torbay Aircraft Museum
United Kingdom Atomic Energy Authority
Wales Tourist Board
Martin Weaver
Welshpool and Llanfair Light Railway
Roy Westlake
Sir Mortimer Wheeler
The Castle, Winchester
Dean and Chapter of Winchester Cathedral
Winchester City Museums
Warden and Fellows of Winchester College
City Art Gallery, York
Merchant Adventurers' Hall, York

The publishers also acknowledge their indebtedness to the following books and journals which were consulted for reference.

Abbeys R. Gillyard-Beer (HMSO)
Ancient Monuments I-VI (HMSO)
Atlas of the British Flora F. H. Perring and S. M. Walters (Thomas Nelson)
Berkshire L. Yarrow (Robert Hale)
Blue Guide to England (Ernest Benn Ltd)
Blue Guide to Wales (Ernest Benn Ltd)
Britain's Heritage (Automobile Association)
A Butterfly Book E. Sanders (Oxford University Press)
Castles in Britain Stuart Barton (Lyle)
The Cathedrals of Britain A. Clifton-Taylor (Thames & Hudson)
Chalkways of South and South East England E. G. Pyatt (David & Charles)
Chambers's Encyclopaedia (Newnes)
Chilterns to Black Country W. G. Hoskins (Collins)
Collins Pocket Guide to England
Companion Guide to Kent and Sussex K. Spence (Collins)
Companion Guide to the West Highlands of Scotland W. H. Murray (Collins)
Cumbria R. Millward and A. Robinson (Macmillan)
Dictionary of National Biography (Oxford University Press)
Discovering Castles in England and Wales J. Kinross (Shire)
Discovering Crosses G. H. Haines (Shire)
East Anglian Forestry Commission (HMSO)
Encyclopaedia Britannica (Encyclopaedia Britannica)
English Cathedrals J. Harvey (B. T. Batsford Ltd)
English Cathedrals M. Hurlmann (Thames & Hudson)
The English Country House O. Cook (Thames & Hudson)
Finding Wild Flowers R. S. R. Fitter (Collins)
Follies Sir Hugh Casson (Chatto & Windus)
Hadrian's Wall A. R. Birley (HMSO)
Heart of England L. Wright and J. Priddey (Robert Hale)
Historic Houses, Castles and Gardens ABC Historic Publication
Illustrated Road Book of England and Wales (Automobile Association)
Illustrated Road Book of Scotland (Automobile Association)
Isle of Mull P. A. Macnab (David & Charles)
Lake District M. J. B. Baddeley (Ward Lock)

Lake District/A Geographer's Guide (Geographia Ltd)
The Lake District R. Millward and A. Robinson (Eyre & Spottiswoode)
Lancashire Villages J. Lofthouse (Robert Hale)
Letts Guides to Counties in England and Wales (Charles Letts)
The Lost Roads of Wessex C. Cochrane (Pan)
Monuments Sir Hugh Casson (Chatto & Windus)
Mountains and Moorlands W. H. Pearsall (Collins/Fontana)
Nature Trails in Britain (BTA)
Nicholson's Guides to Great Britain (R. Nicholson Public Ltd)
Nicholson's Guides to the Waterways (British Waterways Guide)
Odd Aspects of England G. Hogg (David & Charles)
Old Customs of Britain (BTA)
Old English Towns F. R. Banks (B. T. Batsford Ltd)
Oxfordshire D. M. Barrett and D. G. Vaisey (Blackwells)
The Pennine Way T. Stephenson (HMSO)
Pocket Guide to English Parish Churches John Betjeman (Collins)
Portrait of Dorset R. Wightman (Robert Hale)
Portrait of Durham County P. A. White (Robert Hale)
Portrait of York R. Willis (Robert Hale)
Properties of the National Trust (National Trust)
Red Guides (Ward Lock)
Salisbury R. L. P. Jowitt (B. T. Batsford Ltd)
Scottish Border and Northumberland J. T. White (Eyre Methuen)
Shell Guide to Britain (Ebury Press)
Shell Guide to England (Michael Joseph)
Shell Guide to Scotland (Ebury Press & Rainbird)
Shell Guide to Wales (Michael Joseph)
Shell Guides to the Counties of England (Faber)
Staffordshire V. Bird (B. T. Batsford Ltd)
Story of Carmarthenshire A. G. Prys-Jones (Christopher Davies)
Survey Gazetteer of the British Isles (Bartholomew)
Sussex J. Burke (B. T. Batsford Ltd)
Travellers Guides ed. by Sean Jennett (Darton, Longman & Todd)
Trees and Bushes H. Vedel and J. Lange (Methuen)
Warwickshire V. Bird (B. T. Batsford Ltd)
Where to Watch Birds J. Gooders (Sphere Books Ltd)
Wonders of Yorkshire M. Hartley and J. Ingilby
Woodlands W. Condry (Collins)
Yorkshire Dales M. Hartley and J. Ingilby

THE MAPS OF THE TOURS HAVE BEEN DERIVED FROM ORDNANCE SURVEY MATERIAL WITH THE SANCTION OF THE CONTROLLER OF HER MAJESTY'S STATIONERY OFFICE (CROWN COPYRIGHT RESERVED)

CARTOGRAPHERS: FAIREY SURVEYS LTD, MAIDENHEAD

Paper, printing and binding by:

Bowater Paper Sales Ltd; Brown Knight & Truscott Ltd, Tonbridge; Hazell Watson & Viney Ltd, Aylesbury; Northampton Phototypesetters Ltd, Northampton; Petty & Sons Ltd, Leeds; Reprocolor Llovet, Barcelona; Schwitter Ltd, Zurich; Typesetting Services Ltd, Glasgow.